Best Wishes
Barry

THE PFA FOOTBALLERS' WHO'S WHO

2005/2006

Editor and St

Barry J Hugman

Assistant Editor

Ian Nannestad

Photographs by

Getty Images

QUEEN ANNE PRESS

First published in Great Britain in 2005 by
Queen Anne Press
a division of Lennard Associates Limited
Mackerye End, Harpenden
Hertfordshire AL5 5DR

A CIP catalogue record for this book
is available from the British Library

ISBN 1 85291 662 1

Typeset and designed by
Typecast (Artwork & Design)

Printed and bound in Great Britain by
Butler & Tanner, London and Frome

Foreword

Welcome once again to the Footballers' Who's Who – a definitive guide to every one of the PFA members playing first-team football throughout the Premier League and the Football League in England and Wales.

As ever, I am extremely pleased to give the PFA's full endorsement and recommendation to this unique publication which is now in its 11th year. Since the inception of the Who's Who, interest in the modern game – at all levels – has continued to grow at a remarkable rate, and this book once again reflects that growth.

Packed full of statistics and profiles on all PFA members, the Footballers' Who's Who provides the background to what the game is all about – the players. Having to deal with 4,000 PFA members, the book gives me a valuable source of information in an easily accessible, attractive and enjoyable format – as it does anybody involved in the game, whether it be an administrator, player, manager, spectator or commentator. It is especially invaluable for any football 'Brain of Britain' or football quiz aspirant!

The publication is compiled by Barry Hugman, whose record in this field is unsurpassed, and he is aided by a team of close on 100 people who provide him with the invaluable aspects of local information, which gives this book such credibility. It's a fascinating read and an unequalled source of reference. We hope you enjoy it.

Gordon Taylor
PFA Chief Executive

PROFESSIONAL FOOTBALLERS' ASSOCIATION
PFA
ACCIDENT INSURANCE
EDUCATION
YOUTH TRAINING
PERSONAL REPRESENTATION
COMMERCIAL AFFAIRS
PENSIONS
TRANSFERS
LEGAL ADVICE
FINANCIAL HELP
CONTRACTS
PLAYERS UNITED
THE OUTCASTS F.C.
TEN DECADES' SERVICE TO FOOTBALL
FOUNDED AT THE IMPERIAL HOTEL, MANCHESTER IN 1907, THE PROFESSIONAL FOOTBALLERS' ASSOCIATION TODAY COMMANDS AN ENVIABLE REPUTATION AS THE WORLD'S LONGEST-ESTABLISHED PROFESSIONAL SPORTSMEN'S UNION.
This status stands as testament to the unswerving determination, dedication and commitment of all its contributors, from its earliest forefathers such as Billy Meredith right through to its current Management Committee.
The result is that the PFA is now involved in every aspect of a player's career, from financial management and pensions, to education and training, coaching, commercial, accident insurance and medical & benevolent assistance.
The PFA is also a key factor in both the Youth Training/Football Scholarship Scheme and Football In The Community Programme, ensuring that the players of tomorrow receive the best possible start to their careers.
THE PFA - PROTECTING THE PLAYERS, PROTECTING THE GAME.
PROFESSIONAL FOOTBALLERS ASSOCIATION
20 Oxford Court, Bishopsgate, Manchester M2 3WQ
THE PFA SAYS LET'S KICK RACISM OUT OF FOOTBALL
it's only
the colou
of the shirt
that counts

Acknowledgements

Formerly known as the *Factfile* and now in its 11th edition, we believe that the *Who's Who* has become an invaluable part-work which, in due course, will cover the season-by-season career record of all professional footballers operating at that time in the Premier and Football Leagues. To this end, I would once again like to express my thanks to **Gordon Taylor**, the chief executive, and all those at the PFA who are genuinely supporting and helping to establish the *Footballers' Who's Who*. Their help is invaluable and much appreciated.

The massive task of editing the text this year was again carried out by the assistant editor, **Ian Nannestad**, who has also been a long-standing contributor to the publication on matters regarding Lincoln City.

For the past few years it has been my pleasure to work on the statistical side of the book with **Michael Joyce**, the author of *Football League Players' Records, 1888 to 1939*. This title, which is still available from SoccerData, 4 Adrian Close, Beeston, Nottingham NG9 6FL, slots in perfectly with my post-war *Premier and Football League Players' Records*. Michael, who despite now living in Norfolk has supported Arsenal for as long he can remember, has accumulated data for a complete Football League database over many years and used it to produce the player indexes for the Definitive series of club histories and several other publications. He provides statistical information for the website: since 1888.co.uk.

The editorial team were also lucky to be able to call upon **David Barber** (English FA), **Sandy Bryson** (Scottish FA), **Rebecca Burnett** (FA Premier League), **Ceri Stennett** (FA of Wales), and **Marshall Gillespie** (editor of the Northern Ireland Football Yearbook). Others who gave their time were **Alan Platt** (Where Did They Go?) and **Jenny Hugman** (proof reading), and many Premier and Football League members up and down the country.

For details provided on players, I have listed below, in alphabetical order, the names of the team, without whose help this book would not have been possible to produce. Once again, I thank every one of them for all the hard work they put in.

Audrey Adams (Watford): Has supported Watford since primary school days and currently provides the results and statistics for the BBC's Sports Report on Radio 5 Live. Audrey was also the club statistician for *The Ultimate Football Guide*. Regardless of how the club performed last season her devotion to the Hornets remains undimmed.

Geoff Allman (Walsall): A retired university lecturer, having worked for 49 years without taking a day off, he saw his first ever game in February 1944, Walsall versus Wolves. Has written for Walsall's programme for over 30 seasons and, at one time or another, has provided articles for more than half of the clubs currently in the Premiership and Football League. A keen cricketer, he says that although making few runs he prided himself on being able to hold his end up. Geoff is also a Methodist local preacher and press officer.

Stuart Basson (Chesterfield): As the club's official historian, Stuart has written for the *Who's Who* since its inception and is the author of three successful books about the club. He also produces previews and reports for the club's official website and is the regular summariser for home match commentaries on the club's Spireites World site.

Harry Berry (Blackburn Rovers): As a season ticket holder ever since starting work, Harry has followed Blackburn Rovers for over 50 years, having been born only three miles from Ewood Park and living within 15 miles all his life. Has been a road runner for many years and has completed a few marathons. By profession a financial director, prior to retirement he worked for the largest manufacturer in Blackburn.

Tony Bluff (Doncaster Rovers): First watched the Rovers in 1953. The club historian and statistician for over 20 years, Tony has contributed to the programme for many of those years but now contributes to the web site and club newspaper with historical data and match reports for the first team and reserves. Is co-author of the official history of the club.

Eddie Brennan (Sunderland): Eddie, who has followed Sunderland's fortunes for nearly 30 years and seen many highs and lows on Wearside, is delighted that the Black Cats have made a triumphant return to the Premiership. He is also a former contributor to the *Football League Directory*.

Jim Brown (Coventry City): As the club's official statistician/historian and contributor to the programme, Jim pens a weekly column in the *Coventry Evening Telegraph* answering readers' queries. He is also the author of *Coventry City: The Elite Era* (1998 and 2001) and *The Illustrated History* (2000), in addition to being the co-author of the Breedon *Complete Record* (1991). Has been a Coventry fan since 1962 and has an almost complete collection of Coventry programmes since the war, as well as having a large library of football writings. Away from City, Jim has carried out research for a number of commercial bodies and has also written critically acclaimed books on *Huddersfield Town's Glory Years (1923-26)* and *The Busby Era at Old Trafford (1946-71)*.

Mark Brown (Plymouth Argyle): Helped by his wife, Nicola, in putting together the profiles for this publication, Mark has been supporting the club for over 25 years, having been introduced to them at the tender age of five by his Argyle-mad family. Follows most of their games, whether home or away, and is a member of the travel club. Is the proud father of Libby Margaret, who, with brother Ben, is almost certain to become a Pilgrim!

Gavin Buckland (Everton): A life-long Everton supporter of over 30 years and co-author of *Everton: The Ultimate Book of Stats and Facts* and two other football quiz books, Gavin has also worked as a researcher and question setter on several TV quiz programmes. As the club statistician, he has a trivia and facts column in every Everton home programme and provides factual data for Radio Merseyside.

Trevor Bugg (Hull City): A supporter of the Tigers for over 30 years, Trevor contributes to Hull City's official web site as well as the matchday programme and also continues to pursue a career in football statistics.

Bob Cain (Fulham): Bob has supported Fulham for 34 years, during which time he has not missed a single home match in any first team competition. In all he has clocked up over 1,600 first team games. A strong advocate of all seater stadiums, he has been a contributor to the club programme for over a decade.

Tim Carder (Brighton & Hove Albion): Tim is chairman of both the Supporters' Club and the Albion's Collectors' and Historians' Society. Along with Roger Harris, he co-authored *Seagulls: The Story of Brighton and Hove Albion FC* and *Albion A to Z: A Who's Who of Brighton and Hove Albion FC*. He is also a respected local historian on matters ranging far beyond the Albion.

Wallace Chadwick (Burnley): A Clarets' supporter for well over 40 years, through extremes of thick and thin, and a programme contributor from 1987 to 2004, Wallace has assisted on several publications about the club. He has been a member of the AFS since 1980 and retains a keen interest in all matters statistical as well as remaining committed to a club who in their time have been just about everything but predictable.

Gary Chalk and **Dave Juson** (Southampton): Both are official historians of Southampton FC and members of Hagiology, a collective dedicated to publishing accurate and informative works on the Saints. Gary is co-author, with Duncan Holley, of *Saints: a complete History, 1885-1987*, *The Alphabet of Saints* (1992) and the lectern-crushing, *In That Number: A Post War History of Southampton FC*. Dave is a regular contributor to the Saints' programme and was co-author, with David Bull, of *Full-Time at The Dell* (2001), a narrative history of the Saints, now in its third edition, and, along with Gary, a major contributor to *Match of the Millennium* (2000). Dave's next publication will be *Saints v Pompey*, in collaboration with Clay Aldworth, David Bull and Barry Bendel.

Paul Clayton (Charlton Athletic): Author of the book *The Essential History of Charlton Athletic*, Paul wrote a regular feature in the club programme between 1993 and 1998, having previously written other articles for the now defunct Charlton Athletic magazine and *Valiant's Viewpoint* (Supporters Club newsletter/fanzine). He has also provided the Charlton statistics for a number of publications, including the *Ultimate Football Guide* from 1987 to its final publication in 1999, along with the Charlton player information for the *Factfile/Who's Who* since its inception in 1995. An AFS member, Paul is a long-standing season ticket holder at The Valley, and rarely misses a game, home or away, despite living in Wiltshire.

David Copping (Barnsley): Is a life-long Barnsley fan who has been a regular columnist in the club matchday programme for many seasons. He also is one of the club statisticians and is currently involved in setting up a museum at the club. For many seasons he commentated on both hospital radio and the club videos.

Frank Coumbe (Brentford): Celebrated his 750th consecutive Brentford home match at Griffin Park last April, a record that was acknowledged when Frank, and dad Syd, were guests of the club for the Bristol City game and met Martin Allen and the players in the dressing room. On the field, an exciting season ultimately ended in defeat in the play-offs. Frank continued to contribute to the Brentford matchday programme, TW8, throughout 2004-05 and has been the club statistician for this publication since its inception.

Peter Cullen (Bury): A life-long Bury fan, 45 year old Peter is a former secretary of Bury FC Supporters' Association and was also the official club historian for a number of years. He acted as programme editor for 12 seasons and contributed articles to the programme for more than 20 years. Has written three books on the Shakers – the last of which was the definitive *Bury FC – The Official History* in 1999. When Bury gained promotion to Division One in 1997, Peter took up a full-time post at Gigg Lane as ticket office manager/programme editor for a three year spell. It is very fitting that the late Brian Turner – a man who made 455 appearances for Bury and is second only to Norman Bullock in the club's all-time appearance list – was the uncle of Peter's wife, Sue.

Mick Cunningham (AFC Bournemouth): Mick celebrated ten years of being both programme editor and club photographer at the club in March 2005. A supporter since the mid '60s, Mick has now been to every game for the last 12 years.

John Curtis (Scunthorpe United): A life-long Scunthorpe fan, John is a former editor of the award-winning club matchday programme. He also covered the club's affairs for the *Scunthorpe Telegraph*, where he now works as the chief sub editor.

Carol Dalziel (Tranmere Rovers): Carol has been variously either having her heart broken or being made deliriously happy on a regular basis by Tranmere Rovers since watching them play for the first time in 1968 against Shrewsbury Town. A former contributor to and assistant editor of the club's matchday programme, she has also been Rovers' electronic scoreboard operator for the last 15 years.

Denise Dann (Aston Villa): In her own words, Denise is a mad, crazy Villa supporter, who follows them up and down the country without fail. With the *PFA Footballers' Factfile/ Who's Who* since its inception, her only previous football work was to help with the club's profiles required for the *Premier League: The Players* publication.

Gareth Davies (Wrexham): Gareth is the co-author of the Who's Who on *Welsh International Footballers* (1991) with Ian Garland; editor/compiler of *Coast of Soccer Memories*, the centenary publication of the North Wales Coast FA (1994); co-author of *The Racecourse Robins* with Peter Jones; *Who's Who of Wrexham FC*, 1921-99 (1999); co-author of Tempus' *Images of Sport: Wrexham FC, 1872-1950* (2000) with Peter Jones and *Wrexham FC, 1950-2001* (2001) with Peter Jones. He is also a contributor to the Wrexham official programme, *The Holyhead* Hotspur (Cymru Alliance), as the club's press officer, and the Welsh Football magazine, while producing various articles and info for other magazines and books.

David Downs (Reading): David is employed by Reading FC as the club's Welfare and Child Protection Officer and is also a regular contributor to the matchday programme with a series of flashback articles. Away from football, he works as a television and film extra and can be seen as a Netherfield Ball guest in Pemberley Pictures' production of Pride and Prejudice, due for cinema release in September 2005.

Ray Driscoll (Chelsea): A life-long Blues' fan, born and bred two miles away from Stamford Bridge, his 47 years' spectating encompasses the era from Roy Bentley to John Terry and it was a dream come true to see both these stalwarts from different eras lift the Premiership trophy on the Stamford Bridge turf. In Bentley's case it was 50 years on. An all-round sports 'nut', he has contributed to many football books as well as other sports such as cricket, golf, rugby and tennis. Has also contributed to more 'cerebral' literature such as reference books.

Brian Ellis (Luton Town): Brian has just purchased his 25th consecutive season ticket after first being taken to see Luton Town in 1967 and seeing many of the dramas that have taken place over the years. The winning of the League One Championship is the third title win he has witnesed and the sixth promotion, yet despite that the winning double of the Football Combination League and Cup has equally given him great satisfaction . Brian has written several articles on Luton Town and is continuing his work on a Luton Town Who's Who.

Dean Enderby and Eddie Collins (Nottingham Forest): A season ticket holder at Forest, this is the first book Dean has contributed to but would like to assist in others in the future. Eddie has been watching Forest since 1956 and derives much pleasure from being involved in this publication. He is also a member of the AFS.

Colin Faiers (Cambridge United): A Cambridge United fan for over 30 years, Colin has witnessed their rise from non-league football. A chartered accountant in the day, he is the club statistician and occasional contributor to the club programme and web site.

Harold Finch (Crewe Alexandra): Having endured the tension of the 2004-05 campaign, Harold is now looking forward to his 71st year of supporting Crewe Alexandra. Still a regular contributor to the official programme, he also supplies statistics of the players' appearances. Has so far written two books on the club, *Crewe Alexandra FC - A Pictorial History of the Club* and also *Crewe Alexandra FC – 100 Greats*. Has an extensive collection of club programmes, photographs, press cuttings and other memorabilia.

Mick Ford and **Richard Lindsay** (Millwall): After 53 years of following Millwall faithfully, to get to the FA Cup Final and

Europe was a dream come true for Mick, something he never thought he would see in his lifetime. It has been a tremendous five years at The New Den with what the club has achieved but, for Mick, nothing will match the '60s in terms of what Millwall is all about. Pride, passion and very difficult to beat at home, hence the still proud record of 59 home matches unbeaten. Having now moved to Spain (with selected memorabilia), he still manages to go to all weekend home fixtures and run the programme shop. Being a Millwall supporter means it is not just supporting them- it's a way of life and in Sue he is proud to acknowledge her as such an understanding and supportive wife who endures his passion. Meanwhile, his *Who's Who* partner, Richard, the author of *Millwall: A Complete Record*, continues to help establish the Millwall FC Museum at the New Den.

Andrew Frazier (Kidderminster Harriers): Has been following the Harriers since 1978, and hasn't missed a game, home or away, for over ten years. Is a contributor to the club programme, is the club statistician, and a member of the Association of Football Statisticians.

Jon Gibbes (Torquay United): Saw his first game on Boxing Day 1970 aged seven, and it was the beginning of an unhealthy obsession with Torquay United, which at times leads to the woeful neglect of wife, Julie, and children, Rosie and Tommy. After having disproved the long-held belief that the club was formed in 1898, Jon co-wrote *Torquay United FC: The Official Centenary History, 1899-1999* with Leigh Edwards and John Lovis.

Harry Glasper (Middlesbrough): Harry realises he is now reaching the veteran stage when it comes to watching his favourite team – his only team! The 2005-06 season will be his 38th and his programme contributions have also reached a memorable milestone for his first contributions (written with ink and a goose quill on A4 parchment) surfaced in 1975. Who would have thought that the new and unforgettable thrill of the 2004 Carling Cup win would be almost equalled the following season. Admittedly, MFC (meekly, in Harry's humble opinion) surrendered the Carling Cup, but what a season despite the lack of silverware. Around Christmas time the club was experiencing the learning curve of UEFA games and also hanging on to a possible Champions' League spot in the most demanding league in the world – the Premiership. But the injury crisis just imploded and, at one point, the club could have fielded a full team of crocks, so dire was the situation. Fortunately, from the club's vantage point (and for the committed fans) the season ended triumphantly when Mark Schwarzer saved Robbie Fowler's penalty in the dying seconds of the season, literally the last kick of a long, long season. Wow. The club has gone to a different level in the last two years and Boro's hardened fans expect success in one form or another. Harry is one of those fans.

Paul Godfrey (Cheltenham Town): Paul watched his first Cheltenham Town game at the age of ten – the Robins losing 2-1 to Yeovil Town in an FA Cup Fourth Qualifying Round match. He followed similar near misses and disappointments religiously before events took a dramatic turn in the late 1990s. Having become the club's programme editor in 1990, he was able to witness at first hand the transformation at Whaddon Road brought about by Steve Cotterill and the Board, headed by the chairman, Paul Baker. Having joined the club on a full-time basis in 2001, he now combines managing the club's website with his role as the secretary, while continuing to struggle manfully with the task of compiling the club history.

Frank Grande (Northampton Town): A supporter for 50 years and club historian and statistician for the past 25 years, Frank has contributed to the programme for 25 years and written five books on the club and its players. Over the years he has been instrumental in reunions and events involving ex players, plus fund raising events for the club.

Roy Grant (Oxford United): A life-long Oxford United fan, Roy previously produced the Oxford United matchday programme and had a spell as the club statistician. A contributor in this publication since its first issue, Roy has also written for several football club programmes as well as contributing to football websites and productions such as *The Official Football League Yearbook* and *The Ultimate Football Guide*.

Michael Green (Bolton Wanderers): Despite being a fanatical Newcastle United supporter, Michael covers Bolton for this publication and continues to produce informative copy. Has a yearning to get involved in the area of freelance journalism, preferably concerning football or popular entertainment (music, films etc).

Alan Harding (Swindon Town): Alan has been supporting Swindon Town since 1968, is a season ticket holder, travels home and away, and has been researching match stats and line-up details, plus details of players, since 1981. Is also a member of the AFS.

Roger Harrison (Blackpool): A life-long supporter who has seen the Pool play every other league side, both home and away, and joint programme editor and club statistician, Roger has contributed to other publications, including *Rothmans Football Yearbook* and *The Ultimate Football Guide*.

Richard Hayhoe (Tottenham Hotspur): Involved since the start of this publication, Richard is happy to write about the men who play for his favourite team and hopes that Spurs can get among the elite in the forthcoming season. He is still delighted to be with the *Who's Who*, despite giving up his season ticket after 15 years. Whilst football and Spurs remain a great love, spending all his free time with his daughter, Holly, now six years old, is his most enjoyable pastime.

Des Hinks (Stockport County): Des has now been following his beloved Hatters for over 40 years and, along with updating the club's website on a daily basis, he also plays a key role in the production of their official matchday magazine. He's also a member of the independent team that produced County's award-winning reserve team programme. His son, **Des (junior)**, who also worked on the *Who's Who*, works with his father updating the club's official website on a daily basis and producing their matchday programme. Now 20 he has been following County from the tender age of four and rarely misses a game, either home or away.

Adrian Hopper (Yeovil Town): Joined Yeovil Town as media manager in 2002 after a long association through a local newspaper he owned. Also known as 'Fat Harry', Adrian is now a devoted Yeovil Town supporter attending every game, but has been known to have a slight leaning towards a certain team that plays in red at a Theatre!

Martin Jarred (Leeds United): Martin saw his first Leeds United game in 1966, a 2-1 midweek home win against West Brom and was hooked. A member of the AFS for many years, he collaborated with Malcom MacDonald on several Leeds' books published by Breedon Books, which include four editions of the *Complete Record*, two *Leeds Story Books*, a *Leeds United Cup Book* and *Leeds United, The Complete European Record*. He is also the co-author, with Dave Windross, of *Citizens and Minstermen, a Who's Who of York City*. A previous sports editor of the *Scarborough Evening News*, he is currently the sports editor of the *Evening Press, York*.

Mike Jay (Bristol Rovers) Mike, a longstanding supporter of over 38 years and a regular programme contributor since 1977, is also the official club historian. He has had four books published on Rovers, his latest being a joint collaboration with Stephen Byrne, titled *Bristol Rovers: The Definitive History 1883-2003*. Stephen and Mike are currently working on updating their *Pirates in Profile, Who's Who,* which was first published in 1994. Mike has watched Rovers on over 125 different league grounds and now has just one more current league club, Chelsea to visit to complete his tour of all 92 grounds. It may be a while before Rovers return to Stamford Bridge!

Colin Jones (Swansea City): A fan since the early 1960s, and a contributor to the club programme for seven years, four of which were spent as editor, Colin played non-league football before being involved in training and coaching. Prior to the start of the 2000-01 season, he also made a significant contribution in setting out all the stats in grid form for David Farmer's book, *The Swans, Town & City*.

Andrew Kirkham (Sheffield United): A Blades' supporter since 1953, and a regular contributor to the club programme and handbook since 1984, Andrew is a member of the AFS and 92 Club. He was also a contributor to *Sheffield United: The First 100 Years*, and co-author of *A Complete Record of Sheffield United Football Club, 1889-1999*.

Geoff Knights (*Macclesfield*): Geoff is a retired bank manager who has supported Macclesfield Town since the late 1980s. Describing himself as an ordinary supporter from the terraces, and one who enjoys the friendly atmosphere of a small club, he keeps detailed statistics and records on the club, which are used in response to media and other enquiries.

Geoffrey Lea (Wigan Athletic): A life-long supporter for over 30 seasons who first started watching the club during the non-league days, Geoff has been the editor of the matchday programme for the last ten seasons. He is also the official matchday clubcall reporter and, as the club's statistician, he performs a number of jobs for Wigan as a labour of love. Has missed only a handful of games over the last 13 seasons and has also worked for a number of local radio stations and newspapers following the club's progress.

Mark Lea (Rushden & Diamonds): Mark has been covering Diamonds full-time for the *Northamptonshire* Evening *Telegraph* over the last six seasons, charting two championships, one runners-up spot in the Conference, a trip to the Millennium stadium for the Division Three play-off final and two successive relegation battles and the club's financial problems. Born in Boston, he also follows the fortunes of his hometown club, along with those of West Ham United.

Gordon Macey (Queen's Park Rangers): Gordon has supported Rangers since the early '60s and has been compiling statistics on all levels at the club for many years. As the club's official historian he is recognised by many areas of the media as the 'expert' on all matters to do with QPR and has published three books on the club's history, including the successful *Complete Record*. He is also involved with his local club, Aldershot Town, including helping out in various roles for the Shots' reserve team. Whenever away on business, Gordon tries to arrange his trips so that he can take in a local football match and has seen many games in various countries around the world on his travels.

John Maguire (Manchester United): A one-club man since the *Who's Who* began, John continues to work on several sports related projects during 2005. Having launched three 'e-books' on www.amazon.co.uk he also looks to nurture other avenues for writing.

Carl Marsden (Oldham Athletic): A life-long supporter, Carl has been involved with his beloved Athletic on several levels. Once the chairman of SAFE (Secure Athletic's Future Existence), a website editor and regular fanzine contributor, he now fronts the sports coverage of the *Oldham Advertiser* newspaper as the paper's sports editor and does live radio commentary on the club's matches for the Latics Live service. He can be reached by email on OldhamSport@gmwn.co.uk

Carl Marston (Colchester United): Has been reporting on the fortunes of Colchester United since they regained their Football League status in 1992, both for the *East Anglian Daily Times* and the *Green 'Un* newspapers. Carl has only missed a few games during those last 13 years, usually when abroad trekking up mountains or running ultra-races and missed two games last season while running the Marathon des Sables in the Sahara Desert.

Tony Matthews (West Bromwich Albion): The official statistician and curator at The Hawthorns, his 60 plus publications include complete records/histories of Aston Villa, Birmingham City, Stoke City, Walsall, West Bromwich Albion and Wolverhampton Wanderers; The Essential Histories of Leicester City and Wolverhampton Wanderers, also assisting with same on Aston Villa and West Bromwich Albion; A-Z Encyclopaedias of Aston Villa, Birmingham City, Bolton Wanderers, Manchester United, Sheffield United, Stoke City, Tottenham Hotspur, West Bromwich Albion, Wolverhampton Wanderers and *Devon Football* (featuring Exeter City, Plymouth Argyle & Torquay United and published in 2002); Who's Whos of Villa, Blues, Manchester United (1945-85), Nottingham Forest, Stoke City, Albion and Wolves; *A Who's Who of England World Cup Players/Managers, The World Cup History: 1930-2002*; wartime and photographic books; *Smokin' Joe: The Cyrille Regis Story* (2002); he also contributes to programmes of Premiership/Nationwide League clubs. His most recent works were a *Who's Who of Aston Villa* (up-dated to 2004) and Everton (1878-2004), *125 years of West Midland's Soccer 1879-2004* and following on will be books on Soccer *Firsts*, *Football* Oddities, Liverpool and Sheffield Wednesday.

Peter Miles and David Goody (Southend U): Peter has just had his eighth football book published, a joint effort once again with fellow historian, David Goody, for whom it is his fifth book, titled *Southend United: 50 Classic Matches*, which is another in the Tempus series tracing great moments in football club histories. Both are life-long Southend supporters; Peter is still a regular at home and away matches, whilst Dave sticks to matches at Roots Hall. Peter and Dave are now undertaking the mammoth task which will see the clubs' *Official Centenary History* published in May 2006 to coincide with the 100th anniversary of the clubs' formation.

Ian Mills (Arsenal): An Arsenal fan for 29 years, Ian first visited 'The Home of Football' in 1982 and has been a regular contributor to the premier Arsenal fanzine, *The Gooner*, since 1997. As the chairman and secretary, he also writes and publishes a *fanzine* for his local Sunday football team, Rushden United, entitled *Sunday Bloody* Sunday. Always to be found in the North Bank Upper Tier at Highbury on matchdays, he also gets to away games when he can and is a keen historian on Arsenal. This is Ian's second year being involved with the *Who's Who* and were are dlighted to have him on board.

Paul Morant (Leyton Orient): Working for an insurance company in London, Paul is an out-and-out Orient fan who rarely misses a game, home or away, and takes great pride in being this publication's Orient contributor. Recently married.

Gerald Mortimer (Derby County): Gerald first went to the Baseball Ground in 1946 and, from 1970, covered the club on behalf of the *Derby Evening Telegraph* for 32 years. He was the main author in two versions of *Derby County: The Complete Record* and, last year, produced a revised and updated version of the club's *Who's Who*. His latest project was a DVD of Derby's 100 top players and another version of the *Complete Record* is on the cards.

Donald Nannestad (Boston United): Reporting on the fortunes of the Pilgrims for Raymonds Press Agency since the club's entry to Division Three, Donald, who is a journalist by profession, has a second role in life as a local councillor in Lincoln.

Ian Nannestad (Lincoln City): Ian has followed the Imps for nearly 40 years and is co-author with his brother, Donald, of *A Who's Who of Lincoln City, 1892-1994* and *Lincoln City: The Official History*. A freelance writer and book editor, in April 2002 he established a new quarterly magazine devoted to the history of the game, titled *Soccer History*. Readers wishing to know more about the magazine can contact Ian by writing to 52 Studland Road, Hall Green, Birmingham, B28 8NW. He was previously editor of the AFS Report.

John Northcutt (West Ham United): Has supported the Hammers since 1959 and is the co-author of *West Ham: A Complete Record* and *The Illustrated History*. A regular contributor to the club programme, John was the club adviser to The *Ultimate Football Guide*. He also answers all the questions put to the Vintage Claret section on the club's web site and has recently produced *The West Ham Definitive*, which can be purchased at SoccerData Publications.

Richard Owen (Portsmouth): A life-long supporter and official club historian for Portsmouth, Richard performs several jobs for the club as a labour of love. A regular contributor to the club programme for the past 27 years, missing only a handful of away games in the past 29 years, he has watched Pompey on 111 league grounds. An avid programme collector, with an almost complete set of post-war Portsmouth home and away issues, in 1998 he co-published *The Centenary Pictorial History of Portsmouth FC* and *A Team Collection*, which featured every team picture of Pompey since 1898. His third book, *Pompey's Rise to the Premiership* was published in July 2003 and he is currently working on two further titles. Richard has now built up a full library of club histories on all British Football League clubs.

Simon Parker (Bradford City): Simon has followed the club's fortunes for five years on behalf of the *Bradford Telegraph & Argus* and enjoyed being able to focus on the pitch this season after all the club's financial problems off it in recent times.

Steve Peart and **Dave Finch** (Wycombe Wanderers): A former programme editor of the club and a supporter for over 30 years, Steve put together the player profiles, while the club statistics were supplied by Dave, the official Wycombe statistician. Both were authors of *Wycombe Wanderers, 1887-1996: The Official History*, published in 1996. Dave has supported Wycombe regularly since 1964 and has been a member of the club's programme editorial team since 1990.

Steve Phillipps (Rochdale): A Rochdale supporter for over 40 years, and the club's official historian, Steve is the author of *The Survivors: The Story of Rochdale AFC* (1990), *The Definitive Rochdale* (1995) and, more recently, *The Official History of Rochdale AFC*. A founder member of the AFS, away from football he is a university professor.

Terry Phillips (Cardiff City): Terry is the chief sports writer for the *South Wales Echo*, mainly covering City home and away, and a sports journalist for over 30 years – *Kent Evening Post* (1970-1977), *Derby Evening Telegraph* (1977-1986), *Gloucester Citizen* (1986-1994) – he has previously covered clubs at all levels, including Brian Clough's Nottingham Forest, Derby County, Gillingham, and Gloucester City. His specialist subjects are Cardiff City FC and Cardiff Devils (Ice Hockey). This year we were helped out by **Gavin Allen**, also of the *South Wales Echo*, who was called up at the very last moment due to unforseen circumstances and produced excellent copy in Terry's absence.

Alan Platt (Liverpool): A dedicated football statistician and follower of Liverpool FC since 1960, whilst resident in London he was a member and official of the London branch of the LFC Supporters Club. He has assisted Barry Hugman in an editorial capacity on all his football publications since 1980, namely five updates of the post-war *Football* (now titled *Premier & Football) League Players' Records*, the two editions of *Premier League: The Players* and, for the last seven years, the *PFA Footballers' Who's Who* (formerly *The Factfile*) when not working overseas in his profession of transport planner. Now resident in Manchester, his main interest today is in non-league football and he keeps detailed records on all the senior semi-professional leagues, having compiled a database of over 6,000 players participating in that level of football.

Kevan Platt (Norwich City): As City's former programme editor and now club secretary, Kevan has always had an interest in football statistics and he combines his role with that of in-house club historian and statistician. Now in his 26th year of employment with the club, having first watched the Canaries in 1968, he has enjoyed and endured the many ups and downs City have had in those 37 years. Co-authored, with Mike Davage, the club's centenary book, *Canary Citizens*.

Mike Purkiss (Crystal Palace): Having supported Palace since 1950 and producing stats on them since 1960, Mike is the author of *Crystal Palace: A Complete History, 1905-1989*. Was the club statistician for *The Ultimate Football Guide* and also contributed to *Premier League: The Players*.

Mick Renshaw (Sheffield Wednesday): Has followed Wednesday for over 40 years, despite all the ups and downs of a club that won the First Division title four times in past years, and will continue to do so regardless. Mick, who is a great supporter of European soccer, also produced the club section for *The Ultimate Football Guide*.

Mick Robinson (Peterborough United): Another life-long fan, for a number of years Mick has contributed to the club programme and was the joint editor of *The Posh*, the official Peterborough history. Was also club statistician for *The Ultimate Football Guide*.

Phil Sherwin (Port Vale): Phil is the Port Vale club statistician and has contributed to the club programme for many years as well as various books about the club. He has also written articles for the local newspaper and has featured on local radio.

Mike Slater (Wolverhampton Wanderers): The Wolves' contributor to this publication since its inception, Mike wrote a book on the club's history called *Molineux Memories*, which he published in 1988. Well-known as the compiler of *The* Brain of Wolves' Quiz, he also produced a booklet in 1996 containing all of Wolves' competitive results and records against every other club. As a follow-up to *Molineux Memories*, Mike produced a booklet, *Took 14 Years, It Only Took 14 Years*, on Wolves' efforts to get back to the top flight from 1989 (when it was Division 1) to 2003.

Gordon Small (Hartlepool United): Gordon has supported the Pool since October 1965 and for over 30 years collected and compiled statistics on his adopted club. He has also contributed to all 11 editions of the *PFA Footballers' Who's Who* and, in 1998, was the author of *The Definitive Hartlepool United FC*. Has a wide range of football interests and, in particular, has ambitions to produce books on the history of soccer in Lancashire.

Dave Smith (Leicester City): Dave has been the official Leicester City statistician and historian for many years and is a regular contributor to both the club programme and the club's extensive media guide. He is also the co-author of both *Of Fossils and Foxes* and *The Foxes Alphabet* and was editor of both *Farewell to Filbert Street* and *Keeping the Faith*, which together charted the final season at Filbert Street and the first campaign at the Walkers Stadium.

Phil Smith (Wimbledon): A supporter of Wimbledon FC for over 20 years, Phil continued to follow the club throughout its troubled start at its new home and is looking forward to continuing his involvement with the renamed Milton Keynes Dons for the 2005-06 season. Is a regular contributor to the club's official programme.

Gerry Somerton (Rotherham United): Gerry, the club's full time media manager, has contributed to the *Who's Who* every year since its inception and is also the programme editor and the club's historian. Has followed the Millers throughout his life and, as one of his multitude of tasks, broadcasts a full match commentary on the website, something he has done for every game for the last four seasons. Has missed just three Rotherham matches in the last 25 years, home or away.

Paul Stead (Huddersfield Town): A life-long supporter of his hometown football club, and a regular spectator both home and away, over the last five years watching Huddersfield Town they have been involved in two relegations and two play offs, along with missing out on the play offs by a point on the last day of the 2005 season. Has been fortunate in seeing Huddersfield promoted from both Wembley and the Millennium Stadium. Now in his eighth year with the *Factfile/Who's Who*.

Richard Stocken (Shrewsbury Town): Has followed Shrewsbury through thick and mainly thin for almost 50 years. Back in the line up this season after a years rest in the Conference, Richard is a collector of all things Shrewsbury and has contributed to a number of books and programmes over the years. In his spare time he is a senior manager with one of the big four banks.

Chas Sumner (Chester City): Chas has been a supporter of Chester City for nearly 40 years, having seen his first game in 1967. The club's official historian and statistician, he is the author of three books on Chester including *On the Borderline, the Official History of Chester City Football Club* published in 1997 and *Images of Sport: Chester City Football Club* published in 2002. A long time programme contributor, he has also written regularly for the *Chester Evening Leader* and supplies material for the award winning website.

Bill Swann *(Newcastle United) :* A supporter since the Jackie Milburn days of the early 1950s, and a long-term shareholder in the club along with his wife and three children, all season ticket holders, he is a keen collector of memorabilia connected with United. Consolidating his information on club matches, teams, scorers, and players into a data base for easy access and analysis, he has assisted in the production of the club's volume in the *Complete Record* series and is a co-author of the *Essential History of Newcastle United*. This is his tenth year as a contributor to this publication.

Colin Tattum (Birmingham City): Colin is the chief sports writer on the *Birmingham Evening Mail* newspaper,with more than 15 years experience in his field and has special responsibility to cover the day-to-day fortunes of Birmingham City.

Paul Taylor (Mansfield Town): A Mansfield Town supporter for over 35 years, Paul has contributed to many publications over the last few years, most notably the club's centenary history in 1997. He is the club's official historian, president of the Stags' Supporters Association and a life member of the AFS. Paul is always happy to help other statisticians and club historians with information concerning his beloved team.

Richard and **Sarah Taylor** and **Ian Mills** (Notts County): Richard is a life-long Notts County fan from a Notts County family, travelling the length and breadth of the land in following the Magpies, and has seen them on all but a few current league grounds and many non-current grounds too. In the summer, he umpires cricket matches to while away the close season. Sarah, like her father and two brothers, became a dedicated fan at an early age and has made regular excursions home from university to support the Magpies. Having seen his first game at Gay Meadow in 1959-60, Ian, who once ran the matchday programme sales, has been hooked ever since and has now completed 1000 consecutive games for County, being presented with a momento by Chris Hull of Nationwide on the pitch in 2002-03. He now sits in the press box at County doing the press officer's job, after 22 seasons of programme involvement and wanting a change.

Les Triggs (Grimsby Town): A retired librarian, Les first saw the Mariners in a wartime league match whilst the club was in exile at Scunthorpe's Old Show Ground and has been a regular supporter since their days as a then First Division club. He first became involved in the historical side of the club when asked to assist in the staging of the Centenary Exhibition in 1978 and is the co-author of *Grimsby Town: A Complete Record*. He was also the Grimsby statistician for *The Ultimate Football Guide* and has been an occasional contributor to the club fanzine.

Roger Triggs (Gillingham): Roger has been a Gillingham supporter for over 40 years and has been collecting statistics and records on the club since he was a schoolboy. Co-author of the highly acclaimed centenary book, *Home of the Shouting Men*, published in 1993, Roger has since produced his images collection in conjunction with Tempus Publishing Company and, in August 2001, brought out *The Complete Who's Who of Gillingham's Football League Players, 1920-1938 & 1950-2001*.

Frank Tweddle (Darlington): The club's official historian and statistician, Frank has regularly contributed articles to the Darlington programme for the last 30 seasons and has avidly supported the Quakers home and away for over 50 years. As well as being a member of the 92 Club and the AFS, he is the author of *Darlington's Centenary History*, published in 1983, and *The Definitive Darlington 1883 - 2000*, as well as producing work for various other football publications. Now early-retired, Frank can devote even more time to delving into Darlington's fascinating if mainly undistinguished past 122 years!

Paul Voller (Ipswich Town): Has been a life-long Town fan and started attending matches at Portman Road in 1963. A member of the Ipswich Town Supporters' Media Committee, he edits the supporters' page in the matchday magazine and the supporters' weekly page in the local *Evening Star*. Was the Ipswich statistician for the *Rothmans Football Yearbook* and the *Football Club Directory* during the 1990s and was joint author of *The Essential History of Ipswich Town*.

Andrew Waldon (Manchester City): A Manchester City supporter of some 29 years, Andrew has contributed to many publications over the last few years and in that time has had four books published about his favourite team.He is the club's reserve team reporter and makes regular contributions to his side's official matchday programme and web site. This is Andrew's second season when he has contributed to *Who's Who*.

Tony Woodburn and **Martin Atherton** (Preston North End): Both being North End fans for well over 30 years, Tony and Martin provide statistical and historical information on the club for various outlets and maintain the National Football Museum's permanent Preston North End collection, as well as writing for the club programme and, of course, the *Who's Who*.

David Woods (Bristol City): An Ashton Gate regular since March 1958, and a shareholder since 1972, David has been involved with seven books on Bristol City, the most recent being *Bristol City: The Early Years, 1894-1915*, published by Desert Island. Was also involved in a history on the Bristol Bulldogs Speedway side. A life-member of the AFS, he belongs to the 92 Club on visiting all the Football League grounds following a match at Lincoln on 18 April 1970. David is also the club's official historian. A graduate of the Open University, his other interests include geology, history, cricket (Gloucestershire), rugby (Bristol), speedway (Somerset Rebels) and tennis.

Peter Wyatt (Stoke City): Peter has been a Stoke supporter for over 45 years, the highlight being the League Cup win over Chelsea in 1972. Best players seen at Stoke are Denis Smith, Gordon Banks, Stanley Matthews and the brilliant Alan Hudson, while the hope for the future is that the club continue to play a more entertaining, attacking game.

Finally, on the production side of the book, my thanks go to **Jean Bastin**, of Typecast (Artwork & Design) for her patience and diligent work on the typesetting and design, which again went far beyond the call of normal duty and was much appreciated.

Frank Lampard, the Football Writers' Player of the Year, who also received the PFA Fans' Premiership award

Editorial Introduction

Following on from last year's edition, the Who's Who portrays the statistical career record of every FA Barclaycard Premiership and Coca-Cola League player who made an appearance in 2004-05, whether it be in league football, the Football League Cup (Carling Cup), FA Cup (Sponsored by AXA), Community Shield (formerly the Charity Shield), UEFA Champions League, UEFA Cup, Inter-Toto Cup, LDV Trophy, or in the Play Offs. Not included are Welsh Cup matches. It goes beyond mere statistics, however, with a write up on all of the 2,300 plus players involved, and also records faithfully last season's playing records separately by club.

The work falls into three sections, all inter-relating. Firstly, the main core, PFA Footballers' Who's Who: A-Z (pages 13 to 452); secondly, FA Barclaycard Premiership and Coca-Cola League Clubs: Summary of Appearances and Goals for 2004-2005 (pages 453 to 474); and thirdly, Where Did They Go? (pages 475 to 479); lists all players shown in the previous edition who either moved on or did not play in 2004-05. Below is an explanation on how to follow the PFA Footballers' Who's Who.

As the title suggests, all players are listed in alphabetical order and are shown by Surnames first, followed by full Christian names, with the one the player is commonly known by shown in bold. Any abbreviation or pseudonym is bracketed.

Birthplace/date: You will note that several players who would be predominately classified as British, were born in places like Germany and India, for example. My book, Premier and Football League Players' Records, which covers every man who has played league football since the war, has, in the past, used the family domicile as a more realistic 'birthplace'. But, for our purposes here, I have reverted to that which has been officially recorded.

Height and Weight: Listed in feet and inches, and stones and pounds, respectively. It must be remembered that a player's weight can frequently change and, on that basis, the recorded data should be used as a guide only, especially as players are weighed several times during the season.

Club Honours: Those shown, cover careers from the Conference and FA Trophy upwards. For abbreviations, read:- European Honours: UEFACL (UEFA Champions League, formerly known as the European Cup), ESC (European Super Cup), ECWC (European Cup Winners' Cup, not contested since 1999) and UEFAC (UEFA Cup, formerly Fairs Cup). English Honours: FAC (FA Cup), FLC (Football League Cup), CS (Community Shield), FMC (Full Members Cup, which took in the Simod and Zenith Data sponsorships), AMC (Associated Members Cup – Freight Rover, Sherpa Van, Leyland DAF, Autoglass, Auto Windscreens and LDV Vans), AIC (Anglo-Italian Cup), GMVC (GM Vauxhall Conference), FC (Football Conference), NC (Nationwide Conference), FAT (FA Trophy), FAYC (FA Youth Cup). Scottish Honours: SPD (Scottish Premier Division), S Div 1/2 (Scottish Leagues), SC (Scottish Cup), SLC (Scottish League Cup). Please note that medals awarded to P/FL, FLC, and AMC winners relate to players who have appeared in 25%, or over, of matches, while FAC, UEFACL, ESC, ECWC and UEFAC winners' medals are for all-named finalists, including unused subs. For our purposes, however, Community Shield winners' medals refer to men who either played or came on as a sub. Honours applicable to players coming in from abroad are not shown at present, but the position continues to be reviewed.

International Honours: For abbreviations, read:- E (England), NI (Northern Ireland), S (Scotland), W (Wales) and RoI (Republic of Ireland). Under 21 through to full internationals give total appearances (inclusive of subs), while schoolboy (U16s and U18s) and youth representatives are just listed. The cut-off date used for appearances was up to and including 1 July 2005.

Player Descriptions: Gives position and playing strengths and, in keeping the work topical, a few words on how their season went in 2004-05. This takes into account, in a positive fashion, key performances, along with value to the team, injuries, honours, and other points of interest, etc. Since 1999-2000, trainees were gradually superseded by scholars under the new scholarship scheme, but for our purposes the young players who come through the club are still denoted as trainees.

Career Records: Full appearances, plus substitutes and goals, are given for all FA Barclaycard Premiership and Coca-Cola League games and, if a player who is in the book has played in any of the senior Scottish Leagues, his appearances with the club in question will also be recorded at the point of signing. Other information given, includes the players' source (clubs in the non-leagues, junior football, or from abroad), registered signing dates (if a player signs permanently following a loan spell, for our purposes, we have shown the initial date as being the point of transfer. Also, loan transfers are only recorded if an appearance is made) and transfer fees (these are the figures that have been reported in newspapers and magazines and should only be used as a guide to a player's valuation). Appearances, substitutions and goals are recorded by P/FL (Premiership and Football League), PL (Premier League), FL (Football League), FLC (Football League Cup), FAC (FA Cup), and Others. Other matches take in the Play Offs, LDV Vans Trophy, Community Shield, and European competitions, such as the European Champions League, UEFA Cup, European Super Cup and Inter-Toto Cup. All of these matches are lumped together for reasons of saving space. Scottish appearances for players on loan to P/FL clubs in 2004-05 are shown at the point of transfer and do not include games following their return to Scotland. That also applies to players transferred from England to Scotland. FA Cup appearances, subs and goals are only recorded when they are made playing for a P/FL club and do not cover appearances made by Conference sides prior to joining or after relegation from the Football League.

Career statistics are depicted as
Appearances + Substitutes/Goals

Whether you wish to analyse someone for your fantasy football team selection or would like to know more about a little-known player appearing in the lower reaches of the game, the PFA Footballers' Who's Who should provide you with the answer.

Barry J. Hugman, Editor, PFA Footballers' Who's Who

A

ABBEY George Peterson
Born: Port Harcourt, Nigeria, 20 October 1978
Height: 5'10" **Weight:** 11.13
International Honours: Nigeria: 16
George spent the first half of last season on trial with a number of clubs before joining Port Vale towards the end of the year. He made his debut as a substitute against Oldham and went on to become a regular in the team, helping them to keep away from the relegation zone. A pacy and strong defender, he missed the game at Hull because he was away on international duty with Nigeria and was forced to sit out the last three games of the season with a hamstring strain.
Macclesfield T *(Signed from Sharks FC, Port Harcourt, Nigeria, on 20/8/1999) FL 79+21/1 FLC 5+1 FAC 5+4 Others 2 (Freed during 2004 close season)*
Port Vale *(Free, following various trials, on 17/12/2004) FL 16+2*

ABBEY Nathanael (Nathan)
Born: Islington, 11 July 1978
Height: 6'1" **Weight:** 12.0
Nathan had an excellent first season as goalkeeper with League Two club Boston United missing just two first-team games both as a result of a fractured finger. He was always dominant inside his own penalty area and produced many excellent reaction saves. Nathan is the brother of striker Zema Abbey who, for a brief loan period, played alongside him for the Pilgrims.
Luton T *(From trainee on 2/5/1996) FL 54+1 FLC 3 FAC 8 Others 2*
Chesterfield *(Free on 10/8/2001) FL 46 FLC 1 FAC 3 Others 3*
Northampton T *(Free on 6/8/2002) FL 4+1 FLC 1 Others 2 (Free to Stevenage Borough during 2003 close season)*
Boston U *(Free, via St Albans C, trials at Luton T, Macclesfield T, Ipswich T, Burnley, on 6/8/2004) FL 44 FLC 2 FAC 4 Others 1*

ABBEY Zema
Born: Luton, 17 April 1977
Height: 6'1" **Weight:** 12.11
This stocky striker joined his brother Nathan at Boston United last August after signing on a month's loan from Premiership club Norwich City. Zema, who had just recovered from a groin injury, scored with a close-range header in his second appearance against Chester City but struggled to impress. Soon after returning to Carrow Road he was released and joined Wycombe on a short-

Nathan Abbey

term deal, but he failed to register a goal and his next port of call was Valley Parade. He made a dramatic entrance, scoring a superb goal in the opening minutes of his debut and then receiving a red card. Zema spent the closing months of the season on another short-term contract at Torquay, scoring a vital winner at MK Dons, but nevertheless he was unable to lead the Gulls away from the relegation zone and was released once more in the summer.
Cambridge U *(Signed from Hitchin T on 11/2/2000) FL 16+6/5 FLC 1+1 FAC 1 Others 1*
Norwich C *(£350,000 on 15/12/2000) FL 30+29/7 FLC 1 FAC 1+2/1*
Boston U *(Loaned on 26/8/2004) FL 3+2/1*
Wycombe W *(Free on 7/10/2004) FL 3+2 Others 1*
Bradford C *(Free on 19/11/2004) FL 6/1*
Torquay U *(Free, via trial at Stoke C, on 2/3/2005) FL 2+4/1*

ABBOTT Pawel Tadeusz Howard

Born: York, 2 December 1981
Height: 6'1" **Weight:** 11.12
International Honours: Poland: U21
This young striker started the 2004-05 campaign on the substitutes' bench for Huddersfield, and duly rewarded the Galpharm faithful with a last-minute winner at Stockport. Once back in the line-up Pawel netted a hat-trick in the away win at Port Vale. The pacy front man showed great control and passing skills, and when on form he proved to be a real handful for opposition defenders. A very healthy return of 27 goals made him top scorer for the season at the club.
Preston NE *(£125,000 + from LKS Lodz, Poland on 16/2/2001) FL 8+17/6 FLC 0+1 FAC 1+3*
Bury *(Loaned on 9/8/2002) FL 13/5 FLC 2 Others 1*
Bury *(Loaned on 18/3/2003) FL 4/1*
Huddersfield T *(Signed on 16/2/2004) FL 48+9/31 FLC 1 FAC 1/1 Others 1+2*

ACHTERBERG John

Born: Utrecht, Holland, 8 July 1971
Height: 6'1" **Weight:** 13.8
This tall goalkeeper continued to be first choice at Tranmere last term, with the only hiccup in his season coming when he was forced to sit out a run of matches at the turn of the year after suffering a knee injury. Dedicated in the extreme, John is always putting in extra training as well as sessions in the gym, and he signed a new contract with the club just before the end of the season, with the intention of also taking on some School of Excellence coaching. John's calm authority, reliability and dominance around the box continue to inspire confidence in his defence, and he is particularly adept with his distribution.
Tranmere Rov *(Free from Eindhoven FC, Holland, ex NAC Breda, on 22/9/1998) FL 219+3 FLC 16+1 FAC 22 Others 8*

ADAGGIO Marco

Born: Malaga, Spain, 6 October 1987
Height: 5'8" **Weight:** 12.4
This young striker spent much of last season in the Shrewsbury reserve team, but after netting a hat-trick against Carlisle he was given his senior debut as a substitute in the 3-0 home win over Oxford at the beginning of April. Marco made four further appearances, and became an instant favourite of the Gay Meadow crowd.
Shrewsbury T *(From juniors on 31/3/2005) FL 0+5*

ADAMS Daniel (Danny) Benjamin

Born: Manchester, 3 January 1976
Height: 5'8" **Weight:** 13.9
Danny was Stockport's first-choice left back for most of the 2004-05 campaign, and it was not until October that he missed a game for the club. He celebrated his first and only goal for County with a superb left-foot strike in the home defeat by, Hull in January. Soon afterwards he was snapped up by Huddersfield and quickly settled in, providing some telling crosses for the strikers to feed off. A strong tackler, what he lacks in pace he more than makes up for in his reading of the game.
Macclesfield T *(£25,000 from Altrincham on 31/8/2000) FL 146+2/1 FLC 5+1 FAC 12 Others 3/1*
Stockport Co *(Signed on 5/3/2004) FL 39/1 FLC 1 FAC 2 Others 1*
Huddersfield T *(Free on 24/3/2005) FL 5*

ADAMS Stephen (Steve) Marc

Born: Plymouth, 25 September 1980
Height: 6'0" **Weight:** 11.10
Club Honours: Div 3 '02; Div 2 '04
Steve started the first five games of the 2004-05 season in his favoured position of central midfield for Plymouth Argyle, but then played in a number of different roles, his best performances coming when he lined up just in front of the back four. Steve scored his only goal for Plymouth in the defeat against Ipswich in September, but a lack of regular first-team action saw him move on to Sheffield Wednesday where he linked up with his former manager Paul Sturrock once more. Strong in the tackle and a good reader of the game, he looked to be a useful addition to the Owls' squad.
Plymouth Arg *(From trainee on 6/7/1999) FL 131+26/7 FLC 4 FAC 7+3 Others 4+2*
Sheffield Wed *(Free on 9/3/2005) FL 8+1 Others 0+1*

ADAMSON Christopher (Chris)

Born: Ashington, 4 November 1978
Height: 6'1" **Weight:** 11.12
Chris joined Sheffield Wednesday during the January transfer window as cover for injured goalkeeper David Lucas. However, he had few chances to impress during his stay at Hillsborough, managing only two first-team appearances, one of which came from the bench.
West Bromwich A *(From trainee on 2/7/1997) FL 12 FAC 2 (Freed on 7/4/2003)*
Mansfield T *(Loaned on 30/4/1999) FL 2*
Halifax T *(Loaned on 1/7/1999) FL 7*
Plymouth Arg *(Loaned on 10/1/2002) FL 1*
Sheffield Wed *(Free from St Patricks on 28/1/2005) FL 1+1*

ADEBOLA Bamberdele (Dele)

Born: Lagos, Nigeria, 23 June 1975
Height: 6'3" **Weight:** 12.8
This tall Coventry centre forward went on loan to Bradford City for the first two months of the 2004-05 campaign, forming an effective strike partnership with Dean Windass. Dele scored four goals, including a superbly taken winner at MK Dons in stoppage time and looked set to sign for the Yorkshire club but could not agree terms. However, on his return to Highfield Road he deservedly won a regular place in the team and his 100 per cent effort not only won the fans over, but also made him something of a cult hero. He netted six goals for the Sky Blues including brilliant solo efforts against Nottingham Forest and Derby and an excellent header against his old club Crewe on the last day of the season.
Crewe Alex *(From trainee on 21/6/1993) FL 98+26/39 FLC 4+3/2 FAC 8+2/3 Others 10+1/2*
Birmingham C *(£1,000,000 on 6/2/1998) FL 86+43/31 FLC 13+4/8 FAC 2+1/2 Others 1+2/1*
Oldham Ath *(Loaned on 20/3/2002) FL 5*
Crystal Palace *(Free on 15/8/2002) FL 32+7/5 FLC 5/2 FAC 4*
Coventry C *(Free on 2/7/2003) FL 33+20/7 FLC 2/1 FAC 2+2/1*
Burnley *(Loaned on 25/3/2004) FL 0+3/1*
Bradford C *(Loaned on 13/8/2004) FL 14+1/3 Others 1/1*

ADVICE-DESRUISSEAUX Frederic

Born: Paris, France, 12 January 1983
Height: 5'9" **Weight:** 11.7

Frédéric signed for Kidderminster in the summer of 2004 following a successful pre-season trial when he featured at both right back and in midfield. The step-up to the League Two football, however, proved a little too much and he was not so successful in competitive matches. Following a change in management he was released by Harriers in December.
Kidderminster Hrs *(Free from OSC Lille, France on 6/8/2004) FL 9 FLC 1*

AGOGO Manuel (Junior)

Born: Accra, Ghana, 1 August 1979
Height: 5'10" **Weight:** 11.7
International Honours: E: SP-3
Junior was in excellent form for Bristol Rovers last term and finished the season as leading scorer with a tally of 22 goals. Perhaps his best strikes were the winner at Mansfield Town on the opening day of the season and a superb volley at Southend in the LDV Vans Southern Area final. His pace and ability to run at defenders proved real assets for the team as was his ability to work alongside a series of different partners throughout the campaign.
Sheffield Wed *(Free from Willesden Constantine on 8/10/1996) PL 0+2 FAC 0+1 (Free to Colorado Rapids, USA on 2/2/2000)*
Oldham Ath *(Loaned on 18/7/1999) FL 2*
Chester C *(Loaned on 3/9/1999) FL 10/6*
Chesterfield *(Loaned on 11/11/1999) FL 3+1*
Lincoln C *(Loaned on 17/12/1999) FL 3/1*
Queens Park Rgrs *(Free from San Jose Earthquakes, USA on 28/3/2002) FL 0+2 (Free to Barnet on 4/7/2002)*
Bristol Rov *(£110,000 + on 1/7/2003) FL 65+16/25 FLC 2+1 FAC 2 Others 2+2/2*

AGYEMANG Patrick

Born: Walthamstow, 29 September 1980
Height: 6'1" **Weight:** 12.0
International Honours: Ghana: 1
A pacy, skilful striker, great things were expected of Patrick during the 2004-05 season. Unfortunately the signings of Iwan Roberts and Darren Byfield meant he found himself on the bench for a great majority of the time, although he did score twice in a 2-2 draw at Coventry. In November he moved on to Preston, where he made a good impact, but only managed two goals in 13 starts before dropping to the bench. He was then brought on regularly to give run at tiring defences, in which capacity he contributed the clinching goal at Upton Park in March.
Wimbledon *(From trainee on 11/5/1999) FL 68+53/20 FLC 3+2/1 FAC 8+3/1*
Brentford *(Loaned on 18/10/1999) FL 3+9 FAC 1*
Gillingham *(£200,000 on 13/1/2004) FL 29+4/8 FLC 1*
Preston NE *(£350,000 on 17/11/2004) FL 15+12/4 FAC 1 Others 0+3*

AHMED Adnan Farooq

Born: Burnley, 7 June 1984
Height: 5'10" **Weight:** 11.12
Adnan made a couple of appearances from the bench for Huddersfield in the LDV Vans Trophy ties last season, scoring a blistering long-range goal in the defeat at Blackpool. After some impressive displays for the reserves he stepped in for a run of first-team matches and never let the team down. The industrious midfielder improved with each appearance. Strong, creative and a good passer of the ball, he was always at the hub of the action. Adnan scored his first League goal in the emphatic home win over Stockport County and also won the 'Reserves Player of the Year' award.
Huddersfield T *(From trainee on 22/8/2003) FL 16+3/1 Others 0+2/1*

AHMED Shahed

Born: East Ham, 13 September 1985
Height: 5'10" **Weight:** 11.2
This pacy striker or wide midfielder made a surprise senior debut for Wycombe as a substitute on the opening day of the 2004-05 season at home to Cambridge. Later in August he scored at Kidderminster with a far post knock-in, but after five appearances, all from the bench, he drifted out of manager Tony Adams plans.
Wycombe W *(From trainee at Wimbledon on 1/7/2004) FL 0+4/1 Others 0+1*

AINSWORTH Gareth

Born: Blackburn, 10 May 1973
Height: 5'9" **Weight:** 12.5
This wide-right midfield player started the 2004-05 season in exactly the same way as the previous one, by scoring after just five minutes of the opening game. In his second outing he suffered a serious leg injury which kept him out of the side for three months. Gareth was then a regular, either starting or coming on from the bench and missed just one game in four months before his season ended in March with a knee injury.
Preston NE *(Signed from Northwich Vic, ex Blackburn Rov YTS, on 21/1/1992) FL 2+3 Others 1/1*
Cambridge U *(Free on 17/8/1992) FL 1+3/1 FLC 0+1*
Preston NE *(Free on 23/12/1992) FL 76+6/12 FLC 3+2 FAC 3+1 Others 8+1/1*
Lincoln C *(£25,000 on 31/10/1995) FL 83/37 FLC 8/3 FAC 2 Others 4/1*
Port Vale *(£500,000 on 12/9/1997) FL 53+2/10 FLC 2/1 FAC 2*
Wimbledon *(£2,000,000 on 3/11/1998) P/FL 21+15/6 FLC 1+1 FAC 5+2/1*
Preston NE *(Loaned on 28/3/2002) FL 3+2/1*
Walsall *(Loaned on 5/12/2002) FL 2+3/1*
Cardiff C *(£50,000 on 17/3/2003) FL 9*
Queens Park Rgrs *(Free on 17/7/2003) FL 35+16/8 FLC 2+1/1 FAC 2 Others 2*

AISTON Samuel (Sam) James

Born: Newcastle, 21 November 1976
Height: 6'1" **Weight:** 12.10
Club Honours: Div 1 '96
International Honours: E: Sch
This skilful left winger had something of a mixed season at Shrewsbury last term when he was not always a first choice in the line-up and he contributed just a single goal, netting in the 4-0 home win over Darlington. A player with excellent ball control and a great turn of speed he left many defenders for dead, but was not always able to deliver a quality ball into the box. Sam was released by Shrewsbury in the summer.
Sunderland *(From Newcastle U juniors on 14/7/1995) P/FL 5+15 FLC 0+2 FAC 0+2*
Chester C *(Loaned on 21/2/1997) FL 14 Others 2*
Chester C *(Loaned on 27/11/1998) FL 11 Others 1*
Stoke C *(Loaned on 6/8/1999) FL 2+4 FLC 1*
Shrewsbury T *(Loaned on 24/12/1999) FL 10*
Shrewsbury T *(Free on 21/7/2000) FL 99+34/7 FLC 3 FAC 2+2 Others 1+3*

AKINBIYI Adeola (Ade) Oluwatoyin

Born: Hackney, 10 October 1974
Height: 6'1" **Weight:** 12.9
International Honours: Nigeria: 1
Fast and direct, Ade quickly became the fan's favourite at Stoke last season. He was played mainly as a lone striker but never wavered in his determination and was top scorer before his transfer to Burnley early in the new year. His impact for the Clarets was twice delayed, firstly by a thigh strain which postponed his debut, and secondly by being suspended following his sending off in only the third minute of his debut, in the home game against Sunderland. Even in that brief appearance, though, there was enough to suggest that he could be the answer to the team's goal shortage, and his first strike duly arrived on his first full appearance, away at Sheffield United. His sheer physical presence is sufficient to disturb most Championship defenders, and Ade looks set to be the leader of the front line that the Clarets lacked for much of the 2004-05 season.
Norwich C *(From trainee on 5/2/1993) P/FL 22+27/3 FLC 2+4/2 FAC 0+2 Others 0+1*

Ade Akinbiyi

Hereford U *(Loaned on 21/1/1994) FL 3+1/2*
Brighton & Hove A *(Loaned on 24/11/1994) FL 7/4*
Gillingham *(£250,000 on 13/1/1997) FL 63/28 FLC 2 FAC 2/1 Others 0+1*
Bristol C *(£1,200,000 on 28/5/1998) FL 47/21 FLC 5/4 FAC 1*
Wolverhampton W *(£3,500,000 on 7/9/1999) FL 36+1/16 FAC 3*
Leicester C *(£5,000,000 on 28/7/2000) PL 49+9/11 FLC 1/1 FAC 5+1/1 Others 2*
Crystal Palace *(£2,200,000 + on 6/2/2002) FL 11+13/3 FAC 0+4*
Stoke C *(Loaned on 27/3/2003) FL 4/2*
Stoke C *(Free on 15/9/2003) FL 52+7/17 FLC 0+1 FAC 2*
Burnley *(£600,000 on 24/2/2005) FL 9+1/4*

AKINFENWA Saheed Adebayo

Born: Nigeria, 10 May 1982
Height: 5'11" **Weight:** 13.0
A summer signing from Doncaster, Adebayo's early displays for Torquay showed a lack of fitness and discipline. A match-winning two-goal performance, marred by a red card for over-celebrating the winner, against Yeovil in the LDV Vans Trophy turned the tide. Benefiting from the guidance of manager Leroy Rosenior, he developed into an extremely effective centre forward, ending the campaign as the supporters' 'Player Of The Season' with 16 goals to his name. Immensely strong and powerful, with good close control and surprising speed for a man so big, he has the natural attributes to progress further.
Boston U *(Free from Barry T, ex FK Atlantas, on 15/10/2003) FL 2+1 Others 1/1*
Leyton Orient *(Free on 31/10/2003) FL 0+1 FAC 0+1*
Rushden & Diamonds *(Free on 11/12/2003)*
Doncaster Rov *(Free on 18/2/2004) FL 4+5/4*
Torquay U *(Free on 1/7/2004) FL 28+9/14 FLC 0+1 FAC 1 Others 1+1/2*

ALBRECHTSEN Martin

Born: Copenhagen, Denmark, 31 March 1980
Height: 6'1" **Weight:** 12.13
International Honours: Denmark: 3; U21-14; Yth
This tall full back became West Bromwich Albion's-joint record signing when he signed for the club in the summer of 2004. After taking time to settle at the Hawthorns, he finally established himself in the right-wing-back position following the arrival of new boss Bryan Robson. A powerful competitor, quick in recovery and with a terrific engine, he then

enjoyed a long run in the side right through to the end of the season.
West Bromwich A *(£2,700,000 from FC Copenhagen, Denmark, on 30/6/2004) PL 20+4 FLC 1 FAC 3*

ALBRIGHTON Mark Christopher
Born: Nuneaton, 6 March 1976
Height: 6'1" **Weight:** 12.7
Club Honours: Div 3 '04
An essential pillar of strength in the previous season's success Mark started the 2004-05 campaign out of the Doncaster team as new signing Nicky Fenton was preferred in the centre of defence. However, he had a brief run in the side in the autumn and then returned to the line-up for the Boxing Day win over Milton Keynes. He remained there until mid-February when a leg injury struck to rule him out for the remainder of the campaign.
Doncaster Rov *(Signed from Telford U, ex Nuneaton Borough, Atherstone U, on 5/7/2002) FL 42+3/4 FLC 1 FAC 1 Others 2*

ALEXANDER Gary George
Born: Lambeth, 15 August 1979
Height: 5'11" **Weight:** 13.0
Gary struggled with an injury for the first part of the 2004-05 season before having an operation in October, and this ruled him out of the Leyton Orient line-up for three months. A hard-working centre forward with an eye for a goal, he forged a useful partnership with fellow striker Lee Steele. Gary finished the season on a high by registering doubles against Wycombe and Mansfield to reach a tally of ten goals.
West Ham U *(From trainee on 6/7/1998)*
Exeter C *(Loaned on 19/8/1999) FL 37/16 FLC 1 FAC 3/1 Others 4/2*
Swindon T *(£300,000 on 11/8/2000) FL 30+7/7 FLC 3 FAC 2+1 Others 2+1/2*
Hull C *(£160,000 on 21/6/2001) FL 64+4/23 FLC 3/2 FAC 3/2 Others 4/3*
Leyton Orient *(Signed on 27/1/2003) FL 81+8/26 FLC 1+1 FAC 2/1 Others 1+2/1*

Martin Albrechtsen

ALEXANDER Graham
Born: Coventry, 10 October 1971
Height: 5'10" **Weight:** 12.7
Club Honours: Div 2 '00
International Honours: S: 16; B-1
One of Preston's senior pros, Graham had a renaissance under Billy Davies and was once again rewarded by selection for the PFA Championship team of the season. His form was uncertain early on and he found himself relegated to the bench for a couple of games around Christmas, but he marked his return to form with a recall to the Scotland squad. By the season's end, the right back was close to 700 career games and 100 goals. Sadly Graham missed the play-off semi-finals through injury and only made a late substitute appearance at the Millennium Stadium.
Scunthorpe U *(From trainee on 20/3/1990) FL 149+10/18 FLC 11+1/2 FAC 12/1 Others 13+4/3*
Luton T *(£100,000 on 8/7/1995) FL 146+4/15 FLC 17/2 FAC 7+1 Others 6+2*
Preston NE *(£50,000 on 25/3/1999) FL 266+1/43 FLC 19/5 FAC 14/4 Others 6+1*

ALEXANDER Neil
Born: Edinburgh, 10 March 1978
Height: 6'1" **Weight:** 11.0
Club Honours: S Div 2 '99; S Div 1 '01
International Honours: S: B-1; U21-10
When the 2004-05 season began Neil was third-choice 'keeper at Cardiff, but then a dip in form by Tony Warner and an injury to Martyn Margetson meant Neil was thrust back into the starting line-up in mid-January. After a steady start he began to excel as the season drew to a close and turned in a trio of stunning performances against Preston, Leicester and Reading in April that were massively significant in Cardiff's survival.
Stenhousemuir *(Free from Edina Hibs on 8/8/1996) SL 48 SLC 1 SC 1 Others 1*
Livingston *(Signed on 22/8/1998) SL 60 SLC 2 SC 8 Others 5*
Cardiff C *(£200,000 on 6/8/2001) FL 127+1 FLC 4 FAC 8 Others 5*

ALIADIERE Jeremie
Born: Rambouillet, France, 30 March 1983
Height: 6'0" **Weight:** 11.8
Club Honours: FAYC '01; PL '04; CS '04
International Honours: France: U21; Yth
Jeremie suffered a knee ligament injury in the FA Community Shield victory over Manchester United and this ruined his season for Arsenal. The pacy striker fought his way back to return as an extra-time substitute in the FA Cup fifth round replay at Bramall Lane and almost won the tie within seconds of his arrival on the pitch. He continued to make fleeting appearances from the bench for the rest of the campaign as he built up his match fitness.
Arsenal *(From trainee on 4/4/2000) PL 3+15/1 FLC 3+2/4 FAC 1+2 Others 0+2*

ALJOFREE Hasney
Born: Manchester, 11 July 1978
Height: 6'0" **Weight:** 12.1
Club Honours: Div 2 '04
International Honours: E: Yth
Hasney had a frustrating time with injuries last term and these reduced his impact at Plymouth. Early on he linked up with his former boss Paul Sturrock in a loan move to Sheffield Wednesday, but after some impressive performances he returned to Home Park with an injury. He eventually made his first start for the Pilgrims in February and then went on to cement his place in the heart of the defence, but even then he managed to miss the final two games of the campaign after suffering a broken nose.
Bolton W *(From trainee on 2/7/1996) P/FL 6+8 FLC 4+2 FAC 0+2*
Dundee U *(Signed on 9/6/2000) SL 52+2/4 SLC 5+1 SC 5+1/3*
Plymouth Arg *(Signed on 30/8/2002) FL 51+4/2 FLC 2 FAC 1 Others 2*
Sheffield Wed *(Loaned on 23/9/2004) FL 2 Others 1*

ALLEN Damien Samuel
Born: Cheadle, 1 August 1986
Height: 5'11" **Weight:** 11.4
A product of Stockport's youth scheme, Damien made a big impact in the first team last season producing a number of impressive displays. He scored his first goal for the club during the 4-2 victory at home to Doncaster in April and his performances provided a rare highlight in an otherwise disappointing season for County. Damian is an energetic and committed midfielder.
Stockport Co *(From trainee on 12/7/2004) FL 14+7/1 FAC 1 Others 1*

ALLEN Graham
Born: Bolton, 8 April 1977
Height: 6'1" **Weight:** 12.8
International Honours: E: Yth
This no-nonsense central defender was virtually ever-present for Rushden last term until a hip operation ruled him out of the final weeks of the club's successful battle against relegation. Graham scored his first goal for the Nene Park club against Wycombe just before his injury problems. He will be hoping to play a key role again in 2005-06 after making a full recovery to fitness.
Everton *(From trainee on 10/12/1994) PL 2+4*
Tranmere Rov *(Free on 28/8/1998) FL 193+7/10 FLC 14+2/1 FAC 19 Others 3*
Rushden & Diamonds *(Free on 12/7/2004) FL 25+1/1 FAC 2 Others 1*

ALLISON Wayne Anthony
Born: Huddersfield, 16 October 1968
Height: 6'1" **Weight:** 12.6
Club Honours: Div 2 '96
Wayne became one of the oldest-ever debutants for Chesterfield when he played, and scored, against Brentford on the opening day of the 2004-05 campaign. He subsequently rolled back the years to produce a series of fine performances as an old-fashioned centre forward. His presence had a beneficial effect both on and off the pitch, and his experience and maturity were invaluable in helping bring on some of the younger members of the squad.
Halifax T *(From trainee on 6/7/1987) FL 74+10/23 FLC 3/2 FAC 4+1/2 Others 8+1/3*
Watford *(£250,000 on 26/7/1989) FL 6+1*
Bristol C *(£300,000 on 9/8/1990) FL 149+46/48 FLC 4+5/2 FAC 12+1/5 Others 6+2/3*
Swindon T *(£475,000 on 22/7/1995) FL 98+3/31 FLC 9/3 FAC 7/2 Others 3*
Huddersfield T *(£800,000 on 11/11/1997) FL 71+3/15 FLC 3+1/2 FAC 6/2*
Tranmere Rov *(£300,000 on 3/9/1999) FL 85+18/26 FLC 4+3/1 FAC 6+1/5 Others 1*
Sheffield U *(Free on 30/7/2002) FL 29+44/7 FLC 7+1/1 FAC 4+4/2 Others 0+2*
Chesterfield *(Free on 30/7/2004) FL 27+11/6 Others 1*

ALLOTT Mark Stephen
Born: Manchester, 3 October 1977
Height: 5'11" **Weight:** 12.6
Mark made the position on the right side of Chesterfield's midfield his own last term. He can tackle, pass with either foot and has the vision to spot colleagues in good positions some distance away. His long throw caused disruption in many an opposition defence and he earned the full respect of all Spireites' supporters.
Oldham Ath *(From trainee on 14/10/1995) FL 105+49/31 FLC 7+3/2 FAC 8+7 Others 2+3*
Chesterfield *(Free on 19/12/2001) FL 123+16/8 FLC 3+1/2 FAC 3 Others 3+2/1*

ALLSOPP Daniel (Danny)
Born: Melbourne, Australia, 10 August 1978
Height: 6'1" **Weight:** 12.0
International Honours: Australia: U23-7; Yth
After enjoying tremendous success in 2003-04, Danny was always going to struggle to repeat such an outstanding campaign particularly as his established strike partner Ben Burgess missed most of the season through injury. However, the natural predator still made a telling contribution of seven goals as Hull completed a second successive promotion. Danny left the Tigers shortly before the end of the season after agreeing a deal with Melbourne Victory of the new Hyundai A-League.
Manchester C *(£10,000 from Carlton, Australia, ex South Melbourne Lakers, on 7/8/1998) P/FL 3+26/4 FLC 0+7/1 Others 1+1/1*
Notts Co *(Loaned on 5/11/1999) FL 3/1*
Wrexham *(Loaned on 25/2/2000) FL 3/4*
Bristol Rov *(Loaned on 12/10/2000) FL 4+2*
Notts Co *(£300,000 on 22/11/2000) FL 97+8/42 FLC 3/4 FAC 8/4 Others 2+2/3*
Hull C *(£100,000 on 7/5/2003) FL 45+19/22 FLC 1 FAC 1+1*

ALMUNIA Manuel
Born: Pamplona, Spain, 19 May 1977
Height: 6'4" **Weight:** 11.8
Club Honours: FAC '05
This Spanish goalkeeper suddenly found himself thrust into the first-team spotlight for Arsenal last December when he made his Premiership debut at home to Birmingham City. He started 11 consecutive games, keeping five clean sheets in the process, before losing out to Jens Lehmann again. Manuel enjoyed his best moment of season in the FA Cup fifth round replay at Sheffield United when he kept a clean sheet throughout and then made two stunning penalty saves as the Gunners triumphed in the shoot-out.
Arsenal *(£500,000 from Celta Vigo, Spain, on 19/7/2004) PL 10 FLC 3 FAC 2 Others 1*

ALNWICK Benjamin (Ben) Robert
Born: Prudhoe, 1 January 1987
Height: 6'2" **Weight:** 13.12
International Honours: E: Yth
This teenaged goalkeeper sat on the bench on 28 occasions last term before an injury crisis at Sunderland handed him

Xabi Alonso

his League debut in April. Ben's first appearance saw him turn in a superb performance at the Stadium of Light against Leicester as the Wearsiders clinched promotion back to the Premiership, and he followed this up by performing admirably away at West Ham a week later as the Championship title was secured. Tall and extremely agile, Ben belies his age when commanding his penalty area and looks to have an exciting career ahead of him.
Sunderland *(From trainee on 13/3/2004) FL 3*

ALONSO Xabi

Born: Tolosa, Spain, 25 November 1981
Height: 6'0" **Weight:** 11.2
Club Honours: UEFACL '05
International Honours: Spain: 17
One of the most gifted Spanish players of his generation, Xabi was the biggest of the signings made by new Liverpool manager Rafael Benitez in the summer of 2004. A holding midfielder he is noted for his ball control and accurately weighted passes over short and long range and is already an automatic selection for the Spanish national team. After a slow start to his Anfield career his first notable contribution came at Fulham in October when, as a half-time substitute, he orchestrated a second-half turn around and scored his first goal for the Reds with a deflected free kick in the 4-2 victory. He also played a starring role in the stunning last-gasp victory over reigning champions Arsenal in December, scoring the opening goal. Just as he was running into top form his season was cut short by an ankle injury incurred at home to Chelsea on New Year's Day. Happily Xabi returned to action in time for the climactic end-of-season games in the European Champions' Cup. His come-back match away to Juventus in Turin was probably his best performance of the season, dictating the pace of the game with his ball retention and short passes and thus preventing the Italian team building any momentum to score the single goal they needed to win the tie. In the final in Istanbul his coolness under pressure was crucial to Liverpool's amazing comeback and although his penalty to bring the scores level at 3-3 was saved he had the presence of mind to follow up and place the rebound high into the net.
Liverpool *(Signed from Real Sociedad, Spain, on 27/8/2004) PL 20+4/2 Others 7+1/1*

ALSOP Julian Mark

Born: Nuneaton, 28 May 1973
Height: 6'4" **Weight:** 14.0
Club Honours: Div 3 '00

Julian Alsop

This big striker featured for Oxford at the start of the 2004-05 campaign under Graham Rix but failed to manage a goal in his five appearances and was soon on his way following a well-publicised training-ground incident. He joined Northampton on a short-term contract, where he was mostly used as a substitute before moving on again to sign for Conference outfit Forest Green Rovers.
Bristol Rov *(£15,000 from Halesowen on 14/2/1997) FL 20+13/4 FLC 2/1 FAC 1/1 Others 2*
Swansea C *(Loaned on 20/1/1998) FL 5/2*
Swansea C *(£30,000 on 12/3/1998) FL 73+12/14 FLC 4+2 FAC 6+1/1 Others 5*
Cheltenham T *(Free on 3/7/2000) FL 99+18/35 FLC 4+1 FAC 8+2/6 Others 6+1/3*
Oxford U *(Free on 8/7/2003) FL 29+5/5 FLC 1 FAC 1*
Northampton T *(Free on 22/10/2004) FL 1+6/1 FAC 0+1 Others 2/1*

AMANKWAAH Kevin Osei-Kuffour
Born: Harrow, 19 May 1982
Height: 6'1" **Weight:** 12.0
Club Honours: Div 2 '05
International Honours: E: Yth
This tall, rangy right back or central defender again failed to fulfil his potential at Bristol City last term, when he was restricted to sporadic appearances in the first half of the campaign. In February he moved on to join League Two promotion candidates Yeovil Town and featured regularly in the match squad for the remainder of the campaign.
Bristol C *(From trainee on 16/6/2000) FL 35+19/1 FLC 2+1/1 FAC 1+1/2 Others 7+2/1*
Torquay U *(Loaned on 25/1/2003) FL 6*
Cheltenham T *(Loaned on 16/8/2003) FL 11+1*
Yeovil T *(Signed on 3/2/2005) FL 10+5*

AMBROSE Darren Paul
Born: Harlow, 29 February 1984
Height: 5'11" **Weight:** 10.5
International Honours: E: U21-5; Yth
Darren is a hard-working player who was used mainly on the right of Newcastle's midfield last term, and occasionally in the centre. His first-team opportunities were limited, not helped by suffering a knee injury during the pre-season, and for most of the first half of the campaign he warmed the bench, being used only occasionally. Darren displayed his attacking flair at Bolton in October when he scored with a stunning strike from 30 yards, but this failed to secure him a start. However, he was in the line-up at Old Trafford in April when he scored a fine goal after a penetrating run and ended the season with a spell in the side. He continued to be a regular selection for the England U21 squad.
Ipswich T *(From trainee on 3/7/2001) P/FL 20+10/8 FLC 2/1 FAC 1+1/1 Others 3+1/1*
Newcastle U *(£1,000,000 on 25/3/2003) PL 18+19/5 FLC 1+1 FAC 0+2 Others 8+7/1*

AMEOBI Foluwashola (Shola)
Born: Zaria, Nigeria, 12 October 1981
Height: 6'2" **Weight:** 12.0
International Honours: E: U21-21
Shola is a highly rated striker who displays excellent ball skills for such a tall player but needs to impose himself on the opposition and improve his strike rate if he is to fully realise his potential. Injuries restricted his opportunities for Newcastle early on last season, but after Craig Bellamy left for Celtic in January he was given a run in the starting line-up. He came off the bench in the UEFA Cup tie at Panionios to gain a match-winning penalty, but his best game of the season was at home to Arsenal. He also netted the club's only goal in the FA Cup semi-final defeat by Manchester United.
Newcastle U *(From trainee on 19/10/1998) PL 59+61/16 FLC 4+2/3 FAC 5+5/3 Others 24+12/10*

AMOO Ryan Lee
Born: Leicester, 11 October 1983
Height: 5'10" **Weight:** 9.12
Club Honours: FAYC '02
Ryan had something of a disappointing time at Northampton last term and after suffering an early-season suspension he found it difficult to win his place back as the midfield took on a settled look. He found himself well down the pecking order and was released shortly before the end of the season.
Aston Villa *(From trainee on 26/7/2001)*
Northampton T *(Free on 23/3/2004) FL 2+4*

AMORUSO Lorenzo
Born: Bari, Italy, 28 June 1971
Height: 6'2" **Weight:** 13.10
Club Honours: SPD '99, '00, '03; SC '98, '99, '02, '03; SLC '99, '02, '03
Although he made the starting line-up for the opening Premiership game of the season, Lorenzo soon lost his place at Blackburn and thereafter only made sporadic appearances, and none at all after October. The experienced defender missed three months of the season with a heel injury but will be hoping for much better fortunes in 2005-06.
Glasgow Rgrs *(£5,000,000 from Fiorentina, Italy, ex Bari, on 29/5/1997) SL 149/13 SLC 13/2 SC 21+2/5 Others 41/4*
Blackburn Rov *(£1,400,000 on 15/7/2003) PL 16+2/3 FLC 1 Others 2*

ANACLET Edward (Eddie) Bahati Obara
Born: Arusha, Tanzania, 31 August 1985
Height: 5'9" **Weight:** 10.5
This versatile Southampton youngster featured both as a striker and at right back for the club's reserve team last season. Eddie made the step-up to full professional status during the campaign and made his bow in senior football during a loan spell at Chester when he came on as a substitute for striker Robbie Booth in the FA Cup tie at Halifax. Soon after returning to St Mary's he suffered a broken ankle, but he was back in action for Saints' second string shortly before the end of the season.
Southampton *(From trainee on 8/12/2004)*
Chester C *(Loaned on 3/12/2004) FAC 0+1*

ANDERSEN Stephan Maigaard
Born: Copenhagen, Denmark, 26 November 1981
Height: 6'2" **Weight:** 13.0
International Honours: Denmark: 1; U21-21; Yth
Stephan was signed by Charlton as cover for Dean Kiely, and had spent the entire season on the bench until he was surprisingly named in the starting line-up for the home game against Manchester United in May. He performed very well, despite a 0-4 defeat, and kept his place for the away game at Chelsea the following week. Again he made some excellent saves, even keeping out Claude Makelele's penalty, before unfortunately being beaten by the follow up. Stephan is tall and well built and is surprisingly agile for such a big man. He is a good shot-stopper, comfortable with crosses and not afraid to come of his line when necessary. He also has a very long throw. Recalled to the full Denmark international squad at the end of the season, Stephan will be pushing Dean Kiely all the way in 2005-06.
Charlton Ath *(£720,000 from AB Copenhagen, Denmark on 6/7/2004) PL 2*

ANDERSON Ijah Massai
Born: Hackney, 30 December 1975
Height: 5'8" **Weight:** 10.6
Club Honours: Div 3 '99
This experienced left-sided defender was out of the first-team picture at Bristol Rovers last term and soon after the start of the season he was released. After a brief trial with Oldham, he signed a monthly contract for Swansea and eventually won a longer deal with the club. Ijah was regularly included in the Swans' squad, and occasionally featured in a left-sided midfield position.
Southend U *(From trainee at Tottenham H on 2/8/1994)*

Brentford *(Free on 31/7/1995) FL 196+6/4 FLC 19/1 FAC 5+3 Others 12+1*
Wycombe W *(Loaned on 27/11/2002) FL 5*
Bristol Rov *(Free on 7/2/2003) FL 51+2 FLC 1 Others 1*
Swansea C *(Free on 26/11/2004) FL 8+5 FAC 1+1*

ANDERSON John

Born: Greenock, 2 October 1972
Height: 6'2" **Weight:** 12.2
Club Honours: S Div 2 '95; S Div 1 '01
This experienced central defender added a much needed physical presence to the Bristol Rovers rearguard last term. After failing to hold down a place early in the season John asked to be placed on the transfer list, and was then sidelined for several weeks by a groin injury after getting back in the side. However, he was back in the line-up for the final third of the campaign.
Morton *(Signed from Gourock YAC on 25/1/1994) SL 97+3/18 SLC 5/1 SC 9/2 Others 5+1/1*
Livingston *(Signed on 5/6/2000) SL 42+1/3 SLC 3 SC 7/2 Others 4/2*
Hull C *(Free on 17/6/2002) FL 42+1/1 FLC 1 FAC 1*
Bristol Rov *(Free on 25/3/2004) FL 36+6/1 FLC 1 Others 4*

ANDERSON Stuart

Born: Banff, 22 April 1986
Height: 6'0" **Weight:** 11.9
International Honours: S: Yth
After failing to break into the first team at Southampton this young midfielder moved on to join Blackpool last December. Stuart was a regular in the reserve team and stepped up to make his senior debut at Swindon in January, later featuring in three games at the very end of the season.
Southampton *(From trainee on 24/4/2004)*
Blackpool *(Free on 17/12/2004) FL 1+3*

ANDERTON Darren Robert

Born: Southampton, 3 March 1972
Height: 6'1" **Weight:** 12.5
Club Honours: FLC '99
International Honours: E: 30; B-1; U21-12; Yth
Signed initially on a 'pay-as-you play' deal, Darren earned a contract for Birmingham City after proving his fitness and performing impressively. His accurate passing and clever positioning added a calming dimension to the Blues' midfield. He scored the goal at Liverpool in November that ended a winless run and helped ease the Blues away from the foot of the table.
Portsmouth *(From trainee on 5/2/1990) FL 53+9/7 FLC 3+2/1 FAC 7+1/5 Others 2*
Tottenham H *(£1,750,000 on 3/6/1992) PL 273+26/34 FLC 30+1/8 FAC 26+2/6*
Birmingham C *(Free on 11/8/2004) PL 9+11/3 FLC 2 FAC 2*

ANDRADE Diogo

Born: Lisbon, Portugal, 23 July 1985
Height: 5'9" **Weight:** 12.0
International Honours: Portugal: Yth
This skilful midfielder came to Bournemouth on trial during the summer of 2004 and was given a short-term contract. He made his debut in the Carling Cup win at Blackburn and also turned out in the LDV Vans Trophy tie at Shrewsbury. Diogo went on loan to Dorchester Town in the autumn and remained with the Conference South outfit until the end of the season after being released by the Cherries at the end of the year.
Bournemouth *(Free from Belenenses, Portugal, on 10/9/2004) FLC 0+1 Others 0+1*

ANDREW Calvin

Born: Luton, 19 December 1986
Height: 6'0" **Weight:** 12.11
Calvin impressed enough in the youth and reserve teams to earn himself a call-up to the Luton Town first-team squad last term. A striker with good balance, he made his senior debut in the LDV Vans Trophy tie against Swansea in September. Calvin was also a member of the Hatters' team that won the Pontin's Combination League Cup and had the distinction of scoring the winner in the 2-1 win over Reading at the Madejski Stadium.
Luton T *(From trainee on 25/9/2004) FL 2+6 FAC 0+2 Others 1*

ANDREWS Keith Joseph

Born: Dublin, 13 September 1980
Height: 5'11" **Weight:** 11.5
This well-built midfielder hoped to finally establish himself at Molineux last season and duly scored his first Wolves' goal, in the Carling Cup tie against Rochdale at the end of August. However, although he had a brief run in the side under Glenn Hoddle when he played the 'holding' role in a diamond formation he had somewhat mixed fortunes. Later he had a few more starts, including a tidy outing at right back before a hernia operation brought his season to an early end.
Wolverhampton W *(From trainee on 26/9/1997) P/FL 41+24 FLC 3/1 FAC 4*
Oxford U *(Loaned on 10/11/2000) FL 4/1 Others 1*
Stoke C *(Loaned on 9/8/2003) FL 16*
Walsall *(Loaned on 13/3/2004) FL 10/2*

ANDREWS Wayne Michael Hill

Born: Paddington, 25 November 1977
Height: 5'10" **Weight:** 11.12
A hot-shot striker with electric pace, Wayne began the season in fine form for Colchester, scoring two in the first three games. Early in September he made the step-up to the Premiership, linking up with his former Oldham manager Iain Dowie at Selhurst Park. He spent much of the remainder of the season developing in the Eagles' reserve team, for whom he scored six goals, but also featured from the bench on a number of occasions at first-team level.
Watford *(From trainee on 5/7/1996) FL 16+12/4 FLC 3+2/1 FAC 0+2 Others 2/1 (Free to St Albans C during 1999 close season)*
Cambridge U *(Loaned on 2/10/1998) FL 1+1*
Peterborough U *(Loaned on 5/2/1999) FL 8+2/5*
Oldham Ath *(Free from Chesham U on 30/5/2002) FL 28+9/11 FLC 1+2 FAC 2+1 Others 3/1*
Colchester U *(Free on 9/8/2003) FL 36+10/14 FLC 1 FAC 4+1 Others 3+1/2*
Crystal Palace *(Signed on 9/9/2004) PL 0+9*

ANELKA Nicolas

Born: Versailles, France, 14 March 1979
Height: 6'0" **Weight:** 12.3
Club Honours: PL '98; FAC '98; CS '98
International Honours: France: 28
There was no doubt about Nicolas's ability in front of goal and he continued to find the net at an impressive rate for Manchester City last term, but constant tabloid speculation linked him with a host of clubs. It was subsequent comments in the French newspaper *L'Equipe* casting doubts on City as a big club that back fired on him and he moved to Turkish side Fenerbahce during the January transfer window for a club record transfer fee.
Arsenal *(£500,000+ from Paris St Germain on 6/3/1997) PL 50+15/23 FLC 3 FAC 13+1/3 Others 7+1/2 (£22,900,000 to Real Madrid, Spain on 20/8/1999)*
Liverpool *(Loaned from Paris St Germain on 24/12/2001) PL 13+7/4 FAC 2/1*
Manchester C *(£13,000,000 from Paris St Germain, France on 16/7/2002) PL 87+2/37 FLC 4 FAC 5/4 Others 5/4*

ANGEL Juan Pablo

Born: Medellin, Colombia, 24 October 1975
Height: 6'0" **Weight:** 11.6
International Honours: Colombia: 30
A striker with plenty of technical ability, Juan Pablo is strong in the air and a cool finisher. He has the ability to score

spectacular goals as well as 'bread and butter' tap-ins. His intelligence and movement off the ball and in and around the area make him a difficult opponent to face. He suffered a recurrence of a knee injury during the 2004 close season and was advised to rest, causing him to miss the first game of the new campaign, before making a late appearance from the bench in the second game at West Brom. Thereafter he was more or less ever-present and went on to score nine goals in all competitions. Perhaps the best of these came in the 3-0 victory over Portsmouth in November when he neatly controlled a cross, added two touches and a feint past a Pompey defender and unleashed an unstoppable shot into the net. Juan Pablo also featured regularly for Colombia in their World Cup qualifying campaign.

Aston Villa *(£9,500,000 + from River Plate, Argentina, ex Atletico Nacional, on 19/1/2001) PL 104+17/37 FLC 8+3/10 FAC 5/1 Others 2+2/4*

ANGUS Stevland (Stev) Dennis

Born: Westminster, 16 September 1980
Height: 6'0" **Weight:** 12.0
Club Honours: FAYC '99

Stev started the 2004-05 season as first choice at full back for Cambridge, but lost his place at the end of September, and after falling out of favour at the Abbey Stadium he spent the remainder of the campaign out on loan. He provided defensive cover at Hull during the busy Christmas and New Year period, then moved on to Scunthorpe. Stev immediately forced his way into the starting line-up for the Iron, switching from right back to centre back, where his electric pace and assurance on the ball made him a valuable asset in the promotion push.

West Ham U *(From trainee on 2/7/1999)*
Bournemouth *(Loaned on 11/8/2000) FL 7+2*
Cambridge U *(Free on 19/7/2001) FL 134+1/1 FLC 5 FAC 10 Others 10+1*
Hull C *(Loaned on 15/12/2004) FL 1+1 FAC 1*
Scunthorpe U *(Loaned on 31/1/2005) FL 9*

ANSELIN Cedric

Born: Lens, France, 24 July 1977
Height: 5'9" **Weight:** 11.4

This experienced midfielder played briefly for Mildenhall Town early on last term before joining Cambridge United on non-contract forms. He made his debut for the U's at Notts County in November and also featured in the home game with Scunthorpe before leaving the Abbey Stadium. He subsequently spent time training with Southend and had a brief association with Gravesend & Northfleet, before finishing the season playing for Norwich United.

Norwich C *(£250,000 from Bordeaux, France, on 25/3/1999) FL 22+4/1 FLC 2 FAC 1 (Freed on 19/6/2001)*
Ross Co *(Free on 17/11/2001) SL 7+3 SC 1 (Freed on 1/6/2002)*
Cambridge U *(Free from Mildenhall T, ex Oriente Petrolero, on 25/11/2004) FL 2*

ANTHONY Byron Joseph

Born: Newport, 20 September 1984
Height: 6'1" **Weight:** 11.0
International Honours: W: U21-3; Yth

Following hot on the heels of Wales centre halves Danny Gabbidon and James Collins the Bluebirds believe they have another defensive star of the future on their hands in Byron. The trainee made his full debut for Cardiff in the 4-1 Carling Cup win at MK Dons in September and followed up with an appearance from the bench in the next round against Bournemouth. Byron also represented Wales at U21 level during the campaign.

Cardiff C *(From trainee on 7/7/2003) FLC 1+1/1*

ANYA Ikechi

Born: Glasgow, 3 January 1988
Height: 5'5" **Weight:** 11.4

At 16 years and 279 days old Ikechi became the youngest ever Wycombe Wanderers player to appear in the Football League when he came off the bench at Scunthorpe in October. Two more substitute appearances followed and this exciting winger was rewarded with a professional contract. Ikechi also won the club's 'First Year Scholar of the Season' award.

Wycombe W *(Trainee) FL 0+3 Others 0+1*

ANYINSAH Joseph (Joe) Greene

Born: Bristol, 8 October 1984
Height: 5'8" **Weight:** 11.0

An exciting wing man with all the skills to make a real impact in the game, Joe is a product of Bristol City's youth policy. He made his first-team debut from the bench in the opening game against Torquay and featured on a number of occasions during the campaign, mostly as a substitute. Joe also had a short spell on loan with Conference club Hereford United.

Bristol C *(From trainee on 24/10/2001) FL 2+5 Others 0+2*

APPLEBY Andrew (Andy)

Born: Seaham, 11 October 1985
Height: 5'10" **Weight:** 11.1

A hard-working Hartlepool striker whose game improved tremendously during 2004-05, Andy made his first-team breakthrough early on with a couple of appearances as a substitute. He then had a successful work placement with Blyth Spartans, and on his return was restored to the squad adding a string of appearances from the bench. He endeared himself to the Pools' supporters when he scored a late goal to clinch a 3-2 victory over Bournemouth after the team had been two goals in arrears.

Hartlepool U *(Trainee) FL 0+15/2 FAC 1+2 Others 0+1*

APPLEBY Matthew (Matty) Wilfred

Born: Middlesbrough, 16 April 1972
Height: 5'8" **Weight:** 11.12

Matty's disappointing spell with Oldham Athletic finally ended last March when he re-joined one of his former clubs, Darlington. The experienced midfielder, whose Boundary Park career was beset with a succession of injury woes, was largely confined to the bench at Oldham. He had made just 13 starts in League One before agreeing a severance deal on his contract. Matty immediately slotted into central midfield for the Quakers, showing his wealth of experience with strong tackling and calm and positive distribution of the ball. He played in the final ten games of the season but just failed to inspire the club to another play-off attempt.

Newcastle U *(From trainee on 4/5/1990) P/FL 18+2 FLC 2+1 FAC 2 Others 2+2*
Darlington *(Loaned on 25/11/1993) FL 10/1 Others 1*
Darlington *(Free on 15/6/1994) FL 77+2/7 FLC 2 FAC 4 Others 8/3*
Barnsley *(£200,000 on 19/7/1996) P/FL 131+8/7 FLC 10+3 FAC 6+2 Others 3*
Oldham Ath *(Free on 15/1/2002) FL 36+10/2 FLC 1 FAC 1 Others 2/1*
Darlington *(Free on 11/3/2005) FL 10*

APPLEBY Richard (Richie) Dean

Born: Middlesbrough, 18 September 1975
Height: 5'9" **Weight:** 11.4
Club Honours: Div 3 '00
International Honours: E: Yth

After recovering from injury Richie joined Kidderminster on non-contract terms in the summer of 2004. However, he managed just a handful of games before being released in October to join up with Forest Green in the Conference. The

highlight of his time at Aggborough came when he scored the winner from the penalty spot in the victory over Macclesfield.
Newcastle U *(From trainee on 12/8/1993) Others 2*
Ipswich T *(Free on 12/12/1995) FL 0+3 Others 1*
Swansea C *(Free on 16/8/1996) FL 90+30/11 FLC 4+4 FAC 5+1/2 Others 3+4/1*
Kidderminster Hrs *(Free on 9/11/2001) FL 18+1/4 FAC 1*
Hull C *(Free on 3/7/2002) FL 6 FLC 1 (Freed on 4/12/2003)*
Kidderminster Hrs *(Free, after recovering from injury, on 30/7/2004) FL 6+3/1 FLC 0+1*

ARANALDE Zigor

Born: Guipuzcoa, Spain, 28 February 1973
Height: 6'1" **Weight:** 13.5
Zigor was again happier going forward than when defending for Walsall last term. At his best his directional heading and tackling were impressive and he took his appearance tally for the Saddlers well past the 200-mark before joining Sheffield Wednesday on a short-term contract in March. He made a handful of appearances for the Owls, but his attempts to win a longer deal were hampered by a period of suspension.
Walsall *(Free from CD Logrones, Spain, ex Albacete, Marbella, Seville, on 11/8/2000) FL 183+12/5 FLC 12/1 FAC 12 Others 5*
Sheffield Wed *(Free on 24/3/2005) FL 1+1*

ARBER Mark Andrew

Born: Johannesburg, South Africa, 9 October 1977
Height: 6'1" **Weight:** 12.11
Mark arrived at Boundary Park in the summer of 2004 as one of Brian Talbot's key signings but the move quickly turned sour. The no-nonsense centre back struggled to find form and was dropped in mid-November after a series of disappointing displays. Frustrated by the lack of first-team action, Mark agreed to return to former club Peterborough United on loan in December and the switch became permanent the following month. Despite some sterling performances and playing the last few games while carrying an injury, Mark failed to stop Posh slipping to relegation.
Tottenham H *(From trainee on 27/3/1996)*
Barnet *(£75,000 on 18/9/1998) FL 123+2/15 FLC 4 FAC 3 Others 8/1*
Peterborough U *(Free on 9/12/2002) FL 67+2/5 FLC 1 FAC 3 Others 2*
Oldham Ath *(Free on 27/7/2004) FL 13+1/1 FLC 2 Others 1*
Peterborough U *(Free on 21/12/2004) FL 21 FAC 2/1*

Julio Arca

ARCA Julio Andres
Born: Quilmes Bernal, Argentine, 31 January 1981
Height: 5'10" **Weight:** 11.6
Club Honours: Ch '05
International Honours: Argentina: Yth (World Yth '01)
Sunderland's exciting left winger enjoyed another excellent season at the Stadium of Light as the club returned to the Premiership after winning the Championship title. Julio can also operate at left back but his talents are best used in an advanced role where his dribbling skills and superb crossing ability can come to the fore. As well as creating chances for others, Julio hit the net nine times last term, most notably away at West Ham in April when a 2-1 victory gave the Black Cats the title. A huge favourite with the Sunderland fans, Julio continued to have an almost telepathic understanding with left back George McCartney and for the second season running he was chosen by his fellow professionals in the PFA Championship team of the season.
Sunderland *(£3,500,000 from Argentinos Juniors, Argentine, on 31/8/2000) P/FL 123+10/16 FLC 5/2 FAC 13/3*

ARDLEY Neal Christopher
Born: Epsom, 1 September 1972
Height: 5'11" **Weight:** 11.9
International Honours: E: U21-10
Neal was Watford's most creative player and the leading provider of goals in the whole Championship at the turn of the year. Operating mainly in left midfield, he produced a series of excellent crosses and perfectly weighted passes, and was a key man at dead-ball situations. He also contributed four goals, including a gem of a volley at Queen's Park Rangers. Unfortunately, just when his value to the team was at last being fully appreciated, he became unsettled and his contract was terminated abruptly in the wake of Ray Lewington's sudden departure. Neil subsequently joined Cardiff and played a useful role in ensuring the Bluebirds avoided relegation. A highlight was a beautiful 18-yard free kick past Ian Walker to help the team salvage a draw at Leicester.
Wimbledon *(From trainee on 29/7/1991) P/FL 212+33/18 FLC 22+3/5 FAC 27+4/3*
Watford *(Free on 9/8/2002) FL 105+6/7 FLC 7+1 FAC 8+1*
Cardiff C *(Free on 23/3/2005) FL 8/1*

ARMSTRONG Alun
Born: Gateshead, 22 February 1975
Height: 6'1" **Weight:** 11.13
Club Honours: Div 1 '98
This strong running and skilful forward joined Darlington last September and soon struck up a good understanding with Clyde Wijnhard. Alun showed good aerial ability and scored a hat-trick against Southend United in his third game for the club. He went on to bag 11 goals for the season, which was unfortunately interrupted by injury thus ruling him out of the crucial last few games.
Newcastle U *(From trainee on 1/10/1993)*
Stockport Co *(£50,000 on 23/6/1994) FL 151+8/48 FLC 22/8 FAC 10+1/5 Others 7*
Middlesbrough *(£1,500,000 on 16/2/1998) P/FL 10+19/9 FLC 4*
Huddersfield T *(Loaned on 23/3/2000) FL 4+2*
Ipswich T *(£500,000 + on 8/12/2000) P/FL 50+29/14 FLC 2+2/1 FAC 2+1/1 Others 5+3/3*
Bradford C *(Loaned on 27/12/2003) FL 6/1 FAC 1*
Darlington *(Free on 15/9/2004) FL 31+1/9 FAC 2/2*

Alun Armstrong

ARMSTRONG Christopher (Chris) David
Born: Ripon, 8 November 1984
Height: 6'1" **Weight:** 13.9
Chris started the 2004-05 season with Queen of the South before moving on to Stockport during the January transfer window, making his debut as a late substitute in the 3-0 defeat of Luton Town later that month. The young striker featured on a number of occasions thereafter and scored once, netting during the 2-2 home draw with Bournemouth in February. Chris was released at the end of the season.
Leeds U *(From trainee on 12/11/2001)*
Queen of the South *(Free, via trial at Rochdale, on 3/8/2004) SL 2+4 SLC 0+1 Others 1*
Stockport Co *(Free on 14/1/2005) FL 9+2/1*

ARMSTRONG Christopher (Chris) Peter
Born: Newcastle, 19 June 1971
Height: 6'0" **Weight:** 13.3
Club Honours: Div 1 '94; FLC '99
International Honours: E: B-1
This experienced striker struggled to make any real impact last term and was more of a peripheral figure in the Wrexham squad as the season wore on. Injury problems did not help his cause, but he showed that he still possessed the ability to test defences as his eight goals in the League suggests. It was no real surprise when he was released in May.
Wrexham *(Free from Llay Welfare on 3/3/1989) FL 40+20/13 FLC 2+1 FAC 0+1 Others 5+1/3*
Millwall *(£50,000 on 16/8/1991) FL 11+17/5 FLC 3+1/2 FAC 0+1 Others 0+1*
Crystal Palace *(£1,000,000 on 1/9/1992) P/FL 118/45 FLC 8/6 FAC 8/5 Others 2/1*
Tottenham H *(£4,500,000 on 30/6/1995) PL 117+24/48 FLC 15/10 FAC 9+5/4 Others 3*
Bolton W *(Free on 28/8/2002) FLC 1*
Wrexham *(Free on 22/7/2003) FL 37+22/13 FLC 1 FAC 1+2/1 Others 1+1/1*

ARMSTRONG Steven **Craig**
Born: South Shields, 23 May 1975
Height: 5'11" **Weight:** 12.10
Craig was again out of the first-team picture at Sheffield Wednesday last term and in January he moved on to join Bradford City on a short-term contract, making his debut as a substitute on the left-hand side of midfield against Barnsley. He started four games at left back but struggled after a long spell away from first-team football and was released in the summer.
Nottingham F *(From trainee on 2/6/1992) P/FL 24+16 FLC 6+2/2 FAC 1*
Burnley *(Loaned on 29/12/1994) FL 4*
Bristol Rov *(Loaned on 8/1/1996) FL 4+1*
Bristol Rov *(Loaned on 28/3/1996) FL 9*
Gillingham *(Loaned on 18/10/1996) FL 10 FLC 2 Others 1*
Watford *(Loaned on 24/1/1997) FL 3*
Watford *(Loaned on 14/3/1997) FL 12*
Huddersfield T *(£750,000 on 26/2/1999) FL 101+6/5 FLC 7+1 FAC 2 Others 1+1*
Sheffield Wed *(£100,000 on 15/2/2002) FL 29+6/1 FLC 3 Others 2*
Grimsby T *(Loaned on 24/2/2004) FL 9/1*
Bradford C *(Free on 20/1/2005) FL 4+3*

ARMSTRONG Ian
Born: Kirkby, 16 November 1981
Height: 5'7" **Weight:** 10.2
International Honours: E: Yth; Sch
Ian made a great start to the 2004-05 season with Port Vale, scoring twice in the first home game against MK Dons. A tricky left winger he was unfortunately affected by a series of injuries thereafter, including a spell of mumps, and these restricted his appearances. Ian returned in March at Oldham, but ten minutes after coming on as a substitute he was forced to limp off after a heavy challenge. He was released on a free transfer in the summer.
Liverpool *(From trainee on 16/12/1998)*
Port Vale *(Free on 2/7/2001) FL 50+39/14 FLC 1+1 FAC 1+3 Others 5+2/3*

ARTELL David (Dave) John
Born: Rotherham, 22 November 1980
Height: 6'2" **Weight:** 13.9
Dave produced some solid early-season displays in the centre of defence for Mansfield last term and contributed a valuable goal against Yeovil. His consistent form meant that he was not easily displaced, but an ankle injury kept him out of the line-up. This could have had more serious consequences after he was rushed to hospital with a suspected DVT and led to a more prolonged absence. He was hampered by further ankle problems in the second half of the campaign.
Rotherham U *(From trainee on 1/7/1999) FL 35+2/4 FAC 3 Others 1*
Shrewsbury T *(Loaned on 26/9/2002) FL 27+1/1 FAC 3 Others 5*
Mansfield T *(Free on 7/8/2003) FL 43+2/5 FLC 2 FAC 5+1 Others 1+1*

ARTETA Mikel
Born: San Sebastian, Spain, 26 March 1982
Height: 5'9" **Weight:** 10.12
Club Honours: SPD '03; SLC '03
Signed on a short-term loan deal until the summer this technically gifted midfielder, with fine passing skills over any distance and strength on the ball, made a great impression on both fans and staff at Everton in the second half of the season. After joining in January Mikel put in several fine performances, including sublime displays at Villa Park and in the home win over Crystal Palace, when he had the bonus of scoring his first goal from a superb free kick.
Glasgow Rgrs *(£5,800,000 from Paris St Germain, France, ex Barcelona, on 1/7/2002) SL 49+1/12 SLC 5 SC 6/1 Others 7/1 (Transferred to Real Sociedad, Spain on 9/7/2004)*
Everton *(Loaned from Real Sociedad, Spain, on 31/1/2005) PL 10+2/1 FAC 1*

ASABA Carl Edward
Born: Westminster, 28 January 1973
Height: 6'2" **Weight:** 13.4
A pacy striker who is good at running at defenders with the ball at his feet, Carl began the 2004-05 season on the bench for Stoke, eventually breaking into the starting line-up in an unfamiliar role on the right-hand side of midfield. His performances gradually dropped and it was no surprise that he was left out of the side. A transfer deadline move to Coventry fell through and at the time of writing he seemed to be about to depart for pastures new.
Brentford *(Free from Dulwich Hamlet on 9/8/1994) FL 49+5/25 FLC 5 FAC 4 Others 7/2*
Colchester U *(Loaned on 16/2/1995) FL 9+3/2*
Reading *(£800,000 on 7/8/1997) FL 31+2/8 FLC 7+2/3 FAC 3/1*
Gillingham *(£600,000 on 28/8/1998) FL 65+12/36 FLC 3/2 FAC 1+1 Others 9/2*
Sheffield U *(£92,500 + on 8/3/2001) FL 52+15/23 FLC 6+1/1 FAC 2+1 Others 3*
Stoke C *(Free on 6/8/2003) FL 40+30/9 FLC 2/1 FAC 2+1*

ASAMOAH Derek
Born: Ghana, 1 May 1981
Height: 5'6" **Weight:** 10.12
This tricky winger was soon a favourite with the Mansfield fans last term, his electric pace proving useful for both making and scoring goals. Derek gave a 'Man of the Match' performance against his former club Northampton, when he scored the first goal and made the second. However, he fell out of favour at Field Mill and in March he moved on to join Lincoln City. Used as a right-sided striker by the Imps, he provided an injection of pace into the attack. Derek played in a three-man strike force at Sincil Bank and was unlucky not to find the net in the run-in to the end of the campaign. He finished the season by

coming off the bench to play in the League Two play-off final at the Millennium Stadium.
Northampton T *(Free from Slough T, ex Barking, Hampton & Richmond Borough, on 26/7/2001) FL 27+86/10 FLC 0+3 FAC 6+3/2 Others 5+3/1*
Mansfield T *(Free on 5/8/2004) FL 24+6/5 FAC 1 Others 0+1*
Lincoln C *(Free on 15/3/2005) FL 8+2 Others 1+2*

ASHBEE Ian

Born: Birmingham, 6 September 1976
Height: 6'1" **Weight:** 13.7
International Honours: E: Yth
Ian became the first player to captain Hull City in two consecutive promotion campaigns as he led the Tigers into the Championship for 2005-06. With his infectious will to win, his leadership from the middle of midfield ensured City were always difficult to beat and often grabbed vital points through sheer determination. To the delight of both colleagues and supporters, Ian finally grabbed his first goal on Hull soil with the opener in the 6-1 win against Tranmere in December.
Derby Co *(From trainee on 9/11/1994) FL 1*
Cambridge U *(Free on 13/12/1996) FL 192+11/11 FLC 7 FAC 15 Others 9+1*
Hull C *(Free on 3/7/2002) FL 110/4 FLC 3/1 FAC 4 Others 1*

ASHBY Barry John

Born: Park Royal, 2 November 1970
Height: 6'2" **Weight:** 13.8
Club Honours: FAYC '89
Barry was once again a steady and reliable performer in the centre of the defence for Gillingham last term, although injury problems reduced his appearances. Despite his advancing years, he showed the younger players around him that there was still a role for experience in the team.
Watford *(From trainee on 1/12/1988) FL 101+13/3 FLC 6 FAC 4 Others 2+1*
Brentford *(Signed on 22/3/1994) FL 119+2/4 FLC 11 FAC 9/1 Others 11+1*
Gillingham *(£140,000 on 8/8/1997) FL 270+3/7 FLC 18 FAC 19/1 Others 10/1*

ASHDOWN Jamie Lawrence

Born: Wokingham, 30 November 1980
Height: 6'3" **Weight:** 14.10
This promising young 'keeper joined Portsmouth in the summer of 2004 but to begin with he was restricted to appearances in the Carling Cup ties. However, he made his Premiership debut against Manchester City in November and enjoyed to extended runs in the line-up. Jamie has immense confidence in his own abilities and is capable of pulling off some spectacular saves.

Jamie Ashdown

Reading *(From trainee on 26/11/1999) FL 12+1 FAC 1 Others 2*
Bournemouth *(Loaned on 22/8/2002) FL 2*
Rushden & Diamonds *(Loaned on 14/11/2003) FL 19*
Portsmouth *(Signed on 2/7/2004) PL 16 FLC 4 FAC 1*

ASHTON Dean
Born: Crewe, 24 November 1983
Height: 6'1" **Weight:** 13.11
International Honours: E: U21-6; Yth
Dean was once again in prolific form for Crewe and his tally of 20 goals in all competitions made him easily the club's leading scorer for the season, despite the fact that he had departed for Norwich in January. He became the Canaries' most expensive signing, but quickly won over a whole new army of fans with his goal-scoring exploits and style of play during the club's stirring end to the season. The powerfully built England U21 international has all the attributes necessary to succeed as a striker in the Premiership. He acts as an excellent target man, being able to hold the ball up and bring others into the game and is a natural goal-scorer, packing a fearsome shot in both feet, as well as having the anticipation required to find space in the most crowded of penalty areas.
Crewe Alex *(From trainee on 6/2/2001) FL 131+28/60 FLC 6+1/3 FAC 6+3/5 Others 3/5*
Norwich C *(£3,000,000 + on 11/1/2005) PL 16/7*

ASHTON Jonathan (Jon) James
Born: Nuneaton, 4 October 1982
Height: 6'2" **Weight:** 13.7
Jon was in impressive form at the centre of the Oxford defence last term when he was a regular in the line-up. He was consistent throughout the campaign and was often able to use his speed and ability to read the game and to bridge the holes that appeared in the back line.
Leicester C *(From trainee on 29/1/2001) P/FL 3+6 FLC 0+1*
Notts Co *(Loaned on 8/11/2002) FL 4*
Oxford U *(Free on 8/8/2003) FL 60+4 FLC 3 FAC 1 Others 1*

ASHTON Neil John
Born: Liverpool, 15 January 1985
Height: 5'10" **Weight:** 11.12
This young Tranmere Rovers defender was unable to break into the first team last term and in December he joined Shrewsbury Town in a loan deal that lasted until the end of the season. He added some much needed balance to the Gay Meadow line-up, featuring mostly on the left-hand side of midfield, and was such a success that he was voted as the club's 'Young Player of the Year'.
Tranmere Rov *(From trainee on 10/4/2003) FL 0+1*
Shrewsbury T *(Loaned on 9/12/2004) FL 22+2*

ATHERTON Peter
Born: Orrell, 6 April 1970
Height: 5'11" **Weight:** 13.12
International Honours: E: U21-1; Sch
Peter's injury problems reared up again when he broke his ankle playing for Bradford City reserves last August and this ruled him out for three months. The steady defender enjoyed a ten-match run at right back at the turn of the year when Darren Holloway was sidelined, but then lost his place and was not offered a new contract at the end of the season.
Wigan Ath *(From trainee on 12/2/1988) FL 145+4/1 FLC 8 FAC 7 Others 12+1*
Coventry C *(£300,000 on 23/8/1991) P/FL 113+1 FLC 4 FAC 2*
Sheffield Wed *(£800,000 on 1/6/1994) PL 214/9 FLC 16 FAC 18 Others 3*
Bradford C *(Free on 6/7/2000) P/FL 90+4/3 FLC 3 FAC 2 Others 4*
Birmingham C *(Loaned on 15/2/2001) FL 10 Others 2*

ATIENO Taiwo Leo
Born: Brixton, 6 August 1985
Height: 6'2" **Weight:** 12.13
In his first season as a professional Taiwo showed himself to be a lively attacker with good movement and ability in the air during his brief appearances for Walsall. He also impressed in loan spells with Rochdale and Chester, finding the net for both clubs. He will be looking to break into the side at Bescot in 2005-06.
Walsall *(From trainee on 2/7/2004) FL 0+3 FLC 1*
Rochdale *(Loaned on 22/10/2004) FL 6+7/2 FAC 1+1 Others 1*
Chester C *(Loaned on 1/2/2005) FL 3+1/1*

ATKINSON Robert (Rob) Guy
Born: Beverley, 29 April 1987
Height: 6'1" **Weight:** 12.0
Rob was again a regular member of the Barnsley reserve team last term. He was also included in the first-team squad on a number of occasions, but only managed one brief appearance as a substitute, coming on at Port Vale in April. A promising defender or midfielder, he will be looking for more opportunities in the 2005-06 season.
Barnsley *(Trainee) FL 0+2*

ATOUBA Thimothee Essama
Born: Douala, Cameroon, 17 February 1982
Height: 6'3" **Weight:** 12.6
International Honours: Cameroon: 23
Favouring a left-sided midfield role, Thimothee also has the versatility to play in defence. He is a strong yet agile player who has good control and pace enough to cause problems for opposition defences. The latter was best demonstrated with a spectacular long-range winning effort against Newcastle at St James' Park securing all three points for Spurs. Vastly experienced across all levels of competition, Thimothee will look to improve upon his 20 or so appearances last season and secure a regular first-team spot in 2005-06.
Tottenham H *(Signed from FC Basle, Switzerland on 13/8/2004) PL 15+3/1 FLC 1 FAC 5*

AUSTIN Kevin Levi
Born: Hackney, 12 February 1973
Height: 6'0" **Weight:** 14.0
International Honours: Trinidad & Tobago: 1
Kevin played most of his games for Swansea at left back last term, but deputised in central defence on occasions when Garry Monk was unavailable. An experienced campaigner, his defensive qualities and consistency were evident on numerous occasions throughout the season, with not many opponents getting the better of him.
Leyton Orient *(Free from Saffron Walden on 19/8/1993) FL 101+8/3 FLC 4/1 FAC 6 Others 7*
Lincoln C *(£30,000 on 31/7/1996) FL 128+1/2 FLC 9 FAC 6 Others 4*
Barnsley *(Free on 5/7/1999) FL 3 FLC 2+1*
Brentford *(Loaned on 27/10/2000) FL 3*
Cambridge U *(Free on 21/11/2001) FL 4+2 Others 1*
Bristol Rov *(Free on 12/7/2002) FL 52+4 FAC 4+1*
Swansea C *(Free on 2/7/2004) FL 41+1 FLC 1 FAC 5 Others 2*

AUSTIN Neil Jeffrey
Born: Barnsley, 26 April 1983
Height: 5'10" **Weight:** 11.11
International Honours: E: Yth
This Barnsley defender had something of a frustrating season at Oakwell last time around. Injuries did not help his cause, but when fit he had to wait patiently in the wings due mainly to the form of Bobby Hassell. When he did get his chance he never let the team down, always giving 100 per cent and tackling combatively. Neil will be hoping for more opportunities in 2005-06.
Barnsley *(From trainee on 27/4/2000) FL 73+13 FLC 0+1 FAC 5+1 Others 0+1*

B

BABAYARO Celestine
Born: Kaduna, Nigeria, 29 August 1978
Height: 5'8" **Weight:** 11.0
Club Honours: FLC '98; ESC '98; FAC '00; CS '00
International Honours: Nigeria: Full; U23 (OLYM '96); Yth (World-U17 '93)
Celestine started just four matches for Chelsea under Jose Mourinho, mainly because of the excellent form shown by Wayne Bridge and William Gallas who shared the left-back slot, and eventually joined Newcastle during the January transfer window to replace the departing Olivier Bernard at left back. A skilful and athletic player with a good left foot and a penchant for attacking down the wing, he quickly settled in with a series of impressive displays, scoring his first goal in the FA Cup tie against Coventry. He picked up a knee injury at the end of February which troubled him for the rest of the season, and although he returned for the home UEFA Cup tie against Sporting Lisbon in April he missed the following two games, returning for the FA Cup semi-final, when he was replaced at half time.
Chelsea *(£2,250,000 from Anderlecht, Belgium on 20/6/1997) PL 118+14/5 FLC 14+2 FAC 16+1 Others 29+3/3*
Newcastle U *(£1,000,000 on 1/1/2005) PL 7 FAC 4/1 Others 2*

BAIDOO Shabazz Kwame
Born: Hackney, 13 April 1988
Height: 5'8" **Weight:** 10.7
International Honours: E: Yth
Shabazz is an exciting young striker who is a product of the Queen's Park Rangers Academy. He made his debut, eight days short of his 17th birthday, in the home game against Gillingham at the beginning of April when coming on as a substitute. Two weeks later he made his starting debut at Burnley. Shabazz had an impressive first full season in the juniors, being voted 'Academy Player of the Year' by the supporters.
Queens Park Rgrs *(Trainee) FL 2+2*

BAILEY Alexander (Alex) Christopher
Born: Newham, 21 September 1983
Height: 5'9" **Weight:** 11.3
Club Honours: FAYC '01
This pacy, assured full back joined Chesterfield in the summer of 2004 hoping for a first-team chance and ended up playing the full 90 minutes in all but two of the club's fixtures. Alex reads the game well enough to be left as the sole defender when others push forward and he has the beating of most opposing backs when overlapping.
Arsenal *(From trainee on 2/7/2001)*
Chesterfield *(Free on 30/7/2004) FL 45/1 FLC 1 FAC 1 Others 1*

BAILEY Mark
Born: Stoke, 12 August 1976
Height: 5'10" **Weight:** 12.0
Mark signed for Macclesfield in the 2004 close season, going straight into the team, and was ever present until mid-October when he suffered an ankle injury that required surgery, keeping him sidelined until his return in March. A useful right wing back, Mark always has a positive approach to his play, uses his pace to attack down the right flank. He is an expert crosser of the ball and scored two well-taken goals.
Stoke C *(From trainee on 12/7/1994)*
Rochdale *(Free on 10/10/1996) FL 49+18/1 FLC 3+1 FAC 1 Others 4 (Free to Winsford U during 1999 close season)*
Lincoln C *(Free from Northwich Vic, ex Lancaster C on 8/10/2001) FL 97+1/1 FLC 1 FAC 3+1 Others 8/3*
Macclesfield T *(Free on 2/7/2004) FL 20+1/2 FLC 1 Others 3*

BAILEY Matthew (Matt) John
Born: Crewe, 12 March 1986
Height: 6'5" **Weight:** 11.6
This promising young striker joined Scunthorpe on loan on the eve of the 2004-05 season and started the first two games of the campaign as a target man, showing a decent touch in his link-up play. He added three more appearances for the Iron before returning to Edgeley Park at the end of the month. Matt then made his debut for County in the LDV Vans Trophy tie against Wrexham and also featured in the home defeat by Chesterfield before joining Conference club Northwich on loan for the closing stages of the campaign.
Stockport Co *(From trainee on 8/7/2003) FL 0+1 Others 0+1*
Scunthorpe U *(Loaned on 6/8/2004) FL 2+2 FLC 1*

BAILEY Stefan Kyon Lloyd
Born: London, 10 November 1987
Height: 5'11" **Weight:** 12.8
Stefan is a right-sided midfielder who has graduated through the youth scheme at Queen's Park Rangers. His debut came in the home game against Sheffield United in April when he came on as a substitute. An impressive performance earned him a position in the starting line-up for the next game. Stefan was a regular in the reserve side and earned his first-team opportunity as a result of some consistent performances.
Queens Park Rgrs *(Trainee) FL 1+1*

BAINES Leighton John
Born: Liverpool, 11 December 1984
Height: 5'8" **Weight:** 11.10
International Honours: E: U21-3
This Wigan Athletic defender enjoyed a fine season when he was first choice at left back for the majority of the time. Showing remarkably maturity for his age, he put in a series of consistent performances and netted his first goal for the club with a 40-yard cracker in the away game at Ipswich. Leighton became the club's first player to gain international honours with England following his debut for the U21s against Austria in September.
Wigan Ath *(From trainee on 4/1/2003) FL 70+3/1 FLC 3+1 FAC 3 Others 1+1*

BAKER Matthew (Matt) Christopher
Born: Harrogate, 18 December 1979
Height: 6'0" **Weight:** 14.0
Club Honours: AMC '05
International Honours: E: SP-4
Matt joined Wrexham in the summer of 2004 and stepped into the breach when regular 'keeper Andy Dibble was injured, eventually holding his place through to December. However, he then became Danny Wilson's first permanent signing for MK Dons, claiming a regular starting berth in early February and quickly proving himself to be a superb shot-stopper. He produced penalty saves in successive games against Swindon and Bournemouth earning crucial points for the Dons in the fight against relegation. Not the tallest of 'keepers, he sometimes seemed unsure when venturing off his line to collect crosses, but all told he played a key part in helping the club retain its League One status.
Hull C *(From trainee on 16/7/1998) FL 0+2 FLC 0+1 Others 1 (Free to Hereford U on 18/8/2000)*
Wrexham *(Free from Hereford U on 8/7/2004) FL 11+2 FLC 1 FAC 2 Others 3*
MK Dons *(Free on 17/12/2004) FL 20*

BAKER Thomas (Tom)
Born: Salford, 28 March 1985
Height: 5'5" **Weight:** 9.0
Tom progressed to the senior ranks with Barnsley in the summer of 2004, but spent most of last season as a regular in the club's reserve side. A hard-working player who is comfortable both in

midfield and up front, he made a handful of appearances for the first team from the bench in the closing stages of the campaign. Tom was released by Barnsley at the end of the season.

Barnsley *(From trainee on 2/7/2004) FL 0+4*

BAKKE Eirik

Born: Sogndal, Norway, 13 September 1977

Height: 6'2" **Weight:** 12.9

International Honours: Norway: 25; U21-34; Yth

Norwegian international midfielder Eirik was restricted to just three minutes of Championship action after snapping a cruciate ligament and sustaining cartilage damage in Leeds' pre-season game against Pitea in Sweden. He returned as a substitute in the 1-1 draw with Brighton at Elland Road in and was promptly booked. A knee problem later flared up prompting further frustration for Eirik.

Leeds U *(£1,000,000 + from Sogndal, Norway on 13/7/1999) P/FL 107+23/8 FLC 6/1 FAC 9+1/6 Others 31+3/5*

BALDWIN Patrick (Pat) Michael

Born: City of London, 12 November 1982

Height: 6'2" **Weight:** 10.12

Centre half Pat deservedly claimed a clean-sweep of Colchester United's 'Player of the Season' awards. He spent most of August on the bench, but was called up to the side for the terrific Carling Cup victory over West Brom in September, after which he missed just three matches. The youngster will now be looking to score his first-ever goal in 2005-06, to add to his excellent defensive qualities.

Colchester U *(Free from trainee at Chelsea on 16/8/2002) FL 49+12 FLC 4 FAC 6 Others 1+2*

BANGURA Alhassan (Al)

Born: Sierra Leone, 24 January 1988

Height: 5'8" **Weight:** 10.7

Al made a surprise first-team debut for Watford in the penultimate match of the season at the age of 17 years and 96 days, making him the fifth youngest player ever to represent the club. A left-footed central-midfield player who had played only six reserve matches since arriving from Sierra Leone, Al took his chance with poise and confidence. He did even better in the next match, demonstrating sinuous movement combined with tenacious tackling and a willingness to shoot on sight.

Watford *(Trainee) FL 1+1*

BANKOLE Ademola (Ade)

Born: Abeokuta, Nigeria, 9 September 1969

Height: 6'3" **Weight:** 12.10

Ade joined Brentford in February with a dual role as a player and goalkeeping coach after spells earlier in the season with Lewes, Maidenhead and Windsor & Eton. He kept a clean sheet on his debut against MK Dons the same month and added two further League One appearances before the end of the campaign.

Crewe Alex *(Free from Shooting Stars, Ibadan, Nigeria, via trials at Doncaster Rov, Leyton Orient, on 25/9/1996) FL 6 FLC 1*

Queens Park Rgrs *(£50,000 on 2/7/1998) FL 0+1*

Crewe Alex *(£50,000 on 19/7/2000) FL 51+1 FLC 1+1 FAC 5+1 Others 4 (Free to Lewes during 2004 close season)*

Brentford *(Free from Maidenhead U, ex Windsor & Eton, on 3/2/2005) FL 3*

BANKS Steven (Steve)

Born: Hillingdon, 9 February 1972

Height: 6'0" **Weight:** 13.2

Steve was first-choice goalkeeper for Gillingham at the beginning of last season, but lost his place in October and it was not until the end of the year that he returned to the line-up. He was then an ever-present until Jason Brown

Steve Banks

replaced him in March. A popular figure at the club, it will be interesting to see which 'keeper gets the nod for the Gills once the 2005-06 season gets under way.
West Ham U *(From trainee on 24/3/1990) Others 1*
Gillingham *(Free on 25/3/1993) FL 67 FAC 7 Others 2*
Blackpool *(£60,000 on 18/8/1995) FL 150 FLC 13 FAC 8 Others 11*
Bolton W *(£50,000 on 25/3/1999) P/FL 20+1 FLC 7 FAC 5 Others 3*
Rochdale *(Loaned on 14/12/2001) FL 15*
Bradford C *(Loaned on 30/8/2002) FL 8+1*
Stoke C *(Free on 6/12/2002) FL 14 FAC 2*
Wimbledon *(Free on 1/8/2003) FL 24 FLC 1 FAC 3*
Gillingham *(Free on 12/3/2004) FL 39 FAC 1*

BARACLOUGH Ian Robert
Born: Leicester, 4 December 1970
Height: 6'1" **Weight:** 12.2
Club Honours: Div 3 '98
International Honours: E: Yth
Ian joined Scunthorpe in the summer of 2004 and enjoyed an outstanding season, playing a major role in taking United to promotion. After playing at left back for most of his career, Ian returned to the centre of midfield for the start of the campaign and revelled in this role, orchestrating United's play with his cultured left foot. A hard-working player, he missed just one match, and chipped in with four goals from midfield, including a stunning 30-yarder against Mansfield in September. Ian won one of the club's 'Player of the Year' awards in May.
Leicester C *(From trainee on 15/12/1988) FAC 1 Others 0+1*
Wigan Ath *(Loaned on 22/3/1990) FL 8+1/2*
Grimsby T *(Loaned on 21/12/1990) FL 1+3*
Grimsby T *(Free on 13/8/1991) FL 1*
Lincoln C *(Free on 21/8/1992) FL 68+5/10 FLC 7/1 FAC 4 Others 7*
Mansfield T *(Free on 6/6/1994) FL 47/5 FLC 7 FAC 4 Others 4*
Notts Co *(Signed on 13/10/1995) FL 107+4/10 FLC 5+1/1 FAC 8 Others 5*
Queens Park Rgrs *(£50,000 on 19/3/1998) FL 120+5/1 FLC 7 FAC 6*
Notts Co *(Free on 5/7/2001) FL 93+8/5 FLC 6 FAC 6+1 Others 3+1*
Scunthorpe U *(Free on 2/8/2004) FL 45/3 FLC 1 FAC 3/1*

BARKER Christopher (Chris) Andrew
Born: Sheffield, 2 March 1980
Height: 6'0" **Weight:** 11.8
This left back was out of favour at Cardiff early on last season, but moved out on loan to Stoke where he showed some fine form. The spell effectively re-ignited his career, for he returned a transformed player. The best parts of his game came to the fore: aggression, energy and consistency, and his subsequent performances earned him the 'Player of the Year' award.
Barnsley *(Signed from Alfreton on 24/8/1998) FL 110+3/3 FLC 11+1 FAC 4 Others 0+1*
Cardiff C *(£600,000 on 12/7/2002) FL 103+15 FLC 6 FAC 7 Others 4*
Stoke C *(Loaned on 6/8/2004) FL 4*

BARKER Richard (Richie) Ian
Born: Sheffield, 30 May 1975
Height: 6'0" **Weight:** 13.5
International Honours: E: Yth; Sch
An ever-willing worker, Richie's efforts rarely reaped the reward they deserved

Chris Barker (back) attempts to tackle Leicester's Stephen Hughes

for Rotherham last term, his only goal came in the Carling Cup tie against Chesterfield. In November he moved on to Mansfield and went straight into the Stags' line-up. Although he took a while to get on the score sheet he ended the season with a double-figure tally. Two of these efforts stood out: firstly a spectacular overhead kick to earn a draw at Rochdale and secondly a header at Notts County which proved to be the winner in the local 'derby'. He unsettled opposing defences and provided goal-scoring opportunities for those around him too.
Sheffield Wed *(From trainee on 27/7/1993) Others 1+1 (Free to Linfield on 22/8/1996)*
Doncaster Rov *(Loaned on 29/9/1995) FL 5+1 Others 0+1*
Brighton & Hove A *(Free on 19/12/1997) FL 48+12/12 FLC 1+1/1 FAC 1/1 Others 1*
Macclesfield T *(Free on 5/7/1999) FL 58/23 FLC 6/2 FAC 3 Others 1/1*
Rotherham U *(£60,000 on 3/1/2001) FL 69+71/12 FLC 8+2/3 FAC 5/2*
Mansfield T *(Free on 26/11/2004) FL 28/10*

BARKER Shaun
Born: Nottingham, 19 September 1982
Height: 6'2" **Weight:** 12.8
A young player who had progressed through the juniors ranks at Millmoor, Shaun was a regular in the first team last season. What's more he showed his versatility by occupying a number of different positions, playing at right back, in the centre of defence and in midfield where his ability to tackle strongly stood him in good stead. Shaun can also deliver long throws into the opposing penalty area and he is very useful in supporting free kicks and corners, as demonstrated when he scored the only goal in the 1-0 win at Leicester City.
Rotherham U *(From trainee on 10/7/2002) FL 77+3/4 FLC 4 FAC 2*

BARLOW Matthew (Matty) John
Born: Oldham, 25 June 1987
Height: 5'11" **Weight:** 10.2
This young striker continues to make steady progress after working his way through Oldham Athletic's youth ranks. A consistent performer and an industrious worker, Matty had made his senior debut in the final game of the previous season. He went on to make his full debut at Swindon Town last October and is seen as a promising future prospect by the Boundary Park coaching staff.
Oldham Ath *(Trainee) FL 1+9 FLC 0+2*

BARLOW Stuart
Born: Liverpool, 16 July 1968
Height: 5'10" **Weight:** 11.0
Club Honours: AMC '99
This veteran striker had to settle for a mixture of starts and substitute appearances at Edgeley Park last season. Goals were also hard to come by and he only managed four, two of which came in dramatic 3-3 draws. He scored the crucial third in the comeback against Swindon Town at Edgeley Park in October and the second goal in the amazing fight back at Barnsley in December.
Everton *(Free from Sherwood Park on 6/6/1990) P/FL 24+47/10 FLC 3+5/1 FAC 4+3/2 Others 0+2*
Rotherham U *(Loaned on 10/1/1992) Others 0+1*
Oldham Ath *(£450,000 on 20/11/1995) FL 78+15/31 FLC 5+1 FAC 6+1/1 Others 1*
Wigan Ath *(£45,000 on 26/3/1998) FL 72+11/40 FLC 6/3 FAC 5/3 Others 9+3/6*
Tranmere Rov *(Free on 5/7/2000) FL 62+32/19 FLC 6+3/3 FAC 5+5/3 Others 1+1/2*
Stockport Co *(Free on 8/8/2003) FL 26+35/11 FLC 1+1/1 FAC 1+3 Others 3+2/4*

BARMBY Nicholas (Nick) Jonathan
Born: Hull, 11 February 1974
Height: 5'7" **Weight:** 11.3
Club Honours: FLC '01; UEFAC '01; CS '01
International Honours: E: 23; B-2; U21-4; Yth; Sch
Despite dropping into League One with Hull City last term, Nick emphatically proved the doubters wrong as he inspired the Tigers to a second promotion in a row. Usually employed in an advanced attacking role, his skill, touch, vision and movement gave City an extra dimension. His hard work and determination provided outstanding examples to his colleagues. Nick has already earned a place in the City record books with a goal after seven seconds against Walsall (the quickest in the club's history) and he was voted in to 15th place in a poll of the Tigers' 100 greatest-ever players.
Tottenham H *(From trainee on 9/4/1991) PL 81+6/20 FLC 7+1/2 FAC 12+1/5*
Middlesbrough *(£5,250,000 on 8/8/1995) PL 42/8 FLC 4/1 FAC 3/1*
Everton *(£5,750,000 on 2/11/1996) PL 105+11/18 FLC 2+3/3 FAC 12/3*
Liverpool *(£6,000,000 on 19/7/2000) PL 23+9/2 FLC 3+4/1 FAC 2+3/1 Others 10+4/4*
Leeds U *(£2,750,000 on 8/8/2002) PL 17+8/4 FLC 1 FAC 0+2 Others 3/1*
Nottingham F *(Loaned on 27/2/2004) FL 6/1*
Hull C *(Free on 6/7/2004) FL 38+1/9 FAC 2*

BARNARD Donny Gary
Born: Forest Gate, 1 July 1984
Height: 6'0" **Weight:** 11.3
Donny began the 2004-05 season as a regular at right back for Leyton Orient before losing his place to Justin Miller. He also featured in central midfield for the O's ,contributing a single goal in the 2-0 home win over Notts County. Donny is effective at breaking up opposition moves and when supporting his colleagues in attack.
Leyton Orient *(From trainee on 4/3/2003) FL 67+28/1 FLC 0+2 FAC 2+2 Others 6/1*

BARNARD Lee James
Born: Romford, 18 July 1984
Height: 5'10" **Weight:** 10.10
This young Tottenham striker suffered a broken collar bone during the 2004 close season, but once he had recovered fitness he went out on loan to Leyton Orient, where he was required as cover for injuries. However, although he showed some neat touches he failed to find the net and returned to White Hart Lane. A second loan spell saw him turn out for Northampton where he proved to be an aggressive front man, capable of shaking up opposition defences. He failed to find the net at Sixfields too, but Lee more than made up for this with his performances for Spurs reserves, and he finished the campaign as second-top scorer in the Barclays Reserve League South with a tally of 17 goals.
Tottenham H *(From trainee on 3/7/2002)*
Exeter C *(Loaned on 1/11/2002) FL 3 Others 1*
Leyton Orient *(Loaned on 5/11/2004) FL 3+5 FAC 1 Others 1*
Northampton T *(Loaned on 4/3/2005) FL 3+2*

BARNES Philip (Phil) Kenneth
Born: Sheffield, 2 March 1979
Height: 6'1" **Weight:** 11.1
Club Honours: AMC '02
Phil jumped at the chance to join Sheffield United as cover for goalkeeper Paddy Kenny and was a regular in the reserves last term. In February he signed for Torquay on a month's loan. He looked an extremely capable 'keeper but an injury to Kenny saw him recalled to Bramall Lane later the same month. Phil made his debut for the club in the 'derby' match against Rotherham, keeping a clean sheet as the Blades won 1-0.
Rotherham U *(From trainee on 25/6/1997) FL 2*
Blackpool *(£100,000 on 22/7/1997) FL 141 FLC 7 FAC 7 Others 14*
Sheffield U *(Free on 2/7/2004) FL 1*
Torquay U *(Loaned on 3/2/2005) FL 5*

BARNESS Anthony
Born: Lewisham, 25 March 1973
Height: 5'10" **Weight:** 13.1
Club Honours: Div 1 '00
A competent right back, Anthony found his first team-chances at Bolton limited last season. After making only two Premiership starts during the first half of the campaign, Anthony started three consecutive games in February as a result of an injury to Nicky Hunt. Despite performing admirably he lost his place when Hunt returned to fitness and was allowed to leave the club at the end of the season.
Charlton Ath *(From trainee on 6/3/1991) FL 21+6/1 FLC 2 FAC 3 Others 1+1/1*
Chelsea *(£350,000 on 8/9/1992) PL 12+2 FLC 2 Others 2+1*
Middlesbrough *(Loaned on 12/8/1993) Others 1*
Southend U *(Loaned on 2/2/1996) FL 5*
Charlton Ath *(£165,000 on 8/8/1996) P/FL 83+13/3 FLC 5 FAC 3+1 Others 1+1*
Bolton W *(Free on 6/7/2000) P/FL 73+20 FLC 9+2 FAC 7+2 Others 3*

BARNET Leon Peter
Born: Stevenage, 30 November 1985
Height: 6'1" **Weight:** 11.3
This promising young defender made his bow in senior football when he featured for Luton in the LDV Vans Trophy tie against Swansea City last September. That was to be the only first-team experience for this tall commanding centre half during the season. Leon had a spell on loan at Aylesbury United towards the end of the year, but otherwise featured for the Hatters' reserve team, being included in the team that defeated Reading to win the Pontin's Combination League Cup.
Luton T *(From trainee on 28/9/2004) FAC 1 Others 3+1*

BAROS Milan
Born: Valasske Mezirici, Czech Republic, 28 October 1981
Height: 6'0" **Weight:** 11.12
Club Honours: FLC '03; UEFACL '05
International Honours: Czech Republic: 39; U21-19; Yth
When Michael Owen left Anfield for Real Madrid in the summer of 2004, it was expected that Milan would take on the mantle of leading scorer at Anfield. Indeed he did, but with a paltry 13 goals compared to Owen's usual haul of 25 to 30 goals. Whilst his form was reasonable in the first three months of the campaign – a hat-trick against Crystal Palace in November took his total to ten – a hamstring injury then disrupted his season. Milan made little impact in the European Cup final in Istanbul and was substituted late in the game.
Liverpool *(£3,400,000 from Banik Ostrava, Czech Republic, on 24/12/2001) PL 45+21/19 FLC 3+5/4 FAC 0+3 Others 18+11/4*

BARRAS Anthony (Tony)
Born: Billingham, 29 March 1971
Height: 6'3" **Weight:** 14.9
Tony was signed by Macclesfield in the 2004 close season and went straight into the team where he was ever present until late November when he was sidelined for four months with an achilles injury, returning briefly in March and then for the League Two play-off semi-final. Tony usually played on the left side of a three-man central defence, showing good aerial ability.
Hartlepool U *(From trainee on 6/7/1989) FL 9+3 FLC 2 FAC 1*
Stockport Co *(Free on 23/7/1990) FL 94+5/5 FLC 2 FAC 7 Others 19+1*
Rotherham U *(Loaned on 25/2/1994) FL 5/1*
York C *(£25,000 on 18/7/1994) FL 167+4/11 FLC 16/2 FAC 10/1 Others 8+1/1*
Reading *(£20,000 on 19/3/1999) FL 4+2/1*
Walsall *(£20,000 on 16/7/1999) FL 91+14/9 FLC 9+2/2 FAC 5/1 Others 4*
Plymouth Arg *(Loaned on 22/11/2002) FL 4*
Notts Co *(Free on 7/8/2003) FL 38+2/2 FLC 3/1 FAC 2/1 Others 0+1*
Macclesfield T *(Free on 2/7/2004) FL 22+2/1 FLC 1 FAC 2 Others 4/1*

BARRASS Matthew (Matt) Robert
Born: Bury, 28 February 1980
Height: 5'11" **Weight:** 12.0
Matt endured something of an injury-hit season with Bury last term. The club's longest-serving player started the campaign in the right-wing-back berth, but then lost his place after being sidelined with a calf injury. Although he soon returned to the bench he never really established himself in the side and later on found his appearances restricted by knee problems.
Bury *(From trainee on 19/5/1999) FL 77+7/2 FLC 3+1 FAC 2 Others 4*

BARRETT Adam Nicholas
Born: Dagenham, 29 November 1979
Height: 5'10" **Weight:** 12.0
An inspirational performer from the moment he broke into the Southend United team last September, Adam scored a remarkable tally of ten goals from centre back. A natural leader, he deputised as captain on the occasions when Kevin Maher was absent. A series of superb performances saw him voted into the PFA League Two team of the season, whilst he also won the overall PFA Fan's League Two 'Player of the Year' award, was a landslide winner in the clubs' own 'Player of The Year' award and was voted as the 'Players' Player of the Year' by his colleagues.
Plymouth Arg *(Free from USA football scholarship, ex trainee at Leyton Orient, on 13/1/1999) FL 47+5/3 FLC 4 FAC 6+1 Others 1*
Mansfield T *(£10,000 on 1/12/2000) FL 34+3/1 FAC 3 Others 2*
Bristol Rov *(Free on 2/7/2002) FL 90/5 FLC 2 FAC 5/1 Others 2*
Southend U *(Free on 5/7/2004) FL 42+1/11 FLC 1 FAC 1 Others 10*

BARRETT Graham
Born: Dublin, 6 October 1981
Height: 5'10" **Weight:** 11.7
Club Honours: FAYC '00
International Honours: RoI: 6; U21-24; Yth (UEFA-U16 '98); Sch
After a promising start as first-choice left-sided midfielder Graham suffered a disappointing season at Coventry last term. His skill and speed were key strengths but he was often intimidated by stronger defenders. Despite some excellent performances for the reserve team, including several goals, he was rarely given a chance to play in his favoured striking role in the first team and on transfer-deadline day he went on loan to Sheffield Wednesday. He scored on his debut for the Owls against Torquay, but never really established himself in the side. Graham also added a couple more caps for the Republic of Ireland during the campaign.
Arsenal *(From trainee on 14/10/1998) PL 0+2 FLC 1*
Bristol Rov *(Loaned on 15/12/2000) FL 0+1*
Crewe Alex *(Loaned on 11/9/2001) FL 2+1 FLC 0+1*
Colchester U *(Loaned on 14/12/2001) FL 19+1/4*
Brighton & Hove A *(Loaned on 29/8/2002) FL 20+10/1 FAC 1*
Coventry C *(Free on 3/7/2003) FL 32+23/6 FLC 2+2/1*
Sheffield Wed *(Loaned on 24/3/2005) FL 5+1/1*

BARRON Michael (Micky) James
Born: Chester-le-Street, 22 December 1974
Height: 5'11" **Weight:** 11.9
Last term was something of a disappointing season for Hartlepool's captain and longest-serving player. Micky missed the start of the campaign while

Milan Baros

BENTLEY David Michael
Born: Peterborough, 27 August 1984
Height: 5'10" **Weight:** 11.0
International Honours: E: U21-3; Yth
David spent the entire 2004-05 campaign on loan at Carrow Road from Arsenal where his first-team opportunities had been limited. Obviously blessed with excellent technique, he made a good impression at the start of the season, playing mainly on the left-hand side of midfield. He later switched to a more central role before picking up a knee injury in the FA Cup tie at West Ham in January. His return to the Canaries' squad coincided with their end-of-season improvement and his quality on the ball was there for everyone to see. David has the ability to beat his opponent with clever footwork and is excellent at dead-ball situations.
Arsenal *(From trainee on 8/9/2001) PL 1 FLC 4 FAC 0+3/1 Others 0+1*
Norwich C *(Loaned on 28/6/2004) PL 22+4/2 FLC 0+1 FAC 1*

BENTLEY Mark James
Born: Hertford, 7 January 1978
Height: 6'2" **Weight:** 13.0
Mark enjoyed a tremendous first full season in the professional game at Southend last term. An integral part of the club's successful campaign, he forged an excellent central-midfield partnership with captain Kevin Maher, impressing with his strength on the ball and attacking runs into opponents' penalty areas. Mark's overall contribution to the team cannot be underestimated and with a bit more luck he would have scored more than the six goals he managed.
Southend U *(Signed from Dagenham & Redbridge on 15/1/2004) FL 50+10/7 FLC 1 FAC 0+1 Others 10/1*

BERESFORD David
Born: Middleton, 11 November 1976
Height: 5'5" **Weight:** 11.4
International Honours: E: Yth; Sch
An effective utility man, David can play out wide on either the right or left flank, but prefers the former. A hamstring injury seriously restricted his season, and he remained largely on the periphery of the Tranmere squad, his only sustained run coming in the closing matches. Better known as a provider of useful crosses into the box, David still grabbed two League goals of his own but, apart from these, he will be remembered by Tranmere fans for scoring the last-gasp goal against Hartlepool in the second leg of the League One play-off semi-final which took the tie to extra time. Out of contract at the end of the 2004-05 season, he was released by the club as soon as their interest in promotion came to an end.
Oldham Ath *(From trainee on 22/7/1994) P/FL 32+32/2 FLC 3+3 FAC 0+1 Others 3*
Swansea C *(Loaned on 11/8/1995) FL 4+2*
Huddersfield T *(£350,000 on 27/3/1997) FL 24+11/3 FLC 2+3 FAC 1+1*
Preston NE *(Loaned on 17/12/1999) FL 1+3 FAC 0+1 Others 1*
Port Vale *(Loaned on 15/9/2000) FL 4*
Hull C *(Free on 4/7/2001) FL 33+8/1 FLC 2 FAC 1 Others 3*
Plymouth Arg *(Free on 23/7/2002) FL 6+11 Others 2*
Macclesfield T *(Loaned on 2/10/2003) FL 5 Others 0+1*
Tranmere Rov *(Free on 5/11/2003) FL 21+23/3 FLC 1+1 FAC 6 Others 0+3/1*

BERESFORD Marlon
Born: Lincoln, 2 September 1969
Height: 6'1" **Weight:** 13.6
Club Honours: Div 1 '05
This experienced goalkeeper gave Luton's shaky defence the stability it had previously lacked. Marlon commanded his area well, marshalling his defenders effectively, and kept a total of 14 clean sheets during the campaign. A key figure in the Hatters' championship-winning

Mark Bentley

side, he was also rewarded with a place in the PFA League One team of the season.
Sheffield Wed *(From trainee on 23/9/1987)*
Bury *(Loaned on 25/8/1989) FL 1*
Northampton T *(Loaned on 27/9/1990) FL 13 Others 2*
Crewe Alex *(Loaned on 28/2/1991) FL 3*
Northampton T *(Loaned on 15/8/1991) FL 15*
Burnley *(£95,000 on 28/8/1992) FL 240 FLC 18 FAC 20 Others 16*
Middlesbrough *(£500,000 on 10/3/1998) P/FL 8+2 FLC 3*
Sheffield Wed *(Loaned on 12/1/2000) FL 4*
Burnley *(Free on 31/1/2002) FL 13*
York C *(Free on 5/8/2002) FL 6*
Burnley *(Free on 10/10/2002) FL 33+1 FLC 4 FAC 5*
Bradford C *(Free on 15/9/2003) FL 5*
Luton T *(Free on 24/10/2003) FL 11 FAC 5 Others 1*
Barnsley *(Free on 26/1/2004) FL 14*
Luton T *(Signed on 5/7/2004) FL 38 FLC 1 FAC 2*

BERGER Patrik

Born: Prague, Czech Republic, 10 November 1973
Height: 6'1" **Weight:** 12.6
Club Honours: FAC '01; UEFAC '01; CS '01
International Honours: Czech Republic: 44; Czechoslovakia: 2; Yth (UEFA-U16 '90)
This vastly experienced and very talented midfielder was a regular for Portsmouth in Premiership action last term. Cool, confident and often the catalyst behind Pompey's attacking moves he scored three goals during the campaign, all in the early weeks of the season. However, he was out of contract at Fratton Park during the summer and at the time of writing it seemed likely that he would be on his way elsewhere.
Liverpool *(£3,250,000 from Borussia Dortmund, Germany, ex Slavia Prague, on 15/8/1996) PL 106+42/28 FLC 9+2/3 FAC 4+4 Others 17+12/4*
Portsmouth *(Free on 12/7/2003) PL 50+2/8 FLC 3+2 FAC 3*

Patrik Berger

BERGKAMP Dennis Nicolaas

Born: Amsterdam, Holland, 18 May 1969
Height: 6'0" **Weight:** 12.5
Club Honours: PL '98, '02, '04; FAC '02, '03, '05; CS '98, '02, '04
International Honours: Holland: 79; U21
Dennis remained a huge part of the Arsenal first team last term despite his advancing years. He lifted the Community Shield in Cardiff following the 3-1 win over Manchester United and scored the Gunners' opening goal of the campaign in the 4-1 romp over Everton at Goodison Park. His fine early form continued as he added further goals against Middlesbrough and Norwich City. Once more though he suffered periods of injury, but returned to register in three of his next four games. At the season's close he produced a sublime performance against Everton in which he set up three goals and added one of his own, and a further strike at Birmingham.
Arsenal *(£7,500,000 from Inter Milan, Italy, ex Ajax, on 3/7/1995) PL 245+46/85 FLC 15/8 FAC 33+5/14 Others 40+8/10*

BERKOVIC Eyal

Born: Haifa, Israel, 2 April 1972
Height: 5'7" **Weight:** 10.6
Club Honours: SLC '00; Div 1 '02
International Honours: Israel: 78; U21
This influential midfield playmaker featured only intermittently for Pompey last term and never enjoyed a regular presence in the side. His final appearance came as a substitute against Chelsea at the end of the year and soon afterwards his contract was cancelled by mutual consent. Eyal subsequently returned to Israel and signed for Maccabi Tel Aviv.
Southampton *(Loaned from Maccabi Tel Aviv, Israel on 11/10/1996) PL 26+2/4 FLC 5+1/2 FAC 1*
West Ham U *(£1,700,000 on 30/7/1997) PL 62+3/10 FLC 6 FAC 7+1/2*
Glasgow Celtic *(£5,500,000 on 20/7/1999) SL 29+3/9 SLC 0+2 SC 1 Others 3+3*
Blackburn Rov *(Loaned on 9/2/2001) FL 4+7/2 FAC 3*

Dennis Bergkamp

Manchester C (£1,500,000 on 2/8/2001) P/FL 48+8/7 FLC 3+2/1 FAC 3+1/1 Others 2
Portsmouth (Free on 9/1/2004) PL 16+6/2 FLC 2/1 FAC 4

BERMINGHAM Karl Joseph Kevin
Born: Dublin, 6 October 1985
Height: 5'10" **Weight:** 12.7
International Honours: RoI: Yth
This speedy striker did well for Manchester City reserves last term and after netting four goals in the 5-1 defeat of rivals Manchester United in a Manchester Senior Cup tie he was given his first taste of senior football on loan to League Two club Lincoln City. Karl was introduced from the substitutes' bench for his debut at Rochdale but found it difficult to win a place in the Imps' line-up. His only other appearance was when he came on with Lincoln three goals down at home to Wycombe Wanderers. Karl played his part in a revival which saw the Imps almost snatch an improbable draw. At the end of his loan spell Karl returned to the City of Manchester Stadium to continue his development.
Manchester C (From trainee on 10/10/2002)
Lincoln C (Loaned on 11/2/2005) FL 0+2

BERNARD Olivier
Born: Paris, France, 14 October 1979
Height: 5'9" **Weight:** 12.6
Olivier was first-choice left back in Newcastle's back four in the first half of last season. Strong and quick with an attacking flair and a good left foot, he displayed his versatility by performing well on the left side of midfield at home to Sporting Lisbon in December's UEFA Cup tie. His understanding with Laurent Robert was an important factor in providing the side with a good balance, and he was sorely missed after his transfer to Southampton in January. Brought in by Saints to add pace to the back four, Olivier made a good early impression and looked at his best when playing behind Graeme Le Saux, forming a useful attacking partnership down the left wing.
Newcastle U (Signed from Lyon, France, on 26/10/2000) PL 82+20/6 FLC 6 FAC 5 Others 26+6
Darlington (Loaned on 13/3/2001) FL 9+1/2
Southampton (£400,000 on 31/1/2005) PL 12+1 FAC 3

BERSON Mathieu
Born: Vannes, France, 23 February 1980
Height: 5'9" **Weight:** 11.6
International Honours: France: U21
A good solid midfielder, Mathieu's uncompromising style and hard tackling brought an extra edge to Villa's midfield, while he also showed he could link the play quickly between midfield and attack. After making his debut from the bench in the Carling Cup tie against Queen's Park Rangers, he had to wait until December for his bow in the Premiership. Altogether Matthieu had a relatively quiet time last term and more will be expected of him in the 2005-06 campaign.
Aston Villa (£1,600,000 from Nantes, France, on 11/8/2004) PL 7+4 FLC 0+1 FAC 0+1

BERTOS Leonida (Leo) Christos
Born: Wellington, New Zealand, 20 December 1981
Height: 6'0" **Weight:** 12.6
International Honours: New Zealand: 7 Full; U23; Yth; Sch
Leo had something of a mixed start to the 2004-05 season, scoring Rochdale's first goal of the campaign and then being sent off the following week. He took a short while to win his place back, but once in the side again he netted a spectacular goal in the 2-1 win against Boston at the end of November. Playing more as a third striker than in his previous role as a winger, he continued to be a regular in the line-up, but he was released at the end of the season. Leo again featured for the New Zealand national side during the campaign.
Barnsley (Signed from Wellington Olympic, New Zealand on 1/9/2000) FL 4+8/1 FAC 0+1
Rochdale (Free on 25/7/2003) FL 73+9/13 FLC 1 FAC 3+1/1 Others 2

BEST Leon Julian Brendan
Born: Nottingham, 19 September 1986
Height: 6'1" **Weight:** 13.3
International Honours: RoI: Yth
The striking star of the Saints U19 side, Leon was, as a result of an injury plague, chucked in at the deep end at Everton last October, leading the attack with fellow youth-team graduate Dexter Blackstock. However, as his teammates were concentrating harder on stopping goals than making them service was at something of a premium, but he impressed with his hard work, smooth running and confidence. Leon was loaned to Queen's Park Rangers in December, where he made just a handful of appearances before returning to St Mary's to lead the young Saints attack as they progressed to the final of the FA Youth.
Southampton (From trainee on 21/9/2004) PL 1+2 FLC 1+1
Queens Park Rgrs (Loaned on 17/12/2004) FL 2+3

BESWETHERICK Jonathan (Jon) Barry
Born: Liverpool, 15 January 1978
Height: 5'11" **Weight:** 11.4
Club Honours: Div 3 '02
This experienced left-sided defender began the 2004-05 season on a short-term contract at Bristol Rovers, but made just one first-team appearance, lining up for the Carling Cup tie against Norwich City. He subsequently moved on to Kidderminster on non-contract terms and featured regularly in a struggling side. However, he was released following a change in management and spent the remainder of the campaign with Conference outfit Forest Green Rovers.
Plymouth Arg (From trainee on 27/7/1996) FL 133+13 FLC 3 FAC 14+2 Others 4
Sheffield Wed (Free on 6/6/2002) FL 9+2 FAC 2+1 Others 1+1
Swindon T (Loaned on 21/2/2003) FL 3
Macclesfield T (Loaned on 16/1/2004) FL 3+1
Bristol Rov (Free on 30/7/2004) FLC 1
Kidderminster Hrs (Free on 4/11/2004) FL 10 FAC 1

BETSY Kevin Eddie Lewis
Born: Seychelles, 20 March 1978
Height: 6'1" **Weight:** 11.12
International Honours: E: SP-1
This powerful right-sided midfielder or striker started the season on loan at Hartlepool from Barnsley, and showed signs that he could be a useful acquisition. He seemed to be about to sign a permanent deal, but then accepted an offer from Oldham where he made a dream debut, netting, ironically, against Pools. Latics' deepening injury problems soon meant Kevin was asked to play up-front with a variety of partners and his form was affected. However, a return to his favoured position wide on the right later in the season under Ronnie Moore wrought a transformation in confidence.
Fulham (£80,000 + from Woking on 16/9/1998) P/FL 3+12/1 FLC 2+1 FAC 0+1 Others 1
Bournemouth (Loaned on 3/9/1999) FL 1+4
Hull C (Loaned on 26/11/1999) FL 1+1 Others 1
Barnsley (£200,000 on 28/2/2002) FL 84+10/15 FLC 2 FAC 6/1 Others 3
Hartlepool U (Loaned on 6/8/2004) FL 3+3/1 FLC 1
Oldham Ath (Free on 10/9/2004) FL 34+2/5 FAC 3 Others 5

BEVAN Scott Anthony
Born: Southampton, 16 September 1979
Height: 6'6" **Weight:** 15.10
Scott missed the first few games of the

2004-05 season through injury but then took his starting place at the end of August on the day the MK Dons won their first game of the season against Torquay. He then missed out again through injury and although he reclaimed the number one spot in November a trio of shaky performances meant that he failed to get another start once new manager Danny Wilson took over in early December. A very tall 'keeper, he sometimes looked unsure when the ball was crossed into the box.
Southampton *(From trainee on 16/1/1998)*
Huddersfield T *(Loaned on 27/7/2002) FL 30 FLC 2 FAC 1 Others 1*
Wycombe W *(Loaned on 16/1/2004) FL 5*
Wimbledon/MK Dons *(Free on 12/3/2004) FL 17 FLC 1 Others 1*

BEWERS Jonathan (Jon) Anthony
Born: Wellingborough, 10 September 1982
Height: 5'9" **Weight:** 10.2
International Honours: E: Yth; Sch
Jon had a short spell on the books of Walsall at the beginning of last season making a single appearance when he featured on the right-hand side of the defence in the 1-1 draw with Sheffield Wednesday. He subsequently departed for Conference South outfit Kettering Town where he spent the remainder of the campaign.
Aston Villa *(From trainee on 16/9/1999) PL 0+1*
Notts Co *(Free on 25/3/2004) FL 0+3*
Walsall *(Free on 9/9/2004) FL 1*

BIGNOT Marcus
Born: Birmingham, 22 August 1974
Height: 5'10" **Weight:** 11.2
Club Honours: Div 3 '03
International Honours: E: SP-1
A right-sided defender who can also operate as a wing back when required, Marcus had a very successful season for Queen's Park Rangers last term when he made the right-back position his own. Although he likes to push forward he did not score any goals, but was a good source of chances for the front players.
Crewe Alex *(£150,000 + from Kidderminster Hrs on 1/9/1997) FL 93+2 FLC 8 FAC 3*
Bristol Rov *(Free on 7/8/2000) FL 26/1 FLC 5/2 FAC 1 Others 3*
Queens Park Rgrs *(Signed on 16/3/2001) FL 49+5/1 FLC 1 FAC 1 Others 1*
Rushden & Diamonds *(Free on 8/8/2002) FL 68/2 FLC 1+1 FAC 4 Others 3*
Queens Park Rgrs *(Free on 25/3/2004) FL 47+2 FLC 2*

BIGNOT Paul Junior
Born: Birmingham, 14 February 1986
Height: 6'1" **Weight:** 12.3
Paul has progressed through the youth set-up at Crewe and made his Championship debut at Rotherham in September when he lined up as a full back, although he possesses the necessary skills to play in a range of defensive positions. Paul is the brother of the Queen's Park Rangers player Marcus Bignot.
Crewe Alex *(From trainee on 1/3/2005) FL 3+2 FLC 0+1*

BIMSON Stuart James
Born: Liverpool, 29 September 1969
Height: 5'11" **Weight:** 11.12
This tough-tackling left back found himself out of favour at Cambridge early on last term and he was loaned out to Accrington Stanley in the autumn. However, he won a surprise recall for the FA Cup tie at Halifax and enjoyed a brief run in the side which lasted into the new year before dropping out of contention again. A qualified UEFA coach, he added aggression and experience towards the U's ultimately unsuccessful fight against relegation.
Bury *(£12,500 from Macclesfield T on 6/2/1995) FL 36 FLC 5 Others 3*
Lincoln C *(Free on 29/11/1996) FL 157+18/4 FLC 2 FAC 7+2 Others 14+1/1*
Cambridge U *(Free on 31/7/2003) FL 37+6 FLC 1 FAC 2*

Marcus Bignot

BIRCH Gary Stephen
Born: Birmingham, 8 October 1981
Height: 5'10" **Weight:** 11.6
Gary battled away tirelessly up front for Walsall in the first part of the 2004-05 season, holding up the ball well and proving a handful for any defence. He scored only once, a late winner against Swindon when the Saddlers came back from a two-goal deficit to win 3-2, and moved on to Kidderminster in December. Gary scored for the Harriers in the 3-1 win at Cambridge and followed up with another in the next game at Scunthorpe before knee surgery kept him out for six weeks.
Walsall *(From trainee on 31/10/1998) FL 42+26/7 FLC 1+2 FAC 1 Others 4+1/1*
Exeter C *(Loaned on 22/3/2001) FL 6+3/2*
Exeter C *(Loaned on 10/8/2001) FL 5+10 Others 1*
Barnsley *(Loaned on 25/3/2004) FL 8/2*
Kidderminster Hrs *(Free on 15/12/2004) FL 11+3/4*

BIRCHALL Adam Stephen
Born: Maidstone, 2 December 1984
Height: 5'7" **Weight:** 11.8
International Honours: W: U21-9
A prolific goal-scorer with Arsenal's reserve and youth teams, Adam spent most of the first half of last season on loan at Wycombe where he was used as a left winger rather than in his more familiar role as a striker. After a slow start he scored a brace of headers at home to Grimsby and three more goals followed, his intelligent link up play and cool finishing endearing himself to the Chairboys' fans. The end of his loan spell coincided with the departure of Tony Adams and he returned to Highbury. Although an injury kept him on the sidelines for a while he was back in action in March when he added to his tally of U21 caps for Wales.
Arsenal *(From trainee on 2/7/2002)*
Wycombe W *(Loaned on 20/8/2004) FL 11+1/4 FLC 1 Others 2/1*

BIRCHALL Christopher (Chris)
Born: Stafford, 5 May 1984
Height: 5'9" **Weight:** 12.12
International Honours: Trinidad & Tobago: 4
This all-action right winger really came to the fore with Port Vale last season when he became a regular in the first team. He first made the breakthrough in October and after scoring the winner against Swindon Town he was there to stay. A brace of superb goals in the 3-1 victory over promotion-chasing Tranmere preceded an excellent December for Chris, when his pace caused plenty of problems for opposing defenders. Altogether he scored seven goals, the best being a 25-yard effort against Barnsley that won the club's 'Goal of the Season' award. Chris also received Vale's 'Young Player of the Year' prize.
Port Vale *(From trainee on 1/5/2004) FL 30+17/6 FLC 0+2 FAC 2+3 Others 1+1/1*

BIRCHAM Marc Stephen John
Born: Wembley, 11 May 1978
Height: 5'10" **Weight:** 12.4
Club Honours: Div 2 '01
International Honours: Canada: 17; U23-1
This central midfield player was a regular for Queen's Park Rangers last season. A competitive player, Marc coped well with the regular changes to his partner in the middle of the park. He has never been a prolific goal-scorer, and netted just once last term, in the final home game of the season against Nottingham Forest.
Millwall *(From trainee on 22/5/1996) FL 86+18/3 FLC 3+1 FAC 6+1/1 Others 5+1*
Queens Park Rgrs *(Free on 10/7/2002) FL 102+7/5 FLC 3+1 FAC 2 Others 5*

BIRD David Alan
Born: Gloucester, 26 December 1984
Height: 5'8" **Weight:** 12.2
David established himself as a regular member of the Cheltenham Town first-team squad last term. Operating either in the centre of midfield or wide on either flank, his energy and determination enabled him to cover a lot of ground during matches and he was a quiet but highly effective presence in the team, winning tackles and playing simple passes. He was unlucky not to score on a number of occasions.
Cheltenham T *(Signed from Cinderford T on 1/2/2001) FL 56+16 FLC 2 FAC 3 Others 2+1*

BISCAN Igor
Born: Zagreb, Croatia, 4 May 1978
Height: 6'3" **Weight:** 12.8
Club Honours: FLC '01, '03; ESC '01; CS '01
International Honours: Croatia: 15
Although this central midfielder played fewer games for Liverpool in 2004-05 than in the previous season, he enjoyed arguably his best season at Anfield and finally winning over the sceptical Reds' supporters. Starting the season as a regular substitute, in which role he scored his first-ever Premiership goal at Fulham in October, a commanding performance in the crucial European Champions' League match away to Deportivo La Coruna convinced new manager Rafael Benitez that he was a worthy stand-in for Steven Gerrard. Sidelined for six weeks with a calf injury in December, following his return to fitness in January he played in nearly every significant match thereafter, including all the crucial Champions' Cup ties with the exception of the final. Out of contract in the summer his future was unclear at the time of writing.
Liverpool *(£3,500,000 from Dynamo Zagreb, Croatia, ex Samobar, on 7/12/2000) PL 50+22/2 FLC 12+3/1 FAC 5+2 Others 14+10*

BISCHOFF Mikkel
Born: Denmark, 3 February 1982
Height: 6'4" **Weight:** 13.5
International Honours: Denmark: U21-4; Yth
After recovering from a series of injuries Mikkel joined Wolves on loan in the autumn looking to re-ignite his career. He began to forge a useful partnership with Jolean Lescott in the centre of defence, and even produced a glancing header that proved the winner against Nottingham Forest. However, he then dislocated a shoulder and returned to the City of Manchester Stadium to recuperate. Mikkel returned to Molineux for another loan spell in March, with a view to a permanent transfer, but with Lescott and Jody Craddock in good form he had to settle for a couple of games at right back.
Manchester C *(£750,000 from FC Copenhagen, Denmark on 2/7/2002) PL 1 Others 1*
Wolverhampton W *(Loaned on 30/9/2004) FL 7/1*
Wolverhampton W *(Loaned on 24/3/2005) FL 2+2*

BISGAARD Morten
Born: Randers, Denmark, 25 June 1974
Height: 6'1" **Weight:** 12.4
International Honours: Denmark: 8; U21-8; Yth
Morten was fresh from helping FC Copenhagen to win a domestic double when he joined Derby County, one of several shrewd dips the Rams made into the European market. He made a slow start at Pride Park, hampered by early-season calf and foot injuries. After playing his way back in the reserves, the Danish international became a regular on the right of midfield. He has a good touch and an alert football brain, but a shift of position brought out the best in him. As Derby's bid for the play-offs gathered momentum, George Burley gave Morten a more fluid supporting role in midfield. This helped him to add goals,

including an important winner against Sheffield United at Bramall Lane.
Derby Co *(Signed from FC Copenhagen, Denmark, ex Udinese, on 6/8/2004) FL 31+5/4 FAC 3 Others 2*

BJORKLUND Joachim
Born: Vaxjo, Sweden, 15 March 1971
Height: 6'1" **Weight:** 12.10
Club Honours: SPD '97; SLC '96
International Honours: Sweden: 75
A surprise signing for Wolves, this quick and experienced centre back had not had a 'pre-season' to speak of. Joachim promptly pulled a hamstring in his second match and did not appear until late September, before slipping out of the first-team picture altogether. He was only selected once under Glenn Hoddle, featuring as a man-marker in the FA Cup tie at Highbury.
Glasgow Rgrs *(Signed from Vicenza, Italy, ex Osters, Brann Bergen, Goteborg, on 15/7/1996) SL 59 SLC 5 SC 8 Others 13 (Transferred to Valencia, Spain during 1998 close season)*
Sunderland *(£1,500,000 from Venezia, Italy on 1/2/2002) P/FL 49+8 FLC 1 FAC 4+1 Others 1+1*
Wolverhampton W *(Free on 5/8/2004) FL 2+1 FLC 1 FAC 1*

BLACK Thomas (Tommy) Robert
Born: Chigwell, 26 November 1979
Height: 5'7" **Weight:** 11.4
On the fringes of the Crystal Palace first-team squad, Tommy spent a month on loan at Sheffield United as cover for the injured Andy Liddell. After five lively performances, mainly as a wide midfielder, and a goal in the 1-1 draw against Coventry City, he returned to Selhurst Park. However, soon afterwards the unfortunate winger suffered a broken leg playing for Palace reserves against Arsenal and this kept him out of action for the remainder of the campaign.
Arsenal *(From trainee on 3/7/1998) PL 0+1 FLC 1*
Carlisle U *(Loaned on 25/8/1999) FL 5/1*
Bristol C *(Loaned on 17/12/1999) FL 4*
Crystal Palace *(£250,000 + on 21/7/2000) FL 67+59/10 FLC 13+3/5 FAC 3+1/2*
Sheffield U *(Loaned on 17/9/2004) FL 3+1/1 FLC 1*

BLACKBURN Lee Charles
Born: Hornchurch, 1 October 1985
Height: 5'8" **Weight:** 10.5
Lee began last term as a third-year scholar with Norwich City, but in the new year it was announced he was to be released at the end of the season. He subsequently had a trial with Notts County before transferring his scholarship to Cambridge United where he soon won a call-up to the first team, making his debut from the substitutes' bench at Bury in March. A competitive midfielder, he added two further appearances as a substitute before the end of the season.
Cambridge U *(Trainee, ex trainee at Norwich C) FL 0+3*

BLACKSTOCK Dexter Anthony
Born: Oxford, 20 May 1986
Height: 6'2" **Weight:** 13.0
International Honours: E: Yth
Slick, fast and determined, Dexter is a natural penalty-box predator. He got his chance to claim a first-team place for Saints due to injuries, making his debut, at Everton in October. A little over a week later he came on as a substitute in the Carling Cup game against Colchester United at St Mary's, and ran up a hat-trick. With James Beattie, Kevin Phillips and Peter Crouch all fit, and, later, with the signing of Henri Camara, Dexter's first-team opportunities were limited and he was loaned to Plymouth, where he prospered. He scored his first Argyle goal against Sheffield United at Home Park and went on to net three more during his short stay with Argyle. Dexter also represented England at U19 level during the season.
Southampton *(From trainee on 24/5/2004) PL 8+1/1 FLC 0+2/4*
Plymouth Arg *(Loaned on 13/2/2005) FL 10+4/4*

BLACKWOOD Michael Andrew
Born: Birmingham, 30 September 1979
Height: 5'10" **Weight:** 11.10
This attacking left back signed for Lincoln City in the summer of 2004 after doing well in pre-season. Michael started in the first six games of the campaign but then suffered a stomach injury and lost his place to Kevin Sandwith. When fit again he was restricted to the occasional appearance from the substitutes' bench and he was released at the end of the season.
Aston Villa *(From trainee on 14/4/1998)*
Chester C *(Loaned on 3/9/1999) FL 9/2*
Wrexham *(Free on 18/7/2000) FL 24+22/2 FLC 1 FAC 1+1 Others 1 (Free to Stevenage Borough)*
Lincoln C *(Free from Telford U, ex Halesowen T, on 15/7/2004) FL 5+4 FLC 1*

BLAKE Nathan Alexander
Born: Cardiff, 27 January 1972
Height: 5'11" **Weight:** 13.2
Club Honours: WC '92, '93; Div 3 '93, Div 1 '97
International Honours: W: 29; B-1; U21-5; Yth
This veteran striker was one of seven players to make their bow for Leicester on the opening day of the season at home to West Ham. He opened his goal-scoring account for the Foxes in the Carling Cup defeat at home to Preston, but failed to earn a regular starting spot and joined Leeds on loan in January. Nathan netted in his second game – a 2-1 victory at Coventry – but 19 minutes into his next match, a third round FA Cup tie at Birmingham, he ruptured a hamstring and returned to the Foxes who released him at the end of the season.
Cardiff C *(From trainee at Chelsea on 20/8/1990) FL 113+18/35 FLC 6+2 FAC 10/4 Others 13+2/1*
Sheffield U *(£300,000 on 17/2/1994) P/FL 55+14/34 FLC 3+1/1 FAC 1 Others 1*
Bolton W *(£1,500,000 on 23/12/1995) P/FL 102+5/38 FLC 10+1/8 FAC 6/2*
Blackburn Rov *(£4,250,000 on 30/10/1998) P/FL 37+17/13 FLC 3/1 FAC 5+3/2*
Wolverhampton W *(£1,400,000 on 13/9/2001) P/FL 70+5/24 FLC 3/1 FAC 2 Others 5/1*
Leicester C *(Free on 2/8/2004) FL 4+10 FLC 1/1*
Leeds U *(Loaned on 31/12/2004) FL 2/1 FAC 1*

BLAKE Robert (Robbie) James
Born: Middlesbrough, 4 March 1976
Height: 5'9" **Weight:** 12.6
Installed as Burnley's captain last term, Robbie carried the responsibility well despite often playing as a lone figure up front. His tricky skills continued to delight the Clarets' faithful and for the first half of the season Burnley relied heavily on his goals, which were frequently spectacular, none more so than a superbly struck free kick from distance in the home match against Preston. That game proved to be Robbie's last appearance at Turf Moor as he was sold to Birmingham in January. Robbie scored his first Blues' goal from the penalty spot in a vital defeat of Southampton at St Andrew's when he pulled the strings up front with his elusive dribbling, good movement and creative passing. He was mainly used from the bench by manager Steve Bruce, coming on in a variety of attacking positions.
Darlington *(From trainee on 1/7/1994) FL 54+14/21 FLC 4+2/1 FAC 3+1 Others 3+1/1*
Bradford C *(£300,000 on 27/3/1997) P/FL 109+44/40 FLC 8+3/4 FAC 7/1 Others 3+1/2*
Nottingham F *(Loaned on 22/8/2000) FL 9+2/1 FLC 1*
Burnley *(£1,000,000 + on 25/1/2002) FL 103+17/42 FLC 11/5 FAC 6+1/4*
Birmingham C *(£1,250,000 on 5/1/2005) PL 2+9/2 FAC 1+1*

BLATHERWICK Steven (Steve) Scott
Born: Hucknall, 20 September 1973
Height: 6'1" **Weight:** 14.6
Steve enjoyed another commanding season at the centre of Chesterfield's defence last term, forming a fine partnership with Ian Evatt. He also posed huge problems for the opposition when going forward at set pieces, and weighed in with four goals of his own to double his tally for the club.
Nottingham F *(From trainee at Notts Co on 2/8/1992) P/FL 10 FLC 2 FAC 1 Others 2*
Wycombe W *(Loaned on 18/2/1994) FL 2 Others 1*
Hereford U *(Loaned on 11/9/1995) FL 10/1 Others 2*
Reading *(Loaned on 27/3/1997) FL 6+1*
Burnley *(£150,000 on 18/7/1997) FL 16+8 FLC 5 FAC 1+1 Others 3*
Chesterfield *(Loaned on 18/9/1998) FL 2*
Chesterfield *(£50,000 on 1/12/1998) FL 184+9/8 FLC 8+1 FAC 3+1 Others 10/1*

BLAYNEY Alan
Born: Belfast, 9 October 1981
Height: 6'2" **Weight:** 13.12
International Honours: NI: U23-1; U21-4
The third-choice goalkeeper at St Mary's at the beginning of the 2004-05 season, injuries to Antti Niemi and Paul Smith meant that Alan had the misfortune to deputise for two of the more maladroit defensive performances staged by the Saints during the campaign. With both Niemi and Smith fit he went out on loan to Rushden, where he kept two clean sheets before a change in the management meant a return to St Mary's. Alan then spent the last seven matches of the campaign on loan at Brighton, playing a big part in the Seagulls' successful fight against relegation. Brave on the ground and confident in the air, he gave several 'Man of the Match' performances, instilling a new confidence in an Albion defence which had declined in the absence of regular 'keeper Michel Kuipers.
Southampton *(From trainee on 13/7/2001) PL 3 FLC 1*
Stockport Co *(Loaned on 29/10/2002) FL 2 Others 1*
Bournemouth *(Loaned on 24/12/2002) FL 2*
Rushden & Diamonds *(Loaned on 7/1/2005) FL 4*
Brighton & Hove A *(Loaned on 24/3/2005) FL 7*

BLEWITT Darren Lee
Born: Newham, 3 September 1985
Height: 6'2" **Weight:** 13.0
This young West Ham defender stepped up to the professional ranks in the summer of 2004 and featured as an unused substitute in the Carling Cup tie against Southend United. He went on to captain the Hammers' reserve team on occasions and in the new year went out on loan to Southend as cover for injuries. However, the only first-team action he saw for the Roots Hall club was when he came on as a last-minute substitute at Cheltenham. He subsequently returned to Upton Park to continue his football development.
West Ham U *(From trainee on 5/7/2004)*
Southend U *(Loaned on 16/3/2005) FL 0+1*

BLINKHORN Matthew David
Born: Blackpool, 2 March 1985
Height: 5'11" **Weight:** 10.10
Club Honours: AMC '04
This young Blackpool striker spent the early months of the 2004-05 campaign out on loan to Luton. However, he was used as a back-up for regulars Steve Howard and Rowan Vine during his spell at Kenilworth Road and only featured from the bench. On his return to the Seasiders he had a brief run in the side, scoring twice in the LDV Vans Trophy victory over Huddersfield before a shoulder injury brought his campaign to a premature close in December.
Blackpool *(From trainee on 28/6/2003) FL 9+17/3 FAC 1+1 Others 3+5/4*
Luton T *(Loaned on 31/7/2004) FL 0+2 FLC 0+1*

BLIZZARD Dominic John
Born: High Wycombe, 2 September 1983
Height: 6'2" **Weight:** 13.5
Dominic proved a valuable member of the Watford first-team squad last term as a hard-working central-midfield player with an unfussy and effective style. Tall and strong with a distinctive, coltish running gait, he tackled firmly and showed an encouraging improvement in his passing. A product of the Watford Academy, he was rewarded with a new contract in December.
Watford *(From trainee on 19/4/2002) FL 13+6/2 FLC 2+2 FAC 1*

BLOOMER Matthew (Matt) Brian
Born: Grimsby, 3 November 1978
Height: 6'0" **Weight:** 13.0
Matt again showed his versatility for Lincoln City last term and was used in a number of different positions. Although primarily a defender appearing as a right back or centre half, he was also pushed up front as an extra striker. He is a good squad player who fitted into whatever role he was given.
Grimsby T *(From juniors on 3/7/1997) FL 3+9 FLC 0+2 Others 0+1*
Hull C *(Free on 5/7/2001) FL 0+3 FLC 1*
Lincoln C *(Loaned on 22/3/2002) FL 4+1*
Lincoln C *(Free on 31/12/2002) FL 48+29/3 FLC 3 FAC 3/1 Others 4+4*

BLOOMFIELD Matthew (Matt) James
Born: Ipswich, 8 February 1984
Height: 5'9" **Weight:** 11.3
International Honours: E: Yth
This skilful Wycombe midfielder had an unfortunate start to the 2004-05 campaign when he twisted his knee in a collision with a colleague in a pre-season friendly. After surgery he returned to the first team in December, but then pulled a hamstring in January, which kept him out for another five weeks. Matt finished as one of the strongest players in the team: hard working, quick-footed and able to take the game to the opposition.
Ipswich T *(From trainee on 3/7/2001) FLC 0+1*
Wycombe W *(Free on 24/12/2003) FL 30+8/3 FAC 0+2 Others 2*

BLUNDELL Gregg Steven
Born: Liverpool, 3 October 1977
Height: 5'10" **Weight:** 12.2
Club Honours: Div 3 '04
This talented striker found it harder to score goals for Doncaster in League One last season, but still finished the campaign as the club's second-top scorer with a tally of 11 in all competitions. He served the team well throughout, and also occasionally featured in a role out on the right flank from where he was able to set up chances for his colleagues.
Tranmere Rov *(From trainee on 9/7/1996. Free to Knowsley U on 30/11/1996)*
Doncaster Rov *(Free from Northwich Vic on 27/3/2003) FL 74+11/27 FLC 4/2 FAC 3/2*

BOA MORTE Luis
Born: Lisbon, Portugal, 4 August 1977
Height: 5'10" **Weight:** 11.5
Club Honours: PL '98; Div 1 '01; CS '98, '99
International Honours: Portugal: 21; U21-28; Yth
Luis gave a number of outstanding performances for Fulham last term and on his day he is single-handedly capable of turning a match on its head. A very skilful player with excellent ball control and speed off the mark, he is at his most effective when playing wide on the left. He was outstanding in the 4-1 win at Newcastle and also in the home win over Portsmouth. Luis hit nine goals in all competitions and won a recall to the Portugal squad after missing out on Euro 2004.

***Arsenal** (£1,750,000 + from Sporting Lisbon, Portugal on 25/6/1997) PL 6+19 FLC 3/2 FAC 2+3/1 Others 2+4/1*
***Southampton** (£500,000 + on 27/8/1999) PL 6+8/1 FLC 0+2 FAC 1*
***Fulham** (£1,700,000 on 31/7/2000) P/FL 122+33/38 FLC 10+4/5 FAC 15+1/2 Others 10+2/2*

BOARDLEY Stuart James
Born: Ipswich, 14 February 1985
Height: 5'10" **Weight:** 11.0
A product of Ipswich Town's youth set-up, Stuart joined Torquay United in the summer of 2004 and made his senior debut in the LDV Vans Trophy tie against Yeovil at the end of September. He featured in a handful of first-team games thereafter, but his last appearance came in February as injuries restricted his availability. A promising left-sided midfielder, Stuart was released by the Gulls in the summer.
***Torquay U** (From trainee at Ipswich T on 13/9/2004) FL 2+4 FAC 0+1 Others 2*

BOATENG George
Born: Nkawkaw, Ghana, 5 September 1975
Height: 5'9" **Weight:** 11.7
Club Honours: FLC '04
International Honours: Holland: 2; U21-18
George had a magnificent season at the Riverside despite a three-month interruption with a broken toe. Boro's hard-tackling midfielder was never renowned as a goal-scorer which prompted Don Mackay – Boro's head of Football Recruitment – to promise George 12 bottles of champagne if he scored three goals last season. George accepted the former Blackburn Rovers' manager's challenge and responded, of course, with three successful strikes – against Blackburn Rovers, Bolton Wanderers and the vital winner at the Riverside, albeit from a Ledley King deflection, against Tottenham Hotspur.
***Coventry C** (£250,000 from Feyenoord, Holland, ex Excelsior, on 19/12/1997) PL 43+4/5 FLC 3/1 FAC 8/1*
***Aston Villa** (£4,500,000 on 22/7/1999) PL 96+7/4 FLC 9+1/1 FAC 9 Others 13*
***Middlesbrough** (£5,000,000 on 8/8/2002) PL 88/3 FLC 6 FAC 2 Others 4*

BOCANEGRA Carlos
Born: Alta Loma, USA, 25 May 1979
Height: 6'0" **Weight:** 12.4
International Honours: USA: 36
Carlos was first choice at left back for Fulham for much of last season. A committed, wholehearted defender who never shirks a challenge, he likes to join the attack and scored his first goal for the club with a diving header early in the season at Portsmouth. Solid in the challenge he links well with Luis Boa Morte on the left-hand side. Carlos continued to feature for the USA international side, appearing in a number of World Cup qualifiers during the campaign.
***Fulham** (Free from Chicago Fire, USA on 14/1/2004) PL 41+2/1 FLC 3 FAC 8*

BODKIN Matthew (Matt) James
Born: Chatham, 23 November 1983
Height: 5'6" **Weight:** 11.5
A speedy and tricky winger, Matt was a virtual ever-present for Gillingham's reserves last season. He made the starting line-up for the FA Cup tie at Portsmouth, when he did not let the team down, and also featured in the two following Championship games from the bench.
***Nottingham F** (From trainee on 4/1/2003)*
***Gillingham** (Free on 14/8/2004) FL 0+2 FAC 1*

BOERTIEN Paul
Born: Haltwhistle, 21 January 1979
Height: 5'10" **Weight:** 11.2
The 2004-05 campaign proved to be a season of utter frustration for Paul at Derby. He worked hard through the summer to recover from an operation on cruciate knee ligaments and was in the reserves by November. He returned to

Carlos Bocanegra

senior action at left back against Wigan Athletic in the FA Cup but suffered severe bruising on a knee in the fourth round replay at Fulham. The injury was slow to clear and further surgery ended his campaign.
Carlisle U *(From trainee on 13/5/1997) FL 16+1/1 FLC 0+2 FAC 1 Others 1*
Derby Co *(£250,000 on 25/3/1999) P/FL 82+21/2 FLC 4+1 FAC 5+2*
Crewe Alex *(Loaned on 11/2/2000) FL 2*
Notts Co *(Loaned on 23/1/2004) FL 5*

BOJIC Pedrag (Pedji)
Born: Sydney, Australia, 9 April 1984
Height: 5'11" **Weight:** 11.12
International Honours: Australia: Yth
Pedji came to the attention of Northampton Town when he appeared for an Australian U23 side against them in a pre-season friendly and he was offered terms soon afterwards. He established himself in the side at right back and made some exciting dashes down the flank, linking up well with Josh Low. His wholehearted play resulted in numerous crosses into the opposition box and he also chanced his arm with a few shots at goal himself.
Northampton T *(Signed from Sydney Olympic, Australia, on 6/8/2004) FL 25+11 FLC 2 FAC 2+1 Others 2*

BOLAND William (Willie) John
Born: Ennis, 6 August 1975
Height: 5'9" **Weight:** 11.2
International Honours: RoI: B-1; U21-11; Yth; Sch
Willie began the 2004-05 season as a first choice alongside Graham Kavanagh in the centre of the Cardiff midfield, but a poor run of results saw manager Lennie Lawrence draft in midfield reinforcements. Willie battled briefly with loan signing Gary O'Neil for a starting spot before suffering an injury against Watford in December. This ruled him out until April when he returned to lend a timely hand in ensuring the Bluebirds avoided relegation.
Coventry C *(From juniors on 4/11/1992) PL 43+20 FLC 6+1 FAC 0+1*
Cardiff C *(Free on 24/6/1999) FL 176+18/3 FLC 11+1 FAC 11+4/1 Others 6*

BOLDER Adam Peter
Born: Hull, 25 October 1980
Height: 5'8" **Weight:** 11.0
In a Derby County side essentially geared to going forward, Adam's industry became increasingly important last term. He understands that his job is to cover, tackle and harass but still managed to get up to support the strikers effectively when a chance presented itself. He scored a fine goal in the final match at Highfield Road although, by then, Coventry City were on the way to a crushing victory. Adam's style is much appreciated by other players and there were occasions when he was distinctly unfortunate to be left out. Always, though, he is prepared to battle back and prove a point.
Hull C *(From trainee on 9/7/1999) FL 18+2 Others 2+1*
Derby Co *(Signed on 3/4/2000) P/FL 75+43/9 FLC 3 FAC 4+1 Others 1+1*

BOLLAND Paul Graham
Born: Bradford, 23 December 1979
Height: 5'11" **Weight:** 11.0
One of the longest-serving players at Meadow Lane, Paul is often referred to as one of the unsung heroes of the Notts County side for his quiet, unspectacular performances. An industrious hard-running ball winner in midfield, most of his best performances last term were on the right flank, where his determination and pace often carried him into positions from which he could create chances for his colleagues.
Bradford C *(From trainee on 20/3/1998) FL 4+8 FLC 2*
Notts Co *(£75,000 on 14/1/1999) FL 153+19/6 FLC 3+6 FAC 7+1 Others 2+3/1*

BOLLAND Philip (Phil) Christopher
Born: Liverpool, 26 August 1976
Height: 6'2" **Weight:** 13.8
Club Honours: NC '04
This tall central defender was Chester City's most consistent defensive player in 2004-05. A change in formation to a flat back four, saw Phil line up alongside a succession of different partners in City's first season back in the Football League. A calm, assured centre half he is excellent in the air, while his seemingly telescopic legs frequently came to the rescue with last-ditch tackles. Phil scored one goal, netting in the 2-1 win at Scunthorpe.
Oxford U *(Free from Southport, ex Altrincham, Salford C, Trafford, Knowsley U, Altrincham, on 9/7/2001) FL 20/1 FLC 1 FAC 1 Others 1*
Chester C *(Free on 4/3/2002) FL 42/1 FLC 1 FAC 2 Others 3*

BOND Kain
Born: Torquay, 19 June 1985
Height: 5'8" **Weight:** 10.10
A graduate of Torquay United's youth policy, this young striker failed to make the expected breakthrough at Plainmoor last season. After just two appearances from the bench the young striker was released in October and soon afterwards he signed for Taunton Town.
Torquay U *(From trainee on 2/7/2003) FL 0+3 FAC 0+1 Others 0+1*

BONNER Mark
Born: Ormskirk, 7 June 1974
Height: 5'10" **Weight:** 11.0
Mark endured a frustrating campaign in 2004-5 at Boundary Park. After picking up an early-season hamstring injury, the busy midfield grafter then suffered a broken foot in his comeback game against former club Blackpool. During his absence, Latics drafted in youngsters Mark Hughes and Neil Kilkenny on loan from Premiership clubs and both excelled. Mark subsequently struggled to regain his first-team place upon his return to action - making just two late-season starts - and is a man with a point to prove to new boss Ronnie Moore in 2005-06.
Blackpool *(From trainee on 18/6/1992) FL 156+22/14 FLC 15+3 FAC 11 Others 10+3/1*
Cardiff C *(Free on 17/7/1998) FL 113+30/2 FLC 8 FAC 7+1 Others 8+3/1*
Hull C *(Loaned on 8/1/1999) FL 1/1*
Oldham Ath *(Free on 25/3/2004) FL 21+5 FLC 1 Others 2*

BOOK Steven (Steve) Kim
Born: Bournemouth, 7 July 1969
Height: 5'11" **Weight:** 11.1
Club Honours: FAT '98; NC '99
International Honours: E: SP-3
This experienced goalkeeper spent the 2004-05 season providing cover for Rhys Evans at Swindon. Steve's outings were limited to a first round Carling Cup tie at Rushden and two early rounds of the LDV Vans Trophy, before making an unexpected League appearance from the bench when Evans suffered an injury during the defeat at home to Bournemouth in early March. Steve eventually received a full League outing against Wrexham later that month but was not retained at the end of the season.
Cheltenham T *(Signed from Forest Green Rov on 23/7/1997) FL 171+1 FLC 7 FAC 12 Others 8*
Swindon T *(Free on 5/8/2004) FL 1+1 FLC 1 Others 2*

BOOTH Andrew (Andy) David
Born: Huddersfield, 6 December 1973
Height: 6'0" **Weight:** 13.0
International Honours: E: U21-3
Andy Booth is Huddersfield Town through and through, a rare commodity these days, and he enjoyed another good season in 2004-05. Now approaching the end of his career, he still managed to cause problems for opposing defenders

with his aerial skills, while his striking partner Pawel Abbott benefited from his unselfish displays. Andy often helped out in defence at set pieces and was occasionally used as an emergency defender. He is now the fourth-highest scorer in the Terriers' history, a fitting reward for a great servant of the club.
Huddersfield T *(From trainee on 1/7/1992) FL 109+14/54 FLC 10+1/3 FAC 8/3 Others 12+1/4*
Sheffield Wed *(£2,700,000 on 8/7/1996) P/FL 124+9/28 FLC 10+1/1 FAC 9+1/5*
Tottenham H *(Loaned on 30/1/2001) PL 3+1*
Huddersfield T *(£200,000 on 22/3/2001) FL 131+12/43 FLC 4/1 FAC 3 Others 12/3*

BOOTH Robert (Robbie) Paul
Born: Liverpool, 30 December 1985
Height: 5'7" **Weight:** 11.8
Robbie joined Chester City as a third-year scholar after being released by Everton. An attacking right-sided midfielder he made his full debut against Oxford United in November and went on to sign a professional contract in March. Robbie scored a vital well-taken goal in the home game against Boston and ended the campaign playing up front alongside Ryan Lowe and Robbie Foy. However, he was released at the end of the season.
Chester C *(From trainee, ex Everton trainee, on 15/5/2005) FL 7+4/1 FAC 1+1 Others 2+1*

BOPP Eugene
Born: Kiev, Ukraine, 5 September 1983
Height: 5'10" **Weight:** 12.4
This young Nottingham Forest midfielder again failed to make a breakthrough into regular first-team football last term and was mostly used from the bench. Eugene finished the campaign on something of a high with goals against Queen's Park Rangers and Gillingham, and will be looking to feature more regularly in the starting line-up in 2005-06.
Nottingham F *(From trainee on 11/9/2000) FL 37+28/7 FLC 3+4/2 FAC 2*

BORROWDALE Gary Ian
Born: Sutton, 16 July 1985
Height: 6'0" **Weight:** 12.1
International Honours: E: Yth
A versatile left-sided who can feature in midfield or at full back, Gary found his path to the Crystal Palace first team blocked by Danny Granville last term and he made only intermittent appearances in the Premiership. The youngster signed a new long-term contract for the club and continued to progress at international level, stepping up to play for England U20's.
Crystal Palace *(From trainee on 6/12/2002) P/FL 24+19 FLC 4+4 FAC 1+1*

BOSHELL Daniel (Danny) Kevin
Born: Bradford, 30 May 1981
Height: 5'11" **Weight:** 11.10
Danny was hoping for more regular first-team football at Boundary Park last term and the early signs were good until he lost his place after the team began to struggle. The cultured midfielder dropped out of the first-team picture following a change in management at Boundary Park was subsequently farmed out on-loan to Bury. Comfortable on the ball, and with good passing ability, Danny slotted in well to the Shakers' midfield in a handful of appearances.
Oldham Ath *(From trainee on 10/7/1998) FL 45+25/2 FLC 6/1 FAC 3+3 Others 3/1*
Bury *(Loaned on 24/3/2005) FL 2+4*

BOSSU Bertrand (Bert)
Born: Calais, France, 14 October 1980
Height: 6'7" **Weight:** 14.0
Bert was third-choice 'keeper for Gillingham at the start of the 2004-05 season and was loaned out to Torquay United. However, after just two appearances for the League One club he suffered a knee injury and this prompted an early return. Bert then went out on loan again to Oldham, where he failed to add to his senior experience. He subsequently featured for the Gills in the 3-1 defeat at Cardiff and also came off the bench to replace Steve Banks in the home win over Stoke.
Barnet *(Signed from RC Lens, France on 21/10/1999) Others 0+1 (Transferred to Hayes on 3/8/2001)*
Gillingham *(Free on 9/9/2003) FL 4+2 FAC 2*
Torquay U *(Loaned on 3/8/2004) FL 2*

BOSVELT Paul
Born: Doetinchem, Holland, 26 March 1970
Height: 6'0" **Weight:** 13.3
International Honours: Holland: 24
Paul made the holding midfield role for Manchester City his own last season showing consistency in the position and enjoying an excellent campaign. His influence in the middle of the park has grown enormously since he first arrived at the club and he is now a popular figure with the supporters. He is also well respected by his colleagues for his contribution on the pitch. Out of contract in the summer, his future was uncertain at the time of writing.
Manchester C *(Signed from Feyenoord, Holland, ex GAE Deventer, Twente Enschede, on 29/7/2003) PL 50+3/2 FLC 2 FAC 5/1 Others 4+1*

BOTHROYD Jay
Born: Islington, 7 May 1982
Height: 6'3" **Weight:** 13.6
Club Honours: FAYC '00
International Honours: E: U21-1; Yth; Sch
This talented striker returned to spend the whole of the 2004-05 season on loan at Blackburn. At times he showed the ability to hold the ball up and led the line elegantly, but after being sidelined by a thigh injury he rarely featured at all in the second half of the campaign. Jay scored once for Rovers, netting in the 2-2 draw with Liverpool at Ewood Park.
Arsenal *(From trainee on 8/7/1999)*
Coventry C *(£1,000,000 on 13/7/2000) P/FL 51+21/14 FLC 1+5/2 FAC 5/1 (Transferred to Perugia, Italy on 14/7/2003)*
Blackburn Rov *(Loaned on 9/9/2004) PL 6+5/1 FLC 1 FAC 0+1*

BOUAZZA Hameur
Born: Evry, France, 22 February 1985
Height: 5'10" **Weight:** 12.0
Hameur brought pace, skill and strength to Watford's left flank last term, and cemented his place in the first-team squad, albeit often as a substitute. He suffered a dislocated shoulder in November, which sidelined him for six weeks and seemed to cost him a little confidence on his return. Shuttling between midfield and attack, Hameur was never afraid to have a shot, and he scored a spectacular volleyed goal against Southampton during the Carling Cup run.
Watford *(From trainee on 2/7/2004) FL 16+21/2 FLC 4+2/2 FAC 2*

BOUCAUD Andre Christopher
Born: Enfield, 9 October 1984
Height: 5'10" **Weight:** 11.4
International Honours: Trinidad & Tobago: 6
This skilful ball-playing midfielder had something of a frustrating time at Peterborough last season, for although he featured in almost half the club's League One fixtures he was never given a decent run in the starting line-up. Andre is best used in a central-midfield role, where he always seems to have plenty of time on the ball.
Reading *(From trainee on 25/3/2002)*
Peterborough U *(Loaned on 27/3/2003) FL 5+1*
Peterborough U *(Loaned on 25/7/2003) FL 7+1/1 FLC 1*
Peterborough U *(Free on 1/7/2004) FL 13+9/1 FAC 1 Others 1*

BOULDING Michael (Mick)
Thomas
Born: Sheffield, 8 February 1976
Height: 5'10" **Weight:** 11.4
Despite scoring twice against Luton early in the season Mick found himself mainly on the substitutes' bench for Barnsley at that stage. When manager Paul Hart changed the style of play he was paired with Michael Chopra up front and the team enjoyed a good run of results with Mick finding himself on the score sheet regularly. Sharp in and around the box he worked tirelessly but following a change in management he was allowed to join Cardiff City on loan. However, Mick made little impact at Ninian Park and was subsequently released by Barnsley in the summer.
Mansfield T *(Signed from Hallam FC on 2/8/1999) FL 28+38/12 FLC 2+2 FAC 2+1 Others 1+1*
Grimsby T *(Free on 24/8/2001) FL 24+11/11 FLC 0+2 FAC 0+2*
Aston Villa *(Free on 9/7/2002) Others 2/1*
Sheffield U *(Loaned on 29/9/2002) FL 3+3 FLC 1/1*
Grimsby T *(Free on 10/1/2003) FL 37+2/16 FLC 1 FAC 1/1 Others 0+1*
Barnsley *(£50,000 on 12/2/2004) FL 27+8/10 FLC 1+1 Others 0+1*
Cardiff C *(Loaned on 23/3/2005) FL 0+4*

BOUMSONG Jean-Alain
Somkong
Born: Douala, Cameroon, 14 December 1979
Height: 6'3" **Weight:** 13.3
Club Honours: SPD '05; SLC '05
International Honours: France: 11
Brought in during the January transfer window to stiffen the centre of Newcastle's defence Jean-Alain made his debut in the FA Cup tie at Yeading and he quickly settled in to become a key member of the team. Tall and strong he reads the game well and has the important quality of bringing the best out of his colleagues, it being noticeable how much Titus Bramble improved playing alongside him. Always comfortable on the ball he is a good organiser and is the leader of the defence, a figure which his club has needed for so long now. He added three caps for France during the season.
Glasgow Rgrs *(Signed from Auxerre, France, ex Le Havre, on 30/6/2004) SL 18/2 SLC 2 Others 8*
Newcastle U *(£8,000,000 on 4/1/2005) PL 14 FAC 4*

BOWDITCH Benjamin (Ben)
Edward
Born: Bishops Stortford, 19 February 1984
Height: 5'10" **Weight:** 12.0
Ben was hoping to break into the Colchester United line-up last term, but in the end had to be content with just a few appearances as a substitute. He is a central midfielder who showed promise

Andre Boucaud (left)

during pre-season, with his late runs into the penalty area. The older brother of Ipswich striker Dean Bowditch, Ben was sidelined by injury from the new year.
Tottenham H *(From trainee on 20/2/2001)*
Colchester U *(Free on 7/8/2004) FL 0+5 FLC 0+1 FAC 0+1*

BOWDITCH Dean Peter
Born: Bishops Stortford, 15 June 1986
Height: 5'11" **Weight:** 11.7
International Honours: E: Yth
This pacy striker did not make the progress expected of him at Ipswich last term, partly because opportunities were limited by the success of the partnership between Darren Bent and Shefki Kuqi. He made only six starts during the campaign and spent most of the remaining time on the bench. He spent the last two months of the season on loan at Burnley, making his Clarets debut in the home game against Rotherham. Used up front or occasionally out wide, he proved a skilful player with an eye for goal, and could easily have had more to show than his one appearance on the score sheet, at home to Watford.
Ipswich T *(From trainee on 28/7/2003) FL 13+29/7 FLC 3+1/1 FAC 0+1 Others 0+2*
Burnley *(Loaned on 11/3/2005) FL 8+2/1*

BOWER Mark James
Born: Bradford, 23 January 1980
Height: 5'10" **Weight:** 11.0
Mark began the 2004-05 season competing with Jason Gavin for a position as the regular partner for David Wetherall in the centre of the Bradford defence. He finished it as the club's 'Player of the Year' having started every game. He learned well from Wetherall and plays in a similar cool and unflustered manner. Strong in the air and deceptively quick, Mark also ended a two-year goal drought by scoring three times from set pieces.
Bradford C *(From trainee on 28/3/1998) P/FL 103+7/4 FLC 4 FAC 3+1 Others 2*
York C *(Loaned on 16/2/2000) FL 15/1*
York C *(Loaned on 30/11/2000) FL 21/1 FAC 3 Others 0+1*

BOWRY Robert (Bobby) John
Born: Hampstead, 19 May 1971
Height: 5'9" **Weight:** 10.8
Club Honours: Div 1 '94
International Honours: St Kitts & Nevis
This experienced midfielder suffered a season of injury woe at Layer Road last term. Bobby started Colchester United's first two games, before succumbing to injury, both to his groin and his hip. The former Palace and Millwall man started just seven more games, although he did at least return to fitness before the end of the season, and was on the bench for the last few fixtures. He is best at breaking up opposing attacks.
Crystal Palace *(Free from Carshalton on 4/4/1992) P/FL 36+14/1 FLC 10 FAC 1*
Millwall *(£220,000 on 5/7/1995) FL 125+15/5 FLC 9+1 FAC 6 Others 4*
Colchester U *(Free on 25/7/2001) FL 85+21/2 FLC 2+3 FAC 4+2 Others 6+1*

BOWYER Lee David
Born: Canning Town, 3 January 1977
Height: 5'9" **Weight:** 10.6
International Honours: E: 1; U21-13; Yth
Lee is a feisty midfield terrier with a terrific engine, a biting tackle, and an intense will to win. Playing in the centre of Newcastle's midfield he reads the game well and is a very effective box-to-box player able to find space in the tightest of situations. He scored several goals including a stunning fourth-minute strike at home to Portsmouth in December, the winner at Heerenveen with a back-heel flick, and a fine headed goal at home to Bolton. However, he was sent off three times during the season, one of which involved a well-publicised incident with team mate Kieron Dyer.
Charlton Ath *(From trainee on 13/4/1994) FL 46/8 FLC 6+1/5 FAC 3/1 Others 2*
Leeds U *(£2,600,000 on 5/7/1996) PL 196+7/38 FLC 7+1/1 FAC 16/3 Others 38/13*
West Ham U *(£100,000 on 8/1/2003) PL 10 FAC 1*
Newcastle U *(Free on 7/7/2003) PL 43+8/5 FLC 0+1 FAC 2/1 Others 8+2/3*

BOYACK Steven
Born: Edinburgh, 4 September 1976
Height: 5'9" **Weight:** 10.7
International Honours: S: U21-1
After starting the 2004-05 campaign with SPL club Livingston Steven signed for Boston United during the January transfer window as part of a deal which saw Greg Strong move in the opposite direction. He was brought in to provide experience on the right side of midfield but struggled to hold down a regular place in a team disrupted by injury and suspensions. After a couple of appearances from the bench he scored on his first start at Bristol Rovers but was only given one more chance before leaving to sign for League One club Blackpool. However, he managed only one first-team appearance for the Seasiders, coming on as a substitute at Torquay, and he was released in the summer.
Glasgow Rgrs *(From juniors on 1/7/1993) SL 0+1*
Hull C *(Loaned on 27/2/1998) FL 12/3*
Dundee *(£25,000 on 22/2/1999) SL SL 40+4/3 SLC 3/2 SC 2*
Ayr U *(Loaned on 11/10/2000) SL 10/3*
Heart of Midlothian *(£50,000 on 12/1/2001) SL 37+26/1 SLC 2 SC 6 Others 1*
Livingston *(Free on 12/5/2004) SL 4+2 SLC 1*
Boston U *(Free on 31/1/2005) FL 2+2*
Blackpool *(Free on 24/3/2005) FL 0+1*

BOYCE Emmerson Orlando
Born: Aylesbury, 24 September 1979
Height: 5'11" **Weight:** 11.10
Emmerson was one of the success stories of Crystal Palace's Premiership campaign last time around. A pre-season injury to Danny Butterfield provided him with an opportunity at right back, and he grabbed it with both hands, making the position his own for most of the campaign. Emmerson missed the closing stages of the season with a foot injury and then a hernia operation.
Luton T *(From trainee on 2/4/1998) FL 171+15/8 FLC 11 FAC 9+3/1 Others 3*
Crystal Palace *(Free on 9/7/2004) PL 26+1 FLC 1*

BOYD Adam Mark
Born: Hartlepool, 25 May 1982
Height: 5'9" **Weight:** 10.12
A skilful player with a good turn of speed, 2004-05 proved to be the season that this Hartlepool striker really came of age. Adam was a consistent goal-scorer throughout the campaign and was also the recipient of the Hartlepool 'Player's Player of the Year' award for 2004-05. He scored his first senior hat-trick in the 3-0 win over Sheffield Wednesday, the third goal being voted as the club's 'Goal of the Season'. Adam also produced a fine performance in the play-off semi-final first leg against Tranmere, scoring two well-taken goals.
Hartlepool U *(From trainee on 20/9/1999) FL 77+46/49 FLC 3/1 FAC 6+2/3 Others 9+4/3*
Boston U *(Loaned on 14/11/2003) FL 14/4*

BOYD Marc Edward
Born: Carlisle, 22 October 1981
Height: 5'10" **Weight:** 12.4
Marc moved on to join Gretna in the summer of 2004, but found it difficult to win a regular place in the side. He spent the second half of the campaign on loan at Macclesfield Town making a handful of appearances in the centre of midfield where his steady approach and good distribution served the team well.
Newcastle U *(From trainee on 22/10/1998)*
Port Vale *(Free on 1/7/2002) FL 39+3/3 FLC 1 FAC 4 Others 2+1/1*

Carlisle U *(Free on 18/3/2004) FL 9/1*
Gretna *(Free on 30/7/2004) SL 1+1 Others 0+1*
Macclesfield T *(Loaned on 28/1/2005) FL 4+1*

BRACKSTONE John
Born: Hartlepool, 9 February 1985
Height: 5'11" **Weight:** 10.8
This strong-tackling left back always performed well when called into the Hartlepool first-team squad last season. A first-year professional, he had two short spells in the line-up before his campaign ended prematurely with a bout of glandular fever.
Hartlepool U *(From trainee on 16/3/2004) FL 13+2 FAC 2/1 Others 2*

BRADBURY Lee Michael
Born: Isle of Wight, 3 July 1975
Height: 6'2" **Weight:** 13.10
International Honours: E: U21-3
Lee arrived at Oxford United during the summer of 2005 and was appointed as captain by manager Graham Rix. He started the season playing in his usual striker's role, but struggled to score goals, before being moved into the centre of midfield where he appeared more comfortable. However, a change in management saw him moved around, nevertheless he still managed five goals, including a couple of penalties and a real cracker in the 3-3 draw at Rushden on Boxing Day.
Portsmouth *(Free from Cowes on 14/8/1995) FL 41+13/15 FLC 1+2 FAC 4/2*
Exeter C *(Loaned on 1/12/1995) FL 14/5*
Manchester C *(£3,000,000 + on 1/8/1997) FL 34+6/10 FLC 6/1*
Crystal Palace *(£1,500,000 on 29/10/1998) FL 28+4/6 FLC 3+1/1 FAC 1/1*
Birmingham C *(Loaned on 25/3/1999) FL 6+1 Others 1+1*
Portsmouth *(£380,000 on 14/10/1999) FL 90+9/28 FLC 3+2 FAC 2/1*
Sheffield Wed *(Loaned on 24/12/2002) FL 2+1*
Sheffield Wed *(Loaned on 1/3/2003) FL 8/3*
Derby Co *(Loaned on 14/8/2003) FL 1*
Derby Co *(Loaned on 20/11/2003) FL 6*
Walsall *(Free on 25/3/2004) FL 7+1/1*
Oxford U *(Free on 12/7/2004) FL 39+2/4 FLC 1 FAC 1/1 Others 1*

Marc Boyd

BRADLEY Mark Simon
Born: Dudley, 14 January 1988
Height: 6'0" **Weight:** 11.5
International Honours: W: Yth
This 17-year old midfielder was brought into the Walsall side for the last game of the season against Stockport County and in his 57 minutes of action showed himself full of running and possessing real composure on the ball.
Walsall *(Trainee) FL 1*

BRAIN Jonathan (Jonny) Robert
Born: Carlisle, 11 February 1983
Height: 6'2" **Weight:** 12.4
Jonny started the 2004-05 season as first choice in goal for Port Vale. A tall, commanding 'keeper, he produced a series of competent displays and one of his best performances came at windswept Blackpool early in the New Year when Vale won 2-0. A bout of mumps ended Jonny's run in the first team in February, but unfortunately from his point of view this also coincided with Mark Goodlad's return to full fitness and thereafter he added just one more appearance.
Port Vale *(Free from trainee at Newcastle U, via trials at Carlisle U, on 21/8/2003) FL 58+1 FLC 1 FAC 5 Others 3*

BRAMBLE Tesfaye (Tes) Walda Simeon
Born: Ipswich, 20 July 1980
Height: 6'1" **Weight:** 13.10
This young striker struggled to make much of an impact at Southend last term and he often found himself on the substitutes' bench, managing only two goals for the club during the season. Perhaps his most memorable performance came when he took over in goal after the sending off of goalkeeper Daryl Flahavan in the 2-1 home victory over Boston in October. Tes finished the season on loan at League Two strugglers

Cambridge United, where he added some much-needed bite to the front line. He scored a fantastic 40-yard goal in the home win over Wycombe and was credited with netting U's last goal during their spell in the Football League, slotting home a penalty in the 1-0 win at Rushden.

Southend U *(Signed from Cambridge C on 19/1/2001) FL 101+38/29 FLC 1+3 FAC 13+1/7 Others 13+2/4*

Cambridge U *(Loaned on 11/3/2005) FL 9/3*

BRAMBLE Titus Malachi
Born: Ipswich, 21 July 1981
Height: 6'1" **Weight:** 13.10
International Honours: E: U21-10

Playing at the centre of Newcastle's back four Titus is powerful and strong with a good touch and his long accurate passes out of defence have become a feature of his game. Starting the season with an injury he did not secure a regular start until November when he looked a fine defender, but one who made occasional lapses in concentration. However with the arrival of Jean-Alain Boumsong in January he achieved consistency of a very high standard, one of his most outstanding performances coming in the FA Cup tie against Chelsea. He missed several games in the second half of the campaign as a result of a hernia problem.

Ipswich T *(From trainee on 24/8/1998) P/FL 41+7/1 FLC 4+1/2 FAC 4+1 Others 4/1*

Colchester U *(Loaned on 29/12/1999) FL 2*

Newcastle U *(£5,000,000 on 19/7/2002) PL 58+6/1 FLC 3 FAC 5 Others 25+1/3*

BRAMMER David (Dave)
Born: Bromborough, 28 February 1975
Height: 5'10" **Weight:** 12.0
Club Honours: AMC '01

This experienced central midfielder joined Stoke City in the summer of 2004 and was a near ever-present in the starting line-up throughout the campaign. A player with excellent distribution, his only goal of the season came from a 25-yard drive against Leicester which was subsequently voted 'Goal of the Season' by the club's fans.

Wrexham *(From trainee on 2/7/1993) FL 118+19/12 FLC 6+2 FAC 8+2/1 Others 12+1/1*

Port Vale *(£350,000 + on 24/3/1999) FL 71+2/3 FLC 2 FAC 2/1 Others 7*

Crewe Alex *(£500,000 on 10/8/2001) FL 86+1/4 FLC 6/1 FAC 8/1 Others 2*

Stoke C *(Free on 13/7/2004) FL 42+1/1 FLC 0+1*

BRANCH Graham
Born: Liverpool, 12 February 1972
Height: 6'2" **Weight:** 12.2

Now Burnley's longest-serving player, Graham remained a regular on the Clarets' team sheet, his versatility more of an asset than ever in view of the small squad available to manager Steve Cotterill. Always a player subject to peaks and troughs, he had some of both during 2004-05 but ended the campaign on a fine run of form which no doubt contributed to his being offered a further contract. Employed mainly wide on the left but sometimes in a more central role, either up front or behind a lone striker, he proved as adaptable as ever and had an uncharacteristic scoring run either side of Christmas, his most notable effort being the rapturously-received Turf Moor winner against Wigan.

Tranmere Rov *(Free from Heswall on 2/7/1991) FL 55+47/10 FLC 4+8/1 FAC 1+2 Others 2+1*

Bury *(Loaned on 20/11/1992) FL 3+1/1 Others 1*

Wigan Ath *(Loaned on 24/12/1997) FL 2+1*

Stockport Co *(Free on 31/7/1998) FL 10+4/3 FLC 1*

Burnley *(Free on 31/12/1998) FL 179+43/15 FLC 12+3/1 FAC 9+7 Others 1*

BRANCH Paul **Michael**
Born: Liverpool, 18 October 1978
Height: 5'10" **Weight:** 11.7
International Honours: E: U21-1; Yth; Sch

Last term proved to be something of a stop-start season for Michael as he suffered a series of minor injuries that prevented him from having an extended run in the Chester side. Despite these problems the skilful and speedy striker showed glimpses of the form that had made him such a hot property earlier in his career and he finished the season as the club's leading scorer with 13 goals. Among the highlights of his campaign were doubles against Grimsby and in the FA Cup tie against Halifax, and a magnificent coolly-taken finish against Rochdale to give City a late point.

Everton *(From trainee on 24/10/1995) PL 16+25/3 FLC 0+1 FAC 1+2*

Manchester C *(Loaned on 29/10/1998) FL 4*

Wolverhampton W *(£500,000 + on 25/11/1999) FL 61+11/10 FLC 2+1 FAC 4*

Reading *(Loaned on 21/3/2002) FL 0+2*

Hull C *(Loaned on 4/10/2002) FL 6+1/3*

Bradford C *(Free on 17/7/2003) FL 29+4/6 FLC 1 FAC 0+1*

Chester C *(Signed on 1/7/2004) FL 31+2/11 FLC 1 FAC 1/2 Others 0+1*

BRANCO Serge
Born: Douala, Cameroon, 11 October 1980
Height: 5'9" **Weight:** 11.11
International Honours: Cameroon (OLYM '00)

This central midfield player joined Queen's Park Rangers in mid-September on a monthly contract. He had appeared in a pre-season match but initially started the season with Leeds United. He made his debut in the Carling Cup match at Villa Park but was never a regular first teamer. Although his monthly contract was renewed three times, Serge was released in January and linked up with Russian club Shinnik Yaroslavl.

Queens Park Rgrs *(Free from VfB Stuttgart, Germany, ex Eintracht Brunswick, Eintracht Frankfurt, on 21/9/2004) FL 3+4 FLC 1 FAC 1*

BRANDON Christopher (Chris) William
Born: Bradford, 7 April 1976
Height: 5'7" **Weight:** 10.3

This lively winger proved to be a valuable asset for Huddersfield Town last term, producing some lively displays of all-out attacking football. He became a fans' favourite from the off with his explosive runs and trickery when taking on opposing defenders. A great striker of the ball he was never afraid to have a shot at goal when the opportunity came. Chris flourished in his wide-midfield role and produced a healthy return of six goals for the season.

Torquay U *(Free from Bradford PA on 5/8/1999) FL 64+7/8 FLC 4/1 FAC 5/1 Others 3*

Chesterfield *(Free on 9/7/2002) FL 74+5/11 FLC 2+1/1 FAC 2 Others 4/4*

Huddersfield T *(Free on 5/7/2004) FL 42+2/6 FLC 1 FAC 1*

BRANIFF Kevin Robert
Born: Belfast, 4 March 1983
Height: 5'11" **Weight:** 12.0
International Honours: NI: U23-1; U21-10; Yth; Sch

There was plenty of excitement around Nene Park last summer when Rushden secured this young striker on loan from Millwall for three months, but unfortunately things didn't quite work out for him. He scored in successive wins over Lincoln City and Grimsby Town in August to lift Diamonds briefly into fourth place in League Two, but only managed one more goal. Kevin was dropped to the bench soon afterwards and then went out on loan to Nationwide Conference club Canvey Island. Kevin made two appearances from the bench for Millwall at the start of the new year, but then faded from the scene and later had an extended trial at Darlington without making the first team.

Millwall *(From trainee on 12/4/2000) FL 14+19/1 FLC 3+2/1 FAC 3+6/1*

Rushden & Diamonds *(Loaned on 6/8/2004) FL 11+1/3 FLC 1 Others 1*

BRANSTON Guy Peter Bromley
Born: Leicester, 9 January 1979
Height: 6'0" **Weight:** 13.12
This tough-as-teak centre half was brought in to bolster the Sheffield Wednesday defence. However, he soon lost his place in the side and in the new year he moved out on loan to Peterborough. The competitive defender contributed to an upturn in fortunes during his stay at London Road, but in the end opted for a permanent move to Oldham. Although Latics manager Brian Talbot then departed almost immediately his replacement was Ronnie Moore, whom Guy had worked with at Rotherham, and he featured in the line-up on several occasions during the final run-in.
Leicester C *(From trainee on 3/7/1997)*
Colchester U *(Loaned on 9/2/1998) FL 12/1 Others 1*
Colchester U *(Loaned on 7/8/1998) FL 0+1*
Plymouth Arg *(Loaned on 20/11/1998) FL 7/1 Others 1*
Lincoln C *(Loaned on 10/8/1999) FL 4 FLC 2*
Rotherham U *(£50,000 on 15/10/1999) FL 101+3/13 FLC 5+1 FAC 4 Others 2*
Wycombe W *(Loaned on 19/9/2003) FL 9 Others 2/1*
Peterborough U *(Loaned on 25/2/2004) FL 14*
Sheffield Wed *(Signed on 2/7/2004) FL 10+1 FLC 1 FAC 1*
Peterborough U *(Loaned on 31/12/2004) FL 4/1*
Oldham Ath *(Free on 18/2/2005) FL 6+1/1 Others 1*

BRECKIN Ian
Born: Rotherham, 24 February 1975
Height: 6'0" **Weight:** 12.9
Club Honours: AMC '96
This no-nonsense central defender enjoyed an excellent campaign in the heart of the Wigan Athletic defence playing in all but four matches as the club gained promotion to the top flight. Strong in the air, he was an outstanding performer in the Championship's tightest defence, putting in some classy performances alongside Matt Jackson. An honest and committed performer, the final game of the season against Reading also saw him celebrate his 100th start for the club.
Rotherham U *(From trainee on 1/11/1993) FL 130+2/6 FLC 6 FAC 5 Others 11*
Chesterfield *(£100,000 on 25/7/1997) FL 208+4/8 FLC 16/1 FAC 9/1 Others 12/1*
Wigan Ath *(£150,000 on 25/6/2002) FL 92+4 FLC 4 FAC 3+1 Others 1*

BREEN Gary Patrick
Born: Hendon, 12 December 1973
Height: 6'2" **Weight:** 12.0
Club Honours: Ch '05
International Honours: RoI: 62; U21-9
Sunderland's centre back and skipper capped an excellent season by leading the side to the Championship title. A current Republic of Ireland international, Gary is a commanding presence at the heart of the Black Cats' defence and his ability to read the game allows him to cover for colleagues across the back four with vital interceptions. Gary is always a danger at set pieces and his two goals last term included a vital strike against Cardiff in February that helped the team clinch a narrow 2-1 win. Gary was selected by his fellow professionals for the PFA Championship team of the season.
Maidstone U *(From Charlton Ath juniors on 6/3/1991) FL 19*
Gillingham *(Free on 2/7/1992) FL 45+6 FLC 4 FAC 5 Others 1*
Peterborough U *(£70,000 on 5/8/1994) FL 68+1/1 FLC 6 FAC 6 Others 6/1*
Birmingham C *(£400,000 on 9/2/1996) FL 37+3/2 FLC 4 FAC 1*
Coventry C *(£2,400,000 on 1/2/1997) P/FL 138+8/2 FLC 10+3 FAC 12*
West Ham U *(Free on 30/7/2002) PL 9+5 FLC 2 FAC 2*
Sunderland *(Free on 7/8/2003) FL 72/6 FLC 1 FAC 4 Others 2*

BRENNAN James (Jim) Gerald
Born: Toronto, Canada, 8 May 1977
Height: 5'9" **Weight:** 12.5
Club Honours: Div 1 '04
International Honours: Canada: 38 (Gold Cup '00); U23-1
Jim struggled to make an impact in his second season with Norwich City as a combination of injuries and the form of others restricted him to just 11 first-team appearances. An attacking left back who can also play on the left-hand side of midfield, he is particularly effective when moving forward and possesses a powerful left-foot shot. Jim continued to add to his tally of caps for Canada and will be hoping for a positive season in 2005-06.
Bristol C *(Free from Sora Lazio, Canada on 25/10/1994) FL 51+4/3 FLC 6 FAC 1*
Nottingham F *(£1,500,000 on 29/10/1999) FL 117+6/1 FLC 6 FAC 6 Others 2*
Huddersfield T *(Loaned on 21/3/2001) FL 0+2*
Norwich C *(Free on 7/7/2003) P/FL 13+12/1 FAC 2/1*

BREVETT Rupis (Rufus) Emanuel
Born: Derby, 24 September 1969
Height: 5'8" **Weight:** 11.6
Club Honours: Div 2 '99; Div 1 '01
Rufus started the campaign as first-choice left back at West Ham, and having missed the whole of the previous season he was keen to return to the action. Strong challenges and a keenness to get forward made him a fans' favourite. He scored his first goal for the club with an unstoppable shot at Crewe in August but then lost his place in the side towards the end of the year after Chris Powell arrived at Upton Park.
Doncaster Rov *(From trainee on 8/7/1988) FL 106+3/3 FLC 5 FAC 4 Others 10+1*
Queens Park Rgrs *(£250,000 on 15/2/1991) P/FL 141+11/1 FLC 9+1 FAC 8*
Fulham *(£375,000 on 28/1/1998) P/FL 171+2/1 FLC 14+2/1 FAC 14 Others 12*
West Ham U *(Signed on 31/1/2003) P/FL 24+1/1 FLC 4*

BRIDGE Wayne Michael
Born: Southampton, 5 August 1980
Height: 5'10" **Weight:** 11.11
Club Honours: FLC '05; PL '05
International Honours: E: 20; U21-8; Yth
The England full back, until last season a byword for durability, had an injury-ravaged 2004-05 and for the first time in his career was forced to endure lengthy spells on the sidelines. The campaign had begun brightly for Wayne, who was seen as a vital component of Chelsea's cast iron defence which conceded just eight Premiership goals in the first 27 matches. A virus laid him low either side of Christmas but his season came to a premature end in February when he suffered a broken ankle in the FA Cup fifth round tie at Newcastle. Wayne's attacking combinations down the left flank with Damien Duff and Arjen Robben were potent factors in Chelsea's offensive armoury and the lack of a natural left-footer at left back was a real blow. Wayne was also used successfully as a wide-left midfield player when on international duty for England.
Southampton *(From trainee on 16/1/1998) PL 140+12/2 FLC 10+1 FAC 11*
Chelsea *(£7,000,000 + on 21/7/2003) PL 45+3/1 FLC 4 FAC 4 Others 15+2/2*

BRIDGE-WILKINSON Marc
Born: Nuneaton, 16 March 1979
Height: 5'6" **Weight:** 11.8
Club Honours: AMC '01
A new signing in the summer, this midfielder found it hard to settle in at Edgeley Park last term. He was dropped from the side for a few weeks but shortly after his return he scored against Oldham and then a couple of weeks later he fired County in front at Wrexham with an excellent curling free kick. Even this couldn't kick start his County career and

after a few more appearances he was loaned out to Bradford City for the rest of the season. Marc fared much better at Valley Parade and signed permanently on transfer-deadline day. A very versatile midfielder, he has already operated on both wings but looked most effective playing alongside Steve Schumacher in the middle. Marc scored two fine goals in the 4-1 thrashing of Brentford.

Derby Co *(From trainee on 26/3/1997) PL 0+1*
Carlisle U *(Loaned on 5/3/1999) FL 4+3*
Port Vale *(Free on 4/7/2000) FL 111+13/31 FLC 3/1 FAC 2+2/1 Others 9/3*
Stockport Co *(Free on 2/8/2004) FL 19+3/2 FLC 1 FAC 2*
Bradford C *(Free on 25/2/2005) FL 12/3*

BRIDGES Michael
Born: North Shields, 5 August 1978
Height: 6'1" **Weight:** 10.11
Club Honours: Div 1 '96, '99; Ch '05
International Honours: E: U21-3; Yth; Sch
Unable to get a game at Bolton, this popular striker returned to Sunderland for what was initially a loan period but the switch was later made permanent. Although Michael found it hard to cement a place in the Black Cats' starting line-up, he made numerous appearances from the bench and showed he still possessed the ball-playing skills apparent when he made his debut as a teenager in the mid-'90s. Tall and strong on the ball, Michael came off the bench at Stoke in November to score the only goal of the game and clinch a vital three points. With the Wearsiders clinching the Championship title, Michael collected his third winners' medal with Sunderland.

Sunderland *(From trainee on 9/11/1995) P/FL 31+48/16 FLC 8+3/5 FAC 2*
Leeds U *(£4,500,000 + on 29/7/1999) PL 40+16/19 FLC 3+2 FAC 1+1 Others 17+2/2*
Newcastle U *(Loaned on 2/2/2004) PL 0+6 Others 1+2*
Bolton W *(Free on 1/7/2004)*
Sunderland *(Free on 23/9/2004) FL 5+14/1 FAC 0+2*

BRIGGS Keith
Born: Glossop, 11 December 1981
Height: 5'10" **Weight:** 11.6
Keith was out of the first-team picture at Norwich last term and spent a short period on loan at Crewe at the start of the season. In January he made a welcome return to Edgeley Park and received a superb ovation from the County fans when he made his debut in the 3-0 defeat at Luton Town. A week later he scored in the 2-2 draw at home to Barnsley. Keith was used in a number of different positions during the remainder of the season but always gave his all and produced battling and committed displays in a side that was already heading towards relegation. He also scored in the 2-1 defeat at MK Dons.

Stockport Co *(From trainee on 27/8/1999) FL 47+11/2 FLC 4/1 FAC 3+1 Others 2/1*
Norwich C *(£65,000 on 16/1/2003) FL 2+3*
Crewe Alex *(Loaned on 5/8/2004) FL 3*
Stockport Co *(Free on 14/1/2005) FL 14+2/2*

BRIGHTON Thomas (Tom) James
Born: Kilmarnock, 28 March 1984
Height: 5'10" **Weight:** 11.11
International Honours: S: U21-4; Yth
After impressing pre-season in a match against the Iron, Tom joined Scunthorpe United on a four-month loan. A skilful player, who can operate on the left wing or up front, he found opportunities limited at Glanford Park, making just six appearances for the club before returning to Ibrox. Tom finished the campaign with somewhat mixed fortunes, featuring for Scotland U21s against Moldova and Belarus, but finding himself released by Rangers.

Glasgow Rgrs *(From juniors on 1/7/2003) SL 1*
Scunthorpe U *(Loaned on 31/8/2004) FL 2+3 Others 1*

BRIGHTWELL Ian Robert
Born: Lutterworth, 9 April 1968
Height: 5'10" **Weight:** 12.8
International Honours: E: U21-4; Yth
This experienced defender was appointed as Macclesfield Town reserve-team manager at the start of last term and was also registered as a player in case of need. Following injuries to first-choice defenders, Ian made eight senior appearances in the first half of the season on the right side of the defence, playing for the full 90 minutes on two occasions.

Manchester C *(From juniors on 7/5/1986) P/FL 285+36/18 FLC 29+2 FAC 19+4/1 Others 4+3*
Coventry C *(Free on 2/7/1998) FLC 1*
Walsall *(Free on 11/2/2000) FL 77+4 FLC 6 FAC 5 Others 3*
Stoke C *(Free on 28/3/2002) FL 3+1 Others 0+1*
Port Vale *(Free on 8/8/2002) FL 36+1 FLC 1 FAC 1 Others 2*
Macclesfield T *(Free on 27/7/2004) FL 3+3 FAC 1+1*

BRISCO Neil Anthony
Born: Wigan, 26 January 1978
Height: 6'0" **Weight:** 11.5
Club Honours: AMC '01
Neil was expected to be the key addition to Rochdale's midfield last term after arriving at Spotland in the summer. However, he was injured during the pre-season period and then dropped out of the side after only three games. After regaining fitness he had another brief spell in the line-up, but was left out when Scott Warner returned after injury. Neil went out on loan to Northwich Victoria for three months, but on his return was restored to the squad, coming on as a late substitute against Swansea and immediately setting up Dale's equaliser.

Manchester C *(From trainee on 4/3/1997)*
Port Vale *(Free on 7/8/1998) FL 105+13/2 FLC 2 FAC 4+1 Others 8+1*
Rochdale *(Free on 29/7/2004) FL 6+5 Others 0+1*

BRISCOE Michael James
Born: Northampton, 4 July 1983
Height: 6'1" **Weight:** 11.7
Michael joined Macclesfield in the 2004 close season making his Football League debut in the first match of the season at Leyton Orient. He was a regular in the senior side during the first two months of the campaign, usually playing in the centre of a back-three formation, often in the role of sweeper. With good ball control and excellent distribution Michael made an immediate impact, but lost out to more experienced players and, later, new signings. He spent a month on loan at Conference club Burton Albion towards the end of the season.

Coventry C *(Free from Harpole on 28/4/2003)*
Macclesfield T *(Free on 2/7/2004) FL 12+2 FLC 1 FAC 0+1 Others 1+2*

BRITTON Leon James
Born: Merton, 16 September 1982
Height: 5'5" **Weight:** 9.10
International Honours: E: Yth
Despite starting the campaign in midfield, Leon had to be content with mainly a substitute's role for Swansea City for most of the 2004-05 season, although he started in the away victory at Bury when the Swans sealed automatic promotion. Playing a number of games as a wide right-sided midfielder, it was only when he reverted to his customary central midfield role that his ability and skill on the ball became evident.

West Ham U *(From juniors on 21/9/1999)*
Swansea C *(Free on 13/12/2002) FL 83+14/4 FLC 2 FAC 7+1 Others 0+1*

BRKOVIC Ahmet
Born: Dubrovnik, Croatia, 23 September 1974
Height: 5'7" **Weight:** 10.8
Club Honours: Div 1 '05
This talented midfielder was in excellent form for League One champions Luton Town last season, scoring a total of 16 goals in all competitions. His tally included a vital last-minute winner against Hull which took the Hatters to the top of the table and a brilliant overhead kick against Bradford City, which won the club's 'Goal of the Season' award. His close ball control skills, clever runs with the ball and intelligent passes ensured he was a key figure in the side. Ahmet was one of six Luton players selected for the PFA League One team of the season.
Leyton Orient *(Free from HNK Dubrovnik, Croatia on 14/10/1999) FL 59+10/8 FLC 3/2 FAC 4+2 Others 2+2*
Luton T *(Free on 4/10/2001) FL 109+22/20 FLC 3 FAC 11/4 Others 5/3*

BROAD Joseph (Joe) Reginald
Born: Bristol, 24 August 1982
Height: 5'11" **Weight:** 12.7
Joe had a useful pre-season at Walsall and played in several early games in midfield, showing himself to be a useful box-to-box player ready to adapt to a number of different roles. Although he appeared only occasionally in the latter part of the campaign he was given a contract for 2005-06.
Plymouth Arg *(From trainee on 15/2/2002) FL 2+10 FLC 0+1 Others 2*
Torquay U *(Free on 25/9/2003) FL 4+10 Others 1*
Walsall *(Free on 3/8/2004) FL 5+5 FLC 1 Others 1*

BROADHURST Karl Matthew
Born: Portsmouth, 18 March 1980
Height: 6'1" **Weight:** 11.7
Karl was enjoying his finest season so far for Bournemouth before his campaign was cut short when he underwent a hernia operation in February. After the departure of Carl Fletcher, Karl was handed the captain's armband and he grew in stature with each game. The highlight of this fine centre half's campaign was leading the side out in the Carling Cup tie at Blackburn and scoring against the Premiership side.
Bournemouth *(From trainee on 3/7/1998) FL 148+10/3 FLC 8+1/1 FAC 16/1 Others 7+1*

Karl Broadhurst

BROMBY Leigh
Born: Dewsbury, 2 June 1980
Height: 6'0" **Weight:** 11.8
International Honours: E: Sch
Out of contract with neighbours Wednesday, Leigh signed for the Blades in the summer and went on to become an ever-present in competitive fixtures last term. He was drafted in as a right wing back for the opening game of the season and quickly adapted to his new role, being quick with good anticipation, and causing problems coming forward. In February he moved to his more accustomed role as a central defender where he equipped himself equally well. His long throw was used to good effect and his tally of five goals more than doubled his career total. Many felt he was unlucky to be only a runner-up in the 'Player of the Year' award.
Sheffield Wed *(Free from Liversedge on 9/7/1998) FL 98+2/2 FLC 8 FAC 6+1 Others 5*
Mansfield T *(Loaned on 10/12/1999) FL 10/1 Others 1*
Norwich C *(Loaned on 24/2/2003) FL 5*
Sheffield U *(Free on 5/7/2004) FL 46/5 FLC 3 FAC 5*

BROOKER Paul
Born: Hammersmith, 25 November 1976
Height: 5'8" **Weight:** 10.0
Club Honours: Div 3 '01; Div 2 '02
Although he operated on both flanks during the season, Paul was never an automatic choice for either of the wide-midfield places at Reading, and he rarely completed the full 90 minutes. His crossing of the ball was precise, but he did not score a goal and at the end of the season he was told he could leave on a free transfer if another club came in for him, despite having a year left on his contract.
Fulham *(From trainee on 1/7/1995) FL 13+43/4 FLC 1+2/1 FAC 1+3/1 Others 3+3*
Brighton & Hove A *(£25,000 on 18/2/2000) FL 102+32/15 FLC 5+1 FAC 3+3 Others 3/1*
Leicester C *(Free on 5/7/2003) PL 0+3 FLC 2 FAC 0+1*
Reading *(Loaned on 27/2/2004) FL 5+6*
Reading *(Free on 5/7/2004) FL 22+9 FLC 2 FAC 0+1*

BROOKER Stephen (Steve) Michael Lord
Born: Newport Pagnell, 21 May 1981
Height: 5'10" **Weight:** 12.4
Club Honours: AMC '01
This combative striker began the 2004-05 season in fine style for Port Vale, scoring five goals in his first six games including one against Bristol City. This led to a bid for his services from the Ashton Gate club and he was duly transferred. Steve went on to prove his worth for City with many important goals and he registered a total of 16 for the club, establishing a productive partnership up front with Leroy Lita.
Watford *(From trainee on 9/7/1999) PL 0+1 FAC 0+1*
Port Vale *(£15,000 on 5/1/2001) FL 120+11/35 FLC 5 FAC 4/1 Others 9+2/3*
Bristol C *(£150,000 on 30/9/2004) FL 33/16 FAC 1*

BROOKS Jamie Paul
Born: Oxford, 12 August 1983
Height: 5'9" **Weight:** 10.9
Oxford United fans were delighted to see Jamie Brooks back in action last term after the best part of two seasons on the sidelines recovering from the serious illness which had halted a very promising career. He returned to the first team for the FA Cup tie at Rochdale in November and he soon laid to rest his injury problems with goals against Wycombe and Darlington in the new year. Jamie was mostly used out on the left wing, but his season was ended early due to the need for a hip operation.
Oxford U *(From trainee on 13/12/2000) FL 27+14/13 FAC 1+1 Others 1*

BROOKS Lewis Raymond
Born: Boston, 4 September 1987
Height: 5'10" **Weight:** 11.6
This schoolboy spent most of the 2004-05 campaign in Boston United's youth team but got his senior chance at centre back late in the season. Lewis had just a handful of reserve games behind him when he was drafted on to the substitutes' bench for the home game against Kidderminster because of injuries and suspension. He received his first taste of Football League action when the experienced Alan White was carried off late in the first half. Lewis gave a confident performance in the middle of the defence and was retained for the following game at Mansfield Town, only losing his place when White returned to fitness.
Boston U *(Associated Schoolboy) FL 1+1*

BROOMES Marlon Charles
Born: Birmingham, 28 November 1977
Height: 6'0" **Weight:** 12.12
International Honours: E: U21-2; Yth; Sch
Marlon struggled with injury throughout the 2004-05 season, twice coming on as an early substitute for Preston only to be replaced himself within a few minutes. At his best a solid, two-footed defender with good pace and strong in the air, he never really established a regular place for himself in the side and will be hoping for better fortune and fitness in the 2005-06 season.
Blackburn Rov *(From trainee on 28/11/1994) P/FL 24+7/1 FLC 3 FAC 4*
Swindon T *(Loaned on 22/1/1997) FL 12/1*
Queens Park Rgrs *(Loaned on 25/10/2000) FL 5*
Grimsby T *(Loaned on 7/9/2001) FL 13+2 FLC 3/2*
Sheffield Wed *(Free on 13/12/2001) FL 18+1 FAC 1*
Preston NE *(Free, via trial at Burnley, on 9/8/2002) FL 59+10 FLC 4 FAC 2 Others 0+2*

BROUGH John Robert
Born: Ilkeston, 8 January 1973
Height: 6'0" **Weight:** 13.0
Club Honours: NC '99
The 2004-2005 season was a swansong for this player who has proved to be a great servant for Cheltenham Town. A fiercely competitive player with an exemplary attitude to playing and training, John spent the opening stages of the campaign in the centre of a back four but was forced out of the FA Cup first round tie against Swansea City with an ankle injury that eventually required an operation. John returned to action with the reserves towards the end of the season but was released at the end of his contract.
Notts Co *(From trainee on 9/7/1991)*
Shrewsbury T *(Free on 6/7/1992) FL 7+9/1 FLC 1+1 FAC 1 Others 2 (Free to Telford U during 1994 close season)*
Hereford U *(Free on 4/11/1994) FL 70+9/3 FLC 5 FAC 4/1 Others 4+2*
Cheltenham T *(Signed on 16/7/1998) FL 83+53/6 FLC 2+1 FAC 9+2/1 Others 3+1/1*

BROUGHTON Drewe Oliver
Born: Hitchin, 25 October 1978
Height: 6'3" **Weight:** 12.10
This old-fashioned centre forward featured in a handful of games for Southend at the beginning of last season, but soon found himself loaned out to Rushden. He impressed at Nene Park, writing his name into the record books when he netted the club's fastest-ever goal inside ten seconds of the home match against Notts County before proceeding to register a hat-trick in the 5-1 victory. In December he went out on loan again, this time to Wycombe, but injury and suspension restricted his appearances before he signed for Rushden on a permanent basis. The bustling striker netted twice more for the Diamonds, including a vital equaliser against local rivals Northampton Town in March.

Norwich C *(From trainee on 6/5/1997) FL 3+6/1*
Wigan Ath *(Loaned on 15/8/1997) FL 1+3*
Brentford *(£100,000 on 30/10/1998) FL 1*
Peterborough U *(£100,000 on 17/11/1998) FL 19+16/8 FLC 2 Others 1+1/1*
Kidderminster Hrs *(£50,000 on 22/1/2001) FL 70+24/19 FLC 2 FAC 2/2 Others 5/2*
Southend U *(Free on 13/6/2003) FL 31+13/2 FLC 2/1 FAC 0+2 Others 4+4/5*
Rushden & Diamonds *(Loaned on 14/10/2004) FL 9/4 FAC 1/1*
Wycombe W *(Loaned on 17/12/2004) FL 2+1*
Rushden & Diamonds *(Free on 11/2/2005) FL 11+1/2*

BROWN Aaron Wesley
Born: Bristol, 14 March 1980
Height: 5'10" **Weight:** 11.12
Club Honours: AMC '03
International Honours: E: Sch
This midfielder spent much of last season recovering from a broken leg before linking up with Queen's Park Rangers early in the new year. Aaron played in a number of reserve-team games and had done enough to demonstrate to the management team that he had fully recovered from his time out. He subsequently had a loan spell at Torquay to help his return to full match fitness and was then recalled to Loftus Road, making his debut for Rangers as a substitute against Wigan in April.
Bristol C *(From trainee on 7/11/1997) FL 135+25/12 FLC 3+2 FAC 10+1 Others 12+4*
Exeter C *(Loaned on 6/1/2000) FL 4+1/1*
Queens Park Rgrs *(Free on 5/1/2005) FL 0+1*
Torquay U *(Loaned on 22/3/2005) FL 5*

BROWN Adam James
Born: Sunderland, 17 December 1987
Height: 5'10" **Weight:** 10.10
A scholar on the books at Doncaster, Adam was given a run of appearances in the reserve team towards the end of last season before making it onto the bench for the game at Stockport in April. He replaced the injured David Mulligan after half an hour and performed excellently, netting the final goal in the 4-2 victory when he timed his run to perfection to meet a cross and turn it into the net.
Doncaster Rov *(Trainee) FL 0+3/1*

BROWN Christopher (Chris) Alan
Born: Doncaster, 11 December 1984
Height: 6'1" **Weight:** 13.4
Club Honours: Div 3 '04; Ch '05
International Honours: E: Yth
A young Sunderland striker, Chris is following in his father Alan's footsteps by making a name for himself on Wearside. A tall, pacy, powerful forward with an excellent first touch, Chris has been a real find for Sunderland, scoring twice on his debut in the Carling Cup tie at Crewe in September. Although his League appearances tended to be from the bench, he still hit five important goals towards the club's Championship success, including vital strikes against Coventry in March and away at Queen's Park Rangers in April.
Sunderland *(From trainee on 9/8/2002) FL 13+24/5 FLC 1/2 FAC 0+2*
Doncaster Rov *(Loaned on 3/10/2003) FL 17+5/10*

BROWN Daniel (Danny)
Born: Bethnal Green, 12 September 1980
Height: 6'0" **Weight:** 12.0
Danny had a somewhat frustrating time at Oxford last season, for after featuring regularly in the squad in the opening fixtures he was sidelined by a toe injury which kept him out of action for most of the campaign. A left-footed player who can play either in midfield or at full back, he was released by the club in the summer.
Leyton Orient *(From trainee on 5/5/1998) Others 1*
Barnet *(Free on 25/5/1999) FL 42+11/3 FLC 0+1 FAC 1+1 Others 5*
Oxford U *(Free on 29/7/2003) FL 15+1 FLC 2 Others 1*

BROWN Gary
Born: Darwen, 29 October 1985
Height: 5'6" **Weight:** 10.2
Gary was a regular in Rochdale's reserve team last term and featured as an unused substitute on a number of occasions. He went on to make his senior debut when called up to replace Wayne Evans at right back in the final game of the season at Boston. A tenacious tackler, despite his rather small stature, Gary was voted as the supporters' 'Young Player of the Year' and was offered a professional contract for the 2005-06 campaign.
Rochdale *(Trainee) FL 1*

BROWN Jason Roy
Born: Southwark, 18 May 1982
Height: 5'11" **Weight:** 13.3
International Honours: W: U21-7; Yth
Gillingham's Wales U21 'keeper was hampered by a number of injuries last season and these restricted his appearances. Firstly he pulled a hamstring in training and then in February he suffered a muscle tear in his right leg. Jason replaced Steve Banks in mid-March and was an ever-present until the end of the campaign.
Gillingham *(Free from trainee at Charlton Ath on 19/3/2001) FL 87 FLC 6 FAC 3*

BROWN Marvin Robert
Born: Bristol, 6 July 1983
Height: 5'9" **Weight:** 11.1
International Honours: E: Yth
This skilful young striker spent most of the 2004-05 campaign playing in the Conference with Forest Green and Tamworth before having a brief spell at Weymouth. He made a return to the Football League when signing for Yeovil in March but managed just two outings from the bench for the West Country club.
Bristol C *(From trainee on 18/7/2000) FL 2+17 FLC 0+1 FAC 0+2 Others 2+3 (Free to Forest Green Rovers on 12/8/2004)*
Torquay U *(Loaned on 26/9/2002) FL 2+2*
Cheltenham T *(Loaned on 30/1/2003) FL 11+4/2*
Yeovil T *(Free from Weymouth, ex Tamworth, on 22/3/2005) FL 0+2*

BROWN Michael
Born: Preston, 27 February 1985
Height: 5'11" **Weight:** 11.5
This promising midfielder stepped up to the professional ranks at Preston during the summer of 2004 and after featuring regularly for the club's reserve team he spent the second half of the campaign out on loan with Chester City. A constructive player with good vision, Michael initially took Ben Davies' place in central midfield until he was stretchered off at Swansea after suffering concussion. With Davies restored to the midfield Michael was unable to regain his place in the side, and although he made intermittent appearances he was mainly confined to a role as substitute.
Preston NE *(From trainee on 3/8/2004)*
Chester C *(Loaned on 24/12/2004) FL 11+7 FAC 1*

BROWN Michael Robert
Born: Hartlepool, 25 January 1977
Height: 5'9" **Weight:** 11.8
International Honours: E: U21-4
A versatile midfielder most comfortable in a central role, Michael cemented his place in the Tottenham side under Martin Jol and became a good provider for the attack. Pace and tenacity afford him the ability to be creative in his central role and allow him the opportunity to support the attack with his ability to run with the ball at his feet. Michael likes to find space and penetrate opponents' defences, and has the confidence to shoot for goal from well outside the box. He linked up well

with new signing Michael Carrick in a threatening partnership which will provide more opportunity as their understanding grows.
Manchester C *(From trainee on 13/9/1994) P/FL 67+22/2 FLC 2+4 FAC 10+1/2 Others 4*
Hartlepool U *(Loaned on 27/3/1997) FL 6/1*
Portsmouth *(Loaned on 19/11/1999) FL 4*
Sheffield U *(Signed on 17/12/1999) FL 146+5/27 FLC 13+1/3 FAC 6/3 Others 3/2*
Tottenham H *(£500,000 on 31/12/2003) PL 37+4/2 FLC 3+1/1 FAC 8*

BROWN Nathaniel (Nat) Levi
Born: Sheffield, 15 June 1981
Height: 6'2" **Weight:** 12.6
This no-nonsense Huddersfield Town defender found himself well down the pecking order for places once the 2004-05 season commenced. Nat always worked hard, showing himself to be solid in the tackle and linking up well when pushing forward. Yet to find his true role in defence, the amiable player fits into both the central and full-back roles equally well.
Huddersfield T *(From trainee on 8/7/1999) FL 56+20 FLC 1+2 FAC 1+1 Others 2+1*

BROWN Paul Henry
Born: Liverpool, 10 September 1984
Height: 5'8" **Weight:** 12.2
After signing his first professional contract in the summer of 2004, Paul made his debut for Tranmere last November, coming on as a substitute during the home game with MK Dons. He went on to make a handful more appearances from the bench and started his first, and so far only, full game in the Easter Monday fixture against Doncaster. Very composed and effective on the wing, he can play on either side of the park, and has been a regular member of the Rovers' reserve side since progressing through the club's youth set-up.
Tranmere Rov *(From trainee on 3/6/2004) FL 1+3*

BROWN Ryan Anthony
Born: Stoke, 15 March 1985
Height: 5'9" **Weight:** 10.12
Ryan competed with Craig James for the left-back berth at Port Vale last term. He fought his way into the line-up in October but was never able to recapture his form of the previous campaign. He has a great left foot, demonstrated by his accurate free kicks, and his best game of the season was probably the 3-1 victory over Tranmere Rovers. Ryan also appeared on a few occasions in midfield, performing equally well in the role, but then injuries forced him out of the side and he only played twice after the defeat at Sheffield Wednesday in January. He was released by Vale in the summer.
Port Vale *(From trainee on 22/8/2003) FL 33+5 FLC 2 FAC 2 Others 2*

BROWN Scott
Born: Runcorn, 8 May 1985
Height: 5'7" **Weight:** 10.3
Discarded by Everton, this industrious midfielder failed to impress previous Bristol City boss Danny Wilson when on trial at the end of the 2003-04 season. A change of management, however, saw new manager Brian Tinnion sign the youngster and his faith was rewarded when Scott burst onto the first-team scene, and he went on to feature regularly in the line-up in the closing stages. The only slight disappointment was that he failed to register a goal for the club, but he will be looking to rectify this in 2005-06.
Everton *(From trainee on 16/5/2002)*
Bristol C *(Free on 10/8/2004) FL 13+6 FAC 0+1 Others 0+2*

BROWN Simon Alexander
Born: West Bromwich, 18 September 1983
Height: 5'10" **Weight:** 11.0
Simon began last season on loan at Kidderminster where he was one of the brighter performers in the side in the opening games. A highlight was netting the equaliser in the Carling Cup tie against Cardiff, but he broke a bone in his leg soon afterwards, which kept him out of action for four weeks. In December he made a permanent move to Mansfield for what was a substantial fee for the League Two club. Simon showed electric pace, most usefully being employed on the right-hand side of midfield by the Stags.
West Bromwich A *(From trainee on 9/7/2003)*
Kidderminster Hrs *(Loaned on 25/3/2004) FL 8/2*
Kidderminster Hrs *(Loaned on 19/7/2004) FL 11+2 FLC 1/1 Others 1*
Mansfield T *(£50,000 on 6/12/2004) FL 16+5/2*

BROWN Wayne Larry
Born: Southampton, 14 January 1977
Height: 6'1" **Weight:** 11.12
Club Honours: NC '04
Chester City's longest-serving player started his testimonial season as first-choice 'keeper at the Saunders Honda Stadium. However, a series of niggling injuries meant that he shared the goalkeeping duties with Chris MacKenzie for much of the campaign and by the end of the season he had surrendered the number one spot to his rival. A 'keeper who loves the big games, Wayne is an excellent shot-stopper who is rarely beaten from distance and can be an intimidating presence for opposing forwards in and around the six-yard box. He was released in the summer.
Bristol C *(From trainee on 3/7/1995) FL 1 (Free to Weston-super-Mare during 1996 close season)*
Chester C *(Free on 30/9/1996) FL 107 FLC 8 FAC 7 Others 3*

BROWN Wayne Lawrence
Born: Barking, 20 August 1977
Height: 6'0" **Weight:** 12.6
Left-sided central defender Wayne led by example for Colchester United last term, only missing a handful of games all season. The Essex club may have only finished 15th in League One, but they had the second-best defensive record in the division, behind champions Luton Town. That was down to a well-organised defence, with Wayne marshalling matters as the skipper and the most experienced of the centre halves. He celebrated his first goal for the club with a close-range effort in the 2-2 draw at Wrexham in February.
Ipswich T *(From trainee on 16/5/1996) P/FL 28+12 FLC 3 FAC 2 Others 4+1/1*
Colchester U *(Loaned on 16/10/1997) FL 0+2*
Queens Park Rgrs *(Loaned on 22/3/2001) FL 2*
Wimbledon *(Loaned on 14/9/2001) FL 17/1*
Watford *(Loaned on 30/1/2002) FL 10+1/3*
Watford *(Free on 18/12/2002) FL 24+1/1 FAC 1*
Gillingham *(Loaned on 19/9/2003) FL 4/1*
Colchester U *(Signed on 17/2/2004) FL 54+2/1 FLC 3 FAC 2+1 Others 1+1*

BROWN Wesley (Wes) Michael
Born: Manchester, 13 October 1979
Height: 6'1" **Weight:** 12.4
Club Honours: UEFACL '99; PL '99, '01, '03; FAC '04
International Honours: E: 8; U21-8; Yth; Sch
A solid central defender, who is commanding in the air, with pace and confidence to match, Wes was a missing link for United throughout most of the first half of the season. Having made only eight Premiership appearances up to the new year, the signing of the Argentine defender Gabriel Heinze only added to his concerns. To complicate matters, a contractual dispute lingered on until Wes eventually signed a new long-term deal. Returning to first-team action with added

impetus, he was a consistent performer in the Champions' League, whilst missing only five Premiership games until the end of the campaign. A landmark goal came in the Premiership match against Newcastle at Old Trafford in April, which kept intact the Reds 36-year unbeaten home run against the Magpies. This was Wes's first-ever League goal for the club, and only his second for the first team. With much to look forward to on the domestic front with United, Wes will be hoping that his England aspirations continue to show the same kind of promise.

Manchester U *(From trainee on 13/11/1996) PL 107+14/1 FLC 9+1 FAC 15+2 Others 31+6/1*

BROWNING Marcus Trevor
Born: Bristol, 22 April 1971
Height: 6'0" **Weight:** 12.10
International Honours: W: 5
Now in the veteran stage of his career, Marcus again proved to be a very important member of the Bournemouth squad last term. Over half of his appearances came from the bench, but he remained a big part of the Cherries' squad throughout the season and scored a spectacular goal in the Carling Cup win at Leyton Orient.

Bristol Rov *(From trainee on 1/7/1989) FL 152+22/13 FLC 7+3 FAC 8/1 Others 13+5/3*
Hereford U *(Loaned on 18/9/1992) FL 7/5*
Huddersfield T *(£500,000 on 17/2/1997) FL 25+8 FLC 2+2*
Gillingham *(Loaned on 20/11/1998) FL 1*
Gillingham *(£150,000 on 25/3/1999) FL 60+17/3 FLC 6+1 FAC 3+3 Others 0+1*
Bournemouth *(Free on 9/8/2002) FL 98+27/1 FLC 3+1/2 FAC 8+4/2 Others 7*

BRUCE Alexander (Alex) Stephen
Born: Norwich, 28 September 1984
Height: 6'0" **Weight:** 11.6
Alex joined Oldham Athletic on loan from Blackburn in December 2004 and quickly began to enjoy his first taste of senior football. Equally at home at right back or in the centre of defence, a personal highlight came when he capped an outstanding performance by netting the penalty shoot-out winner against Tranmere to earn Latics a place in the LDV Vans Trophy Northern final. His father, Steve, then negotiated his move to Birmingham as part of the Robbie Savage deal and Alex was recalled to St Andrew's in March. Within days he had been sent back out on-loan, this time to promotion-chasing Sheffield Wednesday for the remainder of the season, featuring for the Owls in the League One play-off final success over Hartlepool at the Millennium Stadium.

Blackburn Rov *(From trainee on 4/7/2002)*
Oldham Ath *(Loaned on 23/12/2004) FL 3+3 FAC 1 Others 1*
Birmingham C *(Signed on 26/1/2005)*
Oldham Ath *(Loaned on 28/1/2005) FL 5+1 FAC 1 Others 1*
Sheffield Wed *(Loaned on 10/3/2005) FL 5+1 Others 3*

BRUNT Christopher (Chris)
Born: Belfast, 14 December 1984
Height: 6'1" **Weight:** 11.8
International Honours: NI: 2; U23-1; U21-1
This young left-sided player had a reasonable, if not spectacular, season for Sheffield Wednesday last term. His best performances came when he was played out wide on the left and he also showed considerable ability when taking free kicks.

Middlesbrough *(From trainee on 6/7/2002)*
Sheffield Wed *(Free on 2/3/2004) FL 35+16/6 FLC 1+1 FAC 1 Others 2+2/1*

BUARI Malik
Born: Accra, Ghana, 21 January 1984
Height: 5'11" **Weight:** 11.11
A near ever-present in the Fulham reserve side last term, usually operating as a right winger, Malik made one first-team appearance, featuring in the Carling Cup tie at Boston. He is a skilful player who has a powerful shot, which he demonstrated to great effect with a spectacular winning goal against Derby reserves.

Fulham *(From trainee on 10/7/2003) PL 1+2 FLC 2*

BUCHANAN David Thomas Hugh
Born: Rochdale, 6 May 1986
Height: 5'8" **Weight:** 10.8
International Honours: NI: Yth
David spent much of the 2004-05 season as skipper of Bury reserves, for whom he turned out at left wing back. However, he finally made his first-team debut for the Shakers in the closing stages of the game at Kidderminster in April, featuring in a more familiar role on the left-hand side of midfield. He produced a couple of surging runs and impressive crosses, showing tremendous enthusiasm and tenacity throughout. David also earned Northern Ireland U19 honours during the season, scoring in the 1-1 draw away against Italy in December.

Bury *(Trainee) FL 0+3*

BULL Ronald (Ronnie) Rodney
Born: Hackney, 26 December 1980
Height: 5'8" **Weight:** 10.12
This left-sided defender joined Grimsby Town after a successful pre-season trial when he impressed with his work rate. Although Ronnie was confined to a role on the bench for most of the early part of the campaign, he commanded a regular place in the starting line-up from November onwards. A combative tackler who sometimes aroused the displeasure of referees, Ronnie also featured occasionally in a ball-winning midfield role.

Millwall *(From trainee on 12/5/1999) FL 37+13 FLC 0+2 Others 3*
Yeovil T *(Loaned on 3/9/2003) FL 7*
Brentford *(Signed on 7/1/2004) FL 20*
Grimsby T *(Free on 19/7/2004) FL 22+5/2 FLC 0+1 Others 1*

BULLARD James (Jimmy) Richard
Born: Newham, 23 October 1978
Height: 5'10" **Weight:** 11.10
Club Honours: Div 2 '03
A consistent performer in the heart of the midfield with a terrific engine and a wide range of passes, Jimmy was an ever-present for Wigan Athletic as they gained promotion into the Premiership. Very much the playmaker in the side, pulling the strings and directing the pattern of the game, he earned himself a place in the PFA Championship team of the season. An inspirational campaign saw him net three goals - all spectacular efforts -against Leeds United, Crewe Alexandra and Brighton.

West Ham U *(£30,000 from Gravesend & Northfleet on 10/2/1998)*
Peterborough U *(Free on 6/7/2001) FL 62+4/11 FLC 2 FAC 6/1 Others 3/2*
Wigan Ath *(£275,000 on 31/1/2003) FL 109/6 FLC 4/1 FAC 1+1*

BULLEN Lee
Born: Edinburgh, 29 March 1971
Height: 6'1" **Weight:** 12.8
This experienced defender proved to be a great signing for Sheffield Wednesday last term. Lee adjusted straight away to the demands of League One football and whether he was employed at full back or in central defence he looked solid and reliable. A good leader, he successfully took over the captaincy when Chris Marsden was ruled out. Lee is very effective in the air and was often pushed up front when the Owls were chasing the game.

Meadowbank *(Signed from Penicuik Ath on 10/1/1990) SL 5+7 Others 0+1*
Stenhousemuir *(Signed on 13/11/1990) SL 15+7/4 SC 1 (Free to Whitburn Juniors on 10/10/1991)*
Dunfermline Ath *(Signed from PAE Kalamata on 3/2/2000) SL 104+26/22 SLC 5+2/1 SC 10+4/1*
Sheffield Wed *(Free on 6/7/2004) FL 46/7 FLC 2 Others 4*

Martin Bullock

BULLOCK Lee
Born: Stockton, 22 May 1981
Height: 5'9" **Weight:** 11.7
In a very testing season for Cardiff City, particularly in the central-midfield department, Lee was unable to establish himself in the line-up. After starting the first three games he lost his place and did not start another Championship game until November (when he began two in a row). For the rest of the season he was restricted to substitute appearances coming on to some effect, for he finished up with a total of five goals for the season.
York C *(From trainee on 29/6/1999) FL 156+15/24 FLC 5+1/1 FAC 10+2/2*
Cardiff C *(£75,000 + on 11/3/2004) FL 12+20/6 FLC 3+1/2 FAC 0+1*

BULLOCK Martin John
Born: Derby, 5 March 1975
Height: 5'5" **Weight:** 10.7
Club Honours: AMC '02, '04
International Honours: E: U21-1
This dangerous winger featured regularly for Blackpool early on last season before suffering a torn hamstring during the match at Swindon in September. It was another three months before he returned to action and although he regained his place in the side in the new year, he struggled to find his best form. Out of contract in the summer, he was released by the Seasiders.
Barnsley *(£15,000 from Eastwood T on 4/9/1993) P/FL 108+77/4 FLC 14+4 FAC 4+11/3 Others 1*
Port Vale *(Loaned on 14/1/2000) FL 6/1*
Blackpool *(Free on 10/8/2001) FL 128+25/4 FLC 4+3 FAC 10+1 Others 13+1/3*

BUNJEVCEVIC Goran Petar
Born: Karlovac, Croatia, 17 February 1973
Height: 6'3" **Weight:** 12.6
International Honours: Serbia: 17
A central defender who favours a sweeper-like role, Goran's season was wrecked early on by a recurring thigh injury and he finished the campaign having made only four appearances. His absence robbed Spurs of a player flexible enough to fill most defensive or midfield positions and his much anticipated return to full fitness neared completion just as the season drew to an end leaving little opportunity to make a real impact.
Tottenham H *(£1,400,000 from Red Star Belgrade, Yugoslavia, ex FK Crvena, Zuezda, on 25/7/2001) PL 41+10 FLC 6+1/2*

BURCHILL Mark James
Born: Broxburn, 18 August 1980
Height: 5'8" **Weight:** 10.2
Club Honours: SLC '00; Div 1 '03

International Honours: S: 6; U21-15; Sch

Out of the first-team picture at Portsmouth, Mark spent a brief spell on loan at Rotherham in the early part of the season. The diminutive striker played just three times, scoring once before an injury meant that he returned to Fratton Park. In the January transfer window he moved permanently to Hearts, where he enjoyed better fortunes, scoring four times from seven starts.

Glasgow Celtic *(From Celtic BC on 3/6/1997) SL 17+34/21 SLC 3+2 SC 1+2/1 Others 4+1/3*
Birmingham C *(Loaned on 22/9/2000) FL 4+9/4 FLC 3+1/1*
Ipswich T *(Loaned on 22/1/2001) PL 2+5/1*
Portsmouth *(£600,000 on 24/8/2001) FL 9+15/8 FLC 1+1*
Dundee *(Loaned on 31/1/2003) SL 7+4/2 SC 1+3/1*
Wigan Ath *(Loaned on 21/8/2003) FL 1+3*
Sheffield Wed *(Loaned on 24/12/2003) FL 4+1*
Rotherham U *(Loaned on 24/9/2004) FL 3/1*

BURGESS Andrew (Andy) John

Born: Bozeat, 10 August 1981
Height: 6'2" **Weight:** 11.6
Club Honours: NC '01; Div 3 '03

Andy was a near ever-present for Rushden last term, when his silky skills in midfield once again created plenty of entertaining football. He was forced to play on the left wing instead of a central role and only managed one goal, netting in the 4-1 home defeat by Southend in September. Andy was placed on the transfer list at his own request in the summer.

Rushden & Diamonds *(From juniors on 3/7/1999) FL 121+17/10 FLC 3+1 FAC 4+1 Others 4+2*

BURGESS Benjamin (Ben) Keiron

Born: Buxton, 9 November 1981
Height: 6'3" **Weight:** 14.4
International Honours: RoI: U21-2; Yth

Ben spent the majority of the 2004-05 campaign recovering from a serious knee ligament injury suffered towards the end of the previous campaign. He eventually made his come back in Hull's final home game against Sheffield Wednesday on a day when the Tigers were celebrating their promotion to the Championship. Ben signed a new contract for the club and will be looking forward to re-establishing himself in the side in 2005-06.

Blackburn Rov *(From trainee on 25/11/1998) FL 1+1 FLC 1*
Brentford *(Loaned on 16/8/2001) FL 43/17 FLC 2 FAC 2/1 Others 4*
Stockport Co *(£450,000 on 5/8/2002) FL 17+2/4 FLC 0+1 FAC 1+1/2 Others 2*
Oldham Ath *(Loaned on 10/1/2003) FL 6+1*
Hull C *(£100,000 on 27/3/2003) FL 51+2/22 FLC 1 FAC 1*

BURGESS Daryl

Born: Birmingham, 24 January 1971
Height: 5'11" **Weight:** 12.4

This veteran Rochdale defender shared centre-back duties with the equally experienced Gareth Griffiths and Greg Heald last term, despite a number of niggling injuries. After contributing to Dale's excellent defensive record during the season, Daryl passed 500 senior games before missing the last couple of months with an ankle injury. He was released by the club in May.

West Bromwich A *(From trainee on 1/7/1989) FL 317+15/10 FLC 20+2/3 FAC 9 Others 14*
Northampton T *(Free on 5/7/2001) FL 60+1/2 FLC 1 FAC 4 Others 3*
Rochdale *(Free on 6/8/2003) FL 52+4 FLC 2 FAC 3 Others 2*

BURNELL Joseph (Joe) Michael

Born: Bristol, 10 October 1980
Height: 5'10" **Weight:** 11.1
Club Honours: AMC '03

This industrious Wycombe central midfielder suffered an injury-hit season last term. After starting the first five games, glandular fever ruled him out until October, then an ankle injury kept him out until January and he also suffered from hamstring problems. When fully fit his midfield partnership with Matt Bloomfield blossomed and was a key feature of the Chairboys' performances. Joe also featured at left back during the campaign.

Bristol C *(From trainee on 24/7/1999) FL 117+14/1 FLC 3+2 FAC 4+3 Others 17+1/2*
Wycombe W *(Free on 7/7/2004) FL 23+1 FLC 1*

BURNS Jacob Geoffrey

Born: Sydney, Australia, 21 January 1978
Height: 5'9" **Weight:** 11.12
International Honours: Australia: 2; U23-19

Jacob signed a new contract prior to the start of the 2004-05 campaign, but the early part of his season was disrupted by a period of suspension. However, he went on to become a fixture in midfield for Barnsley. A high work rate and the ability to get around the pitch were his main assets, and he also showed that he possesses a fierce shot, ably demonstrated by his 25-yard winner against Blackpool in November.

Leeds U *(£250,000 from Parramatta Power, Australia, ex Sydney U, on 31/8/2000) PL 5+1 FLC 1 Others 3+1*
Barnsley *(Free, via trial at Feyenoord, Holland, on 17/10/2003) FL 49+7/3 FLC 1 FAC 4+1 Others 1+1*

BURNS Jamie Daniel

Born: Blackpool, 6 March 1984
Height: 5'9" **Weight:** 10.11
Club Honours: AMC '04

Jamie was a regular on the bench for Blackpool in the first half of the 2004-05 campaign and came on to score twice in extra time in the 6-4 LDV Vans Trophy win over Huddersfield in November. The exciting left winger featured regularly in the starting line-up after Christmas but failed to add to his tally of goals for the Seasiders.

Blackpool *(From trainee on 1/7/2003) FL 26+15 FAC 2+2/1 Others 4+3/2*

BURNS Liam

Born: Belfast, 30 October 1978
Height: 6'0" **Weight:** 12.12
International Honours: NI: U21-13; Yth

Liam had something of a varied campaign last term when he appeared for five different clubs. He began the season on non-contract terms with Bristol Rovers, for whom he made a handful of appearances before joining Shrewsbury Town on a similar basis and adding a couple more outings. The tall central defender then had a brief association with Kidderminster before joining Forest Green Rovers and soon after this he signed for Eircom First Division side Sligo Rovers.

Port Vale *(From trainee on 2/7/1997) FL 94+24 FLC 1 FAC 7+1/1 Others 4+1*
Bristol Rov *(Free on 13/8/2004) FL 3 FAC 1 Others 0+1*
Shrewsbury T *(Free on 10/12/2004) FL 1+1*
Kidderminster Hrs *(Free on 24/12/2004) FL 0+1*

BURTON Deon John

Born: Ashford, 25 October 1976
Height: 5'9" **Weight:** 11.9
Club Honours: Div 1 '03
International Honours: Jamaica: 49

Deon joined Brentford in the summer of 2004 and got off to a good start, netting in the first home game against Chesterfield. He proved to be an excellent target man with good close control and capable of bringing other players into the game. Deon finished the season as leading scorer for the Bees with ten goals, the best of which was a cracking volley against Sheffield

Wednesday in February. He also featured at international level for Jamaica during the season.
Portsmouth *(From trainee on 15/2/1994) FL 42+20/10 FLC 3+2/2 FAC 0+2/1*
Cardiff C *(Loaned on 24/12/1996) FL 5/2 Others 1*
Derby Co *(£1,000,000 + on 9/8/1997) P/FL 78+47/25 FLC 6+2/3 FAC 9+1/3*
Barnsley *(Loaned on 14/12/1998) FL 3*
Stoke C *(Loaned on 21/2/2002) FL 11+1/2 Others 2+1/2*
Portsmouth *(Loaned on 9/8/2002) FL 6/3*
Portsmouth *(£75,000 + on 12/12/2002) P/FL 5+5/1 FAC 1+1*
Walsall *(Loaned on 12/9/2003) FL 2+1 FLC 1*
Swindon T *(Loaned on 17/10/2003) FL 4/1*
Brentford *(Free on 4/8/2004) FL 38+2/10 FLC 1 FAC 7 Others 2*

BURTON Paul David
Born: Enfield, 30 November 1985
Height: 6'0" **Weight:** 11.12
This hard-working midfielder made a breakthrough to first-team action with Oxford last term when he received his debut in senior football in the Carling Cup tie against Reading. One of several scholars at the club to make the senior squad, Paul also featured from the substitutes' bench in the final game of the season against Chester, when he gave an impressive performance.
Oxford U *(Trainee) FL 0+1 FLC 0+1*

BURTON Steven (Steve) Peter Graham
Born: Hull, 10 October 1982
Height: 6'1" **Weight:** 11.5
Steve started the 2004-05 season as first choice in the left-back position for Kidderminster, but lost his place to Jon Beswetherick in November following a change in management. After playing in midfield in the FA Cup defeat at Port Vale he did not feature again until the penultimate game of the season. Steve was placed on the transfer list by Harriers in the summer.
Hull C *(From trainee on 11/7/2002) FL 2+9 FAC 1 Others 2*
Kidderminster Hrs *(Loaned on 24/10/2003) FL 6+1 FAC 1/1*
Kidderminster Hrs *(Free on 25/3/2004) FL 19+1 FLC 1 FAC 1 Others 1*

BURTON-GODWIN Osagyefo (Sagi) Lenin Ernesto
Born: Birmingham, 25 November 1977
Height: 6'2" **Weight:** 13.6
Club Honours: AMC '01
International Honours: St Kitts
The 2004-05 campaign proved to be an injury-hit season for this Peterborough defender. After just three games he dislocated his shoulder and although he returned to first-team action in October another injury sidelined him for most of the second half of the campaign. Sagi is a tough-tackling central defender who shows plenty of skill when on the ball.
Crystal Palace *(From trainee on 26/1/1996) P/FL 19+6/1 FLC 1 FAC 0+1 Others 0+1*
Colchester U *(Free on 26/5/1999) FL 9 FLC 2*
Port Vale *(Free, via trial at Sheffield U, on 14/1/2000) FL 76+10/2 FLC 3/1 FAC 3 Others 6+1/1*
Crewe Alex *(Free on 8/8/2002) FL 1*
Peterborough U *(Free on 29/8/2002) FL 71+6/2 FLC 2 FAC 5 Others 2/1*

BUTCHER Richard Tony
Born: Peterborough, 22 January 1981
Height: 6'0" **Weight:** 12.12
Richard had an outstanding season in the centre of midfield for Lincoln City in 2004-05. He worked tremendously hard and achieved the rarity these days of appearing in every minute of every match played by the Imps. He was an effective winner of the ball in the centre of the park and his distribution set up a healthy supply of chances. Richard's only goal was a scrambled effort which contributed to an important win over Macclesfield Town late in the regular season. At the end of the campaign he chose to leave Sincil Bank and signed a contract with League One club Oldham Athletic.
Rushden & Diamonds *(From trainee at Northampton T on 26/11/1999. Freed on 1/10/2001)*
Lincoln C *(Free from Kettering T on 19/11/2002) FL 95+9/11 FLC 3 FAC 3 Others 12/1*

BUTLER Andrew (Andy) Peter
Born: Doncaster, 4 November 1983
Height: 6'0" **Weight:** 13.6
This commanding centre half dominated Scunthorpe's 'Player of the Season' awards for the second successive season as he played a massive part in the club's promotion to League One. The left-sided defender continued to flourish, commanding in the air and strong on the ground, in the meanest defence in the division. He was also a major goal-scoring threat at set pieces, coming forward from defence to net ten times by the end of February. An ankle ligament injury at the start of March threatened to end his season early, but he returned to play in the final four games, helping his team to four successive clean sheets.
Scunthorpe U *(From trainee on 2/7/2003) FL 70+2/12 FLC 2 FAC 7 Others 3*

BUTLER Philip **Anthony (Tony)**
Born: Stockport, 28 September 1972
Height: 6'2" **Weight:** 12.0
Club Honours: AMC '03
This battling centre half was a regular in the Bristol City line-up during the first half of last season and even scored a rare goal in the 2-1 win at Stockport on Boxing Day. Tony was sorely missed when he rejoined Blackpool in February. A tall, steady defender who is good in the air he produced some solid displays for the Seasiders but missed several games with an injury.
Gillingham *(From trainee on 13/5/1991) FL 142+6/5 FLC 12 FAC 12+1 Others 5+1/1*
Blackpool *(£225,000 on 30/7/1996) FL 98+1 FLC 7 FAC 4 Others 4/1*
Port Vale *(£115,000 on 25/3/1999) FL 19*
West Bromwich A *(£140,000 on 23/3/2000) FL 65+5/1 FLC 7 FAC 1+1 Others 2*
Bristol C *(Free on 30/8/2002) FL 97+1/4 FLC 5 FAC 6 Others 15*
Blackpool *(Free on 7/2/2005) FL 6+2*

BUTLER Martin Neil
Born: Wordsley, 15 September 1974
Height: 5'11" **Weight:** 11.9
One of the main reasons for Rotherham United's poor season was due to the fact that Martin had to miss much of the campaign after being struck by the hepatitis during the summer. That meant he was out of action until November and even then it was felt he had returned too early as he struggled to find his best form. However, he still managed to remain as the club's leading scorer despite missing the last few games of the season. His cause was not helped by the fact that he played alongside a number of different partners.
Walsall *(From trainee on 24/5/1993) FL 43+31/8 FLC 2+1 FAC 2+5/2 Others 2+2/2*
Cambridge U *(£22,500 on 8/8/1997) FL 100+3/41 FLC 9/6 FAC 9+2/5 Others 3+1/1*
Reading *(£750,000 + on 1/2/2000) FL 85+18/32 FLC 4+1 FAC 5/2 Others 4+1/2*
Rotherham U *(£150,000 on 2/9/2003) FL 57+1/21 FLC 1 FAC 1+1*

BUTLER Paul John
Born: Manchester, 2 November 1972
Height: 6'2" **Weight:** 13.0
Club Honours: Div 2 '97; Div 1 '99
International Honours: RoI: 1; B-1
Despite being offered a new contract by Wolves, Paul left Molineux in summer 2004 to join Leeds on a 'Bosman' and was promptly appointed skipper. He was a model of consistency in a squad which saw no less than 37 players pull on a first-team shirt. Centre-back Paul's only

goal of the campaign gave Leeds their first away win – 1-0 at Plymouth in September. The season almost ended in tragedy for Paul as he swallowed his tongue in a collision with his own goalkeeper Neil Sullivan in the 4-0 home defeat against Sheffield United in April. Only the prompt action of physio Dave Hancock prevented anything more serious than concussion which ruled Paul out of the starting line-up for the last five games.

Rochdale *(From trainee on 5/7/1991) FL 151+7/10 FLC 8+1 FAC 6+2 Others 12+1*
Bury *(£100,000 on 22/7/1996) FL 83+1/4 FLC 8 FAC 2 Others 3/1*
Sunderland *(£600,000 + on 15/7/1998) P/FL 78+1/3 FLC 11+1/1 FAC 4*
Wolverhampton W *(Loaned on 17/11/2000) FL 5*
Wolverhampton W *(£1,000,000 on 31/1/2001) P/FL 118+1/3 FLC 5 FAC 7 Others 5*
Leeds U *(Free on 2/7/2004) FL 39 FLC 2*

Paul Butler

BUTLER Thomas Anthony
Born: Dublin, 25 April 1981
Height: 5'8" **Weight:** 10.8
International Honours: RoI: 2; U21-14; Yth

This tricky left winger spent most of the 2004-05 season with SPL club Dunfermline Athletic. On his release he trained with Sheffield Wednesday and later with Hartlepool, showing sufficiently impressive form to be offered a short-term contract by the latter just before the transfer deadline. Thomas was soon involved in first-team action, and twice got his name on the score sheet.

Sunderland *(From trainee on 25/6/1998) P/FL 16+15 FLC 1+3 FAC 0+1*
Darlington *(Loaned on 13/10/2000) FL 8 FAC 2*
Dunfermline Ath *(Free on 10/9/2004) SL 6+6 SLC 2*
Hartlepool U *(Free on 24/3/2005) FL 5+4/1 Others 1+1*

BUTT Nicholas (Nicky)
Born: Manchester, 21 January 1975
Height: 5'10" **Weight:** 11.3
Club Honours: FAYC '92; CS '96, '97, '03; PL '96, '97, '99, '00, 01, '03; FAC '96, '04; UEFACL '99
International Honours: E: 39; U21-7; Yth; Sch

Nicky immediately added quality at Newcastle last term playing a midfield anchor role. Early season proved dramatic with a 'Man of the Match' opener against Middlesbrough and a red card in the UEFA Cup at home to Hapoel two minutes after coming on as a substitute. A hamstring injury incurred against Sochaux in November followed by a twisted ankle led to a two -month absence and on his return, despite an outstanding showing against Chelsea in the FA Cup, he seemed to have lost his sharpness. A calf injury brought his season to a premature end in mid-April. Highly rated at international level, he won several more caps during the season.

Manchester U *(From trainee on 29/1/1993) PL 210+60/21 FLC 7+1 FAC 23+6/1 Others 67+13/4*
Newcastle U *(£2,500,000 on 30/7/2004) PL 16+2/1 FLC 1 FAC 2 Others 4+1*

CAMP Lee Michael John
Born: Derby, 22 August 1984
Height: 5'11" **Weight:** 11.11
International Honours: E: U21-2; Yth
Derby supporters were taken by surprise when George Burley opened the season with Lee in goal. The decision was amply justified by Lee's outstanding form as the Rams pressed for a play-off place. He is agile and capable of electrifying saves but even more impressive was his consistency. Young goalkeepers tend to waver in form but Lee made good decisions and was remarkably free of error. He missed only one game, having been sent off at Wolverhampton, and graduated to the England U21 team with two appearances as substitute. Lee signed a new contract in May, was Derby's 'Young Player of the Year' and has the talent to make a big impact in the game.
Derby Co *(From trainee on 16/7/2002) FL 45+1 FLC 1 FAC 3 Others 2*
Queens Park Rgrs *(Loaned on 12/3/2004) FL 12*

Lee Camp

CAMPBELL Andrew (Andy) Paul
Born: Stockton, 18 April 1979
Height: 5'11" **Weight:** 11.7
International Honours: E: U21-4; Yth
Andy had a disappointing campaign in 2004-05. He was expected to take centre stage when Robert Earnshaw was sold to West Brom at the start of the season, but injury disrupted his run in the first team and he failed to score a goal. He rarely featured thereafter and a loan spell at Doncaster in the new year was cut short by injury.
Middlesbrough *(From trainee on 4/7/1996) P/FL 28+28/4 FLC 5+5/1 FAC 2+3/2*
Sheffield U *(Loaned on 10/12/1998) FL 5/1*
Sheffield U *(Loaned on 25/3/1999) FL 6/2*
Bolton W *(Loaned on 9/3/2001) FL 3+3*
Cardiff C *(£950,000 on 25/2/2002) FL 30+43/12 FLC 3+3/1 FAC 2+5/2 Others 2+5/2*
Doncaster Rov *(Loaned on 27/1/2005) FL 1+2*

CAMPBELL Kevin Joseph
Born: Lambeth, 4 February 1970
Height: 6'1" **Weight:** 13.8
Club Honours: FAYC '88; FLC '93; FAC '93; ECWC '94; Div 1 '98
International Honours: E: B-1; U21-4
Kevin brought a close on a fine career at Everton when he moved to the Hawthorns during the transfer window, after the arrival of Marcus Bent and James Beattie limited his first-team opportunities. He was regarded as a hero at Goodison and he left with the best wishes of all concerned, and a trophy awarded to him by fans when Everton visited West Brom showed how well he was appreciated. A great success with the Baggies, he scored with a sweet right-foot drive on his home debut against Manchester City. Given the captain's armband by manager Bryan Robson late in the season, he slotted straight in alongside Geoff Horsfield. Strong in all aspects of forward play, Kevin's approach to the game certainly gave his fellow colleagues an enormous boost in morale. He was outstanding as Albion produced the 'Great Escape' by retaining their Premiership status after being bottom of the table at Christmas.
Arsenal *(From trainee on 11/2/1988) P/FL 124+42/46 FLC 14+10/6 FAC 13+6/2 Others 15+4/5*
Leyton Orient *(Loaned on 16/1/1989) FL 16/9*
Leicester C *(Loaned on 8/11/1989) FL 11/5 Others 1/1*
Nottingham F *(£3,000,000 on 1/7/1995) P/FL 79+1/32 FLC 2 FAC 11/3 Others 3 (£2,500,000 to Trabzonspor, Turkey on 7/8/1998)*
Everton *(£3,000,000 on 25/3/1999) PL 125+20/45 FLC 5+4/3 FAC 9+1/3*
West Bromwich A *(Free on 11/1/2005) PL 16/3 FAC 1+1*

CAMPBELL Stuart Pearson
Born: Corby, 9 December 1977
Height: 5'10" **Weight:** 10.8
Club Honours: FLC '97, '00
International Honours: S: U21-14

Stuart was one of several players recruited by Bristol Rovers in the summer of 2004. He quickly established himself in the right-wing berth where he proved a real asset, contributing some accurate crosses to set up chances for his colleagues. Unfortunately a hernia problem required surgery and this kept him out of action for the final three months of the campaign.
Leicester C *(From trainee on 4/7/1996) PL 12+25 FLC 2+5 FAC 3+3*
Birmingham C *(Loaned on 23/3/2000) FL 0+2*
Grimsby T *(£200,000 on 15/9/2000) FL 154+1/12 FLC 6/1 FAC 7 Others 0+1*
Bristol Rov *(Free on 5/7/2004) FL 21+4 FLC 2 FAC 2 Others 4+1*

CAMPBELL Sulzeer (Sol) Jeremiah
Born: Newham, 18 September 1974
Height: 6'2" **Weight:** 14.1
Club Honours: FLC '99; PL '02, '04; FAC '02, '05; CS '02
International Honours: E: 65; B-1; U21-11; Yth (UEFA-U18 '93)
Sol endured an injury-ravaged campaign and made just 21 appearances in total in all competitions. Arsenal's back four suffered in his absence once the club's record breaking 49-game unbeaten run was ended at Old Trafford. He initially returned in November and contributed his only goal of the season with a fine long-range strike to win the game at Fratton Park, but it was not until April that he returned to full fitness, by which time the emergence of Phillippe Senderos had ensured he was not guaranteed a first-team place. Sol did come back into the side for the amazing 7-0 victory over fourth-placed Everton and the final game of the campaign away to Birmingham but yet more disappointment was to follow as he was left on the bench for the FA Cup final. Sol was included in England's end-of-season tour to the USA as captain however an ankle injury picked up in the opening game ended his campaign in frustrating fashion.
Tottenham H *(From trainee on 23/9/1992) PL 246+9/10 FLC 28/4 FAC 28+2/1 Others 2*
Arsenal *(Free on 10/7/2001) PL 113+2/6 FAC 18/2 Others 35*

CAMPBELL-RYCE Jamal Julian
Born: Lambeth, 6 April 1983
Height: 5'7" **Weight:** 11.10
International Honours: Jamaica: 1
Few loan players can have had the impact of Jamal during his spell at Chesterfield. His frightening pace and fine close control up either wing saw him terrorise opposing full backs, and he was a prolific shooter, too. His success alerted other clubs and he declined the Spireites' contract offer to go to Rotherham. Jamal made an immediate impression at Millmoor, too with thanks to his tricky footwork and dribbling skills. He picked up a string of 'Man of the Match' awards and was voted as the club's 'Young Player of the Year'.
Charlton Ath *(From trainee on 9/7/2002) PL 0+3 FLC 0+2*
Leyton Orient *(Loaned on 10/8/2002) FL 16+1/2 FLC 2/1*
Wimbledon *(Loaned on 6/2/2004) FL 3+1*
Chesterfield *(Loaned on 20/8/2004) FL 14 FLC 1 Others 1/1*
Rotherham U *(Signed on 30/11/2004) FL 23+1 FAC 1*

Jamal Campbell-Ryce (right)

CAMPO Ramos Ivan
Born: San Sebastian, Spain, 21 February 1974
Height: 6'1" **Weight:** 12.11
International Honours: Spain: 4
Ivan began the 2004-05 campaign as the holding midfielder for Bolton, protecting the back-four unit, a role which he adopted during the previous season. This position allowed him to fully demonstrate his sumptuous passing abilities, and he was in excellent form. However, this fruitful period was brought to an abrupt halt following a nasty clash of heads in the home victory over Crystal Palace in October. Ivan had minor surgery for muscular damage around the eye and returned to first-team action a month later, where he remained until losing his place to Fernando Hierro for the final three months of the season. Ivan showed his versatility when covering the right-back position during the FA Cup victory over Ipswich and will be looking to reclaim his place in the starting line-up at the start of 2005-06.
Bolton W *(Free from Real Madrid, Spain, ex CD Logrones, Alaves, Vallencia, Valladolid, Real Mallorca, on 31/8/2002) PL 85+11/6 FLC 7 FAC 3+1*

CANDELA Vincent
Born: Bedarieux, France, 24 October 1973
Height: 5'10" **Weight:** 11.10
International Honours: France: 40
Vincent began the 2004-05 season with Roma and played in their initial Champions' League matches before falling out of favour. He subsequently joined Bolton on deadline day of the January transfer window and made his Wanderers' debut in the FA Cup victory over Fulham. Vincent soon adapted to the style of the Premiership and figured

regularly during the closing stages of the season, primarily at left back, though also at right back, when necessary. He regularly displayed why the Roma fans nicknamed him 'The Musketeer', advancing up the field at every opportunity and proving to be a useful attacking option.
Bolton W *(Free from AS Roma, Italy on 31/1/2005) PL 9+1 FAC 1+1*

CANERO Peter
Born: Glasgow, 18 January 1981
Height: 5'9" **Weight:** 11.4
International Honours: S: 1; B-3; U21-17
This highly rated young full back or wide midfielder was dogged by injury at Leicester last term and he only made a handful of starts, mostly at right back. Peter looked to have first claim on that position when Craig Levein took over the managerial reins but injury once more halted his progress after a further three games.
Kilmarnock *(From juniors on 16/10/1997) SL 96+21/9 SLC 3+1/1 SC 5+1/1 Others 2+1*
Leicester C *(£250,000 on 20/1/2004) P/FL 8+5*

CANOVILLE Lee
Born: Ealing, 14 March 1981
Height: 6'1" **Weight:** 11.3
International Honours: E: Yth; Sch
After playing a key role in the previous season's promotion side, this talented attacking right back found life in League One far more difficult than expected. A series of niggling injuries further undermined his confidence and saw Lee released by the Gulls at the end of the season.
Arsenal *(From trainee, having earlier been transferred from Millwall juniors for an undisclosed fee, on 3/7/1998) FLC 0+1*
Northampton T *(Loaned on 26/1/2001) FL 2*
Torquay U *(Free on 14/9/2001) FL 107+5/2 FLC 2 FAC 3 Others 4*

CAPALDI Anthony (Tony) Charles
Born: Porsgrunn, Norway, 12 August 1981
Height: 6'0" **Weight:** 11.8
Club Honours: Div 2 '04
International Honours: NI: 11; U21-14; Yth
Tony again had another good season with Plymouth Argyle last term, despite missing a run of matches with a leg injury in the autumn. However, he was soon back in the side once more operating as the creative left-sided player in Argyle's midfield. Tony also featured for Northern Ireland last term, where he was employed in the left-back berth and he was magnificent in the 2-2 draw against Wales at the Millennium Stadium.
Birmingham C *(From trainee on 9/7/1999)*
Plymouth Arg *(Free on 3/5/2003) FL 54+15/9 FLC 2 FAC 1 Others 0+2*

CARBON Matthew (Matt) Phillip
Born: Nottingham, 8 June 1975
Height: 6'2" **Weight:** 13.6
International Honours: E: U21-4
Matt was Barnsley manager Paul Hart's first signing during the 2004 close season. He proved to be a more-than-useful centre back, but found his campaign badly disrupted by injury. A commanding figure in the air he was always a danger at set plays. He will be looking to stay injury-free in 2004-05.
Lincoln C *(From trainee on 13/4/1993) FL 66+3/10 FLC 4/1 FAC 3 Others 4+3*
Derby Co *(£385,000 on 8/3/1996) P/FL 11+9 FLC 1 FAC 0+1*
West Bromwich A *(£800,000 on 26/1/1998) FL 106+7/5 FLC 7+2 FAC 4*
Walsall *(Free on 23/7/2001) FL 49+6/2 FLC 1 FAC 5*
Lincoln C *(Loaned on 24/10/2003) FL 1*
Barnsley *(Free on 5/7/2004) FL 16+10 FLC 1 FAC 1*

CARDEN Paul Andrew
Born: Liverpool, 29 March 1979
Height: 5'8" **Weight:** 11.10
Club Honours: NC '04
Chester City's captain and driving force in the centre of midfield, Paul again impressed with a series of commanding performances last term. Although he struggled to find a place in the line-up under caretaker manager Ray Matthias at the start of the season, the arrival of Ian Rush saw him regain his position alongside Ben Davies. A player who is always in the thick of the action and never one to shirk a challenge, Paul's leadership qualities were crucial in what proved to be a disappointing campaign for the club. Selected as City's 'Player of the Year', he was surprisingly released at the end of the season.
Blackpool *(From trainee on 7/7/1997) FL 0+1 FAC 0+1 Others 1*
Rochdale *(Free on 3/3/1998) FL 30+15 FLC 0+2 FAC 3+1 Others 3+1*
Chester C *(Free on 10/3/2000) FL 45+6 FLC 0+1 FAC 3 Others 3*

CAREY Brian Patrick
Born: Cork, 31 May 1968
Height: 6'3" **Weight:** 14.4
International Honours: RoI: 3; U21-1
This central defender got off to a good start for Wrexham last term, when he was his usual rock-like self at the heart of defence. However, he suffered a knee injury at Walsall in mid-October and that was effectively the end of his season. He was sorely missed and the team suffered for the absence of his vast experience, awareness and sheer presence. Although released in May manager Denis Smith has hinted that there may be a possible coaching position for him at the club.
Manchester U *(£100,000 from Cork C on 2/9/1989)*
Wrexham *(Loaned on 17/1/1991) FL 3*
Wrexham *(Loaned on 24/12/1991) FL 13/1 FAC 3 Others 3*
Leicester C *(£250,000 on 16/7/1993) P/FL 51+7/1 FLC 3 FAC 0+1 Others 4*
Wrexham *(£100,000 on 19/7/1996) FL 282+6/15 FLC 14 FAC 22 Others 8+2*

CAREY Louis Anthony
Born: Bristol, 20 January 1977
Height: 5'10" **Weight:** 11.10
Club Honours: AMC '03
International Honours: S: U21-1
Signed by Peter Reid on a free transfer in the summer this experienced full back took time to settle at Coventry and his form lacked consistency. Little was seen of his skill at overlapping as Reid played a defensive formation, but following a change in management at Highfield Road he took the opportunity to move back to Bristol City at the end of January. However, although the cool and cultured defender featured regularly on his return to Ashton Gate he was unable to guide City into the League One play-offs.
Bristol C *(From trainee on 3/7/1995) FL 301+11/5 FLC 15+1 FAC 18+1 Others 21+2/1*
Coventry C *(Free on 16/7/2004) FL 23 FLC 3 FAC 1*
Bristol C *(Free on 1/2/2005) FL 14*

CARLISLE Clarke James
Born: Preston, 14 October 1979
Height: 6'1" **Weight:** 12.10
International Honours: E: U21-3
After helping Queen's Park Rangers to promotion to the Championship in 2003-04, central defender Clarke hankered after a move back North because of personal reasons. Leeds offered him that chance and he proved a key member of the defence, often weighing in with vital goals, including a late point-saver against Watford and another against the Hornets in the 2-1 win at Vicarage Road.
Blackpool *(From trainee on 13/8/1997) FL 85+8/7 FLC 4+1 FAC 3/1 Others 5*
Queens Park Rgrs *(£250,000 on 25/5/2000) FL 93+3/6 FLC 5 FAC 6 Others 5*
Leeds U *(Free on 12/7/2004) FL 29+6/4 FLC 3*

CARLISLE Wayne Thomas
Born: Lisburn, 9 September 1979
Height: 6'0" **Weight:** 11.6
International Honours: NI: U21-9; Yth; Sch
Wayne joined Leyton Orient during the summer of 2004 and featured regularly during the first half of the campaign, a highlight coming with his two goals at Northampton in August. On his day he is a flying right winger with an eye for goal, but he struggled with an injury during the latter part of the season, although he was back in first-team action for the closing fixtures.
Crystal Palace *(From trainee on 18/9/1996) FL 29+17/3 FLC 4+3 FAC 1*
Swindon T *(Loaned on 12/10/2001) FL 10+1/2 FAC 2*
Bristol Rov *(Free on 28/3/2002) FL 62+9/14 FLC 2 FAC 3+2/1 Others 1*
Leyton Orient *(Free on 27/7/2004) FL 24+4/3 FLC 1 FAC 2/1 Others 3/1*

CARPENTER Richard
Born: Sheerness, 30 September 1972
Height: 6'0" **Weight:** 13.0
Club Honours: Div 3 '01; Div 2 '02
Still the midfield dynamo after five years at Brighton, Richard again had a consistent season despite missing the first six weeks following a knee operation. With his vast experience, he was just the man to have around in a season-long battle to remain in the Championship. A redoubtable tackler and good passer, Richard is renowned for his long-range shooting. He notched three vital goals in the League and also hit the back of the net with a trademark free-kick to equalise in the FA Cup tie at Tottenham in January.
Gillingham *(From trainee on 13/5/1991) FL 107+15/4 FLC 2+1 FAC 9+1 Others 7/1*
Fulham *(£15,000 on 26/9/1996) FL 49+9/7 FLC 4/1 FAC 2/1 Others 2*
Cardiff C *(£35,000 on 29/7/1998) FL 69+6/2 FLC 3+1 FAC 8+1 Others 1*
Brighton & Hove A *(Free on 4/7/2000) FL 197+8/18 FLC 7+1 FAC 8/2 Others 7/2*

CARR Stephen
Born: Dublin, 29 August 1976
Height: 5'9" **Weight:** 12.2
Club Honours: FLC '99
International Honours: RoI: 37; U21-12; Yth; Sch
Stephen was signed to bolster Newcastle's suspect defence and turned in a series of solid performances playing on the right of the back four. A regular in the team he enjoyed raiding down the wing to supplement his attack. Stephen scored his first goal for the club with a superb 30-yard winner at Southampton, but a knee injury in November sidelined him for three months. He returned to action at the end of January, but with injuries depleting the squad he was occasionally moved into a holding midfield role. He continued as a regular in the Republic of Ireland side during the season.
Tottenham H *(From trainee on 1/9/1993) PL 222+4/7 FLC 23/1 FAC 16+1 Others 6*
Newcastle U *(£2,000,000 on 12/8/2004) PL 26/1 FAC 4 Others 9*

CARRAGHER James (Jamie) Lee Duncan
Born: Bootle, 28 January 1978
Height: 6'1" **Weight:** 13.0
Club Honours: FAYC '96; FLC '01, '03; FAC '01; UEFAC '01; ESC '01; CS '01; UEFACL '05
International Honours: E: 17; B-2; U21-27; Yth
For eight years an unsung hero in Liverpool's defence, playing mostly at full back under previous manager Gerald Houllier, Jamie's switch to central defence was a master stroke by incoming manager Rafael Benitez and he responded with performances which elevated him to the level of the all-time greats at centre half for Liverpool. Considered by his manager to be one of the best central defenders in the country, few were arguing against him after

Stephen Carr

Jamie's heroic displays at the climax of the Reds' European Champions' League campaign. His close marking, block tackles, last-ditch clearances and cool distribution under pressure against some of the most powerful teams in Europe ranked among the best performances by a Liverpool player in recent times. Along with Steven Gerrard, Jamie is the heart and soul of Liverpool FC, and for sheer consistency alone he was the most crucial player for the Reds in 2004-05.
Liverpool *(From trainee on 9/10/1996) PL 242+12/2 FLC 19+3 FAC 18 Others 65+1*

CARRAGHER Matthew (Matt)

Born: Liverpool, 14 January 1976
Height: 5'9" **Weight:** 12.12
Club Honours: Div 3 '97; AMC '01
Matt missed the first two months of last season for Macclesfield Town with a stress fracture of the tibia, but after his return played in the majority of matches in the role of sweeper in a three-man defence although, towards the end of the season, he deputised at right-wing-back. Matt is a reliable player and always reads the game well.
Wigan Ath *(From trainee on 25/11/1993) FL 102+17 FLC 6+1/1 FAC 10+1/2 Others 7+1*
Port Vale *(Free on 3/7/1997) FL 190+4/1 FLC 9 FAC 5 Others 12/1 (Free to Stafford Rgrs during 2003 close season)*
Macclesfield T *(Free on 25/11/2003) FL 44+5 FAC 3 Others 4+1*

CARRICK Michael

Born: Wallsend, 28 July 1981
Height: 6'0" **Weight:** 11.10
Club Honours: FAYC '99
International Honours: E: 3; U21-14; Yth
This hugely talented central midfielder continues to grow in stature at both club and international level. Spurs beat a host of Premiership clubs to Michael's signature and he appears to have put recurring injuries behind him to demonstrate some of his best form of late. Creative on the ball with plenty of pace to penetrate opponents' defences, Michael is a real threat going forward. As a playmaker he is accurate in his passing and happy to take opponents on with the ball at his feet. He covers the pitch well and finds space in attack, whilst never shy in his defensive responsibilities. Michael is the type of talent you can build a team around and, with youth on his side, is a fabulous prospect at both club and international level.
West Ham U *(From trainee on 25/8/1998) P/FL 128+8/6 FLC 8 FAC 11 Others 3+1*
Swindon T *(Loaned on 12/11/1999) FL 6/2*
Birmingham C *(Loaned on 23/2/2000) FL 1+1*
Tottenham H *(£3,000,000 on 24/8/2004) PL 26+3 FLC 2+1 FAC 5+1*

CARROLL Roy Eric

Born: Enniskillen, 30 September 1977
Height: 6'2" **Weight:** 12.9
Club Honours: AMC '99; PL '03; FAC '04
International Honours: NI: 17; U21-11; Yth
Roy is a highly accomplished goalkeeper, who possesses great presence, and a safe pair of hands. Having superseded Tim Howard in the first team in September against Liverpool, however, Roy only conceded nine goals in the Premiership up until Christmas. He always produced the goods when needed and in the Premiership alone he kept goal in 17 undefeated games, before Tim Howard was recalled following the Manchester 'derby' in February. With limited appearances in the first team for the rest of the campaign, Roy's future at Old Trafford looked bleak. However, after being reinstated to the side in April in preference to Howard, he played in United's last four Premiership games, and the FA Cup final. Despite this, at the time of writing, his immediate future was still undecided.
Hull C *(From trainee on 7/9/1995) FL 46 FLC 2 FAC 1 Others 1*
Wigan Ath *(£350,000 on 16/4/1997) FL 135 FLC 11 FAC 8 Others 15*
Manchester U *(£2,500,000 on 27/7/2001) PL 46+3 FLC 5 FAC 7+1 Others 10*

CARRUTHERS Christopher (Chris) Paul

Born: Kettering, 19 August 1983
Height: 5'10" **Weight:** 12.3
International Honours: E: Yth
Chris had something of a disappointing time at Northampton last season when he spent much of the time on the injury list and managed just a handful of appearances, all from the substitutes' bench. Most of his first-team action therefore came in loan spells, which saw him feature for Hornchurch, Kettering and Bristol Rovers. He filled in at left-wing-back and also on the left-hand side of midfield for the Pirates, but failed to make much of an impression.
Northampton T *(From trainee on 9/4/2002) FL 52+22/1 FLC 2+1 FAC 7 Others 3+2*
Bristol Rov *(Loaned on 24/3/2005) FL 2+3*

CARRUTHERS Martin George

Born: Nottingham, 7 August 1972
Height: 5'11" **Weight:** 12.0
Martin signed for Boston United in the summer and began the 2004-05 season in the starting line-up, forming a partnership up front with Jason Lee. Martin worked hard but failed to get on the score sheet and lost his place after just four games. After a few more appearances as a substitute he moved to neighbours Lincoln City but struggled to find his form at Sincil Bank and failed to win a regular place in the Imps' starting line-up. He was loaned out to Cambridge in the new year, but failed to add to his appearances on his return and was released at the end of the season.
Aston Villa *(From trainee on 4/7/1990) P/FL 2+2 FAC 0+1 Others 0+1*
Hull C *(Loaned on 31/10/1992) FL 13/6 Others 3*
Stoke C *(£100,000 on 5/7/1993) FL 60+31/13 FLC 7+3/1 FAC 3+1 Others 10+4/6*
Peterborough U *(Signed on 18/11/1996) FL 63+4/21 FLC 5+1/2 FAC 6/4 Others 6*
York C *(Loaned on 29/1/1999) FL 3+3*
Darlington *(Signed on 25/3/1999) FL 11+6/2 FLC 0+2*
Southend U *(£50,000 on 17/9/1999) FL 69+1/26 FLC 2 FAC 5 Others 5+1/3*
Scunthorpe U *(£20,000 on 22/3/2001) FL 80+6/34 FLC 2 FAC 6/4 Others 5+1/1*
Macclesfield T *(Free on 4/7/2003) FL 30+9/8 FLC 1 FAC 3+1/2 Others 1*
Boston U *(Free on 5/8/2004) FL 4+2 FLC 0+1*
Lincoln C *(Free on 21/9/2004) FL 7+4 Others 1*
Cambridge U *(Loaned on 28/1/2005) FL 5*

CARSLEY Lee Kevin

Born: Birmingham, 28 February 1974
Height: 5'10" **Weight:** 11.11
International Honours: RoI: 29; U21-1
A pleasantly surprising feature of Everton's renaissance last season was the inspiring form of this feisty and committed midfielder, who felt the benefits of retiring from international football for the Republic of Ireland. Employed as a holding player in front of the defence in a five-man midfield, Lee also scored some memorable goals, most notably the winner in the Merseyside derby and a curling free kick at Newcastle. At his best when in tandem with Thomas Gravesen, he still maintained a consistent level of performance when the Dane left for Real Madrid. Lee is widely regarded as being a credit to his profession, being actively involved in several charities and he is the patron of the Down's Syndrome Association of Solihull.
Derby Co *(From trainee on 6/7/1992) P/FL 122+16/5 FLC 10+3 FAC 12 Others 3*

Blackburn Rov *(£3,375,000 on 23/3/1999) P/FL 40+6/10 FLC 4/1 FAC 4/1*
Coventry C *(£2,500,000 on 1/12/2000) P/FL 46+1/4 FLC 2/1 FAC 3*
Everton *(£1,950,000 on 8/2/2002) PL 79+10/10 FLC 6/1 FAC 6*

CARSON Scott Paul
Born: Whitehaven, 3 September 1985
Height: 6'3" **Weight:** 13.7
Club Honours: UEFACL '05
International Honours: U21-11; Yth
Already established as the England U21s first-choice 'keeper, Scott was signed by Liverpool manager Rafael Benitez during the January transfer window. However, following injuries to both of Liverpool's first-choice 'keepers he was quickly thrown into first-team action, making his debut in March away to Newcastle United. A few weeks later he was again pressed into service in the Reds' European Champions' Cup quarter-final match at home to Juventus, when he produced a near-flawless performance. Scott will be hoping for plenty more opportunities at Anfield in 2005-06.
Leeds U *(From trainee on 5/9/2002) PL 2+1*
Liverpool *(£750,000 + on 21/1/2005) PL 4 Others 1*

CARSS Anthony (Tony) John
Born: Alnwick, 31 March 1976
Height: 5'10" **Weight:** 12.0
This creative midfielder made a fine start to the season at Huddersfield last term and was rewarded with a brilliant 30-yard free-kick goal in the opening day win at Stockport County. The left-sided player produced some all-out attacking displays and even featured in a defensive role occasionally, turning out as an emergency left wing back. However, he was also affected by injuries and cartilage and groin problems kept him out of action for lengthy spells.
Blackburn Rov *(From trainee at Bradford C on 29/8/1994)*
Darlington *(Free on 11/8/1995) FL 33+24/2 FLC 5/1 FAC 2+1 Others 4*
Cardiff C *(Free on 28/7/1997) FL 36+6/1 FLC 2 FAC 5+1 Others 1*
Chesterfield *(Free on 7/9/1998) FL 26+9/1 FLC 2 FAC 1 Others 1+1*
Carlisle U *(Free on 11/8/2000) FL 6+1 FLC 2*
Oldham Ath *(Free on 13/10/2000) FL 58+17/5 FLC 3/1 FAC 3 Others 1+2*
Huddersfield T *(Free on 7/8/2003) FL 58+5/3 FLC 4/1 Others 2*

CARTER Darren Anthony
Born: Solihull, 18 December 1983
Height: 6'2" **Weight:** 12.5
International Honours: E: Yth
This tall and rangy left-sided midfielder spent a three-month loan spell at Sunderland early on last term, scoring on his debut against Preston in September and proving himself to be an exciting prospect. Although Black Cats' boss Mick McCarthy was keen to sign Darren permanently, he returned to St Andrew's where he was thrown straight back into 'derby' at Villa in December. His strong running and tackling helped the Blues to a 2-1 win that kick-started their season. Darren was a threat when surging late into the penalty area from central midfield and scored twice in the FA Cup defeat of Leeds United. Darren also played wide on the left and did a decent job for the team.
Birmingham C *(From trainee on 13/11/2001) P/FL 28+17/3 FLC 1 FAC 2+3/2 Others 1+1*
Sunderland *(Loaned on 17/9/2004) FL 8+2/1*

CARTLEDGE Jonathan (Jon) Robert
Born: Carshalton, 27 November 1984
Height: 6'2" **Weight:** 13.0
This young centre half found his first-team opportunities at Bury strictly limited last term, starting only once for the Shakers – in the defeat at Rushden in February when he stepped into a struggling team that was lacking confidence. Jon featured on the bench for much of the second half of the campaign from where he was called into the action on four occasions.
Bury *(From trainee on 6/8/2004) FL 8+8/1*

CARTWRIGHT Lee
Born: Rawtenstall, 19 September 1972
Height: 5'8" **Weight:** 11.0
Club Honours: Div 3 '96; Div 2 '00
Lee played in the majority of Stockport's games up until the end of November

Lee Cartwright (left)

when he picked up a serious injury that ruled him out until mid-April. He scored his first goal for the club in the opening away game at Colchester with an angled drive from the edge of the area.
Preston NE *(From trainee on 30/7/1991) FL 312+85/22 FLC 19+4/2 FAC 18+6/1 Others 20+5/1*
Stockport Co *(Free on 29/1/2004) FL 32+2/1 FLC 1 FAC 1 Others 2*

CARVALHO Alberto **Ricardo**
Born: Amarante, Portugal, 18 May 1978
Height: 6'0" **Weight:** 12.6
Club Honours: FLC '05; PL '05
International Honours: Portugal: 16
When legendary central defender Marcel Desailly called time on his glittering career Chelsea were in the fortunate position of being able to recruit another world-class performer to take his place. Jose Mourinho made a trip back to Porto to take another member of his successful Champions' League back four, the brilliant Ricardo Carvalho. Ricardo enjoyed an incredible 12-month period, winning the Champions' League with Porto, the Premiership and Carling Cup with Chelsea and playing superbly for runners-up Portugal in Euro 2004 – a string of performances which deservedly brought him inclusion in UEFA's Team of the Year for 2004. He adapted rapidly to the faster-paced English Premiership and became an integral part of Chelsea's 'Iron Curtain' defence, which yielded a miserly 15 goals during the 38-match programme. His power in the air, speed, reading of play and clean tackling perfectly complemented John Terry and William Gallas and this impregnable trio provided the backbone of the Blues' record-breaking squad. Ricardo suffered a broken toe against Arsenal in December which forced him to miss 14 matches and five games into his comeback scored his only goal so far for Chelsea – and what an important one it was. His header from a corner at Carrow Road wrapped up a crucial victory on the day that the Blues' two closest rivals slipped up and established an 11-point lead.
Chelsea *(£16,500,000 + from FC Porto, Portugal, ex Leca, on 30/7/2004) PL 22+3/1 FLC 3 FAC 1 Others 10*

CASH Brian Dominick
Born: Dublin, 24 November 1982
Height: 5'9" **Weight:** 12.0
International Honours: RoI: U21-4; Yth
This young winger again made little impact at Nottingham Forest last term and spent time on loan at Rochdale in the early weeks of the season. Brian filled in on the right-hand side and providing a series of telling crosses for his strikers during his spell at Spotland. He was released by Forest shortly before Christmas and then had a brief association with Bristol Rovers as a non-contract player, making a single appearance from the bench. After trials with Hearts and St Johnstone he signed for Eircom League side Derry City.
Nottingham F *(From trainee on 15/12/1999) FL 0+7 FLC 0+1*
Swansea C *(Loaned on 19/10/2002) FL 5 Others 1*
Rochdale *(Loaned on 20/8/2004) FL 6 FLC 1*
Bristol Rov *(Free on 17/12/2004) FL 0+1*

CASKEY Darren Mark
Born: Basildon, 21 August 1974
Height: 5'8" **Weight:** 11.9
International Honours: E: Yth (UEFA-U18 '93); Sch
Darren spent the early part of last season with Conference South outfit Hornchurch, before joining Peterborough on a short-term contract at the turn of the year. The talented midfielder featured in four games for Posh before moving on to sign for USL First Division side Virginia Beach Mariners.
Tottenham H *(From trainee on 6/3/1992) PL 20+12/4 FLC 3+1/1 FAC 6+1*
Watford *(Loaned on 27/10/1995) FL 6/1*
Reading *(£700,000 on 28/2/1996) FL 180+22/35 FLC 10+2/4 FAC 9+1/5 Others 8+1/1*
Notts Co *(Free on 4/7/2001) FL 101+13/10 FLC 5 FAC 7 Others 2+2/1 (Freed on 25/3/2004)*
Peterborough U *(Free from Hornchurch, via trial at Bristol C, on 29/11/2004) FL 2+2*

CATON Andrew (Andy) James
Born: Oxford, 3 December 1987
Height: 6'0" **Weight:** 12.3
A tall, pacy forward, Andy received a surprise introduction to senior football when he came off the bench for Swindon on the opening day of the 2004-05 season and netted a late consolation goal in the 2-1 defeat at Wrexham. Thereafter he was used sparingly throughout the campaign before making his full League debut in the final game, a 1-1 draw with Chesterfield. Andy is the son of former Manchester City star Tommy Caton.
Swindon T *(Trainee) FL 1+7/1 Others 1*

CECH Petr
Born: Plzen, Czech Republic, 20 May 1982
Height: 6'5" **Weight:** 14.3
Club Honours: FLC '05; PL '05
International Honours: Czech Republic: 32
It is rare for an overseas player to rewrite the record books in his first season in the Premiership but Chelsea's goalkeeper Petr Cech did just that in the Blues' incredible 2004-05 campaign. From 12 December until 5 March the brilliant Cech kept 10 consecutive clean sheets during an amazing 1,025-minute spell without conceding a goal – overtaking the record of Peter Schmeichel. The new record was established at Ewood Park where a super penalty save from Paul Dickov put Petr within minutes of the old mark. Overall, the Blues conceded just 15 goals in the 38-match Premiership programme – yet another record. These phenomenal achievements earned Petr a place in the PFA Premiership team of the season and a nomination for PFA Player of the Year. Petr has all the attributes for a great 'keeper having an imposing physique, great agility and handling and domination of his penalty area. He can also kick box-to-box with booming left-foot efforts. Petr made one of the saves of the season when he sprang away to his right to claw away a header from compatriot Milan Baros in the Champions' League semi-final first leg.
Chelsea *(£9,000,000 from Stade Rennais, France, ex Chmel Blsany, on 19/7/2004) PL 35 FLC 2 Others 11*

CERNY Radek
Born: Prague, Czech Republic, 18 February 1974
Height: 6'3" **Weight:** 13.5
International Honours: Czech Republic: 3
Radek is best known as number two to Petr Cech in the Czech Republic national side. He finally got his chance of first-team action in April when a knock in the game against arch rivals Arsenal forced Paul Robinson to finish his season and provide Radek with two-and-a-half games to demonstrate his ability. He showed a good presence, great shot-stopping ability and experience in organising the defence and will hope for further opportunities in 2005-06.
Tottenham H *(Loaned from SK Slavia Prague, Czech Republic on 28/1/2005) PL 2+1*

CHADWICK Luke Harry
Born: Cambridge, 18 November 1980
Height: 5'11" **Weight:** 11.0
Club Honours: PL '01
International Honours: E: U21-13; Yth
This tricky right winger signed for West Ham in the summer of 2004. On his day he can be one of the most exciting wingers in the country, but he tended to fade from the picture on too many

occasions. Luke had his best games for the club in December. Firstly came a lively performance at Sunderland when he set up the opening goal as the Hammers won 2-0. A week later he starred against Leeds scoring in the 1-1 draw.
Manchester U *(From trainee on 8/2/1999) PL 11+14/2 FLC 5 FAC 1+2 Others 1+5*
Reading *(Loaned on 7/2/2003) FL 15/1 Others 1+1*
Burnley *(Loaned on 15/7/2003) FL 23+13/5 FLC 2/1 FAC 1+1*
West Ham U *(Free on 5/8/2004) FL 22+10/1 FLC 1 FAC 3*

CHADWICK Nicholas (Nicky) Gerald
Born: Market Drayton, 26 October 1982
Height: 6'0" **Weight:** 12.8
This young striker had limited opportunities at Goodison last term, although he curiously scored more goals (six) than he made first-team starts (four). A good finisher, he left in January to move to Home Park after scoring there against Plymouth in the FA Cup. Powerful and pacy, he impressed the Argyle fans with his willingness for hard work and soon became a great favourite. He has good touch and vision, and scored his first goal for the club against Brighton in March.
Everton *(From trainee on 29/10/1999) PL 3+11/3 FLC 1+3/2 FAC 0+3/1*
Derby Co *(Loaned on 28/2/2003) FL 4+2*
Millwall *(Loaned on 26/11/2003) FL 6/2*
Millwall *(Loaned on 18/3/2004) FL 5+4/2*
Plymouth Arg *(£250,000 on 9/2/2005) FL 11+4/1*

CHALKIAS Konstantinos
Born: Larisa, Greece, 30 May 1974
Height: 6'6" **Weight:** 15.4
International Honours: Greece: 5
This towering goalkeeper featured in Champions' League action for Panathinaikos during the first half of last season, before joining Portsmouth in the January transfer window. He made his debut for Pompey in the dramatic FA Cup fourth round defeat by local rivals Southampton, and enjoyed a brief run in the side over the next few weeks before losing his place.
Portsmouth *(£100,000 from Panathinaikos, Greece, on 28/1/2005) PL 5 FAC 1*

CHALLINOR David (Dave) Paul
Born: Chester, 2 October 1975
Height: 6'1" **Weight:** 12.6
International Honours: E: Yth; Sch
Signed following a successful loan spell during the 2003-04 campaign, Dave was immediately installed as captain of the Bury team last term. His experience and influence shone through at the centre of the defence and he missed just three games during the season. Dave scored just one goal for the Shakers, netting in the 1-1 draw at home to Boston United in October.
Tranmere Rov *(Signed from Brombrough Pool on 18/7/1994) FL 124+16/6 FLC 17+1 FAC 9+2 Others 1*
Stockport Co *(£120,000 on 11/1/2002) FL 78+3/1 FLC 3 FAC 2 Others 4+1*
Bury *(Loaned on 9/1/2004) FL 15*
Bury *(Signed on 30/7/2004) FL 43/1 FLC 1/1 FAC 1/1 Others 1*

CHALLIS Trevor Michael
Born: Paddington, 23 October 1975
Height: 5'9" **Weight:** 11.4
International Honours: E: U21-2; Yth
This vastly experienced and committed left back was a regular in the Shrewsbury Town line-up last season and provided some much-needed balance to the side. Although Trevor had a dip in form at the turn of the year he quickly returned to the line-up and produced a number of solid performances in the closing stages of the campaign. Out of contract in the summer, it was announced that he would not be offered a new deal for the 2005-06 season.
Queens Park Rgrs *(From trainee on 1/7/1994) P/FL 12+1 FAC 2*
Bristol Rov *(Free on 15/7/1998) FL 137+8/1 FLC 7 FAC 14+1 Others 5 (Free to Telford U on 6/8/2003)*
Shrewsbury T *(Signed on 25/3/2004) FL 38 FAC 1 Others 1*

CHAMBERLAIN Alec Francis Roy
Born: March, 20 June 1964
Height: 6'2" **Weight:** 13.9
Club Honours: Div 1 '96; Div 2 '98
Embarking on his 23rd year as a professional, Alec lost his first-team place at Watford as the result of a rib injury suffered in a pre-season friendly. However, he soon had new challenges to face. He was appointed acting goalkeeping coach in October on the departure of Kevin Hitchcock, and continued to turn out for the reserves. In December, he returned to first-team action when Richard Lee was injured against Coventry, becoming the oldest player to represent Watford for over 50 years. He also played in the two FA Cup ties against Fulham. Confirmed as player/goalkeeping coach in March, he again returned to the first team for the last four games of the season, when his ability to organise the defence proved invaluable.
Ipswich T *(Free from Ramsey T on 27/7/1981)*
Colchester U *(Free on 3/8/1982) FL 188 FLC 11 FAC 10 Others 12*
Everton *(£80,000 on 28/7/1987)*
Tranmere Rov *(Loaned on 1/11/1987) FL 15*
Luton T *(£150,000 on 27/7/1988) FL 138 FLC 7 FAC 7 Others 7*
Sunderland *(Free on 8/7/1993) FL 89+1 FLC 9 FAC 8 Others 1*
Watford *(£40,000 on 10/7/1996) P/FL 240+4 FLC 16+1 FAC 16 Others 3*

CHAMBERS Adam Craig
Born: West Bromwich, 20 November 1980
Height: 5'10" **Weight:** 11.8
International Honours: E: Yth
Adam was confined to reserve-team football for West Bromwich Albion last term before being released early in the new year, subsequently joining Kidderminster on non-contract terms. After recovering match fitness he finally made his debut for Harriers at right back in the penultimate game against Grimsby and then played in midfield in the final game of the season.
West Bromwich A *(From trainee on 8/1/1999) P/FL 38+18/1 FLC 4+2 FAC 5+1 Others 0+1*
Sheffield Wed *(Loaned on 19/2/2004) FL 8+3 Others 1*
Kidderminster Hrs *(Free on 24/3/2005) FL 2*

CHAMBERS James Ashley
Born: West Bromwich, 20 November 1980
Height: 5'10" **Weight:** 11.8
International Honours: E: Yth
James joined Watford on a month's loan from West Bromwich Albion last August, and made his debut less than two hours after arriving at Vicarage Road. Playing at right back, he made an immediate impression with his pace and athleticism and was subsequently signed permanently, making him Watford's first transfer outlay for over two years. James also appeared at left back and on the right-hand side of midfield, where he was able to give full rein to his attacking instincts. He scored his first senior goals – a brace– in the Carling Cup against Southampton.
West Bromwich A *(From trainee on 8/1/1999) P/FL 54+19 FLC 5+1 FAC 1*
Watford *(Loaned on 9/8/2004) FL 40 FLC 5/2 FAC 2*

CHAMBERS Luke
Born: Kettering, 29 August 1985
Height: 5'11" **Weight:** 11.0
Luke featured regularly in defence for Northampton last term, although never

able to call any one of the four back positions his own. A cool and calculating player he is good in the air, has plenty of pace and is not afraid to put in a tackle. He will be looking to firmly establish himself in the line-up in 2005-06.
***Northampton T** (From trainee on 3/11/2003) FL 38+14 FLC 3+1 FAC 1+3 Others 4+1*

CHAPLOW Richard David
Born: Accrington, 2 February 1985
Height: 5'9" **Weight:** 9.3
International Honours: E: U21-1; Yth
Starting Burnley's season as an automatic choice, and scoring his first England goal at U20 level, all seemed rosy on the horizon for Richard until injury sidelined him for two months between October and December. On his return, he only occasionally looked the driving midfield force he had previously been, but there was less scope for his naturally attacking instincts in the new and tighter Clarets' formation under Steve Cotterill. Just as the transfer window was closing in January he moved on to Premiership strugglers West Bromwich Albion. Settling into his new surroundings by playing in the reserves, he finally made his first-team debut as a substitute in the 4-1 win at Charlton almost three months after joining. He then gave an excellent performance at White Hart Lane on his first start for the club.
***Burnley** (From trainee on 13/9/2003) FL 48+17/7 FLC 3+1 FAC 5*
***West Bromwich A** (£1,500,000 on 31/1/2005) PL 3+1*

CHARLES Wesley **Darius** Donald
Born: Ealing, 10 December 1987
Height: 5'11" **Weight:** 11.10
This Brentford scholar spent most of last season developing in the club's youth team. He was called up to make his senior debut in the final match of the season against Hull when he gave an assured performance at left back. Darius will be looking to gain more first-team experience for the Bees in 2005-06.
***Brentford** (Trainee) FL 1*

CHARLTON Simon Thomas
Born: Huddersfield, 25 October 1971
Height: 5'8" **Weight:** 11.10
International Honours: E: Yth
Simon signed for Norwich City whilst the club was on tour in Malaysia and he was introduced to his colleagues, and the media, in a Kuala Lumpur hotel. Nigel Worthington brought him to add Premiership experience to his squad and some sterling displays at the heart of the Canaries' defence during the opening weeks of the season showed exactly that. His ability to read the game and his superb positional play soon earned him the respect of City fans. He later switched to his more familiar left-back position before a toe injury forced him out of the reckoning in March.
***Huddersfield T** (From trainee on 1/7/1989) FL 121+3/1 FLC 9/1 FAC 10 Others 14*
***Southampton** (£250,000 on 8/6/1993) PL 104+10/2 FLC 9+4/1 FAC 8+1*
***Birmingham C** (£250,000 on 5/12/1997) FL 69+3 FLC 3 FAC 3*
***Bolton W** (Free on 12/7/2000) P/FL 108+12 FLC 6+2 FAC 3+1 Others 3*
***Norwich C** (£250,000 on 13/7/2004) PL 22+2/1 FLC 1 FAC 1*

CHILLINGWORTH Daniel (Dan) Thomas
Born: Cambridge, 13 September 1981
Height: 6'0" **Weight:** 12.6
This promising striker struggled to find his best form at Cambridge last term and at the turn of the year he went out on loan to Leyton Orient where he was required as cover for injuries. On his return to the Abbey Stadium there had been a change in management and Dan seemed to perform much better. The highlight of his season was registering a double in the U's 2-2 draw with Northampton Town in February.
***Cambridge U** (From trainee on 14/2/2000) FL 53+34/13 FLC 1+2 FAC 1+4 Others 5+6/1*
***Darlington** (Loaned on 19/11/2001) FL 2+2/1 FAC 1/1*
***Leyton Orient** (Loaned on 6/12/2004) FL 8/2*

Simon Charlton

CHILVERS Liam Christopher
Born: Chelmsford, 6 November 1981
Height: 6'1" **Weight:** 13.5
Club Honours: FAYC '00
Defender Liam was a key member for Colchester United for virtually the whole season, both as a centre half and left back. He even weighed in with his first goal for the club, with a late equaliser at Huddersfield. When Pat Baldwin and Wayne Brown were the favoured centre half partnership, Liam shifted to left back to good effect with a succession of solid performances. He is comfortable on the ball and good in the air.
Arsenal *(From trainee on 18/7/2000)*
Northampton T *(Loaned on 22/12/2000) FL 7*
Notts Co *(Loaned on 1/11/2001) FL 9/1 FAC 2*
Colchester U *(Loaned on 24/1/2003) FL 6*
Colchester U *(Loaned on 26/8/2003) FL 29+3 FLC 1 FAC 7 Others 5*
Colchester U *(Free on 6/8/2004) FL 40+1/1 FLC 2 FAC 4+1*

Michael Chopra

CHOPRA Rocky **Michael**
Born: Newcastle, 23 December 1983
Height: 5'8" **Weight:** 9.6
International Honours: E: U21-1; Yth
This promising Newcastle United striker initially joined Barnsley on loan for a month, but this was later extended until the end of the 2004-05 season. After a slow start he began to find the net regularly and his work rate was second to none. He finished as the club's leading scorer with 17 goals, including hat-tricks against Peterborough and Huddersfield, thus becoming the first Reds' player to register a treble since Craig Hignett during the 1999-2000 season. Michael's pace and eye for goal made him a constant threat and his work rate was second to none. He returned to St James' Park at the end of the season and made a 15-minute substitute appearance in the final Premiership game at home to Chelsea, insufficient to make any judgement on his form.
Newcastle U *(From trainee on 4/1/2001) PL 1+7 FLC 0+1 Others 0+2*
Watford *(Loaned on 25/3/2003) FL 4+1/5 FAC 1*
Nottingham F *(Loaned on 6/2/2004) FL 3+2*
Barnsley *(Loaned on 27/8/2004) FL 38+1/17 FLC 1 FAC 1 Others 1*

CHORLEY Benjamin (Ben) Francis
Born: Sidcup, 30 September 1982
Height: 6'3" **Weight:** 13.2
Club Honours: FAYC '01
Ben began the 2004-05 season in a midfield holding role for MK Dons, but after three months reverted to his more customary central-defensive slot. Once he had settled in he produced a string of performances that ultimately earned him both the supporters' and the club's 'Player of the Year' awards. Totally committed in everything he did, the confidence on the ball he picked up whilst in midfield greatly benefited his defenders, and as an inspirational skipper late on in the campaign he was a huge part of the successful fight against relegation.
Arsenal *(From trainee on 2/7/2001)*
Brentford *(Loaned on 14/8/2002) FL 2 FLC 1*
Wimbledon/MK Dons *(Free on 3/3/2003) FL 82+4/4 FLC 3 FAC 3+1 Others 2*

CHRISTIANSEN Jesper
Born: Denmark, 18 June 1980
Height: 6'3" **Weight:** 13.6
This talented striker never really settled into life in the rough-and-tumble world of League Two football. Last term he briefly found a new lease of life in midfield, starring in the 3-2 home win

over Scunthorpe, but after Jan Molby left Kidderminster the club made use of a clause in Jesper's contract that allowed him to leave if Molby departed. In the January transfer window he moved on to SPL club Dunfermline Athletic, for whom he featured regularly in the closing stages of the campaign.
Kidderminster Hrs *(Free from Odense BK, Denmark on 2/1/2004) FL 22+16/1 FLC 1 FAC 2+1 Others 1*

CHRISTIE Iyseden
Born: Coventry, 14 November 1976
Height: 6'0" **Weight:** 12.6
Iyseden was still recovering from a foot injury when he arrived at Kidderminster in the summer of 2004 and a series of complications meant that he did not make his debut for Harriers until September. Unfortunately he then suffered a reaction which restricted him to just one more appearance as a substitute before March. When he eventually returned to action it was from the bench and it was not until the final game of the season at Northampton that he featured in the starting line-up.
Coventry C *(From trainee on 22/5/1995) PL 0+1 FLC 0+1*
Bournemouth *(Loaned on 18/11/1996) FL 3+1*
Mansfield T *(Loaned on 7/2/1997) FL 8*
Mansfield T *(Free on 16/6/1997) FL 44+37/18 FLC 4/5 FAC 0+4 Others 2+1*
Leyton Orient *(£40,000 on 2/7/1999) FL 32+26/12 FLC 4+1/1 FAC 1+2/1 Others 1*
Mansfield T *(Free on 9/8/2002) FL 53+11/26 FLC 2 FAC 4+1/2 Others 1*
Kidderminster Hrs *(Free on 6/8/2004) FL 1+7*

CHRISTIE Malcolm Neil
Born: Stamford, 11 April 1979
Height: 5'6" **Weight:** 11.4
International Honours: E: U21-11
Last term proved to be another frustrating and disappointing season for Boro's popular striker. His comeback from a broken leg lasted eight minutes when he replaced Szilard Nemeth in the club's UEFA cup clash away to Czech side Banik Ostrava, but a stress fracture was diagnosed after the match. It meant another five long months on the sidelines for the England U21 marksman but he returned to the Boro' starting line-up at Portsmouth in February and, looking sharper than ever, he scored the first goal of the game but nevertheless Pompey won the game 2-1. Sadly Malcolm's personal injury jinx struck again four days later when tests revealed he had picked up a stress fracture of his left foot in the 1-0 win over Blackburn Rovers.
Derby Co *(£50,000 + from Nuneaton Borough on 2/11/1998) P/FL 90+26/30 FLC 6+2/3 FAC 5/2*
Middlesbrough *(£1,500,000 + on 31/1/2003) PL 20+4/6 FLC 0+1/1 Others 0+1*

CISSE Aliou
Born: Zinguinchor, Senegal, 24 March 1976
Height: 5'11" **Weight:** 12.8
International Honours: Senegal
This hard-tackling midfielder joined Portsmouth in the summer of 2004, but it was some time before he settled in at Fratton Park. However, he finally secured a first-team place in January, operating in a variety of positions including midfield and at full back. Aliou has yet to score his first goal for Pompey.
Birmingham C *(£1,500,000 from Montpelier, France, ex Lille, Sedan, Paris St Germain, on 26/7/2002) PL 26+10 FLC 1 FAC 0+1*
Portsmouth *(£300,000 on 6/8/2004) PL 12+8 FLC 3+1 FAC 1*

CISSE Djibril
Born: Arles, France, 12 August 1981
Height: 6'0" **Weight:** 13.0
Club Honours: UEFACL '05
International Honours: France: 20
Gerald Houllier's parting gift to Liverpool was this promising striker, whose transfer in the summer had been agreed almost a year earlier. However, the jury will remain out for some time on the wisdom of this signing as his first season at Anfield was wrecked early in the season by a double fracture of the leg at Blackburn in October. His season seemed over as new manager Rafael Benitez offered no prospect of an early return before next season, but incredibly his recovery was so rapid that he was available for the closing weeks of the season, making eight appearances from the bench before starting the final Premiership game against Aston Villa when he scored twice. He came off the bench in the closing stages of the European Cup final in Istanbul and converted one of the Reds' penalties in the decisive shoot-out.
Liverpool *(£14,000,000 from Auxerre, France on 16/7/2004) PL 10+6/4 Others 4+5/1*

CLAPHAM James (Jamie) Richard
Born: Lincoln, 7 December 1975
Height: 5'9" **Weight:** 10.11
Jamie started the season out of favour at Birmingham, had a knee injury and did not win his place back until January. He went on to put together a series of consistent displays from left back. Always reliable, Jamie performed with intelligence defensively and went forward with more much more urgency and determination than usual.
Tottenham H *(From trainee on 1/7/1994) PL 0+1 Others 4*
Leyton Orient *(Loaned on 29/1/1997) FL 6*
Bristol Rov *(Loaned on 27/3/1997) FL 4+1*
Ipswich T *(£300,000 on 9/1/1998) P/FL 187+20/10 FLC 19+1/4 FAC 4+3/1 Others 16+2/1*
Birmingham C *(£1,000,000 + on 10/1/2003) PL 56+12 FLC 2+1 FAC 1+2*

CLARE Daryl Adam
Born: Jersey, 1 August 1978
Height: 5'9" **Weight:** 11.12
Club Honours: AMC '98; NC '02, '05
A great deal was expected of this exciting striker last term after his goals had helped the club win a return to the Football League the previous campaign. However, an injury in pre-season required surgery and although he returned briefly to the team he was transferred to Boston United soon afterwards. Daryl struggled to make an impression at York Street to begin with, finding it difficult to force his way into the starting line-up. He found goals hard to come by, but will be looking to play a more significant role in Boston's fortunes in 2005-06.
Grimsby T *(From trainee on 9/12/1995) FL 34+45/9 FLC 1+8/1 FAC 1+4 Others 4+2*
Northampton T *(Loaned on 12/11/1999) FL 9+1/3*
Northampton T *(Loaned on 24/11/2000) FL 3+1 Others 0+1*
Cheltenham T *(Loaned on 30/12/2000) FL 4*
Boston U *(Free on 26/7/2001) FL 7/1 FLC 1*
Chester C *(Free on 1/11/2002) FL 3+4/1 FAC 1 Others 1*
Boston U *(Signed on 19/11/2004) FL 14+5/3*

CLARE Robert (Rob)
Born: Belper, 28 February 1983
Height: 6'1" **Weight:** 11.7
International Honours: E: Yth
This talented centre half joined Blackpool in the summer of 2004 and was a first choice in the line-up in the opening stages of the campaign. However, he lost his place when Peter Clarke arrived and as the season progressed he drifted out of the first-team picture at Bloomfield Road. Rob was released in the summer.
Stockport Co *(From trainee on 10/3/2000) FL 107+10/3 FLC 4/1 FAC 4 Others 3*
Blackpool *(Free on 5/8/2004) FL 19+4 FLC 1 FAC 4 Others 2*

CLARIDGE Stephen (Steve) Edward
Born: Portsmouth, 10 April 1966
Height: 5'11" **Weight:** 12.10
Steve began the 2004-05 season as

player-manager of Weymouth, but when his reign came to an abrupt end he sought to resurrect his playing career. First stop was Brighton, where the veteran striker showed his customary enthusiasm and added some much-needed experience to the forward line. He subsequently accepted a longer deal at Brentford but made little impact with the West London club and in the new year he moved on to Wycombe, initially on loan. His usefulness to the side was immediately apparent, particularly his ability to hold and distribute the ball, and he was soon signed until the end of the season. Steve's four goals all came in a purple three-game run and his fitness was remarkable for a 38-year old.

Bournemouth *(Signed from Fareham T on 30/11/1984) FL 3+4/1 Others 1 (£10,000 to Weymouth in October 1985)*
Crystal Palace *(Signed from Basingstoke T on 11/10/1988)*
Aldershot *(£14,000 on 13/10/1988) FL 58+4/19 FLC 2+1 FAC 6/1 Others 5/2*
Cambridge U *(£75,000 on 8/2/1990) FL 56+23/28 FLC 2+4/2 FAC 1 Others 6+3/1*
Luton T *(£160,000 on 17/7/1992) FL 15+1/2 FLC 2/3 Others 2/1*
Cambridge U *(£195,000 on 20/11/1992) FL 53/18 FLC 4/3 FAC 4 Others 3*
Birmingham C *(£350,000 on 7/1/1994) FL 86+2/35 FLC 14+1/2 FAC 7 Others 9+1/5*
Leicester C *(£1,200,000 on 1/3/1996) P/FL 53+10/16 FLC 8/2 FAC 4/1 Others 3+1/1*
Portsmouth *(Loaned on 23/1/1998) FL 10/2*
Wolverhampton W *(£400,000 on 26/3/1998) FL 4+1 FAC 1*
Portsmouth *(£200,000 on 10/8/1998) FL 94+10/34 FLC 4+2 FAC 2+2/1*
Millwall *(Free on 21/3/2001) FL 76+15/29 FLC 1+2/1 FAC 4+1/3 Others 1+1 (Free to Weymouth on 30/6/2003)*
Brighton & Hove A *(Free on 12/11/2004) FL 5*
Brentford *(Free on 17/12/2004) FL 3+1*
Wycombe W *(Free on 13/1/2005) FL 14+5/4*

CLARK Benjamin (Ben)

Born: Consett, 24 January 1983
Height: 6'2" **Weight:** 13.0
International Honours: E: Yth; Sch

A central defender or midfielder, Ben started the 2004-05 season in the first team at Sunderland, but he made only two full appearances before being allowed to join near neighbours Hartlepool. Although Ben took some time to settle in his versatility proved a great asset for Pools and he featured regularly in the starting line-up during the remainder of the campaign. He took a little time to settle into his new surroundings, but due to his versatility has proved himself to be a great asset to the first-team squad.

Sunderland *(From trainee on 5/7/2000) P/FL 3+5 FLC 4 FAC 2*
Hartlepool U *(Signed on 22/10/2004) FL 21+4 FAC 5+1 Others 1*

CLARK Christopher (Chris) James

Born: Shoreham, 9 June 1984
Height: 6'0" **Weight:** 10.12

This young midfielder was a regular in Portsmouth's reserve team last season and spent the final three months of the campaign on loan at Stoke City. Signed mainly as cover he made just two substitute appearances during his stay and was released shortly after returning to Fratton Park.

Portsmouth *(From trainee on 26/3/2003)*
Stoke C *(Loaned on 3/2/2005) FL 0+2*

CLARK Ian David

Born: Stockton, 23 October 1974
Height: 5'11" **Weight:** 11.7

Ian's fourth season with the Quakers was frustrated by a leg injury at Christmas and after featuring regularly in the first half of the campaign he failed to reappear until the final game of the season when he came on as a substitute against Cheltenham Town. He again proved his versatility, being used at left back and also on the left side of midfield, and weighed in with two more goals including the winner against Grimsby in the opening game. Ian was released at the end of the season.

Doncaster Rov *(Free from Stockton on 11/8/1995) FL 23+22/3 FLC 1+2 FAC 1+1 Others 4/1*
Hartlepool U *(Free on 24/10/1997) FL 109+29/17 FLC 4 FAC 4+2 Others 11+2/1*
Darlington *(£10,000 on 14/11/2001) FL 84+35/26 FLC 3+1 FAC 7+2/1 Others 1+1*

CLARK Lee Robert

Born: Wallsend, 27 October 1972
Height: 5'8" **Weight:** 11.7
Club Honours: Div 1 '93, '99, '01
International Honours: E: U21-11; Yth; Sch

Last term proved to be very much a season of two halves for the Fulham club captain who did not appear in first-team action until New Year's Day. Lee suffered both achilles and calf problems throughout the first half of the campaign, which eventually necessitated a small operation. After returning to the side he wasted no time in re-establishing his influence on the team. A combative player who is an excellent ball winner and passer of the ball, his only goal of the season was a last-minute equaliser at home to Aston Villa. Lee was out of contract in the summer and his future was unclear at the time of writing.

Newcastle U *(From trainee on 9/12/1989) P/FL 153+42/23 FLC 17 FAC 14+2/3 Others 7+5/1*
Sunderland *(£2,750,000 on 25/6/1997) FL 72+1/16 FLC 4+1 FAC 4 Others 3*
Fulham *(£3,000,000 on 13/7/1999) P/FL 141+8/20 FLC 15/2 FAC 11+1 Others 1+1*

CLARKE Andrew (Andy) Weston

Born: Islington, 22 July 1967
Height: 5'10" **Weight:** 11.7
Club Honours: GMVC '91
International Honours: E: SP-2

This veteran striker was a regular in the Peterborough United squad last term, although most of his appearances came from the bench. He added three more goals to his tally, making him equal fifth in the all-time Football League goal-scorers for Posh. Despite his age Andy was as enthusiastic as ever, but nevertheless he was released on a free transfer at the end of the campaign.

Wimbledon *(£250,000 from Barnet on 21/2/1991) P/FL 74+96/17 FLC 13+12/4 FAC 9+8/2*
Port Vale *(Loaned on 28/8/1998) FL 2+4*
Northampton T *(Loaned on 15/1/1999) FL 2+2*
Peterborough U *(Free on 4/5/1999) FL 170+60/57 FLC 4+2/2 FAC 15+3/7 Others 10/5*

CLARKE Bradie Jason

Born: Cambridge, 26 May 1986
Height: 6'2" **Weight:** 13.10

This promising young 'keeper spent most of the 2004-05 season as understudy to Chris Tardif and Simon Cox at Oxford. Injuries allowed him a brief run of first-team action at the turn of the year, when he generally did well, and he returned to add a further appearance from the substitutes' bench at Swansea in April.

Oxford U *(Trainee) FL 3+1*

CLARKE Clive Richard

Born: Dublin, 14 January 1980
Height: 6'1" **Weight:** 12.3
Club Honours: AMC '00
International Honours: RoI: 2; U21-11; Yth

Stoke City's captain again performed a useful role on the left-hand side of midfield last term. Clive, who has also featured at left back and in the centre of defence, scored just once during the season, netting from the penalty spot against Wolves in the opening game.

Stoke C *(From trainee on 25/1/1997) FL 205+18/9 FLC 12+3 FAC 8+1 Others 17/1*

CLARKE Darrell James
Born: Mansfield, 16 December 1977
Height: 5'10" **Weight:** 11.6
This attacking right-sided Hartlepool midfielder spent the first half of last season recovering from a knee operation. Darrell was loaned out to Stockport in January linking up with his former Pools boss Chris Turner once more. However, he limped out of the action after just 32 minutes with what was later diagnosed as cartilage damage, ending his four-week loan spell before it had really started.
Mansfield T *(From trainee on 3/7/1996) FL 137+24/24 FLC 7/2 FAC 4+1/1 Others 2+2*
Hartlepool U *(Signed on 17/7/2001) FL 92+19/19 FLC 3+1 FAC 2+2/1 Others 3+2/2*
Stockport Co *(Loaned on 12/1/2005) FL 1*

CLARKE James (Jamie) William
Born: Sunderland, 18 September 1982
Height: 6'2" **Weight:** 12.9
Jamie joined Rochdale in the summer of 2004 to provide defensive cover, particularly at right back. However, in only the second game of the season he had to fill-in in midfield and did so well that he held down that position for much of the campaign. He displayed excellent passing ability and was often Dale's most creative player. Jamie scored his first goal for the club when thrown on up front in the last few minutes of the game at Lincoln and his ability to play at right back or centre back when required also proved valuable. Jamie is the son of former Sunderland and Newcastle centre back Jeff Clarke.
Mansfield T *(From trainee on 5/7/2002) FL 29+5/1 FLC 2 FAC 3+1 Others 2*
Rochdale *(Free on 5/7/2004) FL 32+9/1 FLC 1 FAC 3 Others 1+1*

CLARKE Leon Marvin
Born: Birmingham, 10 February 1985
Height: 6'2" **Weight:** 14.2
It was nice to see a local youngster getting his opportunity at Molineux last term, even if this was partly because of injuries to other Wolves' strikers. Leon came off the bench during the opening game against Stoke and then made his full debut three days later against Preston when he netted an equaliser. After a short run in the line-up he returned to the bench, then had another run in the side in the closing stages. He scored consistently for the reserves, 13 in all, in addition to his tally of eight from 12 starts for the first team.
Wolverhampton W *(From trainee on 5/3/2004) P/FL 11+17/7 FLC 1+3/1 FAC 0+2*
Kidderminster Hrs *(Loaned on 25/3/2004) FL 3+1*

CLARKE Matthew Paul
Born: Leeds, 18 December 1980
Height: 6'3" **Weight:** 12.7
This giant central defender completed his third season at Darlington last term. He impressed with a series of consistent displays on the left side of the defence and his ability to strike up a good understanding with a variety of partners at the back. He is very strong in the air and exhibits tricky footwork for a big man, overlapping effectively down the left flank to deliver telling crosses.
Halifax T *(From trainee at Wolverhampton W on 5/7/1999) FL 42+27/2 FAC 5+1 Others 2+2*
Darlington *(Free on 9/7/2002) FL 121+5/10 FLC 4 FAC 5 Others 3*

CLARKE Nathan
Born: Halifax, 30 July 1983
Height: 6'2" **Weight:** 11.5
Nathan finally came of age for Huddersfield last term. The talented defender was in the side for most of the season, only the odd injury keeping him out of the starting line-up. He was awarded the captaincy of the team and showed an awareness of the game well beyond his years with his strong tackling and no-nonsense approach. At the end of the season Nathan received the 'Player of the Year' awards from both the supporters and his fellow players.
Huddersfield T *(From trainee on 6/9/2001) FL 100+2/2 FLC 2 FAC 3 Others 5*

CLARKE Peter Michael
Born: Southport, 3 January 1982
Height: 6'0" **Weight:** 12.0
International Honours: E: U21-8; Yth; Sch
Peter joined Blackpool shortly after the start of the season and proved a revelation. The talented central defender went straight into the line-up and immediately added some much-needed steel to the back line. He was in outstanding form throughout the campaign and was the key figure in turning round the club's fortunes. Peter also contributed six valuable goals and swept the board at the club's end-of-season awards' ceremony.
Everton *(From juniors on 19/1/1999) PL 6+3 FLC 0+1 FAC 4*
Blackpool *(Loaned on 8/8/2002) FL 16/3*
Port Vale *(Loaned on 20/2/2003) FL 13/1*
Coventry C *(Loaned on 13/2/2004) FL 5*
Blackpool *(Signed on 18/9/2004) FL 38/5 FAC 4/1 Others 0+1*

CLARKE Ryan Anthony
Born: Sutton Coldfield, 22 January 1984
Height: 5'11" **Weight:** 12.4
Ryan found his way into Boston's first-team squad blocked by more experienced defenders last term, and his only appearance was in the LDV Vans Trophy tie against Cambridge United. Although the Pilgrims went out of the competition Ryan had an excellent game at centre back, making a number of important tackles which earned him the 'Man of the Match' award. He was loaned out to Southern League club King's Lynn in October and shortly after returning he went on a three-month loan to Conference strugglers Leigh RMI, signing for them on a permanent basis in March.
Boston U *(From trainee at Notts Co on 11/7/2003) FL 1+3 Others 3*

CLARKE Ryan James
Born: Bristol, 30 April 1982
Height: 6'1" **Weight:** 12.0
Ryan was unable to dislodge Kevin Miller as first-choice 'keeper for Bristol Rovers last term and he spent two spells out on loan to gain some match action. The first of these came at Southend, when he covered for one match for suspension and injury to the club's regular 'keepers. Ryan also covered for the injured Jon Danby at Kidderminster, where he impressed the fans with some sound performances. In the new year he stepped up to a place in the Pirates' first team following an injury to Miller and did well enough to retain his place for the remainder of the season.
Bristol Rov *(From trainee on 4/7/2001) FL 22+1 Others 3*
Southend U *(Loaned on 14/10/2004) FL 1*
Kidderminster Hrs *(Loaned on 12/11/2004) FL 6 FAC 1*

CLARKE Thomas (Tom)
Born: Halifax, 21 December 1987
Height: 5'11" **Weight:** 12.2
Tom started the season in the Huddersfield youth team, but with a growing reputation in hand he stepped into the first-team limelight like a seasoned professional. He gained a first start away at MK Dons in the right-back berth, and looked both solid and comfortable. Battered and bruised he bounced back after each encounter with greater aplomb. Quick, sharp and a great tackler, he looked even more confident when partnering his elder brother Nathan in the centre of defence. Tom was voted as the club's 'Most Improved Player' at the end of the season.
Huddersfield T *(From trainee on 18/1/2005) FL 12*

CLEMENCE Stephen Neal
Born: Liverpool, 31 March 1978
Height: 5'11" **Weight:** 11.7
Club Honours: FLC '99
International Honours: E: U21-1; Yth; Sch
It was not until the turn of the year that Stephen forced his way back into the Birmingham City midfield, taking advantage of Robbie Savage's sale. He played with great drive and kept things simple, but to good effect. When he was in the Blues' team he tended to help knit them together and they were more stable. His highlight was a colossal performance against Villa at St Andrew's when he almost suffered a serious chest injury after throwing himself into blocking a shot.
Tottenham H *(From trainee on 3/4/1995) PL 68+22/2 FLC 7+1 FAC 7+1/1 Others 2+1*
Birmingham C *(£250,000 + on 10/1/2003) PL 60+12/4 FLC 3 FAC 3+1/1*

CLEMENT Neil
Born: Reading, 3 October 1978
Height: 6'0" **Weight:** 12.3
International Honours: E: Yth; Sch
Neil began the 2004-05 season in midfield for West Bromwich Albion where he performed with aggression and commitment, scoring important goals at Blackburn and home to Aston Villa in the first two games of the campaign. With Paul Robinson established at left back, he eventually switched to the centre of Albion's defence at the expense of Darren Purse. Here he continued to produce some sterling displays alongside Thomas Gaardsoe as the relegation battle at the foot of the Premiership hotted up and also found space to head his third goal in a 2-0 home win over Birmingham City. Blessed with a terrific left foot, he was once again one of Albion's more consistent players.
Chelsea *(From trainee on 8/10/1995) PL 1 FLC 0+2 FAC 0+1*
Reading *(Loaned on 19/11/1998) FL 11/1 Others 1*
Preston NE *(Loaned on 25/3/1999) FL 4*
Brentford *(Loaned on 23/11/1999) FL 7+1*
West Bromwich A *(£100,000 + on 23/3/2000) P/FL 191+13/19 FLC 11+2/3 FAC 11/2 Others 2*

CLICHY Gael
Born: Paris, France, 26 February 1985
Height: 5'9" **Weight:** 10.0
Club Honours: PL '04; CS '04
International Honours: France: U21
This young left back again made progress at Arsenal during the season yet probably not as quickly as he would have liked due to injury. However, he did start seven

Brian Close

Premiership games and made a further eight appearances as a substitute. Gael also featured in every minute of the Gunners' FA Cup campaign until the semi-final stage. Whilst doubts remain over Ashley Cole's future many Arsenal fans believe they have a ready-made replacement in the teenaged Frenchman.
Arsenal *(£250,000 from Cannes, France on 5/8/2003) PL 14+13 FLC 6 FAC 6+3 Others 2+2*

CLINGAN Samuel (Sammy) Gary
Born: Belfast, 13 January 1984
Height: 5'11" **Weight:** 11.6
International Honours: NI: U23-1; U21-5; Yth; Sch
This talented Wolves' youngster featured as an unused substitute last term, but enjoyed a spell of regular first-team action when on loan to Chesterfield. There was more to Sammy's central midfield play than breaking up opponents' moves, as his screaming point-winning goal at Hillsborough in October proved. His influence on the side was huge, and the club came within a whisker of claiming him as their own on transfer-deadline day, only for Wolves to have second thoughts. Sammy represented Northern Ireland at U21 level during the campaign.
Wolverhampton W *(From trainee on 8/7/2001)*
Chesterfield *(Loaned on 8/10/2004) FL 15/2*

CLOSE Brian Aidan
Born: Belfast, 27 January 1982
Height: 5'10" **Weight:** 12.6
International Honours: NI: U23-1; U21-10; Yth
Brian established himself as a regular in the Darlington defence last term. He is extremely quick to cover ground and a strong tackler with positive distribution to the midfield and forwards. Although he possesses a fierce shot he has yet to find the net for the Quakers in more than 50 appearances.
Middlesbrough *(Free from St Oliver Plunkett BC on 11/10/1999) FLC 0+1*
Chesterfield *(Loaned on 7/3/2003) FL 8/1*
Darlington *(Free on 5/3/2004) FL 45+5 FLC FAC 2 Others 1*

CLYDE Mark Graham
Born: Limavady, 27 December 1982
Height: 6'1" **Weight:** 12.0
International Honours: NI: 3; U21-5
Mark featured more regularly in the starting line-up for Wolves last term although he never really managed to make any one position his own. He was mainly employed at right back, but was perhaps more at home in the centre of defence. He managed a good run of matches at the start of the season before injuring an ankle and was back in the team again in the new year before knee problems forced him to undergo an operation. Mark also enjoyed success on the international front, winning his first full caps for Northern Ireland.
Wolverhampton W *(From trainee on 6/8/2001) P/FL 38+6 FLC 2 FAC 4+1*
Kidderminster Hrs *(Loaned on 13/9/2002) FL 4*

COCHRANE Justin Vincent
Born: Hackney, 26 January 1982
Height: 6'0" **Weight:** 11.8
Justin has now completed his second season at Crewe since his move from Hayes. A hard-tackling midfield player, his appearances in the 2004-05 season mainly came in the first half of the campaign, although he remained a regular member of the first-team squad throughout. He is still waiting to score his first goal for the club, a post at Gillingham having denied him last term.
Queens Park Rgrs *(From trainee on 16/7/1999) FL 0+1 (Free to Hayes on 12/8/2002)*
Crewe Alex *(£50,000 on 19/7/2003) FL 58+10 FLC 4+1*

COGAN Barry
Born: Sligo, 4 November 1984
Height: 5'9" **Weight:** 9.0
International Honours: RoI: U21-1
This tricky, pacy winger started the 2004-05 season in good form and was a regular member of the first-team squad at Millwall. However a back injury put him on the sidelines from October and it was not until February that he returned to action for the club's reserves.
Millwall *(From trainee on 28/11/2001) FL 2+8 FAC 0+1 Others 0+2*

COHEN Christopher (Chris) David
Born: Norwich, 5 March 1987
Height: 5'11" **Weight:** 10.11
International Honours: E: Yth
A regular for the reserve team this promising left back played the full 90 minutes for West Ham in their opening home game against Reading. Chris tackles hard and has a good shot when coming forward. He came on as a substitute on ten occasions last term and was also called up for the England U18 squad.
West Ham U *(From trainee on 1/4/2004) FL 2+16 FLC 1+1 FAC 0+1*

COID Daniel (Danny) John
Born: Liverpool, 3 October 1981
Height: 5'11" **Weight:** 11.7
Club Honours: AMC '02, '04
After a few early-season injury problems were resolved, Danny settled in to become a regular in the Blackpool line-up last term. His versatile skills meant that he was employed in several different roles, notably at full back and in midfield. He was in good form in the second half of the campaign as the Seasiders turned their fortunes around.
Blackpool *(From trainee on 24/7/2000) FL 176+25/9 FLC 8+1 FAC 17/1 Others 18+1/3*

COKE Giles Christopher
Born: Westminster, 3 June 1986
Height: 5'11" **Weight:** 11.10
This youngster began the 2004-05 campaign with Ryman Premier club Kingstonian, joining Mansfield Town in March following a short trial period. A tall midfielder with a cultured left foot, Giles made an impressive debut in the thrilling 4-4 draw at Bristol Rovers in March. This form was maintained in subsequent matches, which made it difficult to believe he was a newcomer to senior football and he was quickly signed up on a more permanent basis by the Stags.
Mansfield T *(From Kingstonian on 17/3/2005) FL 7+2*

COLBECK Philip **Joseph (Joe)**
Born: Bradford, 29 November 1986
Height: 5'10" **Weight:** 10.12
This right winger was a surprise addition to the bench for Bradford City's Carling Cup tie with Notts County last term, having previously made just a handful of appearances for the reserves. Joe came on in extra time, but was unable to turn the game around for the Bantams.
Bradford C *(Trainee) FLC 0+1*

COLDICOTT Stacy
Born: Redditch, 29 April 1974
Height: 5'8" **Weight:** 11.8
This tenacious midfielder was one of only a handful of players to remain at Blundell Park after the club's second successive relegation. Although he avoided the injuries that had hampered him in the previous campaign, Stacy had something of a disappointing time during the first half of the season when he mostly featured as a substitute, and it was not until the new year that he was able to command a regular starting place. However, he went on to play a vital role in enabling the Mariners reach the relative respectability of a mid-table position in League Two.

West Bromwich A *(From trainee on 4/3/1992) FL 64+40/3 FLC 6+1 FAC 2+2/1 Others 7+3*
Cardiff C *(Loaned on 30/8/1996) FL 6*
Grimsby T *(£125,000 on 6/8/1998) FL 189+32/4 FLC 12+1/2 FAC 6+1 Others 1*

COLE Andrew (Andy) Alexander

Born: Nottingham, 15 October 1971
Height: 5'11" **Weight:** 11.12
Club Honours: Div 1 '93; PL '96, '97, '99, '00, '01; FAC '96, '99; CS '97; UEFACL '99; FLC '02
International Honours: E: 15; B-1; U21-8; Yth, Sch
Andy returned to Craven Cottage after a 13-year absence and made an immediate impact with two goals in the opening home game against Bolton. He continued to score regularly throughout the season and ended as Fulham's top scorer with 13 goals in all competitions. Currently the second highest-ever scorer in the Premiership he is a predator in the box and linked well with Brian McBride, although he was also asked to play alone up front on a number of occasions.
Arsenal *(From trainee on 18/10/1989) FL 0+1 Others 0+1*
Fulham *(Loaned on 5/9/1991) FL 13/3 Others 2/1*
Bristol C *(£500,000 on 12/3/1992) FL 41/20 FLC 3/4 FAC 1 Others 4/1*
Newcastle U *(£1,750,000 on 12/3/1993) P/FL 69+1/55 FLC 7/8 FAC 4/1 Others 3/4*
Manchester U *(£6,000,000 on 12/1/1995) PL 161+34/94 FLC 2 FAC 19+2/9 Others 49+8/19*
Blackburn Rov *(£7,500,000 on 29/12/2001) PL 74+9/27 FLC 8/7 FAC 5/3 Others 2+2*
Fulham *(Free on 21/7/2004) PL 29+2/12 FLC 3/1 FAC 5*

COLE Ashley

Born: Stepney, 20 December 1980
Height: 5'8" **Weight:** 10.8
Club Honours: FAC '02, '03, '05; PL '02, '04; CS '02; '04
International Honours: E: 41; U21-4; Yth
Ashley Cole enjoyed another fine campaign for club and country. He netted the winner away to Manchester City in September and scored his only other goal of the season in a 3-1 win at Villa Park. He also found the net in the FA Cup penalty shoot-outs against Sheffield United in the fifth round and in the final against Manchester United as the club clinched the trophy in dramatic style. However, a well-publicised incident, later the subject of an FA investigation, has since put his career at Highbury in some doubt. Ashley was again named in the PFA Premiership team of the season.
Arsenal *(From trainee on 23/11/1998) PL 142+3/8 FLC 2+1 FAC 19+1 Others 42+3/1*
Crystal Palace *(Loaned on 25/2/2000) FL 14/1*

COLE Carlton Michael

Born: Croydon, 12 November 1983
Height: 6'3" **Weight:** 13.4
International Honours: E: U21-12; Yth
This powerful young striker joined Aston Villa in a season-long loan from Chelsea and made a dream start against Southampton when he got on the score sheet. Although occasionally included on the bench, he was involved in most games during the campaign and produced a series of hard-working displays.
Chelsea *(From trainee on 23/10/2000) PL 4+12/4 FLC 1/2 FAC 0+2/1*
Wolverhampton W *(Loaned on 28/11/2002) FL 5+2/1*
Charlton Ath *(Loaned on 20/8/2003) PL 8+13/4 FAC 1/1*
Aston Villa *(Loaned on 12/7/2004) PL 18+9/3 FLC 1+1 FAC 1*

COLE Joseph (Joe) John

Born: Islington, 8 November 1981
Height: 5'9" **Weight:** 11.0
Club Honours: FAYC '99; FLC '05; PL '05
International Honours: E: 23; U21-8; Yth; Sch
One of England's finest midfield talents, Joe had a roller coaster 2004-05 season but enjoyed a positive ending with his first senior domestic silverware. The opening half of the campaign seemed to be a repeat of his previous season when he was making sporadic cameo appearances from the bench as new boss Mourinho preferred less individualistic midfielders. Even so, Joe came on to score four crucial goals. Following Arjen Robben's broken ankle in February, Joe was given the responsibility of taking over the Dutchman's role by Mourinho and he repaid his boss's faith in full, particularly in one three-match spell. He was outstanding in the Carling Cup final against Liverpool; won 'Man of the Match' plaudits and scored a brilliant opener in the crucial Premiership match at Carrow Road; and ran the Barcelona defence ragged in the epic 5-4 aggregate victory in the Champions' League last-16 tie. These performances clinched the 'Barclays Player of the Month' award for March. Never a man to pull his punches, Jose Mourinho has waxed lyrical over Joe's sublime ball skills but demands more discipline and awareness when his team are not in possession. The signs are that Joe is responding to these 'suggestions' and is capable of lifting his game to another level and becoming a complete midfield player. England also benefited from Joe's improved form when he was chosen for the problematic wide-left midfield berth and he produced two superb performances in the World Cup qualifiers over the Easter period.
West Ham U *(From trainee on 11/12/1998) PL 108+18/10 FLC 7+1/1 FAC 10+1/2 Others 2+3*
Chelsea *(£6,600,000 on 6/8/2003) PL 37+26/9 FLC 6+3/2 FAC 5+1 Others 11+7*

COLEMAN Dean Samuel

Born: Dudley, 18 September 1985
Height: 6'1" **Weight:** 14.3
This 19-year old goalkeeper made a sensational first-team debut for Walsall at Blackpool last March when he took over after Joe Murphy was sent off and saved a penalty with his first touch. Later in the game he saved another penalty although this time the opposition scored from the rebound. A week later he again acquitted himself well in the home defeat by Bournemouth, impressing with his safe handling and calmness under pressure. Dean was voted as the Saddlers' 'Young Player of the Season'.
Walsall *(From juniors on 7/8/2003) FL 1+1*

COLES Daniel (Danny) Richard

Born: Bristol, 31 October 1981
Height: 6'1" **Weight:** 11.5
Club Honours: AMC '03
Danny had something of a disappointing season at Bristol City last term, despite being a regular in the line-up throughout the campaign. However, the promising central defender knuckled down to some hard work and by the end of the season his form was back to somewhere near his best.
Bristol C *(From trainee on 7/6/2000) FL 141+7/5 FLC 4/1 FAC 8+1 Others 19/1*

COLGAN Nicholas (Nicky) Vincent

Born: Drogheda, 19 September 1973
Height: 6'1" **Weight:** 13.6
International Honours: RoI: 8; B-1; U21-9; Yth; Sch
Nicky started the 2004-05 campaign as first-choice 'keeper for Barnsley. He showed he was a good shop-stopper, but found himself out of the team when manager Paul Hart brought in Ross Turnbull. Nicky moved on loan to Dundee United during the January transfer window, however, after just two appearances an injury curtailed his season. Amazingly while at Oakwell he faced three penalties, saved them all, only for all three to be retaken successfully.

oe Cole

Chelsea *(From trainee on 1/10/1992) PL 1*
Brentford *(Loaned on 16/10/1997) FL 5*
Reading *(Loaned on 27/2/1998) FL 5*
Bournemouth *(Free on 9/7/1998)*
Hibernian *(Free on 29/7/1999) SL 121 SLC 8 SC 16 Others 2*
Stockport Co *(Loaned on 8/8/2003) FL 14+1 FLC 2*
Barnsley *(Free on 20/7/2004) FL 12+1 FLC 2 Others 1*
Dundee U *(Loaned on 28/1/2005) SL 1 SLC 1*

COLLINS Daniel (Danny) Lewis
Born: Buckley, 6 August 1980
Height: 6'2" **Weight:** 12.1
Club Honours: NC '04; Ch '05
International Honours: W: 1; E: SP-2
The talented left-sided defender had been one of Chester's star performers in the Conference and had no problems making the step up to League Two. Comfortable on the ball and strong in the tackle it was no surprise when he was transferred to Sunderland in October. Although he acted primarily as cover in the Black Cats' squad, he impressed the supporters with some composed displays when called upon. Indeed, in January he enjoyed a short spell in the first team alongside namesake Neill. Danny also collected his first full international cap for Wales in February against Hungary.
Chester C *(Signed from Buckley T on 27/12/2001) FL 12/1 FLC 1*
Sunderland *(£140,000 on 13/10/2004) FL 6+8 FAC 1*

COLLINS James Michael
Born: Newport, 23 August 1983
Height: 6'2" **Weight:** 13.0
International Honours: W: 6; U21-8; Yth
The emergence of James as a centre back to partner Danny Gabbidon was one of the prime reasons Cardiff avoided relegation in the 2004-05 season. Comfortable on the ball, commanding in the air and with an ability to hit long passes he has caught the eye of many clubs. James was also prominent at international level, captaining Wales U21s against Germany in February then partnering his colleague Gabbidon against Austria later in the campaign.
Cardiff C *(From trainee on 5/4/2001) FL 49+17/3 FLC 5 FAC 4+5/3 Others 4+2*

COLLINS Michael Anthony
Born: Halifax, 30 April 1986
Height: 6'0" **Weight:** 10.12
International Honours: RoI: Yth
This Huddersfield Town youngster made his senior debut in the 2-1 win over Blackpool last February and went on to feature in a number of games towards the end of the campaign. The promising midfielder showed himself to be a good passer of the ball and displayed maturity with some good runs and accurate crossing. Michael grafts hard and will be looking to establish himself in the side in 2005-06.
Huddersfield T *(From trainee on 11/5/2005) FL 7+1*

COLLINS Neill William
Born: Irvine, 2 September 1983
Height: 6'3" **Weight:** 13.0
Club Honours: Ch '05
International Honours: S: U21-2
Neill was signed to provide cover for the central defensive pairing of Gary Breen and Steve Caldwell at Sunderland last term. When called upon he performed admirably showing himself to be excellent in the air, a good tackler, and with sound positional sense. Neill collected a Championship winners medal following the Wearsiders' promotion back to the Premiership.
Queen's Park *(From juniors on 20/3/2001) SL 30+2 SLC 1 SC 2*
Dumbarton *(Free on 22/7/2002) SL 62+1/4 SLC 3 SC 2 Others 4*
Sunderland *(£25,000 on 13/8/2004) FL 8+3 FLC 1 FAC 2*

COLLINS Patrick Paul
Born: Oman, 4 February 1985
Height: 6'2" **Weight:** 12.7
International Honours: E: Yth
This versatile defender impressed for Sheffield Wednesday last term when he featured both at centre half and at right back. Tall and commanding with a fair bit of pace, Patrick is a really outstanding prospect. He was a regular in the line-up until December when he picked up a leg injury, which kept him out for several weeks. When he recovered fitness, he found it hard to regain his place, but he eventually got back in during March and carried on his good work for the team.
Sunderland *(From trainee on 8/3/2002)*
Sheffield Wed *(Free on 9/7/2004) FL 25+3/1 FLC 2 FAC 1 Others 1+1*

COLLINS Samuel (Sam) Jason
Born: Pontefract, 5 June 1977
Height: 6'3" **Weight:** 14.0
A regular in the centre of defence for Port Vale last term, Sam was again the cornerstone of the back line before he suffered a knee injury against Torquay in November which led to a spell on the sidelines. Big and uncompromising, Sam scored two goals netting in the home wins over Hull and Doncaster. However, his knee injury flared up again and he missed the last two games of the season to enable him to have an operation.
Huddersfield T *(From trainee on 6/7/1994) FL 34+3 FLC 6+1 FAC 3*
Bury *(£75,000 on 2/7/1999) FL 78+4/2 FLC 5 FAC 0+2 Others 1*
Port Vale *(Free on 15/7/2002) FL 120/11 FLC 3 FAC 5 Others 5*

COLLIS Stephen (Steve) Philip
Born: Harrow, 18 March 1981
Height: 6'2" **Weight:** 13.0
This young 'keeper was restricted to the occasional appearance deputising for Chris Weale in the first half of the season at Yeovil last term. However, he came into the side for the last half-dozen games and acquitted himself well.
Barnet *(From juniors on 27/8/1999)*
Nottingham F *(Free on 11/7/2000)*
Yeovil T *(Free on 6/8/2001) FL 20 Others 2*

COMINELLI Lucas
Born: Buenos Aires, Argentina, 25 December 1976
Height: 6'1" **Weight:** 12.6
This hard-tackling midfielder joined Oxford following a change in management at the club, but took a while to settle into League Two football. However, he proved to be a skilful player who is comfortable on the ball. Lucas scored once, netting with a long-range effort following a clever free kick in the home defeat by Grimsby Town.
Oxford U *(Free from Pahang FA, Malaysia, ex Argentinos Juniors, Grenada (Spain), Newcastle U (loan), Platense, Los Andes, Sarmiento, on 20/1/2005) FL 11+5/1*

COMMONS Kristian (Kris) Arran
Born: Mansfield, 30 August 1983
Height: 5'6" **Weight:** 9.8
Kris joined Nottingham Forest in the summer of 2004 but his debut was delayed by a hamstring problem. However, he was back in action by the end of August and featured regularly in the match squad, though often on the bench. He scored seven goals during the campaign including a great 30-yarder in the FA Cup tie against Queen's Park Rangers and an impressive strike in the home game with Preston. Kris is a left-sided defender or midfielder with terrific pace and a bullet-like shot.
Stoke C *(From trainee on 25/1/2001) FL 20+21/5 FLC 1+2 FAC 0+1 Others 1*
Nottingham F *(Free on 2/7/2004) FL 19+11/6 FLC 2+1 FAC 3/1*

COMYN-PLATT Charlie
Born: Manchester, 2 October 1985
Height: 6'2" **Weight:** 12.0
This young Bolton defender failed to make a breakthrough to the senior squad at the Reebok last term but experienced first-team football during a loan spell with Wycombe during the autumn. A versatile player who featured both as a centre half and at left back, he impressed with his composure and passing skills. Charlie was released by Bolton in the summer.
Bolton W *(From trainee on 17/9/2004) FLC 0+1 FAC 2*
Wycombe W *(Loaned on 18/9/2004) FL 3+1 Others 1*

CONLON Barry John
Born: Drogheda, 1 October 1978
Height: 6'3" **Weight:** 13.7
International Honours: RoI: U21-7
Barry soon became a favourite with the Barnsley fans last term. When the team struggled in the opening period he never shirked the challenge and his link up play was of an excellent standard. He had netted seven times before a troublesome groin caused him to miss a number of games. During his absence manager Paul Hart changed the formation and on his return to fitness he had to settle for a place on the bench. Before long the groin problem reappeared and put an early end to his season.
Manchester C *(From trainee at Queens Park R on 14/8/1997) FL 1+6 FLC 0+1*
Plymouth Arg *(Loaned on 26/2/1998) FL 13/2*
Southend U *(£95,000 on 4/9/1998) FL 28+6/7 FAC 1 Others 1*
York C *(£100,000 on 20/7/1999) FL 33+15/11 FLC 2+2 FAC 1 Others 0+1*
Colchester U *(Loaned on 9/11/2000) FL 23+3/8 FAC 1 Others 1*
Darlington *(£60,000 on 6/7/2001) FL 114+1/39 FLC 4 FAC 4/3 Others 2*
Barnsley *(Free on 5/7/2004) FL 17+7/6 FLC 2/1 FAC 1 Others 1*

CONNELL Alan John
Born: Enfield, 15 February 1983
Height: 5'11" **Weight:** 10.8
Last term proved to be a frustrating season for this young Bournemouth striker. He started ten games and came on as a substitute over 30 times. A regular in the reserve side, he netted in six consecutive matches in the Combination. Alan scored four goals for the first team, showing his talent with a marvellous effort against Bradford.
Bournemouth *(From Ipswich T juniors on 9/7/2002) FL 18+36/8 FLC 1+3/1 FAC 3+2/2 Others 0+1*

CONNELLY Sean Patrick
Born: Sheffield, 26 June 1970
Height: 5'10" **Weight:** 11.10
This ever-reliable right back made a big impression at Rushden last term and picked up three end-of-season awards after producing a series of consistent performances throughout what was a troubled campaign. He achieved the landmark of 500 career appearances in the Good Friday game against Lincoln City. Although he was released by the club in the summer, his chartered physiotherapy qualification secures a long-term future once his playing days are over.
Stockport Co *(Free from Hallam on 12/8/1991) FL 292+10/6 FLC 29/1 FAC 15+2 Others 15+1*
Wolverhampton W *(Free on 21/3/2001) FL 11+3 FLC 1*
Tranmere Rov *(Free on 11/10/2002) FL 66+4 FLC 2 FAC 6 Others 4*
Rushden & Diamonds *(Free on 12/7/2004) FL 40+2 FLC 1 FAC 2 Others 1*

CONNOLLY Adam James
Born: Manchester, 10 April 1986
Height: 5'9" **Weight:** 12.4
This emerging young midfield player made his first-team debut for Cheltenham in the game at Boston last April and went on to make the starting line-up at Bury. Adam is a strong, hard-working central midfielder who can pass, tackle and support the attack. His breakthrough into the senior squad was rewarded with the offer of a full-time contract at the end of the season.
Cheltenham T *(Trainee) FL 1+3*

CONNOLLY David James
Born: Willesden, 6 June 1977
Height: 5'8" **Weight:** 11.4
International Honours: RoI: 40; U21
This hard-running striker joined Leicester in the summer of 2004. His hard work and unselfish effort up front made him popular with the fans, but David will be disappointed in his overall strike rate for the season. He still managed to contribute a few crucial goals along the way including a last-gasp effort to deny local rivals Nottingham Forest at the City Ground, but his confidence was certainly tested by the number of near misses that mounted up. Even so, a late scoring burst sealed his place at the head of the Foxes' charts, with his goal at home to Derby being the strike that confirmed City's Championship status for another season.
Watford *(From trainee on 15/11/1994) FL 19+7/10 FLC 1 FAC 3+3/4 Others 1/1 (Free to Feyenoord, Holland during 1997 close season)*
Wolverhampton W *(Loaned on 21/8/1998) FL 18+14/6 FLC 2 FAC 0+1*
Wimbledon *(Free from Feyenoord, Holland on 27/7/2001) FL 63/42 FLC 1 FAC 4*
West Ham U *(£285,000 on 8/8/2003) FL 37+2/10 FLC 2/2 FAC 4/2 Others 3*
Leicester C *(£500,000 on 22/7/2004) FL 43+1/13 FAC 3+2*

CONNOLLY Paul
Born: Liverpool, 29 September 1983
Height: 6'0" **Weight:** 11.9
Club Honours: Div 2' 04
Paul initially had to bide his time whilst David Worrell started as Plymouth Argyle's right back at the beginning of the 2004-05 season. His first appearance was not until September and thereafter he was in and out of the first team. A tough-tackling right back who is strong in the air, he has good pace and enjoys overlapping down the flank to deliver crosses into the box. Paul will be looking to cement his place in the Argyle first team during the 2005-06 campaign.
Plymouth Arg *(From trainee on 23/7/2002) FL 49+2 FAC 1 Others 1*

CONNOR Paul
Born: Bishop Auckland, 12 January 1979
Height: 6'1" **Weight:** 11.5
Club Honours: AMC '00
A hard-working striker, Paul took some time before scoring his first goal of the season for Swansea last term. He then suffered a dead leg and this kept him out of action for a few games. However, he later signed an extension to his contract and by the end of the campaign had scored a total of 13 League and Cup for the Swans and forged a good understanding with Lee Trundle up front.
Middlesbrough *(From trainee on 4/7/1996)*
Hartlepool U *(Loaned on 6/2/1998) FL 4+1*
Stoke C *(Free on 25/3/1999) FL 18+18/7 FLC 3+3/3 FAC 0+1 Others 2+3*
Cambridge U *(Loaned on 9/11/2000) FL 12+1/5 FAC 1*
Rochdale *(£100,000 on 9/3/2001) FL 76+18/28 FLC 3 FAC 8+1/3 Others 0+2*
Swansea C *(£35,000 on 12/3/2004) FL 46+6/15 FAC 5/3 Others 1*

CONSTANTINE Leon
Born: Hackney, 24 February 1978
Height: 6'2" **Weight:** 11.10
Posh snapped up Leon during the summer of 2004, but even though the team was struggling to score goals he was given few chances to shine during his stay at London Road. In October he was sent out on loan to Torquay and scored on his debut at Swindon. He

returned briefly to Posh but soon afterwards made a permanent move to Plainmoor. However, after a memorable Boxing Day hat-trick at Brentford, goals and confidence dried up. As Torquay adapted to 4-5-1, he was forced to abandon his favoured role as a central striker to play wider and deeper.
Millwall *(Signed from Edgware T on 31/8/2000) FL 0+1 Others 1*
Leyton Orient *(Loaned on 27/8/2001) FL 9+1/3 Others 0+1*
Partick T *(Loaned on 11/1/2002) SL 2 SC 1*
Brentford *(Free on 8/8/2002) FL 2+15 FLC 1+1*
Southend U *(Free on 21/8/2003) FL 40+3/21 FAC 2+1 Others 6+1/4*
Peterborough U *(Free on 2/7/2004) FL 5+6/1 Others 1*
Torquay U *(Loaned on 29/10/2004) FL 4/3 FAC 1*
Torquay U *(£75,000 on 10/12/2004) FL 20+3/6*

CONTRA Cosmin Marius
Born: Timisoara, Romania, 15 December 1975
Height: 5'11" **Weight:** 11.9
International Honours: Romania: 46
A strong, determined right-wing-back or midfielder, Cosmin never got much of a chance at the Hawthorns last term. He was substituted on his debut in the Carling Cup tie at Colchester and then made a decent first start in the Premiership in the 2-1 home defeat by Middlesbrough (manager Bryan Robson's first game in charge). A groin injury affected his game for a while but after that he was generally overlooked. He did not get another chance in the first team and in the January transfer window he returned to Atletico Madrid.
West Bromwich A *(Loaned from Atletico Madrid, Spain, ex Dinamo Bucharest, on 31/8/2004) PL 5 FLC 1*

CONVERY Mark Peter
Born: Newcastle, 29 May 1981
Height: 5'6" **Weight:** 10.5
Mark ended his fourth full season with the Quakers operating mainly as a substitute, his injection of pace down the right flank and effective crosses often bringing success late in the game. His most consistent spell of first-team action came in February and March, but at the end of the season his club total of substitute appearances had again overtaken his starts. He failed to add to his tally of goals for the club and was released at the end of the season.
Sunderland *(From trainee on 24/3/1999)*
Darlington *(Free on 30/1/2001) FL 38+38/3 FLC 1+1 FAC 0+3 Others 1+3*

CONVEY Robert (Bobby)
Born: Phliladelphia, USA, 27 May 1983
Height: 5'9" **Weight:** 11.4
International Honours: USA: 31
The signing of Bobby Convey from DC United represented a major investment for Reading, but the young winger failed to live up to expectations, and clearly needs more time to adjust to the physical demands of the English game. His best displays came in the FA Cup ties against Swansea, and he filled in as an emergency left back on occasions, but remained on the periphery of the team for most of the campaign.
Reading *(£850,000 from DC United, USA, on 4/8/2004) FL 4+14 FLC 1+1 FAC 2*

COOK Lee
Born: Hammersmith, 3 August 1982
Height: 5'9" **Weight:** 11.7
This wide-left midfield player joined Queen's Park Rangers at the start of the season from Watford and became a fixture in the side. A quick player with good ball control he soon became popular with fans (probably due to his being a QPR supporter in his school days). Lee only scored two goals during the campaign, but his surging runs down the left flanks caused defenders problems and often led to goal-scoring chances for his colleagues. Lee was voted as the club's 'Young Player of the Year'.
Watford *(Signed from Aylesbury U on 19/11/1999) FL 31+28/7 FLC 0+2 FAC 2+1*
York C *(Loaned on 2/10/2002) FL 7/1 Others 1/1*
Queens Park Rgrs *(Loaned on 20/12/2002) FL 13/1*
Queens Park Rgrs *(Free on 3/7/2004) FL 38+4/2 FLC 1+1 FAC 1*

COOKE Andrew (Andy) Roy
Born: Shrewsbury, 20 January 1974
Height: 6'0" **Weight:** 12.8
This hard-working striker joined Bradford City during the January transfer window after a spell in South Korea. He forged a good partnership with Dean Windass and despite scoring only four goals himself set up numerous chances for his attacking partner. Andy is a very strong target man who can hold off defenders and also has the knack of finding the right pass for colleagues running into the penalty area.
Burnley *(Signed from Newtown on 1/5/1995) FL 134+37/52 FLC 8+2/6 FAC 7+3/2 Others 9+2/2*
Stoke C *(£350,000 on 1/12/2000) FL 71+17/21 FLC 1+1 FAC 2+2/1 Others 4+4/1 (Free to Busan Icons on 22/7/2003)*
Bradford C *(Free on 7/1/2005) FL 20/4*

COOKE Stephen Lee
Born: Walsall, 15 February 1983
Height: 5'8" **Weight:** 9.8
International Honours: E: Yth
This promising central-midfield playmaker spent much of last season in the Aston Villa reserve team. At the turn of the year he enjoyed a successful loan spell with League Two outfit Wycombe Wanderers before he was sidelined by an ankle injury. A player who possesses great skill and vision, Stephen was out of contract in the summer and looked to be on his way out of Villa Park at the time of writing.
Aston Villa *(From trainee on 22/2/2000) PL 0+3 Others 0+1*
Bournemouth *(Loaned on 8/3/2002) FL 6+1*
Bournemouth *(Loaned on 6/1/2004) FL 3*
Wycombe W *(Loaned on 10/12/2004) FL 4+2*

COOKSEY Ernest (Ernie) George
Born: Bishops Stortford, 11 June 1980
Height: 5'9" **Weight:** 11.4
Although a cult figure with supporters, this tenacious midfielder was allowed to leave Boundary Park just weeks into the 2004-05 season. After failing to make a first-team appearance since the opening day, he moved on to join neighbours Rochdale in September. Initially playing as part of a five-man midfield, he subsequently took the left-hand midfield role when Dale had more success with a 4-3-3 formation. He scored his first goal in the 3-0 victory over Macclesfield and cracked in Rochdale's 'Goal of the Season' against Boston.
Oldham Ath *(Signed from Crawley T, ex Colchester U trainee, Heybridge Swifts, Bishops Stortford, Bromley, Chesham U, on 8/8/2003) FL 23+14/4 FAC 2/2 Others 1+1*
Rochdale *(Free on 17/9/2004) FL 27+7/5 FAC 3 Others 2*

COOPER Colin Terence
Born: Sedgefield, 28 February 1967
Height: 5'10" **Weight:** 11.9
Club Honours: Div 1 '98; FLC '04
International Honours: E: 2; U21-8
Colin, still soldiering on in the Premiership at the age of 38, achieved some personal milestones during the season and played his 400th career game for Boro' against Arsenal at Highbury in the amazing 5-3 defeat. Admittedly, Colin probably played more games last term than the Riverside management had originally envisaged because of the injury crisis at the club, but he responded magnificently every time his services were called upon. He also holds the distinction of being both the youngest and the oldest captain in the club's history.

***Middlesbrough** (From juniors on 17/7/1984) FL 183+5/6 FLC 18 FAC 13 Others 19+1/3*
***Millwall** (£300,000 on 25/7/1991) FL 77/6 FLC 6 FAC 2 Others 2*
***Nottingham F** (£1,700,000 on 21/6/1993) P/FL 179+1/20 FLC 14/2 FAC 12/1 Others 7*
***Middlesbrough** (£2,500,000 on 22/8/1998) PL 139+18/5 FLC 14+1 FAC 5+1 Others 3*
***Sunderland** (Loaned on 12/3/2004) FL 0+3*

COOPER Kenny

Born: Baltimore, USA, 21 October 1984
Height: 6'3" **Weight:** 14.1
This promising striker arrived on loan at Oldham with an impressive goal-scoring record for Manchester United's reserve and youth sides. Earlier in the season he had a stint on loan at top-flight Portuguese club Academia before agreeing the switch to Boundary Park. Quick-footed and a composed finisher, Kenny netted against Swindon Town in only his second start. His loan spell was then extended for a second month and he returned to Old Trafford having netted three times in nine appearances, including a double against Port Vale.
***Manchester U** (Signed from Dallas Mustangs, USA on 2/1/2004)*
***Oldham Ath** (Loaned on 28/1/2005) FL 5+2/3 FAC 0+1 Others 1*

COOPER Kevin Lee

Born: Derby, 8 February 1975
Height: 5'7" **Weight:** 10.7
Kevin struggled to win a place in the Wolves line-up at the beginning of the 2004-05 campaign when he mostly featured on the bench. He eventually got a run of games towards the end of the year, scoring both goals in the 2-0 win over Derby, but after Boxing Day he made the starting line-up only once more. However, he ended the season on a high after coming on to score against Sheffield United in the final game of the season.
***Derby Co** (From trainee on 2/7/1993) P/FL 0+2 FLC 0+2 Others 0+1*
***Stockport Co** (£150,000 on 24/3/1997) FL 146+22/21 FLC 7+5/2 FAC 6 Others 1*
***Wimbledon** (£800,000 + on 15/3/2001) FL 50+1/13 FLC 1 FAC 2*
***Wolverhampton W** (£1,000,000 on 26/3/2002) P/FL 32+30/9 FLC 1 FAC 0+1 Others 2+1/1*
***Sunderland** (Loaned on 6/1/2004) FL 0+1*
***Norwich C** (Loaned on 19/3/2004) FL 6+4*

COOPER Shaun David

Born: Isle of Wight, 5 October 1983
Height: 5'10" **Weight:** 10.10
Shaun failed to make a breakthrough to the first team at Portsmouth last term, although he was a regular in the club's reserve team. He featured regularly at right back during a loan spell with League Two outfit Kidderminster Harriers, the highlight of his time at Aggborough coming when he set up the winning goal in the thrilling 3-2 victory over Scunthorpe in October. Shaun was released by Pompey in the summer.
***Portsmouth** (From trainee on 7/4/2001) FL 3+4*
***Leyton Orient** (Loaned on 17/10/2003) FL 9*
***Kidderminster Hrs** (Loaned on 24/9/2004) FL 10 FAC 1 Others 1*

COPPINGER James (Jamie)

Born: Middlesbrough, 10 January 1981
Height: 5'7" **Weight:** 10.6
International Honours: E: Yth
Signed in the summer of 2004 from Conference club Exeter City, Jamie's consummate skills on the right flank were much appreciated by the Doncaster fans last season. He was dogged with injury throughout the season, reflecting the attention he received from opposing defenders, but the only real disappointment was that he failed to register a goal.
***Newcastle U** (£250,000+ from trainee at Darlington on 27/3/1998) PL 0+1*
***Hartlepool U** (Loaned on 10/3/2000) FL 6+4/3 Others 1*
***Hartlepool U** (Loaned on 25/1/2002) FL 14/2*
***Exeter C** (Free on 2/8/2002) FL 35+8/5 FLC 1 FAC 3 Others 2*
***Doncaster Rov** (£30,000 on 7/7/2004) FL 27+4 FLC 1+2 FAC 1+1 Others 2*

CORBETT James (Jim) John

Born: Hackney, 6 July 1980
Height: 5'10" **Weight:** 12.0
Jim suffered the frustration of another injury-ravaged season for Southend last term when he made the starting line-up on just one occasion. Equally at home in midfield or up front, he has excellent ball control and a good turn of pace. Jim was released by the Roots Hall club at the end of the campaign.
***Gillingham** (From trainee on 13/1/1998) FL 8+8/2 FLC 0+1 Others 0+1*
***Blackburn Rov** (£525,000 + on 22/5/1998)*
***Darlington** (Loaned on 28/2/2003) FL 9+1/2*
***Southend U** (Free on 15/7/2003) FL 14+9/2 FLC 1 FAC 3+1/1 Others 1+2/1*

CORBO Mateo Andres

Born: Montevideo, Uruguay, 21 April 1976
Height: 5'11" **Weight:** 12.7
This tough-tackling defender added some much needed bite to the Oxford back line at a time when goals seemed to be leaking from several areas. Mateo was more or less a regular in the United side but seemed to attract the attention of the officials more than was warranted and accumulated a number of yellow cards. He was not retained by the club at the end of the season.
***Barnsley** (£250,000 from Real Oviedo, Spain, ex River Plate, on 29/8/2000) FL 10+8 FLC 2/1 FAC 0+1 (Freed in February 2002)*
***Oxford U** (Free from Olimpia Asuncion on 13/1/2005) FL 13*

CORDEN Simon Wayne

Born: Leek, 1 November 1975
Height: 5'9" **Weight:** 11.3
Wayne began the 2004-05 season in his usual position wide on the left for Mansfield but was dropped after a couple of appearances. However, he was soon back in the side and scored his first two goals of the campaign in the impressive home win over Northampton. He lost his place once more in October and after falling out of favour he moved on to League Two rivals Scunthorpe in the new year. Although struggling for match fitness, he made eight appearances in the run-in, helping his new club to promotion. An out-and-out left winger, who likes to attack players and is an excellent crosser of the ball, Wayne is expected to have a big part to play in the 2005-06 season.
***Port Vale** (From trainee on 20/9/1994) FL 30+36/1 FLC 4 FAC 2+1/1*
***Mansfield T** (Free on 3/7/2000) FL 173+19/35 FLC 8/2 FAC 9+1/1 Others 8*
***Scunthorpe U** (Free on 18/2/2005) FL 3+5*

CORT Carl Edward Richard

Born: Southwark, 1 November 1977
Height: 6'4" **Weight:** 12.7
International Honours: E: U21-12
Carl missed the opening stages of the 2004-05 season for Wolves with a hamstring injury, but was back in action by the middle of September and netted a fine double in the 2-1 win over Queen's Park Rangers. The rangy striker often found himself playing out wide, but carried on scoring throughout, finishing with a tally of 16 in all competitions. He missed several games towards the end of the campaign as a result of a thigh strain.
***Wimbledon** (From trainee on 7/6/1996) PL 54+19/16 FLC 8+2/7 FAC 6+4/2*
***Lincoln C** (Loaned on 3/2/1997) FL 5+1/1*
***Newcastle U** (£7,000,000 on 6/7/2000) PL 19+3/7 FLC 3/1 FAC 2 Others 0+1*
***Wolverhampton W** (£2,000,000 on 28/1/2004) P/FL 47+6/20 FLC 1 FAC 2/1*

CORT Leon Terence Anthony
Born: Bermondsey, 11 September 1979
Height: 6'2" **Weight:** 13.4
Leon struggled to find his best form in his early weeks at Hull but any doubts were soon forgotten as he established a formidable central-defensive partnership with Damien Delaney. It became the cornerstone of City's first-ever back-to-back promotion with Leon dominant in the air and making countless vital blocks and clinical tackles. The quality of his defending is demonstrated by the fact that despite playing in 48 games he did not pick up a single yellow card. He also honed his skills as a goal-scorer, netting four times in the final 13 games. Leon was voted runner-up in the club's 'Player of the Year' awards and had the honour of being named 'Players' Player of the Year'.
Millwall *(Free from Dulwich Hamlet on 23/1/1998)*
Southend U *(Free on 11/7/2001) FL 135+2/11 FLC 3 FAC 13/1 Others 8*
Hull C *(Free on 7/7/2004) FL 43+1/6 FLC 1 FAC 3*

COTTERILL David Rhys George Best
Born: Cardiff, 4 December 1987
Height: 5'10" **Weight:** 10.11
International Honours: W: U21-2; Yth
This exciting winger broke through from Bristol City's Academy ranks last season, making his debut when coming on as substitute in the 0-0 draw at home to Colchester United in October. A real crowd pleaser he was also capped for Wales at U21 level during the campaign.
Bristol C *(From trainee on 5/1/2005) FL 8+4 Others 0+1*

COUGHLAN Graham
Born: Dublin, 18 November 1974
Height: 6'2" **Weight:** 13.6
Club Honours: S Div 1 '01; Div 3 '02; Div 2 '04
Graham was once again a near ever-present at the heart of Plymouth Argyle's defence last term. A central defender who is extremely strong in the air, Graham possesses great determination and prides himself on his performance, which is all about commitment and hard work. He scored two goals for the Pilgrims during the campaign, netting in the vital wins against Nottingham Forest and Sheffield United.
Blackburn Rov *(£100,000 from Bray W on 14/10/1995)*
Swindon T *(Loaned on 25/3/1997) FL 3*
Livingston *(Free on 29/3/1999) SL 53+3/2 SLC 4 SC 2 Others 5*
Plymouth Arg *(Free on 21/6/2001) FL 177/25 FLC 4 FAC 10 Others 2/1*

Carl Cort

COULSON Mark David
Born: Huntingdon, 11 February 1986
Height: 5'8" **Weight:** 10.3
One of several promising youngsters on the books at Peterborough, Mark made his senior debut as a substitute in the 5-0 defeat at Tranmere in March and then featured regularly in the squad in the closing stages of the campaign. A hard-tackling left-sided defender, he agreed an extension to his contract with Posh during the season.
Peterborough U *(From trainee on 20/3/2003) FL 2+5*

COUNAGO Pablo
Born: Pontevedra, Spain, 9 August 1979
Height: 5'11" **Weight:** 11.12
Pablo had a disappointing season for Ipswich in 2004-05. He was not fully fit at the start of the campaign and when he was ready to play found the attacking positions filled by Darren Bent and Shefki Kuqi. On top of this he did not see eye to eye with the management and found himself training and playing with the reserves for a time. He received two offers of loan spells at other Championship sides but turned them down and eventually got back into the first-team squad for the last few games. However, his contract expired in the summer and at the time of writing it seemed unlikely that he would remain at Portman Road.
Ipswich T *(Free from Celta Vigo, Spain on 19/7/2001) P/FL 51+49/31 FLC 7/2 FAC 4+2 Others 7+2/3*

COUTTS James Ryan
Born: Weymouth, 15 April 1987
Height: 5'8" **Weight:** 9.7
This young Bournemouth midfielder had a busy season last term when he featured for the first team, the reserves and the U18s. A tidy player who puts in a great deal of work, he made his senior debut at Brentford in September and also appeared in the LDV Vans Trophy tie at Shrewsbury. James will be hoping for more first-team action in the 2005-06 season.
Bournemouth *(From Southampton juniors on 12/7/2004) FL 0+1 Others 0+1*

COWAN Gavin Patrick
Born: Hanover, Germany, 24 May 1981
Height: 6'4" **Weight:** 14.4
International Honours: E: SP-2
This tall central defender spent much of last season with Conference outfit Canvey Island before joining Shrewsbury Town in March. An injury to Dave Walton allowed Gavin to make his Football League debut in the 1-1 draw at Cheltenham in early April and he retained his place for the remainder of the campaign. Despite his inexperience he quickly fitted in and looked comfortable throughout.
***Shrewsbury T** (Free from Canvey Island, ex Braintree T, on 22/3/2005) FL 5*

COX Ian Gary
Born: Croydon, 25 March 1971
Height: 6'0" **Weight:** 12.2
International Honours: Trinidad & Tobago: 12
This experienced defender began the 2004-05 season as a regular for Gillingham but lost his place after being sent off against Wolves and it was not until Stan Ternent, his old manager at Burnley, was appointed that he was able to force his way back into the line-up. Ian's performances from January onwards were superb and there is no doubt he would have won the 'Player of the Year' trophy if he had been a regular all season.
***Crystal Palace** (£35,000 from Carshalton on 8/3/1994) P/FL 2+13 FAC 1+2/1*
***Bournemouth** (Free on 28/3/1996) FL 172/16 FLC 14 FAC 10 Others 11/1*
***Burnley** (£500,000 on 4/2/2000) FL 107+8/5 FLC 7 FAC 8+1*
***Gillingham** (Free on 6/8/2003) FL 61+3/2 FLC 4 FAC 2*

COX Neil James
Born: Scunthorpe, 8 October 1971
Height: 6'0" **Weight:** 13.7
Club Honours: FLC '94; Div 1 '95
International Honours: E: U21-6
A veteran of over 450 League appearances, Neil had to draw on all his experience during a difficult season at Vicarage Road last term. He was a constant factor in central defence, where his steadiness and ability to read the game proved invaluable, and continued to lead by example even after he had resigned the captaincy. Neil reserved his best performances for the cup matches against Premiership opposition and was outstanding in defeat at Liverpool and Fulham. Like several of his colleagues, his form dipped towards the end of the season, and he was made available for transfer.
***Scunthorpe U** (From trainee on 20/3/1990) FL 17/1 FAC 4 Others 4+1*
***Aston Villa** (£400,000 on 12/2/1991) P/FL 26+16/3 FLC 5+2 FAC 4+2/1 Others 2*
***Middlesbrough** (£1,000,000 on 19/7/1994) P/FL 103+3/3 FLC 14+1 FAC 5/1 Others 1+1*
***Bolton W** (£1,200,000 on 27/5/1997) P/FL 77+3/7 FLC 9/1 FAC 1+1 Others 3*
***Watford** (£500,000 on 5/11/1999) P/FL 215+4/20 FLC 18/1 FAC 11*

COX Simon Peter
Born: Clapham, 24 March 1984
Height: 5'11" **Weight:** 11.0
International Honours: RoI: Yth
Simon had a disappointing time at Oxford last season when he was second-choice 'keeper to Chris Tardif throughout the campaign. He proved a useful stand-in on the occasions he was called upon, but will be looking to gain more regular first-team action in the 2005-06 campaign.
***Oxford U** (From trainee on 8/7/2003) FL 7+1*

COYNE Christopher (Chris) John
Born: Brisbane, Australia, 20 December 1978
Height: 6'1" **Weight:** 13.10
Club Honours: Div 1 '05
International Honours: Australia: U23
Chris was one of the outstanding players in Luton Town's League One championship winning side last term. A solid rock at the back, he is quick to cover ground and a good reader of the game. He also provided a useful physical presence when moving up to join the attack for set pieces and contributed five goals during the campaign. Chris was one of six Luton players named in the PFA League One team of the season.
***West Ham U** (£150,000 from Perth SC, Australia on 13/1/1996) PL 0+1*
***Brentford** (Loaned on 21/8/1998) FL 7 FLC 1*
***Southend U** (Loaned on 25/3/1999) FL 0+1*
***Dundee** (Free on 31/3/2000) SL 16+4 SLC 0+2 SC 4 Others 2*
***Luton T** (£50,000 on 18/9/2001) FL 150+5/11 FLC 4/1 FAC 10 Others 3*

COYNE Daniel (Danny)
Born: Prestatyn, 27 August 1973
Height: 5'11" **Weight:** 13.0
International Honours: W: 8; B-1; U21-9; Yth; Sch
Welsh international 'keeper Danny joined Burnley from Leicester shortly before the start of the 2004-05 season and was promptly installed as first choice between the posts. It was soon easy to see why, as he hardly made a mistake during the first two months of the Clarets' season, always seeming calm and in command, and spectacular when necessary. However, a bad injury sustained in the match at Queen's Park Rangers in October sidelined him for some three months, and on his return to fitness he found his predecessor Brian Jensen in such consistently fine form that there was no easy way back into the side. He returned in April, as Steve Cotterill rotated the two 'keepers for the final few matches of the season, and looked generally as solid as ever. It will be interesting to see who emerges as first choice in 2005-06.
***Tranmere Rov** (From trainee on 8/5/1992) FL 110+1 FLC 13 FAC 2 Others 2*
***Grimsby T** (Free on 12/7/1999) FL 181 FLC 13 FAC 7*
***Leicester C** (Free on 4/7/2003) PL 1+3 FLC 1*
***Burnley** (£25,000 on 4/8/2004) FL 20 FLC 2*

COZIC Bertrand Edern
Born: Quimper, France, 18 May 1978
Height: 5'10" **Weight:** 12.6
Bertrand settled into the Northampton midfield last season, chasing hard and tackling effectively. However, after a period of suspension he found it hard to get back into the side with the midfield four taking on a settled look. He was released from his contract and signed for Kidderminster early in the new year. Normally a central-midfield player he found himself pushed wide onto the right wing for most of his appearances at Aggborough, but never let the team down. He was one of a number of Harriers' players who were out of contract at the end of the season and whose future had yet to be resolved at the time of writing.
***Cheltenham T** (Free from Team Bath on 8/8/2003) FL 7/1 FLC 0+1 (Free to Hereford U in March 2004)*
***Northampton T** (Free on 3/8/2004) FL 8+6 FLC 1 FAC 1+1 Others 1+1*
***Kidderminster Hrs** (Free on 2/2/2005) FL 13+2*

CRADDOCK Darren
Born: Bishop Auckland, 23 February 1985
Height: 6'0" **Weight:** 12.2
A first-year professional with Hartlepool last season, Darren showed that he is developing into a useful right back. For much of the campaign he took a back seat while more experienced players were used in the position, but in the closing stages he performed well in a short first-team run. Later on he got a brief taste of big-time football in the League One play-off final when he came on as a substitute following Micky Barron's injury.
***Hartlepool U** (From trainee on 6/7/2004) FL 18+2 FLC 1 FAC 0+1 Others 0+4*

CRADDOCK Jody Darryl
Born: Redditch, 25 July 1975
Height: 6'1" **Weight:** 12.4
This tall centre half struggled with the responsibility of being the senior defender in the early games of last season for Wolves. He lost his place for a while, but returned to the line-up and once Glenn Hoddle took over as manager his form improved tremendously. Jody made numerous crucial tackles and blocks, most notably a vital, lunging challenge at Crewe, and was careful in his distribution. He also popped up with a goal at Preston, his only strike of the season.
Cambridge U *(Free from Christchurch on 13/8/1993) FL 142+3/4 FLC 3/1 FAC 6 Others 5*
Sunderland *(£300,000 + on 4/8/1997) P/FL 140+6/2 FLC 8+2 FAC 7+2 Others 3*
Sheffield U *(Loaned on 27/8/1999) FL 10*
Wolverhampton W *(£1,750,000 on 15/8/2003) P/FL 71+3/2 FLC 5/1 FAC 4+1*

CRAIG Tony Andrew
Born: Greenwich, 20 April 1985
Height: 6'0" **Weight:** 10.13
Tony joined Wycombe on loan from Millwall last October and saw plenty of first-team action during a three-month spell with the Chairboys. A competent left back who likes to push forward, he is strong in the challenge and reads the game well. Recalled to the New Den he became established in the left-back berth and acquitted himself well in the period to the end of the season.
Millwall *(From trainee on 13/3/2003) FL 19+2/1 FLC 1*
Wycombe W *(Loaned on 22/10/2004) FL 14 FAC 2 Others 2*

CRAINEY Stephen Daniel
Born: Glasgow, 22 June 1981
Height: 5'9" **Weight:** 9.11
Club Honours: SPD '02
International Honours: S: 6; B-1; U21-7
Stephen became Leeds' first cash signing in two years when Kevin Blackwell snapped him up from Southampton. He initially came on loan in time to make his debut in the 0-0 draw at Wolves, signing permanently a few days later. After settling in at left back he showed an increasing willingness to get forward and shoot. But just as the former Celtic and Scottish international defender was finding his best form he sustained knee ligament damage in October and missed the rest of the season.
Glasgow Celtic *(From juniors on 3/7/1997) SL 18+2/1 SLC 6+1/1 SC 2+3 Others 3+2*
Southampton *(£500,000 + on 31/1/2004) PL 5*
Leeds U *(£200,000 on 6/8/2004) FL 9 FLC 1*

CRAINIE Martin James
Born: Yeovil, 23 September 1986
Height: 6'0" **Weight:** 12.4
International Honours: E: Yth
The skipper of the England U19s, as well as the fulgent Saints' side that reached the FA Youth Cup final in 2004-05, Martin is a calm, intelligent player, at his happiest in the centre of the defence, where he shines at breaking-up attacks and launching counter offensives. In his few first-team appearances he was usually deployed as a wing back, a position in which he looked comfortable, but he has yet to be given an extended run. Martin also had a loan spell at Bournemouth in the autumn, but his appearances were limited due to his involvement in the England youth set up.
Southampton *(From trainee on 29/9/2004) PL 4 FLC 0+1 FAC 1+1*
Bournemouth *(Loaned on 29/10/2004) FL 2+1*

CRAMB Colin
Born: Lanark, 23 June 1974
Height: 6'0" **Weight:** 12.6
Club Honours: B&Q '93
This experienced striker fell out of favour at Shrewsbury after just a handful of early-season appearances and in September he joined Grimsby Town on a non-contract basis. However, despite a moderately successful spell at Blundell Park, Colin opted to move on to join Hamilton Academical early in the new year. He went on to score two goals in nine appearances for the Scottish Division One side.
Hamilton Academical *(From juniors on 1/6/1993) SL 29+19/10 SC 0+1 Others 1+3*
Southampton *(£75,000 on 8/6/1993) PL 0+1*
Falkirk *(Signed on 30/8/1994) SL 6+2/1 SLC 0+1*
Heart of Midlothian *(Signed on 1/3/1995) SL 3+3/1*
Doncaster Rov *(£25,000 on 15/12/1995) FL 60+2/25 FLC 2/1 FAC 1/1 Others 1/1*
Bristol C *(£250,000 on 10/7/1997) FL 38+15/9 FLC 3+1 FAC 1/1 Others 1+1*
Walsall *(Loaned on 27/2/1999) FL 4/4 Others 2*
Crewe Alex *(£200,000 on 6/8/1999) FL 43+7/10 FLC 5+1/1 FAC 2 (Free to Fortuna Sittard, Holland on 16/7/2001)*
Notts Co *(Loaned on 11/9/2000) FL 2+1*
Bury *(Loaned on 16/2/2001) FL 15/5*
Bury *(Free from Fortuna Sittard, Holland, on 24/1/2003) FL 17+1/3 Others 2*
Shrewsbury T *(Free on 27/6/2003) FL 0+2 FLC 0+1*
Grimsby T *(Free on 10/8/2004) FL 7+4/2 FAC 0+1 Others 1/1*

CRANE Anthony (Tony) Steven
Born: Liverpool, 8 September 1982
Height: 6'1" **Weight:** 12.6
International Honours: E: Yth
Tony had the misfortune to suffer a serious cartilage injury during the pre-season period and this kept him out of action for much of the 2004-05 campaign. Recovery was quicker than expected, but apart from a brief outing from the bench in February his full appearances were restricted to the last two games of the season when he proved that he had lost none of his class. When fully fit he is a powerfully built central defender who is both combative and effective.
Sheffield Wed *(From trainee on 15/9/1999) FL 24+25/4 FLC 3+5/1 FAC 1+3*
Grimsby T *(Free on 7/7/2003) FL 39+1/3 FLC 1 FAC 2*

CRAWFORD Stephen (Stevie)
Born: Dunfermline, 9 January 1974
Height: 5'10" **Weight:** 10.7
Club Honours: S Div 1 '93; SLC '94; S Div 1 '99
International Honours: S:25; U21-19
Stevie signed for Plymouth Argyle during the 2004 close season and got off the mark with a goal against Sunderland in August. However, although he scored seven times for the Pilgrims, the experienced striker failed to settle in the West Country and during the January transfer window he returned to Scotland to sign for Dundee United, where he featured in the line-up for the Scottish Cup final defeat by Celtic.
Raith Rov *(Free from Rosyth Rec on 13/8/1992) SL 82+33/22 SLC 4+3/1 SC 6/3 Others 7+2/2*
Millwall *(Signed on 4/7/1996) FL 40+2/11 FLC 1 FAC 2/1 Others 2/3*
Hibernian *(£360,000 on 1/8/1997) SL 64+9/23 SLC 5+1/1 SC 2+1*
Dunfermline Ath *(Signed on 29/10/1999) SL 168+1/63 SLC 10/4 SC 15/6*
Plymouth Arg *(Free on 2/7/2004) FL 19+7/6 FLC 1/1*

CREGG Patrick Anthony
Born: Dublin, 21 February 1986
Height: 5'9" **Weight:** 10.4
International Honours: RoI: U21-1; Yth
This young Arsenal midfield prospect made the step-up to the senior team last term, featuring in the Carling Cup ties against Everton and Manchester United. Patrick will be hoping to continue to make progress at Highbury in 2005-06.
Arsenal *(From trainee on 24/2/2003) FLC 0+2*

CRESSWELL Richard Paul Wesley
Born: Bridlington, 20 September 1977
Height: 6'0" **Weight:** 11.8
International Honours: E: U21-4
After a barren season in 2003-04, Richard rediscovered his goal-scoring touch with a vengeance last term. A hard-working striker, he netted 21 goals all told, including a hat-trick in the 3-2 Carling Cup victory over Leicester at the Walker Stadium. He obviously enjoyed the experience, as he repeated the feat with a first half treble on New Year's Day against Sunderland and saw a powerful header cleared off the line in the play-off final. He had several partners during the campaign, but he worked best with David Nugent.
York C *(From trainee on 15/11/1995) FL 72+23/21 FLC 3+3 FAC 4+2/3 Others 4*
Mansfield T *(Loaned on 27/3/1997) FL 5/1*
Sheffield Wed *(£950,000 + on 25/3/1999) P/FL 7+24/2 FLC 1+1/1 FAC 0+3*
Leicester C *(£750,000 on 5/9/2000) PL 3+5 FLC 1 FAC 0+2/1 Others 0+2*
Preston NE *(£500,000 on 12/3/2001) FL 161+23/49 FLC 8+2/5 FAC 2+1/3 Others 4+2/1*

CROFT Gary
Born: Burton-on-Trent, 17 February 1974
Height: 5'9" **Weight:** 11.8
International Honours: E: U21-4
Gary's 2004-05 season was wrecked almost immediately when he sustained a serious knee injury in mid-August having made just one appearance for Cardiff City, featuring as a substitute in the opening day draw at Crewe. Gary's rehabilitation was long and arduous and the full back spent a week training at the FA facility in Lilleshall at the turn of the year in a bid to accelerate his return. However, a series of setbacks meant he did not play again in the campaign. He was released in the summer.
Grimsby T *(From trainee on 7/7/1992) FL 139+10/3 FLC 7 FAC 8+2/1 Others 3*
Blackburn Rov *(£1,700,000 on 29/3/1996) PL 33+7/1 FLC 6 FAC 4+2*
Ipswich T *(£800,000 on 21/9/1999) P/FL 20+9/1 FLC 3+1 FAC 1 Others 2+1*
Wigan Ath *(Loaned on 17/1/2002) FL 7*
Cardiff C *(Free on 28/3/2002) FL 65+12/3 FLC 2 FAC 3+2 Others 2+2*

CROFT Lee David
Born: Wigan, 21 June 1985
Height: 5'9" **Weight:** 13.1
International Honours: E: Yth
Manchester City have no player with more international appearances than Lee on their books. He has been an England regular at most age groups and progressed to the England U20 side last season. The right-sided attacking midfielder tasted first-team action whilst on loan at Oldham Athletic where he was instrumental in the club's mid-season burst of form and particularly outstanding in the FA Cup exit at the hands of Bolton Wanderers. On his return to City Lee made his first-team debut when coming on as a second half substitute, once more against Bolton.
Manchester C *(From trainee on 2/7/2002) PL 0+7*
Oldham Ath *(Loaned on 12/11/2004) FL 11+1 FAC 3/1 Others 2/1*

CROFTS Andrew Lawrence
Born: Chatham, 29 May 1984
Height: 5'9" **Weight:** 10.8
International Honours: W: U21-3; Yth
This promising young midfielder gained a regular first-team spot for Gillingham last September and never looked back. Good in the air and tireless in his work rate, he will be looking to make further progress in 2005-06. Andrew signed a new contract for the Gills in January on the day he scored the winning goal against Plymouth.
Gillingham *(From trainee on 6/8/2003) FL 26+10/2 FLC 0+2 FAC 1*

CRONIN Lance
Born: Brighton, 11 September 1985
Height: 6'1" **Weight:** 13.4
This young Crystal Palace goalkeeper found himself out of the first-team picture at Selhurst Park last term and in March he joined League Two outfit Wycombe Wanderers on loan as cover for injured second-string 'keeper Steve Williams. Lance was rewarded with his full debut at Bristol Rovers in the last game of the season, when he gave a capable performance despite the Chairboys 1-0 defeat.
Crystal Palace *(From juniors on 27/9/2002)*
Wycombe W *(Loaned on 18/3/2005) FL 1*

CROOKS Lee Robert
Born: Wakefield, 14 January 1978
Height: 6'0" **Weight:** 12.1
International Honours: E: Yth
This tough-tackling central midfielder played more than 30 games in his first season with Bradford, when he proved to be an effective foil for the more attack-minded Steve Schumacher. Lee, who scored once against Doncaster, missed the last month of the campaign after tearing his groin.
Manchester C *(From trainee on 14/1/1995) P/FL 52+24/2 FLC 5+2 FAC 5 Others 3*
Northampton T *(Loaned on 26/12/2000) FL 3*
Barnsley *(£190,000 on 2/3/2001) FL 50+17 FLC 2 FAC 2 Others 2*
Bradford C *(Free on 6/8/2004) FL 30+2/1 FLC 1 Others 1*

CROOKS Leon Everton George
Born: Greenwich, 21 November 1985
Height: 6'1" **Weight:** 11.12
Leon made his Football League debut for MK Dons as a substitute in the 3-0 defeat at Oldham last August, and then featured intermittently before being given a surprise call-up to the left-back berth by new manager Danny Wilson in the memorable 4-1 win at Bradford City. Despite being a natural central defender he kept his spot for the next 13 games, showing some good awareness and a surprising willingness to get forward. Although he reverted to the bench for the final two key games, he made a very solid contribution to the successful fight against relegation.
MK Dons *(From trainee on 23/7/2004) FL 15+2 FLC 1 Others 1*

CROSBY Andrew (Andy) Keith
Born: Rotherham, 3 March 1973
Height: 6'2" **Weight:** 13.7
Club Honours: Div 3 '01
A summer signing from League Two rivals Oxford, Andy had an inspirational season as Scunthorpe skipper last term, and was deservedly voted into the PFA divisional team of the season. A brilliant leader and strong centre half, he organised the division's meanest defence and led by example, forming a rock-solid partnership with youngster Andy Butler. Dominant in the air and calm in possession, he netted three times, including twice from the penalty spot to maintain his 100 per cent record.
Doncaster Rov *(From trainee at Leeds U on 4/7/1991) FL 41+10 FLC 1+1 FAC 2 Others 4+1/1*
Darlington *(Free on 10/12/1993) FL 179+2/3 FLC 10 FAC 11/1 Others 9*
Chester C *(Free on 8/7/1998) FL 41/4 FLC 3 FAC 1 Others 1*
Brighton & Hove A *(£10,000 on 28/7/1999) FL 64+8/5 FLC 3 FAC 1+1 Others 7*
Oxford U *(Free on 13/12/2001) FL 109+2/12 FLC 5 FAC 4 Others 2/1*
Scunthorpe U *(Free on 2/8/2004) FL 43+1/4 FLC 1 FAC 3*

CROSS Scott Keith
Born: Northampton, 30 October 1987
Height: 5'10" **Weight:** 11.0
This promising young striker came on as a substitute for Northampton in the home match against Bury last Christmas

and showed the fans a sample of his talents. Although just two months past his 17th birthday, he showed no fear and got stuck in against experienced defenders. He then spent the second half of the campaign on loan at Kettering Town, where he found the net on a regular basis.
Northampton T *(Trainee) FL 0+1*

CROSSLEY Mark Geoffrey
Born: Barnsley, 16 June 1969
Height: 6'0" **Weight:** 16.0
International Honours: W: 8; B-1; E: U21-3
Although again deputy to Edwin van der Sar for much of the season Mark earned a recall to the Fulham line-up following a fine display in the Carling Cup tie at Birmingham. He followed this with an even more impressive game at Newcastle when some of his saves defied belief in a performance which will be remembered for many a season. After a brief run in the side he sustained a groin injury against Blackburn and though he recovered quickly he once more found himself on the bench. In spite of his lack of club action he was a regular in the Wales squad early in the season.
Nottingham F *(From trainee on 2/7/1987) P/FL 301+2 FLC 39+1 FAC 32 Others 18*
Millwall *(Loaned on 20/2/1998) FL 13*
Middlesbrough *(Free on 25/7/2000) PL 21+2 FLC 5 FAC 3*
Stoke C *(Loaned on 29/11/2002) FL 1*
Stoke C *(Loaned on 6/3/2003) FL 11*
Fulham *(£500,000 on 14/8/2003) PL 6 FLC 4*

CROUCH Peter James
Born: Macclesfield, 30 January 1981
Height: 6'7" **Weight:** 11.12
Club Honours: Div 1 '04
International Honours: E: 1; U21-6; Yth
If anybody was impressed by the signing of this beanpole striker last summer, it was not immediately evident. It was not until Harry Redknapp arrived at St Mary's, in December, that Peter was able to get a run in the first team. He found an instant rapport with Kevin Phillips, and both strikers prospered, despite poor support from their midfield. Height is his most obvious attribute, one he employs with panache, but his first touch, overall ball control and dribbling are exemplary, and he won the Saints' 'Player of the Year' award at a canter. It is as a target man that he excels, but he is no mean striker, and his call up to the England squad to tour the USA in the summer was well deserved.
Tottenham H *(From trainee on 2/7/1998)*
Queens Park Rgrs *(£60,000 on 28/7/2000) FL 38+4/10 FLC 1+1 FAC 3/2*
Portsmouth *(£1,250,000 on 11/7/2001) FL 37/18 FLC 1/1 FAC 1*
Aston Villa *(£4,000,000 + on 28/3/2002) PL 20+17/6 FLC 1+1 Others 4*
Norwich C *(Loaned on 8/9/2003) FL 14+1/4*
Southampton *(£2,000,000 on 14/7/2004) PL 18+9/12 FLC 1 FAC 5/4*

CROW Daniel (Danny) Stephen
Born: Great Yarmouth, 26 January 1986
Height: 5'10" **Weight:** 11.4
A product of the Norwich City youth set-up, this enthusiastic and hard-working striker was rewarded for his efforts with his first professional contract last September and, following a succession of injuries to the club's senior strikers, he made his Premiership debut at Middlesbrough in December, almost scoring with his first touch. Three more senior games followed before he enjoyed a loan spell at Northampton, where he scored a couple of opportunist goals and showed plenty of skill. Unfortunately his loan came to an abrupt end after suffering injury in a reserve game.
Norwich C *(From trainee on 29/9/2004) PL 0+3 FAC 0+1*
Northampton T *(Loaned on 15/2/2005) FL 4+6/2*

CROWE Jason William Robert
Born: Sidcup, 30 September 1978
Height: 5'9" **Weight:** 10.9
Club Honours: Div 1 '03
International Honours: E: Yth
Although only in his second season with Grimsby Town, Jason is already one of the club's longest-serving professionals. A versatile player who is comfortable in almost any position, he is highly rated by the Mariners' fans. Jason is very effective when bringing the ball forward and contributed four useful goals during the campaign.
Arsenal *(From trainee on 13/5/1996) FLC 0+2 FAC 0+1*
Crystal Palace *(Loaned on 10/11/1998) FL 8*
Portsmouth *(£750,000 + on 7/7/1999) FL 67+19/5 FLC 4 FAC 1+2*
Brentford *(Loaned on 12/9/2000) FL 9 FLC 2*
Grimsby T *(Free on 7/8/2003) FL 64+5/4 FLC 3 FAC 3 Others 1*

CROWELL Matthew (Matty) Thomas
Born: Bridgend, 3 July 1984
Height: 5'9" **Weight:** 10.12
Club Honours: AMC '05
International Honours: W: U21-5; Yth
Matty continued to show progress in Wrexham's midfield last term and was involved in more than half the club's competitive fixtures. He was more prominent in the second half of the season, when he made the starting line-up for the Racecourse club in the LDV Vans Trophy final against Southend at Cardiff. A player who likes to make his presence felt in the engine room at the heart of battle and does not shirk his responsibilities, he was also a member of the Wales U21 squad during the campaign.
Southampton *(From trainee on 13/7/2001)*
Wrexham *(Free on 15/7/2003) FL 31+12/1 FLC 0+1 FAC 1 Others 6+2*

CUDICINI Carlo
Born: Milan, Italy, 6 September 1973
Height: 6'1" **Weight:** 12.3
Club Honours: FAC '00; CS '00; FLC '05
International Honours: Italy: U21; Yth
With the well-publicised goalkeeping problems of Chelsea's main rivals, the Blues were in the fortunate position of having perhaps the best two 'keepers in the Premiership on their books. The arrival of the excellent Petr Cech saw Carlo Cudicini demoted to number two in the goalkeeping pecking order and no other club could boast of such an embarrassment of riches. Whilst Cech took over for Premiership and Champions' League duties, Carlo was pressed into service whenever the Blues fielded a 'shadow' side and he showed that he had lost none of his sharpness. He played brilliantly in Chelsea's run to the Carling Cup final, particularly in a tough fourth round tie at St. James' Park, where his heroics took the match into extra time allowing the Blues to snatch two late goals and a dramatic victory. Carlo's second appearance at Newcastle, in the FA Cup fifth round tie, had a much unhappier end result when an injury-time red card deprived him of an appearance against Liverpool at the Millennium Stadium the following weekend. During the season Carlo kept his 74th clean sheet from 170 appearances – a tremendous ratio and a total which put him fourth in the Blues all-time goalkeeping list.
Chelsea *(£160,000 from Castel di Sangro, Italy, ex AC Milan, Prato, Lazio, on 6/8/1999) PL 116+2 FLC 13 FAC 22 Others 16+1*

CULLIP Daniel (Danny)
Born: Bracknell, 17 September 1976
Height: 6'1" **Weight:** 12.7
Club Honours: Div 3 '01; Div 2 '02
After a slow start at Brighton Danny found his feet after a few weeks of Championship football only to be then sidelined by a hernia operation. He soon rediscovered his form but with his contract due to expire at the end of the

season he chose to move on to Sheffield United in December. Danny went straight into the centre of defence for the Blades, playing with determination and commitment, being particularly strong in the air. However, following a spell on the sidelines with an injury he went out on loan to Watford to assist in their battle against relegation.
Oxford U *(From trainee on 6/7/1995)*
Fulham *(Free on 5/7/1996) FL 41+9/2 FLC 8 FAC 2 Others 1*
Brentford *(£75,000 on 17/2/1998) FL 15 FLC 2*
Brighton & Hove A *(£50,000 on 17/9/1999) FL 216+1/7 FLC 8/1 FAC 11/2 Others 6/1*
Sheffield U *(£250,000 on 17/12/2004) FL 11 FAC 4/1*
Watford *(Loaned on 24/3/2005) FL 4*

CUMMINGS Warren
Born: Aberdeen, 15 October 1980
Height: 5'9" **Weight:** 11.8
International Honours: S: U21-9
This left back enjoyed an excellent season for Bournemouth in 2004-05 and was named in the PFA League One team of the year. A popular player with the supporters and his colleagues, his season was cut short in March when he broke his ankle in the win at Swindon and he was sorely missed in the run-in.
Chelsea *(From trainee on 5/7/1999)*
Bournemouth *(Loaned on 20/10/2000) FL 10/1 Others 1*
West Bromwich A *(Loaned on 21/3/2001) FL 1+2*
West Bromwich A *(Loaned on 25/7/2001) FL 6+8 FLC 0+2*
Dundee U *(Loaned on 23/8/2002) SL 7+1 SLC 1*
Dundee U *(Loaned on 16/11/2002) SL 0+3*
Bournemouth *(Free on 3/2/2003) FL 92/4 FLC 3/1 FAC 7+1 Others 4*

CUMMINS Michael (Micky) Thomas
Born: Dublin, 1 June 1978
Height: 6'0" **Weight:** 11.11
Club Honours: AMC '01
International Honours: RoI: U21-2; Yth
This dependable Port Vale midfield player once again gave his all for the club in 2004-05. Micky was mainly used in a central-midfield role, which seemed to suit him well. Injuries to others left him as one of the senior players and he was forced to sit back a bit more than normal which reduced his tally of goals and he scored only twice. For most of the season he was hampered by a shoulder injury, but deferred an operation until the team was safe from relegation worries.
Middlesbrough *(From trainee on 1/7/1995) PL 1+1*
Port Vale *(Free on 17/3/2000) FL 211+3/21 FLC 6 FAC 9/1 Others 16/1*

CUNNINGHAM Kenneth (Kenny) Edward
Born: Dublin, 28 June 1971
Height: 6'0" **Weight:** 11.8
International Honours: RoI: 68; B-2; U21-4; Yth
Kenny was a Premiership ever-present for Birmingham last term after missing the first two matches due to suspension. An exceptional reader of the game, the Blues' captain produced quiet but highly efficient performances. He provided a steadying presence at the back during some of the fraught games for the Blues when the pressure was on, making key tackles and interceptions.
Millwall *(Signed from Tolka Rov on 18/9/1989) FL 132+4/1 FLC 10 FAC 1 Others 5+1/1*
Wimbledon *(£650,000 on 9/11/1994) P/FL 249+1 FLC 22+1 FAC 32+1*
Birmingham C *(£600,000 on 18/7/2002) PL 103 FLC 3 FAC 5*

CURETON Jamie
Born: Bristol, 28 August 1975
Height: 5'8" **Weight:** 10.7
International Honours: E: Yth
Jamie, who can play either in central midfield or as a striker, never really became an established member of the Queen's Park Rangers team last season. His appearances seemed to come in groups of five or six games at a time. His main opportunity came when Tony Thorpe was injured and Kevin Gallen had moved back into a midfield role. He scored four goals during the campaign including a hat-trick in the 4-1 win over Coventry in September.
Norwich C *(From trainee on 5/2/1993) P/FL 13+16/6 FLC 0+1 FAC 0+2*
Bournemouth *(Loaned on 8/9/1995) FL 0+5 Others 0+1*
Bristol Rov *(£250,000 on 20/9/1996) FL 165+9/72 FLC 7+1/2 FAC 10/2 Others 6/3*
Reading *(£250,000 on 21/8/2000) FL 74+34/50 FLC 4+1/1 FAC 5+2/2 Others 6+1/2 (Free to Busan Icons, South Korea during 2003 close season)*
Queens Park Rgrs *(£95,000 on 2/2/2004) FL 20+23/6 FLC 2/1 FAC 1*

CURLE Thomas (Tom) Keith
Born: Bristol, 3 March 1986
Height: 5'10" **Weight:** 10.0
Tom was called up for his first appearance of the 2004-05 season for Mansfield in the LDV Vans Trophy tie against Darlington at Field Mill in September. Playing on the left-hand side of midfield he showed some good touches and played his part in the Stags eventual victory. However, the departure of his father as the club manager led to his being released by mutual consent and after training with Macclesfield he accepted a contract with Conference North outfit Bradford Park Avenue in March.
Mansfield T *(Trainee) FL 0+1 Others 2*

CURRIE Darren Paul
Born: Hampstead, 29 November 1974
Height: 5'11" **Weight:** 12.7
Brighton manager Mark McGhee took a chance on this ball-playing winger and offered him a contract in the Championship in the summer of 2004. Able to turn out on either flank, Darren made a slow start but showed the passing and crossing ability that would make him useful at any level. Using his intricate skills to beat opponents and make up for a lack of pace, he brought quality and creativity to the side and soon attracted the interest of promotion contenders Ipswich. With Albion strapped for cash, Darren was sold to the Suffolk club. He made an immediate impression on his debut from the bench at Queen's Park Rangers, setting up an equaliser and then putting his team in front with a crisp drive. He continued to do well during the remainder of the campaign and was also occasionally employed as a central playmaker.
West Ham U *(From trainee on 2/7/1993)*
Shrewsbury T *(Loaned on 5/9/1994) FL 10+2/2*
Shrewsbury T *(Loaned on 3/2/1995) FL 5*
Leyton Orient *(Loaned on 16/11/1995) FL 9+1*
Shrewsbury T *(£70,000 on 7/2/1996) FL 46+20/8 FLC 2+1/1 FAC 3*
Plymouth Arg *(Free on 26/3/1998) FL 5+2*
Barnet *(Free on 13/7/1998) FL 120+7/19 FLC 5/1 FAC 3/2 Others 6*
Wycombe W *(£200,000 on 11/7/2001) FL 109+17/14 FLC 5 FAC 6+1/5 Others 5*
Brighton & Hove A *(Free on 5/8/2004) FL 21+1/2 FLC 1*
Ipswich T *(£250,000 on 10/12/2004) FL 19+5/3 FAC 1 Others 1+1*

CURTIS John Charles Keyworth
Born: Nuneaton, 3 September 1978
Height: 5'10" **Weight:** 11.9
Club Honours: FAYC '95; FLC '02
International Honours: E: B-1; U21-16; Yth; Sch
This stylish full back made just a single appearance as a substitute for Pompey at the beginning of last season before being farmed out on loan to Preston. He

impressed the Deepdale fans with his obvious class, but a permanent move fell through following the change in management at Fratton Park. However, John eventually moved on to join Nottingham Forest on a short-term contract in February, but he was unable to prevent the City Ground club from slipping to relegation.
Manchester U *(From trainee on 3/10/1995) PL 4+9 FLC 5 Others 0+1*
Barnsley *(Loaned on 19/11/1999) FL 28/2 Others 1+1*
Blackburn Rov *(£2,250,000 on 1/6/2000) P/FL 61 FLC 10 FAC 6 Others 1*
Sheffield U *(Loaned on 3/3/2003) FL 9+3 FAC 1 Others 3*
Leicester C *(Free on 15/8/2003) PL 14+1 FLC 1 FAC 1*
Portsmouth *(Free on 2/2/2004) PL 5+2*
Preston NE *(Loaned on 10/9/2004) FL 12*
Nottingham F *(Free on 3/2/2005) FL 11 FAC 2*

CURTIS Thomas (Tom) David
Born: Exeter, 1 March 1973
Height: 5'8" **Weight:** 11.7
This midfield ball winner had a difficult time at Mansfield in the early part of last season when he found it hard to match the tremendous form he had shown during the previous campaign and failed to win a regular place in the line-up. However, his no-nonsense approach and all-out effort made him a valued member of the first-team squad, before a knee injury put him on the sidelines at the end of March.
Derby Co *(From juniors on 1/7/1991)*
Chesterfield *(Free on 12/8/1993) FL 235+5/12 FLC 20/1 FAC 14/1 Others 11+1*
Portsmouth *(£150,000 on 4/8/2000) FL 7+6 FLC 1+1*
Walsall *(Loaned on 20/9/2001) FL 3+1*
Tranmere Rov *(Loaned on 30/8/2002) FL 8 FLC 2 Others 1*
Mansfield T *(Free on 20/12/2002) FL 83+10 FLC 2 FAC 5/1 Others 3/1*

Darren Currie

CUTLER Neil Anthony
Born: Cannock, 3 September 1976
Height: 6'1" **Weight:** 12.0
International Honours: E: Yth; Sch
The tall goalkeeper was one of Stockport's summer signings and looked a promising capture. However, he never really settled in the line-up, often looking shaky behind the County defence and he was eventually replaced by James Spencer.
West Bromwich A *(From trainee on 7/9/1993)*
Chester C *(Loaned on 27/3/1996) FL 1*
Crewe Alex *(Signed on 30/7/1996)*
Chester C *(Loaned on 30/8/1996) FL 5*
Chester C *(Free on 8/7/1998) FL 23 FLC 1 FAC 1 Others 1*
Aston Villa *(Signed on 30/11/1999) PL 0+1*
Oxford U *(Loaned on 15/12/2000) FL 11*
Stoke C *(Free on 24/7/2001) FL 65+4 FLC 3 FAC 6+1 Others 3*
Swansea C *(Loaned on 28/2/2003) FL 13*
Stockport Co *(Free on 12/7/2004) FL 22 FLC 1 FAC 1+1 Others 2*

CYGAN Pascal
Born: Lens, France, 19 April 1974
Height: 6'3" **Weight:** 13.10
Club Honours: PL '04; CS '04
After making steady progress during the previous season, Pascal had a disappointing campaign by comparison in 2004-05. The tall centre back still made 23 appearances in total, including 15 in the Premiership, yet he featured in many games where Arsenal's defensive frailties were all too evident. Pascal also suffered with injury and whilst he was sidelined Philippe Senderos took full advantage to become a first teamer in his absence for the final four months of the season.
Arsenal *(£2,100,000 from Lille, France, ex Valenciennes, Wasquehal, on 8/8/2002) PL 41+10/1 FLC 4 FAC 4+1 Others 15+3*

DABIZAS Nikolaos (Nikos)
Born: Amyndaeo, Greece, 3 August 1973
Height: 6'1" **Weight:** 12.7
International Honours: Greece: 69; U21; Yth
This experienced central defender started the 2004-05 season wearing the captain's armband for Leicester under Micky Adams and managed an early goal in the home win over Sheffield United. However, an inconsistent spell of form plus a mixture of defensive partners, made things harder as the campaign progressed. Nikos headed home the important opening goal in City's fine FA Cup win at the Valley, but nevertheless was released by the Foxes at the end of the campaign. He also added to his tally of Greek caps during the season.
Newcastle U *(£1,300,000 from Olympiakos, Greece on 13/3/1998) PL 119+11/10 FLC 6 FAC 17+1/2 Others 21+1/1*
Leicester C *(Free on 2/1/2004) P/FL 51/1 FLC 1 FAC 5/1*

DADI Eugene
Born: Abidjan, Ivory Coast, 20 August 1973
Height: 6'2" **Weight:** 12.11
A tall but surprisingly skilful striker, Eugene struggled to reproduce his exceptional form of the 2003-04 season for Tranmere last term. He won back his regular first-team place in February, scoring twice in three games, but although most of his appearances were from the bench, he still contributed nine goals in the push for promotion. Eugene has plenty of natural ability, easily unsettling opposing defenders with his bustling, determined style of play and he is adept at snapping up any half-chance. Off the field, Eugene runs his own fashion-design label and designed the official suits for the Tranmere team.
Aberdeen *(Signed from Toulouse, France, ex Laval, Sete, ASK Linz, on 24/8/2001) SL 20+8/4 SLC 1+1/1 SC 3*
Livingston *(Signed on 23/7/2002) SL 16+7/3 SLC 2/1 Others 1+1*
Tranmere Rov *(Free on 8/8/2003) FL 44+25/25 FLC 2+2/1 FAC 6+2/2 Others 2+3*

Nikos Dabizas

DAGNALL Christopher (Chris)
Born: Liverpool, 15 April 1986
Height: 5'8" **Weight:** 11.9
Chris is another product of the successful Tranmere youth policy, and has represented the club at every level from U13s onwards. He possesses an extremely powerful shot and is capable of scoring memorable goals, but likes nothing better than getting behind defenders to challenge in the box. Unfortunately, Chris did not enjoy as full a season as he would have liked; his over-enthusiastic goal celebrations against Hartlepool earned him an early red card whilst a fractured cheekbone sustained in October kept him out of the first team for two months and his appearances in the latter half of the season were mostly from the bench. A firm favourite with the Tranmere fans, he shows much promise for the future.
Tranmere Rov *(From trainee on 11/7/2003) FL 18+15/7 FLC 0+1 Others 1+1*

DAILLY Christian Eduard
Born: Dundee, 23 October 1973
Height: 6'0" **Weight:** 12.10
Club Honours: SC '94
International Honours: S: 55; B-1; U21-34; Yth; Sch
The West Ham captain was sorely missed after being out for most of the season with a knee ligament problem. The experienced central defender played in the opening two games of the campaign before a swelling on his knee made surgery necessary. Christian battled hard all year to return to the action and was rewarded with substitute appearance in the final two play-off games.

Dundee U *(From juniors on 2/8/1990) SL 110+33/18 SLC 9/1 SC 10+2 Others 8+1/1*
Derby Co *(£1,000,000 on 12/8/1996) PL 62+5/4 FLC 6 FAC 4+1*
Blackburn Rov *(£5,300,000 on 22/8/1998) P/FL 60+10/4 FLC 5+1 FAC 4 Others 2*
West Ham U *(£1,750,000 on 18/1/2001) P/FL 117+5/2 FLC 5 FAC 10+2 Others 3+2/1*

DAKINAH Kofi

Born: Denmark, 1 February 1980
Height: 6'3" **Weight:** 12.11
International Honours: Denmark: Yth
This tall defender made several pre-season appearances for Walsall and came close to scoring against Manchester United with an opportunist header. His only first-team appearances after that, however, were both against Sheffield Wednesday in the Carling Cup and in the League One fixture but he was injured in the first half of the latter game and did not appear again. In his brief outings his bravery in the tackle was not quite matched by his positional sense. Kofi subsequently returned to Denmark and signed for Nordsjaelland.
Walsall *(Signed from Herfolge, Denmark on 30/7/2004) FL 1 FLC 1*

DALEY Omar

Born: Jamaica, 25 April 1981
Height: 5'10" **Weight:** 11.0
International Honours: Jamaica
This Jamaican wide man joined Preston on a season-long loan last term, but failed to establish himself in the starting line-up. Quick and tricky on the right wing, his only starts came in the Carling Cup tie at Mansfield, in which he recorded his only goal of the campaign, and the home draw with Millwall. His contract was cancelled on transfer-deadline day.
Reading *(Signed from Portmore U, Jamaica on 19/8/2003) FL 0+6 FLC 0+1*
Preston NE *(Free on 3/8/2004) FL 1+13 FLC 1+2/1*

DALY Jonathan (Jon) Marvin

Born: Dublin, 8 January 1983
Height: 6'1" **Weight:** 12.4
International Honours: RoI: U21-9; Yth
The tall striker found himself slightly out of favour at the start of last season at Stockport and he only made a few appearances during the opening three

Jon Daly

months of the campaign, scoring once in the LDV Vans Trophy win over Bury. He was then loaned out to Grimsby, as the Mariners sought to solve their lack of fire power. However, the loan was abruptly ended when he received a red card in the 'derby' match against Scunthorpe. Jon subsequently moved on to Hartlepool where he added an extra dimension to the strike force. Short of match fitness, he initially struggled to win a first team place, but with Joel Porter injured he got his chance and scored two important goals. The first came at Bournemouth helping Pools get a draw in the last game of the season to ensure that they reached the play-offs. The second came at the Millennium Stadium, when he scored from a header with his first touch of the ball after coming off the bench.
Stockport Co *(From trainee on 18/1/2000) FL 65+26/14 FLC 3+1/1 FAC 4/1 Others 1+1/1*
Bury *(Loaned on 2/1/2004) FL 7/1*
Grimsby T *(Loaned on 22/10/2004) FL 3/1*
Hartlepool U *(Signed on 11/2/2005) FL 4+8/1 Others 2+1/1*

DANBY John Robert
Born: Stoke, 20 September 1983
Height: 6'2" **Weight:** 14.7
John was one of the few bright spots in what was otherwise a very disappointing season for Kidderminster last term. He made the goalkeeper's jersey his own and began his campaign with three consecutive clean sheets. A broken toe kept him out of the side for nine games, and later in the season a dislocated finger caused him some discomfort. John could be pleased with his performances throughout the campaign and was deservedly named 'Junior Supporters Club Player of the Year'.
Kidderminster Hrs *(From juniors on 14/12/2001) FL 46+2 FLC 1 Others 1*

[DANI] FERREIRA RODRIGUES Daniel
Born: Madeira, Portugal, 3 March 1980
Height: 6'0" **Weight:** 11.8
International Honours: Portugal: U21
Striker Dani returned to Bournemouth in the summer of 2004 and started the season as a regular, before a series of injuries restricted his appearances. A player with great technique, as he proved with a superb goal at Blackpool which many regard as the best strike of the season, Dani played in less than half the games and will be hoping to prove himself in the 2005-06 campaign.
Bournemouth *(Loaned from CS Farense, Portugal on 1/10/1998) FL 0+5 Others 0+2*
Southampton *(£170,000 on 3/3/1999) PL 0+2*
Bristol C *(Loaned on 3/10/2000) FL 3+1*
Bristol C *(Loaned on 31/12/2001) FL 0+4 Others 0+1*
Walsall *(Free on 6/8/2002) FL 0+1 (Freed on 13/1/2003)*
Yeovil T *(Free from Ionikos, Greece on 25/3/2004) FL 3+1/4*
Bournemouth *(Free on 19/7/2004) FL 10+13/3 FLC 1 FAC 0+2/1 Others 1*

DANIELS David (Dave) William
Born: Bedford, 14 September 1985
Height: 5'8" **Weight:** 10.10
This intelligent young midfielder spent much of last season developing in Cambridge United's reserve and youth teams. He stepped up to make his debut in senior football when he featured as a substitute in the LDV Vans Trophy tie against Leyton Orient in November, this being his only first-team appearance during the campaign.
Cambridge U *(Trainee) FL 0+1 Others 0+1*

DANN Scott
Born: Liverpool, 14 February 1987
Height: 6'2" **Weight:** 12.0
Walsall's tall teenaged defender gave a composed display in the pre-season draw against Manchester United, but his only League One appearance was a brief substitute appearance against Chesterfield in January. He then had a successful loan spell in Denmark with Koge BK but returned towards the end of the season. His composure under pressure makes him one of Walsall's bright young hopes.
Walsall *(From trainee on 6/8/2004) FL 0+1*

DANNS Neil Alexander
Born: Liverpool, 23 November 1982
Height: 5'9" **Weight:** 12.1
This central midfielder was a revelation at Colchester United, initially arriving on a two-month loan from Blackburn, before making the move permanent around the turn of the year. Attack-minded Neil scored four goals in his first stint, including a brace in the 2-1 home win over Port Vale, and U's supporters were delighted when he returned at the end of December. The goals flowed aplenty. There was another brace at basement dwellers Stockport to secure a vital 2-1 victory, the winner arriving in injury-time to ease the U's relegation fears. He ended the campaign with an impressive tally of 12 goals, and was second to Pat Baldwin in most of Colchester's 'Player of the Season' categories.
Blackburn Rov *(From trainee on 3/7/2000) PL 1+2 FLC 2 FAC 1 Others 1*
Blackpool *(Loaned on 7/8/2003) FL 12/2 FLC 2 Others 1*
Hartlepool U *(Loaned on 12/3/2004) FL 8+1/1 Others 0+2*
Colchester U *(Signed on 9/9/2004) FL 32/11 FLC 2/1 FAC 1 Others 1*

DANZE Anthony
Born: Perth, Australia, 15 March 1984
Height: 6'0" **Weight:** 12.0
International Honours: Australia: U23-7; Yth
This young midfielder signed for Crystal Palace last October but his only first-team experience came in the Carling Cup tie against Manchester United the following month. Anthony joined the MK Dons on loan in December and had the misfortune to make his debut in a cold Boxing Day hammering at Doncaster. He showed up much better in the next game at home to Wrexham but was injured after 30 minutes, which forced his quick return to Selhurst Park. He went on to score three goals for the reserves but has yet to make his debut in League competition for Palace.
Crystal Palace *(Free from Perth Glory on 6/10/2004) FLC 1*
MK Dons *(Loaned on 23/12/2004) FL 2*

DARBY Duane Anthony
Born: Birmingham, 17 October 1973
Height: 5'11" **Weight:** 12.6
Club Honours: NC '01; Div 3 '03
After being one of the heroes of Shrewsbury Town's promotion via the Conference play-offs in 2003-04, Duane had something of a disappointing time at Gay Meadow last season. He managed just a single goal in eight starts before a groin problem brought his campaign to a premature close in February. The experienced striker spent much of the campaign on the transfer list and will be hoping for an improvement in his fortunes in the 2005-06 season.
Torquay U *(From trainee on 3/7/1992) FL 60+48/26 FLC 4+3/1 FAC 1+4 Others 5+3/2*
Doncaster Rov *(£60,000 on 19/7/1995) FL 8+9/4 FLC 2 FAC 0+1 Others 1+1*
Hull C *(Signed on 27/3/1996) FL 75+3/27 FLC 5/1 FAC 4/6 Others 4/2*
Notts Co *(Free on 2/7/1998) FL 22+6/5 FLC 3+1/1*
Hull C *(Loaned on 25/3/1999) FL 4+4*
Rushden & Diamonds *(Free on 21/6/2000) FL 61+18/23 FLC 1+2/1 FAC 4+1 Others 0+1*
Shrewsbury T *(Free on 13/11/2003) FL 8+8/1 Others 1*

DARLINGTON Jermaine Christopher
Born: Hackney, 11 April 1974
Height: 5'7" **Weight:** 10.10
Jermaine came to Watford on a free transfer at the start of the 2004-05

campaign. At first he lacked fitness, having missed the pre-season build-up, but he came into the first team in October and kept his place until a dip in form towards the end of the season. Able to kick with either foot, Jermaine is comfortable on the ball and enjoys going forward. He played mainly at left back, although he was equally adept on the right flank. He was transfer-listed at the end of the season.
Charlton Ath *(From trainee on 30/6/1992) FL 1+1 (Free to Dover Ath on 23/9/1993)*
Queens Park Rgrs *(£25,000 from Aylesbury U on 25/3/1999) FL 70+1/2 FLC 2 FAC 6*
Wimbledon *(£200,000 on 16/7/2001) FL 97+8/3 FLC 3+1 FAC 4*
Watford *(Free on 9/8/2004) FL 25+1 FLC 7 FAC 2*

DAVENPORT Calum Raymond Paul
Born: Bedford, 1 January 1983
Height: 6'4" **Weight:** 14.4
International Honours: E: U21-7; Yth
This tall and commanding central defender was destined to move to the Premiership and after six games in which he consistently shone for Coventry he joined Tottenham. Calum's superb but moving final appearance for the Sky Blues in the home win over West Ham deservedly won him the 'Man of the Match' award. Almost immediately afterwards he was loaned out to the Hammers where he proved to be a class act before being recalled due to an injury crisis. Calum made his only appearance of the season for Spurs as a late substitute at Villa Park in November, before spending the second half of the campaign on loan at Southampton. Brought in with the hope of adding much needed pace to the heart of a sluggish Saints' defence, Calum exhibited admirable character and persistence within a back four which failed to gel. A confident player, both in the air and on the deck, his only shortcoming was a lack of experience.
Coventry C *(From trainee on 6/1/2000) P/FL 64+11/3 FLC 3 FAC 5+1*
Tottenham H *(£1,100,000 + on 31/8/2004) PL 0+1*
West Ham U *(Loaned on 9/9/2004) FL 10*
Southampton *(Loaned on 4/1/2005) PL 5+2 FAC 4+1*

DAVIDSON Callum Iain
Born: Stirling, 25 June 1976
Height: 5'10" **Weight:** 11.8
Club Honours: S Div 1 '97
International Honours: S: 17; U21-2
Callum's catalogue of injuries at Preston last term would have taxed the staunchest of resolves, and he was only able to show his defensive capabilities in short bursts. He twice had to leave the field in the opening quarter of an hour with injuries and he also had to withdraw during the warm-up against Cardiff. Predominantly left-sided, he looked solid at left back and also combined well on the overlap with Eddie Lewis and Matt Hill. His only goal was the winner over Crewe, and he will be looking forward to a fresh start to his North End career in 2005-06.
St Johnstone *(From juniors on 8/6/1994) SL 39+5/4 SLC 1 Others 3*
Blackburn Rov *(£1,750,000 on 12/2/1998) P/FL 63+2/1 FLC 3+1 FAC 6 Others 1+1*
Leicester C *(£1,700,000 on 12/7/2000) P/FL 90+11/2 FLC 5+1 FAC 5+1 Others 0+1*
Preston NE *(Free on 6/8/2004) FL 16+3/1 FLC 1+1*

DAVIES Adam Glen
Born: Peterborough, 27 March 1987
Height: 6'2" **Weight:** 13.5
International Honours: W: Yth
This promising Cambridge United youngster made his senior debut as a substitute in the LDV Vans Trophy victory over Boston last September. Adam went on to feature twice more from the bench during the campaign. Although a midfield player earlier in his career he has since developed into a talented defender who can play either at centre half or at right back.
Cambridge U *(Trainee) FL 0+2 Others 0+1*

DAVIES Andrew John
Born: Stockton, 17 December 1984
Height: 6'3" **Weight:** 14.8
International Honours: E: U21-1; Yth
This promising central defender struggled to win a place in the Middlesbrough line-up last term and was loaned out to Queen's Park Rangers to get some first-team games under his belt. He remained at Loftus Road almost until the end of the season, forming a solid central defensive partnership with Danny Shittu and prompting manager Ian Holloway to enquire about a permanent transfer.
Middlesbrough *(From trainee on 6/7/2002) PL 11+3 FLC 3*
Queens Park Rgrs *(Loaned on 12/1/2005) FL 9*

DAVIES Arron Rhys
Born: Cardiff, 22 June 1984
Height: 5'9" **Weight:** 10.0
Club Honours: Div 2 '05
International Honours: W: U21-3
This promising winger was only ever on the fringes of the Southampton first-team squad last term and in December he made a permanent move to Yeovil. He proved to be an immediate hit at Huish Park, scoring on his debut at Leyton Orient and netting nine goals from 15 starts. Arron was also called up to the Wales U21 squad during the campaign.
Southampton *(From trainee on 11/7/2002)*
Barnsley *(Loaned on 13/2/2004) FL 1+3*
Yeovil T *(Signed on 16/12/2004) FL 15+8/8 FAC 0+2/1*

DAVIES Benjamin (Ben) James
Born: Birmingham, 27 May 1981
Height: 5'6" **Weight:** 10.7
Club Honours: NC '04
A tigerish whole-hearted player Ben is a big favourite with the Chester fans and formed a formidable partnership with Paul Carden in the centre of the park last season. Like his midfield partner, Ben fell out of favour under caretaker manager Ray Matthias, but was restored to the team under Ian Rush. Strong in the tackle and never one to give less than 100 per cent, he chipped in with important goals against Kidderminster and Southend. Ben was also used as cover at right back following injuries to Darren Edmondson and loan signing Ian Hillier.
Walsall *(From trainee at Stoke C on 11/8/1999)*
Kidderminster Hrs *(Free on 1/3/2000) FL 11+1 FLC 1 Others 1*
Chester C *(Free on 7/5/2002) FL 38+6/2 FLC 0+1 FAC 2 Others 1+1*

DAVIES Craig Martin
Born: Burton-on-Trent, 9 January 1986
Height: 6'2" **Weight:** 13.5
International Honours: W: U21-2; Yth
Craig had an excellent season at Oxford last term and deservedly won the club's 'Young Player of the Year' award. He found the net on a regular basis for the youth team early on and was quickly promoted to the first-team squad, making his senior debut at Notts County in August. He had to wait a while longer for another game but when he broke through he scored five times in a run of nine appearances. A striker who is very quick and with an eye for goal, he has great self-confidence and was able to retain his place in the side for a lengthy spell. Craig also featured for Wales at U21 level during the campaign.
Oxford U *(Trainee) FL 13+15/6 Others 0+1*

DAVIES Curtis Eugene
Born: Waltham Forest, 15 March 1985
Height: 6'1" **Weight:** 11.13
Club Honours: Div 1 '05
This young central defender continued to improve his game at Luton last term and

matured well over the season. A pacy player who times his tackles well, he impressed with his ability to play the ball out when under pressure rather than use a more direct approach. His partnership at the back with Chris Coyne was one of the cornerstones on which the Hatters' League One championship side was built. Curtis was selected for the PFA League One team of the season.
Luton T *(From trainee on 2/7/2004) FL 48+2/1 FLC 1 FAC 3 Others 0+1*

DAVIES Gareth
Born: Chesterfield, 4 February 1983
Height: 6'1" **Weight:** 12.13
Despite starting only a handful of League One games last term Chesterfield's utility player can look on 2004-5 with some pride. With resolute defending and an eye for a quick break, Gareth was completely reliable whenever he was called upon, and he was rewarded with a new contract as the season closed.
Chesterfield *(Free from Buxton on 20/8/2001) FL 54+27/2 FLC 2+1 FAC 2+1/2 Others 4*

DAVIES Kevin Cyril
Born: Sheffield, 26 March 1977
Height: 6'0" **Weight:** 13.6
International Honours: E: U21-3; Yth
Following an excellent first season with Bolton, Kevin picked up where he had left off and produced a number of impressive displays last term. A centre forward of the traditional English variety, he proved to be a handful for many of the Premiership's finest defenders. Playing as the focal point of what was often a three-pronged attack (using attacking wingers who would double up as supporting strikers), Kevin's strength and ability to hold onto the ball were particular assets and he struck up a particularly effective understanding with El-Hadji Diouf, finishing the season just one goal behind his striking colleague.
Chesterfield *(From trainee on 18/4/1994) FL 113+16/22 FLC 7+2/1 FAC 10/6 Others 9+2/1*
Southampton *(£750,000 on 14/5/1997) PL 20+5/9 FLC 3+1/3 FAC 1*
Blackburn Rov *(£7,250,000 on 2/6/1998) P/FL 11+12/1 FLC 3 FAC 2/1 Others 1*
Southampton *(Signed on 18/8/1999) PL 59+23/10 FLC 3+2/1 FAC 3+5/2*
Millwall *(Loaned on 13/9/2002) FL 6+3/3*
Bolton W *(Free on 25/7/2003) PL 71+2/17 FLC 5+2/1 FAC 4/1*

DAVIES Simon
Born: Haverfordwest, 23 October 1979
Height: 5'10" **Weight:** 11.4
International Honours: W: 24; B-1; U21-10; Yth
Simon is a pacy, intelligent midfielder who favours the right side and he impressed again last season with his bridge play between midfield and attack. Well established for both club and country, he has confidence in abundance and energy to match. Injury meant a stop-start season which hindered his usual fluidity.
Peterborough U *(From trainee on 21/7/1997) FL 63+2/6 FLC 4 FAC 3 Others 3*
Tottenham H *(£700,000 on 10/1/2000) PL 99+22/13 FLC 10+3/3 FAC 10+3/2*

DAVIS Claude
Born: Jamaica, 6 March 1979
Height: 6'3" **Weight:** 14.4
International Honours: Jamaica
Preston's Jamaican international defender was a regular up to Christmas, despite a couple of periods out injured, but then featured from the bench until recalled for the final few games. 'Man of the Match' in two of the play-off games, he is incredibly strong at holding players off and prefers to shepherd both opponents and the ball away from danger. His unusual high-stepping stride masks his great pace in recovery and he has an almost telescopic tackling ability. A particularly powerful header of the ball, he was very unlucky not to feature in the goal-scoring charts during the season.
Preston NE *(Signed from Portmore U, Jamaica on 15/8/2003) FL 37+17/1 FLC 3 FAC 2 Others 3*

DAVIS Kelvin Geoffrey
Born: Bedford, 29 September 1976
Height: 6'1" **Weight:** 14.0
International Honours: E: U21-3; Yth
Although it does not show in the goals against column, Kelvin did as much as anyone to help Ipswich to the upper echelons of the table in 2004-05. An excellent shot-stopper he made numerous brilliant saves to keep Town in the game or preserve their lead. Sheffield United manager Neil Warnock was particularly eulogistic about Kelvin's performance at Bramall Lane while in the first leg of the play-off semi-final he, somehow, managed to tip Ferdinand's close-range header over the bar. Kelvin was selected for the PFA Championship team of the season by his fellow professionals.
Luton T *(From trainee on 1/7/1994) FL 92 FLC 7 FAC 2 Others 6*
Torquay U *(Loaned on 16/9/1994) FL 2 FLC 1 Others 1*
Hartlepool U *(Loaned on 8/8/1997) FL 2 FLC 1*
Wimbledon *(£600,000 + on 14/7/1999) FL 131 FLC 7 FAC 8*
Ipswich T *(Free on 6/8/2003) FL 84 FLC 2 FAC 3 Others 4*

DAVIS Sean
Born: Clapham, 20 September 1979
Height: 5'10" **Weight:** 12.0
Club Honours: Div 1 '01
International Honours: E: U21-11
Sean is a tough-tackling midfielder who suffered set backs due to injury throughout last season's campaign. He joined Spurs as the first signing of Jacques Santini who was attracted by his ability to play a holding role in the middle or as an attacking midfielder. A good range and accuracy in his passing had taken Sean to the brink of an England call-up and an injury-free season could well see him realise that opportunity again in 2005-06.
Fulham *(From trainee on 2/7/1998) P/FL 128+27/14 FLC 9+5/3 FAC 15+2/2 Others 12/1*
Tottenham H *(£3,000,000 on 10/7/2004) PL 11+4 FLC 1*

DAVIS Solomon (Sol) Sebastian
Born: Cheltenham, 4 September 1979
Height: 5'8" **Weight:** 11.0
Club Honours: Div 1 '05
This Luton Town defender improved his game in leaps and bounds last term, showing a greater maturity in his play. Consistent throughout the campaign, he impressed with some well-timed tackles and his probing runs down the left-hand side. Sol was a near ever-present for the League One champions and will be looking to continue in similar vein in 2005-06.
Swindon T *(From trainee on 29/5/1998) FL 100+17 FLC 7 FAC 5+1 Others 1*
Luton T *(£600,000 + on 16/8/2002) FL 113+2/2 FLC 4+1 FAC 8 Others 4*

DAVIS Steven
Born: Ballymena, 1 January 1985
Height: 5'7" **Weight:** 9.7
International Honours: NI: 4; U23-1; U21-3; Yth; Sch
A hard-working midfielder who has come through the youth ranks at Villa, Steven was included on the bench for the first time early on last season and went on to make his senior debut as a substitute at Norwich. Introduced slowly, it was not until the end of November that he received his first start but from then on he featured regularly in the side. Steven turned out to be one of the success stories of Villa's season and quickly became a firm favourite with the fans. He drilled home his first senior goal to seal victory away at Southampton in April. Steven stepped up to make his debut for Northern Ireland as a full international during the campaign.
Aston Villa *(From trainee on 15/1/2002) PL 19+9/1 FAC 0+1*

DAVISON Aidan John
Born: Sedgefield, 11 May 1968
Height: 6'1" **Weight:** 13.12
Club Honours: AMC '98
International Honours: NI: 3; B-1
Experienced 'keeper Aidan enjoyed a solid first campaign with Colchester, combining first-team action with coaching his young understudy Dean Gerken. He missed only 16 games all season, through injury, and contributed much to the U's excellent defensive record – second best in League One.
Notts Co *(Signed from Billingham Synthonia on 25/3/1988) FL 1*
Bury *(£6,000 on 7/10/1989)*
Millwall *(Free on 14/8/1991) FL 34 FLC 3 FAC 2 Others 2*
Bolton W *(£25,000 on 26/7/1993) P/FL 35+2 FAC 8 Others 4*
Hull C *(Loaned on 29/11/1996) FL 9 Others 1*
Bradford C *(Free on 14/3/1997) FL 10*
Grimsby T *(Free on 16/7/1997) FL 77 FLC 10 FAC 7 Others 10*
Sheffield U *(Free on 6/8/1999) FL 1+1*
Bradford C *(Free on 4/1/2000) P/FL 49+2 FLC 6 FAC 1 Others 2+1*
Grimsby T *(Free on 8/8/2003) FL 32 FLC 1 FAC 2 Others 1*
Colchester U *(Free on 12/7/2004) FL 33 FLC 2 FAC 3 Others 1*

DAWSON Andrew (Andy)
Born: Northallerton, 20 October 1978
Height: 5'9" **Weight:** 10.2
Both of Andy's seasons at Hull have now culminated in promotion and last term, as in 2003-04, he gave a series of assured performances to maintain his place as one of the favourites amongst the KC Stadium crowd. Rather than undermine his authority, the introduction of Roland Edge was an addition of worthy competition and meant that the Hull squad is very fortunate to have two top quality left-backs.
Nottingham F *(From trainee on 31/10/1995) FLC 1*
Scunthorpe U *(£70,000 on 18/12/1998) FL 192+3/8 FLC 6 FAC 12/1 Others 12/2*
Hull C *(Free on 1/7/2003) FL 66+1/3 FLC 0+1 FAC 4*

Aidan Davison

DAWSON Kevin Edward
Born: Northallerton, 18 June 1981
Height: 6'0" **Weight:** 10.10
Kevin was forced to sit out the first half of the 2004-5 campaign through injury. By the time he returned Chesterfield's back four was well established and the competitive and likeable full back made only one League One appearance, at Walsall in January. Typically, he performed well in that game, but he was released by the Spireites in the summer.
Nottingham F *(From trainee on 25/6/1998) FL 8+3 FAC 1*
Barnet *(Loaned on 9/3/2001) FL 5*
Chesterfield *(Free on 8/8/2002) FL 49+2/1 FLC 3 FAC 2 Others 2*

DAWSON Michael Richard
Born: Northallerton, 18 November 1983
Height: 6'2" **Weight:** 12.12
International Honours: E: U21-7; Yth
This young Nottingham Forest central defender had a late start to the season due to injury. When he returned to the side in October he was reappointed captain and continued to impress with some mature performances in a struggling Championship side. He was allowed to move to Tottenham in the January transfer window but his debut in the Premiership was delayed due to a shin injury. Full of confidence on the ball and good aerial ability, Michael possesses a good footballing brain and natural leadership qualities.
Nottingham F *(From trainee on 23/11/2000) FL 82+1/7 FLC 5 FAC 2 Others 1*
Tottenham H *(Signed on 31/1/2005) PL 5*

DAY Christopher (Chris) Nicholas
Born: Walthamstow, 28 July 1975
Height: 6'3" **Weight:** 13.6
International Honours: E: U21-6; Yth (UEFA-U18 '93)
This experienced goalkeeper was first choice for Queen's Park Rangers at the start of last season and did not miss a game until early January. However, he then lost his place to Simon Royce and in February he was loaned out to Preston where he covered for injuries. He impressed during his stay at Deepdale but

a longer-term deal could not be arranged and he returned to Loftus Road.
Tottenham H *(From trainee on 16/4/1993) Others 4*
Crystal Palace *(£225,000 + on 9/8/1996) FL 24 FLC 2 FAC 2*
Watford *(£225,000 on 18/7/1997) P/FL 11 FLC 1 Others 1*
Lincoln C *(Loaned on 4/12/2000) FL 14 Others 4*
Queens Park Rgrs *(Free on 24/7/2001) FL 87 FLC 6 FAC 2 Others 5*
Preston NE *(Loaned on 23/2/2005) FL 6*

DAY Jamie Robert
Born: High Wycombe, 7 May 1986
Height: 5'9" **Weight:** 10.7
This talented Peterborough youngster spent much of last term developing in the reserves and also had a loan spell with Crawley Town early in the campaign. Jamie stepped up to make his senior debut in the home game against Doncaster Rovers in February when he came on as a second-half substitute. The skilful left winger missed the closing stages of the season with a cartilage injury.
Peterborough U *(From trainee on 19/8/2003) FL 0+1*

DAY Rhys
Born: Bridgend, 31 August 1982
Height: 6'2" **Weight:** 13.6
Club Honours: AMC '02
International Honours: W: U21-11; Yth
Although a favourite of the Mansfield Town fans, Rhys was left out of the team at the start of last term in favour of Dave Artell. However, he returned to the line-up when Alex John-Baptiste was moved into midfield, stepping into his favoured central defensive position. Illness and injury then kept him out from October and it was not until March that he returned to action. A talented central defender who is effective in the air, he was particularly missed at set pieces where his surges forward regularly unsettle opposing defences.
Manchester C *(From trainee on 21/9/1999)*
Blackpool *(Loaned on 31/12/2001) FL 4+5 FAC 0+1 Others 3*
Mansfield T *(Free on 29/11/2002) FL 74+8/10 FLC 1+1 FAC 5+1 Others 5/2*

DEANE Brian Christopher
Born: Leeds, 7 February 1968
Height: 6'3" **Weight:** 12.7
International Honours: E: 3; B-3
Brian returned to Leeds at the age of 36 after a seven-year break from Elland Road. He was expected to be cover for the attack but more often than not ended up leading the line. Goals were few and far between for the veteran target man but he enjoyed one glorious November afternoon with a four-goal haul in the 6-1 rout of Queen's Park Rangers. He often played through the pain barrier and spent some time in an oxygen chamber after sustaining a hamstring injury during the 2-2 home draw against Watford just four days after his demolition of QPR. He also suffered a nasty shoulder injury but made a rapid recovery much to the delight of manager Kevin Blackwell who hailed Brian as a model professional. On transfer-deadline day Brian made a surprise move to Premiership-bound Sunderland to add his vast experience to the Wearsiders' promotion push. He proved his worth in only his second game when he entered the fray as a substitute in the vital promotion clash at Ipswich and almost immediately set up Stephen Elliott's equaliser.
Doncaster Rov *(From juniors on 14/12/1985) FL 59+7/12 FLC 3 FAC 2+1/1 Others 2+2*
Sheffield U *(£30,000 on 19/7/1988) P/FL 197/82 FLC 16/11 FAC 23+1/11 Others 2/2*
Leeds U *(£2,900,000 on 14/7/1993) PL 131+7/32 FLC 8+3/2 FAC 13+3/4 Others 3*
Sheffield U *(£1,500,000 on 29/7/1997) FL 24/11 FLC 4/2 FAC 1 (£1,000,000 to Benfica, Portugal on 15/1/1998)*
Middlesbrough *(£3,000,000 on 16/10/1998) PL 72+15/18 FLC 4+1 FAC 3/1*
Leicester C *(£150,000 on 30/11/2001) P/FL 44+8/19 FLC 2 FAC 2*
West Ham U *(Free on 31/10/2003) FL 9+17/6 FAC 3/1 Others 0+3*
Leeds U *(Free on 23/7/2004) FL 23+8/6 FLC 1+1/1*
Sunderland *(Free on 24/3/2005) FL 0+4*

DEARDEN Kevin Charles
Born: Luton, 8 March 1970
Height: 5'11" **Weight:** 13.4
Whilst concentrating on his coaching role, this experienced 'keeper filled in for Torquay when required, despite his mobility being limited by continuing knee problems that finally led to his retirement from the game. An excellent shot-stopper who also communicates well and marshals his back four effectively, his professional attitude made him a popular player throughout his lengthy career.
Tottenham H *(From trainee on 5/8/1988) P/FL 0+1 FLC 1*
Cambridge U *(Loaned on 9/3/1989) FL 15*
Hartlepool U *(Loaned on 31/8/1989) FL 10*
Swindon T *(Loaned on 23/3/1990) FL 1*
Peterborough U *(Loaned on 24/8/1990) FL 7*
Hull C *(Loaned on 10/1/1991) FL 3*
Rochdale *(Loaned on 16/8/1991) FL 2*
Birmingham C *(Loaned on 19/3/1992) FL 12*
Brentford *(Free on 30/9/1993) FL 205 FLC 17 FAC 13 Others 19*
Barnet *(Loaned on 5/2/1999) FL 1*
Wrexham *(Free on 4/6/1999) FL 81 FLC 3 FAC 6*
Torquay U *(Free on 9/8/2001) FL 98+2 FLC 3 FAC 1 Others 2+1*

DE BOLLA Grant **Marcus (Mark)**
Born: Camberwell, 1 January 1983
Height: 5'7" **Weight:** 11.9
A striker with pace and a powerful shot, Mark formed promising partnerships with a series of colleagues at Chesterfield last term. His maiden goal – against Sheffield Wednesday in February – was met with widespread relief, since he had done everything but score in the months before! Mark missed the season's end through injury but will be back to fight for a place in 2005-06.
Aston Villa *(From trainee on 17/4/2000)*
Charlton Ath *(Signed on 25/1/2001)*
Chesterfield *(Loaned on 11/9/2003) FL 2+1 Others 1*
Chesterfield *(Free on 5/3/2004) FL 16+17/4 FLC 1 FAC 0+1 Others 0+1*

DEEN Ahmed Nuru
Born: Sierra Leone, 30 June 1985
Height: 5'9" **Weight:** 11.5
One of several promising youngsters on the books at Peterborough, Ahmed spent time on loan with Hornchurch last season, featuring in their line-up for the FA Cup first round tie against Boston United. He made his senior debut with a brief appearance as a substitute at Torquay in February and featured in a handful of games towards the end of the campaign. Ahmed is a left back who reads the game well and is quick to recover in the tackle when required.
Peterborough U *(From trainee at Leicester C on 9/8/2004) FL 4+1*

DEENEY Saul
Born: Londonderry, 12 March 1983
Height: 6'1" **Weight:** 12.10
International Honours: RoI: U21-2; Yth
This rapidly developing young 'keeper made excellent progress with Notts County last term, establishing himself as first choice at Meadow Lane and producing some wonderful match-winning performances. Saul made some truly outstanding reaction saves and was rewarded in June when he received his first start for the Republic of Ireland U21s against Israel.
Notts Co *(From trainee on 8/9/2000) FL 41+1 FLC 2 FAC 4*

Jermain Defoe

DEFOE Jermain Colin
Born: Beckton, 7 October 1982
Height: 5'7" **Weight:** 10.4
International Honours: E: 12; U21-23; Yth; Sch
Last term proved to be another superb season for this prolific striker who now features as a regular in the full England international squad. Minor injuries prevented his selection in all 38 Premiership games but nonetheless he netted 22 goals in all competitions. Jermain is quick, possesses good ball control and can play the role of provider to his strike partner. He can score goals from long range but is just as happy to take on the last defender. However, he needs to maintain his consistency across a whole campaign for Spurs to fully benefit from his immense talent.
West Ham U *(£400,000 + from trainee at Charlton Ath on 15/10/1999) P/FL 62+31/29 FLC 6+1/6 FAC 4+1/6*
Bournemouth *(Loaned on 26/10/2000) FL 27+2/18 FAC 1/1 Others 1*
Tottenham H *(£7,000,000 + on 2/2/2004) PL 42+8/20 FLC 2+2/5 FAC 5/4*

DE GOEY Eduard (Ed) Franciscus
Born: Gouda, Holland, 20 December 1966
Height: 6'6" **Weight:** 15.0
Club Honours: FLC '98; ECWC '98; ESC '98; FAC '00; CS '00
International Honours: Holland: 31; U21-17
This experienced 'keeper remained as first choice for Stoke last season, only losing his place due to an unfortunate injury at Reading. A good shot-stopper and strong in the air, he gave many a fine performance in the Potters' goal but was a permanent resident on the bench after Steve Simonsen established himself.
Chelsea *(£2,250,000 from Feyenoord, Holland, ex Sparta Rotterdam, on 10/7/1997) PL 123 FLC 5 FAC 13+1 Others 37*
Stoke C *(Free on 1/8/2003) FL 54 FLC 1*

DE LA CRUZ Bernardo **Ulises**
Born: Piqulucho, Ecuador, 8 February 1974
Height: 5'11" **Weight:** 11.12
International Honours: Ecuador: 78
Ulises is a right-sided player with attacking instincts who is capable of playing in midfield or at full back. He is strong defensively and is most effective when played in a wing-back role, moving down the flank to deliver an accurate cross into the box. He enjoyed an extended run in the team last term when Martin Laursen suffered a knee problem,

necessitating a defensive reshuffle with Mark Delaney moving into the middle, and responded with some steady, reliable performances. Ulises was once again a regular at international level for Ecuador.
Hibernian *(£700,000 from Liga Deportiva Universitaria, Ecuador, on 18/6/2001) SL 25+7/2 SLC 2 SC 2+2/1 Others 2*
Aston Villa *(£1,500,000 on 2/8/2002) PL 62+20/1 FLC 6+1/1 FAC 2*

DELANEY Damien
Born: Cork, 20 July 1981
Height: 6'3" **Weight:** 13.10
International Honours: RoI: U21-1; Yth
Peter Taylor's first signing for Hull again proved to be an extremely sound investment as Damien was one of the stalwarts of the Tigers historic second successive promotion in their centenary season. He missed only three games in City's League One campaign due to undergoing keyhole surgery to a knee injury in September. Damien provided the left side of an outstanding central-defensive partnership with Leon Cort as the young duo applied themselves with admirable determination to establish the necessary foundation for promotion. Damien's only goal came in the impressive 4-0 win at Bournemouth.
Leicester C *(£50,000 from Cork C on 9/11/2000) PL 5+3 FLC 1 FAC 1+1*
Stockport Co *(Loaned on 15/11/2001) FL 10+2/1*
Huddersfield T *(Loaned on 28/3/2002) FL 1+1*
Mansfield T *(Loaned on 6/9/2002) FL 7*
Hull C *(£50,000 on 18/10/2002) FL 119/4 FLC 2 FAC 5*

DELANEY Mark Anthony
Born: Fishguard, 13 May 1976
Height: 6'1" **Weight:** 11.7
International Honours: W: 33
Mark is a tough-tackling defender who normally plays at right back for Aston Villa. He is reliable, defensively composed and strong when it comes to going forward. His trademark is without doubt his sliding tackles and steady defending. He adds a different dimension to the right flank with his darting forward bursts and accurate in-swinging crosses. Early on last term Mark was switched to a role in the centre of the Villa defence playing alongside Olof Mellberg and he adjusted well, impressing with some very accomplished displays. In general he was a regular last season with the exception of a spell on the sidelines with a knee injury. Mark continued to represent Wales at international level during the campaign.
Cardiff C *(Free from Carmarthen on 3/7/1998) FL 28 FLC 2 FAC 5/1*
Aston Villa *(£250,000 + on 10/3/1999) PL 132+14/1 FLC 9+3 FAC 5+1 Others 13*

DELAP Rory John
Born: Sutton Coldfield, 6 July 1976
Height: 6'0" **Weight:** 12.10
Club Honours: AMC '97
International Honours: RoI: 11; B-1; U21-4
A quality footballer, good in the tackle, Rory can hit a well-struck pass and moves the ball effectively, but sometimes seems to have a need to develop more focus. A near fixture in a dysfunctional Southampton midfield last term under the management of Paul Sturrock and Steve Wigley, the highlight of his season was a brace of headed goals in the 2-2 draw at Arsenal in October. Soon after Harry Redknapp arrived at St Mary's Rory was given an extended run as right wing back, although this was not a huge success.
Carlisle U *(From trainee on 18/7/1994) FL 40+25/7 FLC 4+1 FAC 0+3 Others 12+2*
Derby Co *(£500,000 + on 6/2/1998) PL 97+6/11 FLC 7/2 FAC 2+1*
Southampton *(£3,000,000 + on 21/7/2001) PL 106+10/5 FLC 7+1 FAC 7+1 Others 1+1*

DELOUMEAUX Eric Jean
Born: Montbeliard, France, 12 May 1973
Height: 5'10" **Weight:** 11.13
This Coventry City midfielder had a

Mark Delaney

hamstring injury in the early part of the 2004-05 season and when he recovered his fitness he was given few chances to stake a claim for a place, starting just twice. He was released in January and signed for SPL club Livingston where he featured more regularly, scoring his only goal in the 1-1 draw at Dundee United in April.
Motherwell *(£100,000 from Le Havre, France, ex Gueugnon, on 9/11/2001) SL 22+1 SC 1*
Aberdeen *(£50,000 on 12/7/2002) SL 40+3/4 SLC 4+1/1 SC 2 Others 4*
Coventry C *(Free on 16/1/2004) FL 20+1/1 FLC 1 FAC 2*

DE MERIT Jay Michael
Born: Green Bay, Wisconsin, USA, 4 December 1979
Height: 6'1" **Weight:** 13.5
Watford's 'find of the season', Jay came on trial after impressing for Ryman League club Northwood in a pre-season friendly. He proved a quick learner and signed a long-term contract in November. A strong tackler, good in the air, Jay earned the chance of a run in the first team in January and seemed to improve with every match. He was 'Man of the Match' against Fulham in the FA Cup, and outstanding against Liverpool in the Carling Cup, when his direct opponent was Champions' League winner Fernando Morientes. His cup performances won him the 'Carling New Talent' award for the season.
Watford *(Free from Northwood, ex University of Illinois, Chicago Fire, on 13/8/2004) FL 22+2/3 FLC 5+1 FAC 2*

DEMPSTER John
Born: Kettering, 1 April 1983
Height: 6'0" **Weight:** 11.10
Club Honours: Div 3 '03
International Honours: S: U21-1; Yth
John's first-team opportunities were fairly limited at Rushden last term. At the start of the season he was used in midfield with some success, notably producing a 'Man of the Match' display against Cheltenham. However, he is more comfortable operating in the centre of the defence, but competition from more experienced players meant that he spent much of the season on the substitutes' bench.
Rushden & Diamonds *(From juniors on 24/7/2001) FL 31+21/1 FLC 1+2 FAC 1+1 Others 2*

DENTON Samuel (Sam) Elliot
Born: Kippax, 31 July 1986
Height: 6'2" **Weight:** 13.2
This young centre half was given his Bradford City debut in the LDV Vans Trophy tie against Accrington last season. Selected at right back, Sam was spared from criticism after the League One side went out of the competition and later in the campaign he was loaned out to Unibond League outfit Guiseley to gain some first-team experience.
Bradford C *(Trainee) Others 1*

DE PEDRO Javier Francisco
Born: Logrono, Spain, 4 August 1973
Height: 5'11" **Weight:** 12.3
International Honours: Spain: 12
Javier's long absence from top class football was evident in the pre-season period, when he suffered an injury, but he was still selected on the left wing for Blackburn's opening game against West Brom. Unable to adjust to the pace he was taken off at half time and apart from a brief substitute appearance and a Carling Cup game, he never played again, joining Perugia in January. Javier's casual, almost walking, style looked alien to the Rovers but he had a left foot that could open up a defence with one quick flick.
Blackburn Rov *(Free from Real Sociedad, Spain, on 16/7/2004) PL 1+1 FLC 1*

DERBYSHIRE Matthew (Matt) Anthony
Born: Great Harwood, 14 April 1986
Height: 5'10" **Weight:** 11.1
It was something of a surprise when this slim, mobile youngster was given a first-team squad number for Blackburn at the end of the season, but it was just reward for his goals at reserve-team level. A prolific scorer throughout his career Matt was given a brief outing with the first team in the last Premiership home game against Fulham.
Blackburn Rov *(Signed from Great Harwood T on 20/4/2004) PL 0+1*

Shaun Derry

DERRY Shaun Peter
Born: Nottingham, 6 December 1977
Height: 5'10" **Weight:** 10.13
Club Honours: Div 3 '98
This hard-working central midfielder made one just one Premiership start for Crystal Palace against Manchester City in September, plus a few outings from the bench before going on loan to Nottingham Forest in December. Shaun impressed at the City Ground with his combative play and was on the verge of extending his stay when he was recalled by Palace who sold him to Leeds in February. He became an instant hero for the Whites after netting with a late winner on his home debut against West Ham. That was followed by a point-saving free kick against Wolves in his next Elland Road outing. But his season came to an early end when he received a three-match ban after being sent off in the penultimate away game of the campaign at Queen's Park Rangers.
Notts Co *(From trainee on 13/4/1996) FL 76+3/4 FLC 4+1 FAC 6+1/1 Others 3*
Sheffield U *(£700,000 on 26/1/1998) FL 62+10 FLC 4 FAC 7/1*
Portsmouth *(£300,000 + on 16/3/2000) FL 48+1/1 FLC 4 FAC 1+1*
Crystal Palace *(£400,000 on 6/8/2002) P/FL 62+21/3 FLC 9 FAC 4 Others 1+2*
Nottingham F *(Loaned on 24/12/2004) FL 7 FAC 1*
Leeds U *(Signed on 18/2/2005) FL 7/2*

DEVANEY Martin Thomas
Born: Cheltenham, 1 June 1980
Height: 5'10" **Weight:** 11.12
This long-serving Cheltenham Town player matured last season, showing himself to be an inventive player with greater awareness and much-improved decision making. Midway through the season manager John Ward switched him to the left-hand side of midfield and as a result he proved highly effective and a regular source of goals as both provider and finisher. Martin ended the campaign as joint-top scorer for the Robins with ten goals.
Coventry C *(From trainee on 4/6/1997)*
Cheltenham T *(Free on 5/8/1999) FL 154+49/38 FLC 5+1/1 FAC 6+3/2 Others 8+2/2*

DEVLIN Paul John
Born: Birmingham, 14 April 1972
Height: 5'9" **Weight:** 11.5
Club Honours: AIC '95
International Honours: S: 10; B-1
Paul's season was disrupted by a serious hamstring injury in September, along with an ongoing toe problem. He returned to the Watford right wing in December, but after a three-month lay-off he lacked his normal pace and the confidence to take on opponents, although he played well at Anfield in the Carling Cup semi-final. In March he finally bowed to the inevitable and underwent an operation on his toe that ruled him out for the rest of the season.
Notts Co *(£40,000 from Stafford R on 22/2/1992) FL 132+9/25 FLC 11+1/1 FAC 8/1 Others 17+2/6*
Birmingham C *(Signed on 29/2/1996) FL 61+15/28 FLC 8+1/4 FAC 3+1/2*
Sheffield U *(£200,000 + on 13/3/1998) FL 122+25/24 FLC 9+3/4 FAC 8/1 Others 2*
Notts Co *(Loaned on 23/10/1998) FL 5*
Birmingham C *(£200,000 on 8/2/2002) P/FL 31+16/4 FAC 1 Others 2*
Watford *(£150,000 on 12/9/2003) FL 54+2/4 FLC 4+1 FAC 4*

DE VOS Jason Richard
Born: Ontario, Canada, 2 January 1974
Height: 6'4" **Weight:** 13.7
Club Honours: Div 2 '03
International Honours: Canada: 49; (Gold Cup 2000); U23-14; Yth
Jason joined Ipswich during the summer of 2004 and played in every Championship game apart, ironically, from the away trip to Wigan which he missed because he was suspended. He provided a calming influence at the heart of the defence and won most of the aerial challenges. Jason took over as team captain when Jim Magilton was rested and built up a good defensive understanding with Richard Naylor. He also added further appearances for Canada in their efforts to qualify for the next World Cup, but once that failed he decided he would retire from the international scene.
Darlington *(Free from Montreal Impact, Canada on 29/11/1996) FL 43+1/5 FLC 3/1 FAC 4 Others 1*
Dundee U *(£400,000 on 12/10/1998) SL 91+2/2 SLC 5+1 SC 12*
Wigan Ath *(£500,000 on 8/8/2001) FL 87+3/15 FLC 6 FAC 2*
Ipswich T *(Free on 2/6/2004) FL 45/3 FLC 1 FAC 1 Others 2*

DE VRIES Mark
Born: Paramaribo, Surinam, 24 August 1975
Height: 6'3" **Weight:** 12.1
This tall striker featured regularly for SPL club Hearts last term before signing for Leicester along with his colleague Alan Maybury during the January transfer window. Injuries earlier in the campaign meant that it took Mark a while to reach full fitness. He has a good touch for such a tall man and is adept at turning his marker and unleashing a fierce shot on goal. Sometimes used as a lone striker, he was always willing to work selflessly for the team, and finally broke his goal-scoring duck with a close-range header in the home win over Millwall in April. With a full pre-season under his belt, Mark will be hoping to show the City fans his best form in 2005-06.
Heart of Midlothian *(Free from Dordrecht 90, Holland on 1/6/2002) SL 62+10/29 SLC 6/1 SC 3 Others 8+1/4*
Leicester C *(Signed on 16/1/2005) FL 9+7/1 FAC 2+2*

DE ZEEUW Adrianus (Arjan) Johannes
Born: Castricum, Holland, 16 April 1970
Height: 6'1" **Weight:** 13.11
Club Honours: Div 1 '03
Arjan continued to make good progress at Portsmouth last term when he was also the club captain. A firm favourite of the Pompey fans, he was a rock at the heart of the defence and produced a series of fine performances to lead the club away from the relegation zone to a position of safety. He scored three Premiership goals, including one in the 4-1 victory over local rivals Southampton in April.
Barnsley *(£250,000 from Telstar, Holland, ex Vitesse 22, on 3/11/1995) P/FL 138/7 FLC 12 FAC 14*
Wigan Ath *(Free on 2/7/1999) FL 126/6 FLC 8 FAC 6 Others 6*
Portsmouth *(Free on 3/7/2002) P/FL 103+3/5 FLC 6 FAC 6*

DIALLO Drissa
Born: Nouadhibou, Mauritania, 4 January 1973
Height: 6'1" **Weight:** 12.0
International Honours: Guinea
Drissa was a vital part of the Ipswich defence for the first half of last season. Slotting in at right back, his aerial ability was an asset at set pieces and he settled in well alongside Jason De Vos and Richard Naylor. However, he picked up a hamstring injury in the game at Queen's Park Rangers which proved difficult to overcome and virtually ruled him out for the rest of the campaign. He made a a few substitute appearances at the end and played in the first leg of the play-off semi-final but, after missing so many games, he was not really match fit.
Burnley *(Free from KV Mechelen, Belgium, ex RC Tilleur, Sedan, AS Brevannes, on 9/1/2003) FL 14/1 FAC 4/1*
Ipswich T *(Free on 6/6/2003) FL 39+6 FLC 3 Others 1*

DIAO Salif Alassane
Born: Kedougou, Senegal, 10 February 1977
Height: 6'0" **Weight:** 11.7
Club Honours: FLC '03
International Honours: Senegal
Always a bit-part squad player since his arrival at Anfield three years ago, this midfielder remained an occasional performer for Liverpool last season with only four starts in the Premiership to show for his efforts, although he scored a rare goal in the Reds' 3-0 victory at Millwall in the Carling Cup. In January he was farmed out on loan to Birmingham City and made his debut in the 2-1 home defeat by Fulham when he looked neat and tidy but lacking in match fitness. A nagging calf injury then limited his participation to just one more game.
Liverpool *(£5,000,000 from Sedan, France, ex Monaco, on 9/8/2002) PL 19+18/1 FLC 7+1/1 FAC 1+1 Others 8+6/1*
Birmingham C *(Loaned on 18/1/2005) PL 2*

DIAZ Ramon **Emiliano**
Born: Naples, Italy, 22 June 1983
Height: 5'7" **Weight:** 10.2
Emiliano is a skilful midfield player who linked up with his father Ramon Diaz at Oxford last term and made a handful of first-team appearances in April. Used mostly in a wide-right role, he showed plenty of talent on the ball, but found it difficult to adjust to the physical demands of League Two football.
Oxford U *(Free from Deportivo Colonia, Uruguay, ex River Plate, Avellino (loan), River Plate, on 18/2/2005) FL 2+5*

DIBBLE Andrew (Andy) Gerald
Born: Cwmbran, 8 May 1965
Height: 6'3" **Weight:** 16.8
International Honours: W: 3; U21-3; Yth; Sch
This experienced goalkeeper did not enjoy the best fortune with injuries at Wrexham last term. Andy suffered a dislocated finger at Tranmere in September, and although regaining his place between the sticks from Matt Baker in early December, a thigh strain suffered in the League match at Sheffield Wednesday at the turn of the year proved to be his final appearance of the season. He was released by the club in May.
Cardiff C *(From apprentice on 27/8/1982) FL 62 FLC 4 FAC 4*
Luton T *(£125,000 on 16/7/1984) FL 30 FLC 4 FAC 1 Others 1*
Sunderland *(Loaned on 21/2/1986) FL 12*
Huddersfield T *(Loaned on 26/3/1987) FL 5*
Manchester C *(£240,000 on 1/7/1988) P/FL 113+3 FLC 14 FAC 8+1 Others 2*
Aberdeen *(Loaned on 20/10/1990) SL 5*
Middlesbrough *(Loaned on 20/2/1991) FL 19 Others 2*
Bolton W *(Loaned on 6/9/1991) FL 4 Others 1*
Bolton W *(Loaned on 27/9/1991) FL 9*
West Bromwich A *(Loaned on 27/2/1992) FL 9*
Glasgow Rgrs *(Signed on 11/3/1997) SL 7*
Luton T *(Free on 15/9/1997) FL 1 FLC 2*
Middlesbrough *(Free on 30/1/1998) FL 2 (Free to Altrincham during 1998 close season)*
Hartlepool U *(Free on 25/3/1999) FL 6 FLC 2 Others 2+1*
Carlisle U *(Loaned on 8/10/1999) FL 2*
Stockport Co *(Free on 10/8/2000) FL 22+1 FLC 0+1 FAC 1*
Wrexham *(Free on 9/8/2002) FL 83 FLC 3 FAC 1 Others 1*

DICHIO Daniele (Danny) Salvatore Ernest
Born: Hammersmith, 19 October 1974
Height: 6'3" **Weight:** 12.3
Club Honours: Div 1 '99
International Honours: E: U21-1; Sch
This experienced striker scored some valuable goals for Millwall last term, finishing the campaign with a respectable tally of ten strikes in Championship matches. Tall and with good strength, Danny leads the front line with ability. He can hold the ball up and direct headers perfectly to bring in supporting players.
Queens Park Rgrs *(From trainee on 17/5/1993) P/FL 56+19/20 FLC 6/2 FAC 3+3 (Free to Sampdoria, Italy during 1997 close season)*
Barnet *(Loaned on 24/3/1994) FL 9/2*
Sunderland *(£750,000, via loan spell at Lecce, Italy on 28/1/1998) P/FL 20+56/11 FLC 11+1/6 FAC 3+3/1 Others 1+2*

Danny Dichio

West Bromwich A *(Loaned on 23/8/2001) FL 3/2*
West Bromwich A *(£1,250,000 on 30/11/2001) P/FL 47+16/12 FLC 3+1 FAC 6/4*
Derby Co *(Loaned on 17/10/2003) FL 6/1*
Millwall *(£200,000 + on 13/1/2004) FL 42+4/17 FAC 5/1 Others 0+1*

DICKINSON Carl Matthew
Born: Swadlincote, 31 March 1987
Height: 6'0" **Weight:** 12.0
This versatile midfielder or left back was a regular for Stoke's reserves last term and caught the eye with his determined play. He featured just once at first-team level, coming on as a last-minute substitution against Coventry in December.
Stoke C *(Trainee) FL 0+1*

DICKMAN Jonjo
Born: Hexham, 22 September 1981
Height: 5'8" **Weight:** 10.8
This pacy young midfielder was a regular in Sunderland's reserve team last term, captaining the side on occasions. However, he elected to move on to Darlington, for whom he made his debut against Boston United in early March. He impressed with some enthusiastic play in the centre of the park and after a brief spell out with injury he returned to score his first goal for the Quakers with a stunning volley against Cheltenham Town on the final day of the season. Jonjo also displayed uncanny perception when intercepting opponents' passes.
Sunderland *(From juniors on 2/11/1998) PL 0+1*
York C *(Loaned on 25/2/2004) FL 2*
Darlington *(Free on 28/2/2005) FL 8/1*

DICKOV Paul
Born: Livingston, 1 November 1972
Height: 5'6" **Weight:** 11.9
Club Honours: ECWC '94
International Honours: S: 10; U21-4; Yth; Sch
In an age when spectators are sceptical about whether players earn their wages no one begrudged Paul a penny of his rewards for Blackburn last term. Isolated up front he ran non-stop, always seeking to make himself available and close down defenders throughout the game. Incredibly for much of the season he was nursing a groin strain that made training difficult. Despite not playing in the last half-dozen games he finished comfortably as top scorer. At the Reebok he not only scored a goal of great quality, but also gave a display of totally committed energy that can seldom have been bettered.
Arsenal *(From trainee on 28/12/1990) PL 6+15/3 FLC 2+2/3*
Luton T *(Loaned on 8/10/1993) FL 8+7/1*
Brighton & Hove A *(Loaned on 23/3/1994) FL 8/5*
Manchester C *(£1,000,000 on 23/8/1996) P/FL 105+51/33 FLC 9+4/5 FAC 5+4/1 Others 3/2*
Leicester C *(Signed on 22/2/2002) P/FL 81+8/32 FLC 4/2 FAC 4/3*
Blackburn Rov *(£150,000 on 16/6/2004) PL 27+2/9 FAC 6/1*

DICKSON Ryan Anthony
Born: Saltash, 14 December 1986
Height: 5'10" **Weight:** 11.5
A product of Plymouth Argyle's youth set-up, Ryan made his first-team debut from the bench against Wigan last September and went on to make his full debut in the following game against Rotherham. Although the cultured left-sided midfield player added one further appearance all season, he will have learnt plenty from his experiences.
Plymouth Arg *(Trainee) FL 2+1*

DIMECH Luke Anthony
Born: Malta, 11 January 1977
Height: 5'11" **Weight:** 13.4
International Honours: Malta: 37
Luke started the 2004-05 season on the bench for Mansfield, and after an unsuccessful spell at right back he settled into the centre-half position where he played well as cover for injured regulars Rhys Day and Dave Artell. He never gave less than 100 per cent and was always a reliable replacement when required. Luke also continued to represent Malta at international level during the campaign. He was released in the summer at the end of his contract.
Mansfield T *(Free from Shamrock Rov, ex Lincoln C trainee, Sliema, Birkirkara, on 7/8/2003) FL 36+9/1 FLC 2 FAC 3+1 Others 2*

DINNING Tony
Born: Wallsend, 12 April 1975
Height: 6'0" **Weight:** 12.11
Club Honours: Div 2 '03; AMC '04
This composed midfield player found himself surplus to requirements at Wigan last term and began the season on loan at Ipswich where he covered for Jim Magilton. In October he went out on loan again and enjoyed an impressive spell at Bristol City, prompting a permanent transfer. However, his form then dipped and he was loaned once more, this time to Port Vale. Tony made an impressive debut in the 2-2 draw at Hull and proceeded to guide the team away from the relegation zone. He scored three goals, including a blistering free kick in the 5-0 win over Barnsley.
Newcastle U *(From trainee on 1/10/1993)*
Stockport Co *(Free on 23/6/1994) FL*

Luke Dimech

159+32/25 FLC 12+5/3 FAC 4+7 Others 6+1/2
***Wolverhampton W** (£600,000 + on 22/9/2000) FL 35/6 FLC 1/1 FAC 1*
***Wigan Ath** (£750,000 on 7/9/2001) FL 79+5/12 FLC 5 FAC 3*
***Stoke C** (Loaned on 27/3/2002) FL 5 Others 3*
***Walsall** (Loaned on 20/11/2003) FL 2+3*
***Blackpool** (Loaned on 23/1/2004) FL 10/3 Others 3*
***Ipswich T** (Loaned on 9/8/2004) FL 3+4 FLC 2*
***Bristol C** (Free on 28/10/2004) FL 15+4 Others 1*
***Port Vale** (Loaned on 23/3/2005) FL 7/3*

DIOP Pape Bouba
Born: Dakar, Senegal, 28 January 1978
Height: 6'4" **Weight:** 15.7
International Honours: Senegal
This powerfully built midfielder made an immediate impact at Fulham last term. Normally operating in a defensive-midfield role, he proved to be an effective ball winner and also capable of scoring goals, as demonstrated by spectacular long-range efforts in the home games against Chelsea and Manchester United. His height proved useful and he headed crucial goals against West Brom and at Birmingham. He was also a regular in the Senegal international side throughout the season.
***Fulham** (Signed from RC Lens, France, on 30/7/2004) PL 29/6 FLC 3 FAC 3/1*

El Hadji Diouf

DIOP Youssouph (Youssou)
Born: Zinguinchor, Senegal, 5 May 1980
Height: 6'1" **Weight:** 12.7
This tall striker joined Kidderminster in the summer of 2004 after a successful pre-season trial. Competitive football, however, proved to be a different matter and he struggled to adapt to life in League Two. Following a change in management Youssou was released in December.
***Kidderminster Hrs** (Free from Toulouse, France, ex Laval, on 26/7/2004) FL 7+3 Others 0+1*

DIOUF El Hadji Ousseynou
Born: Dakar, Senegal, 15 January 1981
Height: 5'11" **Weight:** 11.11
Club Honours: FLC '03
International Honours: Senegal
One of the shrewdest signings of the season, El-Hadji had fallen out of favour at Liverpool and joined Bolton in a season-long loan deal last August. He made his debut as a substitute in the pressure-cooker atmosphere of a local 'derby' against Manchester United, and scored his first goal for the club in what was to be the first of many match-winning performances, in the 2-1 victory over Newcastle. He was at the peak of his game when the much publicised sending off against Portsmouth coincided with a downturn in Bolton's fortunes. Promptly restored to the starting line-up upon the completion of a ban, El-Hadji was the catalyst for a magnificent run of results during the final four months of the season. 'Man of the Match' performances in the victories over Birmingham and Arsenal, as well as several match-winning goals, ensured that he became a firm favourite with the Bolton fans. He finished the campaign as the club's top scorer with nine goals whilst continuing to feature for the Senegal national team.

iverpool *(£10,000,000 from RC Lens, ance, ex Sochaux, Rennes, on 17/7/2002) L 41+14/3 FLC 7/3 FAC 4 Others 9+5*
olton W *(Loaned on 20/8/2004) PL 23+4/9 C 2 FAC 1+2*

ISLEY Craig Edward
orn: Worksop, 24 August 1981
eight: 5'10" **Weight:** 11.0
raig enjoyed a fine pre-season with ristol Rovers, but unfortunately picked p an ankle injury, which meant that it as not until November that he made his rst start for the club. He proved an fective force in the centre of the park, s close control and forward runs aking him a firm favourite with the rates' supporters. Craig contributed five oals during the campaign including the pening strike in the 4-1 win over hester in December.
ansfield T *(From trainee on 23/6/1999) FL 06+35/16 FLC 2 FAC 9+1 Others 5*
istol Rov *(Free on 13/7/2004) FL 18+10/4 C 0+1 FAC 1 Others 5/1*

ISTIN Sylvain
orn: Paris, France, 16 December 1977
eight: 6'4" **Weight:** 13.10
left-footed centre back of composure nd authority, Sylvain was an ever-present r Manchester City in the Premiership st term when he was also club captain. e is a powerful, quick athlete who has oved himself at the highest level. He njoyed an impressive season and formed ne of the best central-defensive artnerships in the Premiership alongside chard Dunne.
ewcastle U *(Loaned from Paris St ermain, France, ex Tours, Guegnon, on /9/2001) PL 20+8 FLC 2 FAC 5*
anchester C *(£4,000,000 from Paris St ermain, France on 4/7/2002) PL 110/3 FLC FAC 7/1 Others 5*

IXON Jonathan (Jonny) mes
orn: Muria, Spain, 16 January 1984
eight: 5'9" **Weight:** 11.2
ycombe's young striker or winger ntinued to warm the bench last term, it the arrival of manager John Gorman November saw him spend two loan ells with Conference side Aldershot, nere he was a big success. After scoring ne goals in 12 games he was recalled in nuary and netted with a penalty for the nairboys in his first start of the season ainst Boston. Jonny continued to be a uad player, but started the last two mes of the campaign and subsequently cepted a new contract with the Adams rk club.
ycombe W *(From trainee on 14/2/2003) 20+26/6 FAC 1 Others 0+3/1*

DJE Ludovic
Born: Paris, France, 22 July 1977
Height: 6'4" **Weight:** 14.6
This giant central defender linked up with Stockport early in the new year and after signing a short-term deal he was a surprising inclusion in the line-up for the trip to Bradford City in March. He played 57 minutes of the game at Valley Parade before being replaced by Damien Allen. He made a substitute appearance in the 1-0 defeat at Tranmere shortly afterwards, before ending the season with a second start in the final day defeat at Walsall.
Stockport Co *(Free from Royal Francs Borains, Belgium, via trials at Grimsby T, Woking, Gillingham, ex Poissy, Creteil, Saint Denis/Saint Lev, Argentan, US Marseilles-Endoume-Catalans, Vreil, Paris St Germain, France on 24/3/2005) FL 2+1*

DJEMBA DJEMBA Eric Daniel
Born: Douala, Cameroon, 4 May 1981
Height: 5'9" **Weight:** 11.13
Club Honours: CS '03; FAC '04
International Honours: Cameroon: 26
A tough-tackling midfielder, Eric played in the opening four games of both the Premiership and Champions' League campaign for the Reds before being confined mostly to Carling Cup duties. His last performance came in the two FA

Craig Disley

Cup games against Exeter before he was transferred to Aston Villa during the January transfer window. However, he did not get his wish of more regular first-team football at Villa Park for he suffered a pulled hamstring in training and was mostly on the sidelines in the closing stages of the campaign.

Manchester U *(£3,500,000 + from Nantes, France on 29/7/2003) PL 13+7 FLC 5/1 FAC 2+1 Others 7+4/1*

Aston Villa *(£1,350,000 + on 31/1/2005) PL 4+2*

DJORKAEFF Youri

Born: Lyon, France, 9 March 1968
Height: 5'11" **Weight:** 11.6
International Honours: France: 82

When Blackburn manager Mark Hughes wanted to strengthen his side outside of the transfer windows he could only sign free agents, which was how Youri came to Ewood Park. A delightfully created goal for Brett Emerton on his debut against Aston Villa paled when he was part of the team which lost the next two games by four goals. A serious hamstring injury received in training kept him out for weeks and the club decided not to renew his contract when it expired at the end of December.

Bolton W *(Free from Kaiserslautern, Germany, ex Grenoble, Strasbourg, AS*

Scott Dobie (left)

ecember when Kirkland succumbed to ack problems. Although doubts were xpressed about his level of consistency, erzy's heroics in the European hampions' Cup final will ensure his lace in the club's history after his iraculous point-blank double save from ndrii Shevchenko at the end of extra me plus his two saves in the ensuing enalty shoot-out which put the seal on e Reds' amazing recovery from a 3-0 eficit at half time.

verpool (£4,850,000 from Feyenoord, olland, ex GKS Tychy, Sokol Tychy, on /8/2001) PL 119 FLC 9 FAC 7+1 Others 38

UDFIELD Lawrence .awrie) George
orn: Southwark, 7 May 1980
eight: 6'1" **Weight:** 13.9
though having to play something of a t-part role for Southend season behind st-choice strikers Freddy Eastwood and ayne Gray, Lawrie's hard work and eye r goal meant that he made some luable contributions from the bstitutes' bench. Possibly the most tural goal-scorer on the books at Roots ll, Lawrie just couldn't find the form to lodge either player from the line-up. will be hoping to win a regular place the side in 2005-06.

icester C *(Signed from Kettering T on /1997) PL 0+2*
coln C *(Loaned on 15/9/2000) FL 2+1*
esterfield *(Loaned on 14/12/2000) FL 10/3 Others 3+1/1*
ll C *(£190,000 on 2/7/2001) FL 39+20/13 2 FAC 2/2 Others 3*
rthampton T *(Signed on 14/3/2003) FL +9/4 FLC 1+1/1 FAC 0+1 Others 0+2/2*
uthend U *(Signed on 5/2/2004) FL +20/9 FLC 1 Others 4+5/3*

UFF Damien Anthony
rn: Dublin, 2 March 1979
ight: 5'10" **Weight:** 12.0
b Honours: FLC '02, '05; PL '05
ernational Honours: RoI: 54; B-1; ; Sch
bben or Duff?' That was the question many lips when the mercurial Dutch winger joined Chelsea but Jose urinho had the perfect solution – both them! The 'wing wizards' terrorised ences with their bewildering dribbling intuitive switching of flanks and even en Damien was forced onto his aker right side he was still standing. The magical winger scored sistently throughout the season – ably a clutch of very early goals – but saved his best effort for a late winner Old Trafford which ensured Chelsea's sage into the Carling Cup final. Unfortunately, Damien's injury jinx returned with a vengeance when a hamstring strain forced him to miss both legs of the crucial Champions' League semi-final against Liverpool, when his guile and wing wizardry were sadly missed. Carling Cup and Premiership-winners' medals were a fair reward for a dazzling season from a player who has developed into a cult hero with Blues' fans in his two seasons at Stamford Bridge.

Blackburn Rov *(Signed from Lourdes Celtic on 5/3/1996) P/FL 157+27/27 FLC 16+1/5 FAC 13+5/2 Others 4/1*
Chelsea *(£17,000,000 on 26/7/2003) PL 45+8/11 FLC 7+1/2 FAC 1+2 Others 15+6/3*

DUFF Michael James
Born: Belfast, 11 January 1978
Height: 6'1" **Weight:** 11.8
Club Honours: FAT '98; NC '99
International Honours: NI: 4
Burnley manager Steve Cotterill returned to his former club Cheltenham to sign Michael, and the apparent gamble of moving the player two divisions up the League certainly paid off, as he became an integral part of the Clarets' solid back line. Most often appearing at right back, he also stood-in on occasions in central defence and played a few games in a more forward role in midfield. An enthusiastic competitor with no shortage of skill, he certainly benefited from the experience of John McGreal and Frank Sinclair alongside him at the back and can only improve further as he gains more Championship experience.

Cheltenham T *(From trainee on 17/8/1996) FL 201/12 FLC 6 FAC 15 Others 9*
Burnley *(£30,000 on 8/7/2004) FL 37+5 FLC 4 FAC 2*

DUFF Shane Joseph
Born: Wroughton, 2 April 1982
Height: 6'1" **Weight:** 12.10
International Honours: NI: U21-1
One of the success stories of Cheltenham Town's 2004-05 season, Shane graduated to first choice centre back following the departure of his brother Michael in the close season. He took his chance and displayed growing confidence and maturity, combining a thoughtful and composed attitude to defending with determination and competitiveness. He was a near ever-present in the side and established a fine partnership at the back with newcomer Gavin Caines. At the end of the season Shane received both the supporters' and players' 'Player of the Season' awards.

Cheltenham T *(From juniors on 20/10/2000) FL 73+5/2 FLC 1 FAC 1+1 Others 3*

DUFFY Richard Michael
Born: Swansea , 30 August 1985
Height: 5'10" **Weight:** 10.4
International Honours: W: U21-6; Yth
An early example of Steve Cotterill's Midas touch in the loan market, Richard joined Burnley from Portsmouth in September, and proved a talented and adaptable player during his two-month stay at Turf Moor. Primarily a defender, he was also called on in midfield and enjoyed the highlight of his Clarets' career playing as an emergency left winger when he scored the winning goal at Elland Road. Although most often named on the bench, he was a valuable squad member prior to his return to Fratton Park in November. Later in the season he went out on loan to Coventry where he featured regularly in the closing months showing himself to be a classy defender with cool distribution and good positional play.

Swansea C *(From trainee on 3/9/2002) FL 16+2/1 FAC 3+1 Others 1*
Portsmouth *(£300,000 on 26/1/2004) PL 0+1*
Burnley *(Loaned on 24/9/2004) FL 3+4/1 FLC 2*
Coventry C *(Loaned on 27/1/2005) FL 14 FAC 1*

DUFFY Robert James
Born: Swansea, 2 December 1982
Height: 6'1" **Weight:** 12.6
Club Honours: Div 3 '03
Robert managed just one first-team appearance for Rushden last term, fittingly against his hometown club Swansea City at Nene Park. The promising striker struggled to overcome a knee problem and then needed a hernia operation after returning from a loan spell with Southern League club Stamford. He was released by the club in the summer.

Rushden & Diamonds *(From juniors on 7/7/2000) FL 8+21/1 FLC 0+1 FAC 3+1/3 Others 1*

DUKE David
Born: Inverness, 7 November 1978
Height: 5'10" **Weight:** 11.3
David was once again in consistent form for Swindon last term when he was a near ever-present in the line-up. Usually employed on the left-hand side, either as a wing back or wide midfielder, he was always looking to get forward when opportunities arose.

Sunderland *(Free from Redby CA on 3/7/1997)*
Swindon T *(Free on 10/8/2000) FL 181+23/7 FLC 9+1 FAC 10+2/1 Others 7+2*

Damien Duff

DUKE Matthew (Matt)
Born: Sheffield, 16 June 1977
Height: 6'5" **Weight:** 13.4
Hull were left with only one senior 'keeper as the 2004-05 season approached and Matt eagerly accepted the offer of another chance in League football after a successful trial in a pre-season friendly at Alfreton. Although Boaz Myhill's consistent form meant he was largely restricted to the bench – making a total of four appearances – Matt nonetheless became an important member of the Hull squad that won promotion to the Championship at the first attempt.
Sheffield U *(Free from Alfreton T on 26/8/1999)*
Hull C *(£60,000 from Burton A on 23/7/2004) FL 1+1 FLC 1 Others 0+1*

DUNCAN Andrew (Andy)
Born: Hexham, 20 October 1977
Height: 5'11" **Weight:** 13.0
International Honours: E: Sch
Cambridge United's longest-serving player was a near ever-present last term and did his best to add some solidity to the U's defence. His consistent displays won him the supporters' 'Player of the Year' award, which was some consolation following the disappointment of the club's relegation to the Conference.
Manchester U *(From trainee on 10/7/1996)*
Cambridge U *(£20,000 on 9/1/1998) FL 233+9/6 FLC 10+2/1 FAC 16 Others 16*

DUNCAN Derek Henry Junior
Born: Newham, 23 April 1987
Height: 5'9" **Weight:** 10.12
This Leyton Orient youngster was mainly used as cover for Andy Scott last term and made the starting line-up on only a handful of occasions. Derek, who is a flying left winger with the ability to go past players and cross the ball, will be looking to break through to become a regular member of the first-team squad in 2005-06.
Leyton Orient *(Trainee) FL 6+10 FAC 0+1 Others 0+3*

DUNCUM Samuel (Sam)
Born: Sheffield, 18 February 1987
Height: 5'9" **Weight:** 11.2
A product of the Rotherham United youth scheme, Sam made his debut as a substitute in the 3-1 home defeat at the hands of Gillingham in March and went on to gain his first start in the final match of the season against Leeds. Sam is a speedy left-footed winger who is equally comfortable on either flank.
Rotherham U *(Trainee) FL 1+1*

DUNFIELD Terence (Terry)
Born: Vancouver, Canada, 20 February 1982
Height: 5'10" **Weight:** 11.6
International Honours: Canada: U23-1; Yth; E: Yth
Bury's attacking midfielder was used mainly as a substitute in the opening months of last season. Terry was then in and out of the side as the campaign progressed, starting seven games when he mainly deputised for David Flitcroft. The highlight of his season came in the game at Darlington in October when he capped a fine individual performance with his only goal of the season. In January he was stretchered off with a knee ligament injury in a home game against Leyton Orient, and he was eventually referred to the Lilleshall Rehabilitation Centre in a bid to clear up the problem.
Manchester C *(From trainee on 5/5/1999) PL 0+1*
Bury *(Loaned on 16/8/2002) FL 15/2 FLC 3*
Bury *(Free on 13/12/2002) FL 48+11/3 FLC 0+1 Others 3+1/1*

DUNN David John Ian
Born: Great Harwood, 27 December 1979
Height: 5'10" **Weight:** 12.3
Club Honours: FLC '02
International Honours: E: 1; U21-20; Yth
David's 2004-05 season was cut short because of hamstring trouble. Eventually he underwent back surgery in an attempt to cure the problem once and for all. His absence was a major blow for Birmingham City. When he was in the side, mainly at left midfield, he was dynamic, creative and made them more of a threat. His passing and interplay with Emile Heskey was mesmerising in the win at Villa Park in December when he scored the Blues' second goal.
Blackburn Rov *(From trainee on 30/9/1997) P/FL 120+16/30 FLC 14+3/5 FAC 11+2/3 Others 3+1*
Birmingham C *(£5,500,000 on 9/7/2003) PL 29+3/4 FLC 1+1 FAC 3*

DUNNE Alan James
Born: Dublin, 23 August 1982
Height: 5'10" **Weight:** 12.0
Alan began last season in the right-back position for Millwall, but later in the campaign he switched to the right-hand side of midfield and proved to be a revelation. He produced some excellent performances and scored his first senior goal against Gillingham with a fine left-foot finish. He showed a good turn of pace and strength in the tackle before his season was cut short by an injury.
Millwall *(From trainee on 17/3/2000) FL 22+10/3 FLC 1+1 FAC 1*

DUNNE Richard Patrick
Born: Dublin, 21 September 1979
Height: 6'1" **Weight:** 14.0
Club Honours: FAYC '98; Div 1 '02
International Honours: RoI: 23; B-1; U21-4; Yth (UEFA-U18 '98); Sch
This Republic of Ireland powerhouse holds the record for most League appearances in the current Manchester City squad after completing his 150th appearance against Birmingham City in April. He was a constant tower of strength at the heart of the defence last term and produced consistently impressive performances winning him several 'Man of the Match' awards. Richard recently penned a new deal that will keep him at City for the near future and deservedly won the club's 'Player of the Year' trophy.
Everton *(From trainee on 8/10/1996) PL 53+7 FLC 4 FAC 8*
Manchester C *(£3,000,000 on 20/10/2000) P/FL 152+5/3 FLC 6 FAC 12 Others 3+1*

DYCHE Sean Mark
Born: Kettering, 28 June 1971
Height: 6'0" **Weight:** 13.10
Club Honours: Div 2 '01
Watford's battling captain and centre half was ruled out for most of the second half of last season because of a persistent groin problem, and his commitment and inspiring leadership were badly missed. A veteran of more than 450 senior matches, he was made available for transfer at the end of the season.
Nottingham F *(From trainee on 20/5/1989)*
Chesterfield *(Free on 1/2/1990) FL 219+12/8 FLC 9 FAC 13/1 Others 16*
Bristol C *(£350,000 on 11/7/1997) FL 14+3 FLC 2+1*
Luton T *(Loaned on 4/1/1999) FL 14/1 Others 1*
Millwall *(£150,000 on 5/7/1999) FL 69/3 FLC 2+1 FAC 4*
Watford *(Free on 12/7/2002) FL 68+4 FLC 5 FAC 1*

DYER Bruce Antonio
Born: Ilford, 13 April 1975
Height: 6'0" **Weight:** 11.3
International Honours: E: U21-11
Bruce plays in the style of an old-fashioned centre forward who leads the line well and holds up the ball for colleagues. An unselfish player, honest and hard working, he has now made over 400 League appearances for three different clubs. Last term he again

reached double figures in the goal-scoring lists, including braces at Leeds and Sunderland. Despite featuring in every first-team squad bar one he was released at the end of the season.
Watford *(From trainee on 19/4/1993) FL 29+2/6 FLC 4/2 FAC 1 Others 2/1*
Crystal Palace *(£1,100,000 on 10/3/1994) P/FL 95+40/37 FLC 9+5/1 FAC 7+3/6 Others 3+2*
Barnsley *(£700,000 on 23/10/1998) FL 149+33/59 FLC 11+1/4 FAC 5+2/3 Others 2+1/3*
Watford *(Free on 10/7/2003) FL 39+29/12 FLC 6+2/2 FAC 1+2*

DYER Kieron Courtney
Born: Ipswich, 29 December 1978
Height: 5'7" **Weight:** 9.7
International Honours: E: 28; B-2; U21-11; Yth
This talented Newcastle midfielder had rather a difficult season in 2004-05. A hamstring injury sidelined him for two months but he returned for new manager Graeme Souness in a wide role and a series of wholehearted performances characterised by blistering pace, good control and tireless running won over the fans. A much-publicised incident with teammate Lee Bowyer saw him receive a red card in the home game with Villa incurring a ban which excluded him from the FA Cup semi final. Recurring hamstring problems then restricted his availability in the closing stages of the campaign.
Ipswich T *(From trainee on 3/1/1997) FL 79+12/9 FLC 11/1 FAC 5 Others 5+1/2*
Newcastle U *(£6,000,000 on 16/7/1999) PL 145+12/18 FLC 5+2/3 FAC 13+1/3 Others 26+3/4*

DYER Lloyd Richard
Born: Birmingham, 13 September 1982
Height: 5'10" **Weight:** 11.4
Lloyd was unable to get any joy in West Bromwich Albion's first team last season, making only one start, in the disappointing Carling Cup defeat at Colchester in September. A fast-raiding left-sided midfielder who loves to run at defenders, he joined Coventry City on loan for the final month of the campaign. His tricky style gave City some extra options but his final ball was often inconsistent.
West Bromwich A *(Signed from Aston Villa juniors on 9/7/2001) P/FL 2+19/2 FLC 2 FAC 0+1*
Kidderminster Hrs *(Loaned on 5/9/2003) FL 5+2/1*
Coventry C *(Loaned on 22/3/2005) FL 6*

Lloyd Dyer

ADEN Nicholas (Nicky)
ɜremy
orn: Sheffield, 12 December 1972
eight: 5'9" **Weight:** 12.8
lub Honours: Div 2 '03
nis consistent right back made the berth is own at Wigan Athletic from the end f November after starting the 2004-05 ɜason on the bench. His positional sense ʋas excellent and he worked the flanks nselfishly, producing some solid displays. teady and undemonstrative, the season lso saw him pass his century of Football eague appearances for the club in anuary. Nicky deservedly earned a new ontract with the Latics.
arnsley *(From juniors on 4/6/1991) P/FL 81+12/10 FLC 18+3/3 FAC 20 Others 4+1*
irmingham C *(Free on 6/7/2000) FL 8+6/3 FLC 13/1 FAC 1 Others 1+1/1*
Vigan Ath *(Signed on 20/9/2002) FL 116+6 LC 8 FAC 4 Others 1*

AGLES Christopher (Chris)
 Λark
orn: Hemel Hempstead, 19 November 985
leight: 6'0" **Weight:** 10.8
lub Honours: FAYC '03
nternational Honours: E: Yth
A talented right-sided midfielder who is ighly regarded for his dribbling and close control, Chris was given only a leeting chance to shine in the Manchester United first team last term notably in the Carling Cup, and one solitary appearance in the Champions' League against Dinamo Bucharest. He moved on loan to Watford in January and soon demonstrated his class at Championship level, bringing pace and vision to the right of midfield. He also scored his first goal in senior football, a fine individual effort against Gillingham.
Manchester U *(From trainee on 25/7/2003) FLC 1+4 FAC 1 Others 1+2*
Watford *(Loaned on 21/1/2005) FL 10+3/1*

EARNSHAW Robert
Born: Zambia, 6 April 1981
Height: 5'8" **Weight:** 10.10
International Honours: W: 19; U21-10; Yth
Cardiff City's record goal-scorer played just five games for the Bluebirds in the 2004-05 season before Premiership new boys West Bromwich Albion finally took the plunge and signed him for a substantial fee. Quick over the ground and alert, he has the knack of sneaking into the danger-zone when least expected. He made his debut for Albion as a second-half substitute at Liverpool a fortnight after moving to the Hawthorns. Although never a regular in the side, he proved to be a very useful asset when called off the bench and ended the season as Albion's top-scorer with 14 goals. Robert also had the distinction of scoring the club's first Premiership hat-trick after coming off the bench in the 4-1 win at Charlton in March. He continued to add to his caps for Wales during the campaign.
Cardiff C *(From trainee on 4/8/1998) FL 141+37/85 FLC 6+2/10 FAC 11+2/9 Others 5+1/1*
Morton *(Loaned on 20/1/2000) SL 3/2 SC 1*
West Bromwich A *(£3,500,000 + on 1/9/2004) PL 18+13/11 FAC 2+1/3*

EASTER Jermaine Maurice
Born: Cardiff, 15 January 1982
Height: 5'8" **Weight:** 12.4
International Honours: W: Yth
This busy striker featured regularly for Cambridge United early on last season and his tally of six goals made him the club's joint-top scorer. In March he moved on to Boston United where he burst on the scene in dramatic style, coming off the bench to score twice in the home victory over Notts County. Jermaine was paired with several different strike partners in his remaining appearances but managed just one more goal for the Pilgrims and was not offered a new contract. In May he was reported to have signed for Stockport County, linking up again with manager Chris Turner with whom he had worked at Hartlepool.
Wolverhampton W *(From trainee on 6/7/2000)*
Hartlepool U *(Free on 17/3/2001) FL 0+27/2 Others 0+3*
Cambridge U *(Free on 6/2/2004) FL 25+14/8 FLC 1 FAC 1 Others 2/1*
Boston U *(Free on 15/3/2005) FL 5+4/3*

EASTON Clint Jude
Born: Barking, 1 October 1977
Height: 5'11" **Weight:** 10.8
Club Honours: Div 2 '98
International Honours: E: Yth
This left-footed midfielder added some much-needed class for Wycombe Wanderers last term. Able to deliver defence-splitting passes, he was sorely missed when a knee injury kept him out of the side during the autumn. He returned, a little surprisingly, as a left back, a position he quickly made his own with some superb performances. Dominant in the air and an excellent tackler, he is very comfortable bringing the ball out of defence.
Watford *(From trainee on 5/7/1996) P/FL 50+14/1 FLC 4+4/1 FAC 3+1 Others 3*
Norwich C *(£200,000 on 19/6/2001) FL 41+9/5 FLC 2 FAC 0+2 Others 3*
Wycombe W *(Free on 20/7/2004) FL 29+4/1 FLC 1 Others 1*

EASTWOOD Freddy
Born: Epsom, 29 October 1983
Height: 5'11" **Weight:** 12.0
After earning a reputation as a prolific goal-scorer in non-League football, Freddy made a sensational start to his senior career with Southend following his arrival on loan. Making his debut against League Two leaders Swansea City, he netted within eight seconds and went on to complete a hat-trick. Unsurprisingly he was hastily signed up and his scoring exploits were pivotal in the club's most successful campaign for many years. In the latter part of the season he netted in seven consecutive games, thus equalling Brett Angell's post-war club record. Freddy finished on a high by netting the vital opening goal in extra time of the play-off final against Lincoln, to set the team on their way to promotion. His tremendous first touch and ability to score with either foot will ensure he will inevitably come under the watchful eye of bigger clubs.
Southend U *(Signed from Grays Ath, ex trainee at West Ham U, on 4/10/2004) FL 31+2/19 FAC 1 Others 6+2/5*

EATON Adam Paul
Born: Wigan, 2 May 1980
Height: 5'11" **Weight:** 11.2
Club Honours: FAYC '98
After missing almost all of the previous season with a groin injury Adam started the 2004-05 campaign in his customary left-back position. Unfortunately he was not there for long, however, as he was once again struck down by injury early in the campaign and, following two operations on his hip, he did not play again until the summer.
Everton *(From trainee on 2/6/1997)*
Preston NE *(Free on 29/6/1999) FL 7+7 FLC 2 FAC 1 Others 0+1*
Mansfield T *(Loaned on 10/12/2002) FL 6*
Mansfield T *(Signed on 4/2/2003) FL 19 Others 3*

EBANKS-BLAKE Sylvan Augustus
Born: Cambridge, 29 March 1986
Height: 5'10" **Weight:** 13.4
Club Honours: FAYC '03
A pacy young striker with an eye for a goal, Sylvan made his Manchester United

Freddy Eastwood

debut as a second-half substitute against Crewe Alexandra in the Carling Cup at Gresty Road. Having produced some impressive displays in United's youth and reserve teams, Sir Alex Ferguson was certainly pleased by his efforts on the big stage. Unfortunately any hope of a late recall to the first team was ended when Sylvan suffered a broken leg in a reserve-team game against Middlesbrough. However, once fit again his great promise will be tested in 2005-06.

Manchester U *(From trainee on 24/2/2005) FLC 0+1*

E'BEYER Mark Edward
Born: Stevenage, 21 September 1984
Height: 5'11" **Weight:** 11.5
Mark became one of Graham Rix's first signings for Oxford when he joined in the summer of 2004, but despite producing some neat and tidy midfield displays he never became a regular in the side. He scored his only goal to date in the 3-1 win at Chester in November, before being sidelined by injury for much of the second half of the campaign.

Oxford U *(From trainee at Milton Keynes Dons on 1/7/2004) FL 6+4/2 FAC 1*

EBOUE Emmanuel
Born: Abidjan, Ivory Coast, 4 June 1983
Height: 5'10" **Weight:** 11.3
International Honours: Ivory Coast
After impressing on loan in pre-season, Emmanuel arrived permanently in the January transfer window from Arsenal's feeder club, Beveren. The right back made his debut in the FA Cup third round win over Stoke City and played in the next two rounds. Emmanuel will be looking to add to his first-team appearance total for the Gunners in 2005-06.

Arsenal *(£1,540,000 from Beveren, Belgium, ex ASEC Mimosas Abidjan, on 1/1/2005) PL 0+1 FAC 3*

ECHANOMI Efe
Born: Nigeria, 27 September 1986
Height: 5'7" **Weight:** 11.7
This young striker started the 2004-05 season playing for the Leyton Orient youth team, but injuries to more experienced players allowed him to break into the first-team squad and he made his senior debut from the bench against Southend in December. Efe scored in his second appearance for the O's against Yeovil and added four more goals before the end of the campaign as he regularly found himself used as a substitute.

Leyton Orient *(Trainee) FL 4+14/5*

EDDS Gareth James
Born: Sydney, Australia, 3 February 1981
Height: 5'11" **Weight:** 10.12
International Honours: Australia: U23-2; Yth
Gareth's 2004-05 season at MK Dons turned around when an injury to on-loan midfielder Paul Mitchell created a vacancy for a defensive midfielder that he grabbed with both hands. Previously used to average effect in the right-back berth, he immediately showed his ability to cover every blade of grass twice over and his vital goals against Bournemouth and Oldham proved to be mere appetisers for his two-goal salvo in the final match against Tranmere that secured the club's League One survival. Put simply, he had an excellent last three months of the season.

Nottingham F *(From trainee on 19/2/1998) FL 11+5/1 FAC 1*
Swindon T *(Free on 9/8/2002) FL 8+6 FLC 0+1 FAC 1 Others 2*
Bradford C *(Free on 14/7/2003) FL 19+4 FLC 1*
MK Dons *(Free on 23/7/2004) FL 37+2/5 FLC 2 FAC 2 Others 1*

EDGE Lewis John Spencer
Born: Lancaster, 12 January 1987
Height: 6'2" **Weight:** 12.10
This promising young Blackpool goalkeeper spent most of last season developing in the club's reserve team. He made his first-team debut in the FA Cup replay against Leicester when the club's other 'keepers were unavailable and produced an excellent performance. Lewis made several fine saves and was only beaten by a super strike as the Seasiders went out of the competition.

Blackpool *(Trainee) FL 1 FAC 1*

EDGE Roland
Born: Gillingham, 25 November 1978
Height: 5'9" **Weight:** 11.12
Roland returned south to team up with his former Gillingham manager, Peter Taylor, at Hull. Although dropping down to League One and facing competition for the left-back berth from Andy Dawson, it proved to be a wise move for all involved as the Tigers completed back-to-back promotions and both players produced a series of thoroughly reliable performances when called upon. Initially, Roland had to be patient but he posted a fine debut in the 3-0 win over leaders Luton at the KC Stadium in October. A shoulder injury restricted his further involvement until the second half of the campaign. A tenacious defender, Roland is not always given enough credit for his attacking and distribution skills.

Gillingham *(From trainee on 10/7/1997) FL 93+9/1 FLC 6 FAC 12+1 Others 5*
Hibernian *(Free on 1/7/2003) SL 20 SLC 4*
Hull C *(Free on 7/7/2004) FL 13+1 FLC 1 Others 1*

EDGHILL Richard Arlon
Born: Oldham, 23 September 1974
Height: 5'9" **Weight:** 11.5
International Honours: E: B-1; U21-3
Richard, who can play on either side of defence, signed a new contract for Queen's Park Rangers last term, but after just a couple of substitute appearances he missed two months with an injury. Once fit again he became a permanent member of the line-up, playing in different roles in the defence where his versatility was very definitely an asset.

Manchester C *(From trainee on 15/7/1992) P/FL 178+3/1 FLC 17 FAC 8+1 Others 3*
Birmingham C *(Loaned on 14/11/2000) FL 3*
Wigan Ath *(Free on 21/10/2002) Others 1*
Sheffield U *(Free on 17/1/2003) FL 0+1*
Queens Park Rgrs *(Free on 22/8/2003) FL 28+12 FLC 3 FAC 1 Others 1+1*

EDMAN Erik Kenneth
Born: Huskvarna, Sweden, 11 November 1978
Height: 5'10" **Weight:** 12.4
International Honours: Sweden: 30
This left-sided defender possesses great pace and strength and loves to get forward. Having impressed in Portugal at the Euro 2004 finals, Erik proved to be a fabulous signing for Spurs adding width and depth behind the ball and an extra dimension going forward. Erik demonstrated a good eye for goal and a powerful let foot. A solid and reliable defender, he adapted to the Premiership well and looks comfortable on the left side, which had previously been a weak area for Spurs.

Tottenham H *(£1,300,000 from SC Heerenveen, Holland, ex Helsingborg, on 5/8/2004) PL 28/1 FAC 2+1*

EDMONDSON Darren Stephen
Born: Coniston, 4 November 1971
Height: 6'0" **Weight:** 12.11
Club Honours: Div 3 '95; AMC '97
This experienced defender became a regular at right back for Chester following the appointment of Ian Rush as manager. Darren's presence steadied a vulnerable looking City defence and coincided with a ten-game unbeaten run. However, an ankle injury put him out of action for two months and when he returned to the line-up he struggled to regain his early-season form.

Richard Edghill

Carlisle U (From trainee on 17/7/1990) FL 205+9/9 FLC 15/1 FAC 15/3 Others 22/3
Huddersfield T (£200,000 + on 3/3/1997) FL 28+9 FLC 2 FAC 2+2
Plymouth Arg (Loaned on 11/9/1998) FL 4
York C (Free on 23/3/2000) FL 126+5/6 FLC 5 FAC 10 Others 1
Chester C (Free on 5/8/2004) FL 26+1 FAC 2

[EDU] GASPAR Eduardo Cesar Daud
Born: Sao Paulo, Brazil, 15 May 1978
Height: 6'1" **Weight:** 11.4
Club Honours: FAC '02, '05; PL '02, '04; CS '02
International Honours: Brazil: 15
Central midfielder Edu's season at Arsenal was a tale of injuries and contract wrangles. He made just 12 Premiership appearances in total as he failed to build on the great form shown in the club's unbeaten Premiership campaign. It was widely expected that he would depart in the January transfer window, but he stayed and eventually returned to the side. However, having declared his intention to leave Highbury in the summer he scored an emotional last goal for the club from the penalty spot in the 7-0 hammering of Everton in May. His final appearance came as a substitute in the FA Cup final success over Manchester United.
Arsenal (£6,000,000 from Corinthians, Brazil on 18/1/2001) PL 41+38/7 FLC 8/2 FAC 13+4/3 Others 14+9/3

EDWARDS Andrew (Andy) David
Born: Epping, 17 September 1971
Height: 6'3" **Weight:** 12.10
Club Honours: Div 3 '03
This experienced central defender returned to Roots Hall in the 2004 close season but despite his huge experience he found himself on the substitutes' bench on a regular basis. This was primarily due to the fantastic form of regular centre-back partners, Adam Barrett and Spencer Prior, but also to a string of niggling injuries. However, when called upon Andy served the Shrimpers well during a highly successful campaign.
Southend U (From trainee on 14/12/1989) FL 141+6/5 FLC 5 FAC 4 Others 9/2
Birmingham C (£400,000 on 6/7/1995) FL 37+3/1 FLC 12/1 FAC 2 Others 5/1
Peterborough U (Signed on 29/11/1996) FL 266/10 FLC 12 FAC 21/1 Others 17/2
Rushden & Diamonds (Free on 5/3/2003) FL 40+1/4 FLC 1 FAC 1 Others 2
Southend U (Free on 5/7/2004) FL 9+3/1 FLC 1 FAC 0+1 Others 2+2

EDWARDS Akenhaton **Carlos**
Born: Port of Spain, Trinidad, 24 October 1978
Height: 5'11" **Weight:** 11.9
Club Honours: AMC '05
International Honours: Trinidad & Tobago: 38
This wing back was conspicuous by his absence from the Wrexham line-up in the opening stages of the 2004-05 campaign, a result of a knee injury suffered playing for Trinidad & Tobago in a World Cup qualifying match against the Dominican Republic in June 2004. Carlos eventually returned for the home game with Tranmere in mid-January but was unable to keep the Racecourse side in League One. His wing play again caused havoc in opponents' defences and he maintained his knack of scoring spectacular goals, although he managed just one for the season, netting in the 4-1 win at Stockport. He was reported to have signed for Luton during the summer.
Wrexham (£125,000 from Defence Force, Trinidad on 8/8/2000) FL 144+22/23 FLC 4+2/1 FAC 3 Others 6/1

EDWARDS Christian Nicholas Howells
Born: Caerphilly, 23 November 1975
Height: 6'2" **Weight:** 12.8
International Honours: W: 1; B-2; U21-7

Carlos Edwards

This experienced central defender was once again a regular at the heart of the Bristol Rovers' rearguard last term. He produced some fine displays including a 'Man of the Match' performance in the narrow victory over his former club Swansea City. Christian proved effective in the air and scored his first and only goal for the club against Notts County. Transfer listed by Rovers in March, despite having a further one-year contract, his future may well be away from the Memorial Stadium.
Swansea C *(From trainee on 20/7/1994) FL 113+2/4 FLC 5 FAC 4 Others 8*
Nottingham F *(£175,000 + on 26/3/1998) P/FL 44+10/3 FLC 1 FAC 1*
Bristol C *(Loaned on 11/12/1998) FL 3*
Oxford U *(Loaned on 24/2/2000) FL 5/1*
Crystal Palace *(Loaned on 16/11/2001) FL 9*
Tranmere Rov *(Loaned on 17/9/2002) FL 12 FLC 1 FAC 2 Others 2*
Oxford U *(Loaned on 17/1/2003) FL 5+1*
Bristol Rov *(Free on 4/7/2003) FL 79+5/2 FLC 3 FAC 3 Others 5*

EDWARDS David Alexander
Born: Pontesbury, 3 February 1986
Height: 5'11" **Weight:** 11.2
International Honours: W: Yth
This young right-sided midfielder enjoyed an excellent season for Shrewsbury last term. David makes intelligent use of the ball and possesses a tremendous shot, which enabled him to bag a total of five goals, including three in consecutive matches at the turn of the year. He was again involved in the Wales U19 set up during the campaign.
Shrewsbury T *(From trainee on 5/1/2004) FL 16+12/5 FLC 1 FAC 1 Others 0+1*

EDWARDS Michael (Mike)
Born: Hessle, 25 April 1980
Height: 6'1" **Weight:** 12.0
This highly capable and experienced Notts County defender had the misfortune to suffer a serious injury early on last season in the Carling Cup at West Ham and this was his last experience of first-team action during the campaign. Mike's loss to the team was incalculable, but he went on to make a full recovery and will be looking to regain his place in the line-up in 2005-06.
Hull C *(From trainee on 16/7/1998) FL 165+13/6 FLC 8+1 FAC 11/2 Others 9+1*
Colchester U *(Free on 27/3/2003) FL 3+2*
Grimsby T *(Free on 7/8/2003) FL 32+1/1 FAC 2 Others 1*
Notts Co *(Free on 2/7/2004) FL 8+1 FLC 2*

EDWARDS Neil Ryan
Born: Aberdare, 5 December 1970
Height: 5'9" **Weight:** 11.10
International Honours: W: U21-1; Yth; Sch
Neil began the 2004-05 season as Rochdale's first choice 'keeper and, apart from a couple of LDV Vans Trophy games, was ever present until missing out through injury against Cambridge in November. However, with understudy Matt Gilks grabbing his chance, Neil had to settle for a place on the bench when he returned. A hernia operation then led to another spell out of action. Neil has now reached the top-ten of all-time Football League appearances for Dale.
Leeds U *(From trainee on 10/3/1989) Others 1*
Stockport Co *(£5,000 on 3/9/1991) FL 163+1 FLC 11 FAC 11 Others 31*
Rochdale *(£25,000 on 3/11/1997) FL 239 FLC 9 FAC 16+1 Others 12*

EDWARDS Paul
Born: Manchester, 1 January 1980
Height: 5'11" **Weight:** 10.12
This pacy winger joined Blackpool during the summer of 2004 but missed the start of the new campaign with an ankle injury. He took his place in the side at the end of August, but never really established himself during his stay at Bloomfield Road and was released in May.
Doncaster Rov *(Free from Ashton U on 2/2/1998) FL 5+4*
Swindon T *(Free from Altrincham, ex Knutsford T, on 17/8/2001) FL 14+6 FLC 0+1 FAC 1/1 Others 1*
Wrexham *(Free on 12/7/2002) FL 73+6/4 FLC 3 FAC 0+1 Others 3*
Blackpool *(Free on 26/7/2004) FL 22+6/3 FAC 1 Others 2*

EDWARDS Robert (Robbie)
Born: Manchester, 23 February 1970
Height: 5'9" **Weight:** 12.4
Even though Robbie is at the veteran stage of his career, the gritty left-sided defender showed some fine battling qualities for Huddersfield early on last season and was rewarded with a great strike in the win against Hull City. He was always willing to encourage the youngsters in the team, and although a calf injury kept him out for large chunks of the season he showed total commitment. The fans' favourite was rewarded with the final goal of the season at the Galpharm Stadium in the win over Swindon Town. After proving an excellent servant for the Terriers he was released in the summer.
Crewe Alex *(From trainee on 11/7/1988) FL 110+45/44 FLC 8/5 FAC 13+5/5 Others 9+7/5*
Huddersfield T *(£150,000 on 8/3/1996) FL 109+29/14 FLC 12+1/1 FAC 7+1/1*
Chesterfield *(£20,000 on 8/9/2000) FL 89+5/7 FLC 2+1 FAC 5 Others 8*
Huddersfield T *(Free on 7/8/2003) FL 32+9/3 FLC 2 Others 2+1/1*

EDWARDS Robert (Rob) Owen
Born: Telford, 25 December 1982
Height: 6'1" **Weight:** 12.0
International Honours: W: 7; Yth
Rob was substitute for Wolves in their opening fixture last term then looked promising in the next four games only t be injured. A swollen ankle led to tests and a diagnosis that he had suffered ligament damage. This caused a lengthy absence and he did not return to action until February. However, he then settled down and was involved in most of the remaining fixtures, featuring either at right back or as a central defender in a well-organised back four.
Aston Villa *(From trainee on 4/1/2000) PL 7+1 FAC 1*
Crystal Palace *(Loaned on 21/11/2003) FL 6+1/1*
Derby Co *(Loaned on 9/1/2004) FL 10+1/1*
Wolverhampton W *(£150,000 + on 26/7/2004) FL 15+2 FLC 1*

EDWARDS Robert (Rob) William
Born: Kendal, 1 July 1973
Height: 6'0" **Weight:** 12.2
Club Honours: Div 2 '00
International Honours: W: 4; B-2; U21-17; Yth
This experienced defender joined Blackpool during the 2004 close season and featured in a midfield role in the early fixtures before switching to left back. However, he then moved to the centre of the defence, partnering Peter Clarke, and the pair went on to form an effective partnership at the back. Rob was rewarded for his efforts with an extension of his contract in the summer.
Carlisle U *(From trainee on 10/4/1990) FL 48/5 FLC 4 FAC 1 Others 2+1*
Bristol C *(£135,000 on 27/3/1991) FL 188+28/5 FLC 16+3/1 FAC 13+2 Others 12+1/2*
Preston NE *(Free on 5/8/1999) FL 156+13/4 FLC 13 FAC 10 Others 5/1*
Blackpool *(Free on 2/8/2004) FL 24+2/1 FLC 1 FAC 3+1 Others 3*

EDWORTHY Marc
Born: Barnstaple, 24 December 1972
Height: 5'8" **Weight:** 11.10
Club Honours: Div 1 '04
Marc faced stiff competition for the Canaries' right-back berth last season from Thomas Helveg. He was kept out of the side for the first two Premiership

Neil Edwards

games before reclaiming his place and displaying, once again, tremendous enthusiasm and defensive capabilities. A solid all-round defender with great positional awareness, his attacking bursts on the right flank gave an extra weapon to City's armoury. In early April Helveg once again earned the manager's vote at right back. Marc was released by Norwich at the end of the season.
Plymouth Arg *(From trainee on 30/3/1991) FL 52+17/1 FLC 5+2 FAC 5+2 Others 2+2*
Crystal Palace *(£350,000 on 9/6/1995) P/FL 120+6 FLC 8+1/1 FAC 8 Others 8*
Coventry C *(£850,000 + on 28/8/1998) P/FL 62+14/1 FLC 5 FAC 4*
Wolverhampton W *(Free on 23/8/2002) FL 18+4 FLC 1*
Norwich C *(Free on 8/8/2003) P/FL 69+2 FLC 2+1 FAC 2*

EHIOGU Ugochuku (Ugo)

Born: Hackney, 3 November 1972
Height: 6'2" **Weight:** 14.10
Club Honours: FLC '96, '04
International Honours: E: 4; B-1; U21-15
Ugo saw his 2004-05 season with Middlesbrough frequently blighted by injury. By the turn of the year knee and calf problems had restricted the England international to just three first-team appearances, two Premiership games and the Carling Cup victory over Coventry City. The new year was just as unlucky for him as the previous one had been. He found it frustrating that when he was match fit he was sitting the match out on the bench unable to oust Chris Riggott. He was forced to hobble off after just 18 minutes of Boro's 1-1 draw with Everton at the Riverside in January with a further knee problem, but managed to end the season on a high note by featuring in the closing games of the Premiership campaign as the club secured seventh place and a position in the UEFA Cup competition for 2005-06.
West Bromwich A *(From trainee on 13/7/1989) FL 0+2*
Aston Villa *(£40,000 on 12/7/1991) P/FL 223+14/12 FLC 23+1/1 FAC 22+2/1 Others 18/1*
Middlesbrough *(£8,000,000 on 20/10/2000) PL 106+2/7 FLC 5 FAC 7/1*

EINARSSON Gylfi

Born: Iceland, 27 October 1978
Height: 6'0" **Weight:** 12.8
International Honours: Iceland: 15; Yth
Midfielder Gylfi signed for Leeds at the end of the year, although he actually arrived at Elland Road two months earlier. The Iceland international, who also had trials at Cardiff, impressed manager Kevin Blackwell during a short trial period, but was unable to complete his move from Norwegian club Lillestrom until the transfer window opened. He scored 16 goals in his last season in Norway and was always eager to get into the box. He opened his Leeds account by getting the winner with a flying header in United's 1-0 victory at Burnley in February. He is gradually imposing himself at international level and scored in Iceland's famous 2-0 friendly win over Italy in August 2004.
Leeds U *(Free from Lillestrom, Norway, ex Fylkir, on 31/12/2004) FL 6+2/1*

EL-ABD Adam Mohamad

Born: Brighton, 11 September 1984
Height: 5'11" **Weight:** 13.9
A strapping, no-nonsense defender, Adam was a fringe member of the Brighton squad for much of the season-long battle against relegation from the Championship in 2004-05, but he stepped into the breach whenever required and performed admirably either at full back or as a central defender. One of a number of excellent products of the Brighton youth system, Adam will have benefited hugely from the experience gained during the successful fight to avoid the drop.
Brighton & Hove A *(From trainee on 22/12/2003) FL 20+7 Others 2*

EL KARKOURI Talal

Born: Casablanca, Morocco, 8 July 1976
Height: 6'1" **Weight:** 12.3
International Honours: Morocco
Talal was probably Alan Curbishley's best buy for Charlton during the 2004 close season. A versatile player able to feature at right back, central defence or midfield, he started out in the centre of the park but was switched to central defence at the end of October and became a fixture in that position. Tall, strong and athletic, Talal is excellent in the air and is one of the best distributors of the ball at the club. He reads the game well and has good ball control. He also possesses an incredibly powerful shot, and is deadly at set pieces, particularly from long range. He hit five goals during the season, with four of them coming in an incredible six game spell, not bad for a central defender! He scored against Birmingham City at the Valley with an incredible free kick from almost the halfway line, and his 30-yard free kick against Arsenal on New Year's Day won the club's 'Goal of the Season' award, chosen by the supporters. Something of a cult hero at the Valley, Talal was runner-up to Luke Young as the supporters' 'Player of the Year'.
Sunderland *(Loaned from Paris St Germain, France, ex Raja Casablanca, on 31/1/2003) PL 8 FAC 0+1*
Charlton Ath *(£1,000,000 from Paris St Germain, France, on 11/7/2004) PL 28+4/5 FLC 1 FAC 3*

EL KHOLTI Abdelhalim (Abdou)

Born: Annemasse, France, 17 October 1980
Height: 5'10" **Weight:** 11.2
A versatile player, who is capable of playing in both defence and midfield, Abdou featured regularly for Cambridge United in the first half of last season. However, he fell out of favour following a change in management and rarely featured at all in the second half of the campaign. He was one of several players released by the U's in the summer.
Yeovil T *(Free from Raja Casablanca, Morocco on 9/10/2002) FL 19+4/1 FLC 0+1 FAC 0+1 Others 1*
Cambridge U *(Free on 6/7/2004) FL 13+2 FLC 1 FAC 0+1 Others 2*

ELDERSHAW Simon

Born: Stoke-on-Trent, 2 December 1983
Height: 5'10" **Weight:** 11.7
This Port Vale striker was always behind Billy Paynter and Lee Matthews in the pecking order, but gave his all when called upon to do so. Simon made three substitute appearances before his first start of the season at Luton in December. He held his place for the next two games and scored his first senior goal at Huddersfield on Boxing Day. Despite that he was limited to a further two starts a month later and a few more appearances from the bench. Tall with an eye for goal, the lack of a reserve team hampered his progress, as he could never get a run of games. He was released on a free transfer in the summer.
Port Vale *(From trainee on 1/7/2003) FL 5+10/1*

ELLEGAARD Kevin Stuhr

Born: Copenhagen, Denmark, 23 May 1983
Height: 6'5" **Weight:** 15.0
International Honours: Denmark: U21-9; Yth
Kevin found himself well down the pecking order of goalkeepers at Manchester City last term and his only first-team action came during a brief spell at Blackpool at the turn of the year. At international level he stepped up to the Denmark U21 squad and was the regular first choice during the campaign winning nine caps. He was released by City during the summer.

Manchester C *(£750,000 from Farum, Denmark on 16/11/2001) PL 2+2 FLC 1 FAC 2*
Blackpool *(Loaned on 31/12/2004) FL 2 FAC 1*

ELLENDER Paul

Born: Scunthorpe, 21 October 1974
Height: 6'1" **Weight:** 12.7
Club Honours: NC '02
International Honours: E: SP-1
This experienced central defender was a tower of strength at the back for League Two club Boston United in 2004-05. Paul captained the team and led very much by example. He was powerful in the air and always a danger when pushed up front at set pieces, while opposition strikers found it difficult to get past him on the ground.
Scunthorpe U *(From trainee on 8/4/1993. Freed during 1994 close season)*
Boston U *(Signed from Scarborough, ex Gainsborough Trin, Altrincham, on 17/8/2001) FL 106+1/6 FLC 5/1 FAC 5/1 Others 2*

ELLINGTON Nathan Levi Fontaine

Born: Bradford, 2 July 1981
Height: 5'10" **Weight:** 12.10
Club Honours: Div 2 '03
An exceptionally quick striker who has an unerring eye for goal, Nathan finished the season as top scorer in the Championship with 24 goals for Wigan. His tally of goals was a justification of the trickery, skill and total commitment that he showed and included spectacular strikes against Sheffield United and Coventry City. Nathan finished as the Latics' top scorer for the third consecutive season and also equalled a club record when he scored in six consecutive League matches. He was deservedly named in the PFA Championship team of the season.
Bristol Rov *(£150,000 from Walton & Hersham on 18/2/1999) FL 76+40/35 FLC 7/2 FAC 6+1/4 Others 6+1/3*
Wigan Ath *(£750,000 + on 28/3/2002) FL 130+4/59 FLC 6+1/6 FAC 3+1/2 Others 0+1*

ELLIOT Robert (Rob)

Born: Chatham, 30 April 1986
Height: 6'3" **Weight:** 14.10
This young Charlton Athletic goalkeeper spent the early part of last season on loan at Bishop's Stortford and in January he went out on loan again, this time to League Two outfit Notts County, where he was required to provide cover during an injury crisis. Rob was thrown in at the deep end behind a struggling County back line, making his debut in the home game with Kidderminster in March. He had a baptism of fire but showed great strength of character when under pressure and went on to make three more appearances before returning to the Valley to continue his development.
Charlton Ath *(From trainee on 27/1/2005)*
Notts Co *(Loaned on 28/1/2005) FL 3+1*

ELLIOTT Marvin Conrad

Born: Wandsworth, 15 September 1984
Height: 5'11" **Weight:** 12.2
Although still young Marvin firmly established himself in the Millwall first-team squad last term producing some outstanding performances in the middle of the park and at right back when called upon. An attacking midfielder he scored his first goal for the club in the 4-3 win over Crewe in April.
Millwall *(From trainee on 6/2/2002) FL 46+17/1 FLC 1 FAC 2+3 Others 2*

ELLIOTT Matthew (Matt) Stephen

Born: Wandsworth, 1 November 1968
Height: 6'3" **Weight:** 14.10
Club Honours: FLC '00
International Honours: S: 18
This right-footed central defender and club captain managed only a couple of outings for Leicester City at the end of October, before injury ended his season and, by March, his distinguished playing career. Matt will always be fondly remembered around Leicester for his match-winning efforts in the 2000 League Cup.
Charlton Ath *(£5,000 from Epsom & Ewell on 9/5/1988) FLC 1*
Torquay U *(£10,000 on 23/3/1989) FL 123+1/15 FLC 9/2 FAC 9/2 Others 16/1*
Scunthorpe U *(£50,000 on 26/3/1992) FL 61/8 FLC 6 FAC 2 Others 8*
Oxford U *(£150,000 on 5/11/1993) FL 148/21 FLC 16/1 FAC 11/2 Others 6*
Leicester C *(£1,600,000 on 18/1/1997) P/FL 239+6/27 FLC 20+2/3 FAC 18+1/3 Others 4*
Ipswich T *(Loaned on 16/3/2004) FL 10 Others 2*

ELLIOTT Robert (Robbie) James

Born: Gosforth, 25 December 1973
Height: 5'10" **Weight:** 11.6
International Honours: E: U21-2; Yth
Last term proved to be a renaissance season for local boy Robbie as he returned to Newcastle's first team for the first time in 20 months. He featured regularly in the squad, captaining the side at home to Hapoel in the UEFA Cup in September and playing at centre back or his more accustomed position on the left of the back four until undergoing surgery for a cartilage injury in January. He returned briefly in April but limped off again in the home game against Crystal Palace at the end of the month with a thigh strain. A wholehearted player and a strong tackler he used his experience well to compensate for his reduced pace and earned himself a new contract for 2005-06.
Newcastle U *(From trainee on 3/4/1991) P/FL 71+8/9 FLC 5 FAC 7+3 Others 5+1*
Bolton W *(£2,500,000+ on 2/7/1997) P/FL 71+15/5 FLC 4+1/2 FAC 5 Others 5+2*
Newcastle U *(Free on 11/7/2001) PL 41+5/2 FLC 3+1 FAC 3+1 Others 11+1/1*

ELLIOTT Stephen William

Born: Dublin, 6 January 1984
Height: 5'8" **Weight:** 11.8
Club Honours: Ch '05
International Honours: RoI: 3; U21-10; Yth
When Sunderland boss Mick McCarthy signed this striker from Manchester City few fans had heard his name but by the season's end they were predicting an extremely bright future for him. Stephen is quick, strong, possesses an excellent first touch and is surprisingly good in the air for a relatively small man, while his 15 goals contributed immensely to the Black Cats winning the Championship title. A Republic of Ireland U21 international who holds his country's scoring record at that level, Stephen picked up his first full cap against Croatia in November.
Manchester C *(From trainee on 17/1/2001) PL 0+2*
Sunderland *(Signed on 6/8/2004) FL 29+13/15 FLC 0+2/1 FAC 2*

ELLIOTT Steven (Steve) William

Born: Swadlincote, 29 October 1978
Height: 6'1" **Weight:** 14.0
Club Honours: AMC '04
International Honours: E: U21-2
This experienced central defender established himself in Bristol Rovers rearguard with some impressive and commanding displays last season when he was a near ever-present in the side. Steve also successfully deputised at left back when required and contributed two goals during the campaign, netting against Macclesfield and Darlington.
Derby Co *(From trainee on 26/3/1997) P/FL 58+15/1 FLC 8+1 FAC 3+2*
Blackpool *(Free on 14/11/2003) FL 28 Others 5*
Bristol Rov *(Free on 5/7/2004) FL 40+1/2 FLC 2 FAC 1 Others 5*

ELLIOTT Stuart

Born: Belfast, 23 July 1978
Height: 5'10" **Weight:** 11.9
International Honours: NI: 27; U21-3

Stuart enjoyed an absolutely sensational campaign as Hull claimed their second successive promotion and he fell only one goal short of 30 goals. A man of strong religious beliefs, the club's 'Player of the Year' would be the first to admit that Hull are not a one-man team. With the required striking powers of a lethal left foot and prodigious heading ability, Stuart achieved this from a position wide on the left of midfield. Top scorer in League One, he was also selected for the PFA divisional team of the year.
Motherwell *(£100,000 from Glentoran on 20/7/2000) SL 50+20/22 SLC 2+1 SC 1+1/1*
Hull C *(£175,000 on 12/7/2002) FL 107+7/53 FLC 1+1 FAC 2+2/1 Others 0+1/1*

ELLIOTT Wade Patrick
Born: Eastleigh, 14 December 1978
Height: 5'9" **Weight:** 11.1
International Honours: E: Sch
This popular right-sided midfielder enjoyed arguably his finest campaign for Bournemouth in 2004-05. A broken toe in his foot ruled him out early on and coincided with a bad run for the side. However, the wing wizard recovered quickly and was ever-present for the remainder of the season with some eye-catching displays.
Bournemouth *(£5,000 from Bashley on 4/2/2000) FL 178+42/31 FLC 6+1 FAC 19/5 Others 9+2/1*

ELLISON Kevin
Born: Liverpool, 23 February 1979
Height: 6'1" **Weight:** 12.8
This left-sided midfielder was one of the few successes in the first half of Chester's 2004-05 campaign. Deceptively quick for such a tall player Kevin has a powerful shot and is extremely dangerous at set pieces. He hit a purple patch of goal-scoring form with a series of sensational long-distance goals around the turn of the year and was eventually snapped up by his former manager Peter Taylor at Hull City. His enthusiastic approach assisted City in their remarkable rise to the Championship.
Leicester C *(£50,000 + from Altrincham on 13/2/2001) PL 0+1*
Stockport Co *(£55,000 on 30/11/2001) FL 33+15/2 FLC 1 FAC 1 Others 2*
Lincoln C *(Loaned on 12/3/2004) FL 11 Others 2*
Chester C *(Free on 6/8/2004) FL 24/9 FLC 1 FAC 3/1 Others 2/1*
Hull C *(£100,000 on 12/1/2005) FL 11+5/1*

Wade Elliott

ELOKOBI George Nganyuo
Born: Cameroon, 31 January 1986
Height: 6'0" **Weight:** 13.2
This big defender joined Colchester United in the summer of 2004 and featured regularly in the reserves last season, with the occasional appearance in the first-team squad as an unused substitute. His only experience of senior football during the campaign came during a loan spell with League Two outfit Chester City in the new year. George initially lined up at right back in a four-man defensive set up, however, he looked far more comfortable when moved to a central-defensive role as cover for the injured Phil Bolland, his heading strength and ability to attack the ball proving more effective.
Colchester U *(Free from Dulwich Hamlet on 12/7/2004)*
Chester C *(Loaned on 27/1/2005) FL 4+1*

EMANUEL Lewis James
Born: Bradford, 14 October 1983
Height: 5'8" **Weight:** 11.12
International Honours: E: Yth
This promising youngster featured at left back and on the left-hand side of midfield for Bradford last term. Lewis enjoyed a three-month run in the side in mid-season when Wayne Jacobs was injured but then lost his regular slot to on-loan defender Paul Tierney.
Bradford C *(From trainee on 5/7/2001) FL 79+23/2 FLC 4 FAC 2+1 Others 1*

EMBLEN Neil Robert
Born: Bromley, 19 June 1971
Height: 6'1" **Weight:** 13.11
Neil skippered the Walsall side through a rather uncertain start to the 2004-05 campaign. His best spell was in mid-season and his strength in the tackle was as great as ever although he could

sometimes be beaten for pace by a ball over the top. Always ready to go forward he headed a neat equaliser against Bradford City in February. At the end of the season he signed for Hyundai-A League side New Zealand Knights.

Millwall *(£175,000 from Sittingbourne on 8/11/1993) FL 12 Others 1*
Wolverhampton W *(£600,000 on 14/7/1994) FL 80+8/9 FLC 2+2/1 FAC 7+2 Others 2+1*
Crystal Palace *(£2,000,000 on 21/8/1997) PL 8+5 FAC 1+1/2*
Wolverhampton W *(£900,000 on 26/3/1998) FL 102+12/7 FLC 8+1/1 FAC 6+1*
Norwich C *(£500,000 + on 12/7/2001) FL 6+8 FLC 0+1*
Walsall *(Loaned on 10/1/2003) FL 2+2*
Walsall *(Free on 2/5/2003) FL 62+14/7 FLC 2 FAC 2 Others 2*

EMERTON Brett

Born: Sydney, Australia, 22 February 1979
Height: 6'1" **Weight:** 13.5
International Honours: Australia: 40; U23; Yth

This talented Blackburn winger had something of a mixed season last term, when he struggled to find consistency in his form. Capable of beating a man on the outside he appeared reluctant to do this often and his finishing was often wayward. Nevertheless he worked hard and was always the chief outlet for the ball played up field. Brett was a regular in the Rovers line-up, contributing four Premiership goals.

Blackburn Rov *(£2,200,000 from Feyenoord, Holland, ex Sydney Olympic, on 21/7/2003) PL 64+10/6 FLC 1+1/1 FAC 4+2 Others 2/1*

ENCKELMAN Peter

Born: Turku, Finland, 10 March 1977
Height: 6'2" **Weight:** 12.5
International Honours: Finland: 6; U21-15

Peter was back-up 'keeper to Brad Friedel last term when he was an ever-present on the bench without being called upon for Premiership action. His only first-team appearance for Blackburn came in the Carling Cup defeat by Bournemouth when Rovers slipped to a surprise defeat. Peter only featured in a handful of games for the reserves too, as he competed with David Yelldell and then Steve Drench for a place in the side.

Aston Villa *(£200,000 from TPS Turku, Finland on 1/2/1999) PL 51+1 FLC 6 FAC 1 Others 7+1*
Blackburn Rov *(£150,000 on 7/11/2003) PL 2 FLC 1*

ETHERINGTON Matthew

Born: Truro, 14 August 1981
Height: 5'10" **Weight:** 11.2
International Honours: E: U21-3; Yth

Last term proved to be a great season for the West Ham left winger who has plenty of pace and an extensive repertoire of tricks. The sight of Matthew jinking past his marker and creating openings was one of the highlights for the Hammers' faithful in 2004-05. He is a 'big game' player and against Ipswich in the play-offs he was in brilliant form, setting up three of the goals and causing nightmares for the opposition defenders. Again in the play-off final he was the danger man providing a constant supply of crosses one of which set up Bobby Zamora to score the winner.

Peterborough U *(From trainee on 15/8/1998) FL 43+8/6 FLC 1+1 FAC 2+1 Others 2*
Tottenham H *(£500,000 on 10/1/2000) PL 20+25/1 FLC 3+1 FAC 1+1/1*
Bradford C *(Loaned on 23/10/2001) FL 12+1/1*
West Ham U *(£1,000,000 on 8/8/2003) FL 71+3/9 FLC 5 FAC 4 Others 6/1*

ETUHU Dickson Paul

Born: Kano, Nigeria, 8 June 1982
Height: 6'2" **Weight:** 13.4
Club Honours: Div 1 '02

A young midfielder with bags of potential, Dickson will be disappointed with his progress at Preston last term. A steady start was spoilt with a dismissal at Wolves in August, but two goals on his return suggested he had not lost form whilst away. However, a number of frustrating performances saw him lose his starting place from December. Strong in the tackle and when running with the ball, Dickson will be looking to make significant strides forward in more ways than one in 2005-06.

Manchester C *(From trainee on 23/12/1999) FL 11+1 FLC 1*
Preston NE *(£300,000 on 24/1/2002) FL 94+27/15 FLC 8 FAC 4/1 Others 0+3*

EUELL Jason Joseph

Born: Lambeth, 6 February 1977
Height: 5'11" **Weight:** 11.0
International Honours: Jamaica: 1; E: U21-6

Jason had a disappointing season, for after starting the first five games for Charlton he only made the line-up on three more occasions during the campaign, being used mainly as a late substitute and being given few chances to shine. He scored in the second game at home to Portsmouth, but he added only one more goal, when coming off the bench against Norwich City at in November. When Jason did play it was usually in a midfield role, not in his preferred striker's position. He is strong, good in the air, and holds the ball up well, although his first touch sometimes lets him down. His unselfish play brings others into the game and playing in midfield, just behind the front two, seemed to give him more goal-scoring opportunities. Jason won his first cap for Jamaica in November when he came on as a substitute against the USA in Columbus, Ohio.

Wimbledon *(From trainee on 1/6/1995) P/FL 118+23/41 FLC 15+2/4 FAC 14+5/2 Others 2+2*
Charlton Ath *(£4,750,000 on 16/7/2001) PL 97+32/33 FLC 4+3/1 FAC 5+3/2*

EUSTACE John Mark

Born: Solihull, 3 November 1979
Height: 5'11" **Weight:** 11.12

This tough-tackling midfield general's influence was sorely missed at Stoke last season. A troublesome groin injury received during the 2003-04 campaign remained a problem and it was not until just before Christmas that John returned to the side. After just one start and five substitute appearances he fell victim to a knee problem which kept him out until the end of the season. The Stoke midfield needs his presence and it is hoped that he will be ready to reclaim his place in the side for the start of 2005-06.

Coventry C *(From trainee on 5/11/1996) P/FL 62+24/7 FLC 6+2/2 FAC 3+2/1*
Dundee U *(Loaned on 17/2/1999) SL 8+3/1 SC 2*
Middlesbrough *(Loaned on 17/1/2003) PL 0+1*
Stoke C *(Free on 4/8/2003) FL 28+5/5 FLC 2 FAC 2+1/1*

EVANS Gareth Joseph

Born: Leeds, 15 February 1981
Height: 6'0" **Weight:** 11.12
Club Honours: AMC '04
International Honours: E: Yth

This useful defender broke into the Blackpool squad in September and featured regularly thereafter. He enjoyed a decent run in the side only to succumb to a knee injury in February and this brought his campaign to a premature close. Nevertheless he was offered an extension to his contract for the Seasiders in the summer.

Leeds U *(From trainee on 26/3/1998) PL 0+1 Others 0+1*
Huddersfield T *(Free on 9/8/2001) FL 35 FLC 1 Others 5*
Blackpool *(Free on 19/8/2003) FL 43+2 FLC 2 FAC 3+1 Others 4+2*

EVANS Michael (Micky) James
Born: Plymouth, 1 January 1973
Height: 6'1" **Weight:** 13.4
Club Honours: Div 3 '02; Div 2 '04
International Honours: RoI: 1
Micky was again an integral member of Plymouth Argyle's first-team squad last term. A strong and powerful centre forward he led the line excellently especially when manager Bobby Williamson decided to play with only one forward. Extremely good in the air Micky provided his opposition defenders with many a difficult afternoon. However, his goal tally of four was a little disappointing and he will be looking to increase this in 2005-06.
Plymouth Arg *(From trainee on 30/3/1991) FL 130+33/38 FLC 8+1 FAC 10+2/3 Others 10/2*
Southampton *(£500,000 on 4/3/1997) PL 14+8/4 FLC 2+1/1*
West Bromwich A *(£750,000 on 27/10/1997) FL 35+28/6 FLC 3+3/2 FAC 2+2/1*
Bristol Rov *(£250,000 on 18/8/2000) FL 19+2/4 FLC 2 Others 3/2*
Plymouth Arg *(£30,000 on 22/3/2001) FL 143+33/30 FLC 2+1/1 FAC 9/1 Others 1+2/2*

EVANS Paul Simon
Born: Oswestry, 1 September 1974
Height: 5'8" **Weight:** 11.6
Club Honours: Div 3 '94, '99
International Honours: W: 2; U21-4; Yth
This tough-tackling central midfielder was a regular in the Nottingham Forest squad last term with the exception of a spell in mid-season when he was sidelined by injury. Paul scored four goals during the campaign including a penalty in the 2-2 home draw with East Midlands rivals Derby County.
Shrewsbury T *(From trainee on 2/7/1993) FL 178+20/26 FLC 12+2/4 FAC 12+1/2 Others 12/4*
Brentford *(£110,000 on 3/3/1999) FL 130/31 FLC 8 FAC 3 Others 13/3*
Bradford C *(Free on 9/8/2002) FL 36+6/5 FLC 2 FAC 1*
Blackpool *(Loaned on 17/1/2003) FL 10/1*
Nottingham F *(Signed on 25/3/2004) FL 42+5/4 FLC 3 FAC 3*

EVANS Rhys Karl
Born: Swindon, 27 January 1982
Height: 6'1" **Weight:** 12.2
International Honours: E: U21-2; Yth; Sch
Rhys was first choice in goal for Swindon last term and missed just one first-team game during the campaign. He again showed that he is a fine shot-stopper making many excellent saves, throughout the season. Tall and confident he is a competent handler of the ball and not afraid to compete for crosses.
Chelsea *(From trainee on 8/2/1999)*
Bristol Rov *(Loaned on 25/2/2000) FL 4*
Queens Park Rgrs *(Loaned on 6/11/2001) FL 11*
Leyton Orient *(Loaned on 10/8/2002) FL 7*
Swindon T *(Free on 28/7/2003) FL 86 FLC 2+1 FAC 4 Others 3*

EVANS Thomas (Tommy) Raymond
Born: Doncaster, 31 December 1976
Height: 6'0" **Weight:** 13.2
International Honours: NI: Yth
After five seasons as Scunthorpe United's number one, Tommy found himself restricted to the role of reserve 'keeper throughout the 2004-05 season. A good shot-stopper and reliable last line of defence, he made just one senior appearance during the campaign, featuring in the LDV Vans Trophy defeat at Hereford in September.
Sheffield U *(From trainee on 3/7/1995)*
Crystal Palace *(Free on 14/6/1996)*
Scunthorpe U *(Free on 22/8/1997) FL 226+1 FLC 7 FAC 20 Others 13*

EVANS Duncan **Wayne**
Born: Abermule, 25 August 1971
Height: 5'10" **Weight:** 12.5
Wayne was yet again a consistent performer at right back for Rochdale last term. Playing in a very experienced back four, the timing of his tackles made up for any lack of pace and also ensured he had a good disciplinary record. Wayne was just short of 300 senior appearances for Dale when he was released by the club in the summer.
Walsall *(Free from Welshpool on 13/8/1993) FL 173+10/1 FLC 14+1/1 FAC 15+1 Others 12+3*
Rochdale *(Free on 2/7/1999) FL 259/3 FLC 9/1 FAC 18 Others 11*

EVATT Ian Ross
Born: Coventry, 19 November 1981
Height: 6'3" **Weight:** 13.11
Ian had a fine season for Chesterfield last term when he was a near ever-present in the line-up. Powerful and resolute, he relishes a physical battle with opposing strikers but has the skill to play football, too. A force in the air, he also likes to get forward to help out in attack.
Derby Co *(From trainee on 3/12/1998) P/FL 19+15 FLC 0+2/1 FAC 1*
Northampton T *(Loaned on 10/8/2001) FL 10+1 FLC 2*
Chesterfield *(Free on 4/8/2003) FL 84/9 FLC 2 FAC 2/1 Others 1+1*

EYRE John Robert
Born: Hull, 9 October 1974
Height: 6'0" **Weight:** 12.7
Despite starting the season firmly in Brian Talbot's plans, John left Oldham Athletic for a second time in summer 2005. A model professional, his versatility perhaps proved his undoing as he has operated up front, in the middle, out wide and even in the back four since returning to Boundary Park. John was chiefly deployed on the right of midfield last term, being a virtual ever-present until the Latics started to struggle in November. Three young midfielders were then brought in on long-term loan deals from the Premiership and his involvement was largely confined to the substitutes' bench thereafter. With the player's contract due to expire, new boss Ronnie Moore opted to release him in April.
Oldham Ath *(From trainee on 16/7/1993) P/FL 4+6/1 FLC 0+1*
Scunthorpe U *(Loaned on 15/12/1994) FL 9/8*
Scunthorpe U *(£40,000 on 4/7/1995) FL 151+13/43 FLC 9/2 FAC 12/3 Others 8+1/3*
Hull C *(Free on 5/7/1999) FL 43+9/13 FLC 5/3 FAC 4+1/2 Others 3+2/1*
Oldham Ath *(Free on 25/7/2001) FL 98+20/14 FLC 7/1 FAC 8+1/1 Others 6+3/1*

EYRES David
Born: Liverpool, 26 February 1964
Height: 5'11" **Weight:** 11.8
Club Honours: Div 2 '00
Despite Oldham Athletic's struggles in 2004-5 this was another excellent campaign for David, the oldest outfield player in the Football League. Incredibly, the wily 41-year-old left winger made 51 appearances – more than any other player at the club – and again picked up a clutch of awards. A personal highlight came when he scored the Latics' 'Goal of the Season', a 45-yard strike against Tranmere Rovers in the LDV VansTrophy in January. After stepping in as joint caretaker-boss with Tony Philliskirk following Brian Talbot's departure in March, David also scooped the supporters' 'Player of the Year' accolade. Out of contract in the summer, his future was unclear at the time of writing.
Blackpool *(£10,000 from Rhyl on 15/8/1989) FL 147+11/38 FLC 11+1/1 FAC 11/2 Others 13+2/4*
Burnley *(£90,000 on 29/7/1993) FL 171+4/37 FLC 17/7 FAC 14/8 Others 9/3*
Preston NE *(£80,000 on 29/10/1997) FL 85+23/19 FLC 3+4 FAC 10/3 Others 5/3*
Oldham Ath *(Free on 13/10/2000) FL 172+14/32 FLC 8/2 FAC 14+1/4 Others 8+1/4*

F

FABREGAS Francesc (Cesc)
Born: Barcelona, Spain, 4 May 1987
Height: 5'9" **Weight:** 10.8
Club Honours: CS '04; FAC '05
International Honours: Spain: U21; Yth
Without doubt the find of the season for Arsenal, this youngster stood shoulder-to-shoulder with more senior players in Premiership and European games and did not look out of place. Having started in the FA Community Shield win over Manchester United, he made his Premiership bow at Goodison Park in the opening game of the Gunners' title defence. His clever passing game, eye for goal and tremendous energy in midfield were a joy to behold and all this while still a teenager. He grabbed a first Premiership goal against Blackburn in August and another against Liverpool in May. He also made regular appearances in the Champions' League, the highlight of which was a marvellous goal against Rosenborg at Highbury.
Arsenal *(From trainee on 14/9/2004) PL 24+9/2 FLC 3+1/1 FAC 4+2 Others 5+1/1*

FACEY Delroy Michael
Born: Huddersfield, 22 April 1980
Height: 5'11" **Weight:** 13.10
After suffering a foot injury at the end of the 2003-04 campaign, Delroy missed most of the pre-season build-up with his new club so it was not until October that he came to the fore at Hull. His pace and power caused all sorts of problems for League One defences as City established their promotion credentials, but unfortunately, his progress was then hampered by a hamstring injury. With Hull increasing their attacking options, the popular striker was allowed to return to Huddersfield on loan in February, where he produced some powerful displays and was unlucky not to find the back of the net before making a permanent move to Oldham on transfer-deadline day. A powerful striker with searing pace, he had a frustrating introduction to life at Boundary Park with Ronnie Moore unwilling to break up the prolific partnership of Chris Killen and Luke Beckett. Delroy finally made his first start in the penultimate game of the season at Chesterfield.
Huddersfield T *(From trainee on 13/5/1997) FL 40+35/15 FLC 1+1 FAC 1+2 Others 2*
Bolton W *(Signed on 4/7/2002) PL 1+9/1 FAC 4*
Bradford C *(Loaned on 8/11/2002) FL 6/1*
Burnley *(Loaned on 1/9/2003) FL 12+2/5 FLC 2*
West Bromwich A *(£100,000 on 30/1/2004) FL 2+7*
Hull C *(Free on 1/7/2004) FL 12+9/4 FLC 1 FAC 2/2 Others 1*
Huddersfield T *(Loaned on 26/2/2005) FL 4*
Oldham Ath *(Free on 24/3/2005) FL 1+5*

FADIGA Khalilou
Born: Dakar, Senegal, 30 December 1974
Height: 6'0" **Weight:** 12.2
International Honours: Senegal
Primarily a left-sided midfielder, Khalilou signed for Bolton last September. He made his first appearance as a substitute against Crystal Palace, but suffered health problems in October and had a defibrillator fitted to his heart. Although some medical experts predicted he would never play the game again, he returned to reserve-team action in December. He made his first Bolton start in the FA Cup victory over Ipswich and, after a 19-month absence returned to the Senegal national team early in 2005. A player of undoubted quality, Khalilou will be looking to make his mark on the Premiership during the 2005-06 campaign.
Bolton W *(Free from Inter Milan, Italy on 1/10/2004) PL 0+5 FAC 3*

FAGAN Craig Anthony
Born: Birmingham, 11 December 1982
Height: 5'11" **Weight:** 11.12
Craig proved himself to be one of the most talented players ever to don a

Craig Fagan

Colchester United shirt, and he bemused opposing defences with his speed and trickery up front before finally signing for League One promotion certainties Hull City in February. Craig was the U's top scorer with 15 goals, scoring six times in the first 11 fixtures. He found the net within minutes of his debut for Hull, netting in the crucial 3-1 win at Tranmere. Craig soon became a key figure as the Tigers clinched their second consecutive promotion with his superb performance as a lone striker in the fine 2-0 victory at Bradford in April especially catching the eye.

Birmingham C *(From trainee on 20/12/2001) PL 0+1 FLC 0+2 FAC 0+1*
Bristol C *(Loaned on 16/1/2003) FL 5+1/1 Others 1*
Colchester U *(Free on 5/8/2003) FL 55+8/17 FLC 5/3 FAC 10/4 Others 4*
Hull C *(Signed on 28/2/2005) FL 11+1/4*

FALLON Rory Michael
Born: Gisbourne, New Zealand, 20 March 1982
Height: 6'2" **Weight:** 11.10
International Honours: E: Yth
Much was expected of Rory at Swindon during 2004-05 and the pressure seemed to get to him during the early part of the season. He kept plugging away and benefited hugely from a loan spell at Yeovil, where he scored on his debut against Scunthorpe. Rory came back to Swindon revitalised and put in several good performances towards the end of the campaign. A tall and strong striker, he causes defenders problems with his physical presence but also possesses a good touch.

Barnsley *(From trainee on 23/3/1999) FL 33+19/11 FLC 2+1 FAC 1 Others 2*
Shrewsbury T *(Loaned on 14/12/2001) FL 8+3*
Swindon T *(£60,000 on 14/11/2003) FL 18+32/9 FLC 1+1 FAC 1+2 Others 3+2/2*
Yeovil T *(Loaned on 22/2/2005) FL 2+4/1*

FARRELL David William
Born: Birmingham, 11 November 1971
Height: 5'10" **Weight:** 11.9
This talented left winger had something of a difficult time at Peterborough last term. David made the starting line-up in less than half the club's League Two fixtures and managed just two goals, netting at Colchester and in the 4-0 home win over Port Vale. He will be hoping to return to his best form in 2005-06 as Posh seek to return to League One at the first time of asking.

Aston Villa *(£45,000 from Redditch U on 6/1/1992) PL 5+1 FLC 2*
Scunthorpe U *(Loaned on 25/1/1993) FL 4+1/1 Others 2*
Wycombe W *(£100,000 on 14/9/1995) FL 44+16/8 FLC 6 FAC 3+2 Others 2*
Peterborough U *(Free on 21/7/1997) FL 248+60/36 FLC 10+3/2 FAC 21+1/3 Others 13/5*

FAULCONBRIDGE Craig Michael
Born: Nuneaton, 20 April 1978
Height: 6'1" **Weight:** 13.0
Injuries continued to plague this tall Wycombe striker last term. A knee injury, picked up in March 2004, kept him sidelined until November, and he then had a run of ten games without a goal before his knee broke down again. A January operation was reported as being a success but kept him out of action until the summer when his contract was due to end.

Coventry C *(From trainee on 5/7/1996)*
Dunfermline Ath *(Loaned on 27/3/1998) SL 1+12/1 SLC 0+1*
Hull C *(Loaned on 18/12/1998) FL 4+6 FAC 1 Others 1+1*
Wrexham *(Free on 6/8/1999) FL 92+19/31 FLC 4+1/1 FAC 4+2/1 Others 4/1*
Wycombe W *(Free on 24/7/2002) FL 46+12/8 FLC 2 FAC 3+1 Others 4+1*

FAYADH Jassim
Born: Baghdad, Iraq, 1 July 1975
Height: 5'9" **Weight:** 10.7
International Honours: Iraq
This talented left-sided player winger first came to the notice of the owners of Macclesfield Town when he appeared in the Iraqi national side during their 2004 close season tour in a match at Moss Rose. After signing for Macclesfield he spent time in the reserves, eventually making his Football League debut from the substitutes' bench in the home match against Notts County in October, thus becoming the first-ever Iraqi national to play at this level in England. He made one further substitute appearance before he was granted compassionate leave in November so that he could return to Baghdad to be with his family. Subsequently he was released from his contract by mutual consent and later signed for the Police Club of Iraq.

Macclesfield T *(Free from Al Jawiya, Iraq, ex Al Zawraa, on 27/8/2004) FL 0+1 Others 0+1*

FAYE Amdy Mustapha
Born: Dakar, Senegal, 12 March 1977
Height: 6'1" **Weight:** 12.4
International Honours: Senegal
This tenacious, hard-tackling, defensive midfielder was a regular for Portsmouth in the first half of the 2004-05 season before being sold to Newcastle during the January transfer window. He had a fine debut in the FA Cup tie against Coventry and quickly established himself as a key member of the side until an ankle injury forced his substitution in the FA Cup semi final against Manchester United. Amdy mostly featured in a role as a shield in front of the back four, using his tidy distribution to turn defence into attack. He added two further caps for Senegal during the season.

Portsmouth *(£1,500,000 from Auxerre, France on 14/8/2003) PL 44+3 FLC 2 FAC 2+1*
Newcastle U *(£2,000,000 on 25/1/2005) PL 8+1 FAC 3 Others 5*

FEATHERSTONE Lee Paul
Born: Chesterfield, 20 July 1983
Height: 6'0" **Weight:** 12.8
This versatile left-sided player who can operate at wing back, as a winger or up front was restricted to just two appearances for Scunthorpe United during 2004-05. After his final game, the LDV Vans Trophy defeat at Hereford in September, he was loaned out to Barrow where his month was cut short by a calf problem. Another loan at Harrogate Town followed and his contract was cancelled by mutual consent at the start of March after which he signed for Alfreton Town.

Sheffield U *(From trainee on 4/7/2001)*
Scunthorpe U *(Free on 11/10/2002) FL 17+15 FLC 1 FAC 3+3 Others 1+3*

FEENEY Warren James
Born: Belfast, 17 January 1981
Height: 5'10" **Weight:** 11.6
International Honours: NI: 5; U21-8; Yth; Sch
Warren became an immediate favourite with the Stockport fans last term, netting on his debut in the opening day victory over Huddersfield and finishing up with an impressive tally of 17 goals for the season, including an impressive hat-trick in his farewell appearance against Huddersfield. The pacy striker moved on to Luton on transfer-deadline day, but took time to settle in and failed to add to his tally of goals before the end of the season.

Leeds U *(Signed from St Andrew's BC on 26/1/1998)*
Bournemouth *(Free on 22/3/2001) FL 83+25/36 FLC 1+1 FAC 6+4 Others 3+2/1*
Stockport Co *(Free on 29/7/2004) FL 31/15 FAC 2/2*
Luton T *(£175,000 on 24/3/2005) FL 1+5*

FENTON Nicholas (Nicky) Leonard
Born: Preston, 23 November 1979
Height: 5'10" **Weight:** 10.4
International Honours: E: Yth
Nicky joined Doncaster Rovers in the summer of 2004 and replaced fans' favourite Mark Albrighton in the centre of the defence. Although dropped after the heavy home defeat by Sheffield Wednesday just before Christmas, he regained his place in February when Albrighton was injured and went from strength to strength, proving to be a fine signing for the club.
Manchester C *(From trainee on 26/11/1996) FL 15 FLC 3+1 Others 1*
Notts Co *(Loaned on 7/10/1999) FL 13/1 Others 1*
Bournemouth *(Loaned on 23/3/2000) FL 8*
Bournemouth *(Loaned on 11/8/2000) FL 4+1*
Notts Co *(£150,000 on 18/9/2000) FL 153+2/9 FLC 7 FAC 12/2 Others 4*
Doncaster Rov *(Free on 27/7/2004) FL 37+1/1 FLC 3 FAC 2/1 Others 2*

FERDINAND Anton Julian
Born: Peckham, 18 February 1985
Height: 6'0" **Weight:** 11.0
International Honours: E: U21-3; Yth
Last term proved to be the season when Anton established himself in the West Ham starting line-up. He was Initially played as a full back but once he reverted to the centre-back position he never looked back. He struck up an excellent partnership with another youngster, Elliott Ward, and the two received plenty of acclaim. Anton is composed and dominant, and deserves to play at the top level like his more famous brother Rio. In the final Championship game of the regular season at Watford he scored his first goal with a stunning volley. In August he gained his first England U21 cap against Ukraine and followed this up with another against Austria the following month.
West Ham U *(From trainee on 15/8/2002) FL 33+16/1 FLC 3+1 FAC 6 Others 3*

FERDINAND Leslie (Les)
Born: Acton, 8 December 1966
Height: 5'11" **Weight:** 13.5
Club Honours: FLC '99
International Honours: E: 17; B-1
A Premiership legend, Les made his Bolton debut in the opening-day victory over Charlton. He scored his first goal in the 2-2 draw with Manchester United and made his first start in the Carling Cup victory at Yeovil. Despite his undoubted pedigree, Les made just one Premiership start for Bolton, generally figuring in games only as a substitute, and it came as no surprise when he signed for Reading during the January transfer window. Recruited in an attempt to bolster the Royals' injury-hit strike force, he scored only once in 14 appearances and never completed a full 90 minutes. Nevertheless he was immensely popular with the fans, and showed some sublimely skilful touches.
Queens Park Rgrs *(£15,000 from Hayes on 12/3/1987) P/FL 152+11/80 FLC 11+2/7 FAC 6+1/3 Others 1*
Brentford *(Loaned on 24/3/1988) FL 3*
Newcastle U *(£6,000,000 on 7/6/1995) PL 67+1/41 FLC 6/3 FAC 4+1/2 Others 5/4*
Tottenham H *(£6,000,000 on 5/8/1997) PL 97+21/33 FLC 11+4/5 FAC 15+1/1*
West Ham U *(£200,000 on 21/1/2003) PL 12+2/2*
Leicester C *(Free on 15/7/2003) PL 20+9/12 FAC 1+1/1*
Bolton W *(Free on 7/7/2004) PL 1+11/1 FLC 1+1/1*
Reading *(Free on 6/1/2005) FL 4+8/1 FAC 2*

Anton Ferdinand

FERDINAND Rio Gavin
Born: Peckham, 7 November 1978
Height: 6'2" **Weight:** 12.1
Club Honours: PL '03; CS '03
International Honours: E: 38; U21-5; Yth
A consummate central defender, who possesses great strength in the air and neat skills on the ground, Rio stepped back onto the Premiership stage against Liverpool in September, and his subsequent performances for the Reds suggested he'd ever been away. With his much-publicised ban now firmly behind him, his cool, reliable, solid and dependable presence kick-started what had been a rather laboured start to the season by United. Putting together a run of 17 consecutive Premiership games, Rio was rewarded with a place in the PFA Premiership team of the season. At the Millennium Stadium in May, he had a 'goal' marginally ruled out for offside – what a first of the season that might have been! Planting the seed that he wanted to succeed Roy Keane as United's next captain, the only stalling point at the time of writing was Rio signing a new long-term contract.
West Ham U *(From trainee on 27/11/1995) PL 122+5/2 FLC 12+1 FAC 9 Others 9*
Bournemouth *(Loaned on 8/11/1996) FL 10 Others 1*
Leeds U *(£18,000,000 on 27/11/2000) PL 54/2 FLC 2 FAC 3 Others 14/1*
Manchester U *(£29,100,000 + on 22/7/2002) PL 78+1 FLC 5 FAC 8 Others 23*

FERGUSON Barry
Born: Glasgow, 2 February 1978
Height: 5'11" **Weight:** 11.1
Club Honours: SPD '99, '00, '03; SLC '98, '00, '03; SC '00, '02, '03
International Honours: S: 29; U21-12
Appointed captain of Blackburn Rovers under manager Graeme Souness, Barry never seemed comfortable with the role early on last season and struggled to impose himself on matches. The arrival of new boss Mark Hughes made him reconsider his future, and in the January transfer window he moved back to his former club Rangers. He went on to assist the Ibrox club to a surprise last-gasp success in winning the SPL title and also continued to represent Scotland during the campaign.
Glasgow Rgrs *(From juniors on 6/7/1994) SL 151+2/24 SLC 15/3 SC 23+2/6 Others 46+1/2*
Blackburn Rov *(£7,500,000 on 30/8/2003) PL 35+1/3 FLC 1/1 FAC 1*

FERGUSON Darren
Born: Glasgow, 9 February 1972
Height: 5'10" **Weight:** 11.10
Club Honours: PL '93; AMC '05
International Honours: S: U21-5; Yth
This central midfield remained a key figure at the heart of Wrexham's midfield engine-room last season, although he did not always show his best form. Darren is never more happy than when he is acting as midfield general, dictating the play from the centre of the park. He notched the second goal in Wrexham's 2-0 LDV Vans Trophy success against Southend United at Cardiff's Millennium Stadium.
Manchester U *(From trainee on 11/7/1990) P/FL 20+7 FLC 2+1*
Wolverhampton W *(£250,000 on 13/1/1994) FL 94+23/4 FLC 13+2/3 FAC 9+2/3 Others 6*
Wrexham *(Free on 17/9/1999) FL 237+1/22 FLC 8/2 FAC 11/1 Others 12+1/2*

FERGUSON Duncan Cowan
Born: Stirling, 27 December 1971
Height: 6'4" **Weight:** 14.6
Club Honours: SL '94; SLC '94; FAC '95
International Honours: S: 7; B; U21-7; Yth; Sch
This big centre forward enjoyed one of his finest seasons in the royal blue jersey of Everton, staying injury-free for the most part, and he remained a major influence both on and off the pitch at Goodison. David Moyes got the best out of the Scot by employing him as a substitute and he could usually be relied upon to make things happen when entering the fray. Of his five Premiership goals, three were winners and one was a late equaliser against Birmingham. Duncan's power in the air is legendary but he is also more than adept when the ball is kept on the floor and he has a much underrated football brain. He was offered a new contract near the end of the season, partly as a reward for his efforts during the campaign.
Dundee U *(Signed from Carse Thistle on 1/2/1990) SL 75+2/28 SLC 2+1/2 SC 8/6*
Glasgow Rgrs *(£4,000,000 on 20/7/1993) SL 8+6/2 SLC 2+2/3 SC 0+3 Others 1*
Everton *(£4,400,000 on 4/10/1994) PL 110+6/37 FLC 8/1 FAC 8+1/4*
Newcastle U *(£7,000,000 + on 25/11/1998) PL 24+6/8 FAC 6+2/3 Others 2+1/1*
Everton *(£3,750,000 on 19/8/2000) PL 45+51/22 FLC 5+1/4 FAC 5/3*

FERNANDES Fabrice
Born: Paris, France, 29 October 1979
Height: 5'9" **Weight:** 11.7
Club Honours: Div 1 '01
International Honours: France: U21
When Harry Rednapp became Saints' manager in December he quickly identified why his side were struggling: lack of pace! Which should have been good news for 'Fab', who can be electrifying. Left footed, he is at his best on the right wing, cutting in to create scoring opportunities, or pulling the ball back to cross, but he has the tendency to promise more than he delivers, and he failed to impress Redknapp. Minor injuries limited Fabrice's availability in February and March, but he was not even allocated bench-warming duties after January.
Fulham *(Loaned from Rennes, France on 3/8/2000) FL 23+6/2 FLC 4+2/1 FAC 1/1*
Glasgow Rgrs *(Loaned on 16/3/2001) SL 0+4/1*
Southampton *(£1,100,000 from Rennes, France on 27/12/2001) PL 76+15/5 FLC 4+1/1 FAC 6+2 Others 2*

FERREIRA Renato **Paulo**
Born: Cascais, Portugal, 18 January 1979
Height: 6'0" **Weight:** 11.13
Club Honours: FLC '05; PL '05
International Honours: Portugal: 22
For the second time in two years Jose Mourinho signed this attacking right back. Mourinho obviously has great faith in Ferreira and the dashing defender settled immediately into English football following a surprisingly hesitant Euro 2004 tournament. He is adventurous, solid in the tackle, comfortable on the ball and played a large part in Chelsea's record-breaking season. He is also adaptable, occasionally switching to the left flank, with no noticeable discomfort, to cover for the absent Wayne Bridge. Unfortunately, Paulo missed the season's climax when he became the third victim of Chelsea's broken metatarsal jinx following Arjen Robben and Scott Parker. Paulo sustained his injury on international duty for Portugal in their World Cup qualifier in Slovakia.
Chelsea *(£13,200,000 from FC Porto, Portugal, on 20/7/2004) PL 29 FLC 5 FAC 0+1 Others 6+1*

FERRELL Andrew (Andy) Eric
Born: Newcastle, 9 January 1984
Height: 5'8" **Weight:** 11.5
Andy joined Watford on a free transfer before the start of the 2004-05 season. A left-footed midfield player, he made his first-team debut as a substitute against Cambridge in the Carling Cup and marked the occasion with a spectacular match-winning goal. But despite playing consistently for the reserves, he made only one further appearance for the first team and was released at the end of the season.
Newcastle U *(From trainee on 5/12/2002)*
Watford *(Free on 21/7/2004) FLC 0+2/1*

Duncan Ferguson (right)

Alan Fettis

FETTIS Alan William
Born: Belfast, 1 February 1971
Height: 6'2" **Weight:** 13.10
International Honours: NI: 25; B-3; Yth; Sch
This vastly experienced 'keeper was signed by Macclesfield in the 2004 close season and immediately became the club's first choice. Last term he was sidelined through injury on three separate occasions and despite making a quick recovery there were times when he was kept on the substitutes' bench because of the good form of Steve Wilson. Nevertheless, Alan commands his area well, distributes the ball thoughtfully and is good in the air.
Hull C *(£50,000 from Ards on 14/8/1991) FL 131+4/2 FLC 7+1 FAC 5 Others 7*
West Bromwich A *(Loaned on 20/11/1995) FL 3*
Nottingham F *(£250,000 on 13/1/1996) P/FL 4 FLC 1 FAC 0+1*
Blackburn Rov *(£300,000 on 12/9/1997) P/FL 9+2 FAC 1*
York C *(Free on 1/3/2000) FL 125 FLC 3 FAC 12*
Hull C *(Free on 23/1/2003) FL 20 FLC 1 Others 2*
Sheffield U *(Loaned on 5/12/2003) FL 2+1*
Grimsby T *(Loaned on 11/3/2004) FL 11*
Macclesfield T *(Free on 2/7/2004) FL 28 FAC 1 Others 4*

FILAN John Richard
Born: Sydney, Australia, 8 February 1970
Height: 5'11" **Weight:** 13.2
Club Honours: Div 2 '03
International Honours: Australia: 2; U23
John remained a vital member of the Wigan Athletic defence last term, as demonstrated by his being an ever-present as the club gained promotion to the top flight for the first time in their history. A strong figure between the posts he enjoyed another exceptional season with terrific form as the last line of defence. The campaign saw him celebrate his 150th League start for the club in February. A top shot-stopper, his positional sense and handling ability were impressive throughout. He was reported to have signed a new contract, which will keep him at the JJB Stadium for the foreseeable future.
Cambridge U *(£40,000 from Budapest St George, Australia on 12/3/1993) FL 68 FLC 6 FAC 3 Others 5*
Coventry C *(£300,000 on 2/3/1995) PL 15+1 FLC 2*
Blackburn Rov *(£700,000 on 10/7/1997) P/FL 61+1 FLC 6 FAC 5*
Wigan Ath *(£450,000 on 14/12/2001) FL 162 FLC 6 FAC 5 Others 1*

FINNAN Stephen (Steve) John
Born: Limerick, 20 April 1976
Height: 5'10" **Weight:** 11.6
Club Honours: Div 3 '98; Div 2 '99; Div 1 '01; UEFACL '05
International Honours: RoI: 36; B-1; U21-8
After a disappointing first season at Anfield, the Republic of Ireland international right back enjoyed a more convincing and consistent 2004-05 campaign playing in nearly all of Liverpool's significant Premiership and European Champions' League games. At the beginning of the season his usual full-back slot was allocated to Josemi, a summer signing by new manager Rafael Benitez, and he was handed the right-midfield role from which position he scored his first (and to date) only goal for the Reds at home to West Brom in September. From November onwards, however, he held down the right-back berth and tightened up his defensive play. In the unforgettable European Cup final, in common with his colleagues, he was overwhelmed by the rampant AC Milan team and was substituted at half time, thus playing no part in Liverpool's stunning recovery.
Birmingham C *(£100,000 from Welling U on 12/6/1995) FL 9+6/1 FLC 2+2 Others 2+1*
Notts Co *(Loaned on 5/3/1996) FL 14+3/2 Others 3/1*
Notts Co *(£300,000 on 31/10/1996) FL 71+9/5 FLC 4 FAC 7/1 Others 1*
Fulham *(£600,000 on 13/11/1998) P/FL 171+1/6 FLC 10+1 FAC 18/1 Others 6*
Liverpool *(£3,500,000 on 30/6/2003) PL 48+7/1 FLC 4+1 FAC 3 Others 17+3*

FINNIGAN John Francis
Born: Wakefield, 29 March 1976
Height: 5'8" **Weight:** 10.11
Cheltenham Town's club captain enjoyed another highly consistent season in the centre of midfield last term. An energetic figure who never stops running and chasing, John is also comfortable in possession and a good passer. He mostly partnered Grant McCann in the centre of a four-man midfield for the Robins, leading the team to the fringes of the battle for a play-off spot. He also contributed four goals, including a brace in the 3-2 win at Leyton Orient over Easter.
Nottingham F *(From trainee on 10/5/1993)*
Lincoln C *(£50,000 on 26/3/1998) FL 139+4/3 FLC 7 FAC 8+1/1 Others 7*
Cheltenham T *(Free on 7/3/2002) FL 109+5/7 FLC 2 FAC 6 Others 5/2*

FISH Mark Anthony
Born: Cape Town, South Africa, 14 March 1974
Height: 6'4" **Weight:** 13.2
International Honours: South Africa: 62 (ANC '96)
Mark's 2004-05 season at Charlton was wrecked by persistent knee injury problems. He started out as first choice in central defence, playing in the first four games, but made only four more appearances throughout the rest of the campaign. Although he can play at right back, Mark is at his best in the centre of the defence, where his height and presence are best suited. He is very calm when under pressure and is strong, very good in the air and extremely comfortable on the ball. A vastly experienced player he is an asset to the side when fully fit.
Bolton W *(£2,500,000 from Lazio, Italy, ex Orlando Pirates, on 16/9/1997) P/FL 102+1/3 FLC 12+1/1 FAC 6 Others 5*
Charlton Ath *(£700,000 on 10/11/2000) PL 101+1/2 FLC 4 FAC 4+1*

FISH Nicholas (Nicky) James
Born: Cardiff, 15 September 1984
Height: 5'10" **Weight:** 11.4
International Honours: W: U21-2; Yth
A product of the youth policy at Ninian Park, this central midfielder was a mainstay of Cardiff City's successful reserve team last term. He was named in the senior squad for the first time at the start of the campaign and he made his full debut in the Carling Cup tie at Bournemouth in October, which proved to be his only first-team appearance of the season.
Cardiff C *(From trainee on 6/3/2002) FLC 1*

FISKEN Gary Stewart
Born: Watford, 27 October 1981
Height: 6'0" **Weight:** 12.7
A creative midfield player, Gary was mainly used as a substitute by Swansea City during the opening half of the 2004-05 season, finally making his first start in a suspension and injury-depleted side against Bury at the Vetch Field in late November. He had a loan spell at Cambridge City in early April, scoring on his debut and helping the club reach the final of the Conference South play-offs.
Watford *(From trainee on 8/2/2000) FL 15+7/1 FLC 3+2 FAC 1*
Swansea C *(Signed on 6/8/2004) FL 1+4 FLC 0+1 FAC 0+1*

FITZGERALD John Desmond
Born: Dublin, 10 February 1984
Height: 6'2" **Weight:** 12.13
International Honours: RoI: U21-11; Yth

This young defender continued to make progress with Blackburn's reserve team last season and in January he joined Bury on loan, making his debut in the 2-0 home win over Northampton. A commanding centre half who is powerful in the air, John remained an automatic choice throughout the three months of his loan, during which time the Shakers' fortunes improved greatly. He continued to represent Republic of Ireland at U21 level during the campaign.
Blackburn Rov *(From trainee on 16/2/2001)*
Bury *(Loaned on 21/1/2005) FL 14*

FITZGERALD Scott Brian
Born: Westminster, 13 August 1969
Height: 6'0" **Weight:** 12.12
International Honours: RoI: B-1; U21-4
After helping Brentford avoid relegation in 2003-04, while on loan, Scott joined the Bees on a permanent contract in the summer. He started the season at centre half but suffered neck and thigh injuries in September and these led to a spell on the sidelines. He only made occasional appearances thereafter due to the form of Michael Turner and Sam Sodje. Scott will be Brentford's youth-team manager in 2005-06.
Wimbledon *(From trainee on 13/7/1989) P/FL 95+11/1 FLC 13 FAC 5 Others 1*
Sheffield U *(Loaned on 23/11/1995) FL 6*
Millwall *(Loaned on 11/10/1996) FL 7*
Millwall *(£50,000 + on 28/7/1997) FL 79+3/1 FLC 4 FAC 2 Others 5*
Colchester U *(Free on 17/10/2000) FL 114+2 FLC 3 FAC 5 Others 4*
Brentford *(Free on 16/3/2004) FL 21 FLC 1 FAC 1 Others 1*

FITZGERALD Scott Peter
Born: Hillingdon, 18 November 1979
Height: 5'11" **Weight:** 11.6
Scott failed to make a first-team start for Watford last term and embarked on a series of loan transfers, with mixed success. He joined Swansea in September, but although he showed some neat touches he had little chance to shine. Next stop was Leyton Orient where he had the misfortune to be sent off on his debut and his final port of call was Brentford. He thus became the second 'Scott Fitzgerald' on the club's books. A goalmouth poacher Scott scored all his four goals away from home, including two on his full debut at Oldham and the goal that took the Bees into the play-offs at Wrexham.
Watford *(Free from Northwood on 5/3/2003) FL 29+26/11 FLC 0+3/1 FAC 0+1*
Swansea C *(Loaned on 28/9/2004) FL 0+3 Others 1*
Leyton Orient *(Loaned on 14/1/2005) FL 1*
Brentford *(Signed on 4/3/2005) FL 7+5/4 Others 1*

FLAHAVAN Darryl James
Born: Southampton, 28 November 1978
Height: 5'10" **Weight:** 12.1
After starting the 2004-05 campaign as understudy to new signing Bart Griemink, Darryl ended the season back as first choice 'keeper for Southend. The two both enjoyed useful runs in the side until Griemink's injury against Notts County in January finally left Darryl in charge, and he took his chance well. Although only small in stature, he shook off his reputation for not coming off his line and became much more dominating in the box, a testament to his work with Shrimpers' goalkeeping coach Lee Turner.
Southampton *(From trainee on 14/5/1996. Free to Woking on 13/8/1998)*
Southend U *(Free from Chesham U on 16/10/2000) FL 174+2 FLC 2 FAC 17 Others 25*

FLAMINI Mathieu
Born: Marseille, France, 7 March 1984
Height: 5'10" **Weight:** 11.12
International Honours: France: U21
Mathieu made the now well-worn route from France to London as Arsene Wenger added another fellow countryman to the

Mathieu Flamini

Gunners' squad in the close season. His game is based on his ability to seemingly cover every blade of grass in midfield. He formed an impressive central-midfield partnership with Cesc Fabregas for the home games with Chelsea in the Premiership and Rosenborg in the Champions League and grabbed his first Arsenal goal in the 7-0 romp over Everton in May.
Arsenal *(Signed from Marseilles, France, on 11/8/2004) PL 9+12/1 FLC 3 FAC 4 Others 2+2*

FLEETWOOD Stuart Keith
Born: Gloucester, 23 April 1986
Height: 5'10" **Weight:** 11.8
International Honours: W: U21-2; Yth
Noted for his excellent pace and ability to get behind full backs on the flanks, this promising striker is highly rated at Cardiff City. Stuart waited patiently for his chance last term and it duly arrived in September when he was selected for a starting place ahead of Alan Lee. He began brightly, but unfortunately suffered an ankle injury shortly before half time. This kept him out until December and a series of niggling injuries thereafter prevented him from recovering sufficient fitness to progress in the senior team.
Cardiff C *(From trainee on 2/2/2004) FL 1+7 FLC 0+3*

FLEMING Craig
Born: Halifax, 6 October 1971
Height: 6'0" **Weight:** 12.10
Club Honours: Div 1 '04
Craig extended his proud record of not missing a game for the Canaries to an impressive 92 games and played every single minute of his team's first Premiership campaign in nine years. A much underrated central defender he thrives on the direct confrontation and battle with his opponent, always competing for the high ball and being prepared to throw his body in the way of shots and crosses. He moved into the club's all-time top-20 appearance makers during the 2004-05 season, which represents an excellent return on Norwich's investment back in 1997.
Halifax T *(From trainee on 21/3/1990) FL 56+1 FLC 4 FAC 3 Others 3+2*
Oldham Ath *(£80,000 on 15/8/1991) P/FL 158+6/1 FLC 12+1 FAC 11 Others 4*
Norwich C *(£600,000 on 30/6/1997) P/FL 290+7/11 FLC 19 FAC 10+1 Others 3*

FLEMING Curtis
Born: Manchester, 8 October 1968
Height: 5'11" **Weight:** 12.8
Club Honours: Div 1 '95
International Honours: RoI: 10; U23-2; U21-5; Yth
This vastly experienced defender returned to the North-East last term to link up with several former Middlesbrough team-mates at Darlington. Curtis immediately impressed with his calm play at the back and ability to bring the ball out of defence to set up attacks. He suffered a couple of spells out through injury but overall was a steadying influence in the heart of the defence.
Middlesbrough *(£50,000 from St Patricks on 16/8/1991) P/FL 248+18/3 FLC 24+2/1 FAC 16+1 Others 7+1*
Birmingham C *(Loaned on 16/11/2001) FL 6*
Crystal Palace *(£100,000 on 31/12/2001) FL 41+4 FLC 2+1 FAC 1*
Darlington *(Free on 5/8/2004) FL 24+3 FLC 1*

FLEMING Terence (Terry) Maurice
Born: Marston Green, 5 January 1973
Height: 5'9" **Weight:** 10.9
This experienced, gritty midfielder signed for Grimsby Town after impressing in the pre-season programme and soon gained a regular place in the starting line-up. Terry showed his versatility by appearing in a variety of positions, although he was mainly used on the right-hand side of midfield. He also netted a couple of goals, which were much appreciated in a season when the Mariners failed to come up with a regular goal-scorer.
Coventry C *(From trainee on 2/7/1991) P/FL 8+5 FLC 0+1*
Northampton T *(Free on 3/8/1993) FL 26+5/1 FLC 2 FAC 0+1 Others 0+1*
Preston NE *(Free on 18/7/1994) FL 25+7/2 FLC 4 FAC 0+1 Others 3+2*
Lincoln C *(Free on 7/12/1995) FL 175+8/8 FLC 11+1/2 FAC 11/2 Others 4*
Plymouth Arg *(Free on 4/7/2000) FL 15+2 FLC 2 FAC 2 Others 0+2*
Cambridge U *(Free on 8/3/2001) FL 96+9/4 FLC 3 FAC 7 Others 8+2/1*
Grimsby T *(Free on 12/7/2004) FL 43/2 FLC 2 FAC 1 Others 0+1*

FLETCHER Carl Neil
Born: Camberley, 7 April 1980
Height: 5'10" **Weight:** 11.7
International Honours: W: 8
Carl started the 2004-05 season as Bournemouth captain in fine style, netting twice in the opening seven games before making his last appearance at the end of August at Luton after which he was sold to West Ham. A versatile player who can feature either in midfield or as a defender, he is very much a leader on the pitch. Carl made an impressive debut for the Hammers at Sheffield United and contributed goals in successive fixtures against Derby and Cardiff City. After losing his place in the side in March he came back with a vengeance, producing an awesome display at Ipswich in the play-off semi-final. Carl also added to his tally of caps for Wales during the campaign.
Bournemouth *(From trainee on 3/7/1998) FL 186+7/19 FLC 6 FAC 15+1/1 Others 9+1/3*
West Ham U *(£250,000 on 31/8/2004) FL 26+6/2 FAC 3 Others 1*

FLETCHER Darren Barr
Born: Edinburgh, 1 February 1984
Height: 6'0" **Weight:** 13.5
Club Honours: FAC '04
International Honours: S: 15; B-1; U21-2
An elegant midfielder, who possesses good touch and passing skills, Darren continued to show promise despite his somewhat limited first-team opportunities for Manchester United in 2004-05. A handy statistic that might have gone unnoticed by many Reds fanatics was that Darren was only on the losing side twice for the Reds in all four major competitions - against Chelsea in the last home Premiership game of the season, and against Arsenal in the FA Cup final. Although not a regular goal-scorer, he did manage two efforts throughout the campaign, the first against Middlesbrough in January, and the second against Charlton in May.
Manchester U *(From trainee on 3/2/2001) PL 35+5/3 FLC 5 FAC 5+3 Others 8+6*

FLETCHER Steven (Steve) Mark
Born: Hartlepool, 26 June 1972
Height: 6'2" **Weight:** 14.9
Last term proved to be a record-breaking season for this big Bournemouth striker who lived up to his reputation of being one of the best target men in the lower divisions. He scored the first senior hat-trick of his 15-year career, passed the 100-goal mark, the 500-appearance mark for the Cherries, and in April broke the all-time League appearance record for the club with his 424th outing at Bradford, beating present manager Sean O'Driscoll's record.
Hartlepool U *(From trainee on 23/8/1990) FL 19+13/4 FLC 0+2/1 FAC 1+2 Others 2+2/1*
Bournemouth *(£30,000 on 28/7/1992) FL 393+32/83 FLC 28/3 FAC 28+2/7 Others 18+3/4*

FLINDERS Scott Liam
Born: Rotherham, 12 June 1986
Height: 6'4" **Weight:** 14.0
International Honours: E: Yth

Darren Fletcher

Scott spent much of the 2004-05 campaign developing in Barnsley's reserve team and was given his chance when Ross Turnbull was injured. The promising 'keeper looked comfortable in the role and proved a good shot-stopper, doing well enough to retain his place in the line-up until the end of the season. He was called up to the England U20 squad in the summer.
Barnsley *(From trainee on 2/4/2005) FL 11*

FLITCROFT David (Dave) John
Born: Bolton, 14 January 1974
Height: 5'11" **Weight:** 13.5
A committed hard-tackling central midfield player, Dave was a preferred choice of Bury manager Graham Barrow throughout the 2004-05 season. He generally played in a 'holding' role that allowed his midfield partners to push forward to great effect. He scored just one goal during the campaign, netting an important last-minute winner against bottom club Cambridge in March, thus ending a run of seven without a win for the Shakers and triggering an improvement in form which saw the team climb away from the lower reaches of the League Two table.
Preston NE *(From trainee on 2/5/1992) FL 4+4/2 FLC 0+1 Others 0+1*
Lincoln C *(Loaned on 17/9/1993) FL 2 FLC 0+1*
Chester C *(Free on 9/12/1993) FL 146+21/18 FLC 10+1 FAC 7 Others 8/1*
Rochdale *(Free on 5/7/1999) FL 141+19/4 FLC 5+2 FAC 7+4 Others 9+1*
Macclesfield T *(Free on 11/7/2003) FL 14+1 Others 1*
Bury *(Free on 30/1/2004) FL 49+4/3 FLC 1 FAC 2 Others 1*

FLITCROFT Garry William
Born: Bolton, 6 November 1972
Height: 6'0" **Weight:** 12.2
Club Honours: FLC '02
International Honours: E: U21-10; Yth; Sch
This combative Blackburn midfielder was hampered by injuries last term and started less than half the club's Premiership games. Garry was at his best when the team was under pressure and it required a tough man to get a boot in. His finest display was in the 1-0 win at Bolton over the Christmas period, when he consistently made tackles and picked up loose balls.
Manchester C *(From trainee on 2/7/1991) PL 109+6/13 FLC 11+1 FAC 14/2*
Bury *(Loaned on 5/3/1992) FL 12*
Blackburn Rov *(£3,200,000 on 26/3/1996) P/FL 230+14/14 FLC 10+3/1 FAC 15+2/4 Others 4/1*

FLOOD William (Willo) Robert
Born: Dublin, 10 April 1985
Height: 5'6" **Weight:** 9.11
International Honours: RoI: U21-10; Yth
A right winger who loves to take on the full back and make a dash to the flank, Willo made a big impact for Manchester City in his first season in the Premiership following a dream debut in the Blues 7-1 rout of Barnsley in the Carling Cup. He further enhanced his claims to a regular place in the first team by scoring on his Premiership debut. During the season Willo was named the Republic of Ireland's U19 'Player of the Year' and he also featured in the U21 squad during the campaign.
Manchester C *(From trainee on 13/4/2002) PL 4+5/1 FLC 2/1 FAC 0+1 Others 1*
Rochdale *(Loaned on 15/3/2004) FL 6*

FLYNN Michael (Mike) Anthony
Born: Oldham, 23 February 1969
Height: 6'0" **Weight:** 11.0
Club Honours: AMC '04
This veteran defender was in and out of the Blackpool line-up last term as the team struggled defensively. However, he fell out of contention following the arrival of Peter Clarke and at the end of September he moved on to join Conference outfit Accrington Stanley, featuring regularly in their line-up for the remainder of the campaign.
Oldham Ath *(From apprentice on 7/2/1987) FL 37+3/1 FLC 1+1 FAC 1 Others 2*
Norwich C *(£100,000 on 22/12/1988)*
Preston NE *(£125,000 on 4/12/1989) FL 134+2/7 FLC 6 FAC 6+1/1 Others 13*
Stockport Co *(£125,000 on 25/3/1993) FL 386+1/16 FLC 34/2 FAC 20/1 Others 19*
Stoke C *(Loaned on 12/1/2002) FL 11+2*
Barnsley *(Free on 15/3/2002) FL 20+1*
Blackpool *(Free on 10/1/2003) FL 55+2/1 FLC 1 FAC 2+1 Others 6+1*

FLYNN Michael John
Born: Newport, 17 October 1980
Height: 5'10" **Weight:** 12.10
Club Honours: Div 2 '03
International Honours: W: SP
This versatile performer found first-team opportunities limited at Wigan Athletic and was loaned out to Blackpool to gain experience. Particularly effective at supporting the forwards when employed in the middle of the park, his only goal for the Latics came in the home win over Coventry City in his first appearance of the season. He started his only game in the home draw against Watford before joining Gillingham, where he settled in well and produced a 'Man of the Match' performance when the two clubs met at Priestfield.
Wigan Ath *(£50,000 from Barry T, ex Newport Co, on 25/6/2002) FL 5+33/2 FLC 0+4 FAC 1+2/1 Others 2*
Blackpool *(Loaned on 20/8/2004) FL 6 FLC 1*
Gillingham *(Signed on 3/2/2005) FL 16/3*

FOLAN Caleb Colman
Born: Leeds, 26 October 1982
Height: 6'1" **Weight:** 12.12
This young Chesterfield striker built on the promise of the previous season and enjoyed a fine start to the 2004-05

Michael Flynn (Gillingham)

campaign. His pace and height caused problems for opposition defenders and he scored six goals, a tally that will surely increase with experience. Caleb was probably the best foil for the experienced Wayne Allison and the pair looked the most dangerous of the club's forward combinations.
Leeds U *(From trainee on 2/11/1999)*
Rushden & Diamonds *(Loaned on 5/10/2001) FL 1+5 Others 1*
Hull C *(Loaned on 30/11/2001) FL 0+1*
Chesterfield *(Free on 14/2/2003) FL 30+22/7 FAC 1*

FOLEY David John
Born: South Shields, 12 May 1987
Height: 5'4" **Weight:** 8.9
This promising young Hartlepool striker received few first-team opportunities in 2004-05. An injury crisis allowed him a place in the starting line-up at Oldham, but otherwise he was restricted to substitute appearances. David was a member of the Hartlepool reserve team which won the Durham Challenge Cup.
Hartlepool U *(Trainee) FL 1+2 FAC 0+1 Others 0+1*

FOLEY Kevin Patrick
Born: Luton, 1 November 1984
Height: 5'9" **Weight:** 11.2
Club Honours: Div 1 '05
International Honours: RoI: U21-4
This versatile Luton Town player lined up at right back at the start of the 2004-05 campaign. His passing, sense of position and speed in getting forward all contributed to the Hatters' water-tight defence. Kevin also appeared in midfield and on the left side of the defence when required. He featured for the Republic of Ireland at U21 level during the campaign.
Luton T *(From trainee on 8/3/2004) FL 70+4/3 FLC 2/2 FAC 5 Others 1+1*

FOLKES Peter Alexander
Born: Birmingham, 16 November 1984
Height: 6'0" **Weight:** 12.2
Peter continued to gain experience after his move to Lincoln City and was given his senior debut when he was included at right back in the Imps' LDV Vans Trophy first round tie. Peter, who was also used at centre back in the reserves, was included on the substitutes' bench on a regular basis in the first half of the season, but his only other action was when he came on as a late substitute in the FA Cup tie at Hartlepool. He was briefly loaned to Southern League club Stamford in March and at the end of the season he accepted the offer of a new contract with the Imps.
Bradford C *(From trainee at Bristol C on 6/8/2003)*
Lincoln C *(Free on 4/8/2004) FAC 0+1 Others 1*

FOLLY Yoann
Born: Togo, 6 June 1985
Height: 5'11" **Weight:** 11.0
International Honours: France: Yth
After a noteworthy start to his Premiership career towards the conclusion of the 2003-04 season, Yoann started last term in the centre of midfield at Villa Park, was substituted at half time, and made just three more appearances for Saints thereafter. A refined, dexterous player, with fine anticipation and adroit distribution skills, he spent the latter half of the season on loan, firstly at Nottingham Forest and then at Preston, but although he showed fine potential at both clubs he made few appearances.
Southampton *(£250,000 from St Etienne, France on 31/7/2003) PL 10+2 FLC 0+1*
Nottingham F *(Loaned on 7/1/2005) FL 0+1 FAC 1/1*
Preston NE *(Loaned on 14/3/2005) FL 0+2*

FONTAINE Liam Vaughan Henry
Born: Beckenham, 7 January 1986
Height: 6'3" **Weight:** 12.2
Club Honours: Div 2 '05
A young central defender with a promising future Liam made his first-team debut for Fulham as a substitute at Southampton and was then selected to start in the FA Cup third round tie at Watford when he gave an assured performance. This followed an early-season loan spell at Yeovil where he shone in the back line alongside Terry Skiverton. Later in the campaign he spent time on loan with SPL club Kilmarnock before returning early with a back injury.
Fulham *(From trainee on 5/3/2004) PL 0+1 FAC 1*
Yeovil T *(Loaned on 13/8/2004) FL 15 FLC 2 Others 1*
Kilmarnock *(Loaned on 28/1/2005) SL 3 SC 2*

FORBES Adrian Emmanuel
Born: Ealing, 23 January 1979
Height: 5'8" **Weight:** 11.10
International Honours: E: Yth
Adrian joined Swansea City with a reputation for playing either as a central striker, or as a wide-right-sided midfielder. He initially struggled to make a breakthrough for the Swans but after impressing against his former club Luton Town in the LDV Vans Trophy tie, he scored his first goal in the next home game against Mansfield Town. He was sidelined in late January with a knee injury, which kept him out of action for a few weeks, but he scored in the last two games to help ensure an automatic promotion place for the Swans.
Norwich C *(From trainee on 21/1/1997) FL 66+46/8 FLC 1+4 FAC 2+2*
Luton T *(£60,000 on 16/7/2001) FL 39+33/14 FLC 1 FAC 5/6 Others 0+1*
Swansea C *(Free on 2/7/2004) FL 36+4/7 FLC 1 FAC 5 Others 2*

FORBES Terrell Dishan
Born: Southwark, 17 August 1981
Height: 6'0" **Weight:** 12.8
Club Honours: FAYC '99
This right-sided defender started the 2004-05 campaign on a monthly contract for Queen's Park Rangers, although he had been on the list of released players. His contract was not renewed at the end of August and he moved on to join League Two outfit Grimsby Town. Despite well-publicised off-the-field problems in the early part of the season this right-sided defender was one of the most consistent players in what was generally a somewhat indifferent season for the Mariners.
West Ham U *(From trainee on 2/7/1999)*
Bournemouth *(Loaned on 18/10/1999) FL 3 FAC 1*
Queens Park Rgrs *(Free on 24/7/2001) FL 113+1 FLC 6 FAC 3+1 Others 6*
Grimsby T *(Free on 15/9/2004) FL 33 Others 1*

FORLAN Corazo **Diego**
Born: Montevideo, Uruguay, 19 May 1979
Height: 5'8" **Weight:** 11.11
Club Honours: PL '03; CS '03
International Honours: Uruguay: 27
This talented young striker made three appearances from the bench for Manchester United early on last season before moving on to join Villarreal in August. Diego proved a tremendous success, helping the Spanish club qualify for the European Champions' Cup and finishing the season as leading scorer in La Liga with 25 goals. He also continued to assist Uruguay in their campaign to qualify for the 2006 World Cup finals during the campaign.
Manchester U *(£7,500,000 from Independiente, Uruguay on 23/1/2002) PL 23+40/10 FLC 4+2/3 FAC 2+2/1 Others 8+17/3*

FORREST Daniel (Danny) Paul Halafihi
Born: Keighley, 23 October 1984
Height: 5'10" **Weight:** 11.7
International Honours: E: Yth

A back injury suffered during the summer meant that Danny's 2004-05 season did not really kick off until November. However, the tenacious forward then made an early impact by coming off the bench to score in Bradford's win at Brentford. He saw off the competition to become the back-up striker to Dean Windass and Andy Cooke and will be looking to win a regular place in the starting line-up in 2005-06.
Bradford C *(Trainee) FL 16+34/5 FLC 1 FAC 0+1*

FORRESTER Jamie Mark
Born: Bradford, 1 November 1974
Height: 5'6" **Weight:** 11.0
Club Honours: FAYC '93
International Honours: E: Yth (UEFA-U18 '93); Sch
This experienced striker had long been a target for Bristol Rovers and eventually joined the West Country club during the summer of 2004. Jamie was a regular in the side in the first half of the season and netted several important goals, including a fine effort at Cheltenham. He took over as captain in the absence of Kevin Miller, but in the second half of the campaign he mostly featured from the substitutes' bench.
Leeds U *(£60,000 from Auxerre, France on 20/10/1992) PL 7+2 FAC 1+1/2*
Southend U *(Loaned on 1/9/1994) FL 3+2*
Grimsby T *(Loaned on 10/3/1995) FL 7+2/1*
Grimsby T *(Signed on 17/10/1995) FL 27+14/6 FLC 0+1 FAC 3+1/3*
Scunthorpe U *(Signed on 21/3/1997) FL 99+2/37 FLC 6/1 FAC 7/4 Others 7 (Free to FC Utrecht, Holland on 1/6/1999)*
Walsall *(Loaned on 30/12/1999) FL 2+3*
Northampton T *(£150,000 on 21/3/2000) FL 109+12/45 FLC 5/1 FAC 7/2 Others 3/2*
Hull C *(Signed on 22/1/2003) FL 17+15/7 FAC 0+1 Others 1/1*
Bristol Rov *(Free on 5/7/2004) FL 20+15/7 Others 3+1/2*

FORSSELL Mikael Kaj
Born: Steinfurt, Germany, 15 March 1981
Height: 6'1" **Weight:** 12.8
International Honours: Finland: 32; U21-8; Yth
It was hoped that Mikael would forge a prolific partnership with Emile Heskey for Birmingham City after he re-signed on loan. However, the young Chelsea striker made just four appearances before a serious knee injury cut short his stay at St Andrew's. He eventually recovered and the Stamford Bridge fans had the opportunity to welcome him back when he made a surprise substitute appearance against Bayern Munich in the Champions' League quarter-final in April. It was the striker's first appearance in a Chelsea shirt for 19 months. He then had a 20-minute run out in the final home match of the season against Charlton as he tried to regain match sharpness.
Chelsea *(Free from HJK Helsinki, Finland on 18/12/1998) PL 6+27/5 FLC 1+4/2 FAC 3+6/5 Others 2+4*
Crystal Palace *(Loaned on 23/2/2000) FL 13/3*
Crystal Palace *(Loaned on 30/6/2000) FL 31+8/13 FLC 8/2 FAC 1+1*
Birmingham C *(Loaned on 29/8/2003) PL 32/17 FLC 0+1 FAC 3+1/2*
Birmingham C *(Loaned on 1/7/2004) PL 4*

FORSTER Nicholas (Nicky) Michael
Born: Caterham, 8 September 1973
Height: 5'10" **Weight:** 11.5
International Honours: E: U21-4
Although he missed chunks of the season through injury, Nicky still formed Reading's most effective spearhead when he played alongside Dave Kitson in attack. He has lost none of his pace, ability to turn quickly, or close control, and he netted some spectacular goals. He was the subject of transfer speculation on several occasions during the campaign, but at the time of writing appeared to be committed to Reading for at least one more season.
Gillingham *(Signed from Horley T on 22/5/1992) FL 54+13/24 FLC 3+2 FAC 6/2*
Brentford *(£100,000 on 17/6/1994) FL 108+1/39 FLC 11/3 FAC 8/1 Others 7+1/4*
Birmingham C *(£700,000 on 31/1/1997) FL 24+44/11 FLC 2+2/1 FAC 3+1*
Reading *(£650,000 on 23/6/1999) FL 157+30/60 FLC 10+1/4 FAC 7+1/2 Others 5+4/2*

FORTE Jonathan Ronald James
Born: Sheffield, 25 July 1986
Height: 6'2" **Weight:** 11.4
International Honours: E: Yth
Jonathan failed to make a real breakthrough into the Sheffield United first team last season. Although a regular squad member he made two starts in the Carling Cup and several appearances from the bench in the Championship before his first start in April. A fast and tricky attacking player and a useful crosser of the ball, he managed one goal at Leicester. Jonathan will hope for more consistency and a regular place in 2005-06.
Sheffield U *(From trainee on 7/7/2004) FL 2+27/1 FLC 2+1 FAC 0+3*

FORTUNE Clayton Alexander
Born: Forest Gate, 10 November 1982
Height: 6'3" **Weight:** 13.10
Clayton did not really establish himself in the Bristol City line-up until the closing stages of the 2004-05 campaign, stepping in due to the drop in form of more experienced players at the club. A nephew of Doncaster Rovers striker Leo Fortune-West, the young defender will be looking to gain more regular first-team experience in 2005-06.
Bristol C *(From trainee at Tottenham H on 22/3/2001) FL 25+22 FLC 1+2 FAC 1 Others 4+2*

FORTUNE Jonathan (Jon) Jay
Born: Islington, 23 August 1980
Height: 6'2" **Weight:** 11.4
Jon had another good season in the heart of the Charlton defence in 2004-05, the accomplished central defender coping adequately with the Premiership's best strikers. Quick and good in the air, Jon is strong and is a formidable opponent. He started the season as first choice along side Mark Fish and then Chris Perry, but lost his place to Talal El Karkouri, before replacing Perry. Jon lost his place again in February, but finished the season as first choice once more. As a former striker he likes to get into the opposing penalty area for corners, and possesses a powerful shot as well as his aerial ability. He scored with headers in the away defeat at Portsmouth and also in the home win over Crystal Palace in the final game of the season, adding a volley in the 4-1 FA Cup win over Rochdale.
Charlton Ath *(From trainee on 2/7/1998) PL 85+19/5 FLC 6+1/1 FAC 7+1/1*
Mansfield T *(Loaned on 18/2/2000) FL 4*
Mansfield T *(Loaned on 31/8/2000) FL 14*

FORTUNE Quinton
Born: Cape Town, South Africa, 21 May 1977
Height: 5'11" **Weight:** 11.11
Club Honours: CS '03
International Honours: South Africa: 47; U23-18
A top-class forward or midfielder with pace and good ball skills to match, Quinton's first-team opportunities for Manchester United were limited to just seven outings from August to December. His opener in the FA Cup fifth round at Everton in February turned the tie in United's favour. Coming more and more into the fray as the season reached its climax, an FA Cup final appearance was ample reward for a player who has been jinxed by injuries during his time at Old Trafford. Now hopeful that those worries

are behind him, maybe 2005-06 will be the season when he finally establishes himself in the side.
Manchester U *(£1,500,000 from Atletico Madrid, Spain on 27/8/1999) PL 53+23/5 FLC 8 FAC 8+1/1 Others 19+14/4*

FORTUNE-WEST Leopold (Leo) Paul Osborne
Born: Stratford, 9 April 1971
Height: 6'3" **Weight:** 13.10
Club Honours: Div 3 '04
It looked as if this big striker's days at Doncaster were numbered when Neil Roberts was brought in from Wigan Athletic last October and replaced him in the first team. Then after a few appearances on the bench Leo received an injury, which kept him out of football until early March. However, when Roberts was injured Leo stepped back into the line-up and scored four goals in a run of four starts. He signed a new contract for Rovers at the end of April.
Gillingham *(£5,000 from Stevenage Borough on 12/7/1995) FL 48+19/18 FLC 3+1/2 FAC 3+1/2*
Leyton Orient *(Loaned on 27/3/1997) FL 1+4*
Lincoln C *(Free on 6/7/1998) FL 7+2/1 FLC 2*
Rotherham U *(Loaned on 8/10/1998) FL 5/4*
Brentford *(£60,000 on 17/11/1998) FL 2+9 FAC 0+1 Others 2+1/1*
Rotherham U *(£35,000 on 26/2/1999) FL 59/26 FLC 4 FAC 2 Others 2*
Cardiff C *(£300,000 on 11/9/2000) FL 53+39/23 FLC 2+1 FAC 7+6/3 Others 5/2*
Doncaster Rov *(Free on 24/7/2003) FL 44+19/17 FLC 5/2 FAC 1 Others 1+1*

FOSTER Benjamin (Ben) Anthony
Born: Leamington Spa, 3 April 1983
Height: 6'2" **Weight:** 12.6
Club Honours: AMC '05
Ben was third-choice 'keeper at Stoke last term and his only first-team action came during loan spells at other clubs. He appeared twice for Kidderminster in the autumn when covering for the injured John Danby and then spent the second half of the campaign at Wrexham. He proved to be a class act and produced several excellent displays, none more so than in the FAW Premier Cup tie at Bangor City. Ben was also a member of the Wrexham team that defeated Southend to lift the LDV Vans Trophy at the Millennium Stadium.
Stoke C *(Signed from Racing Club Warwick on 25/4/2001)*
Kidderminster Hrs *(Loaned on 29/10/2004) FL 2*
Wrexham *(Loaned on 24/1/2005) FL 17 Others 4*

FOSTER James **Ian**
Born: Liverpool, 11 November 1976
Height: 5'7" **Weight:** 11.0
Club Honours: NC '00, '04
International Honours: E: SP-1; Sch
Despite starting only 16 games in Kidderminster's fateful 2004-05 campaign, Ian still ended up as joint-leading scorer with six goals. A knee injury curtailed his season in February, although he returned for a substitute appearance in the final game of the season. Perhaps if he had been fit for more of the campaign there would have been a better outcome as four of his six goals came in the wins over Darlington, Scunthorpe and Rochdale.
Hereford U *(Free from Liverpool juniors on 15/7/1996) FL 4+15 FLC 2+1 Others 0+1 (Free to Barrow during 1998 close season)*
Kidderminster Hrs *(Free on 13/8/1999) FL 37+35/11 FLC 3 FAC 3+1 Others 4+2 (Freed during 2003 close season)*
Kidderminster Hrs *(Free from Chester C on 10/2/2004) FL 25+13/9 FLC 0+1 FAC 0+1 Others 1*

FOSTER Stephen (Steve)
Born: Mansfield, 3 December 1974
Height: 6'1" **Weight:** 12.0
Club Honours: FAT '97; Div 3 '04
Steve began the 2004-05 season as club captain and a regular in the centre of the defence for Doncaster Rovers. However, he suffered an ankle injury in the LDV Vans Trophy match at Lincoln, which kept him out of action for three months. After making his come back on Boxing Day he remained at the heart of the Rovers' back line for the remainder of the campaign, playing as if he had never been away. Unfortunately he injured his ankle once more in the final game against Luton.
Mansfield T *(From trainee on 15/7/1993) FL 2+3 FLC 2 (Free to Telford U on 22/1/1994)*
Bristol Rov *(£150,000 from Woking on 23/5/1997) FL 193+4/7 FLC 14 FAC 13 Others 11*
Doncaster Rov *(Free on 1/8/2002) FL 78/2 FLC 4 Others 2*

FOSTER Stephen (Steve) John
Born: Warrington, 10 September 1980
Height: 5'11" **Weight:** 11.8
International Honours: E: Sch
Steve is another of the players to have come up through the youth system at Crewe and he has now become a regular member of the first team operating in a defensive role. A dominant player whose height is an advantage at set pieces, he missed the closing stages of the 2004-05 season after undergoing remedial surgery.
Crewe Alex *(From trainee on 19/9/1998) FL 164+15/12 FLC 9+1/2 FAC 10+1/1 Others 4*

FOWLER Jason Kenneth George
Born: Bristol, 20 August 1974
Height: 6'3" **Weight:** 11.12
After battling illness and injury, this exceptionally gifted midfielder was finally forced to retire in mid-season due to continuing hip problems. Jason possesses the vision and awareness to dominate games from centre midfield, but his fitness problems meant that his contributions for Torquay were patchy with moments of brilliance and he struggled to complete 90 minutes, although his commitment and professionalism were never in doubt.
Bristol C *(From trainee on 8/7/1993) FL 16+9 FLC 1+1 Others 1+1*
Cardiff C *(Signed on 19/6/1996) FL 138+7/14 FLC 8/1 FAC 12+2/4 Others 3/1*
Torquay U *(Free on 30/11/2001) FL 85+12/7 FLC 3 FAC 4/1 Others 2+1*

FOWLER Jordan Michael
Born: Barking, 1 October 1984
Height: 5'9" **Weight:** 11.0
This young Arsenal midfielder began last season in the club's reserves before enjoying a spell of regular first-team football during a loan period with Chesterfield. Jordan showed some promising touches and composure for the Spireites, but returned to Highbury after suffering an injury.
Arsenal *(From trainee on 1/7/2002)*
Chesterfield *(Loaned on 11/1/2005) FL 4+2*

FOWLER Lee Anthony
Born: Cardiff, 10 June 1983
Height: 5'7" **Weight:** 10.8
International Honours: W: U21-9; Yth
Lee had something of a disappointing season at Huddersfield last term when he never really established himself in the line-up. The solid midfield playmaker never shirked a tackle, and he used his strong running and excellent distribution skills to the best effect, always seeming capable of delivering a defence-splitting pass. Towards the end of the campaign he grabbed the opportunity when it was presented and produced some tenacious displays. Lee was also involved with the Wales U21 squad during the campaign.
Coventry C *(From trainee on 7/7/2000) FL 6+8 FAC 1+1/1*
Huddersfield T *(Signed on 11/8/2003) FL 35+14 FLC 3 FAC 0+1 Others 2+1/1*

FOWLER Robert (Robbie) Bernard
Born: Liverpool, 9 April 1975
Height: 5'11" **Weight:** 11.10
Club Honours: FLC '95, '01; FAC '01; UEFAC '01; ESC '01
International Honours: E: 26; B-1; U21-8; Yth (UEFA-U18 '93)

Robbie was in fine form for Manchester City last term and looked as sharp and hungry as at any time during his career with the Blues. He is now a firm crowd favourite and produced some outstanding all-round displays. The former England star is just as happy setting up goals as he is taking them but still finished joint-top scorer at the club with 11 goals in all, while he became only the third player in the history of the Premiership to score 150 goals when he netted twice against Norwich City.
Liverpool *(From trainee on 23/4/1992) PL 210+26/120 FLC 32/27 FAC 21+3/12 Others 26+12/11*
Leeds U *(£11,000,000 on 30/11/2001) PL 24+6/14 FAC 1+1 Others 0+1*
Manchester C *(£3,000,000 + on 30/1/2003) PL 63+13/20 FLC 3/2 FAC 4/1 Others 4/1*

FOX David Lee
Born: Leek, 13 December 1983
Height: 5'9" **Weight:** 12.2
International Honours: E: Yth
David returned to Old Trafford after a spell on loan with Royal Antwerp, but spent most of last season in the United reserve team. In October he gained his first experience of senior football during a loan spell at Shrewsbury, scoring in his second appearance at Leyton Orient. The young midfielder ended the season on a high as a member of the Reds' reserve team that defeated Charlton in the FA Premier Reserve League play-off.
Manchester U *(From trainee on 18/12/2000)*
Shrewsbury T *(Loaned on 8/10/2004) FL 2+2/1 Others 1*

FOX Michael James Stephen Neil
Born: Mansfield, 7 September 1985
Height: 5'11" **Weight:** 11.0
This promising young striker spent much of the 2004-05 campaign developing in Chesterfield's youth team. Michael went on to make his debut as a substitute in the closing stages of the final match of the season at Swindon. There was little chance for fans to see the pace and crossing ability that has been so evident at youth level, but a huge long throw was used to good effect.
Chesterfield *(Trainee) FL 0+1*

FOY Robert (Robbie) Andrew
Born: Edinburgh, 29 October 1985
Height: 5'6" **Weight:** 9.9
International Honours: S: U21-5
This promising youngster was a regular in

Robbie Fowler

Liverpool's reserve team last term and was an unused substitute for the Carling Cup quarter-final tie with Tottenham. The lightening-fast winger was loaned to League Two side Chester City during the second half of the campaign where he was used in a more central role by manager Ian Rush, although his lightweight build appeared best suited to a wide position. On his day Robbie can be a real handful for any full back. He also added to his total of U21 caps for Scotland during the campaign.
Liverpool *(From trainee on 27/1/2003)*
Chester C *(Loaned on 18/2/2005) FL 13*

FRAMPTON Andrew (Andy) James Kerr
Born: Wimbledon, 3 September 1979
Height: 5'11" **Weight:** 10.10
The 2004-05 season proved to be the breakthrough at Brentford and became the team's regular left back. He missed a few games in October due to a swollen knee and a hip injury sidelined him for spells in January and February, but otherwise he was a fixture in the side, scoring a consolation goal in the play-offs against Sheffield Wednesday. Andy is a fine all-round player and his tackling, heading and passing are all of a good quality.
Crystal Palace *(From trainee on 8/5/1998) FL 19+9 FLC 3+1 FAC 2*
Brentford *(Free on 28/10/2002) FL 53+13 FLC 2 FAC 10+1/2 Others 7/1*

FRANCE Ryan
Born: Sheffield, 13 December 1980
Height: 5'11" **Weight:** 11.11
A regular figure on the right side of midfield for Hull, Ryan had been on the books of Sheffield Wednesday as a youngster, and so he eagerly awaited the Tigers visit to Hillsborough last December. In front of a crowd of over 28,000, it proved to be a memorable night as City won 4-2 in a pivotal game of another successful season. Although hindered by a neck injury in the latter stages, Ryan's contract was extended during the campaign.
Hull C *(£15,000 from Alfreton T on 24/9/2003) FL 29+30/4 FLC 1/1 FAC 1+1/1 Others 2/1*

FRANCIS Damien Jerome
Born: Wandsworth, 27 February 1979
Height: 6'1" **Weight:** 11.2
Club Honours: Div 1 '04
International Honours: Jamaica: 1
Damien enjoyed a fantastic season with the Canaries, winning praise from all quarters with his powerful and energetic midfield displays. His performances in the first half of the campaign in particular were of the highest order as he combined the physical side of his game with a rich vein of goal-scoring form as he powered forward, often arriving late into the penalty area, in search of goals. An unfortunate training ground clash left him with a fractured cheekbone in late November, but he made a scoring return at Portsmouth on New Year's Day. Damien was voted as runner-up in the Canaries' 'Player of the Season' awards.
Wimbledon *(From trainee on 6/3/1997) P/FL 80+17/15 FLC 7+4 FAC 9*
Norwich C *(Signed on 23/7/2003) P/FL 71+2/14 FLC 3 FAC 2*

FRANCIS Simon Charles
Born: Nottingham, 16 February 1985
Height: 6'0" **Weight:** 12.6
International Honours: E: Yth
Last season was something of a disappointment for Simon at Sheffield United. Expected to play in his role as a right wing back in the opening game he contracted glandular fever. Once recovered, a medial ligament injury kept him out until February and his second appearance of the season was as a substitute for England U20s against Russia. He then made occasional appearances whilst he regained full fitness.
Bradford C *(From trainee on 3/5/2003) FL 49+6/1 FLC 1 FAC 1*
Sheffield U *(£200,000 on 16/3/2004) FL 6+5 FAC 0+1*

FRANDSEN Per
Born: Copenhagen, Denmark, 6 February 1970
Height: 6'1" **Weight:** 12.6
Club Honours: Div 1 '97
International Honours: Denmark: 23; U21; Yth
A calming influence and key man in the middle of the Wigan Athletic midfield, Per's tenacity complemented an effective partnership alongside the flair and skill of Jimmy Bullard. He netted his only goal in the home win over Brighton before a torn cruciate ligament brought his season to a premature finish after just nine matches. Out of contract at the end of the season, he announced his retirement from the game and returned to Denmark to become a football agent.
Bolton W *(£1,250,000 from FC Copenhagen, Denmark, ex Lille, on 7/8/1996) P/FL 129+1/17 FLC 15+1/4 FAC 4+1 Others 3/1*
Blackburn Rov *(£1,750,000 + on 22/9/1999) FL 26+5/5 FAC 4/1*
Bolton W *(£1,600,000 on 24/7/2000) P/FL 116+19/13 FLC 5+1 FAC 3+3 Others 2+1/1*
Wigan Ath *(Free on 20/7/2004) FL 9/1*

FRECKLINGTON Lee Craig
Born: Lincoln, 8 September 1985
Height: 5'8" **Weight:** 11.0
This tenacious young central-midfield player continued to increase his first-team experience with League Two club Lincoln City in 2004-05. Lee was regularly included in the squad in the second half of the season and made his Football League debut when he came on as a substitute at Rochdale in February. He made further brief appearances from the bench at Cheltenham and Yeovil and at the end of the season accepted the offer of a new contract.
Lincoln C *(Trainee) FL 0+3 Others 1+1*

FREEDMAN Douglas (Dougie) Alan
Born: Glasgow, 21 January 1974
Height: 5'9" **Weight:** 11.2
International Honours: S: 2; B-1; U21-8; Sch
This popular and experienced striker struggled to make much of an impact at Crystal Palace in the Premiership last term and only featured in the starting line-up intermittently. He scored twice in Carling Cup ties but only one goal in Premiership action, netting in the final game of the season at Charlton. Dougie finished as leading scorer for the club's reserve team with seven goals.
Queens Park Rgrs *(From trainee on 15/5/1992)*
Barnet *(Free on 26/7/1994) FL 47/27 FLC 6/5 FAC 2 Others 2*
Crystal Palace *(£800,000 on 8/9/1995) P/FL 72+18/31 FLC 3+2/1 FAC 2+1 Others 3+2/2*
Wolverhampton W *(£800,000 on 17/10/1997) FL 25+4/10 FAC 5+1/2*
Nottingham F *(£950,000 on 12/8/1998) P/FL 50+20/18 FLC 8+1/4 FAC 3+1/1*
Crystal Palace *(£600,000 on 23/10/2000) P/FL 107+43/54 FLC 11/7 FAC 1+4 Others 0+1*

FRIARS Emmet Charles
Born: Londonderry, 14 September 1985
Height: 6'1" **Weight:** 11.5
International Honours: NI: U21-2; Yth
Another talented youngster brought through into senior football by the Notts County Centre of Excellence, this tall left-sided centre back seized his opportunity when the left-back berth became vacant due to injury. Emmet reads the game well and shows composure in possession, and will be looking to establish himself in the first-team squad in 2005-06.
Notts Co *(From trainee on 28/2/2004) FL 4+5 Others 1*

FRIEDEL Bradley (Brad) Howard
Born: Lakewood, USA, 18 May 1971
Height: 6'3" **Weight:** 14.7
Club Honours: FLC '02
International Honours: USA: 82
Brad was an ever-present for Blackburn in Premiership fixtures last term, performing best once Ryan Nelsen and Andy Todd were paired in front of him, and by the end of the season he had few superiors in the Premiership. His outstanding individual displays came in the two games against Manchester United and in the FA Cup semi-final against Arsenal at Cardiff, while he managed to keep a total of 15 clean sheets in Premiership matches. Brad showed remarkable concentration at times because the efficiency of the back four meant that he was only called into action on odd occasions in any particular game.
Liverpool *(£1,000,000 from Columbus Crew, USA on 23/12/1997) PL 25 FLC 4 Others 1+1*
Blackburn Rov *(Free on 7/11/2000) P/FL 174/1 FLC 10 FAC 20 Others 6*

FRIIO David
Born: Thionville, France, 17 February 1973
Height: 6'0" **Weight:** 11.7
Club Honours: Div 3 '02; Div 2 '04
This extremely popular playmaker continued to please the Plymouth Argyle faithful last term with a fine array of passing and some trademark runs into the box. However, after turning down a new contract with the Pilgrims during the season he was surprisingly transferred to relegation rivals Nottingham Forest in February. David was restricted by a calf injury in the closing stages of the campaign, very much reducing the impact he made at the City Ground.
Plymouth Arg *(Free from ASOA Valence, France, ex Epinal, Nimes, on 30/11/2000) FL 158+9/39 FLC 1+3 FAC 9+1/4 Others 4/1*
Nottingham F *(£100,000 on 14/2/2005) FL 5*

FRY Adam George
Born: Bedford, 9 February 1985
Height: 5'8" **Weight:** 10.7
Adam made his first-team debut for Peterborough as a late substitute in the LDV Vans Trophy game against Bristol City last term and went on to feature in the starting line-up in three end-of-season matches. A ball-playing midfielder, he is the son of Posh manager Barry Fry.
Peterborough U *(From trainee on 2/7/2004) FL 3 Others 0+1*

David Friio

FRY Russell Harok
Born: Hull, 4 December 1985
Height: 6'2" **Weight:** 12.1
After making his now traditional annual appearance in the LDV Vans Trophy for Hull, this highly rated midfielder was finally handed his League debut in the Tigers' final game of the season. It proved to be a disappointing day as City slumped to a 2-1 defeat at Brentford, while Russell lasted only 32 minutes after being injured. He was a stalwart of the City reserve team that won the Pontin's Holidays League Premier Division title.
Hull C *(From trainee on 16/12/2002) FL 1 FAC 0+1 Others 0+2*

FRYATT Matthew (Matty) Charles
Born: Nuneaton, 5 March 1986
Height: 5'10" **Weight:** 11.0
International Honours: E: Yth
Matty enjoyed an excellent first full season at Bescot and ended up as Walsall's leading scorer with 15 goals. Although of modest build he showed the ability to twist and turn through tight defences and netted a hat-trick against Huddersfield in January. He also snatched a vital late equaliser against Torquay in April within seconds of coming on as a substitute. Matty was voted as the Saddlers' 'Player of the Season' at the end of the campaign.
Walsall *(From trainee on 28/4/2003) FL 26+21/16 FLC 0+1 FAC 1 Others 1+1*
Carlisle U *(Loaned on 18/12/2003) FL 9+1/1*

FULLER Ashley John
Born: Bedford, 14 November 1986
Height: 5'9" **Weight:** 10.10
A skilful and tricky left-footed midfielder, Ashley spent much of last term developing in Cambridge United's youth team. However, his performances won him a call-up to the senior squad and he went on to make two first-team appearances from the substitutes' bench in mid-season.
Cambridge U *(Trainee) FL 0+3*

FULLER Ricardo Dwayne
Born: Kingston, Jamaica, 31 October 1979
Height: 6'3" **Weight:** 13.3
International Honours: Jamaica
Ricardo began last term at Preston, but after scoring in North End's first away game of the season he moved up to the Premiership, signing for Portsmouth. He went on to become a regular in the

Pompey match squad, although many of his appearances came from the substitutes' bench and he managed just a single goal. A talented striker with powerful heading ability and good skills on the ground, he will be hoping to register a higher tally of goals in the 2005-06 season.
Crystal Palace *(£1,000,000 from Tivoli Gardens, Jamaica on 19/2/2001) FL 2+6*
Heart of Midlothian *(Loaned on 19/10/2001) SL 27/8 SC 2/2*
Preston NE *(£500,000 on 1/7/2002) FL 57+1/27 FLC 2+1/2 FAC 2/2*
Portsmouth *(£200,000 + on 27/8/2004) PL 13+18/1 FLC 3+1 FAC 1+1*

FULOP Marton
Born: Budapest, Hungary, 3 May 1983
Height: 6'6" **Weight:** 14.7
International Honours: Hungary: 1; U21
Marton found himself third-choice goalkeeper for Tottenham last term and although he occasionally warmed the bench he did not feature at first-team level. He experienced regular first-team football during a loan spell at Chesterfield where he displayed confidence in controlling his box and looked safe in the air. Marton also featured for Hungary at U21 level during the campaign and stepped up to make his full international debut as a second-half substitute against France at the end of May.
Tottenham H *(Signed from MTK Hungaria, Hungary on 8/6/2004)*
Chesterfield *(Loaned on 11/3/2005) FL 7*

FURLONG Paul Anthony
Born: Wood Green, 1 October 1968
Height: 6'0" **Weight:** 13.8
Club Honours: FAT '88
International Honours: E: SP-5
This experienced striker started the 2004-05 campaign as a regular partner for Kevin Gallen in the Queen's Park Rangers attack. Paul had a remarkable goal-scoring record in September, hitting the back of the net seven times in just five matches and he continued to score regularly, ending the campaign with a total of 18 Championship goals. Paul collected a trio of awards at the end of the season: fans' 'Player of the Year', 'Player's Player of the Year' and 'Goal of the Season' (for his effort at Sunderland in August).
Coventry C *(£130,000 from Enfield on 31/7/1991) FL 27+10/4 FLC 4/1 FAC 1+1 Others 1*
Watford *(£250,000 on 24/7/1992) FL 79/37 FLC 7/4 FAC 2 Others 3*
Chelsea *(£2,300,000 on 26/5/1994) PL 44+20/13 FLC 3+1 FAC 5+5/1 Others 7/3*
Birmingham C *(£1,500,000 on 17/7/1996) FL 104+27/50 FLC 11+2/3 FAC 5/3 Others 4*
Queens Park Rgrs *(Loaned on 18/8/2000) FL 3/1*
Sheffield U *(Loaned on 8/2/2002) FL 4/2*
Queens Park Rgrs *(Free on 8/8/2002) FL 97+12/47 FLC 3+1 FAC 1 Others 4+1/1*

Paul Furlong

FUTCHER Benjamin (Ben) Paul
Born: Manchester, 20 February 1981
Height: 6'4" **Weight:** 12.4
This giant central defender had another good campaign as League Two club Lincoln City reached the play-offs for the third consecutive season. Ben used his height to win plenty of balls in the air, but was surprisingly effective on the ground for such a tall player. He also provided an added danger to opposing defences when pushed forward at set pieces. Ben, who missed a run of ten games after suffering a fractured cheekbone, spent most of the season on the transfer list and at the end of the campaign signed for Boston United.
Oldham Ath *(From trainee on 5/7/1999) FL 2+8 FAC 0+1 (Free to Stalybridge Celtic on 3/1/2000)*
Lincoln C *(Free from Doncaster Rov on 7/8/2002) FL 119+2/13 FLC 3 FAC 4/1 Others 14/2*

FYFE Graham
Born: Dundee, 7 December 1982
Height: 5'6" **Weight:** 10.6
A small, but quick and skilful, player who can operate at either left back or on the left-hand side of midfield, Graham was mostly restricted to reserve-team football at Cheltenham last term. A popular figure with the supporters for his bubbly character and great enthusiasm, Graham left Whaddon Road at the end of the season with a return to his native Scotland among the possibilities for the next stage of his career.
Glasgow Celtic *(From juniors on 13/7/1999)*
Raith Rov *(Free on 1/1/2003) SL 8+2/1*
Cheltenham T *(Free on 7/8/2003) FL 16+7 FLC 1 Others 1+1*

GAARDSOE Thomas
Born: Randers, Denmark, 23 November 1979
Height: 6'2" **Weight:** 12.8
International Honours: Denmark: 2; U23-10
Initially partnering new signing Darren Purse at the heart of West Bromwich Albion's defence, Thomas then had Darren Moore as his aide before losing his position in the side. However, following an injury to Moore and the arrival of new boss Bryan Robson, he regained his position before a red card scuppered his chances of a prolonged run in the side. Later on Thomas returned to partner Neil Clement in the Baggies' back division, going on to produce some fine displays as the team successfully avoided relegation from the Premiership.
Ipswich T *(£1,300,000 from AAB Aalborg on 31/8/2001) P/FL 40+1/5 FLC 2+1/1 FAC 1/1 Others 2+2*
West Bromwich A *(£520,000 on 5/8/2003) P/FL 70+4/4 FLC 6 FAC 2*

GABBIDON Daniel (Danny) Leon
Born: Cwmbran, 8 August 1979
Height: 6'1" **Weight:** 11.2
International Honours: W: 26; U21-17; Yth
This highly rated centre back continued to develop his elegant interpretation of the role in a season essentially free from injury. Danny's reputation was further enhanced last season by the emergence of colleague James Collins with whom he formed a formidable partnership at the back for Cardiff. Danny took over the captaincy in March after the sale of Graham Kavanagh and continued to impress. Now established as a first choice for his country too, he added to his tally of caps throughout the season.
West Bromwich A *(From trainee on 3/7/1998) FL 20 FLC 4+1 FAC 2*
Cardiff C *(£175,000 + on 10/8/2000) FL 194+3/10 FLC 8 FAC 11 Others 3*

GABRIELI Emanuele
Born: L'Aquila, Italy, 31 December 1980
Height: 5'11" **Weight:** 12.8
After a promising month's trial with the Blades, Emanuele was signed on a four-month deal as cover for the central defence. A regular in the reserves, scoring three times, he made just one substitute appearance at Gillingham. Released at the end of January he joined Boston United on another short-term deal. Brought in by the Pilgrims as cover for injuries and suspensions, he made a confident debut in the away win at Wycombe. However, he lacked match fitness and struggled at times to cope with English lower division football, despite showing plenty of skill on the ball. Emanuele was released at the end of his contract and subsequently returned to Italy.
Sheffield U *(Free from Cavese, Italy, ex Chieti, on 1/10/2004) FL 0+1*
Boston U *(Free on 4/2/2005) FL 4*

GAIN Peter Thomas
Born: Hammersmith, 11 November 1976
Height: 6'1" **Weight:** 11.0
International Honours: RoI: U21-1; Yth
Peter had another excellent season in the centre of midfield for League Two club Lincoln City. He linked well with Richard Butcher and his performances led to interest from a number of higher division clubs. His most outstanding display was at Darlington where he completely dominated midfield and was the inspiration for a memorable 3-0 victory. At the end of the season Peter was out of contract and his future was undecided at the time of writing.
Tottenham H *(From trainee on 1/7/1995)*
Lincoln C *(Loaned on 31/12/1998) FL 0+3 Others 1*
Lincoln C *(£15,000 on 26/3/1999) FL 195+29/21 FLC 7+1 FAC 9+1/1 Others 14+2*

GALBRAITH David James
Born: Luton, 20 December 1983
Height: 5'8" **Weight:** 11.0
This left-sided midfield player made most of his appearances as a substitute for Northampton last season. The skilful winger provided new options when

Thomas Gaardsoe (left)

coming off the bench and scored a memorable late equaliser in the home game with Darlington in January.
Northampton T *(From trainee at Tottenham Hotspur on 16/1/2004) FL 9+16/1 FLC 2 FAC 0+1 Others 2*

GALL Kevin Alexander
Born: Merthyr Tydfil, 4 February 1982
Height: 5'9" **Weight:** 11.1
Club Honours: Div 2 '05
International Honours: W: U21-8; Yth; Sch
This pacy young striker opened up many a League Two defence with his tremendous speed last term. Kevin was a near ever-present in the Yeovil squad, although making a number of appearances from the bench, but he scored only three goals during the campaign.
Newcastle U *(From trainee on 29/4/1999)*
Bristol Rov *(Free on 22/3/2001) FL 28+22/5 FLC 2 FAC 2+2 Others 2+2*
Yeovil T *(Free on 4/2/2003) FL 69+17/11 FLC 2+1 FAC 7+1/1 Others 3/1*

GALLACHER Paul James
Born: Glasgow, 16 August 1979
Height: 6'0" **Weight:** 11.8
International Honours: S: 8; U21-7
Paul won full international recognition for Scotland in the summer of 2004 and was signed by Norwich City in June as cover for goalkeeper Robert Green. An unfortunate pre-season back injury saw him slip to third choice and in fact his only first-team experience during the campaign came during loan spells elsewhere. He made three appearances for Gillingham at Christmas time, covering for injuries and then went to Sheffield Wednesday where he performed well in the closing stages of the regular season.
Dundee U *(Signed from Lochee U on 2/9/1997) SL 120+1 SLC 7 SC 10*
Airdrie *(Loaned on 19/11/1999) SL 9*
Norwich C *(Signed on 3/6/2004)*
Gillingham *(Loaned on 10/12/2004) FL 3*
Sheffield Wed *(Loaned on 18/3/2005) FL 8*

GALLAGHER Paul
Born: Glasgow, 9 August 1984
Height: 6'1" **Weight:** 12.0
International Honours: S: 1; B-1; U21-4
This young striker never really made the impact expected of him for Blackburn last season. He managed few starts and with most of his appearances coming from the bench he was often forced to come on in emergencies and assume a variety of roles. Paul's snappy finish against Fulham was striking at its best but his work rate was not impressive and he will be looking to make real progress at Ewood Park in 2005-06.
Blackburn Rov *(From trainee on 5/2/2003) PL 17+26/5 FLC 0+2/1 FAC 4+1*

GALLAS William
Born: Paris, France, 17 August 1977
Height: 6'1" **Weight:** 12.7
Club Honours: FLC '05; PL '05
International Honours: France: 30; U21
Along with Claude Makelele another unsung hero of Chelsea's record-breaking 2004-05 season was defender William Gallas who put in an excellent campaign. Since being paired with John Terry in 2001 the two young defenders have developed into the most effective partnership in the Premiership. William was alongside his skipper in central defence as the Blues shattered the previous records of ten consecutive clean sheets and 1,025 minutes without conceding a goal. Comfortable in any position along the back four, William was pressed into service, albeit reluctantly, as an emergency left back for the last third of the season following Wayne Bridge's broken ankle. Although lacking the England star's attacking élan he proved to be a reliable deputy and, overall, his athleticism, tackling, heading and anticipation made him a major factor in the remarkable statistic of just 15 goals conceded during the Premiership season – yet another record. He also moved upfield to poach valuable goals in consecutive away matches against West Brom and Fulham to confirm a brilliant season. Now a regular in the French side, he has the opportunity to emulate his mentor the great Marcel Desailly and accumulate a century of caps for *Les Bleus*.
Chelsea *(£6,200,000 from Marseilles, France, ex SM Caen, on 4/7/2001) PL 114+11/7 FLC 13 FAC 14/1 Others 28/1*

GALLEN Kevin Andrew
Born: Chiswick, 21 September 1975
Height: 5'11" **Weight:** 12.10
International Honours: E: U21-4; Yth (UEFA-U18 '93); Sch
A striker who can also play in any central midfield position, Kevin was an ever-present for Queen's Park Rangers last term. A popular choice to replace the departed Steve Palmer as captain, he began as the partner to Paul Furlong in attack, but moved back into midfield when other players were injured or otherwise unavailable. Kevin finished the season with just ten goals and was rewarded with an extended contract during the campaign.
Queens Park Rgrs *(From trainee on 22/9/1992) P/FL 126+45/36 FLC 9+3/2 FAC 6+2/2*
Huddersfield T *(Free on 10/8/2000) FL 30+8/10 FAC 1*
Barnsley *(Free on 27/7/2001) FL 8+1/2 FLC 0+1*
Queens Park Rgrs *(Free on 20/11/2001) FL 156+2/47 FLC 5+1/2 FAC 2+1 Others 5+2*

GALLIMORE Anthony (Tony) Mark
Born: Nantwich, 21 February 1972
Height: 5'11" **Weight:** 12.6
Club Honours: Div 3 '95; AMC '98
After missing much of the previous season through injury, Tony was given a trial at Rochdale and on proving his fitness was offered a contract. Playing at left back, he was often the youngest member of a highly experienced back four, responsible for Dale's excellent defensive record during the campaign. Tony also showed his versatility during a stint in central defence. He claimed his first goal for the club when his shot cannoned off the post and into the net off the goalkeeper for a last-minute winner against Oxford, but unfortunately for Tony the records show it as an own goal!
Stoke C *(From trainee on 11/7/1990) FL 6+5*
Carlisle U *(Loaned on 3/10/1991) FL 8*
Carlisle U *(Loaned on 26/2/1992) FL 8*
Carlisle U *(£15,000 on 25/3/1993) FL 124/9 FLC 8 FAC 8/1 Others 24/1*
Grimsby T *(£125,000 on 28/3/1996) FL 263+10/4 FLC 20/2 FAC 15 Others 10*
Barnsley *(Free on 8/8/2003) FL 20 FLC 1 FAC 2 Others 2*
Rochdale *(Free on 19/8/2004) FL 32+2 FLC 1 FAC 2 Others 2*

GARCIA Luis Javier
Born: Barcelona, Spain, 24 June 1978
Height: 5'6" **Weight:** 10.5
Club Honours: UEFACL '05
International Honours: Spain: 2
Joint-top scorer for Liverpool with 13 goals (including five in the European Champions' League) this right winger or striker nevertheless flattered to deceive at times last season. Two of his goals were candidates for 'Goal of the Season', a strike at home to Charlton in October and the dipping volley from 25 yards which gave Liverpool a 2-0 half time lead at home to Juventus in the Champions' Cup quarter-final first leg in March. Luis also scored the controversial goal against Chelsea in the semi-final which carried Liverpool to their sixth European Cup final. Having done so much to propel Liverpool into the final, his performance in Istanbul was somewhat low key, his

most significant contribution being a goal-line clearance early in the game.
Liverpool *(£6,000,000 from Barcelona, Spain, on 27/8/2004) PL 26+3/8 FLC 2+1 Others 12/5*

GARCIA Richard
Born: Perth, Australia, 4 September 1981
Height: 6'1" **Weight:** 11.2
Club Honours: FAYC '99
International Honours: Australia: U23; Yth
After one substitute appearance for West Ham against Coventry in August this young midfielder joined Colchester United the following month. Although injury, notably a hip problem, disrupted his campaign, he scored six goals for the U's. Richard showed his versatility by appearing as a striker, on the right wing and in the centre of midfield, but was most effective playing wide.
West Ham U *(From trainee on 16/9/1998) P/FL 4+12 FLC 0+5 FAC 0+1*
Leyton Orient *(Loaned on 11/8/2000) FL 18/4 FLC 3*
Colchester U *(Signed on 3/9/2004) FL 20+4/4 FLC 1+1 FAC 3/1 Others 1/1*

GARDNER Anthony
Born: Stone, 19 September 1980
Height: 6'5" **Weight:** 13.8
International Honours: E: 1; U21-1
A career dogged by injury to date has robbed Spurs of this talented defender's full potential. Just 14 starts gave little opportunity for the youngster to demonstrate his great aerial ability, good possession play and strong tackling. Anthony will need to return to full fitness to capitalise on his talents.
Port Vale *(From trainee on 31/7/1998) FL 40+1/4 FLC 2 FAC 1*
Tottenham H *(£1,000,000 on 28/1/2000) PL 68+17/1 FLC 10/1 FAC 8+1*

GARDNER Ricardo Wayne
Born: St Andrews, Jamaica, 25 September 1978
Height: 5'9" **Weight:** 11.0
International Honours: Jamaica: 60
One of the longest serving members of the Bolton squad, last season was perhaps Ricardo's most effective yet. Starting out on the left of what was primarily a flat back four, Ricardo turned in some assured and competent displays, with his electric pace proving to be a particular asset. This impressive run of form was abruptly ended when he picked up a knee injury in November. He returned to the starting line-up in the new year and remained a constant fixture in the side for the rest of the season. Towards the end of the campaign he struck up a particularly effective left-flank partnership with Vincent Candela, which allowed Ricardo to exploit his natural attacking instincts on many occasions.
Bolton W *(£1,000,000 from Harbour View, Jamaica on 17/8/1998) P/FL 182+27/15 FLC 14+4/2 FAC 9+4 Others 6/2*

GARDNER Ross
Born: South Shields, 15 December 1985
Height: 5'8" **Weight:** 10.6
International Honours: E: Yth
This left-sided midfielder made good progress at Nottingham Forest last term and enjoyed an extended run of first-team action early in the new year. Ross produced some very promising displays and will be hoping to finally establish himself in the line-up at the City Ground in the 2005-06 season.

Luis Garcia

Newcastle U *(From trainee on 15/5/2002)*
Nottingham F *(Signed on 11/8/2003) FL 10+6*

GARNER Darren John
Born: Plymouth, 10 December 1971
Height: 5'9" **Weight:** 12.7
Club Honours: AMC '96

This experienced midfielder was a regular for Rotherham early on last season, but from mid-October he was hampered by a number of niggling injuries and struggled to maintain a presence in the side. In March he joined Torquay United on loan to assist in their fight against relegation from League One and impressed with his no-nonsense professional approach. He was happy to sit fairly deep in midfield and proved an excellent foil to Alex Russell with solid tackling and simple but effective distribution.

Plymouth Arg *(From trainee on 15/3/1989) FL 22+5/1 FLC 2+1 FAC 1 (Free to Dorchester T on 19/8/1994)*
Rotherham U *(£20,000 on 26/6/1995) FL 248+16/23 FLC 15+2 FAC 15+2/6 Others 9/1*
Torquay U *(Loaned on 14/3/2005) FL 8+1*

GARNER Glyn
Born: Pontypool, 9 December 1976
Height: 6'2" **Weight:** 13.6

Bury's goalkeeper experienced a highly eventful campaign last term. In the opening months he struggled to find his best form, but nevertheless saved four of the six early-season penalties that he faced. In October he enjoyed impressive performances against Leyton Orient and Mansfield, but then succumbed to a niggling knee injury and then a cartilage operation kept him out of action for four months. Glyn returned for the home game against Cambridge in March and was a major factor in the team's improved performances in the closing stages of the season.

Bury *(Free from Llanelli on 7/7/2000) FL 124+2 FLC 5 FAC 3 Others 10*

Glyn Garner

GARRARD Luke Edward
Born: Barnet, 22 September 1985
Height: 5'10" **Weight:** 11.9

This slightly built right-sided defender broke into the Swindon first team at right wing back following a 'Man of the Match' performance in the LDV Vans Trophy victory over Bristol City. Luke enjoyed a brief run in the line-up at the turn of the year before dropping out of contention once more.

Swindon T *(From Tottenham H juniors on 8/7/2002) FL 8+3 FLC 1 FAC 1+1 Others 2+1*

GASCOIGNE Paul John
Born: Gateshead, 27 May 1967
Height: 5'10" **Weight:** 11.12
Club Honours: FAYC'85; FAC'91. SPL'96,'97; SLC'97; SC'96
International Honours: E: 57; B-4; U21-13; Yth

One of England's most outstanding midfield players of the last 50 years appeared to finally bring down the curtain on his career with a brief spell at Boston United. Paul's decision to sign as player-coach for the tiny Lincolnshire club was a surprise move and it was clear from his first appearances in pre-season friendlies that he needed to build up his fitness to be able to compete at League Two level. Paul finally saw action when he came on as a substitute for the final ten minutes of the Pilgrims' 1-0 defeat at Cheltenham, making his first start on August Bank Holiday Monday. He fitted into a central-midfield role and although lacking stamina showed he still had plenty of skill on the ball. His most successful game for Boston was when he came on as a second-half substitute at neighbours Lincoln when United were two goals down and heading for defeat. He transformed the team and they went on to score twice in the final seven minutes for a share of the points. Paul's final appearance was in Boston's 4-1 Carling Cup defeat at home to Premiership Fulham. He left the club in early October.

Newcastle U *(From apprentice on 13/5/1985) FL 83+9/21 FLC 8/1 FAC 4/3 Others 2+1*
Tottenham H *(£2,000,000 on 18/7/1988) FL 91+1/19 FLC 13+1/8 FAC 6/6 (£5,500,000 to Lazio, Italy on 1/5/1992)*
Glasgow Rgrs *(£4,300,000 on 10/7/1995) SL 64+10/30 SLC 7/4 SC 7+1/3 Others 16/2*

ddlesbrough (£3,450,000 on 27/3/1998)
. 39+2/4 FLC 3+2 FAC 2
erton (Free on 20/7/2000) PL 18+14/1
: 1+1 FAC 3+1
rnley (Free on 18/3/2002) FL 3+3 (Freed
ing 2002 close season)
ston U (Free from Gansa Tianma on
7/2004) FL 2+2 FLC 1

AVIN Jason Joseph
rn: Dublin, 14 March 1980
ight: 6'1" **Weight:** 12.7
ernational Honours: RoI: U21-6; Yth
EFA-U18 '98)
son suffered an ankle injury in Bradford
y's first pre-season friendly and this
pt him on the sidelines for a while.
ice fit he found his opportunities
nited by the form of Mark Bower and
ly made one League appearance when
featured at right back. After being
formed that his contract would not be
newed at the end of the campaign he
oved on to join Eircom League side
amrock Rovers.
ddlesbrough (From trainee on
/3/1997) PL 19+12 FLC 5+1 FAC 1+2
imsby T (Loaned on 1/11/2002) FL 8+2
ddersfield T (Loaned on 14/3/2003) FL
)/1
adford C (Free on 16/7/2003) FL 38+3
C 1 FAC 0+1 Others 1

AYLE Marcus Anthony
orn: Hammersmith, 27 September 1970
eight: 6'1" **Weight:** 12.9
ub Honours: Div 3 '92
ternational Honours: E: Yth. Jamaica:
4
larcus was beset by injuries for most of
e 2004-05 season and his height and
uthority in the centre of the Watford
efence were sorely missed. He missed
ost of the pre-season with an achilles
roblem, and then suffered a calf strain
hat kept him out until November. After a
andful of substitute appearances, he
uccumbed to a hamstring problem in
he New Year. In March Marcus returned
ome to Brentford, 11 years after leaving.
layed predominantly on the left wing,
e made a useful contribution and
howed his crossing ability was as good
s ever by whipping in some dangerous
alls.
rentford (From trainee on 6/7/1989) FL
18+38/22 FLC 6+3 FAC 6+2/2 Others
4+6/3
Vimbledon (£250,000 on 24/3/1994) P/FL
98+38/37 FLC 23+1/7 FAC 18+7/3
ilasgow Rgrs (£900,000 on 9/3/2001) SL
8+8/4
Vatford (£900,000 on 8/8/2001) FL
0+12/5 FLC 4+1/2 FAC 8/2
rentford (Free on 24/3/2005) FL 4+2
Others 1+1

GEARY Derek Peter
Born: Dublin, 19 June 1980
Height: 5'6" **Weight:** 10.8
This right back showed his class straight away for Stockport last term with some energetic and committed displays in the back four. Such good form earned him a quick move to Bramall Lane where he was a regular member of the Blades' squad. Hard working and using his speed both in defence and when pushing forward he was used mainly as a left or right wing back, but occasionally featured in a midfield role. Derek scored his first-ever senior goal with a volley at Millwall.
***Sheffield Wed** (Signed from Cherry Orchard on 17/11/1997) FL 95+9 FLC 12+2 FAC 4 Others 5*
***Stockport Co** (Free on 2/8/2004) FL 12+1 FLC 1 Others 1*
***Sheffield U** (£25,000 on 22/10/2004) FL 15+4/1 FAC 4+1*

GEMMILL Scot
Born: Paisley, 2 January 1971
Height: 5'11" **Weight:** 11.6
Club Honours: FMC '92; Div 1 '98
International Honours: S: 26; B-2; U21-4
This cultured midfielder was snapped up for Leicester on a short-term contract in August 2004, and subsequently saw his deal extended to the end of the season. A model professional who enjoyed a smattering of appearances he never quite grabbed a starting spot of his own. Scot never let the Foxes down though, and was a great help to the younger midfielders as they emerged during the campaign. Nevertheless, he was released at the end of the season as the Foxes looked to reduce their overall wage bill.
***Nottingham F** (From trainee on 5/1/1990) P/FL 228+17/21 FLC 29+2/3 FAC 19+2/1 Others 13+1/4*
***Everton** (£250,000 on 25/3/1999) PL 79+18/5 FLC 3+1 FAC 7+2*
***Preston NE** (Loaned on 12/3/2004) FL 7/1*
***Leicester C** (Free on 6/8/2004) FL 11+6 FAC 1*

GERA Zoltan
Born: Pecs, Hungary, 22 April 1979
Height: 5'11" **Weight:** 11.3
International Honours: Hungary: 30
Zoltan made his debut in the Premiership as a second-half substitute for West Bromwich Albion at Blackburn on the opening day of the season. He then scored after just three minutes when starting a game for the first time against Spurs shortly afterwards. Quickly becoming a firm favourite with the Baggies' fans, he netted some marvellous goals including a wonderful effort at home to Bolton Wanderers to earn Albion their first win of the campaign. He also netted with a cracking header from a left-wing cross that defeated Everton, and beat Chelsea 'keeper Petr Cech with a beauty from the edge of the box in a 4-1 defeat. Captain of Hungary, he produced some excellent performances in Albion's midfield, always looking to get into the penalty area while not being afraid to shoot from any distance.
***West Bromwich A** (£1,500,000 from Ferencvaros, Hungary on 9/8/2004) PL 31+7/6 FLC 1 FAC 3*

[GEREMI] N'JITAP FOTSO Geremi Sorele
Born: Cameroon, 20 December 1978
Height: 5'11" **Weight:** 12.8
Club Honours: PL '05
International Honours: Cameroon: 69
This vastly experienced Cameroon international became a peripheral figure under the regime of Jose Mourinho, featuring in a mere handful of matches during 2004-05. He started the first two Premiership fixtures, both 1-0 victories, but thereafter he was confined to short substitute appearances until the dying embers of the season when a full-back crisis gave him a chance to claim a Premiership-winner's medal. His cause wasn't helped by the recruitment of two outstanding players who play down his favoured right flank – Paulo Ferreira and Arjen Robben.
***Middlesbrough** (Loaned from Real Madrid, Spain, ex Racing Baffousam, Cerro Porteno, Genclerbirligi, on 31/7/2002) PL 33/7 FAC 1*
***Chelsea** (£7,000,000 on 1/8/2003) PL 25+13/1 FLC 4 FAC 3 Others 8+6*

GERKEN Dean Jeffery
Born: Southend, 22 May 1985
Height: 6'3" **Weight:** 13.0
Teenaged 'keeper Dean enjoyed his first extended runs in the Colchester line-up last term in the absence of the injured Aidan Davison. He kept three clean sheets in a row during January, and particularly enjoyed the 2-0 win at Hull City in the third round of the FA Cup. Dean showed maturity beyond his years, and is being groomed as the U's future long-term number one.
***Colchester U** (From trainee on 12/7/2004) FL 14 FLC 1 FAC 2*

GERRARD Anthony
Born: Liverpool, 6 February 1986
Height: 6'2" **Weight:** 13.1
Anthony spent much of last season developing with Everton's reserve team and managed an outing as an unused substitute for the first team. The

promising defender spent a brief spell on loan at Accrington early on before joining Walsall on a similar basis in March. He immediately settled into a central-defensive position at Bescot and was signed up on a more permanent basis at the end of the campaign. An excellent reader of the game for one so young, his positional play was a major factor in tightening up the Saddlers back line. Anthony is a cousin of Liverpool's Steven Gerrard.
Everton *(From trainee on 10/7/2004)*
Walsall *(Loaned on 24/3/2005) FL 8*

GERRARD Paul William
Born: Heywood, 22 January 1973
Height: 6'2" **Weight:** 14.4
International Honours: E: U21-18
After being on loan at the end of the previous campaign, Paul returned to the City Ground to sign permanently for Nottingham Forest in the summer of 2004. He immediately established himself as the club's number one 'keeper and went on to become a near ever-present for the season. Paul is a fine shot-stopper and will be looking to assist Forest to promotion at the first attempt in 2005-06.
Oldham Ath *(From trainee on 2/11/1991) P/FL 118+1 FLC 7 FAC 7 Others 2*
Everton *(£1,000,000 + on 1/7/1996) PL 89+1 FLC 6 FAC 3*
Oxford U *(Loaned on 18/12/1998) FL 16*
Ipswich T *(Loaned on 16/11/2002) FL 5*
Sheffield U *(Loaned on 29/8/2003) FL 16*
Nottingham F *(Free on 25/3/2004) FL 50 FLC 4 FAC 3*

GERRARD Steven George
Born: Huyton, 30 May 1980
Height: 6'2" **Weight:** 12.4
Club Honours: FLC '01, '03; FAC '01; UEFAC '01; ESC '01; UEFACL '05
International Honours: E: 34; U21-4; Yth
The Liverpool captain and England midfielder returned from a disappointing Euro 2004 campaign in Portugal with speculation raging about his future with the club. Happily new manager Rafael Benitez persuaded him to stay at Anfield assuring him that the club had every intention of challenging for major honours in the years ahead. By his own admission Steven's form blew hot and cold during the season yet this is only to judge by his own high standards. He stood head and shoulders above any other Liverpool player last season, with the exception of the immaculate Jamie Carragher, and the sheer effort required to drive his team forward almost single-handedly in match after match inevitably took its toll in some games. As in previous seasons his campaign was disrupted by injury, a fractured bone in his foot sidelining him for two months, but he returned to action with no after effects. His haul of 13 goals was outstanding for a midfielder and his best seasonal total ever for the Reds. Steven scored at least two candidates for 'Goal of the Season' – the pile driver from 25 yards against Olimpiakos in December which ensured Liverpool's continuance in the European Champions' League at the very last gasp and a 30-yard swerving volley against Middlesbrough in April. It was only fitting therefore that Steven should end the season with the performance of his life in the European Champions' Cup final with AC Milan in Istanbul. With the teamtrailing the Italian giants 3-0 at half time he led the second-half counter attack superbly, scoring the goal which gave his team some hope and then, after Vladimir Smicer' second goal, winning the penalty with a forward drive, from which Liverpool incredibly drew level. In perhaps his shrewdest tactical move Benitez switched Steve to right back in extra time to counter Milan's potential match winner Serginho and although in his own words he was running on empty, Steven blocked and tackled the talented winger as though his life depended on it. He was also selected for the PFA Premiership team of the season.
Liverpool *(From trainee on 26/2/1998) PL 179+21/27 FLC 14+1/4 FAC 11+2/1 Others 53+2/9*

GIANNAKOPOULOS Stilianos (Stelios)
Born: Athens, Greece, 12 July 1974
Height: 5'8" **Weight:** 11.0
Club Honours: Div 2 '04
International Honours: Greece: 54
Stelios began last season on a high, having been an integral part of the Greek national team who sensationally won the 2004 European Championship. He struggled to replicate this form at club level early on, though he burst into life after Christmas, proving to be a key figure in the Wanderers' line-up. Working most effectively as an attacking winger, Stelios' form in the second half of the season coincided with an impressive run which saw Bolton claim that elusive UEFA Cup spot for the first time in their history, and his natural skill and eye for goal certainly played their role. In stark contrast to the first half of the season, when he netted a solitary Premiership goal, Stelios scored six in the second half of the campaign, including a sensational strike against Arsenal that was voted Bolton's 'Goal of the Season'.
Bolton W *(Free from Olympiakos, Greece on 15/7/2003) PL 45+20/9 FLC 5+3/2 FAC 4/1*

GIBB Alistair (Ally) Stuart
Born: Salisbury, 17 February 1976
Height: 5'9" **Weight:** 11.7
Ally had a frustrating time at Bristol Rovers last term when his campaign was disrupted by injuries. A niggling back problem affected him in the early months of the season and then he suffered a knee injury in the game at Lincoln in January and did not return to first-team action until the penultimate fixture at Scunthorpe. When fit he made a valuable contribution from the right flank, creating a series of goal-scoring opportunities for his colleagues with some fine crosses from the wing.
Norwich C *(From trainee on 1/7/1994)*
Northampton T *(Loaned on 22/9/1995) FL 9/1 Others 2*
Northampton T *(£30,000 on 5/2/1996) FL 51+71/3 FLC 8+4 FAC 5+3 Others 4+3*
Stockport Co *(£50,000 on 18/2/2000) FL 157+8/1 FLC 6 FAC 6 Others 3*
Bristol Rov *(Free on 25/3/2004) FL 24+7/1 FLC 2 FAC 0+1*

GIDDINGS Stuart James
Born: Coventry, 27 March 1986
Height: 6'0" **Weight:** 11.8
International Honours: E: Yth
The young Coventry City left back displaced Steve Staunton in the line-up last October after some impressive displays in a brief run in the team. Niggling ankle injuries blighted his campaign but after Micky Adams' arrival in January he again looked set to be first choice. However, in his second game back against Wigan he suffered a bad hamstring injury which curtailed his season.
Coventry C *(From trainee on 16/6/2004) FL 11+2 FLC 2 FAC 1*

GIER Robert (Rob) James
Born: Bracknell, 6 January 1980
Height: 5'9" **Weight:** 11.7
A hat-trick of awards from the Rushden supporters showed just what they thought of Rob's performances for the club last term. Despite being smaller than many centre halves, he compensated with some superb positional play and reading of the game. Rob also got forward to score his first senior goal in the 2-0 home win over Leyton Orient in January and followed up with another strike against Bury.
Wimbledon *(From trainee on 11/5/1999) FL 67+4 FLC 4+3 FAC 4*
Rushden & Diamonds *(Free on 12/7/2004) FL 30+2/2 FLC 1 FAC 0+1*

GIGGS Ryan Joseph
Born: Cardiff, 29 November 1973
Height: 5'11" **Weight:** 10.9
Club Honours: ESC '91; FAYC '92; FLC '92; PL '93, '94, '96, '97, '99, '00, '01, '03; CS '93, '94, '96, '97, '03; FAC '94, '96, '99, '04; UEFACL '99
International Honours: W: 51; U21-1; Yth. E: Sch
An outstanding naturally talented left winger, who can play equally well as a front-line striker, Ryan continued to show why he is still so highly regarded at Old Trafford, despite contractual rumblings casting a cloud over his future for most of the season. Perhaps it was ironic that during those negotiations he enjoyed his most prolific goal-scoring spell of the season with Premiership strikes in November and December against Newcastle, Bolton and Aston Villa. Notching a single goal in both the Carling Cup and Champions' League campaigns, Ryan's most notable appearance of the season came not against Arsenal, Chelsea or AC Milan, but against Crystal Palace in the Premiership in December. Before that match, he was presented with a silver salver by United Chief Executive David Gill to mark his 600th game for the club. Despite scoring United's goal against Chelsea in the Carling Cup semi-final in January, he could not prevent the Reds from losing their unbeaten home record in this competition stretching back 35 years. Two months on, his attempted shot against the AC Milan woodwork in the San Siro was the closest United got to progressing further in the Champions' League. As he reached the landmark of 50 caps on the international stage, his biggest reward came in May when he signed a new contract that will keep him at Old Trafford for the remainder of his career.
Manchester U *(From trainee on 1/12/1990) P/FL 396+51/91 FLC 22+5/7 FAC 46+6/9 Others 103+6/22*

GILBERT Peter
Born: Newcastle, 31 July 1983
Height: 5'11" **Weight:** 12.13
International Honours: W: U21-7
Peter was again Plymouth Argyle's regular left back last season when he was a near ever-present in the line-up. A tough-tackling defender, he tried to get forward as much as possible to deliver his left-footed crosses into the box, although he did not manage to get on the score sheet himself during the campaign. In August he was called up to represent Wales at U21level against Latvia and went on to become an integral member of their squad.
Birmingham C *(From trainee on 1/7/2002)*
Plymouth Arg *(Signed on 8/7/2003) FL 78/1 FLC 2 FAC 2 Others 2/1*

[GILBERTO] SILVA Gilberto
Born: Lagoa da Prata, Brazil, 7 October 1976
Height: 6'2" **Weight:** 12.4
Club Honours: CS '02, '04; FAC '03, '05; PL '04
International Honours: Brazil: 31
This was the season that Gilberto's defensive qualities were finally admired by and missed in equal measure by the Arsenal faithful. The season began well enough with the opening goal in the Gunner's 3-1 Community Shield victory over Manchester United. He was forced to seek medical advice in the opening weeks due to a back problem but after a long recovery process he made a welcome return to the first team for the Premiership game with Norwich City in April, some six months after his previous appearance. It was no coincidence that Arsenal's defensive stability improved upon his comeback and he remained a permanent member of the side that ended the season fittingly enough back in Cardiff with victory in the FA Cup final.
Arsenal *(£4,500,000 from Atletico Mineiro, Brazil, ex America-MG, on 9/8/2002) PL 74+6/4 FLC 1 FAC 6+2 Others 19+5/4*

GILCHRIST Philip (Phil) Alexander
Born: Stockton, 25 August 1973
Height: 5'11" **Weight:** 13.12
Club Honours: FLC '00
Phil signed a permanent deal for Rotherham during the summer of 2004 and he was an automatic choice on the left side of the central defence early on before losing his place in mid-October. He then found himself out of favour until a managerial change at the end of January, following which he was appointed captain. Phil produced some fine displays at the back for the Millers but then dislocated a shoulder and this ended his campaign prematurely.
Nottingham F *(From trainee on 5/12/1990)*
Middlesbrough *(Free on 10/1/1992)*
Hartlepool U *(Free on 27/11/1992) FL 77+5 FLC 4+1 FAC 4 Others 5*
Oxford U *(£100,000 on 17/2/1995) FL 173+4/10 FLC 16 FAC 9/1 Others 3*
Leicester C *(£500,000 on 10/8/1999) PL 23+16/1 FLC 6+1 FAC 4+1*
West Bromwich A *(£500,000 on 22/3/2001) P/FL 89+1 FLC 6+1 FAC 5+1 Others 2*
Rotherham U *(Free on 12/3/2004) FL 31+3/1 FLC 1 FAC 0+1*

GILKS Matthew (Matt)
Born: Oldham, 4 June 1982
Height: 6'1" **Weight:** 12.7
Matt was restricted to a couple of appearances in the LDV Vans Trophy games for Rochdale early on last term, but stepped into regular first-team action after first-choice 'keeper Neil Edwards was injured. Once in the side, the big goalkeeper never looked back, recording four clean sheets in a row as Dale ran up six straight wins. By the season's close he had kept an impressive tally of 16 clean sheets and Dale's two 'keepers had between them equalled a post-war record of 20 clean sheets in a League campaign. Matt performed heroics in a number of games, perhaps most notably in the draw against Wycombe, while a flying save in the abandoned game against Grimsby was widely considered one of the best seen at Spotland for many years.
Rochdale *(From trainee on 4/7/2001) FL 82+2 FLC 2 FAC 6+1 Others 3*

GILL Jeremy (Jerry) Morley
Born: Clevedon, 8 September 1970
Height: 5'7" **Weight:** 11.0
International Honours: E: SP-1
This experienced defender was a regular at right back for Cheltenham Town throughout the 2004-05 season, also occasionally being pressed into action as a sweeper in a five-man defence. His tackling, passing, awareness and ability to stay calm under pressure were all consistently evident throughout the campaign and he was rewarded with a contract extension.
Leyton Orient *(Free from Trowbridge T on 16/12/1988. Free to Weston-super-Mare on 1/7/1990)*
Birmingham C *(£30,000 from Yeovil T on 14/7/1997) FL 43+17 FLC 11+1 FAC 3 Others 1*
Northampton T *(Free on 9/8/2002) FL 41 FLC 1 FAC 2 Others 2*
Cheltenham T *(Free on 27/2/2004) FL 48+3 FLC 1 FAC 1 Others 1*

GILL Matthew James
Born: Cambridge, 8 November 1980
Height: 5'11" **Weight:** 12.10
Matthew took time to settle in at Notts County following his arrival in the summer of 2004 but once he had regained his form he was able to hold down a regular place in the side as a midfield anchor man. A ferocious ball winner, he also possesses a powerful long throw and delivered many of the team's set-piece kicks.
Peterborough U *(From trainee on 2/3/1998) FL 121+30/5 FLC 3+1 FAC 6+1 Others 3+4*
Notts Co *(Free on 17/6/2004) FL 38+5 FLC 2 FAC 3+1 Others 1*

GILLESPIE Keith Robert
Born: Bangor, 18 February 1975
Height: 5'10" **Weight:** 11.3
Club Honours: FAYC '92; FLC '02
International Honours: NI: 62; U21-1; Yth; Sch
This right winger started the 2004-05 season as an occasional substitute for Leicester, but was given a new lease of life when Craig Levein took over the manager's chair. Keith's form blossomed to such an extent that he even got back on the score sheet after a lengthy barren spell. His televised 30-yard volley at Upton Park will be long remembered and it was voted the club's 'Goal of the Season'. Keith was also the Supporters' Club choice as 'Player of the Season', but this did not prevent him from being released in the summer.
Manchester U *(From trainee on 3/2/1993) PL 3+6/1 FLC 3 FAC 1+1/1*
Wigan Ath *(Loaned on 3/9/1993) FL 8/4 Others 2*
Newcastle U *(£1,000,000 on 12/1/1995) PL 94+19/11 FLC 7+1/1 FAC 9+1/2 Others 11+5*
Blackburn Rov *(£2,250,000 on 18/12/1998) P/FL 67+46/5 FLC 8+3 FAC 6+4/1 Others 0+3*
Wigan Ath *(Loaned on 1/12/2000) FL 4+1 FAC 2*
Leicester C *(Free on 9/7/2003) P/FL 26+16/2 FLC 0+2 FAC 4*

GILLESPIE Steven
Born: Liverpool, 4 June 1984
Height: 5'9" **Weight:** 11.5
Steven was only on the fringes of the first-team squad at Bristol City last term and made the starting line-up for just a single League One fixture. He fared better during an extended loan spell at Cheltenham during the second half of the campaign. A deceptively quick striker who is sharp around the penalty box and has an eye for goal, Steven scored four times in his first five appearances for the Whaddon Road club including a double in the 3-0 win at Chester.
Bristol C *(From trainee at Liverpool on 6/8/2004) FL 1+7 FLC 0+1 FAC 0+1 Others 1+1*
Cheltenham T *(Loaned on 11/1/2005) FL 10+2/5*

Keith Gillespie

GILROY Keith
Born: Sligo, 8 July 1983
Height: 5'10" **Weight:** 11.4
International Honours: RoI: U21-1; Yth
This talented young midfielder spent much of last term on monthly contracts at Scarborough before returning to the Football League when he signed for Darlington in February. He operated mainly down the right wing but as the Quakers had a surfeit of right-sided attacking players he made only a couple of appearances before being released at the end of the season.
Middlesbrough *(Signed from Sligo Rovers on 5/9/2000. Free to Scarborough on 27/3/2003)*
Darlington *(Free from Scarborough on 24/2/2005) FL 1+1*

GIVEN Seamus (Shay) John James
Born: Lifford, 20 April 1976
Height: 6'0" **Weight:** 13.4
Club Honours: Div 1 '96
International Honours: RoI: 70; U21-5; Yth
As the last line of Newcastle's defence Shay had a busy season last term but performed with distinction. Athletic, with strong wrists and quick feet, his run of 140 consecutive Premiership games came to an end in early November when he was absent to attend the birth of his first child. His 300th game for the club came in the UEFA Cup at Sochaux when he was outstanding, and he became the first Newcastle player to reach 50 European appearances in the home tie against Sporting Lisbon in April. Shay carried his form into the international arena adding several more to his tally of Republic of Ireland caps including a World Cup qualifier against Switzerland in November described by many as his best-ever performance for his country.
Blackburn Rov *(From Glasgow Celtic juniors on 8/8/1994) PL 2 FLC 0+1*
Swindon T *(Loaned on 4/8/1995) FL 5*
Sunderland *(Loaned on 19/1/1996) FL 17*
Newcastle U *(£1,500,000 on 14/7/1997) PL 253 FLC 5+1 FAC 23 Others 51*

Shay Given

GLEESON Daniel (Dan) Edward
Born: Cambridge, 17 February 1985
Height: 6'1" **Weight:** 12.8
This tall, strong Cambridge United defender gained further experience last term when he established himself as a regular in the first-team squad, featuring in over half the club's League Two fixtures. He mostly filled the right-back berth, but is also capable of playing in midfield if required.
Cambridge U *(From trainee on 25/2/2004) FL 24+13 FLC 1 Others 2*

GLEESON Jamie Bradley
Born: Poole, 15 January 1985
Height: 6'0" **Weight:** 12.3
This young midfielder struggled to make a breakthrough at Kidderminster last term and he made just two starts. His prospects looked more promising early in the season when he made his debut in the Carling Cup tie with Cardiff, but he was soon sent out on loan to Ryman League club Eastleigh, and was released from his contract at the end of the campaign.
Southampton *(From trainee on 2/7/2002)*
Kidderminster Hrs *(Free on 4/8/2004) FL 2+5 FLC 0+1*

GNOHERE David **Arthur**
Born: Yamoussoukro, Ivory Coast, 20 November 1978
Height: 6'2" **Weight:** 12.13
This solid centre half started the season as the first choice partner for Danny Shittu in the Queen's Park Rangers defence. However, he only played three games before suffering a serious leg injury, and then when on a comeback for the reserves he suffered a bad knee injury in November. This kept him out of action for the remainder of the season.
Burnley *(Free from SM Caen, France, ex AS Cannes, on 9/8/2001) FL 74+7/6 FLC 7 FAC 5*
Queens Park Rgrs *(Loaned on 4/9/2003) FL 6 Others 1/1*
Queens Park Rgrs *(Free on 19/2/2004) FL 14+1 FLC 1*

GOATER Leonard **Shaun**
Born: Hamilton, Bermuda, 25 February 1970
Height: 6'1" **Weight:** 12.0
Club Honours: AMC '96
International Honours: Bermuda: 19; Yth
Used sparingly during the early part of the season, Shaun spent time languishing in Reading's reserve team before joining Coventry City on loan for the final run-in. The veteran striker started four successive games but looked far from his best, probably due to his lack of first-team action. He played in the crucial wins over Brighton and Nottingham Forest but he had few chances to score, although he made a major contribution in lifting the spirit of the team.
Manchester U *(Free from North Village, Bermuda on 8/5/1989)*
Rotherham U *(Free on 25/10/1989) FL 169+40/70 FLC 13+4/4 FAC 12+3/7 Others 15+4/5*
Notts Co *(Loaned on 12/11/1993) FL 1*
Bristol C *(£175,000 on 17/7/1996) FL 67+8/40 FLC 7/2 FAC 5 Others 5+1/1*
Manchester C *(£400,000 on 26/3/1998) P/FL 164+20/84 FLC 13/9 FAC 9+3/9 Others 3/1*
Reading *(£500,000 on 4/8/2003) FL 32+11/12 FLC 3+1/1 FAC 2/2*
Coventry C *(Loaned on 23/3/2005) FL 4+2*

GOBERN Lewis Thomas
Born: Birmingham, 28 January 1985
Height: 5'10" **Weight:** 11.7
This right-sided midfielder spent much of last season developing in Wolves' reserve team. With chances limited at Molineux, he took the opportunity of first-team football with a loan spell at Hartlepool. Unfortunately he got few chances to prove himself, and after just two games he was sidelined with an ankle injury before returning to the Midlands.
Wolverhampton W *(From trainee on 5/3/2004)*
Hartlepool U *(Loaned on 1/11/2004) FL 1 Others 0+1*

GOLBOURNE Scott Julian
Born: Bristol, 29 February 1988
Height: 5'8" **Weight:** 11.8
International Honours: E: Yth
A product of Bristol City's youth set-up, this teenager impressed after making his first-team debut at Colchester in February. Scott became only the sixth 16-year-old to play League football for City and later took over the full-back position vacated by his cousin Matt Hill who was transferred to Preston. Scott will be looking to firmly establish himself in the squad in 2005-06.
Bristol C *(From trainee on 5/3/2005) FL 7+2*

GOMA Alain
Born: Sault, France, 5 October 1972
Height: 6'0" **Weight:** 13.0
International Honours: France: 2; B-1; U21; Yth
Alain had something of a frustrating season at Fulham last term. He started the season vying with Ian Pearce for first-team selection before sustaining calf and hamstring injuries which kept him out for three months. A commanding central defender who is seldom beaten in the air, he eventually re-established himself as a first choice during the latter part of the campaign.
Newcastle U *(£4,750,000 from Paris St Germain, France, ex Auxerre, on 9/7/1999) PL 32+1/1 FLC 4 FAC 2 Others 2*
Fulham *(£4,000,000 on 16/3/2001) P/FL 102+2 FLC 2 FAC 17+1 Others 13*

GOODALL Alan Jeffrey
Born: Birkenhead, 2 December 1981
Height: 5'9" **Weight:** 11.6
Alan featured for Bangor City in their Inter Toto Cup ties against Romanian side Gloria Bistrita last June before completing a move to Rochdale. He made an excellent impression as an attacking left back in the pre-season games and was handed a place in the starting line-up for the opening game at Scunthorpe. After a spell on the fringes of the side he reappeared around Christmas time and was pretty much a regular thereafter, occasionally featuring on the left-hand side of midfield. Alan scored his first League goal in the draw with Yeovil and his form was rewarded with an extended contract and the supporters' 'Most Improved Player of the Year' award.
Rochdale *(Signed from Bangor C on 30/7/2004) FL 27+7/2 FAC 2 Others 1*

GOODFELLOW Marc David
Born: Swadlincote, 20 September 1981
Height: 5'8" **Weight:** 10.6
This skilful winger fell out of favour at Bristol City last season and had few opportunities to demonstrate his goal-scoring talents. Marc spent much of the campaign out on loan, beginning with a spell at Port Vale, where he covered for injuries. His next stop was Swansea where he scored four goals in a run of six appearances, prompting a bid for his services. However, he was recalled briefly to Ashton Gate to cover for an injury crisis, only to be farmed out again in March, this time to Colchester. He scored a cracking goal in the 3-0 win at Peterborough, but was then relegated to the bench.
Stoke C *(From juniors on 29/1/1999) FL 17+37/6 FLC 3+3/2 FAC 1+6 Others 4/1*
Bristol C *(£50,000 on 9/1/2004) FL 8+12/4 Others 0+2/1*
Port Vale *(Loaned on 6/10/2004) FL 4+1*
Swansea C *(Loaned on 26/11/2004) FL 6/3 FAC 1+1/1*
Colchester U *(Loaned on 17/3/2005) FL 4+1/1*

GOODHIND Warren Ernest
Born: Johannesburg, South Africa, 16 August 1977
Height: 5'11" **Weight:** 11.6

After spending part of the pre-season having trials back in South Africa with Moroka Swallows, Warren returned to Cambridge United only to suffer a tendon injury almost immediately. The versatile defender returned to first-team action towards the end of September and was a regular member of the line-up for the remainder of the campaign.
Barnet *(From trainee on 3/7/1996) FL 73+20/3 FLC 5+2 FAC 2 Others 4/1*
Cambridge U *(£80,000 on 21/9/2001) FL 95+8 FLC 1 FAC 9 Others 6+3*

GOODISON Ian
Born: St James', Jamaica, 21 November 1972
Height: 6'3" **Weight:** 12.10
International Honours: Jamaica
Ian brought vast experience and neat ball control to the Tranmere defence in his first full season at Prenton Park. He is a strong and versatile player, who has shown himself to be readily prepared to take over in any position if the occasion demands. Ian is a persistent, no-nonsense tackler as well as being a valuable, all-round team man. He was a near ever-present during 2004-05, but at the time of writing his future at the club was still unclear.
Hull C *(Free from Olympic Gardens, Jamaica on 22/10/1999) FL 67+3/1 FLC 2 FAC 6+1 Others 5 (Free to Seba U, Jamaica during 2002 close season)*
Tranmere Rov *(Free on 20/2/2004) FL 55+1/1 FLC 1 FAC 3 Others 5*

GOODLAD Mark
Born: Barnsley, 9 September 1979
Height: 6'0" **Weight:** 13.2
Club Honours: AMC '01
Mark returned to the Port Vale line-up last season after missing the whole of the previous campaign through injury. Unfortunately his comeback only lasted five games as he was forced to limp off at Brentford with a leg injury and it was only when 'keeper Jonny Brain went down with mumps in February that he returned to the side. This time Mark managed to cement his status as the club's number one with some excellent displays and he missed only one more game. A good shot-stopper who is efficient rather than spectacular, he signed a new contract in the summer.
Nottingham F *(From trainee on 2/10/1996)*
Scarborough *(Loaned on 5/2/1999) FL 3*
Port Vale *(Free on 23/3/2000) FL 139+2 FLC 5 FAC 5 Others 12*

GOODWIN James (Jim)
Born: Waterford, 20 November 1981
Height: 5'9" **Weight:** 12.2
International Honours: RoI: 1; U21-14
Jim was a near ever-present for Stockport last term and although not the most skilful of footballers, the versatile player more than compensated with his commitment to the cause. A player who will always give his all for the team, he rarely if ever pulls out of a tackle.
Glasgow Celtic *(Signed from Tramore on 25/11/1997) SL 1*
Stockport Co *(Free on 7/6/2002) FL 81+22/7 FLC 3 FAC 6/1 Others 7/1*

GORDON Dean Dwight Joshua
Born: Croydon, 10 February 1973
Height: 6'0" **Weight:** 13.4
Club Honours: Div 1 '94
International Honours: E: U21-13
This experienced defender joined Grimsby on a weekly contract as cover for an early-season injury to new signing Ronnie Bull. Despite being an ever present throughout the first half of the campaign and being one of the club's most consistent performers, Dean departed soon after being left out of the line-up for the Boxing Day game against Macclesfield. He subsequently opted to join Apoel Nicosia in the new year.
Crystal Palace *(From trainee on 4/7/1991) P/FL 181+20/20 FLC 16+3/2 FAC 14+1/1 Others 5+1*
Middlesbrough *(£900,000 on 17/7/1998) PL 53+10/4 FLC 5 FAC 3*
Cardiff C *(Loaned on 23/11/2001) FL 7/2*
Coventry C *(Free on 1/8/2002) FL 33+2/1 FLC 2 FAC 4+1*
Reading *(Loaned on 23/3/2004) FL 0+3*
Grimsby T *(Free on 13/8/2004) FL 20/2 FLC 2 FAC 1*

GORDON Kenyatta **Gavin**
Born: Manchester, 24 June 1979
Height: 6'1" **Weight:** 12.0
This tall and powerful target man formed an effective partnership with Glynn Hurst for Notts County last season, leading the front line well. He scored eight goals himself and set up many chances for his colleagues before an injury brought his campaign to a premature close in February.
Hull C *(From trainee on 3/7/1996) FL 22+16/9 FLC 1+4/1 Others 1+1*
Lincoln C *(£30,000 on 7/11/1997) FL 87+12/28 FLC 2/1 FAC 9/2 Others 4+1*
Cardiff C *(£275,000 + on 18/12/2000) FL 26+24/5 FLC 0+2 FAC 2/1 Others 1+1/6*
Oxford U *(Loaned on 27/9/2002) FL 3+3/1 FLC 0+1*
Notts Co *(Free on 2/7/2004) FL 23+4/5 FAC 4/3 Others 0+1*

GORRE Dean
Born: Surinam, 10 September 1970
Height: 5'8" **Weight:** 11.7
International Honours: Holland: U21
After being released by Barnsley, Dean had a trial period with Blackpool before signing on a short-term contract at the end of August. A creative midfielder with plenty of experience, he made only one first-team appearance during his stay at Bloomfield Road, coming off the bench during the home game with Swindon in September. Dean was released by the club in December.
Huddersfield T *(£330,000 from Ajax, Holland on 16/9/1999) FL 49+13/6 FLC 4/1 FAC 1+1*
Barnsley *(£50,000 on 24/7/2001) FL 48+17/9 FLC 3/1 Others 2*
Blackpool *(Free on 26/8/2004) FL 0+1*

GOSLING Jamie John
Born: Bath, 21 March 1982
Height: 6'0" **Weight:** 10.6
Jamie began last season with Team Bath before joining Torquay United in a short-term deal. He performed well in the centre of midfield showing good passing ability and a willingness to get forward but was not quite able to earn a longer deal and ended the season with Woking.
Yeovil T *(£20,000 from Bath C on 31/7/2003) FL 4+8/1 FLC 1 FAC 0+2 Others 0+2 (Freed during 2004 close season)*
Torquay U *(Free from Team Bath on 2/12/2004) FL 6+1/1*

GOTTSKALKSSON Olafur (Ole)
Born: Keflavik, Iceland, 12 March 1968
Height: 6'3" **Weight:** 13.12
Club Honours: S Div 1 '99
International Honours: Iceland: 9; U21-7; Yth
This former Brentford and Hibernian 'keeper had retired from the professional game due to a back injury but after successful treatment back in Iceland he decided to try a come back. Despite an extended run in the Torquay team, he never really inspired confidence in his back four and it was no surprise when he decided to call it a day once more.
Hibernian *(Signed from Keflavik, Iceland, ex Akranes, KR Reykjavik, on 29/7/1997) SL 64 SLC 4 SC 2*
Brentford *(Free on 11/7/2000) FL 73 FLC 6 FAC 3 Others 7 (Freed on 15/11/2002)*
Torquay U *(Free, following a break from football, on 30/9/2004) FL 15 FAC 1 Others 1*

GOULD Jonathan Alan
Born: Paddington, 18 July 1968
Height: 6'1" **Weight:** 13.7
Club Honours: SPD '98, '01; SLC '98, '00, '01
International Honours: S: 2; B-1

This experienced goalkeeper started the season on the transfer list at Preston where he was well down the pecking order. A lengthy loan spell at Hereford ended when he was needed for the bench following Andy Lonergan's broken hand, and he eventually made four consecutive appearances before losing his place after a heavy defeat at Wigan. His contract was cancelled in February and soon afterwards he signed for Bristol City, but he did not add to his total of first-team appearances during his stay at Ashton Gate.

Halifax T *(Free from Clevedon T on 18/7/1990) FL 32 FLC 2 FAC 5 Others 5*
West Bromwich A *(Free on 30/1/1992)*
Coventry C *(Free on 15/7/1992) PL 25 FLC 1+1*
Bradford C *(Free on 29/3/1996) FL 18 FLC 2 Others 3*
Gillingham *(Loaned on 28/10/1996) FL 3*
Glasgow Celtic *(Signed on 2/8/1997) SL 109+1 SLC 14+1 SC 12 Others 21*
Preston NE *(Free on 9/1/2003) FL 54+1 FLC 1 FAC 3*
Bristol C *(Free on 25/2/2005)*

GOWER Mark
Born: Edmonton, 5 October 1978
Height: 5'11" **Weight:** 11.12
Club Honours: FLC '99
International Honours: E: SP-4; Yth; Sch
Mark had something of a frustrating season at Southend last term, when a pre-season hernia operation hampered his early preparations to reach match fitness. A skilful midfield playmaker, a highlight of his campaign came in the first leg of the LDV Vans Trophy Southern Area final, when with the tie locked at one apiece, Mark unleashed an unstoppable shot from an awkward angle at the edge of the box. The strike was a clear winner of the club's 'Goal of the Season' award.

Tottenham H *(From trainee on 1/4/1997) FLC 0+2*
Motherwell *(Loaned on 12/3/1999) SL 8+1/1*
Barnet *(£32,500 on 19/1/2001) FL 10+4/1 Others 1/1*
Southend U *(£25,000 on 25/7/2003) FL 72+6/12 FLC 2 FAC 6/2 Others 14+1/2*

GRABOVAC Zarko
Born: Ruma, Serbia, 16 March 1983
Height: 6'5" **Weight:** 14.9
After doing well with Dutch amateurs Geldrop AEK, this giant striker signed a short-term contract for Blackpool during the January transfer window. Zarco made two appearances from the bench and then featured in the starting line-up for the 2-0 home win over Oldham in February before fading from the scene. He was released by the Seasiders at the end of the season.

Blackpool *(Free from Geldrop AEK, ex Ronse, TOP Oss, on 14/1/2005) FL 1+2*

GRAHAM Daniel (Danny) Anthony William
Born: Gateshead, 12 August 1985
Height: 5'11" **Weight:** 12.5
International Honours: E: Yth
Danny, an old-fashioned type of centre forward, was a latecomer to professional football, having first made his name with Northern League outfit Chester-le-Street Town. The former window fitter made his debut last October, coming on as a substitute in the 1-1 draw at Manchester United with the Boro' side decimated by injuries. He grabbed his first goal a few weeks later when scoring in the 3-0 Carling Cup victory over Coventry City at the Riverside, but knew little of it after suffering a broke nose whilst netting the ball.

Middlesbrough *(From trainee on 6/3/2004) PL 0+11/1 FLC 0+2/1 FAC 0+2 Others 1+1*
Darlington *(Loaned on 19/3/2004) FL 7+2/2*

GRAHAM David
Born: Edinburgh, 6 October 1978
Height: 5'10" **Weight:** 11.5
International Honours: S: U21-8
A summer signing from Torquay, this striker found his first-team opportunities limited at Wigan last term due to the goal-scoring form of Nathan Ellington and Jason Roberts. David mostly featured on the right-hand side of midfield, netting his only goal in the home win over Coventry City. A good squad player who has the ability to unlock a defence with his skills on the ball, he also has a voracious work rate.

Glasgow Rgrs *(From juniors on 1/7/1995) SL 0+3 Others 1+1*
Dunfermline Ath *(Signed on 15/11/1998) SL 17+23/4 SLC 1 SC 3/1 Others 0+1*
Inverness CT *(Loaned on 5/1/2001) SL 0+2 SC 0+2*
Torquay U *(Free on 22/3/2001) FL 103+17/47 FLC 3+1/2 FAC 4 Others 1+1*
Wigan Ath *(£215,000 on 26/7/2004) FL 13+17/1 FLC 1 FAC 1*

GRANT Anthony (Tony) James
Born: Liverpool, 14 November 1974
Height: 5'10" **Weight:** 10.2
Club Honours: CS '95
International Honours: E: U21-1
Rarely a star man, but as dependable as any player in the Burnley side, Tony was a near automatic choice during 2004-05, usually appearing at the back of the midfield unit, his generally impeccable passing providing the link between the defence and the more attack-minded midfielders, whose composition changed considerably over the course of the campaign. Despite his more defensive role in the side, Tony weighed in with two rare goals late in the campaign. His Burnley contract expired at the end of the season, and he was released after four seasons with the club.

Everton *(From trainee on 8/7/1993) PL 43+18/2 FLC 5+1 FAC 4+4 Others 2+2/1*
Swindon T *(Loaned on 18/1/1996) FL 3/1*
Tranmere Rov *(Loaned on 2/9/1999) FL 8+1 FLC 1/1*
Manchester C *(£450,000 on 24/12/1999) P/FL 11+10 FLC 1 FAC 2+1*
West Bromwich A *(Loaned on 1/12/2000) FL 3+2*
Burnley *(£250,000 on 11/10/2001) FL 121+20/3 FLC 9+1 FAC 15*

GRANT Anthony Paul Shaun Andrew
Born: Lambeth, 4 June 1987
Height: 5'11" **Weight:** 11.3
What a wonderful situation for a young footballer to make his first-team debut: your club has been crowned Premiership champions and are 3-1 up at Old Trafford as you come on as a late substitute. Chelsea midfielder Anthony Grant was the fortunate young man to walk into this scenario. He is very highly thought of by the Stamford Bridge hierarchy having been attached to the club since the age of nine. Originally a right back with the youth team, Anthony has been earning rave reviews for the reserve side in a central holding midfield role à la Claude Makelele.

Chelsea *(Trainee) PL 0+1*

GRANT John Anthony Carlton
Born: Manchester, 9 August 1981
Height: 5'11" **Weight:** 11.9
John arrived at Gay Meadow in the summer of 2004 having spent much of his career playing in the Conference. However, he never quite seemed to make the step-up to League Two football and many of his appearances were from the substitutes' bench. He offered plenty of effort and commitment, but managed only two goals and in March he moved on to join Halifax Town.

Crewe Alex *(From trainee on 7/7/1999) FL 2+5 FLC 1+3 (Free to Hereford U on 19/7/2002)*
Shrewsbury T *(Free from Telford U on 7/8/2004) FL 10+9/2 FLC 1 Others 0+1*

GRANT Lee Anderson
Born: Hemel Hempstead, 27 January 1983
Height: 6'2" **Weight:** 13.4
International Honours: E: U21-4; Yth
Although he played well in his only senior start, Derby County's 2-0 victory over Burnley at Turf Moor when Lee Camp was suspended, Lee had to endure a season on the bench after winning England U21 caps in the previous campaign. Worse came in March, when he suffered a hairline fracture of the right wrist in training, leading to the loan signing of Kevin Miller. The following month, Lee underwent a shoulder operation, so it was a season to forget.
Derby Co *(From trainee on 17/2/2001) FL 63+4 FLC 1 FAC 2*

GRANVILLE Daniel (Danny) Patrick
Born: Islington, 19 January 1975
Height: 5'11" **Weight:** 12.5
Club Honours: FLC '98, ECWC '98; Div 1 '02
International Honours: E: U21-3
Danny was a near ever-present for Crystal Palace last term and missed only three games during the campaign. He scored his first Premiership goal in the 3-1 defeat by Portsmouth in September, then added further strikes against Tottenham and Manchester United. Danny is an experienced defender who is effective when pushing down the flank and a free-kick specialist. Out of contract in the summer his future was uncertain at the time of writing.
Cambridge U *(From trainee on 19/5/1993) FL 89+10/7 FLC 3+2 FAC 2+2 Others 4+2*
Chelsea *(£300,000 + on 21/3/1997) PL 12+6 FLC 3 Others 4+1/1*
Leeds U *(£1,600,000 on 8/7/1998) PL 7+2 FLC 1 FAC 3 Others 0+1*
Manchester C *(£1,000,000 on 7/8/1999) P/FL 56+14/3 FLC 1+4 FAC 5*
Norwich C *(Loaned on 27/10/2000) FL 6*
Crystal Palace *(£500,000 on 28/12/2001) P/FL 102+5/9 FLC 5 FAC 4+3 Others 3*

GRAVES Wayne Alan
Born: Scunthorpe, 18 September 1980
Height: 5'8" **Weight:** 12.10
Last term was a season Wayne will want to forget as a recurring knee injury restricted him to just one first-team appearance for Scunthorpe United as a substitute in the LDV Vans Trophy defeat at Hereford in September. A wholehearted, quick player he can fill in equally well at full back, wing back or in the centre of midfield. He was released by the club at the end of the season.
Scunthorpe U *(From trainee on 24/3/1999) FL 97+38/6 FLC 4+3 FAC 7+5 Others 4+3*

GRAVESEN Thomas
Born: Vejle, Denmark, 11 March 1976
Height: 5'10" **Weight:** 12.4
International Honours: Denmark: 56; U21-6
Thomas enjoyed the best season of his Everton career before moving to Real Madrid in the January transfer window. The new five-man midfield allowed the charismatic midfielder greater freedom and as a result he posed far more of an attacking threat than in previous years - the Dane also displayed greater discipline both when in possession and in the physical aspect of his play. Consequently before Christmas he was a major inspiration behind his side's quest for a Champions' League spot and it was with mixed feelings that he left for Spain.
Everton *(£2,500,000 from SV Hamburg, Germany, ex Vejle BK, on 9/8/2000) PL 131+10/11 FLC 6/1 FAC 6+2*

GRAY Andrew (Andy) David
Born: Harrogate, 15 November 1977
Height: 6'1" **Weight:** 13.0
International Honours: S: 2; B-3; Yth
The Blades' top scorer last season, Andy played in all but three Championship games. For a time in the middle of the campaign he featured in the unaccustomed role of a lone striker, but was happier, and more prolific, playing alongside a partner. Always hard working, he converted a good

Danny Granville

percentage of his chances and held his nerve well with spot kicks, converting twice in shoot-outs and twice with vital last-minute penalties against Arsenal and Queen's Park Rangers. Andy was called up for the full Scotland international squad in August.

Leeds U *(From trainee on 1/7/1995) PL 13+9 FLC 3+1 FAC 0+2*
Bury *(Loaned on 11/12/1997) FL 4+2/1*
Nottingham F *(£175,000 on 2/9/1998) P/FL 34+30/1 FLC 3+4 FAC 4+1*
Preston NE *(Loaned on 23/2/1999) FL 5*
Oldham Ath *(Loaned on 25/3/1999) FL 4*
Bradford C *(Free on 9/8/2002) FL 77/20 FLC 2 FAC 2/1*
Sheffield U *(Signed on 27/2/2004) FL 55+2/24 FLC 2/2 FAC 5/1*

GRAY Ian James

Born: Manchester, 25 February 1975
Height: 6'2" **Weight:** 13.0

This big goalkeeper produced some outstanding saves for Huddersfield in their opening-day win at Stockport. The highlight of his season proved to be an impressive display in the emphatic home win over Hull City at the Galpharm Stadium, when he also saved a penalty. Unfortunately he was then affected by injuries to his hand and to a hamstring and these problems eventually led to his decision to retire from the game shortly before the end of the year.

Oldham Ath *(From trainee on 16/7/1993)*
Rochdale *(Loaned on 18/11/1994) FL 12 Others 3*
Rochdale *(£20,000 on 17/7/1995) FL 66 FLC 4 FAC 5 Others 4*
Stockport Co *(£200,000 + on 30/7/1997) FL 14+2 FLC 3*
Rotherham U *(Free on 10/7/2000) FL 38+2 FLC 2 FAC 3 Others 1*
Huddersfield T *(Free on 7/8/2003) FL 29 FLC 4 FAC 1 Others 1*

GRAY Julian Raymond

Born: Lewisham, 21 September 1979
Height: 6'1" **Weight:** 11.10

Julian was a big success during his first full season in the Premiership at Birmingham. His pace, agility and incredible stamina caused problems down the left-hand side and his form was so good that he was considered for an England call-up. Julian filled in at left back to good effect in emergencies and scored his first goal for the club with a back-post volley in the stirring win over Liverpool in February.

Arsenal *(From trainee on 13/7/1998) PL 0+1*
Crystal Palace *(£250,000 + on 21/7/2000) FL 100+25/10 FLC 5+6/1 FAC 6/2 Others 2*
Cardiff C *(Loaned on 13/10/2003) FL 5+4*
Birmingham C *(Free on 24/6/2004) PL 18+14/2 FLC 2 FAC 2*

GRAY Michael

Born: Sunderland, 3 August 1974
Height: 5'7" **Weight:** 10.10
Club Honours: Div 1 '96, '99
International Honours: E: 3

Michael featured several times for Blackburn early on last term and although be was briefly restored by caretaker manager Tony Parkes he dropped out of the first-team picture. He joined Leeds United on loan for the last three months of the season. Michael made his debut for the Whites in the 1-0 win at Burnley in February but in his sixth game in a United shirt was red-carded against Gillingham. After serving his three-match ban he returned to the side for the last four games of the campaign before injury ruled him out of the final match at home to Rotherham.

Sunderland *(From trainee on 1/7/1992) P/FL 341+22/16 FLC 23+4 FAC 17+1/1 Others 3+1*
Glasgow Celtic *(Loaned on 31/8/2003) SL 2+5 SLC 1 Others 1+1*
Blackburn Rov *(Free on 28/1/2004) PL 23*
Leeds U *(Loaned on 3/2/2005) FL 10*

GRAY Stuart Edward

Born: Harrogate, 18 December 1973
Height: 5'11" **Weight:** 11.2
Club Honours: Div 3 '03
International Honours: S: U21-7

Stuart played a key role for Rushden last term when he was a regular in the line-up and although he rarely received much praise from the supporters, his influence was recognised when he won the club's 'Players' Player of the Year' award. He was disappointed to score just twice - in the FA Cup defeat to Colchester United and, far more importantly, setting up the 2-0 home win over eventual champions Yeovil Town in April. After another difficult year both on and off the pitch at Nene Park, the Diamonds' club captain seemed likely to be seeking a new club for the 2005-06 campaign at the time of writing.

Glasgow Celtic *(Signed from Giffnock North AFC on 7/7/1992) SL 19+9/1 SC 1 Others 2+1*
Morton *(Loaned on 17/10/1997) SL 15/1*
Reading *(£100,000 on 27/3/1998) FL 46+6/2 FLC 8 FAC 1+1 Others 2*
Rushden & Diamonds *(Free on 23/3/2001) FL 116+7/13 FLC 4+1 FAC 6/1 Others 4+1/1*

GRAY Wayne William

Born: Camberwell, 7 November 1980
Height: 5'10" **Weight:** 12.10

Wayne suffered a torrid start to the 2004-05 season with Southend and was briefly dropped from the side by manager Steve Tilson. On his return to the line-up he looked a different player, his speed and unquenchable work rate causing untold problems for opposition defences. His striking partnership with Freddy Eastwood bore some excellent fruit, with Wayne scoring 13 goals and making many more for his colleagues.

Wimbledon *(From trainee on 10/2/1999) P/FL 33+42/6 FLC 1+1 FAC 1+7/1*
Swindon T *(Loaned on 3/3/2000) FL 8+4/2*
Port Vale *(Loaned on 6/10/2000) FL 2+1*
Leyton Orient *(Loaned on 30/11/2001) FL 13+2/5 FAC 2/1*
Brighton & Hove A *(Loaned on 27/3/2002) FL 3+1/1*
Southend U *(Free on 8/7/2004) FL 33+11/11 FLC 0+1 FAC 1 Others 6+4/2*

GRAYSON Simon Nicholas

Born: Ripon, 16 December 1969
Height: 6'0" **Weight:** 13.7
Club Honours: FLC '97; AMC '04

This veteran midfielder was a regular in the Blackpool line-up last term, mostly featuring in the centre of the park. He also contributed two valuable goals, netting winners at Colchester in February and against Chesterfield in the penultimate home game of the season. Simon agreed an extension to his contract at Bloomfield Road and is also likely to be involved in coaching during the 2005-06 campaign.

Leeds U *(From trainee on 13/6/1988) FL 2 Others 1+1*
Leicester C *(£50,000 on 13/3/1992) P/FL 175+13/4 FLC 16+2/2 FAC 9 Others 13+1*
Aston Villa *(£1,350,000 on 1/7/1997) PL 32+16 FLC 1+1 FAC 4+1/2 Others 6+3*
Blackburn Rov *(£750,000 + on 29/7/1999) FL 31+3 FLC 1+1 FAC 2+1*
Sheffield Wed *(Loaned on 11/8/2000) FL 5*
Stockport Co *(Loaned on 12/1/2001) FL 13 FAC 1*
Notts Co *(Loaned on 6/9/2001) FL 10/1 FLC 1 Others 2*
Bradford C *(Loaned on 15/2/2002) FL 7*
Blackpool *(Free on 1/8/2002) FL 104+10/6 FLC 4+1 FAC 9 Others 7+1*

GREAVES Mark Andrew

Born: Hull, 22 January 1975
Height: 6'1" **Weight:** 13.0

Mark had another steady season at Boston United for whom he was used in a number of different positions. He was perhaps most effective playing in front of the back four where his ability to win the ball provided a solid base for the team. Mark was used both as a right-sided and central midfield player and also appeared at centre back and right back. He suffered a back injury in January, which led to him undergoing an operation and this kept him out of action for the remainder of the season.

Hull C *(Free from Brigg T on 17/6/1996) FL 152+25/10 FLC 8/1 FAC 11/1 Others 6+2*
Boston U *(Free on 29/8/2002) FL 79+6/1 FLC 3 FAC 5 Others 3*

GREEN Adam
Born: Hillingdon, 12 January 1984
Height: 5'9" **Weight:** 10.11
This calm and composed left-sided defender gained an early-season run of five consecutive matches during the absence of Carlos Bocanegra. In January he had a loan spell with Sheffield Wednesday, where he featured on the left-hand side at both full back and wing back without really settling. There was a similar outcome at Bournemouth, where he ended his loan spell on the bench before returning to Fulham.
Fulham *(From trainee on 4/7/2003) PL 8 FLC 2 FAC 2*
Sheffield Wed *(Loaned on 25/1/2005) FL 3*
Bournemouth *(Loaned on 11/3/2005) FL 3*

GREEN Francis James
Born: Nottingham, 25 April 1980
Height: 5'9" **Weight:** 11.6
Francis battled hard up front for Lincoln City in a season when the Imps again narrowly missed out on promotion. He was a key player in the three-man strike force with his bustling style causing problems for opposing defences. An injury caused him to miss the run-in to the end of the season but he came back for the play-offs to give City a boost.
Peterborough U *(£25,000 + from Ilkeston T on 2/3/1998) FL 51+57/14 FLC 4+3 FAC 5 Others 3+4/2*
Lincoln C *(£7,500 on 16/9/2003) FL 56+16/15 FLC 1+1 FAC 1 Others 4+3/1*

GREEN Paul Jason
Born: Pontefract, 10 April 1983
Height: 5'10" **Weight:** 10.12
Club Honours: Div 3 '04
This young Doncaster Rovers midfielder enjoyed another good season at Belle Vue last term, although his form fluctuated a bit towards the end of the campaign. Paul again showed the ability to score goals from the centre of the park, with none better than his fine effort against Stockport in April when Rovers were struggling to get on level terms.
Doncaster Rov *(From trainee on 16/8/2000) FL 76+9/15 FLC 3+1 FAC 3 Others 1*

GREEN Robert Paul
Born: Chertsey, 18 January 1980
Height: 6'2" **Weight:** 12.2
Club Honours: Div 1 '04
International Honours: E: 1; Yth
Robert thoroughly enjoyed his first season of Premiership football and won a whole

Robert Green

new army of admirers with some outstanding displays, particularly at Tottenham and Manchester United. An unflappable character he was a much busier 'keeper than in City's championship-winning season and thrived on the extra responsibilities. A commanding figure, he possesses terrific reflexes and his kicking is particularly reliable. He was also a regular member of the England squad throughout the season.
Norwich C *(From juniors on 3/7/1997) P/FL 180+1 FLC 5 FAC 7 Others 3*

GREEN Scott Paul
Born: Walsall, 15 January 1970
Height: 5'10 **Weight:** 12.5
Club Honours: Div 1 '97; Div 2 '03; AMC '99, '05
Scott recovered from his knee injury problems and after training with Wrexham from October he signed on non-contract forms at the end of the following month. The experienced midfielder helped the Dragons to earn a surprise victory at Huddersfield and then signed up until the end of the season. A good organiser on the pitch who is composed on the ball, and is both physically and mentally strong, he was used mainly as a substitute as the season wore on and was not retained at the end of the campaign.
Derby Co *(From trainee on 20/7/1988)*
Bolton W *(£50,000 on 17/3/1990) P/FL 166+54/25 FLC 19+4/1 FAC 20+3/4 Others 15+4/1*
Wigan Ath *(£300,000 on 30/6/1997) FL 177+22/10 FLC 16+1 FAC 17/1 Others 15+1*
Wrexham *(Free on 14/2/2003) FL 12+3/3 (Free to Telford U on 7/8/2003)*
Wrexham *(Free, following a lengthy injury, on 27/11/2004) FL 5+7 FAC 1 Others 1+2*

GREEN Stuart
Born: Whitehaven, 15 June 1981
Height: 5'10" **Weight:** 11.4
Undoubtedly blessed with fine skills and balance on the ball, Stuart added greater maturity and application to his play to make a considerable contribution to Hull City's second consecutive promotion. He certainly made a notable contribution in the goal-scoring department, his tally of ten only being bettered by the prolific Stuart Elliott. Although he prefers a central-midfield role, his attacking qualities also meant that he was a threat when cutting inside from a position wide on the right. Sadly, Stuart missed the exciting run-in to the end of the season after suffering an ankle injury in March.
Newcastle U *(From trainee on 8/7/1999)*
Carlisle U *(Loaned on 14/12/2001) FL 16/3*
Hull C *(£150,000 on 3/7/2002) FL 91+8/20 FLC 1+1 FAC 4/1 Others 1/1*
Carlisle U *(Loaned on 19/2/2003) FL 9+1/2 Others 3*

GREENACRE Christopher (Chris) Mark
Born: Halifax, 23 December 1977
Height: 5'11" **Weight:** 12.8
This nippy striker was hampered by a series of injuries which restricted his appearances for Stoke last term. After starting the season on the bench he got a run in the side from November onwards but was used mainly either on the right or left side of midfield, rather than his more familiar role up front. He will be looking for better fortune in the 2005-06 season.
Manchester C *(From trainee on 1/7/1995) FL 3+5/1 FAC 0+1*
Cardiff C *(Loaned on 22/8/1997) FL 11/2*
Blackpool *(Loaned on 5/3/1998) FL 2+2*
Scarborough *(Loaned on 10/12/1998) FL 10+2/2 Others 1*
Mansfield T *(Free on 5/11/1999) FL 120+1/49 FLC 5/3 FAC 5/6 Others 2+1*
Stoke C *(Free on 8/7/2002) FL 44+31/7 FLC 2 FAC 5+1/2*

GREENING Jonathan
Born: Scarborough, 2 January 1979
Height: 5'11" **Weight:** 11.7
Club Honours: UEFACL '99; FLC '04
International Honours: E: U21-18; Yth
One of four players to make their debut for West Bromwich Albion in the opening Premiership game of the season at Blackburn, Jonathan went on to have an excellent campaign. Although he failed to score himself, he nevertheless worked tirelessly down both flanks and provided telling crosses from which several chances were created and goals scored.
York C *(From trainee on 23/12/1996) FL 5+20/2 FLC 0+1 Others 1*
Manchester U *(£500,000 + on 25/3/1998) PL 4+10 FLC 6 FAC 0+1 Others 3+3*
Middlesbrough *(£2,000,000 on 9/8/2001) PL 91+8/4 FLC 5 FAC 4+1*
West Bromwich A *(£1,250,000 on 30/7/2004) PL 32+2 FLC 0+1 FAC 2*

GREENWOOD Ross Michael
Born: York, 1 November 1985
Height: 5'11" **Weight:** 11.2
This fine young Sheffield Wednesday prospect made the step-up from youth and reserve-team football to the first-team squad last term. Ross made his debut in the Carling Cup tie against Coventry and followed up with three more substitute appearances. A promising right back, he showed plenty of confidence and did not look out of place.
Sheffield Wed *(Trainee) FL 0+2 FLC 1 Others 0+1*

GREGAN Sean Matthew
Born: Guisborough, 29 March 1974
Height: 6'2" **Weight:** 14.7
Club Honours: Div 2 '00
Persistent Leeds boss Kevin Blackwell finally got his man when the Whites signed Shaun in September. Blackwell had been tracking the West Brom midfielder for several weeks but had to be patient because of the Elland Road club's precarious finances. The tough-tackling player added his experience and physical presence to a youthful squad. Shaun had missed most of the pre-season with the Baggies because of injury and took some time to settle at Leeds. He clicked into form after Christmas and showed his versatility with appearances a centre back at Queen's Park Rangers and at home to Rotherham.
Darlington *(From trainee on 20/1/1991) FL 129+7/4 FLC 8 FAC 7 Others 10+1/1*
Preston NE *(£350,000 on 29/11/1996) FL 206+6/12 FLC 14 FAC 15/1 Others 10*
West Bromwich A *(£1,500,000 on 6/8/2002) P/FL 76+3/2 FLC 4 FAC 2*
Leeds U *(£500,000 on 17/9/2004) FL 34+1 FLC 2 FAC 1*

GREGORIO Adolfo
Born: Turlock, California, USA, 1 October 1982
Height: 5'9" **Weight:** 11.11
After rejecting the offer of a contract with Colorado Rapids, this young midfielder crossed the Atlantic and signed for Darlington following trials with Bristol City and Wigan. He soon made his mark in the Quakers' first team showing skilful close control and a keen eye for a pass, as well as popping in a couple of goals in consecutive games in January. A leg injury kept him out for a couple of spells but he featured in over half the club's League Two fixtures during the campaign.
Darlington *(Free from UCLA on 17/9/2004) FL 19+5/2 Others 1*

GRESKO Vratislav
Born: Pressburg, Slovakia, 24 July 1977
Height: 5'11" **Weight:** 11.5
International Honours: Slovakia: 24
Vratislav started the 2004-05 season as a surprise choice in central midfield by Blackburn manager Graeme Souness. He looked to be in tough-tackling form but was quickly sacrificed to give the team a better shape and thereafter his only first-team appearance came in the surprise Carling Cup defeat by Bournemouth. Vratislav continued to represent Slovakia during the campaign and it was while on

international duty that he suffered the cruciate injury that ended his season prematurely.
Blackburn Rov *(£1,200,000 from Parma, Italy, ex Dukla Banska, Inter Bratislava, Bayer Leverkusen, Inter Milan, on 31/1/2003) PL 34+3/1 FLC 2 FAC 1 Others 2*

GRIEMINK Bart

Born: Holland, 29 March 1972
Height: 6'4" **Weight:** 15.4
This commanding goalkeeper joined Southend on a free transfer during the 2004 close season and was initially installed as number-one choice ahead of regular custodian, Daryl Flahavan. Bart kept his place in the side until suffering a knee injury in the game at Rushden and this kept him sidelined for two months. On his return to the side Bart kept several clean sheets, but his most memorable performance came in a tight encounter at Bury when he made an injury-time penalty save to secure all three points. In December he was voted League Two's 'Player of the Month' primarily due to keeping four clean sheets. However, his season came to a premature end in January after he suffered a further injury to his knee in the home game with Notts County.
Birmingham C *(Free from WK Emmen, Holland on 9/11/1995) FL 20 FLC 3 FAC 1 Others 1+1*
Peterborough U *(£25,000 on 11/10/1996) FL 58 FLC 1 FAC 4 Others 4*
Swindon T *(Loaned on 5/2/2000) FL 4*
Swindon T *(Free on 27/7/2000) FL 118+2 FLC 8 FAC 7 Others 5*
Southend U *(Free on 8/7/2004) FL 19 FLC 1 FAC 1 Others 1*

GRIFFIN Adam

Born: Salford, 26 August 1984
Height: 5'7" **Weight:** 10.5
After being awarded a new contract in the summer of 2004 Adam continued to be Oldham Athletic's first-choice left back under Brian Talbot. A gritty prospect who enjoys getting forward to support the attack, he was a virtual ever-present until the arrival of new boss Ronnie Moore in March. Adam then lost his first-team berth to Marc Tierney just four games after Moore's arrival but he will be chomping at the bit to regain his place in the starting line-up again in 2005-06.
Oldham Ath *(From trainee on 9/8/2003) FL 58+4/3 FLC 2 FAC 4+1 Others 4+1/1*

GRIFFIN Andrew (Andy)

Born: Billinge, 7 March 1979
Height: 5'9" **Weight:** 10.10
International Honours: E: U21-2; Yth
Andy joined Portsmouth during the summer and produced some impressive displays, earning several 'Man of the Match awards'. A versatile full back, he was a regular in the line-up for the first half of the season but a series of niggling injury problems restricted his appearances thereafter. He is a fierce tackler with good stamina who enjoys pushing forward to support the attack.
Stoke C *(From trainee on 5/9/1996) FL 52+5/2 FLC 4+1 FAC 2*
Newcastle U *(£1,500,000 + on 30/1/1998) PL 63+13/2 FLC 8 FAC 6 Others 14/1*
Portsmouth *(Free on 2/7/2004) PL 18+4 FLC 3+1 FAC 1*

GRIFFIN Daniel (Danny) Joseph

Born: Belfast, 19 August 1977
Height: 5'10" **Weight:** 10.5
Club Honours: S Div 1 '97
International Honours: NI: 29; U21-10
Danny was still recovering from injury at the start of last season and had to wait until mid-September for his first appearance in the 3-1 home defeat against leaders Luton Town. The central defender held a regular position in County's back four and scored only his second goal for the club in the FA Cup replay at Swansea City – a superb 30-yard effort that flew into the net. Unfortunately his season came to an early end in January when he picked up an injury against Hull City.
St Johnstone *(Signed from St Andrew's BC on 18/2/1994) SL 101+23/4 SLC 6+1/2 SC 4/2 Others 2*
Dundee U *(£600,000 on 17/12/2000) SL 72+5/4 SLC 4/1 SC 6*
Stockport Co *(Free on 9/1/2004) FL 31/1 FAC 3/1 Others 2*

GRIFFIT Leandre

Born: Maubeuge, France, 21 May 1984
Height: 5'11" **Weight:** 11.1
This talented young Saint was perhaps too inexperienced for last term's relegation battle, but when selected he added more pace to the side. Later in the season he had loan spells at Leeds and then Rotherham but only managed sparse appearances during his stay in the Championship. Leandre is a quick and nimble winger who creates space behind defences and has a knack of scoring classy goals.
Southampton *(Free from Amiens, France on 23/7/2003) PL 2+5/2 FLC 0+1*
Leeds U *(Loaned on 6/1/2005) FL 0+1*
Rotherham U *(Loaned on 9/3/2005) FL 1+1*

GRIFFITHS Gareth John

Born: Winsford, 10 April 1970
Height: 6'4" **Weight:** 14.0
Rochdale's veteran centre half missed the start of the 2004-05 season through injury before re-establishing himself in the side as the team recovered from a poor start. He provided his usual dominating presence in the air at the back, with a string of 'Man of the Match' performances that ultimately earned him the 'Player of the Year' award. Definitely a player you want on your side when the going gets tough, Gareth's future was undecided at the time of writing.
Port Vale *(£1,000 from Rhyl on 8/2/1993) FL 90+4/4 FLC 8 FAC 7/1 Others 7*
Shrewsbury T *(Loaned on 31/10/1997) FL 6*
Wigan Ath *(Free on 2/7/1998) FL 44+9/2 FLC 4/1 FAC 5 Others 5+1*
Rochdale *(Free on 18/7/2001) FL 147+8/12 FLC 3 FAC 8/1 Others 7/3*

GRITTON Martin

Born: Glasgow, 1 June 1978
Height: 6'1" **Weight:** 12.7
This strong and hard-working centre forward led the line well for Torquay and had managed six goals by mid-December when he was allowed to move on to Grimsby for a small fee in the wake of the permanent arrival of Leon Constantine. He quickly established a useful understanding with fellow Mariners' striker Michael Reddy, but after a promising start at Blundell Park, his high work rate did not often reap the rewards it deserved, as the goals dried up.
Plymouth Arg *(Free from Porthleven on 7/8/1998) FL 15+29/7 FLC 2+2/1 FAC 0+4 Others 3/1*
Torquay U *(Signed on 8/8/2002) FL 72+21/23 FLC 2 FAC 2+1/3 Others 2*
Grimsby T *(£5,000 on 24/12/2004) FL 22+1/4*

GRONKJAER Jesper

Born: Nuuk, Denmark, 12 August 1977
Height: 6'1" **Weight:** 12.8
International Honours: Denmark: 55; U21-13
Jesper provided a constant stream of crosses for Birmingham City from the right and helped stretch the opposition with his pace and direct running. However, he was never really appreciated by the fans as the Blues struggled early on and, by his own admission, found it hard to adapt to a more defensively-minded team than he was used to. He always wanted the ball and tried to make things happen, however. He was sold to Atletico Madrid during the January transfer window.
Chelsea *(£7,800,000 from Ajax, Holland, ex Aalborg BK, on 21/12/2000) PL 56+32/7 FLC 3+2 FAC 10+4/3 Others 8+4/1*
Birmingham C *(£2,200,000 on 30/7/2004) PL 13+3 FLC 2/1*

GUDJOHNSEN Eidur Smari
Born: Reykjavik, Iceland, 15 September 1978
Height: 6'1" **Weight:** 13.0
Club Honours: CS '00; FLC '05; PL '05
International Honours: Iceland: 36; U21-11; Yth
With the departure of long-standing strike partner Jimmy-Floyd Hasselbaink plus the return of Hernan Crespo and Adrian Mutu to Italy, Eidur Gudjohnsen was the only striker from 2003-04 to survive into Jose Mourinho's 'Brave New World' and he featured in all but one of Chelsea's Premiership fixtures. He had a great season as the Blues played some bewildering attacking football in the most successful campaign of their 100-year history. Whilst new signing Didier Drogba terrorised defences with his strength and direct approach, Eidur relied on his astute positional sense and deft ball control to drop off into midfield and create space and chances for teammates. One particular domestic highlight was his first senior hat-trick, scored within 11 minutes against Blackburn, a well-deserved achievement. He also made significant contributions in two consecutive cup matches to secure famous victories for the Blues. His extra-time shot being parried into the path of Mateja Kezman who scored the decisive goal in the Carling Cup final and then his exquisite early goal in the Champions' League tie against Barcelona helped the Blues overcome a first-leg deficit and clinch a place in the quarter-finals. His final goal of the season was a superb effort at Old Trafford in the penultimate Premiership fixture, nonchalantly dinking the ball over the advancing 'keeper. Eidur's outstanding form was all the more remarkable considering the fact that he had to shoulder the central attacking burden for large parts of the season owing to Drogba's injury problems. One other memorable victory occurred at international level when he skippered Iceland to a shock 2–0 victory over Italy in Reykjavik in August, scoring one of the goals.
Bolton W *(Free from KR Reykjavik, Iceland, ex Valur, PSV Eindhoven, on 6/8/1998) FL 48+7/18 FLC 8+1/3 FAC 4+1/4 Others 4/1*
Chelsea *(£4,000,000 on 12/7/2000) PL 110+50/52 FLC 7+8/6 FAC 14+8/9 Others 21+8/8*

Martin Gritton

GUDJONSSON Bjarni
Born: Akranes, Iceland, 26 February 1979
Height: 5'9" **Weight:** 11.9
Club Honours: AMC '00
International Honours: Iceland: 15; U21-20; Yth
Bjarni had a disappointing time at Coventry last term when he faded quickly from the first-team picture and despite doing well in the reserves he proved unable to get back in the side. In December he moved on to Plymouth where his fortunes immediately improved. Bjarni showed himself to be a talented and creative player, demonstrating class by scoring for the Pilgrims with a superb volley in the FA Cup defeat at the hands of Everton. He also continued to represent Iceland at international level during the campaign.
Newcastle U *(£500,000 from Akranes, Iceland on 14/7/1997. £125,000 to KRC Genk on 12/11/1998)*
Stoke C *(£250,000 on 10/3/2000) FL 119+13/11 FLC 7/2 FAC 8+1/1 Others 9+4/2 (Freed during 2003 close season)*
Coventry C *(Free from VfL Bochum, Germany on 16/1/2004) FL 20+8/3 FLC 3 FAC 1+1*
Plymouth Arg *(Free on 17/12/2004) FL 12+3 FAC 1/1*

GUDJONSSON Johannes (Joey) Karl
Born: Akranes, Iceland, 25 May 1980
Height: 5'8" **Weight:** 11.5
International Honours: Iceland: 23; U21-10; Yth
This defensive midfielder joined Leicester on a free transfer in the 2004 close season, but his debut was delayed until the second fixture of the new campaign due to the late arrival of his international clearance from Spain. Combative, and with a penchant for trying his luck from long range, he netted with a splendid effort in the FA Cup victory at Blackpool. Joey showed far more subtlety when slotting home a spot kick against Preston in the Carling Cup. He was a regular choice for Iceland during the campaign.
Aston Villa *(Loaned from Real Betis, Spain, ex IA Akranes, KRC Genk, MVV Maastricht, RKC Waalwijk, on 27/1/2003) PL 9+2/2*

Wolverhampton W *(Loaned from Real Betis, Spain on 29/8/2003) PL 5+6 FLC 3/1 FAC 1+1*
Leicester C *(Free from Real Betis, Spain, on 11/8/2004) FL 26+9/2 FLC 1/1 FAC 5/1*

GUDJONSSON Thordur
Born: Akranes, Iceland, 14 October 1973
Height: 5'9" **Weight:** 12.5
International Honours: Iceland: 58; U21-10; Yth
This striker or midfielder managed only a couple of appearances from the bench for Stoke last season and was only ever on the fringes of the first-team squad. Thordur is the son of former Potters' manager Gudjon Thordarsson and brother of Bjarni Gudjonsson.
Derby Co *(Loaned from Las Palmas, Spain, Ex IA Akranes, KA Akureyrar, VfL Bochum, KRC Genk, on 2/3/2001) PL 2+8/1*
Preston NE *(Loaned from Las Palmas, Spain, on 8/2/2002) FL 4+3 FAC 0+1*
Stoke C *(Free from VfL Bochum, Germany on 28/1/2005) FL 0+2*

GUERET Willy July
Born: St Claude, Guadeloupe, 3 August 1973
Height: 6'1" **Weight:** 13.5
Initially a trialist at the Vetch Field in the close season, Willy signed a one-year contract just prior to the start of the 2004-05 campaign. Consistent form saw him miss just two League matches during the season as the Swans maintained a challenge for an automatic promotion place to the very last game at Bury. Willy is a talented 'keeper and although not the most consistent of kickers from hand, his reflex saves were top quality and helped the team become one of the meanest defences in the division.
Millwall *(Free from Le Mans, France on 31/7/2000) FL 13+1 FAC 3 Others 2*
Swansea C *(Free on 5/8/2004) FL 44 FLC 1 FAC 5 Others 2*

GUINAN Stephen (Steve) Anthony
Born: Birmingham, 24 December 1975
Height: 6'1" **Weight:** 13.7
International Honours: E: SP-4
This experienced striker returned to Football League action with Cheltenham Town in the summer of 2004 after a prolific spell in the Conference with Hereford United. A powerful player with good touch and the ability to hold the ball up and bring other players into the action, Steve operated as a lone striker during a spell in the middle of the season. This reliance upon him to work the forward line and help to create chances meant that he was not as prolific with his own scoring as he may have hoped, although he did manage to contribute some important goals to the cause.
Nottingham F *(From trainee on 7/1/1993) P/FL 2+5 FLC 2/1*
Darlington *(Loaned on 14/12/1995) FL 3/1*
Burnley *(Loaned on 27/3/1997) FL 0+6*
Crewe Alex *(Loaned on 19/3/1998) FL 3*
Halifax T *(Loaned on 16/10/1998) FL 12/2*
Plymouth Arg *(Loaned on 24/3/1999) FL 11/7*
Scunthorpe U *(Loaned on 10/9/1999) FL 2+1/1*
Cambridge U *(Free on 24/12/1999) FL 4+2 FAC 0+2 Others 1*
Plymouth Arg *(Free on 23/3/2000) FL 15+15/3 FLC 2 FAC 2 Others 0+1*
Shrewsbury T *(Free on 28/3/2002) FL 4+1 (Free to Hereford U on 15/8/2002)*
Cheltenham T *(Free on 17/5/2004) FL 35+8/6 FLC 1 FAC 1 Others 2/1*

GULLIVER Philip (Phil) Stephen
Born: Bishop Auckland, 12 September 1982
Height: 6'2" **Weight:** 13.6
Phil's first full season at Rushden saw him battle it out with Graham Allen and Rob

Willy Gueret

Gier for the two centre-half positions as Diamonds successfully fought against relegation. It was a big learning curve, but Phil coped admirably well and produced a series of strong performances, particularly in the three-month spell just before Christmas.
Middlesbrough *(From trainee on 7/7/2000)*
Blackpool *(Loaned on 29/11/2002) FL 2+1 FAC 1*
Carlisle U *(Loaned on 31/12/2002) FL 1*
Bournemouth *(Loaned on 27/3/2003) FL 4+2 Others 3*
Bury *(Loaned on 10/10/2003) FL 10 FAC 1*
Scunthorpe U *(Loaned on 16/1/2004) FL 2 Others 1*
Rushden & Diamonds *(Free on 6/8/2004) FL 29+3 FLC 1 FAC 2 Others 1*

GUNNARSSON Brynjar Bjorn
Born: Reykjavik, Iceland, 16 October 1975
Height: 6'1" **Weight:** 11.12
International Honours: Iceland: 50; U21-8; Yth
Brynjar came to Watford on the recommendation of his Icelandic compatriot Heidar Helguson, arriving on a free transfer from Stoke. A steely defensive midfielder who plays the game simply but with great effect, he proved a shrewd acquisition. He dovetailed well with Gavin Mahon in central midfield and also found time to support his forwards, weighing in with some useful goals. Brynjar showed his commitment by playing on while unfit, though he was halted by a knee injury in January.
Stoke C *(£600,000 from Orgryte IS, Sweden on 4/1/2000) FL 128+3/16 FLC 7/1 FAC 7/2 Others 12+1/1*
Nottingham F *(Free on 1/8/2003) FL 9+4 FAC 1*
Stoke C *(Free on 19/3/2004) FL 1+2*
Watford *(Free on 2/7/2004) FL 34+2/3 FLC 5 FAC 1+1*

GUPPY Stephen (Steve) Andrew
Born: Winchester, 29 March 1969
Height: 5'11" **Weight:** 11.12
Club Honours: FAT '91, '93; GMVC '93; FLC '00; SPD '02
International Honours: E: 1; B-1; U21-1; SP-1
After the departure of many big-name stars following relegation from the Premiership, Leeds boss Kevin Blackwell turned to this experienced winger, among others, at the start of the campaign on a trial basis. He had mixed fortunes on his only Championship start, netting against Nottingham Forest at Elland Road but unluckily giving away a late penalty which allowed the visitors to snatch a 1-1 draw. Steve was not signed on a permanent basis, and subsequently had a short spell with Stoke City before rejoining Wycombe, where he was given a hero's welcome on his return. He scored a memorable goal at Swansea before being allowed to leave for the USA and a spell with DC United.
Wycombe W *(Signed from Colden Common on 1/9/1989) FL 41/8 FLC 4 FAC 3 Others 10/2*
Newcastle U *(£150,000 on 2/8/1994) FLC 0+1*
Port Vale *(£225,000 on 25/11/1994) FL 102+3/12 FLC 7 FAC 8 Others 7+1/1*
Leicester C *(£950,000 on 28/2/1997) PL 133+13/9 FLC 15 FAC 9/1 Others 4*
Glasgow Celtic *(£350,000 on 2/8/2001) SL 22+11 SLC 2+1 SC 4 Others 4+5*
Leicester C *(Free on 16/1/2004) PL 9+6*
Leeds U *(Free on 13/8/2004) FL 1+2/1 FLC 1*
Stoke C *(Free on 13/9/2004) FL 0+4*
Wycombe W *(Free on 26/11/2004) FL 12+2/1 FAC 1 Others 1*

GURNEY Andrew (Andy) Robert
Born: Bristol, 25 January 1974
Height: 5'10" **Weight:** 11.6
Andy featured on the right-hand side either in defence or midfield for Swindon at the start of last season and it was something of a surprise when he departed for Swansea City. The experienced defender showed good composure on the ball, and some accurate shooting skills when bursting through from defence for the Swans. His only goal of the season came at the Vetch Field against Rochdale in March. Andy also played a number of games in midfield.
Bristol Rov *(From trainee on 10/7/1992) FL 100+8/9 FLC 7/1 FAC 5 Others 15*
Torquay U *(Free on 10/7/1997) FL 64/10 FLC 6 FAC 5/1 Others 3*
Reading *(£100,000 on 15/1/1999) FL 55+12/3 FLC 5 FAC 5+1 Others 5+1*
Swindon T *(Free on 2/7/2001) FL 132/20 FLC 4/1 FAC 4/2 Others 4+1*
Swansea C *(Free on 1/9/2004) FL 25+3/1 FAC 4 Others 1*

GUTTRIDGE Luke Horace
Born: Barnstaple, 27 March 1982
Height: 5'5" **Weight:** 9.7
This combative midfielder had something of a disappointing season at Cambridge last term when he struggled to overcome the effects of a viral infection. Luke eventually moved on to join Southend just before the transfer deadline where he did well, featuring as a substitute in the LDV Vans Trophy final against Wrexham and helping the club achieve promotion via the play-offs.
Torquay U *(Trainee) FL 0+1*
Cambridge U *(Free on 15/8/2000) FL 127+9/17 FLC 1+3 FAC 6+1/1 Others 9+3/2*
Southend U *(Signed on 18/3/2005) FL 3+2 Others 0+3*

GUY Jamie Lesley
Born: Barking, 1 August 1987
Height: 6'1" **Weight:** 13.0
This teenaged striker was one of the heroes of Colchester United youth team's excellent run in the FA Youth Cup last term. He was rewarded with a succession of places on the bench during February, although he only made two brief appearances as a substitute at home to Blackpool (his senior debut) and at Hull. Jamie is a tigerish front-runner, who hassles defenders with his pace and work-rate.
Colchester U *(Trainee) FL 0+2*

GUY Lewis Brett
Born: Penrith, 27 August 1985
Height: 5'10" **Weight:** 10.8
International Honours: E: Yth
This lively striker had scored regularly for Newcastle's reserve and youth teams, but his only first-team action last term came when he made a 20-minute appearance from the bench in the UEFA Cup tie at home to Sporting Lisbon in December. After being released by the Magpies he signed for Doncaster in March and immediately impressed with his pace and work rate. He had settled in nicely by the end of the season and his two goals against Luton Town in the last game of the season were splendidly taken, providing an illustration of what could well be in store in 2005-06.
Newcastle U *(From trainee on 3/8/2002) Others 0+1*
Doncaster Rov *(Free on 3/3/2005) FL 4+5/3*

GUYETT Scott Barry
Born: Ascot, Australia, 20 January 1976
Height: 6'2" **Weight:** 13.2
Club Honours: NC '04; Div 2 '05
International Honours: E: SP-4
This big central defender had something of a frustrating time at Yeovil last term when his appearances were restricted by injury. Knee problems prevented him from making a first-team appearance before October, but once fit he had an extended run in the line-up. However, a further knee injury then kept him out of action from February.
Oxford U *(Free from Southport, ex Brisbane C, Gresley Rov, on 9/7/2001) FL 20+2 FLC 1 FAC 1 Others 1 (Free to Chester C on 2/8/2002)*
Yeovil T *(Free on 30/7/2004) FL 13+5/2 FAC 5*

HAAS Bernt
Born: Vienna, Austria, 8 April 1978
Height: 6'1" **Weight:** 12.8
International Honours: Switzerland: 36
With Riccy Scimeca installed at right wing back at West Bromwich Albion, Bernt was named in midfield early on but never really adapted to the role and struggled to find his form. He then lost his place in the side and with Marten Albrechtsen seemingly also ahead of him in the selection stakes, he was released by Albion's new boss Bryan Robson during the January transfer window. Soon afterwards he signed for Bastia.
Sunderland *(£750,000 from Grasshopper Zurich, Switzerland, on 10/8/2001) PL 27 FLC 0+1 FAC 1*
West Bromwich A *(£400,000 + on 3/8/2003) P/FL 45+1/1 FLC 5/2 FAC 1*

HACKETT Christopher (Chris) James
Born: Oxford, 1 March 1983
Height: 6'0" **Weight:** 11.6
Chris produced some quality performances for Oxford United last term, when he was a regular in the side under both management regimes. Usually employed in a wide-right midfield role or as an out-and-out winger, he used his pace to good effect. He also occasionally featured as a striker and it was from this position that he netted two goals in the 3-1 win at Mansfield.
Oxford U *(From trainee on 20/4/2000) FL 53+51/7 FLC 0+2 FAC 1+3 Others 2+3*

HADFIELD Jordan Michael
Born: Swinton, 12 August 1987
Height: 5'10" **Weight:** 11.4
A product of Stockport's youth policy, Jordan was handed a surprise debut in the 2-1 defeat at MK Dons in early March. He started the game at the National Hockey Stadium before being replaced by Adam Le Fondre nine minutes into the second half. Jordan did not make another appearance for the club during the final two months of the season but will be hoping to make a bigger impact in the first team in 2005-06.
Stockport Co *(Trainee) FL 1*

HAHNEMANN Marcus Stephen
Born: Seattle, USA, 15 June 1972
Height: 6'3" **Weight:** 16.2
International Honours: USA: 4
The only player to be on the field for every minute of Reading's 51 competitive games last season, Marcus added to his already immense reputation with some superb displays between the posts. Possessed of great agility for such a big man, and totally fearless, he earned a deserved recall to the USA international squad. He has a tremendous clearance kick, which led to several 'route-one' goals.
Fulham *(£80,000 from Colorado Rapids, USA on 9/7/1999) FL 2 FLC 2*
Rochdale *(Loaned on 12/10/2001) FL 5 Others 2*
Reading *(Loaned on 14/12/2001) FL 6*
Reading *(Free on 14/8/2002) FL 123 FLC 7 FAC 7 Others 2*

HAINING William (Will) Wallace
Born: Glasgow, 2 October 1982
Height: 5'11" **Weight:** 10.10
This aerially dominant and determined centre back had another excellent season for Oldham Athletic, culminating in his winning the 'Players' Player of the Year' award. Will – who was handed the captain's armband on several occasions - was easily the club's most consistent defender before his campaign was curtailed by a hamstring injury. Always a threat in the opposition penalty box at set pieces, Will also netted the first goal of the Ronnie Moore era in a 3-0 defeat of Port Vale at Boundary Park.
Oldham Ath *(From trainee on 17/10/2001) FL 90+6/9 FLC 3+1 FAC 4+1/1 Others 7*

HALDANE Lewis Oliver
Born: Trowbridge, 13 March 1985
Height: 6'0" **Weight:** 11.13
This young striker continued to make progress at Bristol Rovers last term when he was a regular goal-scorer for the reserve team. However, his first-team opportunities were somewhat limited and he managed only one start plus a dozen or so appearances from the substitutes' bench. The highlight of his season came when he scored a vital extra-time winner in the LDV Vans Trophy tie at Leyton Orient. Lewis had a spell on loan with Conference club Forest Green Rovers during the closing stages of the campaign. He was selected by the club's supporters as the 'Young Player of the Season'.
Bristol Rov *(From trainee on 13/10/2003) FL 17+23/5 FAC 1+2 Others 1+2/2*

HALFORD Gregory (Greg)
Born: Chelmsford, 8 December 1984
Height: 6'4" **Weight:** 13.10
International Honours: E: Yth
Scouts from bigger clubs queued up to watch promising youngster Greg in action at Colchester last term. They were only put off by the lack of a settled position for the big man – he played at right back, in central midfield, on the right wing and as an effective target man during the course of the season. A player with bags of talent, both in the air and on the ground, Greg scored nine goals before the turn of the year, including a hat-trick in the FA Cup victory at Rushden.
Colchester U *(From trainee on 8/8/2003) FL 59+4/8 FLC 2+1/1 FAC 7/4 Others 5*

HALL Christopher (Chris) Michael
Born: Manchester, 27 November 1986
Height: 6'1" **Weight:** 11.4
A rising forward talent, Chris is one of the youngest-ever players to appear for Oldham. He was just 16 years and 312 days old when making his senior bow at Peterborough the previous term and spent most of last season on the first-team fringes. Tall and pacy, he made two League starts – both against Bournemouth – and did very little wrong. A real handful for defenders, his strength lies in his physical presence and he is very highly rated by the coaching staff at Boundary Park.
Oldham Ath *(Trainee) FL 2+5 FAC 0+1 Others 0+2*

HALL Daniel (Danny) Andrew
Born: Ashton-under-Lyne, 14 November 1983
Height: 6'2" **Weight:** 12.7
This accomplished young central defender endured a somewhat frustrating time at Oldham in the 2004-05 campaign. Having established himself as a first-team regular the previous season Danny made 28 consecutive starts before a serious knee injury ended his season in February.
Oldham Ath *(From trainee on 7/8/2003) FL 48+6/1 FLC 1 FAC 5+1 Others 5*

HALL Fitz
Born: Leytonstone, 20 December 1980
Height: 6'1" **Weight:** 13.4
Fitz followed his former Oldham manager Iain Dowie to Selhurst Park in the summer of 2004 and had a steady season for the Premiership club. He was a near ever-present in the line-up and scored two goals, netting in the home games against West Brom and Southampton. Fitz is a skilful defender with a good touch on the ball who provides a constant threat when joining up with the attack for set pieces.
Oldham Ath *(£20,000 + from Chesham U, ex Staines T, on 15/3/2002) FL 44/5 FLC 4 FAC 3/1 Others 2+1*

Greg Halford

Southampton *(£250,000 + on 14/7/2003) PL 7+4 FLC 1*
Crystal Palace *(£1,500,000 on 12/8/2004) PL 36/2 FAC 1*

HALL Marcus Thomas Jackson
Born: Coventry, 24 March 1976
Height: 6'1" **Weight:** 12.2
International Honours: E: B-1; U21-8
Marcus began the 2004-05 season as first choice at left back for Stoke and put in some fine performances, securing a last-minute winner over Derby at the end of August. However, his performances began to dip mainly due to his carrying an injury. Although he regained his place in January, it was no surprise when he was allowed to return to Coventry the following month. Marcus made an immediate positive impact for the Sky Blues in the home defeat by Wigan when he featured at centre back before proceeding to give a series of consistent performances at left back to help City avoid relegation.
Coventry C *(From trainee on 1/7/1994) P/FL 113+19/2 FLC 14+1/2 FAC 8+2*
Nottingham F *(Free on 7/8/2002) FL 1*
Southampton *(Free on 30/8/2002)*
Stoke C *(Free on 6/12/2002) FL 76+3/1 FLC 3 FAC 5*
Coventry C *(Free on 21/2/2005) FL 10*

HALL Paul Anthony
Born: Manchester, 3 July 1972
Height: 5'9" **Weight:** 11.0
Club Honours: Div 3 '03
International Honours: Jamaica: 41
Paul signed for Tranmere in the 2004 close season following a successful short-term spell at Prenton Park, and alternated easily between right wing and front-running roles last term, being equally happy in either. After a slow start, the goals began to flow and he soon became the favoured striking partner of Iain Hume. Paul has the ability to go past opponents in the central area and to bring others into play but he is also blessed with a good touch, all of which has made him a firm favourite with the Rovers' fans. A prodigiously hard worker, he was the only player to have featured in every game, and deservedly finished as the second-highest scorer with 12 goals.
Torquay U *(From trainee on 9/7/1990) FL 77+16/1 FLC 7 FAC 4+1/2 Others 5+1/1*
Portsmouth *(£70,000 on 25/3/1993) FL 148+40/37 FLC 10+3/1 FAC 7+1/2 Others 5+2/2*
Coventry C *(£300,000 on 10/8/1998) PL 2+8 FLC 2+1/1*
Bury *(Loaned on 18/2/1999) FL 7*
Sheffield U *(Loaned on 17/12/1999) FL 1+3/1*

West Bromwich A *(Loaned on 10/2/2000) FL 4*
Walsall *(Free on 17/3/2000) FL 46+6/10 FLC 4+1 FAC 3/1 Others 3*
Rushden & Diamonds *(Free on 11/10/2001) FL 106+6/26 FLC 3 FAC 4+2 Others 4+2/3*
Tranmere Rov *(Free on 25/3/2004) FL 49+6/13 FLC 2 FAC 1 Others 5/1*

HALLS John

Born: Islington, 14 February 1982
Height: 6'0" **Weight:** 11.4
Club Honours: FAYC '00
International Honours: E: Yth

This young right back or midfielder has become very popular with the Stoke fans, so it was a disappointment to see him succumb to a long-term back injury last January. He was out of the side until a surprise inclusion on the bench for the final home game against Watford. John seemed to suffer no further reaction to his injury and the future remains promising. He was voted as the club's 'Young Player of the Season'.

Arsenal *(From trainee on 18/7/2000) FLC 0+3*
Colchester U *(Loaned on 18/1/2002) FL 6*
Stoke C *(£100,000 on 4/10/2003) FL 54+2 FLC 1 FAC 3*

HAMANN Dietmar (Didi)

Born: Waldsasson, Germany, 27 August 1973
Height: 6'3" **Weight:** 12.2
Club Honours: FLC '01; FAC '01; UEFAC '01; ESC '01; CS '01; UEFACL '05
International Honours: Germany: 58; U21; Yth

The 'metronome' at the heart of Liverpool's midfield, Didi had a relatively subdued season in the final year of his contract with the Reds. With the arrival of Xabi Alonso in August it seemed that his place in the team was under threat but partly due to injuries to others he remained a fixture in the team until March, when he was sidelined with a knee injury for one month. Happily for him and crucially for the team, he returned to fitness at the climax of a tumultuous season playing in the second leg of the epic Champions' Cup semi-final with Chelsea. Although omitted from the starting line-up for the final, his introduction at half time changed the course of the game, allowing Steven Gerrard the freedom to move forward with dramatic impact. Didi's role in the team is usually unspectacular and often unnoticed, protecting the back four, intercepting passes or winning the ball in the tackle before releasing it with a safe pass to ensure the team retains

John Halls

possession. Unspectacular maybe, but the team always performs more fluently when he is in it.
Newcastle U *(£4,500,000 from Bayern Munich, Germany, ex Wacker Munchen, on 5/8/1998) PL 22+1/4 FLC 1 FAC 7/1*
Liverpool *(£8,000,000 on 23/7/1999) PL 161+13/8 FLC 7+4 FAC 14/1 Others 48+4/2*

HAMILTON Lewis Emmanuel
Born: Derby, 21 November 1984
Height: 5'11" **Weight:** 11.6
Lewis is a young right-sided player who normally operates on the right-hand side of the defensive line. However, he can also play at wing back or in midfield. He joined Queen's Park Rangers in the summer of 2004, but suffered a serious knee injury in the reserve game at Woking in October which kept him out of the game for three months. On regaining fitness he was loaned out initially to Kingstonian and then AFC Wimbledon for match experience, before returning to Loftus Road to make a brief appearance as a substitute in the game at Burnley in April.
Queens Park Rgrs *(From trainee at Derby Co on 6/8/2004) FL 0+1*

HAMMOND Dean John
Born: Hastings, 7 March 1983
Height: 6'0" **Weight:** 12.4
Given three months to prove himself at the start of the season, Dean could see his career at Brighton slipping away, but he knuckled down, worked hard, and was given his first opportunity for nearly two years by manager Mark McGhee in August, taking it in some style. Having added some steel to his game, the elegant young midfielder was rewarded with a new contract and, although he became a regular on the substitutes' bench, he was rarely missing from the squad. A creative, attacking player with the ability to ghost into the opposition penalty area, Dean returned to the starting line-up in April and scored a vital equaliser at Burnley. The following week he bettered that by heading both Albion goals in a 2-2 draw against promotion-chasing West Ham at the Withdean Stadium.
Brighton & Hove A *(From trainee on 10/6/2002) FL 21+13/4 FLC 1/1 Others 0+1*
Leyton Orient *(Loaned on 17/10/2003) FL 6+2 FAC 1*

Dean Hammond

HAMMOND Elvis Zark
Born: Accra, Ghana, 6 October 1980
Height: 5'10" **Weight:** 10.10
Elvis made only two substitute appearances for Fulham last term before departing for a loan spell with Dutch side Roosendaal in January. His appearance against Chelsea in the Carling Cup brought an immediate impact when he set up a goal from Brian McBride. Elvis is a centre forward who reacts quickly to situations inside the penalty box and possesses a strong shot.
Fulham *(From trainee on 1/7/1999) P/FL 3+8 FLC 0+2*
Bristol Rov *(Loaned on 31/8/2001) FL 3+4 FLC 0+1*
Norwich C *(Loaned on 14/8/2003) FL 0+4*

HAMSHAW Matthew (Matt) Thomas
Born: Rotherham, 1 January 1982
Height: 5'9" **Weight:** 11.12
International Honours: E: Yth; Sch
Last term proved to be another injury-hit season for this unlucky Sheffield Wednesday midfielder. An honest, enterprising player who gives his all for the team, he is confident when running at opponents with the ball and has a good eye for goal. Matt certainly adds to and improves the team when fit, but he was out of contract in the summer and his future was uncertain at the time of writing.
Sheffield Wed *(From trainee on 5/1/1999) FL 35+39/2 FLC 6+3/2 FAC 2+1/2 Others 2*

HAND Jamie
Born: Uxbridge, 7 February 1984
Height: 5'11" **Weight:** 11.10
International Honours: E: Yth
This young central midfielder failed to make a breakthrough at first-team level with Watford last season and spent much of the campaign out on loan. During his two months at Oxford he became a firm favourite of the club's fans, showing

himself to be a forceful player who was always in the thick of the action. In the new year he was out on loan again, this time to SPL club Livingston where he featured on several occasions without registering a goal.
Watford *(From trainee on 17/4/2002) FL 40+15 FLC 1+2 FAC 1+2*
Oxford U *(Loaned on 27/8/2004) FL 11 Others 1/1*
Livingston *(Loaned on 6/1/2005) SL 5+2 SC 1+1*

HANLON Richard (Richie) Kenneth
Born: Wembley, 26 May 1978
Height: 6'1" **Weight:** 13.7
This central-midfield man began last term in the Conference with Stevenage before signing for Lincoln City in December after injuries left the Imps short of players in the middle of the park. Richie found it hard to win a regular place in the starting line-up but will always be remembered for his cracking 35-yard goal in the local 'derby' clash at Boston United. At the end of the season he was released.
Southend U *(From trainee at Chelsea on 10/7/1996) FL 1+1 (Free to Welling U on 18/9/1997)*
Peterborough U *(Signed from Rushden & Diamonds on 9/12/1998) FL 0+4/1 Others 1 (Free to Welling U on 12/8/1999)*
Peterborough U *(Free on 17/12/1999) FL 30+13/2 FLC 1+1 FAC 0+1 Others 3+2*
Rushden & Diamonds *(£30,000 on 10/9/2001) FL 51+11/7 FLC 0+1 FAC 2+1/2 Others 3 (Free to Stevenage Borough on 29/7/2004)*
Lincoln C *(Free on 17/12/2004) FL 6+6/1*

HANSON Christian
Born: Middlesbrough, 3 August 1981
Height: 6'1" **Weight:** 11.5
International Honours: E: Yth; Sch
This central defender began last season with Havant & Waterlooville before joining Port Vale on a non-contract basis in December. He made his first appearance from the substitutes' bench against Tranmere but was used as cover until March when he was called into action again. Once the club was free from relegation worries Christian was introduced to the starting line-up and looked most comfortable when playing in a back four. He was released at the end of the campaign.
Middlesbrough *(From trainee on 5/8/1998. Freed during 2002 close season)*
Cambridge U *(Loaned on 22/3/2001) FL 8*
Torquay U *(Loaned on 23/11/2001) FL 6*
Port Vale *(Free From Spennymoor U, ex Havant & Waterlooville, on 6/12/2004) FL 3+2*

HARDIKER John David
Born: Preston, 17 July 1982
Height: 6'0" **Weight:** 11.4
John started in more than half the League One fixtures for Stockport last term, but sometimes struggled to find his best form. He was used in a variety of positions in both defence and midfield, but failed to register a goal during the campaign.
Stockport Co *(£150,000 from Morecambe on 28/1/2002) FL 94+9/3 FLC 4+1 FAC 5 Others 6*

HARDING Benjamin (Ben) Scott
Born: Carshalton, 6 September 1984
Height: 5'10" **Weight:** 11.2
Ben began the 2004-05 season in the starting line-up for MK Dons, but was dropped after a home defeat by Bournemouth and soon after picked up a knee injury that kept him out of action for four months. He scored on his return in mid-January against Colchester and then became a key figure for the next three months, showing a deft touch and silky distribution from his central-midfield spot. He faded slightly as the season wore on and lost his starting place for the final few games, but showed enough to give good cause for optimism regarding his future career.
Wimbledon/MK Dons *(From trainee on 15/10/2001) FL 31+10/4 FAC 1*

HARDING Daniel (Dan) Andrew
Born: Gloucester, 23 December 1983
Height: 6'0" **Weight:** 11.11
International Honours: E: U21-4
Dan's first experience of a season at

Dan Harding

Championship level proved somewhat up and down. After an uncertain start he came back strongly towards the end of the campaign and played his part as the club secured its place in the division for another season. In December the young defender scored the first senior goal of his career, the winner against Rotherham at the Withdean Stadium, and he also played a number of games as a left-sided midfielder. In August Dan was called into the England U21 squad for the first time and went on to feature on a number of occasions at left back during the season.
Brighton & Hove A *(From trainee on 28/7/2003) FL 56+11/1 FLC 1+2 FAC 1 Others 4+1*

HAREWOOD Marlon Anderson

Born: Hampstead, 25 August 1979
Height: 6'1" **Weight:** 11.0
The powerful West Ham striker had a fine season netting 17 Championship goals as the Hammers gained promotion to the Premiership via the play-offs. He was sometimes used out on the right but was more effective in the middle. At times he was unstoppable with his strength and pace causing problems for opposition defenders. The best of his goals were a 25-yarder at Sheffield United and a fine individual effort at Wigan. Marlon was awesome in the play-off semi-final against Ipswich scoring once and setting up another for Bobby Zamora.
Nottingham F *(From trainee on 9/9/1996) P/FL 124+58/51 FLC 12+4/3 FAC 3+2/1 Others 2*
Ipswich T *(Loaned on 28/1/1999) FL 5+1/1*
West Ham U *(£500,000 on 25/11/2003) FL 73/30 FLC 3/2 FAC 7/3 Others 6/1*

HARGREAVES Christian (Chris)

Born: Cleethorpes, 12 May 1972
Height: 5'11" **Weight:** 12.2
This barnstorming, all-action midfielder joined Brentford in the 2004 close season and was a regular in the first half of the campaign, driving the side forward and forming an impressive midfield partnership with Stewart Talbot. A calf injury in January and a hernia operation in March curtailed his appearances thereafter, although he did return for the last few games.
Grimsby T *(From trainee on 6/12/1989) FL 15+36/5 FLC 2+2/1 FAC 1+2/2 Others 2+4*
Scarborough *(Loaned on 4/3/1993) FL 2+1*
Hull C *(Signed on 26/7/1993) FL 34+15 FLC 1 FAC 2+1/1 Others 3+1*
West Bromwich A *(Free on 13/7/1995) FL 0+1 Others 0+1*
Hereford U *(Free on 19/2/1996) FL 57+4/6 FLC 3+1 FAC 1 Others 2*
Plymouth Arg *(Free on 20/7/1998) FL 74+2/5 FLC 4 FAC 11/2 Others 1*
Northampton T *(Free on 7/7/2000) FL 144+7/6 FLC 5+1/1 FAC 11/2 Others 8/2*
Brentford *(Free on 2/7/2004) FL 30/2 FLC 1 FAC 6/1 Others 2*

HARKINS Gary

Born: Greenock, 2 January 1985
Height: 6'2" **Weight:** 12.10
This young midfielder spent much of the 2004-05 campaign playing in Blackburn's reserve side before joining Bury on loan in February to replace knee-injury victim Dwayne Mattis. Gary proved to be a strong-tackling midfield player, but sometimes struggled to come to terms with the cut and thrust of League Two football, however, he will have benefited from the experience.
Blackburn Rov *(From trainee on 22/1/2004)*
Huddersfield T *(Loaned on 24/3/2004) FL 1+2*
Bury *(Loaned on 8/2/2005) FL 4+1*

HARKNESS Jonathan (Jon)

Born: Antrim, 18 November 1985
Height: 5'11" **Weight:** 11.12
This young defender did well in Walsall's reserves last term and went on to make his first-team debut in the final game of the season against Stockport. Jon impressed both on the left flank of the defence and in the centre, switching roles after an injury forced Ian Roper off the field.
Walsall *(Trainee) FL 1*

HARLEY Jonathan (Jon)

Born: Maidstone, 26 September 1979
Height: 5'9" **Weight:** 10.3
Club Honours: FAC '00
International Honours: E: U21-3; Yth
Jon signed a long-term deal with Sheffield United in the summer of 2004, after two separate loan spells, thus becoming the first player to join the Blades three times. Missing just two games, he had a solid season operating as a left wing back or in midfield. Hard working and effective in the tackle, he used his speed both in attack and defence but although he produced some searching crosses his final ball was not always the best. Both his goals came from free kicks from outside the box.
Chelsea *(From trainee on 20/3/1997) PL 22+8/2 FLC 0+1 FAC 7 Others 1+3*
Wimbledon *(Loaned on 20/10/2000) FL 6/2*
Fulham *(£3,500,000 on 8/8/2001) PL 19+6/1 FLC 2 FAC 4+1 Others 4*
Sheffield U *(Loaned on 30/10/2002) FL 8+1/1 FLC 2*
Sheffield U *(Loaned on 16/9/2003) FL 5*
West Ham U *(Loaned on 16/1/2004) FL 15/1 FAC 1*
Sheffield U *(Free on 4/8/2004) FL 44/2 FLC 3 FAC 5*

HARLEY Ryan Bernard

Born: Bristol, 22 January 1985
Height: 5'9" **Weight:** 11.0
A product of Bristol City's youth set-up, this young midfielder made his senior debut in an ignominious 3-0 defeat at Port Vale early on last season. He also added a couple of appearances from the bench later in the campaign and will be looking to gain more first-team experience in 2005-06.
Bristol C *(From trainee on 6/7/2004) FL 1+1 Others 0+1*

HARPER James Alan John

Born: Chelmsford, 9 November 1980
Height: 5'10" **Weight:** 11.7
This creative midfield player was a regular in the Reading team until the last quarter of the season, when he lost his place to the more abrasive Ricky Newman. James was in the match squad for every competitive match and contributed a couple of goals, the most important of which was the late winner at home to Nottingham Forest, which kept his team in contention for a play-off spot. James is an exciting young player who has still to realise his full potential.
Arsenal *(From trainee on 8/7/1999)*
Cardiff C *(Loaned on 29/12/2000) FL 3*
Reading *(£400,000 on 28/2/2001) FL 136+18/8 FLC 6+1/1 FAC 8 Others 4+2*

HARPER Kevin Patrick

Born: Oldham, 15 January 1976
Height: 5'6" **Weight:** 10.10
Club Honours: Div 1 '03
International Honours: S: B-1; U21-7; Sch
This right-sided midfielder was only on the fringes of the first-team squad at Portsmouth last term and in September he moved out on loan to Leicester City. Kevin made quite an impression on his debut at Rotherham, but an injury during the warm up for his first home appearance three days later proved crucial. By the time he was fit to return there had been a change in management and he went back to Fratton Park. After featuring from the bench in Pompey's Carling Cup defeat by Watford he was released in the new year and signed for Stoke. Although he struggled for fitness at times he showed glimpses of what he could do with an excellent performance against Brighton before injury struck to hamper his progress.

Hibernian *(Signed from Hutchison Vale BC on 3/8/1992) SL 73+23/15 SLC 4+5 SC 9+1/3*
Derby Co *(£300,000 + on 11/9/1998) PL 6+26/1 FLC 1+5 FAC 0+3/1*
Walsall *(Loaned on 17/12/1999) FL 8+1/1*
Portsmouth *(£300,000 on 6/3/2000) P/FL 85+34/9 FLC 1+3 FAC 5*
Norwich C *(Loaned on 12/9/2003) FL 9*
Leicester C *(Loaned on 9/9/2004) FL 2*
Stoke C *(Signed on 2/2/2005) FL 8+1*

HARPER Lee Charles Phillip
Born: Chelsea, 30 October 1971
Height: 6'1" **Weight:** 13.11
Northampton Town's regular 'keeper last season, Lee was a near ever-present in the side and helped the team reach the play-offs at the end of the campaign. A broken bone in his hand cost him two months out of action following the trip to Scunthorpe at the end of August, but otherwise he proved a reliable last line of defence and an excellent shot-stopper.
Arsenal *(£150,000 from Sittingbourne on 16/6/1994) PL 1*
Queens Park Rgrs *(£125,000 + on 11/7/1997) FL 117+1 FLC 8+1 FAC 4*
Walsall *(Free on 20/7/2001) FL 3 FLC 2*
Northampton T *(Free on 18/7/2002) FL 106 FLC 2 FAC 10 Others 9+1*

HARPER Stephen (Steve) Alan
Born: Easington, 14 March 1975
Height: 6'2" **Weight:** 13.0
Goalkeeper Steve is Newcastle's longest-serving player and continues to provide excellent cover for first choice Shay Given. Agile, with safe hands, he made a couple of substitute appearances in the UEFA Cup, demonstrating his dependability by making crucial saves, and also started in two Premiership matches and in a handful of domestic cup ties.
Newcastle U *(Free from Seaham Red Star on 5/7/1993) PL 31+2 FLC 10 FAC 9+1 Others 9+2*
Bradford C *(Loaned on 18/9/1995) FL 1*
Hartlepool U *(Loaned on 29/8/1997) FL 15*
Huddersfield T *(Loaned on 18/12/1997) FL 24 FAC 2*

HARRAD Shaun Nicholas
Born: Nottingham, 11 December 1984
Height: 5'10" **Weight:** 12.4
This Notts County youngster received a handful of starts last term, but most of his first-team action came from the substitutes' bench. Shaun is a pacy and skilful striker whose preferred position is in a central role up front.
Notts Co *(From trainee on 22/4/2004) FL 4+25/1 FAC 1+2*

HARRIS Andrew (Andy) David Douglas
Born: Springs, South Africa, 26 February 1977
Height: 5'10" **Weight:** 11.11
Club Honours: NC '04
A peripheral figure in Chester's Conference campaign, Andy was given an opportunity in the turmoil following Mark Wright's departure on the eve of the 2004-05 season. A strong, hard-tackling central midfielder, Andy lost his place when Ray Matthias brought in Alan Navarro on loan from Tranmere. However, he continued to make occasional appearances, mainly as a substitute, but was essentially a squad player and spent three months on loan with Forest Green Rovers before returning as a substitute for the final game of the season.
Liverpool *(From trainee on 23/3/1994)*
Southend U *(Free on 10/7/1996) FL 70+2 FLC 5 FAC 3*
Leyton Orient *(Free on 5/7/1999) FL 143+6/2 FLC 11 FAC 9 Others 3+2*
Chester C *(Free on 2/7/2003) FL 9+10 FAC 1+1 Others 3*

HARRIS Neil
Born: Orsett, 12 July 1977
Height: 5'11" **Weight:** 12.9
Club Honours: Div 2 '01
This hard-working centre forward created a piece of history when he scored for Millwall against Cardiff last October, thus equally Teddy Sheringham's all-time record of 93 League goals for the club. However, although he featured regularly for the Lions that was his only goal and in December he joined Cardiff City on loan, where he scored on his full debut before Nottingham Forest came in to sign him on a permanent basis. Neil made 14 first-team appearances for the City Ground club but failed to add to his career tally of goals.
Millwall *(£30,000 from Cambridge C on 26/3/1998) FL 186+47/93 FLC 6+1 FAC 13+2/2 Others 13+1/3*
Cardiff C *(Loaned on 3/12/2004) FL 1+2/1*
Nottingham F *(Free on 22/12/2004) FL 5+8 FAC 0+2*

HARRISON Daniel (Danny) Robert
Born: Liverpool, 4 November 1982
Height: 5'11" **Weight:** 12.5
A solid central midfielder who is a product of the Tranmere youth scheme, Danny was given an extended contract at Prenton Park during the season. He is sound in the tackle, but also enjoys the chance to go forward and although he is not a flamboyant player, Danny has become increasingly reliable, diligent and a good reader of the game as his experience has grown. Frequently rumoured to be a target of other clubs, and despite suffering from a few niggling injuries, Danny had consolidated his position as a first-team regular by the end of the 2004-05 campaign.
Tranmere Rov *(From trainee on 16/5/2002) FL 56+21/2 FLC 1+1 FAC 7+1 Others 5+2/1*

HARRISON Lee David
Born: Billericay, 12 September 1971
Height: 6'2" **Weight:** 12.7
Lee started the 2004-05 season as second choice to Glenn Morris as the Leyton Orient goalkeeper, but by early September he had regained his place in the side. A tremendous shot-stopper, he remained in control of the jersey for most of the remainder of the campaign, but nevertheless he was released by the O's in the summer.
Charlton Ath *(From trainee on 3/7/1990)*
Fulham *(Loaned on 18/11/1991) Others 1*
Gillingham *(Loaned on 24/3/1992) FL 2*
Fulham *(Free on 18/12/1992) FL 11+1 FAC 1 Others 6*
Barnet *(Free on 15/7/1996) FL 183 FLC 9 FAC 3 Others 12*
Peterborough U *(Loaned on 12/12/2002) FL 12*
Leyton Orient *(Signed on 14/3/2003) FL 59+1 FLC 1 FAC 3+1 Others 1*

HARROLD Matthew (Matt) James
Born: Leyton, 25 July 1984
Height: 6'1" **Weight:** 11.10
Brentford striker Matt missed the first six weeks of the campaign with a torn muscle but was then a regular in the squad apart from loan spells at Dagenham & Redbridge and Grimsby. Despite his enthusiasm and skill he was unable to score a goal for the Bees during the season. It was a different story during his spell at Blundell Park, however, where he scored in each of his first two appearances and won several 'Man of the Match' awards.
Brentford *(Free from Harlow T on 12/8/2003) FL 11+21/2 FAC 2+3/3 Others 2*
Grimsby T *(Loaned on 4/3/2005) FL 6/2*

HARSLEY Paul
Born: Scunthorpe, 29 May 1978
Height: 5'9" **Weight:** 11.10
Paul was the only Macclesfield player to be ever present last term, usually featuring on the right side of the midfield. However, he is a versatile player and performed equally well in any of the midfield positions, and, for a few matches, seamlessly moved into a right-wing-back role. A pacy player who never

gives less than 100 per cent, Paul scored four goals last season and as a key figure in the side was rewarded with the 'Player of the Year' award.
Grimsby T *(From trainee on 16/7/1996)*
Scunthorpe U *(Free on 7/7/1997) FL 110+18/5 FLC 6 FAC 4+2/1 Others 5+1*
Halifax T *(Free on 1/7/2001) FL 45/11 FLC 1 FAC 3/1 Others 1*
Northampton T *(Free on 8/7/2002) FL 46+13/2 FLC 2 FAC 3+2/1 Others 2+2*
Macclesfield T *(Free on 13/2/2004) FL 60+2/5 FLC 1 FAC 3 Others 5/1*

HART Gary John
Born: Harlow, 21 September 1976
Height: 5'9" **Weight:** 12.8
Club Honours: Div 3 '01; Div 2 '02
Gary's seventh season with Brighton started uncertainly, but he knuckled down, trained hard, made his first start on Boxing Day and never looked back. Rewarded with an extension to his contract, the never-say-die winger also played as an out-and-out striker on occasion, usually as a tactical switch within a game, so he will probably be disappointed with a return of just two goals. One of these, a last-minute winner against Millwall in February, earned three precious points in the club's successful battle against relegation. Gary will run for 90 minutes and never gives up, making him a great favourite of the Withdean crowd.
Brighton & Hove A *(£1,000 from Stansted on 18/6/1998) FL 239+36/41 FLC 8+3 FAC 9 Others 7+4/1*

HART Charles **Joseph (Joe)** John
Born: Shrewsbury, 19 April 1987
Height: 6'3" **Weight:** 12.9
This promising young Shrewsbury Town goalkeeper spent much of last season in the club's reserve team before being called up for his senior debut in the vital home fixture with Oxford United shortly before the end of the campaign. He produced an excellent performance as the Gay Meadow club ran out 3-0 winners and retained his place in the side for the remaining fixtures. Joe will be looking to gain more first-team experience in 2005-06.
Shrewsbury T *(From trainee on 10/8/2004) FL 6*

HASLAM Steven (Steve) Robert
Born: Sheffield, 6 September 1979
Height: 5'11" **Weight:** 10.10
International Honours: E: Yth; Sch
This experienced defender spent most of last term at Conference club Halifax Town where he was a regular in the line-up. In the early part of the season he had a brief attachment with Northampton Town, where he was used in midfield as cover for injuries. However, although he showed plenty of effort and commitment he managed only a handful of appearances before returning to the Shay.
Sheffield Wed *(From trainee on 12/9/1996) P/FL 115+29/2 FLC 10+1 FAC 9+1 Others 5+1 (Free to Halifax T on 13/8/2004)*
Northampton T *(Free on 27/8/2004) FL 2+1*

HASSELBAINK Jerrel (Jimmy Floyd)
Born: Surinam, 27 March 1972
Height: 6'2" **Weight:** 13.4
Club Honours: CS '00
International Honours: Holland: 23
One of five exciting new summer signings at Middlesbrough, Jimmy signed on a free transfer under the 'Bosman' ruling and with every Riverside fan purring at the prospect of Mark Viduka and Jimmy-Floyd Hasselbaink playing in the same side the start of the season could not come quick enough. Viduka missed the first couple of games courtesy of a suspension carry-over from his time at Leeds but Jimmy didn't wait to start banging in the goals, scoring two in his first two games including a late, late equaliser against Newcastle United on his debut earning Boro' a 2-2 draw. Other goal highlights included a hat-trick at Ewood Park and the club's first-ever goal in European competition (against Banik Ostrava). Jimmy ended the season with a marvellous goal direct from a free kick at Manchester City which set the club up for seventh place in the Premiership. He was also the first striker in Steve McClaren's player portfolio to achieve double figures, netting 16 goals to become the club's leading scorer for the season.
Leeds U *(£2,000,000 from Boavista, Portugal, ex Campomaiorense, on 18/7/1997) PL 66+3/34 FLC 5/2 FAC 9/5 Others 4/1 (£12,000,000 to Atletico Madrid, Spain on 20/8/1999)*
Chelsea *(£15,000,000 on 12/7/2000) PL 119+17/69 FLC 10/7 FAC 16/7 Others 11+4/4*
Middlesbrough *(Free on 12/7/2004) PL 36/13 FAC 2 Others 5+2/3*

HASSELL Robert (Bobby) John Francis
Born: Derby, 4 June 1980
Height: 5'9" **Weight:** 12.6
Bobby took some time to settle in at right back for Barnsley last term, but once he did he became one of the team's most consistent performers. Even when moved to centre back he did not look out of place and made up for his lack of height with his ability to read the game, cutting out many balls before they reached their target.
Mansfield T *(From trainee on 3/7/1998) FL 151+9/3 FLC 6+1 FAC 9 Others 4*
Barnsley *(Free on 5/7/2004) FL 37+2 FLC 2 FAC 1 Others 1*

HATSWELL Wayne Mervin
Born: Swindon, 8 February 1975
Height: 6'0" **Weight:** 13.10
International Honours: E: SP-2
Last term proved to be something of an up-and-down season for Kidderminster skipper Wayne. He was forced to play out of position on a number of occasions, firstly by the arrival of Adie Viveash and then later due to the absence of an in-form left back at Aggborough. As a result his own form suffered and he lost the captaincy. Wayne netted two goals for Harriers including a great 25-yard free kick in the FA Cup tie at Port Vale.
Oxford U *(£35,000 from Forest Green Rov on 1/12/2000) FL 47+1 FLC 1 FAC 1 Others 2 (Free to Chester C on 1/6/2002)*
Kidderminster Hrs *(£15,000 on 16/10/2003) FL 70+2/3 FLC 1 FAC 5/1 Others 1*

HAWKINS Peter Steven
Born: Maidstone, 19 September 1978
Height: 6'0" **Weight:** 11.6
This attacking left back was a near ever-present for Rushden last term. He picked the perfect moment to score his first senior goal by putting Diamonds into an early lead against local rivals Northampton Town on course to a 3-2 home win. Peter probably should have added to that tally as he likes to push forward but often settles for a pass instead of taking a shot himself.
Wimbledon *(From trainee on 6/3/1997) FL 113+7 FLC 6 FAC 9+1*
York C *(Loaned on 22/2/2000) FL 14*
Rushden & Diamonds *(Free on 12/7/2004) FL 41/1 FLC 1 FAC 2 Others 1*

HAWORTH Simon Owen
Born: Cardiff, 30 March 1977
Height: 6'2" **Weight:** 13.8
Club Honours: AMC '99
International Honours: W: 5; B-1; U21-12; Yth
Despite suffering a double fracture of his right leg during the away game at Brentford in January 2004, centre forward Simon signed a new contract with Tranmere in the close season and

had high hopes of regaining his place in the attack. He returned briefly to first-team action in November. However, his recovery did not progress as well as hoped, as even working on his fitness level left Simon in considerable pain and further investigation showed that one of the breaks had not completely healed. As a result, he decided to call at least a temporary halt to his football career to concentrate on his partnership in a sports hospitality business; Simon was already a keen racing fan and part-owner of a horse while still playing.
Cardiff C *(From trainee on 7/8/1995) FL 27+10/9 FLC 4 FAC 0+1 Others 4/1*
Coventry C *(£500,000 on 4/6/1997) PL 5+6 FLC 2/1 FAC 0+1*
Wigan Ath *(£600,000 on 2/10/1998) FL 99+18/44 FLC 8/6 FAC 4/4 Others 12+1/4*
Tranmere Rov *(£125,000 on 28/2/2002) FL 77+2/31 FLC 3/1 FAC 4/2 Others 3*

Peter Hawkins

HAY Alexander (Alex) Neil
Born: Birkenhead, 14 October 1981
Height: 5'10" **Weight:** 11.5
Alex's pacy attacks looked as though they would cause plenty of problems for League Two defences last term, but he struggled for consistent form as Rushden dropped into a relegation battle. He was switched from centre forward to a wide role and also spent some time on the bench, but was released at the end of the season.
Tranmere Rov *(From trainee on 24/3/2000) FL 16+25/3 FLC 2 FAC 0+6 Others 1*
Rushden & Diamonds *(Free on 12/7/2004) FL 29+13/3 FLC 1 FAC 2 Others 1*

HAYES Paul Edward
Born: Dagenham, 20 September 1983
Height: 6'0" **Weight:** 12.2
After a frustrating 2003-04 campaign, Scunthorpe striker Paul was entrusted with a place in the starting line-up at the beginning of last season and repaid manager Brian Laws' faith with an electric opening three months. He had netted 14 goals by the end of November - including a run of 11 in 10 games - to bring the scouts flocking to Glanford Park. A strong centre forward, who is an excellent finisher, he went off the boil a bit and, despite firing his side into a shock lead at Premiership champions Chelsea in January, the goals dried up. He was dropped to the bench for five matches but still reached 20 goals for the season as the Iron won promotion to League One.
Scunthorpe U *(From trainee at Norwich C on 22/3/2003) FL 68+31/27 FLC 2+1/2 FAC 6+2/4 Others 3+3/1*

HAYLES Barrington (Barry) Edward
Born: Lambeth, 17 May 1972
Height: 5'9" **Weight:** 13.0
Club Honours: GMVC '96; Div 2 '99; Div 1 '01
International Honours: Jamaica: 10; E: SP-2
Barry joined Sheffield United in the 2004 close season with the aim of providing leadership to the front line. However, things did not work out and after just five games without a goal he returned to London and signed for Millwall. A competitive player who uses his experience and physique to gain a yard on defenders, he is a deadly finisher

inside the box and scored 12 Championship goals including one which earned the Lions their first victory over Gillingham in ten games.
Bristol Rov *(£250,000 from Stevenage Borough on 4/6/1997) FL 62/32 FLC 4/1 FAC 5/2 Others 3+2/1*
Fulham *(£2,100,000 on 17/11/1998) P/FL 116+59/44 FLC 10+2/5 FAC 12+7/6 Others 2+5/2*
Sheffield U *(Free on 26/6/2004) FL 4 FLC 1*
Millwall *(Signed on 1/9/2004) FL 28+4/12 FAC 1*

HAYTER James Edward
Born: Sandown, 9 April 1979
Height: 5'9" **Weight:** 11.2
This Bournemouth striker enjoyed his best season to date in 2004-05, building on his achievements of the previous campaign. Despite missing games through injury, he managed to find the net on 22 occasions and also showed how his game has developed with his unselfish play to provide chances for his colleagues.
Bournemouth *(From trainee on 7/7/1997) FL 218+52/64 FLC 6+3/4 FAC 14+3/3 Others 10+4/5*

HEALD Gregory (Greg) James
Born: Enfield, 26 September 1971
Height: 6'1" **Weight:** 12.8
International Honours: E: SP-1; Sch
Greg suffered an injury-hit time at Rochdale in 2004-05. The tough-tackling centre back was injured in only the sixth game of the season and managed just three more appearances before December. Reclaiming a regular spot as Dale lost only once in a dozen games to move into play-off contention, Greg netted a key goal in the victory against fellow contenders Lincoln. However, he damaged a hamstring against Grimsby and only reappeared for five games at the end of the season, signing off with a goal in the 5-1 win over Oxford before being released.
Peterborough U *(£35,000 from Enfield on 8/7/1994) FL 101+4/6 FLC 8 FAC 8+1 Others 11/2*
Barnet *(Signed on 8/8/1997) FL 141/13 FLC 8/1 FAC 4 Others 7/1*
Leyton Orient *(£9,000 on 27/3/2003) FL 9/1*
Rochdale *(Free on 15/3/2004) FL 39/3 FLC 1 FAC 2*

David Healy

HEALY David Jonathan
Born: Downpatrick, 5 August 1979
Height: 5'8" **Weight:** 11.0
International Honours: NI: 43; B-1; U21-8; Yth; Sch
David scored five goals in twelve appearances for Preston last term before a lengthy transfer saga ended with a transfer to Elland Road. Coincidentally he opened his scoring account for United with a double strike on his return to Deepdale in the 4-2 United win in November. Although a penalty-box predator, he was deployed largely out wide or occupied a floating role behind Brian Deane or Rob Hulse. A clever forward with a sharp footballing brain, he also proved astute at bending in crosses to the box for his colleagues. His long-range lobbed winner in the 2-1 home victory over Plymouth was voted the club's 'Goal of the Season'. David missed the final five Championship games with an ankle injury. On the international front, he broke the Northern Ireland goal-scoring record with a couple of goals against Trinidad and Tobago in June 2004 and netted a wonder goal in the 3-3 draw with Austria in October.
Manchester U *(From trainee on 28/11/1997) PL 0+1 FLC 0+2*
Port Vale *(Loaned on 25/2/2000) FL 15+1/3*
Preston NE *(£1,500,000 on 29/12/2000) FL 104+35/44 FLC 7+1 FAC 7+1 Others 3/1*
Norwich C *(Loaned on 30/1/2003) FL 5/1*
Norwich C *(Loaned on 13/3/2003) FL 5+3/1*
Leeds U *(Signed on 29/10/2004) FL 27+1/7 FAC 1*

HEALY Joseph (Joe) Benjamin
Born: Sidcup, 26 December 1986
Height: 6'0" **Weight:** 12.4
A talented youngster who has developed through Millwall's youth set-up, Joe was in excellent form for the club's reserve and youth teams last season. The pacy striker made his senior debut as a substitute in the Carling Cup tie against Liverpool and added a handful more appearances from the bench later in the season, acquitting himself well. Joe also had a spell on loan with Conference club Crawley Town at the end of the campaign.
Millwall *(From juniors on 20/4/2004) FL 0+2 FLC 0+1 FAC 0+1*

HEARN Charles (Charley) Richard
Born: Ashford, Kent, 5 November 1983
Height: 5'11" **Weight:** 11.9
This young Millwall midfielder joined Northampton Town on loan last December and stayed at Sixfields until the end of the season. The Cobblers fans quickly took him to their hearts as he impressed with an all-action style of play that added flair to the middle of the park. He seemed to cover almost every blade of grass in each game he played and weighed in with his first-ever League goal in the 3-1 victory over Macclesfield.
Millwall *(From trainee on 27/4/2001) FL 9+9 FLC 1+1 FAC 2+2*
Northampton T *(Loaned on 3/12/2004) FL 21+3/1 FAC 1+1 Others 2*

HEATH Colin
Born: Matlock, 31 December 1983
Height: 6'0" **Weight:** 13.1
This promising young Manchester United striker returned from a spell in Belgium with Beveren and spent much of last season developing in the club's reserve team. In December he joined League Two strugglers Cambridge United on loan, making his senior debut in the home defeat by Scunthorpe. He featured in five more games for the U's showing he could hold the ball up well, but without registering a goal, and eventually returned to old Trafford.
Manchester U *(From trainee on 4/1/2001)*
Cambridge U *(Loaned on 6/12/2004) FL 5+1*

HEATH Matthew (Matt) Philip
Born: Leicester, 1 November 1981
Height: 6'4" **Weight:** 13.13
This promising young defender was never quite able to lock down a regular spot at the heart of the Foxes' defence last term. Bizarrely, Matt found the net at both ends in the home clash with Ipswich scoring with a sharp left-foot volley from the edge of the box before firmly planting a late header past Kevin Pressman when trying to clear for a corner. He was still an important squad member after Craig Levein's arrival, although not an automatic first choice.
Leicester C *(From trainee on 17/2/2001) P/FL 42+9/6 FLC 3 FAC 5+2*
Stockport Co *(Loaned on 24/10/2003) FL 8 Others 2*

HECKINGBOTTOM Paul
Born: Barnsley, 17 July 1977
Height: 5'11" **Weight:** 12.0
This experienced left back had a good campaign for Sheffield Wednesday in 2004-05. He arrived during the close season and was a near ever-present apart from a spell out injured in September and October. Effective defensively and very attack-minded he provided good balance on the left and also chipped in with some useful goals.
Sunderland *(From trainee at Manchester U on 14/7/1995)*
Scarborough *(Loaned on 17/10/1997) FL 28+1 Others 1*
Hartlepool U *(Loaned on 25/9/1998) FL 5/1*
Darlington *(Free on 25/3/1999) FL 111+4/5 FLC 4 FAC 8/1 Others 8*
Norwich C *(Free on 5/7/2002) FL 7+8 FLC 0+1*
Bradford C *(Free on 17/7/2003) FL 43 FLC 1 FAC 1*
Sheffield Wed *(Free on 12/7/2004) FL 37+1/4 FLC 1 Others 3*

HEFFERNAN Paul
Born: Dublin, 29 December 1981
Height: 5'10" **Weight:** 10.7
International Honours: RoI: U21-3
Paul was more often than not used as a substitute last term, and although he managed a respectable tally of seven goals he never established himself in the line-up for Bristol City due to the success of the partnership between Steve Brooker and Leroy Lita. The talented young striker will be hoping for more regular first-team action at Ashton Gate in 2005-06.
Notts Co *(Signed from Newtown, Co Wicklow on 22/10/1999) FL 74+26/36 FLC 2+3/1 FAC 2+2/1 Others 2+3*
Bristol C *(£125,000 + on 16/7/2004) FL 10+17/5 FLC 0+1 FAC 1/1 Others 2/1*

HEGARTY Nicholas (Nick) Ian
Born: Hemsworth, 25 June 1986
Height: 5'9" **Weight:** 11.7
This promising Grimsby Town scholar produced a series of impressive performances for the club's reserve team last term and was rewarded with an appearance from the substitutes' bench in the penultimate match of the season against Kidderminster. Nick is a left-sided midfield player or striker and will be looking for more senior experience in 2005-06.
Grimsby T *(Trainee) FL 0+1*

HEINZE Gabriel Ivan
Born: Crespo, Argentina, 19 April 1978
Height: 5'10" **Weight:** 12.4
International Honours: Argentina: 26
A tough-tackling left-footed centre back with a real bite in the tackle, Gabriel arrived at Old Trafford in the summer of 2004. Although he missed the opening stages of the Premiership campaign on Copa America and Olympic Games duty with Argentina, he soon became a solid immovable force in the Reds' defence. Opening his United career with a debut goal against Bolton Wanderers in September, he cemented a reputation as the new hero of the Stretford End from thereon in. Playing a major part in all competitions, he was lauded by Sir Alex Ferguson for his passion and commitment. Unfortunately just when United needed him the most at the vital run in to the campaign, Gabriel was a missing link with injury in five of the last eight Premiership games and the FA Cup final. Having solved United's problem left-back position in a season of much promise, Gabriel also proved he can slot into a central-defensive role when required.
Manchester U *(£6,900,000 from Paris St Germain, France, on 7/7/2004) PL 26/1 FLC 2 FAC 4 Others 7*

HELGUSON Heidar
Born: Akureyri, Iceland, 22 August 1977
Height: 6'0" **Weight:** 12.2
International Honours: Iceland: 34; U21-6; Yth
Watford's 'Player of the Season' and leading scorer with 20 goals, Heidar was outstanding for the Hornets in 2004-05. Over the last five years Watford fans have had good reason to be grateful for the Icelander's prodigious work rate, goal-scoring expertise, particularly in the air, and total commitment to the cause. His importance to the club was reflected in the fact that he won three awards in all, a unique achievement. As well as being voted 'Player of the Season' – by a landslide – his volleyed goal against Southampton in the Carling Cup and his display in the same match were also rated the best of the season. Modest

and unassuming off the pitch, Heidar continued to perform with distinction for the Iceland international team.
Watford *(£1,500,000 from SK Lillestrom, Norway, ex Throttur, on 13/1/2000) P/FL 132+42/55 FLC 8+7/5 FAC 8+2/4*

HELVEG Thomas Lund
Born: Odense, Denmark, 24 June 1971
Height: 5'10" **Weight:** 12.4
International Honours: Denmark: 95; U21-3
Denmark's international skipper signed for the Canaries in the summer, fresh from his exploits at Euro 2004, Thomas was signed to add some real experience and quality to the Canaries' squad as they re-entered the top flight of English football. Like so many international imports, initially at least, he found it tough to pick up on the pace of the game and it was not until the second half of the season that Norwich fans saw the best of him. Very strong in the tackle and a tremendous passer of the ball, he displayed all the attributes that had allowed him to survive in Serie A for 11 seasons. Thomas played at right back and in midfield for the Canaries and continued to lead his country as they strove to qualify for the 2006 World Cup.
Norwich C *(Free from Inter Milan, Italy, ex OB Odense, Udinese, on 3/8/2004) PL 16+4 FLC 1+1 FAC 1*

HENCHOZ Stephane
Born: Billens, Switzerland, 7 September 1974
Height: 6'1" **Weight:** 12.10
Club Honours: FLC '01, '03; FAC '01; UEFAC '01; ESC '01; CS '01
International Honours: Switzerland: 72; U21; Yth
Once a key figure in the Liverpool back line, this talented central defender became something of a forgotten man under new manager Rafael Benitez and played only four games for the Reds last season (and none in the Premiership) before he moved on to Glasgow Celtic in the January transfer window. Curiously, in his final competitive match for Liverpool he scored his first and only goal for the club in six seasons – a successful conversion in a penalty shoot-out in the Carling Cup tie at Tottenham.
Blackburn Rov *(£3,000,000 from Hamburg, Germany, ex FC Bulle, Neuchatel Xamax, on 14/7/1997) PL 70 FLC 3+1 FAC 6 Others 2*
Liverpool *(£3,750,000 on 20/7/1999) PL 132+3 FLC 16 FAC 15 Others 38+1*
Glasgow Celtic *(Loaned on 31/1/2005) SL 2+4 SC 2*

HENDERSON Darius Alexis
Born: Sutton, 7 September 1981
Height: 6'0" **Weight:** 12.8
This big, bustling forward enjoyed a successful loan spell at Swindon early on last season. Darius scored five goals in six appearances for the Robins, including a double in the West Country 'derby' at Ashton Gate. Back at Priestfield he soon got off the mark with a goal for the Gills at Plymouth and went on to finish the campaign as the team's leading scorer with a total of nine goals, despite a spell on the sidelines with an abdominal injury.
Reading *(From trainee on 15/12/1999) FL 5+66/11 FLC 2+2/2 FAC 1+2 Others 4+1/2*
Brighton & Hove A *(Loaned on 8/8/2003) FL 10/2*
Gillingham *(£25,000 on 2/1/2004) FL 31+5/9 FAC 2+1/1*
Swindon T *(Loaned on 20/8/2004) FL 6/5*

HENDERSON Ian
Born: Bury St Edmunds, 24 January 1985
Height: 5'8" **Weight:** 10.10
Club Honours: Div 1 '04
International Honours: E: Yth
Ian retained his place in the England international set-up, having progressed to being a leading member of the U20 side in 2004-05. His opportunities at Premiership level were restricted to just three substitute outings, due to the seniority of others and an ankle injury which kept him out of action for four months either side of Christmas. A graduate of the Norwich youth set-up, he is a hard-working and inventive front-runner who can also play on the right-hand side of midfield. Ian has a terrific attitude and never ever gives up, being prepared to chase seemingly lost causes for the benefit of his team.
Norwich C *(From trainee on 3/2/2003) P/FL 18+24/5 FLC 1+1 FAC 0+3*

HENDERSON Paul
Born: Sydney, Australia, 22 April 1976
Height: 6'1" **Weight:** 12.6
Paul was a real find for Bradford after turning up in pre-season and asking for a trial. He caught the eye straight away and earned the starting spot in goal at the expense of Donovan Ricketts. Paul was a superbly consistent shot-stopper during a run of 42 successive appearances, including excellent performances in the away games at Port Vale and Barnsley. However, he turned down the chance to stay at Valley Parade and found himself on the bench for the final month of the season.
Bradford C *(Signed from Northern Spirit, Australia, ex Sutherland, on 10/8/2004) FL 40 FLC 1 FAC 1 Others 1*

HENDERSON Wayne
Born: Dublin, 16 September 1983
Height: 5'11" **Weight:** 12.2
Club Honours: FAYC '02
International Honours: RoI: U21-10; Yth
This young Aston Villa 'keeper spent time on loan at Notts County in the early part of last season when he was required to cover during an injury crisis. He quickly showed himself to be a very talented custodian and on his return to Villa Park he featured as an unused substitute in the Premiership clash against Arsenal in October. Wayne had a second loan spell at Meadow Lane in December, when he made a couple more appearances before returning to continue his development with the Midlands club. He also represented the Republic of Ireland at U21 level during the campaign.
Aston Villa *(From trainee on 27/9/2000)*
Wycombe W *(Loaned on 23/4/2004) FL 3*
Notts Co *(Loaned on 9/8/2004) FL 9 Others 1*
Notts Co *(Loaned on 3/12/2004) FL 2*

HENDRIE Lee Andrew
Born: Birmingham, 18 May 1977
Height: 5'10" **Weight:** 10.3
International Honours: E: 1; B-1; U21-13; Yth
Lee is a quick-witted midfielder who also has the feet to make things happen when moving forward. He worked hard throughout the 2004-05 season and was never short of commitment. After overcoming some niggling injuries early on he became a regular in the line-up, contributing five Premiership goals. One of the highlights of the season for Villa was his spectacular strike against Crystal Palace when he curled an inch-perfect 25-yard shot into the top corner, but all of his goals were of the spectacular, long-range variety.
Aston Villa *(From trainee on 18/5/1994) PL 195+39/26 FLC 15+2/3 FAC 10+8 Others 14+5/2*

HENRY Karl Levi Daniel
Born: Wolverhampton, 26 November 1982
Height: 6'1" **Weight:** 10.13
International Honours: E: Yth
A tenacious midfielder with good distribution, Karl produced his best performances for Stoke last season in the left-back berth. He continued to grow in confidence and featured in the majority of Championship games during the campaign, albeit often as a substitute.
Stoke C *(From trainee on 30/11/1999) FL 52+44/1 FLC 3+1 FAC 4+2 Others 1+1*
Cheltenham T *(Loaned on 13/1/2004) FL 8+1/1*

HENRY Thierry
Born: Paris, France, 17 August 1977
Height: 6'1" **Weight:** 12.2
Club Honours: FAC '02, '03; PL '02, '04; CS '02, '04
International Honours: France: 70 (UEFA '00); Yth (UEFA-U18 '96)
Thierry had another fine season in the Premiership as he finished as the top-flight's leading scorer for the third time in four seasons. He also became the first player ever to win the European Golden Slipper two seasons running as his 25 league goals tied him with Diego Forlan. To add to his array of awards he was runner-up in the 'World Player of the Year' and France's 'Sportsman of the Year' once more. In total the fleet-footed star was on target 30 times with his five other strikes all coming in the Champions' League. Usually a player who suffers little with injury Thierry started and finished the campaign on the sidelines. He lasted only the first half of the FA Community Shield victory over Manchester United in August and missed Arsenal's run-in as they claimed runners-up spot in the Premiership and won the FA Cup on a penalty shoot-out. Thierry was again named in the PFA Premiership team of the season.
Arsenal *(£8,000,000 from Juventus, Italy, ex Monaco, on 6/8/1999) PL 189+16/137 FLC 2/1 FAC 15+6/6 Others 65+5/37*

HERIVELTO Moreira
Born: Tres Rios, Brazil, 23 August 1975
Height: 5'10" **Weight:** 11.6
This speedy striker had a brief trial period with Walsall last December, but he failed to make the same impact as in his previous spell at Bescot. He managed just a single first-team appearance as a late substitute in the game at Brentford before departing once more.
Walsall *(Free from Cruzeiro, Brazil, ex Flamenco, CS Maritimo, on 9/8/2001) FL 11+17/5 FLC 2+1/1 FAC 1+1 (Free to Ionikos, Greece, during February 2003)*
Walsall *(Free on 21/12/2004) FL 0+1*

HERON Daniel (Danny) Craig
Born: Cambridge, 9 October 1986
Height: 5'11" **Weight:** 10.9
This promising young striker was called into first-team action for Mansfield Town in the Carling Cup tie defeat at home to Preston due to injuries. He had previously shown up well in the pre-season friendly matches with Leeds and Wolves. Danny was offered a new contract in March and was given his full debut in the last home match of the season against Boston when he partnered Ritchie Barker in the Stags' frontline.
Mansfield T *(Trainee) FL 1+2 FLC 0+1 FAC 0+1*

HERVE Laurent
Born: Quimper, France, 19 June 1976
Height: 5'10" **Weight:** 11.7
On the evidence of his season with MK Dons it is clear that Laurent is a very skilful central midfielder with a very good eye for a pass. Unfortunately, when he played his upright style often left the team short of midfield tackling ability, a key requirement in League One football, and this lack of physical presence meant that he was in and out of the side in the first half of the season and rarely featured after Danny Wilson took over in December.
MK Dons *(Signed from Guingamp, France, on 6/8/2004) FL 15+5 FLC 2 FAC 2 Others 1+1*

HESKEY Emile William Ivanhoe
Born: Leicester, 11 January 1978
Height: 6'2" **Weight:** 13.12
Club Honours: FLC '97, '00, '01, '03; FAC '01; UEFAC '01; ESC '01; CS '01
International Honours: E: 43; B-1; U21-16; Yth
'Player of the Season' and 'Players' Player of the Season', Emile was a huge hit after signing for Birmingham City in the summer of 2004. Used in his preferred role as a traditional centre forward, the team played to his strengths and reaped the rewards. He had eight different front partners and took upon himself to carry the burden throughout. His powerful, muscular play allied to good use of the ball caused nightmares for some of the best defenders in the world. He scored some terrific goals, including a pile driver at Fulham, a long-range effort at Everton and the winner in the last game of the season against Arsenal, which brought up double figures in the Premiership.
Leicester C *(From trainee on 3/10/1995) P/FL 143+11/40 FLC 25+2/6 FAC 11 Others 5*
Liverpool *(£11,000,000 on 10/3/2000) PL 118+32/39 FLC 7+5/2 FAC 9+5/6 Others 42+5/13*
Birmingham C *(£3,500,000 + on 2/7/2004) PL 34/10 FLC 2 FAC 2/1*

HESSENTHALER Andrew (Andy)
Born: Gravesend, 17 August 1965
Height: 5'7" **Weight:** 11.5
International Honours: E: SP-1
Andy had something of a difficult time at Gillingham last term and resigned as player-manager at the beginning of December. The experienced midfielder remained on the club's playing staff but was out of favour under new boss Stan Ternent and joined League One promotion chasers Hull on loan in January. When Andy made his Tigers' debut at Chesterfield he broke a club record to become the team's oldest debutant at 39 years 168 days. His experience both on and off the field boosted City's ambitions, whilst his enthusiasm and energy in the centre of midfield belied his advancing years.
Watford *(£65,000 from Redbridge Forest on 12/9/1991) FL 195/12 FLC 13/1 FAC 5/2 Others 4*
Gillingham *(£235,000 on 7/8/1996) FL 259+28/19 FLC 22+2/3 FAC 18+2/2 Others 9+1/3*
Hull C *(Loaned on 31/1/2005) FL 6+4*

HESSEY Sean Peter
Born: Whiston, 19 September 1978
Height: 5'10" **Weight:** 12.6
A no-nonsense central defender, Sean was one of several players signed by Mark Wright in preparation for Chester's return to the Football League. Competition for places meant that Sean spent much of the season playing out of position at left back and although he performed to the best of his abilities he looked more comfortable on the occasions when he could attack the ball from the centre of defence. Sean contributed a single goal, netting with a tremendous free kick against Rushden.
Leeds U *(From Liverpool juniors on 15/9/1997)*
Wigan Ath *(Free on 24/12/1997)*
Huddersfield T *(Free on 12/3/1998) FL 7+4 FAC 1 (Freed on 30/6/1999)*
Kilmarnock *(Free on 31/8/1999) SL 38+6/1 SLC 2 SC 1*
Blackpool *(Free on 12/2/2004) FL 4+2 Others 0+1*
Chester C *(Free on 2/7/2004) FL 31+3/1 FLC 1 FAC 3 Others 2/1*

HEWLETT Matthew (Matt) Paul
Born: Bristol, 25 February 1976
Height: 6'2" **Weight:** 11.3
International Honours: E: Yth
Last term proved to be a slightly disappointing season for Matt who failed to capture his form of the previous campaign for Swindon. A competitive player with good passing skills who operates in the centre of midfield, he was eventually released in the summer.
Bristol C *(From trainee on 12/8/1993) FL 111+16/9 FLC 10+2 FAC 4+1/2 Others 7+2/1*
Burnley *(Loaned on 27/11/1998) FL 2 Others 1*
Swindon T *(Free on 27/7/2000) FL 175+4/6 FLC 11/1 FAC 5 Others 5*

HEYWOOD Matthew (Matty) Stephen
Born: Chatham, 26 August 1979
Height: 6'2" **Weight:** 14.0
Knee surgery at the start of the season delayed Matty's first League One appearance for Swindon until last October when he came on in an unfamiliar full-back role at Stockport. After regaining his fitness he resumed his place at the heart of the Town defence where he looked comfortable as a central defender either in a back three or four. Tall and strong he is good in the air and a committed tackler, although he rarely falls foul of referees.
Burnley *(From trainee on 6/7/1998) FL 11+2 FAC 1 Others 1*
Swindon T *(Free on 22/1/2001) FL 176+7/8 FLC 5+1 FAC 9/1 Others 10/1*

HIBBERT Anthony (Tony) James
Born: Liverpool, 20 February 1981
Height: 5'8" **Weight:** 11.3
Club Honours: FAYC '98
The local-born defender was yet another Everton player who re-discovered his best form during the successful 2004-05 season, when he established himself as one of the best defensive right backs in the Premiership. Tony was an automatic selection and he reached the landmark of 100 appearances during the campaign, although he has yet to score his first goal. His main strengths are crisp and tough tackling, especially at pace, and excellent technique on the ball.
Everton *(From trainee on 1/7/1998) PL 90+8 FLC 7+1 FAC 5*

HIBBERT David (Dave) John
Born: Eccleshall, 28 January 1986
Height: 6'2" **Weight:** 12.6
This tall Port Vale striker experienced the highs and lows of football last season. He made his debut from the bench at Chesterfield in August before impressing on his full debut against Barnsley in the LDV Vans Trophy. Unfortunately Dave then damaged a knee ligament which kept him out of action for four months. He made a sensational full League debut against Luton in February, scoring twice in the 3-1 victory. A couple of weeks later he was knocked unconscious during the game at MK Dons and had to be airlifted to hospital in an air ambulance. Fortunately there was no lasting damage but he was forced to miss the remainder of the season as a precaution.
Port Vale *(Trainee) FL 2+7/2 Others 1*

HICKS David Christopher
Born: Enfield, 13 November 1985
Height: 5'10" **Weight:** 10.8
David had a frustrating time at Northampton last season when injury restricted his availability and he managed just two starts for the Cobblers. A workhorse in the centre of midfield, David also had a brief spell on loan at Conference South club Hornchurch in the autumn.
Northampton T *(From trainee at Tottenham Hotspur on 26/2/2004) FL 1+2 FLC 1 Others 0+1*

HIERRO Fernando
Born: Velez, Malaga, Spain, 23 March 1968
Height: 6'2" **Weight:** 13.3
International Honours: Spain: 89
A true legend in the modern game, eyebrows were none-the-less raised when Sam Allardyce persuaded the former Real Madrid stalwart to move to Bolton at the age of 36, following a season spent playing in Qatar. Fernando made his first start in the Carling Cup victory at Yeovil, though he had to wait until November for a first Premiership start. Fleeting appearances from the bench were the order of the day until Hierro was awarded a rare first-team start, replacing Ivan Campo in the away fixture at Newcastle in February. He subsequently retained his place in the side, starting the final 11 Premiership games in the midfield holding role. It was in this role that Hierro showed his undoubted class, dictating the play in many games and providing a quality of distribution rarely seen at the Reebok Stadium. Phenomenal technical abilities, allied with an almost innate ability to read the game, led to Sam Allardyce attempting to persuade Hierro to play on for one more season.

Danny Higginbotham

After much deliberation, Fernando decided to retire and, quite fittingly, a magnificent playing career drew to a close with a 'Man of the Match' performance in the final-day victory against Everton.
Bolton W *(Free from Al Rayyan, Qatar, ex Real Valladolid, Real Madrid, on 28/7/2004) PL 15+14/1 FLC 2 FAC 4*

HIGDON Michael
Born: Liverpool, 2 September 1983
Height: 6'1" **Weight:** 11.5
A product of the Crewe Alexandra youth scheme, Michael is a very versatile player who can operate either in a defensive role or in one of the striking positions. Last term he made just one appearance in the starting line-up in Championship fixtures, but featured on many occasions from the substitutes' bench. He scored three times during the campaign including a vital strike in the decisive victory over Coventry City on the last day of the season to help ensure that Alexandra avoided relegation.
Crewe Alex *(From trainee on 6/2/2001) FL 8+22/4 FLC 0+1 FAC 1*

HIGGINBOTHAM Daniel (Danny) John
Born: Manchester, 29 December 1978
Height: 6'1" **Weight:** 12.6
As the 2004-05 season dawned Danny was expected, in the absence of the injured Michael Svensson, to make a comfortable fist of partnering Claus Lundekvam in the centre of the defence, but the Saints' back four struggled from the start and he was dropped from the line-up. Regaining the left-back berth early in Harry Redknapp's managerial reign, Danny was then supplanted when Olivier Bernard was introduced to the side. However, strong, hard working and persistent, he featured prominently and honourably, in the club's futile Premiership last stand, bringing hopes of survival by scoring a dramatic last-gasp equaliser at Crystal Palace in the penultimate match of the season.
Manchester U *(From trainee on 10/7/1997) PL 2+2 FLC 1 Others 1+1*
Derby Co *(£2,000,000 on 12/7/2000) P/FL 82+4/3 FLC 7+1/1 FAC 3+1*
Southampton *(Signed on 31/1/2003) PL 47+10/1 FLC 3 FAC 6 Others 1*

HIGGS Shane Peter
Born: Oxford, 13 May 1977
Height: 6'2" **Weight:** 12.12
This tall confident goalkeeper enjoyed another highly consistent season with Cheltenham Town and played in all 50 of the club's first-team matches. A fine shot-stopper with a long-range kick and safe

Shane Higgs

at handling crosses under pressure, Shane displayed some excellent form and was attracting scouts from higher division clubs towards the end of the campaign.
Bristol Rov *(From trainee on 17/7/1995) FL 10 Others 2 (Free to Worcester C on 11/7/1998)*
Cheltenham T *(£10,000 on 21/6/1999) FL 98+2 FLC 1 FAC 4 Others 5*

HIGNETT Craig John
Born: Prescot, 12 January 1970
Height: 5'9" **Weight:** 11.10
Club Honours: Div 1 '95; FLC '02
This vastly experienced striker joined Darlington last September and immediately showed his goal-poaching instinct by scoring in his first two games. Craig's ability to make space for himself in the box and create shooting opportunities was a joy to behold and he went on to score nine goals in all, despite being hampered by a series of niggling injuries. He was also used in midfield where his clever footwork and vision indicated his pedigree.
Crewe Alex *(From trainee at Liverpool on 11/5/1988) FL 108+13/42 FLC 9+1/4 FAC 11+1/8 Others 6+1/3*
Middlesbrough *(£500,000 on 27/11/1992) P/FL 126+30/33 FLC 19+3/12 FAC 10+2/3 Others 5+1*
Aberdeen *(Free on 1/7/1998) SL 13/2 SLC 2*
Barnsley *(£800,000 on 26/11/1998) FL 62+4/28 FLC 2 FAC 6/5 Others 3/2*
Blackburn Rov *(£2,250,000 on 14/7/2000) P/FL 20+33/8 FLC 5+1/3 FAC 4+4/3 Others 1*
Coventry C *(Loaned on 1/11/2002) FL 7+1/2 FLC 1*
Leicester C *(Free on 25/7/2003) PL 3+10/1 FLC 1 FAC 1*
Crewe Alex *(Loaned on 20/2/2004) FL 11+4*
Darlington *(Free, via trial at Leeds U, on 10/9/2004) FL 17+2/9*

HILL Clinton (Clint) Scott
Born: Huyton, 19 October 1978
Height: 6'0" **Weight:** 11.6
This tall no-nonsense central defender had his first season at Stoke decimated by injury. However, after starting last term on the bench he came into the side towards the end of September and kept his place, featuring mostly at left back as the season continued. Although his campaign ended in disappointment after he was sidelined by a knee injury, Clint received consolation when he was voted as the fans' 'Player of the Season'.
Tranmere Rov *(From trainee on 9/7/1997) FL 138+2/16 FLC 18/3 FAC 11+1/1*
Oldham Ath *(Signed on 16/7/2002) FL 17/1 FLC 4 FAC 2 Others 2*
Stoke C *(£120,000 on 22/7/2003) FL 40+4/1 FLC 1*

HILL Kevin
Born: Exeter, 6 March 1976
Height: 5'8" **Weight:** 10.3
This hard-working honest professional started the season in an attacking role on the left-hand side of midfield for Torquay, but was later asked to play as a ball-winner in the centre of midfield and he also filled-in when needed at left back and as a second striker. Kevin found League One football challenging, but worked hard at his game to remain competitive. He scored a bizarre goal at home to Stockport when he hid behind the 'keeper, waited for the ball to be put down, sneaked in and beat the goalie with a sharp turn before netting in an open goal.
Torquay U *(Free from Torrington on 8/8/1997) FL 290+36/39 FLC 12+1/1 FAC 14+1/2 Others 8+2/1*

HILL Matthew (Matt) Clayton
Born: Bristol, 26 March 1981
Height: 5'7" **Weight:** 12.6
Club Honours: AMC '03
This young defender contributed plenty of exuberance and honest commitment for Bristol City last term and was badly missed when he was sold to Preston mid-way through the campaign. An intelligent player who is comfortable anywhere in the back four or on the left side of midfield, Matt uses his space well and has an amazing leap for someone of his height. Matt shared the left-hand side

Matt Hill

with Callum Davidson and Eddie Lewis at Deepdale and built excellent partnerships with both.
Bristol C *(From trainee on 22/2/1999) FL 182+16/6 FLC 8 FAC 15 Others 19+5*
Preston NE *(£100,000 on 10/1/2005) FL 11+3 Others 3*

HILLIER Ian Michael
Born: Neath, 26 December 1979
Height: 6'0" **Weight:** 11.10
International Honours: W: U21-5
This versatile player found himself out of favour at Luton again last term and his only senior action came during a loan spell with Chester City at the turn of the year. Originally signed as a replacement for the injured Darren Edmondson at right back, Ian in turn suffered injury and on his recovery he briefly returned to the side in a midfield role. He went back to Kenilworth Road in February and was released at the end of the season.
Tottenham H *(From trainee on 2/7/1998)*
Luton T *(Free on 18/8/2001) FL 31+25/1 FLC 0+2 FAC 3+2 Others 5*
Chester C *(Loaned on 16/12/2004) FL 7+1*

HILLIER Sean Philip
Born: Hanwell, 19 April 1986
Height: 5'10" **Weight:** 11.10
A third-year scholar with Brentford, Sean stepped up to make his senior debut at centre back in the LDV Vans Trophy tie against MK Dons back in September. Although he gave a competent performance he was not offered professional terms by the Bees at the end of the season.
Brentford *(Trainee) Others 1*

HILLS John David
Born: Blackpool, 21 April 1978
Height: 5'9" **Weight:** 11.2
Club Honours: AMC '02
This talented left back continued to cause endless problems for the opposition with his runs down the flank and crossing ability in the early stages of the 2004-05 season. However, under new manager Stan Ternent he found himself out of favour and used mainly as a substitute. John was out of contract in the summer and his future was unclear at the time of writing.
Blackpool *(From trainee on 27/10/1995)*
Everton *(£90,000 on 4/11/1995) PL 1+2*
Swansea C *(Loaned on 30/1/1997) FL 11*
Swansea C *(Loaned on 22/8/1997) FL 7/1*
Blackpool *(£75,000 on 16/1/1998) FL 146+16/16 FLC 5 FAC 12/2 Others 13+1/2*
Gillingham *(Free on 6/8/2003) FL 47+5/2 FLC 3/1 FAC 2*

HINDS Richard Paul
Born: Sheffield, 22 August 1980
Height: 6'2" **Weight:** 11.0
After starting the first three games of the season in his familiar right-back berth, Richard soon became a peripheral figure at Hull as their 2004-05 promotion season progressed. The tall defender produced a reliable performance when called upon – notably in the Yorkshire derby at Doncaster in January, before joining Scunthorpe United on loan for the closing two months of the campaign. He settled in well in League Two's meanest defence, operating either at right back or centre half. Good in the air and on the ground, his versatility made him a useful acquisition for the Iron.
Tranmere Rov *(From juniors on 20/7/1998) FL 42+13 FLC 3+5 FAC 5 Others 1*
Hull C *(Free on 1/7/2003) FL 40+5/1 FLC 1 FAC 1 Others 1+1*
Scunthorpe U *(Loaned on 17/3/2005) FL 6+1*

HINSHELWOOD Adam
Born: Oxford, 8 January 1984
Height: 5'10" **Weight:** 12.10
In the season he turned 21, Adam also came of age in his professional career, becoming a regular at the heart of the Brighton defence alongside veteran Guy Butters. Still learning with every game, he makes up for a lack of experience with enthusiasm, strong tackling and a good turn of pace. Adam also enjoyed a handful of outings in midfield and as a man-marker, but his season was cruelly ended in March when he sustained a cruciate ligament injury against Reading.

Richard Hinds

Nevertheless, he can look back with satisfaction on a season which saw him score his first goal (against Queen's Park Rangers), earn a call-up as a reserve into the England U21 squad, and sign an extension to his contract at the Withdean Stadium. Adam also finished third in the club's 'Player of the Season' vote.
Brighton & Hove A *(From trainee on 28/7/2003) FL 57+5/1 FLC 3 FAC 2 Others 1+1*

HINTON Craig

Born: Wolverhampton, 26 November 1977
Height: 6'0" **Weight:** 12.0
Club Honours: NC '00
Craig quickly established himself in the right-back berth at Bristol Rovers last term, producing some solid performances. Always prepared to link up with the attack he could be relied upon to defend solidly, and occasionally filled in as a central defender. Craig missed the closing stages of the campaign with injury but will be looking to resume his place in the side in 2005-06.
Birmingham C *(From trainee on 5/7/1996)*
Kidderminster Hrs *(Free on 12/8/1998) FL 172+1/3 FLC 5 FAC 10 Others 8*
Bristol Rov *(Free on 20/7/2004) FL 33+5 FLC 2 FAC 2 Others 6*

HIRSCHFELD Lars

Born: Edmonton, Canada, 17 October 1978
Height: 6'4" **Weight:** 13.8
International Honours: Canada: 18; U23-1
Lars began last season as second-choice 'keeper for Dundee United before joining Leicester as a back-up goalkeeper in the January transfer window. Lars was capped for Canada against Portugal in March, prior to making his debut for the Foxes in the closing fixture at Home Park, when he duly delivered a clean sheet.
Tottenham H *(Free from Calgary Storm, Canada, ex Edmonton Drillers, Energie Cottbus, via trial at Portsmouth, on 31/8/2002)*
Luton T *(Loaned on 22/2/2003) FL 5*
Gillingham *(Loaned on 27/2/2004) FL 2*
Dundee U *(Free on 1/8/2004) SL 1+1 SLC 1*
Leicester C *(Free on 28/1/2005) FL 1*

HISLOP Neil Shaka

Born: Hackney, 22 February 1969
Height: 6'4" **Weight:** 14.4
Club Honours: Div 2 '94; Div 1 '03
International Honours: Trinidad & Tobago: 21; E: U21-1
Shaka was Portsmouth's first-choice 'keeper for the opening half of the 2004-05 campaign, but eventually lost his place to new signing Jamie Ashdown. A tall goalkeeper with a vast frame, he has excellent reactions and shows a good command of his penalty area. Shaka did not feature in the Pompey line-up after mid-January and was released at the end of the campaign. He received the PFA's Special Merit Award for the season.
Reading *(Signed from Howard University, USA on 9/9/1992) FL 104 FLC 10 FAC 3 Others 9*
Newcastle U *(£1,575,000 on 10/8/1995) PL 53 FLC 8 FAC 6 Others 4*
West Ham U *(Free on 8/7/1998) PL 105 FLC 11 FAC 7 Others 9*
Portsmouth *(Free on 3/7/2002) P/FL 93 FLC 2 FAC 5*

HITZLSPERGER Thomas

Born: Munich, Germany, 5 April 1982
Height: 6'0" **Weight:** 12.5
International Honours: Germany: 9; U21-20; Yth
Thomas is a midfielder who has a powerful left-foot shot on him from open play or set pieces and displays an impressive ability to score spectacular goals from distance. However, last term he struggled to gain a regular place in the Aston Villa line-up and spent as much time on the bench as he did on the pitch. He scored just twice during the campaign including a stunning volley from the edge of the box to secure victory at Bolton. Thomas won the Midland Football Writers' 'Young Player of the Year' award, but in April he revealed that he would be returning to Germany in the summer once his contract expired. Thomas won his first full caps for his country during the campaign.
Aston Villa *(Free from Bayern Munich, Germany on 8/8/2000) PL 74+25/8 FLC 4+6/4 FAC 0+1 Others 4*
Chesterfield *(Loaned on 27/10/2001) FL 5 Others 1*

HJELDE Jon Olav

Born: Levanger, Norway, 30 July 1972
Height: 6'1" **Weight:** 13.7
Club Honours: Div 1 '98
This central defender rejoined Nottingham Forest following a trial in August 2004 after a spell in South Korea. He was a regular during the early part of the season until the return to fitness of Michael Dawson in October and continued to be a useful member of the squad, but did not feature again after receiving a red card against Cardiff in January. Jon Olav was released by Forest at the season's close and soon afterwards was reported to be on trial with Denmark's AGF Aarhus.
Nottingham F *(£600,000 from Rosenborg on 8/8/1997) P/FL 136+21/4 FLC 11/2 FAC 5 Others 0+1 (Free to Busan Icons, South Korea, during 2003 close season)*
Nottingham F *(Free on 12/8/2004) FL 13+1 FLC 1*

HOBBS Jack

Born: Portsmouth, 18 August 1988
Height: 6'0" **Weight:** 12.0
This highly-rated teenaged defender became Lincoln City's youngest post-war Football League player at 16 years and 149 days when he was given his debut in January. Jack slotted in at right back for the closing few minutes of the Imps' home draw with Bristol Rovers showing some neat touches. He was included on the bench on five other occasions without seeing action but was a regular in the reserve and youth teams. Jack, a first-year scholar who has been with Lincoln's academy since the age of 9, suffered an ankle injury in late April which kept him out for the final couple of weeks of the season. He was selected as the Imps' ' Young Player of the Year'.
Lincoln C *(Trainee) FL 0+1*

HOCKLESS Graham

Born: Hull, 20 October 1982
Height: 5'7" **Weight:** 10.6
This young Grimsby midfielder had something of a disappointing time last season when most of his football was played in the club's reserve team, with a spell on loan at Leigh RMI in the autumn. Graham enjoyed a brief run of first-team action in February when he was used in a midfield role, playing just behind the front two strikers. A firm favourite with the fans, he is a tricky little player who adds a different dimension to the Mariners' midfield when given the opportunity.
Grimsby T *(From Hull C juniors on 9/7/2001) FL 8+12/2 FLC 0+1 Others 1*

HOCKLEY Matthew (Matt)

Born: Paignton, 5 June 1982
Height: 5'10" **Weight:** 11.7
This tough-tackling committed Torquay player began the season as a central-midfield ball-winner, where he had been remarkably successful in the previous season's promotion side, but he found life in League One tough, particularly when his experienced partner Alex Russell was missing through injury. After losing his regular starting place, he went back to a utility role, filling-in in defence or midfield as required, before regaining a first-team place at right back for the run-in.
Torquay U *(From trainee on 4/7/2000) FL 105+32/9 FLC 2 FAC 6 Others 5*

HODGES Lee Leslie
Born: Epping, 4 September 1973
Height: 6'0" **Weight:** 12.1
Club Honours: Div 3 '02; Div 2 '04
International Honours: E: Yth
The 2004-05 season proved to be an extremely frustrating one for Lee as injury ruled him out for a major part of the campaign. However, it all started brightly as he made the line-up for the first six games to assist the Pilgrims to a place at the head of the Championship table. Thereafter he was mainly used from the bench with only the occasional first-team start. Good in the air and with a cultured left foot, Lee suffered a back injury in January and this ended his campaign early.
Tottenham H *(From trainee on 29/2/1992) PL 0+4*
Plymouth Arg *(Loaned on 26/2/1993) FL 6+1/2*
Wycombe W *(Loaned on 31/12/1993) FL 2+2 FAC 1 Others 1*
Barnet *(Free on 31/5/1994) FL 94+11/26 FLC 6+1 FAC 6+1/4 Others 4+1*
Reading *(£100,000 on 29/7/1997) FL 58+21/10 FLC 7+3 FAC 7+1/1 Others 0+2*
Plymouth Arg *(Free on 17/8/2001) FL 119+21/11 FLC 3 FAC 8+1 Others 2+1*

HODGSON Richard James
Born: Sunderland, 1 October 1979
Height: 5'10" **Weight:** 11.8
Richard began the 2004-05 season out of favour with Stevenage and spent time on loan with Forest Green Rovers. After being released in September he had a brief spell with Crawley Town without making an appearance and then made a return to the Football League when he signed for League Two strugglers Cambridge United. He made an impressive start at the Abbey Stadium and scored two goals before a change in management saw him leave the club. He subsequently took the opportunity to continue his career in Malaysia with Pahang, but was reported to have signed for Crawley once more in the summer.
Nottingham F *(From trainee on 8/10/1996)*
Scunthorpe U *(Free on 9/3/2000) FL 1*
Darlington *(Free on 7/8/2000) FL 66+32/6 FLC 3+1 FAC 8+1/3 Others 5+1/1 (Free to Farnborough T on 12/8/2003)*
Cambridge U *(Free from Crawley T, ex Stevenage Borough, on 28/10/2004) FL 9+1/2 FAC 0+1*

HOLDEN Dean Thomas John
Born: Salford, 15 September 1979
Height: 6'0" **Weight:** 11.0
International Honours: E: Yth
Dean was appointed Oldham Athletic skipper in the summer of 2004 but suffered from the club's widespread defensive inconsistency. A solid attacking right back, he made 48 appearances but did not hit the heights he had shown the previous term. Dean was also unfortunate enough to suffer ankle ligament damage that deprived him of involvement in the Latics' epic FA Cup derby battles against Manchester City and Bolton. New manager Ronnie Moore retained Dean as captain but he was out of contract in the summer and his future was uncertain at the time of writing.
Bolton W *(From trainee on 23/12/1997) P/FL 7+6/1 FLC 3+1 FAC 3+1*
Oldham Ath *(Free on 12/10/2001) FL 98+10/10 FLC 2+1 FAC 5 Others 8+1/1*

HOLDSWORTH Andrew (Andy)
Born: Pontefract, 29 January 1984
Height: 5'9" **Weight:** 11.2
Andy established himself as a valued member of the Huddersfield Town squad last term. Used as a wing back or in midfield, the youngster produced some very astute displays. Strong on the ball and a very good crosser of the ball, he grew in stature as the season progressed. A pacy player who links well with the frontline when pushing forward, Andy was an ever-present in the side apart from the odd spell out injured.
Huddersfield T *(From trainee on 6/12/2003) FL 69+7 FLC 3/1 FAC 2 Others 5*

Andy Holdsworth

Chris Holland

HOLGATE Ashan Bayyan Sellasse
Born: Swindon, 9 November 1986
Height: 6'2" **Weight:** 12.0
A tall striker who can also play on the right-hand side of midfield, Ashan added more steel to his game during the course of the 2004-05 campaign and was rewarded with two substitute appearances at the end of the season. He featured regularly for Swindon's U18s and netted a late equaliser at Burnley as they overcame their hosts on penalties to lift the Football League Youth Alliance Cup. Ashan also scored a cracking goal in the pre-season friendly against Millwall.
Swindon T *(Trainee) FL 0+2*

HOLLAND Christopher (Chris) James
Born: Clitheroe, 11 September 1975
Height: 5'9" **Weight:** 11.5
International Honours: E: U21-10; Yth
Chris had a mixed season in Boston United's midfield in 2004-05, finding it difficult to win a regular place in the first half of the campaign. He was transfer-listed but responded with some excellent performances in the centre of the park. Chris ended up being voted 'Players' Player of the Season' by his colleagues and was offered a new contract at the end of the campaign.
Preston NE *(Trainee) FL 0+1 Others 1*
Newcastle U *(£100,000 on 20/1/1994) PL 2+1 FLC 0+1*
Birmingham C *(£600,000 on 5/9/1996) FL 39+31 FLC 7+5 FAC 4 Others 1+1*
Huddersfield T *(£150,000 on 3/2/2000) FL 113+7/2 FLC 4 FAC 5 Others 9+1/1*
Boston U *(Free on 22/3/2004) FL 33+4 FLC 1 FAC 3 Others 1*

HOLLAND Matthew (Matt) Rhys
Born: Bury, 11 April 1974
Height: 5'9" **Weight:** 11.12
International Honours: RoI: 46; B-1
Matt suffered an ankle injury early in Charlton's opening fixture at Bolton Wanderers, but after returning to the side he did not miss another game. He partnered Danny Murphy in the centre of the midfield throughout the season and they built up a good understanding. Although equally comfortable on the right of midfield, a central role looks his most effective position. A strong tackler with good positional sense, Matt is very comfortable on the ball and has good passing ability. Once again, he chipped in with some valuable goals. He scored the winners at both West Brom and Everton with his trademark long-range efforts, and hit another from the edge of the box

Matt Holland (right)

against Middlesbrough at the Valley. Matt also featured for the Republic of Ireland international side.
West Ham U *(From trainee on 3/7/1992)*
Bournemouth *(Signed on 27/1/1995) FL 97+7/18 FLC 6 FAC 3 Others 3*
Ipswich T *(£800,000 on 31/7/1997) P/FL 259/38 FLC 23+1/6 FAC 12 Others 17+2/2*
Charlton Ath *(£750,000 on 17/6/2003) PL 69+1/9 FLC 3 FAC 4*

HOLLIS Jermain Phydell
Born: Nottingham, 7 October 1986
Height: 5'10" **Weight:** 11.0
International Honours: Jamaica: Yth
A product of the youth team at Kidderminster Jermain made his debut in the last four minutes of the final game of the season at Northampton, playing as a striker rather than in his normal position on the right wing. He also represented Jamaica at U20 level on a number of occasions during the campaign.
Kidderminster Hrs *(Free from Eastwood T on 21/11/2004) FL 0+1*

HOLLOWAY Darren
Born: Crook, 3 October 1977
Height: 5'10" **Weight:** 12.2
International Honours: E: U21-1
A solid, unflustered right back who is happy to play his way out of trouble, Darren grabbed the limelight with a ferocious 30-yard volley in Bradford City's televised win at Hull - even more remarkable because he struck it with his left foot. He missed ten games with a torn calf suffered against Torquay but returned in time for the Easter programme and played the entire run-in.
Sunderland *(From trainee on 12/10/1995) P/FL 46+12 FLC 3 FAC 2 Others 3*
Carlisle U *(Loaned on 29/8/1997) FL 5*
Bolton W *(Loaned on 14/12/1999) FL 3+1*
Wimbledon *(£1,250,000 on 2/10/2000) FL 84+8 FLC 4 FAC 6*
Scunthorpe U *(Loaned on 27/2/2004) FL 5/1*
Bradford C *(Free on 6/8/2004) FL 33/1 FLC 1 FAC 1*

HOLMES Derek
Born: Lanark, 18 October 1978
Height: 6'0" **Weight:** 13.2
This tall striker made most of his appearances for Bournemouth from the bench last term. Derek always gave 100 per cent and scored three goals during the season before signing for Carlisle United. He went on to assist the Cumbrian side to promotion back to the Football League via the Conference play-offs.
Heart of Midlothian *(From juniors on 5/1/1995) SL 1+6/1 SLC 0+2/2 Others 0+3/1*
Cowdenbeath *(Loaned on 21/11/1997) SL 13/5*
Raith Rov *(Loaned on 8/1/1999) SL 13+1/6*
Ross Co *(Free on 15/10/1999) SL 39+19/14 SLC 1+1/1 SC 1+1 Others 3*
Bournemouth *(£40,000 on 14/9/2001) FL 63+52/16 FLC 2+3 FAC 2+7/2 Others 5+2*

HOLMES Lee Daniel
Born: Mansfield, 2 April 1987
Height: 5'7" **Weight:** 10.6
International Honours: E: Yth
Lee found it hard to break into Derby County's squad and, curiously, the only senior start for the left winger was on the right in a Carling Cup defeat at Lincoln. He continued in England's U19 team and was a big hit during three months on loan to Swindon Town where he produced some impressive displays on the left flank. Lee was rewarded for his efforts when he was chosen as 'Young Player of the Year' by one of the Swindon supporters' groups.
Derby Co *(From trainee on 15/5/2004) FL 17+11/2 FLC 1 FAC 0+2*
Swindon T *(Loaned on 22/12/2004) FL 14+1/1 Others 1*

HOLMES Peter James
Born: Bishop Auckland, 18 November 1980
Height: 5'10" **Weight:** 10.6
Club Honours: Div 1 '05
International Honours: E: Yth; Sch
Luton Town's longest-serving player, Peter was never much more than a squad player last term. A skilful midfield player who can appear on the right-hand side or in a more central role, he is one of the best passers of the ball on the club's books.
Sheffield Wed *(From trainee on 2/12/1997)*
Luton T *(Free on 1/8/2000) FL 48+29/9 FLC 3+2 FAC 5+2 Others 5+1/1*

HOLT Andrew (Andy)
Born: Stockport, 21 May 1978
Height: 6'1" **Weight:** 12.7
Club Honours: AMC '05
Not many would argue against the opinion that Andy has been manager Denis Smith's best signing for Wrexham since he has been at the club. The left-sided wing back took the 'Man of the Match' honours on a number of occasions, often popping up with important goals, including the opener in the 2-1 win at Huddersfield in November. A powerful player who always showed total commitment, he swept the board winning all the various 'Player of the Year' awards for the Racecourse club at the end of the season.
Oldham Ath *(From trainee on 23/7/1996) FL 104+20/10 FLC 8 FAC 6+4 Others 3*
Hull C *(£150,000 on 15/3/2001) FL 45+26/3 FLC 1 FAC 1 Others 5+1*
Barnsley *(Loaned on 15/8/2002) FL 4+3 FLC 1*
Shrewsbury T *(Loaned on 27/3/2003) FL 9*
Wrexham *(Free on 3/8/2004) FL 45/6 FLC 2 FAC 2/1 Others 6*

HOLT Gary James
Born: Irvine, 9 March 1973
Height: 6'0" **Weight:** 12.11
Club Honours: SC '98; Div 1 '04
International Honours: S: 10
Gary continued to add to his tally of Scotland caps in 2004-05 and his all-action midfield displays again made him a firm fans' favourite at Carrow Road. Always first to the tackle and to close down his opponent, he is also very adept at breaking forward at pace when in possession of the ball. A real team player, his contribution should not be measured by the number of goals he scores, but by the number of opposition attacks he snuffs out. His season was badly affected by a serious illness which saw him hospitalised in November with a chest infection. His amazing powers of recovery saw him back in action in January.
Stoke C *(From Glasgow Celtic N/C on 20/10/1994)*
Kilmarnock *(Free on 18/8/1995) SL 138+13/9 SLC 10+1 SC 13 Others 8*
Norwich C *(£100,000 on 22/3/2001) P/FL 161+7/3 FLC 5 FAC 6 Others 3*

HOLT Grant
Born: Carlisle, 12 April 1981
Height: 6'1" **Weight:** 12.7
This big bustling striker was in excellent form for Rochdale last term when he finished the season as the club's leading scorer with a total of 24 goals. Indeed, when the whole side clicked into gear from the end of October, Grant was at the head of the League Two scoring charts for a while. However, he also accumulated a significant number of yellow cards and this is an area of his game where he needs to show improvement. Grant was selected as Dale's 'Players' Player of the Season' at the end of the campaign.
Halifax T *(Signed from Workington on 16/9/1999) FL 0+6 FLC 1/1 Others 1 (Free to Barrow during 2001 close season)*
Sheffield Wed *(Free on 27/3/2003) FL 12+12/3 FLC 0+1 FAC 2/1 Others 1+2*
Rochdale *(Signed on 30/1/2004) FL 54/21 FLC 1/1 FAC 3/5 Others 1/1*

HOPE Christopher (Chris) Jonathan
Born: Sheffield, 14 November 1972
Height: 6'1" **Weight:** 12.7
This cool and calm central defender

struggled to find his best form for Gillingham last term, although he was a regular in the starting line-up. Chris remained a dangerous threat at set pieces and scored two goals during the campaign.

Nottingham F *(From Darlington juniors on 23/8/1990)*
Scunthorpe U *(£50,000 on 5/7/1993) FL 278+9/19 FLC 13+1 FAC 18/1 Others 18/2*
Gillingham *(£250,000 on 12/7/2000) FL 210+2/12 FLC 13 FAC 10+1/2*

HOPE Richard Paul
Born: Stockton, 22 June 1978
Height: 6'2" **Weight:** 12.6
Richard was one of several experienced players signed to bolster Chester's squad in the summer of 2004 following their promotion from the Conference. A solid defender he came into the side in October following Danny Collins' transfer to Sunderland and lined up in the middle of the back four alongside Phil Bolland. Although Richard lost his place in the side at the turn of the year following the arrival of Dave Bayliss, he was back in the line-up again in February. Strong in the air, he scored one goal for the club when he was thrust up front in the LDV Vans Trophy against Sheffield Wednesday. Richard was released at the end of the season.

Blackburn Rov *(From trainee on 9/8/1995)*
Darlington *(Free on 17/1/1997) FL 62+1/1 FLC 3 FAC 1 Others 0+1*
Northampton T *(Signed on 18/12/1998) FL 13+22/7 FLC 3 FAC 5+3 Others 7+1*
York C *(Free on 8/8/2003) FL 36/2 FLC 1 FAC 1 Others 1*
Chester C *(Free on 30/7/2004) FL 26+2 FAC 1 Others 1+2/1*

HORLOCK Kevin
Born: Erith, 1 November 1972
Height: 6'0" **Weight:** 12.0
Club Honours: Div 2 '96; Div 1 '02
International Honours: NI: 32; B-2
Kevin arrived at Ipswich during the summer of 2004 and quickly established himself as a regular in the side, playing in a defensive midfield role just in front of the back line. His place in the team came under threat following the arrival of Darren Currie and in the second half of the season he found himself on the substitutes' bench as much as he was in the starting line-up.

West Ham U *(From trainee on 1/7/1991)*
Swindon T *(Free on 27/8/1992) P/FL 151+12/22 FLC 15+2/1 FAC 12/3 Others 5+2*
Manchester C *(£1,250,000 on 31/1/1997) P/FL 184+20/37 FLC 15+1/3 FAC 9/1 Others 3/1*
West Ham U *(£300,000 on 15/8/2003) FL 23+4/1 FLC 2 FAC 4*
Ipswich T *(Free on 9/7/2004) FL 33+8 FLC 0+1 FAC 1 Others 1*

HORNUSS Julien
Born: Paris, France, 12 June 1986
Height: 5'10" **Weight:** 11.0
A fleet-footed and very skilful young striker, Julien made his Football League debut as a substitute on the opening day of the season for MK Dons against Barnsley, and then featured regularly on the bench for the next couple of months before injury cost him his place. Once fit he was unable to get back into the match squad, but he still showed enough to be kept on the retained list at the end of the season.

MK Dons *(Signed from Sedan Ardennes, France on 23/7/2004) FL 0+3 FLC 0+1 Others 0+1*

HORSFIELD Geoffrey (Geoff) Malcolm
Born: Barnsley, 1 November 1973
Height: 5'10" **Weight:** 11.0
Club Honours: FC '98; Div 2 '99
This old-fashioned centre forward had to work long and hard at his game throughout the 2004-05 season - perhaps the toughest of his professional career. He was never a regular first choice in West Bromwich Albion's attack but was always totally committed and a constant threat in and around the penalty area. He scored three Premiership goals during the season: the first in the 3-1 defeat at Newcastle United in late September, his second, the opener in a 4-1 win at Charlton and his third, the breakthrough, in the final home fixture against Portsmouth which Albion won 2-0 to retain their top-flight status.

Scarborough *(From juniors on 10/7/1992) FL 12/1 FAC 1 Others 0+2 (Free to Halifax T on 31/3/1994)*
Halifax T *(Free from Witton A on 8/5/1997) FL 10/7 FLC 4/1*
Fulham *(£325,000 on 12/10/1998) FL 54+5/22 FLC 6/6 FAC 8+1/3*
Birmingham C *(£2,000,000 + on 12/7/2000) P/FL 75+33/23 FLC 10+1/3 FAC 1+1 Others 5/2*
Wigan Ath *(Signed on 6/9/2003) FL 16/7 FLC 1*
West Bromwich A *(£1,000,000 on 18/12/2003) P/FL 38+11/10 FLC 1/1 FAC 2+1*

HORWOOD Evan David
Born: Billingham, 10 March 1986
Height: 6'0" **Weight:** 11.2
This young Sheffield United defender progressed to the Blades' reserve team last season and in March he was loaned out to Stockport County, initially for a month before this was extended to cover the remainder of the campaign. Evan did well during his stay at Edgeley Park, making the left-back position his own.

Sheffield U *(From trainee on 12/11/2004)*
Stockport Co *(Loaned on 11/3/2005) FL 10*

HOSKINS William (Will) Richard
Born: Nottingham, 6 May 1986
Height: 5'11" **Weight:** 11.2
International Honours: E: Yth
This promising Rotherham striker did well with England U19s last term, but the majority of his appearances at club level were from the bench. Will scored just two goals, netting at Gillingham in December and against Preston towards the end of the season. He will be expecting to feature much more prominently for the Millers in their League One campaign in 2005-06.

Rotherham U *(From trainee on 16/2/2005) FL 6+20/4 FLC 0+1 FAC 0+2*

HOULT Russell
Born: Ashby-de-la-Zouch, 22 November 1972
Height: 6'3" **Weight:** 14.9
For the third season in succession goalkeeper Russell Hoult was generally outstanding between the posts for West Bromwich Albion, despite suffering with a niggling back injury. Confident on his line, strong and safe in the air, he produced some stunning saves to keep the Baggies in with a shout in several games when defeat looked a foregone conclusion. Russell reached two personal milestones at club level during the campaign: 400 senior appearances and 350 League appearances.

Leicester C *(From trainee on 28/3/1991) FL 10 FLC 3 Others 1*
Lincoln C *(Loaned on 27/8/1991) FL 2 FLC 1*
Bolton W *(Loaned on 3/11/1993) FL 3+1 Others 1*
Lincoln C *(Loaned on 12/8/1994) FL 15 Others 1*
Derby Co *(£300,000 on 17/2/1995) P/FL 121+2 FLC 8 FAC 7*
Portsmouth *(£300,000 + on 21/1/2000) FL 40 FLC 4*
West Bromwich A *(£500,000 on 5/1/2001) P/FL 175 FLC 8 FAC 10 Others 2*

HOWARD Brian Richard William
Born: Winchester, 23 January 1983
Height: 5'8" **Weight:** 11.1
International Honours: E: Yth
Brian was an ever-present for Swindon Town until mid-January, but thereafter featured mostly as a substitute and was absent for a while after it was discovered he had broken a bone in his foot. A left-

Steve Howard

footed midfielder who can also play up front, he likes to get forward and weighed in with some useful goals.
Southampton *(From trainee on 27/1/2000)*
Swindon T *(Free on 6/8/2003) FL 49+21/9 FLC 3+1 FAC 4/1 Others 4+1*

HOWARD Steven (Steve) John

Born: Durham, 10 May 1976
Height: 6'2" **Weight:** 14.6
Club Honours: Div 1 '05

A traditional-style centre forward, big and strong, Steve's main strength is his ability in the air. A regular for League One champions Luton Town last term, he finished as the club's leading scorer with a total of 22 goals in all competitions and is now fifth in the all-time list of scorers for the club. One of six Hatters' players selected for the PFA League One team of the season, Steve was out of contract in the summer and his future was undecided at the time of writing.
Hartlepool U *(Free from Tow Law on 8/8/1995) FL 117+25/26 FLC 7+1/1 FAC 5/2 Others 7/3*
Northampton T *(£120,000 on 22/2/1999) FL 67+19/18 FLC 4 FAC 2+1 Others 2*
Luton T *(£50,000 on 22/3/2001) FL 169/81 FLC 6/2 FAC 7/4 Others 1*

HOWARD Timothy (Tim) Matthew

Born: North Brunswick, USA, 6 March 1979
Height: 6'3" **Weight:** 14.12
Club Honours: CS '03; FAC '04
International Honours: USA: 12

A solid goalkeeper, who is quick off his line, Tim discovered that one good season at Old Trafford doesn't necessarily bring permanence in the next - particularly when your luck is down. Little more than a year after being hailed as the heir apparent to Fabian Barthez, Tim was just five games into the new campaign when an error against Lyons in a Champions' League fixture led to his demotion in favour of Roy Carroll. Resigned to keeping goal for the Carling Cup campaign, he eventually earned a reprieve when Sir Alex Ferguson brought him back to regular Premiership action starting against Portsmouth in February. He seemed to have earned a permanent place in the team, but once again Roy Carroll blocked his path. The signing of a new contract showed that Sir Alex Ferguson certainly has confidence in Tim's abilities.
Manchester U *(£2,300,000 from New York/New Jersey Metrostars, USA, on 22/7/2003) PL 44 FLC 5 FAC 8 Others 14*

HOWARTH Russell Michael
Born: York, 27 March 1982
Height: 6'1" **Weight:** 13.10
International Honours: E: Yth
Once again Russell's first-team opportunities at Tranmere were severely restricted by the form and fitness of regular goalkeeper John Achterberg. When he did get his chance, due to injury to his rival, he proved himself to be a more than competent deputy, but was unfortunate to be substituted himself due to concussion following a clash of heads shortly after being called on as Achterberg's replacement in the game at Hull. Very assured for a relatively young 'keeper, Russell is confident coming out of the box, kicking and distributing well, but he quietly spent the majority of what must have been another frustrating season for him on the bench. His contract with Rovers was not renewed at the end of the campaign.
York C *(From trainee on 26/8/1999) FL 6+2 FLC 3 Others 3*
Tranmere Rov *(Free on 5/11/2002) FL 10+2 FAC 0+1 Others 1*

HOWE Edward (Eddie) John Frank
Born: Amersham, 29 November 1977
Height: 5'10" **Weight:** 11.10
International Honours: E: U21-2
This popular player rejoined Bournemouth on loan from Portsmouth at the start of the 2004-05 season. He remained for three months and when he returned to Fratton Park the Cherries' supporters raised £16,000 in less than 24 hours to help secure his permanent return. He is a steady and solid centre half, who was a fixture in the starting line-up when fit.
Bournemouth *(From trainee on 4/7/1996) FL 183+17/10 FLC 12+1/1 FAC 12/2 Others 3+2*
Portsmouth *(£400,000 on 28/3/2002) FL 2*
Bournemouth *(Free on 6/8/2004) FL 33+2/1 FLC 2 FAC 3*

HOWEY Stephen (Steve) Norman
Born: Sunderland, 26 October 1971
Height: 6'2" **Weight:** 11.12
Club Honours: Div 1 '93, '02
International Honours: E: 4
This experienced centre half returned from a spell in the MLS and spent time training firstly with Oldham and then Hartlepool. He was signed on by Pools just before the transfer deadline to provide cover in defence. Short on match fitness, he made just one first-team appearance, playing half a game after coming on as substitute for the injured Michael Nelson.
Newcastle U *(From trainee on 11/12/1989) P/FL 167+24/6 FLC 14+2/1 FAC 21+2 Others 10+2*
Manchester C *(£2,000,000 + on 14/8/2000) P/FL 94/11 FLC 6 FAC 3*
Leicester C *(£300,000 on 4/7/2003) PL 13/1 FLC 2*
Bolton W *(Free on 30/1/2004) PL 2+1 (Freed during 2004 close season)*
Hartlepool U *(Free from New England Revolution, USA on 24/3/2005) FL 0+1*

HOWIE Scott
Born: Motherwell, 4 January 1972
Height: 6'2" **Weight:** 13.7
Club Honours: S Div 2 '93
International Honours: S: U21-5
Scott was first-choice 'keeper for Shrewsbury Town from the beginning of last season, guiding the team through the difficult early days of their return to the Football League when clean sheets were hard to come by. Equally efficient in the air and as a shot-stopper, he retained his place following a change in management until being replaced for the last few games of the campaign. At the time of writing he seemed set to leave Gay Meadow, being out of contract and with no offer of a new deal.
Clyde *(Signed from Ferguslie U on 7/1/1992) SL 55 SLC 3 SC 4 Others 1*
Norwich C *(£300,000 on 12/8/1993) PL 1+1*
Motherwell *(£300,000 on 13/10/1994) SL 69 SLC 4 SC 5 Others 1*
Reading *(£30,000 on 26/3/1998) FL 84+1 FLC 6 FAC 4 Others 7*
Bristol Rov *(Free on 2/8/2001) FL 90 FLC 3 FAC 10 Others 3*
Shrewsbury T *(Free on 15/8/2003) FL 40 FLC 1 FAC 1 Others 2*

HOYTE Justin Raymond
Born: Waltham Forest, 20 November 1984
Height: 5'11" **Weight:** 10.10
Club Honours: CS '04
International Honours: E: U21-7; Yth
Justin made 12 appearances in all competitions in a right-back position that is keenly contested at Highbury. Five of those games came in the Premiership with four of those as starts. He also featured in the Champions' League clashes with PSV Eindhoven and Rosenborg and played in all three Carling Cup matches the Gunners contested.
Arsenal *(From trainee on 1/7/2002) PL 4+3 FLC 5 FAC 0+1 Others 1+2*

HREIDARSSON Hermann
Born: Iceland, 11 July 1974
Height: 6'1" **Weight:** 13.1
Club Honours: Div 3 '99
International Honours: Iceland: 61; U21-6
One of manager Alan Curbishley's most successful signings, Hermann was again a regular at left back for Charlton last term until a cruciate ligament injury cut short his season with three games to go. Tall and uncompromising, he is good in the air, skilful on the ground and very strong. He also possesses a long throw. Hermann is very quick and likes to overlap down the left wing and get in an accurate cross. He linked up particularly well with Paul Konchesky on the left flank. Hermann found the net on one occasion, with his trusty left foot in the 2-0 win over Everton at the Valley. He was also a regular for the Iceland international side during the season, and in mid-December was voted runner-up to Chelsea's Eidur Gudjonsson as his country's 'Player of the Year' for 2004.
Crystal Palace *(Signed from IBV, Iceland on 9/8/1997) P/FL 32+5/2 FLC 5/1 FAC 4 Others 2*
Brentford *(£850,000 on 24/9/1998) FL 41/6 FLC 2 FAC 2/1 Others 3/1*
Wimbledon *(£2,500,000 on 14/10/1999) P/FL 25/1 FAC 2*
Ipswich T *(£4,000,000 + on 19/8/2000) P/FL 101+1/2 FLC 11 FAC 6 Others 9/1*
Charlton Ath *(£500,000 + on 27/3/2003) PL 66+1/3 FLC 3/1 FAC 4*

HUCKERBY Darren Carl
Born: Nottingham, 23 April 1976
Height: 5'10" **Weight:** 11.12
Club Honours: Div 1 '02, '04
International Honours: E: B-1; U21-4
Norwich City's 'Player of the Season' for 2004-2005, Darren continued to excite Canary fans with his blinding pace and mazy runs which troubled many a top-flight defence. He netted City's first Premiership goal in nine years in the opening game against Crystal Palace and was the creator of the majority of the club's goals all season. Darren was used as an out-and-out striker and also as an attacking midfielder on the left-hand side, from where his ability to run at defenders, causing them to back-pedal, was a constant threat.
Lincoln C *(From trainee on 14/7/1993) FL 20+8/5 FLC 2 Others 1/2*
Newcastle U *(£400,000 on 10/11/1995) PL 0+1 FAC 0+1*
Millwall *(Loaned on 6/9/1996) FL 6/3*
Coventry C *(£1,000,000 on 23/11/1996) PL 85+9/28 FLC 2+1 FAC 12/6*
Leeds U *(£4,000,000 on 12/8/1999) PL 11+29/2 FLC 1+1/2 FAC 1+2 Others 1+11/2*
Manchester C *(£2,250,000 + on 29/12/2000) P/FL 44+25/22 FLC 2+3/6 FAC 6+1/2 Others 1/1*
Nottingham F *(Loaned on 24/2/2003) FL 9/5 Others 2*
Norwich C *(£750,000 on 12/9/2003) P/FL 72+1/20 FLC 2/1 FAC 2*

HUDDLESTONE Thomas (Tom) Andrew
Born: Nottingham, 28 December 1986
Height: 6'3" **Weight:** 14.12
International Honours: E: U21-3; Yth
It was typical for Tom that, on his England U21 debut at Pride Park, he spent 45 minutes in midfield and the second half in defence. A great deal has been asked of Derby County's young prodigy who, in the transfer window, signed a pre-contract agreement with Tottenham Hotspur. Although he turned 18 only in December, Tom left Derby with 95 appearances in his two seasons in the senior side. Many were in defence last season, because of injuries to Mo Konjic, although he prefers to be in midfield. Tom's technical ability gives him great potential. He has fine control, however the ball comes to him, and can pass long or short. Tom was also named in the PFA divisional team of the season.
Derby Co *(From trainee on 27/2/2004) FL 84+4 FLC 2 FAC 3 Others 2*

HUDSON Mark
Born: Bishop Auckland, 24 October 1980
Height: 5'10" **Weight:** 11.3
Mark began the 2004-05 season in good form in the centre of Chesterfield's midfield, putting in tackles and setting up attacks with vision. He scored twice in the Spireites' 3-2 win at Bristol City in January, but seemed to lose his way in the new year.
Middlesbrough *(From trainee on 5/7/1999) PL 0+5 FAC 0+1*
Chesterfield *(Loaned on 13/8/2002) FL 15+1/1 FLC 1 FAC 0+1 Others 0+1*
Carlisle U *(Loaned on 10/12/2002) FL 14+1/1*
Chesterfield *(Free on 21/3/2003) FL 72+5/8 FLC 1 FAC 1 Others 3*

Darren Huckerby

HUDSON Mark Alexander
Born: Guildford, 30 March 1982
Height: 6'3" **Weight:** 12.6
Mark joined Crystal Palace in the summer of 2004 but after a handful of early-season appearances he lost his place in the side. Soon afterwards the young defender was injured and spent six months on the sidelines before making a comeback in the game against Middlesbrough in April. Mark will be seeking more regular first-team action in 2005-06.
Fulham *(From trainee on 6/4/1999) FLC 2+1*
Oldham Ath *(Loaned on 25/8/2003) FL 15 Others 1*
Crystal Palace *(£550,000 on 16/1/2004) P/FL 21/1 FLC 2*

HUGHES Aaron William
Born: Cookstown, 8 November 1979
Height: 6'0" **Weight:** 11.2
International Honours: NI: 43; B-2; Yth
Aaron is versatile member of the Newcastle defence, always steady and composed, a good reader of the game, and he was a fixture in the side for most of the 2004-05 season, featuring at various times in both full-back positions and at centre back. His best performance was probably in the home game with Arsenal when he dealt capably with the Gunners' prolific attack, although he was also excellent when appearing as a substitute in the UEFA Cup tie at Heerenveen. His season was brought to a premature end in April by a hernia operation.
Newcastle U *(From trainee on 11/3/1997) PL 193+12/4 FLC 9+1 FAC 15+4/1 Others 39+5/1*

HUGHES Andrew (Andy) John
Born: Manchester, 2 January 1978
Height: 5'11" **Weight:** 12.1
Club Honours: Div 3 '98
Andy had to play in a number of positions for Reading last term, including both full-back berths, centre of midfield, and as a wide, almost old-fashioned winger on both flanks. Despite making the occasional error, his enthusiasm and all-action style endeared him to the supporters, and he was a vital member of Reading's small yet tight-knit squad. One

of the most experienced players at the club, he is an excellent example to the younger members of the squad.
Oldham Ath *(From trainee on 20/1/1996) FL 18+15/1 FLC 1+1 FAC 3+1 Others 1+2*
Notts Co *(£150,000 on 29/1/1998) FL 85+25/17 FLC 6+1/1 FAC 10/2 Others 2*
Reading *(Free on 16/7/2001) FL 157+9/18 FLC 7/1 FAC 6+1 Others 3*

HUGHES Bryan
Born: Liverpool, 19 June 1976
Height: 5'9" **Weight:** 11.2
Club Honours: WC '95
Bryan joined Charlton Athletic in the close season from Birmingham City in an attempt to bolster the midfield. An intelligent player, he is equally comfortable in a central role or out on the left and he likes to get forward. Bryan reads the game well and is very skilful on the ball. He was used sparingly by Alan Curbishley during the campaign, and despite his attacking style of play, only found the net in the final Premiership game of the season against Crystal Palace. He came into his own however, in the FA Cup, scoring three goals in three appearances, two of these coming in the 4-1 win over Rochdale.
Wrexham *(From trainee on 7/7/1994) FL 71+23/12 FLC 2 FAC 13+3/7 Others 6+1/1*
Birmingham C *(£750,000 + on 12/3/1997) P/FL 197+51/34 FLC 17+5/3 FAC 8+5/4 Others 6+2/1*
Charlton Ath *(Free on 2/7/2004) PL 10+7/1 FLC 1+1 FAC 3/3*

HUGHES Christopher (Chris)
Born: Sunderland, 5 March 1984
Height: 6'0" **Weight:** 11.6
Chris' second season with Darlington saw him used mainly as a substitute, coming on to inject a bit of pace down the right-hand side of the field with his dashing runs and strong crosses. These limited opportunities meant that he failed to add to his goal tally and he was not retained by the club.
Darlington *(From trainee on 1/7/2003) FL 29+16/2 FLC 2+1 FAC 1 Others 1*

HUGHES Mark Anthony
Born: Dungannon, 16 September 1983
Height: 5'10" **Weight:** 12.4
International Honours: NI: U23-1; U21-11; Yth; Sch
Mark spent most of last season away from White Hart Lane in loan deals. He covered for injury at Northampton early on in the campaign before moving to Boundary Park on an initial one-month loan deal in November. A cultured midfielder who is strong in the air, breaks up attacks and distributes immaculately, he quickly impressed enough for Latics to extend the deal for a further two months. Despite a series of stirring central-midfield displays, Spurs then indicated they were prepared to release the player and he joined the club for the remainder of the season.
Tottenham H *(From trainee on 12/7/2001)*
Northampton T *(Loaned on 27/8/2004) FL 3*
Oldham Ath *(Free on 19/11/2004) FL 25+2 FAC 3 Others 1+3*

HUGHES Michael Eamonn
Born: Larne, 2 August 1971
Height: 5'7" **Weight:** 10.13
International Honours: NI: 71; U23-2; U21-1; Yth; Sch
This diminutive hard-working midfielder signed a new contract for Palace in the summer and had a brilliant campaign last term, when he was a near ever-present in the club's Premiership line-up. Michael was appointed club captain in December and also added to his total of caps for Northern Ireland during the season.
Manchester C *(From trainee on 17/8/1988) FL 25+1/1 FLC 5 FAC 1 Others 1 (£450,000 to RS Strasbourg, France on 3/8/1992)*
West Ham U *(Loaned on 29/11/1994) PL 15+2/2 FAC 2*
West Ham U *(Loaned on 2/10/1995) PL 28 FLC 2 FAC 3/1*
West Ham U *(Free on 12/8/1996) PL 33+5/3 FLC 5 FAC 2*
Wimbledon *(£1,600,000 on 25/9/1997) P/FL 99+16/13 FLC 5+1/2 FAC 8+1/2*
Birmingham C *(Loaned on 28/3/2002) FL 3*
Crystal Palace *(Free on 14/8/2003) P/FL 68+2/5 FLC 3 FAC 2 Others 3*

Michael Hughes (right)

HUGHES John **Paul**
Born: Hammersmith, 19 April 1976
Height: 6'0" **Weight:** 12.10
International Honours: E: Sch
Paul showed all his determination and class for Luton during the pre-season friendlies, but once the campaign proper started he was only on the fringes of the squad. His only first-team appearance came in the LDV Vans Trophy tie against Swansea. The gifted midfield player was also affected by a mystery virus, but will be hoping to come back strongly in 2005-06.
Chelsea *(From trainee on 11/7/1994) PL 13+8/2 FAC 1 Others 1*
Stockport Co *(Loaned on 17/12/1998) FL 7*
Norwich C *(Loaned on 24/3/1999) FL 2+2/1*
Southampton *(Free on 23/3/2000)*
Luton T *(Free, via trial at Burnley, on 10/8/2001) FL 62+17/6 FLC 5 FAC 1 Others 3*

HUGHES Richard Daniel
Born: Glasgow, 25 June 1979
Height: 5'9" **Weight:** 9.12
International Honours: S: 4; U21-9; Yth
This combative midfielder was rewarded for his patience at Portsmouth last term when he finally won through to feature regularly in the line-up in the closing stages of the campaign. Richard is a committed player who always gives 100 per cent effort in the cause of the team.
Arsenal *(Free from Atalanta, Italy on 11/8/1997)*
Bournemouth *(£20,000 on 5/8/1998) FL 123+8/14 FLC 9+1 FAC 8/2 Others 5*
Portsmouth *(£100,000 on 13/6/2002) P/FL 25+8 FLC 2+1 FAC 4+2/1*
Grimsby T *(Loaned on 21/2/2003) FL 12/1*

HUGHES Stephen David
Born: Motherwell, 14 November 1982
Height: 5'11" **Weight:** 9.6
International Honours: S: U21-12; Yth
This highly-rated midfielder started out last season in the SPL with Rangers before Leicester manager Craig Levein snapped him up during the January transfer window. Stephen took a while to get fully match fit, but his class was soon evident to all. He was used both in central midfield and on the flanks, where his ability to kick with either foot proved an asset. Stephen scored once for the Foxes, netting at Watford after an incisive passing move with David Connolly.
Glasgow Rgrs *(From juniors on 12/7/1999) SL 41+23/7 SLC 3+4 SC 4+3 Others 7+4*
Leicester C *(£100,000 + on 31/1/2005) FL 13+3/1 FAC 1+1*

HUGHES Stephen John
Born: Reading, 18 September 1976
Height: 6'0" **Weight:** 12.12
Club Honours: FAYC '94; PL'98; CS '98
International Honours: E: U21-8; Yth; Sch
The former Arsenal and Everton midfielder was given a contract by Coventry manager Peter Reid in the summer of 2004 and exceeded all expectations. Once match-fit he was the star man and after being handed the captain's armband in Tim Sherwood's absence showed strong leadership qualities, allied with some skilful passing and strong positional play. In the home game with Stoke Stephen became the first Coventry outfield player to go into goal for 16 years after Ian Bennett was sent off and kept a clean sheet for over 45 minutes with a string of good saves. He finished the season in a rich vein of form and deservedly won the main 'Player of the Season' awards for the Sky Blues.
Arsenal *(From trainee on 15/7/1995) PL 22+27/4 FLC 5+3/1 FAC 7+7/1 Others 2+4/1*
Fulham *(Loaned on 26/7/1999) FL 3 FLC 1*
Everton *(£500,000 + on 10/3/2000) PL 27+2/1 FLC 1+1 FAC 2/1*
Watford *(Free on 12/7/2001) FL 11+4 FLC 2*
Charlton Ath *(Free on 14/8/2003)*
Coventry C *(Free on 6/7/2004) FL 39+1/4 FLC 2/1 FAC 2*

HUKE Shane
Born: Reading, 2 October 1985
Height: 5'11" **Weight:** 12.7
This combative Peterborough midfielder spent the early part of the 2004-05 campaign out on loan, firstly at Cambridge City and then at Hornchurch, where he featured in the FA Cup first round tie against Boston United. Shane made his senior debut for Posh as a substitute at Bradford City, when he was played out of position as a centre forward, and went on to feature in the starting line-up on several occasions before succumbing to a virus. He was reported to have suffered a broken ankle during the summer but he will be looking to gain more first-team experience at London Road in 2005-06.
Peterborough U *(From trainee on 10/10/2003) FL 6+2*

HULBERT Robin James
Born: Plymouth, 14 March 1980
Height: 5'9" **Weight:** 10.5
International Honours: E: Yth; Sch
This central-midfield player was a regular in the Port Vale line-up during the first half of the 2004-05 season and generally did well as the team made a good start. A leg injury hampered his progress in November but he returned to the team at Christmas. Robin is a busy player, more active in a defensive role than when going forward, and always gave 100 per cent when he played. He suffered a hamstring strain in February and only played one more game after that.
Swindon T *(From trainee on 25/9/1997) FL 12+17 FLC 1+1 FAC 2*
Bristol C *(£25,000 on 23/3/2000) FL 21+18 FLC 1+4 Others 5+3 (Free to Telford U on 21/11/2003)*
Shrewsbury T *(Loaned on 27/3/2003) FL 4+3*
Port Vale *(Free on 29/7/2004) FL 23+1 FAC 1+1 Others 1*

HULSE Robert (Rob) William
Born: Crewe, 25 October 1979
Height: 6'1" **Weight:** 11.4
Rob never really figured in West Bromwich Albion's plans during 2004-05, although an early-season stomach injury did not help matters, and he only featured on the bench for the Baggies before manager Bryan Robson allowed him to move to Elland Road. He made a dream start to his Leeds career with a two-goal debut in the 3-1 home win over Reading – both spectacular long-range strikes. Rob then cemented his hero status with the Elland Road faithful with goals in three successive matches against West Ham, Millwall and Gillingham. Sure of touch, the possessor of a thumping shot and good in the air, Rob looked at home at Elland Road. He was scheduled to return to the Hawthorns at the end of the season but Leeds thrashed out a deal with the Baggies which made Rob a permanent signing.
Crewe Alex *(From trainee on 25/6/1998) FL 97+19/46 FLC 6+1/2 FAC 5+1 Others 2/4*
West Bromwich A *(£750,000 + on 8/8/2003) P/FL 29+9/10 FLC 5+1/3 FAC 1+1*
Leeds U *(Loaned on 8/2/2005) FL 13/6*

HUME Iain
Born: Brampton, Canada, 31 October 1983
Height: 5'7" **Weight:** 11.2
International Honours: Canada: 11; Yth
Iain is a spectacular performer, scoring some extraordinary goals, and although he can occasionally experience a brief lapse in concentration, nonetheless, he continued to attract the attention from other clubs during the 2004-05 season. The swift and resourceful striker was mostly paired with Paul Hall up-front for Rovers, and this proved to be the club's most successful attacking combination. Iain was a regular in the Canadian international side and was voted Tranmere's 'Player of the Season' by the supporters. Dazzling when on form, he finished the season as the club's top scorer in all competitions.

Tranmere Rov *(From juniors on 6/11/2000) FL 95+49/31 FLC 4+3 FAC 8+2/3 Others 6+3/2*

HUMPHREYS Richard (Richie) John
Born: Sheffield, 30 November 1977
Height: 5'11" **Weight:** 14.6
International Honours: E: U21-3; Yth
Last term proved to be another great season for Hartlepool's left-sided midfield playmaker. He was once again an ever-present in the side and when Micky Barron was indisposed he took over as captain. Richie also had the distinction of scoring the winning penalty at Tranmere to take Hartlepool through to the League One play-off final.
Sheffield Wed *(From trainee on 8/2/1996) P/FL 34+33/4 FLC 4+2 FAC 5+4/5*
Scunthorpe U *(Loaned on 13/8/1999) FL 6/2*
Cardiff C *(Loaned on 22/11/1999) FL 8+1/2 FAC 1 Others 1*
Cambridge U *(Free on 2/2/2001) FL 7/3*
Hartlepool U *(Free on 18/7/2001) FL 180+4/22 FLC 6 FAC 12/1 Others 11+1*

HUNT David
Born: Dulwich, 10 September 1982
Height: 5'11" **Weight:** 11.9
David began the 2004-05 season as a first choice in central midfield for Leyton Orient alongside Michael Simpson but lost his place to Daryl McMahon and thereafter rarely featured. In March he joined Northampton Town on a short-term contract where he mostly appeared at right back, although he was also occasionally employed in midfield after coming off the bench. David proved to have an effective long throw but failed to register a goal during his brief spell at Sixfields.
Crystal Palace *(From trainee on 9/7/2002) FL 2 FLC 0+1*
Leyton Orient *(Signed on 11/7/2003) FL 57+8/1 FLC 2 FAC 3/1 Others 3+1*
Northampton T *(Free on 24/3/2005) FL 2+2 Others 0+1*

HUNT James Malcolm
Born: Derby, 17 December 1976
Height: 5'8" **Weight:** 10.3
This experienced central midfielder followed his former manager Ian Atkins to Bristol Rovers during the summer of 2004. James impressed as a ball winner, breaking up opponents' attacks and chipping in with important goals in the home games with Yeovil, Northampton and Grimsby. James reached the landmark of 300 Football League appearances during the season and was selected as the Supporters Club 'Player of the Season'.
Notts Co *(From trainee on 15/7/1994) FL 15+4/1 FAC 0+1 Others 2+2/1*
Northampton T *(Free on 7/8/1997) FL 150+22/8 FLC 8+2 FAC 7+3/1 Others 10+1/1*
Oxford U *(Free on 12/7/2002) FL 75+5/3 FLC 4/1 FAC 3*
Bristol Rov *(Free on 5/7/2004) FL 41/4 FLC 2 FAC 2 Others 4*

HUNT Lewis James
Born: Birmingham, 25 August 1982
Height: 5'11" **Weight:** 12.8
Talented and athletic, Lewis can play equally well in midfield or centre back, however, he was tried at right back by Southend manager Steve Tilson last term and went on to make the position his own. Unfortunately his campaign ended prematurely in March after he suffered a torn cartilage in the game at Chester City and this subsequently required surgery.
Derby Co *(From trainee on 17/2/2001) FL 8+3 FLC 0+2*
Southend U *(Free on 28/10/2003) FL 50+7 FAC 4 Others 9+1*

HUNT Nicholas (Nicky) Brett
Born: Westhoughton, 3 September 1983
Height: 6'1" **Weight:** 10.8
International Honours: E: U21-7
One of the promising youngsters from the previous campaign, Nicky made the right-back position at Bolton his own during the first half of last season with a series of assured performances. Recognition soon arrived in the form of a

Richie Humphreys

call-up to the England U21 squad with whom he acquitted himself well. A tough-tackling defender, with a tendency to make surging runs down the wing, the second half of his campaign was interrupted by niggling injuries.
Bolton W *(From trainee on 7/7/2001) P/FL 57+4/1 FLC 7 FAC 5+2*

HUNT Stephen (Steve)
Born: Port Laoise, 1 August 1980
Height: 5'7" **Weight:** 12.6
International Honours: RoI: U21-1
After being a mainstay of the Brentford line-up for the previous three years Steve's 2004-05 campaign was cruelly disrupted by groin injuries. Nevertheless when he did play the skilful left winger created his usual number of chances and contributed four League One goals. His first, an opportunist effort against Swindon, and the third, a well-converted chance to equalise against Sheffield Wednesday, both brought the house down at Griffin Park.
Crystal Palace *(From trainee on 29/6/1999) FL 0+3*
Brentford *(Free on 6/8/2001) FL 126+10/25 FLC 2+2 FAC 8+3/2 Others 9/3*

HUNT Stephen James
Born: Southampton, 11 November 1984
Height: 6'1" **Weight:** 13.0
It could only get better for this Colchester United left back, when his senior debut dramatically ended within a matter of seconds. Appearing as a substitute at Chesterfield in August, Stephen was sent off almost straight away. However, the former Southampton trainee recovered from this disastrous first taste of senior football, and he went on to make more than 20 appearances for his new club, all at left back.
Colchester U *(From trainee at Southampton on 19/7/2004) FL 16+4/1 FLC 2 FAC 1+1 Others 1*

HUNTER Barry Victor
Born: Coleraine, 18 November 1968
Height: 6'3" **Weight:** 13.2
Club Honours: Div 3'03
International Honours: NI: 15; B-2; Yth
One substitute appearance for Rushden throughout the whole of the 2004-05 campaign doesn't even begin to tell the full story for the former Northern Ireland international defender who is now entering his first full season in management. Barry was disappointed to be left out of the Diamonds' squad by previous boss Ernie Tippett, although he agreed to stay and also helped out coaching some of the club's promising youngsters. However, in January he took over for his second spell as caretaker-boss and soon afterwards he was given the job on a full-time basis.
Newcastle U *(Signed from Coleraine on 2/11/1987. Freed during 1988 close season)*
Wrexham *(£50,000 from Crusaders on 20/8/1993) FL 88+3/4 FLC 6 FAC 7+1/1 Others 8*
Reading *(£400,000 on 12/7/1996) FL 76+8/4 FLC 5/1 FAC 3+1/1 Others 6+1*
Southend U *(Loaned on 12/2/1999) FL 5/2*
Rushden & Diamonds *(Free on 14/9/2001) FL 106+1/6 FLC 2 FAC 5*

HURST Glynn
Born: Barnsley, 17 January 1976
Height: 5'10" **Weight:** 11.10
This talented striker took a short while to settle in at Notts County last term, but the supply of goals soon began to flow at a steady rate. His final tally was 15 in all competitions, with the highlight coming when he notched a hat-trick in the 3-0 win at Rochdale at the end of September. Glynn is a lively front man who is capable of leaving defenders in his wake with his exciting bursts of pace.
Barnsley *(From trainee at Tottenham H on 13/7/1994) FL 0+8 FLC 1 (Freed on 27/3/1997)*
Swansea C *(Loaned on 15/12/1995) FL 2/1*
Mansfield T *(Loaned on 18/11/1996) FL 5+1 Others 0+1*
Ayr U *(£30,000 from Emley on 23/3/1998) SL 78/49 SLC 6/2 SC 10 Others 1+2*
Stockport Co *(£150,000 on 16/2/2001) FL 22+4/4 FLC 0+1*
Chesterfield *(Free on 14/12/2001) FL 77+7/29 FLC 1 FAC 0+1*
Notts Co *(Free on 5/7/2004) FL 36+5/14 FLC 2 FAC 2+1 Others 1/1*

HURST Kevan James
Born: Chesterfield, 27 August 1985
Height: 6'0" **Weight:** 11.7
Kevan failed to break through into the Blades' first team last term, making just three hard-working, lively substitute appearances in a forward role. A regular in the reserves, he moved on loan to Stockport County in February where he played in every game for the rest of the season. The tricky winger made his debut in the superb 2-1 'derby' victory at Oldham, and scored the opening goal shortly before the interval.
Sheffield U *(From trainee on 24/3/2004) FL 0+1 FLC 0+3*
Boston U *(Loaned on 25/3/2004) FL 3+4/1*
Stockport Co *(Loaned on 18/2/2005) FL 14/1*

HURST Paul Michael
Born: Sheffield, 25 September 1974
Height: 5'4" **Weight:** 9.4
Club Honours: AMC '96
There can rarely have been such a wholehearted player who has given better service to Rotherham United's cause over the years than Paul, a loyal one-club player who always gives his best. Paul figured regularly on the left side of the back four last term and after a spell on the sidelines at the start of the season he made the position his own.
Rotherham U *(From trainee on 12/8/1993) FL 335+44/13 FLC 10+3 FAC 21+2/3 Others 14+1*

HURST Thomas (Tom) William
Born: Leicester, 23 September 1987
Height: 6'1" **Weight:** 11.0
This young defender made his Football League debut for Boston United when he came on as a late substitute at Rushden last April. Tom gave a solid performance in the short time he was on the pitch, working hard both at the back and when pushed forward for set pieces. He was close to a debut goal with a flashing header, but suffered a groin injury in the following reserve game and this ruled him out of further first-team action.
Boston U *(Trainee) FL 0+1*

HUSBANDS Michael Paul
Born: Birmingham, 13 November 1983
Height: 5'9" **Weight:** 9.13
Club Honours: FAYC '02
Michael started the 2004-05 season with great hopes, his speed and skill on the ball promising much. However, although he came off the bench in the opening game against Southend, he only featured once more during the campaign, also from the bench, as one injury seemed to make way for another. He left the Roots Hall club by mutual consent in April.
Aston Villa *(From trainee on 2/4/2002)*
Southend U *(Free on 31/7/2003) FL 3+8 FLC 1 FAC 0+2 Others 0+2*

HUTCHINSON Edward (Eddie) Stephen
Born: Kingston, 23 February 1982
Height: 6'1" **Weight:** 12.7
Brentford's box-to-box midfielder didn't appear last term until December due to a hip injury. He was then a regular in the line-up with the highlight of his campaign coming when he fired home the opener in the FA Cup fifth round replay against Southampton. Eddie missed several more matches in April due to a hamstring injury.
Brentford *(£75,000 from Sutton U on 21/7/2000) FL 78+12/6 FLC 3 FAC 6+2/1 Others 3+2*

HUTCHINSON Jonathan (Joey)
Born: Middlesbrough, 2 April 1982
Height: 6'0" **Weight:** 12.0
This classy young central defender had the misfortune to suffer a serious knee injury playing for Darlington at Rochdale last September and this required an operation, which ruled him out for the rest of the campaign. This was a major blow to the Quakers' defence as his quick tackling, perceptive reading of the game and timely interceptions were sorely missed in the rearguard.
Birmingham C *(From trainee on 1/7/2000) P/FL 1+3 FLC 2 FAC 1*
Darlington *(Free on 8/8/2003) FL 46+1 FLC 2 FAC 0+1 Others 1*

HUTCHISON Donald (Don)
Born: Gateshead, 9 May 1971
Height: 6'1" **Weight:** 11.8
International Honours: S: 26; B-2
Last term was a season to forget for this experienced West Ham midfielder. A persistent knee problem caused him problems throughout the campaign and meant that he played in only five Championship games, including three when he came off the bench. Out of contract in the summer he looked to be on his way from Upton Park at the time of writing.
Hartlepool U *(From trainee on 20/3/1990) FL 19+5/2 FLC 1+1 FAC 2 Others 1*
Liverpool *(£175,000 on 27/11/1990) P/FL 33+12/7 FLC 7+1/2 FAC 1+2 Others 3+1/1*
West Ham U *(£1,500,000 on 30/8/1994) PL 30+5/11 FLC 3/2 FAC 0+1*
Sheffield U *(£1,200,000 on 11/1/1996) FL 70+8/5 FLC 3+2 FAC 5/1 Others 2+1*
Everton *(£1,000,000 + on 27/2/1998) PL 68+7/10 FLC 4+1/1 FAC 9*
Sunderland *(£2,500,000 on 19/7/2000) PL 32+2/8 FLC 2/2 FAC 3*
West Ham U *(£5,000,000 on 31/8/2001) P/FL 36+27/5 FLC 2+1 FAC 3+1 Others 0+1*

HUTH Robert
Born: Berlin, Germany, 18 August 1984
Height: 6'2" **Weight:** 12.12
Club Honours: PL '05
International Honours: Germany: 11; U21-2; Yth
In the light of Germany's disappointing showing at Euro 2004 new boss Jurgen Klinsmann's remedy was to rebuild his defence around Chelsea's giant young centre back Robert Huth. The great irony being that the brilliant youngster played more international football than domestic fare as two nasty injuries interrupted his season. An ankle injury laid him low before Christmas and he was unable to start a match until the FA Cup fourth round tie against Birmingham which brought him mixed fortunes to say the least! He galloped upfield to open the scoring with a bullet header from a corner but limped off in the second half with a knee injury. Robert then made a dramatic reappearance eight matches later in the second leg of the Champions' League last-16 tie when he came off the bench to ease Chelsea's passage into the quarter-finals. Robert played twice against his boyhood heroes Bayern Munich, once in an unfamiliar right-back role, as the Blues progressed to their second successive semi-final.
Chelsea *(From trainee on 23/8/2001) PL 16+13 FLC 1 FAC 1+2/1 Others 3+5/1*

HUTTON Rory Neil
Born: Ely, 3 May 1985
Height: 5'9" **Weight:** 10.4
International Honours: RoI: Yth
This promising left back or midfielder was only on the fringes of the Cambridge United first-team squad last term. He featured as a substitute in the early-season games against Swansea and Darlington, but was released soon afterwards and signed for Southern League outfit Hitchin Town. Later in the season he played for both Waterbeach and Dunstable Town.
Peterborough U *(From trainee on 8/3/2004)*
Cambridge U *(Free on 27/8/2004) FL 0+2*

Micah Hyde

HYDE Micah Anthony
Born: Newham, 10 November 1974
Height: 5'9" **Weight:** 11.5
Club Honours: Div 2 '98
International Honours: Jamaica: 16
A pre-season signing from Watford, Micah marked his Burnley debut with a goal in the season's opener at home to Sheffield United. His only other strike will be far better remembered, though, a magnificent equaliser at Ewood Park in the FA Cup replay against Blackburn which won most of the club's 'Goal of the Season' awards. Goals were not his main contribution to the side, however; Micah is a combative and highly committed midfield man whose form seemed to get steadily better throughout the season. On many occasions, he was the driving force in the middle of the park, both breaking up opposition attacks and setting them up for the Clarets.
Cambridge U *(From trainee on 19/5/1993) FL 89+18/13 FLC 3 FAC 7+2 Others 4+1*
Watford *(£225,000 on 21/7/1997) P/FL 235+18/24 FLC 16+1/4 FAC 13 Others 3*
Burnley *(Free on 23/7/2004) FL 37+1/1 FLC 4 FAC 4/1*

HYYPIA Sami
Born: Porvoo, Finland, 7 October 1973
Height: 6'4" **Weight:** 13.5
Club Honours: FLC '01, '03; FAC '01; UEFAC '01; ESC '01; CS '01; UEFACL '05
International Honours: Finland: 69; U21-27; Yth
Liverpool's Finland international central defender has never quite recaptured the heights of form he touched in his early seasons at Anfield in partnership with Stephane Henchoz. Even though he found a worthy partner in Jamie Carragher last season he occasionally looked fallible in the air at set pieces. He lost his place for a while to new signing Mauricio Pellegrino for four games, but returned in triumph for the European Champions' Cup quarter-final at home to Juventus when he opened the scoring for Liverpool at a corner, not with a trademark header, but with a controlled volley just inside the far post. Two weeks later he scored an even better goal, the equaliser in the 2-2 home draw with Tottenham, a turn and volley from the edge of the penalty box. Together with the peerless Jamie Carragher he defended stoutly in the closing stages of the European Champions' Cup competition, including in the final against AC Milan in Istanbul.
Liverpool *(£2,600,000 from Willem II, Holland, ex MyPa, on 7/7/1999) PL 216/17 FLC 15/1 FAC 18 Others 64/6*

Sami Hyypia

IBE Okezie (Kezie) Enyeribenyam
Born: Camden Town, 6 December 1982
Height: 5'10" **Weight:** 12.0
This diminutive Yeovil striker spent much of the 2004-05 campaign out on loan with Taunton Town and then Exeter City. He made two appearances from the bench for the Glovers early in the season and also featured as a substitute against Bristol Rovers in February.
Yeovil T *(Free from Staines T on 6/8/2004) FL 0+3*

IBEHRE Jabo Oshevire
Born: Islington, 28 January 1983
Height: 6'2" **Weight:** 12.10
This exciting young striker began last term on the bench for Leyton Orient, but then broke into the first team following a series of injuries to his colleagues. Jabo scored two goals from ten starts but then suffered a knee injury, which required an operation and forced him to miss the rest of the season.
Leyton Orient *(From trainee on 18/7/2001) FL 60+55/17 FLC 2+3/2 FAC 5+3/1 Others 8+1/2*

IDE Charlie Joe
Born: Sunbury, 10 May 1988
Height: 5'8" **Weight:** 10.6
A striker who is on Brentford's books as a scholar, Charlie spent last season developing in the youth team. He stepped up to make his senior debut when coming off the bench to play the last few minutes of the final game of the season against Hull.
Brentford *(Trainee) FL 0+1*

IDIAKEZ Inigo
Born: San Sebastian, Spain, 8 November 1973
Height: 6'0" **Weight:** 12.2
Inigo's skill from free kicks was vital to Derby County and prompted manager George Burley to call him the best exponent he had encountered in his long career in the game. Six of his 11 goals came from free kicks, two from penalties and one directly from a corner. In addition, he hit post or bar, sometimes from open play, a remarkable 13 times. His willingness to play the ball from midfield, especially when he adjusted to the English tempo, impressed the Rams' supporters who voted him 'Player of the Year'. A training-ground injury appeared to rule him out of the play-offs but he was back for the second leg. Inigo was voted into the PFA Division One team of the season.
Derby Co *(Signed from Rayo Vallecano, Spain, ex Real Sociedad, Real Oviedo, on 27/7/2004) FL 41/9 FLC 1/1 FAC 3/1 Others 1*

IFIL Jerel Christopher
Born: Wembley, 27 June 1982
Height: 6'1" **Weight:** 12.11
After making a permanent move to the County Ground in the summer of 2004, Jerel enjoyed something of a mixed season last term. He rarely hit the form that he had shown in his previous loan spells, but still showed signs of developing into a useful defender, performing excellent man-marking jobs on League One danger men Leroy Lita and Stuart Elliott. Jerel is a strong-tackling central defender with great pace.
Watford *(From trainee on 8/2/2000) FL 10+1*
Huddersfield T *(Loaned on 28/3/2002) FL 1+1 Others 2*
Swindon T *(Loaned on 30/1/2003) FL 5+4*
Swindon T *(Loaned on 4/9/2003) FL 6*
Swindon T *(Loaned on 14/11/2003) FL 10*
Swindon T *(£70,000 on 14/7/2004) FL 31+4 FLC 2 FAC 2 Others 3*

IFIL Philip Nathan
Born: Willesden, 18 November 1986
Height: 5'9" **Weight:** 10.8
International Honours: E: Yth
A Spurs youth-team regular, Philip impressed in his first-team defensive debut looking pacy, confident on the ball and composed. He went on to make just two full and one substitute appearance but promises much for the future and Martin Jol may well consider a future loan spell to gain more experience to reap the full benefit of the youngster's potential.
Tottenham H *(From trainee on 19/11/2004) PL 2 FLC 0+1*

IFILL Paul
Born: Brighton, 20 October 1979
Height: 6'0" **Weight:** 12.10
Club Honours: Div 2 '01
International Honours: Barbados
This popular Millwall player was dogged by injury throughout the 2004-05 season and played only a handful of games. Paul can play as a winger or an out-and-out striker and at his best he is full of pace, trickery and unpredictability.
Millwall *(From trainee on 2/6/1998) FL 188+42/40 FLC 5/1 FAC 15/2 Others 9+2*

IGOE Samuel (Sammy) Gary
Born: Staines, 30 September 1975
Height: 5'6" **Weight:** 10.0
This busy little right-sided midfielder had a consistent season for Swindon Town last term when he was a near ever-present in the line-up. One of the most skilful players on the club's books he has quick feet and the ability to run at defenders with the ball. Sammy was clearly delighted with his spectacular late strike which brought a 1-0 victory over Bradford at the end of September.
Portsmouth *(From trainee on 15/2/1994) FL 100+60/11 FLC 7+5 FAC 2+3*
Reading *(£100,000 on 23/3/2000) FL 53+34/7 FLC 4+1 FAC 4+2 Others 6+1*
Luton T *(Loaned on 27/3/2003) FL 2*
Swindon T *(Free on 14/7/2003) FL 75+4/9 FLC 3+1 FAC 3 Others 3+1*

ILIC Sasa
Born: Melbourne, Australia, 18 July 1972
Height: 6'4" **Weight:** 14.0
International Honours: Yugoslavia: 2
This experienced 'keeper stepped in to sign for Blackpool shortly before the start of the 2004-05 campaign with cover required for the injured Lee Jones. He featured in the first three games, but his only appearances thereafter came in the LDV Vans Trophy games. Sasa was released at the end of his short-term contract and later had spells as back-up for both Aberdeen and Leeds United without adding to his total of senior appearances.
Charlton Ath *(Free from St Leonards Stamcroft on 5/10/1997) P/FL 51 FLC 3 FAC 2 Others 3 (Freed on 30/6/2002)*
West Ham U *(Loaned on 24/2/2000) PL 1*
Portsmouth *(Loaned on 7/9/2001) FL 7*
Portsmouth *(Free from Zalaegerszegi, Hungary on 20/2/2003)*
Barnsley *(Free on 8/8/2003) FL 25 FLC 1 FAC 5 Others 2*
Sheffield U *(Free on 26/2/2004)*
Blackpool *(Free on 6/8/2004) FL 3 Others 2*
Aberdeen *(Free on 13/1/2005)*
Leeds U *(Free on 24/3/2005)*

IMPEY Andrew (Andy) Rodney
Born: Hammersmith, 30 September 1971
Height: 5'8" **Weight:** 11.2
Club Honours: FLC '00
International Honours: E: U21-1
This right-sided midfielder started the 2004-05 season as a regular in the Nottingham Forest line-up but made his last appearance for the side against West Ham in December after which he was frozen out of the first-team picture following a change of manager. He was loaned out to Millwall in March for the rest of the season. Signed as cover for the right-hand side, he made a handful of appearances from the bench during his stay at the New Den. Andy was out of contract at the end of the season and his future was uncertain at the time of writing.

Queens Park Rgrs *(£35,000 from Yeading on 14/6/1990) P/FL 177+10/13 FLC 15+1/3 FAC 7+3/1 Others 0+2/1*
West Ham U *(£1,300,000 on 26/9/1997) PL 25+2 FLC 4 FAC 3*
Leicester C *(£1,600,000 on 25/11/1998) P/FL 132+20/1 FLC 9+4 FAC 10+1 Others 2*
Nottingham F *(Free on 13/2/2004) FL 33+3/1 FLC 3*
Millwall *(Loaned on 11/3/2005) FL 0+5*

INAMOTO Junichi

Born: Kagoshima, Japan, 18 September 1979
Height: 5'11" **Weight:** 11.13
International Honours: Japan: 57
After a long and tedious fight to regain fitness following a last-minute broken leg mishap when playing for Japan against England in June 2004, this strong-running midfielder was farmed out on loan to Cardiff City just before Christmas. Junichi took a few games to find his match legs but became a central influence as his three-month spell progressed. Back at the Hawthorns he finally made his debut for Albion against Tottenham in April and featured on two more occasions before the season's end.
Arsenal *(Loaned from Gamba Osaka, Japan on 24/7/2001) FLC 2 Others 0+2*
Fulham *(Loaned from Gamba Osaka, Japan on 23/7/2002) PL 9+10/2 FLC 2 FAC 1+1 Others 3+7/4*
Fulham *(Loaned on 1/7/2003) PL 15+7/2 FLC 1 FAC 2/1*
West Bromwich A *(£200,000 from Gamba Osaka, Japan on 31/8/2004) PL 0+3*
Cardiff C *(Loaned on 23/12/2004) FL 13+1 FAC 2*

INCE Clayton

Born: Trinidad, 13 July 1972
Height: 6'3" **Weight:** 14.2
International Honours: Trinidad & Tobago
Clayton started the 2004-05 season as deputy to Ben Williams in goal for Crewe, but then regained the number one spot in November. A broken finger caused him to miss a number of games but he again forced his way back into the side. Clayton is a very capable 'keeper and in the vital game against Coventry City when safety from relegation was clinched, he was received the 'Man of the Match' award. Clayton was also a regular at international level for Trinidad.
Crewe Alex *(£50,000 from Defence Force, Trinidad on 21/9/1999) FL 120+3 FLC 6 FAC 8*

Clayton Ince

INCE Paul Emerson Carlyle

Born: Ilford, 21 October 1967
Height: 5'11" **Weight:** 12.2
Club Honours: CS '93, '94; FAC '90, '94; ECW '91; ESC '91; FLC '92; PL '93, '94
International Honours: E: 53; B-1; U21-2; Yth
Paul started slowly for Wolves last term before hitting a cracking goal in the Carling Cup tie at Rochdale. There was another strike in September against Cardiff, but the combative midfielder was not at his best and was dropped. He then suffered problems with a toe, which required minor surgery. Returning to the line-up for the FA Cup tie against Millwall, his leadership qualities and sheer presence seemed to lift the team. A goal a week later against West Ham made his day, and he played superbly throughout 2005, netting a long-range drive against Burnley. Paul was runner-up in the club's 'Player of the Season' vote.
West Ham U *(From apprentice on 18/7/1985) FL 66+6/7 FLC 9/3 FAC 8+2/1 Others 4/1*
Manchester U *(£1,000,000 on 14/9/1989) P/FL 203+3/25 FLC 23+1/2 FAC 26+1/1 Others 24/1 (£8,000,000 to Inter Milan, Italy on 13/7/1995)*
Liverpool *(£4,200,000 on 22/7/1997) PL 65/14 FLC 6/1 FAC 3/1 Others 7/1*
Middlesbrough *(£1,000,000 on 3/8/1999) PL 93/7 FLC 6/1 FAC 7/1*
Wolverhampton W *(Free on 6/8/2002) P/FL 92+5/7 FLC 4+1/1 FAC 6/1 Others 3*

INGHAM Michael (Mike) Gerard

Born: Preston, 7 September 1980
Height: 6'4" **Weight:** 13.12
International Honours: NI: 1; U21-4; Yth
Mike was fourth-choice goalkeeper at Sunderland last term but enjoyed a loan spell at Doncaster in the autumn where he was required as cover for Andy Warrington. He managed a couple of appearances before returning to Wearside, but it was a real surprise when he was called upon to make a long overdue League debut for the Black Cats against Reading in April. The next match, a vital promotion clash at Ipswich saw him make a brilliant late save to preserve a vital point. Mike also won his first full cap for Northern Ireland, featuring in the friendly against Germany in June.
Sunderland *(£30,000 from Cliftonville on 28/7/1999) P/FL 1+1 FLC 2*
Carlisle U *(Loaned on 1/10/1999) FL 7*
Stockport Co *(Loaned on 23/8/2002) FLC 1*
Darlington *(Loaned on 22/11/2002) FL 3*
York C *(Loaned on 24/1/2003) FL 17*

Wrexham (Loaned on 16/3/2004) FL 11
Doncaster Rov (Loaned on 2/11/2004) FL 1 Others 1

INGIMARSSON Ivar
Born: Iceland, 20 August 1977
Height: 6'0" **Weight:** 12.7
International Honours: Iceland: 16; U21-14; Yth
Up until the away game at Sunderland, when he was somewhat harshly blamed for the home side's goal and substituted, Ivar had been a regular in the heart of the Reading defence, partnering first Adrian Williams then Ibrahima Sanko. A tough yet composed centre back, he also weighed in with some vital goals, none better than a spectacular last-minute volley in the FA Cup tie against Swansea City, which earned a replay. Ivar has retired from the Iceland international squad to concentrate on his young family and his club football.
***Torquay U** (Loaned from IBV Vestmannaeyjar, Iceland on 21/10/1999) FL 4/1*
***Brentford** (£150,000 from IBV Vestmannaeyjar, Iceland on 18/11/1999) FL 109+4/10 FLC 6 FAC 3 Others 13/1*
***Wolverhampton W** (Free on 2/7/2002) FL 10+3/2 FLC 2*
***Brighton & Hove A** (Loaned on 10/2/2003) FL 15*
***Reading** (£100,000 + on 23/10/2003) FL 67+2/4 FLC 4 FAC 4/1*

INNES Mark
Born: Glasgow, 27 September 1978
Height: 5'10" **Weight:** 12.1
This naturally left-footed midfielder was a regular for Chesterfield at the start of the 2004-05 season, but lost his place after suffering injury and suspension in the autumn. Despite his obvious ability he was released by the Spireites in March and Port Vale moved quickly to sign him. After three substitute appearances he made his full debut for Vale against Wrexham and was offered a new contract at the season's end.
***Oldham Ath** (From trainee on 10/10/1995) FL 52+21/1 FLC 4+3 FAC 4+2 Others 3+1*
***Chesterfield** (Free on 19/12/2001) FL 62+14/2 FLC 1 Others 0+1*
***Port Vale** (Free on 24/3/2005) FL 2+3*

IPOUA Guy
Born: Douala, Cameroon, 14 January 1976
Height: 6'1" **Weight:** 12.2
This experienced target man joined Doncaster in the summer of 2004 following a spell in the Middle East, but spent most of his time at Belle Vue playing for the reserves. A loan spell at Mansfield saw him make an impressive debut against Notts County before his form tailed off. In February he was out on loan again at Lincoln where he worked hard but had no luck in front of goal. Guy was released by Rovers shortly before the end of the season.
***Bristol Rov** (Free from Seville, Spain, ex Atletico Madrid, Novelda, on 7/8/1998) FL 15+9/3 FLC 1+1 FAC 3+1 Others 1*
***Scunthorpe U** (Free on 27/8/1999) FL 50+15/23 FAC 5/4 Others 2*
***Gillingham** (£25,000 on 19/3/2001) FL 42+40/13 FLC 4+2/1 FAC 2+4/2*
***Livingston** (Free on 1/7/2003) SL 0+1 SLC 0+1 (Freed on 19/2/2004)*
***Doncaster Rov** (Free from Al Shaab, Dubai on 6/8/2004) FL 1+8 FLC 1 FAC 0+1*
***Mansfield T** (Loaned on 15/10/2004) FL 4+1*
***Lincoln C** (Loaned on 11/2/2005) FL 0+6*

IRELAND Craig Robert
Born: Dundee, 29 November 1975
Height: 6'3" **Weight:** 13.9
This experienced central defender joined Peterborough in the summer of 2004, but although he was a regular starter in the first half of the season he was allowed to go on loan to Bristol City at the turn of the year. Craig impressed during his spell at Ashton Gate and the signing looked about to be made permanent, but eventually fell through.
***Aberdeen** (From juniors on 5/10/1994) SLC 1*
***Dunfermline Ath** (Free on 12/2/1996) SL 61+6/2 SLC 0+2 SC 0+1*
***Dundee** (Free on 27/10/1999) SL 14/1 SC 1*
***Airdrie** (Loaned on 12/10/2000) SL 12/2 Others 1*
***Notts Co** (£50,000 on 2/2/2001) FL 77+3/2 FLC 2 FAC 1*
***Barnsley** (Free on 8/8/2003) FL 43/3 FLC 1 FAC 5 Others 2*
***Peterborough U** (Free on 3/8/2004) FL 22+1 FLC 1 FAC 1 Others 1*
***Bristol C** (Loaned on 10/1/2005) FL 5*

IRIEKPEN Ezomo (Izzy)
Born: London, 14 May 1982
Height: 6'1" **Weight:** 12.4
Club Honours: FAYC '99
International Honours: E: Yth
Izzy missed most of the first half of the 2004-05 season after suffering an ankle injury in pre-season training and then a knee injury in November. However, after regaining his first-team place he showed the form that placed him high in the ratings as one of the most consistent central defenders in League Two. Dangerous at set-piece situations, both of his goals contributed to away wins for the Swans.
***West Ham U** (From trainee on 25/5/1999)*
***Leyton Orient** (Loaned on 22/10/2002) FL 5/1 FAC 1 Others 2/1*
***Cambridge U** (Loaned on 28/2/2003) FL 13/1*
***Swansea C** (Free on 22/8/2003) FL 62+1/3 FAC 7 Others 0+1*

ISTEAD Steven Brian
Born: South Shields, 23 April 1986
Height: 5'8" **Weight:** 11.4
An attacking winger with a good turn of speed, Steven continued his football education on the first-team bench for Hartlepool during the 2004-05 season. He regularly made a late appearance in games, coming on to add pace to a tiring attack. Although still a scholar, he has now been involved in over 60 first-team games, yet he must be disappointed to have started in only two of them.
***Hartlepool U** (Trainee) FL 1+53/1 FLC 0+3/1 FAC 0+8 Others 1+1*

IZZET Kemal (Kem)
Born: Whitechapel, 29 September 1980
Height: 5'8" **Weight:** 10.5
Central midfielder Kem's 2004-05 season was ruined by injury. After picking up a groin injury in pre-season he was then plagued by two ankle problems, which restricted him to just three starts, all in October. Eventually, an operation sorted out his ankle woe and Kem returned as a substitute for Colchester United's last game of the season, when he appeared as a late substitute to warm applause from the Layer Road faithful. The U's missed his bustling presence in the middle of the park, and will welcome his return in 2005-06.
***Charlton Ath** (From trainee on 11/1/1999)*
***Colchester U** (Signed on 22/3/2001) FL 130+9/15 FLC 5/1 FAC 8 Others 7/2*

IZZET Mustafa (Muzzy) Kemal
Born: Mile End, 31 October 1974
Height: 5'10" **Weight:** 10.12
Club Honours: FLC '97, '00
International Honours: Turkey: 9
Muzzy started the season brightly for Birmingham, passing the ball well and moving into good positions from central midfield. He scored a thunderous volley at Bolton playing just off the front, a role the Blues used him in on a couple of occasions. After jarring his knee against Newcastle in October he required two rounds of surgery, but returned to the team only to be sent off on his final appearance, for handling on the goal line, against Everton the following month.
***Chelsea** (From trainee on 19/5/1993)*
***Leicester C** (£650,000 + on 28/3/1996) P/FL 265+4/38 FLC 24+3/4 FAC 16/4 Others 7/1*
***Birmingham C** (Free on 2/7/2004) PL 10/1*

Izzy Iriekpen

JAASKELAINEN Jussi
Born: Vaasa, Finland, 19 April 1975
Height: 6'3" **Weight:** 12.10
International Honours: Finland: 21; U21-14; Yth
The longest-serving player in the Reebok ranks, last season saw Jussi's already acclaimed reputation rise even further. Already established as one of the Premiership's finest shot-stoppers, his all-round game seemed to advance to another level. Commanding his box more effectively than he had done previously, Jussi marshalled his defence exceptionally well, especially in the new year when the team kept six clean sheets in a run of eight Premiership games. His finest performance came in the 1-1 draw with Aston Villa in April. Coming at such a crucial stage of the season, this was a virtuoso display, with Jussi repelling almost everything the Villa players could throw at him.
Bolton W *(£100,000 + from VPS Vassa, Finland, ex MPS, on 14/11/1997) P/FL 240+1 FLC 13 FAC 9 Others 2*

JACK Rodney Alphonso
Born: Kingstown, St Vincent, 28 September 1972
Height: 5'7" **Weight:** 10.9
International Honours: St Vincent & Grenadines
Widely hailed as Oldham Athletic's key close-season signing in summer 2004, Rodney's season was subsequently a big disappointment for both club and player. After netting twice in the opening three games he was relegated to the substitutes' bench before disaster struck in October. Away on international duty playing for St Vincent against St Kitts, Rodney suffered a knee injury and never figured again. Although approaching full fitness again towards the end of the season, new manager Ronnie Moore opted to pay the remainder of his contract up and he departed by mutual consent in April.
Torquay U *(Free from Lambada, St Vincent on 10/10/1995) FL 82+5/24 FLC 6/1 FAC 6 Others 6/3*
Crewe Alex *(£650,000 on 14/8/1998) FL 140+23/33 FLC 12/5 FAC 8+2 Others 3/4*
Rushden & Diamonds *(Free on 21/7/2003) FL 44+1/12 FLC 1 FAC 1 Others 2/1*
Oldham Ath *(Free on 3/7/2004) FL 5+5/2 FLC 0+1*

JACKMAN Daniel (Danny) James
Born: Worcester, 3 January 1983
Height: 5'5" **Weight:** 10.2
Danny was a regular name on the Stockport team sheet last term, playing mainly on the left-hand side of the field both in defence and midfield. He started the season well, scoring in the 4-0 win at Blackpool with a clinical finish from inside the area. He was also on the score sheet at the start of February when he equalised for the Hatters during the 2-1 defeat at Peterborough United with a close-range effort.
Aston Villa *(From trainee on 4/4/2001)*
Cambridge U *(Loaned on 14/2/2002) FL 5+2/1 Others 1+1*
Stockport Co *(£70,000 on 31/10/2003) FL 51+9/4 FLC 1 FAC 1 Others 4*

JACKSON Benjamin (Ben) Robert
Born: Peterlee, 20 October 1985
Height: 5'9" **Weight:** 11.5
Ben started the 2004-05 season in great style scoring goals galore for the Doncaster Rovers youth team. He was given his debut for the first team when he came on as a substitute in the LDV Vans Trophy match at Lincoln towards the end of September. Ben went on to make his Football League debut from the bench against Wrexham, but then suffered an injury. Later he was loaned out to Conference club York City before being released in the summer.
Doncaster Rov *(From trainee at Newcastle U on 20/1/2004) FL 0+1 Others 0+2*

JACKSON John (Johnnie)
Born: Camden, 15 August 1982
Height: 6'1" **Weight:** 13.0
International Honours: E: Yth
This promising young striker had a brief run of first-team action at Tottenham early on last term before joining Watford on a three-month loan in December. He was immediately thrown into the hectic Christmas programme without any chance to acclimatise, and at first found it difficult to settle, especially as he started playing wide left of midfield. He looked far more comfortable when he was switched to the centre and proved a real asset with his hard-working attitude and assured touch on the ball.
Tottenham H *(From trainee on 23/3/2000) PL 12+7/1 FLC 1 FAC 1+2*
Swindon T *(Loaned on 13/9/2002) FL 12+1/1 FAC 2 Others 2/1*
Colchester U *(Loaned on 11/3/2003) FL 8*
Coventry C *(Loaned on 21/11/2003) FL 2+3/2*
Watford *(Loaned on 23/12/2004) FL 14+1*

JACKSON Mark Graham
Born: Barnsley, 30 September 1977
Height: 6'0" **Weight:** 11.12
International Honours: E: Yth
Scunthorpe's club captain found himself out of favour at Glanford Park last term and, apart from a run-out in the LDV Vans Trophy match at Hereford, he had to wait until the new year to make the starting line-up. That turned out to be his final appearance for the Iron and the centre half, who is strong in the air and comfortable on the ball, joined League Two rivals Kidderminster on a free transfer in the middle of February. He soon became a vital player in the heart of the defence alongside Johnny Mullins and eventually took over the captain's armband from Wayne Hatswell. Nevertheless he was unable to prevent Harriers from being relegated to the Conference.
Leeds U *(From trainee on 1/7/1995) PL 11+8 FAC 4*
Huddersfield T *(Loaned on 29/10/1998) FL 5*
Barnsley *(Loaned on 14/1/2000) FL 1*
Scunthorpe U *(Free on 9/3/2000) FL 127+9/4 FLC 3 FAC 11 Others 8+1/1*
Kidderminster Hrs *(Free on 18/2/2005) FL 13*

JACKSON Mark Philip
Born: Preston, 3 February 1986
Height: 5'11" **Weight:** 11.9
Preston's young midfielder or striker continued to show steady development last term, with the highlight of his five appearances being his full debut at Leicester in the Carling Cup. Playing up front he demonstrated excellent awareness and close control. He returned to the reserves after Christmas and will have benefited from more first-team involvement.
Preston NE *(From trainee on 3/8/2004) FL 0+3 FLC 1+2 FAC 0+1*

JACKSON Matthew (Matt) Alan
Born: Leeds, 19 October 1971
Height: 6'1" **Weight:** 12.12
Club Honours: FAC '95; Div 2 '03
International Honours: E: U21-10; Sch
Matt played a captain's innings as he guided Wigan Athletic to history following their promotion to the Premiership, marshalling the defence superbly and leading by example. A composed and impressive central defender, he produced a series of reliable and impressive performances alongside Ian Breckin, reading the game well and tackling under pressure. A polished and experienced performer, his only goal

came in the draw at Wolves. Matt was rewarded with a new contract during the campaign.
Luton T *(From juniors on 4/7/1990) FL 7+2 FLC 2 Others 0+1*
Preston NE *(Loaned on 27/3/1991) FL 3+1 Others 1*
Everton *(£600,000 on 18/10/1991) P/FL 132+6/4 FLC 9 FAC 14/2 Others 4*
Charlton Ath *(Loaned on 26/3/1996) FL 8 Others 2*
Queens Park Rgrs *(Loaned on 20/8/1996) FL 7*
Birmingham C *(Loaned on 31/10/1996) FL 10*
Norwich C *(£450,000 on 24/12/1996) FL 158+3/6 FLC 6 FAC 5*
Wigan Ath *(Free on 19/10/2001) FL 129+2/3 FLC 8 FAC 4+1 Others 2*

JACKSON Michael James

Born: Runcorn, 4 December 1973
Height: 6'0" **Weight:** 13.8
Club Honours: Div 2 '97, '00
International Honours: E: Yth
Michael eventually joined Tranmere in the close season, having previously spent a successful loan spell at Prenton Park in 2002. He fitted straight away into a young defence, where his experience and maturity were both needed and appreciated; a tenacious tackler and a ready 'talker', he was a near ever-present in the line-up. In the absence of Jason McAteer, Michael took over as captain on the field and never failed to lead by example; he surprised even himself by netting five goals despite not being a naturally attacking player.
Crewe Alex *(From trainee on 29/7/1992) FL 5 FLC 1 FAC 1 Others 2*
Bury *(Free on 13/8/1993) FL 123+2/9 FLC 9/1 FAC 3 Others 12*
Preston NE *(£125,000 on 26/3/1997) FL 237+8/17 FLC 16/2 FAC 14 Others 8*
Tranmere Rov *(Loaned on 18/12/2002) FL 6*
Tranmere Rov *(Free on 2/7/2004) FL 43/5 FLC 1 FAC 1 Others 5*

JACKSON Richard

Born: Whitby, 18 April 1980
Height: 5'8" **Weight:** 10.12
Richard was unlucky with injuries last term, notably a torn calf muscle in Derby County's home win over Leeds United at the end of January. At the time, he was nicely settled at left back, having again demonstrated his ability to play on either side of the defence. While both Richard and Jamie Vincent were out of action, Derby signed Chris Makin from Leicester City. Richard was back for the victory over Preston North End that clinched Derby's play-off place and will be hoping for a winter free of injuries in 2005-06.
Scarborough *(From trainee on 27/3/1998) FL 21+1 FLC 2*
Derby Co *(£30,000 + on 25/3/1999) P/FL 75+12 FLC 3 FAC 1 Others 2*

JACKSON Simeon Alexander

Born: Kingston, Jamaica, 28 March 1987
Height: 5'9" **Weight:** 11.0
Simeon spent much of last term developing in the youth and reserve teams at Rushden. However, he made two early-season appearances from the bench and also featured as a substitute in the final match of the campaign at Macclesfield. He will be looking to gain further senior experience in the 2005-06 season.
Rushden & Diamonds *(Trainee) FL 0+3*

JACOBS Wayne Graham

Born: Sheffield, 3 February 1969
Height: 5'9" **Weight:** 11.2
This popular left back began his testimonial season as a regular in the Bradford side, but a knee injury required surgery and cost him his place in the line-up. He played only three more matches, against Bournemouth and Walsall in December and a farewell appearance as a substitute in the final home game. Wayne has been a loyal servant to the Valley Parade club, but was released in the summer.
Sheffield Wed *(From apprentice on 3/1/1987) FL 5+1 FLC 3 Others 1*
Hull C *(£27,000 on 25/3/1988) FL 127+2/4 FLC 7 FAC 8 Others 6*
Rotherham U *(Free on 5/8/1993) FL 40+2/2 FLC 4 FAC 1 Others 2*
Bradford C *(Free on 5/8/1994) P/FL 302+16/12 FLC 17+2 FAC 13/2 Others 7*

JAGIELKA Philip (Phil) Nikodem

Born: Manchester, 17 August 1982
Height: 5'11" **Weight:** 12.8
International Honours: E: U21-6; Yth
Phil had another splendid season for Sheffield United in 2004-05. The supporters' 'Player of the Year', and ever-present in the Championship and cup matches he played in three different roles during the campaign, as well as taking the captain's arm band on occasions. He began as a central defender, but in December switched to an attacking midfield role. An athletic and hard-working player, he is good in the air and in the tackle and has good anticipation. Due to Paddy Kenny's dismissal and a later injury, Phil spent more than 100 minutes in goal, equipping himself well despite conceding three goals.
Sheffield U *(From trainee on 8/5/2000) FL 147+23/6 FLC 16/2 FAC 13/2 Others 3*

JAIDI Radhi Ben Abdelmajid

Born: Tunis, Tunisia, 30 August 1975
Height: 6'4" **Weight:** 14.0
International Honours: Tunisia
Despite winning the African Nations Cup with Tunisia in February 2004, Radhi was still an unfamiliar name when he signed for Bolton in July of the same year. This soon changed though, as a series of excellent performances at the heart of the back four propelled him into the limelight. An outstanding debut in the victory at Southampton was soon followed by his first goal in English football, with Radhi using his considerable build to power home a header at Arsenal. A huge physical presence, he also possesses a considerable amount of skill on the ball: a rare commodity for someone so powerful. His size also posed a threat in opposing penalty areas and he weighed in with five Premiership goals, the highlight coming in the draw with Birmingham, when he controlled the ball on his chest before turning and volleying home an unstoppable shot.
Bolton W *(Free from Esperance de Tunis, Tunisia, on 14/7/2004) PL 20+7/5 FAC 0+1*

JAKOBSSON Andreas

Born: Lund, Sweden, 6 October 1972
Height: 6'2" **Weight:** 13.0
International Honours: Sweden: 36
An accomplished and commanding centre back, Andreas arrived at St Mary's last September, when it became obvious that Michael Svensson's long-term injury was going to be even longer term than anticipated. The initial signs were promising, and Andreas can hardly be blamed for lacking the one attribute the Saints' defence so desperately needed: pace! Having to hold the centre behind a midfield with a tendency to usher swift attackers through rather than impede, he was often left horribly exposed, and he was rotated with Danny Higginbotham and Calum Davenport in an effort to find the best defensive combination.
Southampton *(£1,000,000 from Brondby, Denmark, ex Teckomatorps SK, Landskrona, Helsingborgs, Hansa Rostock, on 31/8/2004) PL 24+3/2 FLC 3 FAC 2+1*

JAMES Craig Peter

Born: Middlesbrough, 15 November 1982
Height: 6'2" **Weight:** 11.8
This left back began last season as a regular in the Port Vale line-up and scored his only goal of the season in the 3-0 victory over Bristol City in August with a direct free kick. Craig suffered a leg injury in early November and did not

start another game for three months, but then returned to his regular role. An expert dead-ball kicker who causes problems for the opposition with his forays down the wing, Craig featured in midfield on occasions during the campaign.
Sunderland *(From trainee on 12/7/2000) FL 1 FLC 1*
Hibernian *(Loaned on 29/8/2002) SL 20+2/2 SLC 1 SC 2*
Darlington *(Loaned on 14/11/2003) FL 10/1*
Port Vale *(Signed on 19/3/2004) FL 31+7/1 FLC 1 Others 2*

JAMES David Benjamin
Born: Welwyn Garden City, 1 August 1970
Height: 6'5" **Weight:** 14.5
Club Honours: FAYC '89; FLC '95
International Honours: E: 32; B-1; U21-10; Yth
David enjoyed a consistent season at club level for Manchester City although he lost his position as his country's first choice after an error in England's opening 2006 World Cup qualifier against Austria. He continued to impress City fans with his assured, confident handling and was one of the main reasons why the side conceded so few goals during the Premiership campaign. In the final game of the season David made a cameo appearance as a striker late on as the Blues strove to find the winning goal at home to Middlesbrough that would have enabled them to qualify for the UEFA Cup.
Watford *(From trainee on 1/7/1988) FL 89 FLC 6 FAC 2 Others 1*
Liverpool *(£1,000,000 on 6/7/1992) PL 213+1 FLC 22 FAC 19 Others 22*
Aston Villa *(£1,800,000 on 23/6/1999) PL 67 FLC 6 FAC 8 Others 4*
West Ham U *(£3,500,000 on 17/7/2001) P/FL 91 FLC 5 FAC 6*
Manchester C *(£1,300,000 + on 14/1/2004) PL 55 FAC 1*

JAMES Kevin Ernest
Born: Southwark, 3 January 1980
Height: 5'9" **Weight:** 10.7
Kevin made a couple of early-season appearances from the bench for Nottingham Forest before being sidelined by an injury and whilst on his way back to full fitness he joined Boston United on loan. He was used on the right side of midfield and on occasions as a wing back at York Street. Kevin showed awareness on the ball but when pushing forward was out of luck in his attempts to get on the score sheet. He managed to fit in eight appearances in his short time with the Pilgrims being used at right back in his final game before returning to the City Ground where he had a brief run of first-team action before losing his place at the beginning of April.
Charlton Ath *(From trainee on 2/7/1998)*
Gillingham *(Free on 21/8/2000) FL 18+31/4 FLC 1+2 FAC 1+1*
Nottingham F *(Free on 26/6/2004) FL 2+5*
Boston U *(Loaned on 30/12/2004) FL 6 FAC 2*

JANSEN Matthew (Matt) Brooke
Born: Carlisle, 20 October 1977
Height: 5'11" **Weight:** 10.13
Club Honours: AMC '97; FLC '02
International Honours: E: U21-6; Yth
Matt continued his rehabilitation back into football last term following the serious head injury he suffered in 2002. Given his chance by new manager Mark Hughes he responded with a goal against Portsmouth to earn Blackburn their first win of the season and he also scored in the 3-3 home draw with Birmingham. However, he then dropped out of the first-team picture and was told to take a three-month break from the game to try and get back to full fitness.
Carlisle U *(From trainee on 18/1/1996) FL 26+16/10 FLC 4+1/3 FAC 1+3 Others 3+3*
Crystal Palace *(£1,000,000 + on 12/2/1998) P/FL 23+3/10 FLC 4 FAC 0+1 Others 2*
Blackburn Rov *(£4,100,000 on 19/1/1999) P/FL 103+46/44 FLC 9+4/8 FAC 8+4/4 Others 2+1/1*
Coventry C *(Loaned on 13/2/2003) FL 8+1/2*

JARMAN Nathan George
Born: Scunthorpe, 19 September 1986
Height: 5'10" **Weight:** 12.8
A strong, lively striker, Nathan did well with Barnsley's reserves last season when he scored a number of goals. He made his senior debut for the Reds as a substitute at Oldham in November, and featured on several occasions towards the end of the campaign, receiving his first start at Port Vale at the end of April. Nathan will be looking to appear more regularly for the first team in 2005-06.
Barnsley *(From trainee on 10/5/2005) FL 1+5*

JAROSIK Jiri
Born: Usti Nad Lebem, Czech Republic, 27 October 1977
Height: 6'4" **Weight:** 13.3
Club Honours: FLC '05; PL '05
International Honours: Czech Republic: 22
Two months after playing impressively against Chelsea for CSKA Moscow in the Champions' League Jiri Jarosik became the Blues' only transfer window acquisition when he put pen to paper to confirm a contract. Jiri was a teammate of Petr Cech at Sparta Prague before leaving for CSKA in a Russian record transfer deal in 2003. He is essentially an attacking midfielder with neat ball control and accurate distribution but has the versatility to play anywhere across the midfield and has even filled in occasionally in central defence and in attack where his height is a great asset. He could hardly have had a more exciting start to his career in England – featuring in the two-legged Carling Cup semi-final against Manchester United and the subsequent final against Liverpool when he won his first English medal within six weeks of his arrival! Jiri gives Chelsea further flexibility in an already powerful midfield department and proved to be a very useful addition to the squad.
Chelsea *(£3,000,000 from CSKA Moscow, Russia, ex Sparta Prague, on 6/1/2005) PL 3+11 FLC 1+2 FAC 2+1*

JARRETT Albert Ojumiri
Born: Sierra Leone, 23 October 1984
Height: 5'11" **Weight:** 11.2
Arriving in Brighton via Conference South club Lewes following his release by Wimbledon, Albert proved to be an exciting young winger. With a long-term contract under his belt he started the season in the first-team line-up, but fell away after three months and didn't figure in the squad again. In March he moved to Stevenage on loan and largely warmed the bench as the Hertfordshire club fought its way into the Conference play-offs. Albert has shown he can beat an opponent and will surely improve with experience.
Wimbledon *(Signed from Dulwich Hamlet on 17/4/2003) FL 3+6 FLC 0+1*
Brighton & Hove A *(Free on 5/8/2004) FL 3+9/1 FLC 1*

JARRETT Jason Lee Mee
Born: Bury, 14 September 1979
Height: 6'0" **Weight:** 12.4
Club Honours: Div 2 '03
An energetic box-to-box player, Jason suffered a broken leg in a pre-season friendly for Wigan Athletic last term. Loaned out to Stoke City to improve his fitness, he made his first start of the season for the Potters in the FA Cup tie against Arsenal in January. Involved in the first team on his return to the JJB Stadium, he started the last three matches of the season, putting in a 'Man of the Match' in the final game of as the Latics gained promotion. Jason was rewarded with the offer of a new contract following the club's rise to the Premiership.

David James

***Blackpool** (From trainee on 3/7/1998) FL 2 FAC 0+1 Others 1*
***Wrexham** (Free on 8/10/1999) FL 1*
***Bury** (Free on 13/7/2000) FL 45+17/4 FLC 0+1 FAC 2+2 Others 3/1*
***Wigan Ath** (£75,000 on 27/3/2002) FL 67+28/1 FLC 7/2 FAC 3 Others 1+1/1*
***Stoke C** (Loaned on 7/1/2005) FL 2 FAC 1*

JARVIE Paul
Born: Aberdeen, 14 June 1982
Height: 6'0" **Weight:** 12.3
This young 'keeper started out the 2004-05 as second choice for Dundee United and made a few appearances when Tony Bullock was injured. He was released during the new year and after a trial with Bristol City he signed for Torquay on a short-term deal. His only first-team appearance for the Gulls came in the defeat at Barnsley at the end of February after which Andy Marriott was brought in. Paul spent the remainder of the season warming the bench before being released in the summer.
***Dundee U** (From juniors on 25/5/1999) SL 10+1 SLC 1*
***Stenhousemuir** (Loaned on 24/11/2001) SL 5*
***Torquay U** (Free on 3/2/2005) FL 1*

JARVIS Matthew (Matt) Thomas
Born: Middlesbrough, 22 May 1986
Height: 5'8" **Weight:** 11.7
This promising attacking midfield player featured regularly at first-team level for Gillingham last term although the majority of his appearances came from the bench. The pacy youngster scored his first senior goal against Wolves in October and will be looking to win a regular place in the starting line-up in 2005-06.
***Gillingham** (From trainee on 13/5/2004) FL 14+26/3 FLC 1 FAC 0+1*

JARVIS Ryan Robert
Born: Fakenham, 11 July 1986
Height: 5'11" **Weight:** 11.0
Club Honours: Div 1 '04
International Honours: E: Yth
Ryan made just a handful of first-team appearances for Norwich last season when he worked hard to dislodge the more experienced strikers ahead of him. He scored a spectacular goal against Liverpool at Carrow Road in January and finished the season as leading scorer for the reserves. Ryan was farmed out on loan to Colchester at the back-end of the campaign. He played both as a striker and a winger, but he found it difficult to make a strong impression, especially with the Essex club operating with just one man up front for away games.
***Norwich C** (From trainee on 5/8/2003) P/FL 3+16/2 FLC 1 FAC 0+2*
***Colchester U** (Loaned on 24/3/2005) FL 2+4*

JASZCZUN Antony (Tommy) John
Born: Kettering, 16 September 1977
Height: 5'10" **Weight:** 10.10
Club Honours: AMC '02, '04
Tommy's season was disrupted by injury at Northampton last term and as a result he was in and out of the side. A talented left back, his forays down the flank excited the fans and often ended with a telling cross. However, his season came to a premature end after he required surgery to correct a knee problem.
***Aston Villa** (From trainee on 5/7/1996) FLC 0+1*
***Blackpool** (£30,000 on 20/1/2000) FL 107+15 FLC 7 FAC 5/1 Others 12/1*
***Northampton T** (Free on 8/7/2004) FL 24+8 FLC 2 FAC 3 Others 1*

JEANNIN Alexandre (Alex)
Born: Troyes, France, 30 December 1977
Height: 6'1" **Weight:** 11.12
Alex was a regular for Conference outfit Exeter City last term, contributing three goals. However, he was released at the end of the season and subsequently answered a call to play for Bristol Rovers in their final match of the campaign against Wycombe. He featured in a central-midfield role, nearly scored with a spectacular lob and left a good impression on the home supporters.
***Darlington** (Free from Troyes, France on 22/3/2001) FL 22 Others 2 (Freed to Troyes, France on 22/1/2002)*
***Bristol Rov** (Free from Exeter C on 5/5/2005) FL 1*

JEFFERS Francis
Born: Liverpool, 25 January 1981
Height: 5'9" **Weight:** 10.7
Club Honours: FAYC '98
International Honours: E: 1; U21-16; Yth; Sch
Signed by Alan Curbishley during the 2004 close season, Francis was given a chance by Charlton to resurrect his promising career. After coming on as substitute in the first two games, he was named in the starting line-up against Aston Villa at the Valley and scored two fine goals in a 3-0 win. The fans had great expectations, but Francis was to score only once more in the Premiership, although he did manage one in each of the cup competitions. In fairness to the striker, he rarely started and was used mainly as a late substitute. He sustained several niggling injuries, but part of the problem was a tendency to play a lone striker in a 4-5-1 formation, which did not really suit his game. Francis is a goal poacher who likes the ball to feet in the penalty area and is a great finisher, his strike against Bolton at the Valley providing a perfect example.
***Everton** (From trainee on 20/2/1998) PL 37+12/18 FLC 2+2/1 FAC 6+1/1*
***Arsenal** (£8,000,000 + on 27/6/2001) PL 4+18/4 FLC 1/1 FAC 7+1/3 Others 1+7*
***Everton** (Loaned on 1/9/2003) PL 5+13 FLC 1 FAC 0+3/2*
***Charlton Ath** (£2,600,000 on 12/8/2004) PL 9+11/3 FLC 2/1 FAC 2/1*

JELLEYMAN Gareth Anthony
Born: Holywell, 14 November 1980
Height: 5'10" **Weight:** 10.6
International Honours: W: U21-1; Yth
This left wing back began last season on loan at Boston and he was included in United's starting line-up in the opening day victory over Oxford United when he produced some forceful runs down the flank giving the team an extra attacking option. Gareth featured on a number of occasions for Peterborough on his return but was always on the fringes of the first-team squad and at the turn of the year he moved on to Mansfield. He made an impressive debut at left back for the Stags and proved to a useful acquisition, although injuries restricted his appearances towards the end of the campaign.
***Peterborough U** (From trainee on 5/8/1998) FL 80+21 FAC 7+2 Others 12+1*
***Boston U** (Loaned on 6/8/2004) FL 3*
***Mansfield T** (Free on 21/1/2005) FL 14*

JENAS Jermaine Anthony
Born: Nottingham, 18 February 1983
Height: 5'11" **Weight:** 11.2
International Honours: E: 12; U21-9; Yth
Jermaine is an important part of Newcastle's midfield with his good control and sound reading of the game increasingly allowing him to make telling runs into the opposition box. He started well, netting to earn a point at Birmingham, but his form then dipped leading to a spell on the bench in February and March. Although most effective in a central role, he occasionally appeared wide right, dropping to right back during the home with Fulham, whilst in the FA Cup tie against Spurs he made a substitute appearance at left back. His form was recovering when he pulled a calf muscle in the UEFA Cup tie at Sporting Lisbon. Jermaine also continued to represent England at international level and was selected for the close season visit to the USA.

Nottingham F *(From trainee on 19/2/2000) FL 29/4 FLC 2 FAC 2*
Newcastle U *(£5,000,000 on 5/2/2002) PL 83+23/9 FLC 3/1 FAC 6+1/1 Others 27+4/1*

JENKINS Lee David
Born: Pontypool, 28 June 1979
Height: 5'9" **Weight:** 11.0
Club Honours: Div 3 '00
International Honours: W: U21-9; Yth; Sch
Always dependable, Lee was a crucial part of the Kidderminster squad last season, when he featured at right back and in midfield. He was a regular in the side for most of the campaign but failed to register a goal for Harriers. Lee was one of a number of out-of-contract players whose future at Aggborough had yet to be decided at the time of writing.
Swansea C *(From trainee on 20/12/1996) FL 125+44/3 FLC 3+1 FAC 3+1 Others 9+1*
Kidderminster Hrs *(Free on 12/12/2003) FL 36+3 FLC 1 FAC 0+1 Others 0+1*

JENKINS Stephen (Steve) Robert
Born: Merthyr Tydfil, 16 July 1972
Height: 5'11" **Weight:** 12.3
Club Honours: AMC '94
International Honours: W: 16; U21-2; Yth
This experienced defender lost out last term when Peterborough opted for a 3-5-2 formation with no room for full backs. In October he joined Swindon Town on loan, where he proved to be a steady and reliable performer. Steve settled down well in the right-back slot and his transfer was eventually made permanent.
Swansea C *(From trainee on 1/7/1990) FL 155+10/1 FLC 12+1 FAC 10+1 Others 22*
Huddersfield T *(£275,000 on 3/11/1995) FL 257+1/4 FLC 18 FAC 14 Others 5*
Birmingham C *(Loaned on 15/12/2000) FL 3 FLC 1*
Cardiff C *(Free on 5/2/2003) FL 4*
Notts Co *(Free on 8/8/2003) FL 17 FLC 3 FAC 2 Others 1*
Peterborough U *(Free on 15/1/2004) FL 11+3/1 Others 1*
Swindon T *(Free on 29/10/2004) FL 24 FAC 2/1*

JENNINGS Steven (Steve) John
Born: Liverpool, 28 October 1984
Height: 5'7" **Weight:** 11.7
Steve is best known as a midfielder who has been with Tranmere since being released by Everton at the age of 14. He has been a cornerstone of a young reserve-team set-up, playing mostly in the middle, but he has appeared with some distinction at right back as well when required. Although relatively small in footballing terms, Steve is a deceptively strong and determined player who also has an eye for grabbing spectacular goals. He was a regular member of Brian Little's first-team squad in season 2004-05, although he was used mostly from the bench in the push for promotion, getting just a handful of League One starts.
Tranmere Rov *(From trainee on 28/10/2002) FL 5+10 FLC 0+1 FAC 1 Others 1+1*

Steve Jenkins

JENSEN Brian
Born: Copenhagen, Denmark, 8 June 1975
Height: 6'1" **Weight:** 12.4
Demoted to Burnley's second-choice 'keeper and deprived of his number one shirt following the arrival of Danny Coyne, Brian's chance arose when Coyne was injured at Queen's Park Rangers and he proved a revelation. Undoubtedly helped by the transformation in the defence in front of him, he was a consistently solid figure between the posts, seldom if ever prone to the recklessness that had marred his first season with the Clarets. Brian was secure in the position when Coyne returned to fitness, and he retained his place until the last few games of the season when Steve Cotterill decided to alternate the two 'keepers. Few would confidently bet on who will start the 2005-06 season as first choice.
West Bromwich A *(£100,000 from AZ Alkmaar, Holland, ex B93, Hvidovre, on 3/3/2000) FL 46 FLC 4*
Burnley *(Free on 18/7/2003) FL 72+1 FLC 5 FAC 7*

JENSEN Claus William
Born: Nykobing, Denmark, 29 April 1977
Height: 5'11" **Weight:** 12.6
International Honours: Denmark: 37; U21-17
This experienced midfielder joined Fulham in the summer of 2004, but his appearances were restricted by a series of injuries and the form of others in the side. A skilful midfielder who is an accurate passer of the ball, he linked well with the forwards and used this to good effect to score his only goal of the season in the FA Cup tie against Derby. Claus continued to be selected for the Denmark international squad when fit.

Bolton W *(£1,600,000 from Lyngby, Denmark, ex Naestved, on 14/7/1998) FL 85+1/8 FLC 12/2 FAC 6 Others 5*
Charlton Ath *(£4,000,000 on 21/7/2000) PL 112+10/16 FLC 7/1 FAC 4*
Fulham *(£1,250,000 on 27/7/2004) PL 10+2 FLC 1 FAC 0+2/1*

JEROME Cameron Zishan
Born: Huddersfield, 14 August 1986
Height: 6'1" **Weight:** 13.5
Cameron made his debut for Cardiff as a second half substitute against Leeds United at Ninian Park last October. His powerful build, skill and raw pace quickly marked him out as a talent to watch and he netted his first senior goal for the Bluebirds at Bournemouth in the Carling Cup later that month. One of the jewels in Cardiff's crown of young talent, the promising striker finished with an encouraging tally of seven goals for the season.
Cardiff C *(Free, following trials at Huddersfield T, Grimsby T, Sheffield Wed, Middlesbrough, on 14/1/2004) FL 21+8/6 FLC 0+2/1 FAC 1*

JESS Eoin
Born: Aberdeen, 13 December 1970
Height: 5'9" **Weight:** 11.10
Club Honours: SLC '89
International Honours: S: 18; B-2; U21-14
This attacking midfielder was an ever-present for Nottingham Forest until the end of October when he dropped down to the substitutes' bench. However, a groin injury then sidelined him for several months although he returned to action for the reserves during the closing stages of the campaign. Eoin was out of contract at the season's close and his future was unclear at the time of writing.
Aberdeen *(From Glasgow R juniors on 13/11/1987) SL 167+34/50 SLC 19+2/4 SC 14+2/3 Others 8+2/6*
Coventry C *(£1,750,000 on 24/2/1996) PL 28+11/1 FLC 1 FAC 4/2*
Aberdeen *(£700,000 on 3/7/1997) SL 108+3/29 SLC 8+1/1 SC 6/1*
Bradford C *(Free on 29/12/2000) P/FL 60+2/17 FLC 2 FAC 2*
Nottingham F *(Free on 9/8/2002) FL 54+32/7 FLC 3+4*

JEVONS Philip (Phil)
Born: Liverpool, 1 August 1979
Height: 5'11" **Weight:** 11.10
Club Honours: FAYC '98; Div 2 '05
Phil featured in every League Two match for Yeovil last term and finished the campaign as the leading goal-scorer in the division with a tally of 27. A lively striker with a great eye for goal, he was also deadly from the penalty spot. Phil

Phil Jevons

was one of five Yeovil players selected for the PFA League Two team of the season.
Everton *(From trainee on 10/11/1997) PL 2+6 FLC 1*
Grimsby T *(£150,000 + on 26/7/2001) FL 46+17/18 FLC 4/2 FAC 3/1*
Hull C *(Loaned on 5/9/2002) FL 13+11/3 FLC 1 FAC 1*
Yeovil T *(Free on 21/7/2004) FL 45+1/27 FLC 2 FAC 4/2*

JIHAI Sun
Born: Dalian, China, 30 September 1977
Height: 5'10" **Weight:** 10.12
International Honours: China
This versatile Manchester City midfielder had the misfortune to suffer a bad knee injury in the game against Chelsea last October and this ruled him out of action for the rest of the season. Jihai can play at left back, right back or in midfield and City sorely missed the option of having him around the squad. With his contract due to expire in the summer City offered the popular utility player an extension to his current deal.
Crystal Palace *(£500,000 from Dalian Wanda, China on 10/9/1998) FL 22+1 FLC 1 FAC 1 (£500,000 to Dalian Wanda, China on 27/7/1999)*
Manchester C *(£2,000,000 on 26/2/2002) P/FL 60+14/3 FLC 4 FAC 4 Others 5/1*

JOACHIM Julian Kevin
Born: Boston, 20 September 1974
Height: 5'6" **Weight:** 12.2
International Honours: E: U21-9; Yth; (UEFA-U18 '93)
Fleet-footed Julian looked the part in his early games with Leeds when he partnered both Michael Ricketts and Brian Deane. He finally got off the mark when he stabbed the ball in from close range for the final goal in the 3-0 win against his former club, Coventry, in September. His only other Championship goal came in the 3-2 Boxing Day victory at Sunderland. With the arrival of David Healy and Rob Hulse, Julian's opportunities became more limited and he was loaned to Walsall where he rediscovered his scoring form with a hat-trick against promotion contenders Hull City.
Leicester C *(From trainee on 15/9/1992) P/FL 77+22/25 FLC 7+2/3 FAC 4+1/1 Others 4+2/2*
Aston Villa *(£1,500,000 on 24/2/1996) PL 90+51/39 FLC 10+1/3 FAC 8+4/2 Others 6+3/1*
Coventry C *(Signed on 11/7/2001) FL 41+15/11 FLC 1 FAC 4/3*
Leeds U *(Free on 2/7/2004) FL 10+17/2 FLC 3 FAC 0+1*
Walsall *(Loaned on 24/3/2005) FL 8/6*

JOB Josephe-Desire
Born: Lyon, France, 1 December 1977
Height: 5'10" **Weight:** 11.3
Club Honours: FLC '04
International Honours: Cameroon: 48 (ANC '00)
Josephe-Desire was another Middlesbrough squad player who, perhaps, would not have played as many games had it not been for the club's incredible injury list. Always capable of scoring goals he found the back of the net on seven occasions. In early April he returned from international duty with a knee injury which required corrective surgery. He had played in Cameroon's World Cup qualifying game against Sudan and was ruled out for the remainder of the season after loose bone was removed from his knee.
Middlesbrough *(£3,000,000 from RC Lens, France, ex Lyon, on 7/8/2000) PL 62+29/16 FLC 4+4/1 FAC 4+1/2 Others 4+2/2*

JOHANSSON Andreas
Born: Vanersborg, Sweden, 5 July 1978
Height: 5'10" **Weight:** 12.0
International Honours: Sweden: 12
Wigan Athletic recruited the Sweden international on a three-and-a-half year deal during the January transfer window. Small but strong and difficult to shake off

Nils-Eric Johansson

the ball, the left-sided player is at his best when playing behind the two main strikers. Andreas was limited to just one appearance from the bench last term, but has been acclimatising in preparation for the Latics' Premiership campaign in 2005-06.
Wigan Ath *(Signed from Djurgaarden, Sweden, on 7/1/2005) FL 0+1*

JOHANSSON Jonatan (JJ)
Lillebror
Born: Stockholm, Sweden, 16 August 1975
Height: 6'1" **Weight:** 12.8
Club Honours: SPL '99, '00; SLC '99
International Honours: Finland: 64; U21-7
JJ had his most successful campaign for some time, featuring in most of Charlton's games throughout the season and becoming the most capped player in the history of the club. Although used mainly as a striker in the past, JJ played the majority of his games wide on the left in a five-man midfield. He is no stranger to this role, as it is where he usually plays for his country. JJ is an excellent crosser of the ball, and worked hard, using his pace to get behind the opposition defence to support the lone striker. He found the net on four occasions, two of those coming in the 4-0 home win over Norwich City in November. He is very quick and possesses a powerful shot and is able to set up goals for other players using his pace and ability to turn a defender.
Glasgow Rgrs *(From FC Flora Tallinn, Estonia, ex TPS Turku, on 13/8/1997) SL 22+25/14 SLC 4/1 SC 2+4/3 Others 9+8/7*
Charlton Ath *(£3,250,000 + on 1/8/2000) PL 89+55/27 FLC 7+2/3 FAC 5+3/2*

JOHANSSON Nils-Eric
Born: Stockholm, Sweden, 13 January 1980
Height: 6'1" **Weight:** 12.7
Club Honours: FLC '02
International Honours: Sweden: 3; U21-21
Although Nils-Eric received several opportunities in his preferred position of centre back he failed to establish himself as a dominant player for Blackburn last term, losing out when Aaron Mokoena and Ryan Nelsen were signed. Instead he found himself playing at left back and although he produced some useful performances he was eventually replaced by Dominic Matteo.
Blackburn Rov *(£2,700,000 from Nuremburg, Germany, ex Brommapojkarna, AIK Solna, Bayern Munich, on 5/10/2001) PL 59+27 FLC 8+2/1 FAC 8+2/1 Others 4*

JOHN Collins
Born: Zwandru, Liberia, 17 October 1985
Height: 6'0" **Weight:** 12.11
International Honours: Holland: U21; Yth
An opportunist striker with an eye for goal, Collins was in fine form for Fulham late in the season, scoring a well-taken goal at Chelsea and a vital strike in the next game against Everton. A confident player who believes in his own ability he won a number of caps at U21 level for Holland, scoring against England at Pride Park just days after claiming an FA Cup goal on the same ground. Strong and quick off the mark, he was used as a substitute on more than 20 occasions in 2004-05.
Fulham *(£600,000 from Twente Enschede, Holland on 31/1/2004) PL 16+19/8 FLC 0+2 FAC 1+4/2*

JOHN Stern
Born: Tunapuna, Trinidad, 30 October 1976
Height: 6'1" **Weight:** 12.12
International Honours: Trinidad & Tobago
Stern made just three Premiership appearances as substitute before Birmingham opted to sign Dwight Yorke which forced his exit to Coventry City. Although suffering an injury soon after arriving at Highfield Road, he returned to the side some six weeks later. Stern took some time to settle in with the Sky Blues,

Stern John

but overcame his critics with a strong vein of form which saw him net several excellent goals including the winner at Reading and superb strikes against Wolves and Derby.
Nottingham F *(£1,500,000 + from Columbus Crew, USA on 22/11/1999) FL 49+23/18 FLC 3/2 FAC 4+1*
Birmingham C *(Free on 8/2/2002) P/FL 42+35/16 FLC 2/3 FAC 1+2/1 Others 3/1*
Coventry C *(£200,000 on 14/9/2004) FL 25+5/11 FLC 1 FAC 2/1*

JOHN-BAPTISTE Alexander (Alex) Aaron
Born: Sutton-in-Ashfield, 31 January 1986
Height: 5'11" **Weight:** 11.7
This highly promising youngster signed an extension to his contract for Mansfield in the summer of 2004 and started last season in his usual position in the centre of a four-man defence. When the midfield was deemed to require a bit more steel, Alex moved to a position in the centre of the park, but following a change in management he was restored to the defence and handed the club captaincy for the FA Cup tie with Colchester. At the age of 18 years and 287 days this made him the youngest skipper in the club's history.
Mansfield T *(From trainee on 5/2/2003) FL 59+3/1 FLC 1 FAC 2/1 Others 5+1*

JOHNSEN Jean **Ronny**
Born: Norway, 10 June 1969
Height: 6'2" **Weight:** 13.2
Club Honours: PL '97, '99, '01; CS '97; FAC '99; UEFACL '99
International Honours: Norway: 61
Ronny was manager Graeme Souness' first signing for Newcastle when he joined as a free agent in September on a short-term contract. A composed central defender who is calm under pressure and comfortable on the ball, he found that injuries limited his opportunities and he only made five appearances, his Premiership debut coming against his former club Manchester United in November. His contract expired at the end of 2004 and he subsequently announced his retirement from the game.
Manchester U *(£1,200,000 from Besiktas, Turkey, ex Lyn, Lillestrom, on 26/7/1996) PL 85+14/7 FLC 3 FAC 8+2/1 Others 35+3/1*
Aston Villa *(Free on 29/8/2002) PL 46+3/1 FLC 5+1 FAC 1*
Newcastle U *(Free on 17/9/2004) PL 3 FLC 2*

JOHNSON Adam
Born: Sunderland, 14 July 1987
Height: 5'9" **Weight:** 9.11
Club Honours: FAYC '04
Adam, a natural left-sided midfielder, was thrilled to have been on the substitutes' bench in one of the biggest-ever games in Middlesbrough's long history, the UEFA Cup tie at the Riverside against Sporting Lisbon in March. Manager Steve McClaren gave him his debut a week later in the second leg when he replaced Doriva for the final 11 minutes of the game.
Middlesbrough *(From trainee on 12/5/2005) Others 0+1*

JOHNSON Andrew (Andy)
Born: Bedford, 10 February 1981
Height: 5'9" **Weight:** 9.7
International Honours: E: 2; Yth
Andy had a superb season in the Premiership for Crystal Palace, featuring in almost every game and scoring 21 goals, although many came from the penalty spot. The pacy striker was rewarded for his efforts with the club's 'Player of the Year' award and he also made the PFA Premiership team of the season. Further honours came his way when he made his England debut from the bench against Holland in February and he won his first full cap against the USA during the summer. Andy signed a new long-term contract for the Eagles, but at the time of writing there was much speculation about his future.
Birmingham C *(From juniors on 11/3/1998) FL 44+39/8 FLC 6+9/5 FAC 1 Others 1+3*
Crystal Palace *(£750,000 on 5/8/2002) P/FL 104+3/59 FLC 6/7 FAC 5 Others 3/1*

JOHNSON Andrew (Andy) James
Born: Bristol, 2 May 1974
Height: 6'0" **Weight:** 13.0
Club Honours: Div 1 '98
International Honours: W: 15; E: Yth
An aggressive midfielder who enjoys a challenge, Andy once more worked overtime in West Bromwich Albion's engine room until a serious knee injury ruled him out from mid-January. Prior to that he had produced some excellent displays in the centre of the park, although a lack of goals again let him down. He added to his collection of caps for Wales, but announced his retirement from international football in October.
Norwich C *(From trainee on 4/3/1992) P/FL 56+10/13 FLC 6+1/2 FAC 2*
Nottingham F *(£2,200,000 on 4/7/1997) P/FL 102+17/9 FLC 6+1/1 FAC 2*
West Bromwich A *(£200,000 on 19/9/2001) P/FL 113+11/7 FLC 4+1 FAC 7/1*

JOHNSON Bradley (Brad) Paul
Born: Hackney, 28 April 1987
Height: 6'0" **Weight:** 12.10
A quick, strong and energetic left-footed midfielder, Brad spent much of last season developing in Cambridge United's reserve and youth teams. He received a call-up to the first-team squad for the game against Scunthorpe in December and came off the bench to make his debut in senior football in the closing stages. Brad was reported to have signed for Northampton Town during the summer.
Cambridge U *(From juniors on 17/11/2004) FL 0+1*

JOHNSON Damien Michael
Born: Lisburn, 18 November 1978
Height: 5'9" **Weight:** 11.2
Club Honours: FLC '02
International Honours: NI: 43; U21-11; Yth
An unsung hero for Birmingham City, Damien's high-energy performances and aggression in the tackle earned him the tag of 'Mr Reliable'. He rose to the challenge after Jesper Gronkjaer and Jermaine Pennant arrived at St Andrew's and played in a variety of positions. After Robbie Savage's sale, he was particularly useful in central midfield, where he closed down the opposition and passed the ball accurately.
Blackburn Rov *(From trainee on 2/2/1996) P/FL 43+17/3 FLC 12+3/1 FAC 3+4 Others 0+1*
Nottingham F *(Loaned on 29/1/1998) FL 5+1*
Birmingham C *(Signed on 8/3/2002) P/FL 104+5/3 FLC 1+2 FAC 5 Others 1*

JOHNSON David Anthony
Born: Kingston, Jamaica, 15 August 1976
Height: 5'6" **Weight:** 12.3
Club Honours: FAYC '95; Div 2 '97
International Honours: Jamaica: 4; E: B-1; Sch
David had a disappointing season with Nottingham Forest for although he started out as captain he struggled to find his form. He had his best spell in November when he netted in two consecutive Championship games but was dropped after the following match and then had a public falling out with the manager. Not long afterwards he was loaned to Sheffield United, but the return of Steve Kabba and the signing of Danny Webber meant he was restricted to a few lively appearances from the bench.
Manchester U *(From trainee on 1/7/1994)*
Bury *(Free on 5/7/1995) FL 72+25/18 FLC 8+3/4 FAC 1+1 Others 3+2/1*
Ipswich T *(£800,000 on 14/11/1997) P/FL 121+10/55 FLC 13/5 FAC 7/2 Others 7*

Nottingham F *(£3,000,000 + on 12/1/2001) FL 110+21/43 FLC 9/2 FAC 2+2 Others 2/2*
Sheffield Wed *(Loaned on 5/2/2002) FL 7/2*
Burnley *(Loaned on 12/3/2002) FL 8/5*
Sheffield U *(Loaned on 11/3/2005) FL 0+4*

JOHNSON Edward (Eddie) William
Born: Chester, 20 September 1984
Height: 5'10" **Weight:** 13.7
Club Honours: FAYC '03
International Honours: E: Yth
This Manchester United youngster joined Coventry City on a season-long loan deal and manager Peter Reid made him his first choice striker at the start of 2004-05. Eddie scored a good goal on his debut against Sunderland but otherwise the stocky but skilful front man struggled to find the net. However, he always put himself about and showed strong energy levels. Eddie lost his place when Stern John arrived in September but returned when John was injured. After Micky Adams' arrival he made only three substitute appearances, but was hampered by achilles problems.
Manchester U *(From trainee on 4/10/2001) FLC 0+1*
Coventry C *(Loaned on 16/7/2004) FL 20+6/5 FLC 1+1 FAC 0+1*

JOHNSON Gavin
Born: Stowmarket, 10 October 1970
Height: 5'11" **Weight:** 12.0
Club Honours: Div 2 '92; Div 3 '97
Left-sided specialist Gavin defied his advancing years to enjoy one of the best seasons of his career last term. He put a nightmarish injury spell behind him to score 11 goals for Colchester, his biggest haul in any one campaign. Gavin was sidelined for more than a year with a broken leg, before making a big impact towards the end of the 2003-04 season. He improved still further last term, operating as a left-sided midfielder, but also occasionally as a left back and in central midfield.
Ipswich T *(From trainee on 1/3/1989) P/FL 114+18/11 FLC 10+1/2 FAC 12+1/2 Others 3+1/1*
Luton T *(Free on 4/7/1995) FL 4+1*
Wigan Ath *(£15,000 on 15/12/1995) FL 82+2/8 FLC 4 FAC 3 Others 1*
Dunfermline Ath *(Free on 1/7/1998) SL 18 SC 0+1*
Colchester U *(Free on 12/11/1999) FL 134+13/13 FLC 6+1/1 FAC 8 Others 3+2*

JOHNSON Glen McLeod
Born: Greenwich, London, 23 August 1984
Height: 6'0" **Weight:** 12.0
Club Honours: FLC '05; PL '05
International Honours: E: 4; U21-12; Yth
The 2004-05 season was a step sideways for Glen Johnson as the young England right back was superseded by Jose Mourinho's protégé, the classy Paulo Ferreira. Glen was limited to sporadic appearances for the majority of the season as his rival fitted seamlessly into a defensive unit which shattered all existing records. However, Glen did have the satisfaction of appearing in his first major domestic final and made a telling contribution too – his long throw being turned home by Didier Drogba for Chelsea's second goal in their Carling Cup triumph over Liverpool. Ferreira was sidelined by injury in March, and Glen filled-in admirably for the season's climax, showing one memorable piece of skill at Southampton by dribbling past four defenders and laying on a goal for Eidur Gudjohnsen.
West Ham U *(From trainee on 25/8/2001) PL 14+1 FAC 0+1*
Millwall *(Loaned on 17/10/2002) FL 7+1*
Chelsea *(£6,000,000 on 22/7/2003) PL 30+6/3 FLC 5+1 FAC 4 Others 12+3/1*

JOHNSON Jemal Pierre
Born: New Jersey, USA, 3 May 1984
Height: 5'8" **Weight:** 11.5
This quick-footed young striker was added to the Blackburn Rovers' first-team squad around the turn of the year and scored on his first full start in the FA Cup fourth round tie against Colchester. Jemal showed he could hold the ball under pressure and link the play.
Blackburn Rov *(From trainee on 10/5/2002) PL 0+3 FAC 1+2/1*

JOHNSON Jermaine
Born: Kingston, Jamaica, 25 June 1980
Height: 5'9" **Weight:** 11.5
International Honours: Jamaica
Jermaine had a frustrating season at Boundary Park when he struggled to establish himself. Although an extremely skilful and pacy front man, his finishing was wayward at times and he underachieved with a tally of just four goals. He suffered a knee injury and had his contract paid up in February before new manager Ronnie Moore offered him a second chance. Jermaine re-signed on a pay-as-you-play deal but made just one more start before being released again in May.
Bolton W *(£750,000 from Tivoli Gardens, Jamaica on 19/9/2001) PL 4+8 FLC 3 FAC 1+1*
Oldham Ath *(Free on 28/11/2003) FL 31+8/9 FLC 2 FAC 1/1 Others 1*

JOHNSON Lee David
Born: Newmarket, 7 June 1981
Height: 5'6" **Weight:** 10.7
Club Honours: FAT '02; NC '03; Div 2 '05
International Honours: E: SP-5
Lee was a key figure in the Yeovil side last term when he was a near ever-present and netted a total of 11 goals in all competitions. Playing alongside Darren Way in the centre of midfield he was very much the heartbeat of the side and demonstrated a phenomenal work rate. One of his best performances came in the Carling Cup tie against Plymouth when he netted a great hat-trick. Lee was one of five Yeovil players selected for the PFA League Two team of the season.
Watford *(From trainee on 3/10/1998)*
Brighton & Hove A *(Free on 4/9/2000) Others 1/1*
Brentford *(Free on 22/3/2001)*
Yeovil T *(Free on 12/7/2001) FL 89/12 FLC 3/3 FAC 8/1 Others 2+1*

JOHNSON Leon Dean
Born: Shoreditch, 10 May 1981
Height: 6'0" **Weight:** 12.4
This assured central defender made a brief run of appearances for Gillingham in the autumn without ever letting the team down. However, he only featured on one occasion in the second half of the campaign, coming off the bench in the 3-1 win at Rotherham in March. Leon was out of contract in the summer and his future was uncertain at the time of writing.
Southend U *(From trainee on 17/11/1999) FL 43+5/3 FLC 1 FAC 1+3 Others 8*
Gillingham *(Free on 15/8/2002) FL 32+14 FLC 2 FAC 1+1*

JOHNSON Michael Owen
Born: Nottingham, 4 July 1973
Height: 5'11" **Weight:** 11.12
Club Honours: AIC '95
International Honours: Jamaica: 14
Michael's commitment never flags and he is able to shrug off most of the bruises that come from playing in central defence. He challenges and competes for everything, an attitude greatly appreciated by other members of the team. A more serious injury, in Derby's FA Cup replay against Fulham at Craven Cottage, kept him out for seven games. Irritatingly, damaged knee ligaments stemmed from a collision with co-defender Pablo Mills. He came back well but the knee went again in the first leg of the play-off semi-final against Preston at Deepdale.
Notts Co *(From trainee on 9/7/1991) FL 102+5 FLC 9 FAC 4 Others 15+1*

Birmingham C *(£225,000 on 1/9/1995) P/FL 227+35/13 FLC 25+6/5 FAC 6+4 Others 11*
Derby Co *(Signed on 15/8/2003) FL 74+1/2 FLC 1 FAC 3 Others 1*

JOHNSON Richard Mark
Born: Newcastle, Australia, 27 April 1974
Height: 5'11" **Weight:** 12.4
Club Honours: Div 2 '98
International Honours: Australia: 1
Richard established a useful partnership with Marcus Bean for Queen's Park Rangers in the opening stages of the 2004-05 season, before joining the injury list at Loftus Road. In October he joined MK Dons on loan, where he linked play well and showed some impressive shooting ability from distance. Richard's contract was cancelled in January and he returned to Australia to sign for Newcastle Jets of the new Hyundai A League.
Watford *(From trainee on 11/5/1992) P/FL 210+32/20 FLC 14+1/1 FAC 13+2/1 Others 5+1*
Northampton T *(Loaned on 7/2/2003) FL 5+1/1*
Colchester U *(Free on 27/10/2003) Others 0+1*
Stoke C *(Free on 17/11/2003) FL 3+4 FAC 1+1*
Queens Park Rgrs *(Free on 18/2/2004) FL 16+1 FLC 1*
MK Dons *(Loaned on 28/10/2004) FL 2 Others 0+1*

JOHNSON Roger
Born: Ashford, 28 April 1983
Height: 6'3" **Weight:** 11.0
Roger had a real season of two halves at Wycombe in 2004-05. He was unsettled early on, when he was sometimes dropped from his position as a central defender or asked to play out of position at left back. However, he enjoyed a new lease of life when John Gorman took charge, going on to captain the side. His gritty, inspirational performances have made him hugely popular with the fans who love to see him pushed up as a central striker when the Chairboys are chasing the game. Roger finished the campaign as the club's second-top scorer with seven goals, many of which came from far-post headers.
Wycombe W *(From trainee on 10/7/2001) FL 101+11/12 FLC 4 FAC 5/1 Others 6+3/1*

JOHNSON Seth Art Maurice
Born: Birmingham, 12 March 1979
Height: 5'10" **Weight:** 11.0
International Honours: E: 1; U21-15; Yth
It was another frustrating season at Elland Road for former England midfielder Seth. Bedevilled by injuries since his big-money move from Derby, the 2004-05 season was no exception. He finally made the long haul back from a serious knee injury with his first start of the campaign against Wolves in April. A fortnight later he scored in the 1-1 draw at Queen's Park Rangers, but was then left out of the side until the end of the season.
Crewe Alex *(From trainee on 12/7/1996) FL 89+4/6 FLC 5 FAC 2/1 Others 0+3*
Derby Co *(£3,000,000 on 21/5/1999) PL 73/2 FLC 6+1 FAC 0+1*
Leeds U *(£7,000,000 + on 19/10/2001) P/FL 43+11/4 FLC 1 FAC 3+1*

JOHNSON Simon Ainsley
Born: West Bromwich, 9 March 1983
Height: 5'9" **Weight:** 12.0
International Honours: E: Yth
All of this young striker's appearances for Leeds in 2004-05 came in the space of nine days. He featured in the side knocked out of the Carling Cup by Portsmouth in October, kept his place for the Championship home defeat against Wigan and came off the bench against Burnley the following Wednesday, A speedy forward who found the net regularly at reserve level, he earlier spent time on loan at Sunderland and later in the campaign he was farmed out again, this time to Doncaster. Although initially used on the right-hand side of midfield, when switched to a role as an out-and-out striker he responded with two goals against MK Dons. Simon finished the season on loan once more at Barnsley, where he again played mainly as a wide man.
Leeds U *(From trainee on 7/7/2000) P/FL 3+8 FLC 1*
Hull C *(Loaned on 12/8/2002) FL 4+8/2 FLC 0+1*
Blackpool *(Loaned on 13/12/2003) FL 3+1/1 FAC 0+1*
Sunderland *(Loaned on 10/9/2004) FL 1+4*
Doncaster Rov *(Loaned on 6/12/2004) FL 8+3/3*
Barnsley *(Loaned on 24/2/2005) FL 10+1/2*

JOHNSON Thomas (Tommy)
Born: Newcastle, 15 January 1971
Height: 5'11" **Weight:** 12.8
Club Honours: FLC '96; SPD '01; SLC '00; SC '01
International Honours: E: U21-7
This veteran striker was again dogged by injuries at Gillingham last term, making just a handful of appearances and scoring twice, against Crewe and Nottingham Forest in November. His contract was eventually cancelled by mutual consent and he joined the coaching staff at Bramall Lane, also registering as a player. Tommy made just one appearance for the Blades, featuring against Rotherham at the end of February.
Notts Co *(From trainee on 19/1/1989) FL 100+18/47 FLC 7+2/5 FAC 3+2/1 Others 14+3/4*
Derby Co *(£1,300,000 on 12/3/1992) FL 91+7/30 FLC 9+1/2 FAC 5/1 Others 16/8*
Aston Villa *(£1,450,000 on 6/1/1995) PL 38+19/13 FLC 5/2 FAC 5+2/1 Others 1+1/1*
Glasgow Celtic *(£2,400,000 on 27/3/1997) SL 23+12/18 SLC 3+1/3 SC 2+4 Others 0+3/1*
Everton *(Loaned on 24/9/1999) PL 0+3*
Sheffield Wed *(Free on 8/9/2001) FL 8/3 FLC 1*
Kilmarnock *(Free on 22/12/2001) SL 7+3/7 SC 1+1*
Gillingham *(Free on 7/8/2002) FL 20+29/7 FLC 0+4/1 FAC 2+1/1*
Sheffield U *(Free on 10/2/2005) FL 1*

JONES Bradley (Brad)
Born: Armadale, Australia, 19 March 1982
Height: 6'3" **Weight:** 12.3
Club Honours: AMC '04
International Honours: Australia: U23-4; Yth
With senior 'keepers Mark Schwarzer and Carlo Nash both struggling with injuries, Brad was recalled by Middlesbrough from his long-term loan with Blackpool where he had starred for the Seasiders in a dozen or so games. He was informed he was in goal for the Riverside game against Arsenal in April only 20 minutes before the kick-off and played a total of five Premiership games – conceding only three goals - before he succumbed to chicken-pox and the return from injury of Mark Schwarzer.
Middlesbrough *(From trainee on 26/3/1999) PL 6 FAC 1*
Stockport Co *(Loaned on 13/12/2002) FL 1*
Blackpool *(Loaned on 4/11/2003) FL 5 Others 2*
Blackpool *(Loaned on 5/11/2004) FL 12*

JONES David Frank Llwyd
Born: Southport, 4 November 1984
Height: 5'11" **Weight:** 10.10
Club Honours: FAYC '03
International Honours: E: U21-1; Yth
A hard-working young midfielder David has made giant strides at Old Trafford in recent seasons, and last term he made his senior bow in the Reds' goalless FA Cup third round tie against non-league Exeter City in January. He will be looking to feature again at first-team level in 2005-06.
Manchester U *(From trainee on 18/7/2003) FLC 0+1 FAC 1*

ONES Gary Roy
rn: Birkenhead, 3 June 1977
ight: 5'10" **Weight:** 12.0
ter missing the start of the 2004-05 ason through injury, Gary returned with ang, netting a double for Rochdale in eir 2-0 home win over Southend to ng Dale their first points. Although still ubled by an old foot injury, he re-tablished himself as an automatic oice in the centre of midfield, while a mbination of his powerful shooting d responsibility as penalty taker made n the side's second-highest scorer. ary has now played 200 Football ague games for the club during two ells at Spotland.
vansea C *(Signed from Caernarfon T on /7/1997) FL 3+5 FLC 0+1*
chdale *(Free on 15/1/1998) FL 123+17/22 C 4+1 FAC 6+3 Others 7+2/3*
rnsley *(£175,000 on 30/11/2001) FL 56/2 C 1*
chdale *(Free on 13/11/2003) FL 65/12 C 1 FAC 4 Others 1*

ONES Gary Steven
orn: Chester, 10 May 1975
eight: 6'3" **Weight:** 14.0
ersatile, tall and tenacious, Gary is omfortable playing in defence, midfield nd up front. A good team man, he was gain generous in sharing his experience eely to assist his younger colleagues and pplied himself to perform to the best of is ability in whatever role he found imself called upon to fulfil. Gary's resence has always been effective in ausing confusion in the opposition anks, but a troublesome toe injury everely limited his first-team ppearances in the 2004-05 season. Gary urned down a loan move to Chester in Aarch, but at his own request and nowing that he would not be retained t the end of the season, he asked for his ontract with Tranmere to be cancelled in arly May. Off the field, Gary has an nterest in an electrical contracting usiness.
ranmere Rov *(From trainee on 5/7/1993) L 117+61/28 FLC 17+4/3 FAC 9+2/3 Others +1*
Nottingham F *(Free on 3/7/2000) FL ?4+12/2 FLC 1+1 FAC 1*
ranmere Rov *(Free on 29/8/2002) FL 31+11/16 FLC 4 FAC 9+1/2 Others 4+1/2*

JONES Graeme Anthony
Born: Gateshead, 13 March 1970
Height: 6'0" **Weight:** 13.0
Club Honours: Div 3 '97; AMC '99
Graeme was signed by Bury to add experience, strength and physical presence to the forward line. Able to hold up the ball well, he was seen as the big man that the other forwards could play off, and his initial introduction to the team couldn't have been better as he scored the Shakers' third goal after coming off the bench in the opening game against Yeovil. However, injuries kept him on the sidelines for most of the next four months and at the end of the year his contract was terminated by mutual consent. He subsequently joined Clyde, netting the winner on his debut against Airdrie United and featuring regularly for the rest of the season.
Doncaster Rov *(£10,000 from Bridlington T on 2/8/1993) FL 80+12/26 FLC 4+1/1 FAC 2+1/2 Others 5/1*
Wigan Ath *(£150,000 on 8/7/1996) FL 76+20/44 FLC 4+3/1 FAC 4/1 Others 6+2/6*
St Johnstone *(£100,000 on 19/11/1999) SL 31+10/7 SLC 2 SC 1*
Southend U *(£35,000 on 30/7/2002) FL 18+3/2 FLC 1 FAC 2+1 Others 1/1*
Boston U *(Free on 21/3/2003) FL 33+3/7 FLC 0+1*
Bury *(Free on 6/7/2004) FL 1+2/1*

JONES Kenwyne Joel
Born: Trinidad, 5 October 1984
Height: 6'2" **Weight:** 13.6
International Honours: Trinidad & Tobago: 18
This Trinidad & Tobago striker joined Saints during the summer of 2004, but had not made an appearance in the first team before he was loaned out to Sheffield Wednesday in December. Kenwyne proved to be a pacy, well built striker and made a terrific impact at Hillsborough, scoring in his first six games, but also showing strong leadership of the line and a high work rate. On his return to St Mary's he featured in a couple of games at the turn of the year before joining Stoke on loan, where he again found the net on his debut. However, he found goals harder to come by after that and only added two more before the end of the campaign.
Southampton *(Signed from W-Connection on 20/5/2004) PL 1+1 FAC 0+1*
Sheffield Wed *(Loaned on 17/12/2004) FL 7/7*
Stoke C *(Loaned on 14/2/2005) FL 13/3*

JONES Lee
Born: Pontypridd, 9 August 1970
Height: 6'3" **Weight:** 14.4
Club Honours: AMC '94; '04
This experienced 'keeper was first choice for Blackpool for most of the 2004-05 campaign. He was absent for a spell in mid-season as a result of an injury, when namesake Brad Jones took over, but returned to produce some excellent form

Mark Jones

in the closing stages. Lee was rewarded for his efforts when he was offered an extension to his contract in the summer.
Swansea C *(£7,500 from AFC Porth on 24/3/1994) FL 6 Others 1*
Bristol Rov *(Signed on 7/3/1998) FL 76 FLC 6 FAC 7 Others 4*
Stockport Co *(£50,000 on 19/7/2000) FL 72+3 FLC 5 FAC 4*
Blackpool *(Free on 8/8/2003) FL 50 FLC 3 FAC 4 Others 5*

JONES Mark Alan
Born: Wrexham, 15 August 1983
Height: 5'11" **Weight:** 10.10
Club Honours: AMC '05
International Honours: W: U21-2
This central midfielder showed fine control and the ability to find a colleague with a pinpoint pass in his displays for Wrexham last season. He scored four goals for the Dragons, the highlight of which was a superb 20-yard strike in the home game with Chesterfield in December. Mark was voted as the club's 'Young Player of the Season' for 2004-05.
Wrexham *(From trainee on 9/7/2003) FL 17+23/4 FLC 0+1 FAC 1+1 Others 7+2/2*

JONES Michael
Born: Liverpool, 3 December 1987
Height: 6'3" **Weight:** 13.0
This young Wrexham goalkeeper made his Football League debut when replacing Xavi Valero at Chesterfield last January. Although just turned 17 Michael coped adequately with everything thrown at him. The first-year scholar broke a bone in his arm as a result of a freak training ground accident in February, however, he was back to take his seat on the bench for the FAW Premier Cup final against Swansea City at the end of the season.
Wrexham *(Trainee) FL 0+1*

JONES Nathan Jason
Born: Rhondda, 28 May 1973
Height: 5'7" **Weight:** 10.12
Club Honours: Div 3 '01
With the majority of his appearances during 2004-05 coming from the bench, Nathan's involvement in Brighton's battle against relegation from the Championship was largely that of a substitute. Kept out of the side by the likes of Darren Currie, Dan Harding and Kerry Mayo, the winger or full back must have found it a frustrating experience, but he remained an excellent character to have in the squad. Always enthusiastic and keen to get forward at every opportunity, Nathan was released at the end of the season after five years at the Withdean Stadium.
Luton T *(£10,000 from Merthyr Tydfil on 30/6/1995. Freed on 20/12/1995)*
Southend U *(Free from Numancia, Spain on 5/8/1997) FL 82+17/2 FLC 6+2 FAC 3+1/1 Others 0+3*
Scarborough *(Loaned on 25/3/1999) FL 8+1*
Brighton & Hove A *(Free on 7/7/2000) FL 109+50/7 FLC 5+3/1 FAC 6+1 Others 8+1*

JONES Paul Steven
Born: Chirk, 18 April 1967
Height: 6'3" **Weight:** 14.8
International Honours: W: 43
Paul was first-choice 'keeper for Wolves in the opening matches of the 2004-05 campaign before making way for Andy Oakes. In December he moved out on loan to Watford and after a nervous start he established himself as a commanding presence behind the defence. His experience was particularly valuable in the Carling Cup semi-final against Liverpool, which allowed Paul a sentimental return to the club he supported as a boy.
Wolverhampton W *(£40,000 from Kidderminster Hrs on 23/7/1991) FL 33 FLC 2 FAC 5 Others 4*
Stockport Co *(£60,000 on 25/7/1996) FL 46 FLC 11 FAC 4 Others 4*
Southampton *(£900,000 on 28/7/1997) PL 192+1 FLC 16+1 FAC 11+1 Others 1*
Liverpool *(Loaned on 9/1/2004) PL 2*
Wolverhampton W *(£250,000 on 29/1/2004) P/FL 26*
Watford *(Loaned on 24/12/2004) FL 9 FLC 2*

JONES Robert (Rob) William
Born: Stockton, 30 November 1979
Height: 6'7" **Weight:** 12.2
This tall centre back joined Grimsby Town on a 12-month contract after being released by Stockport. However, although he began the campaign in the starting line-up, he was injured in his second outing against Boston United and once fit again found it difficult to regain a permanent place in the team. Nevertheless, Rob was reported to have signed a further contract with the Mariners at the end of the campaign.
Stockport Co *(Signed from Gateshead on 9/4/2003) FL 14+2/2 FLC 2 Others 1*
Macclesfield T *(Loaned on 31/10/2003) FL 1*
Grimsby T *(Free on 30/7/2004) FL 18+2/1 FAC 1 Others 1*

JONES Stephen (Steve) Graham
Born: Londonderry, 25 October 1976
Height: 5'4" **Weight:** 10.9
International Honours: NI: 16
Steve worked hard once again for Crewe Alexandra in 2004-05 and finished as the club's second-highest scorer with 13 goals in all competitions. The most important of these was the winning strike against Coventry in the final game of the season, which ensured that Crewe retained their place in the Championship. A regular in the Northern Ireland squad, he has good pace and works extremely hard as the leader of the attack.
Blackpool *(Free from Chadderton on 30/10/1995)*
Bury *(Free on 23/8/1996. Free to Sligo Rov during 1997 close season)*
Crewe Alex *(£75,000 + from Leigh RMI, ex Bray W, Chorley, on 4/7/2001) FL 86+32/34 FLC 4+1/4 FAC 4+1/1 Others 2+2/1*
Rochdale *(Loaned on 5/2/2002) FL 6+3/1*

JONES Stuart Clive
Born: Bristol, 24 October 1977
Height: 6'1" **Weight:** 14.0
Stuart joined Doncaster Rovers in the summer of 2004 as cover for regular goalkeeper Andy Warrington. Apart from the LDV Vans Trophy game against Lincoln, the only other first-team action he saw came early in the new year when he had a brief run in the line-up. Stuart was then injured in training and did not fully recover before the end of the season when he was released.
Sheffield Wed *(£20,000 + from Weston super Mare on 26/3/1998)*
Torquay U *(£30,000 on 3/2/2000) FL 32 FLC 2 FAC 2 Others 1 (Free to Hereford U on 26/10/2001)*
Brighton & Hove A *(Free from Weston super Mare on 6/2/2004) FL 2+1*
Doncaster Rov *(Free on 6/8/2004) FL 3+1 Others 1*

JONES Stuart John
Born: Aberystwyth, 14 March 1984
Height: 6'0" **Weight:** 11.8
International Honours: W: U21-1; Yth
Despite starting in the opening League Two game of the 2004-05 season, this young defender featured in the line-up for just one more first-team game for Swansea, plus a few appearances from the substitutes' bench. Stuart missed the closing stages of the campaign after suffering sprained knee ligaments. He made his first appearance at U21 level for Wales against Azerbaijan last September.
Swansea C *(From trainee on 28/7/2003) FL 23+11 FLC 1 FAC 1 Others 2*

JONES William (Billy)
Born: Shrewsbury, 24 March 1987
Height: 5'11" **Weight:** 13.0
International Honours: E: Yth
Billy is another of the players on the books at Gresty Road who have developed through the club's youth set-up. Although illness and injury caused

him to miss some games he generally made good progress during the campaign. Billy is a versatile defender who distributes the ball accurately.
Crewe Alex *(From trainee on 13/7/2004) FL 13+4/1 FLC 2 FAC 1*

JONES William (Billy) Kenneth
Born: Chatham, 26 March 1983
Height: 6'0" **Weight:** 11.7
Billy found himself out of the first-team picture at Leyton Orient last term and in January he opted for a move to Kidderminster. He soon settled into the side at left back and proved particularly useful in dead-ball situations, although he didn't quite manage to find the net with any of his free kicks. He lost his place to Wayne Hatswell for a while, but forced his way back into the side before the end of the season.
Leyton Orient *(From trainee on 10/7/2001) FL 68+4 FLC 2 FAC 3+1 Others 0+1*
Kidderminster Hrs *(Free on 7/1/2005) FL 10+2*

JONSON Mattias
Born: Orebro, Sweden, 16 January 1974
Height: 5'11" **Weight:** 11.9
International Honours: Sweden: 46
Mattias is a regular member of the full Sweden international set-up and scored the controversial late goal in Euro 2004 which ensured a 2-2 draw against Denmark and eliminated Italy from the competition. An attacking midfield player, comfortable on either flank, he can also play as a striker. His robust and hard-working style is well suited to the English game as is his commitment and ability in the air. One of several Norwich players whose season was interrupted by a series of niggling injuries, he will be hoping to win a regular starting place in 2005-06.
Norwich C *(Signed from FC Brondby, Denmark, ex Helsingborg, on 10/8/2004) PL 19+9 FLC 1 FAC 1*

JORDAN Stephen (Steve) Robert
Born: Warrington, 6 March 1982
Height: 6'0" **Weight:** 11.13
Following injury to Manchester City's first-choice left back, Ben Thatcher, Steve established himself on the left-hand side of the back four last term and performed with distinction and maturity. In only his second full senior game he had the distinction of earning the 'Man of the Match' award for his display against Manchester United.
Manchester C *(From trainee on 11/3/1999) PL 19+3 FLC 0+2*
Cambridge U *(Loaned on 4/10/2002) FL 11 Others 3*

JORGENSEN Claus Beck
Born: Holstebro, Denmark, 27 April 1979
Height: 5'11" **Weight:** 11.0
International Honours: Faroe Islands: 5
After being told that he was surplus to requirements towards the end of the 2003-04 campaign, Claus worked his way back to become a regular member of the Coventry City squad by the end of last season. The winger was rarely seen during Peter Reid's reign but under Micky Adams he featured on either wing or as a midfield marker. A cracked rib kept him out for some time, but he scored three goals including a stunning 20-yard effort at Watford and a crucial late equaliser at Millwall. Claus stepped up to make his international debut for the Faroes during the season.
Bournemouth *(Free from AC Horsens, Denmark on 12/7/1999) FL 77+10/14 FLC 6/1 FAC 6 Others 1+1*
Bradford C *(Free on 23/7/2001) FL 41+9/12 FLC 2+1 FAC 1*
Coventry C *(Free on 5/8/2003) FL 15+10/3 FLC 1+2 FAC 0+2*
Bournemouth *(Loaned on 23/1/2004) FL 16+1*

[JOSEMI] GONZALEZ Jose Miguel
Born: Malaga, Spain, 15 November 1979
Height: 5'9" **Weight:** 12.8
Club Honours: UEFACL '05
A young right back drafted in by new Liverpool manager Rafael Benitez in the summer, Josemi started his Anfield career as first-choice right back. However, he looked a little out of his depth in the Premiership and was frequently substituted before losing his place to Steve Finnan in November. Shortly afterwards his season was brought to a premature end by a long-term knee injury. Although he returned to action for the final Premiership fixture, lack of match fitness ruled him out of consideration for the European Cup final.
Liverpool *(£2,000,000 from Malaga, Spain, on 29/7/2004) PL 13+2 FLC 1 Others 5+2*

JOSEPH Marc Ellis
Born: Leicester, 10 November 1976
Height: 6'0" **Weight:** 12.10
Marc was once again an important member of the Hull City squad last term as the club advanced towards their second successive promotion With Leon Cort establishing an outstanding central-defensive partnership with Damien Delaney, Marc was usually employed at right back. His season was severely hampered by injury though, as he suffered a hamstring problem, then a back injury and finally a groin strain.
Cambridge U *(From trainee on 23/5/1995) FL 136+17 FLC 7 FAC 5+2 Others 7+1*
Peterborough U *(Free on 3/7/2001) FL 60+1/2 FLC 3 FAC 6 Others 3*
Hull C *(£40,000 on 22/11/2002) FL 79+5/1 FLC 1 FAC 3 Others 1*

JOWSEY James Robert
Born: Filey, 24 November 1983
Height: 6'0" **Weight:** 12.4
After being released by Manchester United at the end of the 2003-04 campaign, this young 'keeper spent the summer months training with Rushden and then on trial at Scarborough. In September he joined Cambridge United on non-contract forms and made a single appearance in the 2-0 home defeat by Grimsby Town later that month before being released.
Manchester U *(From trainee on 27/11/2000. Freed during 2004 close season)*
Cambridge U *(Free from Scarborough on 10/9/2004) FL 1*

JOYNES Nathan
Born: Hoyland, 7 August 1985
Height: 6'1" **Weight:** 12.0
Nathan was a regular goal-scorer for Barnsley reserves last term and registered a hat-trick against Walsall at the beginning of April. Later that month he made his first-team debut when he came off the bench for the second half of the game at Port Vale. Nathan will be looking to gain more experience in the 2005-06 campaign.
Barnsley *(From trainee on 18/2/2005) FL 0+1*

JUDGE Alan Graham
Born: Kingsbury, 14 May 1960
Height: 5'11" **Weight:** 11.6
Oxford United's goalkeeping coach was again forced to step in during an injury crisis last season and produced an excellent performance in the 4-0 defeat at Southend in November. At 44 years of age, he thus extended his own record as the oldest player to appear for the club in senior football.
Luton T *(From juniors on 1/1/1978) FL 11 FLC 1*
Reading *(Loaned on 2/9/1982) FL 3*
Reading *(Free on 1/11/1982) FL 74 FLC 4 FAC 3 Others 3*
Oxford U *(£10,000 on 24/12/1984) FL 80 FLC 11 FAC 5 Others 4*
Lincoln C *(Loaned on 6/11/1985) FL 2*
Cardiff C *(Loaned on 20/10/1987) FL 8 Others 1*
Hereford U *(Free on 25/7/1991) FL 105 FLC 6 FAC 9 Others 8 (Freed during 1994 close season)*

Swindon T *(Free from Banbury U, ex Bromsgrove Rov, Kettering T, on 24/12/2002)*
Oxford U *(Free on 17/3/2003) FL 2*

JULIAN Alan John
Born: Ashford, 11 March 1983
Height: 6'2" **Weight:** 13.5
International Honours: NI: U21-1; Yth
This tall, steady Brentford goalkeeper made just one first-team appearance in 2004-05, starting the LDV Vans Trophy tie against MK Dons only to be replaced at half time. He was released by the Bees in February and subsequently signed a short-term contract with Stevenage. Alan made his debut for Northern Ireland at U21 level back in August and kept a clean sheet against Switzerland.
Brentford *(From trainee on 4/7/2001) FL 16 FLC 0+1 Others 2*

[JULIO CESAR] SANTOS-CORREIA Julio Cesar
Born: Sao Luis, Brazil, 18 November 1978
Height: 6'1" **Weight:** 12.4
An experienced centre half who is equally adept at left back, Julio Cesar arrived at Bolton in the summer of 2004. He made his debut in the opening-day victory over Charlton and despite impressing went on to make just four more Premiership starts, such was the strength in depth and competition for defensive places within the team during the season. He also made two Carling Cup appearances, scoring in the victory over Yeovil, before his brief time with Bolton ended when he was released at the end of the season.
Bolton W *(Free from Real Madrid, Spain, ex Real Sociedad, Real Valladolid, on 13/8/2004) PL 4+1 FLC 2/1*

[JUNIOR] GUIMARAES SANIBIO Jose Luis
Born: Fortaleza, Brazil, 20 July 1976
Height: 6'0" **Weight:** 13.0
Junior needed time to regain full fitness following the previous season's knee operation and was unable to break into Derby County's side as a first-choice striker. There were some useful interventions as a substitute, notably a winner against Wigan Athletic in the FA Cup, and the talented Brazilian also spent time on loan with Rotherham United in mid-season, creating a good impression. He was released at the end of his contract at Pride Park.
Walsall *(Free from Treze, Brazil, via loan spells at Beveren and Ajaccio, ex U.Espanola, Cordoba, Aleanza, Beveren, on 3/8/2002) FL 28+8/15 FLC 3/1 FAC 3*
Derby Co *(Free on 22/8/2003) FL 11+19/4 FLC 0+1 FAC 0+2/1*
Rotherham U *(Loaned on 24/10/2004) FL 12/2*

JUPP Duncan Alan
Born: Guildford, 25 January 1975
Height: 6'0" **Weight:** 12.12
International Honours: S: U21-9
Duncan began last term at right back for Southend, but then lost his place in the side and it was only when Lewis Hunt was injured in March that he returned to the line-up. He added his experience in defence for the promotion-chasing Shrimpers, contributing some solid defending and his trademark attacking overlaps down the flank in tandem with Carl Pettefer. Duncan set up several scoring chances for his colleagues with some quality crosses, and surprised everyone by netting his first goal for several years when he slotted home in the closing stages of the League Two play-off final against Lincoln to clinch a promotion spot for the club.
Fulham *(From trainee on 12/7/1993) FL 101+4/2 FLC 10+2 FAC 9+1/1 Others 9+1/2*
Wimbledon *(£125,000 + on 27/6/1996) P/FL 23+7 FLC 8+2 FAC 3+2*
Notts Co *(Free on 8/11/2002) FL 6+2 FAC 0+1*
Luton T *(Free on 28/2/2003) FL 2+3*
Southend U *(Free on 17/7/2003) FL 67+4 FLC 2 FAC 3 Others 11/1*

Junior

K

KABBA Stephen (Steve)
Born: Lambeth, 7 March 1981
Height: 5'10" **Weight:** 11.12
After being sidelined by a succession of serious injuries, which had effectively kept him out of the game for 17 months, Steve's return to the Blades line-up last season was welcomed. His speed, finishing and ability to do the unexpected added an extra dimension to the attack and his first start produced two goals against Crewe.
Crystal Palace *(From trainee on 29/6/1999) FL 2+8/1 FLC 0+1*
Luton T *(Loaned on 28/3/2002) FL 0+3*
Grimsby T *(Loaned on 23/8/2002) FL 13/6 FLC 1*
Sheffield U *(£250,000 on 15/11/2002) FL 25+12/9 FAC 5/3 Others 1+2/1*

KAKU Blessing
Born: Ughelli, Nigeria, 5 March 1978
Height: 5'11" **Weight:** 12.4
International Honours: Nigeria
Blessing joined Bolton with a reputation as a competent midfield playmaker. He made his first start for the club in the Carling Cup victory at Yeovil, and made his Premiership debut as a substitute in the 2-1 defeat at West Brom. However, he made just one more substitute appearance before joining Derby County on a month's loan. He was unfortunate to make his debut in one of the Rams' worst performances of the season, at Preston, but showed more of his quality in a victory at Plymouth before returning to the Reebok.
Bolton W *(Free from MS Ashdod, Nigeria, on 25/8/2004) PL 0+1 FLC 1+1*
Derby Co *(Loaned on 26/11/2004) FL 3+1*

KAMARA Diomansy Mehdi
Born: Paris, France, 8 November 1980
Height: 6'0" **Weight:** 11.5
International Honours: Senegal
This talented striker signed for Portsmouth shortly before the end of the summer transfer window for what was a then club record fee. He made his debut from the bench in the 3-1 home victory over Crystal Palace and his first goal was Pompey's winner in the Carling Cup tie at Tranmere. Altogether he netted six times during the season, his best strike being a spectacular effort at Middlesbrough. Diomansy, who possesses lightning pace and impressive footwork, will be looking to firmly establish himself in the starting line-up at Fratton Park in 2005-06.
Portsmouth *(£2,000,000 from Modena, Italy on 1/9/2004) PL 15+10/4 FLC 2/2 FAC 2*

KAMARA Malvin Ginah
Born: Southwark, 17 November 1983
Height: 5'11" **Weight:** 13.7
Malvin is a very promising right-sided midfielder but by his own admission did not have the best of seasons for MK Dons in 2004-05. A couple of minor injuries were a factor, but for such a high-energy player he was never really able to get going throughout. Effort was never a problem, but too often crosses failed to find their man and routine passes were misplaced. On the positive side, Malvin remained in good heart throughout and hopefully his fortunes will improve in the 2005-06 campaign.
Wimbledon/MK Dons *(From trainee on 17/7/2003) FL 31+23/3 FLC 0+1/1 FAC 2 Others 1*

KANOUTE Frederic (Fredi)
Born: Sainte Foy Les Lyon, France, 2 September 1977
Height: 6'4" **Weight:** 12.10
International Honours: Mali; France: B-1; U21
A fine run of form at the end of 2004 saw this impressive striker establish himself as a firm favourite with the Spurs' fans. Previous questions over his commitment soon became history as Fredi began to demonstrate some of his best form since joining Spurs. With competition for striker places hotting up, Fredi responded in the best way

Fredi Kanoute

possible and secured his spot with some terrific performances and mature football. Admired not only for his goal-scoring but also his ability to hold the ball up and distribute it, Fredi seemingly became first-choice partner for Jermain Defoe much to the frustration of a competitive Robbie Keane. New coach Martin Jol experimented with all three, and combined all three strikers on a number of occasions, and Fredi continued to respond positively to the challenge.
West Ham U *(£4,000,000 from Lyon, France on 23/3/2000) PL 79+5/29 FLC 3 FAC 5/4*
Tottenham H *(£3,500,000 + on 6/8/2003) PL 41+18/14 FLC 5+2/4 FAC 6/3*

KANU Christopher (Chris)
Born: Owerri, Nigeria, 4 December 1979
Height: 5'8" **Weight:** 11.4
International Honours: Nigeria
Chris was on the fringes of the Peterborough first-team squad last season, and it was only in the closing stages that he displayed his best form. A versatile player who is comfortable either at full back or in a wide midfield role, he was released on a free transfer in the summer.
Peterborough U *(Free from TOP Oss, Holland, ex Eagle Cement, Ajax, on 12/8/2003) FL 25+9 FLC 2 FAC 2+1 Others 2+2*

KANU Nwankwo
Born: Owerri, Nigeria, 1 August 1976
Height: 6'4" **Weight:** 13.3
Club Honours: CS '99; FAC '02, '03; PL '02, '04
International Honours: Nigeria: Full; U23 (OLYM '96); Yth (World-U17 '93)
This established international striker made his debut for West Bromwich Albion on the opening day of the Premiership programme at Blackburn when he partnered Geoff Horsfield in attack. Blessed with exceptional close ball control, he uses both feet with confidence but his canny tricks and talent can be beguiling. At times he displays outrageous ability and wonderful skills, then can be so different, out of the game for long spells, looking disinterested. He did not always figure in manager Bryan Robson's plans - although he did suffer with niggling injuries during the second half of the season.
Arsenal *(£4,500,000 from Inter Milan, Italy, ex Fed Works, Iwuanyanwu National, Ajax, on 4/2/1999) PL 63+56/30 FLC 8/4 FAC 5+12/3 Others 28+26/7*
West Bromwich A *(Free on 30/7/2004) PL 21+7/2 FAC 2/1*

KANYUKA Patrick
Born: Kinshasa, DR Congo, 19 July 1987
Height: 6'2" **Weight:** 13.10
This tall central defender is a product of the Queen's Park Rangers Academy. He showed enough promise to be given a full professional contract on his 17th birthday and after doing well for the U18s and during a loan spell with Kingstonian he stepped up to make his senior debut at Burnley in April. Patrick will be looking to gain more senior experience during the 2005-06 season.
Queens Park Rgrs *(From juniors on 19/7/2004) FL 1*

KARAM Amine
Born: Besancon, France, 3 January 1984
Height: 5'7" **Weight:** 10.8
After beginning the 2004-05 season playing in the lower divisions in France with Sochaux's reserve team, Amine joined Oxford United on a short-term contract following a successful trial. The talented young midfielder looked impressive during both his appearances for the U's, but at the time of writing seemed unlikely to win a contract at the club for the 2005-06 campaign.
Oxford U *(Free from Sochaux, France on 22/3/2005) FL 0+2*

KARBASSIYOON Daniel
Born: Virginia, USA, 10 August 1984
Height: 5'8" **Weight:** 11.7
International Honours: USA: Yth
This youngster featured in all three of Arsenal's Carling Cup games and scored the winning goal in the 2-1 victory at Manchester City. He also made several appearances in the reserves, before being loaned to Ipswich at the turn of the year. An attacking full back capable of delivering some excellent balls into the opposition penalty area, he was released by the Gunners in the summer.
Arsenal *(Signed from Roanoke Star, USA on 29/8/2003) FLC 1+2/1*
Ipswich T *(Loaned on 21/12/2004) FL 3+2 FAC 1*

KAVANAGH Graham Anthony
Born: Dublin, 2 December 1973
Height: 5'10" **Weight:** 12.11
Club Honours: AMC '00
International Honours: RoI: 12; B-1; U21-9; Yth; Sch
Graham endured a tempestuous season at Cardiff last term, but was back to his best form early in the new year before being sold to Wigan. A skilful midfielder, he played a major part in the Latics' promotion campaign adopting a holding role, sitting deep while others got forward. Hard working and with good anticipation he was always at the centre of the team's endeavours and turned in some fine performances. Graham also added to his tally of caps for the Republic of Ireland during the campaign.
Middlesbrough *(Signed from Home Farm on 16/8/1991) P/FL 22+13/3 FLC 1 FAC 2+2/1 Others 7*
Darlington *(Loaned on 25/2/1994) FL 5*
Stoke C *(£250,000 + on 13/9/1996) FL 198+8/35 FLC 16+2/7 FAC 6 Others 15/4*
Cardiff C *(£1,000,000 on 6/7/2001) FL 140+2/28 FLC 6+1 FAC 11/3 Others 5*
Wigan Ath *(Signed on 4/3/2005) FL 11*

KAVIEDES Jaime **Ivan**
Born: Santo Domingo, Ecuador, 24 October 1977
Height: 6'0" **Weight:** 11.9
International Honours: Ecuador: 40
This experienced striker was in the squad on a few occasions early on last term, but his only Premiership start for the Eagles came against Chelsea in August. Although he scored regularly for the club's reserves, he did not feature at all at first-team level after the Carling Cup tie against Manchester United and did not score a first-team goal. Ivan's contract was cancelled by mutual consent in January and he returned to Ecuador, where he remains a regular in the national team.
Crystal Palace *(Loaned from Barcelona de Guayaquil, Ecuador, ex Emelec, Perugia, Celta Vigo, Puebla, FC Porto, on 17/8/2004) PL 1+3 FLC 0+2*

KAY Antony Roland
Born: Barnsley, 21 October 1982
Height: 5'11" **Weight:** 11.8
International Honours: E: Yth
Antony signed a new contract for Barnsley during the 2004-05 close season and was again a regular in the line-up. He showed his versatility by playing in a number of positions, and being effective in most. Good in the air and comfortable with the ball at his feet, he scored six goals during the campaign.
Barnsley *(From trainee on 25/10/1999) FL 92+14/9 FLC 3 FAC 6/1 Others 4*

KAZIM-RICHARDS Colin
Born: Leyton, 26 August 1986
Height: 6'1" **Weight:** 10.10
One of the highlights of Bury's season was the progress made by this strong teenaged striker. Colin made his debut in the LDV Vans Trophy game at Stockport in September and soon afterwards became a regular on the bench. He went on to claim a starting berth in the closing seven games, and looked completely at

ease in League Two, netting his first
ienior goal in the 3-1 win against
Grimsby in March and contributing the
Shakers' 'Goal of the Season' winner
against Cheltenham.
Bury (Trainee) FL 10+20/3 FAC 0+1 Others 1

KEANE Keith Francis
Born: Luton, 20 November 1986
Height: 5'9" **Weight:** 11.1
Club Honours: Div 1 '05
After making a big impression with Luton
during the previous season, Keith found
his path to the first team blocked by
Kevin Foley last term. A versatile player
who is comfortable both at full back and
n midfield, he is a good reader of the
game and his positional sense allows him
o time his tackles to perfection.
***Luton T** (From trainee on 23/8/2004) FL
25+7/1 FAC 1+1 Others 2*

KEANE Ashley **Kieron**
Born: Camden Town, 20 November 1981
Height: 6'0" **Weight:** 12.6
This midfielder or striker was playing in
he Hellenic League at the start of the
2004-05 season before linking up with
Torquay United in the autumn. His single
first-team appearance came in the LDV
Vans Trophy tie with Northampton in
November when he was substituted
midway through the first half. He was
eleased by the Gulls shortly afterwards.
***Torquay U** (Free from Henley T on
1/10/2004) Others 1*

KEANE Michael Thomas Joseph
Born: Dublin, 29 December 1982
Height: 5'7" **Weight:** 10.10
International Honours: RoI: U21-7; Yth
Michael soon made his mark at Hull and
cored in each of his first two games –
against Wrexham in the Carling Cup and
a late winner at Barnsley in League One.
The combative midfielder continued to
assist Hull towards their back-to-back
promotions until he fell out of favour and
was allowed to join Rotherham in March.
A left-sided midfield player, Michael
quickly endeared himself to the Millmoor
upporters with his busy approach and a
willingness to lend a hand in defence.
***Preston NE** (From trainee on 7/8/2000) FL
'9+18/3 FLC 2+1 FAC 5*
***Grimsby T** (Loaned on 27/3/2003) FL 7/2*
***Hull C** (£50,000 on 2/6/2004) FL 12+8/3 FLC
/1 FAC 3/1 Others 1*
***Rotherham U** (Free on 11/3/2005) FL 9+1*

KEANE Robert (Robbie)
David
Born: Dublin, 8 July 1980
Height: 5'9" **Weight:** 11.10
International Honours: RoI: 61; B-1;
Yth; (UEFA-U18 '98)
Last term proved to be another fine, if
unsettled, season for the Spurs' fans
favourite striker. Robbie has been the
most consistent signing since he joined
the club from Leeds United. A really
tenacious forward prepared to take
opponents on, he loves to get inside the
box and reap havoc amongst defences.
He consistently rises to the occasion and
has fought well to keep his place with
Spurs now having four top-class strikers
to choose from. The arrival of Mido from
Roma mid-season saw Robbie raise his
game yet again and towards the end of
the campaign, with Jermain Defoe
experiencing a barren spell, Robbie
became an automatic first choice proving
he is still amongst the best in the
Premiership. With 17 goals at club level
and four at international level for the
Republic of Ireland, Spurs will be anxious
to assure Robbie of his future in their
plans for the club in 2005-06 and will be
aware just how hugely respected he is by
the Spurs' faithful.
***Wolverhampton W** (From trainee on
26/7/1997) FL 66+7/24 FLC 7+2/3 FAC 3+2/2*
***Coventry C** (£6,000,000 on 20/8/1999) PL
30+1/12 FAC 3 (£13,000,000 to Inter Milan,
Italy on 31/7/1999)*
***Leeds U** (£12,000,000 on 22/12/2000) PL
28+18/13 FLC 2/3 FAC 2 Others 6/3*
***Tottenham H** (£7,000,000 on 31/8/2002) PL
83+15/38 FLC 8+2/4 FAC 7+3/4*

KEANE Roy Maurice
Born: Cork, 10 August 1971
Height: 5'10" **Weight:** 12.10
Club Honours: FMC '92; CS '93, '96,
'97, '03; PL '94, '96, '97, '99, '00, '01,
'03; FAC '94, '96, '99, '04
International Honours: RoI: 66; U21-4;
Yth; Sch
An inspirational midfield general who

Roy Keane

possesses excellent skills with a hardened edge to match, Roy showed once again that his engine was far from running dry with many notable performances during another action-packed campaign. Publicly stating that 2005-06 would be his last season in competitive first-team football, Sir Alex Ferguson was quick to rebuff the remark, stating that Roy still had a vital job to play at Old Trafford. Having suffered a fractured rib injury against Chelsea in the opening Premiership game, he quickly returned to the fore to boss the Reds' midfield in a season of many challenges. Itching to notch his 50th goal for the club, it eventually came against Birmingham City in the Premiership match at Old Trafford in February, notably on the 47th anniversary of the Munich Air Disaster. It was Roy's first goal in 14 months, but, like buses, his second effort soon followed when he hit the opener in United's emphatic sixth round FA Cup win at Southampton. Having only really missed out appearance-wise in the Carling Cup campaign, there was little evidence to suggest that his playing days are on the wane.
Nottingham F *(£10,000 from Cobh Ramblers on 12/6/1990) P/FL 114/22 FLC 17/6 FAC 18/3 Others 5/2*
Manchester U *(£3,750,000 on 22/7/1993) PL 305+16/33 FLC 12+2 FAC 44+2/2 Others 92+1/16*

KEARNEY Thomas (Tom) James

Born: Liverpool, 7 October 1981
Height: 5'9" **Weight:** 11.0
Tom looked to have established a regular place in the centre of Bradford City's midfield during the first half of last season. Always a tenacious competitor, he was encouraged to attack more by manager Colin Todd although that first senior goal remained elusive. Unfortunately he suffered a groin injury in the FA Cup tie with Rushden. This was later diagnosed as a double hernia and brought his campaign to a premature close.
Everton *(From trainee on 15/10/1999)*
Bradford C *(Free on 21/3/2002) FL 35+4/1 FLC 1 FAC 2*

KEATES Dean Scott

Born: Walsall, 30 June 1978
Height: 5'6" **Weight:** 10.10
Dean was one of the most consistent performers for Kidderminster last term and deservedly picked up the supporters' 'Player of the Year' award at the end of the season. Tigerish in the centre of midfield, he also proved himself to have nerves of steel when scoring twice from the penalty spot, against different goalkeepers, in the 3-1 win at Notts County. Dean also scored crucial goals in the win at Darlington and the home draw with Bury.
Walsall *(From trainee on 14/8/1996) FL 125+34/9 FLC 15+1/1 FAC 10+4 Others 14+1/3*
Hull C *(Free on 23/8/2002) FL 45+5/4 FLC 1+1 Others 2*
Kidderminster Hrs *(Signed on 10/2/2004) FL 48+1/7 FLC 1 FAC 1 Others 1*

KEENE James Duncan

Born: Wells, Somerset, 26 December 1985
Height: 5'11" **Weight:** 11.8
A prolific goal-scorer at junior and reserve-team level for Portsmouth, James was promoted to the first-team squad last term. The young striker received his senior debut during a loan spell at Kidderminster in the autumn, but he found the challenge of League Two football a big step up and failed to register a goal during his stay at Aggborough. He returned to Fratton Park to continue his development and was rewarded with an appearance on the bench in the penultimate game of the season against Bolton and included in the starting line-up the following week against West Brom. James will be looking to make further progress with Pompey in 2005-06.
Portsmouth *(From trainee on 29/10/2004) PL 1+1*
Kidderminster Hrs *(Loaned on 29/10/2004) FL 5 FAC 1*

KEITH Joseph (Joe) Richard

Born: Plaistow, 1 October 1978
Height: 5'7" **Weight:** 10.6
The 2004-05 season began in terrific fashion for this left-sided player when he curled home a late free kick to seal Colchester United's remarkable 3-0 win at Sheffield Wednesday on the opening day. Joe went on to score three goals in August and was one of the first names on the team-sheet before Christmas. However, he was only a fringe player following the turn of the year, despite another vital goal in the 1-1 draw at Tranmere in February. He was farmed out on loan to Bristol City during April, where he impressed in the win at Torquay, but he returned to Layer Road at the end of his spell.
West Ham U *(From trainee on 9/7/1997)*
Colchester U *(Free on 5/7/1999) FL 178+30/23 FLC 11+2/2 FAC 12+2/2 Others 9+2/1*
Bristol C *(Loaned on 17/3/2005) FL 3*

KEITH Marino

Born: Peterhead, 16 December 1974
Height: 5'10" **Weight:** 12.11
Club Honours: SCC '98; Div 3 '02; Div 2 '04
Marino struggled to hold down a regular first-team starting place for Plymouth Argyle last term and although he scored an injury-time consolation goal against Queen's Park Rangers in September, this was his only strike of the season. In March he dropped down to League One with Colchester and after the talented striker had settled in he went on to find his scoring touch again, netting three times in a run of three matches.
Dundee U *(Free from Fraserburgh on 11/10/1995) SL 0+4 SC 0+1*
Falkirk *(Free on 9/9/1997) SL 53+8/27 SLC 2/1 SC 7/1 Others 1+1*
Livingston *(Signed on 30/7/1999) SL 15+5/7 SLC 1+3 SC 2/3 Others 2*
Plymouth Arg *(Free on 8/11/2001) FL 67+50/30 FLC 2 FAC 4+4 Others 3+1/2*
Colchester U *(Free on 4/3/2005) FL 12/4*

KELL Richard

Born: Crook, 15 September 1979
Height: 6'1" **Weight:** 10.13
International Honours: E: Sch
After his injury problems of previous seasons, Richard established himself as a regular alongside Ian Baraclough in the centre of the Scunthorpe midfield last term. A good passer who likes to get forward, he chipped in with six goals while helping his team win promotion to League One, including the vital winner at Northampton in April. After starting 43 of the first 45 games, disaster struck for the luckless player in the penultimate match of the season when a strong challenge left him with a broken left leg.
Middlesbrough *(From trainee on 2/7/1998)*
Torquay U *(Free on 8/2/2001) FL 15/3*
Scunthorpe U *(Free on 12/9/2001) FL 80+3/8 FLC 3 FAC 9+1 Others 5+2/1*

KELLER Kasey C

Born: Olympia, USA, 27 November 1969
Height: 6'2" **Weight:** 13.12
Club Honours: FLC '97
International Honours: USA: 81
With the arrival of Paul Robinson from Leeds United in the summer and his immediate instalment as first-choice 'keeper, Kasey became unsettled at White Hart Lane. His only first-team appearances for Spurs came in the Carling Cup before he answered an emergency call when Southampton found themselves short of a goalkeeper. Thrown into a local derby against Portsmouth he adapted well and went on to give Saints admirable service. Kasey

/as later released by Tottenham and gned for Borussia Mönchengladbach uring the January transfer window.
Aillwall (Free from Portland University on 0/2/1992) FL 176 FLC 14 FAC 8 Others 4
eicester C (£900,000 on 17/8/1996) PL 99 :C 16 FAC 8 Others 2 (Signed for Rayo 'allecano, Spain during 1999 close season)
ottenham H (Free on 16/8/2001) PL 85 FLC 0 FAC 4
outhampton (Loaned on 12/11/2004) PL 4

KELLY Gary Oliver
orn: Drogheda, 9 July 1974
eight: 5'8" **Weight:** 11.8
nternational Honours: RoI: 52; U21-5; th; Sch
ne-club man Gary has made more ppearances for Leeds than any other ember of the current squad. A survivor f the Elland Road financial upheaval and elegation from the Premiership, the ormer Republic of Ireland right back held ff the challenge of Frazer Richardson to eep his place. He skippered Leeds everal times late on in the season in the bsence of Paul Butler and led the side in friendly at his hometown of Drogheda March. In summer 2004 he had pened a cancer care centre in Drogheda. May 2002 Gary donated a substantial um from his testimonial match against lasgow Celtic to the care centre in emory of his sister, Mandy, who had ied of the illness. He has now set his ghts on reaching 500 appearances for eeds – a rarity in the modern era.
eeds U (Signed from Home Farm on 4/9/1991) P/FL 359+11/2 FLC 26+2 FAC 9+1/1 Others 35+1

KELLY Marcus Philip
orn: Kettering, 16 March 1986
eight: 5'7" **Weight:** 10.0
larcus is a talented winger who can perate on either flank but prefers to ut inside from the left. He made the arting line-up on just three occasions st term, but nevertheless he agreed erms on a new contract with Rushden the summer. He featured as a wing ack in the final game of the season at lacclesfield and will be looking for ore opportunities in the 2005-06 ampaign.
ushden & Diamonds (From juniors on 7/11/2003) FL 7+12 FLC 0+1 FAC 0+1

KELLY Stephen Michael
orn: Dublin, 6 September 1983
eight: 5'11" **Weight:** 12.4
ternational Honours: RoI: U21-15; th
his hard-working young defender clearly enjoyed his season as Spurs new coach Martin Jol experimented with the side and gave opportunities to the younger players. Stephen slotted comfortably into regular first-team action and showed great confidence on the ball and a keen eye for goal, netting two for his efforts. Now also featuring in the senior Republic of Ireland side, Stephen will benefit form playing regularly at the highest level and will add great value to Spurs defence.
***Tottenham H** (From juniors on 11/9/2000) PL 20+8/2 FLC 1 FAC 5*
***Southend U** (Loaned on 30/1/2003) FL 10*
***Queens Park Rgrs** (Loaned on 27/3/2003) FL 7 Others 2*
***Watford** (Loaned on 24/9/2003) FL 13*

KELTIE Clark Stuart
Born: Newcastle, 31 August 1983
Height: 6'0" **Weight:** 12.7
This young Darlington midfielder missed the majority of the second half of last season with a serious injury, making his last substitute appearance in early January. Strong running and solid tackling characterise Clark's game and he possesses a fierce shot, although his only goal of the campaign came with a header after coming on as substitute in the FA Cup tie at home to Yeovil Town in November.
***Darlington** (Free from Walker Central on 19/9/2001) FL 60+23/4 FLC 3 FAC 4+1/1 Others 1+1*

Stephen Kelly

KENDRICK Joseph (Joe)
Born: Dublin, 26 June 1983
Height: 6'0" **Weight:** 11.5
International Honours: RoI: U21-1; Yth
This young left-sided defender returned to the North-East when he signed for Darlington last August. Joe impressed with his composure in the tackle and when bringing the ball forward along the left flank. He opened his goal-scoring account on only his sixth outing in the away game at Chester City but failed to add to this during the remainder of the season.
Newcastle U *(From trainee on 18/7/2000. Freed during 2003 close season)*
Darlington *(Free from TSV Munich on 6/8/2004) FL 19+12/1 FLC 1 FAC 1+1 Others 1*

KENNA Jeffrey (Jeff) Jude
Born: Dublin, 27 August 1970
Height: 5'11" **Weight:** 12.2
International Honours: RoI: 27; B-1; U21-8; Yth; Sch
After an uneasy start to Derby County's season, Jeff settled to play his best football at right back. His experience, so valuable in a battle against relegation when he first joined the club, was now directed towards a bid for the play-offs and he took over as captain when Ian Taylor was out of the side. His mature approach helped to steady a defence that was often liable to error and he found time to help the young players. Jeff grew in authority as the campaign progressed, linking well when he moved forward but is still seeking a first goal for Derby.
Southampton *(From trainee on 25/4/1989) P/FL 110+4/4 FLC 4 FAC 10+1 Others 3*
Blackburn Rov *(£1,500,000 on 15/3/1995) P/FL 153+2/1 FLC 17+2 FAC 13 Others 7*
Tranmere Rov *(Loaned on 20/3/2001) FL 11*
Wigan Ath *(Loaned on 2/11/2001) FL 6/1 FAC 1*
Birmingham C *(Free on 24/12/2001) P/FL 71+4/3 FLC 1 FAC 5 Others 3*
Derby Co *(Free on 11/3/2004) FL 49 FLC 0+1 FAC 2 Others 2*

KENNEDY Jason Brian
Born: Stockton, 11 September 1986
Height: 6'1" **Weight:** 11.10
Club Honours: FAYC '04
Local lad Jason Kennedy has been associated with Middlesbrough since the age of 11 and was part of the club's FA Youth Cup winning side in 2004. Although originally a striker he has now been converted into a midfield player. Jason has, so far in his fledgling football career, played just four minutes of Premiership football for the club. He was awarded his first professional contract in February then he replaced veteran Colin Cooper in the closing stages of the Riverside draw against Fulham in April.
Middlesbrough *(From trainee on 3/2/2005) PL 0+1*

KENNEDY Luke Daniel
Born: Peterborough, 22 May 1986
Height: 6'1" **Weight:** 11.3
Luke established himself in Rushden's reserve team last season and stepped up to make his senior debut from the substitutes' bench in January. He was rewarded with a professional contract in the summer and with a younger squad in place at Nene Park, it seems likely that the gifted midfielder will be given further opportunities to shine in 2005-06.
Rushden & Diamonds *(Trainee) FL 1+2 Others 0+1*

KENNEDY Mark
Born: Dublin, 15 May 1976
Height: 5'11" **Weight:** 11.9
International Honours: RoI: 34; U21-7; Yth; Sch
Mark stood in for Paul Ince as Wolves captain on the opening day of the season, but was then injured in the following match and sidelined for a short spell. Nevertheless he featured fairly regularly in the starting line-up, although rarely in his preferred role as an out-and-out winger, being used at left back and on the left-hand side of midfield.
Millwall *(From trainee on 6/5/1992) FL 37+6/9 FLC 6+1/2 FAC 3+1/1*
Liverpool *(£1,500,000 on 21/3/1995) PL 5+11 FLC 0+2 FAC 0+1 Others 0+2*
Queens Park Rgrs *(Loaned on 27/1/1998) FL 8/2*
Wimbledon *(£1,750,000 on 27/3/1998) PL 11+10 FLC 4+1/1 FAC 2*
Manchester C *(£1,000,000 + on 15/7/1999) P/FL 56+10/8 FLC 5+4/3 FAC 2*
Wolverhampton W *(£1,800,000 on 6/7/2001) P/FL 120+7/10 FLC 2+1 FAC 10/1 Others 3+1/1*

KENNEDY Peter Henry James
Born: Lurgan, 10 September 1973
Height: 5'9" **Weight:** 11.11
Club Honours: Div 2 '98, '03
International Honours: NI: 20; B-1
This experienced winger signed for Peterborough in the summer of 2004 and started last season at full back, where his attacking skills were to the fore. Peter also featured on the flank, but after appearing regularly in the opening months of the campaign he was sidelined by a back injury. He made few first-team appearances in the new year, and was sidelined once more with a knee injury in March.
Notts Co *(£100,000 from Portadown on 28/8/1996) FL 20+2 FLC 1 FAC 2+1/1 Others 0+1*
Watford *(£130,000 on 10/7/1997) P/FL 108+7/18 FLC 9/2 FAC 7/2 Others 3*
Wigan Ath *(£300,000 on 18/7/2001) FL 60+5/2 FLC 6 FAC 4 Others 3*
Derby Co *(Loaned on 31/10/2003) FL 5/1*
Peterborough U *(Free on 3/8/2004) FL 15+2/2 FLC 1 FAC 1+1/1*

KENNEDY Thomas (Tom) Gordon
Born: Bury, 24 June 1985
Height: 5'10" **Weight:** 11.1
Tom was the only ever-present in Bury's 50 competitive fixtures during the 2004-05 season, proving to be a consistent performer in the left-wing-back position. A solid tackler and quality passer of the ball, Tom always tries to get forward and run at opponents. He netted his first-eve League goal with a penalty at Boston in February and showed his adaptability during a late-season injury crisis by playing at centre back at Chester and as a sweeper behind Dave Challinor and Paul Scott at Wycombe.
Bury *(From trainee on 2/11/2002) FL 68+5/ FLC 1 FAC 2 Others 2*

KENNY Patrick (Paddy) Joseph
Born: Halifax, 17 May 1978
Height: 6'1" **Weight:** 14.6
International Honours: RoI: 5
Paddy continued to be Sheffield United's first-choice 'keeper last term, although h had two spells out of the side, one through suspension and the other through injury. He is excellent both as a shot-stopper and in one-on-one situations, and is quick and decisive whe responding to a through ball. Paddy saved four penalties during the season, three in shoot-outs, but he hit the post with his own spot-kick in the shoot-out against Watford. He continued to represent the Republic of Ireland during the season.
Bury *(£10,000 + from Bradford PA on 28/8/1998) FL 133 FLC 5 FAC 7 Others 5*
Sheffield U *(Free on 26/7/2002) FL 112 FLC 11 FAC 13 Others 3*

KENTON Darren Edward
Born: Wandsworth, 13 September 1978
Height: 5'10" **Weight:** 11.11
An injury crisis at St Mary's gave Darren a short run of Premiership action in the autumn, but in March he was shipped out on loan to Leicester. The experienced right back or central defender impressed with his mobility and confidence and looked a solid addition to the squad.

Darren established a useful central-defensive partnership with Paddy McCarthy over the closing weeks before returning to St Mary's.

Norwich C *(From trainee on 3/7/1997) FL 142+16/9 FLC 9+1 FAC 2+2 Others 3*
Southampton *(Free on 19/5/2003) PL 12+4 FLC 2*
Leicester C *(Loaned on 3/3/2005) FL 9+1 FAC 1*

KEOGH Andrew Declan
Born: Dublin, 16 May 1986
Height: 6'0" **Weight:** 11.7
International Honours: RoI: Yth
This young Leeds striker spent the first three months of the season on loan with League Two club Scunthorpe United, coming off the bench to score in his second appearance at Cheltenham. A skilful player, who can operate as a centre forward or in a deeper role, he returned to Elland Road where he received a brief taste of the big time when he came on in the Carling Cup tie at Portsmouth. Later in the season he went on loan to Bury, impressing with his hard-working attitude before Scunthorpe boss Brian Laws came in to sign him on a permanent basis.

Leeds U *(From trainee on 20/5/2003) FLC 0+1*
Scunthorpe U *(Loaned on 6/8/2004) FL 9+3/2*
Bury *(Loaned on 14/1/2005) FL 4/2*
Scunthorpe U *(Signed on 14/2/2005) FL 4+9/1*

KEOWN Martin Raymond
Born: Oxford, 24 July 1966
Height: 6'1" **Weight:** 12.4
Club Honours: PL '98, '02, '04; FAC '98, '02, '03; CS '98, '99, '02
International Honours: E: 43; B-1; U21-8; Yth
This veteran central defender was snapped up by Leicester in the summer of 2004 and became City's oldest-ever debutant on the opening day of the season. He was first choice at the heart of the defence for a while, but was allowed to leave following a change in management at the club. Martin signed for Championship rivals Reading, but was sidelined by injury for much of his time at the Madejski Stadium and made little real impact.

Paddy Kenny (right)

Arsenal *(From apprentice on 2/2/1984) FL 22 FAC 5*
Brighton & Hove A *(Loaned on 15/2/1985) FL 16*
Brighton & Hove A *(Loaned on 6/8/1985) FL 5+2/1 FLC 2/1 Others 2/1*
Aston Villa *(£200,000 on 9/6/1986) FL 109+3/3 FLC 12+1 FAC 6 Others 2*
Everton *(£750,000 on 7/8/1989) P/FL 92+4 FLC 11 FAC 12+1 Others 6*
Arsenal *(£2,000,000 on 4/2/1993) PL 282+28/4 FLC 21+2/1 FAC 32+3 Others 46+8/3*
Leicester C *(Free on 21/7/2004) FL 16+1 FAC 1*
Reading *(Free on 28/1/2005) FL 3+2*

KERLEY Adam Lewis
Born: Sutton-in-Ashfield, 25 February 1985
Height: 5'6" **Weight:** 11.7
This young striker was given his chance by Lincoln City after scoring regularly in reserve-team football in the opening weeks of the 2004-05 season. Adam made his senior debut as a second-half substitute against Doncaster in the LDV Vans Trophy and showed plenty of movement inside the box. He kept his place in the squad but his only other outing was as a late substitute against Kidderminster. Adam was later loaned out to Lincoln United and finished the season on loan at Spalding United. He was released at the end of the season.
Lincoln C *(From trainee on 3/8/2004) FL 0+1 Others 0+1*

KEWELL Harold (Harry)
Born: Sydney, Australia, 22 September 1978
Height: 6'0" **Weight:** 11.10
Club Honours: FAYC '97; UEFACL '05
International Honours: Australia: 17; Yth
After a promising start to his Anfield career, Harry has struggled for both form and fitness and it was the same story at last term. Although he played regularly up to Christmas his form was not of the level expected and the catalogue of niggling injuries seemed to keep on expanding. Strangely, just as he seemed to be running into form with his only goal of the season at Aston Villa in December and a 'Man of the Match' performance against Newcastle, he was then sidelined for two months and played little part in the campaign for the remainder of the season. Surprisingly he was selected for both the Carling Cup final against Chelsea and the European Cup final in Istanbul, in recognition of his match-winning potential, but the gamble misfired as he made little impact in either game.
Leeds U *(Signed from the Australian Academy of Sport on 23/12/1995) PL 169+12/45 FLC 8/4 FAC 16/6 Others 34+3/8*
Liverpool *(£5,000,000 on 9/7/2003) PL 51+3/8 FLC 1+2/1 FAC 3 Others 15+5/3*

KEZMAN Mateja
Born: Belgrade, Yugoslavia, 12 April 1979
Height: 5'11" **Weight:** 11.9
Club Honours: FLC '05; PL '05
International Honours: Serbia & Montenegro: 37
Following a difficult settling-in period in English football, fortune finally turned in Mateja Kezman's favour at the Millennium Stadium in Cardiff when the gangling centre forward scored the decisive goal in extra time to secure Chelsea's Carling Cup victory over Liverpool. Mateja plays with incredible heart as he tries to make the most of his limited opportunities. He seemed to hit the woodwork with maddening frequency and when it seemed that he was fated not to score a Premiership goal he got off the mark in the most impudent fashion – dinking a softly-taken penalty over the Newcastle 'keeper to wrap up a 4—0 victory. A goal at Norwich and a brace against Crystal Palace followed to give him a disappointing Premiership tally of four. Although the goals have not flowed as he would have liked, Mateja made a great contribution to Chelsea's successful season and there is no more popular player with squad-mates and supporters alike.
Chelsea *(£5,000,000 from PSV Eindhoven, Holland, ex Sartid, Partizan Belgrade, on 19/7/2004) PL 6+19/4 FLC 2+2/2 FAC 3/1 Others 3+6*

KIELY Dean Laurence
Born: Salford, 10 October 1970
Height: 6'0" **Weight:** 12.6
Club Honours: Div 2 '97; Div 1 '00
International Honours: RoI: 8; B-1; E: Yth; Sch
Showing his usual consistency, Dean had another fine season in the Charlton goal, keeping 14 clean sheets in all matches. He was rested for two games at the end of the season so that Alan Curbishley could look at his understudy Stephan Andersen, but he started every other game. Dean is an excellent shot-stopper, one of the best in the Premiership, and made some outstanding saves during the campaign. The highlight was probably his penalty save against Crystal Palace at Selhurst Park, when the Addicks went on to score in the last minute to win the game. Dean's kicking can sometimes be a bit wayward and he prefers to stay on his line for corners rather than come out for the ball, which can sometimes cause undue pressure on his defenders, but he is steady and totally reliable under pressure.
Coventry C *(From trainee on 30/10/1987)*
York C *(Signed on 9/3/1990) FL 210 FLC 9 FAC 4 Others 17*
Bury *(£125,000 on 15/8/1996) FL 137 FLC 13 FAC 4 Others 3*
Charlton Ath *(£1,000,000 on 26/5/1999) P/FL 219 FLC 11 FAC 14*

KIGHTLY Michael John
Born: Basildon, 24 January 1986
Height: 5'9" **Weight:** 9.12
This young striker had a disappointing season at Southend last term when his only first-team action came when he appeared as a substitute for hat-trick hero Freddy Eastwood against Swansea. He found himself well down the pecking order at Roots Hall and spent much of the campaign on loan to Conference outfit Farnborough Town.
Southend U *(From trainee on 12/12/2003) FL 2+11 FAC 1+2 Others 2+1/1*

KILBANE Kevin Daniel
Born: Preston, 1 February 1977
Height: 6'0" **Weight:** 12.10
International Honours: RoI: 64; U21-11
Kevin enjoyed a consistent season on the left-hand side of Everton's midfield, wher he became the first outfielder to figure in every League game for 13 years. His consistent displays for his country in a more central role also saw him voted as the Republic of Ireland's 'Player of the Year'. Kevin started the campaign well, scoring his only goal in the victory at Norwich, before he dropped below his normal high standards as the team struggled after Christmas. He came back well when required at the tail-end, producing storming performances in the important home victories over Crystal Palace and Manchester United. Kevin's main strengths are his prodigious work-rate and fine crossing ability from the wing and he is also good in the air.
Preston NE *(From trainee on 6/7/1995) FL 39+8/3 FLC 4 FAC 1 Others 1+1*
West Bromwich A *(£1,000,000 on 13/6/1997) FL 105+1/15 FLC 12/2 FAC 4/1*
Sunderland *(£2,500,000 on 16/12/1999) P/FL 102+11/8 FLC 4 FAC 3+4/1*
Everton *(£750,000 on 2/9/2003) PL 63+5/4 FLC 2 FAC 6/1*

KILGALLON Matthew Shaun
Born: York, 8 January 1984
Height: 6'1" **Weight:** 12.5
International Honours: E: U21-4; Yth
This tall central defender made excellent progress at Leeds throughout the 2004-

05 season. He partnered both Paul Butler and Clarke Carlisle in the heart of the defence but also featured several times at left back. He figured in that position in the opening two games of the season before the arrival of Stephen Crainey and was later used there several times after Crainey was sidelined with an injury. Central defence remains his best position where his aerial power and crisp tackling are at their best. Matthew won his second England U21 cap when he played against Ukraine in August and also came on in the 0-0 draw in Azerbaijan.
Leeds U *(From trainee on 10/1/2001) P/FL 33+3/2 FLC 1 FAC 2 Others 0+1*
West Ham U *(Loaned on 23/8/2003) FL 1+2 FLC 1*

KILKENNY Neil Martin
Born: Middlesex, 19 December 1985
Height: 5'8" **Weight:** 10.8
International Honours: E: Yth
This young midfield prospect made a huge impact at Oldham Athletic after signing on loan from Birmingham City in November 2004. Coming on as a substitute against Barnsley, he set up the winning goal and did even better on his full debut the following weekend. Neil was outstanding at Bradford City, scoring twice as Latics strolled to a comfortable 3-1 win. His loan spell was soon extended for the rest of the season and he became singled out for some rough marking as his reputation spread. A real box of tricks on the ball, his quality consistently stood out and he deservedly won the local Media Writers' 'Player of the Year' award before returning to stake his first-team claims at St Andrew's.
Birmingham C *(From trainee at Arsenal on 27/1/2004)*
Oldham Ath *(Loaned on 19/11/2004) FL 24+3/4 FAC 3 Others 4/1*

KILLEN Christopher (Chris) John
Born: Wellington, New Zealand, 8 October 1981
Height: 5'11" **Weight:** 11.3
International Honours: New Zealand
Chris enjoyed his best season to date with Oldham Athletic in 2004-05 when he finally put his injury problems behind him and began to show his prowess in front of goal. A purple patch in mid-season saw him net ten goals in just six games before groin and hamstring problems struck again. He returned to the side in February, striking up an excellent late-season partnership with on-loan Luke Beckett that ultimately preserved the club's League One status. Also adept at holding the ball up, Chris finished the season as top scorer with 15 strikes – a goal every two games.
Manchester C *(Free from Miramar Rangers, New Zealand on 8/3/1999) FL 0+3*
Wrexham *(Loaned on 8/9/2000) FL 11+1/3*
Port Vale *(Loaned on 24/9/2001) FL 8+1/6 Others 1*
Oldham Ath *(£200,000 + on 31/7/2002) FL 43+23/15 FLC 4+1/1 FAC 3+2/4 Others 2/1*

KING Ledley Brenton
Born: Stepney, 12 October 1980
Height: 6'2" **Weight:** 13.6
International Honours: E: 12; U21-12; Yth
Ledley is a highly rated defender and an accomplished midfielder who continued to impress for both club and country last term. After a hugely successful Euro 2004 Ledley returned home early as a result of the premature arrival of his first child. To that point, Ledley had not put a foot wrong, demonstrating his gritty defensive qualities, confidence in the air and some accurate and effective play making. Having left his England manager with a welcome future selection headache, Ledley went on to appear in all Spurs Premiership fixtures last season, adding experience and composure to the new talent that had been brought in. At club level, Ledley can play in either role but looks most comfortable when just ahead of the defence almost as a fifth midfielder.
Tottenham H *(From trainee on 22/7/1998) PL 143+3/4 FLC 14/1 FAC 16+1/3*

KING Marlon Francis
Born: Dulwich, 26 April 1980
Height: 6'1" **Weight:** 11.12
International Honours: Jamaica: 11
This exciting striker scored for Nottingham Forest on his first appearance of the season against Crewe, and then featured fairly regularly in the line-up, leading the club's scoring charts for some time. However, following a change in management he was allowed to move to Leeds on loan for the remainder of the season. Unfortunately he rarely got a chance to occupy his preferred central-striking role at Elland Road and was deployed wide in a 4-4-3 system. He did not find the net during his stay in Yorkshire and returned to the City Ground at the season's end.
Barnet *(From trainee on 9/9/1998) FL 36+17/14 FLC 0+2 FAC 0+1 Others 2+2*
Gillingham *(£255,000 on 28/6/2000) FL 82+19/40 FLC 6+3/4 FAC 5+1/3*
Nottingham F *(£950,000 on 27/11/2003) FL 40+10/10 FLC 3/3 FAC 3+1/2*
Leeds U *(Loaned on 4/3/2005) FL 4+5*

KINSELLA Mark Anthony
Born: Dublin, 12 August 1972
Height: 5'9" **Weight:** 11.8
Club Honours: GMVC '92; FAT '92; Div 1 '00
International Honours: RoI: 48; B-1; U21-8; Yth
This experienced midfielder mostly featured in a role just in front of the back four for Walsall last term. His quality showed through in his neat and tidy work, but he missed a number of games through injury, returning for the 3-1 win at Hartlepool at the end of April.
Colchester U *(Free from Home Farm on 18/8/1989) FL 174+6/27 FLC 11+1/3 FAC 9/2 Others 12+2/5*
Charlton Ath *(£150,000 on 23/9/1996) P/FL 200+8/19 FLC 4+2 FAC 8+1/3 Others 3*
Aston Villa *(£750,000 on 23/8/2002) PL 17+4 FLC 2+2 FAC 1*
West Bromwich A *(Free on 15/1/2004) FL 15+3/1*
Walsall *(Free on 29/7/2004) FL 21+1 Others 1*

KIRALY Gabor Ferenc
Born: Szombathely, Hungary, 1 April 1976
Height: 6'3" **Weight:** 13.6
International Honours: Hungary: 57
This experienced 'keeper started the 2004-05 season as second choice to Julian Speroni. However, he came into the line-up for the Carling Cup tie against Hartlepool and went on to retain his place for the remainder of the campaign, producing many fine performances. Gabor continued to represent Hungary at international level during the campaign.
Crystal Palace *(Free from Hertha Berlin, Germany on 12/8/2004) PL 32 FLC 1 FAC 1*

KIRK Andrew (Andy) Robert
Born: Belfast, 29 May 1979
Height: 5'11" **Weight:** 11.7
International Honours: NI: 8; U21-9; Yth; Sch
Andy's much anticipated link-up with fellow striker Jason Lee at Boston was delayed until the end of September by injury, but once fit he quickly settled in and proved a prolific scorer for the League Two club. His anticipation and ability to be in the right place at the right time brought him 20 goals and he became the first player in the history of the club to win a full international cap when he was recalled by Northern Ireland for their friendly against Canada in February. Soon afterwards he was sold to Northampton for what was a record fee for the Cobblers. He went on to establish a further record when he became the

first player to net in his first four outings for the club en route to scoring seven times in eight starts.
Heart of Midlothian *(£50,000 from Glentoran on 19/2/1999) SL 64+50/30 SLC 5+4/2 SC 5+2 Others 1+3*
Boston U *(Signed on 22/7/2004) FL 25/19 FLC 1 FAC 4/2 Others 0+1*
Northampton T *(£125,000 on 11/3/2005) FL 8/7 Others 2*

KIRKLAND Christopher (Chris)

Born: Barwell, 2 May 1981
Height: 6'6" **Weight:** 11.7
Club Honours: FLC '03
International Honours: E: U21-8; Yth
This young Liverpool 'keeper must sometimes feel that every season is 'groundhog day' for him, as in each of the last three campaigns he has established himself as first choice at Anfield ahead of Jerzy Dudek only to lose his place through injury. In 2004-05 he was sidelined with a back injury until October, returned to action in the Premiership fixture away to Chelsea and played regularly in the two months up to the local 'derby' game away to Everton. Then the back problem flared up again requiring surgery which ruled him out for the remainder of the season.
Coventry C *(From trainee on 6/5/1998) P/FL 24 FLC 3+1 FAC 1*
Liverpool *(£6,000,000 + on 31/8/2001) PL 25 FLC 6 FAC 3 Others 11*

KISHISHEV Radostin Prodanov

Born: Bulgaria, 30 July 1974
Height: 5'10" **Weight:** 12.4
International Honours: Bulgaria: 57
Radostin had another good season in the heart of Charlton's midfield and at times looked the team's most influential player. The skilful and versatile player is a strong tackler who is very comfortable on the ball and is not afraid to try something unexpected, such as a 40-yard pass to switch the play. He also likes to get forward and has a powerful shot, although he failed to find the net during the season. Radostin deputised for Luke Young at right back for three games and acquitted himself well. However, although he can play either right- or central-midfield, he looks more at ease when playing in the middle where he has more room to express himself. He was recalled into Bulgaria's international squad and played a further six games for his country during the season.
Charlton Ath *(£300,000 + from Liteks Lovech, Bulgaria, ex Neftokhimik Burgas, Bursapor, on 14/8/2000) PL 109+19/2 FLC 3+1 FAC 5+1*

Andy Kirk

KITAMIRIKE Joel Derick

Born: Kampala, Uganda, 5 April 1984
Height: 5'10" **Weight:** 13.1
International Honours: E: Yth
This talented youngster spent time on trial at Walsall in the early part of last term before joining Mansfield Town on a non-contract basis shortly before Christmas as cover for injuries and suspension. Joel made his debut at right back at Southend and did very well as the defence kept a clean sheet, but his stay at Field Mill was short-lived as he signed a long-term deal with Dundee in January. Nominally a centre back, he is quick and tackles very strongly.
Chelsea *(From trainee on 6/4/2001) Others 1 (Freed during 2004 close season)*
Brentford *(Loaned on 19/9/2003) FL 21+1 FAC 1 Others 2*
Mansfield T *(Free from Hornchurch on 16/12/2004) FL 2*

KITCHEN Benjamin (Ben)

Born: Bolton, 19 August 1986
Height: 5'9" **Weight:** 11.7
A regular for Rochdale's reserve side last term, Ben sat on the bench as an unused substitute on several occasions in the middle of the campaign. He eventually made his first-team debut in the last game of the season at Boston, impressing after coming off the bench. A couple of days later he was in the Dale side that won the Lancashire Senior Cup. A speedy winger, he has been offered a professional contract for 2005-06.
Rochdale *(Trainee) FL 0+1*

KITSON David (Dave) Barry

Born: Hitchin, 21 January 1980
Height: 6'3" **Weight:** 12.11

Joel Kitamirike

Averaging a goal every other game, striker Dave Kitson was deservedly voted as 'Player of the Season' by the Reading fans last term. Had he not missed a lengthy spell through a knee injury the club might well have been promotion candidates rather than finishing outside the play-offs. The highlight of his season was of course his hat-trick in the 3-1 home defeat of West Ham United, and there is undoubtedly much more to come from this hugely talented young man.
Cambridge U *(Signed from Arlesey T on 16/3/2001) FL 97+5/40 FLC 4/1 FAC 9/2 Others 7+1/4*
Reading *(£150,000 on 30/12/2003) FL 47+7/24 FLC 1*

[KLEBERSON] PEREIRA KLEBERSON Jose
Born: Urai, Brazil, 19 June 1979
Height: 5'9" **Weight:** 10.5
International Honours: Brazil: 27
An industrious and creative midfielder, Kleberson was only given a few opportunities to shine last term, despite having played in three of Manchester United's opening five Premiership matches of the campaign. Indeed, his performance against Everton at Old Trafford in August was his most notable contribution to the whole campaign. Having also played in the early stages of the Champions' League and Carling Cup campaigns, the new year brought a barren spell for the popular Brazilian, with only two more full first-team appearances in the Premiership against Norwich and West Bromwich Albion in April and May respectively.
Manchester U *(£5,930,000 from Atletico Paranense, Brazil, ex PSTC-Lodrina, on 13/8/2003) PL 16+4/2 FLC 4 FAC 1 Others 3+2*

KLUIVERT Patrick Stephan
Born: Amsterdam, Holland, 1 July 1976
Height: 6'2" **Weight:** 13.3
International Honours: Holland: 79
With an impressive pedigree as Holland's leading all-time international goal-scorer, Patrick's arrival at Newcastle was hailed by many as a major coup and he began in fine style with a goal on his first start at Villa. Several more goals followed, but then a hamstring injury sidelined him for a while during which time he had his wisdom teeth removed. On his return he had his best game of the season against Norwich in the Carling Cup but he was never able to make the impact expected, although his vision and weighting of pass were sublime and he contributed some important goals including the early FA Cup winners against Chelsea and Spurs.

At the end of the season he declared that he would be moving to Spain in the summer.
Newcastle U *(Free from Barcelona, Spain, ex Ajax, AC Milan, on 28/7/2004) PL 15+10/6 FLC 2 FAC 3+1/2 Others 5+1/5*

KNIGHT Leon Leroy
Born: Hackney, 16 September 1982
Height: 5'4" **Weight:** 9.10
International Honours: E: Yth
After scoring 27 goals in Brighton's promotion campaign, Leon found the challenge of Championship football much harder and finished the 2004-05 season with his name on the score sheet just four times. He did not get off to the best of starts, but manager Mark McGhee continued to show faith in his diminutive striker's talent and Leon was never omitted from the squad. As probably the best crosser of a ball at the club and blessed with great close skill, he was played quite effectively as a winger in the latter part of the season. On his day Leon can be a brilliant match-winner, but he will need to show more consistency to succeed at Championship level.
Chelsea *(From trainee on 17/9/1999) Others 0+1*
Queens Park Rgrs *(Loaned on 9/3/2001) FL 10+1*
Huddersfield T *(Loaned on 23/10/2001) FL 31/16 FAC 2/1 Others 4*
Sheffield Wed *(Loaned on 8/7/2002) FL 14+10/3 FLC 2 FAC 0+1*
Brighton & Hove A *(£100,000 on 24/7/2003) FL 76+7/29 FLC 3 FAC 2 Others 6/2*

Leon Knight

KNIGHT Zatyiah (Zat)
Born: Solihull, 2 May 1980
Height: 6'6" **Weight:** 13.8
International Honours: E: 2; U21-4
Zat was a near ever-present for Fulham last term and grew in stature as the season progressed. He provided a commanding presence in the centre of the Fulham defence, being effective in the air and displaying good vision when on the ball. Zat scored his first-ever senior goal in the FA Cup tie at Watford and was called into the full England squad for the post-season tour of the USA.
Fulham *(Signed from Rushall Olympic on 19/2/1999) P/FL 85+8/1 FLC 8 FAC 13+2/1 Others 3+2*
Peterborough U *(Loaned on 25/2/2000) FL 8*

KNIGHTS Darryl James
Born: Ipswich, 1 May 1988
Height: 5'7" **Weight:** 10.1
Club Honours: FAYC '05
After some excellent performances for Ipswich reserves, Darryl was promoted to the first-team squad and made his debut at the Stadium of Light when he came off the bench for the last ten minutes of the match. The highlight of his season was being a member of the club's FA Youth Cup winning side. In both legs of the final he was inspirational, playing as a lone striker.
Ipswich T *(From trainee on 20/5/2005) FL 0+1*

KOLKKA Joonas
Born: Lahti, Finland, 28 September 1974
Height: 5'9" **Weight:** 11.8
International Honours: Finland: 65
This international-class left winger joined Crystal Palace in the summer of 2004 as a replacement for the departed Julian Gray. Joonas featured regularly for the Eagles in the first half of the season, but only sparingly thereafter. He scored three Premiership goals including a brilliant volley in the 3-2 defeat at Anfield which was later voted as the Eagles' 'Goal of the Season'.
Crystal Palace *(£460,000 from Borussia Moenchengladbach, Germany, ex MyPa 47, Willem 11 Tilburg, PSV Eindhoven, on 22/7/2004) PL 20+3/3 FLC 1*

KONCHESKY Paul Martyn
Born: Barking, 15 May 1981
Height: 5'9" **Weight:** 10.12
International Honours: E: 1; U21-15; Yth
Paul enjoyed a good season for Charlton and put in some sterling performances on the left side of midfield. It could well be that this proves to be his best position, as he likes to get forward and seems more comfortable and effective in that role. He is quick, as well as being a strong tackler and can play at either left back, in central defence or on the left side of midfield. He is a good crosser of the ball, has a powerful shot and is a dead-ball specialist. His only goal came in the 4-0 home win over Norwich in November, when he scored Charlton's third with his first touch, after coming on as a late substitute.
Charlton Ath *(From trainee on 25/5/1998) P/FL 91+58/5 FLC 5+4/1 FAC 8+3*
Tottenham H *(Loaned on 1/9/2003) PL 10+2 FLC 2+1*

KONJIC Muhamed (Mo)
Born: Brijesnica Velika, Doboj, Bosnia, 14 May 1970
Height: 6'4" **Weight:** 13.7
International Honours: Bosnia-Herzegovina: 38
Mo established his value to Derby County, a centre half able to attack the ball and win it in the air, but his first season at Pride Park was one long struggle against injuries. He had knee trouble before the campaign was under way and, after five games in September, an operation was necessary. This proved unsuccessful, so there were further consultations and treatment in Italy. He returned in the reserves in February and was pitched into the East Midlands 'derby' against Nottingham Forest later that month. A broken nose caused him double vision and he had groin problems but, although he was creaking, his courage and willingness to compete were never in doubt.
Coventry C *(£2,000,000 from AS Monaco, France, ex Slobada Tuzla, Croatia Belisce, Croatia Zagreb, FC Zurich, on 5/2/1999) P/FL 130+8/4 FLC 9+1 FAC 7*
Derby Co *(Free on 14/5/2004) FL 13+3 Others 2*

KONSTANTOPOULOS Dimitrios (Dimi)
Born: Kalamata, Greece, 29 November 1978
Height: 6'4" **Weight:** 12.2
A tall goalkeeper who takes command of his penalty area, Dimi began 2004-05 as deputy to Jim Provett for Hartlepool, but he was given his initial taste of first-team football early on. He went on to produce a string of outstanding performances and make the goalkeeping position his own. After another spell as reserve, he finished the season strongly back as first-choice custodian. Dimi has a good record for saving penalties, and on two occasions he was a real hero for Hartlepool in penalty shoot-outs.
Hartlepool U *(Free from Deportivo Farense, Portugal, on 22/1/2004) FL 25 FLC 1 FAC 5 Others 6*

KONTE Amadou
Born: Mali, 23 January 1981
Height: 6'3" **Weight:** 13.8
International Honours: Mali: Yth
This towering centre forward made an impressive debut for Cambridge United against Cheltenham last October, showing himself to be athletic, mobile and in possession of some useful skills. He scored three goals for the U's but then fell out of favour following a change in management and moved on to join SPL club Hibernian during the January transfer window. He featured regularly for the Easter Road club during the remainder of the season, although mostly from the substitutes' bench.
Cambridge U *(Free from Paterno Calcio, Italy, ex RC Strasbourg, FC Porto, Vilanovense, on 22/10/2004) FL 6+3/3*

KOO-BOOTHE Nathan Djebril
Born: Westminster, 18 July 1985
Height: 5'11" **Weight:** 12.11
A tall central defender, Nathan made his debut for MK Dons in the 3-0 Carling Cup win at Peterborough, but was given a rough time on his next start four days later at Oldham and failed to feature after that, suffering an illness that kept him out for a couple of months. Later on he was a regular in the reserve side, where his solid tackling and aerial ability were shown to be the strongest parts of his game.
Watford *(Signed from Hayes on 8/2/2003)*
MK Dons *(Free on 23/7/2004) FL 1 FLC 1*

KOSKELA Toni
Born: Finland, 16 February 1983
Height: 6'2" **Weight:** 12.8
International Honours: Finland: U21-5; Yth
Toni joined Cardiff in February on a six-month deal with a view to a longer contract if he impressed. He featured mainly for the reserves as he acclimatised himself to the British game, but when he was handed his chance from the bench in consecutive home games against Crewe and Ipswich he took it. Toni proved himself to be a robust midfielder with quality delivery on set pieces and a good range of passing which meant the club saw enough to offer him a longer deal at Ninian Park.
Cardiff C *(Signed from KooTooPeen on 4/1/2005) FL 0+2*

KOUMAS Jason
Born: Wrexham, 25 September 1979
Height: 5'10" **Weight:** 11.0
International Honours: W: 14
After an excellent 2003-04 season, Jason surprisingly did not figure in either Gary Megson or Bryan Robson's plans for West Bromwich Albion last term. In fact, he made only a dozen or so senior appearances for Albion, starting in just five Premiership games. At his best he is a midfielder blessed with excellent close control and dribbling skills, who creates plenty of chances for his colleagues and scores some wonderful goals.
Tranmere Rov *(From trainee on 27/11/1997) FL 96+31/25 FLC 9+5/2 FAC 9/5*
West Bromwich A *(£2,500,000 on 29/8/2002) P/FL 69+15/14 FLC 5 FAC 4+1*

KOZLUK Robert (Rob)
Born: Mansfield, 5 August 1977
Height: 5'8" **Weight:** 11.7
International Honours: E: U21-2
A foot injury in pre-season training kept Rob out until the new year when he went on loan to Preston to gain match fitness. He was back at Bramall Lane after a couple of outings covering an injury crisis and soon resumed his right-wing-back role for the Blades using his pace and anticipation, both in attack and defence. His long throw posed a threat in the opposition's penalty area.
Derby Co *(From trainee on 10/2/1996) PL 9+7 FLC 3 FAC 2+1*
Sheffield U *(Signed on 12/3/1999) FL 155+12/2 FLC 6+1 FAC 10 Others 3*
Huddersfield T *(Loaned on 7/9/2000) FL 14*
Preston NE *(Loaned on 6/1/2005) FL 0+1 FAC 1*

KUDUZOVIC Fahrudin
Born: Bosnia, 10 October 1984
Height: 6'3" **Weight:** 13.3
Fahrudin had trials with Port Vale before joining Notts County early on last season. A midfield playmaker he caused a buzz of excitement at Meadow Lane and quickly became popular with the fans but he was then injured and he was released during the January transfer window. He subsequently signed for Eircom League side Sligo Rovers.
Notts Co *(From Derby Co trainee on 3/9/2004) FL 0+3*

KUIPERS Michel
Born: Amsterdam, Holland, 26 June 1974
Height: 6'2" **Weight:** 14.10
Club Honours: Div 3 '01; Div 2 '02
Once a marine in the Dutch armed forces, Michel was a courageous last line of defence in Brighton's battle against relegation from the Championship. After missing much of the 2003-04 promotion campaign, he made the jersey his own last term with some outstanding displays and was the club's only ever-present player when, in January, he damaged his shoulder in a game against Nottingham Forest. It was a major blow for the likeable Dutchman, but an even bigger setback for his club which struggled to find a capable deputy.
Bristol Rov *(Free from SDW Amsterdam, Holland on 20/1/1999) FL 1*
Brighton & Hove A *(Free on 4/7/2000) FL 133+1 FLC 4 FAC 7 Others 6*
Hull C *(Loaned on 29/8/2003) FL 3*

KUQI Shefki
Born: Albania, 10 November 1976
Height: 6'2" **Weight:** 13.10
International Honours: Finland: 38
Shefki had probably his most successful season to date at Ipswich, playing regularly in the side and scoring goals consistently throughout the campaign. He finished joint-top scorer with 19 Championship goals and this, together with his tremendous commitment really endeared him to the fans. He is good in the air and has the ability to run at defences at pace, which often leads to scoring opportunities for his colleagues. He also has the knack of being in the box at the right time to pick up rebounds or knock ons. This was best illustrated in the home game with Plymouth when he came off the bench with the side 2-1 down and grabbed a brace of goals to complete an unlikely victory. Shefki was voted as the club's 'Player of the Year' by the supporters.
Stockport Co *(£300,000 from FC Jokerit, Finland, ex HJK Helsinki, on 31/1/2001) FL 32+3/11 FLC 2/1 FAC 1*
Sheffield Wed *(£700,000 + on 11/1/2002) FL 58+6/19 FLC 3 FAC 1*
Ipswich T *(Free on 26/9/2003) FL 69+10/30 FLC 0+2 FAC 2+1/1 Others 3+1/1*

Shefki Kuqi

KUSZCZAK Tomasz
Born: Krosno Odrzanskie, Poland, 20 March 1982
Height: 6'3" **Weight:** 13.3
International Honours: Poland: 2
Signed by West Bromwich Albion as cover for Russell Hoult and Joe Murphy, Tomasz was on the bench for the opening Premiership game of 2004-05 at Blackburn. A well-built, well-proportioned 'keeper, he made his debut in place of the injured Russell Hoult against Fulham, doing well in a 1-1 draw. He then came on as a substitute in the penultimate game of the season and produced some world-class saves as Albion gained a point to set themselves up for the 'Great Escape' act that followed on the final day.
West Bromwich A *(Free from Hertha Berlin, Germany on 2/8/2004) PL 2+1 FLC 1 FAC 0+1*

KYLE Kevin Alistair
Born: Stranraer, 7 June 1981
Height: 6'3" **Weight:** 13.7
International Honours: S: 9; B-3; U21-12
This giant centre forward endured a torrid time with injuries last term. Having spearheaded the Sunderland attack the previous season, Kevin was reduced to only a handful of starts as a persistent hip injury forced him to watch from the sidelines while the Black Cats swept to promotion. Brave and strong in the air, all on Wearside are looking forward to Kevin's eventual return and he signalled his intentions towards the season's end with five goals in a reserve-team outing against Aston Villa.
Sunderland *(Free from Ayr Boswell on 25/9/1998) P/FL 50+26/10 FLC 4+2/5 FAC 7+2/1 Others 2/2*
Huddersfield T *(Loaned on 8/9/2000) FL 0+4*
Darlington *(Loaned on 1/11/2000) FL 5/1 FAC 3/1*
Rochdale *(Loaned on 26/1/2001) FL 3+3*

L

LAKIS Vassilios
Born: Thessaloniki, Greece, 10 September 1976
Height: 5'9" **Weight:** 10.6
International Honours: Greece: 34
This experienced international midfielder arrived at Crystal Palace as a free agent in September after featuring for his country in their successful Euro 2004 campaign. However, Vassilios failed to win a regular place in the Premiership club's line-up and made most of his appearances from the substitutes' bench.
Crystal Palace *(Free from AEK Athens, Greece on 4/10/2004) PL 6+12 FLC 0+1 FAC 1*

LAMBERT Rickie Lee
Born: Liverpool, 16 February 1982
Height: 5'10" **Weight:** 11.2
Rickie struggled to find his best form for Stockport at the start of last season although his fortunes improved at the turn of the year when he netted at Barnsley and then scored both goals in the memorable 2-1 win at Torquay on New Year's Day. He only made a handful of appearances after that and joined Rochdale in February. Playing in midfield or just behind the main strikers, he hit four goals in his first six games, including a superb free-kick winner against Northampton. He later also featured up front when Dale lost their regular strikers through suspension.
Blackpool *(From trainee on 17/7/2000) FL 0+3*
Macclesfield T *(Free on 2/3/2001) FL 36+8/8 FAC 4/2 Others 1*
Stockport Co *(£300,000 on 30/4/2003) FL 88+10/18 FLC 3 FAC 2+1 Others 5+1/1*
Rochdale *(Signed on 17/2/2005) FL 15/6*

LAMBU Goma
Born: Ghana, 10 November 1984
Height: 5'3" **Weight:** 9.8
International Honours: E: Yth
After a good performance in the reserves at Rushden, and with first-choice striker Derek Asamoah reporting ill, Goma was given his debut for Mansfield in the home fixture with Cheltenham. Playing wide on the right he stuck to his task and showed some good touches, causing his opposing full back some problems. However, he did not figure in the first team again, and subsequently joined Conference South side Redbridge.
Millwall *(From trainee on 4/12/2001. Free to Fisher Ath during 2003 close season)*
Mansfield T *(Free from Redbridge, via various trials, ex Tooting & Mitcham, Southall, on 28/1/2005) FL 1*

LAMPARD Frank James
Born: Romford, 20 June 1978
Height: 6'0" **Weight:** 12.6
Club Honours: FLC '05; PL '05
International Honours: E: 32; B-1; U21-19; Yth
How appropriate that Chelsea's two goals at Bolton, which secured their first Championship for 50 years, were scored by Frank Lampard! This rounded off an incredible 12 months for the England midfielder: Chelsea 'Player of the Year' 2004; England fans' 'International Player of the Year'; nominee for both World and European Player of the Year polls; Fans' PFA Premiership 'Player of the Year'. His remarkable performances were recognised by his inclusion in the PFA Premiership team of the season and, ultimately, by the Football Writers' Association who voted him 'Footballer of the Year'. The two-season midfield axis he has formed with Claude Makelele has developed into the most formidable in the Premiership as their very different styles complement perfectly. For a midfield player to top-score for a Premiership-winning side is a great

Rickie Lambert

Richard Langley

achievement and Frank's portfolio of 19 goals contained some brilliant efforts, notably the pile driver against Norwich, a left-footed volley against Bayern Munich and the calmly stroked side-footer against Fulham which turned a potentially difficult match into a vital victory. But perhaps Frank's most noteworthy statistic has been to create a Premiership record of 146 consecutive appearances for an outfield player (playing in every minute of every match) – defying a foot injury which required a close season operation and forced his withdrawal from England's summer tour.

West Ham U *(From trainee on 1/7/1995) PL 132+16/23 FLC 15+1/9 FAC 13/2 Others 10/4*

Swansea C *(Loaned on 6/10/1995) FL 8+1/1 Others 1+1*

Chelsea *(£11,000,000 on 3/7/2001) PL 147+4/34 FLC 11+4/2 FAC 16+3/3 Others 30+2/10*

LANGLEY Richard Barrington Michael

Born: Harlesden, 27 December 1979
Height: 5'10" **Weight:** 11.4
International Honours: Jamaica: 17; E: Yth

Richard is an undoubtedly talented midfielder with vision and the ability to play a killer pass in the final third but he is still to fully establish himself at Cardiff. Used almost entirely on the right side of a midfield four, he is at his best when he drifts inside and is possessed of a fierce shot that makes him dangerous at set pieces. Having sustained a knee injury while on international duty with Jamaica Richard missed virtually the whole of the first half of the season and returned to the starting line-up in January which coincided with a turnaround in form for the Bluebirds.

Queens Park Rgrs *(From trainee on 31/12/1996) FL 123+10/18 FLC 6/2 FAC 7 Others 2/1*

Cardiff C *(£250,000 on 15/8/2003) FL 63+6/8 FAC 3*

LANGMEAD Kelvin Steven

Born: Coventry, 23 March 1985
Height: 6'1" **Weight:** 13.6

A bustling, old-fashioned centre forward, Kelvin had a loan spell at Kidderminster early on last term, where he was a popular addition to the squad and scored a crucial injury-time winner against Scunthorpe. He returned to Preston and went on to make his debut for North End as a substitute in the home draw with Millwall. Shortly afterwards he was allowed to move on to Shrewsbury. He made a good contribution for the Gay

Meadow club and added three goals during the remainder of the season.
Preston NE *(From trainee on 26/2/2004) FL 0+1*
Carlisle U *(Loaned on 27/2/2004) FL 3+8/1*
Kidderminster Hrs *(Loaned on 4/9/2004) FL 9+1/1 Others 1*
Shrewsbury T *(Signed on 26/11/2004) FL 24+4/3*

LAPHAM Kyle Jonathan
Born: Swindon, 5 January 1986
Height: 5'11" **Weight:** 11.0
This Swindon Town youngster was thrown into the fray as a right wing back for the final two games of the 2004-05 season due to an injury crisis. Kyle provided the cross from which Sam Parkin netted in the 1-1 draw with Chesterfield and his assured performances were rewarded with the offer of a professional contract for 2005-06. Kyle can also play as a central defender if required.
Swindon T *(Trainee) FL 2*

LARKIN Colin
Born: Dundalk, 27 April 1982
Height: 5'9" **Weight:** 10.4
International Honours: RoI: Yth
This useful striker made an impressive start to the 2004-05 season with Mansfield, scoring spectacularly when he blasted the ball home from fully 30 yards at Chester. Although his goal-scoring form waned a little as the team's form dipped, his enthusiasm and pace posed problems for more than a few defenders. After being laid low for a month with appendicitis he suffered a loss in form and then fell out of favour following a change in management. Colin was released by the Stags in the summer.
Wolverhampton W *(From trainee on 19/5/1999) FL 1+2 FLC 0+1/1*
Kidderminster Hrs *(Loaned on 14/9/2001) FL 31+2/6 Others 1+1/1*
Mansfield T *(£135,000 on 9/8/2002) FL 61+31/25 FLC 1 FAC 5+1/1 Others 3+4*

LARRIEU Romain
Born: Mont-de-Marsan, France, 31 August 1976
Height: 6'4" **Weight:** 13.11
Club Honours: Div 3 '02
Following his injury-ravaged season in 2003-04, Romain had to wait for his opportunity in goal for Plymouth Argyle last term due to the form of Luke McCormick. He was rewarded with his patience by taking over the number one position against Leeds in September and he then went on to make 24 consecutive appearances for the Pilgrims. A very agile 'keeper, Romain is an excellent shot-stopper and distributes the ball accurately.
Plymouth Arg *(Free from ASOA Valence, France, ex Montpellier, on 30/11/2000) FL 131+1 FLC 3 FAC 9 Others 3*

LARSSON Sebastian Benet
Born: Eskilstuna, Sweden, 6 June 1985
Height: 5'10" **Weight:** 11.4
International Honours: Sweden: U21-5
This defender was another youngster to appear in all three of the Gunners' Carling Cup ties starting on two occasions. He also made the bench for the Champions' League clashes with Panathinaikos, Rosenborg and Bayern Munich and featured as an unused substitute on a handful of occasions in Premiership matches.
Arsenal *(From trainee on 1/7/2002) FLC 2+1*

LASLEY Keith William Robert
Born: Glasgow, 21 September 1979
Height: 5'8" **Weight:** 10.7
This hard-working midfield player put in several excellent pre-season friendly displays for Plymouth and was rewarded with a starting role on the right-hand side of midfield early on last term. Following this initial run in the side Keith had to be satisfied mainly with a place on the bench. Keith came on against Nottingham Forest at the end of August to earn a last-minute penalty from a forceful run into the box, and this resulted in a 3-2 victory for the Pilgrims.
Motherwell *(Signed from Cathkin UBC on 20/3/1999) SL 85+12/9 SLC 4/1 SC 7+1*
Plymouth Arg *(Signed on 18/6/2004) FL 14+10 FLC 1*

LATTE-YEDO Igor
Born: Dabou, Ivory Coast, 14 December 1978
Height: 6'3" **Weight:** 13.0
This giant central defender overcame the disappointment of being red carded on his debut for Cambridge against Wycombe and made a number of appearances in the U's back line. However, following a change in management at the club he found himself pushed up front to add strength to the attack and he spent the second half of the campaign playing as a striker.
Cambridge U *(Free from Marseilles Endoume, France, ex Gap, Beaucaire, AS Cannes, GD Estoril Praia, on 4/8/2004) FL 5+6 Others 1*

[LAUREN] BISAN-ETAME MAYER Laureano
Born: Lodhji Kribi, Cameroon, 19 January 1977
Height: 5'11" **Weight:** 11.4
Club Honours: FAC '02, '03, '05; PL '02, '04; CS '02; '04
International Honours: Cameroon (ANC '00, '02; OLYM '00)
Like many of the Arsenal back four Lauren enjoyed contrasting fortunes throughout the season. He remains very adept at bringing the ball out of defence and is a fine passer and crosser of the ball. However, at times his defensive abilities as well as those of the whole team have been open to question. Lauren remains a strong character though and he was successful in the FA Cup penalty shoot-out victories over Sheffield United and Manchester United. His only goal of the season was a highly important one for his penalty put the Gunners 2-1 ahead at White Hart Lane in a memorable match which eventually finished 5-4 in favour of the away side.
Arsenal *(£7,200,000 from Real Mallorca, Spain, ex Cant Sevilla, Utrera, Seville, Levante, on 16/6/2000) PL 130+7/6 FLC 1 FAC 22/2 Others 44+6/1*

LAURSEN Martin
Born: Silkeborg, Denmark, 26 July 1977
Height: 6'2" **Weight:** 12.5
International Honours: Denmark: 41; U21-14; Yth
This cool and accomplished central defender had something of a disappointing season at Villa last season when he sometimes struggled to adjust to the tempo of Premiership football. He missed a large chunk of the campaign recovering from surgery to a knee and did not return to the line-up until early March. He finished off in commanding form, however. Martin continued to represent Denmark at international level during the campaign.
Aston Villa *(£3,000,000 from AC Milan, Italy, ex Verona, Parma, on 1/7/2004) PL 12/1*

LAVILLE Florent
Born: Valence, France, 7 August 1973
Height: 6'0" **Weight:** 13.0
Bolton's skilful French defender arrived on loan at Coventry towards the end of October, having recovered from his injury problems of the previous campaign. He made an impressive debut in the 3-2 win over Reading and looked like the defensive organiser that the team had lacked. His loan period was extended for a second month but his later performances lacked consistency and he returned to the Reebok after Christmas. Florent was one of several fringe players released by Wanderers at the end of the season.
Bolton W *(£500,000 from Lyon, France on 1/2/2003) PL 15*
Coventry C *(Loaned on 29/10/2004) FL 5+1*

LAWRENCE Denis William
Born: Trinidad, 1 August 1974
Height: 6'7" **Weight:** 12.7
Club Honours: AMC '05
International Honours: Trinidad & Tobago: 55
'Tall-man' Denis remained a big favourite with the Wrexham faithful last term. A virtual ever-present in the line-up, he has good control for such a tall central defender. Famous for his little sorties up field at the Racecourse, he often moves up for set pieces, and contributes to the goal tally. He scored the winner against Bradford City in September and a late leveller against Peterborough in October. Denis also represented Trinidad & Tobago in their World Cup qualifying campaign during the season.
Wrexham *(£100,000 from Defence Force, Trinidad on 10/3/2001) FL 149+7/12 FLC 3 FAC 3+1/1 Others 9/1*

LAWRENCE James (Jamie) Hubert
Born: Balham, 8 March 1970
Height: 5'11" **Weight:** 12.11
Club Honours: FLC '97
International Honours: Jamaica: 23
This experienced midfielder originally joined Brentford on a short-term deal last September but eventually stayed until the end of the season. A player who always gives 100 per cent he appeared in central midfield, on the right wing and even at right back as he filled in for absent colleagues. Unfortunately Jamie suffered a knee injury at Luton in January and did not return until the end of the season. He gained three caps for Jamaica as a Brentford player and one while unattached in August.
Sunderland *(Signed from Cowes on 15/10/1993) FL 2+2 FLC 0+1*
Doncaster Rov *(£20,000 on 17/3/1994) FL 16+9/3 FLC 2 FAC 1 Others 3*
Leicester C *(£125,000 on 6/1/1995) P/FL 21+26/1 FLC 3+4/2 FAC 1+1*
Bradford C *(£50,000 on 17/6/1997) P/FL 133+22/12 FLC 8+1/1 FAC 4+1/1 Others 0+2*
Walsall *(Free on 27/3/2003) FL 12+10/1 FLC 1 FAC 0+1*
Wigan Ath *(Loaned on 20/11/2003) FL 0+4*
Grimsby T *(Free on 23/3/2004) FL 5/1*
Brentford *(Free on 17/9/2004) FL 8+6 FAC 3+1 Others 1*

LAWRENCE Liam
Born: Retford, 14 December 1981
Height: 5'10" **Weight:** 11.3
Club Honours: Ch '05
An fine piece of business by Sunderland boss Mick McCarthy in the close season saw right winger Liam join the Black Cats from Mansfield. An excellent crosser of the ball and deadly with free kicks, Liam weighed in with six goals towards Sunderland's Championship triumph, none better than the two brilliant strikes against Watford at the Stadium of Light in November. The jump from League Two to the Championship did not make much difference to Liam and he will have the chance to impress at Premiership level in 2005-06.
Mansfield T *(From trainee on 3/7/2000) FL 120+16/34 FLC 3 FAC 8/5 Others 4+2*
Sunderland *(Signed on 5/8/2004) FL 20+12/7 FLC 1+1*

LAWRENCE Matthew (Matt) James
Born: Northampton, 19 June 1974
Height: 6'1" **Weight:** 12.12
Club Honours: Div 2 '01
International Honours: E: Sch
Apart from a spell out injured, Matt was an ever-present in defence for Millwall last term, usually playing in his preferred position of centre back. Skippering the side in the latter part of the season he led by example, giving some outstanding performances and spurring on his colleagues. Matt reads the game well and is known for his tough tackling and runs forward.
Wycombe W *(£20,000 from Grays Ath on 19/1/1996) FL 13+3/1 FLC 4 FAC 1 Others 0+1*
Fulham *(Free on 7/2/1997) FL 57+2 FLC 4+1 FAC 2 Others 5*
Wycombe W *(£86,000 + on 2/10/1998) FL 63/4 FLC 4 FAC 7 Others 3*
Millwall *(£200,000 on 21/3/2000) FL 183+10 FLC 8+1 FAC 17 Others 8*

LAWSON James Peter
Born: Basildon, 21 January 1987
Height: 5'9" **Weight:** 10.3
This tall front runner enjoyed a fine season with the Southend United youth team last term. He impressed manager Steve Tilson sufficiently to earn a first-team appearance as a late substitute for Nicky Nicolau in the home game with Rushden on New Year's Day and will be seeking further senior experience in 2005-06.
Southend U *(Trainee) FL 0+1*

LAZARIDIS Stanley (Stan)
Born: Perth, Australia, 16 August 1972
Height: 5'9" **Weight:** 11.12
International Honours: Australia: 56; U23; Yth
Stan began the season at left back for Birmingham, but was injured early on and struggled to recover his fitness thereafter. He returned in December and his free running down the flank helped the Blues become a better attacking force and clinch vital victories at Villa, over West Brom and Middlesbrough before being sidelined again. Defenders always needed to be on their toes with Stan around.
West Ham U *(£300,000 from West Adelaide, Australia on 8/9/1995) PL 53+16/3 FLC 6+1 FAC 9+1 Others 0+1*
Birmingham C *(£1,600,000 on 29/7/1999) P/FL 131+43/8 FLC 12+4 FAC 4+1 Others 2+5*

LEACOCK Dean Graham
Born: Croydon, 10 June 1984
Height: 6'2" **Weight:** 12.4
International Honours: E: Yth
This promising young central defender started last season in Fulham's reserves, but was sent out on loan to Coventry to gain some much-needed first-team experience. He impressed in his debut for the Sky Blues at Leeds, but then suffered a hamstring injury. After returning to fitness the loan period was extended until the end of the campaign, but a subsequent back problem meant that he was not seen in the Coventry first team after the February home defeat by Burnley.
Fulham *(From trainee on 17/7/2002) PL 3+1 FLC 2*
Coventry C *(Loaned on 10/9/2004) FL 12+1 FLC 1 FAC 1+1*

LEADBITTER Grant
Born: Chester-le-Street, 7 January 1986
Height: 5'9" **Weight:** 10.3
International Honours: E: Yth
This young midfielder made one appearance for Sunderland last season in the 3-3 Carling Cup draw at Crewe in September when the Black Cats went on to lose on penalties. Grant continued to represent England at U19 level and his neat play and composed manner could yet see him establish himself at the Stadium of Light.
Sunderland *(From trainee on 9/1/2003) FLC 1+1*

LEARY Michael Antonio
Born: Ealing, 17 April 1983
Height: 5'11" **Weight:** 12.3
International Honours: RoI: Yth
This right-sided attacking midfield player received few first-team opportunities at Luton last term and his only start came in the home defeat by Huddersfield Town in October. However, Michael featured regularly in the Hatters' reserve team and was a member of the side that defeated Reading to win the Pontin's Combination League Cup.
Luton T *(From juniors on 3/8/2001) FL 9+13/2 FLC 0+1 FAC 1+1 Others 3+2/1*

EDLEY Joseph (Joe) nristopher
orn: Cardiff, 23 January 1987
eight: 6'0" **Weight:** 11.7
ternational Honours: W: U21-3; Yth
e made his senior debut for Cardiff as a cond half substitute in the Carling Cup in at MK Dons last September and was nded his full League debut at Brighton e following month. The youngster put gether a decent run in the side tching the eye time after time. Joe arted the season as a left winger but juries gave him a chance in the centre midfield which he took with both nds. His mature decision making oupled with quick feet and a solid left-ot delivery point were key features of s game. Joe was called into the Wales 21 squad in February and made the ep up to the senior squad for a training mp in Spain in May.
***ardiff C** (From trainee on 29/10/2004) FL)+8/3 FLC 2+1 FAC 0+1*

EE Alan Desmond
orn: Galway, 21 August 1978
eight: 6'2" **Weight:** 13.9
ternational Honours: RoI: 8; U21-5
his powerful front man began the 2004-5 campaign as a first choice for Cardiff ut injuries and the sale of players meant nat he partnered three different players three months. Alan never really found is best form and later in the season it vas revealed he had been playing with a roin problem due to Cardiff's lack of vailable players. After undergoing urgery, he returned to the side in ebruary and finished off with a total of even goals in all. Alan added to his tally f caps for the Republic of Ireland during ne campaign.
***ston Villa** (From trainee on 21/8/1995)*
***orquay U** (Loaned on 27/11/1998) FL +1/2 Others 2/1*
***ort Vale** (Loaned on 2/3/1999) FL 7+4/2*
***urnley** (£150,000 on 8/7/1999) FL 2+13 LC 1+1 FAC 0+2 Others 1/1*
***otherham U** (£150,000 on 21/9/2000) FL 05+6/37 FLC 5/2 FAC 4+1/1 Others 1/1*
***ardiff C** (£850,000 + on 15/8/2003) FL 1+20/8 FLC 3/1 FAC 2+1/1*

LEE David John Francis
Born: Basildon, 28 March 1980
Height: 5'11" **Weight:** 11.8
This ball-winning midfielder joined Oldham Athletic on non-contract terms ast October following his release by Brighton the previous summer. He made eight starts for the Latics before the deal was cancelled at the end of November. Following his release, David moved into non-league and had spells at Thurrock Town and Stevenage before signing a contract at Aldershot Town.
***Tottenham H** (From trainee on 17/7/1998)*
***Southend U** (Free on 2/8/2000) FL 37+5/8 FLC 2 FAC 3 Others 5/2*
***Hull C** (Free on 1/6/2001) FL 2+9/1 FLC 0+1 FAC 0+1 Others 0+1*
***Brighton & Hove A** (Free on 11/1/2002) FL 1+5 Others 1 (Freed during 2004 close season)*
***Bristol Rov** (Loaned on 16/10/2002) FL 5 Others 1*
***Oldham Ath** (Free from Thurrock on 30/9/2004) FL 5+2 FAC 1 Others 1*

LEE Graeme Barry
Born: Middlesbrough, 31 May 1978
Height: 6'2" **Weight:** 13.7
Brought from his former club, Hartlepool, by then manager Chris Turner, he has again suffered an injury-ravaged season. Just into 2004-05 he was laid low by a cartilage injury, which led to him having to have an operation. On coming back, he was getting into top form but once again suffered another injury to his leg and his powerful presence was sorely missed at the tail end of the season. A good central defensive player, who is also a real danger in the opponents' box, it is hoped he will be given an extended contract at the end of the season. We would also like to make it clear that Graeme has never suffered from shin splints, as was stated in the previous edition.
***Hartlepool U** (From trainee on 2/7/1996) FL 208+11/19 FLC 7+2/1 FAC 8+1 Others 13+2/2*
***Sheffield Wed** (Free on 2/7/2003) FL 49+3/4 FLC 1/1 FAC 4 Others 3/1*

LEE Jason Benedict
Born: Forest Gate, 9 May 1971
Height: 6'3" **Weight:** 13.8
Club Honours: Div 2 '98
This veteran striker proved a real thorn in the side of opposing defences during his first season with League Two club Boston United. Jason's ability to win the ball in the air and set up plenty of chances proved invaluable. He worked very hard despite playing alongside a number of different partners up front and netted a double-figure tally himself. Jason, who also made a rare appearance at centre back because of an injury crisis, ended the campaign by accepting a new one-year contract and was manager Steve Evans' selection as 'Player of the Season'.
***Charlton Ath** (From trainee on 2/6/1989) FL 0+1 Others 0+2*
***Stockport Co** (Loaned on 6/2/1991) FL 2*
***Lincoln C** (£35,000 on 1/3/1991) FL 86+7/21 FLC 6 FAC 2+1/1 Others 4*
***Southend U** (Signed on 6/8/1993) FL 18+6/3 FLC 1 FAC 1 Others 5+3/3*
***Nottingham F** (£200,000 on 4/3/1994) P/FL 41+35/14 FLC 4+3/1 FAC 0+5 Others 4+2*
***Charlton Ath** (Loaned on 5/2/1997) FL 7+1/3*
***Grimsby T** (Loaned on 27/3/1997) FL 2+5/2*
***Watford** (£200,000 on 16/6/1997) FL 36+1/11 FLC 4 FAC 4 Others 1*
***Chesterfield** (£250,000 on 28/8/1998) FL 17+11/1 FAC 0+2 Others 0+2*
***Peterborough U** (£50,000 on 3/1/2000) FL 49+29/17 FAC 5/1 Others 2+2/1*
***Falkirk** (Free on 1/8/2003) SL 27+2/8 SC 1+1/1 Others 1*
***Boston U** (Free on 6/8/2004) FL 32+7/9 FLC 2/1 FAC 3+1/1*

LEE Richard Anthony
Born: Oxford, 5 October 1982
Height: 6'0" **Weight:** 12.8
International Honours: E: Yth
Watford's young goalkeeper was given his first-team chance at the start of the 2004-05 season and established himself with a string of fine performances. Brave, agile and alert, Richard dealt confidently with crosses and proved a sound shot-stopper, although his kicking was occasionally awry. He was outstanding against Ipswich and Sheffield United, while a tip-over to deny Portsmouth's Patrik Berger was judged 'Save of the Season'. Unhappily, Richard suffered a compound fracture of the cheekbone in an accidental collision with a colleague against Coventry in December. He returned to action after two months, wearing a protective mask and needing to rebuild his confidence. In March he made a fine penalty save at Queen's Park Rangers, but in April he sustained a knee injury which brought his season to a disappointing close.
***Watford** (From trainee on 7/3/2000) FL 37 FLC 5*

LEE Robert (Rob) Martin
Born: West Ham, 1 February 1966
Height: 5'11" **Weight:** 11.13
Club Honours: Div 1 '93
International Honours: E: 21; B-1; U21-2
After leaving West Ham United the previous summer, this veteran midfielder made a surprise move to Boundary Park in November 2004 on non-contract terms. However, after making his debut in the Latics' LDV Vans Trophy win over Hartlepool, he opted to leave the club. He moved on to Wycombe where, after proving his fitness, this veteran midfielder became a regular in the midfield. His class was immediately obvious; he reads the game so well and can still put in a

high work rate over the full 90 minutes. However, an injury ended his short run of first-team action for the Chairboys.
Charlton Ath *(Free from Hornchurch on 12/7/1983) FL 274+24/59 FLC 16+3/1 FAC 14/2 Others 10+2/3*
Newcastle U *(£700,000 on 22/9/1992) P/FL 292+11/44 FLC 22+1/3 FAC 27/5 Others 28/4*
Derby Co *(£250,000 + on 7/2/2002) P/FL 47+1/2 FLC 2*
West Ham U *(Free on 8/8/2003) FL 12+4 FLC 2 FAC 0+1 (Freed during 2004 close season)*
Oldham Ath *(Free, following a short break from football, on 29/11/2004) Others 1*
Wycombe W *(Free on 18/3/2005) FL 6+1*

LE FONDRE Adam

Born: Stockport, 2 December 1986
Height: 5'9" **Weight:** 11.4
This young striker really impressed for Stockport County last season. Adam scored on his debut in the LDV Vans Trophy victory at home to Bury and added four more goals including a superb header against Doncaster. He became a popular player with the fans for his pace, work rate and eye for goal up front.
Stockport Co *(From trainee on 18/2/2005) FL 11+9/4 Others 1+1/1*

Rob Lee

LEGG Andrew (Andy)

Born: Neath, 28 July 1966
Height: 5'8" **Weight:** 10.7
Club Honours: WC '89, '91; AIC '95
International Honours: W: 6
Peterborough United's player-coach was a regular in the line-up for most of the 2004-05 campaign and performed best when included as a sweeper or at full back. Andy also featured in a midfield role, where he battled away for the cause, while his trademark long throw remained an important feature of his game. Andy was diagnosed as having a cancerous lump on his neck towards the end of the campaign and after a bout of surgery he announced he would be hanging up his boots after more than 700 senior appearances.
Swansea C *(Signed from Britton Ferry on 12/8/1988) FL 155+8/29 FLC 9+1 FAC 16/4 Others 15+3/5*
Notts Co *(£275,000 on 23/7/1993) FL 85+4/9 FLC 11 FAC 7+1/2 Others 13+2/3*
Birmingham C *(Signed on 29/2/1996) FL 31+14/5 FLC 3+1 FAC 2+1*
Ipswich T *(Loaned on 3/11/1997) FL 6/1 FLC 1*
Reading *(£75,000 on 20/2/1998) FL 12 FLC 1*
Peterborough U *(Loaned on 15/10/1998) FL 5*
Cardiff C *(Free on 16/12/1998) FL 152+23/12 FLC 8+1 FAC 17+4 Others 4*
Peterborough U *(Free on 8/7/2003) FL 76+5/5 FLC 2 FAC 4+1 Others 1+2*

LEGWINSKI Sylvain

Born: Clermont-Ferrand, France, 6 October 1973
Height: 6'3" **Weight:** 11.7
International Honours: France: B-3; U21
Injury disrupted the 2004-05 season for Sylvain who only managed a decent run in the Fulham starting line-up in the opening stages of the campaign. A combative midfielder who is a good passer of the ball and links well when pushing forward, despite instigating many attacking moves his only goal of the season came in the home game against Birmingham.
Fulham *(£3,500,000 from Bordeaux, France, ex AS Monaco, on 22/8/2001) PL 106+9/8 FLC 3+2/1 FAC 17/1 Others 10+2/2*

LEHMANN Jens

Born: Essen, Germany, 10 November 1969
Height: 6'3" **Weight:** 13.10
Club Honours: PL '04; CS '04; FAC '05
International Honours: Germany: 25

ens Lehmann

Jens had a mixed season very much in keeping with the nature of Arsenal's overall campaign. He started as the undoubted first choice goalkeeper and did not suffer his first-ever Premiership defeat until the visit to Old Trafford which ended a personal run of 47 games unbeaten. However following a 2-1 reverse at Anfield in November, he was dropped in favour of Manuel Almunia and did not return to the side until February. The unwanted absence did him some good though as he kept 11 clean sheets in his last 17 matches of the season. That run included the FA Cup final against Manchester United, when he was a clear 'Man of the Match' making a string of fine saves before producing the crucial stop from Paul Scholes in the penalty shoot-out that helped seal the Gunners' success.

Arsenal *(£1,250,000 from Borussia Dortmund, Germany, ex SW Essen, Schalke 04, AC Milan, on 5/8/2003) PL 66 FAC 10 Others 19*

LEIGERTWOOD Mikele Benjamin

Born: Enfield, 12 November 1982
Height: 6'1" **Weight:** 13.11

This young Crystal Palace star featured occasionally in the autumn, but made a real breakthrough in January, stepping in to replace Aki Riihilahti in the centre of midfield. Mikele adapted well to the new role, impressing with his strong tackling and skills on the ball, and had become a regular in the line-up by the end of the season. He scored one Premiership goal, netting in the 3-0 home win over Tottenham.

Wimbledon *(From trainee on 29/6/2001) FL 55+1/2 FLC 4/1 FAC 5*
Leyton Orient *(Loaned on 19/11/2001) FL 8 FAC 2*
Crystal Palace *(£150,000 on 2/2/2004) P/FL 23+9/1 FLC 2 FAC 1 Others 3*

LEITAO Jorge Manuel

Born: Oporto, Portugal, 14 January 1974
Height: 5'11" **Weight:** 13.4

Jorge took his tally of games for Walsall to well past the 200-mark last term, the main feature of his play again being his tireless running. He operated down both right and left channels in midfield, and occasionally in defence. Jorge netted 11 goals for the Saddlers including doubles in the 3-2 win over Swindon and in the LDV Vans Trophy tie at Cheltenham.

Walsall *(£150,000 from SC Farense, Portugal, ex Avintes, on 10/8/2000) FL 170+37/52 FLC 9/5 FAC 11+1/4 Others 6/3*

LENNIE Joshua (Josh) Nathan

Born: Greenford, 26 March 1986
Height: 6'1" **Weight:** 13.3

This promising young 'keeper made his senior debut for Brentford when he came on as a half-time substitute in the LDV Vans Trophy tie against MK Dons back in September, but spent much of the remainder of the season out on loan at Conference South clubs Carshalton Athletic and Maidenhead United. Josh was not offered a professional contract at the end of the season and was reported to have signed for AFC Wimbledon.

Brentford *(Trainee) Others 0+1*

LENNON Aaron Justin

Born: Leeds, 16 April 1987
Height: 5'5" **Weight:** 9.12
International Honours: E: Yth

Diminutive winger Aaron attracted the attention of a string of Premiership clubs as he hit a streak of red-hot form for Leeds in the new year. Equally good on either flank, his speed and skill tore a succession of defences apart and prompted Elland Road supporters to name him as their 'Young Player of the Year'. He built on his experiences as a Premiership substitute the previous campaign, scoring on his first Championship start in the 3-2 Boxing Day win at champions Sunderland. Not surprisingly he showed signs of fatigue towards the end of the season and was withdrawn from the England U19 squad to preserve his energies for club football.

Leeds U *(Trainee) P/FL 19+19/1 FLC 1+2 FAC 1+1*

LE SAUX Graeme Pierre

Born: Jersey, 17 October 1968
Height: 5'10" **Weight:** 12.2
Club Honours: PL '95; FLC '98; ESC '98; CS '00
International Honours: E: 36; B-2; U21-4

Last term proved to be another season disrupted by injuries, and even when present Graeme's undoubted class and commitment were not enough to make a silk purse out of a Saints' defensive-midfield combination that was palpably inadequate with regards to pace and gumption. After taking over as manager in December Harry Redknapp preferred Graeme in midfield, where he formed a useful partnership with wing back Olivier Bernard – but not useful enough to turn Saints' season around.

Chelsea *(Free from St Paul's, Jersey on 9/12/1987) P/FL 77+13/8 FLC 7+6/1 FAC 7+1 Others 8+1*
Blackburn Rov *(£750,000 on 25/3/1993) PL 127+2/7 FLC 10 FAC 8 Others 6+1*
Chelsea *(£5,000,000 on 8/8/1997) PL 133+7/4 FLC 10/1 FAC 18+2/2 Others 20+2*
Southampton *(£500,000 on 21/7/2003) PL 43+1/1 FLC 1/1 FAC 1 Others 1*

LESCOTT Aaron Anthony

Born: Birmingham, 2 December 1978
Height: 5'8" **Weight:** 10.9

Aaron left Stockport soon after the start of the 2004-05 season, returning to Bristol Rovers for whom he had played on loan in the final two months of the previous campaign. A hard-working central midfielder, he showed his versatility by deputising at both left and right back without letting the team down. Aaron sustained a nasty ankle injury at Rochdale, which kept him out of the squad for several weeks.

Aston Villa *(From trainee on 5/7/1996) FAC 0+1*
Lincoln C *(Loaned on 14/3/2000) FL 3+2*
Sheffield Wed *(£100,000 on 3/10/2000) FL 19+18 FLC 3+1 FAC 2*
Stockport Co *(£75,000 on 14/11/2001) FL 65+7/1 FLC 2+1 FAC 2+1 Others 2+1*
Bristol Rov *(Free on 25/3/2004) FL 32+2 FLC 0+1 FAC 1 Others 5*

LESCOTT Jolean Patrick

Born: Birmingham, 16 August 1982
Height: 6'2" **Weight:** 13.0
International Honours: E: U21-2; Yth

Knee injuries kept this classy centre half out of the whole of the previous campaign, but he made a surprise return for Wolves at Burnley early on last season. Although the intention was to ease him back gradually, he soon became a regular, and by Christmas he was back to his best. A difficult obstacle for opposition forwards to beat, he also produced a series of barnstorming runs up the field which really lifted the Molineux faithful. Jolean ended the season on a high with a goal against Sheffield United. Captain of the team he also won the club's 'Player of the Year' award.

Wolverhampton W *(From trainee on 18/8/1999) FL 160+6/12 FLC 6 FAC 8 Others 5*

LESTER Jack William

Born: Sheffield, 8 October 1975
Height: 5'10" **Weight:** 11.8
Club Honours: AMC '98
International Honours: E: Sch

Jack started the 2004-05 season on the substitutes' bench due to injury then struggled to win a regular place in the Sheffield United line-up, his only goal coming in the Carling Cup tie against Stockport County. Jack returned to Nottingham Forest in November where

Graeme Le Saux

he was employed in a midfield role. He made an instant impression, scoring a late goal on his home debut against Queen's Park Rangers. Unfortunately he suffered a cruciate knee injury against Derby in his next game thus ending his season prematurely.
Grimsby T *(From juniors on 8/7/1994) FL 93+40/17 FLC 13+4/6 FAC 8+1/2 Others 4+4*
Doncaster Rov *(Loaned on 20/9/1996) FL 5+6/1*
Nottingham F *(£300,000 on 28/1/2000) FL 73+26/21 FLC 3/3 FAC 1 Others 0+1*
Sheffield U *(Free on 1/8/2003) FL 26+18/12 FLC 3+1/3 FAC 2/1*
Nottingham F *(£50,000 on 26/11/2004) FL 3/1*

LE TALLEC Anthony
Born: Hennebont, France, 3 October 1984
Height: 6'0" **Weight:** 11.7
International Honours: France: U21; Yth
This young Liverpool midfielder spent the first half of the 2004-05 campaign out on loan with St Etienne, returning to Anfield in January. He soon found himself in the first-team squad, making three appearances from the bench before he made the starting line-up for the crucial European Champions' Cup quarter-final at home to Juventus when he gave a good account of himself, supplying the pass from which Luis Garcia scored a stupendous second goal in the 2-1 victory. However, he made only two more starts and was out of contention in the climax to Liverpool's momentous season.
Liverpool *(Signed from Le Havre, France on 18/7/2003) PL 5+12 FLC 2 FAC 1+3 Others 3+4/1*

LEWINGTON Dean Scott
Born: Kingston, 18 May 1984
Height: 5'11" **Weight:** 11.2
After making his breakthrough the previous season Dean developed into a very solid left back during the season. Particularly strong in the tackle, he always showed a willingness to get forward and his switch to the left-midfield role in early February coincided with the MK Dons' 11-match unbeaten run. He reverted to his customary role for the last two games and was a very consistent performer throughout the season.
Wimbledon/MK Dons *(From trainee on 17/7/2003) FL 71+1/3 FLC 1 FAC 6 Others 1/1*

LEWIS Daniel
Born: Redditch, 18 June 1982
Height: 6'1" **Weight:** 14.0
Daniel was back-up goalkeeper to John Danby at Kidderminster last term and sat on the bench for the whole season until making his debut in the very last game at Northampton Town. He acquitted himself well despite being on the wrong end of a 3-0 defeat.
Kidderminster Hrs *(Signed from Studley on 6/7/2004) FL 1*

LEWIS Edward (Eddie) James
Born: Cerritos, USA, 17 May 1974
Height: 5'9" **Weight:** 11.12
International Honours: USA: 64
Eddie remained as effective as ever on Preston's left wing, although his return of three goals was not as high as he would have liked and he failed to find the net after December. Always a threat out wide with his jinking runs and penetrating crosses, he was a great favourite with the Deepdale fans, not least for his deadly swinging free-kicks. His season seemed over following an emergency appendix operation, but he was back in time for the play-offs. Eddie also continued to represent the USA during the season.
Fulham *(£1,300,000 from San Jose Clash, USA on 17/3/2000) P/FL 8+8 FLC 6/1*
Preston NE *(Signed on 5/9/2002) FL 97+14/15 FLC 5+1/1 FAC 4 Others 3*

LEWIS Karl **Junior**
Born: Wembley, 9 October 1973
Height: 6'5" **Weight:** 12.4
Club Honours: Div 2 '02
After finishing the previous campaign on loan at Hull, Junior duly completed a permanent move to the KC Stadium in the summer of 2004. He proved to be a valuable member of the City team and he was the only player to be selected in the match squad for all 46 League One games as the Tigers successfully completed the notable feat of back-to-back promotions. Often seen as Ian Ashbee's partner in the middle of midfield, Junior's versatility meant he was also used as defensive cover.
Fulham *(From trainee on 3/7/1992) FL 4+2 FAC 1 (Free to Dover Ath during 1993 close season)*
Gillingham *(Free from Hendon on 3/8/1999) FL 47+12/8 FLC 4+2 FAC 7+2 Others 4*
Leicester C *(£50,000 on 30/1/2001) P/FL 24+6/1 FLC 3 FAC 1*
Brighton & Hove A *(Loaned on 8/2/2002) FL 14+1/3*
Swindon T *(Loaned on 19/3/2003) FL 9*
Swindon T *(Loaned on 21/10/2003) FL 4*
Hull C *(Free on 25/2/2004) FL 44+8/3 FAC 1+1 Others 1*

LIDDELL Andrew (Andy) Mark
Born: Leeds, 28 June 1973
Height: 5'7" **Weight:** 11.6
Club Honours: AMC '99; Div 2 '03
International Honours: S: U21-12
Out of contract at Wigan, Andy signed for the Blades in the summer of 2004. A regular member of the side, apart from a spell out injured in early in the season, he played as a wide right-sided attacking midfielder, working hard, using his pace and ability to beat defenders and produce a series of searching crosses. He contributed a useful tally of goals and was always dangerous with free kicks near the box.
Barnsley *(From trainee on 6/7/1991) P/FL 142+56/34 FLC 11+4/3 FAC 5+7/1 Others 2+1*
Wigan Ath *(£350,000 on 15/10/1998) FL 206+11/70 FLC 11/1 FAC 7/1 Others 14+1*
Sheffield U *(Free on 7/7/2004) FL 26+7/3 FLC 1 FAC 5/3*

LIDDLE Craig George
Born: Chester-le-Street, 21 October 1971
Height: 5'11" **Weight:** 12.7
Craig's sixth full season with Darlington was marred by a series of injuries and operations that limited his outings in the team. He remained as club captain throughout the campaign and continued to lead by example, his commitment and dedication proving great motivators for his colleagues. An effective central defender, he is strong in the air, quick into the tackle and a good distributor of the ball from the heart of the defence.
Aston Villa *(From trainee on 4/7/1990. Free to Blyth Spartans in August 1991)*
Middlesbrough *(Free on 12/7/1994) P/FL 20+5 FLC 3+2 FAC 2 Others 2*
Darlington *(Free on 20/2/1998) FL 284+1/17 FLC 11 FAC 15/1 Others 11/3*

LINDEGAARD Andrew (Andy) Rindom
Born: Taunton, 10 September 1980
Height: 5'8" **Weight:** 11.4
Club Honours: FAT '02; NC '03; Div 2 '05
This pacy full back was probably Yeovil's most-improved player last term and featured regularly for the side in the second half of the campaign. He was always willing to offer support when the team was pushing forward, contributing his only goal in the 2-1 win over Kidderminster in December.
Yeovil T *(Signed from Westlands Sports on 5/6/2000) FL 31+21/3 FLC 0+1 FAC 3+2 Others 1*

LINWOOD Paul Anthony
Born: Birkenhead, 24 October 1983
Height: 6'2" **Weight:** 12.8
This central defender suffered a frustrating season at Tranmere last term as complications arising from stomach surgery carried out in the summer

Andy Lindegaard

followed by a series of smaller, niggling injuries severely limited his first-team appearances. Paul is both calm and mature, qualities which mark him out immediately as a natural leader at whatever level he plays, and he will be looking to progress his career in the 2005-06 when fully fit.
Tranmere Rov *(From trainee on 3/4/2002) FL 22+8 FAC 3+1 Others 2*

LIPA Andreas
Born: Vienna, Austria, 26 April 1971
Height: 6'2" **Weight:** 12.4
International Honours: Austria: 1
This midfield player was restricted to just a couple of substitute appearances for Port Vale last season, amounting to ten minutes in total. A succession of hamstring injuries meant that he was rarely available for selection and in November he was released on a free transfer. He subsequently returned to Austria, signing for Austria Lustenau during the January transfer window.
Port Vale *(Free from Xanthi, Greece, ex Austria Vienna, Casino Salzburg, SC Lustenau, Grazer AK, on 14/7/2003) FL 27+5/2 FLC 1 FAC 2*

LISBIE Kevin Anthony
Born: Hackney, 17 October 1978
Height: 5'9" **Weight:** 10.12
International Honours: Jamaica: 9; E: Yth
Kevin had a disappointing time at Charlton last term, missing most of the season with injury problems. It all started well enough with a goal in the opening fixture at Bolton, but this was to be his only strike of the campaign. A hamstring injury kept him out of action for a lengthy period but he was back in action for the closing matches. Kevin has electric pace, is very skilful on the ball and can play as a central striker or wide on the right. He holds the ball up well and is a good crosser of the ball.
Charlton Ath *(From trainee on 24/5/1996) P/FL 61+80/16 FLC 4+8/3 FAC 2+5*
Gillingham *(Loaned on 5/3/1999) FL 4+3/4*
Reading *(Loaned on 26/11/1999) FL 1+1*
Queens Park Rgrs *(Loaned on 1/12/2000) FL 1+1*

LITA Leroy Halirou
Born: DR Congo, 28 December 1984
Height: 5'9" **Weight:** 11.2
International Honours: E: U21-1
New Bristol City manager Brian Tinnion was rewarded for his faith in Leroy's skills with a tally of 29 goals in all competitions last term. The best of these was a brilliant long-range volley at Torquay. The athletic striker also scored on his debut for

England U21s against Holland in February. He was rewarded for his efforts when he won the City supporters' 'Player of the Year' award and a place in the PFA divisional team of the season.
Bristol C *(From trainee on 6/3/2003) FL 44+41/31 FLC 2+1/2 FAC 1+4/3 Others 4+3/2*

LITTLE Glen Matthew
Born: Wimbledon, 15 October 1975
Height: 6'3" **Weight:** 13.0
Glen was a regular in the starting line-up for Reading for most of last season, apart from absence due to injury. He operated mostly on the right flank, occasionally switching sides with either Paul Brooker or Bobby Convey, and showed consistent ability to beat the full back and send over a dangerous cross. To be fully effective, however, he needed to get his name on the score sheet, something he could not accomplish.
Crystal Palace *(From trainee on 1/7/1994. Free to Glentoran on 11/11/1994)*
Burnley *(£100,000 on 29/11/1996) FL 211+35/32 FLC 11+4 FAC 11+6/3 Others 4+1/1*
Reading *(Loaned on 27/3/2003) FL 6/1 Others 1*
Bolton W *(Loaned on 1/9/2003) PL 0+4*
Reading *(Free on 24/5/2004) FL 29+6 FLC 1 FAC 3*

LITTLEJOHN Adrian Sylvester
Born: Wolverhampton, 26 September 1970
Height: 5'9" **Weight:** 11.0
International Honours: E: Yth
This veteran left-sided player joined Lincoln City on a six-month deal at the start of the 2004-05 season but found it difficult to break into the Imps' line-up. Adrian made his only start at Swansea on August Bank Holiday Monday, but he was a regular on the substitutes' bench. He was used either as a wide midfield player or an out-and-out striker but failed to win an extension to his contract and left Sincil Bank in December before signing for League Two rivals Rushden & Diamonds. However, his spell at Nene Park was disrupted by a change in management and after failing to register a goal for the club he was released before the end of the season.
Walsall *(From trainee at West Bromwich A juniors on 24/5/1989) FL 26+18/1 FLC 2+1 FAC 1+1 Others 4+1*
Sheffield U *(Free on 6/8/1991) P/FL 44+25/12 FLC 5+1 FAC 3+2/1 Others 2/1*
Plymouth Arg *(£100,000 on 22/9/1995) FL 100+10/29 FLC 6 FAC 6+2/3 Others 6*
Oldham Ath *(Signed on 20/3/1998) FL 16+5/5 FLC 2/1*
Bury *(£75,000 on 13/11/1998) FL 69+30/14 FLC 4/1 FAC 6/1 Others 2+1*
Sheffield U *(Free on 22/10/2001) FL 1+2 (Freed in December 2001)*
Port Vale *(Free, after spells in China and the USA, via a trial at Barnsley, on 19/2/2003) FL 36+13/10 FLC 1 FAC 3 Others 1*
Lincoln C *(Free on 13/8/2004) FL 1+7 FAC 0+1*
Rushden & Diamonds *(Free on 7/1/2005) FL 8+7*

LIVERMORE David
Born: Edmonton, 20 May 1980
Height: 5'11" **Weight:** 12.1
Club Honours: Div 2 '01
Apart from suspension David was an ever-present in midfield for Millwall last term, operating both centrally and as a wide player. This strong, tough-tackling player gives no quarter and is well

David Livermore

espected by the New Den faithful. David an also play at left back if required.
rsenal *(From trainee on 13/7/1998)*
1illwall *(£30,000 on 30/7/1999) FL 28+4/10 FLC 10/1 FAC 16 Others 7*

IVESEY Daniel (Danny) Richard
Born: Salford, 31 December 1984
Height: 6'2" **Weight:** 13.0
This young Bolton defender joined Blackpool on loan just before the start of the 2004-05 season. However, although he featured in the starting line-up for the opening game at Doncaster he struggled with his fitness and returned to the Reebok early. Later in the season he joined Conference club Carlisle United, initially on loan before the move was made permanent in the new year. He proved a key figure in the centre of defence as the Cumbrians went on to secure a return to the Football League via the play-offs.
Bolton W *(From trainee on 17/8/2002) PL 0+2 FLC 1 FAC 3*
Notts Co *(Loaned on 5/9/2003) FL 9+2 Others 1*
Rochdale *(Loaned on 6/2/2004) FL 11+2*
Blackpool *(Loaned on 4/8/2004) FL 1*

LJUNGBERG Karl **Fredrik (Freddie)**
Born: Sweden, 16 April 1977
Height: 5'9" **Weight:** 11.6
Club Honours: CS '99; PL '02, '04; FAC '02, '03, '05
International Honours: Sweden: 52; U21-12; Yth
Freddie was yet another player to suffer with injury during Arsenal's championship defence, yet he still managed to score 14 goals in all competitions and as ever his unselfish running and combative style mixed with composure in front of goal ensured another fine season from the midfielder. Freddie once more provided some crucial strikes including two away to Charlton Athletic, and point-saving goals at home to Manchester City and at Southampton. He also registered away to both Rosenborg and Panathinaikos in the Champions' League group stage whilst his personal love affair with the FA Cup continued. He scored against Wolves in round four and the match winner away to Bolton in the quarter-final, also successfully converted in the penalty shoot-out victories over Sheffield United and Manchester United as the Gunners claimed the trophy for the tenth time.
Arsenal *(£3,000,000 from BK Halmstad, Sweden on 17/9/1998) PL 151+22/45 FLC 2 FAC 25+4/10 Others 52+9/13*

LLEWELLYN Christopher (Chris) Mark
Born: Swansea, 29 August 1979
Height: 5'11" **Weight:** 11.6
Club Honours: AMC '05
International Honours: W: 3; B-1; U21-14; Yth; Sch
Chris must be about the fittest player on Wrexham's books as he has only missed one League game in the two seasons he has been at the Racecourse. Although brought to the club as a goal-scorer his real value to the side is in his work rate about the pitch, which is outstanding. A valuable player throughout the campaign, he scored seven League One goals including a last-minute winner at Colchester in October.
Norwich C *(From trainee on 21/1/1997) FL 103+39/17 FLC 7+3 FAC 3+3/1*
Bristol Rov *(Loaned on 21/2/2003) FL 14/3*
Wrexham *(Free on 6/8/2003) FL 91/15 FLC 2+1/1 FAC 3/1 Others 8+1/3*

LLOYD Anthony Francis
Born: Taunton, 14 March 1984
Height: 5'7" **Weight:** 11.0
This left back found himself well down the pecking order at Huddersfield last term until opportunity knocked in the away draw at Bristol City. Although he was in and out of the team thereafter, Anthony has plenty of time on his side to develop his full potential. He attacks and defends with some maturity and is a tenacious tackler.
Huddersfield T *(From trainee on 22/8/2003) FL 40+2/3 FAC 2 Others 6*

LLOYD Callum
Born: Nottingham, 1 January 1986
Height: 5'9" **Weight:** 11.4
Mansfield Town's 'Youth Team Player of the Year' in 2003-04, Callum was called into the senior team for his debut for the LDV Vans Trophy tie with Darlington last September. He played wide on the right-hand side of midfield and showed up well, not letting the side down. A very confident player, he forced his way into the first team in March and settled in quite well, contributing several goals. He was offered a new contract in March.
Mansfield T *(From trainee on 28/5/2005) FL 7+3/4 FAC 1 Others 2*

LOCKWOOD Adam Brian
Born: Wakefield, 26 October 1981
Height: 6'0" **Weight:** 12.7
Club Honours: FAT '02; NC '03
International Honours: E: SP-2
Adam was one of several players affected by injury at Yeovil last term. Although he featured a couple of times early on a cartilage injury then put him out for some time. He briefly returned to the side in December but further problems meant that he was not fully fit until March. Adam is a quality full back who is a great favourite of the crowd at Huish Park.
Reading *(From trainee on 19/3/1999)*
Yeovil T *(Free on 17/10/2001) FL 49+4/4 FLC 2 FAC 3 Others 2*

LOCKWOOD Matthew Dominic
Born: Southend, 17 October 1976
Height: 5'9" **Weight:** 10.12
Leyton Orient's longest-serving player was again a first choice at left back for most of last season. Matthew was the club captain and dead-ball specialist, displaying his talents to good effect when he scored with an excellent free kick in the 1-1 home draw with Cambridge in February.
Queens Park Rgrs *(From trainee at Southend U on 2/5/1995)*
Bristol Rov *(Free on 24/7/1996) FL 58+5/1 FLC 2+1 FAC 6 Others 4+2*
Leyton Orient *(Free on 7/8/1998) FL 236+9/31 FLC 14/2 FAC 17/2 Others 14/3*

LOGAN Carlos Sean
Born: Wythenshawe, 7 November 1985
Height: 5'8" **Weight:** 10.5
This promising Manchester City youngster has yet to break into the first team at the City of Manchester Stadium, but enjoyed a run of senior action on loan at Chesterfield last term. Carlos operated as an attacking midfielder, usually on the left flank, and in the style of an old-fashioned winger, with the ability to tease a full back before crossing. He did this to great effect against Tranmere in March, cutting in to rifle home a powerful shot.
Manchester C *(From trainee on 9/7/2004)*
Chesterfield *(Loaned on 3/3/2005) FL 6+3/1*

LOGAN Richard Adam
Born: Washington, 18 February 1988
Height: 6'0" **Weight:** 11.12
This young Darlington striker impressed in the reserves last term and was given his senior debut as a substitute in the home game against Boston United in March when the club's more experienced strikers were either injured or suspended. Richard came on with 20 minutes to go and almost immediately suffered a knock in the face, but soldiered on with some determined harrying and chasing up front in the hard-fought one-goal win.
Darlington *(Trainee) FL 0+1*

LOGAN Richard James
Born: Bury St Edmunds, 4 January 1982
Height: 6'0" **Weight:** 12.5
International Honours: E: Yth; Sch

This powerful striker was out of favour at Peterborough early on last term and joined Shrewsbury Town on loan. Richard scored twice for the Gay Meadow club, including one on his debut against Boston, but subsequently returned to London Road. Thereafter he had something of a mixed season for Posh, finishing the campaign with four goals from 15 League One starts.
Ipswich T *(From trainee on 6/1/1999) P/FL 0+3 FLC 0+1 FAC 0+1*
Cambridge U *(Loaned on 25/1/2001) FL 5/1*
Torquay U *(Loaned on 13/12/2001) FL 16/4*
Boston U *(Free on 30/11/2002) FL 30+5/10 FLC 0+1*
Peterborough U *(Free on 24/9/2003) FL 27+28/11 FAC 4+2/2 Others 1+1/1*
Shrewsbury T *(Loaned on 16/9/2004) FL 5/1 Others 1/1*

LOMAS Stephen (Steve) Martin
Born: Hanover, Germany, 18 January 1974
Height: 6'0" **Weight:** 12.8
International Honours: NI: 45; B-1; Yth; Sch
A committed member of the West Ham team last term, Steve was an influential figure in the middle of the park. Unfortunately throughout the season he suffered a series of niggling injuries which caused him to miss a number of games. When the going got tough at away grounds Steve's battling qualities were in evidence. He was superb in the 2-0 win at Sunderland and also at Plymouth when he scored the Hammers' goal. A calf strain in March sidelined him for the remainder of the season.
Manchester C *(From trainee on 22/1/1991) P/FL 102+9/8 FLC 15/2 FAC 10+1/1*
West Ham U *(£1,600,000 on 26/3/1997) P/FL 179+8/10 FLC 14/2 FAC 10+3/1 Others 13*

LOMAX Kelvin
Born: Bury, 12 November 1986
Height: 5'11" **Weight:** 12.3
This pacy right back got his first taste of senior football last term after progressing through the Boundary Park youth ranks. Brian Talbot handed him his debut as a substitute in the 2-0 defeat at Brentford in October and he made his full debut a fortnight later at home to Swindon Town, the first of eight starts. Comfortable on the ball and remarkably composed for his age, Kelvin did not feature after the arrival of new manager Ronnie Moore in March.
Oldham Ath *(Trainee) FL 7+3 FAC 0+1 Others 1+1*

LONERGAN Andrew (Andy)
Born: Preston, 19 October 1983
Height: 6'4" **Weight:** 13.2
International Honours: RoI: Yth; E: Yth
Andy started the 2004-05 season firmly installed as Preston's first-choice' keeper, saved a penalty on the opening day and then capped that by scoring with a long clearance at Leicester. On the downside, he celebrated his 21st birthday by breaking his hand, which kept him out for nine games. His season then ended early with a serious injury sustained on the training ground. Commanding in his box for such a young player, his reflexes are top class.
Preston NE *(From trainee on 21/10/2000) FL 32/1 FLC 3 FAC 1*
Darlington *(Loaned on 20/12/2002) FL 2*

LONSDALE Richard Paul
Born: Burton-on-Trent, 29 October 1987
Height: 5'9" **Weight:** 10.10
This young midfielder was included on the bench for Mansfield for the LDV Vans Trophy tie against Darlington and was called into action for the last few minutes of extra time when Tom Curle was injured. Although he made the substitutes' bench later on in the season he made no further appearances.
Mansfield T *(Trainee) Others 0+1*

LOPES Osvaldo
Born: Frejus, France, 6 April 1980
Height: 5'10" **Weight:** 11.12
This young midfielder had a brief spell with Cork City before crossing the Irish Sea to sign for Torquay. He had a reasonably successful outing for the Gulls at Huddersfield when he featured as a right wing back but was not offered a longer deal. He subsequently linked up with Conference South outfit Kettering Town in the new year.
Plymouth Arg *(Free from Draguignan, France, ex Montpellier, on 26/8/2002) FL 4+5 FLC 1 FAC 1 Others 2 (Freed during 2003 close season)*
Torquay U *(Free from Cork C, ex ES Frejus, on 6/1/2005) FL 1*

LORAN Tyrone
Born: Amsterdam, Holland, 29 June 1981
Height: 6'2" **Weight:** 13.11
International Honours: Holland: U21
Although a favourite with the Prenton Park crowd, Tyrone struggled to regain his favourite right-back berth at Tranmere early on last season, making only two appearances as substitute. He was loaned out to Port Vale in December to cover an injury crisis and made a promising debut in the FA Cup defeat at Blackpool. Cultured on the ball, he had a short run in the side before returning to Tranmere and he was released soon afterwards. He subsequently returned to Holland, signing for RBC Roosendaal.
Manchester C *(£60,000 from Volendam, Holland on 16/7/2002)*
Tranmere Rov *(Signed on 31/12/2002) FL 42+5 FLC 1 FAC 2 Others 1*
Port Vale *(Loaned on 2/12/2004) FL 6 FAC 1*

LOUIS Jefferson Lee
Born: Harrow, 22 February 1979
Height: 6'2" **Weight:** 13.2
This big striker made just one appearance from the bench for Oxford last term before being loaned out to Conference club Gravesend. On his return he was allowed to leave for Forest Green Rovers and he then spent the second half of the campaign at Woking. Jefferson later answered a call from his former Oxford manager Ian Atkins and became an emergency signing for Bristol Rovers, featuring in the final match of the season against Wycombe. He put in a hard-working performance deputising for leading scorer Junior Agogo as Rovers signed off with a 1-0 victory.
Oxford U *(Free from Thame U, ex Aylesbury U, on 4/3/2002) FL 18+38/8 FLC 1+2/1 FAC 1+3/1 Others 2 (Transferred to Forest Green Rov on 24/9/2004)*
Bristol Rov *(Signed from Woking on 5/5/2005) FL 1*

LOUIS-JEAN Matthieu
Born: Mont St Aignan, France, 22 February 1976
Height: 5'9" **Weight:** 10.12
International Honours: France: U21; Yth
This right-sided defender started the season as a first choice for Nottingham Forest. However, he suffered a couple of niggling hamstring injuries which restricted his impact in the side before coming back into the side against Leeds United when he showed great courage, finishing the game as a member of a three-man central defensive line.
Nottingham F *(Signed from Le Havre, France on 14/9/1998) P/FL 188+10/3 FLC 15+2 FAC 6 Others 2*

LOW Joshua (Josh) David
Born: Bristol, 15 February 1979
Height: 6'1" **Weight:** 12.0
International Honours: W: U21-4; Yth
Josh had something of an up-and-down season with Northampton last term. The speedy right winger delighted the fans with his lightning dashes down the flank, finishing off with either a telling cross or a shot of his own. Indeed, on his day he

d few equals at this level. A highlight his campaign came with the two goals scored in the final game of the regular ason against Kidderminster to ensure e Cobblers reached the play-offs.
istol Rov *(From trainee on 19/8/1996) FL +11 FLC 0+2 FAC 2+2 Others 2*
yton Orient *(Free on 27/5/1999) FL 2+3/1 C 1*
rdiff C *(Free on 20/11/1999) FL 54+21/6 C 1+1 FAC 2+3 Others 3+1*
dham Ath *(Free on 12/8/2002) FL 19+2/3 C 2 FAC 2/1 Others 2*
orthampton T *(£165,000 on 8/8/2003) FL +6/10 FLC 3/1 FAC 4+1/1 Others 6/1*

OWE Keith Stephen
orn: Wolverhampton, 13 September 985
eight: 6'2" **Weight:** 13.3
eith made his debut for Wolves in the arling Cup tie at Rochdale last August hen he featured at right back and went n to feature in a handful of first-team ames in the opening half of the season. incipally a central defender, he always oked very composed on the ball.
Volverhampton W *(Trainee) FL 11 FLC 1+1*

OWE Ryan Thomas
orn: Liverpool, 18 September 1978
eight: 5'11" **Weight:** 11.10
yan failed to win a regular place in the hrewsbury Town line-up last term and is best contributions came from the ubstitutes' bench. He was used mainly n the right-hand side of midfield by the ay Meadow club and scored three oals, including one in the 5-0 win over hester City, to whom he was transferred n March. He created an immediate npression as a hard-working striker at he Saunders Honda Stadium, his nselfish play and off-the-ball running enefiting his colleagues. Ryan scored our goals in the final eight games of the eason including two against Bury and he winner in injury time of the final game against Oxford.
hrewsbury T *(Free from Burscough on 25/7/2000) FL 81+56/23 FLC 2+2 FAC 4+2 Others 7+2/4*
Chester C *(Free on 22/3/2005) FL 8/4*

LOWNDES Nathan Peter
Born: Salford, 2 June 1977
Height: 5'11" **Weight:** 11.6
Club Honours: Div 2 '04
Nathan started the season on the bench for Plymouth but then was out of the first-team picture for a while. He made his one and only start against Wigan Athletic in mid-October and eventually moved on to join Port Vale the following month. Although affected by injury problems, he made a promising start to his career at Vale Park, producing his best performance after coming off the bench in the game at Sheffield Wednesday. He is a talented striker with good pace who is adept at harassing opposition defenders into errors.
Leeds U *(From trainee on 1/4/1995)*
Watford *(£40,000 on 3/10/1995) FL 1+6 FLC 0+1 FAC 1+1 Others 1*
St Johnstone *(£50,000 on 21/8/1998) SL 30+34/14 SLC 2+2/2 SC 4+2 Others 2+1*
Livingston *(Free on 20/7/2001) SL 7+14/3 SLC 0+2 SC 0+2*
Rotherham U *(Loaned on 28/3/2002) FL 2*
Plymouth Arg *(Free on 23/7/2002) FL 25+28/10 FLC 1 FAC 0+1 Others 3+1/2*
Port Vale *(Free on 5/11/2004) FL 7+5/1 FAC 2*

LUA LUA Lomano Tresor
Born: DR Congo, 28 December 1980
Height: 5'8" **Weight:** 12.2
International Honours: DR Congo
Lomano made a permanent move to the South Coast during the summer of 2004 and despite suffering sporadic injury problems he was one of the shining lights in the side last term. A regular in the side when fit, he scored six Premiership goals, but it was his 28-minute display against Southampton in April which will go down in Pompey folklore involving as it did two goals, countless somersaults and a 'Man of the Match' award before he left the pitch with an injury.
Colchester U *(From Leyton College on 25/9/1998) FL 37+24/15 FLC 4/4 FAC 1/1 Others 1*
Newcastle U *(£2,250,000 on 29/9/2000) PL 14+45/5 FLC 2+3 FAC 0+7 Others 5+12/4*
Portsmouth *(£1,750,000 on 3/2/2004) PL 30+10/10 FLC 1*

LUCAS David Anthony
Born: Preston, 23 November 1977
Height: 6'2" **Weight:** 13.10
International Honours: E: Yth
This fine goalkeeper was in great form for Sheffield Wednesday last season. A terrific shot-stopper and great on crosses, David enabled the rest of his defenders to have real confidence in his ability. An overall record of one goal against per game helped send the team into the top six after several barren years. Unfortunately a leg injury against Blackpool in early March ruled him out for a while, but he was back in action for the play-offs as the Owls won promotion after defeating Hartlepool at the Millennium Stadium.
Preston NE *(From trainee on 12/12/1994) FL 117+5 FLC 10 FAC 7 Others 11*
Darlington *(Loaned on 14/12/1995) FL 6*
Darlington *(Loaned on 3/10/1996) FL 7*
Scunthorpe U *(Loaned on 23/12/1996) FL 6 Others 2*
Sheffield Wed *(Loaned on 1/10/2003) FL 17 Others 1*
Sheffield Wed *(£100,000 on 14/6/2004) FL 34 FLC 2 FAC 1 Others 4*

LUCKETTI Christopher (Chris) James
Born: Rochdale, 28 September 1971
Height: 6'0" **Weight:** 13.6
Club Honours: Div 2 '97
Chris continued to be a fixture at the heart of Preston's defence, forming a particularly productive partnership with Youl Mawene. Always leading by example, Chris refuses to give second best to any opponent, using his vast experience to compensate for any loss of pace over the years. A simple and uncomplicated defender, he remains an effective pivot for the defensive line and an inspiration to all around him. He also continues to be a threat at set pieces, his return of four goals not being a fair reflection of his abilities.
Rochdale *(Trainee) FL 1*
Stockport Co *(Free on 23/8/1990)*
Halifax T *(Free on 12/7/1991) FL 73+5/2 FLC 2/1 FAC 2 Others 4*
Bury *(£50,000 on 1/10/1993) FL 235/8 FLC 16 FAC 11/1 Others 15/1*
Huddersfield T *(£750,000 + on 14/6/1999) FL 68/1 FLC 7/1*
Preston NE *(£750,000 on 23/8/2001) FL 161/9 FLC 7 FAC 6 Others 3*

LUNDEKVAM Claus
Born: Norway, 22 February 1973
Height: 6'3" **Weight:** 12.10
International Honours: Norway: 37; U21-16
On his day Claus is an outstanding centre back – very much the foundation upon which a very good Saints' defence has been built in past years – but a number of minor injuries throughout the last 18 months have not helped his game and he has not always looked 100 per cent fit; certainly not fit enough to carry a back-four and midfield which has lacked quality, pace and confidence for over a year. Whatever, it is to be hoped that that he stays at St Mary's, for if he can regain full fitness he will be an important asset in Saints' climb back to the Premiership.
Southampton *(£400,000 from SK Brann, Norway on 3/9/1996) PL 283+7/1 FLC 27+3 FAC 21 Others 2*

LUNT Kenneth (Kenny) Vincent
Born: Runcorn, 20 November 1979
Height: 5'10" **Weight:** 10.0
International Honours: E: Yth; Sch

Kenny was captain of the Crewe Alexandra team in the 2004-05 season. The midfielder, who is the club's longest-serving player, has been a regular in the side since August 1997 and was the only ever-present last term. An excellent penalty taker and also dangerous from free kicks, he always comes high on the list for assists in goal-scoring efforts.
Crewe Alex *(From trainee on 12/6/1997) FL 300+30/31 FLC 20+4/1 FAC 14+1 Others 4/1*

LUPOLI Arturo
Born: Brescia, Italy, 24 June 1987
Height: 5'9" **Weight:** 10.7
International Honours: Italy: Yth
This teenaged forward started all three of Arsenal's Carling Cup ties and scored two goals in the 3-1 home win over Everton. A striker crisis saw Arturo drafted into the first team for the FA Cup fifth round replay victory over Sheffield United, whilst he was also a regular scorer in the reserves.
Arsenal *(£250,000 from Parma, Italy on 16/9/2004) FLC 3/2 FAC 1*

LYNCH Gavin
Born: Chester, 7 September 1985
Height: 5'8" **Weight:** 10.10
A third-year scholar, Gavin joined Chester City after being released by Everton. An out-and-out striker, who was a regular in the reserves, he came off the bench for his senior debut in the FA Cup tie at Halifax. His only other appearance was also as a substitute, at Swansea.
Chester C *(Trainee, ex Everton trainee) FL 0+1 FAC 0+1*

Chris Lucketti

LYNCH Mark John
Born: Manchester, 2 September 1981
Height: 5'11" **Weight:** 11.5
Club Honours: Ch '05
This right back joined Sunderland from Manchester United in the summer of 2004 and collected a Championship winners' medal in his first season on Wearside. Although Mark acted mainly as cover for Stephen Wright, he did not let the side down when called upon, showing a willingness to get forward on the overlap whenever possible. Mark overcame a potentially serious injury sustained at Cardiff in February when he dislocated his kneecap. He has, however, been informed by the Sunderland management that he is free to seek a move away from the Stadium of Light.
Manchester U *(From trainee on 3/7/2001) Others 1*
Sunderland *(Signed on 26/7/2004) FL 5+6 FLC 2*

LYNCH Simon George
Born: Montreal, Canada, 19 May 1982
Height: 6'0" **Weight:** 10.0
International Honours: S: B-2; U21-13
Simon struggled to make an impact at Preston last season, making only two starts and eight appearances from the bench. The lively striker spent three months on loan at neighbours Blackpool later on in the campaign, but failed to register a goal during his stay at Bloomfield Road.
Glasgow Celtic *(From juniors on 13/7/1999) SL 2+1/3 Others 1+1*
Preston NE *(£130,000 on 8/1/2003) FL 14+31/2 FLC 0+1/1*
Stockport Co *(Loaned on 12/12/2003) FL 9/3*
Blackpool *(Loaned on 16/12/2004) FL 5+2 FAC 2*

LYNG Ciaran
Born: Wexford, 24 July 1985
Height: 5'11" **Weight:** 12.8
International Honours: RoI: Yth
This promising youngster spent the early part of last term in Preston's reserve team before moving on to join League Two outfit Shrewsbury Town in December. Ciaran, who can play either on the left-hand side or in the centre of midfield, made his debut as a substitute in the 4-0 home victory against Darlington at the turn of the year and managed a handful more appearances from the bench before the season's end.
Preston NE *(From trainee on 5/9/2003)*
Shrewsbury T *(Free on 23/12/2004) FL 0+4*

M

ΛABIZELA Oldjohn **Mbulelo**
3orn: Pietermaritzburg, South Africa, 16 ›eptember 1980
Ieight: 5'10" **Weight:** 12.6
nternational Honours: South Africa: 37
Λbulelo had another disappointing eason at Tottenham and his only ppearance in the starting line-up in the 'remiership came against Manchester Jnited at the end of September. The enacious defender then left White Hart ane and was reported to have signed for Iorwegian club Valerenga in the new 'ear.
'ottenham H (Signed from Orlando Pirates, 'outh Africa on 26/8/2003) PL 1+6/1 FLC +1

ΛcALISKEY John James
3orn: Huddersfield, 2 September 1984
Ieight: 6'5" **Weight:** 12.7
nternational Honours: RoI: U21-1
ɔhn found first-team opportunities at Iuddersfield limited last term. He nanaged early-season starts in the LDV 'ans Trophy ties against Doncaster and ›lackpool and scored a close-range ›eaded goal at Bournemouth. The big ront man has great close control and ›ood pace, enabling him to torment ›pposition defences. Thrust into the melight at the turn of the year due to njuries, he led the line with great naturity. John was called up to the ₹epublic of Ireland U21 squad against 'ortugal.
Iuddersfield T (From trainee on 1/5/2004) L 12+14/6 FLC 0+1 Others 1+3/1

ΛcANUFF Joel (Jobi) Joshua rederick
3orn: Edmonton, 9 November 1981
Ieight: 5'11" **Weight:** 11.10
nternational Honours: Jamaica: 1
his talented winger made a single ppearance for West Ham on the ›pening day against Leicester before ›eing sold to Cardiff. He quickly became firm favourite of the Bluebirds' fans for ›is exciting style and after he switched to left-wing position in the new year he ›ecame the team's most potent attacking nreat.
Vimbledon (From trainee on 11/7/2000) FL 6+20/13 FLC 2/1 FAC 4+2/1
Vest Ham U (£300,000 on 4/2/2004) FL +9/1 Others 0+1
'ardiff C (£250,000 on 13/8/2004) FL 2+1/2 FLC 3 FAC 2/1

McATEER Jason Wynn
Born: Birkenhead, 18 June 1971
Height: 5'10" **Weight:** 11.12
International Honours: RoI: 52; B-1
Jason was immediately appointed as club captain after arriving at Tranmere during the summer of 2004, but different, recurrent injuries meant that he was used tactically and carefully during the season, and it is fair to say that he probably didn't make quite the impact which might have been hoped for. Still a versatile player, he can operate in central midfield or wide on the right, while his enthusiastic tackling and battle-hardened attitude were the cornerstones of his appearances in a white shirt. Scorer of five goals, he still possesses once of the fiercest shots in the squad. Moved by the news footage from Asia, Jason organised a successful Tsunami benefit game at Anfield in late March, which featured many former Liverpool legends and colleagues.
***Bolton W** (Signed from Marine on 22/1/1992) P/FL 109+5/8 FLC 11/2 FAC 11/3 Others 8+1/2*
***Liverpool** (£4,500,000 on 6/9/1995) PL 84+16/3 FLC 12+1 FAC 11+1/3 Others 12+2*
***Blackburn Rov** (£4,000,000 on 28/1/1999) P/FL 58+14/4 FLC 4 FAC 7*
***Sunderland** (£1,000,000 on 19/10/2001) P/FL 53/5 FAC 6 Others 2*
***Tranmere Rov** (Free on 23/7/2004) FL 32+2/4 FLC 2/1 FAC 1 Others 2*

McAULEY Gareth
Born: Larne, 5 December 1979
Height: 6'3" **Weight:** 13.0
International Honours: NI: 1; B-1; Sch
Gareth had a superb first season in English football after signing for the Imps from Coleraine. He was initially introduced from the substitutes' bench in a striking role but settled into defence producing some excellent performances at both right back and in the middle of a back-five. Gareth netted vital goals in

Gareth McAuley

each of the play-off semi-finals against Macclesfield to see the Imps through to Cardiff. His form earned him his first full Northern Ireland cap when he came on as a late substitute in the friendly against Germany in June.
Lincoln C *(£10,000 from Coleraine, ex Linfield, Crusaders, on 5/8/2004) FL 32+5/3 FLC 2 FAC 1 Others 4/2*

McBRIDE Brian Robert
Born: Arlington Heights, USA, 19 June 1972
Height: 6'1" **Weight:** 12.7
International Honours: USA: 88
A typical old-fashioned centre forward, Brian was often on the bench for Fulham last term, but nevertheless remained a vital part of the team strategy and contributed a number of crucial goals. An excellent header of the ball he linked well with both Andy Cole and Tomasz Radsinzki. A clever opportunist striker who enjoyed his best form towards the end of the season, his headed goal against Everton displayed the hallmark of an accomplished central striker. Brian continued to add to his tally of caps for the USA during the season.
Preston NE *(Loaned from Columbus Crew, USA, ex St Louis University, VFL Wolfsburg, on 15/9/2000) FL 8+1/1 FLC 1 FAC 1*
Everton *(Loaned from Columbus Crew, USA on 5/2/2003) PL 7+1/4*
Fulham *(£600,000 from Columbus Crew, USA on 27/1/2004) PL 20+27/10 FLC 2+2/3 FAC 3+2/1*

McCAFFERTY Neil
Born: Londonderry, 19 July 1984
Height: 5'7" **Weight:** 10.6
Three months on loan with Rushden saw Neil develop into an impressive midfielder who is prepared to make strong tackles despite his size and he can also spot a colleague in space. It took him a while to adapt to the requirements of League Two action compared to reserve-team football where he was the Addicks captain. However, Neil played a big part in helping Diamonds to stay up and he should have few problems finding a club after being released on a free transfer by Charlton when his contract ran out in the summer.
Charlton Ath *(From trainee on 2/8/2001)*
Cambridge U *(Loaned on 23/12/2003) FL 5+1*
Rushden & Diamonds *(Loaned on 28/1/2005) FL 16*

McCALL Andrew **Stuart** Murray
Born: Leeds, 10 June 1964
Height: 5'7" **Weight:** 12.0
Club Honours: Div 3 '85; SPL '92, '93, '94, '95, '96; SLC '92, '93; SC '92, '93, '96
International Honours: S: 40; U21-2
It was expected that Stuart would reduce his playing commitments for Sheffield United last season and he made just two appearances, both in the Carling Cup, when he continued to use his experience in midfield to hold and use the ball to good effect. He was appointed the Blades' assistant manager in September when David Kelly moved to Preston.
Bradford C *(From apprentice on 1/6/1982) FL 235+3/37 FLC 19/3 FAC 11/3 Others 16/3*
Everton *(£850,000 on 1/6/1988) FL 99+4/6 FLC 11/1 FAC 16+2/3 Others 9+1*
Glasgow Rgrs *(£1,200,000 on 15/8/1991) SL 186+8/14 SLC 15/3 SC 25+2 Others 28/2*
Bradford C *(Free on 4/6/1998) P/FL 154+3/8 FLC 5+3/1 FAC 5+1 Others 4*
Sheffield U *(Free on 2/7/2002) FL 69+2/2 FLC 8+1 FAC 9 Others 0+1*

Neil McCafferty

McCAMMON Mark Jason
Born: Barnet, 7 August 1978
Height: 6'5" **Weight:** 14.5
A tall target man, strong and excellent in the air, Mark spent most of his time in Millwall's reserves last term and only managed a handful of appearances in the Championship. He eventually moved on to Brighton in search of regular first-team football firstly on loan and then, from February, permanently. However, despite some fitness problems he scored three goals including the winner against Sunderland.
Cambridge U *(Free from Cambridge C on 1/12/1996) FL 1+3 FAC 0+1 Others 1*
Charlton Ath *(Free on 17/3/1999) FL 1+3 FLC 0+1*
Swindon T *(Loaned on 3/1/2000) FL 4*
Brentford *(£100,000 + on 18/7/2000) FL 46+29/10 FLC 4/1 FAC 3+1/1 Others 3+5/3*
Millwall *(Free on 27/3/2003) FL 15+7/2 FLC 0+1 FAC 0+1 Others 0+1*
Brighton & Hove A *(Free on 16/12/2004) FL 16+2/3*

McCANN Henry **Austin**
Born: Alexandria, 21 January 1980
Height: 5'9" **Weight:** 11.13
This left-sided defender did well in his first season in English football after signing for League Two club Boston United in the summer. Austin slotted in well both at left back and as the left-sided player of a three-man centre-back system. He was decisive in the tackle and always looked to bring the ball forward when given the opportunity. Austin's only goal was a cracking late effort from long range which flew into the top corner to clinch a home victory over Cambridge United. He only missed one League match and was voted 'Player of the Year' by the club's supporters.
Airdrie *(From trainee at Wolverhampton W on 31/7/1997) SL 80+14/7 SLC 7+1/1 SC 2+1/1 Others 8+1*
Heart of Midlothian *(Signed on 16/2/2001) SL 35+4/1 SLC 0+1 SC 4 Others 0+1*
Clyde *(Free on 1/4/2004) SL 6*
Boston U *(Free on 7/8/2004) FL 45/1 FLC 2 FAC 4*

Mark McCammon

McCANN Gavin Peter
Born: Blackpool, 10 January 1978
Height: 5'11" **Weight:** 11.0
International Honours: E: 1
A committed midfielder, tough-tackling and defensive in his stance, Gavin flourished in the centre of the park for Villa last term, when he was just as keen to help out in defence as he was to get forward to support the attack. He was outstanding in the heart of midfield in the home match against Chelsea, producing his best performance to date, constantly breaking up their attacks with biting tackles and fine anticipation as well as distributing the ball intelligently to get Villa moving. Unfortunately knee problems restricted his appearances in the second half of the campaign and he eventually underwent surgery.
Everton *(From trainee on 1/7/1995) PL 5+6*
Sunderland *(£500,000 on 27/11/1998) P/FL 106+10/8 FLC 4+3/2 FAC 11+1/3*
Aston Villa *(£2,250,000 on 31/7/2003) PL 48/1 FLC 8/2 FAC 2*

McCANN Grant Samuel
Born: Belfast, 14 April 1980
Height: 5'10" **Weight:** 12.0
International Honours: NI: 9; U21-11
This talented player enjoyed another season as a first-choice midfielder for Cheltenham Town. A left-footed player with excellent touch, vision and passing ability, Grant operated mostly in the centre of a four- or five-man midfield, but also played a few games wide on the left. He handled the majority of set-piece duties for the team and contributed six goals including a spectacular 30-yard strike at Swansea in August.
West Ham U *(From trainee on 6/7/1998) PL 0+4*

Livingston *(Loaned on 27/8/1999) SL 0+4*
Notts Co *(Loaned on 11/8/2000) FL 2 FLC 1*
Cheltenham T *(Loaned on 17/10/2000) FL 27+3/3 FAC 2 Others 1*
Cheltenham T *(Loaned on 4/10/2002) FL 8 Others 2/1*
Cheltenham T *(£50,000 on 29/1/2003) FL 101/18 FLC 2/1 FAC 3/3 Others 3/1*

McCANN Neil Doherty

Born: Greenock, 11 August 1974
Height: 5'10" **Weight:** 10.4
Club Honours: SPD '99, '00, '03; SC '98, '99, '00, '02, '03; SLC '02
International Honours: S: 23; B-2; U21-9
An industrious and tricky winger, Neil was one of a dozen players rotated by the Saints' three managers in a failed effort to assemble an effective midfield in the 2004-05 season. Scoring a goal in Saints 3–0 win at Northampton in the Carling Cup was not enough to get him a run in the first team, neither was coming on as a substitute and laying on both of Rory Delapp's goals in the 2–2 draw at Arsenal in October. His appearances after Harry Redknapp became the Southampton manager in December were restricted to one Premiership start and the odd cameo from the bench.
Dundee *(Signed from Port Glasgow on 14/5/1992) SL 73+6/5 SLC 5/1 SC 6 Others 4*
Heart of Midlothian *(Signed on 30/7/1996) SL 68+6/19 SLC 8+1/3 SC 10/2 Others 4/2*
Glasgow Rgrs *(£2,000,000 on 14/12/1998) SL 66+47/19 SLC 6+1 SC 18+4/3 Others 13+16/3*
Southampton *(£1,500,000 on 7/8/2003) PL 14+15 FLC 2+2/1 FAC 1+3 Others 0+1*

McCARTHY Patrick (Paddy)

Born: Dublin, 31 May 1983
Height: 6'1" **Weight:** 12.8
International Honours: RoI: U21-7; Yth
With little prospect of gaining first-team football, this highly rated central defender eventually moved on to Leicester in March. Paddy made his debut for the Foxes at Turf Moor and quickly established himself as a first choice at the heart of the defence. He linked up well with loanee Darren Kenton at centre back in the closing fixtures, having shown his adaptability by turning out at right back on a handful of occasions. Tough and uncompromising in the tackle he is a fine reader of the game.
Manchester C *(From trainee on 14/6/2000)*
Boston U *(Loaned on 22/11/2002) FL 11+1*
Notts Co *(Loaned on 23/3/2003) FL 6*
Leicester C *(£100,000 on 4/3/2005) FL 12 FAC 0+1*

McCARTNEY George

Born: Belfast, 29 April 1981
Height: 6'0" **Weight:** 12.6
Club Honours: Ch '05
International Honours: NI: 19; U21-5; Yth; Sch
This left back has been one of Sunderland's most consistent performers for the past two tears and last term saw him collect a Championship winners' medal and also gain selection for the PFA divisional team of the season. George's left-flank partnership with Julio Arca has become a key feature of the Black Cats' play and the two regularly interchange positions down the wing. As well as being a strong tackler, George is adept at putting telling crosses into opponents' penalty areas, although he is somewhat surprisingly still searching for his first Sunderland goal! George capped an excellent season by winning the Sunderland supporters' 'Player of the Year' award.
Sunderland *(From trainee on 28/5/1998) P/FL 104+17 FLC 6+2 FAC 10+3 Others 2*

McCLENAHAN Trent James

Born: Australia, 4 February 1985
Height: 5'9" **Weight:** 11.0
International Honours: Australia: Yth
Trent made his first-team debut for West Ham in August at Crewe and also featured in the line-up for the Carling Cup tie against Southend soon afterwards. Thereafter he was confined to the reserves save for a spell on loan with MK Dons. He quickly claimed the right-back berth for the League One side and showed himself to be a composed all-rounder who worked the length of his flank well. Trent also featured for Australia at U20 level during the campaign.
West Ham U *(From trainee on 6/1/2005) FL 0+2 FLC 1*
MK Dons *(Loaned on 24/3/2005) FL 7+1*

McCOMBE Jamie Paul

Born: Scunthorpe, 1 January 1983
Height: 6'5" **Weight:** 12.6
Jamie began the 2004-05 season in an unfamiliar role as an emergency striker for Lincoln City, but eventually settled into his usual position on the right side of a three-man central defence. Up front he posed problems for opposing defences and showed his finishing power with a clinical strike in the Carling Cup win over Derby County. Once restored to centre back Jamie produced some solid performances using his height and strength to great effect. He was rewarded with a new contract in April.
Scunthorpe U *(From trainee on 28/11/2001) FL 42+21/1 FLC 1 FAC 5+1/2 Others 4+1/1*
Lincoln C *(Free on 11/3/2004) FL 45+4/3 FLC 2/1 FAC 1 Others 5+1*

McCOMBE John Paul

Born: Pontefract, 7 May 1985
Height: 6'2" **Weight:** 12.10
This big stopper centre half made good progress at Huddersfield last term when he made the starting line-up on several occasions, growing in confidence with each appearance. A highlight was scoring with a great header in the LDV Vans Trophy tie against Blackpool. A solid defender who is strong and effective, John has a non-nonsense approach to the game.
Huddersfield T *(From trainee on 5/7/2004) FL 4+2 Others 2*

McCORMACK Alan

Born: Dublin, 10 January 1984
Height: 5'8" **Weight:** 10.0
International Honours: RoI: Yth; Sch
Alan made only two brief substitute appearances for Preston last term but the tigerish midfielder's value was reflected when he was given an extended contract in January. An old-fashioned box-to-box player who provides support at both ends of the field, he wins the ball well and distributes it simply and effectively. Alan joined Southend on loan in March as cover for the suspended Kevin Maher and helped the club's promotion challenge stay on track by scoring twice in the vital 2-1 win at promotion rivals Macclesfield Town.
Preston NE *(Signed from Stella Maris BC on 14/8/2002) FL 2+6 FLC 0+1*
Leyton Orient *(Loaned on 29/8/2003) FL 8+2 Others 1*
Southend U *(Loaned on 17/3/2005) FL 5+2/2 Others 0+1*

McCORMICK Luke Martin

Born: Coventry, 15 August 1983
Height: 6'0" **Weight:** 13.12
Club Honours: Div 2 '04
Luke started the season off as Plymouth Argyle's number one goalkeeper, but soon lost his place to Romain Larrieu and then went out on loan to the Football League's other Pilgrims, Boston United. Luke did well in his two first-team starts at York Street, making some good saves and dominating his area. But once Nathan Abbey regained his fitness Luke was relegated to the bench and returned to Home Park. He worked extremely hard in training to regain the goalkeeping jersey in February and ensured that he kept it for the remainder of the season by delivering some confident displays.
Plymouth Arg *(From trainee on 9/7/2002) FL 66+1 FLC 1 FAC 1 Others 4*
Boston U *(Loaned on 22/10/2004) FL 2*

cCOURT Patrick (Paddy)
nes
rn: Londonderry, 16 December 1983
ight: 5'10" **Weight:** 11.0
ernational Honours: NI: 1; U21-8
chdale boss Steve Parkin gave this gmatic young winger another run in side at the start of last season and ddy appeared in the first half-dozen mes. However, apart from an outing in LDV Vans Trophy and one last cameo pearance in an excellent victory over acclesfield, that proved to be Paddy's ly contribution to Dale's season and after a brief trial at Motherwell he joined Shamrock Rovers in February.
Rochdale *(From trainee on 11/2/2002) FL 31+48/8 FLC 0+3 FAC 2+4/1 Others 1+5*

McCREADY Christopher (Chris) James
Born: Ellesmere Port, 5 September 1981
Height: 6'0" **Weight:** 11.11
Another product of the youth set-up at Crewe, Chris has had to wait patiently before becoming a first-team regular. A confident and thoughtful player who has been unlucky with injuries during his time at Gretsy Road, he normally occupies one of the defensive positions in the side.
Crewe Alex *(From trainee on 30/5/2000) FL 40+11 FLC 1+1 FAC 0+1*

Jamie McCombe

McCULLOCH Lee Henry
Born: Bellshill, 14 May 1978
Height: 6'5" **Weight:** 13.6
Club Honours: Div 2 '03
International Honours: S: 4; B-1; U21-14
Lee is a tall player with great aerial ability, and provided a strong physical presence down the left side of midfield for Wigan last term netting an impressive tally of 14 goals. Named as the 'Players' Player of the Season', he collected his first Scotland cap in the World Cup qualifier against Moldova in October from the bench and made his full debut in Walter Smith's first game in charge against Italy. Lee was rewarded for his efforts with an extension to his contract during the season.
Motherwell *(Signed from Cumbernauld U on 17/8/1995) SL 75+47/28 SLC 5+2/2 SC 11+3/4*
Wigan Ath *(£700,000 on 2/3/2001) FL 140+25/35 FLC 6/1 FAC 2+1 Others 1+1*

McDERMOTT David Anthony
Born: Stourbridge, 6 February 1988
Height: 5'5" **Weight:** 10.0
This skilful little midfielder scored for Walsall in pre-season games against Halesowen and Rushall and at the age of 16 years 191 days he made his first-team debut to become the youngest-ever player to appear for the Saddlers. David showed enough neat touches in his 12 minutes of action to indicate that he will be looking for more first-team experience in 2005-06.
Walsall *(Trainee) FLC 0+1*

McDERMOTT John
Born: Middlesbrough, 3 February 1969
Height: 5'7" **Weight:** 11.0
Club Honours: AMC '98
Despite rumours that Grimsby Town's longest-serving player might be on his way across the Humber during the summer of 2004, John remained a Mariners' player last term when he again extended his record appearance tally for the club. The effects of advancing years were more than compensated for by the experience he contributed, and, keeping almost free of injury, he maintained a regular place in the starting line-up. John took on some coaching duties with the club during the season as he looks to build a career in the game once his playing days are over.
Grimsby T *(From trainee on 1/6/1987) FL 574+18/10 FLC 38+2 FAC 33+1/2 Others 21*

McEVELEY James (Jay) Michael
Born: Liverpool, 11 February 1985
Height: 6'1" **Weight:** 12.11
International Honours: E: U21-1
After recovering from injury Jay was offered a chance in Blackburn's problem left-back spot early on last term. He played with surprising maturity during a brief run in the side and in March he joined Gillingham on loan. Quickly settling into the side he was a key member of the team in the latter stages of the season as the Gills nearly retained their Championship status. Jay then rather surprisingly featured for Rovers in the last game of the season at White Hart Lane.
Blackburn Rov *(From trainee on 8/7/2002) PL 14 FLC 3+1 FAC 2*
Burnley *(Loaned on 15/12/2003) FL 0+4 FAC 1*
Gillingham *(Loaned on 10/3/2005) FL 10/1*

McFADDEN James
Born: Glasgow, 14 April 1983
Height: 5'10" **Weight:** 10.10
International Honours: S: 21; B-1; U21-7
James found it difficult to break into the first-team at Goodison last term, despite being a regular in the Scotland line-up. He was played mostly on the right wing when selected, which is perhaps not his best position as he prefers either the left or behind the strikers, where he can display his considerable ball skills. James had the consolation of scoring his first goal for the club at Spurs and he followed that with two goals in the FA Cup. A good run of first-team football is required to restore his confidence and confirm his reputation as one of the finest young talents produced by Scotland in recent years.
Motherwell *(From juniors on 31/7/1999) SL 52+11/26 SLC 1/1 SC 5+1/5*
Everton *(£1,250,000 on 8/9/2003) PL 18+28/1 FLC 6 FAC 4/2*

McFAUL Shane
Born: Dublin, 23 May 1986
Height: 6'1" **Weight:** 11.10
International Honours: RoI: Yth
This Notts County youngster gained more valuable first-team experience during the season, but he was often played out of position as an emergency full back or defender. His better performances came when he was used in the centre of midfield, where his vision and range of passing ability made him a potential match winner.
Notts Co *(From trainee on 28/2/2004) FL 19+11 FAC 2+1 Others 1*

McGIVERN Leighton Terence
Born: Liverpool, 2 June 1984
Height: 5'8" **Weight:** 11.1
Leighton had played for a string of non-league clubs, most recently Waterloo Dock and Vauxhall Motors, before being given a trial at Rochdale. He impressed as a livewire striker in the pre-season tour of Scotland and was rewarded with a short-term contract, eventually extended for the whole season. Leighton was on the bench for the opening games, scoring his first League goal in stoppage time at Wycombe, before making his first start at Lincoln in October. Thereafter he spent almost the entire season on the bench, being named as substitute on no fewer than 42 occasions, but was not offered a further contract.
Rochdale *(Free from Vauxhall Motors on 30/7/2004) FL 2+23/1 FLC 0+1 FAC 0+2 Others 0+2*

McGLEISH Scott
Born: Barnet, 10 February 1974
Height: 5'9" **Weight:** 11.3
Scott had a good campaign at Northampton last term when he was a near ever-present in the side and finished as the team's leading goal-scorer. Despite his lack of height, he is one of the best headers of the ball on the club's books, possessing the ability to 'hang' in the air and power the ball through. He also has an uncanny knack of being in the right pace at the right time and the ability to score goals from half-chances. A favourite of the fans at Sixfields, he was voted as the club's 'Player of the Season'.
Charlton Ath *(Free from Edgware T on 24/5/1994) FL 0+6*
Leyton Orient *(Loaned on 10/3/1995) FL 4+2/1 Others 1/1*
Peterborough U *(Free on 4/7/1995) FL 3+10 FLC 0+1 FAC 0+1 Others 3+1/2*
Colchester U *(Loaned on 23/2/1996) FL 1+5/2*
Colchester U *(Loaned on 28/3/1996) FL 9/4 Others 2*
Cambridge U *(Loaned on 2/9/1996) FL 10/7 FLC 1*
Leyton Orient *(£50,000 on 22/11/1996) FL 36/7 FLC 3/1 FAC 1 Others 1*
Barnet *(£70,000 on 1/10/1997) FL 106+28/36 FLC 5/4 FAC 3 Others 7+2/2*
Colchester U *(£15,000 on 11/1/2001) FL 118+26/38 FLC 4 FAC 9+1/2 Others 7+2/7*
Northampton T *(Free on 8/7/2004) FL 43+1/13 FLC 2/1 FAC 3/2 Others 4/1*

McGLINCHEY Brian Kevin
Born: Londonderry, 26 October 1977
Height: 5'7" **Weight:** 10.2
Club Honours: Div 3 '01
International Honours: NI: B-1; U21-14; Yth
A highly polished orthodox left back, who likes to get forward but not to the detriment of his defensive duties, Brian was one of Torquay's most consistent performers last term. Unfortunately he was sidelined by a back injury at the beginning of March and had to watch from the sidelines as the Gulls slipped towards relegation.
Manchester C *(From trainee on 4/12/1995)*
Port Vale *(Free on 1/7/1998) FL 10+5/1 FLC 0+1 FAC 1*
Gillingham *(Free on 3/8/1999) FL 7+7/1 FLC 3+1 FAC 4/1 Others 1*
Plymouth Arg *(Free on 1/12/2000) FL 54+14/2 FLC 1 FAC 3+2 Others 4+1*
Torquay U *(Free on 12/9/2003) FL 66+1 FLC 1 FAC 1 Others 2*

McGOVERN Jon-Paul
Born: Glasgow, 3 October 1980
Height: 5'7" **Weight:** 9.6
Club Honours: SLC '04
After joining Sheffield Wednesday in the summer of 2004, Jon-Paul adapted quickly to the demands of League One football, filling in a gap on the right-hand side of midfield. Strong on the ball, with deceptive pace and a good crosser, he led by example in a very young side. Jon-Paul has a very professional attitude to the game and was one of the Owls' most consistent performers throughout the campaign.
Glasgow Celtic *(From Heart of Midlothian juniors on 8/6/2000)*
Sheffield U *(Loaned on 13/8/2002) FL 11+4/1 FLC 2/1 FAC 1/1*
Livingston *(Free on 1/7/2003) SL 12+15 SLC 0+3 SC 0+2*
Sheffield Wed *(Free on 3/6/2004) FL 46/6 FLC 2 FAC 1 Others 4/2*

McGRATH John Matthew
Born: Limerick, 27 March 1980
Height: 5'10" **Weight:** 10.8
International Honours: RoI: U21-5
John was again only ever on the fringes of the first team at Doncaster last term and at the end of August he joined Shrewsbury Town on loan. The young midfielder made an impressive debut against Cheltenham as a replacement for the injured Sam Aiston and stayed two months at Gay Meadow before returning to South Yorkshire. At the turn of the year he joined Kidderminster Harriers on a contract to the end of the season and quickly made the wide-left midfield position his own. John was out of contract in the summer and his future was unclear at the time of writing.
Aston Villa *(Signed from Belvedere YC on 3/9/1999) PL 0+3*
Doncaster Rov *(Free on 10/7/2003) FL 4+7 FLC 1 FAC 1 Others 1*

***rewsbury T** (Loaned on 31/8/2004) FL*
-1
***dderminster Hrs** (Free on 14/1/2005) FL*
'+1

IcGREAL John
orn: Liverpool, 2 June 1972
eight: 5'11" **Weight:** 12.8
eve Cotterill's first signing as Burnley's anager proved to be an inspired one, as hn McGreal was the key man in the ansformation from the leaky defence of e previous two seasons to the tight ıck unit that kept the Clarets ɔmfortably clear of relegation worries in)04-05. John's vast experience at this vel proved invaluable, and he was enerally unflappable at the back, ɔming in with countless saving tackles ; well as showing impeccable positional sense. He also greatly aided the development of the impressive Gary Cahill, his centre-back partner for much of the campaign. A defender first and foremost, John is not averse to venturing forward, particularly at set pieces, and he registered his first Burnley goal in the early-season home fixture against Crewe.
***Tranmere Rov** (From trainee on 3/7/1990) FL 193+2/1 FLC 20+1 FAC 8 Others 7+2*
***Ipswich T** (£650,000 on 4/8/1999) P/FL 120+3/4 FLC 12 FAC 5 Others 10/1*
***Burnley** (Free on 4/8/2004) FL 38+1/1 FLC 3 FAC 3*

McGREGOR Mark Dale Thomas
Born: Chester, 16 February 1977
Height: 5'11" **Weight:** 11.5
This experienced defender was a great success for Blackpool last term when he featured both at right back and in the centre of the defence. His partnership with Peter Clarke in the middle of the back line proved extremely effective and was a key factor in enabling the Seasiders to turn around their fortunes after a poor start to the campaign.
***Wrexham** (From trainee on 4/7/1995) FL 237+7/11 FLC 9 FAC 24+1 Others 11*
***Burnley** (Free on 20/7/2001) FL 46+8/2 FLC 4/1 FAC 5+2*
***Blackpool** (Free on 30/7/2004) FL 36+2 FLC 1 FAC 4 Others 1*

Jon-Paul McGovern

McGURK David Michael
Born: Middlesbrough, 30 September 1982
Height: 6'0" **Weight:** 11.10
This tall young Darlington defender spent the early part of last season on loan at Conference club York City but returned to feature on several occasions after Christmas, contributing two crucial goals from set pieces. David has now made over 50 appearances for the Quakers and when selected can always be relied upon to show some powerful tackling and effectiveness in the air.
***Darlington** (From trainee on 9/8/2002) FL 44+9/6 FLC 3 FAC 1+1 Others 2*

McHALE Christopher (Chris) Mark
Born: Birmingham, 4 November 1984
Height: 6'0" **Weight:** 12.0
A product of the Kidderminster youth team, Chris is comfortable either in defence of midfield. After making his debut in the final three minutes of the previous season he became a regular at the start of last term, mostly featuring at right back. Whenever called upon he could be relied on to give his best and he never let the team down, but he found himself on the fringes of the squad following a change in management and ended the season on the transfer list.
***Kidderminster Hrs** (From juniors on 25/3/2004) FL 11+4 FLC 1 Others 1*

McINDOE Michael
Born: Edinburgh, 2 December 1979
Height: 5'8" **Weight:** 11.0
Club Honours: FAT '02; NC '03; Div 3 '04
International Honours: S: B-1
After enjoying a wonderful campaign for Doncaster Rovers in 2003-04, Michael's form levelled out last season as he came to terms with the higher standard of football required in League One. However, he was still a big threat to opposing defences from the left-hand side of midfield and finished as the club's leading scorer with 12 goals in all competitions.

Luton T *(From trainee on 2/4/1998) FL 19+20 FLC 4+1 FAC 0+3 Others 1 (Free to Hereford U on 20/7/2000)*
Doncaster Rov *(£50,000 from Yeovil T on 5/8/2003) FL 88+1/20 FLC 5/1 FAC 3/1 Others 4*

McINTOSH Austin James
Born: Newham, 5 November 1987
Height: 5'11" **Weight:** 10.9
This Mansfield Town scholar was given his debut in the FA Cup replay with Colchester a few months past his 17th birthday after suspensions decimated the club's small first-team squad. Austin has played at both right back and centre back for the youth team and became a regular on the substitutes' bench for the first team. With nothing at stake, he was given his full senior debut at right back in the final game of the season at Leyton Orient.
Mansfield T *(Trainee) FL 1 FAC 0+1*

McINTOSH Martin Wyllie
Born: East Kilbride, 19 March 1971
Height: 6'2" **Weight:** 12.0
International Honours: S: B-2; Sch
Rotherham's skipper was absent for the start of the 2004-05 season as he was still recovering from a cruciate ligament operation and his commanding presence at the heart of the defence was sorely missed. Martin established himself in the line-up from the end of September and found his scoring touch too, but from the end of January he was out of action again before returning once more in April.
St Mirren *(From trainee at Tottenham H on 30/11/1988) SL 2+2*
Clydebank *(Signed on 17/8/1991) SL 59+6/10 SLC 2 SC 4+1/1 Others 3/1*
Hamilton Academical *(Signed on 1/2/1994) SL 99/12 SLC 5 SC 5 Others 5/1*
Stockport Co *(£80,000 on 15/8/1997) FL 96+3/5 FLC 5+1 FAC 4*
Hibernian *(£250,000 on 10/2/2000) SL 13 SLC 3 SC 2*
Rotherham U *(£125,000 on 17/8/2001) FL 122/16 FLC 6 FAC 4*

McINTYRE Kevin
Born: Liverpool, 23 December 1977
Height: 5'11" **Weight:** 12.2
Club Honours: NC '04
This left wing back suffered more than most in Chester City's poor start to the season, when he was restricted to a purely defensive role, with few opportunities for the overlapping runs that had proved so effective in the Conference championship season. Kevin joined Macclesfield in December where he featured regularly on the left side of midfield, although towards the end of the campaign he filled in at left back and left wing back. Kevin is very much a defensive midfielder but always works tremendously hard in whatever role he is selected.
Tranmere Rov *(From trainee on 6/11/1996) FL 0+2 (Free to Doncaster Rov on 19/1/1999)*
Chester C *(Free on 15/5/2002) FL 9+1 FLC 1 FAC 1+1 Others 3*
Macclesfield T *(Signed on 24/12/2004) FL 21+2 Others 2*

MACKAY David
Born: Rutherglen, 2 May 1981
Height: 6'0" **Weight:** 13.3
David joined Oxford in the summer of 2004 and soon settled into League Two football. A regular throughout the campaign, he missed just two games all season. David is an accomplished defender who is strong in the tackle and likes to get forward to supplement the attack, although he has yet to register his first goal for the club.
Dundee *(Signed from Benburb Thistle on 1/8/1999) SL 82+5/2 SLC 5 SC 9 Others 4*
Brechin C *(Loaned on 3/2/2001) SL 16/1*
Arbroath *(Loaned on 1/7/2001) SL 5 SLC 0+1 Others 1*
Oxford U *(Free on 12/7/2004) FL 44 FLC 1 FAC 1 Others 1*

MACKAY Malcolm (Malky) George
Born: Bellshill, 19 February 1972
Height: 6'1" **Weight:** 11.7
Club Honours: Div 1 '04
International Honours: S: 5
After leading Norwich to promotion in the previous season Malky joined West Ham during the summer. The central defender provided strong leadership both

Kevin McIntyre

n and off the pitch and his experience was of great value to the Hammers' cause. Commanding in the air, he scored against Ipswich and Plymouth, whilst one of his best performances came in the FA Cup tie at Carrow Road. However, he struggled with niggling injuries in March and lost his place in the side.
Queen's Park *(From juniors on 8/12/1989) SL 68+2/6 SLC 3/2 SC 2 Others 2*
Glasgow Celtic *(Signed on 6/8/1993) SL 2+5/4 SLC 5+1 SC 4/1 Others 4+1*
Norwich C *(£350,000 on 18/9/1998) FL 98+14/15 FLC 8+1 FAC 8 Others 3/1*
West Ham U *(£300,000 on 10/9/2004) FL 7+1/2 FLC 1 FAC 3*

MACKEN Jonathan (Jon) Paul
Born: Manchester, 7 September 1977
Height: 5'10" **Weight:** 12.8
Club Honours: Div 2 '00
International Honours: RoI: 1; E: Yth
Injury and a plethora of striking options have limited the number of starts Jon has managed for Manchester City in recent years. He had better fortune last term as his club form won him a call-up to the full Republic of Ireland squad and he won his first cap against Bulgaria last August. A natural target man he excels at holding the ball up and bringing others into the game.
Manchester U *(From trainee on 10/7/1996)*
Preston NE *(£250,000 on 31/7/1997) FL 155+29/63 FLC 12+2/8 FAC 10+5/2 Others 9+3/1*
Manchester C *(£4,000,000 + on 5/3/2002) P/FL 27+24/7 FLC 1+1/3 FAC 2+2/2 Others 1+1*

McKENNA Paul Stephen
Born: Chorley, 20 October 1977
Height: 5'7" **Weight:** 11.12
Club Honours: Div 2 '00
Very much the heartbeat in the Preston team, Paul is now firmly established in the centre of midfield, as illustrated by his selection as the PFA Fans' Championship 'Player of the Season'. A tigerish tackler and precise passer of the ball, Paul is the central pivot of both attack and defence, being tireless in his running to support at both ends of the pitch. He also weighs in with the occasional goal, although his return of two strikes last term does not reflect his shooting abilities.
Preston NE *(From trainee on 2/2/1996) FL 251+20/24 FLC 14 FAC 10+2/2 Others 9+2*

MACKENZIE Christopher (Chris) Neil
Born: Northampton, 14 May 1972
Height: 6'0" **Weight:** 12.6
Snapped up by Mark Wright following Chester City's promotion to League Two, Chris started last term as second choice to Wayne Brown but was soon sharing the goalkeeping duties as City's longest-serving player suffered a series of minor injuries. A 'keeper who likes to control his area Chris proved a steady presence in the Chester goal and by the end of the season had made the goalkeeping jersey his own.
Hereford U *(£15,000 from Corby T on 20/7/1994) FL 59+1/1 FLC 2 FAC 4 Others 8 (Free to Farnborough T in 1997 close season)*
Leyton Orient *(Free on 17/10/1997) FL 30 FLC 3 FAC 5 Others 2 (Free to Nuneaton Borough on 1/8/1999)*
Chester C *(Free from Telford U on 2/7/2004) FL 23+1 FAC 2 Others 1*

McKENZIE Leon Mark
Born: Croydon, 17 May 1978
Height: 5'11" **Weight:** 11.2
Club Honours: Div 1 '04
Leon took a while to find his feet at Premiership level last term. The arrival of Dean Ashton proved to be the turning point in his season as his performance levels improved and the goals began to flow. A tremendously hard-working front-runner, his enthusiasm and willingness to chase seemingly lost causes greatly impressed Norwich fans, who voted him third in their 'Player of the Season' awards. Strong in the air and difficult to dispossess when twisting and turning in and around the penalty area, he had the pleasure of ending Chelsea's run of 11 games without conceding a goal.
Crystal Palace *(From trainee on 7/10/1995) P/FL 44+41/7 FLC 5+2/1 FAC 2+4*
Fulham *(Loaned on 3/10/1997) FL 1+2*
Peterborough U *(Loaned on 13/8/1998) FL 4/3*
Peterborough U *(Loaned on 30/11/1998) FL 10/5 Others 1/1*
Peterborough U *(Free on 13/10/2000) FL 83+7/45 FLC 2 FAC 7+1/1 Others 3/4*
Norwich C *(£325,000 on 15/12/2003) P/FL 36+19/16*

MacKENZIE Neil David
Born: Birmingham, 15 April 1976
Height: 6'1" **Weight:** 12.4
Club Honours: AMC '02
Neil once again impressed the Mansfield Town fans with some accurate passing and thunderous shooting last term. His attacking midfield play always looked likely to create an opening but it also attracted the attentions of Macclesfield and in November he was allowed to go to Moss Rose on a three-month loan, the move later becoming permanent. Despite suffering an achilles injury in his first appearance, which left him sidelined for two months he made a successful return and appeared regularly on the right side of midfield thereafter.
Stoke C *(From trainee at West Bromwich A on 9/11/1995) FL 15+27/1 FLC 1+1 FAC 0+1 Others 0+1*
Cambridge U *(Loaned on 24/3/1999) FL 3+1/1*
Cambridge U *(£45,000 on 14/10/1999) FL 20+8 FLC 1+1 FAC 5 Others 0+1*
Kidderminster Hrs *(Free on 24/11/2000) FL 20+3/3 FAC 0+1 Others 2*
Blackpool *(Free on 9/7/2001) FL 6+8/1 FLC 1+1 FAC 1+3/1 Others 3/2*
Mansfield T *(Free on 6/8/2002) FL 50+21/4 FLC 2+1 FAC 6/3 Others 4+3*
Macclesfield T *(Free on 26/11/2004) FL 16+2*

MACKIE James (Jamie) Charles
Born: Dorking, 22 September 1985
Height: 5'8" **Weight:** 11.2
A very energetic front-runner, Jamie was given few first-team chances at MK Dons last term as both Stuart Murdoch and then Danny Wilson chose to go with more experienced strikers throughout the campaign. His only start was in the LDV Vans Trophy defeat at Bristol City, and he was released at the end of the season.
Wimbledon/MK Dons *(Signed from Leatherhead on 9/1/2004) FL 8+8 FAC 2+1 Others 1*

MACKIE John George
Born: Whitechapel, 5 July 1976
Height: 6'0" **Weight:** 12.6
John started the 2004-05 season as a first choice at centre half for Leyton Orient, but then suffered an injury and this kept him out of action for three months. A tough-tackling defender who leads by example, he often found himself pushed up front when goals were required late on in games and he scored twice during the campaign.
Reading *(Free from Sutton U on 5/11/1999) FL 61+10/3 FLC 3+1 FAC 5+2 Others 1+2*
Leyton Orient *(Free on 13/1/2004) FL 46+1/5 FAC 1 Others 3*

MACKIN Levi Alan
Born: Chester, 4 April 1986
Height: 6'1" **Weight:** 12.0
This promising young midfielder continued his development at Wrexham last season, adding a handful more appearances, mostly in a spell at the turn of the year. Levi was reported to have signed a full professional contract for the Racecourse club during the summer.
Wrexham *(Trainee) FL 6+5 FLC 0+1*

McKINLAY William (Billy)
Born: Glasgow, 22 April 1969
Height: 5'9" **Weight:** 11.6
International Honours: S: 29; B-1; U21-6; Yth; Sch

Billy arrived at Fulham in the summer of 2004 with a brief to assist the development of the reserve-team players. This he did and the second string finished in a respectable position in the table. A combative midfielder with a no-nonsense attitude, he made the occasional first-team appearance although his only Premiership start came in the 'derby' game at Crystal Palace.
Dundee U *(Signed from Hamilton Thistle on 24/6/1985) SL 210+10/23 SLC 21/3 SC 23+3/4 Others 17/2*
Blackburn Rov *(£1,750,000 on 14/10/1995) PL 76+14/3 FLC 4/1 FAC 7+1 Others 1*
Leicester C *(Loaned on 27/10/2000) FLC 1*
Bradford C *(Free on 24/11/2000) PL 10+1 FAC 1*
Clydebank *(Free, via trial at Preston NE, on 24/11/2001) SL 8 SC 1*
Leicester C *(Free on 9/8/2002) P/FL 44+9/1 FLC 1+1 FAC 4*
Fulham *(Free on 1/7/2004) PL 1+1 FLC 1*

McKINNEY Richard
Born: Ballymoney, 18 May 1979
Height: 6'3" **Weight:** 14.0
Richard gave an outstanding display in goal in Walsall's pre-season 2-1 win over Aston Villa and started the 2004-05 season as first choice in League One. However, he remained only briefly in the starting line-up and then an injury in a reserve game prevented him from making any further senior appearances.
Manchester C *(Free from Ballymena U on 25/8/1999)*
Swindon T *(Free on 18/7/2001) FL 1*
Colchester U *(Free on 9/8/2002) FL 25+1 FLC 1 FAC 1 Others 2*
Walsall *(Free on 5/7/2004) FL 3*

McKOY Nicholas (Nick) Paul
Born: Newham, 3 September 1986
Height: 6'0" **Weight:** 12.4
After having featured on a few occasions the previous season, Nick's only appearance for MK Dons last term was as a substitute in the LDV Vans Trophy defeat at Bristol City. He became a regular for the reserve team though, remaining a very promising midfielder.
Wimbledon/MK Dons *(Trainee) FL 1+2 Others 0+1*

McLACHLAN Fraser Malcolm
Born: Manchester, 9 November 1982
Height: 5'11" **Weight:** 12.6
This young midfielder began the 2004-05 season on loan from Stockport to Northwich Victoria, but this was terminated early due to an injury. In November Fraser moved out on loan again, this time to Mansfield Town and he made his debut in the FA Cup tie with Colchester United. He seemed to be settling in when he was injured in the game at Boston United. Highly rated by Carlton Palmer, his loan move was made permanent in January and he retained his place in the starting line-up for the remainder of the campaign.
Stockport Co *(From trainee on 11/7/2001) FL 43+10/4 FLC 1 FAC 2 Others 0+1*
Mansfield T *(Signed on 11/11/2004) FL 16+5 FAC 1*

McLAREN Paul Andrew
Born: High Wycombe, 17 November 1976
Height: 6'0" **Weight:** 13.4
Paul's debut for Rotherham was held back due to a pre-season injury and he was only used as an occasional substitute until the end of October. However, after that he established himself as an automatic choice in midfield for the remainder of the season, taking over as the regular taker of corners and free kicks. He will have been disappointed by the fact that he scored just once, that goal coming with a fine shot to earn a point in a 2-2 draw against Cardiff City.
Luton T *(From trainee on 5/1/1994) FL 137+30/4 FLC 10+4/1 FAC 11/1 Others 9*
Sheffield Wed *(Free on 11/6/2001) FL 83+13/8 FLC 6+1/1 FAC 2 Others 1*
Rotherham U *(Free on 2/8/2004) FL 32+1/1 FAC 1*

MacLEAN Steven (Steve)
Born: Edinburgh, 23 August 1982
Height: 5'10" **Weight:** 11.1
International Honours: S: U21-4
Steve proved to be a very astute signing for Sheffield Wednesday last term. The young striker had a great season and finished the campaign as the team's leading scorer with 20 goals in all competitions. His leading of the line and all-round work rate were much appreciated by his colleagues, while a goal every two games, including a hat-trick at local rivals Doncaster, shot the Owls into a play-off position. Unfortunately a fractured foot suffered in March put him out for several weeks, although he returned for the play-off final against Hartlepool when his penalty took the game into extra time.
Glasgow Rgrs *(From juniors on 17/9/1998) SL 0+3 SC 0+1*
Scunthorpe U *(Loaned on 6/8/2003) FL 37+5/23 FLC 1+1/1 FAC 5 Others 3/1*
Sheffield Wed *(£125,000 on 27/7/2004) FL 36/18 FLC 2 FAC 1 Others 1+1/2*

McLEOD Izale (Izzy) Michael
Born: Birmingham, 15 October 1984
Height: 6'0" **Weight:** 11.2
A lightning-fast striker, Izzy's final goal tally for the season could have been so much more had he taken even half the chances he created for himself. He would also have had many more chances had he been able to stay on his feet for more often than he did, though his very lightweight frame did not help matters there. Undoubtedly capable of being a major player for the club, confidence and consistency will be the key words necessary for Izale's continued progress.
Derby Co *(From trainee on 7/2/2003) FL 24+15/4 FLC 1+1*
Sheffield U *(Loaned on 12/3/2004) FL 1+6*
MK Dons *(£100,000 on 4/8/2004) FL 39+4/16 FLC 2/2 FAC 2+1*

McLEOD Kevin Andrew
Born: Liverpool, 12 September 1980
Height: 5'11" **Weight:** 11.3
This wide left-sided midfield player really established himself as a regular in the line-up for Queen's Park Rangers last term and the vast majority of his outings came from the bench. The vast majority of his appearances were from the bench, when the manager was looking for a fresh pair of legs to get through to the end of the game. In February he moved on, linking up with former Rangers' assistant-manager Kenny Jackett at Swansea. He showed plenty of skill down the flank but went down with a virus shortly after arriving at Vetch Field and this affected his performances.
Everton *(From trainee on 24/9/1998) PL 0+5 FLC 1 FAC 0+1*
Queens Park Rgrs *(Loaned on 21/3/2003) FL 8/2 Others 3*
Queens Park Rgrs *(Signed on 18/8/2003) FL 30+29/4 FLC 3+1/1 FAC 2 Others 1/1*
Swansea C *(Signed on 16/2/2005) FL 7+4*

McMAHON Anthony
Born: Bishop Auckland, 24 March 1986
Height: 5'10" **Weight:** 11.6
Club Honours: FAYC '04
International Honours: E: Yth
Last term was a season of positive progress for this Bishop Auckland-born full back who, initially, got his Premiership chance when Michael Reiziger damaged his shoulder, and what more daunting debut could a teenager have than at Old Trafford and Manchester United against the likes of Ryan Giggs and Christian Ronaldo? At the end of the season the 19-year-old youngster collected Middlesbrough's 'Young Player of the Year Award' and announced that he is prepared to wait patiently in the wings. His time will come and a bright future in the game awaits him.
Middlesbrough *(From trainee on 7/2/2005) PL 12+1 FLC 0+1 FAC 0+1 Others 4*

McMAHON Daryl
Born: Dublin, 10 October 1983
Height: 5'11" **Weight:** 12.2
International Honours: RoI: Yth
This skilful midfield player joined Port Vale on trial last September and made a promising debut as a substitute at Colchester when he was unlucky not to score. Two more appearances from the bench soon followed but although he was offered a short-term deal he opted to join Leyton Orient. Daryl featured for the O's as a left-sided central midfielder and the highlight of his season came with his brace of goals in the game at Boston. He signed a new contract for the Brisbane Road club during the summer.
West Ham U *(From trainee on 16/10/2000)*
Torquay U *(Loaned on 24/3/2004) FL 0+1*
Port Vale *(Free on 28/9/2004) FL 1+4 Others 0+1*
Leyton Orient *(Free on 26/11/2004) FL 22+2/3 FAC 0+1*

McMAHON Lewis James
Born: Doncaster, 2 May 1985
Height: 5'9" **Weight:** 11.4
Lewis was a key member of the Sheffield Wednesday midfield in the early stages of the 2004-05 season, but was dropped briefly after a dip in form. He then suffered a leg injury at the beginning of December which led to a lengthy lay off. However, he was back in action by the end of the season and featured as a second-half substitute in the first leg of the play-off semi-final against Brentford.
Sheffield Wed *(From trainee on 2/7/2004) FL 22+3/2 FLC 1+1 FAC 1 Others 1+2*

McMAHON Stephen Joseph
Born: Southport, 31 July 1984
Height: 5'9" **Weight:** 10.5
Club Honours: AMC '04
Stephen found himself out of favour at Blackpool last term and in September he joined Kidderminster on loan. He proved to be a hard-working and aggressive midfield player, but returned to the Seasiders at the end of his loan spell. Stephen was released by Blackpool at the end of the year and subsequently linked up with his father in Australia joining Perth Glory.
Blackpool *(From trainee on 1/7/2003) FL 10+8 FAC 0+2 Others 3+3*
Kidderminster Hrs *(Loaned on 4/9/2004) FL 3+2 Others 1*

McMANAMAN Steven (Steve)
Born: Bootle, 11 February 1972
Height: 6'0" **Weight:** 11.10
Club Honours: FAC '92; FLC '95
International Honours: E: 37; U21-7; Yth
Steve has been beset by injuries since his arrival at Manchester City from Spanish giants Real Madrid and an achilles problem plagued him throughout the 2004-05 season restricting him to just a handful of starts. An extremely talented winger or central midfield player, he was out of contract in the summer and his future was unclear at the time of writing.
Liverpool *(From trainee on 19/2/1990) P/FL 258+14/46 FLC 32+1/10 FAC 28+1/5 Others 30/5 (Free to Real Madrid, Spain on 1/7/1999)*
Manchester C *(Free on 30/8/2003) PL 25+10 FLC 0+1 FAC 2+2 Others 4*

McMANUS Thomas (Tom) Kelly
Born: Glasgow, 28 February 1981
Height: 5'9" **Weight:** 10.8
International Honours: S: U21-14
Tom had his first taste of English football when he was loaned by SPL club Hibernian to Boston United in August. However, he found it difficult to force his way into the starting line-up, despite showing plenty of movement inside the box when he was given the chance. Tom had little luck in front of goal and only found the back of the net in the FA Cup tie against non-league Hornchurch. He returned to Easter Road in December and the following month was transferred to Dundee.
Hibernian *(From juniors on 10/7/1997) SL 58+51/19 SLC 6+3/2 SC 4+3/2 Others 2+1*
East Fife *(Loaned on 4/3/2000) SL 11/3*
Airdrie *(Loaned on 29/12/2000) SL 1*
Boston U *(Loaned on 7/8/2004) FL 5+3 FLC 1+1 FAC 0+1/2 Others 1*

McMASTER Jamie
Born: Sydney, Australia, 29 November 1982
Height: 5'10" **Weight:** 11.13
International Honours: E: Yth
Hopes that this young striker would make a breakthrough with Leeds in the Championship failed to materialise. Although he came on as a substitute several times his only start came in the Carling Cup victory over Swindon in September. Jamie was subsequently loaned to Swindon, where he scored on his debut, and Peterborough, returning to Elland Road early with injuries. He later signed a short-term deal with Chesterfield but a further injury meant his season ended prematurely. Jamie was released by the Spireites in the summer.
Leeds U *(From trainee on 30/11/1999) P/FL 0+11 FLC 1+1*
Coventry C *(Loaned on 22/11/2002) FL 2*
Chesterfield *(Loaned on 7/1/2004) FL 4+2/2*
Swindon T *(Loaned on 27/9/2004) FL 2+2/1*
Peterborough U *(Loaned on 21/1/2005) FL 3 FAC 1*
Chesterfield *(Free on 4/3/2005) FL 6+2*

McMILLAN Stephen (Steve) Thomas
Born: Edinburgh, 19 January 1976
Height: 5'10" **Weight:** 11.10
Club Honours: Div 2 '03
International Honours: S: U21-4
This injury-jinxed full back was again restricted to just a handful of appearances for Wigan Athletic last term. Second choice behind Leighton Baines, he started the last five games of the season when he looked comfortable in possession and never let the side down. Out of contract at the end of the season, he was offered a new deal by the club.
Motherwell *(Signed from Troon Juniors on 19/8/1993) SL 144+8/6 SLC 9 SC 13+1*
Wigan Ath *(£550,000 on 2/3/2001) FL 81+9 FLC 5 FAC 1*

McNAMARA Niall Anthony
Born: Limerick, 26 January 1982
Height: 5'11" **Weight:** 11.12
International Honours: RoI: Yth
This tall wide-midfield player had been released by Lincoln City in June 2004 but trained with the Imps in pre-season, playing in a number of warm-up matches. He was rewarded with a one-month contract and was included in the squad for the opening-day clash at Shrewsbury. Niall came on as a substitute for the final ten minutes of City's victory but that proved to be his only first-team action. His contract was extended by three months but although a regular in the reserves he left Sincil Bank in December and later signed for Ossett Town.
Nottingham F *(From trainee on 2/2/1999)*
Notts Co *(Free on 5/7/2001) FL 0+4 (Free to Belper T on 30/6/2002)*
Lincoln C *(Free on 5/8/2003) FL 2+9 FLC 1 FAC 1+1 Others 1*

McNAMEE Anthony
Born: Kensington, 13 July 1984
Height: 5'6" **Weight:** 10.0
International Honours: E: Yth
Anthony entered the Watford first-team equation at the turn of the year and was a regular substitute thereafter, making his first start in two years on the last day of the season. A busy, tricky left winger with quick feet, Anthony is a fine crosser of the ball and has the priceless ability to change the course of games. He also showed an improved work rate and a greater awareness of his defensive responsibilities last term.
Watford *(From trainee on 17/4/2002) FL 4+42/1 FLC 0+2 FAC 0+1*

McNIVEN Scott Andrew
Born: Leeds, 27 May 1978
Height: 5'10" **Weight:** 12.1
International Honours: S: U21-1; Yth
This right back signed for Mansfield in the summer of 2004 to replace Bobby Hassell who had departed for Barnsley. A solid performer down the right-hand side, his surging runs were beneficial to both midfield and attack. He was an ever-present until he was diagnosed with testicular cancer in November. Everyone at Field Mill was pleased to welcome him back into training in February. He made an emotional return to the first team against former club Oxford in March. Although not fully fit after this he never let the club down. However, he was surprisingly released at the end of the season.
Oldham Ath *(From trainee on 25/10/1995) FL 204+18/3 FLC 13+1 FAC 18+1/1 Others 9+2*
Oxford U *(Free on 11/7/2002) FL 85/1 FLC 5 FAC 4 Others 1*
Mansfield T *(Free on 23/7/2004) FL 24+1 Others 1*

McPHAIL Stephen John Paul
Born: Westminster, 9 December 1979
Height: 5'10" **Weight:** 12.0
Club Honours: FAYC '97
International Honours: RoI: 10; U21-7; Yth (UEFA-U18 '98)
Stephen was a regular for Barnsley throughout the 2004-05 campaign, but a constant changing of team formation and his own role in the line-up did not always help his cause. Without doubt he is one of the most gifted footballers in the lower divisions, at his best he seemed to control matches with his left foot, notably in the game at Huddersfield in September. Stephen also provided a real danger with his free kicks.
Leeds U *(From trainee on 23/12/1996) PL 52+26/3 FLC 2+4 FAC 3 Others 15+5*
Millwall *(Loaned on 14/3/2002) FL 3*
Nottingham F *(Loaned on 27/8/2003) FL 13+1 FLC 2*
Barnsley *(Free on 5/7/2004) FL 36/2 FLC 1 Others 1*

McPHEE Christopher (Chris) Simon
Born: Eastbourne, 20 March 1983
Height: 5'10" **Weight:** 12.4
After enjoying a breakthrough season in 2003-04, Chris suffered a setback last term when his campaign was severely disrupted by a number of fractures to bones in his feet. After just one start before Christmas, the young centre forward returned to the squad at the end of February, and showed what he can do in the 1-1 draw at Burnley in April when, in company with fellow youth products Jake Robinson and Dean Hammond, he terrorised the home defence. Still learning, Chris needs to add some raw strength to his game to ensure success at Championship level.
Brighton & Hove A *(From trainee on 10/6/2002) FL 25+28/4 FLC 2+2/1 FAC 1/1 Others 2+2/3*

McSHANE Luke
Born: Peterborough, 6 November 1985
Height: 6'1" **Weight:** 10.9
This young Peterborough goalkeeper was understudy to Mark Tyler last term and played most of his football in the club's reserves. However, he made his debut in senior football in the FA Cup third round tie at MK Dons in January when Tyler injured his back during the pre-match

Stephen McPhail

warm-up. Luke had just ten minutes notice before stepping in, but after a nervous start he did well as Posh ran out 2-0 winners.
Peterborough U *(From trainee on 11/7/2003) FAC 1*

McSHANE Paul David
Born: Wicklow, 6 January 1986
Height: 5'11" **Weight:** 11.5
Club Honours: FAYC '03
International Honours: RoI: U21-1; Yth
A regular in Manchester United's reserve-team line-up, Paul joined Walsall on loan shortly before Christmas. He featured on the left-hand side of the defence in his debut against Sheffield Wednesday when he scored with the neatest of headers as the Saddlers went down 3-2. His later appearances came in the centre of the back line where he looked more comfortable and he showed some impressive commitment in the tackle. Paul was later a member of the Reds' reserve team that defeated Charlton Athletic in the FA Premier Reserve League play-off.
Manchester U *(From trainee on 13/1/2003)*
Walsall *(Loaned on 23/12/2004) FL 3+1/1*

McSHEFFREY Gary
Born: Coventry, 13 August 1982
Height: 5'8" **Weight:** 10.10
International Honours: E: Yth
After a disappointing start to the season at Coventry, Gary was dropped and his future at Highfield Road seemed in doubt when he was allowed to go to Luton on a month's loan. However, he was mostly on the bench for the Hatters, unable to break the partnership between Steve Howard and Rowan Vine. On his return to the Sky Blues he was played wide on the left-hand side and looked much sharper. His form took another leap in the New Year and he scored twice in the FA Cup win over Crewe when his running at defenders provided a constant threat. Gary became the penalty king by scoring six from the spot including four in successive home games, many of them from fouls on himself by defenders bemused by his direct-running style. His status as 'Player of the Season' was rubber-stamped with a brilliant opening goal in the final game at Highfield Road.
Coventry C *(From trainee on 27/8/1999) P/FL 62+35/28 FLC 5+2/4 FAC 5+2/3*
Stockport Co *(Loaned on 30/11/2001) FL 3+2/1*
Luton T *(Loaned on 22/8/2003) FL 18/9 FLC 1/1*
Luton T *(Loaned on 18/9/2004) FL 1+4/1*

McSPORRAN Jermaine
Born: Manchester, 1 January 1977
Height: 5'8" **Weight:** 10.10
Jermaine arrived at Doncaster in the summer of 2004 and vied with Jamie Coppinger for a place out wide on the right flank. Just as he was running into top form he received a serious knee injury against Bradford City in March, and this put him out of action for the rest of the season.
Wycombe W *(Signed from Oxford C on 5/11/1998) FL 117+41/30 FLC 9+1/3 FAC 10+2/4 Others 5+2/4*
Walsall *(Free on 25/3/2004) FL 2+4*
Doncaster Rov *(Free on 10/6/2004) FL 15+11/1 FLC 2/1 FAC 1+1*

McVEIGH Paul Francis
Born: Belfast, 6 December 1977
Height: 5'6" **Weight:** 10.5
Club Honours: Div 1 '04
International Honours: NI: 20; U21-11; Yth; Sch
After playing a major part in the Canaries' championship-winning season of 2003-04, Paul struggled to win a regular place in Nigel Worthington's line-

Gary McSheffrey

up last term. His personal highlight would have been scoring at Old Trafford in City's first away game of the season, but in total he started just three Premiership games. A clever player with quick feet and inventive passing skills, he can play wide in midfield, just behind the strikers or as an out-and-out attacker. Paul announced his retirement from the Northern Ireland set-up to concentrate on his club football and, at the end of the season, was told that he could leave Carrow Road if he could find another club to make a fresh start in his playing career.
Tottenham H *(From trainee on 10/7/1996) PL 2+1/1*
Norwich C *(Free on 23/3/2000) P/FL 120+39/29 FLC 2+2 FAC 6/1 Others 3/1*

MADDISON Neil Stanley
Born: Darlington, 2 October 1969
Height: 5'10" **Weight:** 12.0
This experienced midfielder completed his fourth season with the Quakers and continued to show his Premiership class, displaying quality control and accurate passing from midfield. Although he only featured in around half the games last term his vast experience was evident and his commitment unquestionable as he prompted and inspired those around him with commanding displays in the centre of the park. Neil contributed his customary goal by scoring against Macclesfield Town in January.
Southampton *(From trainee on 14/4/1988) P/FL 149+20/19 FLC 9+5 FAC 8+5 Others 1*
Middlesbrough *(£250,000 on 31/10/1997) P/FL 32+24/4 FLC 7+1 FAC 4*
Barnsley *(Loaned on 4/11/2000) FL 3*
Bristol C *(Loaned on 16/3/2001) FL 4+3/1*
Darlington *(Free on 26/7/2001) FL 100+14/4 FLC 3+1 FAC 4+2 Others 4*

MAGILTON James (Jim)
Born: Belfast, 6 May 1969
Height: 6'0" **Weight:** 14.2
International Honours: NI: 52; U23-2; U21-1; Yth; Sch
Jim continued in his role of club captain on and off the field for Ipswich last term and, as always, led by example. His skills as the playmaker who makes the team tick were there for all to see and he was sorely missed when absent. Joe Royle rested him from some games, letting him sit on the substitutes' bench, but often had to bring him on in the second half to turn the game Town's way. After a barren season in terms of goals scored, Jim suddenly hit three in five games during April, all shots from outside the area.
Liverpool *(From apprentice on 14/5/1986)*

Jim Magilton (front)

Oxford U *(£100,000 on 3/10/1990) FL 150/34 FLC 9/1 FAC 8/4 Others 7/3*
Southampton *(£600,000 on 11/2/1994) PL 124+6/13 FLC 12+2/2 FAC 12/3*
Sheffield Wed *(£1,600,000 on 10/9/1997) PL 14+13/1 FLC 2 FAC 1*
Ipswich T *(£682,500 on 15/1/1999) P/FL 218+21/15 FLC 14+1/1 FAC 6+2/1 Others 17+1/3*

MAHER Kevin Andrew
Born: Ilford, 17 October 1976
Height: 6'0" **Weight:** 12.5
International Honours: RoI: U21-4
Southend United's club captain and longest-serving player enjoyed another superb campaign last term, when he eventually led the team to promotion via the League Two play-offs. An excellent passer of the ball and fearsome in the tackle, his midfield skills have long been admired in the lower divisions and it was richly deserved when Kevin was named in the PFA League Two team of the season.
Tottenham H *(From trainee on 1/7/1995)*
Southend U *(Free on 23/1/1998) FL 272+7/16 FLC 11/1 FAC 19 Others 24+1/1*

MAHER Shaun Patrick
Born: Dublin, 20 June 1978
Height: 6'2" **Weight:** 12.6
This centre half overcame a series of injuries to play a major part in Bournemouth's push to the play-offs last term. A confident player who forged an effective partnership with Karl Broadhurst and Eddie Howe, he has developed the knack of being in the right place at the right time from set pieces at the other end of the pitch.
Fulham *(£35,000 from Bohemians on 18/12/1997) Others 2 (Free to Bohemians on 10/9/1998)*
Bournemouth *(Free on 23/8/2001) FL 87+17/5 FLC 5 FAC 3+2/1*

MAHON Alan Joseph
Born: Dublin, 4 April 1978
Height: 5'10" **Weight:** 11.5
Club Honours: FLC '02
International Honours: RoI: 1; U21-18; Yth; Sch
A player of flair and skill, Alan brought a balance to the Wigan Athletic midfield last term. Given his chance after Per Frandsen was injured he made a great impression playing either in the centre of midfield or wide on the left. However, he lost his place after Christmas following the arrival of Graham Kavanagh and was restricted to just three more games. Alan will be looking to be heavily involved in 2005-06 having previously played in the Premiership.
Tranmere Rov *(From trainee on 7/4/1995) FL 84+36/13 FLC 12+6/1 FAC 4+2 (Free to Sporting Lisbon, Portugal on 1/7/2000)*
Blackburn Rov *(£1,500,000 on 14/12/2000) P/FL 25+11/1 FLC 4+3 FAC 10*
Cardiff C *(Loaned on 24/1/2003) FL 13+2/2*
Ipswich T *(Loaned on 5/9/2003) FL 7+4/1 FLC 1*
Wigan Ath *(Free on 6/2/2004) FL 34+7/8 FLC 1 FAC 1/1*

MAHON Gavin Andrew
Born: Birmingham, 2 January 1977
Height: 6'0" **Weight:** 13.2
Club Honours: Div 3 '99
Gavin was one of Watford's most consistent and important players last term, anchoring the side from central midfield and missing only four matches all season. A hard-working and quietly effective performer who concentrated on doing the simple things supremely well, Gavin also captained the side on many occasions. He led by example, never more so than in the Carling Cup semi-final at Anfield, when he was outstanding. However, his failure to find the net all season was a disappointment.
Wolverhampton W *(From trainee on 3/7/1995)*
Hereford U *(Free on 12/7/1996) FL 10+1/1 FLC 4*
Brentford *(£50,000 + on 17/11/1998) FL 140+1/8 FLC 8 FAC 5 Others 12*
Watford *(£150,000 + on 4/3/2002) FL 93+5/2 FLC 8 FAC 8+1/1*

Gavin Mahon

MAIDENS Michael Douglas
Born: Middlesbrough, 7 May 1987
Height: 5'11" **Weight:** 11.4
A midfielder who likes to go forward and take on the opposition, Michael was included in the Hartlepool first-team squad for the pre-season trip to Scotland. After some good displays for the juniors, he got another chance and made his debut as a substitute against Crystal Palace in the Carling Cup. Michael later made a brief appearance from the bench in a League One game and he was also in the team which won the Durham Challenge Cup.
Hartlepool U *(Trainee) FL 0+1 FLC 0+1*

MAIR Lee
Born: Aberdeen, 9 December 1980
Height: 6'0" **Weight:** 11.3
Lee was a summer signing from Dundee but the central defender was prone to mistakes in the heart of Stockport's defence. After the first few weeks of the season, his appearances in the first team became more limited and spread out and he eventually moved on to Dundee United, featuring in a handful of games during the remainder of the campaign.
Dundee *(Signed from Formartine U on 1/7/1999) SL SL 59+6/2 SLC 3 SC 6+1 Others 4*
East Fife *(Loaned on 23/2/2001) SL 13/2*
Falkirk *(Loaned on 20/7/2001) SL 19+1 SLC 2 SC 2 Others 2*
Stockport Co *(Free on 15/6/2004) FL 9+5 FAC 1+1 Others 1*

MAKEL Lee Robert
Born: Sunderland, 11 January 1973
Height: 5'10" **Weight:** 11.12
Club Honours: SLC '04
In the early part of last season Lee enjoyed regular first-team football at Plymouth. Used in the centre of midfield he put in many energetic displays. However he struggled to settle in the West Country and eventually moved back to Scotland signing for Dunfermline in the January transfer window.
Newcastle U *(From trainee on 11/2/1991) FL 6+6/1 FLC 1 Others 0+1*
Blackburn Rov *(£160,000 on 20/7/1992) PL 1+5 FLC 0+3 Others 1+3*
Huddersfield T *(£300,000 on 13/10/1995) FL 62+3/5 FLC 7 FAC 6+1*
Heart of Midlothian *(£75,000 on 13/3/1998) SL 30+19/1 SLC 3+1 SC 2+2 Others 5+1/1*
Bradford C *(Free on 31/8/2001) FL 2+11 FLC 2*
Livingston *(Free on 29/12/2001) SL 73+7/10 SLC 7/3 SC 6 Others 1*
Plymouth Arg *(Free on 8/6/2004) FL 13+6*

MAKELELE Claude
Born: Kinshasa, DR Congo, 18 February 1973
Height: 5'7" **Weight:** 10.12
Club Honours: FLC '05; PL '05
International Honours: France: 35; B-4; U21
While the Chelsea goalkeeper and his defenders rightly take the plaudits for the club's record-breaking achievements in 2004-05 the contribution of Claude Makelele should not be overlooked. Claude occupied the vital midfield role just in front of the back four and snuffed out any danger which loomed through the central area. His reliability and positional discipline allowed Frank Lampard the freedom to rampage forward and influence matches and secure his customary double-figure goal haul. Claude retired from international football after Euro 2004 and seemed destined never to score for the Blues (despite being urged to shoot by the crowd!) until Chelsea were awarded a last-minute penalty against Charlton Athletic in the 'Championship coronation' match. A Makelele goal (albeit a rebound off the 'keeper) followed by the Premiership trophy really made this a red-letter day for the Blues' fans! His covering and tackling make him one of the most effective players in the Premiership and an unsung component in Chelsea's memorable season, although not by Jose Mourinho who singled out Claude for particular praise during the season.
Chelsea *(£16,600,000 from Real Madrid, Spain, ex Brest Armorique, Nantes, Marseilles, Celta Vigo, on 1/9/2003) PL 62+4/1 FLC 5+1 FAC 3 Others 21*

MAKIN Christopher (Chris) Gregory
Born: Manchester, 8 May 1973
Height: 5'10" **Weight:** 11.2
Club Honours: Div 1 '99
International Honours: E: U21-5; Yth; Sch
Chris was a steady performer at right back for Leicester in the first half of the 2004-05 season but was allowed to move on to Derby following a change in management. George Burley was well aware of Chris' capabilities, having once recruited him for Ipswich Town, and was only too happy to step in to sign him. Injuries to Richard Jackson and Jamie Vincent gave Derby a problem at left back but, having quickly wrapped up his contract at the Walkers Stadium, Chris showed all his experience in the push for the play-offs. There is nothing flamboyant about his game but he proved himself a sound professional, especially when the pressure was on, although a heel injury ruled him out of the play-offs.
Oldham Ath *(From trainee on 2/11/1991) P/FL 93+1/4 FLC 7 FAC 11 Others 1+1 (Transferred to Marseilles, France during 1996 close season)*
Wigan Ath *(Loaned on 28/8/1992) FL 14+1/2*
Sunderland *(£500,000 on 5/8/1997) P/FL 115+5/1 FLC 13 FAC 7+1 Others 1+1*
Ipswich T *(£1,250,000 on 7/3/2001) P/FL 78 FLC 4 FAC 2 Others 7+1*
Leicester C *(Free on 2/8/2004) FL 21 FLC 1 FAC 1*
Derby Co *(Signed on 16/2/2005) FL 13*

MAKOFO Serge
Born: Kinshasa, DR Congo, 22 October 1986
Height: 5'11" **Weight:** 12.6
Serge's debut for the MK Dons was one of the highlights of the club's 2004-05 season, scoring on his first touch with a superb overhead kick after coming on a substitute in the LDV Vans Trophy defeat at Bristol City. He made another substitute appearance four days later in a League One match at the same venue, but after the dismissal of manager Stuart Murdoch that weekend he only featured once more on the bench all season. A very skilful left-footed attacker, he was given a professional deal at the end of the season.
MK Dons *(Trainee) FL 0+1 Others 0+1/1*

MALBRANQUE Steed
Born: Mouscron, Belgium, 6 January 1980
Height: 5'8" **Weight:** 11.7
International Honours: France: U21
After missing the start of the 2004-05 season through injury Steed returned to the Fulham squad in late September with a two-goal display in the Carling Cup tie at Boston. A gifted midfielder who displays excellent ball control and links well with his colleagues, he is often the catalyst of attacking moves. He produced an outstanding display in the final away game at Blackburn when he was again on target twice.
Fulham *(£5,000,000 from Lyon, France on 14/8/2001) PL 128+10/26 FLC 5+2/2 FAC 17/7 Others 12+2/3*

MALONEY Jonathan (Jon) Duncan
Born: Leeds, 3 March 1985
Height: 6'0" **Weight:** 11.12
Jon started out last season in Doncaster's reserve team, then spent three months on loan at Conference club York City. The promising central defender did so well at Bootham Crescent that York tried to sign

Steed Malbranque

him, but nevertheless he returned to Belle Vue in March. Jon went on to make two appearances for Rovers towards the end of the campaign, featuring as a substitute at Huddersfield and then at right back at Stockport. He was surprisingly released at the end of the season.
Doncaster Rov *(From trainee on 9/7/2003) FL 1+2 Others 0+1*

MANSARAM Darren Timothy
Born: Doncaster, 25 June 1984
Height: 6'2" **Weight:** 11.7
This young striker began last term on weekly contracts with Grimsby Town, but was nevertheless included in the starting line-up for the opening games, and scored in the 5-1 home victory over Bury. However, he was then loaned out to Halifax and although he made a couple more appearances for the Mariners from the substitutes' bench on his return, he eventually joined the Yorkshire club on a permanent basis early in the new year.
Grimsby T *(From trainee on 16/9/2002) FL 35+38/6 FLC 0+2 FAC 2+1/1 Others 1/1*

MANSELL Lee Richard Samuel
Born: Gloucester, 28 October 1982
Height: 5'9" **Weight:** 10.10
A versatile midfield player who prefers a central role, Lee featured in just a handful of first-team games for Luton last term. He did well in his only League One appearance, as a substitute at Torquay, but otherwise he was restricted to the club's reserves. Lee was a member of the side that defeated Reading to win the Pontin's Combination League Cup. Nevertheless he was released by the Hatters in the summer.
Luton T *(From trainee on 16/5/2001) FL 35+12/8 FLC 2 FAC 6/2 Others 7*

MARCELLE Clinton (Clint) Sherwin
Born: Port of Spain, Trinidad, 9 November 1968
Height: 5'4" **Weight:** 10.6
International Honours: Trinidad & Tobago
This experienced striker followed his former boss from Scarborough to Blundell Park during the summer of 2004 and began the season on short-term contracts. Clint made a handful of appearances for the Mariners, his only start coming in the LDV Vans Trophy defeat at Carlisle. In March he signed for Conference outfit Tamworth, with whom he spent the remainder of the season.
Barnsley *(Free from Felgueiras, Portugal, ex St Francis College (NY), Academica Coimbra, Rio Ave, Vitoria Setubal, on 8/8/1996) P/FL 37+32/8 FLC 3+5 FAC 6+1/1 (Freed on 29/2/2000)*

Scunthorpe U *(Loaned on 10/10/1999) FL 8+2 FAC 1*
Hull C *(Free from Goole AFC on 1/9/2000) FL 16+7/2 FLC 1 FAC 1*
Darlington *(Free on 23/2/2001) FL 8+7 Others 1 (Freed during 2002 close season)*
Grimsby T *(Free from Scarborough, ex Harrogate T, Hucknall T, Stevenage Borough, Ossett T, on 6/8/2004) FL 0+3 FLC 0+1 Others 1*

MARGETSON Martyn Walter

Born: Neath, 8 September 1971
Height: 6'0" **Weight:** 14.0
International Honours: W: 1; B-1; U21-7; Yth; Sch
After finishing the previous campaign in stunning form Martyn began the 2004-05 season as first choice in goal for Cardiff, but after three games he was replaced by new signing Tony Warner. Soon afterwards he suffered injury problems and these ruled him out of contention until April. He regained fitness but was only able to warm the bench for Neil Alexander, although it did not stop John Toshack from selecting Martyn for a Wales training camp in Spain in May.
Manchester C *(From trainee on 5/7/1990) P/FL 51 FLC 2+2 FAC 3 Others 1*
Bristol Rov *(Loaned on 8/12/1993) FL 2+1*
Southend U *(Free on 3/8/1998) FL 32 FLC 4 FAC 1 Others 1*
Huddersfield T *(Signed on 6/8/1999) FL 47+1 FLC 1 FAC 2 Others 8*
Cardiff C *(Free on 2/8/2002) FL 31+1 FLC 3 FAC 2 Others 2*

MARNEY Dean Edward

Born: Barking, 31 January 1984
Height: 5'9" **Weight:** 10.7
International Honours: E: U21-1
A versatile midfielder who can play at right back, central midfield or right midfield Dean joined Gillingham on loan last November and featured in the side at right wing back. On his return to White Hart Lane he made a handful of appearances, performing impressively for Spurs in the 5-2 home victory over Everton when he scored two spectacular goals and provided two assists. Strong and athletic, Dean will look to capitalise on his progress and win a more regular first-team place in 2005-06.
Tottenham H *(From trainee on 3/7/2002) PL 4+4/2 FAC 0+3*
Swindon T *(Loaned on 24/12/2002) FL 8+1*
Queens Park Rgrs *(Loaned on 16/1/2004) FL 1+1 Others 1*
Gillingham *(Loaned on 5/11/2004) FL 3*

MARPLES Simon James

Born: Sheffield, 30 July 1975
Height: 5'10" **Weight:** 11.11
Club Honours: Div 3 '04
International Honours: E: SP-2
Simon started last term as the first-choice right back for Doncaster, but was then laid low with a stomach-muscle problem. He attempted to come back on three separate occasions but was finally forced to rest just before Christmas and did not feature in the line-up thereafter.
Doncaster Rov *(Free from Stocksbridge Park Steels on 13/9/1999) FL 28 FLC 2 FAC 1 Others 1*

MARRIOTT Alan

Born: Bedford, 3 September 1978
Height: 6'1" **Weight:** 12.5
Alan had another excellent campaign as Lincoln City's first-choice goalkeeper missing just one League Two game through injury. He produced some outstanding saves, none more so than in the play-off semi-final at Macclesfield to ensure the Imps went to the Millennium Stadium for the second time in three years. Alan's distribution skills continued to improve making him one of the best 'keepers in the lower divisons.
Tottenham H *(From trainee on 3/7/1997)*
Lincoln C *(Free on 5/8/1999) FL 228 FLC 7 FAC 8 Others 14*

MARRIOTT Andrew (Andy)

Born: Sutton-in-Ashfield, 11 October 1970
Height: 6'1" **Weight:** 12.6
Club Honours: Div 4 '92; FMC '92; WC '95
International Honours: E: U21-1; Yth
This experienced 'keeper had short spells with both Coventry and Colchester at the start of last season, warming the bench for both clubs without seeing any first-team action. In November Andy joined Bury as cover for the injured Glyn Garner on a short-term contract and went on to enjoy a decent run in the line-up. His best performance for the Shakers came in a League Two game against Northampton in which he made several top-class saves and helped the team grab its first win in nine games. In March, with Garner fit again and his contract at an end, he left Gigg Lane and signed for Torquay United. Andy performed solidly throughout the closing stages of the campaign for the Gulls, his confidence on crosses and clean handling inspired confidence in the back four, although he was unable to prevent the team from being relegated.
Arsenal *(From trainee on 22/10/1988)*
Nottingham F *(£50,000 on 20/6/1989) P/FL 11 FLC 1 Others 1*
West Bromwich A *(Loaned on 6/9/1989) FL 3*
Blackburn Rov *(Loaned on 29/12/1989) FL 2*
Colchester U *(Loaned on 21/3/1990) FL 10*
Burnley *(Loaned on 29/8/1991) FL 15 Others 2*
Wrexham *(£200,000 on 8/10/1993) FL 213 FLC 10 FAC 22 Others 13*
Sunderland *(£200,000 + on 17/8/1998) P/FL 2 FLC 3*
Wigan Ath *(Loaned on 1/1/2001) Others 2*
Barnsley *(Free on 13/3/2001) FL 53+1 FLC 2 FAC 1*
Birmingham C *(Free on 13/3/2003) PL 1 (Free during 2003 close season)*
Coventry C *(Free from Beira Mar, Portugal on 6/8/2004)*
Colchester U *(Free on 20/10/2004)*
Bury *(Free on 5/11/2004) FL 19 FAC 2*
Torquay U *(Free on 2/3/2005) FL 11*

MARSDEN Christopher (Chris)

Born: Sheffield, 3 January 1969
Height: 5'11" **Weight:** 10.12
This experienced midfielder arrived at Hillsborough in the summer of 2004 to captain the side and, hopefully, to help revive the fortunes of Sheffield Wednesday. Chris provided a steady influence on the pitch, but just when he had settled in he picked up a nasty hamstring injury in November. This eventually led to him calling a halt to his career, a real blow for the club, the player, and the fans.
Sheffield U *(From apprentice on 6/1/1987) FL 13+3/1 FLC 1 Others 1*
Huddersfield T *(Signed on 15/7/1988) FL 113+8/9 FLC 15+1 FAC 6+2 Others 10*
Coventry C *(Loaned on 2/11/1993) PL 5+2*
Wolverhampton W *(£250,000 on 11/1/1994) FL 8 FAC 3*
Notts Co *(£250,000 on 15/11/1994) FL 10 FLC 1 Others 1/1*
Stockport Co *(£70,000 on 12/1/1996) FL 63+2/3 FLC 13 FAC 4 Others 4/1*
Birmingham C *(£500,000 on 9/10/1997) FL 51+1/3 FLC 5/3 FAC 2*
Southampton *(£800,000 on 2/2/1999) PL 118+11/6 FLC 8+3/1 FAC 10+1/1 Others 1 (Free to Busan Icons, South Korea on 28/1/2004)*
Sheffield Wed *(Free on 16/6/2004) FL 15 FLC 2 Others 1*

MARSHALL Andrew (Andy) John

Born: Bury St Edmunds, 14 April 1975
Height: 6'2" **Weight:** 13.7
International Honours: E: U21-4; Yth (UEFA-U18 '93)
Andy was second-choice goalkeeper for Millwall in the first half of the 2004-05 season before taking over from Graham Stack in February. An excellent shot-stopper who has the vision to turn

defence into attack quickly, he produced some fine performances during the campaign.
Norwich C *(From trainee on 6/7/1993) P/FL 194+1 FLC 18 FAC 5+1*
Bournemouth *(Loaned on 9/9/1996) FL 11*
Gillingham *(Loaned on 21/11/1996) FL 5 FLC 1 Others 1*
Ipswich T *(Free on 4/7/2001) P/FL 53 FLC 2 FAC 4 Others 6*
Wolverhampton W *(Loaned on 18/11/2003) FLC 1*
Millwall *(Signed on 28/1/2004) FL 37+1 FAC 4*

MARSHALL Shaun Andrew
Born: Fakenham, 3 October 1978
Height: 6'1" **Weight:** 12.12
Shaun found himself as second choice to John Ruddy as Cambridge United's goalkeeper last term, but even when his rival was sidelined by injury the management preferred to bring in other players on loan. Shaun's only first-team appearance came in the 2-2 draw with Mansfield Town in September, and later in the season he spent time out on loan with Conference outfit Stevenage.
Cambridge U *(From trainee on 21/2/1997) FL 150+5 FLC 4 FAC 15 Others 8*

MARTIN David Edward
Born: Romford, 22 January 1986
Height: 6'1" **Weight:** 13.7
International Honours: E: Yth
A regular in the England U19 team throughout the season, David made a dozen or so starts and was in possession of the MK Dons number one berth when forced to miss the game at Bradford City in February through international duty. A 4-1 win meant that manager Danny Wilson kept the same team for the next game, which turned out to be the second of an 11-match unbeaten run. Not only that, but the chosen tactic of five outfield players on the bench further restricted the young 'keeper's involvement.
Wimbledon/MK Dons *(From trainee on 19/1/2004) FL 17 FLC 1 FAC 3 Others 1*

MARTIN Russell Kenneth Alexander
Born: Brighton, 4 January 1986
Height: 6'0" **Weight:** 11.8
Wycombe signed this skilful midfielder in the summer of 2004. Used sparingly as a squad player throughout the season, he gave some very capable performances as a busy central midfielder, and his potential was rewarded with a new long-term contract.
Wycombe W *(Free from Lewes on 4/8/2004) FL 1+6 FAC 1 Others 2+1*

MARTINEZ Roberto
Born: Balaguer Lerida, Spain, 13 July 1973
Height: 5'10" **Weight:** 12.2
Club Honours: Div 3 '97
This experienced midfielder lost his place in the Swansea City line-up following the opening day defeat by Northampton Town, but after regaining his place, showed a good level of consistency. A player who possesses good vision and passing ability, he also showed great composure when the team was under pressure.
Wigan Ath *(Free from CFS Vipla Balaguer, Spain on 25/7/1995) FL 148+39/17 FLC 11+1/1 FAC 13+2/4 Others 7+5/2*
Motherwell *(Free on 3/7/2001) SL 8+9*
Walsall *(Free on 13/8/2002) FL 1+5*
Swansea C *(Free on 28/1/2003) FL 77+6/2 FLC 1 FAC 5 Others 2*

MARTYN Antony **Nigel**
Born: St Austell, 11 August 1966
Height: 6'2" **Weight:** 14.7
Club Honours: Div 3 '90; FMC '91; Div 1 '94
International Honours: E: 23; B-6; U21-11
The oldest player to appear regularly in the top-flight last term, Nigel confirmed his reputation as being one of the finest and most consistent 'keepers in the Premiership, regardless of his veteran

Roberto Martinez

Nigel Martyn

status. He was the rock on which Everton built their fine season and his wealth of experience meant he generated an air of confidence that provided reassurance to his colleagues. He was injured at Charlton over Christmas and there was no greater testament to his ability than when he was restored to the team as soon as he regained fitness. A fine shot-stopper, he played his 800th senior game during the campaign, when he also signed an extension to his contract.

Bristol Rov *(Free from St Blazey on 5/8/1987) FL 101 FLC 6 FAC 6 Others 11*
Crystal Palace *(£1,000,000 on 21/11/1989) P/FL 272 FLC 36 FAC 22 Others 19*
Leeds U *(£2,250,000 on 26/7/1996) PL 207 FLC 12 FAC 18 Others 36*
Everton *(£500,000 on 1/9/2003) PL 65+1 FLC 3 FAC 4*

MATIAS Pedro Manuel Miguel
Born: Madrid, Spain, 11 October 1973
Height: 6'0" **Weight:** 12.0
International Honours: Spain: U21
This pacy winger had a trial with Oldham and then a short spell with Bristol Rovers at the start of last season without adding to his tally of competitive appearances. In November he joined Kidderminster on a non-contract basis and got off to a bright start, scoring on his debut at Grimsby. However, he only played four more games before opting to return to Spain at the end of the year.

Macclesfield T *(Free from Logrones, Spain, ex Real Madrid, Almeria, on 3/12/1998) FL 21+1/2 FAC 1*
Tranmere Rov *(Free on 5/8/1999) FL 1+3*
Walsall *(Free on 7/10/1999) FL 105+36/24 FLC 4+3 FAC 6+4/1 Others 4/2*
Blackpool *(Loaned on 25/3/2004) FL 7/1*
Bristol Rov *(Free, via trial at Oldham Ath, on 28/10/2004)*
Kidderminster Hrs *(Free on 19/11/2004) FL 4+1/1*

MATTEO Dominic (Dom)
Born: Dumfries, 28 April 1974
Height: 6'1" **Weight:** 11.12
International Honours: S: 6; E: B-1; U21-4; Yth
This talented central defender featured in a defensive-midfield role for Blackburn during the pre-season period last term. Although given opportunities at centre back, he never really settled, and eventually became first choice at left back under new manager Mark Hughes. Dom's best performance of the season came in the FA Cup semi-final against Arsenal, when in addition to his usual defensive duties he pushed forward more often than usual.

Liverpool *(From trainee on 27/5/1992) PL 112+15/1 FLC 9 FAC 6+2/1 Others 10+1*
Sunderland *(Loaned on 24/3/1995) FL 1*
Leeds U *(£4,750,000 on 24/8/2000) PL 115/2 FLC 2 FAC 6 Others 23/2*
Blackburn Rov *(Free on 7/6/2004) PL 25+3 FAC 4/1*

MATTHEWS Lee Joseph
Born: Middlesbrough, 16 January 1979
Height: 6'3" **Weight:** 12.6
Club Honours: FAYC '97
International Honours: E: Yth
This striker was hampered by injury last season but still managed to finish up as Port Vale's joint-top scorer in League One matches with a tally of ten. His Vale career got off to a good start when he netted on his debut at Walsall on the opening day of the season, but just as he was establishing himself in the line-up he suffered a calf injury which kept him on the sidelines until Christmas. Another leg injury followed but he then hit a purple patch in March and April with five goals in eight appearances, the best of which was a 35-yard lob at Hull. Never afraid to have a go at goal, he has an excellent goals per game ratio and with his injury problems behind him he will be looking for an increased total in 2005-06.

Leeds U *(From trainee on 15/2/1996) PL 0+3*
Notts Co *(Loaned on 24/9/1998) FL 4+1*
Gillingham *(Loaned on 23/3/2000) FL 2+3*
Bristol C *(£100,000 on 16/3/2001) FL 14+29/9 FLC 0+5 FAC 0+2/1 Others 2+2/2*
Darlington *(Loaned on 11/12/2003) FL 6/1*
Bristol Rov *(Loaned on 13/1/2004) FL 9*
Yeovil T *(Loaned on 20/3/2004) FL 2+2*
Port Vale *(Free on 5/7/2004) FL 21+10/10 FLC 1*

MATTIS Dwayne Antony
Born: Huddersfield, 31 July 1981
Height: 6'1" **Weight:** 10.10
International Honours: RoI: U21-2; Yth
This experienced midfielder will have greatly enjoyed his first season at Bury, for whom his consistent displays made him an automatic choice in the line-up. An exciting player who loves to get forward into the opposition penalty area, Dwayne scored seven goals from midfield – the best being a spectacular volley at Swansea in November. He injured a knee in the home game with Darlington in February and was sidelined for a month, but came back strongly and went on to earn the fans' vote as 'Player of the Season'.

Huddersfield T *(From trainee on 8/7/1999) FL 50+19/2 FLC 1+2 FAC 3+1 Others 4/1*
Bury *(Free on 30/7/2004) FL 39/5 FLC 1/1 FAC 2/2*

MAWENE Youl
Born: Caen, France, 16 July 1979
Height: 6'2" **Weight:** 12.6
Youl was simply magnificent in the Preston defence last term, whether playing at right back or in his favoured central position. A superb reader of the game, he prefers subtlety to brute force, is an excellent all-round footballer and has quickly established himself as a fans' favourite. Comfortable on the ball, he marshals colleagues and opponents alike and is strong in the air. Away from football he won plaudits for his community work, to accompany his clean sweep of 'Player of the Year' awards at Deepdale.

Derby Co *(£500,000 from RC Lens, France, ex Caen, on 4/8/2000) P/FL 54+1/1 FLC 2 FAC 4*
Preston NE *(Free on 3/8/2004) FL 46/2 FLC 3 FAC 1 Others 3*

MAWSON Craig John
Born: Keighley, 16 May 1979
Height: 6'2" **Weight:** 13.4
This former Halifax goalkeeper joined the Latics initially on a four-week deal in August as back-up to first-choice Les Pogliacomi. Just after signing a one-month contract extension, he made his home debut in the Carling Cup against Tottenham Hotspur but had to pick the ball out of his net six times in a heavy defeat. He was soon back on the bench following Pogliacomi's return to action in October and was released by the club later that month. He subsequently signed for Conference outfit Hereford United, featuring regularly during the remainder of the campaign.

Burnley *(From trainee on 14/7/1997)*
Halifax T *(Free on 16/2/2001) FL 9 (Freed during 2002 close season)*
Oldham Ath *(Free from Morecambe on 23/8/2004) FL 3+1 FLC 1*

MAXWELL Layton Jonathan
Born: Rhyl, 3 October 1979
Height: 5'8" **Weight:** 11.6
International Honours: W: U21-14; Yth
This young midfielder featured for Rhyl and Newport County in the early part of last season before arriving at Field Mill in December. Layton made his debut for the Stags in midfield at Rochdale in January, but was otherwise a squad player. After being troubled by injury he was released before the end of the season and subsequently joined Welsh Premier League outfit Carmarthen Town.

Liverpool *(From trainee on 17/7/1997) FLC 1/1*
Stockport Co *(Loaned on 17/7/2000) FL 8+12/2 FLC 1+1 FAC 0+1*

Cardiff C *(Free on 7/8/2001) FL 10+24/1 FLC 2+1 FAC 1+3 Others 3+1*
Swansea C *(Free on 25/3/2004) FL 1+2 (Freed during 2004 close season)*
Mansfield T *(Free from Newport Co on 6/12/2004) FL 1*

MAY Benjamin (Ben) Steven
Born: Gravesend, 10 March 1984
Height: 6'1" **Weight:** 12.6
This promising young Millwall striker began the 2004-05 season on an extended loan at Colchester. Although mostly featuring from the bench he became an instant hero for the U's faithful when he scored the goal that knocked West Brom out of the Carling Cup. He subsequently spent three months on loan at Brentford, but only scored one goal. Recalled to the New Den towards the end of the season he looked a much better player and scored the winner in a seven-goal thriller against Crewe.
Millwall *(From juniors on 10/5/2001) FL 8+10/2 FLC 1 FAC 0+1*
Colchester U *(Loaned on 27/3/2003) FL 4+2*
Brentford *(Loaned on 25/8/2003) FL 38+3/7 FAC 1 Others 1*
Colchester U *(Loaned on 6/8/2004) FL 5+9/1 FLC 0+2/1*
Brentford *(Loaned on 3/12/2004) FL 7+3/1 FAC 4+2*

MAY Christopher (Chris) John
Born: Wakefield, 2 September 1985
Height: 5'11" **Weight:** 11.8
With the experienced Ben Roberts sidelined by injury, Chris was Brighton's substitute goalkeeper for most of the 2004-05 campaign. He came off the bench just once, when Michel Kuipers injured a shoulder towards the end of the match against Nottingham Forest at Withdean in January. The youngster had little to do in the few minutes he was on the pitch, but, with Albion battling all season against relegation from the Championship, manager Mark McGhee preferred to entrust the goalkeeper's jersey to someone with a little more experience than the raw youngster. Although he showed promise it was announced in March that he would be released to pursue his career elsewhere.
Brighton & Hove A *(Trainee) FL 0+1*

MAYBURY Alan
Born: Dublin, 8 August 1978
Height: 5'11" **Weight:** 11.12
Club Honours: FAYC '97
International Honours: RoI 10; B-1; U21-8; Yth
This gritty full back, signed for Leicester along with striker Mark de Vries during the January transfer window. Although able to operate on either flank he was more effective when overlapping on the right. Alan quickly established himself as the first-choice successor to Chris Makin and even contributed a couple of goals late in the season: a fine low drive after cutting inside against Wolves and a solo chip after splitting the Sunderland defence. He was also recalled to the Republic of Ireland defence in March for the victory over China in Dublin.
Leeds U *(Free from St Kevin's BC on 17/8/1995) PL 10+4 FLC 1 FAC 2 Others 1*
Reading *(Loaned on 25/3/1999) FL 8*
Crewe Alex *(Loaned on 8/10/2000) FL 6*
Heart of Midlothian *(£100,000 on 12/10/2001) SL 110+2/4 SLC 7 SC 5 Others 10*
Leicester C *(£100,000 on 6/1/2005) FL 17/2 FAC 4+1*

MAYLETT Bradley (Brad)
Born: Manchester, 24 December 1980
Height: 5'8" **Weight:** 10.10
Brad was in competition with Adrian Forbes for a place on the right-hand side of the Swansea midfield last term and struggled to make an impact, being mainly used from the substitutes' bench. A hernia operation kept him out of action for several weeks in the autumn but although he returned to the first-team squad he eventually moved out on loan to Boston United. He proved a useful winger or wing back for the York Street club, giving the Pilgrims a new dimension. His penetrative runs down the flank and his dangerous crosses into the box set up a stream of chances for his colleagues and he soon signed for the club on a more permanent basis.
Burnley *(From trainee on 19/2/1999) FL 3+42 FLC 1+2 FAC 0+1 Others 1*
Swansea C *(Loaned on 14/3/2003) FL 6*
Swansea C *(Free on 17/6/2003) FL 30+19/5 FLC 1+1 FAC 3+1 Others 2*
Boston U *(Signed on 18/3/2005) FL 8+1/3*

MAYO Kerry
Born: Haywards Heath, 21 September 1977
Height: 5'10" **Weight:** 13.4
Club Honours: Div 3 '01; Div 2 '02
With nine seasons as a professional at Brighton under his belt, Kerry can look forward to a well-deserved testimonial season in 2005-06. With Dan Harding occupying the left-back berth for much of the campaign, last term was not the greatest season for the Sussex-born defender as he warmed the bench almost as many times as he was included in the starting line-up, but Kerry always gives of his best whether at left back or when drafted into the centre of defence or midfield. Looking to carry the game to his opponents at every opportunity, the long-serving player scored just once in the successful battle against relegation, the first goal in a vital 2-1 home victory over Watford in January.
Brighton & Hove A *(From trainee on 3/7/1996) FL 277+26/11 FLC 9+1 FAC 9+6/2 Others 7+3*

MAYO Paul
Born: Lincoln, 13 October 1981
Height: 5'11" **Weight:** 11.9
Paul started the 2004-05 season as first-choice left back for Watford, but never looked at ease and lost his place in October. Thereafter he played consistently for the reserves, sometimes at centre half, but made only two further appearances for the first team. He was transfer-listed at the end of the campaign.
Lincoln C *(From trainee on 6/4/2000) FL 92+14/6 FLC 4 FAC 5+1/1 Others 9/2*
Watford *(£100,000 on 8/3/2004) FL 25 FLC 2*

MBOME Herve **Kingsley**
Born: Yaounde, Cameroon, 21 November 1981
Height: 6'4" **Weight:** 13.6
International Honours: Cameroon: Yth
Kingsley arrived at Cambridge in the summer of 2004 and featured regularly in the first-team during the opening stages of the campaign, scoring a vital last-minute equaliser at Kidderminster. However, the defensive midfielder then fell out of favour following a change of management and had trials with other clubs in the new year.
Sheffield U *(Free from AS St Etienne, France, ex Canon Yaounde, trial at Glasgow Celtic, on 17/4/2000. Freed during 2001 close season)*
Cambridge U *(Free from GAP, France on 3/9/2004) FL 12+1/1 FAC 1 Others 1*

MEARS Tyrone
Born: Stockport, 18 February 1983
Height: 5'11" **Weight:** 11.10
Tyrone's time at Preston has been blighted by injury and he missed most of the 2004-05 season with a serious shin injury. After returning to full fitness in March, he was rewarded with a new long-term contract and hopefully this will enable him to realise his full potential. His first appearance for ten months came in the FA Cup tie against West Brom and he also managed a few outings from the bench towards the end of the season. A very pacy player, he will be looking to establish himself in the side at right back in 2005-06.

Manchester C *(From juniors on 5/7/2000) FL 0+1*
Preston NE *(£175,000 on 10/7/2002) FL 23+15/2 FLC 1+2 FAC 1+2*

MEIRELLES Bruno

Born: Leiria, Portugal, 23 February 1982
Height: 6'1" **Weight:** 13.0
This young central midfielder seemed to settle quickly into English football after signing for Torquay during the 2004 close season. He proved a robust performer with good technique, but found a regular starting place elusive and was released in November. In the new year he resurfaced in the lower reaches of the German Leagues, having signed for TUS Koblenz.
Torquay U *(Free from Amadora, Portugal on 10/8/2004) FL 5+4 FLC 1 Others 1*

MELCHIOT Mario

Born: Amsterdam, Holland, 4 November 1976
Height: 6'1" **Weight:** 11.8
Club Honours: FAC '00; CS '00
International Honours: Holland: 13; U21-13; Yth
One of Birmingham City's star performers last term, Mario's powerful attacking forays were a feature of the team. He was encouraged to get forward and given much freedom, and relished in it. His link up with Jermaine Pennant towards the latter stages of the season was at times unstoppable and created countless chances. However, he didn't neglect his defensive duties either as he could always be relied upon to use his physique and strength to blot out opponents.
Chelsea *(Free from Ajax, Holland on 5/7/1999) PL 117+13/4 FLC 9 FAC 14+2 Others 9+1/1*
Birmingham C *(Free on 19/7/2004) PL 33+1/1 FLC 2 FAC 2*

Kingsley Mbome

MELLBERG Erik Olof

Born: Gullspang, Sweden, 3 September 1977
Height: 6'1" **Weight:** 12.10
International Honours: Sweden: 56
Olof is an immense figure in the centre of defence for Aston Villa. His strong tackling and sense of anticipation make him one of the most reliable defenders in the top flight, a fans' favourite and a permanent fixture in the side when fit. He also contributed three valuable goals and at one point early in the campaign he was the club's leading goal-scorer. Olof coped well with a series of different partners in the heart of the defence, before himself succumbing to a knee injury which caused him to miss the closing stages of the campaign. He was once again a regular at international level for Sweden and has now passed the landmark of 50 caps for his country.
Aston Villa *(£5,000,000 from Racing Santander, Spain, ex Degerfors, AIK Solna, on 25/7/2001) PL 133/5 FLC 10 FAC 4 Others 5*

MELLIGAN John (JJ) James

Born: Dublin, 11 February 1982
Height: 5'9" **Weight:** 11.4
Club Honours: Div 3 '04
International Honours: RoI: U21-1; Yth
JJ signed for Cheltenham Town in the summer of 2004 and went straight into the first team, scoring a fine goal in the 2-0 win at Southend on the opening day of the season. He became a regular selection in the centre of a four- or five-man midfield, his natural attacking instincts taking him forward to support the strikers or break out wide to find space for crosses. He produced a number of highly effective performances in the first half of the season, but then struggled with a series of niggling injuries before returning to action for the final weeks of the campaign.
Wolverhampton W *(From trainee on 11/7/2000) FL 0+2*
Bournemouth *(Loaned on 30/11/2001) FL 7+1 FAC 1*
Kidderminster Hrs *(Loaned on 13/9/2002) FL 10/5 Others 2/2*
Kidderminster Hrs *(Loaned on 3/12/2002) FL 18+1/5 Others 1*

Mario Melchiot

Kidderminster Hrs (Loaned on 3/10/2003) FL 5/1 Others 1
Doncaster Rov (Loaned on 17/11/2003) FL 21/2
Cheltenham T (£25,000 on 13/7/2004) FL 23+6/2 FLC 1 FAC 1 Others 2

MELLON Michael (Micky) Joseph
Born: Paisley, 18 March 1972
Height: 5'10" **Weight:** 12.11
This experienced midfielder signed for Kidderminster in the summer of 2004. Unfortunately an achilles injury meant that Harriers' fans were unable to see the best of him and he only managed eight appearances before being released in December following a change in management. In February he linked up with Unibond Premier side Witton Albion.
Bristol C (From trainee on 6/12/1989) FL 26+9/1 FLC 3 FAC 1+1 Others 5+3
West Bromwich A (£75,000 on 11/2/1993) FL 38+7/6 FLC 3+2 FAC 0+1 Others 6/1
Blackpool (£50,000 on 23/11/1994) FL 123+1/14 FLC 9/1 FAC 4 Others 7/2
Tranmere Rov (£285,000 on 31/10/1997) FL 45+12/3 FLC 4 FAC 3+1
Burnley (£350,000 on 8/1/1999) FL 72+12/5 FLC 3+1 FAC 5
Tranmere Rov (Free on 5/3/2001) FL 102+15/3 FLC 7/1 FAC 11+1/3 Others 5
Kidderminster Hrs (Free on 6/8/2004) FL 5+2 FLC 1

MELLOR Neil Andrew
Born: Sheffield, 4 November 1982
Height: 6'0" **Weight:** 13.7
Club Honours: FLC '03
Despite being a prolific scorer for Liverpool's reserve team, Neil must have despaired of ever making the senior squad. However, after being promoted to first-team duty in the Carling Cup he became a regular selection for two months. In the titanic match with reigning champions Arsenal he scored the goal of his life in the third minute of stoppage time when, from a fortuitous knock-down, he arrowed a 25-yard half volley into the corner of the Arsenal net with, quite literally, the last kick of the match. He followed this up with goals in the dramatic 3-1 victory over Olympiakos in the European Champions' League and over Newcastle United in December before he too was laid low by the injury hoodoo, a knee problem which sidelined him for the rest of the season.
Liverpool (From trainee on 8/2/2002) PL 7+5/2 FLC 6/3 FAC 1+1 Others 1+1/1
West Ham U (Loaned on 7/8/2003) FL 8+8/2 FLC 1+1 FAC 0+3

MELTON Stephen (Steve)
Born: Lincoln, 3 October 1978
Height: 5'11" **Weight:** 12.2
Club Honours: Div 3 '01
Steve played in Boston United's midfield in their opening three fixtures of 2004-05 before being hit by injury which plagued him for much of the rest of the campaign. After a brief lay-off he came back into the squad on the substitutes' bench but made just two more League starts. A back problem kept him out towards the end of the season and he underwent an operation in April to correct the problem. When fit he was effective on the right side of midfield both in going forward and in winning the ball.
Nottingham F (From trainee on 9/10/1995) P/FL 2+1 FLC 1
Stoke C (Free on 28/2/2000) FL 0+5 Others 0+2
Brighton & Hove A (Free on 2/8/2000) FL 21+25/3 FLC 1+3 Others 4+1/2
Hull C (Free on 24/12/2002) FL 19+11 FLC 0+1 Others 2
Boston U (Free on 19/3/2004) FL 14+4/2

MELVILLE Andrew (Andy) Roger
Born: Swansea, 29 November 1968
Height: 6'0" **Weight:** 13.10
Club Honours: WC '89; Div 1 '96, '01
International Honours: W: 64; B-1; U21-2
The veteran Welsh defender played in the opening three games of the season for West Ham before losing his place in the side. Thereafter he was only on the fringes of the Hammers' squad when fit

Andy Melville

and in February he joined Nottingham Forest on loan. He featured regularly during an extended stay at the City Ground, but was unable to prevent the club slipping to relegation.
Swansea C *(From trainee on 25/7/1986) FL 165+10/22 FLC 10 FAC 14+1/5 Others 13/2*
Oxford U *(£275,000 on 23/7/1990) FL 135/13 FLC 12/1 FAC 6 Others 6/1*
Sunderland *(£750,000 + on 9/8/1993) P/FL 204/14 FLC 18+1 FAC 11 Others 2*
Bradford C *(Loaned on 13/2/1998) FL 6/1*
Fulham *(Free on 1/7/1999) P/FL 150+3/4 FLC 12+1 FAC 13+2 Others 12*
West Ham U *(Signed on 16/1/2004) FL 14+3 FLC 0+1 Others 3*
Nottingham F *(Loaned on 5/2/2005) FL 13 FAC 2*

MENDES Albert **Junior** Hillyard Andrew
Born: Balham, 15 September 1976
Height: 5'8" **Weight:** 11.4
International Honours: Montserrat
Junior started the 2004-05 campaign as the main striking partner for Pawel Abbott at Huddersfield, but looked more at home when playing out wide. He used his pace and close control effectively to whip past defenders and have a strike on goal. A promising start to the season brought a flourish of goals, notably two outstanding strikes against Luton and a wonderful volley against Milton Keynes. Six goals in as many games heralded a first international start for Montserrat, but on his return he mostly featured from the substitutes' bench.
Chelsea *(From trainee on 1/7/1995)*
St Mirren *(Free on 29/4/1996) SL 98+22/21 SLC 6 SC 4/1 Others 0+2*
Carlisle U *(Loaned on 18/11/1998) FL 5+1/1*
Dunfermline Ath *(£20,000 on 24/7/2000) SL 7+7 SLC 2*
St Mirren *(Free on 22/6/2002) SL 15+2/6 SLC 1 SC 1 Others 3*
Mansfield T *(Free on 30/1/2003) FL 54+3/12 FLC 1 FAC 4/1 Others 3/1*
Huddersfield T *(Free on 5/7/2004) FL 13+12/5 FLC 0+1 FAC 1 Others 1/1*

MENDES Miguel **Pedro**
Born: Guimaraes, Portugal, 26 February 1979
Height: 5'10" **Weight:** 12.4
International Honours: Portugal: 2
Arriving from FC Porto in August, this midfield playmaker added a new creative dimension to the Spurs midfield with great ability on the ball, pace and accurate passing ability. With Martin Jol encouraging the midfield to be more attack minded, Pedro led the line in getting the supply to the forwards and using width to generate playing space in the opposition half. He picked up a toe injury later in the season which saw him miss the last 14 games, but he had already become a huge favourite with the fans.
Tottenham H *(£2,000,000 from FC Porto, ex Vitoria Guimaraes, on 16/7/2004) PL 22+2/1 FLC 2+2 FAC 2*

MENDIETA Gaizka
Born: Bilbao, Spain, 27 March 1974
Height: 5'8" **Weight:** 10.12
Club Honours: FLC '04
International Honours: Spain: 40
Following his season on loan at the Riverside Spanish playmaker Gaizka Mendieta joined Middlesbrough on a long-term contract in the summer of 2004. With the 2006 World Cup finals moving ever closer the midfielder was hoping to impress the Spanish selectors but the club, players and fans were rocked with the news that the influential and gifted player was out for the rest of the campaign with a serious knee injury. He had twisted his right knee in the 1-1 draw at Portsmouth only to discover that his season was over there and then. Corrective surgery in Barcelona eventually followed with months of rehabilitation ahead of him.
Middlesbrough *(Loaned from Lazio, Italy, ex Castellon, Valencia, on 26/8/2003) PL 30+1/2 FLC 6/1 FAC 1*
Middlesbrough *(Loaned on 16/7/2004) PL 7 Others 0+1*

Gaizka Mendieta

MERSON Paul Charles
Born: Harlesden, 20 March 1968
Height: 6'0" **Weight:** 13.2
Club Honours: Div 1 '89, '91, '03; FLC '93; FAC '93; ECWC '94
International Honours: E: 21; B-4; U21-4; Yth
Although there were times when Paul's position as manager of Walsall looked a little shaky he continued to provide defence-splitting passes and inch-perfect crosses in his role as a player. He scored a brilliant goal against Huddersfield but was not in the team when they ended the season on a high with five successive wins. Paul was selected for the PFA League One team of the season and has expressed the desire to continue to play as and when necessary in 2005-06.
Arsenal *(From apprentice on 1/12/1985) P/FL 289+38/78 FLC 38+2/10 FAC 28+3/4 Others 27+2/6*
Brentford *(Loaned on 22/1/1987) FL 6+1 Others 1+1*
Middlesbrough *(£4,500,000 + on 15/7/1997) P/FL 48/11 FLC 7/3 FAC 3/1*
Aston Villa *(£6,750,000 on 10/9/1998) PL 101+16/18 FLC 6+2 FAC 11 Others 8+1/1*
Portsmouth *(Free on 8/8/2002) FL 44+1/12 FLC 2 FAC 1*
Walsall *(Free on 1/8/2003) FL 62+8/6 FLC 3/2 FAC 1 Others 2*

MEZAGUE Valery
Born: Marseille, France, 8 December 1983
Height: 6'1" **Weight:** 13.0
This young defensive midfielder joined Portsmouth in a long-term deal from Montpellier in the summer of 2004. However, he received few opportunities to shine during his stay at Fratton Park making only three starts in Premiership matches, although he was a regular in the club's reserve team throughout the campaign.
Portsmouth *(Loaned from Montpellier, France on 6/9/2004) PL 3+8 FLC 3*

[MIDO] Ahmed Hossam Abdel Hamid
Born: Cairo, Egypt, 23 February 1983
Height: 6'0" **Weight:** 12.10
International Honours: Egypt
This young striker arrived at Spurs in January in an 18-month long loan deal with Roma. Mido joined Spurs with a point to prove having been exiled from the Egypt national side. Nonetheless, he made an immediate impact at White Hart Lane and showed much of his tactical excellence, deft first touch and superb ball skills. Mido worked hard to impress and showed great promise, netting three goals in just a handful of appearances.
Tottenham H *(Loaned from AS Roma, Italy, ex KAA Gent, Ajax, Celta Vigo, Marseilles, on 26/1/2005) PL 4+5/2 FAC 0+2/1*

MIGLIORANZI Stefani
Born: Pocos de Caldas, Brazil, 20 September 1977
Height: 6'0" **Weight:** 11.12
This skilful midfielder had a frustrating season at Swindon last term when injuries restricted his appearances and prevented him from achieving his best form. A classy, skilful player who usually operates in central midfield, he appeared as a central defender in the final game of the season.
Portsmouth *(Free from St John's University, NY, USA on 8/3/1999) FL 25+10/2 FLC 2+4 FAC 1*
Swindon T *(Free on 1/8/2002) FL 89+8/7 FLC 3+1 FAC 2 Others 4/1*

MILDENHALL Stephen (Steve) James
Born: Swindon, 13 May 1978
Height: 6'4" **Weight:** 14.0
A talented and capable 'keeper, Steve featured for Notts County in their opening-day fixture against Chester but then lost his place after suffering a broken hand. He was eventually released and signed for Oldham as back-up to Les Pogliacomi in December. However, the experienced custodian had to wait until the departure of boss Brian Talbot to make his first-team bow. Ronnie Moore picked him to start the 2-2 draw against League One front runners Luton Town in mid-March and he made five more appearances before injury brought his campaign to a premature end. Steve was subsequently released in May.
Swindon T *(From trainee on 19/7/1996) FL 29+4 FLC 2 FAC 2 Others 1*
Notts Co *(£150,000 on 16/7/2001) FL 75+1 FLC 5/1 FAC 6 Others 3*
Oldham Ath *(Free on 1/12/2004) FL 6*

MILES (formerly PLUCK) Colin Ian
Born: Edmonton, 6 September 1978
Height: 6'0" **Weight:** 13.10
Club Honours: FAT '02; NC '03; Div 2 '05
This committed Yeovil central defender was affected by injuries last term and spent long spells on the sidelines. However he battled his way back to fitness and was in good form in the closing stages of the campaign. Colin changed his surname from Pluck to Miles by deed poll during the pre-season period for personal reasons.
Watford *(From trainee on 13/2/1997) FL 1 Others 1*
Morton *(Free on 4/2/2000) SL 3+1 (Free to Stevenage Borough on 1/3/2000)*
Yeovil T *(Free from Dover Ath, ex Hayes, on 30/7/2001) FL 56+1/4 FAC 6/3 Others 2*

MILES John Francis
Born: Bootle, 28 September 1981
Height: 5'10" **Weight:** 12.9
John often found himself on the substitutes' bench for Macclesfield Town last term, initially finding it difficult to break into the senior side with his fellow strikers in good form. However, as the season progressed he was used more often, regularly coming on to change the course of a match. John is at his best when playing just behind the front two although it was necessary for him to play wide left of midfield on several occasions during the campaign.
Liverpool *(From trainee on 27/4/1999)*
Stoke C *(Free on 28/3/2002) FL 0+1*
Crewe Alex *(Free on 16/8/2002) FL 0+5/1 FLC 1 FAC 2 Others 0+2*
Macclesfield T *(Signed on 27/3/2003) FL 44+23/13 FLC 1 FAC 3+2/1 Others 2+3*

MILLER Adam Edward
Born: Hemel Hempstead, 19 February 1982
Height: 5'11" **Weight:** 11.8
This versatile midfielder who can play anywhere along the line, joined Queen's Park Rangers last November from Conference club Aldershot Town. Adam made his debut in the away fixture at Nottingham Forest and quickly became a firm favourite with the fans. By the end of the season he had made some 14 appearances for the club, but had yet to register his first goal.
Queens Park Rgrs *(£50,000 from Aldershot on 15/11/2004) FL 9+5*

MILLER Justin James
Born: Johannesburg, South Africa, 16 December 1980
Height: 6'0" **Weight:** 11.10
This versatile defender uses the ball intelligently and is effective both at breaking down opposition moves and when pushing forward to assist the attack. A favourite of the O's fans, Justin was a near ever-present last term and was reported to have signed a new contract for the club in the summer. An undoubted highlight of his campaign came in the Easter fixture at Oxford when he delivered a 50-yard pass to enable Lee Steele to score the club's fastest-ever goal.
Ipswich T *(From juniors on 26/11/1999)*
Leyton Orient *(Loaned on 13/9/2002) FL 13 FLC 1 FAC 2 Others 2*
Leyton Orient *(Free on 31/1/2003) FL 76+7/2 FLC 2 FAC 2+1 Others 2/1*

MILLER Kenneth (Kenny)
Born: Edinburgh, 23 December 1979
Height: 5'8" **Weight:** 11.3
International Honours: S: 19; B-1; U21-7
Kenny was top scorer for Wolves last term with 20 goals, yet was on the transfer list all season! He scored four in the first six matches, adding two more against leaders Wigan and a winner at Brighton to make his total seven by mid-September. Although he had the occasional barren patch he was back to his goal-scoring best in the new year, registering doubles against West Ham, Crewe and Rotherham. Kenny also continued to represent Scotland during the campaign.
Hibernian *(Signed from Hutchison Vale BC on 22/5/1996) SL 29+16/12 SLC 1+2/1 SC 5/1*
Stenhousemuir *(Loaned on 25/11/1998) SL 11/8*
Glasgow Rgrs *(£2,000,000 on 16/7/2000) SL 12+18/8 SLC 1/1 SC 2+1/1 Others 3+2/1*
Wolverhampton W *(Loaned on 7/9/2001) FL 3+2/2*
Wolverhampton W *(£3,000,000 on 14/12/2001) P/FL 95+32/40 FLC 4+1/3 FAC 8+2/5 Others 3+2/1*

MILLER Kevin
Born: Falmouth, 15 March 1969
Height: 6'1" **Weight:** 13.0
Club Honours: Div 4 '90
This experienced goalkeeper continued to show impressive form for Bristol Rovers last term and was rewarded with the club captaincy. He completed his 600th Football League appearance in the home match with Yeovil in October, but he was sidelined by an ankle injury at the turn of the year. Thereafter he rarely featured in the side and spent the closing stages of the campaign on loan at Derby, where he failed to add to his total of appearances. Kevin was released by the Pirates in the summer.
Exeter C *(Free from Newquay on 9/3/1989) FL 163 FLC 7 FAC 12 Others 18*
Birmingham C *(£250,000 on 14/5/1993) FL 24 FLC 4 Others 2*
Watford *(£250,000 on 7/8/1994) FL 128 FLC 10 FAC 10 Others 3*
Crystal Palace *(£1,000,000 + on 21/7/1997) P/FL 66 FLC 3 FAC 5 Others 2*
Barnsley *(£250,000 on 27/8/1999) FL 115 FLC 11 FAC 4 Others 3*
Exeter C *(Free on 9/8/2002) FL 46 FLC 1 FAC 3 Others 2*
Bristol Rov *(Free on 11/7/2003) FL 72 FLC 3 FAC 3 Others 5*

Kevin Miller

MILLER Lee Adamson
Born: Lanark, 18 May 1983
Height: 6'2" **Weight:** 11.7
Club Honours: S Div 1 '03
This old-fashioned centre forward struggled to make an impact at Bristol City last term and rarely featured in the squad after the end of September. Lee went on loan to Hearts for the second-half of the season and rediscovered his scoring touch, netting 11 times from 22 starts. His form won him a call-up for the full Scotland squad, but he has yet to make his debut on the international scene.
Falkirk *(From juniors on 9/6/2000) SL 61/27 SLC 3/1 SC 6 Others 3/2*
Bristol C *(£300,000 on 30/7/2003) FL 34+15/8 FLC 3+2/1 FAC 3 Others 1*
Heart of Midlothian *(Loaned on 11/1/2005) SL 17+1/8 SLC 1 SC 4/3*

MILLER Liam William Peter
Born: Cork, 13 February 1981
Height: 5'8" **Weight:** 10.6
Club Honours: SPD '04
International Honours: RoI: 9; U21-15
A tenacious midfielder who links up well in the attacking third of the pitch, Liam completed his dream move to Manchester United with a huge task in hand – earmarked as Roy Keane's eventual successor. The youngster wasted no time in marking his debut with a telling contribution, setting up the second goal in United's Champions' League qualifier against Dinamo Bucharest. Indeed, the Champions' League, Carling Cup and FA Cup campaigns provided him with his most consistent spell in the team. He

f first-team action and always seemed ɔ have plenty of time on the ball, the allmark of a quality player. Craig will be ɔoking to firmly establish himself in the :arting line-up in 2005-06.
Vrexham (From trainee on 10/7/2003) FL 3+19/1 FLC 1/1 FAC 1+1 Others 9

IORGAN Daniel (Danny) rederick
orn: Stepney, 4 November 1984
leight: 6'0" **Weight:** 14.0
his young striker joined Oxford in the ımmer of 2004 after netting a hat-trick ı a trial game. However, when the ɘason got under way he received few rst-team opportunities and was ɘstricted to just a handful of ppearances from the substitutes' bench. anny spent the last few months of the ɘason on loan at Southern League club rackley Town.
***xford U** (From trainee at Wimbledon on 2/7/2004) FL 0+3 FLC 0+1*

IORGAN Dean Lance
orn: Enfield, 3 October 1983
eight: 5'11" **Weight:** 11.2
took Dean until November to win a ace in Reading's starting line-up, and he egan a short run of matches before ɘturning to the bench. A tricky, ɔmbative winger who scored a ɘmarkable goal with an improvised ross-shot in the 2-1 win over Cardiff ity, he never played a major part in the anager's plans, and was told he could ave on a free transfer if another club ɿowed an interest in signing him. This as despite still having a year left on his ɔntract.
***olchester U** (From trainee on 8/8/2001) FL 3+48/6 FLC 1 FAC 0+3 Others 1+1*
***eading** (Free on 28/11/2003) FL 13+18/3 .C 0+1 FAC 1+2*

IORGAN Mark **Paul** Thomas
orn: Belfast, 23 October 1978
eight: 6'0" **Weight:** 11.5
ıternational Honours: NI: U21-1
aul was again a vital man for Lincoln ity in the middle of their three-man ɘntre back system. His speed in the ackle and vision ensured he won many ucial challenges. Paul skippered the ıps to their third consecutive top-seven ɔot and was offered a new contract at e end of the season.
***reston NE** (From trainee on 9/5/1997) FLC 1*
***ncoln C** (Free on 17/7/2001) FL 157+2/1 .C 4 FAC 3 Others 9*

IORGAN Westley (Wes) athan
orn: Nottingham, 21 January 1984
eight: 6'2" **Weight:** 14.0
This big Nottingham Forest central defender was a near ever-present in the starting line-up last season. He impressed many with his leadership qualities in a struggling side and his maturity was rewarded when he was appointed captain of the side against Derby County in February.
***Nottingham F** (Signed from Central Midlands League side,Dunkirk, on 5/7/2002) FL 72+3/3 FLC 7 FAC 5*
***Kidderminster Hrs** (Loaned on 27/2/2003) FL 5/1*

MORIENTES Fernando
Born: Caceres, Spain, 5 April 1976
Height: 6'0" **Weight:** 12.4
International Honours: Spain: 24
One of the finest Spanish forwards of his generation, Fernando joined Liverpool from Spanish giants Real Madrid in the January transfer window. A good all-round team player, he has a particular penchant for powerful headers from long range, as he demonstrated with his second goal for the Reds at home to Fulham. Sadly he was ineligible for the Champions' League due to earlier appearances for Real and thus played no part in the Reds' improbable and triumphant campaign in that competition. His three goals from 13 Premiership games were less than hoped for, but in 2005-06, with the benefit of pre-season training, he will be less rusty and provide Liverpool with the reliable and consistent goal-scorer they have recently lacked.
***Liverpool** (£6,300,000 from Real Madrid, Spain, ex Albacete, Real Zaragoza, on 13/1/2005) PL 12+1/3 FLC 2*

MORISON Steven (Steve) William
Born: Enfield, 29 August 1983
Height: 6'2" **Weight:** 12.0
Steve found it hard to make a place for himself in the forward line at Northampton last term and was restricted to the odd appearance as a substitute. The return of Tom Youngs from injury and the arrival of Julian Alsop pushed him further down the pecking order and the pacy striker made a quick exit to Conference South club Bishop's Stortford.
***Northampton T** (From trainee on 7/7/2003) FL 7+16/3 FLC 0+2 Others 0+2*

MORLEY David (Dave) Thomas
Born: St Helens, 25 September 1977
Height: 6'3" **Weight:** 13.8
Club Honours: Div 3 '04
This experienced central defender found himself excess to requirements at Doncaster for much of last term due to the surplus of good centre halves on the club's books. He had a brief run in the line-up from the end of October, but lost his place just before Christmas and soon afterwards moved on to join Macclesfield Town. Dave immediately settled into the side at Moss Rose and, in partnership with Danny Swailes, strengthened the club's three-man back line with some assured performances. His towering presence proved useful especially when defending set pieces and he scored two valuable goals.
***Manchester C** (From trainee on 3/1/1996) FL 1+2/1*
***Ayr U** (Loaned on 14/3/1998) SL 4*
***Southend U** (Signed on 28/8/1998) FL 63+13 FLC 6 FAC 0+2 Others 2*
***Carlisle U** (Free on 26/1/2001) FL 37+4/1 FLC 1 FAC 1 Others 1*
***Oxford U** (Free on 14/12/2001) FL 16+2/3*
***Doncaster Rov** (Free on 5/7/2002) FL 24+6/1 FLC 2 FAC 3 Others 3*
***Macclesfield T** (£15,000 on 14/1/2005) FL 19/2 Others 2*

MORRELL Andrew (Andy) Jonathan
Born: Doncaster, 28 September 1974
Height: 5'11" **Weight:** 12.0
Andy started the 2004-05 season on the bench for Coventry, but quickly became a first-choice striker and notched five goals in six games. A player with a high work rate and natural goal-scoring talents, he performed best when receiving the ball on the ground. He also played in a wide role with some success, but suffered ankle ligament damage in the FA Cup tie at Newcastle and was out for six weeks. After regaining fitness he made a handful of appearances from the bench and never let the side down.
***Wrexham** (Free from Newcastle Blue Star on 18/12/1998) FL 76+34/40 FLC 3/1 FAC 1+2 Others 2+3/2*
***Coventry C** (Free on 2/7/2003) FL 43+21/15 FLC 3+1/1 FAC 4*

MORRIS Glenn James
Born: Woolwich, 20 December 1983
Height: 6'0" **Weight:** 11.3
Glenn started the 2004-05 campaign as first-choice goalkeeper for Leyton Orient, only to lose his place to Lee Harrison early on. He eventually got back in the side towards the end of the season and will be looking to be a regular in the line-up in 2005-06. On his day Glenn is an excellent shot stopper who shows fine technique.
***Leyton Orient** (From trainee on 4/3/2003) FL 63+1 FLC 3+1 FAC 2 Others 7*

MORRIS Jody Steven
Born: Hammersmith, 22 December 1978
Height: 5'5" **Weight:** 10.12
Club Honours: ECWC '98; FAC '00; CS '00
International Honours: E: U21-7; Yth; Sch
Jody signed for Millwall in the summer of 2004 and was given a role in central midfield last term, acquitting himself well. His clever defensive work and midfield control proved valuable assets and he scored five goals including a penalty against his former club Leeds.
Chelsea *(From trainee on 8/1/1996) PL 82+42/5 FLC 10+2/2 FAC 10+5/2 Others 11+1*
Leeds U *(Free on 22/7/2003) PL 11+1*
Rotherham U *(Free on 17/3/2004) FL 9+1/1*
Millwall *(Free on 1/7/2004) FL 35+2/5 FLC 1 FAC 1 Others 2*

MORRIS Lee
Born: Blackpool, 30 April 1980
Height: 5'10" **Weight:** 11.2
International Honours: E: U21-1; Yth
This left-sided midfielder or striker suffered a groin strain in training during the first week of the season that eventually required an operation on a nerve. However, Lee regained his place in the Leicester first-team squad when Craig Levein took over, although generally featuring from the bench before falling victim to another long-term injury.
Sheffield U *(From trainee on 24/12/1997) FL 14+12/6 FAC 2+5/2 Others 0+1*
Derby Co *(£1,800,000 + on 15/10/1999) P/FL 62+29/17 FLC 1+4/1 FAC 2+2*
Huddersfield T *(Loaned on 8/3/2001) FL 5/1*
Leicester C *(£120,000 on 2/2/2004) FL 2+8*

MORRISON Clinton Hubert
Born: Wandsworth, 14 May 1979
Height: 6'1" **Weight:** 11.2
International Honours: RoI: 30; U21-2
Clinton came into his own before the turn of the year when he was given an extended run alongside Emile Heskey. They struck up an instant rapport and he scored four goals in five games and set up several others. His willingness to run unselfishly down the sides and drag defenders out of position made the Blues attack more fluid. Walter Pandiani's arrival on loan in January curtailed his output, but he continued to look sharp when introduced off the bench.
Crystal Palace *(From trainee on 29/3/1997) P/FL 141+16/62 FLC 16+3/9 FAC 4/1 Others 0+1*
Birmingham C *(£4,250,000 + on 3/8/2002) PL 56+30/14 FLC 2+1/1 FAC 6+1/1*

MORRISON James Clark
Born: Darlington, 25 May 1986
Height: 5'10" **Weight:** 10.5
Club Honours: FAYC '04
International Honours: E: Yth
A graduate of the Middlesbrough Academy, James is a strong right-sided midfielder with plenty of pace and was one of several youngsters who, when given the chance, played like men when called upon last term. He scored his first goal for the club and Boro's first-ever away goal in European competition - a late leveller against Czech side Banik Ostrava. Young James relished the European games and also managed to score against FK Partizan and Grazer AK. A double hernia sidelined him for a couple of months in March but he reappeared on the substitutes' bench towards the end of the season, raring to go.
Middlesbrough *(From trainee on 14/7/2003) PL 4+11 FLC 2/1 FAC 2+1 Others 4+1/3*

MORRISON John **Owen**
Born: Londonderry, 8 December 1981
Height: 5'8" **Weight:** 11.12
International Honours: NI: U21-7; Yth; Sch
Owen struggled to find his best form at Stockport last term and made little real impact. Later on he joined Bradford City on loan where he became an instant hero by scoring a long-range winner in the 'derby' match against Huddersfield. A skilful right-footed player, he operated on both flanks but was chiefly employed on the left. The move was eventually made permanent and he will be looking forward to make a major impact at Valley Parade in 2005-06.
Sheffield Wed *(From trainee on 5/1/1999) P/FL 31+25/8 FLC 8+2/3 FAC 1+2*
Hull C *(Loaned on 23/8/2002) FL 1+1*
Sheffield U *(Free on 21/2/2003) FL 3+5*
Stockport Co *(Free on 6/8/2003) FL 11+12/1 FLC 1+1 FAC 0+1 Others 0+2/1*
Bradford C *(Signed on 10/12/2004) FL 17+5/2*

MOSES Adrian (Adie) Paul
Born: Doncaster, 4 May 1975
Height: 5'10" **Weight:** 12.8
International Honours: E: U21-2
Adie is a central defender who has also been called upon to fill the full-back position on occasions. Last term he featured in just under half of Crewe Alexandra's Championship fixtures. A player with plenty of experience at a high level, he has always been a consistent performer in the team.
Barnsley *(From juniors on 2/7/1993) P/FL 137+14/3 FLC 15+1 FAC 15*
Huddersfield T *(£225,000 on 20/12/2000) FL 63+6/1 FLC 1 FAC 2+1/1 Others 5*
Crewe Alex *(Free on 8/7/2003) FL 34+8 FLC 3 FAC 1*

MOSS Darren Michael
Born: Wrexham, 24 May 1981
Height: 5'10" **Weight:** 11.6
International Honours: W: U21-4; Yth
This right back enjoyed an excellent season at Shrewsbury last term. Strong and uncompromising, he is also comfortable going forward, to such an extent that when he was sold to Crewe in February he was the club's leading scorer with six goals. Two of those came in his last game, a vital 4-2 defeat of fellow strugglers Kidderminster, when he drove the team forward as they overturned a two-goal deficit. Darren settled in quickly at Gresty Road and will be aiming to win a regular place in the starting line-up in 2005-06.
Chester C *(From trainee on 14/7/1999) FL 33+9 FLC 1+1 FAC 4 Others 1*
Shrewsbury T *(Free on 24/7/2001) FL 84+13/10 FLC 1+1 FAC 4 Others 8/1*
Crewe Alex *(Free on 2/3/2005) FL 6*

MOSS Neil Graham
Born: New Milton, 10 May 1975
Height: 6'2" **Weight:** 13.10
The 2004-05 campaign proved to be another fine season for this Bournemouth goalkeeper who was ever-present in League One fixtures and the major cup competitions. A tall, commanding 'keeper, he passed the landmark of 100-consecutive appearances for the side. Well respected by players and supporters alike, he seems set to hold on to the number one shirt at the club for some time.
Bournemouth *(From trainee on 29/1/1993) FL 21+1 FLC 1 FAC 3+1 Others 2*
Southampton *(£250,000 on 20/12/1995) PL 22+2 FLC 2*
Gillingham *(Loaned on 8/8/1997) FL 10 FLC 2*
Bournemouth *(Free on 13/9/2002) FL 125 FLC 4 FAC 10 Others 6*

MOSS Ryan James
Born: Dorchester, 14 November 1986
Height: 5'11" **Weight:** 12.4
This big bustling striker was a regular in the Bournemouth U18 side last term and was given a surprise first-team call-up due to an injury crisis. Ryan was on the bench for the game at Luton and came on for the last couple of minutes.
Bournemouth *(Trainee) FL 0+1*

MUGGLETON Carl David
Born: Leicester, 13 September 1968
Height: 6'2" **Weight:** 13.4
International Honours: E: U21-1
Chesterfield's veteran custodian performed well throughout the 2004-05 campaign, despite playing half the season with a niggling cartilage injury that required surgery. A competent shot-stopper he will be looking to retain his place as first choice in 2005-06.
Leicester C *(From apprentice on 17/9/1986) FL 46 FAC 3 Others 5*
Chesterfield *(Loaned on 10/9/1987) FL 17 Others 2*
Blackpool *(Loaned on 1/2/1988) FL 2*
Hartlepool U *(Loaned on 28/10/1988) FL 8 Others 2*
Stockport Co *(Loaned on 1/3/1990) FL 4*
Stoke C *(Loaned on 13/8/1993) FL 6 FLC 1 Others 2*
Glasgow Celtic *(£150,000 on 11/1/1994) SL 12 SC 1*
Stoke C *(£150,000 on 21/7/1994) FL 148+1 FLC 17 FAC 5 Others 6*
Rotherham U *(Loaned on 1/11/1995) FL 6 Others 1*
Sheffield U *(Loaned on 28/3/1996) FL 0+1*
Mansfield T *(Loaned on 9/9/1999) FL 9*
Chesterfield *(Loaned on 9/12/1999) FL 5*
Cardiff C *(Loaned on 15/3/2001) FL 6*
Cheltenham T *(Free on 1/7/2001) FL 7 FLC 1*
Bradford C *(Loaned on 28/12/2001) FL 4 FAC 1*
Chesterfield *(Free on 9/7/2002) FL 109 FLC 4 FAC 3 Others 4*

MUIRHEAD Benjamin (Ben) Robinson
Born: Doncaster, 5 January 1983
Height: 5'9" **Weight:** 10.5
International Honours: E: Yth
A lightning-quick right winger, Ben loves to run at defenders and use his pace to unlock defences. He went into the 2004-05 season with the aim of scoring more goals for Bradford City, but had to settle for the one - an absolute belter after a linking run in the memorable 5-4 win at Tranmere.
Manchester U *(From trainee on 7/1/2000)*
Bradford C *(Free on 6/3/2003) FL 43+33/3 FLC 1+1 FAC 1+1 Others 1*

MULDOWNEY Luke John
Born: Feltham, 31 July 1986
Height: 5'7" **Weight:** 10.6
Luke was one of several promising scholars on the books at Brentford last season. He made his senior debut when he came off the bench in the LDV Vans Trophy tie against MK Dons back in September and played in midfield. Luke also had loan spells at Kingstonian and Staines Town before the end of the season but was not offered a professional contract by the Bees in the summer.
Brentford *(Trainee) Others 0+1*

MULHOLLAND Scott Rene
Born: Bexleyheath, 7 September 1986
Height: 5'8" **Weight:** 10.5
Scott is a midfielder who emerged through the youth set-up at Queen's Park Rangers. He was a regular in both the U18 and reserve sides during the season and made his first-team debut as a substitute in the away game at Burnley in mid-April. He will be looking for more opportunities at first-team level in 2005-06.
Queens Park Rgrs *(Trainee) FL 0+1*

MULLIGAN David (Dave) James
Born: Bootle, 24 March 1982
Height: 5'8" **Weight:** 9.13
Club Honours: Div 3 '04
International Honours: New Zealand: Full; Yth
After starting the season on the right side of midfield and then occupying the bench until Christmas, Dave took over the right-back spot for Doncaster when both Simon Marples and Jamie Price were injured and formed a useful partnership with Jamie Coppinger on the right flank. His surging runs down the wing produced some of the most thrilling moments of the season for Rovers' fans. Dave continued to represent New Zealand at international level during the campaign.
Barnsley *(From trainee on 18/10/2000) FL 59+6/1 FLC 1 FAC 3 Others 1*
Doncaster Rov *(Free on 16/2/2004) FL 41+4/2 FLC 0+2 Others 1+1*

MULLIGAN Gary
Born: Dublin, 23 April 1985
Height: 6'1" **Weight:** 12.3
This young Wolves striker made his debut from the bench at Burnley last August when the squad was decimated by injuries and later in the season he was sent out on loan to Rushden to gain some much-needed experience. His first senior goal - a spectacular overhead kick - earned a 1-1 draw at Wycombe in October and he also struck in the home defeats by Darlington and Scunthorpe before returning to Molineux.
Wolverhampton W *(From trainee on 9/7/2002) FL 0+1*
Rushden & Diamonds *(Loaned on 13/10/2004) FL 12+1/3*

MULLIN John Michael
Born: Bury, 11 August 1975
Height: 6'0" **Weight:** 11.10
A midfield dynamo who loves to launch surging runs, John endured a season of mixed fortunes at Rotherham last term. At his best when used in an attacking role, John willingly played a number of games in a position wide on the right to help the team's cause but this restricted his attacking ability somewhat. He netted just one goal, earning a valuable point in a 1-1 draw at Crewe in January.
Burnley *(From trainee on 18/8/1992) FL 7+11/2 FAC 2*
Sunderland *(£40,000 + on 12/8/1995) P/FL 23+12/4 FLC 5+1 FAC 2+1*
Preston NE *(Loaned on 13/2/1998) FL 4+3 Others 1*
Burnley *(Loaned on 26/3/1998) FL 6*
Burnley *(Free on 20/7/1999) FL 38+39/8 FLC 2+1 FAC 5+1/1 Others 1*
Rotherham U *(£150,000 on 5/10/2001) FL 119+18/10 FLC 5+1 FAC 4/2*

MULLINS Hayden Ian
Born: Reading, 27 March 1979
Height: 6'0" **Weight:** 11.12
International Honours: E: U21-3
A very versatile player, Hayden covered a number of defensive positions for West Ham during the campaign. However, he was best seen in central midfield where he added steel with some gritty hard-tackling performances. He revelled in this role in the play-offs with an outstanding performance at Portman Road, which saw the Hammers progress to the final.
Crystal Palace *(From trainee on 28/2/1997) FL 219+3/18 FLC 24/2 FAC 9 Others 2*
West Ham U *(£600,000 on 22/10/2003) FL 59+5/1 FLC 2 FAC 6+1/1 Others 6*

MULLINS John (Johnny) Christopher
Born: Hampstead, 6 November 1985
Height: 5'11" **Weight:** 12.7
This versatile youngster stepped up to the professional ranks with Reading last term and in December he joined League Two outfit Kidderminster Harriers in a long-term loan deal. Johnny produced a string of outstanding performances at right back and in the centre of the defence, notably in the 2-0 win at Oxford. One of the few consistent players in an under-performing team, he became a firm favourite with the Aggborough faithful before returning to Reading at the end of the season.
Reading *(From trainee on 17/12/2004)*
Kidderminster Hrs *(Loaned on 17/12/2004) FL 21/2*

MULRYNE Phillip (Phil) Patrick
Born: Belfast, 1 January 1978
Height: 5'8" **Weight:** 10.11
Club Honours: FAYC '95; Div 1 '04
International Honours: NI: 26; B-1; U21-3; Yth

Phil's contract at Norwich City was terminated by mutual consent in May 2005 after a frustrating season for the talented playmaker. A series of minor injuries ensured that he played no more than a peripheral role in City's first Premiership campaign in nine years. At his best, Phil can dictate the pace and pattern of play by dominating possession with his excellent range of passing skills. He likes to get forward into the penalty area and can be very dangerous at set-piece situations with his variety of free kicks.

Manchester U *(From trainee on 17/3/1995) PL 1 FLC 3 FAC 0+1*

Norwich C *(£500,000 on 25/3/1999) P/FL 132+29/18 FLC 6+1 FAC 5+2/2 Others 3*

MURDOCK Colin James

Born: Ballymena, 2 July 1975
Height: 6'2" **Weight:** 13.0
Club Honours: Div 2 '00
International Honours: NI: 28; B-3; Yth; Sch

This former Manchester United and Preston North End defender was released by Hibernian in February 2005 and then signed for Crewe until the end of the season. He made his debut for Alexandra at Leicester in February and was a regular in the heart of defence from then on. Colin was also a regular member of the Northern Ireland international side.

Manchester U *(From juniors on 21/7/1992)*

Preston NE *(£100,000 on 23/5/1997) FL 163+14/6 FLC 13+1 FAC 9+2 Others 10*

Hibernian *(Free on 17/7/2003) SL 37/3 SLC 6/1 SC 1 Others 1*

Crewe Alex *(Free on 31/1/2005) FL 15+1*

MURPHY Brian

Born: Waterford, 7 May 1983
Height: 6'0" **Weight:** 13.1
International Honours: RoI: U21-3; Yth

Brian was second choice to regular 'keeper Willy Gueret at Swansea last term and rarely featured at first-team level. His only appearances for the Swans coming in the League Two matches at Boston and Mansfield, and in the FAW Cup games at Caernarfon Town and TNS. Nevertheless he continued to add to his tally of U21 caps for the Republic of Ireland during the campaign.

Manchester C *(From trainee on 13/5/2000. Freed during 2003 close season)*

Peterborough U *(Loaned on 2/5/2003) FL 1*

Swansea C *(Free from Waterford on 8/8/2003) FL 13 FLC 1 Others 1*

MURPHY Christopher (Chris) Patrick

Born: Leamington Spa, 8 March 1983
Height: 5'6" **Weight:** 9.12

This diminutive striker or attacking midfield player signed for Cheltenham Town during the summer of 2004, but although he featured regularly for the reserves he made just a handful of appearances from the substitutes' bench at first-team level. He is an adaptable player who can operate as a striker, out wide on either flank or playing just behind the front two.

Shrewsbury T *(From trainee on 3/7/2002) FL 0+8 FAC 0+1 Others 0+1 (Free to Telford U on 7/7/2003)*

Cheltenham T *(Free on 2/7/2004) FL 0+4*

MURPHY Daniel (Danny) Benjamin

Born: Chester, 18 March 1977
Height: 5'10" **Weight:** 11.0
Club Honours: FLC '01, '03; FAC '01; UEFAC '01; ESC '01; CS '01
International Honours: E: 9; U21-5; Yth; Sch

This vastly experienced player was signed to add some class to Charlton's midfield and he featured in every competitive fixture last term, starting in all but two. Danny took a while to settle, but after a few games built up a good partnership with both Matt Holland and Radostin Kishishev in the centre of the Addicks' midfield. Very comfortable on the ball, he is difficult to dispossess when in possession. He is a dead-ball specialist and took nearly all of the team's corners and most of the free kicks awarded around the box during the season. Danny scored five goals in all competitions, four with free kicks and a fifth with a perfectly executed finish in the home game with Birmingham in January.

Crewe Alex *(From trainee on 21/3/1994) FL 110+24/27 FLC 7 FAC 7/4 Others 15+2/4*

Liverpool *(£1,500,000 + on 17/7/1997) PL 114+56/25 FLC 15+1/11 FAC 11+4/3 Others 38+10/5*

Crewe Alex *(Loaned on 12/2/1999) FL 16/1*

Charlton Ath *(£2,500,000 on 12/8/2004) PL 37+1/3 FLC 2/1 FAC 2+1/1*

MURPHY John James

Born: Whiston, 18 October 1976
Height: 6'2" **Weight:** 14.0
Club Honours: AMC '02, '04

This experienced striker was once again a regular in the Blackpool line-up despite missing a few games with niggling injuries. Although not quite as prolific as in the previous campaign he still managed to score ten goals including doubles in the victories at Brentford and Wrexham.

Chester C *(From trainee on 6/7/1995) FL 65+38/20 FLC 7+3/1 FAC 1+2 Others 3+1*

Blackpool *(Signed on 6/8/1999) FL 201+17/75 FLC 8+2/5 FAC 15/5 Others 15+3/11*

MURPHY Joseph (Joe)

Born: Dublin, 21 August 1981
Height: 6'2" **Weight:** 13.6
International Honours: RoI: 1; U21-14; Yth (UEFA-U16 '98)

Joe found himself as third-choice 'keeper at West Brom last season and although he featured on the bench a couple of times without seeing any action, he spent most of the campaign out on loan at near-neighbours Walsall. He tightened up the Saddlers' defence from the moment he arrived and features of his game included some excellent kicking and safe handling of the ball. He missed only one match in six months until he received a red card at Blackpool in March and then found he could not replace Andy Oakes.

Tranmere Rov *(From trainee on 5/7/1999) FL 61+2 FLC 8 FAC 3 Others 1*

West Bromwich A *(Signed on 17/7/2002) P/FL 3+2 FLC 1*

Walsall *(Loaned on 8/10/2004) FL 25 Others 2*

MURRAY Adam David

Born: Birmingham, 30 September 1981
Height: 5'8" **Weight:** 10.10
International Honours: E: Yth

Adam proved to be a popular signing for Mansfield during the 2004 close season, having previously enjoyed a successful spell at Field Mill. He quickly became an important part of the Stags' midfield with some solid displays during which he displayed tenacious tackling and weighed in with several useful goals. However, he, never really achieved the level of performance that he had previously shown with the club and was allowed to join Conference outfit Carlisle United on transfer-deadline day in March.

Derby Co *(From trainee on 7/10/1998) P/FL 25+31 FLC 3+1 FAC 4 (Free to Solihull Borough on 12/11/2003)*

Mansfield T *(Loaned on 26/2/2002) FL 13/7*

Kidderminster Hrs *(Loaned on 29/8/2003) FL 3*

Notts Co *(Free from Burton A on 27/11/2003) FL 1+2 FAC 0+1*

Kidderminster Hrs *(Free on 9/1/2004) FL 16+3/3*

Mansfield T *(Free on 7/7/2004) FL 27+5/5 FLC 1 FAC 1+1 Others 2*

MURRAY Frederick (Fred) Anthony

Born: Clonmel, 22 May 1982
Height: 5'10" **Weight:** 11.12
International Honours: RoI: Yth

Fred enjoyed a good season at Northampton last term when he was a near ever-present in the side playing either at left back or in the centre of the defence. He always gave 100 per cent

effort but failed to register a goal during the campaign.
Blackburn Rov *(From trainee on 25/5/1999)*
Cambridge U *(Free on 14/12/2001) FL 80+8 FLC 2 FAC 3+2 Others 7*
Northampton T *(Signed on 20/7/2004) FL 38 FAC 2 Others 4*

MURRAY Matthew (Matt) William
Born: Solihull, 2 May 1981
Height: 6'4" **Weight:** 13.10
International Honours: E: U21-5; Yth
Injury had all but wiped out his Premiership season in 2003-04, so goalkeeper Matt was hoping to fare better at Wolves last term. It was slow progress, as he advanced to a regular place on the bench in October but did not make the team until January. The agility and command of his defence were still there, and he kept Wolves' first clean sheet in 16 games. Yet after just one more appearance Matt was injured again, a stress fracture of the foot, and was soon ruled out of the campaign.
Wolverhampton W *(From trainee on 7/5/1998) P/FL 42 FLC 2 FAC 5 Others 3*

MURRAY Scott George
Born: Aberdeen, 26 May 1974
Height: 5'10" **Weight:** 11.0
Club Honours: AMC '03
International Honours: S: B-2
Scott again struggled to find his best form for Bristol City in 2004-05. Whilst a goal return of eight was satisfactory for a winger, his incisive runs down the flanks were all too often missing from his game. He will be looking to rectify this situation in the 2005-06 campaign.
Aston Villa *(£35,000 from Fraserburgh on 16/3/1994) PL 4*
Bristol C *(£150,000 on 12/12/1997) FL 193+31/46 FLC 10+3 FAC 13+1/7 Others 18+2/8*
Reading *(£650,000 on 9/7/2003) FL 25+9/5 FLC 3+1 FAC 2*
Bristol C *(£500,000 on 25/3/2004) FL 35+13/8 FLC 2 FAC 2 Others 3+3*

MURTY Graeme Stuart
Born: Saltburn, 13 November 1974
Height: 5'10" **Weight:** 11.10
International Honours: S: 1; B-1
Reading's longest-serving player signed an extension to his contract at the start of last season, and took over as club captain following the departure of Adrian Williams to Coventry City. A fine full back who can overlap before firing over a cross or cutting in to shoot at goal, Graeme has now completed more than 200 appearances for the club. His only disappointment was in not being able to force his way back into the Scotland squad, but he is still regarded as one of the best defenders outside the Premiership.
York C *(From trainee on 23/3/1993) FL 106+11/7 FLC 10/2 FAC 5+1 Others 6+2*
Reading *(£700,000 on 10/7/1998) FL 204+11/1 FLC 6 FAC 12+1 Others 6+2*

MUSAMPA Kizito (Kiki)
Born: Kinshasa, DR Congo, 20 July 1977
Height: 5'11" **Weight:** 12.0
International Honours: Holland: U21-22
Better known throughout Europe as 'Kiki', this left-sided midfielder joined Manchester City on a six-month loan deal with the option to make a permanent move. Although it took him time to adapt to the English game he began to look sharper by the week and scored his first Premiership goal in the crucial victory at home to Liverpool. He is a fast attacking player who on his day can cause havoc in the opposition defence from either his preferred midfield position or out on the wing.
Manchester C *(Loaned from Atletico Madrid, Spain on 31/1/2005) PL 14/3*

MUSCAT Kevin Vincent
Born: Crawley, 7 August 1973
Height: 5'11" **Weight:** 12.2
Club Honours: SPD '03; SL '03
International Honours: Australia: 45; U23; Yth
This experienced defender was hampered by injuries last term, but still managed to appear in over half of Millwall's Championship fixtures. The tough-tackling right back is a true professional who gives no quarter and is a steadying factor in the defence. He continued to add to his tally of caps for Australia during the campaign and was a member of the squad for the Confederations Cup tournament in the summer.
Crystal Palace *(£35,000 from South Melbourne, Australia on 16/8/1996) P/FL 51+2/2 FLC 4/1 FAC 2 Others 2*
Wolverhampton W *(£200,000 on 22/10/1997) FL 178+2/14 FLC 10/1 FAC 11*
Glasgow Rgrs *(Free on 1/7/2002) SL 22+1 SLC 0+1 SC 3+1 Others 1+1*
Millwall *(Free on 29/8/2003) FL 52+1 FLC 1 FAC 6 Others 2*

MUSSELWHITE Paul Stephen
Born: Portsmouth, 22 December 1968
Height: 6'2" **Weight:** 14.2
Club Honours: AMC '93
Paul made a sentimental return to the club where he started his career and it proved a fairy tale season for the experienced goalkeeper. He won the pre-season fight to be Scunthorpe's first-choice 'keeper and the competition from previous number one Tommy Evans ensured his high standards never dropped during the campaign. A big 'keeper, who is a good shot-stopper and has a commanding presence in the area, Paul was an ever-present, helping the club win promotion to League One. In the 46 League matches, he kept 19 clean sheets and only conceded 42 goals – the best record in the division.
Portsmouth *(From apprentice on 1/12/1986)*
Scunthorpe U *(Free on 21/3/1988) FL 132 FLC 11 FAC 7 Others 13*
Port Vale *(£20,000 on 30/7/1992) FL 312 FLC 15 FAC 21 Others 19*
Sheffield Wed *(Free, via trials at Scunthorpe U, Darlington, on 25/8/2000)*
Hull C *(Free on 19/9/2000) FL 94+1 FAC 4 Others 5*
Scunthorpe U *(Free on 5/8/2004) FL 46 FLC 1 FAC 3*

MUTU Adrian
Born: Calinesti, Romania, 8 January 1979
Height: 5'11" **Weight:** 11.12
International Honours: Romania: 39; U21; Yth
In the space of two weeks Adrian Mutu's faltering Chelsea career went into a tailspin with catastrophic consequences. Already marginalised by Jose Mourinho – he played just 49 minutes in two substitute appearances from the first six matches – then defied the new boss by travelling to the Czech Republic for Romania's World Cup qualifier who then ruled the striker unfit with a knee injury. But worse was to follow when Mutu tested positive for a banned substance and was summarily sacked by the club. Adrian was handed a seven-month ban by the FA but in January was given a chance to resurrect his career back in Serie A by Juventus.
Chelsea *(£15,800,000 + from Parma, Italy, ex Arges Pitesti, Dinamo Bucharest, Inter Milan, Verona, on 19/8/2003) PL 21+6/6 FLC 0+1 FAC 3/3 Others 6+1/1*

MYERS Andrew (Andy) John
Born: Hounslow, 3 November 1973
Height: 5'10" **Weight:** 13.11
Club Honours: FAC '97; ECWC '98
International Honours: E: U21-4; Yth
This experienced left back joined Brentford in the summer of 2004. However, he had a disappointing campaign with the Bees when he was unable to displace Andy Frampton from the line-up and then suffered an ankle injury in January. He was released at the end of the season.
Chelsea *(From trainee on 25/7/1991) P/FL 74+10/2 FLC 2+1 FAC 9+3 Others 4+3*
Bradford C *(£800,000 on 16/7/1999) P/FL 74+15/3 FLC 5 FAC 1 Others 3+1*
Portsmouth *(Loaned on 23/3/2000) FL 4+4*

Paul Musselwhite

Colchester U *(Free on 15/7/2003) FL 21 FLC 1 FAC 2 Others 2*
Brentford *(Free on 2/7/2004) FL 6+4 FLC 1 FAC 1 Others 1*

MYHILL Glyn (Boaz) Oliver

Born: California, USA, 9 November 1982
Height: 6'3" **Weight:** 14.6
International Honours: E: Yth

It is not only the fact that both of Boaz's seasons at Hull have culminated in promotion that have established his reputation of one of the best young 'keepers in the lower divisions, for he was a near ever-present in the line-up and consistent throughout the campaign. Although still learning his trade, he makes the most of his physical presence to dominate his area and is an outstanding shot-stopper.

Aston Villa *(From trainee on 28/11/2000)*
Bradford C *(Loaned on 22/11/2002) FL 2*
Macclesfield T *(Loaned on 8/8/2003) FL 15 FLC 1*
Stockport Co *(Loaned on 22/11/2003) FL 2 Others 1*
Hull C *(£50,000 on 12/12/2003) FL 68 FAC 3 Others 1*

MYHRE Thomas

Born: Sarpsborg, Norway, 16 October 1973
Height: 6'4" **Weight:** 13.12
Club Honours: Ch '05
International Honours: Norway: 40; U21-27; Yth

Norway's first choice international goalkeeper, Thomas had endured a stop-start career at Sunderland until last season when he finally established himself as the Black Cats' number one custodian. After deputising for the injured Mart Poom early on in the campaign, Thomas again stepped in when his rival was sidelined in October and he remained in the side until April when a back strain saw him miss out on the club's promotion and Championship celebrations. By this time, however, his performances had been a major factor in the Wearsiders' success. An imposing figure, Thomas possesses excellent handling skills and marshals his defence with real authority. His experience will be important to Sunderland upon their return to the Premiership.

Everton *(£800,000 from Viking Stavanger, Norway on 28/11/1997) PL 70 FLC 3 FAC 9 (£375,000 to Besiktas, Turkey on 1/11/2001)*
Glasgow Rgrs *(Loaned on 24/11/1999) SL 3 SLC 1 Others 2*
Birmingham C *(Loaned on 31/3/2000) FL 7 Others 2*
Tranmere Rov *(Loaned on 28/11/2000) FL 3 FLC 1*
Sunderland *(Free on 8/7/2002) P/FL 35+2 FLC 3 FAC 2*
Crystal Palace *(Loaned on 24/10/2003) FL 15 FLC 1*

N

NAFTI Mehdi
Born: Toulouse, France, 28 November 1978
Height: 5'9" **Weight:** 11.3
International Honours: Tunisia
Signed on loan from Racing Santander during the January transfer window, Mehdi made a good impression at Birmingham City last term. He debuted at Manchester United the following month, when he held his own in midfield, and went on to become a regular towards the season's end. Although not physically imposing, he got around the pitch quickly to challenge opponents with snappy tackles and proved himself a slick distributor of the ball. He was outstanding in the Blues' 1-1 draw at Chelsea.
Birmingham C *(Loaned from Racing Santander, Spain, on 31/1/2005) PL 7+3*

NALIS Lilian Bernard Pierre
Born: Paris, France, 29 September 1971
Height: 6'1" **Weight:** 13.3
This energetic Leicester midfielder continued to demonstrate good vision with his passing and the rare ability to shoot with stylish technique from anywhere around the box. He actually led the Foxes' goal-scoring chart for a few weeks during the early months, having never had to contribute a tap in. He was handed the captain's armband for the closing minutes of the final home fixture against Leeds, a moment that proved poignant as he was released days later by Craig Levein, as preparations for 2005-06 got underway.
Leicester C *(Free from Chievo, Italy, ex SM Caen, Laval, Guingamp, Le Havre, Bastia, on 6/7/2003) P/FL 43+16/6 FLC 2 FAC 1+4*

NARDIELLO Daniel (Danny) Antony
Born: Coventry, 22 October 1982
Height: 5'11" **Weight:** 11.4
International Honours: E: Yth; Sch
This exciting young forward returned to Barnsley on a season-long loan from Manchester United last season. However, despite scoring at Wrexham early on he found himself mostly used as a substitute. A change in management saw his fortunes improve and after he got a good run in the side the goals began to flow at last.
Manchester U *(From trainee on 1/11/1999) FLC 1+2 Others 0+1*
Swansea C *(Loaned on 24/10/2003) FL 3+1 Others 1/1*
Barnsley *(Loaned on 27/1/2004) FL 14+2/7*
Barnsley *(Loaned on 16/7/2004) FL 11+17/7 FLC 0+2 Others 1*

NASH Carlo James
Born: Bolton, 13 September 1973
Height: 6'5" **Weight:** 14.1
Club Honours: Div 1 '02
The former Manchester City shot-stopper knew that unless something happened to Mark Schwarzer his chances at the Riverside would be limited last term. He fared slightly better than in previous campaigns, playing some four games spread over as many months, but realising that Brad Jones was racing up in his rear-view mirror he accepted a move to Preston North End in March. Carlo took over the goalkeeper's position in Andy Lonergan's absence and made some telling contributions to the play-off effort. Tall and athletic, he had very little to do in his first few games, which did not help him readjust to first-team football after a season on the bench, but he showed his form with some terrific saves in the play-off final, including a brilliant double effort.
Crystal Palace *(£35,000 from Clitheroe on 16/7/1996) FL 21 FLC 1 Others 3*
Stockport Co *(Free on 7/6/1998) FL 89 FLC 5 FAC 4*
Manchester C *(£100,000 on 12/1/2001) P/FL 37+1 FLC 2 FAC 1*

Carlo Nash

***Middlesbrough** (£150,000 on 14/8/2003) PL 3 FLC 2*
***Preston NE** (£175,000 on 24/3/2005) FL 7 Others 3*

NAVARRO Alan Edward
Born: Liverpool, 31 May 1981
Height: 5'11" **Weight:** 11.7
Alan found himself completely out of favour at Tranmere last term and the only first-team action he experienced was whilst out on loan. He became caretaker-manager Ray Mathias' only signing for Chester when he joined the club on a month's loan last August, but then returned to Prenton Park following a change in management. Later he spent time with Macclesfield where he did well in a central-midfield role. Alan produced some gritty and determined performances, strengthening the middle line as a whole and scored a last-minute winner in the home game against Wycombe at the turn of the year, He was released by Tranmere in the summer when his contract expired.

Alan Navarro

***Liverpool** (From trainee on 27/4/1999)*
***Crewe Alex** (Loaned on 22/3/2001) FL 5+3/1*
***Crewe Alex** (Loaned on 9/8/2001) FL 7 FLC 2*
***Tranmere Rov** (£225,000 on 9/11/2001) FL 35+10/1 FAC 4+2/1 Others 0+1*
***Chester C** (Loaned on 20/8/2004) FL 3 FLC 1*
***Macclesfield T** (Loaned on 16/12/2004) FL 11/1*

NAYBET Noureddine
Born: Casablanca, Morocco, 10 February 1970
Height: 6'0" **Weight:** 11.11
International Honours: Morocco: 105
Previously a reported target of Manchester United, Noureddine added strength and experience in what had been a leaky Spurs defence last season. Despite his advancing years, pace and agility were still plentiful. Martin Jol's arrival as a replacement for Jacques Santini early into the campaign suited Noureddine who likes to push the ball out of defence and move up for set pieces.
***Tottenham H** (£700,000 from Deportivo la Coruna, Spain, on 13/8/2004) PL 27/1 FLC 2 FAC 2*

NAYLOR Lee Martyn
Born: Walsall, 19 March 1980
Height: 5'9" **Weight:** 11.8
International Honours: E: U21-3; Yth
This pacy left back missed little action for Wolves early on last season, despite injury concerns. Although dropped for a while in the autumn he was soon back and generally showed steady improvement as the campaign progressed. Lee always gave 100 per cent and he was an ever-present from mid-December, his surging forward runs and crosses being an important part of Wolves' attacking play.
***Wolverhampton W** (From trainee on 10/10/1997) P/FL 229+21/6 FLC 18 FAC 17/1 Others 3/1*

NAYLOR Richard Alan
Born: Leeds, 28 February 1977
Height: 6'1" **Weight:** 13.7
Richard was the only Ipswich player to appear in all 46 Championship games last season. As in the previous campaign he found himself at the heart of the defence where his ability in the air and his experience gave him the edge over opposition forwards. He supported his forwards at set pieces and scored some vital goals including one against each of Town's promotion rivals, Sunderland and Wigan, at Portman Road. Richard also captained the side at Wigan in the absence of Jim Magilton and Jason De Vos.

swich T *(From trainee on 10/7/1995) P/FL 3+84/34 FLC 9+10/1 FAC 4+5/1 Others 6/1*
illwall *(Loaned on 29/1/2002) FL 2+1*
rnsley *(Loaned on 4/3/2002) FL 7+1*

AYSMITH Gary Andrew
orn: Edinburgh, 16 November 1978
eight: 5'7" **Weight:** 11.8
ub Honours: SC '98
ternational Honours: S: 28; B-1; U21-2; Sch
ary had an unfortunate season at verton, when a combination of injury nd the good form of others meant his st-team opportunities were limited. fter starting the campaign in the side he as sent-off at Crystal Palace and then iffered an ankle injury playing for cotland in October. He began just three emiership games for the Blues after is, although he remained a first-choice election for his country, and his future as unclear at the end of the season, hen he was out of contract. Gary can lay either at full back or wing back, roviding good quality crosses when equired, but he may need to move on to urther his career.
eart of Midlothian *(Signed from Whitehill Velfare on 17/6/1996) SL 92+5/3 SLC 5/1 SC 0 Others 7/1*
verton *(£1,750,000 on 20/10/2000) PL 6+16/5 FLC 5+1/1 FAC 11+1*

N'DUMBU-NSUNGU Guylain
orn: Kinshasa, DR Congo, 26 December 982
eight: 6'1" **Weight:** 12.8
Guylain struggled to match his form of he previous campaign for Sheffield Wednesday last term, although he scored early on against Tranmere. The pacy striker then went on loan to Preston where he provided extra attacking options for the side. He returned to Hillsborough but eventually moved on to Colchester on a short-term contract. Guylain scored once for the U's before being released at the end of March.
Sheffield Wed *(Signed from Amiens, France on 9/9/2003) FL 24+11/10 FLC 0+1 FAC 1+1/1 Others 5+1*
Preston NE *(Loaned on 28/9/2004) FL 4+2*
Colchester U *(Free on 20/1/2005) FL 2+6/1 FAC 0+1*

NEAL Christopher (Chris) Michael
Born: St Albans, 23 October 1985
Height: 6'2" **Weight:** 12.4
An injury crisis at Deepdale saw this young 'keeper promoted to the bench for Preston against Burnley last December. Three months later, he found himself called up again and this time he made his debut as a late substitute in the televised clash with Ipswich. An excellent point-blank save was his contribution to the first-team cause, but great things are hoped for from Chris in the future.
Preston NE *(From trainee on 23/12/2004) FL 0+1*

NEAL Lewis Ryan
Born: Leicester, 14 July 1981
Height: 6'0" **Weight:** 11.2
Lewis is a left-sided midfielder who has a good turn of pace and a few tricks in his locker. Unfortunately he is a little on the light side but does get stuck in. Although never a regular for Stoke last term he made a useful contribution and scored his first goal in18 months with a rare header against Crewe in April.
Stoke C *(From juniors on 17/7/1998) FL 29+41/2 FLC 2+1 FAC 3+3 Others 1+2/1*

NEEDHAM Liam Paul
Born: Sheffield, 19 October 1985
Height: 5'11" **Weight:** 12.0
A youngster who developed through Sheffield Wednesday's youth set-up, Liam was on the fringes of the first-team squad last season and made his senior debut in the LDV Vans Trophy tie against Chester. A tricky, speedy midfielder or striker he will be looking to gain more experience in the 2005-06 campaign.
Sheffield Wed *(Trainee) Others 0+1*

NEGOUAI Christian
Born: Fort de France, Martinique, 20 January 1975
Height: 6'4" **Weight:** 13.11
This towering midfielder was unable to force his way into the Manchester City first team last season and was sent off after just minutes of his only Premiership outing of the campaign at Everton on Boxing Day. Christian joined Coventry City on a month's loan in January and played in midfield in the FA Cup defeat at Newcastle before a niggling thigh injury meant that he returned to the City of Manchester Stadium for treatment. He later made a comeback in the reserves playing successfully in a striking role.
Manchester C *(£1,500,000 from RSC Charleroi, Belgium, ex Vaux en Velin, Lyon, Namur, on 16/11/2001) P/FL 2+4/1 FLC 1+1 FAC 0+1 Others 1/1*
Coventry C *(Loaned on 27/1/2005) FL 1 FAC 1*

NEIL Alexander (Alex)
Born: Bellshill, 9 June 1981
Height: 5'8" **Weight:** 12.10
Alex started last season in a central-midfield role for Mansfield Town, but was later moved to a position wide on the right-hand side of midfield. He put in some excellent performances and became a permanent fixture in the side. Although it appeared he was surplus to requirements when new manager Carlton Palmer took over he was switched to right back due to Scott McNiven's illness and proved himself to be a very useful asset, to such an extent that he was offered a new contract. Very popular with the fans he was voted the Stags' Supporters Association's 'Player of the Season'.
Airdrie *(From Dunfermline Ath juniors on 8/7/1999) SL 15+1/5 SC 0+1*
Barnsley *(£25,000 on 11/7/2000) FL 83+38/4 FLC 2+2 FAC 4+2 Others 1*
Mansfield T *(Free on 23/7/2004) FL 40+1/1 FLC 1 FAC 1/1*

NEILL Lucas Edward
Born: Sydney, Australia, 9 March 1978
Height: 6'1" **Weight:** 12.0
Club Honours: Div 2 '01
International Honours: Australia: 13; U23-12; Yth
Never anything other than competitive, Lucas was one of several Blackburn players who improved as Mark Hughes' coaching staff worked on his game. Restricting his inclinations to get forward and be exploited on the counter attack, he concentrated on strong tackling and covering in defence, roles in which he excels. Lucas scored once for Rovers last term, netting a classy effort in the final home game of the season against Fulham.
Millwall *(Free from Australian Academy of Sport on 13/11/1995) FL 124+28/13 FLC 6+1 FAC 4 Others 11+1*
Blackburn Rov *(£1,000,000 on 7/9/2001) PL 129+4/4 FLC 6 FAC 15 Others 5*

NEILSON Alan Bruce
Born: Wegburg, Germany, 26 September 1972
Height: 5'11" **Weight:** 12.10
International Honours: W: 5; B-2; U21-7
This veteran Luton Town defender was used as cover for injuries and suspensions last term. When selected his experience proved invaluable, none more so than in the vital home game against Hull in February when his goal-line clearance prevented the visitors taking the lead. Alan, who has begun working towards gaining his coaching qualifications, was released by the Hatters at the end of the season.
Newcastle U *(From trainee on 11/2/1991) P/FL 35+7/1 FLC 4 Others 4*
Southampton *(£500,000 on 1/6/1995) PL 42+13 FLC 7 FAC 1*

Fulham *(£250,000 on 28/11/1997) FL 24+5/2 FLC 4+2 FAC 4 Others 2*
Grimsby T *(Free on 19/10/2001) FL 8+2 FLC 1 FAC 1*
Luton T *(Free on 22/2/2002) FL 46+11/1 FLC 1+2 FAC 1+1 Others 1*

NELSEN Ryan
Born: Christchurch, New Zealand, 18 October 1977
Height: 6'1" **Weight:** 14.0
International Honours: New Zealand
Ryan was very much the key signing for Blackburn Rovers last term and his arrival transformed the defence from one that leaked goals to one which was difficult to score against. A strong central defender, sound in the air, tough in the tackle and a man who realises that his job is to defend, he played at a consistently high standard.
Blackburn Rov *(Free from DC United, USA on 10/1/2005) PL 15 FAC 4+1*

NELSON Michael John
Born: Gateshead, 28 March 1980
Height: 6'2" **Weight:** 13.12
This rock-solid central defender enjoyed an excellent season for Hartlepool last term. Although he was briefly rested in mid-season, he returned to the line-up and was again outstanding at the heart of the defence, and arguably Hartlepool's most consistent performer as they reached the League One play-off final at the Millennium Stadium.
Bury *(Free from Bishop Auckland on 22/3/2001) FL 68+4/8 FLC 4 FAC 3 Others 5*
Hartlepool U *(£70,000 on 10/7/2003) FL 80+3/4 FLC 4 FAC 8 Others 9*

NELSON Stuart James
Born: Stroud, 17 September 1981
Height: 6'1" **Weight:** 12.12
Stuart firmly established himself as Brentford's first choice goalkeeper last term in his first full season at Griffin Park. A brilliant shot-stopper, whose kicking greatly improved, he kept 21 clean sheets including five in succession in September and October. He also had a goal disallowed from a drop kick at Doncaster in March due to a foul on the opposition 'keeper.
Millwall *(Signed from Cirencester T on 6/10/2000. Free to Des Moines University, USA during 2001 close season)*
Brentford *(£10,000 from Hucknall T, ex Oxford C, Doncaster Rov, on 2/2/2004) FL 52 FLC 1 FAC 9 Others 2*

NELTHORPE Craig Robert
Born: Doncaster, 10 June 1987
Height: 5'10" **Weight:** 11.0
Craig showed good form in Doncaster's reserves last term, where he featured either on the left-hand side of midfield or at left back. He was included on the bench for the final game of the season against Luton Town and made his debut when coming on for Steve Foster, taking over at left back with all the aplomb of a seasoned veteran.
Doncaster Rov *(Trainee) FL 0+1*

NEMETH Szilard
Born: Kamarna, Slovakia, 8 August 1977
Height: 5'10" **Weight:** 10.10
Club Honours: FLC '04
International Honours: Slovakia: 52
Regarded by many Middlesbrough fans as unlucky to miss the 2004 Carling Cup final because of injury Szilard Nemeth always believed in his own abilities and always insisted that he would produce the goals if given the chance. Although not an automatic choice for a first-team place he appeared in most games, although often as a substitute. Despite missing a month's football with a groin injury he started to get regular first-team football towards the end of the season and found his goal-scoring form again.
Middlesbrough *(Signed from Inter Bratislava, Slovakia, ex Slovan Bratislava, Kosice, on 30/7/2001) PL 61+51/23 FLC 6+2/3 FAC 4+3/1 Others 6+2/1*

NETHERCOTT Stuart David
Born: Ilford, 21 March 1973
Height: 6'1" **Weight:** 13.8
Club Honours: Div 2 '01
International Honours: E: U21-8
This commanding central defender was always a first choice for Wycombe under manager Tony Adams last term. However, when John Gorman took over the reins, Stuart mostly found himself on the bench as the preferred defensive partnership consisted of Roger Johnson and Mike Williamson. Stuart never let the side down when selected and his experience and leadership skills both on and off the pitch proved invaluable.
Tottenham H *(From trainee on 17/8/1991) PL 31+23 FAC 5+3/1*
Maidstone U *(Loaned on 5/9/1991) FL 13/1 Others 1*
Barnet *(Loaned on 13/2/1992) FL 3*
Millwall *(Signed on 22/1/1998) FL 206+9/10 FLC 8 FAC 6 Others 13*
Wycombe W *(Free on 2/1/2004) FL 49+2/1 FLC 1 FAC 0+1 Others 1*

NEVILLE Gary Alexander
Born: Bury, 18 February 1975
Height: 5'11" **Weight:** 12.8
Club Honours: FAYC '92; PL '96, '97, '99, '00, '01, '03; FAC '96, '99, '04; CS '96; UEFACL '99
International Honours: E: 76; Yth (UEFA-U18 '93)
A hard-tackling fullback, who is equally as effective in a central-defensive role, Gary continued to give his usual 100 per cent for the Reds in another highly productive campaign. A key figure on the right-hand side of the defence, he was rewarded with a place in the PFA Premiership team of the season. Although his regular supply of crosses, and build up play has often led to an abundance of goals for his fellow Reds, a Gary Neville goal is always highly celebrated when it comes. His effort against Olympique Lyon in the Champions' League in November not only celebrated his first European effort in two seasons, it also came on a landmark night for Sir Alex Ferguson, who was celebrating his 1000th game in charge. A niggling groin strain kept him out of the FA Cup final against Arsenal, and England's tour to the USA in the summer.
Manchester U *(From trainee on 29/1/1993) PL 301+14/5 FLC 11+1 FAC 36+2 Others 99+6/2*

NEVILLE Philip (Phil) John
Born: Bury, 21 January 1977
Height: 5'11" **Weight:** 12.0
Club Honours: FAYC '95; PL '96, '97, '99, '00, '01, '03; FAC '96, '99, '04: CS '96, '97, '03; UEFACL '99
International Honours: E: 52; U21-7; Yth; Sch
A versatile player who is equally comfortable at full back or as a central defender, Phil might have thought his Old Trafford days were numbered particularly when England teammate Nicky Butt was deemed surplus to requirements and sold to Newcastle in the summer. Remaining an experienced asset on the periphery of first-team action, however, Phil enjoyed a flurry of Premiership outings from August to December, and was also an ever-present throughout a fruitful Carling Cup campaign, which saw United reach the semi-final stages before losing to Chelsea. Playing six games as a substitute in the qualifying stages of the Champions' League, Phil's other notable contribution came in United's defence of the FA Cup, where he played in all ties except the semi-final and final.
Manchester U *(From trainee on 1/6/1994) PL 210+53/5 FLC 16+1 FAC 25+6/1 Others 50+25/2*

NEWBY Jonathan (Jon) Philip Robert
Born: Warrington, 28 November 1978
Height: 6'0" **Weight:** 12.4
Club Honours: FAYC '96

This popular Bury striker began last term in the starting line-up before losing his place due to the superb form of David Nugent and Chris Porter. Jon worked hard in the reserve team though and eventually gained a regular run in the side following Nugent's transfer to Preston in January, playing largely in a right-sided role. He missed the closing stages of the campaign after limping off with an achilles injury in March.
Liverpool *(From juniors on 23/5/1997) PL 0+1 FLC 0+1 FAC 0+2*
Crewe Alex *(Loaned on 3/3/2000) FL 5+1*
Sheffield U *(Loaned on 4/8/2000) FL 3+10*
Bury *(£100,000 on 2/2/2001) FL 109/21 FLC 1/1 FAC 3 Others 6/2*
Huddersfield T *(Free on 7/8/2003) FL 10+4 FLC 1*
York C *(Loaned on 25/3/2004) FL 6+1*
Bury *(Free on 6/8/2004) FL 17+19/4 FLC 0+1 FAC 0+2 Others 1*

NEWEY Thomas (Tom) William
Born: Huddersfield, 31 October 1982
Height: 5'10" **Weight:** 10.6
Tom featured regularly as a substitute for Leyton Orient in the first half of the 2004-05 season, but only managed a handful of appearances in the starting line-up, deputising for winger Andy Scott. In January he joined Cambridge United on loan, eventually making a permanent move to the Abbey Stadium in March. He impressed as a classy left back for the U's, showing good defensive skills and the ability to push forward down the flank to deliver a useful cross.
Leeds U *(From trainee on 4/8/2000)*
Cambridge U *(Loaned on 14/2/2003) FL 6 Others 1*
Darlington *(Loaned on 27/3/2003) FL 7/1*
Leyton Orient *(Free on 8/8/2003) FL 34+20/3 FLC 1+1 FAC 2+2 Others 3*
Cambridge U *(Free on 21/1/2005) FL 15+1*

NEWMAN Richard (Ricky) Adrian
Born: Guildford, 5 August 1970
Height: 5'10" **Weight:** 12.6
Ricky warmed the substitutes' bench for Reading until the last quarter of the season, when he was drafted into the centre of midfield to add some much-needed steel to the heart of the team. Throughout the campaign, however, his attitude, whether on the bench, at the training ground, or as one of the older heads in the reserves, was exemplary. At the end of the campaign he was offered a role helping with the development of the younger players, but decided to leave Reading in search of first-team football elsewhere.
Crystal Palace *(From juniors on 22/1/1988) P/FL 43+5/3 FLC 5 FAC 5+2 Others 2*
Maidstone U *(Loaned on 28/2/1992) FL 9+1/1*
Millwall *(£500,000 on 19/7/1995) FL 144+6/5 FLC 11 FAC 5 Others 7*
Reading *(Free on 17/3/2000) FL 98+23/1 FLC 6 FAC 8/1 Others 1+1*

NEWSHAM Marc Anthony
Born: Hatfield, Yorks, 24 March 1987
Height: 5'10" **Weight:** 9.11
A product of the Rotherham United youth policy, this promising striker made a handful of appearances as substitute in the last few weeks of the season. He was a prolific scorer in both the reserves and juniors and his first-team experience should hold him in good stead as he looks to make an impact in 2005-06.
Rotherham U *(Trainee) FL 0+4*

NEWTON Adam Lee
Born: Grays, 4 December 1980
Height: 5'10" **Weight:** 11.6
Club Honours: FAYC '99
International Honours: St Kitts; E: U21-1
This speedy wide player was again used more as a defender than an attacker for Peterborough last term. When allowed to push forward and run with the ball at the opposition he is very effective and capable of unsettling any defence. Adam missed the closing stages of the campaign with an ankle injury, but will be hoping to be back in action for the start of the 2005-06 campaign.
West Ham U *(From trainee on 1/7/1999) PL 0+2 Others 0+1*
Portsmouth *(Loaned on 2/7/1999) FL 1+2 FLC 2*
Notts Co *(Loaned on 22/11/2000) FL 13+7/1 FAC 2*
Leyton Orient *(Loaned on 8/3/2002) FL 10/1*
Peterborough U *(Free on 8/7/2002) FL 86+17/4 FLC 1+1 FAC 5+2/1 Others 3+1*

NEWTON Shaun O'Neill
Born: Camberwell, 20 August 1975
Height: 5'8" **Weight:** 11.7
Club Honours: Div 1 '00
International Honours: E: U21-3
The attacking right-side midfielder scored for Wolves at Burnley early on last term and featured regularly in the first half of the season, occasionally appearing at right back. However, in the new year he was sold to West Ham. Shaun started out in defence for the Hammers but was switched to the wing with some success after a few games. In the play-offs he was full of effort and enthusiasm and his pace and sparkling runs lifted the side. Playing against Preston in the play-off final his probing runs caused no end of trouble and he was on hand to clear a goal-bound header off the line.
Charlton Ath *(From trainee on 1/7/1993) P/FL 189+51/20 FLC 19+1/3 FAC 11+6/2 Others 7+1/2*
Wolverhampton W *(£850,000 + on 8/8/2001) P/FL 115+15/12 FLC 5+2/1 FAC 8+1 Others 4+1*
West Ham U *(£10,000 on 11/3/2005) FL 11 Others 2+1*

N'GOTTY Bruno
Born: Lyon, France, 10 June 1971
Height: 6'1" **Weight:** 13.8
International Honours: France: 6; B-10
Another outstanding season saw Bruno voted Bolton's 'Player of the Year'. A constant at centre half, despite the considerable claims of Tal Ben Haim and Radhi Jaidi, Bruno produced consistent performances of an exceptionally high standard that were instrumental in helping Bolton to their first-ever European campaign. Also able to cover either full-back position when required, Bruno cemented his claim as one of the most influential players at the club. Surprisingly, he did not notch a single goal during the season, though it would be folly to let such a fact cloud what turned out to be a fine campaign.
Bolton W *(Signed from Marseilles, France, ex Lyon, Paris St Germain, AC Milan, Venezia, on 11/9/2001) PL 116+3/4 FLC 8+1/1 FAC 5*

NICHOLAS Andrew Peter
Born: Liverpool, 10 October 1983
Height: 6'2" **Weight:** 12.8
Andrew had a disappointing time at Swindon last term when he never really established himself in his accustomed left-back slot. He had a spell on loan at Chester when manager Ian Rush sought to stem the flood of goals conceded before returning to the County Ground where he was involved in the final three games of the season.
Swindon T *(From trainee at Liverpool on 21/7/2003) FL 36+11/1 FLC 1 FAC 1 Others 4+1/1*
Chester C *(Loaned on 18/3/2005) FL 5*

NICHOLLS Ashley Joseph
Born: Ipswich, 30 October 1981
Height: 5'11" **Weight:** 12.2
International Honours: E: Sch
Ashley was a regular for Cambridge United in the first half of last season, but lost his place following a change in management. However, he eventually earned a return to the line-up in March and featured in the closing fixtures. He is a fit, hard-working, tough-tackling

midfield player who has a good range of passing and also contributes the odd goal.
Ipswich T *(Free from Ipswich W on 5/7/2000)*
Darlington *(Free on 7/8/2002) FL 65+2/6 FLC 2+1 FAC 4/1 Others 2*
Cambridge U *(Free on 11/2/2004) FL 40+4/1 FLC 1 FAC 1 Others 1*

NICHOLLS Kevin John Richard
Born: Newham, 2 January 1979
Height: 6'0" **Weight:** 11.0
Club Honours: Div 1 '05
International Honours: E: Yth
Kevin was a model of consistency for Luton Town from the very first game of the 2004-05 season. The enthusiastic midfielder impressed with his tackling and his ability to develop attacking moves. The season was a memorable one for the club and one of Kevin's main contributions was the number of goals he scored either from dead-ball situations or from outside the box. A near ever-present in the line-up, he was one of six Hatters' players selected for the PFA League One team of the season.
Charlton Ath *(From trainee on 29/1/1996) FL 4+8/1 FLC 2+2*
Brighton & Hove A *(Loaned on 26/2/1999) FL 4/1*
Wigan Ath *(£250,000 + on 22/6/1999) FL 19+9 FLC 2 Others 4/1*
Luton T *(£25,000 + on 3/8/2001) FL 142+1/26 FLC 4/1 FAC 4/1 Others 1*

NICHOLSON Shane Michael
Born: Newark, 3 June 1970
Height: 5'10" **Weight:** 12.2
Club Honours: GMVC '88
Shane won over early doubters with a string of consistent displays at left back for Chesterfield last term, and he was rewarded with 'Player of the Season' awards from both the fans and his colleagues. As befits an experienced player his influence was just as huge off the field, where his openness about a chequered past has seen him become something of a model professional for Chesterfield's younger players.
Lincoln C *(From trainee on 19/7/1988) FL 122+11/7 FLC 8+3 FAC 4/1 Others 7+1*
Derby Co *(£100,000 on 22/4/1992) FL 73+1/1 FLC 4 FAC 4/1 Others 5*
West Bromwich A *(£150,000 on 9/2/1996) FL 50+2 FLC 4 FAC 2 Others 2*
Chesterfield *(Free on 21/8/1998) FL 23+1 Others 1*
Stockport Co *(Free on 4/6/1999) FL 73+4/3 FLC 3 FAC 3*
Sheffield U *(Free on 18/7/2001) FL 21+4/3 FLC 1*
Tranmere Rov *(Free on 17/7/2002) FL 45+9/6 FLC 1 FAC 2+3 Others 3+1/1*
Chesterfield *(Free on 2/7/2004) FL 42+1/7 FLC 1 FAC 1*

Antti Niemi

NICOLAS Alexis Peter
Born: Westminster, 13 February 1983
Height: 5'8" **Weight:** 10.6
International Honours: Cyprus: U21
Alexis joined Brighton on trial in July and impressed manager Mark McGhee enough to be taken on a three-month loan from Chelsea. The tough-tackling midfielder was outstanding in the early stages of the campaign, and was secured on a permanent, deal in October. Alexis suffered an ankle problem in the autumn and his form dipped a little, but a season of Championship football can only have improved his game and increased his experience. Always looking to harass his opponents and take the ball from them, Alexis also added to his tally of U21 caps for Cyprus during the season.
Aston Villa *(From trainee on 4/4/2001)*
Chelsea *(Free on 20/12/2001) PL 1+1 FAC 1*
Brighton & Hove A *(Signed on 6/8/2004) FL 29+4 FLC 1*

NICOLAU Nicky George
Born: St Pancras, 12 October 1983
Height: 5'8" **Weight:** 10.8
Club Honours: FAYC '01
Nicky signed for Southend permanently during the 2004 close season following a successful loan spell towards the end of the previous campaign. An attacking left back, he found himself replaced by the more defensive minded Che Wilson, but thereafter he frequently filled in on the left side of midfield following an injury to Mark Gower. The highlights of the season for Nicky came when he netted a cracking goal at Kidderminster and with a goal scored directly from a corner kick in the LDV Vans Trophy tie with Swindon Town.
Arsenal *(From trainee on 1/7/2002)*
Southend U *(Free on 25/3/2004) FL 24+7/1 FLC 1 Others 5+2/1*

NIEMI Antti
Born: Oulu, Finland, 31 May 1972
Height: 6'1" **Weight:** 13.9
Club Honours: SLC '99
International Honours: Finland: 66; U21-17; Yth
Regarded by many as the best goalkeeper in Saints' history it is difficult to find fault with his game, although he had a torrid season behind a defence that he had – evidently on occasions – lost faith in. If it were not for Antti Saints' chances of Premiership survival would not have lasted until the final game of the season: he consistently postponed the inevitable with a series of world-class performances.
Glasgow Rgrs *(Signed from FC Copenhagen, Denmark, ex HJK Helsinki, on 22/7/1997) SL 13 SLC 1 Others 7+1*
Heart of Midlothian *(£400,000 on 17/12/1999) SL 89 SLC 4 SC 9 Others 4*
Southampton *(£2,000,000 on 28/8/2002) PL 81 FLC 7 FAC 9 Others 1*

NILSSON Mikael
Born: Kristianstad, Sweden, 24 June 1978
Height: 5'10" **Weight:** 12.0
International Honours: Sweden: 25
A neat, skilful player, Mikael arrived at St Mary's during the summer of 2004. At his best, apparently, on the right of the midfield, he also featured at right wing back, but he failed to improve the side demonstrably in either position.
Southampton *(£500,000 from Halmstads, Sweden, ex IFK Gothenburg, on 1/7/2004) PL 12+4 FLC 3 FAC 2*

NIVEN Derek
Born: Falkirk, 12 December 1983
Height: 6'1" **Weight:** 11.2
Derek was the consistent hub of Chesterfield midfield last season, anchoring with determination and bringing others into the game with vision. His runs into space from midfield caused problems for the opposition but brought only one goal, albeit a real belter, against Torquay in March.

Derek Niven

Raith Rov *(From Stenhousemuir juniors on 10/7/2000) SL 0+1*
Bolton W *(Signed on 29/11/2001)*
Chesterfield *(Free on 12/12/2003) FL 60/2 FLC 1 FAC 1*

NOBLE David James
Born: Hitchin, 2 February 1982
Height: 6'0" **Weight:** 12.4
Club Honours: FAYC '00
International Honours: S: B-1; U21-2; E: Yth
This skilful central midfield player continued to gain experience with League Two club Boston United in 2004-05. David's passing ability was the key factor in his game and at times he showed great vision on the ball. Although injury kept him out for several weeks in the middle of the season he came back strongly and was soon back in the Pilgrims' starting line-up.
Arsenal *(From trainee on 13/3/2001)*
Watford *(Loaned on 10/7/2001) FL 5+10/1 FLC 3*
West Ham U *(Free on 31/1/2003) FL 0+3 FLC 1*
Boston U *(Free on 27/2/2004) FL 44+2/5 FLC 1 FAC 2+1/1*

NOBLE Mark James
Born: West Ham, 8 May 1987
Height: 5'11" **Weight:** 12.0
International Honours: E: Yth
After making a couple of substitute appearances this England youth international was given his first full outing for West Ham against Norwich City in the FA Cup. Mark was a breath of fresh air playing in the centre of midfield. He gave the whole side a lift with his exuberance and playmaking. He picked up a hamstring injury against Plymouth which forced him out for a month, but after returning he again starred as West Ham reached the play-offs. Mark deservedly won the 'Young Hammer of the Year' award.
West Ham U *(From trainee on 1/7/2004) FL 10+3 FLC 0+2 FAC 3 Others 0+3*

NOBLE Stuart William
Born: Edinburgh, 14 October 1983
Height: 6'0" **Weight:** 12.9
This young Fulham striker spent a month on loan at Torquay at the start of the 2004-05 campaign, during which he worked hard to lead the line but was unable to find the net. After resuming his place in the Premiership club's reserve side, Stuart went out on loan again in the new year, this time to Northampton Town. He showed some neat touches during his stay at Sixfields but returned early with an injury. He was released by Fulham in the summer.
Fulham *(From trainee on 25/8/2003)*
Torquay U *(Loaned on 24/8/2004) FL 2+1 FLC 1*
Northampton T *(Loaned on 3/2/2005) FL 0+4*

NOEL-WILLIAMS Gifton Ruben Elisha
Born: Islington, 21 January 1980
Height: 6'1" **Weight:** 14.6
Club Honours: Div 2 '98
International Honours: E: Yth
Although hampered by an arthritic condition Gifton was again a near ever-present in the starting line-up for Stoke City in 2004-05 and finished the campaign as the club's top scorer with a tally of 13 goals. Last term he spent time in midfield when manager Tony Pulis decided to play Ade Akinbiyi as a lone striker and his performances dipped, only to revive when Akinbiyi was sold. A haul of six goals from five games during March certainly revived his season. Gifton shows great persistence when holding up the ball waiting for the midfield to arrive and support the attack.
Watford *(From trainee on 13/2/1997) P/FL 107+62/33 FLC 10+2/3 FAC 10+2/5*
Stoke C *(Free on 29/5/2003) FL 81+7/23 FLC 1+1 FAC 1*

NOLAN Kevin Anthony Jance
Born: Liverpool, 24 June 1982
Height: 6'1" **Weight:** 13.5
International Honours: E: U21-1; Yth
Kevin began last season on the bench, such was the quality of the Bolton squad in their fourth consecutive Premiership campaign. He forced his way into the starting line-up at the beginning of September, when he proved to be the scourge of Manchester United by scoring against them yet again. Spending much of the season in the team, it was a disappointment when Kevin lost his place at the tail end of the season, largely due to the magnificent form of others. A combative central midfielder with an eye for goal, Kevin chipped in with four Premiership goals.
Bolton W *(From trainee on 22/1/2000) P/FL 138+38/23 FLC 7+3/2 FAC 7+7/3 Others 2*

NOLAN Matthew (Matt) Lee
Born: Hitchin, 25 February 1982
Height: 6'0" **Weight:** 12.0
This young Peterborough striker featured as a second-half substitute in the Carling Cup tie against Milton Keynes last August, but this proved to be his only first-team action for Posh during the campaign. Matt spent much of the season out on loan, firstly at St Albans City, then Ballymena United and finally at Cambridge City.
Peterborough U *(Signed from Hitchin T on 23/9/2003) FL 0+1 FLC 0+1*

NORRIS David Martin
Born: Stamford, 22 February 1981
Height: 5'7" **Weight:** 11.6
Club Honours: Div 2 '04
David is an extremely popular right-sided midfield player at Plymouth. His enthusiasm and hard work is infectious on his colleagues and he just never stops running. Last term his start to the season was halted by injury and unfortunately he missed the first five games. He chipped in with the odd goal including one in each of the Championship fixtures against Nottingham Forest.
Bolton W *(£50,000 from Boston U on 2/2/2000) FLC 3+1 FAC 1/1*
Hull C *(Loaned on 4/3/2002) FL 3+3/1*
Plymouth Arg *(Free on 8/10/2002) FL 104+9/14 FLC 1 FAC 4 Others 0+1*

NORRIS Robert (Rob) Paul
Born: Radcliffe-on-Trent, 12 October 1987
Height: 5'9" **Weight:** 10.3
This young right-sided midfield player became Boston United's youngest Football League player when he made his debut at the age of 17 in the home draw with Bristol Rovers. Rob, a regular in the club's reserve and youth teams, found it difficult to get into the game but looked much more confident in his subsequent appearances from the substitutes' bench. He was one of a number of youth-team players included in the Boston squad in the closing weeks of the season and will be looking to add to his experience in the campaign ahead.
Boston U *(Trainee) FL 1+1 FAC 0+1*

NORTH Daniel (Danny) Jamie
Born: Grimsby, 7 September 1987
Height: 5'9" **Weight:** 12.2
A product of the Grimsby Town youth set-up, Danny gave some impressive performances at youth and reserve-team level last season. The fast and powerful striker also occasionally featured on the senior bench and was given a brief debut in the away defeat at Bristol Rovers.
Grimsby T *(Trainee) FL 0+1*

NOSWORTHY Nyron Paul Henry
Born: Brixton, 11 October 1980
Height: 6'0" **Weight:** 12.0
This hard-working dynamic right back

was a regular for Gillingham throughout the 2004-05 season, apart from a brief absence through injury. However, Nyron was out of contract in the summer and after reportedly rejecting the offer of a new deal with the Gills he looked to be on his elsewhere during the summer.
Gillingham *(From trainee on 30/12/1998) FL 151+23/5 FLC 6+2/1 FAC 7+7 Others 1+2*

NOWLAND Adam Christopher
Born: Preston, 6 July 1981
Height: 5'11" **Weight:** 11.6
This cultured central midfielder started the 2004-05 season with West Ham, netting the winner against Burnley in August. However, after failing to establish himself in the line-up he was loaned to Gillingham in October, making three appearances and scoring a candidate for 'Goal of the Season' in the 2-1 defeat at Millwall. Soon after returning to Upton Park he was sold to Nottingham Forest but was then affected by hamstring problems and he did not feature in the side after mid-December.
Blackpool *(From trainee on 15/1/1999) FL 18+51/5 FLC 1+5/1 FAC 2+2/1 Others 0+2*
Wimbledon *(Signed on 29/6/2001) FL 35+21/5 FLC 2+1 FAC 2/2*
West Ham U *(£75,000 on 28/1/2004) FL 5+10/1 FLC 2*
Gillingham *(Loaned on 29/9/2004) FL 3/1*
Nottingham F *(£250,000 on 5/11/2004) FL 5 FAC 0+1*

NTIMBAN-ZEH Harry Dave
Born: France, 26 September 1973
Height: 6'1" **Weight:** 12.7
After impressing at the end of the previous season Harry was given a new contract for MK Dons and made 15 starts in the first four months of the 2004-05 season. A poor display at Tranmere in late November cost him his place though, and he was frozen out of the squad once new manager Danny Wilson took over. A right-sided central defender and very composed on the ball, Harry competed well but never looked completely comfortable with the more physical elements of League One football.
Wimbledon/MK Dons *(Signed from Sporting Club Espinho, Portugal, ex Racing Club Paris, on 8/3/2004) FL 20+1 FLC 2 FAC 1 Others 1+1*

N'TOYA-ZOA Tcham
Born: Kinshasa, DR Congo, 3 November 1983
Height: 5'10" **Weight:** 12.8
This explosive and unpredictable striker became a firm favourite at Chesterfield last term when he was the club's leading scorer with eight goals. He caused problems for opposition defences with his pace, control and muscular physique and as he gains more experience his somersaulting goal celebration is likely to be much more in evidence!
Chesterfield *(Free from Troyes, France on 25/3/2004) FL 21+23/8 FLC 1 FAC 0+1*

NUGENT David James
Born: Liverpool, 2 May 1985
Height: 5'11" **Weight:** 12.13
International Honours: E: Yth
David started the season with two goals in Bury's opening fixture of the season at home to Yeovil – and just carried on scoring. Always a player with good pace, skill and enthusiasm, he added physical strength to his game this season and reaped the rewards. He moved on to Preston in January where he was quickly promoted to a starting position alongside Richard Cresswell and the goals soon began to flow. A striker with blistering pace and excellent close control, David is a natural goal-scorer who likes to take chances early, and he finished the season with nine goals for North End.
Bury *(From trainee on 8/3/2003) FL 58+30/18 FLC 2+1 FAC 3+1/1 Others 3+4/1*
Preston NE *(Signed on 11/1/2005) FL 13+5/8 Others 3/1*

NUGENT Kevin Patrick
Born: Edmonton, 10 April 1969
Height: 6'1" **Weight:** 13.3
International Honours: RoI: Yth
Despite initially being given a free transfer, Kevin was later appointed as

David Nugent

Swansea City reserve-team manager with a playing contract, and by the start of the 2004-05 season he found himself in the starting line-up following injuries to Lee Trundle and James Thomas. His vast experience was evident as he led the line with authority and he netted some vital goals, however, cartilage problems saw him undergo surgery in mid-January leaving him sidelined for almost two months.

Leyton Orient *(From trainee on 8/7/1987) FL 86+8/20 FLC 9+3/6 FAC 9/3 Others 9+1/1*
Plymouth Arg *(£200,000 on 23/3/1992) FL 124+7/32 FLC 11/2 FAC 10/3 Others 5+3*
Bristol C *(Signed on 29/9/1995) FL 48+22/14 FLC 2+2 FAC 3+2/1 Others 2+1*
Cardiff C *(£65,000 on 4/8/1997) FL 94+5/29 FLC 8+1/1 FAC 9/6 Others 1+1/1*
Leyton Orient *(Free on 31/1/2002) FL 17+11/4 FLC 1/1 FAC 2 Others 1*
Swansea C *(Free on 17/1/2003) FL 53+20/16 FLC 1+1 FAC 2+3/2 Others 0+2/1*

NUNEZ Antonio

Born: Madrid, Spain, 15 January 1979
Height: 6'0" **Weight:** 12.2
Antonio arrived at Anfield in August as the make weight in the Michael Owen deal between Liverpool and Real Madrid. A right-sided midfielder he was an unknown quantity having only played as a substitute for the Spanish giants and he remained anonymous for several months at Anfield after falling foul of the club's injury hoodoo almost as soon as he arrived. After recovering from a knee injury he made his debut as a substitute against Arsenal in November and his first full appearance the following week. Antonio remained in the first-team squad for the rest of the season but without making much impact. His only goal came in the Carling Cup final against Chelsea, a consolation effort in Liverpool's 3-2 defeat in extra time.

Liverpool *(Signed from Real Madrid, Spain on 18/8/2004) PL 8+10 FLC 2+1/1 FAC 1 Others 2+3*

N'ZOGBIA Charles

Born: France, 28 May 1986
Height: 5'9" **Weight:** 11.0
This left-sided midfielder made his debut for Newcastle in the home game against Blackburn, appearing briefly as a substitute, but a dispute over his transfer meant he then had to wait until December before being cleared to play again. After three substitute appearances, including one at left back against Arsenal, his first start came against West Brom early in January and soon he was winning a regular place in the line-up. He improved with each match, being outstanding against Crystal Palace in April, when his twinkling footwork, accurate distribution, and purposeful play demonstrated why the club was so keen to sign him.

Newcastle U *(Signed from Le Havre, France on 3/9/2004) PL 8+6 FAC 1+1 Others 1+2*

Antonio Nunez

O

OAKES Andrew (Andy) Mark
Born: Northwich, 11 January 1977
Height: 6'4" **Weight:** 12.4
Andy started last season on loan from Derby to Bolton, arriving at the Reebok to challenge Kevin Poole as the pretender to Jussi Jaaskelainen's goalkeeping throne. He made just one appearance, in the home defeat against Aston Villa, when Jaaskelainen was suspended and then returned to Pride Park. It came as no surprise when he signed for Walsall in March and he went on to make a great impact for the Saddlers as he helped the team pull clear of the relegation zone.
Hull C *(Signed from Winsford U, ex Burnley trainee, trial with Bury, Macclesfield T, on 8/12/1998) FL 19 Others 1*
Derby Co *(£460,000 on 7/6/1999) P/FL 43 FLC 2 FAC 1*
Bolton W *(Loaned on 31/8/2004) PL 1*
Walsall *(Free on 18/3/2005) FL 9*

OAKES Michael Christian
Born: Northwich, 30 October 1973
Height: 6'2" **Weight:** 14.6
Club Honours: FLC '96
International Honours: E: U21-6
Michael started the 2004-05 season as understudy to Wolves' 'keeper Matt Murray before winning a recall to the line-up at West Ham in October. Although he briefly lost out to Murray in the new year he subsequently retained his place for the full campaign. He remains a fine shot-stopper, who prefers to stay on his line.
Aston Villa *(From juniors on 16/7/1991) PL 49+2 FLC 3 FAC 2 Others 5*
Scarborough *(Loaned on 26/11/1993) FL 1 Others 1*
Wolverhampton W *(£400,000 + on 29/10/1999) P/FL 182 FLC 9+1 FAC 9 Others 2*

OAKES Stefan Trevor
Born: Leicester, 6 September 1978
Height: 5'11" **Weight:** 12.4
Club Honours: FLC '00
Stefan was the midfield playmaker in the Notts County side last term and once he had established his presence in the side he became one of the key elements in the team. He showed that he possesses as sweet a left foot as anyone in the lower divisions, delivering match-winning passes and scoring a number of spectacular goals, including a cracking 40-yard effort at Yeovil. At the time of writing it appeared that he would be moving on to new pastures for the start of the 2005-06 campaign.
Leicester C *(From trainee on 3/7/1997) P/FL 39+25/2 FLC 7+1/2 FAC 5+2*
Crewe Alex *(Loaned on 17/3/2003) FL 3+4*
Walsall *(Free on 18/7/2003) FL 1+4*
Notts Co *(Free on 17/2/2004) FL 42+3/5 FLC 0+1 FAC 2+1/1*

OAKLEY Matthew (Matt)
Born: Peterborough, 17 August 1977
Height: 5'10" **Weight:** 12.1
International Honours: E: U21-4
Matt spent most of the season recovering from a cruciate ligament injury sustained in September 2003, with a few setbacks in the meantime. None of the four managers incumbent at St Mary's since his injury managed to find an adequate replacement and there must have been some relief among the coaching staff when he began to make fleeting appearances in the first team from December. He was used sparingly in the second half of the campaign, and showed glimpses of his old form, which augers well for the 2005-06 season.
Southampton *(From trainee on 1/7/1995) PL 209+23/12 FLC 21+2/2 FAC 20+3/4 Others 1*

OATWAY Anthony Philip David Terry Frank Donald Stanley Gerry Gordon Stephen James **(Charlie)**
Born: Hammersmith, 28 November 1973
Height: 5'7" **Weight:** 10.10
Club Honours: Div 3 '99, '01; Div 2 '02
Charlie missed a few games for Brighton early on because of a hamstring injury, but was otherwise a regular in the side that battled successfully to remain in the Championship. Always harrying opponents and snapping at their heels, Charlie's game is one of non-stop running and chasing in an effort to win the ball for his more constructive colleagues. What he lacks in skill he makes up for with enthusiasm and leadership, and in December he was handed the captain's armband in the wake of Danny Cullip's departure. Charlie has matured in his six years at the Withdean Stadium and largely learned to control his combativeness. He can look back on the season with contentment, having been rewarded with an extension to his contract.
Cardiff C *(Free from Yeading on 4/8/1994) FL 29+3 FLC 2/1 FAC 1+1 Others 2*
Torquay U *(Free on 28/12/1995) FL 65+2/1 FLC 3 FAC 1*
Brentford *(£10,000 on 21/8/1997) FL 37+20 FLC 1+2/1 FAC 4 Others 0+1*
Lincoln C *(Loaned on 21/10/1998) FL 3*
Brighton & Hove A *(£10,000 on 9/7/1999) FL 183+23/8 FLC 8 FAC 11/1 Others 5*

O'BRIEN Andrew (Andy) James
Born: Harrogate, 29 June 1979
Height: 6'3" **Weight:** 12.4
International Honours: RoI: 21; U21-8; E: U21-1; Yth
After missing the season opener with an eye infection Andy played regularly at the centre of Newcastle's back four until a hamstring injury sidelined him in November. Although not a prolific scorer, he found the net in successive games at Villa and at home to Blackburn during this time. The arrival of Jean-Alain Boumsong in January increased competition for places, but Andy kept his place for most of the rest of the season, occasionally featuring at right back. He continued to represent the Republic of Ireland team at international level, delivering an outstanding performance in the World Cup qualifier against Cyprus in September and scoring his first goal for his country against Portugal in February.
Bradford C *(From trainee on 28/10/1996) P/FL 113+20/3 FLC 5 FAC 8 Others 4*
Newcastle U *(£2,000,000 on 28/3/2001) PL 114+6/6 FLC 4+1 FAC 7+3/1 Others 32+5*

O'BRIEN Joseph (Joey) Martin
Born: Dublin, 17 February 1986
Height: 6'2" **Weight:** 12.2
International Honours: RoI: U21-3; Yth
A graduate of the Bolton youth set-up, Joey made his first-team debut as a substitute in the Carling Cup victory at Yeovil. He then spent a very productive three months on loan at Sheffield Wednesday, scoring on his debut against Hull City. His output, skill and endeavour endeared him to the fans and he became an integral part of the Owls' midfield, also earning a call-up to the Republic of Ireland U21 squad. On his return to the Reebok Joey was rewarded with his first Premiership appearance, again as a substitute, in the final game of the season against Everton.
Bolton W *(From trainee on 17/11/2004) PL 0+1 FLC 0+1*
Sheffield Wed *(Loaned on 3/12/2004) FL 14+1/2*

O'BRIEN Roy Joseph
Born: Cork, 27 November 1974
Height: 6'1" **Weight:** 12.4
Club Honours: NC '03; Div 2 '05
International Honours: RoI: Yth; Sch
This cultured Yeovil Town defender played in a number of the early-season fixtures before losing his place and moving out on loan to Weymouth. However, he only featured a couple more times after his return. Roy is a steady reliable player who is well liked by the fans at Huish Park.

Arsenal *(From trainee on 6/7/1993)*
Bournemouth *(Free on 23/8/1996) FL 1 (Freed on 18/12/1996)*
Yeovil T *(Free from Dorchester T on 8/8/2000) FL 23+4 FLC 2+1 FAC 0+1 Others 1*

O'CONNOR Garreth

Born: Dublin, 10 November 1978
Height: 5'7" **Weight:** 11.0
This Bournemouth midfielder came on in leaps and bounds during the 2004-05 season, scoring 14 goals and winning all the club's 'Player of the Year' awards. Garreth's contribution to the team was immense thanks to his fine consistency and he was sorely missed when he was sidelined for a short spell through injury at the end of the campaign.
Bournemouth *(Free from Bohemians on 5/6/2000) FL 109+59/24 FLC 4+2/1 FAC 14+4/1 Others 11+1/2*

O'CONNOR James Francis Edward

Born: Birmingham, 20 November 1984
Height: 5'10" **Weight:** 12.5
Club Honours: FAYC '02
This stocky defender began last season with Aston Villa reserves but then spent three months on loan at Port Vale. He made a promising debut in the 2-0 victory at Bradford City and kept his place in the side. A good tackler, he always gave 100 per cent and when his loan spell was over, Vale tried to make the move a permanent one. Later he had a spell at Bournemouth where he began at right back before switching to centre half. The move was a success and James signed permanent forms for the Cherries, but missed the final stages of the campaign with a groin injury.
Aston Villa *(From trainee on 24/4/2004)*
Port Vale *(Loaned on 3/9/2004) FL 13 Others 2*
Bournemouth *(Free on 18/2/2005) FL 6*

O'CONNOR James Kevin

Born: Dublin, 1 September 1979
Height: 5'8" **Weight:** 11.6
Club Honours: AMC '00
International Honours: RoI: U21-9; Yth
Lacking first-team opportunities at West Bromwich, James joined Burnley on loan

Kevin O'Connor (left)

in October, making his first start in the Clarets' 2-1 victory at Leeds. A hard-working player, he rarely stopped running and was constantly involved in the action from his midfield position. He returned to the Hawthorns in January but was back at Turf Moor on a permanent basis in March, marking his debut as a full-time Claret with a goal in the home victory against Watford. His sheer application to the cause ensures appreciation, and he scored again with a superb solo effort in the final home match against Plymouth.
Stoke C *(From trainee on 5/9/1996) FL 176/16 FLC 9/3 FAC 8+1 Others 16+1/3*
West Bromwich A *(Signed on 8/8/2003) P/FL 27+3 FLC 5+1 FAC 1+1*
Burnley *(Loaned on 29/10/2004) FL 12+1*
Burnley *(£175,000 on 24/3/2005) FL 8/2*

O'CONNOR Kevin Patrick
Born: Blackburn, 24 February 1982
Height: 5'11" **Weight:** 12.0
International Honours: RoI: U21-6
Kevin started the 2004-05 season on the Brentford bench but came on against Wrexham in August, to score with a stunning right-foot volley from the edge of the box. The following month he took over the right-back role from the injured Michael Dobson and went from strength to strength keeping the position until the end of the season, apart from a two-month absence due to a foot injury in December. Kevin also captained the side on a few occasions and was voted 'Most Improved Player of the Season' by the fans.
Brentford *(From trainee on 4/3/2000) FL 136+31/9 FLC 5+1/3 FAC 11+2/2 Others 5+5/1*

O'CONNOR Martin John
Born: Walsall, 10 December 1967
Height: 5'9" **Weight:** 11.8
International Honours: Cayman Islands: 2
This veteran midfield general also held a coaching role with Shrewsbury Town last term, but was used sparingly at first-team level and often featured on the bench. At his best he is a very busy player in the middle of the park, breaking down attacks and using the ball wisely, involving other players around him. He was released by the Gay Meadow club in the summer.
Crystal Palace *(£25,000 from Bromsgrove Rov on 26/6/1992) FL 2 Others 1+1*
Walsall *(Loaned on 24/3/1993) FL 10/1 Others 2/1*
Walsall *(£40,000 on 14/2/1994) FL 94/21 FLC 6/2 FAC 10/2 Others 3/1*
Peterborough U *(£350,000 on 12/7/1996) FL 18/3 FLC 4 FAC 2*
Birmingham C *(£500,000 + on 29/11/1996) FL 181+6/16 FLC 22+1/3 FAC 7 Others 6*
Walsall *(Free on 8/2/2002) FL 45+3/2 FLC 2 FAC 3*
Shrewsbury T *(Free on 9/8/2003) FL 13+8 FAC 1*

ODEJAYI Olukayode (Kay)
Born: Ibadon, Nigeria, 21 February 1982
Height: 6'2" **Weight:** 12.2
This tall and very quick striker continued to promise much at Cheltenham, but by his own admission, the fulfilment of that promise has yet to fully materialise. He scored his only first-team goal of the season in the opening match against Southend United and spent the majority of the campaign being used as a substitute. His pace and heading ability marked him out as an impact player to be used in the closing minutes of games against tired defences.
Bristol C *(From trainee on 17/7/2000) FL 0+6 Others 1 (Free to Forest Green Rov on 28/9/2002)*
Cheltenham T *(£25,000 on 5/6/2003) FL 24+38/6 FLC 1+1 FAC 0+2 Others 0+1*

O'DONNELL Stephen James
Born: Bellshill, 10 July 1983
Height: 6'0" **Weight:** 11.2
Stephen found himself out of favour at SPL club Dundee United last term, but impressed during a week spent training with Boston United in October. This combative central midfield player with a reputation for scoring goals returned to sign for the Lincolnshire club during the January transfer window. He made his Boston debut in the win at Wycombe but managed only one more start as he struggled to adapt to League Two football. Stephen spent most of the remainder of the season warming the substitutes' bench and was only rarely called in to action. He was not offered a new contract at the end of the campaign.
Dundee U *(From juniors on 1/8/2001) SL 7+10 SLC 1+1/3 SC 0+1/1*
Ross Co *(Loaned on 1/7/2003) SL 14+10/3 SLC 0+1 SC 1 Others 1+2*
Boston U *(Free on 31/1/2005) FL 2+2*

ODUBADE Yemi
Born: Lagos, Nigeria, 4 July 1984
Height: 5'7" **Weight:** 11.7
This lightning quick right-sided striker joined Yeovil Town in the summer of 2004. Yemi went on to make his debut for the Glovers from the bench in the LDV Vans Trophy tie and featured in three more games from the bench, scoring in the FA Cup first round tie against Histon. However, having failed to settle at Huish Park he moved on to Eastbourne Borough in February, netting a hat-trick on his home debut for the Conference South club.
Yeovil T *(Free from Eastbourne U on 30/7/2004) FL 0+4 FAC 0+1/1 Others 0+1*

O'GRADY Christopher (Chris) James
Born: Nottingham, 25 January 1986
Height: 6'1" **Weight:** 12.8
International Honours: E: Yth
This exciting young Leicester City striker spent most of last season developing in the club's reserve side. He had a loan spell with Notts County in the autumn to gain experience of first-team football and featured regularly in the Magpies' first-team squad. He proved to be a big strong forward who is very effective behind the front two, holding up the ball well and delivering accurate passes, however, he returned to Leicester at the turn of the year to continue his development and featured as an unused substitute in the final game of the season against Plymouth.
Leicester C *(From trainee on 3/8/2004) FL 0+1*
Notts Co *(Loaned on 24/9/2004) FL 3+6 FAC 0+1 Others 1*

O'HALLORAN Matthew (Matt) Vincent
Born: Nottingham, 18 November 1982
Height: 5'10" **Weight:** 11.6
This hard-working youngster was given few chances on the right side of Boston United's midfield but produced one of the club's moments of the season. His 35-yard stoppage-time winner against Scunthorpe United at York Street was both speculative and spectacular and will live long in the memories of the Pilgrims' supporters. Matt made just a handful of first-team starts and never made it off the substitutes' bench after Christmas. He moved on to non-league King's Lynn at the end of February.
Derby Co *(From trainee on 16/7/2002)*
Oldham Ath *(Free on 16/8/2003) FL 2+11/1 FLC 0+1 FAC 0+1 Others 1+1*
Chesterfield *(Free on 11/12/2003) FL 1+2*
Boston U *(Free on 6/8/2004) FL 5+3/1 FAC 0+1 Others 0+1*

O'HANLON Sean Philip
Born: Southport, 2 January 1983
Height: 6'1" **Weight:** 12.5
International Honours: E: Yth
Sean had an outstanding season with Swindon Town last term, when he blossomed into an effective central defender. Tall, quick and strong his increasingly mature performances saw

Jay Jay Okocha

him rewarded with the captain's armband for a number of games. He was used almost exclusively as a central defender, but can also play at right back and on one occasion last season he turned out in a midfield role, capping a fine performance against Bournemouth with a goal.
Everton *(From trainee on 26/2/2000)*
Swindon T *(£150,000 on 23/1/2004) FL 57+2/5 FLC 1+1 FAC 3/1 Others 3+1*

O'HARE Alan Patrick James
Born: Drogheda, 31 July 1982
Height: 6'2" **Weight:** 12.2
Alan had something of a testing season at Chesterfield last term after losing his place to Shane Nicholson, but his professionalism shone like a beacon. He remained focussed and never complained. Aside from his obvious ability, his loyalty and work ethic commands respect from players and fans alike.
Bolton W *(From trainee on 24/11/2001)*
Chesterfield *(Loaned on 25/1/2002) FL 19*
Chesterfield *(Free on 9/10/2002) FL 72+11/1 FLC 2 FAC 1 Others 5*

OKOCHA Augustine (Jay Jay) Azuka
Born: Enugu, Nigeria, 14 August 1973
Height: 5'7" **Weight:** 11.2
International Honours: Nigeria
Jay Jay delighted his huge army of Bolton fans by signing new contract with the club prior to the start of last season. He subsequently began the campaign in inspired form, scoring three goals during the first three games. A groin injury picked up at the end of September led to Jay Jay missing a few games, and the injury seemed to coincide with a loss of form upon his return to the side. By his own admission Jay Jay was suffering from tiredness towards the end of the season, although he still ended the campaign with six Premiership goals. A player of sublime and immeasurable skill and ability, he will be hoping to return a fresher player when the new campaign begins, once again wowing crowds with his endless box of tricks.
Bolton W *(Free from Paris St Germain, France, ex Enugu R, B.Nuenkirchen, Eintracht Frankfurt, Fenerbahce, on 3/8/2002) PL 38+9/13 FLC 6+1/4 FAC 1+1*

O'LEARY Kristian Denis
Born: Port Talbot, 30 August 1977
Height: 6'0" **Weight:** 13.4
Club Honours: Div 3 '00
International Honours: W: Yth
Kristian was given a surprise midfield role for Swansea last term, featuring alongside Roberto Martinez. He scored his first goal for four seasons in the FA Cup tie at Cheltenham in November, while his match-winning goal at the Vetch Field against Oxford United set the Swans up for the final push for an automatic promotion place. The positional move was clearly a success for at the end of the campaign he was chosen as the Swans' 'Player of the Year'.
Swansea C *(From trainee on 1/7/1996) FL 202+33/8 FLC 10 FAC 12+2/1 Others 9+2*

O'LEARY Stephen Michael
Born: Barnet, 12 February 1985
Height: 5'10" **Weight:** 11.8
Club Honours: Div 1 '05
International Honours: RoI: Yth
Stephen was a regular in the line-up for Luton in the early stages of the 2004-05 campaign, but then lost his place and was mostly on the fringes of the squad in the second half of the campaign. A versatile midfield player who is comfortable in the centre or on the right-hand side, his only League goal came in the 5-1 win over Wrexham back in November. Stephen was a member of the Hatters' reserve team that defeated Reading to win the Pontin's Combination League Cup.
Luton T *(From trainee on 3/8/2004) FL 15+7/2 FAC 2 Others 2*

OLI Dennis Chiedozie
Born: Newham, 28 January 1984
Height: 6'0" **Weight:** 12.4
This tall striker signed a monthly contract for Swansea during the summer of 2004, but his only first-team appearance came as a substitute in the opening fixture of the season against Northampton. Soon after being released he joined Cambridge United on another short-term deal, getting off to a bright start with a goal on his debut against Mansfield. However, the U's inability to offer him a longer contract saw him move on to Grays Athletic, for whom he starred in their successes in the Conference South and FA Trophy.
Queens Park Rgrs *(From juniors on 24/10/2001) FL 8+15 FLC 0+1 FAC 1+2 Others 2+1*
Swansea C *(Free on 6/8/2004) FL 0+1*
Cambridge U *(Free on 9/9/2004) FL 4/1 Others 1*

OLIVEIRA Filipe
Born: Braga, Portugal, 27 May 1984
Height: 5'10" **Weight:** 11.2
International Honours: Portugal: U21; Yth
In danger of becoming lost in Chelsea's star-studded midfield Filipe went on loan to promotion-chasing Preston North End over the Christmas and New Year period to gain some urgently-needed first-team experience and acquitted himself very well, showing great pace on the ball and excellent vision in one so young. His involvement with Chelsea was confined to the last five minutes of the Premiership season as a substitute at Newcastle. He currently faces very stiff opposition in his bid to claim a regular place at Stamford Bridge.
Chelsea *(£140,000 from FC Porto, Portugal on 11/9/2001) PL 0+5 FLC 0+1 FAC 0+1 Others 0+1*
Preston NE *(Loaned on 16/12/2004) FL 1+4*

OLOFINJANA Seyi George
Born: Lagos, Nigeria, 30 June 1980
Height: 6'4" **Weight:** 11.10
International Honours: Nigeria
Seyi was the main summer arrival at Molineux but took a short while to acclimatise to the requirements of the English game. He showed glimpses of his potential on his debut, but it was well into the season before he achieved real consistency. Seyi is a high-energy player who can adapt well to all the midfield roles. A near ever-present during the campaign, he was brilliant in the 2-1 win at Reading, when his tackling, distribution and passing all came together.
Wolverhampton W *(£1,700,000 from SK Brann Bergen, Norway on 6/8/2004) FL 41+1/5 FLC 1+1 FAC 2*

O'NEIL Brian
Born: Paisley, 6 September 1972
Height: 6'1" **Weight:** 12.4
International Honours: S: 6; U21-7; Yth; Sch
An experienced hand in Preston's midfield, Brian had an excellent campaign as the pick-up man just in front of the defence. After a summer operation, he gradually built up his fitness and stamina and his efforts during a game gave little indication that the passing years were taking a toll. He can play both simple passes and raking balls to pick out colleagues some distance away, and his ability to make room for himself is an excellent example to the younger players at the club. Brian supplemented these gifts with three goals, all of them excellent and important strikes, and earned a surprise recall to the Scotland squad as fitting reward for a consistent season.
Glasgow Celtic *(Free from Porirua Viard U on 10/7/1991) SL 92+27/8 SLC 6+4/1 SC 10/9 Others 8+3/1*
Nottingham F *(Loaned on 18/3/1997) PL 4+1*

Aberdeen *(Free on 3/7/1997) SL 24+4/1 SLC 4 SC 1 (Transferred to Wolfsburg, Germany on 23/7/1998)*
Derby Co *(Signed on 16/11/2000) P/FL 14+3 FLC 1+1 FAC 2*
Preston NE *(Free on 3/1/2003) FL 79+8/4 FLC 3 FAC 3/1 Others 3*

O'NEIL Gary Paul

Born: Bromley, 18 May 1983
Height: 5'10" **Weight:** 11.0
Club Honours: Div 1 '03
International Honours: E: U21-6; Yth
Gary made a couple of first-team appearances for Pompey early on last season before going out on loan to Cardiff at the end of September. His arrival coincided with the Bluebirds' first away win of the season and he transformed the club's play during his short stay at Ninian Park, scoring a superb goal at Millwall. Back at Fratton Park Gary finally began to hold down a first-team place following a change in management and showed that he has the temperament for the big occasion by scoring with a stunning volley at Old Trafford in February. A central midfielder, Gary also captained England U21s during the campaign.
Portsmouth *(From trainee on 5/6/2000) P/FL 69+33/9 FLC 6+3 FAC 3+1*
Walsall *(Loaned on 26/9/2003) FL 7*
Cardiff C *(Loaned on 24/9/2004) FL 8+1/1*

Brian O'Neil

O'NEILL Joseph (Joe)

Born: Blackburn, 28 October 1982
Height: 6'0" **Weight:** 10.12
This tall striker had a spell on loan at Mansfield early on last season to gain more experience of senior football, but made most of his appearances from the bench. On his return to Deepdale he was given his first taste of League action for North End when he featured as a substitute and he went on to make his full debut in the FA Cup tie against West Brom. Joe went out loan again in January, this time to Chester where he scored in his second start against Rushden but otherwise made little real impression.
Preston NE *(From trainee on 2/7/2002) FL 0+2 FAC 1*
Bury *(Loaned on 8/7/2003) FL 10+13/3 FLC 0+1 FAC 0+1 Others 1+1*
Mansfield T *(Loaned on 6/8/2004) FL 3+12 Others 2*
Chester C *(Loaned on 27/1/2005) FL 5+6/1*

O'NEILL Matthew (Matt) Paul

Born: Accrington, 25 June 1984
Height: 5'11" **Weight:** 10.9
A regular on the Burnley bench, particularly in the first half of the season, winger Matt was never given the opportunity to develop the promise previously shown and was loaned out to neighbouring Accrington Stanley where he achieved first-team recognition. He was released from Turf Moor at the end of the season.
Burnley *(From trainee on 2/7/2003) FL 2+11*

ONIBUJE Folawiyo (Fola)

Born: Lagos, Nigeria, 25 September 1984
Height: 6'5" **Weight:** 14.9
This tall striker found it hard to break into the Barnsley first team last season and he was restricted to a couple of outings from the substitutes' bench. During February and early March he had trial spells at Shrewsbury and Mansfield before his contract was cancelled by mutual consent. On transfer-deadline day he signed for Peterborough on a non-contract basis and added a couple more appearances from the bench.
Preston NE *(From Charlton Ath juniors on 13/11/2002)*
Huddersfield T *(Loaned on 21/11/2003) FL 0+2*
Barnsley *(Free on 21/7/2004) FL 0+3 FAC 0+1*
Peterborough U *(Free on 24/3/2005) FL 0+2*

ONUOHA Chinedum (Nedum)
Born: Warri, Nigeria, 12 November 1986
Height: 6'2" **Weight:** 12.4
International Honours: E: Yth
Quick and powerful, this young defender broke through into the first-team ranks at Manchester City last term, thanks to injuries and suspensions to more senior members of the squad. His meteoric rise ensured he was given a new improved contract and he was voted as the club's 'Young Player of the Year'. Nedum celebrated his call up to England's U20 side with a goal in the 2-1 win over Russia at Charlton in February.
***Manchester C** (From trainee on 16/11/2004) PL 11+6 FLC 1*

OPARA Junior **Lloyd**
Born: Enfield, 6 January 1984
Height: 6'1" **Weight:** 13.0
A strong, pacy striker, Lloyd sought to resurrect his Football League career at Swindon last term. He made one appearance in the first round of the Carling Cup at Rushden but was then released from his contract during September. Lloyd subsequently joined St Albans City and later featured for Bishop's Stortford and Redbridge before the end of the season.
***Colchester U** (Trainee) FL 0+6 FLC 0+1 FAC 0+1 Others 0+1*
***Cambridge U** (Free from trainee on 28/4/2003) FL 1+9/1 Others 1 (Freed on 22/10/2003)*
***Swindon T** (Free from Grays Ath, ex Braintree, Hornchurch, on 14/7/2004) FLC 1*

ORMEROD Brett Ryan
Born: Blackburn, 18 October 1976
Height: 5'11" **Weight:** 11.4
Club Honours: AMC '02
Featuring only fitfully in the early stages of the season, and with Dexter Blackstock emerging dramatically into first-team contention, Brett's senior opportunities at St Mary's were limited, and he was loaned to Leeds United in September. The striker had a tough time on his debut for the Whites against Sunderland and failed to score during his spell at Elland Road. Later on he was more impressive during a loan spell at Wigan where he netted twice in the win at Leicester. Returning to St Mary's, and with Peter Crouch suspended, Brett was picked to partner Henri Camara for the season's swansong against Manchester United, Saints needing a win to have any hope of Premiership survival. Brett put in a lot of heart and effort, characteristics of his game, but the match, and Saints' top-flight status, was lost.
***Blackpool** (£50,000 from Accrington Stanley on 21/3/1997) FL 105+23/45 FLC 8/4 FAC 5+1/5 Others 7+2/8*
***Southampton** (£1,750,000 on 7/12/2001) PL 49+31/11 FLC 6/5 FAC 5+4/1*
***Leeds U** (Loaned on 23/9/2004) FL 6*
***Wigan Ath** (Loaned on 18/3/2005) FL 3+3/2*

ORR Bradley James
Born: Liverpool, 1 November 1982
Height: 6'0" **Weight:** 11.12
Bradley joined Bristol City during the summer of 2004 and featured regularly in the squad throughout the campaign, starting in exactly half the club's League One fixtures. A dependable, battling, wholehearted midfielder, he will be looking to build on this promising start in the 2005-06 campaign.
***Newcastle U** (From trainee on 12/7/2001)*
***Burnley** (Loaned on 29/1/2004) FL 1+3*
***Bristol C** (Free on 30/7/2004) FL 23+14 FLC 2 FAC 2 Others 1*

Brett Ormerod

OSBORN Simon Edward
Born: Croydon, 19 January 1972
Height: 5'9" **Weight:** 11.4
In a mixed season at Walsall last term, Simon struggled a little in the early stages while trying to combine a coaching role with his position as a player. He generally played in midfield, just in front of the central defenders and his crunching tackles were a feature of his game. Simon played on for several games with a toe injury and did well enough to earn a further contract at Bescot Stadium.
Crystal Palace *(From trainee on 3/1/1990) P/FL 47+8/5 FLC 11/1 FAC 2 Others 1+3*
Reading *(£90,000 on 17/8/1994) FL 31+1/5 FLC 4 Others 3*
Queens Park Rgrs *(£1,100,000 on 7/7/1995) PL 6+3/1 FLC 2*
Wolverhampton W *(£1,000,000 on 22/12/1995) FL 151+11/11 FLC 7/3 FAC 11+1 Others 2*
Tranmere Rov *(Free on 22/3/2001) FL 9/1*
Port Vale *(Free on 7/9/2001) FL 7 FLC 1*
Gillingham *(Free on 12/10/2001) FL 38+8/5 FAC 2+1*
Walsall *(Free on 18/7/2003) FL 71+10/3 FLC 2 FAC 2 Others 2*

OSBORNE Junior
Born: Watford, 12 February 1988
Height: 5'10" **Weight:** 12.3
Junior, a 17-year-old Watford Academy scholar, made his first-team debut as a second-half substitute in the last match of the season. A local lad, Junior can play anywhere in the defence and is well-built and quick with a good first touch.
Watford *(Trainee) FL 0+1*

OSBORNE Karleigh Anthony Jonathan
Born: Southall, 19 March 1988
Height: 6'2" **Weight:** 12.8
One of several promising scholars on the books at Brentford, Karleigh stepped up to make his first-team debut in the final game of the season against Hull City. A big strong lad he played at centre back and then in the holding role in midfield during the game. He will be looking to gain more senior experience at the club in 2005-06.
Brentford *(Trainee) FL 1*

OSBOURNE Isaac Samuel
Born: Birmingham, 22 June 1986
Height: 5'10" **Weight:** 11.12
This young Coventry City midfielder played a handful of games last term when injuries or suspension affected senior players. He always gave 100 per cent and was not afraid of getting stuck in with the Championship's top players. Isaac's promise was recognised when he

Isaac Osbourne

was voted as the Sky Blues' 'Young Player of the Season'.
Coventry C *(From trainee on 10/7/2003) FL 9+2*

OSEI-KUFFOUR Jonathan (Jo)
Born: Edmonton, 17 November 1981
Height: 5'7" **Weight:** 10.6
Club Honours: FAYC '00
A frustrating season of niggling injuries saw Jo struggle to build on the excellent progress of the previous season, although he still managed eight goals in league and cup. He was often deployed on the left wing rather than in his preferred central striking role where his speed and trickery can create more direct results.
Arsenal *(From trainee on 18/7/2000)*
Swindon T *(Loaned on 24/8/2001) FL 4+7/2 FLC 1 Others 1*
Torquay U *(Free on 18/10/2002) FL 77+28/21 FLC 2/1 FAC 1+1/1 Others 2+1/1*

O'SHEA John Francis
Born: Waterford, 30 April 1981
Height: 6'3" **Weight:** 11.12
Club Honours: PL '03; CS '03; FAC '04
International Honours: RoI: 24; U21-13; Yth (UEFA-U16 '98)
A highly talented young central defender who possesses presence, great composure and silky defensive skills, John continued to make his mark in the Manchester United first team with some solid performances throughout an exciting campaign. After a consistent start to the season, playing in seven of the Reds opening eight Premiership games, John was missing throughout most of October and November, although he made starts in all but one of United's Carling Cup games. On the goal front, he notched his first Premiership goal in 12 months against Crystal Palace in December. Another effort in the FA Cup fourth round against Middlesborough in January was followed by a decisive strike in United's emphatic 4-2 victory over Arsenal at Highbury in the Premiership in February, a result that all but put paid to the defending champions' reign.
Manchester U *(Signed from Waterford U on 2/9/1998) PL 78+19/4 FLC 13 FAC 10+1/1 Others 24+9*
Bournemouth *(Loaned on 18/1/2000) FL 10/1 Others 1*

OSMAN Leon
Born: Billinge, 17 May 1981
Height: 5'8" **Weight:** 11.0
Club Honours: FAYC '98
International Honours: E: Yth; Sch
Leon's first full season in the top-flight was a success. A technically gifted midfielder, who can pass the ball adroitly, he has the happy knack of scoring vital goals. During Everton's successful Premiership campaign he netted late winners in home matches against West Brom, Southampton and Portsmouth as well as two in a fine individual and team performance at Villa Park. He coped well with the physical demands of the game, but his small frame means that he can be injury prone and as a result he struggled on occasions after Christmas. Leon spent most of the season playing in a wide-right position where his good, quick feet meant that he could find space when it was at a premium.
Everton *(From trainee on 18/8/1998) PL 27+8/7 FLC 2+2 FAC 3/1*
Carlisle U *(Loaned on 4/10/2002) FL 10+2/1 Others 3/2*
Derby Co *(Loaned on 26/1/2004) FL 17/3*

OSTER John Morgan
Born: Boston, 8 December 1978
Height: 5'9" **Weight:** 10.8
International Honours: W: 13; B-1; U21-9; Yth
This tricky right winger started last season in the Sunderland first team but was allowed to join Leeds United on loan in November. He gave shot-shy United an extra dimension, operating on the right side of midfield and enjoyed a sparkling debut in the 4-2 win at Preston in November. His only goal came in his final game – a 1-1 draw with Millwall at Elland Road – before he was sent back to Sunderland. He later signed for Burnley, where he proved to have plenty of flair and to be a real crowd pleaser when on form. However, he finished the season on the bench and was released at the end of his short-term contract.
Grimsby T *(From trainee on 11/7/1996) FL 21+3/3 FAC 0+1/1*
Everton *(£1,500,000 on 21/7/1997) PL 22+18/1 FLC 4+1/1 FAC 2+3/1*
Sunderland *(£1,000,000 on 6/8/1999) P/FL 48+20/5 FLC 9+2/1 FAC 7+3 Others 2*
Barnsley *(Loaned on 19/10/2001) FL 2*
Grimsby T *(Loaned on 1/11/2002) FL 10/5*
Grimsby T *(Loaned on 21/2/2003) FL 7/1*
Leeds U *(Loaned on 5/11/2004) FL 8/1*
Burnley *(Free on 28/1/2005) FL 12+3/1 FAC 2+1*

OTSEMOBOR John
Born: Liverpool, 23 March 1983
Height: 5'10" **Weight:** 12.7
International Honours: E: Yth
This young Liverpool full back made his Crewe debut against Watford at Crewe last October after arriving at Gresty Road for an extended loan spell. He was a regular during his three months at the club, scoring his only goal in the 2-2 draw against Leicester. John returned to Anfield when his loan had finished and was released by the Reds in the summer.
Liverpool *(From trainee on 23/3/2000) PL 4 FLC 2*
Hull C *(Loaned on 13/3/2003) FL 8+1/3*
Bolton W *(Loaned on 2/2/2004) PL 1*
Crewe Alex *(Loaned on 30/9/2004) FL 14/1 FLC 1*

OWEN Gareth David
Born: Pontypridd, 21 September 1982
Height: 6'1" **Weight:** 11.6
International Honours: W: Yth
This young Stoke defender started the 2004-05 campaign on loan at Torquay but after a nervous start could not establish himself in the first team and returned to the Midlands with an injury. Gareth then made two appearances from the bench for the Potters before finishing the season out on loan again, this time at Oldham. He was subsequently a rock at the heart of the backline in Latics' final nine League One games. Out of contract at the Britannia Stadium in the summer, his future was unclear at the time of writing.
Stoke C *(From trainee on 5/7/2001) FL 1+4*
Oldham Ath *(Loaned on 16/1/2004) FL 15/1*
Torquay U *(Loaned on 1/7/2004) FL 2+3 FLC 1*
Oldham Ath *(Loaned on 19/3/2005) FL 9*

OWUSU Lloyd Magnus
Born: Slough, 12 December 1976
Height: 6'1" **Weight:** 14.0
Club Honours: Div 3 '99
Injuries to Shaun Goater and Nicky Forster gave Lloyd the chance to establish himself as the first-choice strike partner to Dave Kitson for Reading last term. He took the chance well, scoring in three consecutive games in October, but the goals dried up thereafter and he managed only three more all season, though these included a stunning headed equaliser in the 1-1 draw against champions Wigan Athletic. Despite having a year still to run on his contract, he was informed that he could leave if another club came in for him.
Brentford *(£25,000 from Slough T on 29/7/1998) FL 148+16/64 FLC 3+4/3 FAC 8/2 Others 13+3/4*
Sheffield Wed *(Free on 8/7/2002) FL 24+28/9 FLC 2+1 FAC 3/1 Others 1+1*
Reading *(Signed on 23/12/2003) FL 25+16/10 FLC 1+1 FAC 0+3*

OWUSU-ABEYIE Quincy Jamie
Born: Amsterdam, Holland, 15 April 1986
Height: 5'11" **Weight:** 11.10

International Honours: Holland: Yth
This extravagantly talented youngster finally made his mark in the Arsenal first team in a season of growing maturity. He impressed hugely as a half-time substitute in the FA Cup fifth round replay at Sheffield United and was rewarded with a first Premiership start four days later at home to Portsmouth. He made seven first-team appearances in total and scored in the Carling Cup victory over Everton. Quincy made his Champions' League debut in the home win over Rosenborg.
Arsenal *(From trainee on 2/7/2004) PL 1 FLC 2+4/1 FAC 0+2 Others 0+1*

OYEDELE Ade **Shola**
Born: Kano, Nigeria, 14 September 1984
Height: 5'11" **Weight:** 12.7
Shola is a very steady right-sided defender who was in and out of the MK Dons team last season before slotting into the right-back berth when Gareth Edds was moved into midfield at the end of February. He never did anything too complicated, tackling well and distributing simply, but after a couple of shaky outings he lost his place to loan signing Trent McLenahan and sat out the final month of the season.
Wimbledon/MK Dons *(From trainee on 6/8/2004) FL 27+7 FLC 0+1 FAC 2 Others 2*

Leon Osman

P

PACQUETTE Richard Francis
Born: Paddington, 28 January 1983
Height: 6'0" **Weight:** 12.7
Richard joined the MK Dons on a non-contract basis after being released by Queen's Park Rangers and made his debut as a substitute in the win over Hartlepool. He scored in his next match at Brentford in the LDV Vans Trophy, but generally failed to impress and was released at the beginning of November. The pacy striker subsequently had a brief association with Fisher Athletic then signed a short-term contract for Brentford, appearing for the Bees at Hull. Thereafter he moved around the non-league scene making cameo appearances for a number of clubs including Farnborough, Stevenage, Hemel Hempstead Town, St Albans City and Hampton & Richmond.
Queens Park Rgrs *(From trainee on 1/2/2000) FL 13+18/6 FLC 2+1 FAC 0+1 Others 3+3/1*
Mansfield T *(Loaned on 6/2/2004) FL 3+2/1*
MK Dons *(Free on 24/9/2004) FL 1+4 Others 2/1 (Free to Fisher Ath on 5/11/2004)*
Brentford *(Free on 25/11/2004) FL 1*

PADULA Diego **Gino** Mauro
Born: Buenos Aires, Argentina, 11 July 1976
Height: 5'9" **Weight:** 12.4
This left-sided defender is a favourite of the Queen's Park Rangers fans for his speed, tackling and dangerous crosses. He started the 2004-05 season as the first -choice left back and was a regular until mid-February when the formation of the side was altered. Gino regained his place in April and played through to the end of the season.
Walsall *(Free fron Xerez, Spain, ex River Plate, Argentina, via trial at Bristol Rov, on 11/11/1999) FL 23+2 FAC 2*
Wigan Ath *(Free on 21/7/2000) FL 2+2 FLC 0+1 FAC 2 Others 2/1*
Queens Park Rgrs *(Free on 8/7/2002) FL 81+9/4 FLC 4 FAC 1+2 Others 5+1/1*

PAGE Robert John
Born: Llwynpia, 3 September 1974
Height: 6'0" **Weight:** 12.5
Club Honours: Div 2 '98
International Honours: W: 38; B-1; U21-6; Yth; Sch
Robert completed what seemed to be the ideal move when signing for Cardiff, the club he supported as a boy in the summer of 2004. However, the good form of other squad members added to a problematic knee forced him out of the side and he quickly moved on to Coventry City in search of first-team football. The strong centre half took a few games to look match sharp but then played a key role in the Sky Blues' survival with outstanding performances at West Ham and Plymouth. He brought a sense of order to a defence that had struggled to stop the flow of goals before his arrival. Robert captained Wales for the first time against Hungary at the Millennium Stadium in February.
Watford *(From trainee on 19/4/1993) P/FL 209+7/2 FLC 17 FAC 12+1 Others 6/1*
Sheffield U *(£350,000 on 8/8/2001) FL 106+1/1 FLC 7 FAC 11 Others 3*
Cardiff C *(Free on 3/7/2004) FL 8+1*
Coventry C *(Free on 22/2/2005) FL 9*

PALMER Aiden Witting
Born: Enfield, 2 January 1987
Height: 5'8" **Weight:** 10.4
This promising Leyton Orient scholar did well with the club's reserve and youth teams last season and was given his senior debut in the fixture at Oxford in March. Aiden is a sure-footed left back who likes to keep things simple and will be looking to gain further senior experience in 2005-06.
Leyton Orient *(Trainee) FL 3+2*

PALMER Christopher (Chris) Louis
Born: Derby, 16 October 1983
Height: 5'7" **Weight:** 10.12
This left back or left-sided midfield Notts County player suffered an early-season injury that set him back for a while last

Gino Padula

term and it was not until the closing stages of the campaign that he showed his best form. Chris has lots of ability and is capable of shooting explosively from unexpected positions.
Derby Co *(From trainee on 3/7/2003)*
Notts Co *(Free on 2/7/2004) FL 23+2/4 FAC 4*

PALMER Brian **James (Jamie)**

Born: Feltham, 25 November 1985
Height: 5'9" **Weight:** 11.10
Jamie was one of several promising scholars on the books at Brentford last season. He made his senior debut at right back in the LDV Vans Trophy tie against MK Dons back in September when he gave a competent display. Jamie also had loan spells at Kingstonian and Staines Town before the end of the season but was not offered a professional contract by the Bees in the summer.
Brentford *(Trainee) Others 1*

PALMER Jermaine Ashley Clifton

Born: Derby, 28 August 1986
Height: 6'2" **Weight:** 11.3
This powerful young striker spent the summer of 2004 on loan in Iceland with Vikingur, but when he returned to Stoke last season he seemed to lose his way a bit in the reserves. He made just one appearance for the first team, coming off the bench in the home game against Sunderland in November. Jermaine, who is the son of former Derby player Charlie Palmer, was released in the summer.
Stoke C *(From trainee on 5/1/2005) FL 0+4*

PALMER Stephen (Steve) Leonard

Born: Brighton, 31 March 1968
Height: 6'1" **Weight:** 12.13
Club Honours: Div 2 '92, '98
International Honours: E: Sch
Steve was a regular starter for MK Dons in the first half of the 2004-05 season and although now at the veteran stage was a solid and consistent presence at the heart of the defence. He reverted to mainly bench and coaching duties after the signing of Michel Pensee-Bilong, but was able to complete his 500th Football League appearance in the notable 4-1 win at Bradford City, and started three key games late on when filling in for injury and suspension.
Ipswich T *(Signed from Cambridge University on 1/8/1989) P/FL 87+24/2 FLC 3 FAC 8+3/1 Others 4+2*
Watford *(£135,000 on 28/9/1995) P/FL 222+13/8 FLC 18+1/1 FAC 9+2 Others 7*
Queens Park Rgrs *(Free on 17/7/2001) FL 116+11/9 FLC 3 FAC 4 Others 7+2/1*
MK Dons *(Free on 23/7/2004) FL 27+5/1 FLC 1 FAC 2+1 Others 1*

PAMAROT Louis **Noe**

Born: Paris, France, 14 April 1979
Height: 6'2" **Weight:** 13.0
Noe settled quickly in the Spurs defence last term. His strength and tenacity fit well with the physical nature of the English game and he held his own against the best of midfield and attacking opponents. Strong in the challenge and good at keeping possession, Noe likes to get forward and attack.
Portsmouth *(Loaned from OGC Nice, France, ex Paris St Germain, Martigues, on 7/9/1999) FL 1+1 FLC 0+1*
Tottenham H *(£1,700,000 from OGC Nice, France on 24/8/2004) PL 23/1 FLC 3 FAC 2/1*

PANDIANI Walter Gerardo

Born: Montevideo, Uruguay, 27 April 1976
Height: 6'0" **Weight:** 11.9
International Honours: Uruguay: 3
Walter stepped off the plane from Spain 24 hours before a crucial match against Southampton, had to buy some boots from a local sports shop and headed the opening goal in a 2-1 win for Birmingham City after just 12 minutes, thus becoming an instant folk hero. Aggressive, honest and a hard worker, Walter was always a danger around the

Walter Pandiani

penalty area and never afraid to let rip with a powerful shot. He netted the Blues' first ever Premiership goal against Arsenal on the final day of the season in a 2-1 victory in typical poacher's style.
Birmingham C *(Loaned from Deportivo la Coruna, Spain, ex Progresso, Basanez, Penarol, on 1/2/2005) PL 13+1/4*

PARKER Keigan
Born: Livingston, 8 June 1982
Height: 5'7" **Weight:** 10.5
International Honours: S: U21-1; Yth
This exciting young striker began last season on the bench for Blackpool and it was only really following the departure of Scot Taylor to Plymouth that he blossomed. A fine hat-trick in the 4-0 victory over Torquay in December was a highlight as he finished the campaign in good form and with a tally of 12 goals in all competitions. Keigan missed the last few games after undergoing a hernia operation.
St Johnstone *(From juniors on 1/8/1998) SL 80+44/23 SLC 7+3 SC 3+3 Others 3+1/2*
Blackpool *(Free on 21/7/2004) FL 26+9/9 FLC 1 FAC 3+1/1 Others 3/2*

PARKER Scott Matthew
Born: Lambeth, 13 October 1980
Height: 5'7" **Weight:** 10.7
Club Honours: Div 1 '00; FLC '05
International Honours: E: 2; U21-12; Yth; Sch
PFA 'Young Player of the Year' in the preceding season, Chelsea's dynamic midfielder had a frustrating 2004-05 campaign, his greatest misfortune being that he was in direct competition for a regular place in central midfield with one of the Premiership's most effective performers Claude Makelele. He could only manage fleeting substitute appearances in the first three months of the season fuelling transfer speculation in the press. He was then given a rousing reception when he came on against CSKA Moscow in November. Unfortunately, Scott's fortunes plummeted shortly after when he broke a bone in his foot against Norwich City which sidelined him for three months, thereby ruling him out of the season's

Keigan Parker (left)

Scott Parker

climax as the Blues challenged for honours on four fronts.
Charlton Ath *(From trainee on 22/10/1997) P/FL 104+24/9 FLC 8+2/1 FAC 4+3*
Norwich C *(Loaned on 31/10/2000) FL 6/1*
Chelsea *(£10,000,000 on 30/1/2004) PL 8+7/1 FLC 3 FAC 1 Others 7+2*

PARKER Terence (Terry) James
Born: Southampton, 20 December 1983
Height: 5'9" **Weight:** 11.12
Terry was one of a number of players to sign for Oxford from manager Graham Rix's previous club Portsmouth during the summer of 2004. Primarily a left back, Terry had few chances to displace Matt Robinson in the side, but also featured occasionally on the left-hand side of midfield. He spent the closing months of the campaign on loan at Conference outfit Farnborough.
Portsmouth *(From trainee on 26/3/2003)*
Oxford U *(Free on 22/7/2004) FL 6+2 FLC 0+1*

PARKIN Jonathan (Jon)
Born: Barnsley, 30 December 1981
Height: 6'4" **Weight:** 13.12
This Macclesfield Town striker was in fine form from the beginning of last term scoring six goals in the first five matches. Jon went on to finish the season as the club's leading scorer with 22 League Two goals, establishing a new club record in the process. Perhaps the highlight came when he hit a hat-trick in the magnificent 5-0 win at Meadow Lane at the end of January. Jon also plays an important role in defence where his height and physical presence are used to good effect, especially when defending set pieces.
Barnsley *(From trainee on 5/1/1999) FL 8+2 FLC 1+1 FAC 0+1*
Hartlepool U *(Loaned on 7/12/2001) FL 0+1*
York C *(Free on 7/2/2002) FL 64+10/14 FAC 2 Others 2/1*
Macclesfield T *(Free on 20/2/2004) FL 54/23 FLC 1/1 FAC 3/1 Others 5/2*

PARKIN Samuel (Sam)
Born: Roehampton, 14 March 1981
Height: 6'2" **Weight:** 13.0
International Honours: S: B-1; E: Sch
It was business as usual for 'Super Sam' during the 2004-05 campaign as he weighed in with another 20-plus haul of goals for Swindon. His work rate was always high as he sought to hold up the ball and bring colleagues into play, while his ability to run at defenders was also more evident. Sam is very much a complete striker, able to take chances with his head and both feet, and he walked away with three 'Player of the

Jon Parkin

Season' trophies. He also operated as a loan striker for a number of games last term.

Chelsea *(From juniors on 21/8/1998)*
Millwall *(Loaned on 12/9/2000) FL 5+2/4*
Wycombe W *(Loaned on 24/11/2000) FL 5+3/1 FAC 0+3/1 Others 2/1*
Oldham Ath *(Loaned on 22/3/2001) FL 3+4/3*
Northampton T *(Loaned on 4/7/2001) FL 31+9/4 FLC 2/1 FAC 0+2 Others 2*
Swindon T *(£50,000 on 8/8/2002) FL 120+4/67 FLC 4+1/3 FAC 6 Others 5+2/3*

PARKINSON Andrew (Andy) John

Born: Liverpool, 27 May 1979
Height: 5'8" **Weight:** 10.12

This fast and skilful attacking midfielder was arguably the best of new manager Russell Slade's signings for Grimsby Town last term. His spectacular bursts forward excited the fans and produced several fine goals. Andy was a near ever-present in the Mariners' starting line-up and his tally of nine goals in all competitions made him joint-leading scorer for the club.

Tranmere Rov *(From trainee at Liverpool on 12/4/1997) FL 102+62/18 FLC 15+9/5 FAC 12+2/2 Others 1*
Sheffield U *(Free on 18/7/2003) FL 3+4 FLC 1 FAC 1+1*
Notts Co *(Loaned on 15/1/2004) FL 5/3*
Notts Co *(Loaned on 19/3/2004) FL 5+4*
Grimsby T *(Free on 30/7/2004) FL 43+2/8 FLC 2/1 FAC 1*

PARLOUR Raymond (Ray)

Born: Romford, 7 March 1973
Height: 5'10" **Weight:** 11.12
Club Honours: FLC '93; ECWC '94; PL '98, '02, '04; FAC '93, '98, '02, '03; CS '98, '99, '02
International Honours: E: 10; B-1; U21-12

With a year on his contract left and competition for Highbury places in midfield growing Ray moved on to Middlesbrough on a free transfer in July 2004, taking a huge wage cut in the hope of securing regular first-team football. His arrival at the Riverside strengthened an already impressive midfield with Ray making his debut in the 2-2 home draw with Newcastle United. A non-stop footballer, he managed to appear in 41 of the club's 52 games played during the season, despite missing some games with a hip injury, but surprisingly failed to find the back of the net.

Arsenal *(From trainee on 6/3/1991) P/FL 282+57/22 FLC 23+3 FAC 40+4/4 Others 45+12/6*
Middlesbrough *(Free on 30/7/2004) PL 32+1 FAC 2 Others 6*

Ray Parlour

ARNABY Stuart
orn: Durham, 19 July 1982
eight: 5'11" **Weight:** 11.4
lub Honours: FLC '04
nternational Honours: E: U21-4; Yth; ch
tuart, who can operate in defence or idfield, has missed a lot of games to jury in the last five seasons but he layed regular Premiership football from e beginning of the 2004-05 season. hat is until mid-October when he ollected a hairline fracture of his left bula whilst he was warming up. This eak accident cost him another three onths on the sidelines but he returned the side at the beginning of February a 1-0 Riverside win over Blackburn overs and, apart from a groin injury in pril, he played until the end of the eason.
***liddlesbrough** (From trainee on 1/7/1999) PL 45+8 FLC 2+2 FAC 2 Others +1*
***alifax T** (Loaned on 23/10/2000) FL 6*

ARRY Paul Ian
orn: Chepstow, 19 August 1980
eight: 5'11" **Weight:** 11.12
nternational Honours: W: 4
aul started the 2004-05 season on the ench for Cardiff, but gradually worked is way into the starting line-up with a eries of eye-catching substitute ppearances. Normally a left winger, he dded another string to his bow when he egan playing up front, just behind riker Peter Thorne, where his direct unning proved very dangerous. However, e sustained a serious ankle injury in ecember and this kept him out of ction until April. He returned ramatically, stepping off the bench to core a late equaliser in the crucial elegation game against Gillingham in lay and thus guarantee Cardiff's hampionship status for another year.
***ardiff C** (£75,000 from Hereford U on /1/2004) FL 26+15/5 FLC 3+1*

ARTON Andrew (Andy)
orn: Doncaster, 29 September 1983
eight: 5'10" **Weight:** 11.12
fter being an unused substitute in six of cunthorpe's first seven League Two atches, Andy was unable to force his ay into the first-team reckoning during e remainder of the 2004-05 season. He ade just two substitute appearances - t Nottingham Forest in the Carling Cup August and then in the League match t Mansfield in January. A quick player, ho can operate either up front or on ither wing, he was a regular scorer for e reserves but was loaned out to Conference North outfit Stalybridge in February.
***Scunthorpe U** (From trainee on 2/7/2003) FL 1+12 FLC 0+2 FAC 0+3/1 Others 0+1*

PARTRIDGE Richard (Richie) Joseph
Born: Dublin, 12 September 1980
Height: 5'8" **Weight:** 10.10
International Honours: RoI: U21-8; Yth (UEFA U18'98)
This left winger finally made his debut for Liverpool's first team as a substitute in the Carling Cup tie against Middlesbrough last November and made another appearance from the bench in the following round against Tottenham. However, that was the sum of his senior experience during the campaign.
***Liverpool** (From trainee on 16/9/1997) FLC 1+2*
***Bristol Rov** (Loaned on 22/3/2001) FL 4+2/1*
***Coventry C** (Loaned on 27/9/2002) FL 23+4/4 FLC 2 FAC 2*

PASTON Mark
Born: Hastings, New Zealand, 13 December 1976
Height: 6'5" **Weight:** 14.3
International Honours: New Zealand
Mark had a brief spell of first-team action for Walsall, taking over from Richard McKinney early on in the campaign. His best performances came at Torquay, when he kept a clean sheet, and at Doncaster the following week when he saved a penalty. However, the tall 'keeper dropped out of contention following the arrival of Joe Murphy. Mark was released by the Saddlers in February and later had surgery to repair a thigh injury. He represented New Zealand in their summer friendly against Australia at Craven Cottage and also returned home for a brief spell with Napier City Rovers.
***Bradford C** (Free from Napier C, New Zealand on 5/8/2003) FL 13 FLC 1*
***Walsall** (Free on 14/6/2004) FL 8+1 FLC 1 FAC 1 Others 1*

PATERSON Martin Andrew
Born: Tunstall, 13 May 1987
Height: 5'9" **Weight:** 11.5
A promising young striker who can also play wide on the right or left, Martin was the leading scorer for Stoke City's youth team last term and scored the goal that knocked Manchester United out of the FA Youth Cup. He made three first-team appearances, all as a substitute, and will be looking to feature more regularly in 2005-06. Martin was named as Stoke's 'Academy Player of the Season'.
***Stoke C** (Trainee) FL 0+3*

PATERSON Sean Patrick
Born: Greenock, 26 March 1987
Height: 5'11" **Weight:** 11.5
A scholar on the books at Blackpool, this promising young striker led the scoring charts for the club's reserve and youth teams last season. He made his first-team debut from the bench against Torquay in December and added another appearance as a substitute in the final game against Barnsley.
***Blackpool** (Trainee) FL 0+2*

PAYNTER William (Billy) Paul
Born: Liverpool, 13 July 1984
Height: 6'1" **Weight:** 12.0
This youngster was Port Vale's main striker last term, and was a near ever-present in the side, finishing the season as the team's leading scorer with 13 goals in all competitions. An enthusiastic front man, he sometimes occupied a role wide on the right. One of the highlights of his campaign came in the 5-0 win over Barnsley when he scored twice, including a spectacular 30-yard effort that flew into the top corner. It was arguable whether or not that was better than his strike at Stockport, when he ran from the halfway line and beat two defenders before firing the ball home. Billy won Vale's 'Player of the Year' award at the end of the campaign.
***Port Vale** (From trainee on 1/7/2002) FL 103+25/28 FLC 1+1 FAC 4+2/3 Others 5/1*

PEACOCK Lee Anthony
Born: Paisley, 9 October 1976
Height: 6'0" **Weight:** 12.8
Club Honours: AMC '97, '03
International Honours: S: U21-1; Yth
Lee had something of a disappointing season for Sheffield Wednesday, when he was unlucky with a series of niggling injuries. When fit he was often on the bench and he finished the campaign with just six goals. A powerfully built striker with plenty of experience, he will be hoping for better fortune in 2005-06.
***Carlisle U** (From trainee on 10/3/1995) FL 52+24/11 FLC 2+3 FAC 4+1/1 Others 6+4*
***Mansfield T** (£90,000 on 17/10/1997) FL 79+10/29 FLC 4/1 FAC 4 Others 4/2*
***Manchester C** (£500,000 on 5/11/1999) FL 4+4 FAC 1+1*
***Bristol C** (£600,000 on 10/8/2000) FL 131+13/54 FLC 4/3 FAC 11/1 Others 16/5*
***Sheffield Wed** (Free on 2/7/2004) FL 18+11/4 FLC 1/1 Others 3/1*

PEAD Craig George
Born: Bromsgrove, 15 September 1981
Height: 5'9" **Weight:** 11.6
International Honours: E: Yth
Craig was out of the first-team picture at

Coventry last term and had a spell on loan at Notts County in the autumn. A hard-working midfielder during his stay at Meadow Lane, he returned to Highfield Road when his month was up. In March he went out on loan again, this time to Walsall, where he took time to settle in but eventually came good on the right-hand side of the defence, producing a splendid display in the 3-1 win at play-off candidates Hartlepool.

Coventry C *(From trainee on 17/9/1998) FL 24+18/3 FLC 1 FAC 2*
Notts Co *(Loaned on 10/9/2004) FL 4+1 Others 1*
Walsall *(Loaned on 23/3/2005) FL 8*

PEARCE Ian Anthony
Born: Bury St Edmunds, 7 May 1974
Height: 6'3" **Weight:** 14.4
Club Honours: PL '95
International Honours: E: U21-3; Yth
Ian was unable to win a regular place in the Fulham first team last term, and in fact all of his appearances came in the opening half of the season. His best sequence was a six-game run just prior to Christmas, but thereafter a succession of minor injuries meant that he lost out to Zat Knight and Alain Goma. Ian is an experienced central defender who reads the game well and is effective in the air.

Chelsea *(From juniors on 1/8/1991) P/FL 0+4 Others 0+1*
Blackburn Rov *(£300,000 on 4/10/1993) PL 43+19/2 FLC 4+4/1 FAC 1+2 Others 6+1*
West Ham U *(£1,600,000 + on 19/9/1997) P/FL 135+7/9 FLC 8 FAC 10+1/1 Others 1+1*
Fulham *(£400,000 + on 23/1/2004) PL 23+1 FLC 1*

PEARSON Gregory (Greg) Edward
Born: Birmingham, 3 April 1985
Height: 5'11" **Weight:** 12.0
This young West Ham striker made an immediate impact at Lincoln City when he netted a hat-trick for the reserves. Greg went on to make his Football League debut at Scunthorpe United and added two further appearances from the substitutes' bench. He also netted a spectacular goal in City's Lincolnshire Cup tie with Boston United before returning to Upton Park. On the fringes of the first-team squad for the Hammers he will be hoping for a breakthrough in 2005-06.

West Ham U *(From trainee on 24/5/2004)*
Lincoln C *(Loaned on 20/8/2004) FL 1+2*

PEAT Nathan Neil Martin
Born: Hull, 19 September 1982
Height: 5'9" **Weight:** 10.9
This left-sided defender joined Lincoln City from Hull on a three-month loan which was later extended to the end of the campaign. The move was aimed at increasing his senior experience and he was given a run in Lincoln's first team early in the season before losing his place. Nathan continued to be part of the squad and was used on the left side of midfield or at left back when introduced from the substitutes' bench.

Hull C *(From trainee on 11/7/2002) FL 0+2 FAC 0+1 Others 2+1*
Cambridge U *(Loaned on 24/12/2003) FL 3+3*
Lincoln C *(Loaned on 26/7/2004) FL 6+4 FL 1+1 FAC 1*

PEDERSEN Henrik
Born: Copenhagen, Denmark, 10 June 1975
Height: 6'1" **Weight:** 13.5
International Honours: Denmark: 3
The 2004-05 campaign was certainly a season of two vastly contrasting halves for Henrik. He began in the starting line-up and scored all six of his Premiership

Lee Peacock (left)

goals tally before the end of November. His displays showed a more confident and adventurous side to his game, and this was duly rewarded with a return to the Denmark squad for the early-season World Cup qualifying games. The goals dried up however, and Henrik found himself flitting between the starting line-up and the bench, before surprisingly being placed on the transfer list during the January window. Despite this, Henrik stayed with the club and showed a reminder of his abilities when grabbing two goals in the FA Cup win at Ipswich, although he did not make as many appearances as he would have liked during the latter stages of the season.
Bolton W *(£650,000 from Silkeborg, Denmark on 11/7/2001) PL 68+36/20 FLC 5+6/4 FAC 7+1/3*

PEDERSEN Morten Gamst
Born: Vadso, Norway, 8 September 1981
Height: 5'11" **Weight:** 11.0
International Honours: Norway: 15
Although he was blooded for Blackburn soon after he arrived at the club, this midfielder was initially considered to lack the necessary qualities to survive in the Premiership. However, with great fortitude he underwent conditioning training and when given his chance at the turn of the year was a revelation. He ran and tackled all day, competed superbly in the air and scored goals that were not only vital but of supreme quality. His goals in the vital relegation battles against Southampton and Crystal Palace were crucial, but the quality of some of his finishes notably in the Premiership matches against Portsmouth and Southampton was exceptional. If that was not sufficient his defending was often outstanding. He made a fantastic goal-line clearance against Manchester United and his block in the semi-final after Brad Friedel had made a brilliant save was the mark of a strong and courageous player.
Blackburn Rov *(£1,500,000 from Tromso, Norway on 27/8/2004) PL 19/4 FLC 0+1/1 FAC 7/3*

PEETERS Bob
Born: Lier, Belgium, 10 January 1974
Height: 6'5" **Weight:** 13.12
International Honours: Belgium: 2
Bob spent most of the 2004-05 season on the injury list once more, recovering from an ankle problem and then a broken bone in his foot. However, the tall striker recommenced training in February and went on to make three appearances from the substitutes' bench for Millwall in the closing stages of the campaign. He will be hoping for an improvement in his fortunes in 2005-06.
Millwall *(Signed from Vitesse Arnhem, Holland, ex Lierse, Roda JC, on 19/8/2003) FL 16+7/3*

PEJIC Shaun Melvyn
Born: Hereford, 16 November 1982
Height: 6'1" **Weight:** 12.3
Club Honours: AMC '05
International Honours: W: U21-6; Yth
Shaun established himself in the centre of the Wrexham defence last term following an injury to Brian Carey and made excellent progress. The young central defender took on more responsibility at the back and produced a series of reliable performances throughout the campaign. Although not selected in the starting line-up for the LDV Vans Trophy final against Southend, he was thrust into the action when Steve Roberts was injured and slotted in perfectly for the rest of the game.
Wrexham *(From trainee on 9/8/2002) FL 85+11 FLC 5 FAC 3 Others 7+1/1*

PELLEGRINO Mauricio Andres
Born: Leones, Argentina, 5 October 1971
Height: 6'4" **Weight:** 13.3
International Honours: Argentina: 3
This veteran central defender signed for Liverpool in January on a short-term contract to provide cover following the departure of Stephane Henchoz. His track record with Valencia was exceptional with two 'La Liga' champions' medals, two European Champions' League finalist medals plus a UEFA Cup winners' medal to his name. Although ineligible for the Champions' League with Liverpool he made a dozen Premiership appearances and for a few games he replaced the previously indispensable Sami Hyppia. However, he was sometimes caught out by the pace of the Premiership and therefore it was no surprise that his contract was not extended in the summer.
Liverpool *(Loaned from Valencia, Spain, ex Velez Sarsfield, Barcelona, on 10/1/2005) PL 11+1 FLC 1*

PEMBRIDGE Mark Anthony
Born: Merthyr Tydfil, 29 November 1970
Height: 5'8" **Weight:** 12.0
International Honours: W: 54; B-2; U21-1; Sch
A first choice for much of the season at Fulham, Mark anchored the central midfield well, using his experience to anticipate opposition moves and make decisive tackles. An industrious player who is an excellent dead-ball specialist and creates chances for others, he was particularly outstanding in the local 'derby' at Stamford Bridge. Mark possesses an explosive shot as demonstrated by his stunning 35-yard winner in the Carling Cup tie at Birmingham.
Luton T *(From trainee on 1/7/1989) FL 60/6 FLC 2 FAC 4 Others 4*
Derby Co *(£1,250,000 on 2/6/1992) FL 108+2/28 FLC 9/1 FAC 6/3 Others 15/5*
Sheffield Wed *(£900,000 on 19/7/1995) PL 88+5/11 FLC 6/1 FAC 7/1 Others 1 (Free to Benfica, Portugal on 1/7/1998)*
Everton *(£800,000 on 6/8/1999) PL 82+9/4 FLC 1 FAC 8+1*
Fulham *(£500,000 + on 1/9/2003) PL 35+5/1 FLC 4/1 FAC 2+3*

PENFORD Thomas (Tom) James
Born: Leeds, 5 January 1985
Height: 5'10" **Weight:** 11.3
This young Bradford City central midfielder made only five appearances last season, all from the bench. After coming on as a substitute in four of the opening five games, his only other outing was in the LDV Vans Trophy defeat by Accrington.
Bradford C *(Trainee) FL 3+7 FLC 0+1 Others 0+1*

PENNANT Jermaine
Born: Nottingham, 15 January 1983
Height: 5'6" **Weight:** 10.0
Club Honours: FAYC '00, '01; CS '04
International Honours: E: U21-24; Yth; Sch
After a somewhat disappointing first half of the season at Highbury, Jermaine proved to be a great success after joining Birmingham City on loan in January and the transfer was later made permanent. His ability to cross the ball early and dangerously was impressive, while his great close control, ability to beat defenders and interplay with Mario Melchiot down the right flank made him a massive threat and added a new dimension to the Blues' team.
Notts Co *(Associated Schoolboy) FAC 0+1 Others 0+1*
Arsenal *(From trainee on 16/03/2000, having been signed for £1,500,000 on 14/1/1999) PL 2+10/3 FLC 8+1 FAC 1 Others 1+3*
Watford *(Loaned on 10/1/2002) FL 9/2*
Watford *(Loaned on 15/11/2002) FL 12 FAC 2/1*
Leeds U *(Loaned on 20/8/2003) PL 34+2/2*
Birmingham C *(£3,000,000 on 31/1/2005) PL 12*

PENSEE-BILONG Michel
Born: Cameroon, 16 June 1973
Height: 6'4" **Weight:** 14.2
International Honours: Cameroon

A strongly built and very powerful central defender, Michel was alerted to the MK Dons' need for defensive reinforcements and drove through the night from his Paris home to get a trial with the club. He was quickly signed up, made his debut on a very cold January day at Blackpool and from then on kept his place until the end of the season. A key figure in the massive defensive improvement in the second half of the season, he formed a strong barrier with skipper Ben Chorley and became a very popular figure with the club's supporters.
MK Dons *(Signed from Sanfrecce Hiroshima, Japan, ex Tonerre Yaounde, Tampico, Imiwa Chumna, Deportivo Aves, Anji Makachkala, on 21/1/2005) FL 18/1*

PERCH James Robert
Born: Mansfield, 29 September 1985
Height: 5'11" **Weight:** 11.5
James is the latest player to develop through the Nottingham Forest youth set-up and he was a surprise inclusion as a central defender on the opening day of the season. He went on to feature fairly regularly in the squad throughout the campaign and can be pleased with the progress made. James was mostly employed in midfield, but he also featured at full back and scored his only senior goal to date in the Carling Cup victory over Doncaster Rovers.
Nottingham F *(From trainee on 9/11/2002) FL 17+5 FLC 2+1/1 FAC 2+1*

PERPETUINI David Peter
Born: Hitchin, 26 September 1979
Height: 5'8" **Weight:** 10.8
After recovering from a serious injury this left-sided defender or midfielder made three early-season appearances for Gillingham before being released in January. He subsequently had a brief association with Wycombe before ending the campaign at Walsall. David was out of contract in the summer and his future was unclear at the time of writing.
Watford *(From trainee on 3/7/1997) P/FL 17+2/1 FLC 1+1*
Gillingham *(£100,000 on 9/8/2001) FL 55+31/5 FLC 5+3 FAC 4 (Freed on 10/10/2004)*
Wycombe W *(Free on 27/1/2005) FL 1+1*
Walsall *(Free on 24/3/2005) FL 7*

PERRETT Russell (Russ)
Born: Barton-on-Sea, 18 June 1973
Height: 6'3" **Weight:** 13.2
Club Honours: Div 1 '05
This experienced defender found opportunities hard to come by at Luton last term. Niggling injuries restricted his ability to turn out for the reserves but he had a brief run in the line-up at the turn of the year and also featured against Doncaster on the final day of the season when he scored with a header.
Portsmouth *(Signed from Lymington on 30/9/1995) FL 66+6/2 FLC 5 FAC 4*
Cardiff C *(£10,000 on 21/7/1999) FL 28+1/1 FAC 5/1 Others 1*
Luton T *(Free on 10/8/2001) FL 72+6/8 FLC 3 FAC 1 Others 0+1*

PERRY Christopher (Chris) John
Born: Carshalton, 26 April 1973
Height: 5'9" **Weight:** 11.1
With Mark Fish injured for most of the season it was left for Chris to battle for one of the central defensive positions with Jon Fortune, alongside new signing Talal El Karkouri. Chris featured in half of Charlton's Premiership fixtures, scoring in the home draw with Manchester City. He would probably have made more appearances but for a groin injury mid-season. He is good in the air, although his lack of height can sometimes be a disadvantage against the taller opposition forwards. However, he reads the game well, is very comfortable with the ball and has good distribution skills as well as being a strong tackler.
Wimbledon *(From trainee on 2/7/1991) PL 158+9/2 FLC 21 FAC 24/1*
Tottenham H *(£4,000,000 on 7/7/1999) PL 111+9/3 FLC 13 FAC 9 Others 4/1*
Charlton Ath *(£100,000 on 1/9/2003) PL 42+6/2 FLC 3 FAC 1*

PESCHISOLIDO Paolo (Paul) Pasquale
Born: Scarborough, Canada, 25 May 1971
Height: 5'7" **Weight:** 10.12
Club Honours: Div 2 '99
International Honours: Canada: 53; U23-11; Yth
The arrival of Grzegorz Rasiak, along with competition from Tommy Smith and Marcus Tudgay, led to Paul spending more time on the bench for Derby than he wished. Although disappointed, he remained an excellent team player, always likely to find a goal – eight in the Championship season – and able to link with any of his partners. Whether starting or used as a substitute, Paul gave freshness and vitality to the team. Opposing defenders are not keen to see him because they know he will give them no peace. Paul earned two more caps in the autumn but faded out as Canada's World Cup qualifying campaign faltered.
Birmingham C *(£25,000 from Toronto Blizzards, Canada on 11/11/1992) FL 37+6/16 FLC 2/1 FAC 0+1 Others 1+1*
Stoke C *(£400,000 on 1/8/1994) FL 59+7/19 FLC 6/3 FAC 3 Others 5+1/2*
Birmingham C *(£400,000 on 29/3/1996) FL 7+2/1*
West Bromwich A *(£600,000 on 24/7/1996) FL 36+9/18 FLC 4+1/3 FAC 1*
Fulham *(£1,100,000 on 24/10/1997) FL 69+26/24 FLC 7+1/4 FAC 9+1/2 Others 2*
Queens Park Rgrs *(Loaned on 3/11/2000) FL 5/1*
Sheffield U *(Loaned on 19/1/2001) FL 4+1/2*
Norwich C *(Loaned on 22/3/2001) FL 3+2*
Sheffield U *(£150,000 + on 10/7/2001) FL 35+44/17 FLC 3+5/2 FAC 3+5/2 Others 0+2/1*
Derby Co *(Signed on 12/3/2004) FL 21+22/12 FLC 1 FAC 0+1/1 Others 2*

PETERS Mark
Born: Flint, 6 July 1972
Height: 6'0" **Weight:** 11.8
Club Honours: NC '01; Div 3 '03
Mark had a disappointing season last term, managing just a couple of appearances from the substitutes' bench for Leyton Orient in the early part of the campaign. In November he joined Aldershot on loan, but was then sidelined by a toe injury that kept him out of action until the end of the season. A dominant central defender who is powerful in the air and has a good touch on the ball, he was released by the O's in the summer.
Manchester C *(From trainee on 5/7/1990)*
Norwich C *(Free on 2/9/1992)*
Peterborough U *(Free on 10/8/1993) FL 17+2 FLC 2 Others 2*
Mansfield T *(Free on 30/9/1994) FL 107+1/9 FLC 5/1 FAC 8 Others 7*
Rushden & Diamonds *(Free on 3/7/1999) FL 65+2/1 FLC 4/1 FAC 5 Others 5*
Leyton Orient *(Free on 12/9/2003) FL 39+2/2 FAC 2 Others 2*

PETERS Ryan Vincent
Born: Wandsworth, 21 August 1987
Height: 5'8" **Weight:** 10.8
A scholar on the books at Brentford, Ryan stepped up from the youth team to make his senior debut when he came off the bench in the League One fixture at Peterborough last August. The pacy right winger added several more appearances during the season and scored his first senior goal against Sheffield Wednesday in February. Ryan also had brief loan spells at Gravesend & Northfleet and Windsor & Eton during the campaign. He is highly thought of at Griffin Park and was offered a professional contract in the summer.
Brentford *(Trainee) FL 1+8/1 FLC 1 FAC 0+1 Others 1*

PETTA Robert (Bobby) Alfred Manuel
Born: Rotterdam, Holland, 6 August 1974
Height: 5'7" **Weight:** 11.3
Club Honours: SPD '01, '02; SLC '01
Bobby found himself out of favour at Celtic last term and was released by mutual consent in November. Following trials with a number of clubs he signed a contract with the Quakers in the new year and soon began to show his talents for the League Two club. A left-sided midfielder, he displayed some silky skills, ghosting past defenders as if they weren't there and delivering tantalising crosses. Bobby scored on his debut at Bury, winning the game with a beautiful chip from the edge of the box over the 'keeper, but this was his only goal and he was more of a provider than a scorer in his subsequent appearances.
Ipswich T *(Free from Feyenoord, Holland on 12/6/1996) FL 55+15/9 FLC 8+2 FAC 5+1 Others 3*
Glasgow Celtic *(Free on 10/7/1999) SL 36+16 SLC 3+4/1 SC 3+1/1 Others 14+4/2*
Fulham *(Loaned on 1/1/2004) PL 3+6 FAC 2+3*
Darlington *(Free on 31/1/2005) FL 12/1*

PETTEFER Carl James
Born: Burnham, 22 March 1981
Height: 5'7" **Weight:** 10.5
Carl was the only ever-present in the Southend team in 2004-05, a testament to his total recovery from a serious leg injury towards the end of the previous campaign. A terrific worker down either flank his slight frame belies a fearsome tackle and a great will to win. Primarily Carl was employed as a wide right midfielder and forged a good understanding with overlapping full back, Duncan Jupp, while both Freddy Eastwood and Wayne Gray benefited from some high quality crossing. He also proved his value to the squad by filling-in in the central and wide-left midfield berths when required.
Portsmouth *(From trainee on 23/11/1998) FL 1+2*
Exeter C *(Loaned on 21/10/2002) FL 30+1/1 FAC 4 Others 2*
Southend U *(Free on 10/2/2004) FL 57 FLC 1 FAC 1 Others 11+2/1*

PHILLIPS Kevin Mark
Born: Hitchin, 25 July 1973
Height: 5'7" **Weight:** 11.0
Club Honours: Div 1 '99
International Honours: E: 8; B-1
A class act, Kevin's work rate, energy and sharp eye for goal were among the few redeeming features of a grisly Southampton campaign in 2004-05. It was not until after Harry Redknapp was appointed manager that Kevin teamed up with Peter Crouch in a partnership that promised a lot of goals. However, that hope proved to be short-lived after Kevin sustained an ankle injury and Henri Camara was brought to St Mary's.
Watford *(£10,000 from Baldock on 19/12/1994) FL 54+5/24 FLC 2/1 FAC 2 Others 0+2*
Sunderland *(£325,000 + on 17/7/1997) P/FL 207+1/113 FLC 9+1/5 FAC 14/10 Others 3/2*
Southampton *(£3,250,000 on 14/8/2003) PL 49+15/22 FLC 2/1 FAC 4+1/2 Others 2/1*

PHILLIPS Mark Ian
Born: Lambeth, 27 January 1982
Height: 6'2" **Weight:** 13.0
Mark got his chance to step into the Millwall line-up last November at a time when the defence was stricken by injury problems. He seized the opportunity with both hands and went on to enjoy a decent run in the side. A central defender or right back, he possesses great pace and is effective when pushing forward. Mark scored his first senior goal for the club after a fine run against Sheffield United in December.
Millwall *(From trainee on 3/5/2000) FL 33/1 FLC 1+1 FAC 1*

PHILLIPS Martin John
Born: Exeter, 13 March 1976
Height: 5'10" **Weight:** 11.10
Club Honours: Div 3 '02
Released by Plymouth in the close season, this skilful left-footed winger was snapped up by Torquay. However, a series of niggling injuries, not helped by the absence of a reserve team at Plainmoor, resulted in a lack of regular starts and a lack of match fitness. Towards the end of the season an extended run in the team on the right wing saw him recapture his best form as he tormented full backs to create many chances.
Exeter C *(From trainee on 4/7/1994) FL 36+16/5 FLC 1+2 FAC 2+2 Others 1+5*
Manchester C *(£500,000 on 25/11/1995) P/FL 3+12 FLC 0+1*
Scunthorpe U *(Loaned on 5/1/1998) FL 2+1 Others 1*
Exeter C *(Loaned on 19/3/1998) FL 7+1*
Portsmouth *(£50,000 + on 27/8/1998) FL 4+20/1 FLC 2+2 FAC 0+1*
Bristol Rov *(Loaned on 24/2/1999) FL 2*
Plymouth Arg *(£25,000 on 11/8/2000) FL 90+24/10 FLC 4 FAC 7+2/2 Others 4*
Torquay U *(Free on 15/7/2004) FL 19+11/2 FLC 0+1 Others 2*

PHILLIPS Steven (Steve) John
Born: Bath, 6 May 1978
Height: 6'1" **Weight:** 11.10
Club Honours: AMC '03
Steve had an outstanding season in goal for Bristol City last term when he was an ever-present in first-team matches and made a significant contribution to the team's progress. Whilst his 85th-minute penalty save from Everton's James McFadden in the Carling Cup tie was a highlight there were many other fine performances during the course of the campaign. If he were a little more decisive when dealing with crosses he would surely rank among the very best goalkeepers in the country.
Bristol C *(Signed from Paulton Rov on 21/11/1996) FL 237+1 FLC 11 FAC 16 Others 22*

PHILO Mark William
Born: Bracknell, 5 October 1984
Height: 5'11" **Weight:** 11.5
Wycombe's attacking young midfielder suffered wretched luck when breaking an ankle in a friendly match during the 2004 close season. The injury took several months to heal and it was not until March that he returned to action for the first team. In a handful of substitute appearances he impressed with some strong and skilful displays on the right-hand side of midfield and started the final two games. Mark was rewarded with a new long-term contract with the Chairboys.
Wycombe W *(From trainee on 1/7/2003) FL 6+11*

PIDGELEY Leonard (Lenny) James
Born: Twickenham, 7 February 1984
Height: 6'4" **Weight:** 13.10
International Honours: E: Yth
The most dispiriting job in football must be third-choice goalkeeper behind the top two 'keepers in the Premiership and this was the lot of promising young Chelsea 'keeper Lenny Pidgeley. After a successful loan spell at Watford Lenny made a long-awaited debut for the Blues in the Championship 'coronation' match against Charlton Athletic in May. Although he substituted for Carlo Cudicini for the last eight minutes he made a crucial block which maintained the Blues' unbeaten home record. Lenny's outstanding potential has earned him a long-term contract at Stamford Bridge, a firm indication of the esteem in which he is held by the club's power brokers.
Chelsea *(From trainee on 11/7/2003) PL 0+1*
Watford *(Loaned on 16/9/2003) FL 26+1 FAC 2*

PIERCY John William
Born: Forest Gate, 18 September 1979
Height: 5'11" **Weight:** 12.4
International Honours: E: Yth
Able to play in midfield, on the wing or up front, John was probably one of the most talented players at Brighton last term. He started the Championship campaign on a short-term contract, aiming to prove himself worthy of a longer deal, but it was always a struggle for the former Tottenham youngster. Constantly battling against the debilitating hereditary condition colitis, John enjoyed just two outings in the first team. His only start came at centre forward in the home defeat by Crewe in November, when he showed he had the ball control but lacked the fitness required in the modern game. Sadly, just three days later John admitted defeat to the energy-sapping illness and announced his retirement at the age of just 25.
Tottenham H *(From trainee on 2/7/1998) PL 1+7 FLC 1*
Brighton & Hove A *(Free on 20/9/2002) FL 10+20/4 FLC 1 FAC 0+2 Others 0+3*

PILKINGTON George Edward
Born: Rugeley, 7 November 1981
Height: 5'11" **Weight:** 11.6
International Honours: E: Yth
This dependable Port Vale defender was once again a regular in the back four last season. A near ever-present, he performed with equal aplomb at right back, left back or in the centre of the rearguard. George received several 'Man of the Match' awards and battled through the second half of the campaign with breathing problems before undergoing corrective surgery in the summer.
Everton *(From trainee on 18/11/1998)*
Exeter C *(Loaned on 1/11/2002) FL 7 FAC 4 Others 1*
Port Vale *(Free on 1/7/2003) FL 86+1/1 FLC 2 FAC 5 Others 3*

PILKINGTON Joel Thomas
Born: Accrington, 1 August 1984
Height: 5'8" **Weight:** 10.4
One brief substitute appearance in each of the three major competitions was all that midfielder Joel saw of first-team action for Burnley in 2004-05. Almost invariably named on the bench, he was never likely to be called on when more experienced cover was available, and it was no surprise to see him released at the end of the season.
Burnley *(From trainee on 2/7/2003) FL 0+2 FLC 0+1 FAC 0+1*

PILKINGTON Kevin William
Born: Hitchin, 8 March 1974
Height: 6'1" **Weight:** 13.0
Club Honours: FAYC '92
International Honours: E: Sch
Kevin started last term as captain of Mansfield Town and showed excellent early-season form, notably producing a magnificent performance against Preston in the Carling Cup, when he saved a penalty and prevented a bigger defeat. Although relieved of the captaincy following a change in management he made another vital penalty save at Boston to secure the Stags a point. A true professional he continued to provide a great example to the club's younger players. Kevin was an ever present in the League until his season ended with four matches to go when he dislocated a shoulder in training.
Manchester U *(From trainee on 6/7/1992) PL 4+2 FLC 1 FAC 1*
Rochdale *(Loaned on 2/2/1996) FL 6*
Rotherham U *(Loaned on 22/1/1997) FL 17*
Port Vale *(Free on 1/7/1998) FL 23 FLC 1 FAC 1 (Freed during 2000 close season)*
Mansfield T *(Free from Aberystwyth T, via trials at Macclesfield T and Wigan Ath, on 8/9/2000) FL 167 FLC 4 FAC 11 Others 7*

PINAULT Thomas
Born: Grasse, France, 4 December 1981
Height: 5'10" **Weight:** 11.1
This young midfield playmaker became a firm favourite with the Blundell Park crowd last term after arriving on a 12-month deal during the summer. He impressed with some classy touches and an eye for goal, while his tally of seven goals included a double in the 5-1 win over Bury in August. Out of contract in the summer, his future was undecided at the time of writing.
Colchester U *(Free from AS Cannes, France on 5/7/1999) FL 104+29/5 FLC 4+2/1 FAC 10 Others 8/1*
Grimsby T *(Free on 23/7/2004) FL 32+11/7 FLC 2 FAC 1 Others 1*

PIPE David Ronald
Born: Caerphilly, 5 November 1983
Height: 5'9" **Weight:** 12.4
International Honours: W: 1; U21-12; Yth
David was a regular in the Notts County line-up last term and showed plenty of commitment throughout the campaign. A fast raiding right-sided defender or midfielder he was pressed into service at left back and in central defence when emergencies arose. David also featured for Wales at U21 level, captaining the side on occasions.
Coventry C *(From trainee on 8/11/2000) FL 11+10/1 FLC 1+2 FAC 0+1*
Notts Co *(Free on 15/1/2004) FL 56+3/2 FLC 2 FAC 4 Others 1*

PIPER Matthew (Matt) James
Born: Leicester, 29 September 1981
Height: 6'1" **Weight:** 13.5
Matt is surely one of the unluckiest players ever to pull on a Sunderland shirt having endured three injury-wrecked years on Wearside. He is a powerfully built right winger or central striker who possesses electrifying pace but he was limited to only two substitute appearances last season as recurring knee and groin injuries kept him sidelined.
Leicester C *(From trainee on 12/8/1999) PL 14+2/1 FLC 1 FAC 0+1*
Mansfield T *(Loaned on 20/11/2001) FL 8/1*
Sunderland *(£3,500,000 on 21/8/2002) P/FL 13+11 FLC 1+1 FAC 0+2*

PIQUE Gerard
Born: Barcelona, Spain, 2 February 1987
Height: 6'3" **Weight:** 12.10
International Honours: Spain: Yth
Gerard is a highly regarded young central defender who signed for Manchester United in the summer of 2004. So impressed were the coaching staff at Old Trafford with his early progress, he produced a pleasing 23-minute cameo against Crewe in the Carling Cup barely a week after making his first appearance for the reserves. Having played for Spain at U17 level alongside Arsenal's Cesc Fabregas, Gerard looks to be one of the most exciting prospects Sir Alex has signed in years.
Manchester U *(Trainee) FLC 0+1 FAC 1 Others 0+1*

PIRES Robert
Born: Reims, France, 29 October 1973
Height: 6'1" **Weight:** 12.4
Club Honours: PL '02, '04; FAC '03, '05
International Honours: France: 79 (UEFA '00)
Although Robert did not always find his best form for Arsenal last term, he still contributed 17 goals in total despite injury problems and without always being first choice. In fact he made a habit of coming off the bench to score as strikes against Everton on the opening day of the season, Middlesborough and Sheffield United show. He continued this pattern at White Hart Lane where he struck the winner in that amazing 5-4 win. He ended the season in fantastic form hitting another winner at the Riverside and coming so close to breaching the Chelsea defence at

Robert Pires

Stamford Bridge. Above all else Robert remains a great player, when he plays well Arsenal tend to do the same. He scored with a sublime free kick against Liverpool at Highbury and added two more against Everton three days later.
Arsenal *(£6,000,000 from Olympique Marseilles, France, ex Metz, on 24/7/2000) PL 136+20/55 FLC 1/1 FAC 21+6/8 Others 48+4/9*

PISTONE Alessandro (Sandro)
Born: Milan, Italy, 27 July 1975
Height: 5'11" **Weight:** 12.1
International Honours: Italy: U21 (UEFA-U21 '96)
This cultured and classy defender had a generally sound and largely injury-free season for Everton when he enjoyed his longest run of consecutive games since coming to England. Largely employed in his regular position of left back throughout, he can perform in any position in the back four if required. Sandro gave some tremendous performances, especially in the 'derby' victory over Liverpool in December. The former captain of his country's U21 side has all the attributes of a top player, being a good reader of the game and strong in the tackle when needed.
Newcastle U *(£4,300,000 from Inter Milan, Italy, ex Vicenza, Solbiatese, Crevalcore, on 31/7/1997) PL 45+1/1 FLC 1+1 FAC 8 Others 7*
Everton *(£3,000,000 on 12/7/2000) PL 92+9/1 FLC 6+1 FAC 5+1*

PITT Courtney Leon
Born: Westminster, 17 December 1981
Height: 5'7" **Weight:** 10.12
Courtney signed for Boston United on a short-term deal on the eve of last season, making his debut against one of his former clubs, Oxford United, on the opening day. He earned himself a deal until the end of the campaign, showing plenty of skill on both flanks when used as a wide midfield man. He also appeared in some unfamiliar positions in the

Sandro Pistone

closing fixtures, notably at left back and occasionally as an out-and-out striker, but his speed and skill on the ball proved useful in both positions.
Chelsea *(From trainee on 4/7/2000)*
Portsmouth *(£200,000 on 5/7/2001) FL 29+10/3 FLC 1 FAC 1*
Luton T *(Loaned on 8/8/2003) FL 11+1 FLC 1+1/1*
Coventry C *(Loaned on 28/12/2003) FL 1 FAC 0+1*
Oxford U *(Free on 25/3/2004) FL 5+3*
Boston U *(Free on 6/8/2004) FL 20+12/4 FLC 2/1*

PLATT Clive Linton
Born: Wolverhampton, 27 October 1977
Height: 6'4" **Weight:** 13.0
This lanky striker featured regularly for Peterborough in the first half of the 2004-05 campaign, but never really settled at London Road and in January he was sold to MK Dons. He proved to be one of the key signings of the season for the Dons and his arrival heralded an immediate upturn in the club's fortunes. His superb aerial ability gave the attack a focal point and, perhaps more importantly, his defensive heading at set pieces halted the flow of goals the club had been conceding. Unlikely ever to be a frequent scorer because of his very unselfish attitude to the game, he added strength and determination that more than made up for his goal return.
Walsall *(From trainee on 25/7/1996) FL 18+14/4 FLC 1+2/1 FAC 0+1 Others 1+6*
Rochdale *(£70,000 + on 5/8/1999) FL 151+18/30 FLC 5/1 FAC 13/5 Others 7/1*
Notts Co *(Free on 7/8/2003) FL 19/3 FLC 3 FAC 3/3*
Peterborough U *(Free on 7/1/2004) FL 35+2/6 FLC 1 FAC 1*
MK Dons *(Free on 13/1/2005) FL 20/3*

PLATT Matthew
Born: Crewe, 15 October 1983
Height: 6'0" **Weight:** 11.3
A product of the youth set-up at Crewe, Matthew spent most of last season developing in the club's reserve team. He made just a single appearance for the first team, coming off the bench against Wolves in March. The promising striker left the club by mutual consent in the summer, choosing to seek more regular first-team action elsewhere.
Crewe Alex *(From trainee on 8/7/2002) FL 0+1*

PLUMMER Christopher (Chris) Scott
Born: Isleworth, 12 October 1976
Height: 6'3" **Weight:** 12.9
International Honours: E: U21-5; Yth
After just a handful of games for Conference club Barnet at the beginning of last season Chris was sold to Peterborough. Despite the competition for places he featured regularly in the side thereafter, playing both as a central defender and at left back. Chris will be looking to firmly establish himself in the line-up in 2005-06.
Queens Park Rgrs *(From trainee on 1/7/1994) P/FL 54+8/2 FLC 2 FAC 7 (Freed during 2003 close season)*
Bristol Rov *(Loaned on 7/11/2002) FL 2 FAC 2*
Peterborough U *(£30,000 from Barnet on 3/9/2004) FL 21 FAC 1+2*

POGLIACOMI Leslie (Les) Amado
Born: Perth, Australia, 3 May 1976
Height: 6'4" **Weight:** 14.5
International Honours: Australia: Yth
After declining a move to Crystal Palace in summer 2004, this highly rated goalkeeper signed a new contract with Oldham. His shot-stopping ability was particularly in evidence during the club's third round FA Cup defeat of Manchester City in January. However, playing behind an unsettled defence he found the going tough at times with occasional lapses in confidence and problems with his kicking. After briefly losing his place under new boss Ronnie Moore, Les returned to action in determined mood and ended the season on a personal high: named 'Man of the Match' for a breathtaking display that helped Latics earn a final-day victory over Bradford City and avoid relegation from League One.
Oldham Ath *(Free from Parramatta Power, Australia, ex Marconi Stallions, Wollongong Wolves, Parramatta Power, on 22/7/2002) FL 120 FLC 4 FAC 9 Others 8*

POLLITT Michael (Mike) Francis
Born: Farnworth, 29 February 1972
Height: 6'4" **Weight:** 14.0
There's no doubt that this giant of a 'keeper thoroughly deserved all the various 'Player of the Year' awards that he collected because he showed consistent and outstanding form for Rotherham throughout the whole season. If it had not been for a string of magnificent saves, many of the defeats the Millers suffered would have been more emphatic. The last game of the season saw him make his 300th appearance for the club.
Manchester U *(From trainee on 1/7/1990)*
Bury *(Free on 10/7/1991)*
Lincoln C *(Loaned on 24/9/1992) FL 5 FLC 1*
Lincoln C *(Free on 1/12/1992) FL 52 FLC 4 FAC 2 Others 4*
Darlington *(Free on 11/8/1994) FL 55 FLC 4 FAC 3 Others 5*
Notts Co *(£75,000 on 14/11/1995) FL 10 Others 2*
Oldham Ath *(Loaned on 29/8/1997) FL 16*
Gillingham *(Loaned on 12/12/1997) FL 6*
Brentford *(Loaned on 22/1/1998) FL 5*
Sunderland *(£75,000 on 23/2/1998)*
Rotherham U *(Free on 14/7/1998) FL 92 FLC 4 FAC 7 Others 5*
Chesterfield *(Free on 15/6/2000) FL 46 FLC 3 FAC 1 Others 4*
Rotherham U *(£75,000 on 29/5/2001) FL 175 FLC 11 FAC 6*

POOK Michael David
Born: Swindon, 22 October 1985
Height: 5'11" **Weight:** 11.10
A versatile, strong-running young midfielder able to operate in the centre or down either flank, Michael made a very late appearance for Swindon as a substitute in the Carling Cup tie at Elland Road and then made his full debut in the LDV Vans Trophy tie at Exeter during November. An end-of-season injury crisis saw him start the final three games when he produced some competent performances.
Swindon T *(Trainee) FL 3+2 FLC 0+1 Others 2*

POOLE Kevin
Born: Bromsgrove, 21 July 1963
Height: 5'10" **Weight:** 12.11
Club Honours: FLC '97
This veteran 'keeper made two starts for Bolton in the Carling Cup, and must have assumed that to be the extent of his first-team action last season. However, Kevin replaced Jussi Jaaskelainen in goal during the Premiership match at Middlesborough following the Finn's sending off, and also started against West Brom on New Year's Day. This, however, was Kevin's last appearance for Wanderers, and he was released at the end of the season.
Aston Villa *(From apprentice on 26/6/1981) FL 28 FLC 2 FAC 1 Others 1*
Northampton T *(Loaned on 8/11/1984) FL 3*
Middlesbrough *(Signed on 27/8/1987) FL 34 FLC 4 FAC 2 Others 2*
Hartlepool U *(Loaned on 27/3/1991) FL 12*
Leicester C *(£40,000 on 30/7/1991) P/FL 163 FLC 10 FAC 8 Others 12*
Birmingham C *(Free on 4/8/1997) FL 56 FLC 7 FAC 2 Others 2*
Bolton W *(Free on 25/10/2001) PL 4+1 FLC 7 FAC 4*

POOM Mart
Born: Tallinn, Estonia, 3 February 1972
Height: 6'4" **Weight:** 13.6
Club Honours: Ch '05
International Honours: Estonia: 101

Sunderland's hugely popular goalkeeper had his season ruined by injury last term when he required surgery on a damaged knee cartilage in October. A tall and extremely agile stopper, Mart will face a battle to regain his place in 2005-06 with Thomas Myhre and Ben Alnwick both impressing when given opportunities in his absence.

Portsmouth *(£200,000 from FC Wil, Switzerland, ex Flora, on 4/8/1994) FL 4 FLC 3 (Signed by Tallinn SC, Estonia on 9/5/1996)*
Derby Co *(£500,000 on 26/3/1997) P/FL 143+3 FLC 12 FAC 8*
Sunderland *(£2,500,000 on 23/11/2002) P/FL 58/1 FLC 1+1 FAC 6 Others 2*

POPOVIC Anthony (Tony)

Born: Sydney, Australia, 4 July 1973
Height: 6'4" **Weight:** 13.11
International Honours: Australia: 49; U23; Yth

Tony signed a new contract for Crystal Palace in the summer of 2004 and began last season as team captain. However, he lost his place to new arrival Gonzalo Sorondo in December, before returning to the line-up before the end of the season. Tony is a powerful central defender who is steady and reliable.

Crystal Palace *(£600,000 from Sanfrecce Hiroshima, Japan on 24/8/2001) P/FL 111+2/6 FLC 8/1 FAC 5 Others 3*

PORTER Andrew (Andy) Michael

Born: Holmes Chapel, 17 September 1968
Height: 5'9" **Weight:** 12.0
Club Honours: AMC '93, '99

Port Vale's youth coach was forced back into action during an injury crisis last season. Andy came on as a substitute against Tranmere in December and soon displayed the same tenacity in the tackle that he had shown in his earlier days. It was more than four years since he had played League football, but he also made a telling contribution from the bench at Milton Keynes, helping the younger players around him. The 18-year gap between his debut and final appearance is not surprisingly a club record.

Port Vale *(From trainee on 29/6/1987) FL 313+44/22 FLC 22+1 FAC 20+4/3 Others 26+2/1*
Wigan Ath *(Free on 28/7/1998) FL 8+13/1 FLC 0+3 FAC 1 Others 3+3 (Free to Chester C on 20/10/2000)*
Mansfield T *(Loaned on 22/10/1999) FL 5 FAC 1*
Chester C *(Loaned on 5/2/2000) FL 16*
Port Vale *(From retirement on 26/11/2004) FL 0+2*

PORTER Christopher (Chris)

Born: Wigan, 12 December 1983
Height: 6'1" **Weight:** 13.2

Last season began in promising fashion for Bury's lanky striker who was in fine goal-scoring form during the opening months of the campaign. Chris had scored eight goals by January, but then picked up a knee injury in the game at Scunthorpe, which put him out of action for six weeks. He returned to add a further two goals to his total before the problem returned and he was sidelined once more.

Bury *(Free from Queen Elizabeth Grammar School OB, Blackburn, on 3/3/2003) FL 48+23/18 FLC 2 FAC 2+1/2 Others 2*

PORTER Joel William

Born: Adelaide, Australia, 25 December 1978
Height: 5'9" **Weight:** 11.13
International Honours: Australia: 4

This lively Hartlepool front-runner made good progress last term. Joel established a fine understanding with fellow striker Adam Boyd and, growing in confidence, he himself became a more prolific goal-scorer. His enthusiasm and tireless running ensured he was a favourite of the supporters, and he was voted as Hartlepool's 'Player of the Year'.

Hartlepool U *(Free from Olympic Sharks, Australia on 27/11/2003) FL 54+12/17 FLC 1+1 FAC 6+1/2 Others 6+2/2*

POSTMA Stefan

Born: Utrecht, Holland, 10 June 1976
Height: 6'6" **Weight:** 14.12

Stefan was again second-choice 'keeper for Aston Villa last season and spent the whole of the campaign as back-up to Thomas Sorensen. Although given a couple of first-team outings, when he performed well, he became unsettled and handed in a transfer request.

Aston Villa *(£1,500,000 from De Graafschap, Holland, ex Utrecht, on 28/5/2002) PL 7+4 FLC 1 FAC 1 Others 1*

POTTER Darren Michael

Born: Liverpool, 21 December 1984
Height: 6'0" **Weight:** 12.8
International Honours: RoI: U21-9; Yth

Darren is a young central midfielder from the Liverpool FC Academy who has graduated to the fringe of the first-team squad and is also now a Republic of Ireland U21 international. He made his first-team debut as a substitute in the opening game of the season away to Grazer AK in the qualifying round of the European Champions' League and then made the starting line-up in the second leg at Anfield, also featuring in the domestic cup competitions for the Reds as a wide midfielder. He finally made his Premiership debut (again from the bench) at Charlton in February and can confidently expect further first-team opportunities in 2005-06.

Liverpool *(From trainee on 18/4/2002) PL 0+2 FLC 3+1 FAC 1 Others 1+2*

POTTER Graham Stephen

Born: Solihull, 20 May 1975
Height: 6'1" **Weight:** 12.4
International Honours: E: U21-1; Yth

This experienced left-sided defender was a near ever-present for Macclesfield last term, missing a handful of matches in the closing stages of the campaign as a result of an achilles injury. Graham usually played at left wing back in a back-five formation or left back in a four-man defence, but he performed equally well when asked to play on the left of midfield. He is a reliable player who can defend solidly and attack down the flank, his six goals making him the club's third-highest scorer.

Birmingham C *(From trainee on 1/7/1992) FL 23+2/2 FAC 1 Others 6*
Wycombe W *(Loaned on 17/9/1993) FL 2+1 FLC 1 Others 1*
Stoke C *(£75,000 on 20/12/1993) FL 41+4/1 FLC 3+1 FAC 4 Others 5*
Southampton *(£250,000 + on 23/7/1996) PL 2+6 FLC 1+1*
West Bromwich A *(£300,000 + on 14/2/1997) FL 31+12 FLC 0+3 FAC 1*
Northampton T *(Loaned on 24/10/1997) FL 4 Others 1*
Reading *(Loaned on 2/12/1999) FL 4 Others 1*
York C *(Free on 7/7/2000) FL 108+6/5 FLC 4 FAC 12/3 Others 1*
Boston U *(Free on 9/7/2003) FL 11+1 FLC 1 FAC 1 Others 0+1*
Macclesfield T *(Free on 13/2/2004) FL 55+2/8 FLC 1 FAC 3 Others 2+1*

POUTON Alan

Born: Newcastle, 1 February 1977
Height: 6'0" **Weight:** 12.8

This tough-tackling midfielder featured for Gillingham in their Carling Cup tie against Northampton early on last term before joining Hartlepool on loan. Alan did well in his spell with Pools, turning in some good performances. On his return to Priestfield he featured briefly in the side at the turn of the year, but will be looking to gain regular first-team action in 2005-06.

Oxford U *(From trainee at Newcastle U on 7/11/1995)*
York C *(Free on 8/12/1995) FL 79+11/7 FLC 5+1 FAC 5/1 Others 2*

Grimsby T *(£150,000 on 5/8/1999) FL 100+21/12 FLC 11+2 FAC 1+1*
Gillingham *(£35,000 on 17/1/2004) FL 22+9 FLC 1 FAC 1*
Hartlepool U *(Loaned on 10/9/2004) FL 5 Others 1/1*

POWELL Christopher (Chris) George Robin
Born: Lambeth, 8 September 1969
Height: 5'10" **Weight:** 11.7
Club Honours: Div 1 '00
International Honours: E: 5
Out of the first-team picture at the Valley, Chris made an early-season move to Championship side West Ham. The experienced left back proved to be an astute signing and made a big impact with his calm play under pressure. Chris rarely put a foot wrong in any match and saved his best performance for the play-off final against Preston when he was inspirational, assured and polished throughout.
Crystal Palace *(From trainee on 24/12/1987) FL 2+1 FLC 0+1 Others 0+1*
Aldershot *(Loaned on 11/1/1990) FL 11*
Southend U *(Free on 30/8/1990) FL 246+2/3 FLC 13 FAC 8 Others 21*
Derby Co *(£750,000 on 31/1/1996) P/FL 89+2/1 FLC 5 FAC 5/1*
Charlton Ath *(£825,000 on 1/7/1998) P/FL 190+10/1 FLC 8+1 FAC 8/1*
West Ham U *(Free on 10/9/2004) FL 35+1 FAC 3 Others 3*

Darryl Powell

POWELL Darren David
Born: Hammersmith, 10 March 1976
Height: 6'3" **Weight:** 13.2
Club Honours: Div 3 '99
This experienced defender started out in the Crystal Palace reserve team last season and his only first-team games came in the Carling Cup. In November he joined West Ham on loan, featuring regularly for the Hammers and scoring in the home win over Watford. However, he chose to return to Selhurst Park to fight for his place and was rewarded with a few Premiership appearances in the new year. Darren was out of contract in the summer and his future was undecided at the time of writing.
Brentford *(£15,000 from Hampton on 27/7/1998) FL 128/6 FLC 7 FAC 4 Others 10+1/2*
Crystal Palace *(£400,000 on 8/8/2002) P/FL 53+2/2 FLC 9+1/1 FAC 3 Others 0+3/1*
West Ham U *(Loaned on 19/11/2004) FL 5/1*

POWELL Darryl Anthony
Born: Lambeth, 15 January 1971
Height: 6'0" **Weight:** 12.10
International Honours: Jamaica: 17
After being released by Columbus Crew in the autumn, Darryl returned to England and began training with Nottingham Forest. He eventually signed forms in February and made his debut in the FA Cup tie at White Hart Lane soon afterwards. Thereafter he was a regular in the side although unable to prevent the team slipping to relegation. Darryl is a combative and energetic midfielder with plenty of experience in the game.
Portsmouth *(From trainee on 22/12/1988) FL 83+49/16 FLC 11+3/3 FAC 10 Others 9+5/4*
Derby Co *(£750,000 on 27/7/1995) P/FL 187+20/10 FLC 11+1/1 FAC 7+1*
Birmingham C *(Free on 12/9/2002) PL 3+8 FLC 2 FAC 1*
Sheffield Wed *(Free on 16/1/2003) FL 8 (Freed on 24/6/2003)*
Nottingham F *(Free from Colorado Rapids, USA on 14/2/2005) FL 11 FAC 2*

PRATLEY Darren Antony
Born: Barking, 22 April 1985
Height: 6'0" **Weight:** 10.13
A regular in Fulham's reserves last term, Darren spent the last three months of the season on loan at Brentford. He proved to be a skilful yet hard-working player who was a major contributor to the Bees success in reaching the play-offs. Darren scored his first senior goal when he netted at Blackpool with a hard, low right-foot shot from the edge of the box.
Fulham *(From trainee on 29/4/2002) PL 0+1 FLC 0+1*

Brentford *(Loaned on 22/2/2005) FL 11+3/1 Others 2*

PRESSMAN Kevin Paul
Born: Fareham, 6 November 1967
Height: 6'1" **Weight:** 15.5
International Honours: E: B-3; U21-1; Yth; Sch
This veteran goalkeeper joined Leicester as cover for Ian Walker during the summer of 2004 and enjoyed an extended run in the first team due to his rival's subsequent knee trouble. Kevin enjoyed more outings than he might have expected and will be remembered for a mixture of spectacular saves and the occasional gaffe. After his release he briefly linked up with Leeds United, before rejoining former boss Micky Adams at Highfield Road, although he did not add to his total of first-team appearances at either club.
Sheffield Wed *(From apprentice on 7/11/1985) P/FL 400+4 FLC 46 FAC 21 Others 7*
Stoke C *(Loaned on 10/3/1992) FL 4 Others 2*
Leicester C *(Free on 16/7/2004) FL 13 FLC 1 FAC 1*
Coventry C *(Free, via trial at Leeds U, on 24/3/2005)*

PRICE James (Jamie) Benjamin
Born: Normanton, 27 October 1981
Height: 5'9" **Weight:** 11.0
Club Honours: Div 3 '04
This versatile Doncaster defender went on loan to Burton Albion last September and was so well regarded that Nigel Clough wanted to sign him permanently. However, Jamie decided to fight for his place in the Rovers side and got his chance at right back when Simon Marples was injured at the end of October. He was doing well but in December injury struck in the shape of an ankle and foot problem. By the end of the season he was just getting back to fitness when he was told that he was being released.
Doncaster Rov *(From trainee on 6/8/1999) FL 22+3 FLC 2 FAC 2 Others 1+1*

Darren Pratley (front)

PRICE Jason Jeffrey
Born: Pontypridd, 12 April 1977
Height: 6'2" **Weight:** 11.5
Club Honours: Div 3 '00
International Honours: W: U21-7
Jason struggled to overcome an injury suffered during the 2004 close season, then found it difficult to regain his place on the right of midfield for Hull due to the impressive form of Stuart Green. He continued to be on the fringes of the first team as the Tigers completed back-to-back promotions. Jason's highlight was the goal that gave City the lead in the fine 3-1 win at Tranmere in March. After the disappointment of missing the final games of the season with a hand injury, Jason's input into the team effort was recognised in April when his City contract was extended.
Swansea C *(Free from Aberaman on 17/7/1995) FL 133+11/17 FLC 10/1 FAC 4/1 Others 4+1/1*
Brentford *(Free on 6/8/2001) FL 15/1 FLC 2 Others 1*
Tranmere Rov *(Free on 8/11/2001) FL 34+15/11 FAC 5/4*
Hull C *(Free on 1/7/2003) FL 35+25/11 FLC 2 FAC 2+1/1 Others 2/1*

PRICE Lewis Peter
Born: Bournemouth, 19 July 1984
Height: 6'3" **Weight:** 13.6
International Honours: W: U21-6; Yth
This promising young 'keeper featured for Ipswich in their Carling Cup ties against Brentford and Doncaster early on last term, and then had a brief run of Championship action following an injury to Kelvin Davies. A highlight came in the game at Coventry when he saved a spot kick. Later in the season he went on loan to League Two strugglers Cambridge United where he covered for the injured John Ruddy, and made another penalty save, this time against Notts County.

Lewis also represented Wales at U21 level during the campaign.
Ipswich T *(From Southampton juniors on 9/8/2002) FL 8+1 FLC 2*
Cambridge U *(Loaned on 19/11/2004) FL 6*

PRIET Nicolas (Nicky)
Born: Lyon, France, 31 January 1983
Height: 6'4" **Weight:** 12.10
Nicky is principally a central defender, but played all his first-team games at left back last term due to the competition for places in the middle of the Doncaster defence. Most of his opportunities came as a replacement for Tim Ryan, but he was sidelined himself for a while after injuring a foot at Bournemouth in September. Nicky was released at the end of the season.
Leicester C *(Free from Lyon, France on 29/7/2003) FLC 0+1*
Doncaster Rov *(Free on 27/7/2004) FL 7 FLC 1 Others 2*

PRIMUS Linvoy Stephen
Born: Forest Gate, 14 September 1973
Height: 6'0" **Weight:** 14.0
Club Honours: Div 1 '03
This hard-working defender was again a near ever-present for Portsmouth in their Premiership fixtures last term. A reliable player who is a great favourite of the Pompey fans, he scored once during the campaign, netting the winner at Crystal Palace on Boxing Day.
Charlton Ath *(From trainee on 14/8/1992) FL 4 FLC 0+1 Others 0+1*
Barnet *(Free on 18/7/1994) FL 127/7 FLC 9+1 FAC 8/1 Others 4*
Reading *(£400,000 on 29/7/1997) FL 94+1/1 FLC 9 FAC 6 Others 4*
Portsmouth *(Free on 4/8/2000) P/FL 133+8/3 FLC 9/1 FAC 7+1*

PRIOR Spencer Justin
Born: Southend, 22 April 1971
Height: 6'3" **Weight:** 13.4
Club Honours: FLC '97
Spencer's return to Southend in the summer of 2004 was hailed as a great signing, and his partnership with Adam Barrett in the centre of the defence was one of the reasons for the club's fine season in 2004-05. Spencer's aerial ability and positional sense meant that few opposition forwards were given the opportunity to display their skills, while he also managed to add a couple of goals during the campaign.
Southend U *(From trainee on 22/5/1989) FL 135/3 FLC 9 FAC 5 Others 7/1*
Norwich C *(£200,000 on 24/6/1993) P/FL 67+7/1 FLC 10+1/1 FAC 0+2 Others 2*
Leicester C *(£600,000 on 17/8/1996) PL 61+3 FLC 7 FAC 5 Others 2*
Derby Co *(£700,000 on 22/8/1998) PL 48+6/1 FLC 5 FAC 4*
Manchester C *(£500,000 + on 23/3/2000) P/FL 27+3/4 FLC 4 FAC 2+1*
Cardiff C *(£650,000 on 3/7/2001) FL 72+9/2 FLC 2 FAC 8 Others 5*
Southend U *(Free on 2/8/2004) FL 41/2 FAC 1 Others 8*

PROBETS Ashley
Born: Bexleyheath, 13 December 1984
Height: 5'9" **Weight:** 10.11
This promising young player can play anywhere on the left flank and made his senior debut for Rochdale in the opening game of the 2004-05 season at Scunthorpe. Thereafter Ashley was in the first-team squad for virtually every game until his contract was cancelled by mutual consent at the end of November. Soon afterwards he signed for Conference South outfit Welling United.
Arsenal *(From trainee on 7/7/2003)*
Rochdale *(Free on 22/7/2004) FL 4+5 FLC 1 Others 0+2*

PROCTOR Michael Anthony
Born: Sunderland, 3 October 1980
Height: 5'11" **Weight:** 12.7
The 2004-05 season certainly wasn't as good as Michael would have hoped for and he struggled to establish himself as a regular at Rotherham, with his only goal coming in a Carling Cup game. However, he was not helped by the fact that he played up front with a number of different partners and sometimes was asked to fulfil a role out wide. In February he had a spell on loan at Swindon, where he scored twice before returning to Millmoor.
Sunderland *(From trainee on 29/10/1997) P/FL 15+23/3 FLC 3+1 FAC 4+2/2*
Halifax T *(Loaned on 14/3/2001) FL 11+1/4*
York C *(Loaned on 9/8/2001) FL 40+1/14 FLC 1 FAC 6 Others 1*
Bradford C *(Loaned on 23/8/2002) FL 10+2/4*
Rotherham U *(Signed on 6/2/2004) FL 32+13/7 FLC 2/1 FAC 1*
Swindon T *(Loaned on 23/2/2005) FL 4/2*

PROUDLOCK Adam David
Born: Telford, 9 May 1981
Height: 6'0" **Weight:** 13.0
International Honours: E: Yth
After a slow start to his career at Hillsborough, Adam really established himself as a 'must play' striker last term. He recovered his pace and regained his sharpness in front of goal to become a real asset for the side. Adam scored two in a great win at Bristol City, but unfortunately he also picked up an injury in this game which ruled him out for the rest of the season.
Wolverhampton W *(From trainee on 15/7/1999) FL 42+29/13 FLC 4+2/2 FAC 2+3/2 Others 0+2*
Clyde *(Loaned on 1/8/2000) SL 4/4 SLC 2/1*
Nottingham F *(Loaned on 19/3/2002) FL 3*
Tranmere Rov *(Loaned on 25/10/2002) FL 5 Others 1*
Sheffield Wed *(Loaned on 13/12/2002) FL 3+2/2*
Sheffield Wed *(£150,000 on 6/9/2003) FL 37+7/9 FLC 1+1 FAC 3/3 Others 5+1/3*

PROVETT Robert **James (Jim)**
Born: Stockton, 22 December 1982
Height: 6'0" **Weight:** 13.4
This fearless goalkeeper started the 2004-05 campaign as first-choice 'keeper for Hartlepool, but was unlucky to be dropped after one disappointing performance and his replacement Dimi Konstantopoulos came in and made the position his own. Late in the season Jim was restored as first choice, but when he was ousted for a second time he asked for a transfer, although he later withdrew this request.
Hartlepool U *(From trainee on 3/4/2002) FL 66 FLC 3 FAC 4 Others 3*

PRUTTON David Thomas
Born: Hull, 12 September 1981
Height: 6'1" **Weight:** 11.10
International Honours: E: U21-25; Yth
For his wholehearted commitment and enthusiasm, not to mention his skill, David's contribution to a moribund Saints' midfield might have been one of the few plus points of the season – however, his enthusiasm occasionally spilled over and he missed a lengthy period as a result of suspension. Contrite, he kept himself in admirable trim and was selected to play in the make-or-break end-of-season game against Manchester United. Alas, David's presence was not enough to prevent the inevitable.
Nottingham F *(From trainee on 1/10/1998) FL 141+2/7 FLC 7 FAC 5*
Southampton *(£2,500,000 on 31/1/2003) PL 50+12/2 FLC 3+1/1 FAC 4*

PUGH Daniel (Danny) Adam
Born: Manchester, 19 October 1982
Height: 6'0" **Weight:** 12.10
Left-sided utility player Danny became Kevin Blackwell's first signing as Leeds manager when he arrived at Elland Road as part of the deal which saw striker Alan Smith move to Manchester United. Primarily a left back, he proved anything but a makeweight early in the season with a flurry of goals from the left of

midfield, including both in the 2-2 draw at Crewe and the Carling Cup winner against neighbours Huddersfield. Danny possesses a booming shot to add to his speed and neat touch and quickly established his popularity with the Leeds faithful.
Manchester U *(From trainee on 18/7/2000) PL 0+1 FLC 2 FAC 0+1 Others 1+2*
Leeds U *(Signed on 20/7/2004) FL 33+5/5 FLC 3/1 FAC 0+1*

PULIS Anthony James
Born: Bristol, 21 July 1984
Height: 5'10" **Weight:** 11.10
This young midfielder made his debut in senior football for Pompey as a substitute in the Carling Cup game with Cardiff last November and soon afterwards he was sold to Stoke City. Anthony was loaned out almost immediately to League One outfit Torquay United, but with the Gulls involved in a relegation battle he had few chances to shine at Plainmoor. Anthony is the son of Stoke manager Tony Pulis.
Portsmouth *(From trainee on 26/3/2003) FLC 0+1*
Stoke C *(Free on 23/12/2004)*
Torquay U *(Loaned on 24/12/2004) FL 1+2*

PUNCHEON Jason David Ian
Born: Croydon, 26 June 1986
Height: 5'8" **Weight:** 12.2
A skilful left-sided midfielder, Jason made a number of starts for MK Dons under manager Stuart Murdoch, but once Danny Wilson took over he was only ever asked to contribute from the bench. His first League goal gave the club their opening win of the season, and he was unlucky not to net again, but overall his game lacked the consistency necessary to be a regular starter. Having said that, he is still very young and he does possess an excellent left foot.
Wimbledon/MK Dons *(From trainee on 16/10/2004) FL 14+19/1 FLC 1+1 FAC 1+1 Others 2*

PURCHES Stephen (Steve) Robert
Born: Ilford, 14 January 1980
Height: 5'11" **Weight:** 12.0
This versatile Bournemouth player endured a frustrating campaign that saw him on the sidelines for most of the 2004-05 season. Steve pulled up during a pre-season match and although he attempted a come back in September, it was only in the final run-in he regained his place in the first team. However, he kept up his remarkable record of the Cherries winning every game that he has scored in when he found the net at Wrexham.
West Ham U *(From trainee on 6/7/1998)*
Bournemouth *(Free on 4/7/2000) FL 161+14/9 FLC 5 FAC 14+1 Others 8/2*

PURSE Darren John
Born: Stepney, 14 February 1977
Height: 6'2" **Weight:** 12.8
International Honours: E: U21-2
Generally solid and resilient, Darren made his debut for West Bromwich Albion against Blackburn Rovers on the opening day of the Premiership programme and produced some excellent displays in defence during the opening weeks of the season. He was a regular in the line-up when available until dropping out of contention in February.
Leyton Orient *(From trainee on 22/2/1994) FL 48+7/3 FLC 2 FAC 1 Others 7+1/2*
Oxford U *(£100,000 on 23/7/1996) FL 52+7/5 FLC 10+1/2 FAC 2*
Birmingham C *(£800,000 on 17/2/1998) P/FL 143+25/9 FLC 17+2/2 FAC 6 Others 6+1*
West Bromwich A *(£500,000 + on 18/6/2004) PL 22 FAC 2*

PURSER Wayne Montague
Born: Basildon, 13 April 1980
Height: 5'9" **Weight:** 11.13
Wayne started the 2004-05 season on the bench for Leyton Orient and came on to score a consolation goal against Macclesfield in the opening game. However, soon afterwards he moved on to Conference South club Hornchurch in search of regular first-team football. In November he made a quick return to the Football League signing for Peterborough. Used both as a wide midfielder and out-and-out striker he scored in his first two games for Posh and later on registered a double in the 3-1 win at Chesterfield.
Queens Park Rgrs *(From trainee on 21/4/1997)*
Barnet *(Free on 18/8/2000) FL 4+14/3 FLC 1+1 FAC 0+2 Others 1+1/1*
Leyton Orient *(£9,000 on 27/3/2003) FL 36+14/9 FLC 1 FAC 2/1 Others 1 (£15,000 to Hornchurch on 18/8/2004)*
Peterborough U *(Free on 12/11/2004) FL 15+11/6*

Darren Purse (right)

Q

QUASHIE Nigel Francis

Born: Peckham, 20 July 1978
Height: 6'0" **Weight:** 12.4
Club Honours: Div 1 '03
International Honours: S: 7; E: B-1; U21-4; Yth

A gifted playmaker with an educated left foot, Nigel was a regular for Pompey last term, before making the controversial decision to transfer to neighbours Southampton during the January transfer window. An instant hit with the St Mary's crowd, Nigel appeared to be everywhere at once, marrying his energy and passion with splendid guile. Alas, these admirable qualities were undermined by teammates who failed to match the passion and commitment he brought to the Saints' midfield.

Queens Park Rgrs *(From trainee on 1/8/1995) P/FL 50+7/3 FLC 0+1 FAC 4/2*
Nottingham F *(£2,500,000 on 24/8/1998) P/FL 37+7/2 FLC 7/1 FAC 1+1*
Portsmouth *(£200,000 + on 7/8/2000) P/FL 140+8/13 FLC 8/1 FAC 6+1*
Southampton *(£2,100,000 on 20/1/2005) PL 13/1*

QUEUDRUE Franck

Born: Paris, France, 27 August 1978
Height: 6'0" **Weight:** 12.4
Club Honours: FLC '04

Franck was rewarded for some committed performances for Middlesbrough with an extended contract aat the start of the 2004-05 season. Essentially, Franck is an attacking left back, but he is also able to play in midfield if called upon. He found the back of the net five times last season and in one game scored two – against Norwich City at Carrow Road in an amazing 4-4 draw. His solitary goal at the Riverside in February gave Boro' a much-needed 1-0 win against Blackburn Rovers.

Middlesbrough *(£2,500,000 from RC Lens, France, ex Meaux, on 12/10/2001) PL 119+2/8 FLC 9/1 FAC 11 Others 9*

QUIGLEY Mark

Born: Dublin, 27 October 1985
Height: 5'10" **Weight:** 11.7
International Honours: RoI: U21-1; Yth

Mark is a hard-working striker with good pace, strength and a keen eye for goal. After some excellent performances in Millwall's reserves last term he made his first full start against Brighton when he caused all kinds of problems. He will be looking to feature more regularly at first-team level in 2005-06.

Millwall *(From trainee on 1/11/2002) FL 4+5*

QUINN Alan

Born: Dublin, 13 June 1979
Height: 5'9" **Weight:** 11.7
International Honours: RoI: 6; U21-8; Yth (UEFA-U18 '98)

Out of contract with Wednesday, Alan signed for the Blades in the summer and was a regular member of the side. He worked tirelessly as an attacking midfielder winning the ball well, creating problems when running at defenders, at time showing good distribution and contributing seven, mainly vital, goals. A regular member of the Republic of Ireland squad, he made two substitute appearances.

Sheffield Wed *(Signed from Cherry Orchard on 6/12/1997) P/FL 147+10/16 FLC 14/1 FAC 6+1 Others 2*

Nigel Quashie (right)

Sunderland *(Loaned on 3/10/2003) FL 5+1*
Sheffield U *(Free on 7/7/2004) FL 38+5/7 FLC 2 FAC 1+1*

QUINN Barry Scott
Born: Dublin, 9 May 1979
Height: 6'0" **Weight:** 12.2
International Honours: RoI: 4; U21-17; Yth (UEFA-U18 '98)
Barry proved to be a key component in Oxford United's midfield last term. He operated as a playmaker always involved in the action and trying to make things happen in the centre of the park. He was a regular in the side throughout the campaign apart from injuries and came close to winning the club's 'Player of the Year' award.
Coventry C *(From trainee on 28/11/1996) P/FL 67+16 FLC 5 FAC 2+1*
Rushden & Diamonds *(Loaned on 9/1/2004) FL 4*
Oxford U *(Free on 3/3/2004) FL 39+3 FAC 1*

QUINN Stephen **James**
Born: Coventry, 15 December 1974
Height: 6'1" **Weight:** 12.10
International Honours: NI: 37; B-2; U21-1; Yth
James joined Sheffield Wednesday during the January transfer window and soon settled in at Hillsborough. Once the tall striker had got to grips with the hurly-burly nature of League One football he impressed with some cultured play. He scored the winner at Hull to take Wednesday into the play-offs and will be looking for more goals in the 2005-06 campaign.
Birmingham C *(Trainee) FL 1+3*
Blackpool *(£25,000 on 5/7/1993) FL 128+23/37 FLC 10+4/5 FAC 5+1/4 Others 7+4/2*
Stockport Co *(Loaned on 4/3/1994) FL 0+1*
West Bromwich A *(£500,000 on 20/2/1998) FL 85+29/9 FLC 3+4/1 FAC 2 (Free to Willem II, Holland on 1/7/2002)*
Notts Co *(Loaned on 30/11/2001) FL 6/3 Others 1*
Bristol Rov *(Loaned on 22/3/2002) FL 6/1*
Sheffield Wed *(Free from Willem II, Holland on 14/1/2005) FL 10+5/2 Others 3*

QUINTON Darren Jason
Born: Romford, 28 April 1986
Height: 5'8" **Weight:** 9.11
This promising Cambridge United youngster made good progress last term, featuring regularly at first-team level, although most of his appearances came from the substitutes' bench. A skilful and hard-working midfield player, Darren was rewarded with a professional contract in February.
Cambridge U *(From trainee on 8/2/2005) FL 14+18 FLC 1 Others 1+1*

Barry Quinn

R

RACHUBKA Paul Stephen
Born: San Luis Obispo, USA, 21 May 1981
Height: 6'1" **Weight:** 13.5
International Honours: E: Yth
Unable to get into the line-up at Charlton, Paul spent the first half of the 2004-05 season out on loan. His first port of call was MK Dons, then it was on to Northampton where he covered for the injured Lee Harper, winning many admirers. Finally he linked up with Huddersfield Town, where he again impressed as a quality shot-stopper and this time stayed on a more permanent basis. Paul is a 'keeper who plays with great confidence, commands his area well, and marshals others around him. With great handling and distribution skills and the ability to make outstanding saves, it is no wonder he became first choice for the Terriers.
Manchester U *(From trainee on 7/7/1999) PL 1 FLC 0+1 Others 0+1*
Oldham Ath *(Loaned on 23/11/2001) FL 16 Others 1*
Charlton Ath *(Signed on 20/5/2002)*
Huddersfield T *(Loaned on 2/3/2004) FL 13 Others 3*
MK Dons *(Loaned on 6/8/2004) FL 4*
Northampton T *(Loaned on 3/9/2004) FL 10 FLC 1*
Huddersfield T *(Free on 5/11/2004) FL 29 FAC 1*

RADEBE Lucas Valeriu
Born: Johannesburg, South Africa, 12 April 1969
Height: 6'1" **Weight:** 11.8
International Honours: South Africa: 70 (ANC '96)
Veteran defender Lucas endured an injury-ridden final season at Elland Road. He made just one start for Leeds – the 0-0 draw at Wolves back in Augus , but came off after rupturing an achilles tendon. His comeback ended when he damaged medial knee ligaments in a reserve game against Manchester United in February. He did manage to play for a World XI in the high-profile Tsunami Disaster fund-raiser in Barcelona. His popularity at Leeds was underscored when almost 38,000 watched his testimonial game at Elland Road – the proceeds being shared among nine charities in Great Britain and Africa. Lucas made a fleeting substitute appearance in the final game of the season against Rotherham at Elland Road – his 200th League game – to bring down the curtain on a marvellous career. Although his contract was up at the end of the season he was hoping to stay on at Leeds in a coaching capacity. He was also voted South Africa's 'Player of the Decade' during 2004-05.
Leeds U *(£250,000 from Kaizer Chiefs, South Africa on 5/9/1994) P/FL 180+20 FLC 9+5 FAC 19+2/1 Others 27/2*

RADZINSKI Tomasz
Born: Poznan, Poland, 14 December 1973
Height: 5'9" **Weight:** 11.7
International Honours: Canada: 27; U23-3
Tomasz joined Fulham shortly before the start of the 2004-05 season and soon became a favourite with the Craven Cottage fans. For the most part he operated on the right side of midfield although he also occasionally played as an out-and-out striker. He enjoyed a good goals-to-games ratio, with several notable strikes during the campaign. His best scoring spell came at the turn of the year when he hit five goals in eight games. A consistent threat with his speed off the mark he continued to represent Canada at international level throughout the season.
Everton *(£4,500,000 from Anderlecht, Belgium, ex Germinal Ekeren, on 20/8/2001) PL 78+13/25 FLC 2+3 FAC 5/1*
Fulham *(£1,750,000 on 11/8/2004) PL 25+10/6 FLC 2/4 FAC 4/1*

Paul Rachubka

RAMAGE Peter Iain
Born: Whitley Bay, 22 November 1983
Height: 6'1" **Weight:** 12.2
A product of the Newcastle United Academy, Peter made rapid strides during the season, progressing through the reserves, for whom he was captain, into the first team. He made a surprise appearance in the squad for the season opener at Middlesbrough, and after four more games on the bench his debut came as a substitute in the home UEFA Cup tie against Olympiakos. Although nominally a centre back he fitted in comfortably at right back, and a month later he made his first start at Old Trafford, followed by a 'Man of the Match' performance at home to Middlesbrough, while at home to Palace he played the second half at left back. Tall and strong in the tackle he looks a fine prospect.
Newcastle U *(From trainee on 15/7/2003) PL 2+2 Others 0+1*

RAMSDEN Simon Paul
Born: Bishop Auckland, 17 December 1981
Height: 6'0" **Weight:** 12.4
This defender moved to Grimsby Town along with his Sunderland colleague Michael Reddy during the summer of 2004. Simon made the starting line-up for the season's opening fixtures, but then suffered a serious neck injury at the start of September and this kept him out of action for three months. His return to fitness saw him restored to the side as a utility defender, although his favoured position is at centre half, and his performances were such that he was the first of the Mariners' out-of-contract players to secure a new deal at the end of the campaign.
Sunderland *(From trainee on 7/8/2000) FAC 0+1*
Notts Co *(Loaned on 16/8/2002) FL 21+11 FLC 1 FAC 1*
Grimsby T *(Free on 2/8/2004) FL 23+2 FLC 1*

RANKIN Isaiah (Izzy)
Born: Edmonton, 22 May 1978
Height: 5'10" **Weight:** 11.6
Izzy joined Brentford in the 2004 close season. A striker with pace and a quick turn who always gives 100 per cent, he played in the middle or wide on the right but never quite fulfilled his potential over the campaign. He scored ten goals, including two at Bournemouth and a fine individual effort in the FA Cup fifth round tie at Southampton.
Arsenal *(From trainee on 12/9/1995) PL 0+1*
Colchester U *(Loaned on 25/9/1997) FL 10+1/5 Others 1*
Bradford C *(£1,300,000 on 14/8/1998) P/FL 15+22/4 FLC 2/1 FAC 0+2 Others 1+1/1*
Birmingham C *(Loaned on 19/1/2000) FL 11+2/4*
Bolton W *(Loaned on 11/8/2000) FL 9+7/2 FLC 2*
Barnsley *(£350,000 on 19/1/2001) FL 18+29/8 FLC 1+2/1 FAC 2+1/1 Others 1+1*
Grimsby T *(Signed on 12/2/2004) FL 12/4*
Brentford *(Free on 2/7/2004) FL 33+8/8 FLC 0+1 FAC 8+1/2 Others 0+2*

RANKINE Simon **Mark**
Born: Doncaster, 30 September 1969
Height: 5'9" **Weight:** 12.11
Club Honours: Div 2 '00
Signed up by Tranmere in the close season by his former manager at Hull, Mark proved to be one of the club's most consistent performers last term. He is an experienced defensive midfielder who brings both energy and determination to the role, and was often something of an unsung hero, although his unselfish contribution was duly recognised by his colleagues when they voted him their 'Player of the Season'. The midfield general provided some much-needed stability in the middle of the park, and he was especially good at closing down the opposition, then picking up the resultant loose ball to turn defence into attack. While he may have lost a bit of pace, Mark's reading of the game is still sharp, but at the time of writing he was out of contract and his future at Prenton Park was uncertain.
Doncaster Rov *(From trainee on 4/7/1988) FL 160+4/20 FLC 8+1/1 FAC 8/2 Others 14/2*
Wolverhampton W *(£70,000 on 31/1/1992) FL 112+20/1 FLC 9+1 FAC 14+2 Others 7+1*
Preston NE *(£100,000 on 17/9/1996) FL 217+16/12 FLC 16+4/1 FAC 13/1 Others 6/1*
Sheffield U *(Free on 27/3/2003) FL 11+8 FLC 1 FAC 0+2 Others 3*
Tranmere Rov *(Free on 2/7/2004) FL 41 FLC 2 FAC 1 Others 4*

RANKINE Michael Lee
Born: Doncaster, 15 January 1985
Height: 6'1" **Weight:** 14.12
This big striker started out last season with non-league Barrow but an impressive trial led to Scunthorpe manager Brian Laws rewarding him with a contract until the end of the campaign. Michael made a fairy-tale debut, coming off the substitutes' bench to score an injury-time winner at Bury. He had to settle mainly for a place on the bench, only starting one League match and also the FA Cup tie at Chelsea in January. When used as a target man he has considerable physical strength, which causes problems for opposition defenders.
Scunthorpe U *(Free from Barrow, ex Doncaster Rov, on 15/9/2004) FL 1+20/1 FAC 1+1 Others 1*

RAPLEY Kevin John
Born: Reading, 21 September 1977
Height: 5'9" **Weight:** 10.8
Club Honours: Div 3 '99; NC '04
Kept out of Chester's Conference-winning side by the goal-scoring partnership of Daryl Clare and Darryn Stamp, Kevin was given the chance to lead the attack at the start of the 2004-05. A provider rather than an out-and-out goal-scorer, the hard-working striker was often left to plough a lone furrow up front and was unable to provide the necessary goals. However, he had the distinction of netting City's first goal back in the Football League at Notts County. Kevin subsequently spent time on loan at Forest Green Rovers and Droylsden and was released at the end of the season.
Brentford *(From trainee on 8/7/1996) FL 27+24/12 FLC 3+5/3 FAC 0+2 Others 1*
Southend U *(Loaned on 20/11/1998) FL 9/4*
Notts Co *(£50,000 on 23/2/1999) FL 21+31/4 FLC 0+3 FAC 1+1/1 Others 1*
Exeter C *(Loaned on 1/11/2000) FL 6+1 FAC 1 Others 1*
Scunthorpe U *(Loaned on 17/3/2001) FL 1+4*
Colchester U *(Free on 3/8/2001) FL 40+16/11 FLC 2+1 FAC 3 Others 2*
Chester C *(Free on 28/7/2003) FL 12+9/2 FAC 1+2/2 Others 3*

RAPONI Juan Pablo
Born: Santa Fe, Argentina, 7 May 1980
Height: 5'11" **Weight:** 11.3
Juan Pablo joined Oxford last February after the conclusion of the second half of the season in Argentina. A ball-playing midfielder, he took a while to settle into the requirements of League Two football and only started to shine just as the management team departed. At the time of writing it remained to be seen if he would remain at the club in 2005-06.
Oxford U *(Free from Olimpo de Bahia Blanco, Argentina, ex River Plate, Universidad de Chile, Banfield, on 18/2/2005) FL 5+5*

RASIAK Grzegorz
Born: Szczecin, Poland, 12 January 1979
Height: 6'3" **Weight:** 13.3
International Honours: Poland: 18
Good fortune and sound homework combined to produce an international striker for Derby County. During the

summer, Grzegorz left to join Siena in Italy but the transfer was never registered. Derby's intelligence network was aware of the situation and he moved to Pride Park in September. It was soon obvious that Grzegorz knew the game at centre forward, whether with a partner or, more often, on his own. He gave Derby's attack a focal point, useful in the air and skilful on the ground, as best shown by a dazzling goal in the home victory over Stoke City. He had a hernia operation at the end of the season, with Derby's best goals tally since Dean Sturridge in 1995-96, but returned for the play-off second leg a fortnight later. He added four Polish caps, three of them as a substitute.

Derby Co *(Free from Groclin Dyskobolia, Poland on 24/9/2004) FL 35/16 FAC 2/1 Others 1*

RAVEN David Haydn
Born: Birkenhead, 10 March 1985
Height: 6'0" **Weight:** 11.6
International Honours: E: Yth
David is a young central defender from the Liverpool FC Academy of whom the club have high hopes, and who has already been selected for England youth international honours. He made his first-team debut, along with several other reserve-team members, at right back in the Carling Cup tie at Tottenham in December when the Liverpool youngsters went through in a penalty shoot-out. He also played in the FA Cup defeat at Burnley in January and made his Premiership debut the same week as a substitute at Southampton. With Liverpool now short of central defensive cover he may receive several more first-team opportunities in 2005-06.
Liverpool *(From trainee on 20/5/2002) PL 0+1 FLC 1 FAC 1*

Grzegorz Rasiak

RAVENHILL Richard (Ricky) John
Born: Doncaster, 16 January 1981
Height: 5'10" **Weight:** 11.3
Club Honours: Div 3 '04
Ricky shared the central midfield duties for Doncaster with Paul Green and John Doolan last season. A tough, hard-working player who is uncompromising in the tackle, he added a little more finesse to his repertoire. Ricky was mostly employed in a defensive midfield role last term.
Barnsley *(From trainee on 29/6/1999)*
Doncaster Rov *(Free on 18/1/2002) FL 35+36/6 FLC 2+2/1 FAC 2+1 Others 4*

RAWLE Mark Anthony
Born: Leicester, 27 April 1979
Height: 5'11" **Weight:** 12.0
Mark featured only as a substitute for Oxford last term and in the new year he was allowed to join Conference club Tamworth on loan. Signed by Stuart Watkiss in late February, he came to Kidderminster to bolster a goal-shy attack. He scored his first goal for the Harriers in the 2-0 win at Darlington after coming off the bench and then added another two days later with a real cracker in the home game with Mansfield. The experienced striker was out of contract in the summer and at the time of writing it was unclear where his future lay.
Southend U *(£60,000 + from Boston U on 23/2/2001) FL 69+9/15 FLC 2/1 FAC 6+1/3 Others 2/1*
Oxford U *(Free on 17/7/2003) FL 10+27/8 FLC 1 FAC 0+1*
Kidderminster Hrs *(Free on 24/2/2005) FL 5+6/3*

RAYNER Simon Christopher
Born: Vancouver, Canada, 8 July 1983
Height: 6'4" **Weight:** 15.0
International Honours: Canada: U23-1
Simon was given a one-year contract by Lincoln City in the summer of 2004 and spent most of the campaign as back-up to regular goalkeeper Alan Marriott. He made his senior debut in the home League Two clash with Chester City after Marriott was forced to pull out with an ankle injury. Simon gained in confidence from the experience and retained his

place for the LDV Vans Trophy tie against Doncaster. He produced some excellent saves but lost his place when Marriott returned to fitness. Simon spent the remainder of the campaign in the reserves but was brought back on to the bench for the play-offs.
Lincoln C *(Free from Port Talbot T, ex Barry T, on 10/8/2004) FL 1 Others 1*

RAYNES Michael Bernard
Born: Wythenshawe, 15 October 1987
Height: 6'4" **Weight:** 12.0
This combative young central defender is a product of Stockport County's successful youth scheme. Michael made his debut as a late substitute in the FA Cup defeat at Swansea and featured in the starting line-up for the first time at Torquay on New Year's Day. He went on to feature regularly for the Hatters and was chosen as the club's 'Young Player of the Year'.
Stockport Co *(From trainee on 8/3/2005) FL 15+4 FAC 0+1*

REA Simon
Born: Kenilworth, 20 September 1976
Height: 6'1" **Weight:** 13.2
This experienced defender was used sparingly by Peterborough last term. In January he was loaned out to neighbours Cambridge United, where he fitted in well and contributed to a short run of good results for the U's. Back at London Road he made a handful more appearances before being released at the end of the season. Simon is a centre half who is not afraid to put his head in where it hurts.
Birmingham C *(From trainee on 27/1/1995) FL 0+1 Others 1+1*
Peterborough U *(Free on 24/8/1999) FL 146+13/8 FLC 6+1 FAC 11 Others 6+1*
Cambridge U *(Loaned on 6/1/2005) FL 4*

REBROV Sergei
Born: Gorlovka, Ukraine, 3 June 1974
Height: 5'7" **Weight:** 10.11
International Honours: Ukraine: 65
The little striker joined West Ham at the start of the season but was used on the right side of midfield for most games, even though he seemed more effective as a main striker. He produced a superb performance against Watford in November playing up front, helping the team claw back from a 2-0 deficit. Sergei enjoyed another good performance at Molineux in January when he orchestrated the play, setting up two goals for Bobby Zamora. However, he was sidelined by a calf injury in February and this kept him out of action for two months.
Tottenham H *(£11,000,000 from Dynamo Kiev, Ukraine, ex Shakhtar Donetsk, on 6/6/2000) PL 37+22/10 FLC 4+4/3 FAC 7+1/3*
West Ham U *(Free on 2/8/2004) FL 12+14/1 FLC 2+1/1 FAC 1+1 Others 0+1*

REDDY Michael
Born: Kilkenny City, 24 March 1980
Height: 6'1" **Weight:** 11.7
International Honours: RoI: U21-8; Yth
This pacy striker joined Grimsby Town in the summer of 2004 and was a regular in the first-team squad throughout last season, although he made the starting line-up in just over half of the League Two fixtures. Michael formed a useful second-half-of-the-season partnership with Martin Gritton. Despite a somewhat uneven campaign his tally of nine goals made him joint-top scorer for the Mariners.
Sunderland *(£50,000 from Kilkenny C on 30/8/1999) PL 0+10/1 FLC 2+1/1 FAC 0+1*
Swindon T *(Loaned on 27/1/2001) FL 17+1/4 Others 1+1/1*
Hull C *(Loaned on 21/9/2001) FL 1+4/4*
York C *(Loaned on 1/11/2002) FL 10+1/2*
Sheffield Wed *(Loaned on 30/1/2003) FL 13+2/3*
Sheffield Wed *(Loaned on 3/10/2003) FL 9+3/1 FAC 2 Others 3/1*
Grimsby T *(Free on 2/8/2004) FL 24+16/9 FLC 2 FAC 1 Others 0+1*

REDKNAPP Jamie Frank
Born: Barton-on-Sea, 25 June 1973
Height: 6'0" **Weight:** 12.10
Club Honours: FLC '95; ESC '01
International Honours: E: 17; B-1; U21-19; Yth; Sch
Having arrived at St Mary's in December and assessed his squad, perhaps the most astute of Harry Redknapp's decisions was to recruit his son to bolster a midfield deficient in style and gumption. Jamie certainly demonstrated that it is still possible to put one's foot on the ball and distribute with discernment in modern first-class football. Initially, he appreciably boosted the team's moral, but it also became evident that injuries over the past few years have circumscribed his game and his fitness, at times, was questionable. That said, nobody contributed more to Saints' fragile hopes of Premiership survival.
Bournemouth *(From trainee on 27/6/1990) FL 6+7 FLC 3 FAC 3 Others 2*
Liverpool *(£350,000 on 15/1/1991) P/FL 207+30/30 FLC 26+1/5 FAC 17+1/2 Others 21+6/4*
Tottenham H *(Free on 18/4/2002) PL 37+11/4 FLC 1*
Southampton *(Free on 4/1/2005) PL 16 FAC 1/1*

REED Steven
Born: Barnstaple, 18 June 1985
Height: 5'8" **Weight:** 12.2
This promising young Yeovil Town defender was a regular in the club's reserves last term, but managed only four senior appearances during the campaign. He will be hoping to feature more regularly in the squad in the 2005-06 campaign.
Yeovil T *(From juniors on 26/9/2002) FL 4+4 FLC 0+1 Others 1+1*

REEVES Alan
Born: Birkenhead, 19 November 1967
Height: 6'0" **Weight:** 12.0
This committed veteran central defender was largely confined to a coaching role and reserve-team games for Swindon last term, but found time to add to his tally of appearances and goals. Alan assumed the role of first-team coach at the County Ground following the departure of Mick Harford to Rotherham.
Norwich C *(Free from Heswall on 20/9/1988)*
Gillingham *(Loaned on 9/2/1989) FL 18*
Chester C *(£10,000 on 18/8/1989) FL 31+9/2 FLC 1+1 FAC 3 Others 3*
Rochdale *(Free on 2/7/1991) FL 119+2/9 FLC 12/1 FAC 6 Others 5*
Wimbledon *(£300,000 on 6/9/1994) PL 52+5/4 FLC 2+2 FAC 8*
Swindon T *(Free on 23/6/1998) FL 190+17/12 FLC 11+2/2 FAC 8 Others 6+1*

REEVES Martin Lee
Born: Birmingham, 7 September 1981
Height: 6'0" **Weight:** 11.12
Martin found first team-places at a premium in the centre of the park for Northampton last season. The arrival of Lee Williamson and the loan signing of Charley Hearn pushed the all-action midfield player down the pecking order. Despite putting in some useful performances with the reserves Martin was released from his contract in January and later had trials with both Rushden and Aldershot.
Leicester C *(From trainee on 1/11/2000) P/FL 1+7 FLC 1+1*
Hull C *(Loaned on 7/3/2003) FL 5+3/1*
Northampton T *(Free on 16/6/2003) FL 9+6 FLC 1+1 FAC 2+1 Others 1+2*

REGAN Carl Anthony
Born: Liverpool, 14 January 1980
Height: 6'0" **Weight:** 11.5
International Honours: E: Yth
Carl was a regular for Nationwide North club Droylsden last season and some excellent form earned him a quick recall to senior football when he was snapped up by League Two outfit Chester City in

Jamie Redknapp

March. Signed as competition at right back for Darren Edmondson, he finished the season strongly as first choice in the position.
Everton *(From trainee on 19/1/1998)*
Barnsley *(£20,000 on 15/6/2000) FL 31+6 FLC 5*
Hull C *(Free on 15/8/2002) FL 33+5 FLC 1 FAC 1 Others 1 (Freed on 25/3/2004)*
Chester C *(Free from Droylsden on 18/3/2005) FL 4+2*

REHMAN Zeshan (Zesh)
Born: Birmingham, 14 October 1983
Height: 6'2" **Weight:** 12.12
International Honours: E: Yth
A product of the Fulham youth scheme, Zesh was thrust into first-team action as a substitute at Aston Villa replacing the injured Ian Pearce. Given a chance he kept his place for 11 consecutive games producing some outstanding displays worthy of a more experienced player. A good header of the ball he also displays a terrific positional awareness.
Fulham *(From trainee on 7/6/2001) PL 15+3 FLC 4+1 FAC 2*
Brighton & Hove A *(Loaned on 29/9/2003) FL 6/2 Others 1*

REICH Marco
Born: Meisenheim, Germany, 30 December 1977
Height: 6'0" **Weight:** 11.13
International Honours: Germany: 1
The talented German midfield player had a fitful season for Derby, not helped after the turn of the year by a viral infection coupled with injuries. It took time for him to regain sharpness. When he is on top form, there is no better sight in the Championship than Marco running past defenders and creating danger but he is not a consistent player. Although predominantly right-footed, he usually plays on the left and fans know he can entertain them. Sometimes, he fades from games but is unlikely to change his style. Derby County released him at the end of his contract.
Derby Co *(Free from Werder Bremen, Germany, ex Kaiserslautern, on 16/1/2004) FL 36+14/7 FLC 1 FAC 2 Others 1+1*

REID Andrew (Andy) Matthew
Born: Dublin, 29 July 1982
Height: 5'7" **Weight:** 11.12
International Honours: RoI: 16; U21-15; Yth (UEFA-U16 '98)
This attacking midfielder started the season on the left-hand side of Nottingham Forest's midfield but then switched around the midfield positions before joining Tottenham during the January transfer window. Andy demonstrated a good footballing brain to the White Hart Lane faithful, whilst his ability to read the game give him that vital half-yard start over opponents. Yet to realise his full potential having had only half a season in the top flight to acclimatise, Andy will look to be a regular in the first team in 2005-06 and capitalise on the one goal scored for Spurs in last season's campaign.
Notingham F *(From trainee on 16/8/1999) FL 121+23/21 FLC 6+2/1 FAC 6/2 Others 2/1*
Tottenham H *(Signed on 31/1/2005) PL 13/1*

REID Levi Stanley Junior
Born: Stafford, 19 January 1983
Height: 5'5" **Weight:** 11.1
This diminutive Port Vale midfield player was a regular during the first half of last season as Vale made a decent start to the campaign. Despite being small in stature Levi was not afraid of getting stuck in and was the fulcrum of some of the team's better moves. A lack of goals held him back a bit but when he did get off the mark against Kidderminster it was a superb goal, a 30-yard strike that flew into the back of the net. Levi suffered a leg injury in December and then a period of suspension meant that he was mostly a squad player in the second half of the campaign. He was released on a free transfer in the close season.
Port Vale *(From trainee on 1/7/2003) FL 28+14 FLC 1 FAC 5/1 Others 1*

REID Paul James
Born: Sydney, Australia, 6 July 1979
Height: 5'10" **Weight:** 10.10
Such was Paul's contribution to Brighton's successful battle against relegation from the Championship that he was rewarded with an extension to his contract in February. Although the early part of his season was disrupted by a hernia problem, Paul came back into the side in October and November and shone either as a wing back or as an attacking right back. He scored a vital late equaliser at home to Leicester in April, and made a number of other goals for colleagues as he looked to get forward at every opportunity. With solid defensive work added to his passing ability as a former midfielder, Paul is a very useful man to have in the side.
Bradford C *(Free from Wollongong Wolves, Australia on 7/9/2002) FL 7+1/2*
Brighton & Hove A *(Free on 25/3/2004) FL 37+2/2 FAC 1 Others 2+1*

REID Paul Mark
Born: Carlisle, 18 February 1982
Height: 6'2" **Weight:** 12.4
International Honours: E: Yth
After signing for Barnsley during the 2004 close season, Paul went on to become one of the team's most accomplished performers last term. Whether employed in the centre of defence or in midfield he looked comfortable and his long passing was a delight. He also contributed four valuable goals for the Reds.
Carlisle U *(From trainee on 19/2/1999) FL 17+2 Others 3*
Glasgow Rgrs *(£200,000 on 1/7/2000)*
Preston NE *(Loaned on 29/1/2002) FL 0+1/1*
Northampton T *(Loaned on 31/12/2002) FL 19*
Northampton T *(£100,000 on 19/6/2003) FL 33/2 FLC 2 FAC 3 Others 2+2*
Barnsley *(Signed on 19/7/2004) FL 38+3/3 FLC 1/1 FAC 1 Others 1*

REID Steven John
Born: Kingston, 10 March 1981
Height: 6'1" **Weight:** 12.4
Club Honours: Div 2 '01
International Honours: RoI: 13; U21-2; E: Yth
After starting the 2004-05 season on the sidelines with an injury, Steven came into the Blackburn Rovers line-up last October, initially in a wide-right position, before being moved into the centre of midfield. A player who is both hard to tackle and possesses tremendous energy, he was often delegated to support the lone attacker. Steven managed two Premiership goals during the campaign, the best of which came against Birmingham and was aided by a deflection.
Millwall *(From trainee on 18/5/1998) FL 115+24/18 FLC 5+2 FAC 10/1 Others 10+1*
Blackburn Rov *(£1,800,000 + on 30/7/2003) PL 32+12/2 FLC 1 FAC 2+4 Others 1+1*

REILLY Andrew (Andy) Daniel
Born: Luton, 26 October 1985
Height: 5'10" **Weight:** 12.8
International Honours: S: U21-1; Yth
This promising left back received only one start for Wycombe last term, in the Carling Cup tie against Bristol City. He decided to leave the club in October to pursue his studies, joining Conference side Barnet, before a January move to Southern League club Chesham United.
Wycombe W *(From trainee on 2/4/2004) FL 5 Others 2*

REIZIGER Michael John
Born: Amsterdam, Holland, 3 May 1973
Height: 5'7" **Weight:** 11.0
International Honours: Holland: 72
This vastly experienced player arrived at Middlesbrough on a free transfer from

Barcelona in July 2004. The pacy, right full back had turned down Valencia to try his luck in the Premiership with manager Steve McClaren hoping that his experience would be invaluable in the club's first season in Europe. His Boro' debut came in the 2-2 home draw with Newcastle United on the opening day of the season but a shoulder injury in the remarkable 5-3 defeat at Highbury ruled him out of action for the next three months. A return to first-team action came at the end of November and a few weeks later he was celebrating his first goal for the club, a superb solo effort, in the 3-0 home win over Aston Villa.

Middlesbrough *(Free from Barcelona, Spain, Ex Ajax, Volendam, Groningen, Ajax, AC Milan, on 20/7/2004) PL 15+3/1 FAC 2 Others 4+1*

Michael Reiziger

REO-COKER Nigel Shola Andre
Born: Thornton Heath, 14 May 1984
Height: 5'8" **Weight:** 10.5
International Honours: E: U21-6; Yth
Nigel finally begun to show his full potential at West Ham last term, and after an indifferent spell around November he returned to produce some classy midfield displays. He often ran the show, winning tackles in the centre of the park and producing many fine passes. Nigel showed a maturity beyond his years and as the season reached a vital stage he was handed the captaincy, driving the side forward to victory in the play-off final against Preston.

Wimbledon *(From trainee on 15/7/2002) FL 57+1/6 FLC 2+1 FAC 2+1*
West Ham U *(£575,000 on 23/1/2004) FL 47+7/5 FLC 3 FAC 1+1 Others 3+3*

REPKA Tomas
Born: Slavicin Zlin, Czech Republic, 2 January 1974
Height: 6'0" **Weight:** 12.7
International Honours: Czech Republic: 46
This experienced right back enjoyed a fine season at West Ham and was a key figure in the team's promotion back to the Premiership when he was one of the club's most consistent performers. A strong, hard-tackling character, his experience was beneficial to the youngsters around him. In his final game for the Hammers against Preston he was unlucky not to have scored his first-ever goal for the club when he hit the woodwork.

West Ham U *(£5,500,000 from Fiorentina, Italy, ex Banik Ostrava, Sparta Prague, on 14/9/2001) P/FL 145 FLC 6 FAC 8+1 Others 6*

REYES Jose Antonio
Born: Utrera, Spain, 1 September 1983
Height: 5'9" **Weight:** 11.2
Club Honours: PL '04; CS '04; FAC '05
International Honours: Spain: 12
Jose Antonio started the season in devastating form for Arsenal scoring a goal in the FA Community Shield victory over Manchester United. He added further strikes in his first five Premiership games including a spectacular effort in the 5-3 win over Middlesborough. Yet after some rough treatment from defenders the youngster suffered a loss of form and confidence and did not find the net again until the 5-1 Champions' League mauling of Rosenborg in December. He managed to score nine times in total in the Premiership and also notched the equaliser in the FA Cup third round encounter against Stoke City. His form returned towards the end of the campaign and earned him a starting berth in the FA Cup final.

Arsenal *(£10,500,000 + from Seville, Spain on 30/1/2004) PL 32+11/11 FLC 1 FAC 8+1/3 Others 10+3/3*

REYNA Claudio
Born: Livingston, USA, 20 July 1973
Height: 5'8" **Weight:** 11.3
Club Honours: SPD '00; SC '99
International Honours: USA: 106

After enjoying a good pre-season run and starting in the opening six games of the 2004-05 campaign for Manchester City, Claudio was struck down with a thigh injury in September. The right-sided midfielder made a come back in November but broke down again and was then sent to Germany for further treatment. His eventual return from the long injury lay-off was one of the highlights of City's performances towards the end of the season and he was arguably at his best since joining from Sunderland almost two years previously.
Glasgow Rgrs *(£2,000,000 from VFL Wolfsburg, Germany, ex Virginia University, Beyer Leverkusen, on 31/3/1999) SL 57+6/9 SLC 2/1 SC 6+1 Others 25/1*
Sunderland *(£4,500,000 on 7/12/2001) PL 28/3 FLC 1/1*
Manchester C *(£2,500,000 on 29/8/2003) PL 35+5/3 FLC 1 FAC 3 Others 2+2*

RHODES Alexander (Alex) Graham
Born: Cambridge, 23 January 1982
Height: 5'9" **Weight:** 10.4
Brentford's left-sided attacker was used mainly as a substitute in the early months of the campaign. Coming off the bench and using his speed to unsettle defences he netted three times. Unfortunately his season came to a premature end at the beginning of January when he was injured after clattering into an advertising board and damaged his cruciate ligament.
Brentford *(Signed from Newmarket T on 13/11/2003) FL 4+21/4 FLC 1 FAC 1+3/1 Others 1*

RICHARDS Marc John
Born: Wolverhampton, 8 July 1982
Height: 6'0" **Weight:** 12.7
International Honours: E: Yth
Marc was missing from the Northampton Town line-up for most of last season. He picked up an injury that kept him out from early September to mid-November then his comeback was abruptly ended after he came on as a late substitute against Chester, only to be injured once more. He made a second comeback in March starting with a loan spell at Rochdale. At Spotland he was used as cover for the suspended Paul Tait, and also filled in for Grant Holt. His two goals against Leyton Orient helped keep Dale's play-off hopes alive into the last couple of games before he returned to Sixfields.
Blackburn Rov *(From trainee on 12/7/1999) FLC 1+1*
Crewe Alex *(Loaned on 10/8/2001) FL 1+3 FLC 0+1/1*
Oldham Ath *(Loaned on 12/10/2001) FL 3+2 Others 1/1*
Halifax T *(Loaned on 12/2/2002) FL 5*
Swansea C *(Loaned on 22/11/2002) FL 14+3/7*
Northampton T *(Free on 7/7/2003) FL 35+18/10 FLC 3 FAC 0+4/2 Others 4+2/1*
Rochdale *(Loaned on 24/3/2005) FL 4+1/2*

Claudio Reyna

RICHARDS Matthew (Matt) Lee
Born: Harlow, 26 December 1984
Height: 5'8" **Weight:** 11.0
International Honours: E: U21-1
Last term was something of a disappointing season for Matt who never quite managed to establish himself in the starting line-up at Ipswich. He had a couple of runs in the side as cover for injuries, but later on the manager preferred to introduce loan signings into the left-back berth.
Ipswich T *(From trainee on 31/1/2002) FL 66+15/2 FLC 3+1 FAC 3+1 Others 4+2*

RICHARDSON Frazer
Born: Rotherham, 29 October 1982
Height: 5'11" **Weight:** 12.1
International Honours: E: Yth
Frazer got Leeds United's campaign in the Championship off to a flying start with the winner over Derby in the opening game of the season at Elland Road. It proved his only strike of the campaign. Although a right back by trade he was unable to oust Gary Kelly and so mostly played on the right-hand side of midfield. Always keen to get forward, Frazer's driving runs down the flank became a feature of games at Elland Road.
Leeds U *(From trainee on 2/11/1999) P/FL 30+12/1 FLC 2 FAC 2 Others 0+1*
Stoke C *(Loaned on 10/1/2003) FL 6+1*
Stoke C *(Loaned on 8/11/2003) FL 6/1*

RICHARDSON Ian George
Born: Barking, 22 October 1970
Height: 5'10" **Weight:** 11.1
Club Honours: Div 3 '98
International Honours: E: SP-1
Notts County's longest-serving player experienced a quite memorable season in 2004-05. A natural leader on the field with his courageous approach in both defence and midfield, he featured regularly in the side until suffering a knee injury in September and this virtually ruled him out for the remainder of the campaign. In November he was appointed as caretaker player-manager of the Magpies and successfully led the club to safety from relegation only to find that his contract as manager was not renewed in the summer. At the time of writing he had been offered a contract to remain on the playing staff at Meadow Lane, but his future was yet to be decided.
Birmingham C *(£60,000 from Dagenham & Redbridge on 23/8/1995) FL 3+4 FLC 3+1 FAC 2 Others 1+2*
Notts Co *(Loaned on 19/1/1996) FL 4*
Notts Co *(£200,000 on 22/3/1996) FL 233+16/21 FLC 18/2 FAC 20/2 Others 8/1*

Matt Richards

RICHARDSON Kieran Edward
Born: Greenwich, 21 October 1984
Height: 5'9" **Weight:** 10.11
Club Honours: FAYC '03
International Honours: E: 2; U21-3
An excellent all-round midfielder with good all round skills, Kieran was used during United's short-lived Carling Cup run, playing in both matches against Leeds and West Bromwich Albion. Despite his limited appearances, big things are still expected of him at Old Trafford. He enjoyed a successful loan spell at the Hawthorns during the second half of the campaign, adding life to the centre of midfield with his darting runs, powerful shooting and enthusiasm. He also scored two goals one of them a beauty from a free kick in the 1-1 home draw with Blackburn Rovers. After helping the Baggies avoid relegation on the final day of the season, Kieran had a wonderful international debut for England against the USA in the summer, scoring both goals in the 2-1 victory.
Manchester U *(From trainee on 21/8/2003) PL 0+4 FLC 5+1/2 FAC 2+1 Others 3+5*
West Bromwich A *(Loaned on 29/1/2005) PL 11+1/3*

RICHARDSON Leam Nathan
Born: Leeds, 19 November 1979
Height: 5'7" **Weight:** 11.4
Club Honours: AMC '04
This Blackpool defender was a regular in the squad during the first half of last season, but rarely featured in the side after December. Although primarily a right back he can also play in midfield. Leam was one of several players released by the Seasiders in the summer.
Blackburn Rov *(From trainee on 31/12/1997) FLC 1*
Bolton W *(£50,000 on 13/7/2000) P/FL 5+8 FLC 3+1 FAC 1*
Notts Co *(Loaned on 9/11/2001) FL 20+1 FAC 1*
Blackpool *(Loaned on 20/12/2002) FL 20 FAC 1*
Blackpool *(Free on 15/7/2003) FL 44+7 FLC 2 FAC 1/1 Others 7+2*

RICHARDSON Marcus Glenroy
Born: Reading, 31 August 1977
Height: 6'2" **Weight:** 13.2
This tall awkward striker had a difficult time at Lincoln City early in the season when he was unable to force his way into the starting line-up. Marcus worked hard but had little luck in front of goal. He was loaned out to Rochdale where he made a couple of appearances before signing for Yeovil Town. However, he managed just two starts during his stay at Huish Park and failed to register a goal.

Cambridge U *(Free from Harrow Borough on 16/3/2001) FL 7+9/2 FLC 1*
Torquay U *(£5,000 on 18/9/2001) FL 21+18/8 FLC 0+1 FAC 1 Others 0+1*
Hartlepool U *(Free on 1/10/2002) FL 23+4/5 FAC 2/1*
Lincoln C *(Loaned on 22/8/2003) FL 9+3/4 Others 1/1*
Lincoln C *(Free on 8/12/2003) FL 32+8/10 FLC 0+1 FAC 1 Others 2*
Rochdale *(Loaned on 17/2/2005) FL 1+1*
Yeovil T *(Free on 23/3/2005) FL 2+2*

RICHMOND Andrew (Andy) John

Born: Nottingham, 9 January 1983
Height: 6'3" **Weight:** 12.10
Andy was again second-choice 'keeper at Chesterfield last term. His only League One appearance came at Bournemouth in November when he kept a clean sheet. After several years as the Spireites' regular reserve goalie, Andy was released in March and joined Matlock Town.
Chesterfield *(From trainee on 9/7/2002) FL 7+1 Others 1*

RICKARDS Scott

Born: Sutton Coldfield, 3 November 1981
Height: 5'9" **Weight:** 12.6
Scott had something of a disappointing time at Kidderminster at the start of last term, the speedy forward being limited to just a handful of appearances from the substitutes' bench before being loaned out to Redditch United. Soon afterwards he was released by Harriers and he then made a permanent move to the Conference North outfit.
Kidderminster Hrs *(£5,000 from Tamworth, ex Derby Co trainee, on 12/12/2003) FL 5+12/1 FAC 0+1*

RICKETTS Donovan Damon

Born: Kingston, Jamaica, 7 June 1977
Height: 6'4" **Weight:** 14.7
International Honours: Jamaica
This giant goalkeeper signed for Bradford as first choice during the summer of 2004, but found himself overtaken by Paul Henderson. With his rival's form so consistent, Donovan had to show great patience but his chance finally arrived in the last four games of the season when he impressed with his huge kicking and presence around the penalty area.
Bradford C *(Signed from Village U, Jamaica on 28/8/2004) FL 4*

RICKETTS Michael Barrington

Born: Birmingham, 4 December 1978
Height: 6'2" **Weight:** 11.12
Club Honours: FLC '04
International Honours: E: 1
Michael arrived at Elland Road on a free transfer from Middlesbrough. The big, powerful forward started the opening three Leeds matches but struggled with the pace of the games. He later worked under a personal fitness coach to sharpen himself up but the Championship goals simply would not come. His only strike was a well-taken winner in the Carling Cup against Swindon when he calmly finished Gary Kelly's excellent pass. As the season progressed Michael found himself out of the picture and was loaned to Stoke, but he struggled to make an impression at the Britannia Stadium and subsequently returned to Elland Road.
Walsall *(From trainee on 13/9/1996) FL 31+45/14 FLC 2+4 FAC 2+2 Others 3+1/1*
Bolton W *(£500,000 on 17/7/2000) P/FL 63+35/37 FLC 0+4/3 FAC 4+3/4 Others 1+2/2*
Middlesbrough *(£2,200,000 on 31/1/2003) PL 12+20/3 FLC 3+2/1 FAC 2*
Leeds U *(Free on 8/7/2004) FL 9+12 FLC 2+1/1*
Stoke C *(Loaned on 22/2/2005) FL 1+10*

RICKETTS Rohan Anthony

Born: Clapham, 22 December 1982
Height: 5'9" **Weight:** 11.0
Club Honours: FAYC '01
International Honours: E: Yth
This promising Tottenham midfielder featured in the Carling Cup tie against Oldham before going out on loan to Coventry City where he played in a wide-left role but admitted that the pace of Championship football had been a big surprise to him. Back at White Hart Lane he made a handful more first-team appearances at the turn of the year before going out on loan again, this time to Wolves where he became Glenn Hoddle's first signing for the club. After settling in as a substitute Rohan began to perform well and was particularly influential against Reading when he scored a well-taken winning goal. He is dangerous when running at defenders, and capable of slipping inside a telling pass or having a go himself.
Arsenal *(From trainee on 8/9/2001) FLC 0+1*
Tottenham H *(Free on 11/7/2002) PL 17+13/1 FLC 4+2/1*
Coventry C *(Loaned on 15/10/2004) FL 5+1*
Wolverhampton W *(Loaned on 15/3/2005) FL 3+4/1*

RICKETTS Samuel (Sam) Derek

Born: Aylesbury, 11 October 1981
Height: 6'0" **Weight:** 11.12
International Honours: W: 3; E: SP-4
A versatile defender who is capable of playing at full back on either flank, Sam joined Swansea during the 2004 close season and enjoyed an excellent campaign with the Vetch Field club, being a near ever-present in a side that won automatic promotion. His fine form was recognised on a wider stage when he was called up to the full Wales international squad, making his debut against Hungary in February and was selected for the PFA League Two team of the season.
Oxford U *(From trainee on 20/4/2000) FL 32+13/1 FLC 1 Others 2 (Free to Telford U on 7/7/2003)*
Swansea C *(Free on 22/6/2004) FL 42 FLC 1 FAC 5 Others 2/1*

RIDGEWELL Liam Matthew

Born: Bexley, 21 July 1984
Height: 5'10" **Weight:** 11.0
Club Honours: FAYC '02
International Honours: E: U21-5; Yth
This young Aston Villa central defender was sidelined for three months after suffering a knee injury in the final pre-season tour match in Sweden. However, he was back in action by October, and went on to enjoy a short run in the side during the hectic Christmas programme and sustained a run of eleven games. Liam also continued to represent England at U21 level during the campaign.
Aston Villa *(From trainee on 26/7/2001) PL 17+9 FLC 1+2 FAC 1+1*
Bournemouth *(Loaned on 11/10/2002) FL 2+3*

RIDLER David (Dave) George

Born: Liverpool, 12 March 1976
Height: 6'0" **Weight:** 12.1
This central defender had been a key figure in Shrewsbury's Conference play-off success of 2003-04, but never quite reached the same heights in League Two football last term. Restricted to just a handful of starts, he opted to leave the club before the season ended to seek a contract elsewhere for 2005-06.
Wrexham *(Free from Rocky's on 3/7/1996) FL 104+12/1 FLC 5 FAC 10+2 Others 8+2/1*
Macclesfield T *(Free on 16/7/2001) FL 53+3 FLC 2 FAC 4+1 Others 2*
Shrewsbury T *(Free on 11/7/2003) FL 6+3 FLC 1 Others 2*

RIDLEY Lee

Born: Scunthorpe, 5 December 1981
Height: 5'9" **Weight:** 11.2
Lee's fourth season as a professional finally saw him establish himself as a first choice for Scunthorpe United. A pre-season injury to Kevin Sharp gave him a place in the starting line-up on the opening day and he never looked back,

turning in a string of solid displays as the Iron enjoyed the meanest defensive record in the division. A dependable left back, who can also deputise at centre half, he is tidy in possession and his long throw can cause problems for opposition defences. Lee only scored one goal during the promotion-winning season, the opening strike in the 2-0 televised FA Cup victory over League One Wrexham in December.
Scunthorpe U *(From trainee on 3/7/2001) FL 70+9/1 FLC 1 FAC 6+1/1 Others 0+2*

RIGGOTT Christopher (Chris)

Born: Derby, 1 September 1980
Height: 6'3" **Weight:** 12.2
Club Honours: FLC '04
International Honours: E: U21-8; Yth
Chris cemented his place as a regular first-team choice at the Riverside last term and even managed to score his first goal for the club in 21 months against Liverpool in November. The centre half struggled with a knee injury throughout the latter part of the season, causing him to lose six months on the sidelines, but he had re-established himself prior to undergoing knee surgery in mid-May.
Derby Co *(From trainee on 5/10/1998) P/FL 87+4/5 FLC 7/1 FAC 2/1*
Middlesbrough *(£1,500,000 + on 31/1/2003) PL 38+5/4 FLC 6+1 FAC 2+1 Others 8/1*

RIGOGLIOSO Adriano

Born: Liverpool, 28 May 1979
Height: 5'11" **Weight:** 11.12
Club Honours: Div 3 '04
International Honours: E: SP-1
Adriano had a frustrating time with Doncaster last term when he was restricted to just a couple of starts in League One matches and generally featured from the bench. He is a skilful midfield player who is particularly effective in dead-ball situations, but just needs to add a little more consistency to his game.
Doncaster Rov *(£30,000 from Morecambe, ex Liverpool trainee, Marine, on 6/11/2003) FL 7+22 FLC 0+1 FAC 0+2 Others 1/1*

RIIHILAHTI Aki

Born: Helsinki, Finland, 9 September 1976
Height: 6'1" **Weight:** 12.6
International Honours: Finland: 59; U21-2; Yth
Aki signed a new contract for Crystal Palace during the summer of 2004 and featured regularly in the side last term, scoring four Premiership goals. The tall and skilful midfield player was also a regular at international level for Finland, contributing to their campaign to qualify for the 2006 World Cup finals.
Crystal Palace *(£200,000 from Valerenga, Norway, ex HJK Helsinki, on 22/3/2001) P/FL 121+21/11 FLC 7+3/1 FAC 3 Others 3*

RIISE Jon Arne

Born: Molde, Norway, 24 September 1980
Height: 6'1" **Weight:** 12.6
Club Honours: ESC '01; CS '01; FLC '03; UEFACL '05
International Honours: Norway: 45; U21-17; Yth
After a relatively subdued season in 2003-04 this left-sided defender or midfielder was back to his best form last season. Starting out at left back, as in the previous campaign, he was restored to his more favoured left-wing position in October, in place of Harry Kewell who was labouring with both form and fitness. Jon Arne scored his first Premiership goal in 65 outings against Charlton in October and recorded seven more before the end of the season, most of them powerful drives and volleys from the left side of the penalty box. His best performance came on Boxing Day when he scored twice and played a part in three other goals as the Reds hammered West Brom 5-0. He also scored the opening goal in the first minute of the Carling Cup final with Chelsea in February, although the Reds failed to consolidate their early lead and lost 3-2 in extra time. In the European Champions' Cup final in Istanbul he supplied the cross for Steven Gerrard's header which triggered Liverpool's amazing comeback from a 3-0 half-time deficit.
Liverpool *(£3,770,000 from AS Monaco, France, ex Aalesund, on 26/7/2001) PL 121+19/19 FLC 8+3/1 FAC 5+1 Others 45+2/2*

RIVERS Mark Alan

Born: Crewe, 26 November 1975
Height: 5'11" **Weight:** 11.2
Club Honours: Div 1 '04
After three years away, Mark returned to Crewe last summer after being released by the Canaries. A winger with a direct style and plenty of pace, he is a useful player to have around for he can operate in any of the forward positions if required and is always likely to score goals.
Crewe Alex *(From trainee on 6/5/1994) FL 177+26/43 FLC 14+1/8 FAC 12/5 Others 5+3/3*
Norwich C *(£600,000 on 28/6/2001) FL 54+20/10 FLC 1 FAC 2+2 Others 3/1*
Crewe Alex *(Free on 23/7/2004) FL 26+8/7 FLC 1+2/1 FAC 1*

RIZZO Nicholas (Nicky) Anthony

Born: Sydney, Australia, 9 June 1979
Height: 5'10" **Weight:** 12.0
International Honours: Australia: 1; U23-8
Nicky made his debut for MK Dons in the 4-1 home defeat against Luton, and his lively wing display earned him a regular starting berth for the next couple of months. Confined to bench duties throughout the club's 11-match unbeaten run, he returned to score the crucial opening goal in the penultimate match at Peterborough, and contributed again in the crucial final day win over Tranmere that secured the club's League One status.
Liverpool *(Signed from Sydney Olympic, Australia on 26/9/1996)*
Crystal Palace *(£300,000 on 31/7/1998) FL 15+21/1 FLC 1+3/1 FAC 1 (Free to Ternana on 18/7/2000)*
MK Dons *(Free from Prato on 19/11/2004) FL 13+5/2 FAC 2*

ROBBEN Arjen

Born: Groningen, Holland, 23 January 1984
Height: 5'11" **Weight:** 12.8
Club Honours: FLC '05; PL '05
International Honours: Holland: 14
Despite a season interrupted by three serious foot injuries, Chelsea's brilliant winger had a sensational impact on the Premiership. When Arjen made his delayed debut for the Blues in October the team suddenly found that extra attacking dimension when goals had previously been hard to come by. He exploded onto the Premiership in meteoric fashion scoring brilliant goals against CSKA Moscow, Everton, Newcastle and Fulham in successive matches during a fruitful November when the Blues regularly scored four per match. This sensational entrance into English football earned him the 'Barclays Player of the Month' for November after just four starts! Chelsea were virtually unbeatable either side of the New Year and Arjen's scintillating wing combination in tandem with Damien Duff wreaked havoc in opposing defences and created chances galore for the Blues' strike force. The foot injuries sustained against Blackburn and Romania (whilst on international duty) deprived Arjen of appearances in glamour Champions' League ties against Barcelona and Bayern Munich plus the Carling Cup final. Clearly not fully fit he made substitute appearances against Liverpool in the Champions'

Arjen Robben

eague semi-final and his lack of ıarpness was a major factor in helsea's inability to pierce the Reds' earguard. Even with such an injury-avaged season Arjen still made the PFA remiership team of the season and arned a nomination for PFA 'Young layer of the Year'.
helsea (£13,000,000 from PSV Eindhoven, olland, on 22/7/2004) PL 14+4/7 FLC 3+1/1 AC 0+2 Others 2+3/1

ROBERT Laurent
orn: Saint-Benoit, Reunion, 21 May 975
leight: 5'9" **Weight:** 11.2
nternational Honours: France: 9; B-4
his mercurial player had a mixed season n the left flank of Newcastle's midfield ıst term. On his day he is a threat to any efence and a potential match winner nd his running down the wing against helsea in the FA Cup was exhilarating to vatch, while stunning free kicks won the ome game against Liverpool and the way tie at Olympiakos. However, these erformances were interspersed with onflicts with the club's management, eaving his future under some doubt. He elivers wicked crosses with his left foot nd is a dead-ball specialist, all of his oals during the season coming from free icks.
***lewcastle U** (£10,500,000 from Paris St iermain, France, ex Montpellier, Nancy, on 0/8/2001) PL 110+19/22 FLC 6+1/2 FAC 0/3 Others 29+6/5*

ROBERTS Christian John
orn: Cardiff, 22 October 1979
leight: 5'10" **Weight:** 12.8
lub Honours: AMC '03
nternational Honours: W: U21-1; Yth
his pacy striker only added one goal to is Bristol City account before being ransferred to Swindon Town early on last eason. He scored on his debut for his ıew club to earn a 1-0 victory over Oldham and put in some useful erformances, especially when inspiring he side to overcome a two-goal deficit igainst Sheffield Wednesday. However, ıe suffered an injury during the game igainst Peterborough in December confining him to the sidelines for two nonths, and he struggled to make the ame impact later in the campaign.
***ardiff C** (From trainee on 8/10/1997) FL 5+17/3 FLC 2 FAC 2+3 Others 0+2*
***xeter C** (Free on 24/7/2000) FL 67+12/18 FLC 2+1 FAC 2+1 Others 2*
***ristol C** (Signed on 26/3/2002) FL 55+29/20 FLC 5+1 FAC 4+2/4 Others 10+2/2*
***windon T** (£20,000 on 15/10/2004) FL 18+3/3 FAC 2/1*

ROBERTS Gareth Wyn
Born: Wrexham, 6 February 1978
Height: 5'7" **Weight:** 12.6
Club Honours: FAYC '96
International Honours: W: 8; B-1; U21-10
Gareth has made the left-back position at Tranmere his own, but he has also played in left midfield when required. A consistent but deceptively tough player who fortunately suffers few injuries, he missed only a handful of games and also grabbed four goals during 2004-05, including the 'Goal of the Season', a 20-yard volley in Rovers' 5-1 victory against Wrexham at the Racecourse. Gareth never turns in less than reliable, calm and mature performances week after week, while remaining steadily solid and clean in the tackle; he continued to feature as a part of the Wales international set-up.
***Liverpool** (From trainee on 22/5/1996. £50,000 to Panionios, Greece on 15/1/1999)*
***Tranmere Rov** (Free on 5/8/1999) FL 232+5/11 FLC 21 FAC 20+1 Others 9/2*

ROBERTS Gary Steven
Born: Chester, 4 February 1987
Height: 5'8" **Weight:** 10.5
International Honours: E: Yth
Another product of the youth system at

Gareth Roberts

Crewe, Gary has represented England at U18 level. A regular in the club's Academy side, he also made two full Championship appearances against Sheffield United at home and West Ham away. Gary is an all-action midfield player with a good eye for goal-scoring opportunities.
Crewe Alex *(From trainee on 7/7/2004) FL 2+2*

ROBERTS Iwan Wyn
Born: Bangor, 26 June 1968
Height: 6'3" **Weight:** 14.2
Club Honours: Div 1 '04
International Honours: W: 15; B-1; Yth; Sch
This experienced striker joined Gillingham as a player-coach during the summer of 2004 and scored three times early on last term. However, he was left out of the side following a change in management at Priestfield and in March he joined League One strugglers Cambridge United on loan. Exchanging one relegation battle for another, Iwan scored on his debut for the U's against Bury and featured regularly in the closing stages of the campaign, adding two more goals.
Watford *(From trainee on 4/7/1988) FL 40+23/9 FLC 6+2/3 FAC 1+6 Others 5*
Huddersfield T *(£275,000 on 2/8/1990) FL 141+1/50 FLC 13+1/6 FAC 12/4 Others 14+1/8*
Leicester C *(£100,000 on 25/11/1993) P/FL 92+8/41 FLC 5/1 FAC 5/2 Others 1*
Wolverhampton W *(£1,300,000 + on 15/7/1996) FL 24+9/12 FLC 2 FAC 0+1 Others 2*
Norwich C *(£900,000 on 9/7/1997) FL 232+46/84 FLC 15+3/10 FAC 6+1/2 Others 0+3/1*
Gillingham *(Free on 19/7/2004) FL 11+9/3 FLC 0+1 FAC 0+1*
Cambridge U *(Loaned on 1/3/2005) FL 11/3*

ROBERTS Jason Andre Davies
Born: Park Royal, 25 January 1978
Height: 5'11" **Weight:** 12.7
International Honours: Grenada
A hard-working and purposeful striker with an eye for goal, Jason enjoyed a sensational partnership with Nathan Ellington last term as Wigan Athletic gained promotion to the Premiership. His power, pace and finishing were just too much for opponents to handle at times, while his personal tally of 21 goals made him the second-top scorer in the Championship behind Ellington. Jason's all-round contribution was recognised when he was named as the club's 'Player of the Season', whilst he was also named in the PFA Championship team of the season. Jason suffered a broken leg playing in the final game of the campaign but was expected to be fit for the start of 2005-06.
Wolverhampton W *(£250,000 from Hayes on 12/9/1997)*
Torquay U *(Loaned on 19/12/1997) FL 13+1/6 Others 1*
Bristol C *(Loaned on 26/3/1998) FL 1+2/1*
Bristol Rov *(£250,000 on 7/8/1998) FL 73+5/38 FLC 6/3 FAC 6/7 Others 3*
West Bromwich A *(£2,000,000 on 27/7/2000) P/FL 75+14/24 FLC 3+1/2 FAC 6 Others 2/1*
Portsmouth *(Loaned on 1/9/2003) PL 4+6/1 FLC 2/3*
Wigan Ath *(£2,000,000 on 13/1/2004) FL 59/29 FAC 1*

ROBERTS Mark Alan
Born: Northwich, 16 October 1983
Height: 5'11" **Weight:** 11.12
Mark is a young player who gave some impressive performances for Crewe Alexandra in the pre-season games and was eventually rewarded with some first-team outings in the Championship and also in the Carling Cup tie against Sunderland. Mark suffered an injury in November which required surgery, and as a result he was unable to play again during the campaign. The defender is looking forward to the 2005-06 season with keen anticipation of further experience of senior football.
Crewe Alex *(From trainee on 6/7/2003) FL 3+3 FLC 1*

ROBERTS Neil Wyn
Born: Wrexham, 7 April 1978
Height: 5'10" **Weight:** 11.0
Club Honours: Div 2 '03
International Honours: W: 3; B-1; U21-1; Yth
A striker with a high work rate, Neil found himself restricted to just one start in the Carling Cup for Wigan Athletic last season. Unable to split the striking partnership of Nathan Ellington and Jason Roberts, he was allowed to join Bradford City on loan netting on his debut in a 4-1 win over Bristol City. Unfortunately for the Bantams, he did too well and Doncaster came in with an offer which he quickly accepted much to City's disappointment. Neil proved to be popular with the Rovers' fans for his all-action style of play. He never seems to tire over the 90 minutes and holds the ball up well before laying it off for his partner. He also scored six times for Rovers during the season.
Wrexham *(From trainee on 3/7/1996) FL 58+17/17 FLC 1/1 FAC 11+1/4 Others 2+2/2*
Wigan Ath *(£450,000 on 18/2/2000) FL 64+61/19 FLC 7+3/2 FAC 6/1 Others 3+1*
Hull C *(Loaned on 25/1/2002) FL 3+3*
Bradford C *(Loaned on 17/9/2004) FL 3/1 Others 1*
Doncaster Rov *(Signed on 7/10/2004) FL 30+1/6 FAC 2*

ROBERTS Stephen (Steve) Wyn
Born: Wrexham, 24 February 1980
Height: 6'0" **Weight:** 12.7
Club Honours: AMC '05
International Honours: W: 1; U21-4; Yth
Steve enjoyed an excellent season with Wrexham last term and was a key figure in the centre of the defence. He was never hurried on the ball and provided a strong presence at the back, remaining in the side until an injury in the LDV Vans Trophy final caused him to miss the closing stages of the season. Shortly before this Steve had won his first full cap for Wales when making a brief appearance from the bench for Wales in the friendly international against Hungary at the Millennium Stadium in February.
Wrexham *(From trainee on 16/1/1998) FL 143+7/6 FLC 3 FAC 7+1/1 Others 11+1/1*

ROBERTS Stuart Ian
Born: Carmarthen, 22 July 1980
Height: 5'7" **Weight:** 9.8
International Honours: W: U21-13
Stuart started his Kidderminster career with a bang. The winger, signed on non-contract terms after his release by Swansea, scored after just 35 seconds of his debut at Mansfield, the fastest goal scored by any Harriers' player in the Football League. Stuart played just five more games before being released and subsequently joined Conference outfit Forest Green.
Swansea C *(From trainee on 9/7/1998) FL 58+34/14 FLC 4+3 FAC 4 Others 7+2*
Wycombe W *(£102,500 on 19/10/2001) FL 37+33/4 FLC 2+1 FAC 4+2 Others 2+2*
Swansea C *(Free on 24/2/2004) FL 8+4/1*
Kidderminster Hrs *(Free on 20/8/2004) FL 4+1/1 FLC 1*

ROBERTSON Gregor Aedan
Born: Edinburgh, 19 January 1984
Height: 6'0" **Weight:** 12.4
International Honours: S: U21-10
This young Nottingham Forest defender was used sparingly from the bench in the opening stages of the 2004-05 campaign and it was not until mid-September that he featured in the starting line-up. He appeared fairly regularly thereafter, and also added to his tally of caps for Scotland at U21 level.
Nottingham F *(From Heart of Midlothian juniors on 8/2/2001) FL 25+11 FLC 2+2 FAC 4*

ROBERTSON Hugh Scott
orn: Aberdeen, 19 March 1975
eight: 5'9" **Weight:** 12.7
left back with a powerful shot, Hugh's
ng-range goals have been a feature of
s game at Hartlepool. Last season he
issed a lengthy spell due to a foot injury
nd subsequently struggled to find his
est form. He played some first-team
otball, but the latter part of his
ampaign was also badly disrupted
rough injury.
berdeen *(Signed from Lewis U on 4/8/1993) SL 13+9/2 SLC 0+1 SC 1*
undee *(Signed on 18/1/1997) SL 41+11/3 LC 1+1 SC 1*
rechin C *(Loaned on 20/3/1998) SL 5+2*
verness CT *(Loaned on 3/10/1998) SL 12*
yr U *(Loaned on 3/11/2000) SL 8/2*
oss Co *(Free on 1/2/2001) SL 100+3/12 LC 8 SC 4 Others 5*
artlepool U *(Free on 31/1/2004) FL 5+3/6 FAC 4 Others 2*

ROBERTSON Mark William
orn: Sydney, Australia, 6 April 1977
eight: 5'9" **Weight:** 11.4
nternational Honours: Australia: U23-; Yth
his combative midfielder was plagued by
jury at Stockport last season. He was a
egular in the starting line-up during the
rst half of the campaign but picked up
n injury against MK Dons in December
nd this ruled him out for a couple of
onths. On his return he only managed
x more appearances before another
jury, coincidentally in the return fixture
gainst the Dons, ruled him out for the
emainder of the season.
urnley *(Free from Marconi Stallions, ustralia on 3/10/1997) FL 27+9/1 FLC 1+2 thers 3+2*
windon T *(Loaned on 22/8/2000) FL 4+6/1 .C 2+1*
undee *(Free on 8/3/2001) SL 9+16 SLC 3 C 1+1 Others 1+1*
t Johnstone *(Loaned on 31/1/2003) SL 0/1*
t Johnstone *(Loaned on 29/8/2003) SL +1/1 SLC 3+1*
tockport Co *(Free on 9/1/2004) FL 27+5/1 AC 3 Others 1*

ROBINSON Andrew (Andy) Mark
orn: Birkenhead, 3 November 1979
eight: 5'8" **Weight:** 11.4
his attacking Swansea City midfielder
ound it difficult to emulate his exciting
isplays of the previous campaign during
he early stages of 2004-05.
evertheless, he chipped in with eight
eague Two goals and also netted the
Swans' second goal as they went on to
defeat Wrexham and win the FAW Cup.
Tranmere Rov *(Free from Cammell Laird on 11/11/2002) Others 0+1*
Swansea C *(Free on 14/8/2003) FL 63+11/16 FLC 1 FAC 8+1/2 Others 1*

ROBINSON Anton Dale
Born: Harrow, 17 February 1986
Height: 5'9" **Weight:** 10.3
A product of the successful Millwall youth set-up, Anton performed consistently well for the U18s last term and got his chance to start his first senior game for Millwall in the FA Cup third round tie against Wolves, when the squad was decimated by injuries. The fast and strong midfielder produced a good display and will be looking for more first-team action in 2005-06.
Millwall *(From trainee on 23/4/2004) FAC 1*

ROBINSON Carl Phillip
Born: Llandrindod Wells, 13 October 1976
Height: 5'10" **Weight:** 12.10
Club Honours: Div 1 '03; Ch '05
International Honours: W: 21; B-2; U21-6; Yth
This central midfielder enjoyed an excellent season at Sunderland, picking up a deserved Championship winners' medal. Carl soon established himself as a key player in Mick McCarthy's side, forming a strong partnership with Jeff Whitley in the Black Cats' midfield 'engine room'. A strong tackler, Carl distributes the ball well and can also weigh in with important goals as he demonstrated with a superb strike to clinch three points at Leeds in September and a priceless effort at promotion rivals Ipswich in April that earned a precious draw. Carl also bravely played through the pain barrier after breaking his nose against Rotherham in October and then again against Millwall only a month later.
Wolverhampton W *(From trainee on 3/7/1995) FL 129+35/19 FLC 12+1/1 FAC 14/3*
Shrewsbury T *(Loaned on 28/3/1996) FL 2+2 Others 1*
Portsmouth *(Free on 31/7/2002) P/FL 11+5 FLC 1+1 FAC 0+2*
Sheffield Wed *(Loaned on 17/1/2003) FL 4/1*
Walsall *(Loaned on 20/2/2003) FL 10+1/1*
Rotherham U *(Loaned on 18/9/2003) FL 14 FLC 2*
Sheffield U *(Loaned on 30/1/2004) FL 4+1*
Sunderland *(Free on 25/3/2004) FL 46+1/5 FLC 1 FAC 2 Others 1+1*

ROBINSON Jake David
Born: Brighton, 23 October 1986
Height: 5'9" **Weight:** 10.4
A will-o'-the-wisp striker, Jake repeated his feat of scoring for the Brighton first team, reserves and youth team last term. He enjoyed a great start to the season, netting his first League goal at Reading and quickly becoming a favourite of the Withdean crowd. He fell behind others in the pecking order, though, and in February he joined Conference side Aldershot Town on loan to gain experience. Recalled in April, he played his part in Albion's successful fight against relegation, especially at Burnley where, as a substitute, he transformed the game to earn a precious point. What he lacks in physical stature Jake more than makes up for with intelligent running, pace and a keen eye for goal, and he will be hoping to be given more opportunities in 2005-06.
Brighton & Hove A *(From trainee on 22/12/2003) FL 2+17/1 FLC 0+2 Others 0+1/1*

ROBINSON John Robert Campbell
Born: Bulawayo, Rhodesia, 29 August 1971
Height: 5'10" **Weight:** 11.7
Club Honours: Div 1 '00
International Honours: W: 30; U21-5
This wholehearted midfielder played a handful of games for Cardiff in the early part of last season before returning to live in the South-East, at which point he signed for Gillingham. Unfortunately he tore a hamstring during the warm up at West Ham soon after his arrival and this effectively ended his stay at Priestfield. Later in the season John featured for Conference outfit Crawley Town.
Brighton & Hove A *(From trainee on 21/4/1989) FL 57+5/6 FLC 5/1 FAC 2+1 Others 1+2/2*
Charlton Ath *(£75,000 on 15/9/1992) P/FL 296+36/35 FLC 20+4/5 FAC 17+3/3 Others 5+1*
Cardiff C *(Free on 10/7/2003) FL 39+3/3 FLC 0+1*
Gillingham *(Free on 15/10/2004) FL 2+2*

ROBINSON Marvin Leon St Clair
Born: Crewe, 11 April 1980
Height: 6'0" **Weight:** 12.9
International Honours: E: Sch
This powerful young striker spent last term playing on short-term contracts for a series of clubs. Starting out at Notts County, he moved on to Rushden, where will be remembered for his dramatic, last-minute winner with a diving header at the far post to knock Bradford City out of the FA Cup at Valley Parade. In December he moved on to Walsall where he netted

twice on his home debut, but was eventually released. Marvin ended the season at Stockport where he made little real impact and was released once more in the summer.
Derby Co *(From trainee on 8/7/1998) P/FL 3+9/1*
Stoke C *(Loaned on 13/9/2000) FL 3/1*
Tranmere Rov *(Loaned on 29/11/2002) FL 1+5/1 Others 0+1*
Chesterfield *(Free on 19/9/2003) FL 17+15/6 FAC 1 Others 2/1*
Notts Co *(Free on 10/9/2004) FL 1+1*
Rushden & Diamonds *(Free on 9/11/2004) FL 0+2 FAC 2/1*
Walsall *(Free on 7/12/2004) FL 4+6/4*
Stockport Co *(Signed on 24/3/2005) FL 3*

ROBINSON Matthew Adam
Born: Newmarket, 22 March 1984
Height: 5'10" **Weight:** 11.6
A promising young midfielder who can also play up front, Matthew began the 2004-05 season on short-term contracts with Cambridge United. However, his only start came in the LDV Vans Trophy tie against Leyton Orient and otherwise he was restricted to just a handful of outings from the substitutes' bench. He eventually moved on to join local rivals Cambridge City in the new year, remaining with the Conference South outfit until the end of the season.
Bournemouth *(From trainee at Ipswich T on 31/10/2003)*
Cambridge U *(Free on 9/2/2004) FL 1+6 Others 1+1*

ROBINSON Matthew (Matt) Richard
Born: Exeter, 23 December 1974
Height: 5'11" **Weight:** 11.8
Matt was a regular in the Oxford United line-up last term, mostly featuring at left back, but also occasionally in a left-sided-midfield role. A solid defender who always likes to join the attack, he contributed goals in the away games at Chester and Rochdale. Matt has now been a mainstay for the U's for three seasons and gives a good balance on the left-hand side.
Southampton *(From trainee on 1/7/1993) PL 3+11 FAC 1+2*
Portsmouth *(£50,000 on 20/2/1998) FL 65+4/1 FLC 3+2 FAC 3*
Reading *(£150,000 on 28/1/2000) FL 62+3 FLC 3+1 FAC 2 Others 4*
Oxford U *(Free on 12/7/2002) FL 127/4 FLC 6 FAC 4 Others 2+1*

ROBINSON Paul
Born: Seaton Delaval, 25 May 1983
Height: 6'0" **Weight:** 12.0
This young striker was unable to break into the first team at Tranmere last term and in September he joined Grimsby Town on loan. Paul made his senior debut for the Mariners at Macclesfield, but returned to Prenton Park when his loan spell was over. Shortly afterwards he negotiated an end to his contract with Rovers and subsequently signed for Conference outfit York City.
Tranmere Rov *(From trainee on 29/5/2002)*
Grimsby T *(Loaned on 10/9/2004) FL 1+1 Others 1*

ROBINSON Paul Mark James
Born: Barnet, 7 January 1982
Height: 6'1" **Weight:** 12.1
After being unable to break into the Millwall first team at the start of last season, Paul went out on loan to Torquay just before Christmas. Used mainly as a central defender, he showed great maturity and composure and it was a disappointment when he was recalled to the New Den. He subsequently turned out at full back for Millwall, producing some outstanding performances in the closing stages of the campaign.
Millwall *(From trainee on 25/10/2000) FL 26+4/1 FAC 3+1/1*
Torquay U *(Loaned on 23/12/2004) FL 12*

ROBINSON Paul Peter
Born: Watford, 14 December 1978
Height: 5'9" **Weight:** 11.12
Club Honours: Div 2 '98
International Honours: E: U21-3
This highly efficient attacking left wing back, scored his first goal for West Bromwich Albion three minutes into added time at the end of the local 'derby' with Aston Villa in April, his header from Riccy Scimeca's right-wing cross earning his side a vital point from a 1-1 draw. A gutsy performer, all told he had an excellent season and was certainly the team's most consistent defender over the last third of the campaign. He reached the career milestone of 300 club appearances during the season.
Watford *(From trainee on 13/2/1997) P/FL 201+18/8 FLC 15+1/1 FAC 10+2 Others 5*
West Bromwich A *(£250,000 on 14/10/2003) P/FL 58+3/1 FAC 4*

ROBINSON Paul William
Born: Beverley, 15 October 1979
Height: 6'2" **Weight:** 13.4
Club Honours: FAYC '97
International Honours: E: 12; U21-11
Widely regarded as one of the top goalkeepers in England, Paul finally joined Spurs in the summer of 2004. After displacing Kasey Keller as first-choice 'keeper, Paul became a crowd favourite demonstrating his agility and dominance in the box. Paul has great organisational skills and his presence alone added stability in a Spurs side which suffered not from an ability to score goals, but were conceding too many. Featuring in all bar a handful of games Paul went on to capitalise on his selection for the England squad which travelled to Portugal for Euro 2004 and secured the number one spot for his country early on in the season.
Leeds U *(From trainee on 13/5/1997) PL 93+2 FLC 5/1 FAC 7 Others 12*
Tottenham H *(£1,500,000 on 16/5/2004) F 36 FLC 2 FAC 6*

ROBINSON Stephen (Steve)
Born: Lisburn, 10 December 1974
Height: 5'9" **Weight:** 11.3
Club Honours: Div 1 '05
International Honours: NI: 5; B-4; U21 1; Yth; Sch
Steve started the 2004-05 season in top form for Luton, scoring an important goa against Barnsley. A neat midfield player, he provided balance on the right-hand side and his efficient play enabled Kevin Foley to come forward and overlap dow the flanks. However, his progress was halted by a groin problem, and although he returned to action he had a second spell on the sidelines within another groi injury.
Tottenham H *(From trainee on 27/1/1993) PL 1+1*
Bournemouth *(Free on 20/10/1994) FL 227+13/51 FLC 14/1 FAC 15+1/5 Others 16/3*
Preston NE *(£375,000 on 26/5/2000) FL 6+18/1 FLC 3+1 FAC 0+1*
Bristol C *(Loaned on 18/3/2002) FL 6/1*
Luton T *(£50,000 on 20/6/2002) FL 83+11/ FLC 2+1 FAC 8/1 Others 3*

ROBINSON Steven (Steve) E
Born: Nottingham, 17 January 1975
Height: 5'9" **Weight:** 11.3
This energetic midfielder found himself on the fringes of first-team action for Swindon as the 2004-05 season started, but always gave his usual committed performance when called upon. An injur at Bradford in January looked to have brought an end to his career at the County Ground and he had a brief trial a Boston before an end-of-season injury crisis forced his recall for the last game allowing the chance for fans to thank him for his past efforts in a Town shirt.
Birmingham C *(From trainee on 9/6/1993) FL 53+28 FLC 6+2/1 FAC 2+2/1 Others 2+1*
Peterborough U *(Loaned on 15/3/1996) FL*
Swindon T *(£50,000 on 12/2/2001) FL 128+14/5 FLC 5 FAC 6+1 Others 4/1*

ROBINSON Trevor Kymar
orn: Jamaica, 20 September 1984
leight: 5'9" **Weight:** 12.11
fter impressing in the Millwall reserve nd youth teams, Trevor was given his rst start against Stoke in February when e acquitted himself well. A tricky and acy winger he is another product of the uccessful youth set-up at the New Den.
illwall *(From trainee on 23/1/2004) FL 1+2*

ROBSON Matthew (Matty) ames
orn: Spennymoor, 23 January 1985
leight: 5'10" **Weight:** 11.2
left-sided utility player who is effective oing forward and always prepared to ave a shot a goal, Matty started the 004-05 season in Hartlepool's reserve eam. However, with Hugh Robertson out njured he got an early promotion to the tarting line-up and more than held his wn. Late in the season he was back in he side, and he looked particularly npressive for Hartlepool in the play-off ames.
artlepool U *(From trainee on 16/3/2004) . 39+11/3 FLC 3 FAC 3+1/1 Others 3*

ROCASTLE Craig Aaron
orn: Lewisham, 17 August 1981
leight: 6'1" **Weight:** 12.13
raig was only on the fringes of the quad at Chelsea last term and spent nost of the first half of the campaign out n loan with SPL club Hibernian, for vhom he featured regularly. The tall oungster was eventually allowed to eave Stamford Bridge on a free transfer nd signed for Sheffield Wednesday. A trong box-to-box central midfielder he pened his scoring account against lackpool but failed to add to his tally uring the remainder of the campaign.
helsea *(Free from Slough T, ex Croydon, ravesend & Northfleet, Ashford T, ingstonian, on 1/9/2003)*
arnsley *(Loaned on 13/2/2004) FL 4+1*
incoln C *(Loaned on 25/3/2004) FL 0+2*
ibernian *(Loaned on 31/8/2004) SL 11+2 .C 1*
heffield Wed *(Free on 3/2/2005) FL 9+2/1 thers 3*

ROCHE Barry Christopher
orn: Dublin, 6 April 1982
leight: 6'4" **Weight:** 12.6
nternational Honours: RoI: Yth
arry was again the back-up goalkeeper or Nottingham Forest last term. With aul Gerrard in fine form he received few pportunities, and managed only two rst-team appearances at the beginning f the season. Barry was one of several layers released by Forest in the summer.
ottingham F *(From trainee on 29/6/1999) . 10+3*

ROCHE Lee Paul
Born: Bolton, 28 October 1980
Height: 5'10" **Weight:** 10.12
International Honours: E: U21-1; Yth
In what was a generally disappointing second season at Burnley for Lee Roche, he was more often seen as a right-sided midfielder than in his usual right-back role, which had been taken over by Michael Duff. Rarely an automatic starter, he nevertheless appeared in well over half of the Clarets' games and could seldom be faulted even if his impact on events was sometimes incidental. Never one to shirk a challenge, his attacking instincts were seen to best effect when he scored Burnley's equaliser in the 2-1 win at Leeds. He was released at the end of the season.
Manchester U *(From trainee on 11/2/1999) PL 0+1 FLC 1 Others 1*
Wrexham *(Loaned on 24/7/2000) FL 41 FLC 2 FAC 1 Others 1*
Burnley *(Free on 18/7/2003) FL 38+16/2 FLC 3+2 FAC 4+3*

RODGERS Luke John
Born: Birmingham, 1 January 1982
Height: 5'7" **Weight:** 11.2
International Honours: E: SP-2

Luke Rodgers

Luke is a striker who is small in stature but very strong on the ball, he possesses a great turn of speed and always shows tremendous commitment. He had something of a mixed season with Shrewsbury last term, for although he finished as the club's leading scorer he had an unusually long spell without finding the net. At the time of writing it appeared he was about to leave Gay Meadow, having reportedly declined the offer of a new contract.
Shrewsbury T *(From trainee on 10/7/2000) FL 122+20/52 FLC 3/1 FAC 6+1 Others 9+2/5*

RODIC Alexsander
Born: Serbia, 26 December 1979
Height: 6'2" **Weight:** 12.11
International Honours: Slovenia: 4
This experienced striker joined Portsmouth during the January transfer window and received a swift introduction to Premiership football when he came off the bench in the home win over Middlesbrough. However, he only made one start for Pompey, at Manchester City in April, and featured just twice more from the bench. Nevertheless he was a regular at international level for Slovenia and scored in the World Cup qualifier against Belarus in March.
Portsmouth *(£1,000,000 from NK Gorica, Slovenia on 31/1/2005) PL 1+3*

ROGERS Alan
Born: Liverpool, 3 January 1977
Height: 5'9" **Weight:** 12.6
Club Honours: Div 1 '98
International Honours: E: U21-3
This left-sided defender who is equally happy to play in midfield for Nottingham Forest was a regular in the side at the start of the season, but then faded from contention with the emergence of Gregor Robertson. Alan is a pacy player who links up well with his colleagues down the flank.
Tranmere Rov *(From trainee on 1/7/1995) FL 53+4/2 FLC 1 FAC 1*
Nottingham F *(£2,000,000 on 10/7/1997) P/FL 135+2/17 FLC 15/2 FAC 2+1/1*
Leicester C *(£300,000 on 16/11/2001) P/FL 57+5 FLC 3/2 FAC 4*
Wigan Ath *(Loaned on 1/12/2003) FL 5*
Nottingham F *(Free on 13/2/2004) FL 44+1 FLC 4 FAC 2*

ROGET Leo Thomas Earl
Born: Ilford, 1 August 1977
Height: 6'1" **Weight:** 12.2
Leo joined Oxford in the summer of 2004 and quickly became a regular in the line-up. A strong defender who likes to dominate the penalty area, he used his power to good effect at the other end of the field too, scoring with headers at Wycombe and in the home game with Bristol Rovers. At his best he is a very effective defender who is hard to get past.
Southend U *(From trainee on 5/7/1995) FL 105+15/7 FLC 8 FAC 6/1 Others 3/1*
Stockport Co *(Free on 1/3/2001) FL 28+3/1 FLC 2*
Reading *(Loaned on 14/2/2002) FL 1*
Brentford *(Free on 9/8/2002) FL 29 FLC 1 FAC 1 Others 2*
Rushden & Diamonds *(Free on 30/1/2004) FL 16+1*
Oxford U *(Free on 14/7/2004) FL 35/2 FLC 1*

ROMA Dominic Mark
Born: Sheffield, 29 November 1985
Height: 5'9" **Weight:** 12.4
International Honours: E: Yth
This right-sided player stepped up to the professional ranks at Sheffield United last term but failed to make a breakthrough into the first team. In February he joined Boston United on loan at a time when the Pilgrims were without six defenders due to injury and suspension. Dominic made an effective debut in the visit to Bristol Rovers when he was used on the right side of a three-centre-back system. He retained his place for the following game against Northampton, when he switched to right back in a flat back four, but was sacrificed late on for an extra attacking player. Dominic did not feature again for Boston and later returned to Bramall Lane.
Sheffield U *(From trainee on 7/7/2004)*
Boston U *(Loaned on 18/2/2005) FL 2*

ROMMEDAHL Dennis
Born: Copenhagen, Denmark, 22 July 1978
Height: 5'9" **Weight:** 10.10
International Honours: Denmark: 53; U21-15; Yth
This experienced international was signed at the start of the season but took time to settle into the Charlton side. He made his debut as a substitute in the opening fixture at Bolton Wanderers and started in the next game, but was in the line-up for only half of the club's Premiership fixtures during the campaign. Dennis is a skilful winger who can play on either flank and has electric pace, quite possibly the quickest in the Premiership. It is said he can run 100m in 10.2 seconds. He won over the Charlton fans with a last-minute winner in the local 'derby' at Selhurst Park and also scored an equalising goal at St James' Park to earn a valuable point against Newcastle in February. His performances towards the end of the season seemed more assured and hopefully his best is yet to come in a Charlton shirt, as he is undoubtedly a quality player.
Charlton Ath *(£2,000,000 from PSV Eindhoven, Holland, ex Lyngby, RKC Waalwijk, on 23/7/2004) PL 19+7/2 FAC 1*

[RONALDO] DOS SANTOS AVEIRO Cristiano Ronaldo
Born: Madeira, Portugal, 5 February 1985
Height: 6'0" **Weight:** 12.4
Club Honours: FAC '04
International Honours: Portugal: 21; U21-15; Yth
A prodigiously gifted forward who is comfortable on either flank or up front, Ronaldo continued to live up to Sir Alex Ferguson's praises as one of the most exciting players in the game. A regular in United's first-team squad throughout another action-packed campaign, Ronaldo was the scourge of defences both at home and abroad. Although his party tricks did at times frustrate his own teammates, notably new signing Alan Smith, his tantalising magic was often worth the admission price alone. An absence of goals in the Champions' League was a little surprising but he certainly produced some vital strikes in the Premiership and FA Cup. Kick-starting United's defence of the latter trophy in the replay at Exeter, he added further contributions in successive rounds at Everton and Southampton. Arguably his greatest hits of the season came in that Premiership showdown against the defending Champions' Arsenal at Highbury, when a brace practically ended the Gunners hopes of capturing a second successive Premiership crown.
Manchester U *(£7,700,000 + from Sporting Lisbon, Portugal on 14/8/2003) PL 40+22/9 FLC 3 FAC 11+1/6 Others 10+3*

ROONEY Thomas (Tommy) Anthony
Born: Liverpool, 30 December 1984
Height: 6'0" **Weight:** 12.5
This young Macclesfield Town striker made his Football League debut last November, coming on from the substitutes' bench in the home match against Cheltenham Town. With the established strikers in good form there were no opportunities for Tommy to break into the senior side on a regular basis, although he did make one further brief substitute appearance and finished the season as leading scorer for the club's reserve side. Tommy is cousin of Manchester United's Wayne Rooney.
Macclesfield T *(From trainee at Tranmere Rov on 17/6/2004) FL 0+1 FAC 0+1*

Ronaldo (left)

Wayne Rooney

ROONEY Wayne Mark
Born: Liverpool, 24 October 1985
Height: 5'10" **Weight:** 12.4
International Honours: E: 23; Yth
A highly promising striker or playmaker who has become one of the hottest prospects in European football, Wayne joined United from Everton at the close of the August transfer window. A sensational hat-trick in his first-ever game for the Reds in the Champions' League heralded his arrival on the Old Trafford stage, whilst a highly notable contribution came against Arsenal at Old Trafford in October, which ended the Gunners 49-game unbeaten Premiership run, and on his 19th birthday to boot. Wayne's first return to Merseyside since his transfer was 'warmly' received by the Liverpool fans at Anfield, particularly when he netted the winning goal. Statistically it was the first time that United had completed a hat-trick of wins at Anfield. Wayne's two brilliant goals against Middlesbrough in the FA Cup fourth round put United on the Millennium Stadium trail, whilst his strike in the Manchester 'derby' at Maine Road kept the red half of the city happy. As the season reached its climax, he missed out on his first major honour in the FA Cup final against Arsenal. However, Wayne topped off a magnificent display being rewarded with the 'Man of the Match' award, which went nicely with his PFA 'Young Player of the Year' award.
Everton *(From trainee on 20/2/2003) PL 40+27/15 FLC 4+2/2 FAC 4*
Manchester U *(£20,000,000 + on 31/8/2004) PL 24+5/11 FLC 1+1 FAC 6/3 Others 6/3*

ROPER Ian Robert
Born: Nuneaton, 20 June 1977
Height: 6'3" **Weight:** 13.4
Ian had an unhappy start to the 2004-05 season at Walsall when he ran into problems with referees, however he eventually settled down again and was back to his best form for the second half of the campaign. An effective centre half, his strengths are his power in the air and his firm tackling. Ian is now nearing the 300-appearance mark for his one-and-only club and is due for a testimonial in 2005-06.
Walsall *(From trainee on 15/5/1995) FL 228+26/2 FLC 8+6 FAC 10+3/1 Others 12+3*

ROSE Matthew David
Born: Dartford, 24 September 1975
Height: 5'11" **Weight:** 11.1
Club Honours: FAYC '94
International Honours: E: U21-2
This left-sided defender was a regular starter for Queen's Park Rangers at the beginning of the season. However, he suffered a serious leg injury in the game at Leeds in November and did not fully recover for three months. Once fit he went straight back into the starting line-up and held his place before being injured once more, this time in the return game against Leeds, and missed the final month of the campaign.
Arsenal *(From trainee on 19/7/1994) PL 2+3*
Queens Park Rgrs *(£500,000 on 20/5/1997) FL 195+21/8 FLC 7 FAC 4 Others 4+1*

ROSE Michael Charles
Born: Salford, 28 July 1982
Height: 5'10" **Weight:** 11.2
Club Honours: Div 2 '05
Michael was a regular in the line-up for Yeovil last term, mostly featuring at left back. He is effective when pushing forward on the overlap and can deliver a more-than-useful cross into the penalty area. He netted his first senior goal for the Glovers from a free kick in the 5-2 win against Mansfield in April. Michael was one of five Yeovil players selected for the PFA League Two team of the season.
Manchester U *(From trainee on 9/9/1999. Freed during 2001 close season)*
Yeovil T *(Free from Hereford U, ex Chester C on 14/5/2004) FL 37+3/1 FLC 2 FAC 3+1 Others 0+1*

ROSE Richard Alan
Born: Pembury, 8 September 1982
Height: 6'0" **Weight:** 11.9
This promising Gillingham defender took advantage of the club's injury problems last term to break into the starting line-up. However, the arrival of Jay McEveley on loan from Blackburn meant it was back to the substitutes' bench, but Richard can be satisfied that he gave his all in the club's hour of need.
Gillingham *(From trainee on 10/4/2001) FL 31+13 FLC 1+1 FAC 1*
Bristol Rov *(Loaned on 13/12/2002) FL 9*

ROSENIOR Liam James
Born: Wandsworth, 9 July 1984
Height: 5'9" **Weight:** 11.8
Club Honours: AMC '03
International Honours: E: U21-2; Yth
Liam made his first start for Fulham in the Carling Cup tie at Boston, while his Premiership debut came three months later against Manchester United when he replaced Moritz Volz at right back. He then retained his place in the side, before switching flanks to play at left back later in the campaign. Liam was particularly outstanding in the home games against Manchester United and Everton and was called up for the England U21 squad during the campaign.
Bristol C *(From trainee on 15/8/2001) FL 2+20/2 FAC 0+1 Others 2+3/1*
Fulham *(Free on 7/11/2003) PL 16+1 FLC 1+1 FAC 4*
Torquay U *(Loaned on 19/3/2004) FL 9+1*

ROSS John (Jack) James
Born: Falkirk, 5 June 1976
Height: 6'1" **Weight:** 11.5
Club Honours: S Div 2 '00
A versatile player, Jack was initially used at right back by Hartlepool last term and this was subsequently looked on as his main playing position. He always gave his best, despite being hampered by niggling injuries, but after being stretchered off in the game at Stockport in March, he went back to Scotland to recuperate.
Clyde *(Signed from Camelon Juniors on 30/7/1999) SL 158+1/11 SLC 6+2/1 SC 9+1/1 Others 8/2*
Hartlepool U *(Free on 21/7/2004) FL 21+3 FAC 5+1 Others 1*

ROSSI Generoso
Born: Naples, Italy, 3 January 1979
Height: 6'3" **Weight:** 13.5
Generoso is a tall goalkeeper who joined Queen's Park Rangers last January, although he was unable to play for the club until mid-February due to a ban imposed by the Italian FA. After impressing for Ranger's reserves Generoso was given his first-team debut at Wigan and retained his place for the final three games of the season.
Queens Park Rgrs *(Free from Palermo, Italy, ex Venezia, Lecce, Siena, on 4/2/2005) FL 3*

ROSSI Giuseppe
Born: New Jersey, USA, 1 February 1987
Height: 5'9" **Weight:** 11.3
International Honours: Italy: Yth
An attacking midfielder or winger, Giuseppe may be small in height, but he is excellent in the air. He made his United debut in the Carling Cup tie against Crystal Palace in November, just two weeks after signing professional forms with the club. Although born in the USA, Giuseppe has featured for Italy at U17 and U18 levels.
Manchester U *(From trainee on 3/11/2004) FLC 0+2*

ROUTLEDGE Wayne Neville
Born: Sidcup, 7 January 1985
Height: 5'6" **Weight:** 10.7
International Honours: E: U21-3; Yth
This small, tricky right winger played in every single Premiership game for Crystal Palace last term and scored once, netting in the 2-2 draw at Southampton in November. He also continued to make

progress on the international front during the campaign, featuring for England at both U20 and U21 levels. Wayne was out of contract in the summer and at the time of writing had yet to agree a new deal with the Eagles.
Crystal Palace *(From trainee on 9/7/2002) P/FL 83+27/10 FLC 5+2 FAC 2+1 Others 3*

ROWE James Anthony
Born: Christchurch, 10 March 1987
Height: 5'9" **Weight:** 10.0
This hard-working Bournemouth midfielder was given a first-team squad number for the 2004-05 season, when he was a regular in the reserve and U18 sides. He made his senior debut in the home game against Bristol City and also made an appearance at Brentford, but ended the campaign after suffering a broken foot in a reserve match at Plymouth.
Bournemouth *(From trainee on 12/7/2004) FL 0+2*

ROWLAND Stephen (Steve) John
Born: Wrexham, 2 November 1981
Height: 5'10" **Weight:** 12.4
This Port Vale defender occupied a variety of roles during the 2004-05 campaign. Equally at home at full back or in the centre of the back four, Steve began the season at right back but was left out after a defeat at Chesterfield and then the arrival of James O'Connor on loan kept him out until December. He also had a spell in midfield, being asked to man-mark the opposition's danger man on more than one occasion. In the new year he had a stint at left back, but wherever he was used he always gave 100 per cent.
Port Vale *(From trainee on 2/7/2001) FL 90+13/1 FAC 2+2 Others 5*

Wayne Routledge

ROWLANDS Martin Charles
Born: Hammersmith, 8 February 1979
Height: 5'9" **Weight:** 10.10
Club Honours: Div 3 '99
International Honours: RoI: 3; U21-8
A midfield player who can play on either wing, Martin was in his second season at Queen's Park Rangers last term. He started in a wide-right midfield role and was a regular in the line-up apart from injury throughout the campaign. Although not noted for his goal-scoring exploits, Martin managed to find the net three times during the campaign.
Brentford *(£45,000 from Farnborough T on 6/8/1998) FL 128+21/20 FLC 8+3/1 FAC 7+2 Others 17/2*
Queens Park Rgrs *(Free on 6/8/2003) FL 72+5/13 FLC 4/3 FAC 2 Others 3*

ROWSON David Andrew
Born: Aberdeen, 14 September 1976
Height: 5'10" **Weight:** 11.12
This midfield powerhouse had something of an indifferent season at Northampton last term, although he settled down once a stable midfield had bedded in. A stylish player capable of quality performances, he is always willing to help out colleagues either in attack or defence.
Aberdeen *(Signed from FC Stoneywood on 5/10/1994) SL 120+20/10 SLC 9+3 SC 7/1 Others 2*
Livingston *(Loaned on 24/3/2000) SL 6/1*
Stoke C *(Free on 2/7/2001) FL 8+5 FLC 1 FAC 1+2 Others 1*
Partick T *(Free on 27/1/2003) SL 48/3 SLC 1 SC 3/1*
Northampton T *(Free on 22/7/2004) FL 35+2/2 FAC 3 Others 3*

ROYCE Simon Ernest
Born: Forest Gate, 9 September 1971
Height: 6'2" **Weight:** 11.6
With the signing of Stephan Anderson as cover for Dean Kiely, Simon found himself third-choice 'keeper at the Valley last term and spent the majority of the season out on loan. His only involvement

with the Charlton first-team squad was a place on the bench in the Carling Cup tie at Grimsby Town. At Luton his safe handling and positioning for shots and crosses brought back confidence to a shaky back four. At Loftus Road he enjoyed an extended run in the side with some impressive performances before returning to the Addicks.
Southend U *(£35,000 from Heybridge Swifts on 15/10/1991) FL 147+2 FLC 9 FAC 5 Others 6*
Charlton Ath *(Free on 2/7/1998) PL 8*
Leicester C *(Free on 17/7/2000) PL 16+3 FLC 1 FAC 4*
Brighton & Hove A *(Loaned on 24/12/2001) FL 6*
Queens Park Rgrs *(Loaned on 24/8/2002) FL 16 Others 1*
Charlton Ath *(Free on 4/7/2003) PL 1*
Luton T *(Loaned on 29/10/2004) FL 2*
Queens Park Rgrs *(Loaned on 13/1/2005) FL 13*

RUDDY John Thomas Gordon

Born: St Ives, 24 October 1986
Height: 6'4" **Weight:** 15.4
John had an excellent season in 2004-05 with Cambridge United, despite the team's relegation problems. He firmly established himself as the club's first-choice 'keeper and missed only a handful of games through injury. He produced a series of excellent saves and was rewarded with the club's 'Young Player of the Season' award at the end of the campaign. John was reported to have signed a pre-contractual agreement with Everton in February and was expected to make a permanent move to the Goodison Park club in the close season.
Cambridge U *(From trainee on 3/9/2004) FL 39 FLC 1 FAC 1 Others 2*

RUNDLE Adam

Born: Durham, 8 July 1984
Height: 5'10" **Weight:** 11.2
This pacy left winger spent the summer months playing for Dublin City, but after being released by the Eircom League side he signed for Mansfield Town on an initial one-month deal. Adam quickly impressed manager Carlton Palmer and he was signed up on a deal until the end of the season. A bit raw, he was given his first taste of senior action in the 'derby' games with Lincoln City and Notts County and did well. He opened his goal account at Bury with a simple tap in, and later scored a couple of crackers against Grimsby and Yeovil. Once Adam settled in he became a favourite with the fans and he eventually signed a contract to stay at Field Mill for another year.
Darlington *(Trainee) FL 8+9*
Carlisle U *(Free on 31/12/2002) FL 25+19/1 FLC 1 Others 4+1/2 (Freed on 19/8/2004)*
Mansfield T *(Free from Dublin C on 14/1/2005) FL 18/4*

RUSK Simon Edward

Born: Peterborough, 17 December 1981
Height: 5'11" **Weight:** 12.8
Club Honours: NC '02
Simon began the 2004-05 season on the Boston United substitutes' bench after being handed a three-month contract, but he soon won his way into the starting line-up and his deal was extended until the end of the campaign. Simon, Boston's longest serving player, was used in his favoured central-midfield role in the second half of the season, but also appeared in a wide role on either flank, both at the back and in midfield. His ball-winning skills and ability to push forward were both assets to the team.
Boston U *(Free from Cambridge C on 6/4/2001) FL 50+18/5 FLC 3+1 FAC 3+2 Others 2*

Simon Rusk

RUSSELL Alexander (Alex) John
Born: Crosby, 17 March 1973
Height: 5'9" **Weight:** 11.7
This experienced central midfielder was once again the star of Torquay United's team last season. Always looking to receive the ball, he was the hub of the side, controlling games with his vision and his fast and accurate distribution. A hamstring injury put him out of action for six weeks early in the campaign and on his return he was paired with a variety of midfield partners – key factors in the club's ultimate relegation. Alex really hit top form when Darren Garner arrived to share the workload and then when the club switched to 4-5-1, giving him free attacking license.
Rochdale *(£4,000 from Burscough on 11/7/1994) FL 83+19/14 FLC 5/1 FAC 1+1 Others 2+3*
Cambridge U *(Free on 4/8/1998) FL 72+9/8 FLC 7+1 FAC 6 Others 3*
Torquay U *(Free on 9/8/2001) FL 152+1/21 FLC 4 FAC 4/1 Others 2*

RUSSELL Craig Stewart
Born: Jarrow, 4 February 1974
Height: 5'10" **Weight:** 12.6
Club Honours: Div 1 '96
Craig continued to be used up front by Darlington throughout the 2004-05 season, operating as cover when either of the main strikers was unavailable. His experience in shielding the ball and winning it in the air proved invaluable to the team, but he only managed to add one more to his personal goal tally, netting at Bristol Rovers on Easter Monday. Craig was one of several players released by the club in the summer.
Sunderland *(From trainee on 1/7/1992) P/FL 103+47/31 FLC 7+6/1 FAC 6+3/2 Others 2*
Manchester C *(£1,000,000 on 14/11/1997) FL 22+9/2 FAC 5+1/2*
Tranmere Rov *(Loaned on 7/8/1998) FL 3+1*
Port Vale *(Loaned on 29/1/1999) FL 8/1*
Darlington *(Loaned on 3/9/1999) FL 11+1/2*
Oxford U *(Loaned on 11/2/2000) FL 5+1*
St Johnstone *(Loaned on 29/3/2000) SL 1/1*
St Johnstone *(Free on 12/7/2000) SL 16+19/2 SLC 1+1 SC 1+1/1 Others 2*
Carlisle U *(Free on 16/1/2003) FL 10+9/1 FLC 1/1 FAC 1 Others 4+1*
Darlington *(Free on 16/1/2004) FL 21+19/2 FLC 1 Others 1*

RUSSELL Darel Francis Roy
Born: Stepney, 22 October 1980
Height: 5'11" **Weight:** 11.9
International Honours: E: Yth
This tenacious midfielder was again a near ever-present for Stoke City last season. His main asset was his high work rate, although he also contributed superb long-range goals against Wolves and Plymouth.
Norwich C *(From trainee on 29/11/1997) FL 99+33/7 FLC 8/2 FAC 6+1*
Stoke C *(£125,000 on 8/8/2003) FL 91/6 FLC 3 FAC 3*

RUSSELL Samuel (Sam) Ian
Born: Middlesbrough, 4 October 1982
Height: 6'0" **Weight:** 10.13
This youngster joined Darlington in the summer of 2004 and quickly made the goalkeeper's jersey his own, appearing in all 50 competitive games during the campaign. Sam showed himself to be an excellent all-round stopper and confident gatherer of crosses and corners. He also made a number of crucial penalty saves that helped earn points for the side, including one in the first minute at Mansfield in April when the game ended 1-1.
Middlesbrough *(From trainee on 7/7/2000)*
Darlington *(Loaned on 28/12/2002) FL 1*
Scunthorpe U *(Loaned on 22/8/2003) FL 10 FLC 1 Others 1*
Darlington *(Free on 5/8/2004) FL 46 FLC 1 FAC 2 Others 1*

RUSSELL Simon Craig
Born: Hull, 19 March 1985
Height: 5'7" **Weight:** 10.6
One of the few bright spots in Kidderminster's disappointing season last term was the form of Simon Russell. Signed by Jan Molby in the summer, he made just a couple of substitute appearances under the Dane before being given his chance by Shaun Cunnington in October. Simon was a regular in the team until February, playing mostly on the right wing but also as an attacking midfielder. He scored two goals, including a fine effort in the win at Oxford over the Christmas period.
Hull C *(Trainee) FL 0+1 Others 0+1*
Kidderminster Hrs *(Free on 29/7/2004) FL 18+10/2 FAC 1*

RYAN Keith James
Born: Northampton, 25 June 1970
Height: 5'11" **Weight:** 12.8
Club Honours: FAT '91, '93; GMVC '93
Club captain and veteran midfielder for Wycombe Wanderers, Keith enjoyed an excellent 2004-05 season in the heart of midfield. Forceful, hard working and dominant in the air, he also briefly acted as caretaker-manager following the departure of Tony Adams. He then became first-team coach under new manager John Gorman, but continued to feature in the line-up and became only the fifth player in the club's history to make 500 appearances. Out of contract as a player in the summer, it was unclear at the time of writing whether he would decide to hang up his boots and focus on his coaching career.
Wycombe W *(Signed from Berkhamstead T during 1990 close season) FL 299+52/29 FLC 13+2/3 FAC 22+4/4 Others 17+2/1*

RYAN Oliver Paul
Born: Boston, 26 September 1985
Height: 5'9" **Weight:** 11.0
This young striker gained considerably in experience with Lincoln City after being given his first team-debut in the FA Cup tie at Hartlepool last term. He showed speed and skill on the ball as well as an eye for goal. Oliver was regularly on the substitutes' bench after Christmas, but still awaits his first senior goal despite finishing as top scorer for the Imps' reserve team. At the end of the season he accepted the offer of a new contract.
Lincoln C *(Trainee) FL 0+6 FAC 0+1*

RYAN Robert (Robbie) Paul
Born: Dublin, 16 May 1977
Height: 5'10" **Weight:** 12.0
Club Honours: Div 2 '01
International Honours: RoI: U21-12; Yth; Sch
Robbie took time to settle in at Bristol Rovers last term, but held down a regular place in the side at left back. He showed up well defensively in the last quarter of the season, producing some determined displays, but missed the closing fixtures with an injury.
Huddersfield T *(Free from Belvedere YC on 26/7/1994) FL 12+3 FLC 2*
Millwall *(£10,000 on 30/1/1998) FL 209+17/2 FLC 9 FAC 16 Others 5*
Bristol Rov *(Free on 27/7/2004) FL 39+1 FLC 1 FAC 2 Others 5*

RYAN Timothy (Tim) James
Born: Stockport, 10 December 1974
Height: 5'10" **Weight:** 11.6
Club Honours: Div 3 '04
International Honours: E: SP-14
This wholehearted, popular player enjoyed another great season at Doncaster last term, winning several of the club's 'Player of the Year' awards. His enthusiasm for the game and his excursions down the flank from his position at left back bring the crowd to their feet especially when he hits the back of the net with his spectacular shooting from long range.
Scunthorpe U *(From trainee on 8/4/1993) FL 1+1 (Free to Buxton on 28/11/1994)*
Doncaster Rov *(Free on 8/8/1996) FL 22+6 FLC 0+1 FAC 1 Others 1 (Free to Southport on 5/8/1997)*
Doncaster Rov *(Free on 24/5/2000) FL 79+2/6 FLC 4 FAC 3 Others 1+1*

S

SAAH Brian Ebo
Born: Hornchurch, 16 December 1986
Height: 6'1" **Weight:** 11.0
This promising Leyton Orient youngster gained further experience of senior football last term. A ball-winning central midfielder; he is good at breaking up opposition moves and helping to start attacks for the O's. A highlight of his campaign came when he netted with a 30-yard screamer in the LDV Vans Trophy tie at Woking in September. Brian will be looking to become a first-team regular in 2005-06.
Leyton Orient *(Trainee) FL 13+5 FLC 0+1 FAC 1 Others 3/1*

SABIN Eric
Born: Paris, France, 22 January 1975
Height: 6'1" **Weight:** 12.4
This speedy and talented striker found himself on the bench for Northampton for much of last season, mainly due to the surplus of strikers on the club's books. Fast and skilful, Eric can turn a game with his bursts of speed and ball-playing talents. He also made a major contribution by setting up two goals in the final match of the regular season against Kidderminster to ensure the Cobblers reached the play-offs.
Swindon T *(Free from Wasquehal, France on 13/7/2001) FL 60+13/9 FLC 2 FAC 5 Others 0+1*
Queens Park Rgrs *(Free on 17/7/2003) FL 3+7/1 FLC 0+2 FAC 1 Others 2+1*
Boston U *(Loaned on 3/3/2004) FL 2*
Northampton T *(Free on 12/3/2004) FL 37+14/13 FLC 2/1 FAC 2+1 Others 1+4*

SAFRI Youssef
Born: Morocco, 1 March 1977
Height: 5'10" **Weight:** 11.8
International Honours: Morocco:
Norwich signed this midfielder from Coventry City in the 2004 close season. A strong-tackling player he has the incisive passing skills and necessary vision to make the best use of the ball once he has won it. One of several Canaries to have an injury-interrupted season, Youssef had a hernia repair, he was unable to produce his best form until the latter part of the campaign and Norwich fans will be hoping that he can make a big impact in the Championship in 2005-06. He scored a 'Goal of the Season' contender in the home match against Newcastle United from fully 35 yards.
Coventry C *(Free from Raja Casablanca, Morocco on 25/8/2001) FL 87+4/1 FLC 6 FAC 1*
Norwich C *(£500,000 on 9/7/2004) PL 13+5/1 FLC 1+1/1*

SAHA Louis
Born: Paris, France, 8 August 1978
Height: 5'11" **Weight:** 11.10
Club Honours: Div 1 '01
International Honours: France: 8; U21; Yth (UEFA-U18 '97)
A skilful and pacy striker who is lethal in the air, Louis was constantly hampered by injury problems in a season when Sir Alex Ferguson shored up his attack with the double signings of Alan Smith and Wayne Rooney. Having made only three Premiership appearances from August to December, he returned to play a major part in United's exciting Carling Cup run. Celebrating his first goal of the season against Crystal Palace in that competition in November, his first Premiership goal came against Aston Villa in January. With only fleeting appearances in the side before more injury woes surfaced, a return to first-team action against Norwich at Carrow Road in the Premiership in April was curtailed after barely 20 minutes with further injury woes.
Newcastle U *(Loaned from Metz, France on 8/1/1999) PL 5+6/1 FAC 1/1*
Fulham *(£2,100,000 from Metz, France on 29/6/2000) P/FL 100+17/53 FLC 3+3/6 FAC 10+1/3 Others 5+4/1*
Manchester U *(£12,825,000 on 23/1/2004) PL 16+10/8 FLC 4/1 FAC 0+2 Others 1+3*

Youssef Safri (front)

Louis Saha

SAKIRI Artim
Born: Struga, Macedonia, 23 September 1973
Height: 5'11" **Weight:** 12.0
International Honours: Macedonia: 67
Artim appeared in only three Premiership games for West Bromwich Albion in 2004-05, one of them as a substitute. Unable to establish himself in the side under either of the Baggies' two managers, he languished in the reserves for long periods. He still succeeded in playing regularly for his country and scored a rare goal against Armenia in a World Cup qualifier.
West Bromwich A *(Signed from CSKA Sofia, Bulgaria, ex Varder Skopje, Halmstads, Tennis Borussia, HIT Gorica, Malatyaspar, on 4/8/2003) P/FL 8+20/1 FLC 2+2 FAC 1*

SALAKO John Akin
Born: Nigeria, 11 February 1969
Height: 5'10" **Weight:** 12.8
Club Honours: FMC '91; Div 1 '94, '00
International Honours: E: 5
John joined Brentford in the summer of 2004 and was a regular in the line-up throughout the 2004-05 season. His crossing with either foot was always accurate when he played at outside left, but he also appeared at left back on occasions where he was equally effective. A dead-ball expert, he scored a wonderful goal from a free kick in the FA Cup tie at Bristol City. John also continued to work in the media in addition to his playing commitments.
Crystal Palace *(From apprentice on 3/11/1986) P/FL 172+43/22 FLC 19+5/5 FAC 20/4 Others 11+3/2*
Swansea C *(Loaned on 14/8/1989) FL 13/3 Others 2/1*
Coventry C *(£1,500,000 on 7/8/1995) PL 68+4/4 FLC 9/3 FAC 4/1*
Bolton W *(Free on 26/3/1998) PL 0+7*
Fulham *(Free on 22/7/1998) FL 7+3/1 FLC 2/1 FAC 2+2 Others 1*
Charlton Ath *(£150,000 + on 20/8/1999) P/FL 10+37/2 FLC 1+2 FAC 3+4/1*
Reading *(£75,000 + on 2/11/2001) FL 96+15/13 FLC 4+1/1 FAC 0+4 Others 1*
Brentford *(Free on 2/8/2004) FL 30+5/4 FAC 3+1/1 Others 0+1*

SALL Abdou Hamed
Born: Dakar, Senegal, 1 November 1980
Height: 6'3" **Weight:** 14.2
This giant defender was always something of an enigma at Kidderminster last term. At the top of his game he could cope without just about anything thrown at him, but his form was often inconsistent. He missed the first month of the season through injury and then struggled to win a regular place in the side before being placed on the transfer list late in the campaign.
Kidderminster Hrs *(Free from Toulouse, France on 10/8/2001) FL 31/2 FAC 1 Others 2/1 (Free to Nuneaton Borough on 14/2/2003)*
Oxford U *(Loaned on 29/11/2002) FL 0+1 FAC 0+1*
Kidderminster Hrs *(Free from Revel, France on 12/2/2004) FL 19+2 FAC 1*

SAM Hector McLeod
Born: Mount Hope, Trinidad, 25 February 1978
Height: 5'9" **Weight:** 11.5
Club Honours: AMC '05
International Honours: Trinidad & Tobago: 20
This talented striker was again in enigmatic form for Wrexham last term. Although often used from the bench he remained a crowd pleaser, the highlight of his campaign coming when he netted a hat-trick in the 3-2 win at Oldham back in August. Hector continued to represent Trinidad & Tobago at international level during the campaign.
Wrexham *(£125,000 from CL Financial San Juan Jabloteh, Trinidad, on 8/8/2000) FL 77+73/35 FLC 6+1/1 FAC 4+2/1 Others 6+7/3*

SAM Lloyd Ekow
Born: Leeds, 27 September 1984
Height: 5'8" **Weight:** 9.12
International Honours: E: Yth
Charlton's 'Young Player of the Year', Lloyd was a star performer in the club's successful reserve side before receiving a well-deserved first-team debut in the final game of the season against Crystal Palace at the Valley, when he came on as a late substitute. He had previously been an unused substitute in the away game with Newcastle in February. Lloyd is a skilful winger who likes to take on defenders and is exciting to watch. He also has an eye for goal and finished as the reserve team's leading scorer with eight goals. Lloyd scored for England U20s on his debut at that level, against Russia at the Valley in February.
Charlton Ath *(From trainee on 5/7/2002) PL 0+1*
Leyton Orient *(Loaned on 15/1/2004) FL 5+5*

SAMBROOK Andrew (Andy) John
Born: Chatham, 13 July 1979
Height: 5'10" **Weight:** 12.4
Club Honours: Div 3 '03
International Honours: E: Sch
Andy proved to be a useful member of the Rushden squad last term, although he received few opportunities due to the form of Sean Connelly. A utility player whose best position is at right back, he was sidelined for several months in the new year with an ankle injury. Andy was one of several players released by the club in the summer.
Gillingham *(Associated Schoolboy) FL 0+1*
Rushden & Diamonds *(Free from Hartwick College, USA on 9/8/2001) FL 48+21 FAC 2 Others 2+1*

SAMUEL JLloyd
Born: Trinidad, 29 March 1981
Height: 5'11" **Weight:** 11.4
International Honours: E: U21-7; Yth
Jlloyd is a versatile defender who can play at right back, left back or in a wing-back role. However, being naturally left-footed he is more comfortable when playing on the left-hand side. A steady performer throughout the campaign, his run of playing in every second of every match extended to 56 games before he was substituted with a shoulder injury during the Carling Cup game with Burnley.
Aston Villa *(From trainee on 2/2/1999) PL 128+18/2 FLC 12+1/1 FAC 5 Others 5+2*
Gillingham *(Loaned on 26/10/2001) FL 7+1*

SANASY Kevin Roy
Born: Leeds, 2 November 1984
Height: 5'8" **Weight:** 10.5
This young Bradford City striker made a couple of substitute appearances early on last season but found his opportunities at Valley Parade strictly limited. He twice went out on loan in the Conference and had brief stays at Halifax and Leigh RMI.
Bradford C *(Trainee) FL 2+7/1 FLC 0+1*

SANDWITH Kevin
Born: Workington, 30 April 1978
Height: 5'11" **Weight:** 12.5
Kevin began the 2004-05 season on the bench, but quickly forced his way into the Lincoln City starting line-up and made the left-back position his own. He was always quick to move forward but his most important contribution was his ability to deliver accurate free kicks and corners into opposition danger zones. Kevin accepted a new contract at the end of the season.
Carlisle U *(From trainee on 16/7/1996) FL 2+1 (Free to Barrow on 27/9/1998)*
Lincoln C *(Free from Halifax T, ex Telford U, Doncaster Rov, on 12/3/2004) FL 35+5/2 FAC 1 Others 4*

SANOKHO Amadou
Born: France, 1 September 1975
Height: 6'3" **Weight:** 12.6
This big burly midfielder spent four

months of the season at Burnley but managed only one full appearance, in the Carling Cup home defeat by Tottenham. His size ensured that he was immediately recognisable to supporters and opponents alike, but despite occasionally looking threatening going forward, he rarely did enough to suggest a long-term future at Turf Moor. In March he joined Oldham as new boss Ronnie Moore looked to add more steel to his midfield options. However, Amadou made just one appearance - coming on as a second-half substitute against Sheffield Wednesday in April – before being released.

Burnley *(Free from Sanguistese, ex Nantes, Modena, Rondinella, on 24/9/2004) FL 0+3 FLC 1*

Oldham Ath *(Free on 23/3/2005) FL 0+1*

SANTOS Georges

Born: Marseille, France, 15 August 1970
Height: 6'3" **Weight:** 14.0

Georges joined Queen's Park Rangers as a midfield player, but due to the lack of available central defenders he started the season at the back, playing alongside Danny Shittu. After a shaky start he soon won over the fans with some strong performances and effective tackling. However, when Andrew Davies arrived in January, Georges moved forward to his more familiar midfield role. He scored five goals during the campaign, mostly from set pieces.

Tranmere Rov *(Free from Toulon, France on 29/7/1998) FL 46+1/2 FLC 6 FAC 1*

West Bromwich A *(£25,000 on 23/3/2000) FL 8*

Sheffield U *(Free on 5/7/2000) FL 37+24/6 FLC 2+3 FAC 1+1*

Grimsby T *(Free on 27/9/2002) FL 24+2/1 FAC 1*

Ipswich T *(Free on 1/8/2003) FL 28+6/1 FLC 2*

Queens Park Rgrs *(Free on 3/8/2004) FL 39+4/5 FLC 1+1*

SAUNDERS Mark Philip

Born: Reading, 23 July 1971
Height: 5'11" **Weight:** 11.12

This experienced full back or midfielder featured in the opening games of the season for Gillingham, but his campaign was effectively over before it even started after he suffered a double-fracture of the right leg after just six minutes of the home game with Preston in August. Mark will be hoping to be back in action once more for the Gills in time for the start of the 2005-06 campaign.

Plymouth Arg *(Signed from Tiverton T on 22/8/1995) FL 60+12/11 FLC 1+1 FAC 2+3 Others 2*

Gillingham *(Free on 1/6/1998) FL 117+55/15 FLC 8+2/1 FAC 9+1/1 Others 3+4*

SAVAGE Basir (Bas) Mohammed

Born: Wandsworth, 7 January 1982
Height: 6'3" **Weight:** 13.8

This pacy striker failed to break through into the first team at Reading last term and in September he joined Wycombe Wanderers on loan where he featured regularly without finding the net. In February he had another loan spell, this time with Bury. Bas linked up well in attack with Jon Newby on his debut and had a hand in both goals, earning a penalty. Tall and mobile and, perhaps not surprisingly, good in the air, he subsequently failed to recapture such form and eventually returned to the Madejski Stadium. He was released by Reading in the summer.

Reading *(£20,000 from Walton & Hersham on 7/2/2002) FL 6+10 FLC 1 FAC 1*

Wycombe W *(Loaned on 2/9/2004) FL 2+2 Others 1*

Bury *(Loaned on 11/2/2005) FL 5*

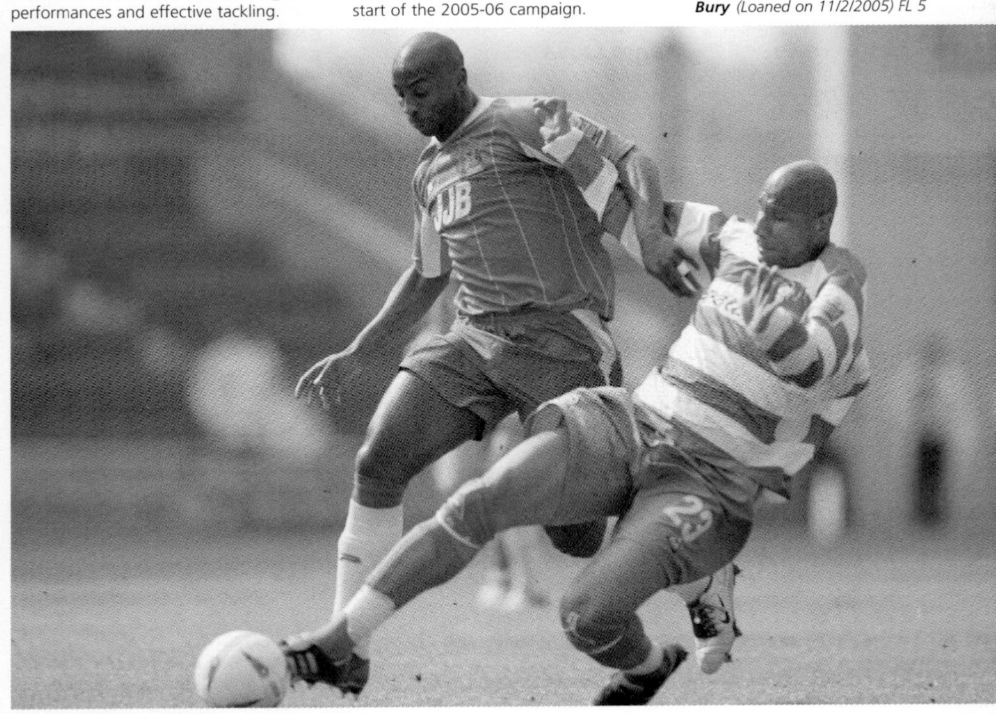

Georges Santos (right)

SAVAGE David (Dave) Thomas Patrick
Born: Dublin, 30 July 1973
Height: 6'1" **Weight:** 12.7
International Honours: RoI: 5; U21-5
After failing to make the starting line-up for Bristol Rovers early on last season this experienced midfielder was placed on the transfer list. However, a couple of impressive performances allowed him to re-establish himself in a wide role, from where he worked hard to create openings for the strikers. He ended his season just short of the landmark total of 400 Football League appearances.
Brighton & Hove A *(Signed from Kilkenny on 5/3/1991. Free to Longford T in May 1992)*
Millwall *(£15,000 on 27/5/1994) FL 104+28/6 FLC 11/2 FAC 6+2/2 Others 2/1*
Northampton T *(£100,000 on 7/10/1998) FL 98+15/18 FLC 3 FAC 5 Others 2+1*
Oxford U *(Free on 18/8/2001) FL 85/5 FLC 4 FAC 4 Others 2*
Bristol Rov *(Free on 1/7/2003) FL 58+7/3 FLC 1+1 FAC 2 Others 2*

SAVAGE Robert (Robbie) William
Born: Wrexham, 18 October 1974
Height: 6'1" **Weight:** 11.11
Club Honours: FAYC '92; FLC '00
International Honours: W: 39; U21-5; Yth; Sch
Robbie began the 2004-05 season in all-action style for Birmingham City and was the driving force behind Blues before it all turned sour. He demanded a transfer in January, was left out of the next match against Bolton Wanderers and ordered to play in the reserves until he eventually got his wish and was sold to Blackburn Rovers. However, he arrived at Ewood Park with a groin strain and struggled throughout to achieve fitness. Indeed he had something of a disappointing second half of the campaign, seldom finding his best form for his new club.
Manchester U *(From trainee on 5/7/1993)*
Crewe Alex *(Free on 22/7/1994) FL 74+3/10 FLC 5 FAC 5 Others 8/1*
Leicester C *(£400,000 on 23/7/1997) PL 160+12/8 FLC 15+2 FAC 12/1 Others 2+1*
Birmingham C *(£2,500,000 on 30/5/2002) PL 82/11 FLC 1/1 FAC 5*
Blackburn Rov *(£3,100,000 on 19/1/2005) PL 9 FAC 3+1*

SCARTISCINI Leandro
Born: Buenos Aires, Argentina, 30 January 1985
Height: 5'11" **Weight:** 12.2
This strong-running Argentine forward earned a short-term contract with Darlington after impressing on trial at the end of the 2003-04 season. A product of the Lanus Youth Academy in Argentina he also had trials with Italian Serie A side, Udinese. However, he made only one appearance as a substitute in the Carling Cup tie with Barnsley in August before being released to return across the Atlantic.
Darlington *(Free from Manfredonia, Italy on 5/8/2004) FLC 0+1*

SCHOFIELD Daniel (Danny) James
Born: Doncaster, 10 April 1980
Height: 5'10" **Weight:** 11.3
Danny featured regularly in the Huddersfield Town squad last term, although he was often used from the substitutes' bench. On his day the tricky wingman is the most dangerous player on the club's books, capable of tormenting defences with his close control and turn of pace. He scored with a fine solo effort in the home defeat by Wrexham and netted with a superb volley directly from a corner in the LDV Vans Trophy tie against Blackpool.
Huddersfield T *(£2,000 from Brodsworth on 8/2/1999) FL 124+23/23 FLC 5+1 FAC 5+1 Others 12+1/6*

SCHOLES Paul
Born: Salford, 16 November 1974
Height: 5'7" **Weight:** 11.10
Club Honours: PL '96, '97, '99, '00, '01, '03; FAC '96, '99, '04; CS '96, '97, '03
International Honours: E: 66; Yth (UEFA-U18 '93)

Paul Scholes

A central midfielder whose imaginative distribution makes him the fulcrum of the Manchester United team, Paul's retirement from the international arena certainly didn't dampen his enthusiasm on the Premiership stage. The rumour mill was suggesting that this might be his last season in top-class football, though such talk was playfully dismissed. Although the 'Scholes Means Goals' slogan seemed to have run dry after nine months of club football without a notable strike, Paul's renaissance came in November with a flurry of goals in five games out of six. His first against Charlton in the Premiership came on his 30th birthday, and this on his 350th appearance for the club. A leading performer in all competitions, he was inspirational in helping the Reds reach their second successive FA Cup final with three goals in the early rounds.
Manchester U *(From trainee on 29/1/1993) PL 259+62/87 FLC 11+5/8 FAC 23+9/12 Others 84+11/20*

SCHUMACHER Steven (Steve) Thomas

Born: Liverpool, 30 April 1984
Height: 5'10" **Weight:** 11.0
International Honours: E: Yth
This young midfielder won a regular place in Bradford City's side last term and impressed with his energetic and consistent performances. A more defensive player at first, his game developed as manager Colin Todd encouraged him to make more runs into the penalty area. This resulted in six goals, including a belting volley against Bournemouth on his 21st birthday.
Everton *(From trainee on 12/5/2001)*
Carlisle U *(Loaned on 31/10/2003) FL 4 FAC 1 Others 1/1*
Bradford C *(Free on 6/8/2004) FL 42+1/6 FLC 1 FAC 1 Others 1*

SCHWARZER Mark

Born: Sydney, Australia, 6 October 1972
Height: 6'5" **Weight:** 13.6
Club Honours: FLC '04
International Honours: Australia: 30; Yth
Mark remained first-choice 'keeper at the Riverside last term, and after interest was rumoured from a number of Premiership rivals he signed a new contract for Boro'. He suffered a back spasm in the 1-0 win at Crystal Palace in early April and was out of action for the next five games. The pinnacle of Mark's 2004-05 Premiership season was, unquestionably, the penalty save from Robbie Fowler at the City of Manchester stadium which earned the club seventh place in the final Premiership table and an automatic qualification for the 2005-06 UEFA Cup.
Bradford C *(£350,000 from Kaiserslautern, Germany, ex Blacktown, Marconi, Dynamo Dresden, on 22/11/1996) FL 13 FAC 3*
Middlesbrough *(£1,500,000 on 26/2/1997) P/FL 270 FLC 23 FAC 15 Others 10*

SCIMECA Riccardo (Riccy)

Born: Leamington Spa, 13 June 1975
Height: 6'1" **Weight:** 12.9
Club Honours: FLC '96
International Honours: E: B-1; U21-9
A player with excellent skills, good control and an appetite for hard work, Riccy was used as an orthodox right back, in central defence and also in midfield for West Bromwich Albion during the course of the 2004-05 season. He made his debut for the Baggies against Blackburn Rovers at Ewood Park on the opening day of the Premiership programme and held his place at right back until early in the new year when Bryan Robson decided to replace him with Martin Albrechtsen. Used thereafter mainly as a substitute, it was from his precise cross that fellow full back Paul Robinson headed Albion's last-gasp equaliser against his former club at Villa Park in April.
Aston Villa *(From trainee on 7/7/1993) PL 50+23/2 FLC 4+3 FAC 9+1 Others 5+2*
Nottingham F *(£3,000,000 on 23/7/1999) FL 147+4/7 FLC 8/1 FAC 5 Others 2*
Leicester C *(Free on 5/7/2003) PL 28+1/1 FLC 1 FAC 1*
West Bromwich A *(£100,000 on 24/5/2004) PL 27+6 FLC 1 FAC 2*

SCOFFHAM Stephen (Steve)

Born: Munster, Germany, 12 July 1983
Height: 5'11" **Weight:** 11.4
This promising young striker spent much

Mark Schwarzer

of last season recuperating from a broken leg suffered at the end of the previous campaign. Steve eventually returned to first-team action in March, coming off the bench in the home game against Bristol Rovers, and featured in a number of games in the closing stages.
Notts Co *(Signed from Gedling T on 14/2/2004) FL 7+15/2*

SCOTT Andrew (Andy)
Born: Epsom, 2 August 1972
Height: 6'1" **Weight:** 11.5
Club Honours: Div 3 '99
Andy returned to match fitness last term and was a valuable member of the Leyton Orient team, scoring more than his fair share of goals from the left wing. A useful target man who can also play as a centre forward when needed, he was unfortunately forced to retire from the game in April due to health problems. Andy was a real crowd pleaser and will be missed by everyone at Brisbane Road.
Sheffield U *(£50,000 from Sutton U on 1/12/1992) P/FL 39+36/6 FLC 5/2 FAC 2+1 Others 3+1/3*
Chesterfield *(Loaned on 18/10/1996) FL 4+1/3*
Bury *(Loaned on 21/3/1997) FL 2+6*
Brentford *(£75,000 on 21/11/1997) FL 109+9/28 FLC 8+1/4 FAC 3 Others 6/3*
Oxford U *(£75,000 on 12/1/2001) FL 77+18/24 FLC 3+1/1 FAC 0+1*
Leyton Orient *(Free on 24/3/2004) FL 45+2/10 FLC 1 FAC 2 Others 2+1*

SCOTT Paul
Born: Wakefield, 5 November 1979
Height: 5'11" **Weight:** 12.8
This central defender signed non-contract forms for Bury last August and made his debut 24 hours later in the home game against Chester, playing alongside Dave Challinor and Danny Swailes in the Shakers' back five. He was soon signed permanently, but after an extended run in the side lost his place to Colin Woodthorpe in October. Paul was in and out of the side for the remainder of the season, but reclaimed a regular berth in the closing weeks. He also deputised in midfield on the odd occasion.
Huddersfield T *(From trainee on 3/7/1998) FL 18+14/2 FLC 1+1 FAC 1 Others 1+1*
Bury *(Free on 20/8/2004) FL 20+3 FLC 1 FAC 0+1 Others 1/1*

SCOTT Robert (Rob)
Born: Epsom, 15 August 1973
Height: 6'1" **Weight:** 11.10
Rob was a near-permanent substitute for Rotherham in the opening stages of the 2004-05 campaign, but then he came into the side on the right of the back four and also slotted into the middle of a back three on occasions. A persistent shoulder injury prevented him from being able to use his ability to throw the ball a long way but he was always a willing worker. Rob was released at the end of the season.
Sheffield U *(£20,000 from Sutton U on 1/8/1993) FL 2+4/1 FLC 0+1 Others 2+1*
Scarborough *(Loaned on 22/3/1995) FL 8/3*
Northampton T *(Loaned on 24/11/1995) FL 5 Others 1*
Fulham *(£30,000 on 10/1/1996) FL 65+19/17 FLC 3+5 FAC 3/1 Others 2+2/1*
Carlisle U *(Loaned on 18/8/1998) FL 7/3*
Rotherham U *(£50,000 on 17/11/1998) FL 160+14/9 FLC 9+1 FAC 9/1 Others 6*

SCOWCROFT James (Jamie) Benjamin
Born: Bury St Edmunds, 15 November 1975
Height: 6'1" **Weight:** 12.2
International Honours: E: U21-5
Jamie can operate either as a striker or in a withdrawn midfield role. A regular choice in both roles under all Leicester managers during the season, he never really found any regular goal-scoring form for the Foxes. He did, though, manage the last gasp header that ousted Reading from the FA Cup. He was allowed to rejoin Ipswich on loan in the new year, and led the line as a replacement for the injured Shefki Kuqi before dropping back to a place on the bench.
Ipswich T *(From trainee on 1/7/1994) P/FL 163+39/47 FLC 21+4/7 FAC 9+1 Others 7+3/1*
Leicester C *(£3,000,000 on 31/7/2001) P/FL 127+6/24 FLC 6+1/1 FAC 7/3*
Ipswich T *(Loaned on 15/2/2005) FL 3+6*

SCULLY Anthony (Tony) Derek Thomas
Born: Dublin, 12 June 1976
Height: 5'7" **Weight:** 11.12
International Honours: RoI: B-1; U21-10; Yth; Sch
This much-travelled enigmatic winger was a regular in the Notts County first-team squad last term, although often featuring from the substitutes' bench as a result of

Tony Scully

struggling to find consistent form. At his best Tony has the capability to change the course of a match with an exceptional and unexpected piece of skill to set up a chance for a colleague, or to score a spectacular goal himself.
Crystal Palace *(From trainee on 2/12/1993) FL 0+3*
Bournemouth *(Loaned on 14/10/1994) FL 6+4 Others 2*
Cardiff C *(Loaned on 5/1/1996) FL 13+1*
Manchester C *(£80,000 on 12/8/1997) FL 1+8*
Stoke C *(Loaned on 27/1/1998) FL 7*
Queens Park Rgrs *(£155,000 on 17/3/1998) FL 20+20/2 FLC 4+1 FAC 0+1*
Cambridge U *(Free on 9/7/2001) FL 20+11/2 FLC 0+1 FAC 2 Others 3*
Southend U *(Loaned on 1/11/2002) FL 8 FAC 4*
Peterborough U *(Free on 26/3/2003) FL 0+3 (Free to Dagenham & Redbridge on 5/9/2003)*
Notts Co *(Free from Tamworth, via Barnet, on 12/2/2004) FL 26+15/5 FLC 2 FAC 2+2/1 Others 0+1*

SEDGEMORE Jake Oliver
Born: Wolverhampton, 10 October 1978
Height: 6'1" **Weight:** 12.10
International Honours: E: SP-5
Jake was in and out of the Shrewsbury line-up last term, mostly featuring in a central-midfield role, although he was occasionally used in defence. Wherever he was employed he always showed great commitment and drive and looked dangerous from free-kick situations in front of goal. He netted a total of five goals including a vital winner at Grimsby in February. Jake was one of several players released by the Gay Meadow club in the summer.
Shrewsbury T *(Signed from Northwich Vic, ex Hednesford T, Hereford U, on 11/7/2003) FL 25+6/5 FAC 1 Others 2*

SEDGWICK Christopher (Chris) Edward
Born: Sheffield, 28 April 1980
Height: 5'11" **Weight:** 10.10
A speedy right winger who came up through the junior ranks at Rotherham, Chris was an automatic first-team choice from the outset last season before moving to Preston in November. A tireless worker when pushing forward he is a dangerous crosser of the ball and weighed in with some useful goals, including one on his return to Millmoor, when his reputation was marked by a standing ovation from all four sides of the ground when substituted near the end.
Rotherham U *(From trainee on 16/8/1997) FL 195+48/17 FLC 10+2/3 FAC 8+5 Others 2+2/1*
Preston NE *(£300,000 on 23/11/2004) FL 24/3 FAC 1 Others 3*

SEMPLE Ryan David
Born: Belfast, 4 July 1985
Height: 5'11" **Weight:** 10.11
This flying winger made a number of appearances for Peterborough last term without ever establishing himself in the side. Ryan is an exciting talent who has yet to reach his full potential and will be looking to do so in the 2005-06 campaign.
Peterborough U *(From trainee on 12/8/2002) FL 4+9 FLC 0+1 FAC 1+2 Others 0+1*

SENDA Daniel (Danny) Luke
Born: Harrow, 17 April 1981
Height: 5'10" **Weight:** 10.0
International Honours: E: Yth
Danny had another excellent season at Wycombe Wanderers in 2004-05. In the early part of the campaign he operated as a wide-right midfielder, but new manager John Gorman alternated with Danny and Gus Uhlenbeek in the right-back and right-midfield roles, finally deciding that Danny was a better defender. As a right back he uses his startling acceleration to close down attackers but is also very comfortable coming forward.
Wycombe W *(From Southampton juniors on 26/1/1999) FL 173+59/9 FLC 4+3 FAC 9+3 Others 9+4*

SENDEROS Philippe
Born: Geneva, Switzerland, 14 February 1985
Height: 6'1" **Weight:** 13.10
Club Honours: FAC '05
International Honours: Switzerland: 2; U21; Yth
This young Swiss central defender finally came to prominence at Highbury having recovered from a catalogue of injuries that had threatened to curtail the great promise shown. Philippe broke through late on in the campaign to partner Kolo Toure in the absence of the injured Sol Campbell and did such a fine job that the England international remained on the bench for several Premiership games as well as the FA Cup final. Arsenal kept 11 clean sheets in the 16 matches he started and lost only once. He gave some tremendous performances in that time notably at home to Bayern Munich in the Champions' League and in the FA Cup final win over Manchester United.
Arsenal *(£2,500,000 from Servette, Switzerland on 18/7/2003) PL 12+1 FLC 3 FAC 6 Others 1*

SENIOR Philip (Phil) Anthony
Born: Huddersfield, 30 October 1982
Height: 5'11" **Weight:** 11.1
Phil spent last season as understudy firstly to Ian Gray and later to Paul Rachubka at Huddersfield. The promising 'keeper managed a handful of first-team appearances, mostly in the first half of the campaign. Phil is capable of marshalling the back line and is also a good shot-stopper.
Huddersfield T *(From trainee on 6/11/1999) FL 37+3 FAC 0+1 Others 2*

SEOL Ki-Hyeon
Born: South Korea, 8 January 1979
Height: 6'0" **Weight:** 11.7
International Honours: South Korea
This South Korean international arrived at Molineux in the summer of 2004 but it was some time before he began to make an impact at first-team level. He eventually settled in a role just behind the strikers and netted four goals in seven games, starting with a 25-yard cracker at home to Plymouth. However, there was to be no summer rest as he began National Service for his country.
Wolverhampton W *(Signed from Anderlecht, Belgium on 1/9/2004) FL 28+9/4 FLC 1/1 FAC 2/1*

SEREMET Dino
Born: Slovenia, 16 August 1980
Height: 6'3" **Weight:** 14.2
Dino was a surprise signing for Luton during the summer of 2004. The giant goalkeeper had a brief run in the line-up during the autumn and also featured in the 3-3 draw with Doncaster on the final day of the season. Dino, who possesses good reflexes and is very brave, will be looking to establish himself as the club's number one 'keeper in 2005-06.
Luton T *(Free from NK Maribor, Slovenia on 26/7/2004) FL 6+1 FAC 1 Others 1*

SERIOUX Adrian Roger
Born: Scarborough, Ontario, Canada, 12 May 1979
Height: 6'0" **Weight:** 12.12
International Honours: Canada: 3
Adrian impressed so much during Millwall's summer tour of Canada that he was given a contract. He is a tough-tackling defender who can also play in midfield. Once he adapted to the pace of the English game he became an asset until injury struck. Adrian possesses an exceptionally long throw that causes opposition defenders all sorts of problems.
Millwall *(Free from Toronto Lynx, Canada on 12/8/2004) FL 10+9 FLC 1*

SESTANOVICH Ashley Shane
Born: Lambeth, 18 September 1981
Height: 6'3" **Weight:** 13.0
This skilful midfield player spent the first half of last season on a long-term loan at Grimsby Town, having previously worked with manager Russell Slade during a loan spell at Scarborough. However, he returned to Bramall Lane in January and soon afterwards joined Chester City on a short-term contract. He demonstrated an excellent range of passing and the ability to make time for himself on the ball, but left the League Two club shortly before the end of the season.
Sheffield U *(Signed from Hampton & Richmond, ex Manchester C N/C, Kingstonian, Royal Antwerp, Mullingar T, on 27/2/2003) FL 0+2*
Grimsby T *(Loaned on 29/6/2004) FL 17+5/2 FLC 2 FAC 1*
Chester C *(Free on 17/2/2005) FL 3+4*

SHAABAN Rami
Born: Stockholm, Sweden, 30 June 1975
Height: 6'4" **Weight:** 14.9
Arriving in Brighton as a free agent after trials with a number of clubs, Rami replaced the on-loan David Yelldell between the Withdean sticks, making his debut in the 2-1 win over future champions Sunderland. It was the custodian's first senior appearance for more than two years following serious injury problems at Arsenal, and he did well enough to convince manager Mark McGhee that he was worth a contract to the end of the season. Playing throughout with a restricting toe injury and looking hesitant at times, Rami kept a clean sheet in his second game, a 1-0 victory over Millwall, but a run of four consecutive defeats persuaded McGhee to opt for Southampton's Alan Blayney, and Rami was relegated to the bench for the rest of the season as the Seagulls just avoided relegation from the Championship.
Arsenal *(Signed from Djurgaarden, Sweden, ex Saltsjobadens, Zamalek, Thadodosman, Nacka FF, on 30/8/2002) PL 3 Others 2 (Freed during 2004 close season)*
Brighton & Hove A *(Free, following trials with Lillestrom, FC Saarbrucken, Tottenham H, on 18/2/2005) FL 6*

SHACKELL Jason Philip
Born: Stevenage, 27 August 1983
Height: 5'11" **Weight:** 11.9
Jason ended the 2004-05 campaign as Craig Fleming's regular partner at the heart of the Norwich defence. A product of City's youth set-up, he impressed many seasoned football watchers with his strong and commanding presence in the back line. He attacks the high ball superbly, is confident when in possession and has a natural leader's instinct for one so young. The experience he gained in the Premiership will stand him in great stead as he seeks to cement his place in the Canaries' line-up for the seasons to come.
Norwich C *(From trainee on 28/1/2003) P/FL 17+2 FLC 1*

SHAKES Ricky Ulric
Born: Brixton, 26 January 1985
Height: 5'10" **Weight:** 12.0
A diminutive but speedy striker, Ricky made his only first-team appearance for Bolton in the Carling Cup victory at Yeovil. He found opportunities hard to come by at the Reebok and spent time on loan at Bristol Rovers and Bury before being released by Bolton at the end of the season. Although he impressed with the Pirates he only featured from the bench. He then became a rather appropriate signing for the Shakers where he fared much better, scoring an injury-time goal at Kidderminster and producing a fine display against Cheltenham, when he scored one goal and also had a hand in creating two more for his colleagues.
Bolton W *(From trainee on 1/7/2004) FLC 1 FAC 0+1/1*
Bristol Rov *(Loaned on 15/2/2004) FL 0+1 Others 0+1*
Bury *(Loaned on 24/3/2005) FL 4+3/2*

SHARP Kevin Phillip
Born: Ontario, Canada, 19 September 1974
Height: 5'9" **Weight:** 11.11
Club Honours: FAYC '93; Div 3 '97; AMC '99
International Honours: E: Yth (UEFA-U18 '93); Sch
This experienced Scunthorpe left back, who is comfortable on the ball and loves to get forward, suffered a disappointing 2004-05 campaign. An ankle injury ruled him out of action until October and the good form of Lee Ridley restricted him to just a handful of appearances during the season. He had to wait until January to make the starting line-up and then after starting three successive games in February he lost his place again and failed to make another appearance during the closing three months of the campaign. He was released at the end of the season.
Leeds U *(£60,000 from Auxerre, France on 20/10/1992) PL 11+6 Others 0+1*
Wigan Ath *(£100,000 on 30/11/1995) FL 156+22/10 FLC 7+2/1 FAC 7+3 Others 18+1/1*
Wrexham *(Free on 2/11/2001) FL 12+3*
Huddersfield T *(Free on 8/8/2002) FL 38+1 FLC 2 FAC 1 Others 1*
Scunthorpe U *(Free on 2/7/2003) FL 41+5/2 FLC 2 FAC 5+1 Others 4*

SHARP William (Billy) Louis
Born: Sheffield, 5 February 1986
Height: 5'8 **Weight:** 12.2
A free scoring striker in the Blades' reserves, Billy made his Championship debut as a substitute in November. In January he moved on loan to Rushden where he did exceptionally well and finished the campaign as the team's leading scorer with nine goals. Billy's first senior goal came in the 3-1 defeat at Chester on his birthday but he had plenty to celebrate later with crucial strikes for the League Two strugglers. His final appearance at Nene Park brought a stunning second-half hat-trick inside 30 minutes to beat Boston United 4-2 while Diamonds' supporters will also fondly recall Billy's last-gasp winner against local rivals Northampton Town. After returning to Bramall Lane, Billy was given a late appearance from the bench on the final day of the season at Wolves.
Sheffield U *(From trainee on 7/7/2004) FL 0+2*
Rushden & Diamonds *(Loaned on 21/1/2005) FL 16/9*

SHARPS Ian William
Born: Warrington, 23 October 1980
Height: 6'4" **Weight:** 13.8
Ian is a central defender and another product of Tranmere's successful youth scheme. Just coming into his prime, he is both outstanding in the air and difficult to shake off the ball, as well as being able to read the game well and distribute the ball accurately. Almost an ever-present in the Rovers' side last term, his main assets are that he is strong, tenacious and hard working.
Tranmere Rov *(From trainee on 5/7/1999) FL 124+7/5 FLC 6 FAC 6 Others 6*

SHAW Jonathan (Jon) Steven
Born: Sheffield, 10 November 1983
Height: 6'1" **Weight:** 12.9
This young striker failed to build on his breakthrough of the previous season and managed just a handful of first-team appearances for Sheffield Wednesday last term. In November he moved on to Conference outfit Burton Albion and began to regain both his form and confidence, netting 11 goals from just 18 starts.
Sheffield Wed *(From trainee on 2/7/2003) FL 8+10/2 FLC 0+1 FAC 0+2 Others 1+2*
York C *(Loaned on 14/11/2003) FL 5+3*

Alan Shearer

HAW Matthew (Matt) Alan
›rn: Blackpool, 17 May 1984
›ight: 6'1" **Weight:** 12.0
att arrived at Wrexham on trial last ıgust and featured regularly for the ıb's reserve team even though he did ›t sign until October, and then only on non-contract basis. The enthusiastic ·iker made one appearance for the ·agons, coming off the bench in the ›sing stages of the 2-1 win at ›lchester. Matt subsequently signed for ackpool and after several appearances a substitute he received his first start in e home game with Hartlepool United ı Easter Monday.
heffield Wed *(From trainee at Stockport › on 15/3/2002. Freed on 17/1/2004)*
/rexham *(Free, via trial at Burnley, on 3/10/2004) FL 0+1*
lackpool *(Free on 17/12/2004) FL 2+8 FAC +1*

;HAW Paul
orn: Burnham, 4 September 1973
leight: 5'11" **Weight:** 12.4
ıternational Honours: E: Yth
aul began his season on loan at /lillmoor, where he played in a role just ehind the front two and scored twice. le was recalled to Bramall Lane due to a triker shortage in September and was a egular in the side until December. Here oo he was most effective when playing ıst behind the front men where he was ıble to hold and lay-off the ball to ›thers. Paul scored a tremendous goal in he 3-3 draw against Wolves in ·Jovember, but fell out of favour towards he end of the campaign.
Arsenal *(From trainee on 18/9/1991) PL 1+11/2 FAC 0+1*
Burnley *(Loaned on 23/3/1995) FL 8+1/4*
Cardiff C *(Loaned on 11/8/1995) FL 6*
Peterborough U *(Loaned on 20/10/1995) FL 12/5 Others 2*
Millwall *(£250,000 on 15/9/1997) FL 88+21/26 FLC 6/2 FAC 2 Others 5+2/4*
Gillingham *(£450,000 on 11/7/2000) FL 118+17/26 FLC 5+3 FAC 8/3*
Sheffield U *(£75,000 on 12/1/2004) FL 20+14/8 FLC 0+2 FAC 1+1*
Rotherham U *(Loaned on 6/8/2004) FL 9/2*

SHAW Richard Edward
Born: Brentford, 11 September 1968
Height: 5'9" **Weight:** 12.8
Club Honours: FMC '91; Div 1 '94
Richard was a virtual ever-present in the heart of Coventry's defence last season until January, playing alongside several different partners, but thereafter his appearances were few and far between. He was always a solid performer using his many years of experience to good effect whilst compensating for a slight slowing down with good positional play. Richard was out of contract in the summer and his future was unclear at the time of writing.
Crystal Palace *(From apprentice on 4/9/1986) P/FL 193+14/3 FLC 28+2 FAC 18 Others 12+1*
Hull C *(Loaned on 14/12/1989) FL 4*
Coventry C *(£1,000,000 on 17/11/1995) P/FL 272+20/1 FLC 21+2 FAC 19+1*

SHEARER Alan
Born: Newcastle, 13 August 1970
Height: 6'0" **Weight:** 12.6
Club Honours: PL '95
International Honours: E: 63; B-1; U21-11; Yth
Alan continued to captain his hometown club Newcastle, leading from the front and displaying all his qualities of passion, commitment, durability, and deadly finishing. Chasing the club scoring record he fell short last season, due in part to an absence of two months with a torn thigh muscle followed by a calf injury. However, he passed numerous other milestones during the season including his 400th Premiership appearance, while no British player has scored more than his 30 European goals. Although not as prolific as in previous campaigns, his goals came at frequent intervals, and his form and overall contribution persuaded him to change his mind about retiring and to sign on for a further year, during which he will be player-coach at the club. This is seen by many as a step towards his becoming the Magpies' manager at some time in the not-too-distant future. Alan was inducted into the National Football Museum's Hall of Fame in November for his outstanding contribution to the game.
Southampton *(From trainee on 14/4/1988) FL 105+13/23 FLC 16+2/11 FAC 11+3/4 Others 8/5*
Blackburn Rov *(£3,600,000 on 24/7/1992) PL 132+6/112 FLC 16/14 FAC 8/2 Others 9/2*
Newcastle U *(£15,000,000 on 30/7/1996) PL 264+7/138 FLC 13+1/6 FAC 33/20 Others 46/28*

SHEARER Scott
Born: Glasgow, 15 February 1981
Height: 6'3" **Weight:** 14.8
International Honours: S: B-1
The giant shot-stopper started last season as Coventry City's first-choice goalkeeper but was dropped after the 3-0 defeat at Leeds. In February he joined Rushden on loan to cover for a goalkeeping crisis but his spell was cut short when he had to cover Ian Bennett's suspension for the Sky Blues at Watford. However, Scott rejoined Diamonds the following week and produced a number of stunning saves, particularly away from home. He was released by Coventry at the end of the season.
Albion Rov *(Signed from Tower Hearts on 6/7/2000) SL 47+2/1 SLC 1 SC 2 Others 1*
Coventry C *(Signed on 7/7/2003) FL 37+1 FLC 3*
Rushden & Diamonds *(Loaned on 18/2/2005) FL 3*
Rushden & Diamonds *(Loaned on 11/3/2005) FL 10*

SHEEHAN Alan Michael Anthony
Born: Athlone, 14 September 1986
Height: 5'11" **Weight:** 11.2
International Honours: RoI: U21-1; Yth
This promising young left back impressed in his outings for Leicester's reserves and Academy teams last season to such an extent that he was given his full debut in the closing fixture away to Plymouth. There he continued to demonstrate his huge potential and he will be looking to gain more first-team experience in 2005-06.
Leicester C *(From trainee on 24/9/2004) FL 1*

SHERINGHAM Edward (Teddy) Paul
Born: Highams Park, 2 April 1966
Height: 5'11" **Weight:** 12.5
Club Honours: Div 2 '88; FMC '92; CS '97; PL '99, '00, '01; FAC '99; UEFACL '99
International Honours: E: 51; U21-1; Yth
This veteran striker proved a great signing for West Ham last term. After snatching a late winner against Reading in the opening home game he maintained high standards throughout the campaign. Teddy hit 20 Championship goals and provided countless assists, often defying his years by playing two and sometimes three games in a week. A model of consistency and professionalism his presence alone helped bring out the best in the club's youngsters. He deservedly won the Hammer of the Year' award and the 'Powerade Championship Player of the Year' trophy. Unfortunately a hamstring injury kept him out of the play-off games although he was on the bench for the final.
Millwall *(From apprentice on 19/1/1984) FL 205+15/93 FLC 16+1/8 FAC 12/5 Others 12+1/5*
Aldershot *(Loaned on 1/2/1985) FL 4+1 Others 1*
Nottingham F *(£2,000,000 on 23/7/1991) P/FL 42/14 FLC 10/5 FAC 4/2 Others 6/2*
Tottenham H *(£2,100,000 on 28/8/1992) PL 163+3/76 FLC 14/10 FAC 17/13*

Teddy Sheringham

Manchester U *(£3,500,000 on 1/7/1997) PL 73+31/31 FLC 1/1 FAC 4+5/5 Others 23+16/9*
Tottenham H *(Free on 16/7/2001) PL 67+3/22 FLC 6+1/3 FAC 3/1*
Portsmouth *(Free on 2/7/2003) PL 25+7/9 FLC 3 FAC 2+1/1*
West Ham U *(Free on 30/7/2004) FL 26+7/20 FLC 0+1 FAC 2/1*

SHERON Michael (Mike) Nigel

Born: St Helens, 11 January 1972
Height: 5'10" **Weight:** 11.13
Club Honours: AMC '04
International Honours: E: U21-16
Mike was a regular member of the Macclesfield side, usually in a three-man attack, until the turn of the year after which he only made a handful of appearances. A highly experienced striker, he scored four goals for the Moss Rose club, but with opportunities limited, his contract was cancelled by mutual agreement in March and shortly afterwards he signed for Shrewsbury Town. However, despite his undoubted skills, he never really seemed to fit in to the Shrews' style of play and he left the club just before the season ended to seek his future elsewhere.
Manchester C *(From trainee on 5/7/1990) P/FL 82+18/24 FLC 9+1/1 FAC 5+3/3 Others 1*
Bury *(Loaned on 28/3/1991) FL 1+4/1 Others 2*
Norwich C *(£1,000,000 on 26/8/1994) P/FL 19+9/2 FLC 6/3 FAC 4/2*
Stoke C *(£450,000 on 13/11/1995) FL 64+5/34 FLC 4/5 FAC 1 Others 2*
Queens Park Rgrs *(£2,750,000 on 2/7/1997) FL 57+6/19 FLC 2+2/1 FAC 2*
Barnsley *(£1,000,000 on 27/1/1999) FL 114+38/33 FLC 10+2/7 FAC 4+3 Others 1*
Blackpool *(Free on 21/7/2003) FL 28+10/8 FLC 2+1 FAC 1+1 Others 7/3*
Macclesfield T *(Free on 5/8/2004) FL 14+12/3 FLC 0+1 FAC 3/1 Others 2+1*
Shrewsbury T *(Free on 15/3/2005) FL 6+1/2*

SHERWOOD Timothy (Tim) Alan

Born: St Albans, 6 February 1969
Height: 6'0" **Weight:** 12.9
Club Honours: PL '95; Div 1 '03
International Honours: E: 3; B-1; U21-4
This former England international was made club captain for Coventry after signing in the 2004 close season, but was still troubled by an ankle problem in his early days at the club. Although Tim had an excellent game in the 4-1 win at Nottingham Forest, Sky Blues' fans rarely saw the best of him in his appearances and in February a scan revealed ongoing trouble with the ankle and he was ruled out for the rest of the campaign.
Watford *(From trainee on 7/2/1987) FL 23+9/2 FLC 4+1 FAC 9 Others 4+1*
Norwich C *(£175,000 on 18/7/1989) FL 66+5/10 FLC 7/1 FAC 4 Others 5+1/2*
Blackburn Rov *(£500,000 on 12/2/1992) P/FL 239+7/25 FLC 24+1/2 FAC 15+2/4 Others 12*
Tottenham H *(£3,800,000 on 5/2/1999) PL 81+12/12 FLC 6+3/2 FAC 13/1 Others 3/1*
Portsmouth *(Free on 29/1/2003) P/FL 24+6/1 FLC 2+1/2*
Coventry C *(Free on 3/8/2004) FL 10+1*

SHIPPERLEY Neil Jason

Born: Chatham, 30 October 1974
Height: 6'1" **Weight:** 13.12
International Honours: E: U21-7
After scoring the goal that took Crystal Palace back to the Premiership in the previous season's play-off final, Neil had a frustrating time with injuries last term and even when fit he was mostly reduced to reserve-team football. The big powerful striker made just three first-team appearances, all from the bench, and will be hoping for better fortune in 2005-06.
Chelsea *(From trainee on 24/9/1992) PL 26+11/7 FLC 4+2/1 FAC 3/1 Others 2*
Watford *(Loaned on 7/12/1994) FL 5+1/1*
Southampton *(£1,250,000 on 6/1/1995) PL 65+1/12 FLC 5+1/2 FAC 10/5*
Crystal Palace *(£1,000,000 on 25/10/1996) P/FL 49+12/20 FLC 3 FAC 2 Others 5/1*
Nottingham F *(£1,500,000 on 22/9/1998) PL 12+8/1 FAC 1*
Barnsley *(£700,000 on 7/7/1999) FL 70+8/27 FLC 4+1/3 FAC 2 Others 3/1*
Wimbledon *(£750,000 on 25/7/2001) FL 82+5/32 FLC 4/3 FAC 4/1*
Crystal Palace *(Signed on 24/7/2003) P/FL 40+1/9 FLC 4+1 FAC 1+1 Others 3/2*

SHITTU Daniel (Danny) Olusola

Born: Lagos, Nigeria, 2 September 1980
Height: 6'3" **Weight:** 16.0
International Honours: Nigeria: 1
This tall and solid central defender started the 2004-05 season on the injured list for Queen's Park Rangers. Although he returned at the end of September he suffered a relapse and was not fully fit until early November. Once he was back in the team he played in every one of the remaining Championship games. A powerful player known for his no-nonsense clearances and strong headers he remained very popular with the fans. Danny scored four goals during the campaign and was runner-up in the 'Player of the Year' award.
Charlton Ath *(Free from Carshalton Ath on 15/9/1999)*
Blackpool *(Loaned on 16/2/2001) FL 15+2/2 Others 2*
Queens Park Rgrs *(£250,000 on 23/10/2001) FL 121+3/13 FLC 5 FAC 2 Others 5*

SHOREY Nicholas (Nicky)

Born: Romford, 19 February 1981
Height: 5'9" **Weight:** 10.10
Always one of the first names on manager Steve Coppell's team sheet, Nicky added to his status as one of the best defenders outside the Premiership with a season of classy displays as an attacking left wing-back for Reading. Strong in the tackle, with the stamina to overlap throughout the 90 minutes, and possessing immaculate timing, he is also a master of the dead-ball situation. Not only does he take corner kicks from both sides of the field, he also scored three important goals, all from precisely struck long-range free kicks.
Leyton Orient *(From trainee on 5/7/1999) FL 12+3 FAC 1*
Reading *(£25,000 on 9/2/2001) FL 154/7 FLC 8 FAC 9 Others 4*

SHORT Craig Jonathan

Born: Bridlington, 25 June 1968
Height: 6'1" **Weight:** 13.8
Club Honours: FLC '02
Generally regarded as the best centre back on the books at Blackburn, this rugged defender simply found that age caught up with him last term, and a series of niggling injuries, particularly to his hamstrings, kept him out of the team. Once Ryan Nelsen and Aaron Mokoena arrived he himself acknowledged that he was not able to play and train at the same intensity. Craig opened the season with an equalising goal against West Brom, his only Premiership strike of the season.
Scarborough *(Free from Pickering T on 15/10/1987) FL 61+2/7 FLC 6 FAC 2 Others 7/1*
Notts Co *(£100,000 on 27/7/1989) FL 128/6 FLC 6/1 FAC 8/1 Others 16/2*
Derby Co *(£2,500,000 on 18/9/1992) FL 118/9 FLC 11 FAC 7/4 Others 7*
Everton *(£2,700,000 on 18/7/1995) PL 90+9/4 FLC 7 FAC 4 Others 3*
Blackburn Rov *(£1,700,000 + on 3/8/1999) P/FL 131+3/4 FLC 4/1 FAC 6 Others 2*

SHOWUNMI Enoch Olusesan

Born: Kilburn, 21 April 1982
Height: 6'3" **Weight:** 14.10
Club Honours: Div 1 '05
This talented young striker provided back-up for Steve Howard and Rowan Vine at

Luton last term. He featured regularly on the substitutes' bench and when he came on showed plenty of skill. An unorthodox player who is difficult to mark, he scored a number of vital goals late-on in matches. Enoch was also a member of the Hatters' successful reserve side and featured in the side that defeated Reading to win the Pontin's Combination League Cup.
Luton T *(Signed from Willesden Constantine on 5/9/2003) FL 25+36/13 FLC 0+1/1 FAC 2+3 Others 3+1/1*

SHUKER Christopher (Chris) Alan
Born: Liverpool, 9 May 1982
Height: 5'5" **Weight:** 10.1
This lively wide-midfield man was a handful for his opponents when playing for Barnsley last term. Chris was always willing to take on his marker and equally, when given the opportunity, to have a shot. In excellent form all season, the highlight of his campaign came when he scored in the magnificent 3-1 win at Luton. Chris was the Reds' 'Player of the Season' for 2004-05.
Manchester C *(From trainee on 21/9/1999) P/FL 1+4 FLC 0+1/1*
Macclesfield T *(Loaned on 27/3/2001) FL 6+3/1*
Walsall *(Loaned on 26/2/2003) FL 3+2*
Rochdale *(Loaned on 7/8/2003) FL 14/1 FLC 1*
Hartlepool U *(Loaned on 13/12/2003) FL 14/1 FAC 1*
Barnsley *(Signed on 17/3/2004) FL 48+6/7 FLC 2/1 FAC 1*

SIBIERSKI Antoine
Born: Lille, France, 5 August 1974
Height: 6'2" **Weight:** 12.8
International Honours: France: Yth
A talented attacking midfielder with an eye for goal, Antoine produced a string of performances packed with guile and endeavour for Manchester City last term. Widely regarded as a good finisher and the best header of a ball at the club, he is a player of vast experience and can operate on the left of midfield or even as a deep-lying striker.
Manchester C *(£700,000 from Lens, France, ex Lille OSC, Auxerre, Nantes, on 7/8/2003) PL 52+16/9 FLC 2+1/2 FAC 4+2/1 Others 1/1*

SIDIBE Mamady
Born: Mali, 18 December 1979
Height: 6'4" **Weight:** 12.4
International Honours: Mali: 7
This talented striker was a regular for Gillingham throughout most of the 2004-05 season, although he was absent for several weeks early in the new year with an achilles injury. Mamady returned to action and under new boss Stan Ternent he looked a much better player. Strong in the air and able to hold the ball up to allow his colleagues to come into the play, he was out of contract in the summer and looked likely to be moving elsewhere.
Swansea C *(Free from CA Paris, France, ex Racing Club Paris, on 27/7/2001) FL 26+5/7 FLC 0+1 FAC 2/1 Others 1*
Gillingham *(Free on 9/8/2002) FL 80+26/10 FLC 4+1/1 FAC 3+1/2*

SIDWELL Steven (Steve) James
Born: Wandsworth, 14 December 1982
Height: 5'10" **Weight:** 11.2
Club Honours: FAYC '00, '01
International Honours: E: U21-5; Yth
The honours continued to accumulate for Steve, who completed another superb season at the heart of Reading's midfield. Voted by a national football magazine as the best player outside the Premiership, he was also named in the PFA Championship team of the season, and he became the youngest captain in Reading's history when he took over from the injured Graeme Murty. Able to do with one touch things which might take other players two or three, he naturally attracted attention from Premiership clubs, most notably Everton. Steve had signed a new, improved contract with Reading at the start of the season, however.
Arsenal *(From trainee on 2/7/2001)*
Brentford *(Loaned on 23/10/2001) FL 29+1/4 FAC 2 Others 3*
Brighton & Hove A *(Loaned on 9/11/2002) FL 11+1/5*
Reading *(£250,000 on 21/1/2003) FL 100/15 FLC 4/1 FAC 3+1 Others 2*

SILK Gary Lee
Born: Newport, Isle of Wight, 13 September 1984
Height: 5'9" **Weight:** 13.7
After impressing in pre-season friendlies, Wycombe signed Gary from Portsmouth on a season-long loan deal. He quickly established himself as a rock-solid right back, with a few appearances at left back, and a fearsome tackler with a big heart. New manager John Gorman was not so enthusiastic and by December he was reduced to a place on the bench. He returned to Fratton Park in February at the Premiership side's request to cover a shortage of players, needing special dispensation to do so.
Portsmouth *(From trainee on 6/1/2004)*
Wycombe W *(Loaned on 6/7/2004) FL 19+3 FLC 1 FAC 2 Others 3*

SILVESTRE Mikael Samy
Born: Chambray-les-Tours, France, 9 August 1977
Height: 6'0" **Weight:** 13.1
Club Honours: PL '00, '01, '03; CS '03; FAC '04
International Honours: France: 36; U21; Yth (UEFA-U18 '96)
A stylish and pacy defender who keeps a cool head under pressure, Mikael was one of Manchester United's most consistent performers throughout another highly productive campaign. Although not renowned for his goal-scoring exploits, his brace against Liverpool in September was celebrated almost like a title win by the Stretford End. Missing only three Premiership games throughout the season, he was a major player throughout the Champions' League and FA Cup runs.
Manchester U *(£4,000,000 from Inter Milan, Italy on 10/9/1999) PL 186+13/4 FLC 7 FAC 13+2/1 Others 58+7/3*

SIMEK Franklin (Frankie) Michael
Born: St Louis, USA, 13 October 1984
Height: 6'0" **Weight:** 11.6
International Honours: USA: Yth
This promising Arsenal central defender spent time on loan at Queen's Park Rangers last term as cover for injuries at Loftus Road. Later in the campaign he had a similar spell at Bournemouth where he impressed at right back before returning to Highbury to continue his career development.
Arsenal *(From trainee on 1/7/2002) FLC 1*
Queens Park Rgrs *(Loaned on 19/10/2004) FL 5*
Bournemouth *(Loaned on 24/3/2005) FL 8*

SIMONSEN Steven (Steve) Preben Arthur
Born: South Shields, 3 April 1979
Height: 6'3" **Weight:** 13.2
International Honours: E: U21-4; Yth
Steve took over the goalkeeping mantle from Ed De Goey for Stoke last season. A magnificent shot-stopper he has tremendous positional sense and once he got in the side he made sure he retained his place with some magnificent displays. He ensured the Potters had the second-best defensive record in the Championship table and was awarded the title of 'Players' Player of the Season' for his efforts.
Tranmere Rov *(From trainee on 9/10/1996) FL 35 FLC 4 FAC 3*
Everton *(£3,300,000 on 23/9/1998) PL 28+2 FLC 2 FAC 5*
Stoke C *(Free on 6/8/2004) FL 29+2 FLC 1 FAC 1*

SIMPSON Joshua (Josh)
Born: Vancouver, Canada, 15 May 1983
Height: 5'10" **Weight:** 12.2
International Honours: Canada: 7
Josh was signed up by Millwall after producing some excellent displays against the club during the pre-season tour of Canada. He can operate at both left back and left midfield and when he adapted to the quicker pace of Championship football he was more prepared to take players on, delivering some sweet crosses and scoring his first goal against Derby with a mazy run and a great finish.
Millwall *(Free from University of Portland, USA on 6/8/2004) FL 22+8/1 FAC 1 Others 2*

SIMPSON Michael
Born: Nottingham, 28 February 1974
Height: 5'9" **Weight:** 10.8
Club Honours: AIC '95
Michael joined Leyton Orient during the summer of 2004 and became a key figure for the O's in the centre of the park, missing just one League Two match. A competitive midfielder who appears to cover every blade of grass during a game, he is always trying to either break up an attack by opponents or start a move for the O's. Michael is a real crowd favourite at Brisbane Road and was voted as the club's 'Player's Player of the Season'.
Notts Co *(From trainee on 1/7/1992) FL 39+10/3 FLC 4+1 FAC 2+1 Others 7+3*
Plymouth Arg *(Loaned on 4/10/1996) FL 10+2*
Wycombe W *(£50,000 on 5/12/1996) FL 267+18/16 FLC 14+1 FAC 24+2/5 Others 14*
Leyton Orient *(Free on 6/7/2004) FL 45/2 FLC 1 FAC 2 Others 3*

SINAMA-PONGOLLE Florent
Born: Saint Pierre, Reunion, 20 October 1984
Height: 5'9" **Weight:** 10.10
International Honours: France: U21; Yth
Very much a fringe player at the start of the season, this young striker was drafted into the Liverpool first-team squad in October, and was a regular performer until January. He became a mini-hero to Reds' fans in December when he not only scored the late penalty in extra time at Tottenham in the Carling Cup to take the match to a penalty shoot-out, but also converted the decisive kick in that shoot-out. A week later he scored one of the goals in Liverpool's thrilling 3-1 victory over Olympiakos in the European Champions' League which ensured their continuance in the competition at the last gasp. Further goals at Christmas against West Brom and Southampton were signs that he was starting to realise his undoubted potential. Unfortunately in January he damaged his knee ligaments in an innocuous tumble in the Carling Cup semi-final at Watford, thus ending his season.
Liverpool *(Signed from Le Havre, France on 18/7/2003) PL 9+22/4 FLC 5+2/1 FAC 2+2 Others 1+6/1*

SINCLAIR Frank Mohammed
Born: Lambeth, 3 December 1971
Height: 5'9" **Weight:** 12.9
Club Honours: FAC '97; FLC '98, '00
International Honours: Jamaica: 24
It was something of a coup for Steve Cotterill when he secured the signature of a player with such vast Premiership experience as Frank, who arrived at Burnley just prior to the start of last

Steve Simonsen

season. Initially partnering John McGreal in a rock-solid central defence, he later often featured at right back as young Gary Cahill became established as an automatic choice in the middle. Frank's experience proved invaluable, and he was a popular choice as captain after the departure of Robbie Blake, but his game was occasionally let down by recklessness. His only goal came in the 2-1 home win against Rotherham.
Chelsea *(From trainee on 17/5/1990) P/FL 163+6/7 FLC 17+1/2 FAC 18/1 Others 13/3*
West Bromwich A *(Loaned on 12/12/1991) FL 6/1*
Leicester C *(£2,000,000 on 14/8/1998) P/FL 153+11/3 FLC 20 FAC 10/1*
Burnley *(Free on 29/7/2004) FL 36/1 FLC 1+1 FAC 4*

SINCLAIR Scott Andrew
Born: Bath, 26 March 1989
Height: 5'10" **Weight:** 10.0
This schoolboy striker was aged just 15 years and 256 days when he came on in injury time on Boxing Day at the Memorial Stadium against Leyton Orient to become the youngest post-war Bristol Rovers player to make a Football League appearance. Scott made another brief substitute appearance against Rushden and was a regular goal-scorer for the club's reserve and youth teams.
Bristol Rov *(Associated Schoolboy) FL 0+2*

SINCLAIR Trevor Lloyd
Born: Dulwich, 2 March 1973
Height: 5'10" **Weight:** 12.10
International Honours: E: 12; B-1; U21-14; Yth
Trevor managed just a handful of appearances for Manchester City last term, his final outing coming in the Carling Cup defeat by Arsenal. During that game he felt discomfort in his knee. A corrective operation was required and he was ruled out for the rest of the season. With a long, hard summer in the gym and on the training pitch planned he hopes to comeback fitter and stronger than ever for 2005-06.
Blackpool *(From trainee on 21/8/1990) FL 84+28/15 FLC 8 FAC 6+1 Others 8+5/1*
Queens Park Rgrs *(£750,000 on 12/8/1993) P/FL 162+5/16 FLC 13/3 FAC 10/2*
West Ham U *(£2,300,000 + on 30/1/1998) PL 175+2/37 FLC 10+1 FAC 8 Others 10/1*
Manchester C *(£2,500,000 on 22/7/2003) PL 22+11/2 FLC 3 FAC 3+1 Others 3/1*

SINGH Harpal
Born: Bradford, 15 September 1981
Height: 5'7" **Weight:** 10.9
Unable to get in the first team at Elland Road, Harpal joined Stockport on loan and made an immediate impact on his debut in the memorable 2-1 win at neighbours Oldham Athletic. He became an instant hit with the County faithful with his mazy runs down the left-hand side and accurate crosses and went on to make a handful of appearances although injury kept him out for a spell. By the end of the season he had made a permanent move to Edgeley Park.
Leeds U *(From trainee on 26/9/1998)*
Bury *(Loaned on 11/9/2001) FL 11+1/2 FAC 2/1 Others 1*
Bristol C *(Loaned on 8/3/2002) FL 3*
Bradford C *(Loaned on 8/11/2002) FL 3*
Bury *(Loaned on 8/8/2003) FL 20+8/2 FLC 1 FAC 1*
Stockport Co *(Signed on 18/2/2005) FL 5+1*

SKIVERTON Terence (Terry) John
Born: Mile End, 26 June 1975
Height: 6'1" **Weight:** 13.6
Club Honours: FAT '02; NC '03; Div 2 '05
International Honours: E: SP-4
Terry was again Yeovil Town's 'Captain Fantastic' last term leading the team by example throughout the campaign. Rarely absent from the side, the big powerful defender contributed four goals including two in the vital win at Boston.
Chelsea *(From trainee on 19/5/1993)*
Wycombe W *(Loaned on 17/2/1995) FL 8+2*
Wycombe W *(Free on 26/3/1996) FL 5+5/1 FAC 0+1 (Free to Welling U on 13/8/1997)*
Yeovil T *(Free on 3/6/1999) FL 61+3/6 FLC 2 FAC 6 Others 2*

SKOPELITIS Giannis Ioannis
Born: Greece, 2 March 1978
Height: 5'11" **Weight:** 11.12
This bustling midfielder joined Pompey during the January transfer window to add determination and bite in the centre of the park. After a settling-in period he became a first-team regular before the end of the season and he will be looking to consolidate his position in the side in 2005-06.
Portsmouth *(£1,000,000 from Aigaleo, Greece on 28/1/2005) PL 9+4*

SKORA Eric
Born: Metz, France, 20 August 1981
Height: 6'1" **Weight:** 11.10
This Preston midfielder featured in the first ten matches of the 2004-05 squad, but then fell out of favour following a change in management. Comfortable on the ball, he mostly appeared on the right hand side of the field, combining crossing ability with defensive duties. A knee injury brought his campaign to a premature close just before Christmas.
Preston NE *(Free from Nancy, France on 22/10/2001) FL 37+14 FLC 3+1/1 FAC 3/1*
Kilmarnock *(Loaned on 23/1/2004) SL 16+1/3 SC 1*

SKUSE Cole
Born: Bristol, 29 March 1986
Height: 6'1" **Weight:** 11.5
This youngster made his debut for Bristol City when he came off the bench during the 2-0 win at Colchester last February. He went on to feature in the starting line-up for the home game against Wrexham in April when he was very impressive in a central-midfield role. Cole received a standing ovation at the end of the game and was also cited as 'Man of the Match'.
Bristol C *(From trainee on 29/4/2005) FL 4+3*

SLABBER Jamie Andrew
Born: Enfield, 31 December 1984
Height: 6'2" **Weight:** 12.2
International Honours: E: Yth
A tall, young, bustling striker, Jamie returned to White Lane following a loan spell at AB Copenhagen, but then missed the opening months of last season with a shoulder injury. After recuperating he went on loan to Swindon where he put in a lot of effort but was unable to find the net. He was subsequently released by Spurs and had a spell at Aldershot where he scored a late equaliser in the Conference play-off semi-final second leg at Carlisle to take the game into extra time.
Tottenham H *(From trainee on 3/1/2002) PL 0+1*
Swindon T *(Loaned on 31/12/2004) FL 4+5 Others 0+1*

SMALL Wade Kristopher
Born: Croydon, 23 February 1984
Height: 5'7" **Weight:** 11.6
A very skilful and speedy attacker with excellent close control, Wade was a regular starter for the MK Dons throughout the 2004-05 season, either wide on the right or as one of the two main strikers. He was calm and composed in front of goal when he needed to be, and scored a couple of screamers from distance. Defensively he also did his fair share, and he deservedly picked up the club's 'Players' Player of the Year' award at the end of the season.
Wimbledon/MK Dons *(From trainee on 17/7/2003) FL 64+7/11 FLC 2 FAC 6/1 Others 1/1*

SMART Allan Andrew Colin
Born: Perth, 8 July 1974
Height: 6'2" **Weight:** 12.10
Club Honours: AMC '97

Allan was given a contract by MK Dons after impressing during pre-season and showed up well early on last term, scoring three goals in the first five games. His ability to lay the ball off was clear for all to see, and despite missing a month through injury he returned to score a couple of key goals for new manager Danny Wilson over the Christmas period. The arrival of Clive Platt in January cost him his starting berth however, and from then on he became a regular on the bench, sitting through eight consecutive games at one stage. He was released at the end of the season.
St Johnstone *(From juniors on 24/1/1991)*
Brechin C *(Free on 30/12/1991)*
Inverness CT *(Free on 28/7/1993) SL 2+2 SLC 1+1*
Preston NE *(£15,000 on 22/11/1994) FL 17+4/6 FAC 2/1 Others 1+1*
Carlisle U *(Loaned on 24/11/1995) FL 3+1*
Northampton T *(Loaned on 13/9/1996) FL 1*
Carlisle U *(Signed on 9/10/1996) FL 41+3/16 FLC 1/1 FAC 4 Others 4+1*
Watford *(£75,000 + on 2/7/1998) P/FL 48+9/12 FLC 1+2 FAC 1 Others 0+3/1*
Hibernian *(Loaned on 14/8/2001) SL 2+3/1*
Stoke C *(Loaned on 6/11/2001) FL 0+2*
Oldham Ath *(£225,000 on 30/11/2001) FL 14+7/6 FAC 1 Others 2/1*
Dundee U *(Free on 19/6/2002) SL 2+15 SLC 0+1*
Crewe Alex *(Free on 15/8/2003) FL 0+6*
MK Dons *(Free on 26/7/2004) FL 15+3/4 FLC 2/1 FAC 2/1*

SMELTZ Shane

Born: Goppingen, Germany, 29 September 1981
Height: 6'1" **Weight:** 12.6
International Honours: New Zealand
After being released by Adelaide United last October, Shane made his way to England and signed a one-month contract for Mansfield. He performed well enough to earn an extended deal, but could not win a regular place in the side and, following a trial with Rushden, he was released from his contract and moved on to AFC Wimbledon in mid-March. A quick and skilful striker, he was used mainly from the bench at Field Mill. Shane continued to be selected for the full New Zealand international squad.
Mansfield T *(Free from Adelaide U, Australia, ex Gold Coast C, Brisbane Strikers, Napier C, Adelaide C, on 10/1/2005) FL 1+4*

Wade Small

SMERTIN Alexei

Born: Barnaul, Russia, 1 May 1975
Height: 5'9" **Weight:** 10.8
Club Honours: PL '05
International Honours: Russia: 49
At least one face of Chelsea's summer 2004 intake of continental stars was familiar – captain of Russia Alexei Smertin reported for duty at Stamford Bridge after a very successful loan period at Portsmouth and in so doing swapped a battle at the foot of the Premiership for a place in Chelsea's record-breaking squad. The wholehearted midfielder proved to be very popular with crowd and teammates alike and demonstrated his versatility by occasionally filling-in at the centre of the defence or at full back. The amazing season at Chelsea was in marked contrast to Russia's dismal showing in Portugal where Alexei's dynamic performances were their only bright spot. He scored just the solitary goal for the Blues but it was a splendid effort – a sweetly-taken half volley against reigning champions Porto which paved the way for an impressive Group H Champions' League victory.
Chelsea *(£3,450,000 from Bordeaux, France, ex Uralan, Lokomotiv Moscow, on 26/8/2003) PL 11+5 FLC 1 FAC 3 Others 4+1/1*
Portsmouth *(Loaned on 27/8/2003) PL 23+3 FLC 2 FAC 5*

SMICER Vladimir (Vlad)

Born: Degin, Czech Republic, 24 May 1973
Height: 5'11" **Weight:** 11.3
Club Honours: FLC '01, '03; FAC '01; UEFAC '01; UEFACL '05
International Honours: Czech Republic: 74; U21-7. Czechoslovakia: 1
After assisting the Czech Republic to the semi-finals of Euro 2004 in Portugal Vlad returned to Anfield only to succumb almost immediately to a long-term knee injury which ruled him out for most of the season. He returned to action in February and, mainly due to the long injury list at Anfield, made 15 appearances mostly from the bench. However, his campaign had something of a fairy-tale ending. In the European Champions' Cup final in Istanbul he was surprisingly thrown into action early on for the limping Harry Kewell and

responded with the second goal, a 25-yard drive, in Liverpool's amazing come-back from a 3-0 deficit, following that with a successful conversion in the penalty shoot-out at the end of the match.
Liverpool *(£3,750,000 from RC Lens, France, ex SK Slavia Praha, on 14/7/1999) PL 69+52/10 FLC 13+2/5 FAC 9+1/1 Others 19+19/3*

SMITH Nathan **Adam**
Born: Huddersfield, 20 February 1985
Height: 6'0" **Weight:** 12.5
Adam began to emerge from the shadows at Chesterfield in the 2004-05 season. The attacking midfielder was given his chance after Jamal Campbell-Ryce left for Rotherham and responded well, producing a string of disciplined performances on the left wing.
Chesterfield *(From trainee on 3/8/2004) FL 6+13 FLC 0+1 FAC 1 Others 1+1*

SMITH Alan
Born: Rothwell, 28 October 1980
Height: 5'9" **Weight:** 11.10
International Honours: E: 15; U21-10; Yth
A bustling, goal-scoring striker who possesses great strength against the Premiership's most formidable defenders, Alan's highly emotive move across the Pennines from Leeds to Manchester in May 2004 certainly ruffled a few feathers! Having became an established part of the first-team from the off, however, the doubters were soon silenced when he kick-started his United career with a crisp strike in the Community Shield against Arsenal. After following this up with a superb volley against Norwich in the Premiership in August and with further strikes against Blackburn, Middlesbrough, Fulham and Crystal Palace, he showed the same gritty determination in Europe, by netting twice against Dinamo Bucharest in the Champions League. Cementing his newly forged alliance with the Stretford End, he won praise for his sheer commitment. After playing a major part in every one of United's Premiership games up to Christmas, the new year brought a seasonal bag of appearances for Alan with no further goals in any competition. That said, he certainly came through his first full season as a Red with flying colours, and more importantly won over the fans in abundance.
Leeds U *(From trainee on 26/3/1998) PL 148+24/38 FLC 4+2 FAC 11+4/4 Others 28+7/14*
Manchester U *(£7,000,000 on 26/5/2004) PL 22+9/6 FLC 1+1/1 FAC 0+3 Others 4+2/3*

SMITH Alexander (Alex)
Philip
Born: Liverpool, 15 February 1976
Height: 5'7" **Weight:** 11.10
Club Honours: NC '04; AMC '05
This technically sound midfielder had a frustrating time with injuries which restricted his appearances for Wrexham during the 2004-05 season. Alex started the campaign impressively but was not always available for selection as much as his manager would have liked. Nevertheless a new deal looked on the cards in the summer.
Everton *(From trainee on 1/7/1994)*
Swindon T *(Free on 12/1/1996) FL 17+14/1*
Huddersfield T *(Free on 6/2/1998) FL 4+2*
Chester C *(Free on 8/7/1998) FL 32/2 FLC 4/1 Others 1*
Port Vale *(£75,000 on 25/3/1999) FL 52+6/2 FLC 2+1 FAC 2 Others 7/1*
Reading *(Free on 19/7/2001) FL 12+2/2 FLC 2/1 FAC 1 Others 1 (Freed during 2003 close season)*
Shrewsbury T *(Loaned on 13/12/2002) FL 13 FAC 2 Others 3*
Wrexham *(Free from Chester C on 13/7/2004) FL 17+7 FLC 2 FAC 0+1 Others 2+1*

SMITH Andrew (Andy)
William
Born: Lisburn, 25 September 1980
Height: 5'11" **Weight:** 12.2
International Honours: NI: 18; B-1
This striker took some time to settle in at Preston, a process not helped by a lack of goals. He was loaned to Stockport in mid-season where he linked up well with Warren Feeney and showed some excellent touches. On his return to Deepdale he made several appearances

Ben Smith

on the bench during the second half of the season. Andy was a regular at international level for Northern Ireland throughout the campaign.
Sheffield U *(Signed from Ballyclare Comrades on 11/9/1999) FL 0+6 FLC 0+4 (Freed in February 2002)*
Bury *(Loaned on 30/11/2000) FL 2 Others 1*
Preston NE *(£150,000 from Glentoran on 30/7/2004) FL 3+11 FLC 2+1*
Stockport Co *(Loaned on 12/11/2004) FL 1 FAC 1*

SMITH Benjamin (Ben) Peter
Born: Chelmsford, 23 November 1978
Height: 5'8" **Weight:** 11.6
This attacking midfielder quickly settled into League Two football at Shrewsbury last term and he opened his goal-scoring account in the second game of the season at Macclesfield. Ben had bagged two more before a dislocated shoulder suffered in the LDV Vans Trophy tie against Bournemouth virtually ended his season in September. He eventually returned to make two more appearances from the bench at the end of the campaign and will be looking to steer clear of injuries in 2005-06.
Reading *(From trainee at Arsenal on 16/4/1997) FL 0+1 (Free to Yeovil T on 6/3/1998)*
Southend U *(Free from Yeovil T on 8/6/2001) FL 0+1 (Freed during 2002 close season)*
Shrewsbury T *(Free from Hereford U on 5/6/2004) FL 10+2/3 FLC 1 Others 1*

SMITH Dean
Born: West Bromwich, 19 March 1971
Height: 6'1" **Weight:** 12.10
This experienced central defender began the 2004-05 campaign as the old head in a very young Port Vale squad. Dean provided a steadying influence at the back as he stood in for the injured Michael Walsh, but he always had one eye on the future. An opportunity in this field came up in December when he was offered the position of youth coach at Leyton Orient, one of his former clubs, and he duly accepted in the new year.
Walsall *(From trainee on 1/7/1989) FL 137+5/2 FLC 10 FAC 4 Others 10*
Hereford U *(£75,000 on 17/6/1994) FL 116+1/19 FLC 10/3 FAC 7 Others 11+1/4*
Leyton Orient *(£42,500 on 16/6/1997) FL 239/32 FLC 18 FAC 19/4 Others 12/1*
Sheffield Wed *(Signed on 21/2/2003) FL 55/1 FLC 1 FAC 1+1 Others 4*
Port Vale *(Free on 3/8/2004) FL 12+1 FLC 1/1 Others 1*

SMITH Gary Stephen
Born: Middlesbrough, 30 January 1984
Height: 5'8" **Weight:** 10.8
A hugely popular player with the MK Dons' supporters, Gary was given a permanent deal after impressing whilst on loan at the end of the 2003-04 season. However, he struggled early on with an injury and then had a frustrating spell on the sidelines during the club's 11-match unbeaten run through February and March. A couple of good substitute appearances in April earned him a starting place for the final few games, and he found his best form in the nick of time, running tirelessly in midfield, tackling hard and constantly threading precise balls through to his speedy forwards.
Middlesbrough *(From trainee on 6/7/2002)*
Wimbledon *(Loaned on 22/3/2004) FL 10+1/3*
MK Dons *(Free on 6/8/2004) FL 20+3/1 FLC 0+1 FAC 3 Others 1*

SMITH Grant Gordon
Born: Irvine, 5 May 1980
Height: 6'1" **Weight:** 12.7
Grant started the 2004-05 season at left back for Swindon but soon found himself out of the team and warming the bench. However, he turned things around in the second half of the campaign after being recalled for the game at Bradford in January. An adaptable left-footed player who can operate in a number of positions, he finished the season as the club's second-top scorer with a tally of ten goals.
Reading *(From trainee at Wycombe W on 7/8/1998)*
Heart of Midlothian *(Free on 19/3/1999)*
Livingston *(Free on 4/7/2000) SL 0+2 SLC 1 Others 1*
Clydebank *(Free on 2/12/2000) SL 16+1/2*
Sheffield U *(Free on 13/7/2001) FL 2+8 FAC 0+1*
Halifax T *(Loaned on 7/9/2001) FL 11 Others 1*
Plymouth Arg *(Loaned on 10/3/2003) FL 4+1/1*
Swindon T *(Free on 25/7/2003) FL 23+14/10 FLC 4 FAC 0+3 Others 4+2*

SMITH Jack David
Born: Hemel Hempstead, 14 October 1983
Height: 5'11" **Weight:** 11.5
Jack made a handful of appearances in both full-back positions for Watford last term, but failed to nail down a regular place and was transfer-listed at the end of the season. Able to kick with either foot, he also turned out at centre half for the reserves. His best moment came in the penalty shoot-out that decided the Carling Cup third round tie at Sheffield United: having never taken a penalty before, he hit the winner.
Watford *(From trainee on 5/4/2002) FL 23+2/2 FLC 0+1 FAC 2*

SMITH James (Jamie) Jade Anthony
Born: Birmingham, 17 September 1974
Height: 5'7" **Weight:** 11.4
This full back impressed with his commitment for Bristol City last term after a shaky start to his Ashton Gate career. Indeed his form improved to such an extent that he was appointed captain midway through the season. Out of contract in the summer, his future was unclear at the time of writing.
Wolverhampton W *(From trainee on 7/6/1993) FL 81+6 FLC 10+1 FAC 2 Others 4/1*
Crystal Palace *(Signed on 22/10/1997) P/FL 136+13/4 FLC 16+1/2 FAC 6+2 Others 1+1*
Fulham *(Loaned on 25/3/1999) FL 9/1*
Bristol C *(Free on 4/8/2004) FL 35+4/2 FLC 2 FAC 1+1*

SMITH Jay Mark
Born: Hammersmith, 29 December 1981
Height: 5'11" **Weight:** 11.7
Despite making three first-team appearances in August, central midfielder Jay knew his days at Brentford were numbered as he had been put on the transfer list in the summer. He left the club in October and subsequently linked up with Conference outfit Farnborough, featuring regularly during the remainder of the campaign.
Brentford *(From trainee on 5/7/2000) FL 37+11 FLC 2 FAC 4 Others 3+3*

SMITH Jeffrey (Jeff)
Born: Middlesbrough, 28 June 1980
Height: 5'10" **Weight:** 11.8
This skilful left winger began the 2004-05 season as a regular for Port Vale and scored in the 2-0 win at Bradford City that took the club into third place in the table at the beginning of September. His trickery certainly caused defenders plenty of problems and the highlight of his campaign came at Barnsley in November. Called from the substitutes' bench with Vale 1-0 down he raced clear within a minute and crossed for Billy Paynter to equalise. Five minutes later another of his crosses led to Robbie Williams, no less, scoring an own goal for the winner. This was the only time all season that Vale turned around a half-time deficit. After Christmas he was used mainly as a substitute but still played his part when called upon and was offered a new contract at the season's end.
Hartlepool U *(From trainee on 3/7/1998) FL 2+1 Others 1 (Free to Barrow in October 1999)*

Martin Smith

***Bolton W** (Free from Bishop Auckland on 21/3/2001) P/FL 1+1 FLC 2 FAC 4*
***Macclesfield T** (Loaned on 23/11/2001) FL 7+1/2*
***Scunthorpe U** (Loaned on 16/1/2004) FL 1*
***Rochdale** (Loaned on 20/2/2004) FL 1*
***Preston NE** (Signed on 4/3/2004) FL 0+5*
***Port Vale** (Free on 5/7/2004) FL 23+11/1 FLC 0+1 FAC 2 Others 0+2*

SMITH Martin Geoffrey

Born: Sunderland, 13 November 1974
Height: 5'11" **Weight:** 12.6
Club Honours: Div 1 '96
International Honours: E: U21-1; Yth; Sch

This talented wide midfield player had a spell out with injury last term but otherwise was a regular in the Northampton Town line-up. The architect of many of the Cobblers goals during the campaign, Martin contributed guile and skill down the left wing and was also the club's set-piece specialist, taking many of the free kicks and corners.

***Sunderland** (From trainee on 9/9/1992) P/FL 90+29/25 FLC 10+6/2 FAC 7+3/1*
***Sheffield U** (Free on 6/8/1999) FL 24+2/10 FLC 3+1/4 FAC 3/1*
***Huddersfield T** (£300,000 on 3/2/2000) FL 72+8/29 FLC 2+1 FAC 1 Others 1*
***Northampton T** (Free on 7/8/2003) FL 74+4/21 FLC 1 FAC 8/3 Others 6+2/1*

SMITH Paul Daniel

Born: Epsom, 17 December 1979
Height: 6'4" **Weight:** 14.0

One of the few bright interludes in what was a very gloomy season for Southampton was the introduction of goalkeeper Paul Smith to first-team duty. A thumb injury kept him out of contention early in the campaign, but, with Antti Niemi requiring a knee operation in February, Paul took his opportunity with aplomb: dominating his line, pulling off some breathtaking saves and, despite having to cope with some hapless defending, exhibiting exemplary self-confidence. Had he been second-choice 'keeper behind anybody but Niemi, he might have had an extended run, but with the Finland international fit, it was back to the bench.

***Charlton Ath** (Free from Walton & Hersham on 2/7/1998. Free to Walton & Hersham during 1999 close season)*
***Brentford** (Free from Carshalton Ath on 27/7/2000) FL 86+1 FLC 3 FAC 6 Others 8+1*
***Southampton** (£250,000 + on 28/1/2004) PL 5+1 FAC 3*

SMITH Paul William

Born: East Ham, 18 September 1971
Height: 5'11" **Weight:** 13.0

Despite a slow start after recovering from

serious knee injury sustained at the end of the 2003-04 campaign, Paul was once again voted Gillingham's 'Player of the Year', and was in tremendous form in the second half of the season. The experienced central midfielder scored three goals during the campaign and also won the 'Away Player of the Year' and 'Goal of the Season' awards. Paul was out of contract in the summer and his future was unclear at the time of writing.

Southend U *(From trainee on 16/3/1990) FL 8+2/1 Others 0+1*
Brentford *(Free on 6/8/1993) FL 159/11 FLC 2/1 FAC 12/3 Others 15/2*
Gillingham *(Signed on 25/7/1997) FL 238+4/21 FLC 18/1 FAC 20/1 Others 9+2/2*

SMITH Ian **Paul**
Born: Easington, 22 January 1976
Height: 6'0" **Weight:** 13.3
Paul had a frustrating time with injuries last term and managed just a handful of appearances for Sheffield Wednesday. The experienced left winger had the misfortune to suffer a bad knee injury and did not feature in the first team after October. He was released by Wednesday in the summer.

Burnley *(From trainee on 10/7/1994) FL 79+33/5 FLC 3+1 FAC 6+1 Others 5*
Oldham Ath *(Loaned on 22/9/2000) FL 3+1 FLC 1*
Hartlepool U *(Free, via trial at Torquay U, on 1/11/2001) FL 45+10/4 FAC 3 Others 2*
Sheffield Wed *(Free on 2/7/2003) FL 9+8/2 FLC 1 Others 3*

SMITH Ryan Craig Matthew
Born: Islington, 10 November 1986
Height: 5'10" **Weight:** 10.10
International Honours: E: Yth
Ryan is a gifted player who can feature anywhere on the left-hand side of the field. Last season he featured in all three of Arsenal's Carling Cup ties before his campaign was curtailed by a serious knee injury.

Arsenal *(From trainee on 26/11/2004) FLC 2+4*

SMITH Thomas (Tommy) William
Born: Hemel Hempstead, 22 May 1980
Height: 5'8" **Weight:** 11.4
International Honours: E: U21-1; Yth
Although dealing exclusively in free transfers, George Burley was able to produce some gems for Derby County, with Tommy high on the list. He scored 11 Championship goals and was a regular provider of chances for others. His kind of adaptability appeals to managers and whether playing in attack or on the flank - it did not matter which one - he always gave a performance. Tommy had few thin days and supporters warmed to his enthusiasm. He is an intelligent footballer, well aware of the team's requirements and capable of further development. Tommy proves there are still bargains to be found and was runner-up to Inigo Idiakez as 'Player of the Year'.

Watford *(From trainee on 21/10/1997) P/FL 114+35/33 FLC 7+3/1 FAC 5+3/2*
Sunderland *(Signed on 25/9/2003) FL 22+13/4 FAC 3+1/4 Others 0+2*
Derby Co *(Free on 29/7/2004) FL 41+1/11 FAC 3 Others 2*

SMYTH Mark Michael
Born: Liverpool, 9 January 1985
Height: 5'8" **Weight:** 10.8
International Honours: E: Yth
Mark is a promising young midfielder from the Liverpool Academy who made his first-team debut as a substitute in the Carling Cup tie at Tottenham last December. However, he was not considered close to a regular breakthrough at senior level and was released in the summer.

Liverpool *(From trainee on 23/4/2002) FLC 0+1*

SOAMES David Michael
Born: Grimsby, 10 December 1984
Height: 5'5" **Weight:** 10.8
This young Grimsby Town striker again failed to make a breakthrough into regular first-team football last term. David mostly featured in the club's reserve team, managing just a handful of first-team outings from the substitutes' bench in the closing stages of the campaign. He will be hoping to see more regular first-team action in the 2005-06 season.

Grimsby T *(From trainee on 29/7/2004) FL 0+24/1 FAC 2*

SOARES Louie Pierre
Born: Reading, 8 January 1985
Height: 5'9" **Weight:** 10.3
Louie spent last season on a 12-month contract at Reading, but failed to make the first team. He spent time on loan at Tamworth in the new year and finished the campaign on loan at Bristol Rovers. An emergency signing by Pirates' boss Ian Atkins, he made a brief appearance as a substitute in the final match of the season against Wycombe. A right-sided midfielder or defender, he was released by the Royals in the summer. Louie is the elder brother of Crystal Palace defender Tom.

Reading *(From trainee on 3/7/2004)*
Bristol Rov *(Loaned on 6/5/2005) FL 0+1*

SOARES Thomas (Tom) James
Born: Reading, 10 July 1986
Height: 6'0" **Weight:** 11.4
International Honours: E: Yth
Tom made excellent progress at Crystal Palace last term, progressing from a fringe player to a regular in the Premiership team's line-up. A fine, strongly built midfield player who can also play in a role just behind the main strikers, Tom was a member of the England U20 squad that took part in the Toulon Tournament in the summer. Tom scored one first-team goal for Palace during the season, netting in the Carling Cup tie against Hartlepool.

Crystal Palace *(From trainee on 9/9/2004) P/FL 16+9 FLC 2+1/1 FAC 0+1*

SOBERS Jerrome Roxin
Born: London, 18 April 1986
Height: 6'2" **Weight:** 13.5
This tall well-built defender joined Brentford on loan from Ipswich on transfer-deadline day but did not make his debut until the final match of the season against Hull. Jerrome lined up at right back and capped a fine display by heading home the equaliser from a Jay Tabb corner.

Ipswich T *(Signed from Ford U on 5/5/2004)*
Brentford *(Loaned on 24/3/2005) FL 1/1*

SODJE Idoro **Akpoeyere (Akpo)** Ujoma
Born: Greenwich, 31 January 1981
Height: 6'2" **Weight:** 12.8
This talented striker made the step up from Erith & Belvedere to the rigours of League One football last term. After scoring freely for Huddersfield reserves he went on to make his full debut in the LDV Vans Trophy win over Morecambe. Akpo showed great pace and control, with a keen eye for goal, but was affected by injuries and on transfer-deadline day he was allowed to move on to Darlington. He immediately added extra zest to the Quakers' attack and rounded off the campaign by scoring against Cheltenham in the final minute of the last game of the season.

Huddersfield T *(Free from Erith & Belvedere on 1/9/2004) FL 1+6 Others 1+1*
Darlington *(Loaned on 24/3/2005) FL 1+6/1*

SODJE Efetobore (Efe)
Born: Greenwich, 5 October 1972
Height: 6'1" **Weight:** 12.0
Club Honours: GMVC '96
International Honours: Nigeria
The 2004-05 season started off strongly for this robust central defender, back at the helm captaining Huddersfield for the

new campaign. Always one for a physical battle, he managed to find the net with a close-range header during against Torquay United at the Galpharm. However, he ran into problems with match officials and after losing the club captaincy moved on to Yeovil on transfer-deadline day. Efe made an immediate impact at Huish Park and scored two vital goals against Lincoln to seal the championship on the last day of the season.

Macclesfield T *(£30,000 from Stevenage Borough on 11/7/1997) FL 83/6 FLC 6 FAC 6/1 Others 1*
Luton T *(Free on 12/8/1999) FL 5+4 FLC 1 FAC 2+1 Others 1*
Colchester U *(Free on 23/3/2000) FL 3*
Crewe Alex *(Free on 21/7/2000) FL 86+12/3 FLC 6+2 FAC 6+3/1 Others 2*
Huddersfield T *(Free on 7/8/2003) FL 61+6/5 FLC 3 FAC 1 Others 4+1*
Yeovil T *(Free on 23/3/2005) FL 6/2*

Sam Sodje

SODJE Samuel (Sam) Okeremute

Born: Greenwich, 29 May 1979
Height: 6'0" **Weight:** 12.0
This Brentford centre back enjoyed an amazingly successful first season in League football. His speed at the back was his major strength and he formed an excellent central-defensive partnership with Michael Turner. His incredible leap saw him win headers at both ends of the field and he contributed eight first-team goals during the campaign. Brentford supporters' 'Player of the Year', he is the brother of Efe and Akpo Sodje.

Brentford *(Free from Margate, ex Stevenage Borough on 2/7/2004) FL 40/7 FAC 8/1 Others 2*

SOFIANE Youssef

Born: Lyon, France, 8 July 1984
Height: 5'8" **Weight:** 11.0
International Honours: France: Yth
This young striker was again unable to make any impact at West Ham last term. Youssef spent four weeks on loan with League Two outfit Notts County in the early part of the season where he displayed impressive talent and netted a superb goal in the LDV Vans Trophy tie against Wrexham. Then in the January transfer window he moved on loan to Roda JC where he featured in a handful of first-team games before returning to Upton Park early.

West Ham U *(Free from Auxerre, France on 26/6/2002) FL 0+1 FLC 1*
Notts Co *(Loaned on 10/9/2004) FL 2+2 Others 1/1*

SOLANO Nolberto (Nobby) Albino

Born: Lima, Peru, 12 December 1974
Height: 5'8" **Weight:** 10.8
International Honours: Peru: 75; Yth
This right-sided midfielder is highly regarded at Villa Park for his set pieces and accurate delivery. Last term he was also a consistent goal-scorer and finished the season as the club's leading scorer in Premiership action with a total of eight. Perhaps the best of these was his wonderful goal in the home match against Tottenham when he controlled the ball, swivelled and hammered it home. At club level he enjoyed one of his best-ever seasons, while he also continued to feature for Peru on the international front.

Newcastle U *(£2,763,958 from Boca Juniors, Argentina, ex Cristal Alianza Lima, Sporting, Deportivo Municipal, on 17/8/1998) PL 158+14/29 FLC 10+2 FAC 19/2 Others 27+4/7*
Aston Villa *(£1,500,000 on 29/1/2004) PL 42+4/8 FLC 2/1 FAC 1*

SOMMEIL David

Born: Point-a-Pitre, Guadeloupe, 10 August 1974
Height: 5'11" **Weight:** 11.6
International Honours: France: B-1
David returned to the City of Manchester Stadium at the start of the 2004-05 campaign following a loan spell at Marseille, but was ruled out for the first month after sustaining a calf injury. Further injuries and a loss of form restricted him to one Premiership appearance at home to Bolton Wanderers and 45 minutes of action in the Carling Cup tie against Barnsley.

Manchester C *(£3,500,000 from Bordeaux, France, ex Caen, Rennes, on 27/1/2003) PL 33/2 FLC 1+1 FAC 2 Others 4/1*

Nobby Solano

SOMNER Matthew (Matt) James
Born: Isleworth, 8 December 1982
Height: 6'0" **Weight:** 13.2
International Honours: W: U21-2
Matt made two early-season appearances at left back for Brentford before dropping out of the first-team picture. In December he joined League Two strugglers Cambridge United and the deal eventually became permanent. A versatile player who can play at full back or midfield, he impressed new manager Steve Thompson and was virtually ever-present to the end of the season.
Brentford *(From trainee on 4/7/2001) FL 72+12/1 FLC 1+1 FAC 3+2/1 Others 2*
Cambridge U *(Free on 3/12/2004) FL 24*

SONKO Ibrahima (Ibu)
Born: Bignola, Senegal, 22 January 1981
Height: 6'3" **Weight:** 13.7
International Honours: Senegal: U21
Ibu had to wait until Adrian Williams left for Coventry City before making a first-team start for Reading. The muscular centre back did so well, and progressed so quickly that he stayed as first choice for the rest of the season. He clears his lines effectively with powerful long-distance headers and volleys, and in the home 0-0 draw with Leicester City, became the first player ever to hoist a clearance onto the roof of the Madejski Stadium! Ibrahima is an important part of the club's plans for the foreseeable future.
Brentford *(Free from Grenoble, France, ex St Etienne, on 9/8/2002) FL 79+1/8 FLC 3/1 FAC 6 Others 2*
Reading *(Free on 5/7/2004) FL 35+4/1 FAC 3*

SONNER Daniel (Danny) James
Born: Wigan, 9 January 1972
Height: 5'11" **Weight:** 12.8
International Honours: NI: 13; B-4
A talented ball-playing midfielder Danny joined Peterborough early on last term, but never really settled in at London Road, rarely featuring after October. In the new year he joined Port Vale on loan and made an impressive debut at Swindon Town. He also did well in the 3-1 victory over Luton Town and kept his place for the remainder of the campaign. Danny added a further cap for Northern Ireland when he featured against Switzerland back in August.
Burnley *(From trainee at Wigan Ath on 6/8/1990) FL 1+5 FLC 0+1/1 Others 0+2 (Free to Preussen Koln, Germany during 1993 close season)*
Bury *(Loaned on 21/11/1992) FL 5/3 FAC 3 Others 1/1*
Ipswich T *(Free from FC Erzgebirge Aue, Germany on 12/6/1996) FL 28+28/3 FLC 6+4/1 FAC 1+1 Others 0+1*
Sheffield Wed *(£75,000 on 15/10/1998) PL 42+11/3 FLC 3+1/1 FAC 4+2*
Birmingham C *(Free on 4/8/2000) FL 32+9/2 FLC 12/1 FAC 1 Others 2*
Walsall *(Free on 5/8/2002) FL 20+4/4 FLC 2 FAC 2*
Nottingham F *(Free on 6/8/2003) FL 19+9 FLC 3 FAC 1*
Peterborough U *(Free on 13/8/2004) FL 11+4 FLC 0+1 Others 1*
Port Vale *(Loaned on 22/2/2005) FL 13*

SORENSEN Thomas
Born: Denmark, 12 June 1976
Height: 6'4" **Weight:** 13.10
Club Honours: Div 1 '99
International Honours: Denmark: 48; B-1; U21-6
Thomas was once again one of the best all-round 'keepers in the Premiership and an important presence in the Villa defence, commanding his box well and making several fine saves. He was a near ever-present in the side and reliable throughout, rarely if ever making an unforced error. Thomas also featured for Denmark during the campaign, adding to his total of caps.
Sunderland *(£500,000 + from Odense BK, Denmark on 6/8/1998) P/FL 171 FLC 13 FAC 13*
Aston Villa *(£2,250,000 on 8/8/2003) PL 74 FLC 8 FAC 2*

SORONDO Amaro **Gonzalo**
Born: Montevideo, Uruguay, 9 October 1979
Height: 5'11" **Weight:** 12.8
International Honours: Uruguay: 26
A regular in the centre of defence for Uruguay, Gonzalo had spent part of the previous season on loan with Standard Liege, and joined Crystal Palace in a season-long loan during the summer of 2004. Although hampered early on by injuries he came back strongly in the second half of the campaign when he featured regularly. The strong-tackling defender regularly fell foul of referees and received two red cards during his stay with the Eagles.
Crystal Palace *(Loaned from Inter Milan, Italy, following a loan spell at Standard Liege, Belgium, ex Defensor Sporting, on 2/9/2004) PL 16+4 FLC 2*

SORVEL Neil Simon
Born: Whiston, 2 March 1973
Height: 6'0" **Weight:** 12.9
Club Honours: GMVC '95, '97; FAT '96
Neil returned to Crewe back in 1999 and has become a regular in the team in a midfield role, indeed he was only absent from the starting line-up on one occasion last term. A hard-working midfielder who can be relied upon to give a good performance without always hitting the headlines, he misses very few games through injury.
Crewe Alex *(From trainee on 31/7/1991) FL 5+4 FAC 1+1 Others 4*
Macclesfield T *(Free on 21/8/1992) FL 79+7/7 FLC 4+1 FAC 5 Others 0+1*
Crewe Alex *(Free on 9/6/1999) FL 229+21/13 FLC 17 FAC 11+1 Others 4*

SOUTHALL Leslie **Nicholas (Nicky)**
Born: Stockton, 28 January 1972
Height: 5'10" **Weight:** 12.12
This experienced midfielder struggled to find his form with Gillingham in the first half of the 2004-05. However, it was a different story after Stan Ternent took over as manager and he really came alive under the new regime. Nicky was one of several Gills players out of contract in the summer and his future had yet to be decided at the time of writing.
Hartlepool U *(From Darlington juniors on 21/2/1991) FL 118+20/24 FLC 6+1/3 FAC 4+4 Others 6+2*
Grimsby T *(£40,000 on 12/7/1995) FL 55+17/6 FLC 3+3/1 FAC 4+3/2*
Gillingham *(Free on 9/12/1997) FL 141+13/17 FLC 6+1/1 FAC 10/3 Others 12*
Bolton W *(Free on 2/7/2001) PL 10+8/1 FLC 4 FAC 2*
Norwich C *(Loaned on 27/9/2002) FL 4+5*
Gillingham *(Free on 6/12/2002) FL 86+6/2 FLC 2 FAC 5*

SOUTHERN Keith William
Born: Gateshead, 24 April 1981
Height: 5'10" **Weight:** 12.6
Club Honours: AMC '04
This young midfielder had the misfortune to suffer an injury during the pre-season period, so it was not until November that he made his first appearance for Blackpool. Once he had settled back he quickly hit top form and he went on to win the PFA Fans' League One 'Player of the Year'.
Everton *(From trainee on 21/5/1999)*
Blackpool *(Free on 8/8/2002) FL 78+15/9 FLC 2+1/1 FAC 6+1/2 Others 6+1/1*

SOUTHGATE Gareth
Born: Watford, 3 September 1970
Height: 6'0" **Weight:** 12.8
Club Honours: Div 1 '94; FLC '96, '04
International Honours: E: 57
Middlesbrough's inspirational captain was a near ever-present last term and signed an extension to his contract at the Riverside during the season. At 34 years

f age Gareth is now one of the game's der statesmen but, nevertheless, he gistered his 400th Premiership game uring the campaign, a magnificent chievement. He led the team into UEFA up action against the might of Europe hich included Lazio and Partizan elgrade before eventually succumbing to porting Lisbon in the tenth game of the ompetition. In a nailbiting finale to the eason Gareth then guided the team to nother season of European football by aiming the vital seventh place in the emiership after Mark Schwarzer saved a st-minute penalty at the City of lanchester Stadium.
rystal Palace (From trainee on 17/1/1989) FL 148+4/15 FLC 23+1/7 FAC 9 Others 6
ston Villa (£2,500,000 on 1/7/1995) PL 91/7 FLC 17/1 FAC 20/1 Others 15
liddlesbrough (£6,500,000 on 14/7/2001) . 136/4 FLC 7 FAC 9 Others 10

PARROW Matthew (Matt) onald
orn: Wembley, 3 October 1981
eight: 5'11" **Weight:** 10.6
latt lost his place in the Scunthorpe arting line-up at the beginning of the 004-05 season and had to wait until the nd of October to regain his place on the ght-hand side. An attacking midfield ayer, who loves to get forward and run t defences, he enjoyed a great second alf of the campaign, finishing with six oals as he helped his team win romotion to League One. Equally at ome in the centre of the park, Matt cored twice in the 4-1 home win over heltenham in March.
cunthorpe U (From trainee on 30/7/2001) . 145+25/22 FLC 3+4 FAC 13/1 Others +1/1

PECTOR Jonathan Michael aul
orn: Chicago, USA, 1 March 1986
eight: 6'0" **Weight:** 12.8
nternational Honours: USA: Yth
regular for the USA at U17 level, and ollowing in the footsteps of Jovan irovski and John Thorrington as mericans who began their professional areers with United, Jonathan certainly ooked the main deal when he showed reat maturity in a run of three games at ft back last August. He also forced his ay into the side against Fenerbahce in ne Champions' League, and showed his ndoubted potential against Everton in ne Premiership at Old Trafford. The rrival of Gabriel Heinze, however, limited is opportunities somewhat.
lanchester U (Signed from Chicago ockers, USA on 13/11/2003) PL 2+1 FLC +1 FAC 1 Others 1+2

SPEED Gary Andrew
Born: Deeside, 8 September 1969
Height: 5'10" **Weight:** 12.10
Club Honours: Div 2 '90, Div 1 '92; CS '92
International Honours: W: 85; U21-3; Yth
A high profile pre-season signing for Bolton, Gary lived up to all expectations. His legendary fitness levels proved vital, as Gary started 37 of the 38 Premiership games during the campaign. A commanding midfield presence, Gary is a typical 'team first' player, with his vision, energy and skill providing a massive contribution to Bolton's quest for UEFA Cup football. Despite coming desperately close on many occasions, Gary had to wait until the end of April to celebrate his first goal for the club: a trademark header at Aston Villa. Gary also played in four World Cup qualifying games for Wales before announcing his retirement from international football following the October defeat by Poland.
Leeds U (From trainee on 13/6/1988) P/FL 231+17/39 FLC 25+1/11 FAC 21/5 Others 14+3/2
Everton (£3,500,000 on 1/7/1996) PL 58/16 FLC 5/1 FAC 2/1
Newcastle U (£5,500,000 on 6/2/1998) PL 206+7/29 FLC 9+2/1 FAC 22/5 Others 39/5
Bolton W (£750,000 on 21/7/2004) PL 37+1/1 FAC 2

SPENCER Damian Michael
Born: Ascot, 19 September 1981
Height: 6'1" **Weight:** 14.5
This tall, immensely powerful striker finished as joint-top scorer for Cheltenham Town last term with ten goals in all competitions. He was particularly influential when coming on as a substitute and ended the campaign on a high note with five goals in the last five matches. His size and physical power make him a difficult proposition for defenders to handle and, when he gets things right, he possesses powerful shooting and heading ability.
Bristol C (From trainee on 14/6/2000) FL 8+5/1 FLC 0+1 Others 1+3/1
Exeter C (Loaned on 22/3/2001) FL 2+4
Cheltenham T (Free on 7/8/2002) FL 53+54/23 FLC 1+1 FAC 4+2/2 Others 1+4/1

SPENCER James Matthew
Born: Stockport, 11 April 1985
Height: 6'5" **Weight:** 15.2
This promising goalkeeper found himself second-choice to Neil Cutler for Stockport at the start of last season, but was soon back in the line-up and went on to enjoy an excellent campaign. Despite the disappointment of relegation James was rewarded on a personal level as he collected the club's 'Player of the Year' award at the end of season gala dinner.
Stockport Co (From trainee on 19/4/2002) FL 41+1 FAC 3 Others 3

SPENDER Simon
Born: Mold, 15 November 1985
Height: 5'8" **Weight:** 11.0
Club Honours: AMC '05
International Honours: W: U21-2; Yth
Simon impressed again at Wrexham last term when coming into the side for the injured Jim Whitley. A wing back or midfielder, he was a permanent fixture in the side from the end of October until mid-December, producing some assured displays. He was used sparingly for the rest of the campaign and was also part of the Wales U21 set-up.
Wrexham (Trainee) FL 12+7 FLC 0+2 FAC 2 Others 2

SPERONI Julian
Born: Buenos Aires, Argentina, 18 May 1979
Height: 6'0" **Weight:** 11.5
This experienced 'keeper arrived at Selhurst Park in the summer of 2004 after playing in Scotland for several seasons. Julian began the new campaign as first choice for Crystal Palace, but after the team made a poor start to their Premiership fixtures he was dropped in favour of Gabor Kiraly in September and thereafter only featured in the Carling Cup matches.
Dundee (Signed from Platense on 1/6/2001) SL 92 SLC 5 SC 12 Others 4
Crystal Palace (£750,000 on 14/7/2004) PL 6 FLC 2

SPICER John William
Born: Romford, 13 September 1983
Height: 5'11" **Weight:** 11.7
International Honours: E: Yth
This promising Arsenal midfielder joined Bournemouth on loan last September and quickly established himself as a regular in the side, missing just one game after his arrival. Thanks to the Cherries' innovative 'Player Share' scheme, the move was made permanent and he became a highly influential member of the squad.
Arsenal (From trainee on 2/7/2001) FLC 0+1
Bournemouth (£10,000 on 10/9/2004) FL 39/6 FLC 2/1 FAC 5/1

SPILLER Daniel (Danny)
Born: Maidstone, 10 October 1981
Height: 5'9" **Weight:** 12.3
Danny was a regular for Gillingham in the first half of the 2004-05 campaign before suffering a leg injury at Cardiff in

December. A great favourite with the fans for his tough tackling and non-stop running, Danny struggled to get back into the side once he had recovered fitness and only featured in a couple more games before the end of the season.
Gillingham *(From trainee on 10/7/2000) FL 56+16/6 FLC 3+2 FAC 2+1*

SPRING Matthew John
Born: Harlow, 17 November 1979
Height: 5'11" **Weight:** 11.5
Patience was the watchword for creative midfielder Matthew in his first season with Leeds. His final few months at Luton had been blighted by injury and it was a similar story at Elland Road where he was troubled by groin problems which required surgery early in the campaign. His first Championship start didn't come until Boxing Day when he put in an excellent display in a 3-2 win at Sunderland and he gained more opportunities towards the end of the season.
Luton T *(From trainee on 2/7/1997) FL 243+7/25 FLC 16/1 FAC 18+1/3 Others 4*
Leeds U *(Free on 2/7/2004) FL 4+9/1 FLC 2*

STACK Graham Christopher
Born: Hampstead, 26 September 1981
Height: 6'2" **Weight:** 12.6
Club Honours: FAYC '00
International Honours: RoI: U21-7; Yth
This young Arsenal 'keeper joined Millwall in a season-long loan deal during the summer of 2004. A good shot-stopper who was particularly effective in one-on-one situations he was the club's first choice 'keeper before losing out towards the end of the year. Graham was particularly effective in the two UEFA Cup ties with Ferencvaros. Later in the season he suffered a back injury which kept him out of the squad.
Arsenal *(From trainee on 18/7/2000) FLC 5*
Millwall *(Loaned on 13/7/2004) FL 25+1 FLC 1 FAC 1 Others 2*

STAFF David Steven
Born: Market Harborough, 8 November 1979
Height: 6'1" **Weight:** 11.7
Although small in stature, David arrived at Boston United in the summer with a record of being a prolific scorer in non-league football. He signed a contract after proving himself in pre-season games, but found it difficult to break through into the first team with more experienced players ahead of him. David's Football League debut came as a late substitute in the home draw with Macclesfield Town at the end of August. His only start was in the LDV Vans Trophy tie against Cambridge United the following month and in October he was loaned back to King's Lynn. He returned to York Street, but after a handful of further appearances as a substitute he rejoined King's Lynn on a full-time basis in March. David was reported to have signed for Nuneaton Borough in the summer.
Boston U *(Free from King's Lynn, ex Rushden & Diamonds, Stamford, on 17/8/2004) FL 0+5 Others 1*

STALLARD Mark
Born: Derby, 24 October 1974
Height: 6'0" **Weight:** 13.6
This intelligent striker found himself surplus to requirements at Barnsley last season. After a handful of outings from the bench early on he went out on loan to Chesterfield where his experience proved valuable but he found goals hard to come by. Later he had a loan spell at Notts County, where he was welcomed back and featured regularly, scoring three times. He was released by Barnsley in the summer.
Derby Co *(From trainee on 6/11/1991) FL 19+8/2 FLC 2+1/2 FAC 2+2 Others 3/2*
Fulham *(Loaned on 23/9/1994) FL 4/3*
Bradford C *(£110,000 on 12/1/1996) FL 33+10/10 FLC 2/1 FAC 0+1 Others 3/2*
Preston NE *(Loaned on 14/2/1997) FL 4/1*
Wycombe W *(£100,000 on 7/3/1997) FL 67+3/23 FLC 5+1/1 Others 2/1*
Notts Co *(£10,000 on 3/3/1999) FL 168+17/67 FLC 13+1/8 FAC 10/3 Others 2*
Barnsley *(Free on 21/1/2004) FL 10+5/1 FLC 0+1*
Chesterfield *(Loaned on 1/10/2004) FL 7+2/2 FAC 1*
Notts Co *(Loaned on 4/2/2005) FL 16/3*

STAM Stefan
Born: Amersfoort, Holland, 14 September 1979
Height: 6'2" **Weight:** 12.9
International Honours: Holland: U21
This versatile Dutchman was one of Brian Talbot's last signings for Oldham Athletic and has subsequently proved to be one of the best. A left-footed player who is accomplished in possession, he starred at both left back and in central defence for the Latics, becoming a virtual ever-present in the latter stages of the League One campaign under Ronnie Moore. Stefan was rewarded with a new contract and Moore also believes he could operate in midfield next season.
Oldham Ath *(Free from Huizen, ex Grasshoppers, AFC 34, AZ67 Alkmaar, PSV Eindhoven, ADO Den Haag, on 16/2/2005) FL 11+2 Others 0+1*

STAMP Darryn Michael
Born: Beverley, 21 September 1978
Height: 6'2" **Weight:** 12.0
Club Honours: NC '04
This big striker suffered a knee injury in a pre-season friendly for Chester and then found it difficult to regain his place in the line-up. In December he was sent on a month's loan to Kidderminster, for whom he netted just once, and in February he joined Conference side Stevenage Borough in a permanent move. A clever striker Darryn is effective in the air and has the ability to hold the ball up and bring other players into the game.
Scunthorpe U *(Signed from Hessle on 7/7/1997) FL 18+39/6 FLC 1+3 FAC 2+2 Others 3+1/1 (Free to Scarborough on 11/6/1901)*
Halifax T *(Loaned on 18/2/2000) FL 5*
Northampton T *(£30,000 + on 28/5/2002) FL 12+10/4 FAC 1+1/1*
Chester C *(Signed on 22/8/2003) FL 2+2 Others 1*
Kidderminster Hrs *(Loaned on 5/11/2004) FL 4/1 FAC 1*

STANDING Michael John
Born: Shoreham, 20 March 1981
Height: 5'10" **Weight:** 10.12
International Honours: E: Yth; Sch
At his best Michael did well in his first season at Walsall. His darting runs enlivened a number of games and his powerful shooting brought him goals against Sheffield Wednesday, Doncaster, Hull and Peterborough. After a spell out of the team the midfielder came back strongly in the last few weeks of the season and he began to add general battling skills to his other qualities.
Aston Villa *(From trainee on 26/3/1998)*
Bradford C *(Free on 19/3/2002) FL 16+14/2 FLC 1 FAC 1*
Walsall *(Free on 28/5/2004) FL 27+5/4 FLC 1 FAC 1 Others 2*

STANTON Nathan
Born: Nottingham, 6 May 1981
Height: 5'9" **Weight:** 11.3
International Honours: E: Yth
Nathan started the 2004-05 season as one of the first names on the Scunthorpe United team sheet, making the right-back berth his own. A very fast player, who can also play in the centre of defence, he started every match until he was red carded in the draw at Leyton Orient at the end of October. He then had to wait six matches before he got back in the team and after a further two starts, his season came to an unfortunate end on New Year's Day when he sustained a knee injury. A minor cartilage operation revealed a cracked bone and this ruled

Nathan Stanton

him out of the final four months of the campaign.
Scunthorpe U *(From trainee on 19/3/1999) FL 194+21 FLC 7 FAC 15+2 Others 11+1/1*

STAUNTON Stephen (Steve)
Born: Drogheda, 19 January 1969
Height: 6'1" **Weight:** 12.12
Club Honours: FAC '89; Div 1 '90; FLC '94, '96
International Honours: RoI: 102; U21-4; Yth
Steve recovered from a knee operation in the 2004 close season to become a regular member of the Coventry City line-up last term. His positional sense and confidence were obvious, whether he played at left back or in the centre of defence, although he looked increasingly more comfortable in the latter position. Steve scored a vital late winner for the Sky Blues against Brighton, netting with a curling, vicious shot at the end of a marauding run upfield.
Liverpool *(£20,000 from Dundalk on 2/9/1986) FL 55+10 FLC 6+2/4 FAC 14+2/1 Others 1/1*
Bradford C *(Loaned on 13/11/1987) FL 7+1 FLC 2 Others 1*
Aston Villa *(£1,100,000 on 7/8/1991) P/FL 205+3/16 FLC 17+2/1 FAC 19+1/1 Others 15+1*
Liverpool *(Free on 3/7/1998) PL 38+6 FLC 5/1 FAC 2 Others 5+2*
Crystal Palace *(Loaned on 20/10/2000) FL 6/1*
Aston Villa *(Free on 7/12/2000) PL 65+8 FLC 5 FAC 4 Others 5/1*
Coventry C *(Free on 15/8/2003) FL 66+4/4 FLC 2 FAC 3*

STEAD Jonathan (Jon)
Graeme
Born: Huddersfield, 7 April 1983
Height: 6'3" **Weight:** 11.7
International Honours: E: U21-8
After a half season when he had shot to fame at Ewood Park in the previous campaign, it was perhaps inevitable that Jon would find the going tougher last term. Despite his lack of success and sometimes his lack of touch he always worked hard and when he finally opened his goal account at Goodison it was perhaps the most crucial strike of the season for Blackburn, bringing a vital 1-0 victory. Although he ended up with only two goals he had little luck, hitting the woodwork twice and forcing many fine saves.
Huddersfield T *(From trainee on 30/11/2001) FL 54+14/22 FLC 5/2 FAC 2 Others 2*
Blackburn Rov *(£1,200,000 on 2/2/2004) PL 32+10/8 FLC 0+1 FAC 1+3*

STEARMAN Richard James
Born: Wolverhampton, 19 August 1987
Height: 6'2" **Weight:** 10.8
A highly promising right-footed full back or central defender, Richard made his senior debut for Leicester at Cardiff last October. He played with a calmness and authority in his outings for the first team and is likely to develop into a classy central defender in due course. Richard opened his goal-scoring account against Millwall in a game that showcased his promise until a wild challenge sent him to the treatment table.
Leicester C *(From trainee on 30/11/2004) FL 3+5/1*

STEELE Lee Anthony James
Born: Liverpool, 2 December 1973
Height: 5'8" **Weight:** 12.7
Club Honours: Div 3 '01; Div 2 '02
This experienced striker quickly became a great favourite of the Leyton Orient fans after arriving at Brisbane Road in the summer of 2004. He got off to a great start and had already reached a double-figure goals tally before injury struck in November. However, he was back in the side at the beginning of the new year and eventually increased his total to 16 goals by the end of the season. Lee scored the fastest-ever goal by an O's player when he netted after just 12 seconds at Oxford on Easter Monday. He was reported to have signed a new contract for the club during the summer.
Shrewsbury T *(£30,000 + from Northwich Vic on 23/7/1997) FL 104+9/37 FLC 5/3 FAC 4+1 Others 3*
Brighton & Hove A *(Free on 19/7/2000) FL 24+36/11 FLC 1+1 FAC 1+4 Others 4/1*
Oxford U *(Free on 12/7/2002) FL 6+20/4 FAC 0+1*
Leyton Orient *(Free on 13/7/2004) FL 37+2/16 FLC 1/1 FAC 1 Others 2*

Jon Stead

STEELE Luke David
Born: Peterborough, 24 September 1984
Height: 6'2" **Weight:** 11.12
Club Honours: FAYC '03
International Honours: E: Yth
Luke initially joined Coventry City on a three-month loan deal from Manchester United, but this was eventually extended until the end of the season. He impressed at Highfield Road with confident handling and shot stopping, but with the Sky Blues' form at a low ebb in February manager Micky Adams gave him a break by bringing in Ian Bennett on loan. Luke picked up a thigh injury in training in the meantime but on Bennett's departure he was back in the team and performing as well as ever.
Peterborough U *(From trainee on 26/9/2001) FL 2*
Manchester U *(£500,000 on 4/3/2002)*
Coventry C *(Loaned on 11/9/2004) FL 32 FLC 2 FAC 2*

STEFANOVIC Dejan
Born: Yugoslavia, 28 October 1974
Height: 6'2" **Weight:** 12.10
International Honours: Serbia: 23
A cultured yet uncompromising left-sided defender, Dejan was once again an automatic choice at the back for Portsmouth last term. A proven consistent professional, he has been an excellent signing for Pompey, although he failed to add to his tally of goals for the club last term.
Sheffield Wed *(£2,000,000 from Red Star Belgrade, Yugoslavia, on 22/12/1995) PL 59+7/4 FLC 2 FAC 4/1 (Free to Vitesse Arnhem, Holland on 1/7/1999)*
Portsmouth *(£1,850,000 on 30/7/2003) PL 64/3 FLC 3+1 FAC 6*

STEPHENS Ross
Born: Llanidloes, 28 May 1985
Height: 5'10 **Weight:** 10.9
This young left back struggled to make an impact at Shrewsbury last term and his only start came in the LDV Vans Trophy tie against Bournemouth. Towards the end of the campaign he had a spell on loan with Conference North outfit

Redditch United, but he was released by the Gay Meadow club in the summer.
Shrewsbury T *(Trainee) FL 0+3 Others 1*

STEWART Gareth John
Born: Preston, 3 February 1980
Height: 6'0" **Weight:** 12.8
International Honours: E: Yth; Sch
This agile and commanding goalkeeper recovered from a lengthy spell injured to take his place on the bench for Bournemouth last season. Gareth made just one first-team appearance, in the LDV Vans Trophy tie at Shrewsbury, but showed excellent form in the reserve side to put pressure on Neil Moss.
Blackburn Rov *(From trainee on 11/2/1997)*
Bournemouth *(Free on 2/7/1999) FL 83+1 FLC 1 FAC 6+1 Others 2*

STEWART Jordan Barrington
Born: Birmingham, 3 March 1982
Height: 5'11" **Weight:** 11.12
International Honours: E: U21-1
Jordan was used more often at full back during the 2004-05 season and his defensive play matured significantly. He also looked to forge the beginnings of a useful left-sided partnership with Danny Tiatto as the campaign unfolded. His seasonal low came when he suffered a recurrence of a shoulder dislocation in the televised fixture at Upton Park after an innocuous late fall, however, he recovered quickly enough to win back his place for the closing fixtures.
Leicester C *(From trainee on 22/3/2000) P/FL 86+24/6 FLC 4+2 FAC 8+3*
Bristol Rov *(Loaned on 23/3/2000) FL 1+3*

STEWART William **Marcus** Paul
Born: Bristol, 7 November 1972
Height: 5'10" **Weight:** 11.0
Club Honours: Ch '05
International Honours: E: Sch
This experienced striker topped the scoring charts for Sunderland last term as the Black Cats won the Championship title. Marcus' 16 League goals included two superb hat-tricks, at Gillingham in September and at home to Watford in February, while his ability to hold the ball up and accurately lay it off was vital to the team's attacking play. Possessing a powerful left-foot shot, Marcus was also Sunderland's regular penalty taker. Before the final game of the season, it was announced that Marcus would not be offered a new contract at the Stadium of Light for 2005-06 and his late substitution saw him receive a standing ovation from a packed Stadium of Light and the applause of his colleagues as he left the field.
Bristol Rov *(From trainee on 18/7/1991) FL 137+34/57 FLC 11/5 FAC 7+1/4 Others 16+1/14*
Huddersfield T *(£1,200,000 + on 2/7/1996) FL 129+4/58 FLC 18/7 FAC 9/3*
Ipswich T *(£2,500,000 on 1/2/2000) P/FL 65+10/27 FLC 4+2/1 FAC 4/2 Others 8/7*
Sunderland *(£3,250,000 on 30/8/2002) P/FL 77+25/31 FLC 5+1/4 FAC 7+2/2 Others 2/2*

ST JUSTE Jason Valentine
Born: Leeds, 21 September 1985
Height: 5'8" **Weight:** 10.5
This darting young left winger began last term playing in the Northern Counties East League with Garforth Town before making the big step up to senior football. He made his debut for Darlington from the substitutes' bench at Cheltenham Town in November and featured on a number of occasions, although his outings were limited after the arrival of the more experienced Bobby Petta. Jason is quick and direct and able to run round defenders and deliver quality crosses into the box.
Darlington *(Free from Garforth T on 30/9/2004) FL 9+6/2*

ST LEDGER-HALL Sean Patrick
Born: Birmingham, 28 December 1984
Height: 6'0" **Weight:** 12.0
This promising youngster made excellent progress at Peterborough last term when he established himself as a regular in the line-up. Given his chance in the LDV Vans Trophy tie at Bristol City at the end of September he seized the opportunity with both hands. The stylish central

Marcus Stewart

defender never looked out of his depth and grew in stature as the season progressed. Sean also featured at full back and won Posh's 'Player of the Year' award at the end of the campaign.
Peterborough U *(From trainee on 18/7/2003) FL 34+2 FAC 4 Others 2*

STOCK Brian Benjamin
Born: Winchester, 24 December 1981
Height: 5'11" **Weight:** 11.2
International Honours: W: U21-4
This Bournemouth midfielder continued to make progression last term when he enjoyed an excellent season. A stylish player with fine passing and distribution skills, Brian was the side's free-kick specialist. His return of eight goals from the centre of the park was more than useful as was his overall contribution to the team.
Bournemouth *(From trainee on 25/1/2000) FL 87+32/13 FLC 3/1 FAC 10 Others 6+3/1*

STOCKDALE Robert (Robbie) Keith
Born: Middlesbrough, 30 November 1979
Height: 5'11" **Weight:** 11.3
International Honours: S: 4; B-2; E: U21-1
Robbie signed for Rotherham on a permanent basis in the summer of 2004 and was an automatic choice in the line-up at right back before making a surprise move to Hull in January. He produced some accomplished performances for the Tigers, also shining when he came off the bench to replace the injured Andy Dawson at left back against Barnsley in April.
Middlesbrough *(From trainee on 2/7/1998) P/FL 62+13/2 FLC 8+1 FAC 7*
Sheffield Wed *(Loaned on 13/9/2000) FL 6*
West Ham U *(Loaned on 23/10/2003) FL 5+2 FLC 1 FAC 1*
Rotherham U *(Free on 20/2/2004) FL 43/1 FLC 2*
Hull C *(Free on 31/1/2005) FL 12+2*

STOCKLEY Samuel (Sam) Joshua
Born: Tiverton, 5 September 1977
Height: 6'0" **Weight:** 12.0
Full back Sam has been dubbed as 'Mr Reliable' at Colchester United, and he again displayed great consistency in 2004-05, despite missing time out through injury. He began the season in a less-accustomed position at left back, but he was always happier playing on the right flank, and that was where he made most of his best displays. He scored on the opening day of the season at Sheffield Wednesday, but did not add to that tally.
Southampton *(From trainee on 1/7/1996)*
Barnet *(Free on 31/12/1996) FL 177+5/2 FLC 10 FAC 4 Others 11*
Oxford U *(£150,000 on 13/7/2001) FL 39+2 FLC 1 FAC 1 Others 1*
Colchester U *(Free on 30/8/2002) FL 108+6/2 FLC 4 FAC 12 Others 6+1*

STOLCERS Andrejs
Born: Latvia, 8 July 1974
Height: 5'10" **Weight:** 11.4
Club Honours: Div 1 '01; Div 2 '05
International Honours: Latvia: 78
After being released by Fulham Andrejs joined Yeovil Town at the beginning of September, linking up once more with his former national team boss. A tricky midfield player with plenty of pace he made a great start for the Glovers, and in his third appearance in netted two goals in the 6-1 thrashing of Oxford. However,

Sean St Ledger-Hall (left)

although he was a regular in the side until the closing stages of the campaign his formed faded away later on.
Fulham *(£2,000,000 + from Shakhtjor Donetsk, Ukraine, ex Olympija Riga, Skonto Riga, on 7/12/2000) P/FL 8+17/2 FLC 3+1/2 FAC 0+2 Others 0+1*
Yeovil T *(Free on 3/9/2004) FL 23+13/5 FLC 1 FAC 4+1/1 Others 1/1*

STONE Steven (Steve) Brian
Born: Gateshead, 20 August 1971
Height: 5'8" **Weight:** 12.7
Club Honours: Div 1 '98, '03
International Honours: E: 9
This experienced midfield campaigner featured regularly for Portsmouth last term, contributing three valuable Premiership goals. He produced some intelligent and composed play and was again an influential figure in the side. Out of contract in the summer, he was surprisingly not offered a new deal by the club.
Nottingham F *(From trainee on 20/5/1989) P/FL 189+4/23 FLC 14+1/2 FAC 11 Others 10/2*
Aston Villa *(£5,500,000 on 12/3/1999) PL 66+24/4 FLC 5+3/1 FAC 5+5/2 Others 10+4*
Portsmouth *(Loaned on 24/10/2002) FL 5/1*
Portsmouth *(Free on 20/12/2002) P/FL 64+4/8 FLC 3+1 FAC 1+2/1*

STONEBRIDGE Ian Robert
Born: Lewisham, 30 August 1981
Height: 6'0" **Weight:** 11.4
Club Honours: Div 3 '02; Div 2 '04
International Honours: E: Yth
Wycombe signed Ian during the summer of 2004, primarily as a strike partner for Nathan Tyson. He registered his first goal early on at Northampton, but only managed a further three all season. However, although his goal tally was a little disappointing, he showed himself to be probably the most naturally gifted player at the club. He reads the game well and has the ability to switch play with visionary first-touch passes.
Plymouth Arg *(From trainee at Tottenham H on 13/7/1999) FL 124+47/38 FLC 2+3/1 FAC 16+2/5 Others 5+2/1*
Wycombe W *(Signed on 5/8/2004) FL 31+7/4 FLC 1 FAC 2 Others 3*

STORY Owen Grant
Born: Burton, 3 August 1984
Height: 5'11" **Weight:** 10.10
After starting out last season with Team Bath, Owen linked up with Torquay shortly before Christmas. The pacy right winger made two brief appearances from the bench for the Gulls, but did not earn a longer deal and he later signed for Bath City.
Rushden & Diamonds *(Trainee) FL 0+5 Others 0+1 (Freed during 2004 close season)*
Torquay U *(Free from Team Bath on 13/12/2004) FL 0+2*

STRACHAN Gavin David
Born: Aberdeen, 23 December 1978
Height: 5'11" **Weight:** 11.7
International Honours: S: U21-8; Yth
A midfield playmaker who is particularly effective from set pieces, Gavin had the distinction of being named in the match squad for every Hartlepool first-team fixture last season, although he often featured on the substitutes' bench. He received more first-team starts in the later stages of the campaign when Mark Tinkler injured, and was back playing his best football as Hartlepool reached the play-off final at the Millennium Stadium.
Coventry C *(From trainee on 28/11/1996) P/FL 5+11 FLC 1+3/1 FAC 2+2*
Dundee *(Loaned on 27/1/1999) SL 4+2*
Peterborough U *(Free on 14/3/2003) FL 1+1*
Southend U *(Free on 27/3/2003) FL 6+1*
Hartlepool U *(Free on 8/8/2003) FL 55+10/6 FLC 4 FAC 4+1 Others 6/1*

Steve Stone

STREET Kevin
Born: Crewe, 25 November 1977
Height: 5'10" **Weight:** 10.8
This busy midfield player was a regular in the Shrewsbury Town squad in the first half of last season but then fell out of favour only to fight his way back into the line-up for the last few games following some excellent displays for the reserves. Kevin, who also occasionally featured as a striker, was nevertheless released by the Gay Meadow club in the summer.
Crewe Alex *(From trainee on 4/7/1996) FL 57+58/9 FLC 4+3 FAC 1+1 (Free to Northwich Vic during 2002 close season)*
Luton T *(Loaned on 20/11/2001) FL 1+1*
Bristol Rov *(Free on 29/11/2002) FL 21+12/2 FLC 1 Others 0+1*
Shrewsbury T *(Free on 16/10/2003) FL 15+6/1 FAC 1 Others 1+1*

STRONG Gregory (Greg)
Born: Bolton, 5 September 1975
Height: 6'2" **Weight:** 12.12
International Honours: E: Yth; Sch
Although this central defender signed for Boston United towards the end of the previous season he was hit by injury and did not make his League debut for the Pilgrims until the opening game of 2004-05. He added strength and experience to the side but was dropped after just five starts and towards the end of the year he was loaned to Macclesfield Town. Greg featured on the left side of a three-man central defence at Moss Rose at a time when the regular defenders were unavailable due to injury. On his return he made a surprise return to the Boston starting line-up as a striker in place of the injured Jason Lee. Greg performed his new role with great effect setting up a goal in his first appearance. He subsequently moved north of the border to join SPL club Livingston at the end of January as part of the deal that saw Stephen Boyack move in the opposite direction.
Wigan Ath *(From trainee on 1/10/1992) FL 28+7/3 FLC 5 FAC 1 Others 3+1*
Bolton W *(Signed on 10/9/1995) P/FL 10+2/1 FLC 8+2*
Blackpool *(Loaned on 21/11/1997) FL 11/1 Others 1*
Stoke C *(Loaned on 24/3/1999) FL 5/1*
Motherwell *(£150,000 on 17/3/2000) SL 73+2/3 SLC 1/1 SC 2*
Hull C *(Free on 17/6/2002) FL 3 Others 2*
Cheltenham T *(Loaned on 4/2/2003) FL 3+1*
Scunthorpe U *(Loaned on 25/3/2003) FL 7 Others 2*
Bury *(Loaned on 1/8/2003) FL 10 FLC 1*
Boston U *(Free on 12/3/2004) FL 8+1 FAC 1 Others 1*
Macclesfield T *(Loaned on 10/12/2004) FL 4*

STUART Graham Charles
Born: Tooting, 24 October 1970
Height: 5'9" **Weight:** 11.10
Club Honours: FAC '95; Div 1 '00
International Honours: E: U21-5; Yth
Graham was unable to gain a regular place in Charlton's midfield at the start of the 2004-05 season and was eventually allowed to leave during the January transfer window. His Premier League experience, particularly at the foot of the table, was seen as an ideal addition to the Canaries' squad at the time. Although he only made eight appearances for City before being released at the end of the season, he did bring a steadying influence to the side at a time when they most needed it. Calm in possession, he seldom gave the ball away, picking out colleagues even in the tightest of situations.
Chelsea *(From trainee on 15/6/1989) P/FL 70+17/14 FLC 11/2 FAC 5+2/1 Others 3+2/1*
Everton *(£850,000 on 19/8/1993) PL 116+20/22 FLC 9/3 FAC 10+3/5 Others 2+1/1*
Sheffield U *(£850,000 on 28/11/1997) FL 52+1/11 FLC 4 FAC 10+1/1 Others 0+1*
Charlton Ath *(£1,100,000 on 25/3/1999) P/FL 136+12/22 FLC 8 FAC 8/2*
Norwich C *(Free on 31/1/2005) PL 7+1*

STUBBS Alan
Born: Liverpool, 6 October 1971
Height: 6'2" **Weight:** 13.10
Club Honours: SPD '98, '00; SLC '97, '99
International Honours: E: B-1
A boyhood fan, this inspirational captain was a key figure in Everton's chase for a Champions' League place, appearing in almost every game until a shoulder injury in April effectively ended his season early. Alan had a superb campaign in the centre of the Blues' back line, defending resolutely when required and he had the bonus of scoring his first-ever goal for the club at Goodison. His main strength is his leadership from the front but he also possesses excellent passing skills (especially over distance) for a central defender and fine heading ability. Alan was out of contract during the summer, when he was considering several offers.
Bolton W *(From trainee on 24/7/1990) P/FL 181+21/9 FLC 23/4 FAC 16+2/2 Others 12+1*
Glasgow Celtic *(£3,500,000 on 10/7/1996) SL 101+5/3 SLC 8+1 SC 11 Others 16+1/2*
Everton *(Free on 13/7/2001) PL 117+7/3 FLC 5+2 FAC 11/1*

STURRIDGE Dean Constantine
Born: Birmingham, 27 July 1973
Height: 5'8" **Weight:** 12.1
This experienced Wolves striker was taken off injured on the opening day of last season, but was back in action in September when he hit a cracking winner at Plymouth. Dean featured only intermittently thereafter, partly due to injury, and later moved on to Loftus Road. However his misfortunes continued here, for after just a couple of outings from the bench he was sidelined by injury once more.
Derby Co *(From trainee on 1/7/1991) P/FL 142+48/53 FLC 9+4/4 FAC 8/2 Others 2*
Torquay U *(Loaned on 16/12/1994) FL 10/5*
Leicester C *(£350,000 on 19/1/2001) PL 20+2/6 FLC 1 FAC 2/1*
Wolverhampton W *(£375,000 on 23/11/2001) P/FL 51+31/31 FLC 1+2 FAC 1+1 Others 2+3/1*
Sheffield U *(Loaned on 2/1/2004) FL 2+2 FAC 1*
Queens Park Rgrs *(Free on 18/3/2005) FL 0+2*

STURROCK Blair David
Born: Dundee, 25 August 1981
Height: 6'0" **Weight:** 11.1
Club Honours: Div 3 '02; Div 2 '04
This young striker was out of the first-team picture at Plymouth last term and in December he moved on to join League Two outfit Kidderminster Harriers. Blair netted on his debut for the Harriers against Swansea on Boxing Day and proved to have a good eye for goal, finishing the campaign as the club's joint-top scorer with six goals. However, his future at the club was unclear at the time of writing.
Dundee U *(From juniors on 5/9/1999)*
Brechin C *(Loaned on 8/8/2000) SL 20+7/6 SC 1+2 Others 3+1/3*
Plymouth Arg *(Free on 26/10/2001) FL 9+54/2 FLC 1/1 FAC 0+5 Others 1+1*
Kidderminster Hrs *(Free on 24/12/2004) FL 17+5/5*

SUFFO Kengne Herve **Patrick**
Born: Ebolowa, Cameroon, 17 January 1978
Height: 5'9" **Weight:** 12.12
International Honours: Cameroon (ANC '02)
This enigmatic striker was a regular on the bench for Coventry during the first half of the 2004-05 season, starting only three games. Patrick scored five goals, including two in the Carling Cup win over Torquay, but rarely looked the same player when included in the starting line-up. He gave some impressive displays for the reserves but soon after Micky Adams' arrival his contract was cancelled allowing him to look for a club in the Middle East. A skilful forward who looks more comfortable playing a slightly withdrawn

ole, he uses his body strength well and is awkward to dislodge from the ball.
Sheffield U *(£150,000 from Nantes, France, ex Tonerre Yaounde, Barcelona, on 20/11/2000) FL 16+20/5 FLC 0+1/1 FAC 0+1 Freed on 3/4/2002)*
Coventry C *(Free from Numancia, Spain on 30/7/2003) FL 22+26/10 FLC 3+2/2 FAC 0+1*

SULLIVAN Neil

Born: Sutton, 24 February 1970
Height: 6'0" **Weight:** 12.1
International Honours: S: 27
Neil was voted Leeds United's 'Player of the Season' after a remarkably consistent campaign. He was the only player at Elland Road to play in every competitive game and his four penalty saves earned Leeds vital points. Neil, who was previously third choice at Chelsea, was the pick of the free-transfer arrivals at Leeds in the summer. He was expected to come under pressure from England U21 keeper Scott Carson but held off the youngster's challenge and Carson eventually moved to Liverpool. Leeds' supporters felt Neil was worthy of an international recall but the nearest he got was a workout with the Scottish training camp ahead of their World Cup qualifying game in Italy in March.
Wimbledon *(From trainee on 26/7/1988) P/FL 180+1 FLC 18 FAC 25*
Crystal Palace *(Loaned on 1/5/1992) FL 1*
Tottenham H *(Free on 5/6/2000) PL 64 FLC 8 FAC 9*
Chelsea *(Free on 29/8/2003) PL 4 FLC 2 FAC 1+1*
Leeds U *(Free on 5/8/2004) FL 46 FLC 3 FAC 1*

SUMMERBEE Nicholas (Nicky) John

Born: Altrincham, 26 August 1971
Height: 5'11" **Weight:** 12.8
Club Honours: Div 1 '99
International Honours: E: B-1; U21-3
This experienced right winger recovered from an indifferent start to play a major part in Bradford City's push for a play-off place last term. At one stage he was second in the goal assists table, chiefly supplying the crosses for Dean Windass, but he also chipped in with two sensational efforts of his own. Both were direct from free kicks, coming in successive games against Tranmere and Blackpool during a run of five straight wins which lifted City up to second in the table.
Swindon T *(From trainee on 20/7/1989) P/FL 89+23/6 FLC 9+1/3 FAC 2+3 Others 7/1*
Manchester C *(£1,500,000 on 24/6/1994) P/FL 119+12/6 FLC 11+2/2 FAC 12/2*
Sunderland *(£1,000,000 on 14/11/1997) P/FL 87+6/7 FLC 6+1 FAC 4+1 Others 3/1*
Bolton W *(Free on 4/1/2001) FL 9+3/1 FAC 3*
Nottingham F *(Free on 9/11/2001) FL 17/2 FAC 1*
Leicester C *(Free on 9/8/2002) FL 7+22 FLC 1+1 FAC 2*
Bradford C *(Free on 12/9/2003) FL 64+4/4 FLC 1 FAC 1*

SUMMERFIELD Luke John

Born: Ivybridge, 6 December 1987
Height: 6'0" **Weight:** 11.0
A product of the Plymouth Argyle youth set-up, Luke was a consistent performer for the club's reserve and junior sides last term. The promising midfielder did well enough to force his way into the first-team squad towards the end of the season and was rewarded with his debut as a substitute against Leicester City on the final day of the season. Luke is the son of former Plymouth Argyle midfielder and assistant manager Kevin Summerfield.
Plymouth Arg *(Trainee) FL 0+1*

SURMAN Andrew Ronald Edward

Born: Johannesburg, South Africa, 20 August 1986
Height: 5'10" **Weight:** 11.5
Andrew established himself in Southampton's reserve team last term before joining Walsall on loan at the end of January. The young midfielder impressed with some quality touches from the moment he came on as a substitute against Wrexham and a week later he scored the winner in his first full game at Bristol City. Creativity was a feature of his game and he also got a fine goal at Hartlepool in the last fixture before his loan spell expired.
Southampton *(From trainee on 23/8/2003)*
Walsall *(Loaned on 28/1/2005) FL 10+4/2*

SVARD Sebastian

Born: Hividovre, Denmark, 15 January 1983
Height: 6'1" **Weight:** 12.11
Club Honours: FAYC '01; CS '04
International Honours: Denmark: U21-9; Yth
The gifted central midfielder was a late substitute for Francesc Fabregas in the FA Community Shield in August. The highly rated Arsenal youngster was then sent on loan to Brondby in September where he remained for the rest of the campaign.
Arsenal *(Signed from FC Copenhagen, Denmark on 1/11/2000) FLC 1+1 FAC 1 Others 0+1*
Stoke C *(Loaned on 1/1/2004) FL 9+4/1 FAC 1*

SVENSSON Anders

Born: Sweden, 17 July 1976
Height: 5'10" **Weight:** 12.11
International Honours: Sweden: 59
Most definitely a bit-part player since December, when Harry Redknapp became manager at St Mary's, Anders is, undoubtedly, a very talented footballer, but of the dozen men rotated in midfield during the season he was among the most disappointing – most especially because he is capable of much more than he is contributed. An elegant ball player and distributor of the ball he is, at his best working his way out of, and exploiting, tight situations. Anders' contract lapsed at the end of the season and his future was unclear at the time of writing.
Southampton *(£750,000 from IF Elfsborg, Sweden, ex Hestrafors, on 16/7/2001) PL 97+30/9 FLC 7/2 FAC 10+1/2 Others 2*

SVENSSON Mathias

Born: Boras, Sweden, 24 September 1974
Height: 6'0" **Weight:** 12.4
Club Honours: Div 1 '00, '04
International Honours: Sweden: 3
Mathias' season with the Canaries seemed to mirror his club's fortunes. He started slowly, losing his place after just two games, but returned in the autumn to score some vital goals, including a brace in the 3-2 home win against Bolton, before suffering a knee injury during the away game at Chelsea. This kept him out of the reckoning until early April and his return to the squad coincided with a run of results which so nearly kept the Canaries in the Premiership. His personal highlight would undoubtedly have been the late winner against his former club, Charlton in April. A bustling striker with two good feet, he is strong in the air and thrives on good service from the flanks. His physical style makes him a handful for even the most experienced of defenders and there can be no doubt that his absence for four months was a major blow to Nigel Worthington's plans.
Portsmouth *(£200,000 from Elfsborg, Sweden on 6/12/1996) FL 34+11/10 FLC 1/1 FAC 3+2/1 (£100,000 to Tirol Innsbruck, Austria on 15/7/1998)*
Crystal Palace *(£100,000 on 29/9/1998) FL 26+6/10 FLC 2 FAC 1*
Charlton Ath *(£600,000 on 28/1/2000) P/FL 42+28/7 FLC 0+2 FAC 2+4/1*
Derby Co *(Loaned on 22/8/2003) FL 9+1/3*
Norwich C *(£50,000 on 19/12/2003) P/FL 26+16/11 FLC 1+1*

SWAILES Christopher (Chris) William
Born: Gateshead, 19 October 1970
Height: 6'2" **Weight:** 12.11
This big central defender is the kind of player every team just loves to have in their line-up, as he would almost run through the proverbial brick wall in the club's cause. Even though he was reaching the twilight of his career, Chris could always be relied upon to give his best for Rotherham last term, although he would have been a little disappointed with his return of just one goal as he regularly helped out in attack for corners and free kicks.
Ipswich T *(From trainee on 23/5/1989)*
Peterborough U *(£10,000 on 28/3/1991. Free to Boston U in August 1991)*
Doncaster Rov *(Free from Bridlington T on 27/10/1993) FL 49 FLC 2/1 FAC 1 Others 2*
Ipswich T *(£225,000 on 23/3/1995) P/FL 34+3/1 FLC 3 Others 2*
Bury *(£200,000 on 14/11/1997) FL 125+1/10 FLC 9 FAC 8 Others 3/1*
Rotherham U *(Free on 1/7/2001) FL 167/14 FLC 11/2 FAC 6*

SWAILES Daniel (Danny)
Born: Bolton, 1 April 1979
Height: 6'3" **Weight:** 13.7
Danny missed the opening five games of the 2004-05 season due to a thigh injury, but marked his first appearance for Bury with a goal at Rochdale. He was guaranteed a starting place throughout the next four months performing consistently before being sold to Macclesfield in the new year for a record fee for the Moss Rose club. Danny made an immediate impact strengthening the three-man central defence and his towering presence led to some dominant performances overall, but narrowly failed to take the club to promotion.
Bury *(From trainee on 9/7/1997) FL 154+10/13 FLC 4+3 FAC 9+1 Others 10+3/1*
Macclesfield T *(£40,000 on 14/1/2005) FL 17 Others 2*

SWEENEY Antony Thomas
Born: Stockton, 5 September 1983
Height: 6'0" **Weight:** 11.9
A strong running midfielder who is also good in the air, Antony firmly established himself as an automatic first-team choice with Hartlepool in 2004-05. A player whose all-round game improved greatly, he emerged a regular scorer with 14 goals over the season. The highlight of his campaign came when he scored a hat-trick in the 3-2 home win over Chesterfield.
Hartlepool U *(From trainee on 10/1/2002) FL 54+7/14 FLC 2/1 FAC 6 Others 8/2*

SWEENEY Peter Henry
Born: Glasgow, 25 September 1984
Height: 6'0" **Weight:** 12.0
International Honours: S: B-1; U21-8; Yth
This pacy skilful winger was in and out of the Millwall line-up last term due to ongoing injury problems. When on the ball he remains a delight to watch as he puts opposition defences under all sorts of pressure. Although he appeared in exactly half of the Lions' Championship matches he scored only twice, netting in the home games against Plymouth and Preston in the second half of the season.
Millwall *(From juniors on 13/12/2000) FL 45+14/5 FAC 3+4 Others 0+1*

SWIFT John Maxwell
Born: Leeds, 20 September 1984
Height: 5'7" **Weight:** 10.6
Right back John made his Bradford City debut against Colchester last November and was not fazed by the step-up from the reserves. Although quite small, he is a quick and confident defender and will be looking to feature more regularly in 2005-06 after signing a new contract for the Bantams.
Bradford C *(From trainee on 4/8/2004) FL 2+3*

SYMES Michael
Born: Great Yarmouth, 31 October 1983
Height: 6'3" **Weight:** 12.4
This young striker joined Bradford City along with midfielder Steve Schumacher but did not feature as often as his former Everton colleague last term. A highlight was scoring two goals in a memorable win over Sheffield Wednesday in October. Michael did not feature in the side after New Year's Day and finished the season with an achilles injury.
Everton *(From trainee on 13/2/2002)*
Crewe Alex *(Loaned on 24/3/2004) FL 1+3/1*
Bradford C *(Free on 6/8/2004) FL 5+7/2 FLC 1 FAC 1 Others 0+1*

Peter Sweeney

T

TABB Jay Anthony
Born: Tooting, 21 February 1984
Height: 5'5" **Weight:** 9.7
International Honours: RoI: U21-7
Although not quite matching his performance level of 2003-04, Jay was a constant threat on the right side of Brentford's attack throughout the season. Cutting in onto his stronger left foot he was always a danger to opposing defences. He scored directly from an in-swinging corner against Walsall in January, but his best goal was a fine individual effort against Hull on the last day of the season. Jay was a regular in the Republic of Ireland U21 team throughout the season.
Brentford *(From trainee on 23/7/2001) FL 53+33/14 FLC 1+1 FAC 7+5/1 Others 4+2/2*

TAGGART Gerald (Gerry) Paul
Born: Belfast, 18 October 1970
Height: 6'1" **Weight:** 13.12
Club Honours: Div 1 '97; FLC '00
International Honours: NI: 51; U23-2; Yth; Sch
This rugged central defender has been a crowd favourite at Stoke since his arrival at the club. His never-say-die attitude rubbed off well on his fellow defenders and contributed to the excellent record for goals conceded. Gerry played the last few matches of the season with a pain-killing injection as he was suffering from a broken toe but still put in some decent performances. His future was in doubt at the time of writing as he was out of contract in the summer.
Manchester C *(From trainee on 1/7/1989) FL 10+2/1 Others 1*
Barnsley *(£75,000 on 10/1/1990) FL 209+3/16 FLC 15/1 FAC 14/2 Others 6/1*
Bolton W *(£1,500,000 on 1/8/1995) P/FL 68+1/4 FLC 8/1 FAC 4*
Leicester C *(Free on 23/7/1998) P/FL 105+12/9 FLC 12+2/2 FAC 8+1 Others 2/1*
Stoke C *(Loaned on 9/12/2003) FL 8/2*
Stoke C *(Free on 27/2/2004) FL 44/2 FAC 1*

TAIT Paul
Born: Newcastle, 24 October 1974
Height: 6'1" **Weight:** 11.10
Paul was signed by Rochdale to partner the less experienced Grant Holt up front and got off to a good start, scoring an excellent goal in the Carling Cup tie against Wolves. However, a League goal proved elusive and then Dale switched to playing just one up front. A further change of style to a front three gave him another chance, and although goals were still scarce and Paul found it hard to win over the fans, he proved a valuable foil for Holt.
Everton *(From trainee on 8/7/1993)*
Wigan Ath *(Free on 22/7/1994) FL 1+4 (Free to Runcorn on 16/2/1996)*
Crewe Alex *(Signed from Northwich Vic on 9/6/1999) FL 31+32/6 FLC 0+1 FAC 1+1*
Hull C *(Loaned on 5/11/2001) FL 0+2*
Bristol Rov *(Free on 12/7/2002) FL 61+13/19 FLC 2 FAC 4/1 Others 1*
Rochdale *(Free on 30/7/2004) FL 27+9/2 FLC 1/1 FAC 3 Others 2*

TALBOT Andrew (Drew)
Born: Barnsley, 19 July 1986
Height: 5'10" **Weight:** 11.0
This young forward enjoyed a great season for Sheffield Wednesday in 2004-05. Drew made his senior debut from the bench at Peterborough in October and went on to feature regularly in the squad, although most of his appearances were as a substitute. A pacy striker with a good eye for goal, he scored five times including an important strike in the game at Hull and another in the play-off final against Hartlepool.
Sheffield Wed *(Signed from Dodworth MW on 19/2/2004) FL 3+18/4 FAC 1 Others 0+3/1*

TALBOT Jason Christopher
Born: Irlam, 30 September 1985
Height: 5'8" **Weight:** 10.1
Jason had to turn professional with Bolton Wanderers in order to complete a loan to Derby County, who wanted cover while Jamie Vincent was suspended. It was a big step for the diminutive left back, although he showed plenty of determination in two appearances at Pride Park. Later in the season he went on loan to Mansfield wher he made an impressive debut against Boston United

Gerry Taggart (left)

but then an infected toe caused him to drop out of the side and he returned to Bolton. He was released by Wanderers in the summer.
Bolton W *(From trainee on 23/9/2004)*
Derby Co *(Loaned on 25/9/2004) FL 2*
Mansfield T *(Loaned on 19/11/2004) FL 2*

TALBOT Stewart Dean
Born: Birmingham, 14 June 1973
Height: 5'11" **Weight:** 13.7
Brentford's midfield holding player, Stewart took over the team captaincy last term when Michael Dobson was injured. He had a fine first half of the campaign alongside Chris Hargreaves, but things got tougher as the season progressed and he often played with niggling injuries. Stewart is more adept at breaking up the play and releasing the simple pass rather than getting forward.
Port Vale *(Signed from Moor Green on 10/8/1994) FL 112+25/10 FLC 4+3 FAC 4+1 Others 2+3/1*
Rotherham U *(Free on 13/7/2000) FL 100+14/8 FLC 6 FAC 6+1*
Shrewsbury T *(Loaned on 11/2/2003) FL 5 Others 2*
Brentford *(Free on 17/2/2004) FL 50+2/3 FLC 0+1 FAC 9/1 Others 2*

TALIA Francesco (Frank)
Born: Melbourne, Australia, 20 July 1972
Height: 6'1" **Weight:** 13.6
Club Honours: Div 2 '96
International Honours: Australia: Sch
Frank re-established himself as the first-choice goalkeeper for Wycombe Wanderers in 2004-05, playing in all but two games and probably having his best season yet with the Chairboys. Frank has always been a great shot-stopper but last term he noticeably improved his command of his area, catching and punching with greater confidence.
Blackburn Rov *(Free from Sunshine George Cross, Australia on 28/8/1992)*
Hartlepool U *(Loaned on 29/12/1992) FL 14 Others 1*
Swindon T *(£150,000 on 8/9/1995) FL 107 FLC 9 FAC 2*
Sheffield U *(Free, via trial at Wolverhampton W on 26/9/2000) FL 6 (Freed during 2001 close season)*
Reading *(Free from Royal Antwerp, Belgium on 15/3/2002)*
Wycombe W *(Free on 9/8/2002) FL 97 FLC 2 FAC 5 Others 5*

TANN Adam John
Born: Fakenham, 12 May 1982
Height: 6'0" **Weight:** 11.5
International Honours: E: Yth
A young defender who is equally comfortable either at right back or in the centre of defence and can even play in midfield if required, Adam featured regularly for Cambridge United throughout the 2004-05 campaign. He performed consistently well, scoring his only goal in the 2-1 defeat at Cheltenham in October, however, he was unable to prevent the U's from being relegated from the Football League.
Cambridge U *(From trainee on 7/9/1999) FL 111+10/4 FLC 2 FAC 9+1/3 Others 15/1*

TAPP Alexander (Alex) Nicholas
Born: Redhill, 7 June 1982
Height: 5'8" **Weight:** 11.10
A hard-tackling left-footed midfielder, Alex returned to the MK Dons first team in early October after recovering from a cruciate ligament injury, but after three months involvement then had the cruel misfortune to suffer a similar injury to his other knee during a reserve game at Luton in January. He consequently missed

Adam Tann

of danger to opposition teams with his ability to beat defenders on the ground and create his own chances. Gary continued to score throughout the season providing Lincoln's 'Goal of the Season' with a delicate chipped shot in the home win over Scunthorpe United. He was released at the end of the campaign and signed for Huddersfield Town.

Hull C *(Loaned from Northwich Vic on 16/3/2001) FL 1+4*
Leyton Orient *(£150,000 from Northwich Vic on 9/7/2001) FL 10+11/1 FLC 1/1 FAC 2*
Lincoln C *(Free on 14/8/2003) FL 77+3/27 FLC 1+1/1 FAC 3 Others 8/3*

TEAGUE Andrew Harry
Born: Preston, 5 February 1986
Height: 6'3" **Weight:** 12.10
A third-year trainee at Macclesfield, Andrew started last season playing as a central defender in the reserve and youth teams. However, after some good performances at this level and with the senior side's defence decimated by injury, Andrew made his Football League debut in the home match against Lincoln City in December. He adapted well, making an excellent contribution before returning to the reserves. Andrew was selected as Macclesfield's 'Youth Team Player of the Year'.
Macclesfield T *(Trainee) FL 5*

TEALE Gary
Born: Glasgow, 21 July 1978
Height: 6'0" **Weight:** 11.6
Club Honours: Div 2 '03
International Honours: S: U21-6
Gary is a fast and skilful winger and an accurate crosser of the ball. A confidence player, he was at times unable to establish himself in the Wigan line-up last term, his best spell coming in January and February, boosted by goals in the away wins at Rotherham United and Coventry City. One of the quickest players in the Championship, he is at his best when running at opposition defenders. Out of contract at the end of the season, he was offered a new deal.
Clydebank *(From juniors on 19/6/1996) SL 52+16/14 SLC 3+1 SC 1 Others 4*
Ayr U *(£70,000 on 2/10/1998) SL 94+7/13 SLC 5+1/1 SC 10/3 Others 4/1*
Wigan Ath *(£200,000 on 14/12/2001) FL 94+32/8 FLC 2+4 FAC 3+1 Others 2/2*

TEBILY Olivier
Born: Abidjan, Ivory Coast, 19 December 1975
Height: 6'1" **Weight:** 13.4
Club Honours: SLC '99
International Honours: Ivory Coast; France: U21
Olivier found it tough to break into a settled Birmingham City defence last term and was primarily used in emergencies. He appeared four times out of position at left back. A physically strong player with pace, he was a formidable barrier for opposition attackers. He was a key part of the team that won four games in a row during December to turn Blues' season around.
Sheffield U *(£175,000 from Chateauroux on 24/3/1999) FL 7+1*
Glasgow Celtic *(£1,250,000 on 8/7/1999) SL 29+9 SLC 4+1/1 SC 2+1 Others 5/1*
Birmingham C *(£700,000 on 22/3/2002) P/FL 45+16 FLC 1 FAC 2+2 Others 3*

TEGGART Neil
Born: Downpatrick, 16 September 1984
Height: 6'2" **Weight:** 12.4
International Honours: NI: U21-2; Yth
This young Sunderland striker failed to make a first-team breakthrough last term and at the turn of the year he had an ill-fated loan spell at Scunthorpe. Neil made his debut on New Year's Day against Darlington and lasted 37 minutes before being sacrificed when a defender was sent off. He then injured his ribs in the warm-up before the game at Mansfield two days later and did not play for the Iron again. Soon after returning to the Stadium of Light Neil was released and subsequently signed for Australian A League side Perth Glory. He also represented Northern Ireland at U21 level during the campaign.
Sunderland *(From trainee on 17/4/2002)*
Darlington *(Loaned on 6/2/2004) FL 9+6*
Scunthorpe U *(Loaned on 31/12/2004) FL 1*

TELFER Paul Norman
Born: Edinburgh, 21 October 1971
Height: 5'9" **Weight:** 11.6
International Honours: S: 1; B-2; U21-3
A highly professional and consistent performer, possessing unflagging stamina and commitment, Paul is at his most effective as a right wing-half. It wasn't until Harry Redknapp's appointment as manager in December that he found a settled place in the side, firstly at right back (where he had spent a good deal of his career at Southampton), then in midfield, before returning to right back for the last two, somewhat disappointing, games of the season – not that he could be held in anyway responsible for the results.
Luton T *(From trainee on 7/11/1988) FL 136+8/19 FLC 5 FAC 14/2 Others 2/1*
Coventry C *(£1,500,000 on 11/7/1995) PL 178+13/6 FLC 15/2 FAC 15+4/4*
Southampton *(Free on 2/11/2001) PL 112+16/1 FLC 5+2 FAC 12 Others 1+1*

Gary Teale

John Terry

TERRY John George
Born: Barking, 7 December 1980
Height: 6'0" **Weight:** 12.4
Club Honours: FAC '00; FLC '05; PL '05
International Honours: E: 16; U21-9
Upon his arrival at Chelsea, one of Jose Mourinho's first decisions was to nominate John Terry as his new captain, and how the England centre back has revelled in the responsibility! Following his two immediate predecessors Marcel Desailly and Dennis Wise may have proved daunting but John loses nothing in comparison as he leads by example with bone-jarring tackles and calm passing out of defence. He marshalled the Blues' defence impeccably as they created Premiership records for longest sequence without conceding a goal (1,025 minutes) and fewest conceded in a season (15). Not content with this, he was also one of the most prolific goal-scoring defenders around with a final total of eight! His tally of four in the Champions' League included the header which wrested the titanic last-16 tie away from Barcelona and secured the 5-4 victory for Chelsea over the star-studded Catalan side. The rock-like young skipper lifted the Carling Cup in February at Cardiff – Chelsea's first trophy for five years; shortly followed, on a memorable weekend, by clinching the club's first Championship for 50 years and being voted PFA 'Player of the Year', as well as gaining a place in the PFA divisional team of the season. John's season came to a premature end as he underwent an operation on a troublesome foot injury – his performances while battling through the pain barrier being all the more remarkable.
Chelsea *(From trainee on 18/3/1998) PL 138+12/10 FLC 17+1 FAC 19+5/7 Others 30/6*
Nottingham F *(Loaned on 23/3/2000) FL 5+1*

TERRY Paul Edward
Born: Dagenham, 3 April 1979
Height: 5'10" **Weight:** 12.6
Club Honours: Div 2 '05
International Honours: E: SP-3
Paul has been a tremendous acquisition for Yeovil and once again proved his worth last season, when he was effective in a variety of different roles. A tough-tackling defender or midfielder, he scored a total of seven goals in all competitions for the Glovers.
Yeovil T *(Signed from Dagenham & Redbridge, ex Charlton Ath trainee, on 20/8/2003) FL 57+16/7 FLC 1+1 FAC 7/1 Others 2+1*

TESSEM Jo
Born: Orlandet, Norway, 28 February 1972
Height: 6'3" **Weight:** 12.10
International Honours: Norway: 9; B-1
Out of favour at Southampton, this experienced utility player joined Millwall on a three-month loan last October to cover for injuries. He was used in a midfield role and while his main strengths were in attack, he also worked hard defensively putting in some good performances and scoring in the home game against Cardiff City. Jo subsequently returned to St Mary's but failed to add to his appearance total for the Saints.
Southampton *(£600,000 from Molde, Norway, ex Lyn, on 19/11/1999) PL 67+43/12 FLC 4+2/1 FAC 7+6/3 Others 0+1*
Millwall *(Loaned on 1/10/2004) FL 11+1/1 FLC 1*

THATCHER Benjamin (Ben) David
Born: Swindon, 30 November 1975
Height: 5'10" **Weight:** 12.7
International Honours: W: 7; E: U21-4; Yth
This committed defender joined Manchester City in the summer of 2004 from Leicester City but was in and out of the side, partly as a result of injuries. He almost joined Fulham during the January transfer window but the deal collapsed at the last minute. Ben is a robust, tough-tackling left back.
Millwall *(From trainee on 8/6/1992) FL 87+3/1 FLC 6 FAC 7 Others 1*
Wimbledon *(£1,840,000 on 5/7/1996) PL 82+4 FLC 12 FAC 5*
Tottenham H *(£5,000,000 on 12/7/2000) PL 29+7 FLC 6+1 FAC 3*
Leicester C *(£300,000 + on 17/7/2003) PL 28+1/1*
Manchester C *(£100,000 on 30/6/2004) PL 17+1 FLC 2 FAC 1*

THELWELL Alton Anthony
Born: Islington, 5 September 1980
Height: 6'0" **Weight:** 12.7
International Honours: E: U21-1
After playing against his old club Tottenham in Hull's official centenary game in July, a season that promised so much was once again blighted by injury. Alton required a cartilage operation in August and, although he made a brief return the following month, knee problems soon flared up again to rule the talented right back out for the remainder of the campaign.
Tottenham H *(From trainee on 27/1/1999) PL 13+5 FAC 0+3*
Hull C *(Free on 1/7/2003) FL 24+5/1 FLC 1 Others 1*

THIRLWELL Paul
Born: Washington, 13 February 1979
Height: 5'11" **Weight:** 11.4
International Honours: E: U21-1
Paul played as a trialist for Sheffield United during the pre-season and signed a long-term deal in August. A regular member of the side until December he played as a defensive midfielder, winning, holding and distributing the ball, and contributing one goal. When Phil Jagielka moved into midfield, Paul, although regularly in the squad, was more frequently on the bench. He scored his first Championship goal against Wolves in November.
Sunderland *(From trainee on 14/4/1997) P/FL 55+22 FLC 6+2/1 FAC 5+2*
Swindon T *(Loaned on 8/9/1999) FL 12*
Sheffield U *(Free on 30/7/2004) FL 24+6/1 FLC 2+1 FAC 2+1*

THOMAS Daniel (Danny) Justin
Born: Leamington, 1 May 1981
Height: 5'7" **Weight:** 11.2
Danny held down a regular starting place in Boston United's line-up throughout the 2004-05 season providing plenty of difficulties for opposing defenders down the flanks. He was mostly used as a left-sided player with his ability to run at defenders and provide accurate crosses setting up chances for colleagues.
Leicester C *(From trainee at Nottingham F on 13/5/1998) PL 0+3*
Bournemouth *(Signed on 8/2/2002) FL 35+24/2 FLC 2/1 FAC 6/1 Others 5+2*
Boston U *(Free on 19/3/2004) FL 40+7/6 FLC 0+1 FAC 4 Others 1*

THOMAS Daniel (Danny) Wayne
Born: Blackwood, 13 May 1985
Height: 5'5" **Weight:** 10.10
International Honours: W: Yth
Danny signed his first professional contract with Cardiff City in July 2004 but made just one appearance for the Bluebirds during the season, coming on as a substitute for Chris Barker in the 1-0 home defeat by Preston. Danny started his career as a striker but has since converted to a central-midfield role. He was released by the club in the summer.
Cardiff C *(From trainee on 27/5/2002) FL 0+1*

THOMAS James Alan
Born: Swansea, 16 January 1979
Height: 6'0" **Weight:** 13.0
International Honours: W: U21-21
After a couple of substitute appearances at the start of the 2004-05 season James encountered knee problems, which

eventually led to him having an operation in November. This effectively brought the pacy striker's campaign to a premature close, although Swans' manager Kenny Jackett invited him to attend pre-season training in July in a bid to earn a new contract.
Blackburn Rov *(From trainee on 2/7/1996) FL 1+3/1 FLC 1/2*
West Bromwich A *(Loaned on 29/8/1997) FL 1+2*
Blackpool *(Loaned on 21/3/2000) FL 9/2*
Sheffield U *(Loaned on 24/11/2000) FL 3+7/1 FAC 0+1*
Bristol Rov *(Loaned on 22/3/2002) FL 7/1*
Swansea C *(Free on 9/7/2002) FL 42+15/16 FLC 1+1/1 FAC 2+3 Others 2/1*

THOMAS Jerome William
Born: Wembley, 23 March 1983
Height: 5'10" **Weight:** 11.10
Club Honours: FAYC '00, '01
International Honours: E: Yth
With only one previous substitute appearance to his name for the Addicks, Jerome broke into the first team in September for the Carling Cup tie against Crystal Palace. and subsequently kept his place for a lengthy run. He is an attacking wingman who can play on either side but feels he is more effective on the left. He is very confident of his own ability and has a bag full of tricks. Jerome likes to run at defenders and get a strike on goal when the opportunity arises, as well as creating chances for others. He scored his first Charlton goal in the away match with Tottenham in only his second Premiership start, and added two more in the home games against Fulham and Tottenham again.
Arsenal *(From trainee on 3/7/2001) FLC 1+2*
Queens Park Rgrs *(Loaned on 27/3/2002) FL 4/1*
Queens Park Rgrs *(Loaned on 29/8/2002) FL 5+1/2*
Charlton Ath *(£100,000 on 2/2/2004) PL 21+4/3 FLC 1 FAC 2+1*

THOMAS Stephen
Born: Hartlepool, 23 June 1979
Height: 5'10" **Weight:** 12.0
International Honours: W: U21-5; Yth
Stephen returned to his native North-East and made his Darlington debut on the opening day of the 2004-05 season against Grimsby Town. He immediately settled into midfield where he impressed with his attacking ability and strong tackling, but unfortunately suffered an injury in October. This kept him out of action for some time, although he returned to the line-up towards the end of the campaign.
Wrexham *(From trainee on 4/7/1997) FL 85+31/7 FLC 2+2 FAC 1+1 Others 5+1/2*
Darlington *(Free on 5/8/2004) FL 11+1 Others 1*

THOMAS Wayne Junior Robert
Born: Gloucester, 17 May 1979
Height: 5'11" **Weight:** 11.12
This highly rated central defender had another useful campaign for Stoke City, for whom he was a near ever-present. Always a favourite with the fans for his never-say-die attitude, he cut down on his errors and his game improved no end. Wayne scored the goal which put the Potters ahead in the FA Cup tie at Arsenal, but missed the last few matches of the season due to injury.
Torquay U *(From trainee on 4/7/1997) FL 89+34/5 FLC 2+1/1 FAC 7/1 Others 6+4*
Stoke C *(£200,000 + on 5/6/2000) FL 188+1/7 FLC 7+1 FAC 10/1 Others 10*

THOME Emerson Augusto
Born: Porto Alegre, Brazil, 30 March 1972
Height: 6'1" **Weight:** 13.4
The powerful built centre half only started 13 games for Wigan Athletic following his move from Bolton Wanderers at the start of last season. A physically domineering defender who certainly takes no prisoners, he was plagued by a persistent hamstring injury during the promotion campaign. Emerson's experience will be important in the club's first season in the Premiership.
Sheffield Wed *(Free from Benfica, Portugal on 23/3/1998) PL 60+1/1 FLC 5+1 FAC 4/1*
Chelsea *(£2,700,000 on 23/12/1999) PL 19+2 Others 1*
Sunderland *(£4,500,000 on 1/9/2000) PL 43+1/2 FLC 4 FAC 5*
Bolton W *(Free on 29/8/2003) PL 25+1 FLC 5 FAC 1*
Wigan Ath *(Free on 6/8/2004) FL 11+4 FLC 1 FAC 1*

THOMPSON David Anthony
Born: Birkenhead, 12 September 1977
Height: 5'7" **Weight:** 10.0
Club Honours: FAYC '96
International Honours: E: U21-7; Yth
Returning after two injury-plagued seasons David was still troubled by a knee problem and was re-introduced gradually to Premiership football for Blackburn. His industry and competitive spirit led to new manager Mark Hughes preferring him to Brett Emerton on the right wing, although he tended to play more in the centre and was often switched there during the game. David scored two goals in the FA Cup replay against Cardiff and created scores more for his colleagues with his right-wing crosses and quickly-hit through balls.
Liverpool *(From trainee on 8/11/1994) PL 24+24/5 FLC 5 FAC 0+1 Others 2*
Swindon T *(Loaned on 21/11/1997) FL 10*
Coventry C *(£3,000,000 on 8/8/2000) P/FL 61+5/15 FLC 3+1/1 FAC 2*
Blackburn Rov *(£1,500,000 on 28/8/2002) PL 44+14/5 FLC 5/1 FAC 7+1/2 Others 5/1*

THOMPSON Glyn William
Born: Telford, 24 February 1981
Height: 6'1" **Weight:** 12.4
After being released by Northampton at the end of the 2003-04 season, Glyn began last term with Walsall and also had brief spells in Denmark and with Stafford Rangers before joining Chesterfield on non-contract forms towards the end of the campaign. He made an unexpected debut in goal in the final match at Swindon, when he showed up well enough without having much to do but his future was unclear at the time of writing.
Shrewsbury T *(From trainee on 14/12/1998) FL 1 FLC 1*
Fulham *(£50,000 on 20/11/1999)*
Mansfield T *(Loaned on 21/1/2000) FL 16*
Northampton T *(Free on 29/11/2002) FL 18+1 FLC 1 FAC 1*
Walsall *(Free on 24/8/2004. Free to Stafford Rgrs in January 2005)*
Chesterfield *(Free from Stafford Rgrs on 24/3/2005) FL 1*

THOMPSON John
Born: Dublin, 12 October 1981
Height: 6'1" **Weight:** 11.11
International Honours: RoI: 1; U21-11; Yth
This young Nottingham Forest player had a late start to the 2004-05 season after dislocating his shoulder during the club's pre-season tour to the USA. His versatility enabled him to cover for a number of positions: although mainly used in the centre of midfield and at right back he also featured in the centre of defence where he played his best football of the season. Unfortunately John suffered a knee injury in the match against Sheffield United at the beginning of April and this brought his campaign to a premature close.
Nottingham F *(Signed from Home Farm, ex River Valley Rgrs, on 6/7/1999) FL 66+14/4 FLC 5+1 FAC 3+2 Others 1+1*

THOMPSON Lee Jonathan
Born: Sheffield, 25 March 1983
Height: 5'7" **Weight:** 11.2
International Honours: E: Sch
This diminutive striker provided Boston United with an extra dimension when

coming off the substitutes' bench to boost the team. He was at his most effective in the Carling Cup tie against Luton Town when he grabbed two late goals to seal an unexpected 4-3 victory over the League One club. Lee always looked dangerous with his busy style causing constant problems for opposition defences. It was surprising he was given few chances in the starting line-up and even more of a shock to Boston supporters when he was not offered a new contract at the end of the campaign.
Sheffield U *(From juniors on 7/7/2000)*
Boston U *(Free on 4/10/2002) FL 40+55/12 FLC 0+2/2 FAC 3+3/1 Others 5/2*

THOMSON Steven (Steve)
Born: Glasgow, 23 January 1978
Height: 5'8" **Weight:** 10.4
International Honours: S: Yth
This industrious combative midfielder featured regularly for Peterborough last term apart from a brief spell in the autumn when he was dropped, but did not always reach his best form. However, he came back strongly in the second half of the campaign, scoring at Hull and in the home draw with Bradford City. Steve was released by Posh at the end of the season.
Crystal Palace *(From trainee on 9/12/1995) FL 68+37/1 FLC 8+4/2 FAC 3+1/1 Others 1+1*
Peterborough U *(Free on 5/9/2003) FL 58+8/3 FLC 1 FAC 5/1 Others 3*

THORNE Peter Lee
Born: Manchester, 21 June 1973
Height: 6'0" **Weight:** 13.6
Club Honours: Div 2 '96; AMC '00
Peter finished the 2004-05 season as Cardiff's leading scorer with 14 goals, despite missing a large part of the campaign after suffering an injury in the pre-season friendly with Real Santander. With the Bluebirds struggling badly for goals following the sale of Robert Earnshaw, Peter's absence was a major loss to the side and when he returned briefly in October it gave Cardiff extra life. That run lasted only five games before he was sidelined once more, but a second comeback in December saw him hit five goals in seven games to spark what would eventually be a successful fight against relegation.
Blackburn Rov *(From trainee on 20/6/1991) Others 0+1*
Wigan Ath *(Loaned on 11/3/1994) FL 10+1*
Swindon T *(£225,000 on 18/1/1995) FL 66+11/27 FLC 5+1/4 FAC 4+2 Others 1+1/1*
Stoke C *(£350,000 + on 25/7/1997) FL 147+11/65 FLC 12+1/6 FAC 5+1 Others 9+3/9*
Cardiff C *(£1,700,000 on 13/9/2001) FL 116+10/46 FLC 4/3 FAC 6+1/1 Others 6/1*

THORNTON Sean
Born: Drogheda, 18 May 1983
Height: 5'10" **Weight:** 11.0
Club Honours: Ch '05
International Honours: RoI: U21-12; Yth
Sean is a talented midfield playmaker who has struggled to win a regular berth in the Sunderland starting line-up, but who always seems to make a positive impact when called upon. An excellent passer, Sean is extremely dangerous from set pieces, a skill he demonstrated when coming off the bench against Rotherham in February and netting with two brilliant free kicks in a 4-1 win. A popular figure with the Sunderland fans, it was therefore something of a surprise when Black Cats' boss Mick McCarthy informed Sean that he was free to look for a move away from the Stadium of Light.
Tranmere Rov *(Trainee) FL 9+2/1 FAC 0+1 Others 0+1*
Sunderland *(Signed on 4/7/2002) P/FL 28+21/9 FLC 4 FAC 5+4 Others 1+1*
Blackpool *(Loaned on 7/11/2002) FL 1+2 Others 1*

THORPE Anthony (Tony) Lee
Born: Leicester, 10 April 1974
Height: 5'9" **Weight:** 12.6
This talented striker was injured in just the second game of the season for Queen's Park Rangers and it was not until November that he regained match fitness. Then when he did return to first-

Sean Thornton

team action he suffered a knee injury almost immediately and was sidelined again for a lengthy period. However, a loan spell at Rotherham got him back on track and he returned to the Rangers' line-up once more at the very end of the campaign.
Luton T *(From trainee at Leicester C on 18/8/1992) FL 93+27/50 FLC 5+4/5 FAC 5+3/2 Others 4+3/3*
Fulham *(£800,000 on 26/2/1998) FL 5+8/3 Others 1+1*
Bristol C *(£1,000,000 on 23/6/1998) FL 102+26/50 FLC 5+2/4 FAC 6+1/3 Others 9/4*
Reading *(Loaned on 5/2/1999) FL 6/1*
Luton T *(Loaned on 25/3/1999) FL 7+1/4*
Luton T *(Loaned on 26/11/1999) FL 3+1/1*
Luton T *(Free on 1/7/2002) FL 30+2/15 FLC 1/1 FAC 1/1 Others 2/2*
Queens Park Rgrs *(£50,000 on 22/8/2003) FL 26+15/10 FAC 1+1 Others 1+2/1*
Rotherham U *(Loaned on 24/3/2005) FL 5/1*

THORPE Lee Anthony
Born: Wolverhampton, 14 December 1975
Height: 6'1" **Weight:** 12.4
Lee worked tirelessly up front for Bristol Rovers last term, creating many chances for his colleagues through his hard work and physical strength. In February he moved on to join promotion-chasing Swansea City, initially on loan before signing a more permanent deal. He netted against one of his former clubs, Leyton Orient, after coming off the bench and by the end of the season he had added two more goals as the Swans achieved an automatic promotion place.
Blackpool *(From trainee on 18/7/1994) FL 2+10 FLC 0+1 FAC 1 Others 1*
Lincoln C *(Free on 4/8/1997) FL 183+9/58 FLC 5+1/1 FAC 14/1 Others 9+1/7*
Leyton Orient *(Free on 3/5/2002) FL 42+13/12 FLC 2/1 FAC 1 Others 1+1*
Grimsby T *(Loaned on 6/2/2004) FL 5+1*
Bristol Rov *(Free on 12/3/2004) FL 25+10/4 FLC 1/1 FAC 0+1 Others 4/1*
Swansea C *(Loaned on 8/2/2005) FL 9+6/3*

[TIAGO] MENDES TIAGO Cardoso
Born: Viana do Castelo, Portugal, 2 May 1981
Height: 6'0" **Weight:** 11.7
Club Honours: FLC '05; PL '05
International Honours: Portugal: 15
This neat midfielder acclimatised very quickly to the demands of English football and had an excellent first season for Chelsea. Tiago obviously made a deep impression on Jose Mourinho as he inspired Benfica to inflict a rare domestic defeat over his all-conquering Porto side in the Portuguese Cup final. Chiefly employed on the right of a midfield three at Benfica, Tiago had a reputation as a defensive player but he likes to support the forwards and scored valuable pre-Christmas goals against Crystal Palace, Fulham and Bolton Wanderers. However, he saved the best till last with a sensational 30-yard pile driver in the penultimate Premiership match at Old Trafford which beat the 'keeper all ends up. A squad member in Portugal's Euro 2004 runners-up team, he formed a good partnership with Frank Lampard and Claude Makelele in Chelsea's engine room which developed into a formidable unit as the season progressed.
Chelsea *(£10,000,000 from Benfica, ex Sporting Braga, on 10/8/2004) PL 21+13/4 FLC 4 FAC 2 Others 4+7*

TIATTO Daniele (Danny) Amadio
Born: Melbourne, Australia, 22 May 1973
Height: 5'7" **Weight:** 12.0
Club Honours: Div 1 '02
International Honours: Australia: 23; U23
This uncompromising left-sided defender or midfielder took over as club captain of Leicester after the retirement of Matt Elliott. Danny's combative approach saw him fall foul of the officials at times, but he scored his first Foxes' goal in the demolition of neighbours Coventry early in Craig Levein's reign. Danny's appearances were restricted by a broken jaw and occasional hamstring problems, and he continued to represent Australia when fully fit.
Stoke C *(Loaned from FC Baden, Switzerland on 25/11/1997) FL 11+4/1*
Manchester C *(£300,000 from FC Baden, Switzerland on 15/7/1998) P/FL 112+28/3 FLC 10/1 FAC 3+1 Others 3+2*
Leicester C *(Free on 3/8/2004) FL 25+5/1 FLC 1 FAC 3*

TIDMAN Ola
Born: Sweden, 11 May 1979
Height: 6'2" **Weight:** 11.13
International Honours: Sweden: U21-2; Yth
Ola had a brief run in the Sheffield Wednesday line-up last October, but never really impressed sufficiently to make himself a regular choice. The young 'keeper eventually departed during the January transfer window, signing for Danish club FC Midtjylland.
Stockport Co *(Free from La Louviere, Belgium, ex BK Kick, Malmo FF, KAA Gent, on 24/1/2003) FL 18*
Sheffield Wed *(Free on 8/7/2003) FL 12+1 FLC 1 Others 2*

TIERNEY Francis (Fran)
Born: Liverpool, 10 September 1975
Height: 5'10" **Weight:** 11.0
Club Honours: Div 3 '04
International Honours: E: Yth
After spending much of the previous season out with injury, Fran had hoped he would put his problems behind him in 2004-05. However, he managed just a single first-team appearance for Doncaster in the LDV Vans Trophy tie against Hereford before announcing his retirement from the full-time game last December. Fran will always be remembered as the man whose golden goal returned the club to the Football League. Towards the end of the season he linked up with Northwich Victoria in the Conference.
Crewe Alex *(From trainee on 22/3/1993) FL 57+30/10 FLC 6 FAC 1+4 Others 5+6/3*
Notts Co *(Free on 2/7/1998) FL 19+14/4 FLC 0+1 FAC 1+4/1 Others 2 (Freed on 30/6/2000)*
Exeter C *(Free from Witton A on 10/11/2000) FL 4+3/1 FAC 0+1 (Free to Witton A on 1/2/2001)*
Doncaster Rov *(Free on 20/3/2001) FL 10+3/3 FLC 0+1 Others 2/1*

TIERNEY Marc Peter
Born: Prestwich, 23 August 1985
Height: 5'11" **Weight:** 11.2
He had to be patient but this exciting and strong running left back finally made an impact for the Latics last term. After appearing to have little future at the club under Brian Talbot, Marc was loaned to Conference side Carlisle United and offered a permanent move. However, after opting to return to Boundary Park, he suddenly found the first-team door had re-opened. New boss Ronnie Moore liked what he saw and Marc, the brother of Manchester United left back Paul Tierney, displaced Adam Griffin, finishing the season with nine starts in the final ten fixtures.
Oldham Ath *(From juniors on 8/8/2003) FL 7+6 FLC 1 Others 1*

TIERNEY Paul Thomas
Born: Salford, 15 September 1982
Height: 5'10" **Weight:** 12.10
International Honours: RoI: U21-7
This Manchester United reserve defender joined Bradford City on loan mid-way through the 2004-05 season and made his debut three days after Christmas at Torquay. An athletic and very quick left back who likes to get forward, he missed several games after tearing his calf at Sheffield Wednesday, but finished the campaign as a regular member of Colin Todd's defence. Paul subsequently

returned to Old Trafford and was a member of the Reds' second-string that defeated Charlton Athletic to win the FA Premier Reserve League play-off.
Manchester U *(From trainee on 18/7/2000) FLC 1*
Crewe Alex *(Loaned on 8/11/2002) FL 14+3/1 FAC 2 Others 3*
Colchester U *(Loaned on 30/1/2004) FL 2 FAC 1 Others 1*
Bradford C *(Loaned on 21/12/2004) FL 14+2*

TIMLIN Michael Anthony
Born: New Cross, 19 March 1985
Height: 5'9" **Weight:** 11.8
International Honours: RoI: U21-1; Yth
Michael is a promising youngster who made his first and so far only senior appearance for Fulham as a substitute in the Carling Cup tie at Boston last season. For the remainder of the campaign he continued to progress at reserve-team level where he usually operated on the left side of midfield. A combative player with a desire to win, he impressed with a double strike in the 5-1 win over Arsenal reserves.
Fulham *(From trainee on 27/7/2002) FLC 0+1*

TINKLER Mark Roland
Born: Bishop Auckland, 24 October 1974
Height: 5'11" **Weight:** 13.3
Club Honours: FAYC '93
International Honours: E: Yth (UEFA-U18 '93); Sch
The most experienced player on the Hartlepool staff, and a midfield general who always gives his best, this effective midfielder was greatly missed when sidelined with an achilles problem towards the end of the season. A good team player, he has signed a new long-term contract with the club.
Leeds U *(From trainee on 29/11/1991) PL 14+11 FLC 1 Others 0+1*
York C *(£85,000 on 25/3/1997) FL 88+2/8 FLC 6 FAC 5 Others 2*
Southend U *(£40,000 on 13/8/1999) FL 55+1/1 FLC 2+1 FAC 1 Others 1*
Hartlepool U *(Free on 2/11/2000) FL 185+5/33 FLC 6 FAC 11/1 Others 11+2/1*

TINNION Brian
Born: Stanley, 23 February 1968
Height: 6'0" **Weight:** 13.0
Club Honours: AMC '03
Starting the 2004-05 campaign as player-manager, this skilful Bristol City midfielder gave up on the playing side some two-thirds of the way through the season. Whilst his effectiveness on the pitch was compromised to some extent by the passing years, he still looked better than many of those who endeavoured to replace him.
Newcastle U *(From apprentice on 26/2/1986) FL 30+2/2 FLC 5 Others 1+1*
Bradford C *(£150,000 on 9/3/1989) FL 137+8/22 FLC 12/1 FAC 9/4 Others 7+1/2*
Bristol C *(£180,000 on 23/3/1993) FL 415+43/36 FLC 26+2 FAC 28+3/6 Others 23+6*

TINSON Darren Lee
Born: Birmingham, 15 November 1969
Height: 6'0" **Weight:** 13.7
Club Honours: GMVC '97
Darren enjoyed an excellent season at Shrewsbury last term, proving to be a rock in the centre of a four-man defence. Physically strong and very effective in the air, he deservedly won the club's 'Player of the Year' award. He was a near ever-present in the line-up and therefore it was something of a surprise when it was announced he was to be released at the end of the season.
Macclesfield T *(£10,000 from Northwich Vic on 14/2/1996) FL 263/5 FLC 15 FAC 14 Others 5*
Shrewsbury T *(Free on 11/7/2003) FL 42+1 FLC 1 FAC 1 Others 1*

TIPTON Matthew John
Born: Conwy, 29 June 1980
Height: 5'10" **Weight:** 13.8
International Honours: W: U21-6; Yth
Matthew formed a productive strike force with Jon Parkin for Macclesfield last term. A barren spell in November and December coincided with a niggling foot injury, however, on making a full recovery he regained form and finished the season with 14 goals including a hat-trick in the home match against Rochdale. Matthew was appointed team captain in January following the departure of Tommy Widdrington.
Oldham Ath *(From trainee on 1/7/1997) FL 51+61/15 FLC 3+4 FAC 4+7/1 Others 3+3/1*
Macclesfield T *(Free on 13/2/2002) FL 114+17/41 FLC 3+1/1 FAC 8+1/5 Others 6+1/3*

TODD Andrew (Andy) John James
Born: Derby, 21 September 1974
Height: 5'10" **Weight:** 11.10
Club Honours: Div 1 '97, '00
Andy had something of a roller-coaster season at Blackburn last term, for having been distinctly out of favour at the start of the campaign he finished off as team captain. Told at the start of the season that he was not wanted and left out of the pre-season tour he ended up as captain. He was brought into the squad by new boss Mark Hughes and quietly and efficiently settled in. A fine reader of play, seldom out of position, his game is based on strength and his stand-up tackling is as good as any player in the Premiership.
Middlesbrough *(From trainee on 6/3/1992) FL 7+1 FLC 1+1 Others 5*
Swindon T *(Loaned on 27/2/1995) FL 13*
Bolton W *(£250,000 on 1/8/1995) P/FL 66+18/2 FLC 14+5/1 FAC 1 Others 3*
Charlton Ath *(£750,000 on 18/11/1999) P/FL 27+13/1 FLC 4 FAC 6+1*
Grimsby T *(Loaned on 21/2/2002) FL 12/3*
Blackburn Rov *(£750,000 on 31/5/2002) PL 52+5/2 FLC 4 FAC 9 Others 2*
Burnley *(Loaned on 4/9/2003) FL 7 FLC 1*

TOGWELL Samuel (Sam) James
Born: Beaconsfield, 14 October 1984
Height: 5'11" **Weight:** 12.4
This young Crystal Palace defender was unable to break into the Premiership side last term and his first-team football came during loan spells with Oxford and Northampton. Sam impressed as an efficient central defender during his stay at the Kassam Stadium before returning to Selhurst Park. At Sixfields he was used at right back, and proved to be good in the air and useful pushing forward down the flank.
Crystal Palace *(From trainee on 31/8/2004) FL 0+1*
Oxford U *(Loaned on 22/10/2004) FL 3+1 FAC 1*
Northampton T *(Loaned on 24/3/2005) FL 7+1 Others 2*

TOLLEY Jamie Christopher
Born: Ludlow, 12 May 1983
Height: 6'0" **Weight:** 11.3
International Honours: W: U21-12
This battling midfielder had something of a mixed season at Shrewsbury last term, although it was noticeable that when he did not play the team seemed to suffer from his absence. Jamie possesses a great shot and is adept at timing his runs into the box to support the attack, but nevertheless he managed just four goals during the campaign. He also featured at U21 level for Wales during the campaign.
Shrewsbury T *(From trainee on 9/1/2001) FL 112+12/10 FLC 1+2 FAC 3+3/1 Others 7+1/1*

TOMLINSON Ezekiel Jeremiah
Born: Birmingham, 9 November 1985
Height: 5'9" **Weight:** 11.0
After starting the season in West Brom's reserve team, Ezekiel moved on to Stockport on transfer-deadline day. He went straight into the squad to face Huddersfield Town the following day

when he replaced Keith Briggs at half time and showed some nice touches during the 5-3 defeat. The young midfielder went on to feature in a handful of games for the League One strugglers before the end of the campaign.
Stockport Co *(From trainee at West Bromwich A on 18/3/2005) FL 2+3*

TONER Ciaran
Born: Craigavon, 30 June 1981
Height: 6'1" **Weight:** 12.4
International Honours: NI: 2; U21-17; Yth; Sch
This left-sided midfield man struggled to get into the Lincoln City starting line-up early in the 2004-05 season, but took his chance when injuries created an opening. He had an excellent spell early in the new year contributing to the team with his skills on the ball. Ciaran was later loaned out to Cambridge United and was released by the Imps at the end of the season.
Tottenham H *(From trainee on 14/7/1999)*
Peterborough U *(Loaned on 21/12/2001) FL 6 FAC 1*
Bristol Rov *(Free on 28/3/2002) FL 6*
Leyton Orient *(Free on 7/5/2002) FL 41+11/2 FLC 2 FAC 1 Others 2*
Lincoln C *(Free on 4/8/2004) FL 10+5/2 FLC 0+1 Others 1*
Cambridge U *(Loaned on 19/3/2005) FL 6+2*

TONGE Dale
Born: Doncaster, 7 May 1985
Height: 5'10" **Weight:** 10.6
Dale stepped up to the professional ranks with Barnsley in the summer of 2004 and broke into the first-team at the end of October, making his senior debut at home to Swindon after the Reds' midfield was decimated by injuries and suspensions. He showed plenty of potential, working hard to change the team's fortunes around before losing his place following a change in management. Further injuries saw him return to the side at right back when he again coped admirably.
Barnsley *(From trainee on 2/7/2004) FL 14+1 FAC 0+1*

TONGE Michael William
Born: Manchester, 7 April 1983
Height: 6'0" **Weight:** 11.10
International Honours: E: U21-2; Yth
Michael had something of a quiet season in 2004-05. A regular in the Blades' line-up, despite missing several games due to ankle injuries, he was used as an attacking midfielder, either in the centre or wide on the left. When at his best his passing created good

Anthony Tonkin (left)

penings and he was dangerous when ttacking down the left flank, producing earching crosses.
heffield U (From trainee on 16/3/2001) FL 47+9/15 FLC 10+1/3 FAC 14 Others 3

TONKIN Anthony Richard
Born: Newlyn, 17 January 1980
Height: 5'11" **Weight:** 12.2
Club Honours: FAT '02
A natural left-sided player, Anthony was he most regular occupant of the left-back position for Crewe Alexandra last erm. He is an assured performer who njoys linking up with the attack whenever possible. However, Anthony is till waiting to score his first goal for the lub.
Stockport Co (£50,000 from Yeovil T on 26/9/2002) FL 23+1 FLC 1 FAC 2
Crewe Alex (£150,000 on 26/8/2003) FL 53+8 FLC 2+1 FAC 1

TORGHELLE Sandor
Born: Budapest, Hungary, 5 May 1982
Height: 6'1" **Weight:** 13.6
International Honours: Hungary: 13
This talented international striker was expected to make a big impact at Selhurst Park last season, but injuries and a loss of form saw him fade from the cene and he only managed a total of hree Premiership starts. His only first-eam goal came in the Carling Cup tie against Charlton, although he netted a hat-trick for the reserves in the 8-0 win over Portsmouth in April.
Crystal Palace (Signed from MTK Hungaria, Hungary on 6/8/2004) PL 3+9 FLC 3/1

TORPEY Stephen (Steve) David James
Born: Islington, 8 December 1970
Height: 6'3" **Weight:** 14.6
Club Honours: AMC '94
Scunthorpe target man Steve had a mixed 2004-05 campaign in helping his club win promotion to League One. A pre-season knee injury ruled him out of the first two months of the campaign but he returned in excellent goal-scoring form, netting eight goals in 11 games. He scored twice on his return from suspension in January but then endured a barren run of 17 games without a goal, which was finally ended when he netted a double in the victory over Bristol Rovers in the penultimate match of the season. Still strong in the air and good at holding the ball up, Steve finished the campaign with 13 goals to his name.
Millwall (From trainee on 14/2/1989) FL 3+4 FLC 0+1
Bradford C (£70,000 on 21/11/1990) FL 86+10/22 FLC 6 FAC 2+1 Others 8/6
Swansea C (£80,000 on 3/8/1993) FL 151+11/44 FLC 9+2/2 FAC 10/5 Others 15+3/5
Bristol C (£400,000 on 8/8/1997) FL 53+17/13 FLC 4+1/1 FAC 3 Others 3+1
Notts Co (Loaned on 7/8/1998) FL 4+2/1 FLC 1+1/1
Scunthorpe U (£175,000 on 3/2/2000) FL 193+6/57 FLC 5/2 FAC 18/7 Others 9+2/5

TOURE Kolo Abib
Born: Ivory Coast, 19 March 1981
Height: 5'10" **Weight:** 11.13
Club Honours: CS '02, '04; FAC '03, '05; PL '04
International Honours: Ivory Coast
After setting such high standards during 2003-04 season Kolo made slightly less progress last term. His form was not helped by Arsenal's numerous injuries at centre back where he played alongside a succession of different partners. Nevertheless he still managed to make the highest number of appearances of all the outfield players at Highbury. He was partnered with Philippe Senderos for the final months of the season and the pair struck up a good understanding as they achieved nine clean sheets together, including the FA Cup final success against Manchester United.
Arsenal (Signed from ASEC Mimosa, Ivory Coast on 18/2/2002) PL 80+18/3 FLC 3 FAC 12+4/2 Others 23+5/1

TOWNSEND Luke Allen
Born: Guildford, 28 September 1986
Height: 6'0" **Weight:** 11.10
This young Queen's Park Rangers striker progressed to first-team level last season after working his way through the reserve and youth teams at Loftus Road. He featured from the bench in the League One fixtures against Burnley and Wolves in April. Earlier in the season Luke was loaned out to Maidenhead United to gain experience of first-team football.
Queens Park Rgrs (Trainee) FL 0+2

TOWNSON Kevin
Born: Liverpool, 19 April 1983
Height: 5'8" **Weight:** 10.3
International Honours: E: Yth
Despite a couple of goals in Rochdale's pre-season tour to Scotland, Kevin made just one early-season appearance in the absence of new striker Paul Tait. After making it on to the substitutes' bench a couple of weeks later, he was relegated permanently to the reserves, spending a month on loan at Scarborough. On transfer-deadline day he moved on loan to Macclesfield to provide cover for the established forwards. There were few opportunities for Kevin but he was called into action during Jon Parkin's suspension when he provided a lively presence.
Rochdale (From Everton juniors on 6/7/2000) FL 41+61/25 FLC 0+3/3 FAC 2+4/1 Others 5+1/1
Macclesfield T (Loaned on 24/3/2005) FL 2+4 Others 1+1

TRAORE Djimi
Born: Paris, France, 1 March 1980
Height: 6'3" **Weight:** 13.10
Club Honours: FLC '03; UEFACL '05
International Honours: Mali; France: U21; Yth
After two months on the fringe of the Liverpool first team Djimi was drafted into the left-back slot when Jon Arne Riise was pushed further forward, and held down his place to the end of the season apart from a short absence with a thigh injury in March. Djimi's form blossomed in the second half of the campaign and in the epic Champions' Cup matches with Juventus and Chelsea he was a tower of strength, in particular when subduing former European Footballer of the Year Pavel Nedved in the second leg of the Juventus tie in Turin. The European Cup final in Istanbul was a microcosm of his season: overwhelmed by a stronger AC Milan team in the first half he rallied in the second half and his goal-line clearance at the end of normal time kept Liverpool in the game after their heroic come-back in the second half.
Liverpool (£550,000 from Laval, France on 18/2/1999) PL 63+10 FLC 12+1 FAC 3 Others 26+2/1

TREMARCO Carl Philip
Born: Liverpool, 11 October 1985
Height: 5'11" **Weight:** 12.3
Carl is a calm and classy defender whose maturity belies his age, but was unfortunate in that the remarkable form and staying power of Gareth Roberts in the left-back berth restricted his first-team chances in the 2004-05 season. Content to plug away as one of the cornerstones in a young reserve team, he finally got his chance right at the end of the season and coped admirably in Roberts' absence. Carl plays with great composure and impressed in his first-team outings.
Tranmere Rov (From trainee on 2/4/2004) FL 2+1 FAC 1

TROLLOPE Paul Jonathan
Born: Swindon, 3 June 1972
Height: 6'0" **Weight:** 12.6
Club Honours: Div 2 '99
International Honours: W: 9; B-1

Djimi Traore

This experienced left-sided midfielder linked up with his former manager Ian Atkins at Bristol Rovers last term. Paul was a regular in the side in the first half of the campaign when he looked comfortable on the ball and his accurate passing was a real asset in midfield. Unfortunately he fell out of favour in the final third of the season when he rarely featured and was eventually placed on the transfer list.

Swindon T *(From trainee on 23/12/1989)*
Torquay U *(Free on 26/3/1992) FL 103+3/16 FLC 9+1/1 FAC 7 Others 8+1*
Derby Co *(£100,000 on 16/12/1994) P/FL 47+18/5 FLC 3+2/1 FAC 3+1*
Grimsby T *(Loaned on 30/8/1996) FL 6+1/1*
Crystal Palace *(Loaned on 11/10/1996) FL 0+9*
Fulham *(£600,000 on 28/11/1997) FL 54+22/5 FLC 9+2 FAC 3+5 Others 4/1*
Coventry C *(Free on 22/3/2002) FL 5+1*
Northampton T *(Free on 31/7/2002) FL 84/8 FLC 3 FAC 7 Others 5+1*
Bristol Rov *(Free on 5/7/2004) FL 26+4/2 FLC 2 FAC 2 Others 5+1*

TRUNDLE Lee Christopher

Born: Liverpool, 10 October 1976
Height: 6'0" **Weight:** 13.3

A knee injury delayed Lee's start to the 2004-05 season for Swansea, but after returning to the squad he scored against Cheltenham at the Vetch Field after coming off the bench. He displayed excellent form from then on, and a tally of 22 League goals by the end of the campaign made him the first Swans' player since Bob Latchford in 1982-83 to score more than 20 League goals in a season. An exciting left-footed striker, Lee was selected by his fellow professionals for the PFA divisional team of the season for the second year in succession.

Wrexham *(£60,000 from Rhyl, ex Burscough, Chorley, Stalybridge Celtic, Southport, on 16/2/2001) FL 73+21/27 FLC 0+2 FAC 1 Others 4+1/3*
Swansea C *(Free on 14/7/2003) FL 70+3/38 FLC 2 FAC 10/6 Others 1+1*

TUDGAY Marcus

Born: Shoreham, 3 February 1983
Height: 6'3" **Weight:** 13.2

Marcus had his best scoring season to date for Derby County and was at his most effective before a shoulder injury interrupted his progress. After that, he suffered from his own versatility and the use of Grzegorz Rasiak as a lone striker. Ideally, Marcus needs to be one of two in attack because he can hold the ball and has the intelligence to link with partners. He does an effective job wide in midfield but is not happy as a solitary striker. The essence of his game is combination but he continues to make significant progress.

Derby Co *(From trainee on 16/7/2002) FL 42+29/15 FLC 1 FAC 4+1/1*

TUDOR Shane Anthony

Born: Wolverhampton, 10 February 1982
Height: 5'8" **Weight:** 11.2

Shane had something of a disappointing season for Cambridge United last term when he was disrupted by a series of injuries. A hard-working midfield player who also featured on the wing, Shane finished the campaign as the U's joint-top scorer with a total of seven goals in all competitions.

Wolverhampton W *(From trainee on 9/8/1999) FL 0+1*
Cambridge U *(Free on 22/11/2001) FL 109+12/21 FLC 4/1 FAC 11/2 Others 12/2*

[TUGAY] KERIMOGLU Tugay

Born: Istanbul, Turkey, 24 August 1970
Height: 5'9" **Weight:** 11.6
Club Honours: SPD '00; SC '00; FLC '02
International Honours: Turkey: 92

With increasing years Tugay was relegated to a bit-part role for Blackburn last season, being used as a deputy or brought from the bench when the team needed someone who could hold the ball and pass it around. He remained the most creative player in the squad and his ability to keep the ball was invaluable when the club needed to defend a lead, even if the consistency of his tackling was variable. With plenty more to offer he signed an extension to his contract at Ewood Park.

Glasgow Rgrs *(Signed from Galatasaray, Turkey on 15/1/2000) SL 26+16/4 SLC 2+1 SC 3+4 Others 6*
Blackburn Rov *(£1,300,000 on 20/7/2001) PL 107+20/5 FLC 11+1 FAC 10+2/1 Others 6*

TURLEY William (Billy) Lee

Born: Wolverhampton, 15 July 1973
Height: 6'4" **Weight:** 15.0
Club Honours: NC '01; Div 3 '03

In the period up to Christmas this experienced shot-stopper was unquestionably on course to become Rushden's 'Player of the Season' for 2004-05 as he produced some stunning performances despite the club's slide towards another relegation battle. However, it all went wrong for Billy at the turn of the year when some well-publicised off-the-field problems saw him receive a lengthy ban from the FA and immediately afterwards he left the Nene Park club.

Northampton T *(Free from Evesham on 10/7/1995) FL 28 FAC 2 Others 4*
Leyton Orient *(Loaned on 5/2/1998) FL 14*
Rushden & Diamonds *(£135,000 on 15/6/1999) FL 133+1 FLC 6 FAC 6 Others 5*

TURNBULL Paul Daniel

Born: Handforth, 23 January 1989
Height: 5'11" **Weight:** 11.0

Paul became the youngest-ever player to make a League appearance for Stockport when he replaced Stuart Barlow after 81 minutes of the League One clash with Wrexham at Edgeley Park in April when aged just 16 years and 97 days. Incredibly, the burly forward had made just one appearance for the youth team and two appearances for the reserves before his big moment in the first team. He will be hoping to continue his progress at Edgeley Park in the 2005-06 season.

Stockport Co *(Associated Schoolboy) FL 0+1*

TURNBULL Ross

Born: Bishop Auckland, 4 January 1985
Height: 6'4" **Weight:** 13.5
International Honours: E: Yth

This Middlesbrough 'keeper answered an emergency call from Bradford City on the eve of the 2004-05 season after the arrival of Paul Henderson and Donovan Ricketts was delayed by red tape. He played a couple of times for the Bantams, then soon after returning to the Riverside he went out on loan to Barnsley. Ross went straight into the first team and produced a string of excellent performances before his season was curtailed after he suffered a broken hand during training.

Middlesbrough *(From trainee on 6/7/2002)*
Darlington *(Loaned on 14/11/2003) FL 1*
Barnsley *(Loaned on 22/4/2004) FL 3*
Bradford C *(Loaned on 6/8/2004) FL 2*
Barnsley *(Loaned on 6/10/2004) FL 23 FAC 1*

TURNBULL Stephen

Born: South Shields, 7 January 1987
Height: 5'10" **Weight:** 11.0

An industrious midfielder, Stephen was captain of the successful Hartlepool junior side which had a great season in 2004-05, winning the Durham Challenge Cup. While his twin brother Phil attracted the attention of the England youth-team set-up, it was Stephen who got a brief taste of first-team football. He was named among the substitutes for five consecutive games, and acquitted himself well in two half-hour appearances.

Hartlepool U *(Trainee) FL 0+2*

TURNER Iain Ross

Born: Stirling, 26 January 1984
Height: 6'3" **Weight:** 12.10
International Honours: S: U21-2

This talented young 'keeper was a regular

in Everton's second string last term and in March he joined Doncaster Rovers on loan to gain further experience of senior football. Due to the fact that both Rovers' regular goalkeepers were out of action Iain featured regularly during his stay at Belle Vue. He also represented Scotland at U21 level during the campaign.
Stirling A *(Signed from Riverside BC on 26/8/2000) SL 13*
Everton *(Signed on 16/1/2003)*
Doncaster Rov *(Loaned on 18/3/2005) FL 8*

TURNER John Andrew James
Born: Harrow, 12 February 1986
Height: 6'2" **Weight:** 11.0
John made good progress at Cambridge United last season, featuring in almost every first-team game, although often from the substitutes' bench, and finishing the campaign as the club's joint-top scorer in League Two matches. The highlight of his season came when he netted a hat-trick against Rushden in November, the first treble by a U's player for over four years. A promising young striker who is good in the air and capable with both feet, he was one of several out-of-contract players at the Abbey Stadium whose future had yet to be determined at the time of writing.
Cambridge U *(From trainee on 3/12/2003) FL 33+42/10 FLC 1 FAC 3/2 Others 1+1*

TURNER Michael Thomas
Born: Lewisham, 9 November 1983
Height: 6'4" **Weight:** 12.6
A quiet, unassuming centre half, Michael initially joined Brentford on loan for a month and this was extended twice before he signed permanently. He formed an excellent central defensive partnership with Sam Sodje and only missed out on being ever-present in the League when he was rested for the final game. He scored one goal, a cracking right-footer into the roof of the net against Tranmere and was named as the Brentford 'Players' Player of the Year'.
Charlton Ath *(From trainee on 6/3/2001)*
Leyton Orient *(Loaned on 26/3/2003) FL 7/1*
Brentford *(Signed on 6/8/2004) FL 45/1 FAC 8 Others 2*

TYLER Mark Richard
Born: Norwich, 2 April 1977
Height: 6'0" **Weight:** 12.9
International Honours: E: Yth
In his tenth season at Peterborough this experienced 'keeper was an ever-present in League One fixtures and the only time he was absent from the line-up came when he was injured during the warm-up of the FA Cup tie at MK Dons. Now third in the all-time list of appearance-makers for Posh, Mark remains a fine shot-stopper and has full command of his penalty box.
Peterborough U *(From trainee on 7/12/1994) FL 314+1 FLC 13 FAC 24 Others 20*

TYSON Nathan
Born: Reading, 4 May 1982
Height: 5'10" **Weight:** 11.12
International Honours: E: Yth
Nathan had an excellent campaign as Wycombe's main striker in 2004-05, netting 22 League Two goals, just one short of equalling the club's record in a season, this in spite of a barren two-month spell early on. His tally included two hat-tricks, in the games at Lincoln and Kidderminster. Typically he is at his most dangerous receiving the ball wide on the left flank, outpacing the defence with his amazing pace, and either delivering a perfectly weighted cross or cutting in to shoot on goal. Not surprisingly he was voted 'Player of the Season' by the club's supporters.
Reading *(From trainee on 18/3/2000) FL 9+24/1 FLC 0+2 FAC 2+1 Others 0+2*
Swansea C *(Loaned on 30/8/2001) FL 7+4/1*
Cheltenham T *(Loaned on 22/3/2002) FL 1+7/1*
Wycombe W *(Free on 2/1/2004) FL 61+2/31 FLC 1 FAC 2 Others 0+2*

Nathan Tyson

UV

'GARTE Juan
orn: San Sebastian, Spain, 7 November
980
eight: 5'10" **Weight:** 11.11
ub Honours: AMC '05
nis exciting striker had a spell with
onference South outfit Dorchester Town
the early part of the 2004-05
ampaign where he scored six goals in
even games. Such prolific form attracted
ne attention of more senior clubs and
fter a try-out with Wrexham's reserves
e signed for the Racecourse club. Juan
ot into the starting line-up at the end of
ovember and from then onwards he
elighted the fans with his goal-scoring
xploits. He accumulated some 26 goals
all competitions, including four hat-
icks, all away from home. He also
qualled a club record when he netted
ve times in the amazing 6-4 win at
artlepool in March.
***/rexham** (Free from Dorchester T, ex Real
ociedad, Barakaldo, on 1/11/2004) FL
3+7/17 FAC 1+1 Others 5+1/6*

HLENBEEK Gustav (Gus)
einier
orn: Paramaribo, Surinam, 20 August
970
eight: 5'10" **Weight:** 12.6
lub Honours: Div 2 '99
us arrived at Wycombe Wanderers in
ne summer of 2004 with a reputation as
pacy right back who likes to push
orward at every opportunity. He did not
isappoint and his thrusting runs quickly
ndeared himself to the fans. New
nanager John Gorman eventually settled
n him playing a wide-right midfield role
o make best use of his attacking skills,
nd he responded with three smartly
aken goals late in the season.
***pswich T** (£100,000 from Tops SV, Holland,
x Ajax, Cambuur, on 11/8/1995) FL 77+12/4
LC 5+3 FAC 4+3 Others 7+1*
***ulham** (Free on 22/7/1998) FL 22+17/1 FLC
+1 FAC 3+2 Others 1*
***heffield U** (Free on 10/8/2000) FL 47+4
LC 5 FAC 3*
***Valsall** (Loaned on 28/3/2002) FL 5*
***radford C** (Free on 9/8/2002) FL 42/1 FLC
FAC 1*
***hesterfield** (Free on 5/8/2003) FL 36+1
Others 1*
***Vycombe W** (Free on 30/7/2004) FL 36+6/4
LC 1 FAC 2 Others 1*

LLATHORNE Robert (Rob)
orn: Wakefield, 11 October 1971
eight: 5'8" **Weight:** 11.3
nternational Honours: E: Yth
This experienced left back was a regular in the Notts County line-up last term showing tremendous commitment by playing on through an injury. He eventually succumbed to surgery, which caused him to miss the closing stages of the campaign. Rob always shows plenty of ability when pushing forward and showed some fine form throughout the campaign.
***Norwich C** (From trainee on 6/7/1990) P/FL 86+8/7 FLC 10+2/1 FAC 7+1 Others 1 (Free to Osasuna, Spain during 1996 close season)*
***Leicester C** (£600,000 on 18/2/1997) PL 28+3/1 FLC 8+1 FAC 2/1*
***Sheffield U** (Free, following an injury and trials at Huddersfield T, Real Zaragoza, Tenerife, Newcastle U, on 1/12/2000) FL 39+1 FLC 2 FAC 2 (Freed on 8/5/2003)*
***Northampton T** (Free, via trials at Stoke C, Walsall, Derby Co, on 20/2/2004) FL 13/1 Others 2*
***Notts Co** (Free on 6/7/2004) FL 34+2 FLC 2/1 FAC 1*

UNDERWOOD Paul Victor
Born: Wimbledon, 16 August 1973
Height: 5'11" **Weight:** 12.8
Club Honours: NC '01; Div 3 '03; Div 1 '05
International Honours: E: SP-4
This cultured left-sided player provided

Paul Underwood

balance to the Luton Town formation last season. Paul was a regular in the side throughout the campaign, the key feature of his game being an ability to deliver corners and free kicks with accuracy. He produced a 'Man of the Match' performance in the opening game against Oldham, when he also scored his team's first goal.
Rushden & Diamonds *(£50,000 from Enfield, ex Kingstonian, Molesey, Sutton U, Carshalton Ath, on 6/6/1997) FL 110/1 FLC 4 FAC 6 Others 6*
Luton T *(Free on 25/3/2004) FL 38/5 FLC 1 FAC 3*

UNSWORTH David Gerald
Born: Chorley, 16 October 1973
Height: 6'1" **Weight:** 14.2
Club Honours: FAC '95; CS '95
International Honours: E: 1; U21-6; Yth
David's first season on the South Coast proved to be something of a mixed bag, for after starring in the first half of the campaign he fell out of favour. Although used in a variety of defensive and midfield positions, his best role was in the centre of defence. However, he dropped out of the reckoning at Fratton Park in January and was shipped out on loan to Ipswich. He made an immediate impact in his debut game at Sheffield United when he cut in from the left wing and smashed the ball into the net to open the scoring. He kept his place until the end of the regular season and although his presence strengthened the defence overall, he never reached the heights of that first performance. The loan agreement did not cover the play-off matches so he returned to Fratton Park once the season had ended.
Everton *(From trainee on 25/6/1992) P/FL 108+8/11 FLC 5+2 FAC 7 Others 4/1*
West Ham U *(£1,000,000 + on 18/8/1997) PL 32/2 FLC 5 FAC 4*
Aston Villa *(£3,000,000 on 28/7/1998)*
Everton *(£3,000,000 on 22/8/1998) PL 164+24/23 FLC 10+1/1 FAC 16+1/4*
Portsmouth *(Free on 16/7/2004) PL 15/2 FLC 3 FAC 1*
Ipswich T *(Loaned on 23/1/2005) FL 16/1*

UNSWORTH Lee Peter
Born: Eccles, 25 February 1973
Height: 5'11" **Weight:** 11.8
Lee enjoyed another steady campaign for Bury last term, despite once again being affected by injuries. He started the season playing as a centre half in the Shakers' back five, but then reverted to right wing back after Matt Barrass suffered an injury. Lee lost his place briefly during January but returned to the side until suffering a groin strain during a home game against

Ryan Valentine

rimsby in March. It was an injury, which ffectively ended his season seven games arly.
rewe Alex (Signed from Ashton U on 0/2/1995) FL 93+33 FLC 10+1/1 FAC 5+1/1 thers 8+2
ury (Free on 4/8/2000) FL 141+7/6 FLC 7 AC 7 Others 9

IPSON Matthew James
orn: Stowmarket, 18 April 1979
eight: 6'1" **Weight:** 11.4
lub Honours: PL '02
ternational Honours: E: 7; U21-11; th
rmingham City's vice-captain, Matthew ppeared in more games than any other utfield player last term. Good in the air, ery quick and strong in the tackle, he ad an excellent season, reaching a high vel of consistency alongside Kenny unningham in the heart of the defence. the pivotal 'derby' win at Villa he was agnificent, repelling everything that ame his way.
uton T (From trainee on 24/4/1996) FL 0+1 thers 1
rsenal (£1,000,000 on 14/5/1997) PL 0+14 FLC 8 FAC 3+1 Others 8+2
ottingham F (Loaned on 8/12/2000) FL 1
rystal Palace (Loaned on 2/3/2001) FL 7
eading (Loaned on 6/9/2002) FL 13+1 .C 1/1
irmingham C (£2,000,000 + on 3/1/2003) PL 80/2 FLC 3 FAC 4

VALENTINE Ryan David
orn: Wrexham, 19 August 1982
eight: 5'10" **Weight:** 11.11
ternational Honours: W: U21-8; Yth
yan was a first choice at full back for arlington up until last December, but hereafter was mainly used as a ubstitute. He can perform on either side f the defence and is quick into the ackle, and particularly effective pushing orward on the overlap and linking up ith midfield. He has now completed ell over 100 games for the Quakers and dded a single goal, netting against ambridge United in August.
verton (From trainee on 1/9/1999)
arlington (Free on 8/8/2002) FL 108+11/4 .C 3 FAC 5 Others 3

VALERO Vincente **Xavier Xavi)**
orn: Castellon, Spain, 28 February 1973
eight: 6'5" **Weight:** 14.2
his giant goalkeeper arrived at Wrexham round the same time as Juan Ugarte, ut had rather different fortunes at the acecourse. He came as a free agent, but id not impress during three appearances or the Dragons and after being replaced by youngster Michael Jones at half time in the game at Chesterfield he left the club. He subsequently returned to Spain and signed for Recreativo Huelva during the January transfer window.
***Wrexham** (Free from Ciudad Murcia, ex Real Mallorca, CD Logrones, Castellon, on 10/1/2005) FL 3*

VALOIS Jean-Louis
Born: Saint-Priest, France, 15 October 1973
Height: 5'11" **Weight:** 11.8
Jean-Louis arrived at Burnley after a brief spell with Clyde, and soon made an impression with his silky skills on the ball, trickery and tremendous shooting ability. On his day, he could be the star man capable of opening up the opposition, and, as at Derby, finding the net with an unstoppable free kick. At other times, he could be a virtual passenger watching the game pass him by, but his crowd-pleasing attributes made him a popular figure with the Turf Moor faithful. With consistency he could be an asset to any club at any level, but the lack of it made him something of a luxury, which is perhaps why he was not retained at the season's end.
***Luton T** (Free from Lille, France ex Auxerre, Gueugnon on 21/9/2001) FL 32+2/6*
***Heart of Midlothian** (Free on 2/8/2002) SL 42+7/2 SLC 4+1/2 SC 1 Others 3+1*
***Clyde** (Free on 31/8/2004) Others 1/1*
***Burnley** (Free on 10/9/2004) FL 18+12/3 FLC 2+1/1 FAC 3+1*

VAN DAMME Jelle
Born: Lokeren, Belgium, 10 October 1983
Height: 6'4" **Weight:** 13.1
International Honours: Belgium: 7
Barely out of his teens, Jelle cuts an imposing figure at left back. He was an instant hit with the St Mary's crowd, coming on as a substitute in the pre-season friendly against Chievo Verona, putting himself about with gusto and scoring with a cracking free kick. In his few appearances after that he demonstrated a reckless attacking streak, which may be why he found himself as fourth-choice left back, behind new signing Olivier Bernard, Danny Higginbotham and Graeme Le Saux.
***Southampton** (£2,500,000 from Ajax, Holland on 5/7/2004) PL 4+2 FLC 2+1*

VAN DER SAR Edwin
Born: Leiden, Holland, 29 October 1970
Height: 6'5" **Weight:** 13.6
International Honours: Holland: 100
Edwin enjoyed yet another consistent season between the posts for Fulham last term. Although unlucky to miss a number of games due to some fine displays from Mark Crossley, once back in the side he kept his place for the rest of the campaign. An effective shot-stopper who shone in one-on-one situations, Edwin enjoyed outstanding performances at West Brom and Blackburn, when he saved a penalty. He also continued to be a first choice for Holland, making a number of appearances in World Cup qualifiers.
***Fulham** (£7,000,000 from Juventus, Italy, ex Noordwijk, Ajax, on 10/8/2001) PL 126+1 FLC 1 FAC 15 Others 11*

VAN HEUSDEN Arjan
Born: Alphen, Holland, 11 December 1972
Height: 6'3" **Weight:** 14.7
Torquay's decision to bring in Bert Bossu on a long-term loan during the close season deal was effectively a vote of no confidence in this big 'keeper and he made arrangements to bring forward his retirement and return to Holland. With Bossu quickly returning to Gillingham and Kevin Dearden suffering injury problems, Arjan agreed to stay on until a new custodian was found and performed reliably until succumbing to a thigh injury which ruled him out of action for a period following which his contract was settled up.
***Port Vale** (£4,500 from VV Noordwijk, Holland on 15/8/1994) FL 27 FLC 4 Others 2*
***Oxford U** (Loaned on 26/9/1997) FL 11 FLC 2*
***Cambridge U** (Free on 4/8/1998) FL 41+1 FLC 6 FAC 1 Others 4*
***Exeter C** (Free on 31/7/2000) FL 74 FLC 2 FAC 4 Others 1*
***Mansfield T** (Free on 27/9/2002) FL 5*
***Torquay U** (Free on 1/11/2002) FL 47 FLC 2 FAC 2 Others 1*

VAN NISTELROOY Rutgerus (Ruud) Johannes Martinus
Born: Oss, Holland, 1 July 1976
Height: 6'2" **Weight:** 12.13
Club Honours: PL '03; CS '03; FAC '04
International Honours: Holland: 44
An archetypal centre forward who is blessed with all-round technique, powerful in the air, and packing a fearsome shot in either foot, Ruud had a somewhat frustrating start to his campaign. Having made an appearance against Bolton in the Premiership at the Reebok, just ten weeks after a hernia operation, he celebrated his 29th European goal against Olympique Lyon to beat Denis Law's old record whilst still not fully match fit. After notching his first Premiership goal of the campaign at

Edwin Van Der Sar

obin Van Persie

Spurs in September, both he and Wayne Rooney ended Arsenal's 49-game unbeaten run at Old Trafford in October. Ruud then entered centre stage by scoring all four goals in United's 4-1 home win against Sparta Prague in the Champions' League in November. It was his first-ever hat-trick in Europe, and his sixth in total for the Reds. The last United player to notch four in Europe, incidentally, was Denis Law against Waterford in 1968-69. Having then scored against Olympique Lyon in Sir Alex Ferguson's 1000th match, Ruud continued to notch important goals despite being sidelined by constant injury problems. Unable to find the magic touch in the vital Champions' League against AC Milan, his two goals against Newcastle in the FA Cup semi-final at the Millennium Stadium gave the Reds their only realistic chance of silverware. Although such hopes were scuppered against Arsenal in the final in May, at least Ruud gave ample warning that he was back to his best.

***Manchester U** (£19,000,000 from PSV Eindhoven, Holland, ex Den Bosch, Heerenveen, on 5/7/2001) PL 109+6/74 FLC 4/1 FAC 9+3/14 Others 39+2/37*

VAN PERSIE Robin

Born: Rotterdam, Holland, 6 August 1983
Height: 6'1" **Weight:** 11.2
Club Honours: CS '04; FAC '05
International Honours: Holland: 2; U21

Another of Arsenal's young guns, Robin arrived at Highbury with a reputation for his ability and passionate nature. He scored his first goal for the club in the 2-1 win at Manchester City in the Carling Cup and was on target in the Champions' League victory over Rosenborg. He also announced himself to the Arsenal faithful in spectacular style when he grabbed an injury-time equaliser in the 2-2 home draw with Southampton. Robin found the net ten times in all from only 18 starts including two clinical strikes in the FA Cup semi-final victory over Blackburn Rovers. Robin has fantastic natural ability and a confident approach in front of goal. His season ended in glorious style as he successfully converted his penalty in the shoot-out success over Manchester United in the FA Cup final.

***Arsenal** (£2,750,000 from Feyenoord, Holland on 17/5/2004) PL 12+14/5 FLC 3/1 FAC 3+2/3 Others 0+7/1*

VARNEY Luke Ivan

Born: Leicester, 28 September 1982
Height: 5'11" **Weight:** 11.7

A young striker with a fine turn of speed, Luke featured in over half of Crewe Alexandra's first-team fixtures last term, scoring four goals. He has been making steady progress since becoming a first-team regular. Hard working and keen to learn, his goal output will undoubtedly increase with experience.

***Crewe Alex** (Signed from Quorn on 25/3/2003) FL 22+12/5 FLC 0+1 FAC 2*

VASSELL Darius

Born: Birmingham, 13 June 1980
Height: 5'7" **Weight:** 12.0
International Honours: E: 22; U21-11; Yth

Darius is a quick and skilful striker who loves to take on defences, although he has never been a prolific scorer at club level. He scored Villa's first goal of the season at home to Southampton, but in October he was stretchered off against Fulham with a broken ankle. Further injury problems with the reserves during his comeback led to surgery and it was not until the end of February that he returned to first-team duties. He provided a much-needed injection of pace up front, but he only added one more Premiership goal, in the local 'derby' against West Brom in April.

***Aston Villa** (From trainee on 14/4/1998) PL 107+55/35 FLC 10+8/5 FAC 4+4/1 Others 3+1/14*

VAUGHAN Anthony (Tony) John

Born: Manchester, 11 October 1975
Height: 6'1" **Weight:** 11.2
International Honours: E: Yth; Sch

Tony was appointed as Barnsley captain by manager Paul Hart after signing up during the 2004 close season, but struggled to find his form in the early weeks of the campaign. However, the experienced defender soon began to show the full range of his skills. He was always a danger at set pieces and scored four times for the Reds. Unfortunately his season ended early due to an injury.

***Ipswich T** (From trainee on 1/7/1994) P/FL 56+11/3 FLC 4+2 FAC 2 Others 4*
***Manchester C** (£1,350,000 on 9/7/1997) FL 54+4/2 FLC 6+1 FAC 3 Others 3+1*
***Cardiff C** (Loaned on 15/9/1999) FL 14 Others 1*
***Nottingham F** (£350,000 on 8/2/2000) FL 38+5/1 FLC 2 FAC 1*
***Scunthorpe U** (Loaned on 26/3/2002) FL 5*
***Mansfield T** (Loaned on 25/10/2002) FL 4*
***Motherwell** (Loaned on 31/1/2003) SL 12/1 SC 3*
***Mansfield T** (Free on 4/8/2003) FL 32/2 FAC 3*
***Barnsley** (Free on 5/7/2004) FL 25+1/4 FLC 1 Others 1*

VAUGHAN David Owen

Born: Abergele, 18 February 1983
Height: 5'7" **Weight:** 10.10
International Honours: W: 2; U21-7; Yth

After coming up through the youth rank at Crewe, David has progressed to become a very versatile player and can occupy any position on the left-hand side of the team. Last term he was a near ever-present in the Championship fixture and managed to get on the score sheet with more regularity, netting a total of six goals in all.

***Crewe Alex** (From trainee on 6/2/2001) FL 112+9/9 FLC 6 FAC 8/1 Others 2/1*

VAUGHAN James Oliver

Born: Birmingham, 14 July 1988
Height: 5'11" **Weight:** 12.8
International Honours: E: Yth

This young forward announced himself to the football world last April when, on his debut against Crystal Palace, he became the youngest player to appear for Everton's first team at 16 years 271 days and also the Premiership's youngest ever scorer when he netted 11 minutes after coming off the bench. A speedy and powerful presence up front, James has been at the club since he was nine years old and he has scored goals at all levels in that time. He made a further senior appearance at Bolton and also played for England in the European U17 Championships in Italy in May.

***Everton** (Trainee) PL 0+2/1*

VAUGHAN Stephen James

Born: Liverpool, 22 January 1985
Height: 5'6" **Weight:** 11.1

This promising young utility player started the 2004-05 season at right back for Chester before losing his place to Darren Edmondson in September. He briefly returned to the side in January playing in a midfield role, where his ability to pass the ball with either foot came to the fore. Stephen will be looking to establish himself in the starting line-up in 2005-06.

***Liverpool** (From trainee on 18/4/2002)*
***Chester C** (Free on 21/6/2004) FL 14+7 FLC 1 FAC 2 Others 3*

VAZ TE Ricardo Jorge

Born: Lisbon, Portugal, 1 October 1986
Height: 6'2" **Weight:** 12.7
International Honours: Portugal: Yth

A striker of real promise who has proved himself as a consistent goal scorer when rising through the Bolton ranks, Ricardo was given some invaluable first-team experience last year. He made his first appearance of the season as a substitute against Aston Villa and was rewarded

James Vaughan

with his only Premiership start in the volatile atmosphere of an Old Trafford local 'derby' on Boxing Day. He also scored his first senior goal for the club, netting the winner in the FA Cup tie at Oldham.
Bolton W *(From trainee on 20/10/2004) PL 1+7 FAC 3+1/1*

VENTOLA Nicola
Born: Bari, Italy, 24 May 1978
Height: 6'3" **Weight:** 12.13
International Honours: Italy: U21
This skilful striker joined Crystal Palace on loan with his colleague Gonzalo Sorondo in a season-long deal. However, after a couple of early appearances from the bench Nicola was sidelined firstly by a knee problem and then by a broken ankle, He added one further appearance as a substitute in the crucial relegation battle against Southampton when he netted his only goal for the Eagles.
Crystal Palace *(Loaned from Inter Milan, Italy on 3/9/2004) PL 0+3/1*

VERNAZZA Paolo Andrea Pietro
Born: Islington, 1 November 1979
Height: 6'0" **Weight:** 11.10
International Honours: E: U21-2; Yth
This skilful midfield player found it difficult to establish himself as an automatic choice at Rotherham last term with his best run in the side being a sequence of four successive starts. Despite his limited opportunities, Paolo never stopped working hard and he always tried his best in the difficult circumstances of a relegation season.
Arsenal *(From trainee on 18/11/1997) PL 2+3/1 FLC 4 Others 1+2*
Ipswich T *(Loaned on 2/10/1998) FL 2*
Portsmouth *(Loaned on 14/1/2000) FL 7*
Watford *(£350,000 + on 15/12/2000) FL 71+25/2 FLC 3/1 FAC 8*
Rotherham U *(Free on 7/7/2004) FL 14+13 FLC 1+1 FAC 1*

VERNON Scott Malcolm
Born: Manchester, 13 December 1983
Height: 6'1" **Weight:** 11.6
This promising young striker endured mixed fortunes during the 2004-05 campaign, including suffering a fractured eye socket. He barely featured at the start of the season before being sent out on loan to League One rivals Blackpool. After finding the net three times at Bloomfield Road, he returned to Boundary Park and was recalled to first-team action. A cool penalty-box predator, the highlight of his season

Scott Vernon

came when he netted the winning goal in Latics' memorable FA Cup third round defeat of Manchester City. Despite operating from the bench for the latter stages of the season, he managed a respectable tally of 13 strikes. Scott was out of contract in the summer and his future was unclear at the time of writing.

Oldham Ath *(From trainee on 3/7/2002) FL 43+32/20 FLC 1 FAC 3+2/1 Others 5+2/6*
Blackpool *(Loaned on 10/9/2004) FL 4/3*

VICTORY Jamie Charles
Born: Hackney, 14 November 1975
Height: 5'10" **Weight:** 12.0
Club Honours: FAT '98; NC '99
International Honours: E: SP-1
Cheltenham Town's longest-serving player passed the 400-appearance mark during season 2004-2005. He was the first-choice left back at Whaddon Road, appearing in every game until a back injury forced him out of the closing matches. His experience proved valuable in a young side and his composure and confidence on the ball were once again important features of the team. A naturally athletic player, Jamie won his fair share of tackles and headers while getting forward to support the attack whenever possible.

West Ham U *(From trainee on 1/7/1994)*
Bournemouth *(Free on 1/7/1995) FL 5+11/1 FLC 1+1 Others 1+1*
Cheltenham T *(Free on 1/7/1996) FL 223+3/19 FLC 8/1 FAC 13 Others 11/1*

VIDMAR Anthony (Tony)
Born: Adelaide, Australia, 15 April 1969
Height: 6'1" **Weight:** 12.10
Club Honours: SPD '99, '00; SLC '99, '02; SC '99, '00, '02
International Honours: Australia: 69; Yth
This experienced defender began the 2004-05 season at left back for Cardiff to accommodate new signing Robert Page, but by September Tony was back in his more familiar role at centre half. However, he lost his place to James Collins following a period of suspension and thereafter was mostly restricted to outings from the bench. Tony was reported to have signed for NAC Breda during the close season.

Glasgow Rgrs *(Free from NAC Breda, Holland, ex Ekeren, Adelaide C, on 30/6/1997) SL 89+18/7 SLC 6+2 SC 15/2 Others 23+6/2*
Middlesbrough *(Free on 5/9/2002) PL 9+3 FLC 2 FAC 1*
Cardiff C *(Free on 22/7/2003) FL 68+5/2 FLC 6 FAC 1+1*

VIDUKA Mark Anthony
Born: Australia, 9 October 1975
Height: 6'2" **Weight:** 13.9
Club Honours: SLC '00
International Honours: Australia: 24; U23; Yth
This tall and powerful striker missed his new club's start to the 2004-05 season because he carried over a suspension from his Leeds United days but, as was hoped by the Boro' management, he struck up an immediate scoring partnership with Jimmy Floyd Hasselbaink when he eventually appeared. Mark's season was regularly interrupted by injury, his last game of 2004 ending with a hamstring injury at St Andrew's which kept him on the sidelines until the following April. His comeback lasted only 12 minutes at Selhurst Park, again a recurrence of the same problem and this brought a premature end to his season.
Glasgow Celtic *(Signed from NK Croatia Zagreb, Croatia, ex Melbourne Knights, on 2/12/1998) SL 36+1/30 SLC 4/1 SC 3/3 Others 4/1*
Leeds U *(£6,000,000 on 25/7/2000) PL 126+4/59 FLC 3/1 FAC 8/5 Others 25/7*
Middlesbrough *(£4,500,000 on 8/7/2004) PL 15+1/5 FLC 1 Others 3+1/2*

VIEIRA Patrick
Born: Dakar, Senegal, 23 June 1976
Height: 6'4" **Weight:** 13.0
Club Honours: PL '98, '02, '04; FAC '98, 02, '05; CS '98, '99, '02
International Honours: France: 79 (WC '98, UEFA '00)
Having just led his side to an historic unbeaten triumph, it seemed as if Patrick would be swapping London for Madrid when it was rumoured that Arsenal had accepted an offer to sell their star midfielder to Real Madrid. Citing bonds that were too strong to break, he eventually turned down the move yet injury kept him out of the early weeks of the campaign. When he did return he looked somewhat less committed than he had appeared before the transfer gossip and took a while to find his form. Despite this Patrick enjoyed his finest goal-scoring season to date with seven goals in total including fine efforts at Anfield, White Hart Lane and St James' Park. His best strike was probably the one at home to Everton when he chipped his former Highbury colleague Richard Wright as Arsenal strolled to their biggest-ever Premiership win – 7-0. He was also a scorer in the two FA Cup penalty shoot-outs at Bramall Lane and the Millennium Stadium and finished the season on a high by lifting the FA Cup in Cardiff.
Arsenal *(£3,500,000 from AC Milan, Italy, ex Cannes, on 14/8/1996) PL 272+7/28 FLC 7 FAC 46+2/3 Others 71+1/2*

VILLIS Matthew (Matt)
Born: Bridgwater, 13 April 1984
Height: 6'3" **Weight:** 12.7
This tall young Plymouth central defender, and occasional right back, spent the 2004-05 season at Torquay on a long-term loan. After a hesitant start, he grew in confidence and maturity as the campaign progressed and showed much promise despite never achieving a regular starting place.
Plymouth Arg *(Signed from Bridgwater T on 26/9/2002)*
Torquay U *(Loaned on 12/7/2004) FL 12+10 Others 2*

VINCENT Ashley Derek
Born: Oldbury, 26 May 1985
Height: 5'10" **Weight:** 11.8
This pacy forward impressed during Cheltenham's pre-season programme and made a number of appearances in the first half of the 2004-05 campaign as a striker or out wide on the left. He scored his first Football League goal in the 2-1 win against Cambridge United in October and produced a particularly impressive performance against Walsall in the LDV Vans Trophy, which earned him another two goals. Ashley was used more sparingly in the second half of the season and given the opportunity to gain more experience in the reserves.
Cheltenham T *(From trainee at Wolverhampton W on 2/7/2004) FL 14+12/1 FLC 0+1 FAC 0+1 Others 1+1/2*

VINCENT Jamie Roy
Born: Wimbledon, 18 June 1975
Height: 5'10" **Weight:** 11.8
After missing the start of the season, Jamie settled into Derby County's left-back slot and scored the winning goal when the Rams reversed a two-goal deficit to beat Rotherham United at Pride Park. At the end of November, Jamie suffered a calf strain and recovery proved to be slow. He was able to return to the reserves in March to regain match fitness but, by then, Derby's defence had a more settled look.
Crystal Palace *(From trainee on 13/7/1993) FL 19+6 FLC 2+1/1 FAC 1*
Bournemouth *(Loaned on 18/11/1994) FL 8*
Bournemouth *(£25,000 + on 30/8/1996) FL 102+3/5 FLC 7+1 FAC 8 Others 9/1*
Huddersfield T *(£440,000 + on 25/3/1999) FL 54+5/2 FLC 3+2 FAC 2*
Portsmouth *(£800,000 on 23/2/2001) FL 43+5/1 FLC 1*
Walsall *(Loaned on 17/10/2003) FL 12 FAC 0+1*
Derby Co *(Free on 16/1/2004) FL 22/2 FLC 1*

VINE Rowan Lewis
Born: Basingstoke, 21 September 1982
Height: 6'1" **Weight:** 12.2
Club Honours: Div 1 '05
This young Portsmouth striker spent the whole of the 2004-05 season out on loan with League One outfit Luton Town. A striker with fine close control and a good first touch, he formed a productive partnership with Steve Howard, netting nine goals himself. He worked consistently hard throughout the campaign and was particularly effective when taking on and passing defenders. After spending the last three seasons out on loan, Rowan will be looking to break into the squad at Fratton Park next term.
Portsmouth *(From trainee on 27/4/2001) FL 3+10*
Brentford *(Loaned on 7/8/2002) FL 37+5/10 FLC 1+1/1 FAC 3/2 Others 3*
Colchester U *(Loaned on 7/8/2003) FL 30+5/6 FLC 1 FAC 5+2/4 Others 4+2/2*
Luton T *(Loaned on 6/8/2004) FL 43+2/9 FLC 1 FAC 3*

VIRGO Adam John
Born: Brighton, 25 January 1983
Height: 6'2" **Weight:** 13.7
International Honours: S: B-1
Brighton's Adam Virgo enjoyed a simply extraordinary season in 2004-05. After starting out at right back, he was switched to centre forward early on in an attempt to add some muscle to the front line and finished top scorer with nine goals. His versatility and adaptability – he also turned out in the centre of defence and had a few forays in midfield – were a huge bonus in a hard-fought battle against relegation, and on many occasions he changed position mid-match as the situation demanded. Blessed with great physical attributes and always willing to chase, Adam's enthusiasm helped Albion defend from the front, but he proved to be a more-than-capable target man with a powerful shot and eye for goal. A clear winner of the club's 'Player of the Season' award, Adam never gives up. In December he earned a first international cap for the Scotland Futures side, and it was fitting that, even though playing as a central defender, it was he who secured Albion's position in the Championship with the equaliser against Ipswich in the last game of the campaign.
Brighton & Hove A *(From juniors on 4/7/2000) FL 65+8/10 FLC 2 FAC 1 Others 4+2/1*
Exeter C *(Loaned on 29/11/2002) FL 8+1*

VIVEASH Adrian Lee
Born: Swindon, 30 September 1969
Height: 6'2" **Weight:** 12.13
This experienced defender was out of the first-team picture at Swindon last term and began the season on loan at Kidderminster. He helped Harriers keep a clean sheet in each of their first three games before returning to the County Ground. However, he was released in December to join Conference outfit Aldershot Town, before moving on to Cirencester Town the following month.
Swindon T *(From trainee on 14/7/1988) FL 51+3/2 FLC 6+1 FAC 0+1 Others 2*
Reading *(Loaned on 4/1/1993) FL 5 Others 1/1*
Reading *(Loaned on 20/1/1995) FL 6*
Barnsley *(Loaned on 10/8/1995) FL 2/1*
Walsall *(Free on 16/10/1995) FL 200+2/13 FLC 12 FAC 15/2 Others 13/1*
Reading *(Free on 6/7/2000) FL 62+1/3 FLC 3+1 FAC 5 Others 7*
Oxford U *(Loaned on 6/9/2002) FL 11 FLC 3 Others 1*
Swindon T *(Free on 14/7/2003) FL 14+1 FLC 1 Others 1*
Kidderminster Hrs *(Loaned on 2/3/2004) FL 7*
Kidderminster Hrs *(Loaned on 6/8/2004) FL 7*

VOLZ Moritz
Born: Siegen, Germany, 21 January 1983
Height: 5'11" **Weight:** 12.10
Club Honours: FAYC '00, '01
International Honours: Germany: U21-10; Yth
Consistent at right back throughout the season, Moritz was a regular for Fulham throughout the campaign. An overlapping right back who likes to join the attack, he was rewarded with a goal against Watford in the FA Cup. Moritz was capped at U21 level for Germany, on one occasion lining up against teammate Liam Rosenior who was playing for England, and also won a call-up to the senior international squad.
Arsenal *(Free from Schalke 04, Germany on 25/1/2000) FLC 1+1*
Wimbledon *(Loaned on 3/2/2003) FL 10/1*
Fulham *(£2,200,000 on 8/8/2003) PL 63+1 FLC 3 FAC 7/1*

Adam Virgo (left)

W

WAINWRIGHT Neil
Born: Warrington, 4 November 1977
Height: 6'0" **Weight:** 11.5
Neil is at his best running at defenders on the right wing and can cut in effectively towards goal, although he only netted three times for Darlington during the 2004-05 season. Over half his appearances were made from the substitutes' bench from where his direct approach and mazy running often altered the course of the game.
Wrexham *(From trainee on 3/7/1996) FL 7+4/3 FAC 1 Others 1*
Sunderland *(£100,000 + on 9/7/1998) P/FL 0+2 FLC 5+1*
Darlington *(Loaned on 4/2/2000) FL 16+1/4*
Halifax T *(Loaned on 13/10/2000) FL 13 FAC 1 Others 2*
Darlington *(£50,000 on 17/8/2001) FL 109+32/16 FLC 1+1 FAC 7+3/2 Others 3*

WALKER Desmond (Des) Sinclair
Born: Hackney, 26 November 1965
Height: 5'11" **Weight:** 11.13
Club Honours: FLC '89, '90; FMC '89, '92
International Honours: E: 59; U21-7
A legendary figure at the City Ground, Des finally bought the curtain down on his career when he took up a coaching job with Nottingham Forest. However, he was still registered as a player in case of emergencies and featured from the bench in the opening game of the season against Wigan. Following the departure of Joe Kinnear he was appointed caretaker assistant-manager, but then left the club when Gary Megson arrived in the new year. Des was awarded a testimonial by Forest in May.
Nottingham F *(From apprentice on 2/12/1983) FL 259+5/1 FLC 40 FAC 28 Others 14 (£1,500,000 to Sampdoria, Italy on 1/8/1992)*
Sheffield Wed *(£2,700,000 on 22/7/1993) P/FL 307 FLC 28 FAC 24 Others 3 (Freed during 2001 close season)*
Nottingham F *(Free, via a spell at Burton A, on 9/7/2002) FL 52+5 FLC 1 FAC 2 Others 2*

WALKER Ian Michael
Born: Watford, 31 October 1971
Height: 6'2" **Weight:** 13.1
Club Honours: FAYC '90; FLC '99
International Honours: E: 4; B-1; U21-9; Yth
A mystery knee problem sidelined Ian from the end of August through to late January, when he returned to claim his regular position between the sticks for Leicester. He made a notable penalty save at Upton Park to help the Foxes to a battling draw at a stage when the club was flirting too closely with the relegation zone and his final act was another spot-kick save, at home to Leeds, just days before he was given his release by Craig Levein.
Tottenham H *(From trainee on 4/12/1989) P/FL 257+2 FLC 22+1 FAC 25 Others 6*
Oxford U *(Loaned on 31/8/1990) FL 2 FLC 1*
Leicester C *(£2,500,000 on 26/7/2001) P/FL 140 FLC 6 FAC 10*

WALKER James (Jimmy) Barry
Born: Sutton-in-Ashfield, 9 July 1973
Height: 5'11" **Weight:** 13.5
This vastly experienced goalkeeper joined West Ham in the summer. He made his first-team debut in the Carling Cup tie at Chelsea and became a instant hero when he saved a penalty. On the night he gave a superb display to thwart the star-studded Blues. He bided his time and was rewarded with a call up to the team in April when his safe and confident handling helped West Ham in their

Ian Walker

promotion cause. Jimmy's experience was invaluable to the two young defenders playing in front of him. In the play-off final against Preston he was unfortunate to be stretchered off after twisting his knee in a bad fall.

Notts Co *(From trainee on 9/7/1991)*
Walsall *(Free on 4/8/1993) FL 401+2 FLC 24+1 FAC 30 Others 19*
West Ham U *(Free on 26/7/2004) FL 10 FLC 3 FAC 1 Others 3*

WALKER Justin Matthew
Born: Nottingham, 6 September 1975
Height: 5'11" **Weight:** 12.12
International Honours: E: Yth; Sch
Justin established himself at the heart of the Cambridge United team last season and was a near ever-present in the line-up. The skilful ball playing-midfielder contributed a single goal, netting in the home draw with Leyton Orient back in August, but was unable to prevent the U's from being relegated to the Conference. Justin was one of several out-of-contract players at the Abbey Stadium whose future had yet to be determined at the time of writing.

Nottingham F *(From juniors on 10/9/1992)*
Scunthorpe U *(Signed on 26/3/1997) FL 126+6/2 FLC 8 FAC 6 Others 7/1*
Lincoln C *(Free on 12/7/2000) FL 68+8/4 FLC 1+2 FAC 3+1 Others 6/1*
Exeter C *(Free on 6/8/2002) FL 35+4/5 FLC 1 FAC 3+1/1 Others 1*
Cambridge U *(Free on 9/6/2003) FL 59/2 FLC 2/1 Others 3*
York C *(Loaned on 6/1/2004) FL 7+2*

Justin Walker

WALKER Richard Martin
Born: Birmingham, 8 November 1977
Height: 6'0" **Weight:** 12.0
Club Honours: AMC '02
Richard was one of several former Oxford players to follow manager Ian Atkins to Bristol Rovers last term. He was a patient squad member early on in the campaign as a series of strikers were paired together and finally got his chance in February when he established himself alongside Junior Agogo. The pair finished the season together, with Richard scoring an impressive ten goals in his final 16 appearances to add to his total of four cup goals.

Aston Villa *(From trainee on 13/12/1995) PL 2+4/2 FLC 1+1 FAC 0+1 Others 1*
Cambridge U *(Loaned on 31/12/1998) FL 7+14/3 Others 1+2/1*
Blackpool *(Loaned on 9/2/2001) FL 6+12/3*
Wycombe W *(Loaned on 13/9/2001) FL 10+2/3 FAC 1/1*
Blackpool *(£50,000 + on 21/12/2001) FL 38+24/12 FLC 0+1 FAC 1+2 Others 3+1/3*
Northampton T *(Loaned on 21/10/2003) FL 11+1/4 FAC 4/2 Others 3/2*
Oxford U *(Free on 17/3/2004) FL 3+1*
Bristol Rov *(Free on 2/8/2004) FL 20+7/10 FLC 1+1/1 FAC 1/1 Others 2+1/2*

WALKER Richard Stuart
Born: Stafford, 17 September 1980
Height: 6'2" **Weight:** 13.0
Another of the talented young players to have come up through the Crewe youth scheme, Richard normally plays in a central-defensive position. Good in the air, he usually gets on the scoring lists each season and is a hard-working and a popular member of the staff.

Crewe Alex *(From trainee on 6/7/1999) FL 65+17/5 FLC 4+1 FAC 2+1 Others 4*

WALLIS Scott Edward
Born: Enfield, 28 June 1988
Height: 5'10" **Weight:** 10.10
Scott was one of several youngsters at Leyton Orient who received a taste of first-team action after doing well in the club's reserve and youth teams. A direct and pacy right winger, he made his senior debut as a substitute in the 2-2 draw at Oxford on Easter Monday and added a couple more appearances from the bench in the closing matches. He will be looking to gain more first-team experience in 2005-06.

Leyton Orient *(Trainee) FL 0+3*

WALLWORK Ronald (Ronnie)
Born: Manchester, 10 September 1977
Height: 5'10" **Weight:** 12.9
Club Honours: FAYC '95; PL '01

International Honours: E: Yth
After being installed as West Bromwich Albion's midfield anchorman last December by new boss Bryan Robson this former England Youth international then proceeded to play perhaps the best football of his career during the second half of the season. This culminated in the Baggies retaining their Premiership status, with Ronnie himself, being voted the club's 'Player of the Year.' He scored his first Premiership goal in January, heading home from close range to clinch a 2-0 home victory over Manchester City. Albion's skipper at times, he is a tidy passer of the ball, enjoys a challenge and when given time and space can deliver a powerful right-foot shot.
Manchester U *(From trainee on 17/3/1995) PL 4+15 FLC 4+1 FAC 1+1 Others 1+1*
Carlisle U *(Loaned on 22/12/1997) FL 10/1 Others 2*
Stockport Co *(Loaned on 18/3/1998) FL 7*
West Bromwich A *(Free on 2/7/2002) P/FL 46+6/1 FLC 2+1 FAC 5*
Bradford C *(Loaned on 22/1/2004) FL 7/4*

WALSH Gary
Born: Wigan, 21 March 1968
Height: 6'3" **Weight:** 15.10
Club Honours: ECWC '91; ESC '91; FAC '94
International Honours: E: U21-2
An experienced campaigner, Gary once again had to be content to sit on the bench for Wigan Athletic for virtually the whole of the 2004-05 season with first-team goalkeeper John Filan in excellent form. Restricted to just one start in the Carling Cup, Gary proved a more than capable back-up 'keeper. A tall and commanding figure, he has signed a new deal with the club and will also coach the goalkeepers at the JJB Stadium.
Manchester U *(From juniors on 25/4/1985) P/FL 49+1 FLC 7 Others 6*
Airdrie *(Loaned on 11/8/1988) SL 3 SLC 1*
Oldham Ath *(Loaned on 19/11/1993) PL 6*
Middlesbrough *(£500,000 on 11/8/1995) PL 44 FLC 9 FAC 4*
Bradford C *(£500,000 + on 26/9/1997) P/FL 131+1 FLC 7 FAC 4 Others 1*
Middlesbrough *(Loaned on 15/9/2000) PL 3*
Wigan Ath *(Free on 14/7/2003) FL 1+2 FLC 3*

WALSH Michael George
Born: Liverpool, 30 May 1986
Height: 5'9" **Weight:** 10.5
This young utility player joined Chester City in the summer of 2004 and signed a professional contract with the club in March. The enthusiastic youngster came off the bench for his debut in the FA Cup tie at Bournemouth and made his first start at Swansea on the left side of midfield. Michael scored a crucial goal in his first full home appearance against high-flying Southend, but was nevertheless released at the end of the season.
Chester C *(Free from Rhyl on 6/1/2005) FL 2+3/1 FAC 0+1*

WALSH Michael Shane
Born: Rotherham, 5 August 1977
Height: 6'0" **Weight:** 13.2
Club Honours: AMC '01
This tall Port Vale defender returned to the fray last season after recovering from a serious neck injury that almost ended his career. Michael made his first start in six months against Swindon in October but his comeback was hampered by a suspension and then a thigh injury. A Christmas return against Sheffield Wednesday heralded a regular place for the remainder of the campaign. The Vale defence looked a lot stronger when he was present and having put his injury problems behind him he will be looking to establish himself once again in 2005-06.
Scunthorpe U *(From trainee on 3/7/1995) FL 94+9/1 FLC 4 FAC 9 Others 5*
Port Vale *(£100,000 on 30/7/1998) FL 144+7/4 FLC 6+1 FAC 4 Others 7*

WALTERS Jonathan (Jon) Ronald
Born: Birkenhead, 20 September 1983
Height: 6'1" **Weight:** 12.0
International Honours: RoI: U21-1; Yth
Jon was largely restricted to substitute duties during the opening months of Hull's second consecutive promotion campaign. It was in the FA Cup that the lively forward made his most dramatic impact when he came off the bench to fire home a late winner against Morecambe at the KC Stadium in November. Jon was allowed to go on loan to Scunthorpe in February where he started three games up front, showing a good touch and hitting the post on his debut against Kidderminster.
Blackburn Rov *(From trainee on 3/8/2001)*
Bolton W *(Signed on 30/4/2002) PL 0+4 FLC 1 FAC 0+1*
Hull C *(Loaned on 24/2/2003) FL 11/5*
Barnsley *(Loaned on 12/11/2003) FL 7+1 FAC 3 Others 0+1*
Hull C *(£50,000 on 5/2/2004) FL 9+28/2 FLC 1 FAC 0+2/1 Others 1*
Scunthorpe U *(Loaned on 4/2/2005) FL 3*

WALTON David (Dave) Lee
Born: Bedlington, 10 April 1973
Height: 6'2" **Weight:** 14.8
Club Honours: Div 3 '94
Dave made a surprise return to Shrewsbury Town last term, and although he took some time to settle in he began to thrive following a change in management. Highly rated by the fans, he offered a strong and uncompromising presence in the centre of the defence. He bagged important goals against Swansea and Leyton Orient and it was no coincidence that his return to form heralded an improvement in defensive fortunes. Injury brought his season to a premature end but he looks set to be a key figure in the back line once more in 2005-06.
Sheffield U *(Free from Ashington on 13/3/1992)*
Shrewsbury T *(Signed on 5/11/1993) FL 127+1/10 FLC 7 FAC 10/1 Others 11/1*
Crewe Alex *(£500,000 + on 20/10/1997) FL 146+9/3 FLC 8+1/1 FAC 7*
Derby Co *(Free on 3/7/2003) FL 3+2*
Stockport Co *(Loaned on 6/2/2004) FL 7*
Shrewsbury T *(Free on 6/8/2004) FL 20+2/2 FLC 1 FAC 0+1*

WALTON Simon William
Born: Sherburn-in-Elmet, 13 September 1987
Height: 6'1" **Weight:** 13.5
Few players will remember their debut quite as much as Simon. He made his senior bow as a 16-year-old in a high-profile pre-season friendly against Spanish giants Valencia and scored from the penalty spot but within minutes was sent off for a second bookable offence. Although the Leeds Academy staff believe he will develop in the future as a centre half, he was used in the Championship as a hard-tackling midfielder. The teenager did remarkably well in a tough arena considering only months earlier he had been studying at Sherburn High School, near Selby. Simon's first senior goal was the equaliser in the 1-1 draw at Reading with the others coming in the 4-2 win at Preston and the 1-1 home draw with Cardiff.
Leeds U *(From trainee on 14/9/2004) FL 23+7/3 FLC 1+1 FAC 1*

WANLESS Paul Steven
Born: Banbury, 14 December 1973
Height: 6'1" **Weight:** 13.12
Although approaching the twilight of his career, Paul was still one of the most committed players in the Oxford United side last term. Mostly employed as a ball-winning midfield player he ended the season at centre back where his ability to read the game helped tremendously. Always a threat at set pieces his only goal came in the 1-1 draw with Macclesfield in April. Paul was released by the club at

the end of his contract in the summer.
Oxford U *(From trainee on 3/12/1991) FL 12+20 FLC 0+3/1 Others 2+2*
Lincoln C *(Free on 7/7/1995) FL 7+1 Others 2*
Cambridge U *(Free on 8/3/1996) FL 264+20/44 FLC 13 FAC 19+2/2 Others 16/3*
Oxford U *(Free on 7/8/2003) FL 56+9/6 FLC 2 FAC 2 Others 0+1*

WARD Ashley Stuart
Born: Manchester, 24 November 1970
Height: 6'2" **Weight:** 13.10
Ashley started the 2004-05 season as a third-choice striker for the Blades and his appearances were from the bench until the departure of Barry Hayles. He was then used as the target man where he used his experience to win, hold and distribute the ball proved invaluable. A knee injury at Wigan in September kept him out for several months and he made just one more substitute appearance in February.
Manchester C *(From trainee on 5/8/1989) FL 0+1 FAC 0+2*
Wrexham *(Loaned on 10/1/1991) FL 4/2 Others 1*
Leicester C *(£80,000 on 30/7/1991) FL 2+8 FLC 2+1 FAC 0+1 Others 0+1*
Blackpool *(Loaned on 21/11/1992) FL 2/1*
Crewe Alex *(£80,000 on 1/12/1992) FL 58+3/25 FLC 4/2 FAC 2/4 Others 7/6*
Norwich C *(£500,000 on 8/12/1994) P/FL 53/18 FLC 6/3 FAC 1*
Derby Co *(£1,000,000 on 19/3/1996) P/FL 32+8/9 FLC 1+1 FAC 2/1*
Barnsley *(£1,300,000 + on 5/9/1997) P/FL 45+1/20 FLC 9/4 FAC 6/1*
Blackburn Rov *(£4,250,000 + on 31/12/1998) P/FL 52+2/13 FLC 2 FAC 4+1*
Bradford C *(£1,500,000 on 18/8/2000) P/FL 75+9/17 FLC 4+1/3 FAC 1*
Sheffield U *(Free on 7/8/2003) FL 25+8/5 FLC 2 FAC 2*

WARD Darren
Born: Worksop, 11 May 1974
Height: 6'2" **Weight:** 14.2
Club Honours: Div 3 '98
International Honours: W: 5; B-1; U21-2
Norwich signed this international goalkeeper from Nottingham Forest in July 2004 to increase pressure on Robert Green for his place in the team. With well over 500 senior appearances behind him, Darren provided the experienced cover required, but, unfortunately for him, Green's consistency kept him on the sidelines apart from a brief substitute appearance at Charlton in November. An extremely consistent performer himself, his previous top-class displays against the Canaries obviously persuaded Nigel Worthington to bring him to Carrow Road. A commanding figure with good shot-stopping skills he regained his place in the Wales squad at the season's end.
Mansfield T *(From trainee on 27/7/1992) FL 81 FLC 5 FAC 5 Others 6*
Notts Co *(£160,000 on 11/7/1995) FL 251 FLC 18 FAC 23 Others 10*
Nottingham F *(Free on 21/5/2001) FL 123 FLC 8 FAC 4 Others 2*
Norwich C *(Signed on 6/8/2004) PL 0+1*

WARD Darren Philip
Born: Harrow, 13 September 1978
Height: 6'0" **Weight:** 12.6
One of the most consistent players at the New Den, Darren enjoyed a great season in the centre of defence for Millwall last term when he formed an excellent partnership with Matt Lawrence. His ability to read the game was again well to the fore, while his strong tackling and runs through the middle made him one of the best central defenders in the Championship. Darren received the club's 'Player of the Year' award for the second time in a row.
Watford *(From trainee on 13/2/1997) P/FL 56+3/2 FLC 6/1 FAC 2 Others 0+1*
Queens Park Rgrs *(Loaned on 17/12/1999) FL 14 FAC 1*
Millwall *(£500,000 on 3/10/2001) FL 135+7/4 FLC 3 FAC 12 Others 4*

WARD Elliott Leslie
Born: Harrow, 19 January 1985
Height: 6'2" **Weight:** 12.0
This giant central defender began the season on loan at Peterborough without making an appearance, but returned to Upton Park and featured in the Carling Cup tie against Southend. Later on he went out on loan again to Bristol Rovers, where he made just a few brief appearances from the bench. Then in March he was given his Championship debut against Crewe. Elliott immediately set up a good partnership with Anton Ferdinand in the middle of the back line and as the season progressed he continued to grow in stature, being particularly outstanding in the play-offs.
West Ham U *(From trainee on 23/1/2002) FL 10+1 FLC 1 Others 3*
Bristol Rov *(Loaned on 29/12/2004) FL 0+3*

WARD Gavin John
Born: Sutton Coldfield, 30 June 1970
Height: 6'3" **Weight:** 14.12
Club Honours: Div 3 '93; WC '93; AMC '00
Gavin joined Preston in the summer as back-up to goalkeeper Andy Lonergan and made his debut in October when Lonergan broke his hand in the game against Queen's Park Rangers. He enjoyed a brief run in the line-up then stepped in when his rival was injured a second time only to suffer an eye injury in the televised clash with Ipswich which saw him out for three weeks. After this he returned to the bench and signed an extension to his contract in April.
Shrewsbury T *(From trainee at Aston Villa on 26/9/1988)*
West Bromwich A *(Free on 18/9/1989) FLC 1*
Cardiff C *(Free on 5/10/1989) FL 58+1 FAC 1 Others 7*
Leicester C *(£175,000 on 16/7/1993) P/FL 38 FLC 3 FAC 0+1 Others 4*
Bradford C *(£175,000 on 13/7/1995) FL 36 FLC 6 FAC 3 Others 2*
Bolton W *(£300,000 on 29/3/1996) P/FL 19+3 FLC 2 FAC 4*
Burnley *(Loaned on 14/8/1998) FL 17*
Stoke C *(Free on 25/2/1999) FL 79 FLC 7 FAC 2 Others 12*
Walsall *(Free on 9/8/2002) FL 5+2*
Coventry C *(Free on 4/8/2003) FL 12 FAC 3*
Barnsley *(Loaned on 29/4/2004) FL 1*
Preston NE *(Free on 6/8/2004) FL 6+1 FLC 1*

WARD Graham William
Born: Dublin, 25 February 1983
Height: 5'8" **Weight:** 11.12
International Honours: RoI: U21-3; Yth
Graham made only two substitute appearances for Cheltenham Town last term, when his worth to the squad was seen largely away from the first team. A hard-working central or wide-right midfield player, he captained the reserve team and helped to bring through some of the younger players at the club. He spent some time on loan at Burton Albion in the Conference towards the end of the season but was reported to have signed for their rivals Tamworth in the summer.
Wolverhampton W *(From trainee on 17/7/2000)*
Kidderminster Hrs *(Free on 8/8/2003) FL 17+4 FLC 1 FAC 2 Others 1*
Cheltenham T *(Free on 4/8/2004) FL 0+2*

WARDLEY Stuart James
Born: Cambridge, 10 September 1975
Height: 5'11" **Weight:** 12.7
Club Honours: Div3 '03
After overcoming a career threatening knee injury, this experienced attacking midfielder received a route back into senior football from Torquay. Although lacking match fitness, he soon settled in to the side, scoring twice in the home game with Brentford. His impressive displays attracted an offer from Leyton Orient, where he spent a brief period covering for injuries. Stuart moved on another short-term deal to Cambridge United before switching to Southern League football with Bedford Town.

***Queens Park Rgrs** (£15,000 from Saffron Walden T on 22/7/1999) FL 72+15/14 FLC 2 FAC 3+2/3 Others 1*
***Rushden & Diamonds** (Signed on 25/1/2002) FL 54+3/10 FLC 2 FAC 3/1 Others 3+1/1*
***Torquay U** (Free on 24/8/2004) FL 5+2/2 FLC 0+1*
***Leyton Orient** (Free on 8/10/2004) FL 4+2 FAC 0+1 Others 0+2*
***Cambridge U** (Free on 7/1/2005) FL 1+2*

WARHURST Paul

Born: Stockport, 26 September 1969
Height: 6'1" **Weight:** 13.6
Club Honours: PL '95
International Honours: E: U21-8
Now in the veteran stages of his career, this versatile player joined Blackpool on a short-term contract following a trial at Preston. Paul featured in a handful of games for the Seasiders before finishing the campaign at Conference outfit Forest Green Rovers.
***Manchester C** (From trainee on 1/7/1988)*
***Oldham Ath** (£10,000 on 27/10/1988) FL 60+7/2 FLC 8 FAC 5+4 Others 2*
***Sheffield Wed** (£750,000 on 17/7/1991) P/FL 60+6/6 FLC 9/4 FAC 7+1/5 Others 5/3*
***Blackburn Rov** (£2,700,000 on 17/8/1993) PL 30+27/4 FLC 6+2 FAC 2+1 Others 4+2*
***Crystal Palace** (£1,250,000 on 31/7/1997) P/FL 27/4 FLC 2 FAC 1*
***Bolton W** (£800,000 on 25/11/1998) P/FL 81+10 FLC 3+3 FAC 3+2 Others 2+2*
***Stoke C** (Loaned on 27/3/2003) FL 4+1/1*
***Chesterfield** (Free on 16/10/2003) FL 3+1 FAC 1 Others 1/1*
***Barnsley** (Free on 12/12/2003) FL 3+1*
***Carlisle U** (Free on 20/2/2004) FL 0+1*
***Grimsby T** (Free on 12/3/2004) FL 5+2*
***Blackpool** (Free, via trial at Preston NE, on 1/11/2004) FL 2+2 FAC 0+1 Others 1*

WARK Scott Andrew

Born: Glasgow, 9 June 1987
Height: 6'3" **Weight:** 13.4
This young centre half made his senior debut as a late substitute in Rushden's 1-0 defeat at Macclesfield Town on the final day of the 2004-05 season, having impressed new manager Barry Hunter with his performances for the reserve team. He will be looking to make further progress in his career during 2005-06 and establish himself in the first-team squad. Scott is the nephew of former Ipswich Town player John Wark.
***Rushden & Diamonds** (Trainee) FL 0+1*

WARNE Paul

Born: Norwich, 8 May 1973
Height: 5'9" **Weight:** 11.2
There can surely be no more willing worker than Paul who would literally run his socks off in the team's cause. For much of the 2004-05 campaign he had to be content with a place on the substitutes' bench but whenever called up he could be relied on to give his best. He was often used in a position out wide, on the right but is at his best up front running at defenders. Paul netted a last gasp goal to give the Millers a 1-0 win against Reading in mid-March. Paul had a successful spell on loan at Mansfield in mid-season and was released by the Millers when his contract expired in the summer.
***Wigan Ath** (£25,000 from Wroxham on 30/7/1997) FL 11+25/3 FLC 0+1 FAC 1 Others 1+2/1*
***Rotherham U** (Free on 15/1/1999) FL 173+57/28 FLC 6+6/1 FAC 10/1 Others 5*
***Mansfield T** (Loaned on 26/11/2004) FL 7/1*

WARNER Anthony (Tony) Randolph

Born: Liverpool, 11 May 1974
Height: 6'4" **Weight:** 13.9
Club Honours: Div 2 '01
Tony joined Cardiff in the summer of 2004 and was installed as first-choice 'keeper shortly after the start of the new campaign. The giant stopper has the reflexes and the frame to play at a higher level, but struggled to show his best form at Ninian Park. He was dropped in January after a 3-2 defeat to Blackburn Rovers in the third round of the FA Cup and did not play again during the season.
***Liverpool** (From juniors on 1/1/1994)*
***Swindon T** (Loaned on 5/11/1997) FL 2*
***Glasgow Celtic** (Loaned on 13/11/1998) SL 3*
***Aberdeen** (Loaned on 31/3/1999) SL 6*
***Millwall** (Free on 16/7/1999) FL 200 FLC 10 FAC 10 Others 5*
***Cardiff C** (Free on 3/7/2004) FL 26 FLC 2 FAC 2*

WARNER Scott John

Born: Rochdale, 3 December 1983
Height: 5'11" **Weight:** 11.11
With Gary Jones injured at the start of last term, young midfielder Scott had the opportunity to make further progress at Rochdale, but he was stretchered off in only the second game of the campaign. Nonetheless, on his return to fitness manager Steve Parkin immediately drafted him back into the first team ahead of more experienced players. His wholehearted displays gradually won over the Dale fans and he played or was on the bench for virtually every game for the rest of the season.
***Rochdale** (From trainee on 29/7/2003) FL 41+8/1 FAC 2+2 Others 2*

WARNOCK Stephen

Born: Ormskirk, 12 December 1981
Height: 5'7" **Weight:** 12.1
International Honours: E: Yth; Sch
After spending the previous season on loan to Coventry City, this former graduate from the Liverpool Academy finally made the breakthrough to the Reds' first-team squad at the beginning of last season and was in the match squad regularly, initially playing on the left side of midfield and, in the second half of the season, standing in for Djimi Traore at left back. Despite this impressive progress he seemed on occasions out of his depth in the Premiership and was substituted in ten of his 17 starts in the team.
***Liverpool** (From trainee on 27/4/1999) PL 11+8 FLC 3+1 FAC 1 Others 2+4*
***Bradford C** (Loaned on 13/9/2002) FL 12/1*
***Coventry C** (Loaned on 31/7/2003) FL 42+2/3 FLC 2 FAC 2+1*

WARRINGTON Andrew (Andy) Clifford

Born: Sheffield, 10 June 1976
Height: 6'3" **Weight:** 12.13
Club Honours: Div 3 '04
Andy once again proved his worth as the last line in the Doncaster Rovers' defence last term. The reliable 'keeper was a first choice in the line-up before succumbing to a hernia problem in March, thus bringing his campaign to a premature halt.
***York C** (From trainee on 11/6/1994) FL 61 FLC 7 FAC 4 Others 4*
***Doncaster Rov** (Free on 8/6/1999) FL 80 FLC 5 FAC 3*

WATERREUS Ronald

Born: Kerkrade, Holland, 25 August 1970
Height: 6'3" **Weight:** 13.3
International Honours: Holland: 7
This experienced 'keeper joined Manchester City on a short-term contract at the beginning of last August, to cover for a goalkeeping crisis at the club. Ronald played in two Carling Cup games and later joined Glasgow Rangers during the January transfer window.
***Manchester C** (Free from PSV Eindhoven, Holland, ex RKWM, Roda JC Kerkrade, on 26/8/2004) FLC 2*

WATSON Andrew (Andy) John

Born: Leeds, 13 November 1978
Height: 5'10" **Weight:** 11.0
This midfielder was signed by Chester boss Mark Wright during the summer of 2004 as part of his programme to rebuild the squad in preparation for the club's

return to the Football League. However, much of Andy's season was blighted by injury and he spent time on loan with Forest Green Rovers in order to improve his fitness. On his return to Chester he required a knee operation that brought a premature end to his season. Andy's only appearance for City came in the LDV Vans Trophy game against Rochdale.
Chester C *(Free from Farsley Celtic, ex Doncaster Rov, Tamworth, on 25/6/2004) Others 1*

WATSON Benjamin (Ben)
Born: Camberwell, 9 July 1985
Height: 5'10" **Weight:** 10.11
International Honours: E: U21-1
This promising young midfield player with good distribution made further progress with Crystal Palace last term, when he featured in over half the club's Premiership games. Ben was rewarded for his efforts by a call-up to the England U21 squad and he made his debut as a half-time substitute against Spain in November.
Crystal Palace *(From trainee on 12/8/2004) P/FL 27+15/1 FLC 3+3 FAC 2*

WATSON Kevin Edward
Born: Hackney, 3 January 1974
Height: 6'0" **Weight:** 12.6
Experienced central midfielder Kevin linked up with his former Reading colleague Phil Parkinson last summer to play at Colchester United. Kevin was the model of consistency, holding the team together with his accurate passing and terrific vision. He netted two goals, the first on his home debut against Stockport, and the second in the 1-1 draw at Blackpool in October. He only missed two games all season, both due to niggling injuries and it was no coincidence that Colchester lost both of these.
Tottenham H *(From trainee on 15/5/1992) PL 4+1 FLC 1+1/1 FAC 0+1 Others 4*
Brentford *(Loaned on 24/3/1994) FL 2+1*
Bristol C *(Loaned on 2/12/1994) FL 1+1*
Barnet *(Loaned on 16/2/1995) FL 13*
Swindon T *(Free on 15/7/1996) FL 39+24/1 FLC 2+2 FAC 1+2*
Rotherham U *(Free on 31/7/1999) FL 109/7 FLC 6/1 FAC 7 Others 3*
Reading *(Loaned on 2/11/2001) FL 6*
Reading *(£150,000 + on 14/3/2002) FL 40+20/2 FLC 2 FAC 0+1 Others 0+1*
Colchester U *(Free on 12/7/2004) FL 44/2 FLC 3 FAC 5 Others 1*

Kevin Watson

WATSON Paul Douglas
Born: Hastings, 4 January 1975
Height: 5'8" **Weight:** 10.10
Club Honours: Div 3 '99, '01; Div 2 '02
After playing in Brighton's pre-season programme, it was October before Paul was able to turn out for the reserves due to a back problem. That was followed by injuries to thigh and ankle, and by the end of the campaign he had added just one start and three appearances as a substitute to his name. With his contract expired, the long-serving full back and dead-ball expert will have to pursue his career away from the Withdean Stadium as he was released at the end of the season.
Gillingham *(From trainee on 8/12/1992) FL 57+5/2 FLC 4 FAC 6 Others 5+3*
Fulham *(£13,000 on 30/7/1996) FL 48+2/4 FLC 3/1 FAC 2 Others 2*
Brentford *(£50,000 on 12/12/1997) FL 37 FLC 2 FAC 2 Others 0+1*
Brighton & Hove A *(£20,000 on 9/7/1999) FL 191+6/14 FLC 8/1 FAC 10/3 Others 6*

WATSON Stephen (Steve) Craig
Born: North Shields, 1 April 1974
Height: 6'0" **Weight:** 12.7
International Honours: E: B-1; U21-12; Yth
Steve had something of an unlucky season at Everton last term, being kept out of the team due to the good form of others at the beginning and then picking up a stomach injury against Manchester City on Boxing Day that sidelined him for three months. When he returned to the team in the spring he showed what a

versatile footballer he is: putting in a tremendous performance at left back in the win over Manchester United and also playing at centre half and in midfield when required. Steve has played in almost every position in his time at Goodison (even as an emergency striker) and his courage and determination were rewarded with the offer of a new contract at the end of the season.
Newcastle U *(From trainee on 6/4/1991) P/FL 179+29/12 FLC 10+6/1 FAC 13+4 Others 18+4/1*
Aston Villa *(£4,000,000 on 15/10/1998) PL 39+2 FLC 8+1/1 FAC 4*
Everton *(£2,500,000 on 12/7/2000) PL 106+20/14 FLC 7+1/1 FAC 2+1/1*

WATT Steven (Steve) Mair
Born: Aberdeen, 1 May 1985
Height: 6'3" **Weight:** 13.12
International Honours: S: B-1; U21-2
'If you're good enough, you're old enough'. That was the maxim employed by Jose Mourinho when he pitched this young central defender into the FA Cup third round tie against Scunthorpe United. In front of a full house, Steve made an accomplished debut as part of an unfamiliar-looking Chelsea team who could have been caught napping by the League Two side. He made his Premiership bow in the final match of the season at Newcastle as a very late substitute. A recent rarity, in as much as he is a graduate from the youth team, Steve has formidable competition ahead of him if he wishes to become a long-term first-team player.
Chelsea *(From trainee on 1/7/2002) PL 0+1 FAC 1*

WATTS Ryan Dale
Born: Greenford, 18 May 1988
Height: 5'9" **Weight:** 10.10
One of several promising youngsters on the books at Brentford, Ryan stepped up to make his senior debut when he came on as a substitute in the last game of the season against Hull. He was used on the left wing, showing flashes of skill, and will be looking to make further progress in the 2005-06 campaign.
Brentford *(Trainee) FL 0+1*

WAY Darren
Born: Plymouth, 21 November 1979
Height: 5'7" **Weight:** 11.0
Club Honours: FAT '02; NC '03; Lge 2 '05
International Honours: E: SP-3
Darren provided the dynamo in midfield for Yeovil Town last term. A tremendous battler in the centre of the park, he was one of the key members of the team and scored nine valuable goals. Darren was rewarded for his efforts with the club's 'Player of the Year' and also won a place in the PFA League Two team of the season.
Norwich C *(From trainee on 11/9/1998)*
Yeovil T *(Free on 19/8/2000) FL 83+1/12 FLC 3 FAC 7/2 Others 2*

WEALE Christopher (Chris)
Born: Chard, 9 February 1982
Height: 6'2" **Weight:** 13.3
Club Honours: FAT '02; NC '03; Lge 2 '05
International Honours: E: SP-4
This talented goalkeeper started the season well for Yeovil and maintained that form until the latter part of the campaign when he was replaced by Steve Collis for the run-in to the League Two title. Chris performed with his usual quality and was one of five Yeovil players selected for the PFA League Two team of the season.
Yeovil T *(From juniors on 5/6/2000) FL 72+1 FLC 3 FAC 8 Others 1*

WEATHERSTONE Simon
Born: Reading, 26 January 1980
Height: 5'10" **Weight:** 12.0
Club Honours: NC '02
International Honours: E: SP-3
This experienced striker was only on the bench for Yeovil last term and in September he moved on to Conference South outfit Hornchurch in search of regular first-team football. Later in the campaign he linked up with Stevenage, scoring twice from 13 starts.
Oxford U *(From trainee on 27/3/1997) FL 25+27/3 FLC 1+3/1 Others 1*
Boston U *(Free on 16/2/2001) FL 57+5/10 FLC 2/1 Others 4/1*
Yeovil T *(£15,000 on 23/1/2004) FL 11+10/1 FLC 0+1*

WEAVER Nicholas (Nick) James
Born: Sheffield, 2 March 1979
Height: 6'3" **Weight:** 13.6
Club Honours: Div 1 '02
International Honours: E: U21-10
Nick's appearances for Manchester City have been restricted over the past few seasons due to injury problems with his right knee. However, he put all that behind him and returned to action for City's reserve side last December. He successfully completed a useful run of appearances and was rewarded for all his hard work and endeavour with a 10-minute outing between the sticks in City's final Premiership game of the season at home to Middlesbrough.
Mansfield T *(Trainee) FL 1*
Manchester C *(£200,000 on 2/5/1997) P/FL 145+2 FLC 14 FAC 11 Others 4*

WEAVER Simon Daniel
Born: Doncaster, 20 December 1977
Height: 6'1" **Weight:** 10.7
This hard-working central defender began the 2004-05 season in Lincoln City's starting line-up but quickly found himself out of favour. Simon was unable to get back into the first-team squad and spent two months on loan at Macclesfield Town as cover for regular defenders who were out injured, usually playing on the right side of a three-man central defence. In December he opted for regular first-team football with Kidderminster. He proved himself to be a brave central defender and shored up the back line for a time. Simon moved to right back after the arrival of Mark Jackson and he generally acquitted himself well.
Sheffield Wed *(From trainee on 24/5/1996. Freed during 1998 close season)*
Doncaster Rov *(Loaned on 14/2/1997) FL 2*
Lincoln C *(Free from Nuneaton Borough, ex Ilkeston T, on 7/8/2002) FL 88/3 FLC 2 FAC 3 Others 8/1*
Macclesfield T *(Loaned on 15/10/2004) FL 7 FAC 2 Others 2*
Kidderminster Hrs *(Free on 9/12/2004) FL 22+1*

WEBB Daniel (Danny) John
Born: Poole, 2 July 1983
Height: 6'1" **Weight:** 11.8
Club Honours: Div 2 '02
Danny had something of a disappointing campaign at Cambridge last season when he never really established himself in the first team. The hard-working striker managed just one goal in over 20 first-team outings, netting against one of his former clubs, Lincoln City, in February.
Southend U *(From trainee at Southampton on 4/12/2000) FL 16+15/3 FLC 1 FAC 1+1 Others 3+2/1*
Brighton & Hove A *(Loaned on 12/12/2001) FL 7+5/1 FAC 1*
Brighton & Hove A *(Loaned on 8/11/2002) FL 0+3*
Hull C *(Free on 13/12/2002) FL 4+12 Others 2/1*
Lincoln C *(Loaned on 14/3/2003) FL 4+1/1*
Cambridge U *(Free on 18/12/2003) FL 34+9/4 FAC 1 Others 0+1*

WEBBER Daniel (Danny) Vaughn
Born: Manchester, 28 December 1981
Height: 5'9" **Weight:** 10.8
International Honours: E: Yth
This inventive striker was largely responsible for Watford's heartening start

to the 2004-05 season and his nine goals by the end of September made him the leading scorer in the Championship at that point. However, he had the misfortune to dislocate his shoulder in November when he collided with a post at Gillingham, and was out of action for two months. On his return, he struggled to regain his earlier sharpness and was loaned to Sheffield United as the transfer deadline approached, with a view to a permanent transfer. He made an immediate impact for the Blades with his speed and direct approach, scoring three times in his first two games.
Manchester U *(From trainee on 7/1/1999) FLC 1+1 Others 0+1*
Port Vale *(Loaned on 23/11/2001) FL 2+2 Others 0+1*
Watford *(Loaned on 28/3/2002) FL 4+1/2*
Watford *(Loaned on 13/8/2002) FL 11+1/2*
Watford *(Signed on 7/7/2003) FL 48+7/17 FLC 3+1 FAC 1+3*
Sheffield U *(Loaned on 24/3/2005) FL 6+1/3*

WEBSTER Adrian

Born: Hawkes Bay, New Zealand, 11 October 1980
Height: 5'8" **Weight:** 10.9
International Honours: New Zealand: 1
This young midfielder joined Darlington shortly after the start of last season and made his full debut in the FA Cup tie against Yeovil Town last November. He runs unselfishly throughout the game and was extremely unlucky not to get his name on the score-sheet with some tremendous bursts into the penalty area. This energetic style of play rewarded him with a regular place in the squad. In the summer he was called up for training with the full New Zealand international squad.
Darlington *(Free from St George, NSW, Australia, ex Macarthur Rams, Blacktown C, Charlton Ath N/C, trial at Colchester U, Ashford T, Folkestone I, Ashford T, Welling U Boreham Wood, Maidstone U, trial at Torquay U, Margate, Maidstone U, on 22/10/2004) FL 16+6 FAC 2*

WEIGHT Scott Aaron

Born: Hounslow, 3 April 1987
Height: 5'11" **Weight:** 10.4
A promising scholar on the books at Brentford, Scott made his senior debut as a substitute in the LDV Vans Trophy tie

Danny Webber

against MK Dons last September when he featured in midfield. He was one of several youngsters not offered professional terms by the Bees in the summer.
Brentford *(Trainee) Others 0+1*

WEIR David (Davie) Gillespie
Born: Falkirk, 10 May 1970
Height: 6'2" **Weight:** 13.7
Club Honours: S Div 1 '94; B&Q '94; SC '98
International Honours: S: 40
After looking perhaps to be nearing the end of his Everton career in 2003-04, this veteran centre half had an admirable season at club level and was restored to the national team under Walter Smith after his self-imposed exile. He also netted his first goal in over three years in the home win over Newcastle. A fine, ball-playing defender, who can also play at right back, he is resolute and brave – qualities he displayed superbly in the memorable home win over Man United. Davie is an intelligent and articulate professional who was out-of-contract during the summer.
Falkirk *(From Glasgow Celtic juniors on 1/8/1992) SL 133/8 SLC 5 SC 6 Others 5*
Heart of Midlothian *(Signed on 29/7/1996) SL 92/8 SLC 10/2 SC 9/2 Others 6*
Everton *(£250,000 on 17/2/1999) PL 189+8/8 FLC 9 FAC 13+2*

WELCH Michael Francis
Born: Winsford, 11 January 1982
Height: 6'3" **Weight:** 11.12
International Honours: RoI: Yth
Michael featured in two-thirds of Macclesfield's matches last season on the right side of a three-man central defence, also occasionally deputising at left back in a four-man defence. He always makes good use of his physical presence, is not afraid to make timely tackles and clears the ball well up field to avert danger. In addition, there is an attacking side to his game and he scored two goals from open play during the campaign.
Macclesfield T *(From trainee at Barnsley on 9/8/2001) FL 108+6/5 FLC 4 FAC 6 Others 4*

WELLENS Richard Paul
Born: Manchester, 26 March 1980
Height: 5'9" **Weight:** 11.6
Club Honours: AMC '02, '04
International Honours: E: Yth
This talented midfielder was a regular in the Blackpool line-up last term until injury and suspension ruled him out of the closing stages of the campaign. He scored five goals for the Seasiders including a spectacular in the FA Cup tie against Tamworth. He was reported to have signed for Oldham Athletic during the summer, thus bringing to an end his five-year stay at Bloomfield Road.
Manchester U *(From trainee on 19/5/1997) FLC 0+1*
Blackpool *(Signed on 23/3/2000) FL 173+15/16 FLC 8+1 FAC 10+2/2 Others 12+5/1*

WELLER Paul Anthony
Born: Brighton, 6 March 1975
Height: 5'8" **Weight:** 11.2
Rochdale offered this former Burnley man a trial at the start of the 2004-05 season and after regaining match fitness Paul made his debut for Dale as a non-contract player. Despite showing his class in midfield over the next few games, he was again injured and the club decided not to pursue a permanent signing. After a short trial with Leek Town he then joined Stalybridge Celtic.
Burnley *(From trainee on 30/11/1993) FL 199+53/11 FLC 12+2 FAC 8+6/2 Others 7*
Rochdale *(Free on 30/9/2004) FL 5*

WELLS Benjamin (Ben)
Born: Basingstoke, 26 March 1988
Height: 5'9" **Weight:** 10.7
A first-year scholar with Swindon Town, Ben made his senior debut as a substitute at Hudddersfield in the final away game of the 2004-05 season due to an injury crisis and did not look overawed by the occasion. He is a promising central midfielder who can also play wide right if required.
Swindon T *(Trainee) FL 0+1*

WELSH Andrew (Andy)
Born: Manchester, 24 November 1983
Height: 5'8" **Weight:** 9.8
International Honours: S: Yth
This popular winger was a regular for Stockport during the first half of last season playing on the left-hand side of midfield. He impressed with his trickery and his mazy runs left defenders in his path. In November he moved on to Sunderland where he made an immediate impact, scoring on his home debut in the FA Cup victory over Premiership Crystal Palace. Although Andy was mainly a squad player for the remainder of the campaign, he came up trumps again at Queen's Park Rangers in April when he volleyed a brilliant equaliser that turned the game in the Black Cats' favour.
Stockport Co *(From trainee on 11/7/2001) FL 44+31/3 FLC 1+2 FAC 2 Others 3+2*
Macclesfield T *(Loaned on 30/8/2002) FL 4+2/2*
Sunderland *(£15,000 on 24/11/2004) FL 3+4/1 FAC 1/1*

WELSH John Joseph
Born: Liverpool, 10 January 1984
Height: 5'7" **Weight:** 11.6
International Honours: E: U21-4; Yth
The captain of Liverpool's reserve team advanced his claims for a regular first-team slot in midfield with seven first-team appearances last season. His first outings were as a substitute in the Carling Cup ties at home to Middlesbrough and at Tottenham. In the latter game he calmly converted one of the penalties in the shoot-out which gave the Reds an unlikely victory. John made his first start in the FA Cup tie away to Burnley in January and his first Premiership start at home to Bolton Wanderers in April, when Liverpool's squad was down to the bare bones through injury. He also became a regular selection in the England U21 team. John will certainly be looking for more first-team opportunities in the 2005-06 campaign.
Liverpool *(From trainee on 29/1/2001) PL 2+2 FLC 0+3 FAC 1 Others 0+2*

WEST Dean
Born: Morley, 5 December 1972
Height: 5'10" **Weight:** 12.2
Club Honours: Div 2 '97
Dean returned to Sincil Bank in the summer of 2004 after a ten-year absence and began the season in the starting line-up at right back. However, he lost his place after just four games and was unable to force his way back before being transferred to neighbours Boston United in September. He slotted in well at right back for the Pilgrims and proved to be a steady player who was keen to take the ball forward down the flank. Dean struggled to hold down a place in the second half of the season and was not offered a new contract at the end of the campaign.
Lincoln C *(From trainee on 17/8/1991) FL 93+26/20 FLC 11/1 FAC 6/1 Others 5+2/1*
Bury *(Signed on 29/9/1995) FL 100+10/8 FLC 6 FAC 3 Others 2+1*
Burnley *(Free on 26/7/1999) FL 145+13/5 FLC 6+2/1 FAC 11 Others 1*
Lincoln C *(Free on 14/7/2004) FL 4*
Boston U *(Free on 21/9/2004) FL 22+2 FLC 1 FAC 2*

WESTCARR Craig Naptali
Born: Nottingham, 29 January 1985
Height: 5'11" **Weight:** 11.8
International Honours: E: Yth
Craig missed the start of the 2004-05 season due to a knee injury and after making his only appearance of the season for Nottingham Forest as a substitute against West Ham in December

he was loaned out to Lincoln City. The skilful striker made an immediate impact at Sincil Bank when he netted the winner on his debut against Bury but then struggled to produce similar performances. On transfer-deadline day he joined MK Dons on loan but although he worked hard he failed to register a goal for the League One club.
Nottingham F *(From trainee on 31/1/2002) FL 2+21/1 FLC 1+1 FAC 0+1*
Lincoln C *(Loaned on 31/12/2004) FL 5+1/1*
MK Dons *(Loaned on 24/3/2005) FL 0+4*

WESTLAKE Ian John
Born: Clacton, 10 July 1983
Height: 5'10" **Weight:** 11.6
After a successful 2003-04 campaign with Ipswich, it was a little disappointing that Ian was unable to maintain his best form throughout the 2004-05 season. Although he had periods when he was on top of his game he was unable to find the consistency of performance over the whole of the season and he was rested from some games. He was still able to chip in with a number of goals from midfield and scored his first headed goal in the home game with Rotherham.
Ipswich T *(From trainee on 9/8/2002) FL 71+17/13 FLC 3+1/1 FAC 2 Others 2*

WESTON Curtis James
Born: Greenwich, 24 January 1987
Height: 5'11" **Weight:** 11.9
A very skilful midfield player who is equally adept with both feet, Curtis made a handful of first-team appearances for Millwall last term. Still in his teens he has time on his side, but he will be looking to feature more regularly in the side in 2005-06.
Millwall *(From trainee on 17/3/2004) FL 2+2 FAC 0+2*

Ian Westlake

WESTON Rhys David
Born: Kingston, 27 October 1980
Height: 6'1" **Weight:** 12.3
International Honours: W: 7; U21-4; E: Yth; Sch
Rhys started the 2004-05 season as the first-choice right back in a back four for Cardiff, but midway through September he picked up an ankle ligament injury that caused him to miss a large chunk of the campaign. This was followed by a series of niggling injuries that delayed his comeback but he eventually returned to the side in December replacing his stand-in, loan signing Darren Williams, to finish the season strongly. Rhys's injury problems restricted his involvement with the Wales squad and he will look to reclaim his international berth in 2005-06.
Arsenal *(From trainee on 8/7/1999) PL 1 FLC 1+1*
Cardiff C *(£300,000 on 21/11/2000) FL 144+8/2 FLC 6 FAC 13+1 Others 7*

WESTWOOD Ashley Michael
Born: Bridgnorth, 31 August 1976
Height: 6'0" **Weight:** 12.8
Club Honours: FAYC '95
International Honours: E: Yth
Ashley was Northampton Town's club captain last season but struggled for much of the campaign with injuries. The central defender performed efficiently when selected and scored his only goal of the campaign with a tap-in from a corner in the 2-0 home win over Shrewsbury in March.
Manchester U *(From trainee on 1/7/1994)*
Crewe Alex *(£40,000 on 26/7/1995) FL 93+5/9 FLC 8 FAC 9/2 Others 10*
Bradford C *(£150,000 on 20/7/1998) P/FL 18+6/2 FLC 1 FAC 2+1 Others 1+1*
Sheffield Wed *(£150,000 + on 10/8/2000) FL 79+3/5 FLC 10+2/4 FAC 2*
Northampton T *(Free on 15/7/2003) FL 27+1/2 FAC 2+1 Others 1*

WESTWOOD Christopher (Chris) John
Born: Dudley, 13 February 1977
Height: 6'0" **Weight:** 12.2
This dependable central defender struggled to find his form for Hartlepool early on in the 2004-05 campaign, but he was soon back to his best, establishing a fine central-defensive

partnership with Michael Nelson. Seldom a goal-scorer, he had a purple patch in mid-season when he scored five goals in five games. Chris was sidelined with a hamstring injury late in the campaign, but was back to help Pools reach the League One play-off final.
Wolverhampton W *(From trainee on 3/7/1995) FL 3+1/1 FLC 1+1 (Freed during 1998 close season)*
Hartlepool U *(Signed from Telford U on 24/3/1999) FL 244+6/7 FLC 8 FAC 15/2 Others 20*

WETHERALL David

Born: Sheffield, 14 March 1971
Height: 6'3" **Weight:** 13.12
International Honours: E: Sch
Bradford City's captain looked a class act in his first season in League One, leading by example and marshalling the defence well. David missed only one game, which represents his most prolific run of matches since his first year at Valley Parade. He also scored four goals and was the club's second top-scorer for a lengthy period.
Sheffield Wed *(From trainee on 1/7/1989)*
Leeds U *(£125,000 on 15/7/1991) P/FL 188+14/12 FLC 19+1/2 FAC 21+3/4 Others 4*
Bradford C *(£1,400,000 on 7/7/1999) P/FL 168+3/10 FLC 7/2 FAC 3 Others 3*

WHALEY Simon

Born: Bolton, 7 June 1985
Height: 5'11" **Weight:** 11.7
A very satisfying first full season of regular first-team football saw this adaptable Bury teenager continue to improve and grow in confidence as the months passed. During the first half of the campaign, he was largely used as a substitute, and generally joined the action in central midfield. He gained a regular berth in the side from January onwards playing as a right wing back, but he also appeared in midfield occasionally. Simon helped himself to three League goals, the pick of which was a superb 30-yard strike against Bristol Rovers in March.
Bury *(From trainee on 30/10/2002) FL 25+25/4 FLC 1 FAC 0+2 Others 0+5*

WHALLEY Gareth

Born: Manchester, 19 December 1973
Height: 5'10" **Weight:** 11.12
Gareth was reunited with his former manager Paul Jewell when he joined Wigan Athletic on a short-term contract last September. He played a peripheral role in the centre of midfield making five consecutive appearances in December and January. A skilful and hard-working player with a wholehearted approach, he quietly went about his work, always willing to accept a pass and deliver a telling ball. Out of contract at the end of the season, he was not offered a new deal.
Crewe Alex *(From trainee on 29/7/1992) FL 174+6/9 FLC 11+1/1 FAC 15+1/3 Others 24/3*
Bradford C *(£600,000 on 24/7/1998) P/FL 99+4/3 FLC 10+2/2 FAC 2 Others 5+1*
Crewe Alex *(Loaned on 28/3/2002) FL 7*
Cardiff C *(Free on 9/7/2002) FL 33+8/2 FLC 2 FAC 1 Others 3*
Wigan Ath *(Free on 14/9/2004) FL 7+1 FAC 1*

WHALLEY Shaun James

Born: Prescot, 7 August 1987
Height: 5'9" **Weight:** 10.7
A striker who had previously been on the books of Southport, Shaun was one of several youngsters introduced to the Chester City squad by Ian Rush. The teenager made his debut as a substitute in the home game against Cambridge United and came off the bench on four other occasions in order to inject some pace into the forward line.
Chester C *(Free from Southport on 17/9/2004) FL 0+3 Others 0+2*

WHEATER David James

Born: Redcar, 14 February 1987
Height: 6'4" **Weight:** 12.12
Club Honours: FAYC '04
International Honours: E: Yth
Last season proved to be one of great progress in Boro's reserve side for this young central defender, yet another potentially great prospect to come through the portals of the club's Rockcliffe Academy. Because of injuries to more senior players David was elevated to the substitutes' bench for the club's historic first away game in European competition against Banik Ostrava in September. He signed a new long-term contract in February and realised his dreams when he made his first-team debut, albeit as a last- minute replacement for Stuart Parnaby against Sporting Lisbon the following month.
Middlesbrough *(From trainee on 16/2/2005) Others 0+1*

WHELAN Glenn David

Born: Dublin, 13 January 1984
Height: 6'0" **Weight:** 12.5
International Honours: RoI: U21-13; Yth
Glenn had a useful first season at Hillsborough in 2004-05. Once he got in the side he cemented his place in midfield, and became a vital member of the squad. He continued to his tally of caps for the Republic of Ireland at U21 level and was also voted as the Republic's 'Young Player of the Year'.
Manchester C *(From trainee on 25/1/2001) Others 0+1*
Bury *(Loaned on 29/9/2003) FL 13 FAC 1 Others 1*
Sheffield Wed *(Free on 7/7/2004) FL 36/2 FLC 2 FAC 1/1 Others 3/1*

WHING Andrew (Andy) John

Born: Birmingham, 20 September 1984
Height: 6'0" **Weight:** 12.0
Andy was second choice at right back for Coventry throughout the 2004-05 season, being kept out firstly by Louis Carey, then after Micky Adams' arrival, by Richard Duffy. His appearances came only because of injury or suspension to others, but he always gave 100 per cent when selected. However, in the final game at Highfield Road against Derby he came off the bench to score with his first touch, a goal which was the final one at the stadium and was voted as the club's 'Goal of the Season'.
Coventry C *(From trainee on 7/4/2003) FL 48+10/2 FLC 1+3 FAC 2*

WHITAKER Daniel (Danny) Phillip

Born: Wilmslow, 14 November 1980
Height: 5'10" **Weight:** 11.2
Danny featured regularly in the Macclesfield line-up in the first half of last season in his favoured central-midfield role, but following the arrival of new signings he often found himself on the substitutes' bench. Danny always worked hard using his pace to good effect with some of his best performances coming when pressing forward which gave him the opportunity to score four goals.
Macclesfield T *(Signed from Wilmslow Sports on 5/7/2000) FL 115+14/19 FLC 4/4 FAC 10/2 Others 6+1/1*

WHITBREAD Zak Benjamin

Born: Houston, USA, 4 March 1984
Height: 6'2" **Weight:** 11.6
International Honours: USA: U23
Zak is a central defender from the Liverpool Academy who, in common with several other youngsters at the club, made his first-team debut in the early rounds of the Carling Cup, firstly at Millwall in October and subsequently at home to Middlesbrough and away to Tottenham. He also played in the FA Cup defeat at Burnley in January. Along with his defensive partner in the reserves, David Raven, he will be looking forward to more outings in the 2005-06 season.
Liverpool *(From trainee on 8/5/2003) FLC 3 FAC 1*

WHITE Alan
Born: Darlington, 22 March 1976
Height: 6'1" **Weight:** 13.2
Alan joined Leyton Orient during the summer of 2004 and proved to be a tall dominant centre half who likes nothing more than to bring the ball down and pass. He showed great vision in the home game with Darlington when his 50-yard pass enabled Lee Steele to score. However, he was unable to win a first-team place towards the end of the season and was allowed to join Boston United. He provided the Lincolnshire club with a much-needed experienced head at the centre of defence. Alan played on the right of a three-man defensive line-up and looked to be an excellent signing. He was solid in the tackle and difficult to beat in the air.
Middlesbrough *(From trainee on 8/7/1994) Others 1*
Luton T *(£40,000 on 22/9/1997) FL 60+20/3 FLC 3+3 FAC 2 Others 4*
Colchester U *(Loaned on 12/11/1999) FL 4 Others 1*
Colchester U *(Free on 19/7/2000) FL 128+11/4 FLC 7+1 FAC 6+2 Others 6*
Leyton Orient *(Free on 6/7/2004) FL 26 FLC 1 FAC 2 Others 2*
Boston U *(Free on 4/3/2005) FL 11*

WHITE Andrew (Andy)
Born: Swanwick, 6 November 1981
Height: 6'4" **Weight:** 13.4
Andy had a short spell on loan at Crewe in 2002 but after his release from Mansfield Town in the summer of 2004 he joined the staff at Gresty Road. The young striker made good progress last term and played his part in the attack when included in the first-team squad, netting four valuable goals.
Mansfield T *(Signed from Hucknall T on 13/7/2000) FL 37+31/10 FLC 1+2/1 FAC 0+3 Others 0+2*
Crewe Alex *(Loaned on 24/10/2002) FL 0+2*
Boston U *(Loaned on 11/9/2003) FL 3+3*
Kidderminster Hrs *(Loaned on 31/10/2003) FL 6+1/1 FAC 2*
Crewe Alex *(Free on 7/6/2004) FL 11+11/4 FLC 0+1 FAC 0+1*

WHITE Jason Lee
Born: Sutton-in-Ashfield, 28 January 1984
Height: 6'3" **Weight:** 12.7
Mansfield Town's second-choice 'keeper started the 2004-05 season with his hand in plaster after breaking his thumb towards the end of the previous campaign. However, he recovered to make his full debut in the LDV Vans Trophy tie at Macclesfield when several youth team and fringe players were given a run out in the first team. His patience as understudy to Kevin Pilkington was finally rewarded when his mentor was injured and he deputised in the last four matches of the season. Excellent with his kicks, he showed some good handling and positioning skills.
Mansfield T *(From trainee on 9/8/2002) FL 4+1 Others 1*

WHITE John Alan
Born: Maldon, 26 July 1986
Height: 5'10" **Weight:** 12.1
A product of Colchester United's youth system, John negotiated the big step up to the senior ranks last term, and proved himself capable of holding his own in League One. He made his first-team debut as a substitute in the Carling Cup first round win over Cheltenham, and made his full League debut a few days later in the 4-1 home win over Doncaster. John deputised in central midfield, due to an injury crisis, but also operated as a left back and even at centre half.
Colchester U *(From trainee on 23/2/2005) FL 16+4 FLC 0+1 FAC 3*

WHITEHEAD Dean
Born: Oxford, 12 January 1982
Height: 5'11" **Weight:** 12.1
Club Honours: Ch '05
This midfielder must surely be one of the Wearsiders' all-time bargain buys and he ended the season with a Championship winners' medal and the accolade of

Dean Whitehead

Players' Player of the Year' at the Stadium of Light. Dean can play wide on the right wing where he is an excellent crosser of the ball, and also filled in at right back last term, but it is in central midfield where he is at his best and he proved himself to be a real box-to-box player, making defensive tackles in his own penalty area one minute and the next having an effort on goal in the opponents' box. Dean weighed in with five goals last season and his strong tackling and boundless energy were crucial to Sunderland's triumphant return to the Premiership.

Oxford U *(From trainee on 20/4/2000) FL 92+30/9 FLC 5+1 FAC 3+2 Others 1+2*
Sunderland *(Signed on 2/8/2004) FL 39+3/5 FLC 1+1 FAC 2*

WHITEHEAD Stuart David
Born: Bromsgrove, 17 July 1976
Height: 5'11" **Weight:** 12.4
This experienced defender was a regular in the Shrewsbury Town line-up last term. He formed effective central defensive partnerships with a number of players, largely in a back-four formation, and was one of the few out-of-contract players at the club to be offered a new deal. Equally effective at full back, Stuart is calm and controlled on the ball and always looks to use possession sensibly.

Bolton W *(Signed from Bromsgrove Rov on 18/9/1995)*
Carlisle U *(Free on 31/7/1998) FL 148+4/2 FLC 7 FAC 4 Others 2*
Darlington *(Free on 3/10/2002) FL 23 FAC 1+1 (Free to Telford U on 7/7/2003)*
Shrewsbury T *(Free on 5/7/2004) FL 37+3 FAC 1 Others 2*

WHITLEY James (Jim)
Born: Zambia, 14 April 1975
Height: 5'9" **Weight:** 11.0
Club Honours: AMC '05
International Honours: NI: 3; B-1
This industrious Wrexham midfielder had a frustrating time with injuries which restricted his appearances last term. A very combative player who makes the opposition wary of his presence, Jim was absent for the final three months of the season and was sorely missed by his colleagues. Off the field Jim is a talented artist and an exhibition of his work was held at the City of Manchester Stadium during the summer.

Manchester C *(From juniors on 1/8/1994) FL 27+11 FLC 3+1/1 FAC 2+1 Others 0+1*
Blackpool *(Loaned on 20/8/1999) FL 7+1 FLC 1*
Norwich C *(Loaned on 24/8/2000) FL 7+1/1*
Swindon T *(Loaned on 15/12/2000) FL 2 FAC 1*
Northampton T *(Loaned on 27/2/2001) FL 13*
Wrexham *(Free on 11/10/2001) FL 125+5/1 FLC 3+1 FAC 3 Others 7+1*

WHITLEY Jeffrey (Jeff)
Born: Zambia, 28 January 1979
Height: 5'8" **Weight:** 11.2
Club Honours: Ch '05
International Honours: NI: 19; B-2; U21-17
A robust central midfielder, powerful in the tackle, Jeff's partnership with Carl Robinson in the engine room at Sunderland last season was an important factor in the club's Championship triumph. Jeff uses the ball sensibly and is often asked to sit in front of the back four to provide extra defensive cover. A regular at international level for Northern Ireland, Jeff's brilliant volleyed goal at the Millennium Stadium against Wales in September will be long remembered. Shortly after the end of the season it was announced that Jeff has been handed a free transfer by Black Cats' boss Mick McCarthy but he left the Stadium of Light with a deserved Championship winners' medal.

Manchester C *(From trainee on 19/2/1996) P/FL 96+27/8 FLC 9+1 FAC 2+2 Others 4*
Wrexham *(Loaned on 14/1/1999) FL 9/2*
Notts Co *(Loaned on 21/3/2002) FL 6*
Notts Co *(Loaned on 18/10/2002) FL 12 FAC 1 Others 1*
Sunderland *(Free on 7/8/2003) FL 65+3/2 FLC 2 FAC 5 Others 2*

WHITLOW Michael (Mike) William
Born: Northwich, 13 January 1968
Height: 6'0" **Weight:** 12.12
Club Honours: Div 2 '90, Div 1 '92; FLC '97
Mike joined Notts County in the summer of 2004 and was seen as the experienced leader around which manager Gary Mills intended to build his side. However, he had something of a difficult season when a series of unfortunate injuries prevented him from producing his own high standards. Nevertheless, Mike remained model professional both on and off the pitch.

Leeds U *(£10,000 from Witton A on 11/11/1988) FL 62+15/4 FLC 4+1 FAC 1+4 Others 9*
Leicester C *(£250,000 on 27/3/1992) P/FL 141+6/8 FLC 12/1 FAC 6 Others 14*
Bolton W *(£500,000 + on 19/9/1997) P/FL 124+8/2 FLC 13+2 FAC 10+1 Others 2+3*
Sheffield U *(Free on 22/7/2003) FL 13+4/1 FLC 1 FAC 1+1*
Notts Co *(Free on 29/7/2004) FL 22+2 FLC 1 FAC 4 Others 1*

WHITMORE Theodore (Theo) Eccleston
Born: St James, Jamaica, 5 August 1972
Height: 6'2" **Weight:** 11.2
International Honours: Jamaica
Signed up by his former Hull manager Brian Little, Theo was used sparingly in the for Tranmere early on last season until he was considered fully match-fit. A veteran midfielder with an eye for a good pass, he can be dangerous in any position and was even pressed into service as an emergency, if not very successful, goalkeeper in the away game at Hull when both the first- and second-choice 'keepers were injured and needed to be substituted in the same match. Theo has an exquisite touch for such a big man, and his best work is in evidence when the play is going forward; his silky skills and ability to snap up opportunist goals have also made him a crowd favourite. At the time of writing he was out of contract and his future at Prenton Park was uncertain.

Hull C *(Free from Seba U, Jamaica on 22/10/1999) FL 63+14/9 FLC 3/1 FAC 7+1 Others 5/1 (Freed during 2002 close season)*
Livingston *(Free from Seba U, Jamaica on 1/8/2003) SL 2+1 (Freed on 7/12/2003)*
Tranmere Rov *(Free from Seba U, Jamaica on 8/7/2004) FL 17+16/5 FLC 1 Others 2+1*

WHITTAKER Daniel (Danny) Stephen
Born: Blackpool, 13 January 1987
Height: 6'0" **Weight:** 11.10
One of several promising youngsters on the books at Bloomfield Road, Danny featured regular for the reserve and youth teams last season. Danny made his first-team debut in the LDV Vans Trophy tie at York in September when he came on to replace Danny Coid in the centre of midfield during the second half.

Blackpool *(Trainee) Others 0+1*

WHITTINGHAM Peter Michael
Born: Nuneaton, 8 September 1984
Height: 5'10" **Weight:** 10.5
Club Honours: FAYC '02
International Honours: E: U21-7; Yth
A lively young midfielder with a powerful shot, Peter has a good left foot and is strong in the tackle. However, he struggled to progress last season and the majority of his appearances came from the bench. He enjoyed a spell on loan at Burnley during the second half of the campaign, where he showed plenty of skill but sometimes struggled to come to terms with the physical aspects of Championship football. Peter also represented England at U21 level during the campaign.

Aston Villa *(From trainee on 2/11/2002) PL 26+23/1 FLC 6+2/1 FAC 1*
Burnley *(Loaned on 14/2/2005) FL 7 FAC 2*

WHITTLE Justin Phillip
Born: Derby, 18 March 1971
Height: 6'1" **Weight:** 12.12
After struggling to achieve a regular spot in the squad at the KC Stadium in 2003-04, defender Justin turned down a contract extension at Hull and opted to cross the River Humber to join local rivals Grimsby Town. The move was a success with Justin retaining a regular place in the Mariners' back four and assisting the club to steer well clear of the relegation positions. He also contributed a single goal, netting the winner against Notts County at Blundell Park in December.
Glasgow Celtic *(Signed from Army during 1994 close season)*
Stoke C *(Free on 20/10/1994) FL 66+13/1 FLC 3+4 FAC 2 Others 2*
Hull C *(£65,000 on 27/11/1998) FL 184+9/2 FLC 9 FAC 8+2 Others 7/1*
Grimsby T *(Free on 2/8/2004) FL 39+1/1 FLC 2 FAC 1*

WIDDRINGTON Thomas (Tommy)
Born: Newcastle, 1 October 1971
Height: 5'10" **Weight:** 12.2
Club Honours: AMC '01
Tommy was appointed Macclesfield team captain at the beginning of last season and until the middle of December was a regular in the side playing in a defensive central-midfield role. However, with the introduction of younger players to the side Tommy found himself on the bench or being substituted. His contract was terminated by mutual consent in January and he joined Port Vale on a non-contract basis in January. Tommy made his debut as a substitute against Brentford and was used mainly as a squad player during an injury crisis. In February an opportunity arose at non-league Salisbury City through contacts from his Southampton days and he moved on once more.
Southampton *(From trainee on 10/5/1990) P/FL 67+8/3 FLC 3+1 FAC 11*
Wigan Ath *(Loaned on 12/9/1991) FL 5+1 FLC 2*
Grimsby T *(£300,000 on 11/7/1996) FL 72+17/8 FLC 10+3 FAC 3+1 Others 1*
Port Vale *(Free on 24/3/1999) FL 77+5/8 FLC 2 FAC 2 Others 3*
Hartlepool U *(Free on 30/7/2001) FL 50+6/5 FLC 1 FAC 1+1 Others 2*
Macclesfield T *(Free on 19/8/2003) FL 55+3 FLC 1 FAC 5 Others 4*
Port Vale *(Free on 14/1/2005) FL 2+4*

WIJNHARD Clyde
Born: Paramaribo, Surinam, 9 November 1973
Height: 5'11" **Weight:** 12.4
Clyde joined Darlington in a bid to resurrect his career after serious injuries had kept him out of action for the whole of the previous campaign. He certainly arrived with a bang, scoring in his first three outings, and continued in a similar vein to end as top scorer with a total of 15 goals, forming a formidable partnership with fellow striker, Alun Armstrong. His great strength in holding off opponents and bustling forward style, coupled with his aerial power made him a firm favourite with the Quakers' fans and always a handful for opposition defences.
Leeds U *(£1,500,000 from Willem II Tilburg, Holland, ex Ajax, Groningen, RKC Waalwijk, on 22/7/1998) PL 11+7/3 FLC 1 FAC 1+1/1 Others 1+3*
Huddersfield T *(£750,000 on 22/7/1999) FL 51+11/16 FLC 7/1 FAC 1 Others 1+1/1*
Preston NE *(Free on 22/3/2002) FL 6/3*
Oldham Ath *(Free on 30/8/2002) FL 24+1/10 FLC 3/2 FAC 2/1 Others 1 (Freed during 2003 close season)*
Darlington *(Free from Vitoria Guimaraes, Portugal, on 1/10/2004) FL 31/14 FAC 2*

WILBRAHAM Aaron Thomas
Born: Knutsford, 21 October 1979
Height: 6'3" **Weight:** 12.4
Although his touch and awareness was apparent, Aaron struggled to find his

Clyde Wijnhard

scoring form for Hull City last term and was allowed to go out to Oldham on loan in October. The burly hit man made an immediate impact at Boundary Park, netting twice on his debut as the Latics won 2-1 at Stockport County. He went on to make four more starts before returning to Hull. His fortunes looked brighter after scoring for the Tigers in the first two games of January, however, the introduction of Craig Fagan meant he was unable to establish a starting place as City eased towards back-to-back promotions.
Stockport Co *(From trainee on 29/8/1997) FL 118+54/35 FLC 5+2/1 FAC 3+1 Others 2*
Hull C *(£100,000 on 9/7/2004) FL 10+9/2 FAC 1*
Oldham Ath *(Loaned on 29/10/2004) FL 4/2 Others 1*

WILCOX Jason Malcolm

Born: Farnworth, 15 July 1971
Height: 5'11" **Weight:** 11.10
Club Honours: PL '95
International Honours: E: 3; B-2
This left-sided midfielder was outstanding for Leicester in the home win over Sheffield United, when he also scored his first Foxes' goal Jason then suffered a cruciate ligament injury in the first post-Adams fixture, at Coventry in mid-October. Modern treatment techniques had him able to turn out for the reserves again by late March, and even taste first-team action once more during April.
Blackburn Rov *(From trainee on 13/6/1989) P/FL 242+27/31 FLC 16+1/1 FAC 18+2/2 Others 7*
Leeds U *(£3,000,000 on 17/12/1999) PL 52+29/4 FLC 3 FAC 6+1 Others 9+6/2*
Leicester C *(Free on 3/8/2004) FL 11+3/1 FLC 0+1*

WILES Simon Peter

Born: Preston, 22 April 1985
Height: 5'11" **Weight:** 11.4
This speedy winger had something of a disappointing time at Blackpool last term, for having made a breakthrough into the first-team squad during the pervious campaign, his only appearances came in the LDV Vans Trophy ties. He will be looking to make a much greater impact at Bloomfield Road in the 2005-06 season.
Blackpool *(From trainee on 10/5/2004) FL 0+4 Others 2+2*

WILKINSON Andrew (Andy) Gordon

Born: Stone, 6 August 1984
Height: 5'11" **Weight:** 11.0
This pacy central defender was loaned out to Partick Thistle for the first half of the 2004-05 season to gain experience and received rave reviews for his performances. On his return he spent two months with Stoke's reserves before making a single substitute appearance at Millwall. Andy then spent the last three months of the season on loan at Shrewsbury where he featured at right back and in midfield, helping them retain their League Two status.
Stoke C *(From trainee on 8/7/2002) FL 1+3 FLC 1 Others 0+1*
Partick T *(Loaned on 13/7/2004) SL 9+3/1 SLC 2 Others 1+2*
Shrewsbury T *(Loaned on 8/3/2005) FL 9*

Andy Wilkinson

WILKINSON Jack Lloyd
Born: Beverley, 12 September 1985
Height: 5'8" **Weight:** 10.8
This promising Hartlepool striker failed to make much of an impression in his few first-team appearances last season. In order to gain more experience he had work placement spells with Bishop Auckland and Whitby Town.
Hartlepool U *(Trainee) FL 3+4/2 FAC 0+2*

WILKINSON Wesley (Wes) Michael
Born: Wythenshawe, 1 May 1984
Height: 5'10" **Weight:** 11.1
Wes was released from his contract with Oldham Athletic at the end of the season after enduring a tough first full campaign in the professional game. A pacy young striker, he had signed for the Latics in March 2004 from non-league Nantwich Town after an impressive trial period. But knee damage sustained towards the end of that campaign persisted and, despite undergoing surgery, the striker suffered a series of setbacks that continually hampered his prospects of first-team football.
Oldham Ath *(Signed from Nantwich T on 4/3/2004) FL 2+4 Others 0+1*

WILKSHIRE Luke
Born: Wollongong, Australia, 2 October 1981
Height: 5'9" **Weight:** 11.5
International Honours: Australia: 4; U23-9; Yth
This midfielder had a somewhat mixed campaign for Bristol City in 2004-05. All too frequently he did not appear to be cut out for the hurly-burly soccer in the lower reaches. However he achieved a creditable return of ten goals, the best of which was a 35-yard volley in the home game against Tranmere. Luke made his full international debut for Australia against the Solomon Islands in October and featured in the squad for the Confederations Cup tournament in the summer.
Middlesbrough *(Signed from AIS, Australia on 12/5/1999) PL 13+8 FLC 2 FAC 1*
Bristol C *(£250,000 on 6/8/2003) FL 70+4/12 FLC 4 FAC 4/1 Others 2+2*

WILLETTS Ryan John
Born: Coventry, 3 November 1984
Height: 5'9" **Weight:** 12.0
After signing professional terms for Walsall during the summer of 2004 Ryan got an early first-team opportunity when he appeared on the right-hand side of the defence in the Carling Cup defeat at Sheffield Wednesday in August. He had some injury problems thereafter, but made several impressive reserve-team appearances.
Walsall *(From trainee on 2/7/2004) FLC 1*

WILLIAMS Adrian
Born: Reading, 16 August 1971
Height: 6'2" **Weight:** 13.2
Club Honours: Div 2 '94
International Honours: W: 13
It was a great surprise and disappointment to Reading fans to learn in October that club captain Adrian would be leaving to join Coventry City on a free transfer. Although approaching the veteran stage, the big centre back had looked as reliable and committed as ever during the opening games of the campaign. However, he had mixed fortunes at Highfield Road. He suffered hamstring problems and tonsillitis in December and on the field seemed to miss a compatible central-defensive partner. Adrian suffered a calf strain in March, which kept him out of the run-in and stopped him partnering his fellow Welsh international Robert Page until the final day of the season.
Reading *(From trainee on 4/3/1989) FL 191+5/14 FLC 17/1 FAC 16/2 Others 14/2*
Wolverhampton W *(£750,000 on 3/7/1996) FL 26+1 FLC 3 FAC 2+2 Others 2/1*
Reading *(Loaned on 15/2/2000) FL 5/1 Others 1*
Reading *(Free on 26/3/2000) FL 130+2/3 FLC 8+1 FAC 3 Others 5*
Coventry C *(Free on 2/11/2004) FL 21/2 FAC 2*

WILLIAMS Anthony Simon
Born: Maesteg, 20 September 1977
Height: 6'1" **Weight:** 13.5
International Honours: W: U21-16; Yth
This reliable if unspectacular goalkeeper joined Grimsby Town in the summer of 2004 as part of new manager Russell Slade's programme for reconstructing a team that had been relegated in two consecutive seasons. He was the only Mariners' player to appear in each of the club's 50 first-team games and he remained unflustered throughout the campaign.
Blackburn Rov *(From trainee on 4/7/1996)*
Macclesfield T *(Loaned on 16/10/1998) FL 4*
Bristol Rov *(Loaned on 24/3/1999) FL 9*
Gillingham *(Loaned on 5/8/1999) FL 2 FLC 2*
Macclesfield T *(Loaned on 28/1/2000) FL 11*
Hartlepool U *(Free on 7/7/2000) FL 131 FLC 2 FAC 4 Others 9*
Stockport Co *(Loaned on 23/1/2004) FL 15*
Grimsby T *(Free on 21/7/2004) FL 46 FLC 2 FAC 1 Others 1*

WILLIAMS Ashley Errol
Born: Wolverhampton, 23 March 1984
Height: 6'0" **Weight:** 11.2
Ashley made more appearances for Stockport last season than any other player. He scored his first goal for the club in the 3-1 victory over Huddersfield Town in the FA Cup in November and was on the score sheet the following month with a late strike that sealed all three points in the relegation battle with MK Dons.
Stockport Co *(Free from Hednesford T on 31/12/2003) FL 54/1 FLC 1 FAC 3/1 Others 1*

WILLIAMS Benjamin (Ben) Philip
Born: Manchester, 27 August 1982
Height: 6'0" **Weight:** 13.4
International Honours: E: Sch
Having previously been on loan at Crewe during the 2003-04 season, Ben signed permanently for the club in the summer and shared the goalkeeper's jersey with Clayton Ince. A young 'keeper who will improve with further experience, he played against his former club Manchester United in the Carling Cup competition.
Manchester U *(From juniors on 3/7/2001)*
Chesterfield *(Loaned on 30/12/2002) FL 14*
Crewe Alex *(Free on 19/3/2004) FL 33 FLC 3*

WILLIAMS Christopher (Chris) Jonathan
Born: Manchester, 2 February 1985
Height: 5'8" **Weight:** 9.6
This young striker had a difficult time at Stockport last season, when he was unable to break the early-season partnership of Luke Beckett and Warren Feeney. After an appearance in the Carling Cup defeat by Sheffield United he had a brief spell on loan at Grimsby. Chris made a handful of appearances on his return to Edgeley Park, but never managed to establish himself in the line-up and failed to register a goal.
Stockport Co *(From trainee on 5/3/2002) FL 11+20/3 FLC 1+1 FAC 1+4 Others 2/1*
Grimsby T *(Loaned on 4/9/2004) FL 1+2*

WILLIAMS Daniel (Danny) Ivor Llewellyn
Born: Wrexham, 12 July 1979
Height: 6'1" **Weight:** 13.0
Club Honours: AMC '05
International Honours: W: U21-9
Danny was a regular for Wrexham in the opening stages of the season, justifying Denis Smith's faith in bringing the combative midfielder back to the Racecourse. However, he then had problems with a persistent back injury

and from then on he was in and out of the side. Danny is a useful squad member who is adept at holding things together in the centre of the park.
Liverpool *(From trainee on 14/5/1997)*
Wrexham *(Free on 22/3/1999) FL 38+1/3 FLC 4 FAC 4/1 Others 1*
Kidderminster Hrs *(Free on 11/7/2001) FL 108+3/8 FLC 2 FAC 7 Others 5+1*
Bristol Rov *(Free on 25/3/2004) FL 6/1*
Wrexham *(Free on 3/8/2004) FL 21 FLC 2 Others 3+1/1*

WILLIAMS Darren
Born: Middlesbrough, 28 April 1977
Height: 5'10" **Weight:** 11.12
Club Honours: Div 1 '99
International Honours: E: B-1; U21-2
This long-serving utility man made two final appearances last season for Sunderland before joining Cardiff City on loan and then moving to Ninian Park permanently. With injuries to several of the Bluebirds' regular defenders Darren quickly established himself at right back and his committed performances won him the respect of the fans. He earned a short-term contract until the end of the season but a bout of flu' at Christmas saw Darren lose his place to Rhys Weston and he made only sporadic appearances after that.
York C *(From trainee on 21/6/1995) FL 16+4 FLC 4+1 FAC 1 Others 3/1*
Sunderland *(£50,000 on 18/10/1996) P/FL 155+44/4 FLC 20+2/2 FAC 11+2 Others 4+1*
Cardiff C *(Free on 23/9/2004) FL 17+3*

WILLIAMS Eifion Wyn
Born: Bangor, 15 November 1975
Height: 5'11" **Weight:** 11.12
International Honours: W: B-1
This hard-working Hartlepool front runner had a mixed time in 2004-05. No longer assured of a position as striker, he remained a regular first-teamer and often featured on the right side of midfield. Eifion always gave his best, but with this change in role he scored fewer goals. His season ended well, when he came on as substitute in the play-off final against Sheffield Wednesday and scored a fine opportunist goal to equalise the score at 1-1 and put Hartlepool back in the game.
Torquay U *(£70,000 from Barry T on 25/3/1999) FL 84+27/24 FLC 4+1 FAC 3 Others 3*
Hartlepool U *(£30,000 on 6/3/2002) FL 119+13/37 FLC 3+2/2 FAC 7+1/1 Others 9+1/3*

WILLIAMS Gareth Ashley
Born: Cardiff, 10 September 1982
Height: 5'10" **Weight:** 11.13
International Honours: W: U21-5; Yth
Front-runner Gareth joined Colchester last August in a deal that saw Wayne Andrews move in the opposite direction to Selhurst Park. He began impressively, netting on his first start in the 3-1 win at Bournemouth. However, he failed to land a regular place in the side throughout the course of the season, despite scoring a further four goals, including one in the FA Cup win at Hull City and another in the 5-0 home thrashing of Walsall. On his day, he is a lethal finisher.
Crystal Palace *(From trainee on 9/7/2002) FL 0+5 FLC 2+1*
Colchester U *(Loaned on 24/1/2003) FL 6+2/6*

Eifion Williams

Cambridge U *(Loaned on 30/10/2003) FL 4/1*
Bournemouth *(Loaned on 20/2/2004) FL 0+1*
Colchester U *(Loaned on 22/3/2004) FL 5+2/2*
Colchester U *(Signed on 3/9/2004) FL 12+17/3 FLC 1 FAC 2+1/2 Others 1*

WILLIAMS Gareth John
Born: Glasgow, 16 December 1981
Height: 5'11" **Weight:** 11.10
International Honours: S: 4; B-1; U21-9; Yth
This stylish midfielder joined Leicester in the summer of 2004 and took a while to settle into his new team. However, he soon found his ability to get into scoring positions from midfield an asset that endeared him to the club's fans. Gareth scored vital goals against both Blackpool and Reading as City progressed in the FA Cup and looked to be more and more indispensable as the season progressed.
Nottingham F *(From trainee on 23/12/1998) FL 132+10/9 FLC 4+1 FAC 5 Others 2*
Leicester C *(£500,000 on 6/8/2004) FL 25+8/1 FLC 1 FAC 5/2*

WILLIAMS Gavin John
Born: Pontypridd, 20 June 1980
Height: 5'10" **Weight:** 11.5
Club Honours: NC '03; Div 2 '05
Gavin was again in fine form on the right-hand side of midfield for Yeovil last term and it was therefore no real surprise when he was sold to West Ham in December. He was the Hammers' star man on New Year's Day at Ipswich and only an ankle injury prevented him from winning his first full cap for Wales.
Yeovil T *(£20,000 from Hereford U on 16/5/2002) FL 54+1/11 FLC 1+1 FAC 5/3 Others 2/1*
West Ham U *(£250,000 on 9/12/2004) FL 7+3/1*

Leroy Williams (left)

WILLIAMS Leroy Daniel
Born: Birmingham, 22 October 1986
Height: 5'7" **Weight:** 11.0
Leroy was still only 17 when he gave impressive displays for Walsall in pre-season friendlies against Manchester United and Aston Villa. His readiness to run at defences earned him a place on the bench for the opening League game against Port Vale and he scored a spectacular goal just a few minutes after coming on the field. Although he started only two games for the Saddlers he netted a vital penalty in the shoot-out at Cheltenham in the LDV Vans Trophy tie in November and also had a successful loan spell with Hereford.
Walsall *(From trainee on 5/8/2004) FL 2+5/1 FLC 0+1 FAC 0+1 Others 0+1*

WILLIAMS Marcus Vincent
Born: Doncaster, 8 April 1986
Height: 5'8" **Weight:** 10.9
Marcus' form in Scunthorpe's reserves won him a two-year professional contract and a few first-team opportunities during the season. His six appearances from the bench included a run-out against Chelsea's Premiership stars in the FA Cup. A utility player who is quick and effective on the ball, he was used at left back, on the left wing and in the centre of midfield.
Scunthorpe U *(Trainee) FL 0+5 FAC 0+1 Others 0+1*

WILLIAMS Mark Stuart
Born: Stalybridge, 28 September 1970
Height: 6'0" **Weight:** 13.0
Club Honours: Div 3 '94
International Honours: NI: 36; B-1
Mark began the 2004-05 season as the MK Dons' skipper, but a series of niggling injuries meant he was never able to recover the form he had shown during his first spell with the club. Still very strong in the tackle, he struggled at times with pacier opponents and after another injury in early January ruled him out for a while he was loaned out to neighbours Rushden to help their relegation struggle. He helped the Diamonds to gain crucial results against Northampton Town and

:idderminster Harriers, but returned to he Dons early for surgery to correct a roin problem. Mark continued to add to is tally of caps for Northern Ireland luring the campaign.
Shrewsbury T *(Free from Newtown on 7/3/1992) FL 96+6/3 FLC 7+1 FAC 6 Others 6/1*
Chesterfield *(£50,000 on 7/8/1995) FL 68/12 FLC 10 FAC 13/1 Others 7/1*
Watford *(Free on 13/7/1999) PL 20+2/1 LC 2*
Wimbledon *(Signed on 26/7/2000) FL 59+1/7 FLC 5/1 FAC 8/1*
Stoke C *(Free on 11/3/2003) FL 5+1 (Freed during 2003 close season)*
Wimbledon/MK Dons *(Signed from Columbus Crew, USA on 6/2/2004) FL 2+2/1 FLC 1 Others 1*
Rushden & Diamonds *(Loaned on /3/2005) FL 7*

WILLIAMS Matthew (Matt)

Born: Flint, 5 November 1982
Height: 5'8" **Weight:** 9.11
International Honours: W: U21-10; Yth
Matt continued to make progress with Notts County last term, featuring in a number of first-team games, although mostly from the substitutes' bench. He featured in a deep role behind the two main strikers and also on the flanks from where he contributed some useful performances. Matt scored his first goal in senior football when he netted for the Magpies in the 2-1 win over Cambridge in November.
Manchester U *(From trainee on 1/2/2000)*
Notts Co *(Free on 18/3/2004) FL 13+12/1 FLC 1+1 FAC 2+1*

WILLIAMS Matthew (Matt)

Born: Bury, 21 June 1988
Height: 5'11" **Weight:** 12.0
This first-year scholar spent much of last term developing in Rochdale's reserve team and was called up to the first-team squad for the final match of the season at Boston United. The promising youngster came off the bench to replace defender Gary Brown in the closing minutes of the match to record his first appearance in senior football.
Rochdale *(Trainee) FL 0+1*

WILLIAMS Robert (Robbie) Ian

Born: Pontefract, 2 October 1984
Height: 5'10" **Weight:** 11.13
Robbie signed his first professional contract for Barnsley during the summer of 2004 but struggled with injuries for much of last season and it was only towards the end of the campaign that he got a decent run in the side. He is a promising left back who is developing into a dead-ball specialist.
Barnsley *(From trainee on 2/7/2004) FL 23+6/2 FLC 1 FAC 2 Others 0+2*

WILLIAMS Ryan Neil

Born: Sutton-in-Ashfield, 31 August 1978
Height: 5'5" **Weight:** 11.4
International Honours: E: Yth
Winger Ryan struggled to make an impact at Bristol Rovers in the early part of last season and was restricted to the odd appearance from the substitutes' bench. In December he moved on loan to Conference club Forest Green Rovers and on his return staked a claim for a new contract with some eye-catching performances. A highlight of his campaign came when he scored a cracking long-range goal in the 3-0 win over Grimsby at the Memorial Stadium in February.
Mansfield T *(Trainee) FL 9+17/3 FLC 2 FAC 0+1*
Tranmere Rov *(£70,000 + on 8/8/1997) FL 2+3*
Chesterfield *(£80,000 on 10/11/1999) FL 69+6/13 FLC 3 FAC 1 Others 5+1/1*
Hull C *(£150,000 on 9/7/2001) FL 40+12/2 FLC 1 FAC 2+1 Others 4+1/1*
Bristol Rov *(Free on 30/10/2003) FL 24+12/4 FAC 1 Others 1+2*

WILLIAMS Steven (Steve)

Born: Oxford, 21 April 1983
Height: 6'4" **Weight:** 12.8
After becoming Wycombe's first-choice 'keeper for a period during the previous season, Steve was disappointed to find himself once again understudying Frank Talia, from the start of 2004-05. He played one full game, acquitting himself well in the LDV Vans Trophy win at Aldershot, and came on for the injured Talia at home to Yeovil in November.
Wycombe W *(From trainee on 12/4/2002) FL 19+1 FLC 2 FAC 1 Others 2*

WILLIAMS Thomas (Tommy) Andrew

Born: Carshalton, 8 July 1980
Height: 6'0" **Weight:** 11.8
Tommy eventually left Birmingham in the summer of 2004, signing for League One outfit Barnsley. An all-action full back, he was a regular throughout the campaign and produced a series of energetic performances. A left-sided player who also featured in midfield and in the centre of the defence, he was particularly impressive when pushing forward to deliver crosses into the opposition danger area.
West Ham U *(£60,000 from Walton & Hersham on 3/4/2000)*
Peterborough U *(Free on 22/3/2001) FL 32+4/2 FLC 1+1 FAC 4+1 Others 1*
Birmingham C *(£1,000,000 on 12/3/2002) FL 4*
Queens Park Rgrs *(Loaned on 8/8/2002) FL 22+4/1 FLC 1 FAC 2 Others 2+2*
Queens Park Rgrs *(Loaned on 4/8/2003) FL 4+1*
Peterborough U *(Free on 1/2/2004) FL 20+1/1 FAC 1*
Barnsley *(Free on 4/6/2004) FL 38+1 FLC 2 FAC 1 Others 1*

WILLIAMSON Lee Trevor

Born: Derby, 7 June 1982
Height: 5'10" **Weight:** 10.4
After a good pre-season, Lee lost his place in the Mansfield line-up following a suspension and then struggled to get back in the side. This situation did not last long, however, as he moved on to Northampton in September. He brought some welcome aggression to the Cobblers' midfield, featuring both in his familiar central role and also out on the flanks.
Mansfield T *(From trainee on 3/7/2000) FL 114+30/3 FLC 3+3 FAC 8+1 Others 7*
Northampton T *(Signed on 9/9/2004) FL 31+6 FLC 1 FAC 2/1 Others 3/1*

WILLIAMSON Michael (Mike) James

Born: Stoke, 8 November 1983
Height: 6'4" **Weight:** 13.3
Wycombe manager Tony Adams secured a season-long loan for this tall and strong Southampton central defender. Mike scored in his second game, at Chester, and formed a very effective central defensive partnership with Roger Johnson. Powerful in the air, cool and comfortable with the ball at his feet, the Saints finally agreed to release him and he won a long-term contract with the Chairboys at the end of the campaign.
Torquay U *(Trainee) FL 3 Others 1*
Southampton *(£100,000 on 21/11/2001)*
Torquay U *(Loaned on 15/9/2003) FL 9+2 Others 1*
Wycombe W *(Loaned on 20/7/2004) FL 32+5/2 FAC 2 Others 2*

WILLMOTT Christopher (Chris) Alan

Born: Bedford, 30 September 1977
Height: 6'2" **Weight:** 11.12
Chris was a near ever-present for Northampton last term and performed well in the centre of defence throughout the campaign. He is good in the air and likes to play the ball from the back rather than rely on 'big-boot' tactics. Injuries

meant that he had a string of partners in the back line during the season but he coped admirably and always gave his best.
Luton T *(From trainee on 1/5/1996) FL 13+1*
Wimbledon *(£350,000 on 14/7/1999) P/FL 50+3/2 FLC 3+1 FAC 2*
Luton T *(Loaned on 1/2/2003) FL 7+1*
Luton T *(Loaned on 8/4/2003) FL 5*
Northampton T *(Free on 7/7/2003) FL 80+1/1 FLC 4 FAC 7 Others 9*

WILLOCK Calum Daniel
Born: Lambeth, 29 October 1981
Height: 5'11" **Weight:** 12.7
International Honours: St Kitts; E: Sch
This talented striker was affected by injuries last term but still managed to finish the campaign as leading scorer for Peterborough with 14 goals in all competitions. Calum is lightning-quick, gets into good positions and can score with his head and both feet. He will be looking to fulfil his undoubted potential at London Road in 2005-06.
Fulham *(From ADT College, Putney on 18/7/2000) P/FL 0+5*
Queens Park Rgrs *(Loaned on 7/11/2002) FL 3*
Bristol Rov *(Loaned on 8/8/2003) FL 0+5*
Peterborough U *(£25,000 on 13/10/2003) FL 51+13/20 FAC 4+1/3 Others 2*

WILNIS Fabian
Born: Surinam, 23 August 1970
Height: 5'8" **Weight:** 12.6
Fabian missed the opening games of the 2004-05 campaign for Ipswich, but quickly forced himself back into the side and remained there for the rest of the season in a variety of roles. His usual position is at right back but he firstly played on the left side of the defence and also had the odd appearance as a centre back. Fabian has sufficient pace and experience to gain the upper hand over most opposing wingers and his overlapping can create scoring opportunities for fellow team members. He has also developed a long throw, which he aims at Jason De Vos, who is usually hovering close by the near post. Fabian was out of contract in the summer and his future was unclear at the time of writing.
Ipswich T *(£200,000 from De Graafschap, Holland, ex NAC Breda, on 6/1/1999) P/FL 194+19/5 FLC 10+3 FAC 10 Others 13+1*

WILSON Brian Jason
Born: Manchester, 9 May 1983
Height: 5'10" **Weight:** 11.0
This pacy right-sided player enjoyed his first full season of senior football at Cheltenham Town last term. Brian began the campaign in the right-back position but soon gave way to the experienced Jerry Gill. He then featured as a substitute, scoring his first Football League goal in the2-1 win at Rochdale in October, before earning himself a place in the team on the right-hand side of midfield. Brian went on to see out the rest of the season and established himself as a solid and consistent performer, capable of getting forward quickly and providing cover for the full back behind him.
Stoke C *(From trainee on 5/7/2001) FL 1+5 FLC 0+1 Others 1*
Cheltenham T *(Loaned on 12/12/2003) FL 7 FAC 1*
Cheltenham T *(Signed on 25/3/2004) FL 42+8/3 FLC 1 FAC 1 Others 2*

WILSON Che Christian Aaron Clay
Born: Ely, 17 January 1979
Height: 5'9" **Weight:** 11.3
An early loss of form by first-choice left back Nicky Nicolau saw Che come into the Southend United first team last autumn and he never looked back, starting every game except one from September until the end of the season. Looking more and more comfortable on the ball with each passing game, Che became 'Mr Dependable' in the Southend rearguard and, although predominantly right-footed, he rarely struggled with any opponent during a fantastically successful season for the club.
Norwich C *(From trainee on 3/7/1997) FL 16+6 FLC 3*
Bristol Rov *(Free on 13/7/2000) FL 74+1 FLC 7 FAC 6 Others 3+1 (Free to Cambridge C during 2002 close season)*
Southend U *(Free on 30/7/2003) FL 51+3 FAC 3 Others 11+2*

WILSON Kelvin James
Born: Nottingham, 3 September 1985
Height: 6'2" **Weight:** 12.3
This young Notts County defender made excellent progress last season when he firmly established himself at first-team level. He was initially selected at right back, but injuries and changes in formation later saw him switch to a role as a central defender where he displayed plenty of confidence and ability.
Notts Co *(From trainee on 20/7/2004) FL 38+6/2 FLC 1+1/1 FAC 4 Others 1*

WILSON Mark Antony
Born: Scunthorpe, 9 February 1979
Height: 5'11" **Weight:** 13.0
International Honours: E: U21-2; Yth; Sch
Mark was out of favour at the Riverside last term and his only first-team appearance came in the Carling Cup tie against Coventry City in October. The young midfield player spent time on loan at Doncaster in the early part of the season, but struggled to adjust to the demands of League One football, then spent most of the second half of the campaign on loan with SPL outfit Livingston, where he featured in a handful of games before returning to Boro'.
Manchester U *(From trainee on 16/2/1996) PL 1+2 FLC 2 Others 3+2*
Wrexham *(Loaned on 23/2/1998) FL 12+1/4*
Middlesbrough *(£1,500,000 on 9/8/2001) PL 6+10 FLC 5/2 FAC 2+1*
Stoke C *(Loaned on 14/3/2003) FL 4*
Swansea C *(Loaned on 12/9/2003) FL 12/2 Others 1*
Sheffield Wed *(Loaned on 22/1/2004) FL 3*
Doncaster Rov *(Loaned on 2/9/2004) FL 1+2 Others 1*
Livingston *(Loaned on 24/1/2005) SL 4+1 SC 1*

WILSON Stephen (Steve) Lee
Born: Hull, 24 April 1974
Height: 5'10" **Weight:** 11.2
As an experienced 'keeper Steve could be considered unlucky to lose the number one spot at Macclesfield at the start of last term. Nevertheless, when called upon, he showed his ability as a proven shot-stopper and there were times when his performances kept his rival Alan Fettis on the bench.
Hull C *(From trainee on 13/7/1992) FL 180+1 FLC 13 FAC 13 Others 11+1*
Macclesfield T *(Free on 22/3/2001) FL 132+2 FLC 3 FAC 13 Others 4*

WINDASS Dean
Born: Hull, 1 April 1969
Height: 5'10" **Weight:** 12.6
Dean, who turned 36 in April, rolled back the years with the most prolific season of his career in 2004-05. He scored 28 goals, 27 of them in the League which was the most by a Bradford player since Harry Green 41 years ago, his haul including a hat-trick against Bournemouth in the final home game. Dean finished level with Hull's Stuart Elliott as the League One leading scorer but surprisingly missed out on a place in the PFA team of the season.
Hull C *(Free from North Ferriby on 24/10/1991) FL 173+3/57 FLC 11/4 FAC 6 Others 12/3*
Aberdeen *(£700,000 on 1/12/1995) SL 60+13/21 SLC 5+2/6 SC 7/3 Others 6/1*
Oxford U *(£475,000 on 6/8/1998) FL 33/15 FLC 2 FAC 3/3*

Bradford C *(£950,000 + on 5/3/1999) P/FL 54+10/16 FLC 6/2 FAC 2 Others 6/3*
Middlesbrough *(£600,000 + on 15/3/2001) PL 16+21/3 FLC 2 FAC 4+3*
Sheffield Wed *(Loaned on 6/12/2001) FL 2*
Sheffield U *(Loaned on 11/11/2002) FL 4/3*
Sheffield U *(Signed on 16/1/2003) FL 16/3 Others 2*
Bradford C *(Free on 14/7/2003) FL 73+4/33 FLC 2/1 FAC 2 Others 1*

WINN Ashley
Born: Stockton, 1 December 1985
Height: 5'11" **Weight:** 11.2
This young midfielder made his senior bow for Oldham as a late substitute at Swindon Town in October but managed just nine minutes of first-team action all season. He was subsequently released in May 2005 as part of manager Ronnie Moore's end-of-season clearout.
Oldham Ath *(Trainee) FL 0+2*

WINTERS Thomas (Tom) Richard
Born: Banbury, 11 December 1985
Height: 5'9" **Weight:** 10.10
Tom continued his development with Oxford last term and added a handful more appearances from the substitutes' bench, despite being affected by a run of injuries. A talented left winger, he scored his first goal after just three minutes of his first appearance in the starting line-up in the LDV Vans Trophy tie against Exeter City. Tom will be looking to make a breakthrough into regular first-team football in the 2005-06 campaign.
Oxford U *(Trainee) FL 0+5 Others 1/1*

WISE Dennis Frank
Born: Kensington, 15 December 1966
Height: 5'6" **Weight:** 10.10
Club Honours: FAC '88, '97, '00; FLC '98; ECWC '98; ESC '98; CS '00
International Honours: E: 21; B-3; U21-1
Dennis only made a limited contribution to the Millwall midfield last term due to a back injury and his presence was sorely missed in the centre of the park. Still a thorn in many an opponent's side he continued to show a great passion for the game lifting both players and fans alike. However, just as he seemed to be forming an excellent managerial partnership with Ray Wilkins, Dennis announced he was resigning as the club's manager at the end of the season.
Wimbledon *(From trainee at Southampton on 28/3/1985) FL 127+8/27 FLC 14 FAC 11/3 Others 5*
Chelsea *(£1,600,000 on 3/7/1990) P/FL 322+10/53 FLC 30/6 FAC 38/8 Others 44+1/8*
Leicester C *(£1,600,000 + on 23/6/2001) PL 15+2/1 FLC 1 FAC 1*
Millwall *(Free on 24/9/2002) FL 70+15/7 FAC 9/1 Others 2/2*

WISEMAN Scott Nigel Kenneth
Born: Hull, 9 October 1985
Height: 6'0" **Weight:** 11.6
International Honours: E: Yth
Although the intensity of Hull's second consecutive successful promotion campaign meant Scott was given limited first-team opportunities, he captained Hull's reserves to the Pontin's Holidays League Premier Division title last term. A tall right back who can also be used in midfield, he joined Boston United on loan in the new year when the Lincolnshire club were struggling with injuries and suspensions. He showed some neat touches when making his debut at right wing back in the 1-1 draw at Bristol Rovers but his only other chance came as a second-half substitute in the following game and he returned early to the KC Stadium.
Hull C *(From trainee on 8/4/2004) FL 2+3 FAC 0+1 Others 0+1*
Boston U *(Loaned on 18/2/2005) FL 1+1*

WOLFENDEN Matthew (Matty)
Born: Oldham, 23 July 1987
Height: 5'9" **Weight:** 11.1
Matty was hoping for more regular first-team involvement at Oldham last term. A hard-working and talented striker, he can also operate in a wide position when required. He was chosen to sit on the bench on seven occasions but only got on the park once, as a second-half substitute against Tranmere Rovers on New Year's Day. A local lad, he will be looking to make more of an impact in 2005-06.
Oldham Ath *(Trainee) FL 0+2 FAC 0+1*

WOLLEASTON Robert Ainsley
Born: Perivale, 21 December 1979
Height: 5'11" **Weight:** 12.2
Robert performed impressively for Oxford in the pre-season games and also in the opening fixtures of the 2004-05 campaign. However, he then lost his place in the side and did not feature after the beginning of January. When on form he is a talented midfield player, capable of bossing play in the centre of the park and always looking to get in a shot.
Chelsea *(From trainee on 3/6/1998) PL 0+1 FLC 0+1*
Bristol Rov *(Loaned on 23/3/2000) FL 0+4*
Portsmouth *(Loaned on 8/3/2001) FL 5+1*
Northampton T *(Loaned on 4/7/2001) FL 2+5 FLC 0+1*
Bradford C *(Free on 14/7/2003) FL 6+8/1 FLC 0+1*
Oxford U *(Signed on 12/7/2004) FL 14+6 FLC 1 Others 1*

WOOD Christopher (Chris) Hayden
Born: Worksop, 24 January 1987
Height: 6'0" **Weight:** 10.11
A second-year scholar who can play at either right back or centre back, this Mansfield Town youngster was given his debut in the FA Cup replay at Colchester. His promotion to senior football came early due to the Stags' small squad being decimated by injury and suspension. The 17-year old was captain of the club's youth team and although his first-team opportunities were limited he was a regular on the substitutes' bench.
Mansfield T *(Trainee) FL 0+1 FAC 0+1*

WOOD Neil Anthony
Born: Manchester, 4 January 1983
Height: 5'10" **Weight:** 13.2
This former Manchester United starlet signed for Coventry City in the summer of 2004. The left-footed midfielder got few opportunities to show his talents for the Sky Blues, however, and was made available on a free transfer at the end of the season.
Manchester U *(From trainee on 7/1/2000)*
Peterborough U *(Loaned on 12/9/2003) FL 2+1/1*
Burnley *(Loaned on 30/1/2004) FL 8+2/1 FAC 1*
Coventry C *(Free on 9/7/2004) FL 6+7 FLC 2 FAC 1*

WOOD Richard Mark
Born: Ossett, 5 July 1985
Height: 6'3" **Weight:** 11.11
This young central defender had a great season at Hillsborough last term. Tall and pacy, he produced some commanding performances and when fit he was an automatic choice for the side. Richard also filled in at full back occasionally.
Sheffield Wed *(From trainee on 7/4/2003) FL 45+4/2 FLC 1/1 FAC 1+1 Others 5+1*

WOODHOUSE Curtis
Born: Beverley, 17 April 1980
Height: 5'8" **Weight:** 11.0
International Honours: E: U21-4; Yth
This competitive midfielder was a regular in the Peterborough line-up last term, but did not always shine in a team that struggled throughout the campaign. A skilful yet hard-working box-to-box player, Curtis scored five goals including a last-minute winner in the FA Cup first round tie against Tranmere. He was

reported to have signed for Hull City during the summer.
Sheffield U *(From trainee on 31/12/1997) FL 92+12/6 FLC 5+3 FAC 10*
Birmingham C *(£1,000,000 on 2/2/2001) P/FL 35+13/2 FLC 3+1 FAC 1 Others 2*
Rotherham U *(Loaned on 1/2/2003) FL 11*
Peterborough U *(Free on 13/10/2003) FL 58+3/11 FLC 1 FAC 6/1 Others 4*

WOODMAN Craig Alan
Born: Tiverton, 22 December 1982
Height: 5'9" **Weight:** 9.11
After a handful of early-season appearances for Bristol City, this young full back or midfielder was farmed out on loan to Mansfield Town at the end of September. He made an impressive debut for the Stags in the top-of-the-table clash at Scunthorpe. A highlight came when he scored with a magnificent shot from fully 25 yards against Notts County. After returning to Ashton Gate he spent most of the remainder of the campaign on loan at Torquay. After some hesitant early performances, an injury to Brian McGlinchey gave him an extended run at left back during which he grew in confidence, becoming more solid defensively and also more adventurous at overlapping.
Bristol C *(From trainee on 17/2/2000) FL 30+12 FLC 3 FAC 3 Others 10*
Mansfield T *(Loaned on 25/9/2004) FL 8/1 Others 1*
Torquay U *(Loaned on 6/12/2004) FL 20+2/1*

WOODS Martin Paul
Born: Airdrie, 1 January 1986
Height: 5'11" **Weight:** 11.11
International Honours: S: Yth
This teenaged winger earned a place in Leeds United's pre-season trip to Dublin after good displays in the reserves and juniors. He did well in a loan spell at Hartlepool and had a brief taste of Championship football when he came on for his Leeds debut in the 3-2 Boxing Day win at Sunderland.
Leeds U *(From trainee on 3/1/2003) FL 0+1*
Hartlepool U *(Loaned on 10/9/2004) FL 3+3 FLC 1 Others 1*

WOODS Stephen (Steve) John
Born: Northwich, 15 December 1976
Height: 5'11" **Weight:** 12.3
This experienced central defender is an excellent organiser, strong in the air and solid on the ground with good distribution skills. He enjoyed a solid season for Torquay United in 2004-05, but found the strikers in League One harder to handle, and only looked at his very best when the club sorted out its goalkeeping problems.
Stoke C *(From trainee on 3/8/1995) FL 33+1 FLC 2 FAC 2 Others 2*
Plymouth Arg *(Loaned on 26/3/1998) FL 4+1*
Chesterfield *(Free on 7/7/1999) FL 22+3 FLC 4 Others 0+1*
Torquay U *(Free on 17/8/2001) FL 125+4/10 FLC 3 FAC 3 Others 2*

WOODTHORPE Colin John
Born: Ellesmere Port, 13 January 1969
Height: 5'11" **Weight:** 11.8
This veteran Bury central defender managed to make the starting line-up for more than half the first-team games last term, despite being affected by suspensions. During the second half of the season he regularly turned out despite being hampered by a back injury. Perhaps lacking a little pace at this stage of his career, Colin still offered great experience to the Shakers' young team and was briefly named as captain when Dave Challinor was out injured for two games.
Chester C *(From trainee on 23/8/1986) FL 154+1/6 FLC 10 FAC 8+1 Others 18/1*
Norwich C *(£175,000 on 17/7/1990) P/FL 36+7/1 FLC 0+2 FAC 6 Others 1+1*
Aberdeen *(£400,000 on 20/7/1994) SL 43+5/1 SLC 5+1/1 SC 4 Others 5+2*
Stockport Co *(£200,000 on 29/7/1997) FL 114+39/4 FLC 12+1/2 FAC 4+1/1*
Bury *(Free on 23/8/2002) FL 98+3 FLC 3+1 FAC 4 Others 9/1*

WOOZLEY David James
Born: Ascot, 6 December 1979
Height: 6'0" **Weight:** 12.10
David joined Oxford in the summer of 2004 but had to wait until he had recovered from injury before he could challenge for a place. A capable centre half or full back, he featured fairly regularly for the U's in the first half of the campaign, but then dropped out of contention. He spent the last few months on loan at table toppers Yeovil but added just one more appearance from the substitutes' bench.
Crystal Palace *(From trainee on 17/11/1997) FL 21+9 FLC 3+1 FAC 0+1*
Bournemouth *(Loaned on 15/9/2000) FL 6*
Torquay U *(Loaned on 28/8/2001) FL 12 FLC 1*
Torquay U *(Free on 27/3/2002) FL 52+8/3 FLC 2 FAC 2 Others 1*
Oxford U *(Free on 12/7/2004) FL 11+2/1 FAC 1 Others 1*
Yeovil T *(Loaned on 21/3/2005) FL 0+1*

WORGAN Lee John
Born: Eastbourne, 1 December 1983
Height: 6'1" **Weight:** 13.10
International Honours: W: U21-2; Yth
Lee made his debut for Wales U21s last term, but found himself mainly on the bench for Rushden. He was the number two behind Diamonds' shot-stopper Billy Turley and finally got his chance with fou festive fixtures. However, Lee only managed three more appearances, all ending in defeats, and was released at the end of his Nene Park contract in the summer.
Wimbledon *(From trainee on 9/4/2003) FL 0+3*
Wycombe W *(Loaned on 12/4/2004) FL 2*
Rushden & Diamonds *(Free on 4/8/2004) FL 7*

WORRELL David
Born: Dublin, 12 January 1978
Height: 5'11" **Weight:** 12.4
Club Honours: Div 3 '02; Div 2 '04
International Honours: RoI: U21-17
David started the 2004-05 season as the first-choice right back in Plymouth Argyle's defence and produced some confident displays early on, linking up well with David Norris on the right-hand side of midfield. However, he lost his place to Paul Connolly in December and did not get back into the side until the last few games. Out of contract in the summer he was released by the Pilgrims.
Blackburn Rov *(Signed from Shelbourne on 12/1/1995)*
Dundee U *(Free on 30/3/1999) SL 13+4 SLC 2*
Plymouth Arg *(Signed on 23/11/2000) FL 147 FLC 3 FAC 9 Others 6*

WORTHINGTON Jonathan (Jon) Alan
Born: Dewsbury, 16 April 1983
Height: 5'9" **Weight:** 11.0
This influential Huddersfield Town midfielder added a very competitive edge to his game last term. Jon is a classic box-to-box midfielder, great at holding the ball, always one for the crunching tackle and putting his heart and soul into performances. Rarely out of the first-team spotlight, he contributed three goals, including an important winner in the local 'derby' with Sheffield Wednesday.
Huddersfield T *(From trainee on 10/9/2001) FL 85+15/6 FLC 3 FAC 3 Others 5*

WOTTON Paul Anthony
Born: Plymouth, 17 August 1977
Height: 5'11" **Weight:** 12.0
Club Honours: Div 3 '02; Div 2 '04
Paul started last term playing in the centre of Plymouth Argyle's defence but during the campaign he moved more into a holding midfield role. Always playing with passion for his hometown club, Paul's enthusiasm for the cause was there

be seen. He was once again top scorer ith an excellent return of 13 goals, any scored from free kicks and the enalty spot. He was awarded with a ew contract for the Pilgrims and was so named as Argyle's 'Player of the eason'.
ymouth Arg *(From trainee on 10/7/1995) 288+31/41 FLC 8+1/1 FAC 22/5 Others +1/2*

VRACK Darren
orn: Cleethorpes, 5 May 1976
eight: 5'9" **Weight:** 12.10
arren was a near ever-present for alsall last term when he took his ppearance tally well past the 300-mark. e featured in various midfield positions, nd also at left back when required, oducing an unstoppable left-foot shot open the scoring in the 3-0 win over hesterfield in January. Darren also etted the vital winning penalty in the DV Vans Trophy shoot-out at heltenham in November.
erby Co *(From trainee on 12/7/1994) FL +22/1 FLC 0+3 FAC 0+2*
rimsby T *(£100,000 + on 19/7/1996) FL +8/1 Others 0+1*
hrewsbury T *(Loaned on 17/2/1997) FL +1 Others 1*
/alsall *(Free on 6/8/1998) FL 240+34/44 C 12+1/1 FAC 14+1/3 Others 10+1/1*

VRIGHT Alan Geoffrey
orn: Ashton-under-Lyne, 28 September 971
eight: 5'4" **Weight:** 9.9
lub Honours: FLC '96
nternational Honours: E: U21-2; Yth; ch
lan began last term as first-choice left ving back for the Blades and used his peed and anticipation to good effect oth in defence and when coming orward. After a spell on the sidelines he eturned in January but in his second full ame he damaged a cruciate ligament which kept him out for the rest of the eason.
lackpool *(From trainee on 13/4/1989) FL 1+7 FLC 10+2 FAC 8 Others 11+2*
lackburn Rov *(£400,000 on 25/10/1991) /FL 67+7/1 FLC 8 FAC 5+1 Others 3*
ston Villa *(£1,000,000 on 10/3/1995) PL 55+5/5 FLC 19 FAC 25 Others 26*
Aiddlesbrough *(Free on 12/8/2003) PL 2*
heffield U *(Free on 31/10/2003) FL 32+3/1 AC 3+1*

VRIGHT David
orn: Warrington, 1 May 1980
leight: 5'11" **Weight:** 10.8
nternational Honours: E: Yth
consistent performer in the heart of the Wigan Athletic defence, David started the 2004-05 season as a regular following his summer move. Playing mainly in the right-back berth, he showed speed and accuracy in the tackle and the ability to use the ball well when coming forward. Due to injuries, his also played in the heart of the defence and as a holding player in midfield when coming of the bench later in the campaign.
Crewe Alex *(From trainee on 18/6/1997) FL 206+5/3 FLC 10+1 FAC 12 Others 3+1*
Wigan Ath *(£500,000 on 28/6/2004) FL 19+12 FAC 1*

WRIGHT Jermaine Malaki
Born: Greenwich, 21 October 1975
Height: 5'9" **Weight:** 11.9
International Honours: E: Yth

David Wright

Experienced midfielder Jermaine was one of eight players to sign for Leeds during Kevin Blackwell's rebuilding of the cash-stricken club. He opted for Elland Road ahead of Everton and was rewarded with a regular starting place. His three Championship goals came in the space of a month. The first of them came against Burnley in November when he scored what is believed to be the quickest Leeds goal ever – coming in 12 seconds. He then found the net in the crushing 6-1 win against Queen's Park Rangers and in the 2-2 home draw against Watford four days later. Jermaine's form dipped towards the end of the season and he temporarily lost his place to new arrival Shaun Derry as competition of midfield places hotted up.

Millwall *(From trainee on 27/11/1992)*
Wolverhampton W *(£60,000 on 29/12/1994) FL 4+16 FLC 1+3/1 Others 0+1*
Doncaster Rov *(Loaned on 1/3/1996) FL 13*
Crewe Alex *(£25,000 on 19/2/1998) FL 47+2/5 FLC 5 FAC 1*
Ipswich T *(£500,000 on 23/7/1999) P/FL 147+37/10 FLC 15+2 FAC 8+1/1 Others 10+1*
Leeds U *(Free on 2/7/2004) FL 33+2/3 FLC 1 FAC 1*

WRIGHT Mark Anthony
Born: Wolverhampton, 24 February 1982
Height: 5'11" **Weight:** 11.4
After several seasons of occasional first-team appearances, Mark won a regular place in the Walsall line-up from September onwards. He had a long spell on the right flank of the defence where he was impressive going forward, but he also appeared on the left-hand side of the back line, in central midfield and in a wide-midfield role. Mark scored a last-minute winner at Swindon in April to set the Saddlers off on a run of five successive wins.

Walsall *(From trainee on 26/1/2001) FL 40+17/4 FLC 1+1 FAC 1 Others 4*

WRIGHT Richard Ian
Born: Ipswich, 5 November 1977
Height: 6'2" **Weight:** 13.0
Club Honours: FAC '02; PL '02
International Honours: E: 2; U21-15; Yth; Sch
Richard had an unfortunate third season at Goodison, when Nigel Martyn firmly established himself as first-choice 'keeper. After appearing only in the early rounds of the Carling Cup, he came into the side when Martyn was injured at Charlton over Christmas, but his spell in goal came when the side had lost confidence and he failed to do himself justice in the five games he played. He appeared in two further matches at the end of the season, one being the 7-0 defeat at Arsenal when he was arguably Everton's 'Man of the Match'. Richard is a fine goalkeeper whose main strength is being an excellent shot-stopper, and he deserves better luck in 2005-06.

Ipswich T *(From trainee on 2/1/1995) P/FL 240 FLC 27 FAC 13 Others 11*
Arsenal *(£6,000,000 on 13/7/2001) PL 12 FLC 1 FAC 5 Others 4*
Everton *(£3,500,000 + on 26/7/2002) PL 43+1 FLC 6 FAC 3*

WRIGHT Stephen John
Born: Liverpool, 8 February 1980
Height: 6'2" **Weight:** 12.0
Club Honours: UEFAC '01; Ch '05
International Honours: E: U21-6; Yth
A tall right back with the ability to make a never-ending run of lung bursting overlaps during any match, Stephen is a popular figure at the Stadium of Light and Sunderland's Championship success last term was just reward for a player who remained loyal to the Black Cats following relegation two years ago. A combative player who is never afraid to go in where it hurts, Stephen's exuberance sometimes landed him in trouble with referees. His only goal of the campaign came at home to Preston in September and delighted his many fans on Wearside.

Liverpool *(From trainee on 13/10/1997) PL 10+4 FLC 1+1 FAC 2 Others 2+1/1*
Crewe Alex *(Loaned on 6/8/1999) FL 17+6 FLC 1*
Sunderland *(£3,000,000 on 15/8/2002) P/FL 84+3/2 FLC 0+2 FAC 10*

WRIGHT Thomas (Tommy) Andrew
Born: Kirby Muxloe, 28 September 1984
Height: 6'0" **Weight:** 11.12
International Honours: E: Yth
A prolific striker with the Leicester City Academy and reserve teams in past seasons, Tommy found first-team opportunities somewhat limited last term. He managed just one Championship start all season, at Turf Moor in March, and will be looking to break into the line up on a more regular basis in 2005-06.

Leicester C *(From trainee on 10/6/2003) P/FL 3+18/2 FLC 1 FAC 0+2*
Brentford *(Loaned on 12/9/2003) FL 18+7/3*

WRIGHT-PHILLIPS Bradley Edward
Born: Lewisham, 12 March 1985
Height: 5'8" **Weight:** 11.0
International Honours: E: Yth
Bradley scored goals for fun for Manchester City reserves last season, finishing as the leading scorer for the whole of the Barclaycard Premiership Reserve League. He featured almost exclusively from the bench at first-team level, scoring on his Premiership debut in the 3-2 defeat at Middlesbrough. Bradley will be looking to win a place in City's starting line-up during the 2005-06 campaign.

Manchester C *(From trainee on 2/7/2002) PL 0+14/1 FLC 0+2 FAC 1*

WRIGHT-PHILLIPS Shaun Cameron
Born: Greenwich, 25 October 1981
Height: 5'6" **Weight:** 10.1
Club Honours: Div 1 '02
International Honours: E: 4; U21-6
Shaun signed a new long-term deal for Manchester City last season when he was one of the stars of the side. A versatile player who is perhaps best used on the right wing, he had phenomenal pace and a fantastic attitude and work rate. He finished joint-top scorer in Premiership matches for City with ten goals and also firmly established himself in the England squad during the campaign. Shaun finished runner-up in the PFA 'Young Player of the Year' award and was voted into the PFA Premiership team of the season.

Manchester C *(From trainee on 28/10/1998) P/FL 130+23/26 FLC 9+4/3 FAC 8+1/1 Others 4+2/1*

WRING Daniel (Danny) Ronald
Born: Portishead, 26 October 1986
Height: 5'10" **Weight:** 10.3
This young Bristol City midfielder possesses good ability on the ball and is the type of player who can go past opponents and open things up with a pass. Danny made his debut in the final game of the 2004-05 season, coming on as a substitute for the last three minutes of City's 3-2 win at Hillsborough.

Bristol C *(Trainee) FL 0+1*

WROE Nicholas (Nicky)
Born: Sheffield, 28 September 1985
Height: 5'11" **Weight:** 10.7
Nicky was in the Barnsley first-team squad from the very start of the 2004-05 season and early on he won a regular place in the starting line-up in a midfield role. Manager Paul Hart gave him a rest during December but he came back and recaptured his place in the side. A hard-working player with plenty of potential, he failed to register a goal during the campaign.

Barnsley *(From trainee on 6/8/2004) FL 28+6/1 FLC 2 FAC 1 Others 1*

XYZ

AKUBU Ayegbeni
orn: Benin City, Nigeria, 22 November
82
eight: 6'0" **Weight:** 13.1
ub Honours: Div 1 '03
ternational Honours: Nigeria
is powerful striker was again in exciting rm for Portsmouth last term and on his ird appearance he netted a hat-trick in e 4-3 win over Fulham. He carried on in nilar vein throughout the campaign to iish as the club's leading scorer with 17 als in all competitions from just 35 pearances. Such prolific form made n the transfer target of rival clubs and iring the summer he was reported to ive signed for Middlesbrough. He is ong in the challenge, fast off the mark d not afraid to take on opponents.
rtsmouth *(£1,800,000 from Maccabi ifa, Israel, ex Okomo Oil, Julius Berger, poel Kfar-Saba, on 13/1/2003) P/FL +5/35 FLC 2+3/4 FAC 6/3*

ATES Steven (Steve)
orn: Bristol, 29 January 1970
eight: 5'11" **Weight:** 12.2
ub Honours: Div 3 '90
nflappable, efficient and solid are just a w of the descriptions which can be plied to this veteran defender. iroughout his career Steve has firmly uck to what he knows, never a shirker, ways a battler and a great leader of hers. Perhaps his only disappointment ill be that injury prevented him from aching the landmark figure of 600 ague appearances last term. The proud efender skippered Huddersfield Town, aking his mark with many a hard-orking display. After the curtain fell on e season, Steve looked to find pastures ew, and all fans at the Galpharm wish m well.
istol Rov *(From trainee on 1/7/1988) FL 96+1 FLC 9 FAC 11 Others 21*
ueens Park Rgrs *(£650,000 on 5/8/1993) P/FL 122+12/2 FLC 8 FAC 7*
anmere Rov *(Free on 5/8/1999) FL 09+4/7 FLC 13+1/2 FAC 10/5*
heffield U *(Free on 4/7/2002) FL 11+1 C 1*
uddersfield T *(Free on 7/8/2003) FL)+2/1 FLC 3 FAC 1 Others 4*

EATES Mark Stephen
orn: Dublin, 11 January 1985
eight: 5'9" **Weight:** 10.7
ternational Honours: RoI: U21-3; Yth
n intelligent striker who can also play in

Ayegbeni Yakubu

Dwight Yorke

idfield, Mark made only two subs ppearances for Tottenham last term, ut showed the pace and technical bility which had facilitated his raduation from the reserves where he as a regular. A product of the Spurs cademy, Mark is a bright prospect. arly on in the season. He enjoyed a an spell at Swindon, where he npressed in a wide-midfield role, before ding slightly.

ottenham H *(From trainee on 25/7/2002) 1+2 FAC 0+1*
righton & Hove A *(Loaned on 4/11/2003) FL 9 Others 1*
windon T *(Loaned on 27/8/2004) FL 3+1*

ELLDELL David Raymond
orn: Stuttgart, Germany, 1 October 981
eight: 6'5" **Weight:** 12.11
rought to Brighton on a month's loan om Blackburn following a serious injury Michel Kuipers in January, David was rust into the cauldron of Elland Road, eeds, for his League debut. The young oalkeeper did well enough in his first ame, but looked nervous in his ubsequent outings. He then warmed the ench as the more experienced Rami naaban was given the jersey and he eturned to Ewood Park at the end of his nonth on the South Coast, but the xperience will have greatly benefited im.

lackburn Rov *(Signed from Stuttgart ickers, Germany on 22/7/2003)*
righton & Hove A *(Loaned on 28/1/2005) 3*

EO Simon John
orn: Stockport, 20 October 1973
eight: 5'10" **Weight:** 11.8
imon had an excellent season up front or Lincoln City last term becoming the lub's first player for a decade to reach 0 League goals. His skill at beating pposition defenders on the ground ogether with an explosive shot proved oo much for many League Two teams, ith the highlight of his season being a at-trick in the Imps 4-1 victory at local vals Grimsby Town. Simon finished the ampaign with 23 goals in all ompetitions and was voted 'Player of e Season' by the Imps' supporters. He as offered a new contract at the end of e campaign but instead chose to sign a eal with New Zealand Knights of the lyundai A-League.

incoln C *(Free from Hyde U on 7/8/2002) L 73+49/37 FLC 2+1/2 FAC 4/1 Others +6/6*

YETTON Stewart David
Born: Plymouth, 27 July 1985
Height: 5'8" **Weight:** 10.3
Stewart made his one and only appearance for Plymouth from the substitutes' bench at Sheffield United last October. A lively striker he scored 10 goals for the reserves and also had a spell on loan at Weymouth. Later in the season Argyle released him from his contract allowing him to sign for Tiverton Town.

Plymouth Arg *(From trainee on 4/8/2004) FL 0+3*

YOBO Joseph
Born: Kano, Nigeria, 6 September 1980
Height: 6'2" **Weight:** 11.6
International Honours: Nigeria
The greatest testament to the veteran centre-half partnership of Alan Stubbs and David Weir is that they succeeded in keeping this highly skilful and pacy international out of the Everton line-up. Joseph did play over 20 Premiership matches, on occasions in a holding role in midfield that is not his best position in fairness. When he did play he showed he has all the attributes of a fine defender: great skill on the ball and superb tackling which relies more on stealing the ball rather than brute strength. Joseph also played regularly for Nigeria in their World Cup qualifying campaign.

Everton *(£4,500,000 from Marseilles, France, ex Mechelen, Standard Liege, on 6/8/2002) PL 68+11/2 FLC 7 FAC 3+1*

YORKE Dwight
Born: Canaan, Tobago, 3 November 1971
Height: 5'10" **Weight:** 12.4
Club Honours: FLC '96; FAC '99; PL '99, '00, '01; UEFACL '99
International Honours: Trinidad & Tobago
Dwight struggled to make an impact at Blackburn at the beginning of the 2004-05 season and was quickly off-loaded to Birmingham City. He made a bright start to his career at St Andrew's, coming off the bench to head the equaliser against Charlton. This earned him instant acceptance from the Blues' fans and he followed up with another strike three games later against Newcastle. However, from then on he faced a battle to break into the line-up as Clinton Morrison and Walter Pandiani were preferred. Dwight was eventually released in April and joined Sydney FC of the new Hyundai A League.

Aston Villa *(£120,000 from Signal Hill, Tobago on 19/12/1989) P/FL 195+36/73 FLC 20+2/8 FAC 22+2/14 Others 10/3*
Manchester U *(£12,600,000 on 22/8/1998) PL 80+16/48 FLC 3/2 FAC 6+5/3 Others 31+11/12*
Blackburn Rov *(£2,000,000 on 26/7/2002) PL 42+18/12 FLC 5/4 FAC 3+1/3 Others 4+1*
Birmingham C *(Signed on 31/8/2004) PL 4+9/2 FLC 2 FAC 0+1*

YOUNG Ashley Simon
Born: Stevenage, 9 July 1985
Height: 5'9" **Weight:** 9.13
Winger Ashley, a player with both flair and intelligence, continued to make encouraging progress and was voted Watford's 'Young Player of the Year' last term. Equally capable with either foot, he is at home on either flank and has an eye for goal, although his failure to score last season was a disappointment. A graduate of the Watford Academy, Ashley has two younger brothers intent on following his example.

Watford *(From juniors on 12/7/2002) FL 15+24/3 FLC 4+1*

YOUNG Gregory (Greg) James
Born: Doncaster, 25 April 1983
Height: 6'1" **Weight:** 12.3
This young Grimsby Town defender began last term in promising fashion with a handful of first-team outings, but overall had a disappointing season. He had two spells out on loan with Northwich in the first half of the campaign before leaving Blundell Park to join Halifax Town on a permanent basis in February.

Grimsby T *(From trainee at Sheffield Wed on 26/7/2002) FL 13+11 FLC 1 FAC 0+1 Others 1+1*

YOUNG Luke Paul
Born: Harlow, 19 July 1979
Height: 5'11" **Weight:** 12.4
Club Honours: FLC '99
International Honours: E: 2; U21-12; Yth
It was an eventful season for Luke, who was a model of consistency in the Charlton defence during the campaign. Comfortable as either an orthodox right full back or at right wing back, he is also able to play in central defence. He scored his first-ever goal for the club in his 100th appearance in the 3-0 home win over Aston Villa and then scored another three weeks later in the away game with Birmingham, earning the Addicks a point. Luke is strong in the tackle and distributes the ball well. He is also a good crosser of the ball, and possesses a long throw, which is put to good use on occasions. He was voted Charlton's 'Player of the Year' by the supporters and

rounded off a fine season by being called into the full England squad for their summer tour of the USA.

Tottenham H *(From trainee on 3/7/1997) PL 44+14 FLC 1+3 FAC 9+2 Others 2+1*
Charlton Ath *(£3,000,000 + on 27/7/2001) PL 120+6/2 FLC 6 FAC 6*

YOUNG Neil Anthony
Born: Harlow, 31 August 1973
Height: 5'9" **Weight:** 12.0
This loyal Bournemouth right back was rewarded with a testimonial match against Charlton in July. Although affected by suspensions in the early part of the campaign, he came back to feature strongly in the side's push for the play-offs. Neil is the elder brother of Charlton's Luke Young.

Tottenham H *(From trainee on 17/8/1991)*
Bournemouth *(Free on 11/10/1994) FL 314+18/4 FLC 21+1 FAC 24 Others 20*

YOUNGS Thomas (Tom) Anthony John
Born: Bury St Edmunds, 31 August 1979
Height: 5'9" **Weight:** 10.4
Tom scored a hat-trick for Northampton during their pre-season tour of Spain, bu despite his all-action style and clever ball play he failed to find the net for the first team. An influx of forwards saw him fall down the pecking order and in the new year he joined Leyton Orient on a short-term contract. Here he was used as cove for Wayne Carlisle. Tom scored on his debut as a right-winger and made a few brief appearances before the end of the season but was released during the summer.

Cambridge U *(From juniors on 3/7/1997) F 118+32/43 FLC 3+3 FAC 10/3 Others 12+3/*

Luke Young

Tom Youngs

Northampton T (£50,000 on 27/3/2003) FL 11+15 FLC 2+1 Others 1+1
Leyton Orient *(Free on 28/1/2005) FL 6+4/1*

ZADKOVICH Ruben Anton
Born: Australia, 23 May 1986
Height: 5'10" **Weight:** 11.7
International Honours: Australia: Yth
Ruben was a regular in the Queen's Park Rangers reserve and youth teams last term but after failing to break into the first team he moved on to Notts County in the new year. He impressed enough to win a call-up to the senior squad and scored on his debut in the 3-2 defeat at Chester. The talented midfielder went on to make his debut for Australia at U20 level in May and featured in the squad for the World Youth championships in the Netherlands during the close season.
Queens Park Rgrs *(Free from Wollongong Rgrs, Australia on 3/9/2004)*
Notts Co *(Free on 18/3/2005) FL 6+2/1*

ZAKUANI Gabriel (Gaby)
Born: Congo, 31 May 1986
Height: 6'0" **Weight:** 10.10
Gaby made good progress at Leyton Orient last term, establishing himself as a regular in the starting line-up. A ball-playing central defender who is quick on the turn and is rarely beaten in the air, he was rarely absent from the side apart from injuries.
Leyton Orient *(Trainee) FL 41+3/2 FLC 1 FAC 2 Others 1*

ZAMORA Robert (Bobby) Lester
Born: Barking, 16 January 1981
Height: 6'0" **Weight:** 11.0
Club Honours: Div 3 '01; Div 2 '02
International Honours: E: U21-6
Bobby tried hard to break into the West Ham line-up last term but was mostly used as a substitute. In the early part of the season he scored a superb goal against Gillingham and followed this up with two more goals at Molineux in January. However when Teddy Sheringham was sidelined in April Bobby grabbed his chance to score some vital goals and silence his critics. Perhaps the most crucial of these were a delicate volley in the play-off semi-final with Ipswich and another in the final against Preston to clinch a place in the Premiership for the Hammers.
Bristol Rov *(From trainee on 1/7/1999) FL 0+4 FLC 0+1 FAC 0+1*
Brighton & Hove A *(Loaned on 11/2/2000) FL 6/6*
Brighton & Hove A *(£100,000 on*

Gaby Zakuani

10/8/2000) FL 117+2/70 FLC 4/2 FAC 6/4 Others 1/1
Tottenham H *(£1,500,000 on 22/7/2003) PL 6+10 FLC 1/1 FAC 0+1*
West Ham U *(Signed on 3/2/2004) FL 30+21/12 FLC 2/2 Others 6/4*

ZENDEN Boudewijn (Bolo)

Born: Maastricht, Holland, 15 August 1976
Height: 5'9" **Weight:** 11.5
Club Honours: FLC '04
International Honours: Holland: 54
After spending the previous campaign on loan at Middlesbrough, Bolo made a permanent move to the Riverside in the summer of 2004. He fractured his left wrist in the 1-0 defeat against Everton at Goodison in September but he was able to play a further six games because he was allowed to wear a soft-cast tape and scored three goals in the process. Bolo missed only two of the 51 games played by the club, while his eight goals lifting him to runner-up to leading scorer Jimmy-Floyd Hasselbaink.
Chelsea *(£7,500,000 from Barcelona, Spain, ex PSV Eindhoven, on 10/8/2001) PL 24+19/4 FLC 2+3 FAC 1+6 Others 3+1*
Middlesbrough *(Free on 30/8/2003) PL 67/9 FLC 6+1/2 FAC 3+1/1 Others 10/3*

ZIEGLER Reto Pirmin

Born: Nyon, Switzerland, 16 January 1986
Height: 6'0" **Weight:** 12.6
International Honours: Switzerland: 3; U21
A midfield playmaker who adds width in attack, Reto joined Spurs in the summer of 2004 and had a positive impact on the team's desire to play creative football. He enjoys getting forward and acting as a provider of accurate long passing, while he has the ability and pace to beat the most accomplished defenders. Reto suffered minor injury and fitness problems but featured in a number of Spurs finest displays last season. Regular first-team action will help him settle in the English game and provide the opportunity to impress at club level and on the international stage.
Tottenham H *(Signed from Grasshoppers Zurich, Switzerland on 31/8/2004) PL 12+11/1 FLC 3 FAC 5*

ZOLA-MAKONGO Calvin

Born: Kinshasa, DR Congo, 31 December 1984
Height: 6'1" **Weight:** 12.0
Signed during the 2004 close season, this

Bobby Zamora

tall striker made an immediate impact at Tranmere. Although appearing ungainly, Calvin has the knack of finding the goal and can lull the opposition into believing that he is merely an awkward player rather than a resourceful one. After a bright start, a successful first season at Prenton Park looked to be on the cards, but from mid-November Calvin was not allowed to take any further part in the club's affairs due to problems over his residency status, an issue that had yet to be resolved by the end of the campaign.

Newcastle U *(From trainee on 17/1/2002)*
Oldham Ath *(Loaned on 30/8/2003) FL 21+4/5 FAC 1/1 Others 2/1*
Tranmere Rov *(Free on 9/7/2004) FL 7+8/2 FLC 1+1/1 FAC 1 Others 1/1*

Bolo Zenden

FA Barclaycard Premiership and Coca Cola League Clubs

Summary of Appearances and Goals for 2004-2005

KEY TO TABLES: P/FL = Premier/Football League. FLC = Football League Cup. FAC = FA Cup. Others = Other first team appearances.
Left hand figures in each column list number of full appearances + appearances as substitute. Right hand figures list number of goals scored.

	P/FL		FLC		FAC		Others	
	App	Goals	App	Goals	App	Goals	App	Goals
ARSENAL (PREM: 2nd)								
ALIADIERE Jeremie	0 + 4				0 + 2		0 + 1	
ALMUNIA Manuel	10		3		2		1	
BERGKAMP Dennis	20 + 9	8			4		5	
CAMPBELL Sol	16	1			1		4	
CLICHY Gael	7 + 8		1		5		1 + 2	
COLE Ashley	35	2			3		8 + 1	
CREGG Patrick			0 + 2					
CYGAN Pascal	15		1		2 + 1		4	
DJOUROU Johan			2 + 1					
EBOUE Emmanuel	0 + 1				3			
EDU	6 + 6	2	1		0 + 1		3 + 1	
FABREGAS Cesc	24 + 9	2	1		4 + 2		5 + 1	1
FLAMINI Mathieu	9 +12	1	3		4		2 + 2	
GILBERTO	13				2		2	1
HENRY Thierry	31 + 1	25			1		9	5
HOYTE Justin	4 + 1		3		0 + 1		1 + 2	
KARBASSIYOON Daniel			1 + 2	1				
LARSSON Sebastian			2 + 1					
LAUREN	32 + 1	1			4		8	
LEHMANN Jens	28				5		8	
LJUNGBERG Freddie	24 + 2	10			5 + 1	2	6	2
LUPOLI Arturo			3	2	1			
OWUSU-ABEYIE Quincy	1		1 + 2	1	0 + 2		0 + 1	
PENNANT Jermaine	1 + 6		3		1		1	
PIRES Robert	26 + 7	14			4 + 2	2	7 + 1	1
REYES Jose Antonio	25 + 5	9			6	1	8 + 1	2
SENDEROS Philippe	12 + 1		3		6		1	
SMITH Ryan			2 + 1					
SVARD Sebastian							0 + 1	
TOURE Kolo	35				5 + 1		9	1
VAN PERSIE Robin	12 +14	5	3	1	3 + 2	3	0 + 7	1
VIEIRA Patrick	32	6			6	1	6	
ASTON VILLA (PREM: 10th)								
ANGEL Juan Pablo	30 + 5	7	2	2	1			
BARRY Gareth	33 + 1	7	1		1	1		
BERSON Mathieu	7 + 4		0 + 1		0 + 1			
COLE Carlton	18 + 9	3	1 + 1		1			
DAVIS Steven	19 + 9	1			0 + 1			
DE LA CRUZ Ulises	30 + 4		1					
DELANEY Mark	30		1		1			
DJEMBA-DJEMBA Eric	4 + 2							
HENDRIE Lee	25 + 4	5	2		1			
HITZLSPERGER Thomas	17 +11	2	0 + 2					
LAURSEN Martin	12	1						
McCANN Gavin	20	1	2		1			
MELLBERG Olof	30	3	2		1			
MOORE Luke	5 +20	1	0 + 1		0 + 1			
MOORE Stefan	0 + 1							
POSTMA Stefan	2 + 1							
RIDGEWELL Liam	12 + 3		1		1			
SAMUEL JLloyd	34 + 1		2		1			
SOLANO Nobby	32 + 4	8	2	1	1			
SORENSEN Thomas	36		2		1			
VASSELL Darius	17 + 4	2	1	1				
WHITTINGHAM Peter	5 + 8	1	2					
BARNSLEY (DIV 1: 13th)								
ATKINSON Rob	0 + 1							
AUSTIN Neil	9 + 6							
BAKER Tom	0 + 3							
BOULDING Mike	22 + 7	10	1 + 1				0 + 1	
BURNS Jacob	33 + 1	2	1		0 + 1		0 + 1	
CARBON Matt	16 +10		1		1			
CHOPRA Michael	38 + 1	17	1		1		1	
COLGAN Nicky	12 + 1		2				1	
CONLON Barry	17 + 7	6	2	1	1		1	
FLINDERS Scott	11							
HASSELL Bobby	37 + 2		2		1		1	
JARMAN Nathan	1 + 5							
JOHNSON Simon	10 + 1	2						
JOYNES Nathan	0 + 1							
KAY Antony	37 + 2	6	2		1		1	
McPHAIL Stephen	36	2	1				1	
NARDIELLO Danny	11 +17	7	0 + 2				1	

	P/FL		FLC		FAC		Others	
	App	Goals	App	Goals	App	Goals	App	Goals
ONIBUJE Fola	0 + 3				0 + 1			
REID Paul	38 + 3	3	1	1	1		1	
SHUKER Chris	39 + 6	7	2	1	1			
STALLARD Mark	0 + 5		0 + 1					
TONGE Dale	14				0 + 1			
TURNBULL Ross	23				1			
VAUGHAN Tony	25 + 1	4	1				1	
WILLIAMS Robbie	13 + 4	1	1		1		0 + 1	
WILLIAMS Tommy	38 + 1		2		1		1	
WROE Nicky	26 + 5		2		1		1	
BIRMINGHAM CITY (PREM: 12th)								
ANDERTON Darren	9 +11	3	2		2			
BLAKE Robbie	2 + 9	2			1 + 1			
CARTER Darren	12 + 3	2			2	2		
CLAPHAM Jamie	18 + 9		1 + 1		1 + 1			
CLEMENCE Stephen	13 + 9		2		2			
CUNNINGHAM Kenny	36		1		1			
DIAO Salif	2							
DUNN David	9 + 2	2	0 + 1					
FORSSELL Mikael	4							
GRAY Julian	18 +14	2	2		2			
GRONKJAER Jesper	13 + 3		2	1				
HESKEY Emile	34	10	2		2	1		
IZZET Muzzy	10	1						
JOHN Stern	0 + 3							
JOHNSON Damien	36		0 + 1					
LAZARIDIS Stan	15 + 5		0 + 1		1			
MELCHIOT Mario	33 + 1	1	2		2			
MORRISON Clinton	13 +13	4	0 + 1	1	1 + 1			
NAFTI Mehdi	7 + 3							
PANDIANI Walter	13 + 1	4						
PENNANT Jermaine	12							
SAVAGE Robbie	18	4	1	1				
TAYLOR Maik	38		2		2			
TAYLOR Martin	4 + 3		1		1			
TEBILY Olivier	9 + 6				0 + 2			
UPSON Matthew	36	2	2		2			
YORKE Dwight	4 + 9	2	2		0 + 1			
BLACKBURN ROVERS (PREM: 15th)								
AMORUSO Lorenzo	5 + 1		1					
BOTHROYD Jay	6 + 5	1	1		0 + 1			
DE PEDRO Javier	1 + 1		1					
DERBYSHIRE Matt	0 + 1							
DICKOV Paul	27 + 2	9			6	1		
DJORKAEFF Youri	3							
DOUGLAS Jonathan	0 + 1		1					
EMERTON Brett	33 + 4	4	1	1	4 + 2			
ENCKELMAN Peter			1					
FERGUSON Barry	21	2			1			
FLITCROFT Garry	17 + 2				3 + 1			
FRIEDEL Brad	38				7			
GALLAGHER Paul	5 +11	2	0 + 1	1	3 + 1			
GRAY Michael	9							
GRESKO Vratislav	2 + 1		1					
JANSEN Matt	3 + 4	2	1					
JOHANSSON Nils-Eric	18 + 4		1		4 + 1			
JOHNSON Jemal	0 + 3				1 + 2	1		
MATTEO Dominic	25 + 3				4	1		
McEVELEY Jay	5							
MOKOENA Aaron	16				5 + 1			
NEILL Lucas	34 + 2	1	1		7			
NELSEN Ryan	15				4 + 1			
PEDERSEN Morten Gamst	19	4	0 + 1	1	7	3		
REID Steven	23 + 5	2			2 + 4			
SAVAGE Robbie	9				3 + 1			
SHORT Craig	13 + 1	1						
STEAD Jon	19 +10	2	0 + 1		1 + 3			
THOMPSON David	11 +13				5 + 1	2		
TODD Andy	26	1			6			
TUGAY	13 + 8		1		4	1		
YORKE Dwight	2 + 2							
BLACKPOOL (DIV 1: 16th)								
ANDERSON Stuart	1 + 3							
BARROWMAN Andrew	0 + 2							

Ashley Cole (Arsenal)

	P/FL		FLC		FAC		Others	
	App	Goals	App	Goals	App	Goals	App	Goals
LINKHORN Matthew	2 + 2				1 + 1		2	3
OYACK Steven	0 + 1							
ULLOCK Martin	24 + 4		1		1			
URNS Jamie	19 + 4				1 + 1		2 + 1	2
UTLER Tony	6 + 2							
LARE Rob	19 + 4		1		4		2	
LARKE Peter	38	5			4	1	0 + 1	
OID Danny	33 + 2		1		4		2	1
ONNELLY Ciaran	4 + 4							
OUGHTY Phil							3	
DGE Lewis					1			
DWARDS Paul	22 + 6	3			1		2	
DWARDS Rob	24 + 2	1	1		3 + 1		3	
LLEGAARD Kevin	2				1			
VANS Gareth	22				1 + 1		0 + 1	
LYNN Mike A	5 + 1							
LYNN Michael J	6		1					
ORRE Dean	0 + 1							
RABOVAC Zarko	1 + 2							
RAYSON Simon	32 + 4	2	1		4		2	
IC Sasa	3						2	
ONES Bradley	12							
ONES Lee	29		1		2		1	
IVESEY Danny	1							
YNCH Simon	5 + 2				2			
IcGREGOR Mark	36 + 2		1		4		1	
IURPHY John	30 + 1	9			1		1	1
ARKER Keigan	26 + 9	9	1		3 + 1	1	3	2
ATERSON Sean	0 + 2							
ICHARDSON Leam	20 + 3		1				2 + 1	
HAW Matt	2 + 8				0 + 1			
OUTHERN Keith	25 + 2	6			2 + 1	1	2	
AYLOR Scott	24	12	1	1	2	1	0 + 1	
ERNON Scott	4	3						
VARHURST Paul	2 + 2				0 + 1		1	
VELLENS Richard	27 + 1	3			2 + 2	2	0 + 2	
VHITTAKER Danny							0 + 1	
VILES Simon							2 + 1	
OLTON WANDERERS (PREM: 6th)								
ARNESS Anthony	5 + 3		1		0 + 2			
EN HAIM Tal	19 + 2	1	2		4			
AMPO Ivan	20 + 7				1 + 1			
ANDELA Vincent	9 + 1				1 + 1			
AVIES Kevin	33 + 2	8	1 + 1		4	1		
IOUF El Hadji	23 + 4	9	2		1 + 2			
ADIGA Khalilou	0 + 5				3			
ERDINAND Les	1 +11	1	1 + 1	1				
ARDNER Ricardo	30 + 3		1		3 + 1			
IANNAKOPOULOS Stelios	28 + 6	7	1 + 1		2	1		
IERRO Fernando	15 +14	1	2		4			
UNT Nicky	29		1		3 + 1			
AASKELAINEN Jussi	36				4			
AIDI Radhi	20 + 7	5			0 + 1			
JLIO CESAR	4 + 1		2	1				
AKU Blessing	0 + 1		1 + 1					
'GOTTY Bruno	37				4			
OLAN Kevin	27 + 9	4	2		2 + 2			
AKES Andy	1							
'BRIEN Joey	0 + 1		0 + 1					
KOCHA Jay Jay	29 + 2	6	1	1	1			
EDERSEN Henrik	13 +14	6	1 + 1	1	3 + 1	2		
OOLE Kevin	1 + 1		2					
HAKES Ricky			1					
PEED Gary	37 + 1	1			2			
AZ TE Ricardo	1 + 6				2	1		
OSTON UNITED (DIV 2: 16th)								
BBEY Nathan	44		2		4		1	
BBEY Zema	3 + 2	1						
EEVERS Lee	31	1	2	1	4		1	
ENNETT Tom	11		2				1	
OYACK Steven	2 + 2							
ROOKS Lewis	1 + 1							
ARRUTHERS Martin	4 + 2		0 + 1					
LARE Daryl	14 + 5	3						
LARKE Ryan							1	
ASTER Jermaine	5 + 4	3						
LLENDER Paul	39	2	2		4	1		
ABRIELI Emanuele	4							
ASCOIGNE Paul	2 + 2		1					
REAVES Mark	21 + 1		1		4			
OLLAND Chris	30 + 2		1		3		1	
URST Tom	0 + 1							

	P/FL		FLC		FAC		Others	
	App	Goals	App	Goals	App	Goals	App	Goals
JAMES Kevin	6				2			
JELLEYMAN Gareth	3							
KIRK Andy	25	19	1		4	2	0 + 1	
LEE Jason	32 + 7	9	2	1	3 + 1	1		
MAYLETT Brad	8 + 1	3						
McCANN Austin	45	1	2		4			
McCORMICK Luke	2							
McMANUS Tom	5 + 3		1 + 1		0 + 1	2	1	
MELTON Steve	5 + 4	1						
NOBLE David	30 + 2	3	1		2 + 1	1		
NORRIS Rob	1 + 1				0 + 1			
O'DONNELL Stephen	2 + 2							
O'HALLORAN Matt	5 + 3	1			0 + 1		0 + 1	
PITT Courtney	20 +12	4	2	1				
ROMA Dominic	2							
RUSK Simon	22 + 9	3	1 + 1		2 + 2		1	
STAFF David	0 + 5						1	
STRONG Greg	8 + 1				1		1	
THOMAS Danny	32 + 7	3	0 + 1		4		1	
THOMPSON Lee	8 +37	3	0 + 2	2	1 + 3	1	1	
WEST Dean	22 + 2		1		2			
WHITE Alan	11							
WISEMAN Scott	1 + 1							
BOURNEMOUTH (DIV 1: 8th)								
ANDRADE Diogo			0 + 1				0 + 1	
BROADHURST Karl	29	1	3	1	5		1	
BROWNING Marcus	17 +23		1 + 1	1	2 + 3		1	
CONNELL Alan	7 +27	2	0 + 3		3 + 2	2	0 + 1	
COUTTS James	0 + 1						0 + 1	
CRAINIE Martin	2 + 1							
CUMMINGS Warren	30	2	2	1	4 + 1		1	
DANI	10 +13	3	1		0 + 2	1	1	
ELLIOTT Wade	43	4	3		5	1	1	
FLETCHER Carl	6	2	1					
FLETCHER Steve	30 + 6	9	1		2 + 1	1		
GREEN Adam	3							
HAYTER James	37 + 2	19	3	3	2 + 1		1	
HOLMES Derek	8 +15	2	1 + 2		2 + 2	1	1	
HOWE Eddie	33 + 2	1	2		3			
MAHER Shaun	29 + 7	2	3		3 + 1	1		
MILLS Matthew	12	3						
MOSS Neil	46		3		5			
MOSS Ryan	0 + 1							
O'CONNOR Garreth	39 + 1	13	2 + 1	1	5		1	
O'CONNOR James	6							
PURCHES Steve	10 + 4	1			1 + 1			
ROWE James	0 + 2							
SIMEK Frankie	8							
SPICER John	39	6	2	1	5	1		
STEWART Gareth							1	
STOCK Brian	39 + 2	6	3	1	4		1	1
YOUNG Neil	23 + 7		2		4		1	
BRADFORD CITY (DIV 1: 11th)								
ABBEY Zema	6	1						
ADEBOLA Dele	14 + 1	3					1	1
ARMSTRONG Craig	4 + 3							
ATHERTON Peter	12 + 4							
BENTHAM Craig	0 + 2							
BOWER Mark	46	2	1		1		1	
BRIDGE-WILKINSON Marc	12	3						
COLBECK Joe			0 + 1					
COOKE Andy	20	4						
CROOKS Lee	30 + 2	1	1				1	
DENTON Sam							1	
EMANUEL Lewis	28 + 8		1		1		1	
FORREST Danny	4 +16	2			0 + 1			
GAVIN Jason	1 + 2		1				1	
HENDERSON Paul	40		1		1		1	
HOLLOWAY Darren	33	1	1		1			
JACOBS Wayne	13 + 1							
KEARNEY Tom	13	1			1			
MORRISON Owen	17 + 5	2						
MUIRHEAD Ben	26 +14	1	1		1		1	
PENFORD Tom	0 + 3		0 + 1				0 + 1	
RICKETTS Donovan	4							
ROBERTS Neil	3	1					1	
SANASY Kevin	0 + 3		0 + 1					
SCHUMACHER Steve	42 + 1	6	1		1		1	
SUMMERBEE Nicky	31 + 2	3	1		1			
SWIFT John	2 + 3							
SYMES Michael	5 + 7	2	1		1		0 + 1	
TIERNEY Paul	14 + 2							

	P/FL		FLC		FAC		Others	
	App	Goals	App	Goals	App	Goals	App	Goals
WETHERALL David	45	4			1			
WINDASS Dean	39 + 2	27	1	1	1		1	
BRENTFORD (DIV 1: 4th)								
BANKOLE Ade	3							
BURTON Deon	38 + 2	10	1		7		2	
CHARLES Darius	1							
CLARIDGE Steve	3 + 1							
DOBSON Michael	13 + 5	1	1		4			
FITZGERALD Scott B	12		1		1		1	
FITZGERALD Scott P	7 + 5	4					1	
FRAMPTON Andy	34 + 1		1		6 + 1	1	2	1
GAYLE Marcus	4 + 2						1 + 1	
HARGREAVES Chris	30	2	1		6	1	2	
HARROLD Matt	6 +13				1 + 3		1	
HILLIER Sean							1	
HUNT Steve	13 + 6	3			1 + 3		1	
HUTCHINSON Eddie	14 + 1	1			5 + 1	1	2	
IDE Charlie	0 + 1							
JULIAN Alan							1	
LAWRENCE Jamie	8 + 6				3 + 1		1	
LENNIE Josh							0 + 1	
MAY Ben	7 + 3	1			4 + 2			
MOLESKI George	0 + 1							
MULDOWNEY Luke							0 + 1	
MYERS Andy	6 + 4		1		1		1	
NELSON Stuart	43		1		9		2	
O'CONNOR Kevin	32 + 5	2	1		4 + 1		1	
OSBORNE Karleigh	1							
PACQUETTE Richard	1							
PALMER Jamie							1	
PETERS Ryan	1 + 8	1	1		0 + 1		1	
PRATLEY Darren	11 + 3	1					2	
RANKIN Isaiah	33 + 8	8	0 + 1		8 + 1	2	0 + 2	
RHODES Alex	4 +18	3	1		1 + 3	1	1	
SALAKO John	30 + 5	4			8 + 1	1	0 + 1	
SMITH Jay	0 + 2		1					
SOBERS Jerrome	1	1						
SODJE Sam	40	7			8	1	2	
SOMNER Matt	1 + 1							
TABB Jay	29 +11	5	0 + 1		5 + 4	1	2 + 1	
TALBOT Stewart	35 + 2	1	0 + 1		9	1	2	
TURNER Michael	45	1			8		2	
WATTS Ryan	0 + 1							
WEIGHT Scott							0 + 1	
BRIGHTON & HOVE ALBION (CHAMP: 20th)								
BLAYNEY Alan	7							
BUTTERS Guy	41	2	1	1	1			
CARPENTER Richard	28 + 4	3			1	1		
CLARIDGE Steve	5							
CULLIP Danny	18		1					
CURRIE Darren	21 + 1	2	1					
DOLAN Joe	3							
EL-ABD Adam	14 + 2							
HAMMOND Dean	20 +10	4						
HARDING Dan	39 + 4	1	1		1			
HART Gary	16 +10	2			1			
HINSHELWOOD Adam	37 + 1	1	1		1			
JARRETT Albert	3 + 9	1	1					
JONES Nathan	3 +16		0 + 1					
KNIGHT Leon	33 + 6	4	1		1			
KUIPERS Michel	30		1		1			
MAY Chris	0 + 1							
MAYO Kerry	21 + 6	1			1			
McCAMMON Mark	16 + 2	3						
McPHEE Chris	6 +10							
MOLANGO Maheta	4 + 1	1	1					
NICOLAS Alexis	29 + 4		1					
OATWAY Charlie	31 + 3	1			1			
PIERCY John	1 + 1							
REID Paul	33 + 1	2			1			
ROBINSON Jake	1 + 9	1	0 + 1					
SHAABAN Rami	6							
VIRGO Adam	36	9	1		1			
WATSON Paul	1 + 3							
YELLDELL David	3							
BRISTOL CITY (DIV 1: 7th)								
AMANKWAAH Kevin	1 + 4						3	
ANYINSAH Joe	2 + 5						0 + 2	
BELL Mickey	26 + 5	1			1		2 + 1	
BROOKER Steve	33	16			1			
BROWN Scott	13 + 6				0 + 1		0 + 2	
BUTLER Tony	22	2	1		2		2	
CAREY Louis	14							
COLES Danny	37 + 1	1	1		1 + 1		2	
COTTERILL David	8 + 4						0 + 1	
DINNING Tony	15 + 4						1	
DOHERTY Tommy	25 + 4	1	2		2		2	
FORTUNE Clayton	17 +13		1 + 1		1		2	
GILLESPIE Steven	1 + 7		0 + 1		0 + 1		1 + 1	
GOLBOURNE Scott	7 + 2							
GOODFELLOW Marc	1 + 4							
HARLEY Ryan	1 + 1						0 + 1	
HEFFERNAN Paul	10 +17	5	0 + 1		1	1	2	
HILL Matt	23		2		2		2 + 1	
IRELAND Craig	5							
KEITH Joey	3							
LITA Leroy	42 + 2	24	2	2	1 + 1	1	3	
MILLER Lee	2 + 5		1 + 1		1			
MURRAY Scott	31 +11	8	2		2		3	
ORR Bradley	23 +14		2		2		1	
PHILLIPS Steve	46		2		2		3	
ROBERTS Chris	6 + 2	1	2					
SKUSE Cole	4 + 3							
SMITH Jamie	35 + 4	2	2		1 + 1			
TINNION Brian	15 + 7	1	0 + 1		1 + 1		2	
WILKSHIRE Luke	35 + 2	10	1		1		2	
WOODMAN Craig	3		1					
WRING Danny	0 + 1							
BRISTOL ROVERS (DIV 2: 12th)								
AGOGO Junior	37 + 6	19	1 + 1		2		2 + 2	
ANDERSON John	28 + 6	1	1				4	
BASS Jon	3							
BESWETHERICK Jon			1					
BURNS Liam	3				1		0 + 1	
CAMPBELL Stuart	21 + 4		2		2		4 + 1	
CARRUTHERS Chris	2 + 3							
CASH Brian	0 + 1							
CLARKE Ryan	18						2	
DISLEY Craig	18 +10	4	0 + 1		1		5	
EDWARDS Christian	39 + 3	2	2		2		4	
ELLIOTT Steve	40 + 1	2	2		1		5	
FORRESTER Jamie	20 +15	7					3 + 1	
GIBB Ally	16 + 7		2		0 + 1			
HALDANE Lewis	1 +12				0 + 2		0 + 2	
HINTON Craig	33 + 5		2		2		6	
HUNT James	41	4	2		2		4	
JEANNIN Alex	1							
LESCOTT Aaron	24 + 2		0 + 1		1		5	
LOUIS Jefferson	1							
MILLER Kevin	28		2		2		4	
RYAN Robbie	39 + 1		1		2		5	
SAVAGE Dave	21 + 6	1	0 + 1		1		1	
SHAKES Ricky	0 + 1						0 + 1	
SINCLAIR Scott	0 + 2							
SOARES Louie	0 + 1							
THORPE Lee	17 + 8	3	1	1	0 + 1		4	
TROLLOPE Paul	26 + 4	2	2		2		5 + 1	
WALKER Richard	20 + 7	10	1 + 1	1	1	1	2 + 1	
WARD Elliott	0 + 3							
WILLIAMS Ryan	9 + 8	3					1 + 2	
BURNLEY (CHAMP: 13th)								
AKINBIYI Ade	9 + 1	4						
BLAKE Robbie	24	10	4	3				
BOWDITCH Dean	8 + 2	1						
BRANCH Graham	39 + 4	3	4	1	1 + 2			
CAHILL Gary	27	1	1		4			
CAMARA Mohamed	45		4	1	4			
CHAPLOW Richard	16 + 5	2	2		2			
COYNE Danny	20		2					
DUFF Michael	37 + 5		4		2			
DUFFY Richard	3 + 4	1	2					
GRANT Tony	37 + 5	2	4		4			
HYDE Micah	37 + 1	1	4		4	1		
JENSEN Brian	26 + 1		2		4			
McGREAL John	38 + 1	1	3		3			
MOORE Ian	30 + 5	4	2		4	2		
O'CONNOR James	20 + 1	2						
O'NEILL Matt	0 + 2							
OSTER John	12 + 3	1			2 + 1			
PILKINGTON Joel	0 + 1		0 + 1		0 + 1			
ROCHE Lee	17 +12	1	2 + 1		1 + 3			
SANOKHO Amadou	0 + 3		1					
SINCLAIR Frank	36	1	1 + 1		4			

	P/FL		FLC		FAC		Others	
	App	Goals	App	Goals	App	Goals	App	Goals
WHITTINGHAM Peter	7				2			
BURY (DIV 2: 17th)								
BARRASS Matt	8 + 1				1		1	
BARRY-MURPHY Brian	43 + 2	6	1		2		1	
BOSHELL Danny	2 + 4							
BUCHANAN David	0 + 3							
CARTLEDGE Jon	1 + 4							
CHALLINOR Dave	43	1	1	1	1	1	1	
DUNFIELD Terry	7 + 8	1	0 + 1				0 + 1	
FITZGERALD John	14							
FLITCROFT Dave	32 + 4	3	1		2		1	
GARNER Glyn	27		1				1	
HARKINS Gary	4 + 1							
JONES Graeme	1 + 2	1						
KAZIM-RICHARDS Colin	10 +20	3			0 + 1		1	
KENNEDY Tom	46	1	1		2		1	
KEOGH Andrew	4	2						
MARRIOTT Andy	19				2			
MATTIS Dwayne	39	5	1	1	2	2		
MOORE David	0 + 3							
NEWBY Jon	17 +19	4	0 + 1		0 + 2		1	
NUGENT David	26	11	1		2	1		
PORTER Chris	29 + 3	9	1		2	1	1	
SAVAGE Bas	5							
SCOTT Paul	20 + 3		1		0 + 1		1	1
SHAKES Ricky	4 + 3	2						
SWAILES Danny	20	1			2		0 + 1	
UNSWORTH Lee	34 + 2	1	1		2			
WHALEY Simon	22 +16	3	1		0 + 2		0 + 1	
WOODTHORPE Colin	29 + 1				2		1	
CAMBRIDGE UNITED (DIV 2: 24th)								
ANGUS Stev	14		1				1	
ANSELIN Cedric	2							
BEECH Tom	0 + 4							
BIMSON Stuart	16 + 3				1			
BLACKBURN Lee	0 + 3							
BRAMBLE Tes	9	3						
CARRUTHERS Martin	5							
CHILLINGWORTH Dan	22 + 6	4	0 + 1				0 + 1	
DANIELS Dave							0 + 1	
DAVIES Adam	0 + 2						0 + 1	
DUNCAN Andy	40 + 2	1	0 + 1		1			
EASTER Jermaine	15 + 9	6	1		1		2	1
EL KHOLTI Abdou	13 + 2		1		0 + 1		2	
FULLER Ashley	0 + 2							
GLEESON Dan	21 + 9		1				2	
GOODHIND Warren	25 + 1				1		1	
GUTTRIDGE Luke	14 + 3		0 + 1					
HEATH Colin	5 + 1							
HODGSON Richard	9 + 1	2			0 + 1			
HUTTON Rory	0 + 2							
JOHNSON Brad	0 + 1							
JOWSEY James	1							
KONTE Amadou	6 + 3	3						
LATTE-YEDO Igor	5 + 6						1	
MARSHALL Shaun	1							
MBOME Kingsley	12 + 1	1			1		1	
NEWEY Tom	15 + 1							
NICHOLLS Ashley	25 + 3		1		1		1	
OLI Dennis	4	1					1	
PRICE Lewis	6							
QUINTON Darren	14 +17		1				1 + 1	
REA Simon	4							
ROBERTS Iwan	11	3						
ROBINSON Matt	0 + 4						1 + 1	
RUDDY John	38		1		1		2	
SOMNER Matt	24							
TANN Adam	34 + 2	1	1		1		2	
TONER Ciaran	6 + 2							
TUDOR Shane	22 + 4	6	1		1	1	1	
TURNER John	16 +22	6	1		1		1	
WALKER Justin	36	1	1				2	
WARDLEY Stuart	1 + 2							
WEBB Danny	15 + 7	1			1		0 + 1	
CARDIFF CITY (CHAMP: 16th)								
ALEXANDER Neil	17		2					
ANTHONY Byron			1 + 1	1				
ARDLEY Neal	8	1						
BARKER Chris	38 + 1		3		2			
BOLAND Willie	18 + 3		3					
BOULDING Mike	0 + 4							
BULLOCK Lee	8 +13	3	3 + 1	2	0 + 1			
CAMPBELL Andy	6 + 6		1 + 1		0 + 1			
COLLINS James	32 + 2	1	4		2	1		
CROFT Gary	0 + 1							
EARNSHAW Rob	4	1	1	1				
FISH Nicky			1					
FLEETWOOD Stuart	1 + 5		0 + 2					
GABBIDON Danny	45	1	2		2			
HARRIS Neil	1 + 2	1						
INAMOTO Junichi	13 + 1				2			
JEROME Cameron	21 + 8	6	0 + 2	1	1			
KAVANAGH Graham	28	3	2 + 1		2			
KOSKELA Toni	0 + 2							
LANGLEY Richard	24 + 1	2			2			
LEDLEY Joe	20 + 8	3	2 + 1		0 + 1			
LEE Alan	24 +14	5	3	1	2	1		
MARGETSON Martyn	3 + 1							
McANUFF Jobi	42 + 1	2	3		2	1		
O'NEIL Gary	8 + 1	1						
PAGE Robert	8 + 1							
PARRY Paul	12 +12	4	3 + 1					
ROBINSON John	8	1	0 + 1					
THOMAS Danny	0 + 1							
THORNE Peter	28 + 3	12	2	2	1 + 1			
VIDMAR Tony	23 + 5	1	4		0 + 1			
WARNER Tony	26		2		2			
WESTON Rhys	23 + 2		2		2			
WILLIAMS Darren	17 + 3							
CHARLTON ATHLETIC (PREM: 11th)								
ANDERSEN Stephan	2							
BARTLETT Shaun	25	6			2	2		
EL KARKOURI Talal	28 + 4	5	1		3			
EUELL Jason	7 +19	2	0 + 2		1 + 2			
FISH Mark	6 + 1				0 + 1			
FORTUNE Jon	28 + 3	2	2		3	1		
HOLLAND Matt	31 + 1	3	1		3			
HREIDARSSON Hermann	33 + 1	1	2	1	3			
HUGHES Bryan	10 + 7	1	1 + 1		3	3		
JEFFERS Francis	9 +11	3	2	1	2	1		
JOHANSSON JJ	15 +11	4	1 + 1		1 + 2			
KIELY Dean	36		2		3			
KISHISHEV Radostin	27 + 4		0 + 1					
KONCHESKY Paul	15 +13	1			1 + 2			
LISBIE Kevin	12 + 5	1	1 + 1					
MURPHY Danny	37 + 1	3	2	1	2 + 1	1		
PERRY Chris	17 + 2	1	2					
ROMMEDAHL Dennis	19 + 7	2			1			
SAM Lloyd	0 + 1							
STUART Graham	4		2					
THOMAS Jerome	21 + 3	3	1		2 + 1			
YOUNG Luke	36	2	2		3			
CHELSEA (PREM: 1st)								
BABAYARO Celestine	3 + 1		1					
BRIDGE Wayne	12 + 3		4		2		4	
CARVALHO Ricardo	22 + 3	1	3		1		10	
CECH Petr	35		2				11	
COLE Joe	19 + 9	8	4 + 2		3		8 + 1	
CUDICINI Carlo	3		4		3		1	
DROGBA Didier	18 + 8	10	3 + 1	1	1 + 1		8 + 1	5
DUFF Damien	28 + 2	6	5 + 1	2	1 + 1		8 + 2	2
FERREIRA Paulo	29		5		0 + 1		6 + 1	
FORSSELL Mikael	0 + 1						0 + 1	
GALLAS William	28	2	5		1		12	
GEREMI	6 + 7		1		2		1 + 3	
GRANT Anthony	0 + 1							
GUDJOHNSEN Eidur	30 + 7	12	1 + 5	1	2 + 1	1	9 + 2	2
HUTH Robert	6 + 4				1	1	1 + 3	
JAROSIK Jiri	3 +11		1 + 2		2 + 1			
JOHNSON Glen	13 + 4		2 + 1		3		4 + 2	
KEZMAN Mateja	6 +19	4	2 + 2	2	3	1	3 + 6	
LAMPARD Frank	38	13	3 + 3	2	0 + 2		12	4
MAKELELE Claude	36	1	4				10	
MORAIS Nuno	0 + 2				1		0 + 1	
MUTU Adrian	0 + 2							
OLIVEIRA Filipe	0 + 1							
PARKER Scott	1 + 3		3				3 + 1	
PIDGELEY Lenny	0 + 1							
ROBBEN Arjan	14 + 4	7	3 + 1	1	0 + 2		2 + 3	1
SMERTIN Alexei	11 + 5		1		3		4 + 1	1
TERRY John	36	3	5		1	1	11	4
TIAGO	21 +13	4	4		2		4 + 7	
WATT Steve	0 + 1				1			

Didier Drogba (Chelsea)

HELTENHAM TOWN (DIV 2: 14th)

	P/FL App	P/FL Goals	FLC App	FLC Goals	FAC App	FAC Goals	Others App	Others Goals
IRD David	26 + 8		1		1		1 + 1	
ROUGH John	11 + 2				1		2	1
AINES Gavin	27 + 2	2			1			
ONNOLLY Adam	1 + 3							
EVANEY Martin	37 + 1	10	1	1	1		2	
UFF Shane	45	1	1		1		2	
INNIGAN John	31 + 1	3					1	1
YFE Graham	1 + 2						0 + 1	
ILL Jerry	43 + 1		1		1		1	
ILLESPIE Steven	10 + 2	5						
UINAN Steve	35 + 8	6	1		1		2	1
IGGS Shane	46		1		1		2	
lcCANN Grant	39	4	1				2	1
IELLIGAN John	23 + 6	2	1		1		2	
IORGAN Alan	8							
IURPHY Chris	0 + 4							
DEJAYI Kay	10 +22	1	0 + 1					
PENCER Damian	14 +27	8	0 + 1		0 + 1	1	0 + 2	1
AYLOR Michael	10 + 3		1					
'ICTORY Jamie	40 + 2	3	1		1		2	
'INCENT Ashley	14 +12	1	0 + 1		0 + 1		1 + 1	2
VARD Graham	0 + 2							
VILSON Brian	35 + 8	3	1		1		2	

HESTER CITY (DIV 2: 20th)

	P/FL App	P/FL Goals	FLC App	FLC Goals	FAC App	FAC Goals	Others App	Others Goals
NACLET Eddie					0 + 1			
TIENO Taiwo	3 + 1	1						
AYLISS Dave	9				1			
ELLE Cortez	17 + 5	1	1		1 + 1	1		
OLLAND Phil	42	1	1		2		3	
OOTH Robbie	7 + 4	1			1 + 1		2 + 1	
RANCH Michael	31 + 2	11	1		1	2	0 + 1	
ROWN Michael	11 + 7				1			
ROWN Wayne	23		1		1		1	
ARDEN Paul	36 + 4		0 + 1		3		3	
LARE Daryl	3 + 4	1			1		1	
OLLINS Danny	12	1	1					
AVIES Ben	38 + 6	2	0 + 1		2		1 + 1	
OYLE Colin							1	
RUMMOND Stewart	44 + 1	6	1		2		1 + 2	
DMONDSON Darren	26 + 1				2			
LLISON Kevin	24	9	1		3	1	2	1
LOKOBI George	4 + 1							
OY Robbie	13							
IARRIS Andy	9 +10				1 + 1		3	
IESSEY Sean	31 + 3	1	1		3		2	1
IILLIER Ian	7 + 1							
IOPE Richard	26 + 2				2		1 + 2	1
OWE Ryan	8	4						
YNCH Gavin	0 + 1				0 + 1			
IACKENZIE Chris	23 + 1				2		1	
lcINTYRE Kevin	9 + 1		1		1 + 1		3	
IAVARRO Alan	3		1					
IICHOLAS Andrew	5							
)'NEILL Joe	5 + 6	1						
APLEY Kevin	12 + 9	2			1 + 2	2	3	
EGAN Carl	4 + 2							
ESTANOVICH Ashley	3 + 4							
TAMP Darryn	2 + 2						1	
'AUGHAN Stephen	14 + 7		1		2		3	
VALSH Michael	2 + 3	1			0 + 1			
VATSON Andy							1	
VHALLEY Shaun	0 + 3						0 + 2	

HESTERFIELD (DIV 1: 17th)

	P/FL App	P/FL Goals	FLC App	FLC Goals	FAC App	FAC Goals	Others App	Others Goals
LLISON Wayne	27 +11	6					1	
LLOTT Mark	45	2	1	1	1		1	
AILEY Alex	45	1	1		1		1	
LATHERWICK Steve	33 + 2	4	0 + 1		1		1	
AMPBELL-RYCE Jamal	14		1				1	1
LINGAN Sammy	15	2						
AVIES Gareth	9 +10	1			0 + 1		1	
AWSON Kevin	1							
E BOLLA Mark	15 +13	3	1		0 + 1		0 + 1	
OWNES Aaron	7 + 2	2					1	
VATT Ian	41	4	1		1			
OLAN Caleb	17 +15	6			1			
OWLER Jordan	4 + 2							
OX Michael	0 + 1							
ULOP Marton	7							
IUDSON Mark	32 + 2	4			1		1	
NNES Mark	18 + 3		1					

	P/FL App	P/FL Goals	FLC App	FLC Goals	FAC App	FAC Goals	Others App	Others Goals
LOGAN Carlos	6 + 3	1						
McMASTER Jamie	6 + 2							
MUGGLETON Carl	37		1		1		1	
NICHOLSON Shane	42 + 1	7	1		1			
NIVEN Derek	38	1	1		1			
N'TOYA-ZOA Tcham	18 +20	8	1		0 + 1			
O'HARE Alan	14 + 7		1				1	
RICHMOND Andy	1							
SMITH Adam	6 +10		0 + 1		1		1	
STALLARD Mark	7 + 2	2			1			
THOMPSON Glyn	1							

COLCHESTER UNITED (DIV 1: 15th)

	P/FL App	P/FL Goals	FLC App	FLC Goals	FAC App	FAC Goals	Others App	Others Goals
ANDREWS Wayne	4 + 1	2	1					
BALDWIN Pat	35 + 3		2		5		1	
BOWDITCH Ben	0 + 5		0 + 1		0 + 1			
BOWRY Bobby	7 + 4		0 + 1		1 + 1		1	
BROWN Wayne	38 + 2	1	3		2 + 1		1	
CADE Jamie	4 + 5		1		0 + 3		0 + 1	
CHILVERS Liam	40 + 1	1	2		4 + 1			
DANNS Neil	32	11	2	1	1		1	
DAVISON Aidan	33		2		3		1	
FAGAN Craig	25 + 1	8	3	2	5	4		
GARCIA Richard	20 + 4	4	1 + 1		3	1	1	1
GERKEN Dean	13		1		2			
GOODFELLOW Marc	4 + 1	1						
GUY Jamie	0 + 2							
HALFORD Greg	43 + 1	4	2 + 1	1	5	4	1	
HUNT Stephen	16 + 4	1	2		1 + 1		1	
IZZET Kemal	3 + 1							
JARVIS Ryan	2 + 4							
JOHNSON Gavin	36 + 1	9	2	1	4		0 + 1	
KEITH Joey	27 + 4	4	3		4 + 1		1	
KEITH Marino	12	4						
MAY Ben	5 + 9	1	0 + 2	1				
N'DUMBU-NSUNGU Guylain	2 + 6	1			0 + 1			
STOCKLEY Sam	33 + 4	1	2		5			
WATSON Kevin	44	2	3		5		1	
WHITE John	16 + 4		0 + 1		3			
WILLIAMS Gareth	12 +17	3	1		2 + 1	2	1	

COVENTRY CITY (CHAMP: 19th)

	P/FL App	P/FL Goals	FLC App	FLC Goals	FAC App	FAC Goals	Others App	Others Goals
ADEBOLA Dele	18 + 7	5			0 + 1	1		
BARRETT Graham	12 +12	4	1 + 1					
BENJAMIN Trevor	6 + 6	1						
BENNETT Ian	6							
CAREY Louis	23		3		1			
DAVENPORT Calum	6		1					
DELOUMEAUX Eric	1 + 1		1					
DOYLE Micky	43 + 1	2	3	1	2			
DUFFY Richard	14				1			
DYER Lloyd	6							
GIDDINGS Stuart	11 + 1		2		1			
GOATER Shaun	4 + 2							
GUDJONSSON Bjarni	3 + 7		3					
HALL Marcus	10							
HUGHES Stephen	39 + 1	4	2	1	2			
JOHN Stern	25 + 5	11	1		2	1		
JOHNSON Eddie	20 + 6	5	1 + 1		0 + 1			
JORGENSEN Claus	11 + 6	3	0 + 1		0 + 2			
LAVILLE Florent	5 + 1							
LEACOCK Dean	12 + 1		1		1 + 1			
McSHEFFREY Gary	31 + 6	12	1 + 1		2	2		
MILLS Matthew	4		1					
MORRELL Andy	24 +10	6	2	1	2			
NEGOUAI Christian	1				1			
OSBOURNE Isaac	7 + 2							
PAGE Robert	9							
RICKETTS Rohan	5 + 1							
SHAW Richard	30 + 3		3		1			
SHEARER Scott	8		1					
SHERWOOD Tim	10 + 1							
STAUNTON Steve	32 + 3	1	1		1			
STEELE Luke	32		2		2			
SUFFO Patrick	2 +19	3	1 + 2	2	0 + 1			
WHING Andy	9 + 7	1	0 + 3					
WILLIAMS Adrian	21	2			2			
WOOD Neil	6 + 7		2		1			

CREWE ALEXANDRA (CHAMP: 21st)

	P/FL App	P/FL Goals	FLC App	FLC Goals	FAC App	FAC Goals	Others App	Others Goals
ASHTON Dean	23 + 1	17	3	2				
BELL Lee	17				1			
BIGNOT Paul	3 + 2		0 + 1					
BRIGGS Keith	3							

	P/FL		FLC		FAC		Others	
	App	Goals	App	Goals	App	Goals	App	Goals
COCHRANE Justin	21 + 8		2 + 1					
FOSTER Steve	34	1	3	1	1			
HIGDON Michael	1 +19	3	0 + 1					
INCE Clayton	23				1			
JONES Billy	20		2					
JONES Steve	24 +12	10	3	3	1			
LUNT Kenny	46	5	3		1			
McCREADY Chris	19 + 1				0 + 1			
MOSES Adie	19 + 2		2		1			
MOSS Darren	6							
MURDOCK Colin	15 + 1							
OTSEMOBOR John	14	1	1					
PLATT Matthew	0 + 1							
RIVERS Mark	26 + 8	7	1 + 2	1	1			
ROBERTS Gary	2							
ROBERTS Mark	3 + 3		1					
SORVEL Neil	45 + 1	3	3		1			
TONKIN Anthony	33 + 2		2					
VARNEY Luke	17 + 9	4			1			
VAUGHAN David	43 + 1	6	3		1			
WALKER Richard	15 + 8	2	1 + 1		1			
WHITE Andy	11 +11	4	0 + 1		0 + 1			
WILLIAMS Ben	23		3					
CRYSTAL PALACE (PREM: 18th)								
ANDREWS Wayne	0 + 9							
BORROWDALE Gary	2 + 5		2 + 1					
BOYCE Emmerson	26 + 1		1					
BUTTERFIELD Danny	7		2		1			
DANZE Anthony			1					
DERRY Shaun	1 + 6		3					
FREEDMAN Dougie	10 +10	1	3	2				
GRANVILLE Danny	35	3	1		1			
HALL Fitz	36	2			1			
HUDSON Mark	7	1	2					
HUGHES Michael	34 + 2	2			1			
JOHNSON Andy	37	21			1			
KAVIEDES Ivan	1 + 3		0 + 2					
KIRALY Gabor	32		1		1			
KOLKKA Joonas	20 + 3	3	1					
LAKIS Vassilios	6 +12		0 + 1		1			
LEIGERTWOOD Mikele	16 + 4	1	2		1			
POPOVIC Tony	21 + 2							
POWELL Darren	4 + 2	1	2 + 1		1			
RIIHILAHTI Aki	28 + 4	4						
ROUTLEDGE Wayne	38		1		1			
SHIPPERLEY Neil	0 + 1		0 + 1		0 + 1			
SOARES Tom	16 + 6		2 + 1	1	0 + 1			
SORONDO Gonzalo	16 + 4		2					
SPERONI Julian	6		2					
TORGHELLE Sandor	3 + 9		3	1				
VENTOLA Nicola	0 + 3	1						
WATSON Ben	16 + 5		2		1			
DARLINGTON (DIV 2: 8th)								
APPLEBY Matty	10							
ARMSTRONG Alun	31 + 1	9			2	2		
BATES Matthew	4							
CLARK Ian	13 +11	2	1		2		0 + 1	
CLARKE Matthew	42 + 1	3	1		2		1	
CLOSE Brian	37 + 1		1		2		1	
CONVERY Mark	10 +13		0 + 1		0 + 1		0 + 1	
DICKMAN Jonjo	8	1						
FLEMING Curtis	24 + 3		1					
GILROY Keith	1 + 1							
GREGORIO Adolfo	19 + 5	2					1	
HIGNETT Craig	17 + 2	9						
HUGHES Chris	5 +10		1				1	
HUTCHINSON Joey	8		1					
KELTIE Clark	10 +11		1		0 + 1	1	0 + 1	
KENDRICK Joe	19 +12	1	1		1 + 1		1	
LIDDLE Craig	19 + 1	1			2			
LOGAN Richard	0 + 1							
MADDISON Neil	21 + 3	1	0 + 1		2		1	
McGURK David	9 + 1	2						
PETTA Bobby	12	1						
RUSSELL Craig	15 +13	1	1				1	
RUSSELL Sam	46		1		2		1	
SCARTISCINI Leandro			0 + 1					
SODJE Akpo	1 + 6	1						
ST JUSTE Jason	9 + 6	2						
THOMAS Steve	11 + 1						1	
VALENTINE Ryan	32 + 4	1			2		1	
WAINWRIGHT Neil	26 +12	4	1		1 + 1		1	

	P/FL		FLC		FAC		Others	
	App	Goals	App	Goals	App	Goals	App	Goa
WEBSTER Adrian	16 + 6				2			
WIJNHARD Clyde	31	14			2			
DERBY COUNTY (CHAMP: 4th)								
BISGAARD Morten	31 + 5	4			3		2	
BOERTIEN Paul					2			
BOLDER Adam	24 +12	2	1		1 + 1		1 + 1	
CAMP Lee	45		1		3		2	
DOYLE Nathan	3				0 + 1			
GRANT Lee	1 + 1							
HOLMES Lee	0 + 3		1					
HUDDLESTONE Tom	42 + 3		1		2		2	
IDIAKEZ Inigo	41	9	1	1	3	1	1	
JACKSON Richard	18 + 1		1		1		2	
JOHNSON Michael	35 + 1	1	1		2		1	
JUNIOR	5 +13		0 + 1		0 + 2	1		
KAKU Blessing	3 + 1							
KENNA Jeff	40		0 + 1		2		2	
KONJIC Mo	13 + 3						2	
MAKIN Chris	13							
MILLS Pablo	15 + 7				3		0 + 1	
PESCHISOLIDO Paul	10 +22	8	1		0 + 1	1	2	
RASIAK Grzegorz	35	16			2	1	1	
REICH Marco	27 +10	6	1		2		1 + 1	
SMITH Tommy	41 + 1	11			3		2	
TALBOT Jason	2							
TAYLOR Ian	25 +14	3	0 + 1		2		1 + 1	
TUDGAY Marcus	22 +12	9	1		2 + 1	1		
VINCENT Jamie	15	1	1					
DONCASTER ROVERS (DIV 1: 10th)								
ALBRIGHTON Mark	15 + 2	1	1				1	
BEARDSLEY Chris	1 + 3		0 + 1		0 + 1		2	
BEECH Chris	2							
BLUNDELL Gregg	33 + 8	9	2		2	2		
BROWN Adam	0 + 3	1						
CAMPBELL Andy	1 + 2							
COPPINGER Jamie	27 + 4		1 + 2		1 + 1		2	
DOOLAN John	32 + 6	2	3	1				
FENTON Nicky	37 + 1	1	3		2	1	2	
FORTUNE-WEST Leo	16 + 8	6	3	1			1	
FOSTER Steve	34	1	2				1	
GREEN Paul	38 + 4	7	2 + 1		2			
GUY Lewis	4 + 5	3						
INGHAM Mike	1						1	
IPOUA Guy	1 + 8		1		0 + 1			
JACKSON Ben	0 + 1						0 + 2	
JOHNSON Simon	8 + 3	3						
JONES Stuart	3 + 1						1	
MALONEY Jon	1 + 1							
MARPLES Simon	12		1					
McINDOE Michael	43 + 1	10	3	1	2	1	2	
McSPORRAN Jermaine	15 +11	1	2	1	1 + 1			
MORLEY Dave	9		1		2		1	
MULLIGAN Dave	27 + 4	1	0 + 2				1 + 1	
NELTHORPE Craig	0 + 1							
PRICE Jamie	5 + 1		1		2		0 + 1	
PRIET Nicky	7		1				2	
RAVENHILL Ricky	21 +14	3	1 + 1	1	2		2	
RIGOGLIOSO Adriano	2 +10		0 + 1		0 + 2		1	
ROBERTS Neil	30 + 1	6			2			
RYAN Tim	38 + 1	4	2		2		0 + 1	
TIERNEY Francis							1	
TURNER Iain	8							
WARRINGTON Andy	34		3		2			
WILSON Mark	1 + 2						1	
EVERTON (PREM: 4th)								
ARTETA Mikel	10 + 2	1			1			
BEATTIE James	7 + 4	1			2	1		
BENT Marcus	31 + 6	6	1 + 1	1	2 + 1			
CAHILL Tim	33	11	2 + 1		1 + 1	1		
CAMPBELL Kevin	4 + 2		0 + 1					
CARSLEY Lee	35 + 1	4	2	1	3			
CHADWICK Nick	0 + 1		0 + 2	1	0 + 2	1		
FERGUSON Duncan	6 +29	5	2	1				
GRAVESEN Thomas	20 + 1	4	1	1	0 + 1			
HIBBERT Tony	35 + 1		3		1			
KILBANE Kevin	37 + 1	1	2		3			
MARTYN Nigel	32				1			
McFADDEN James	7 +16	1	3		3	2		
NAYSMITH Gary	5 + 6		1		3			
OSMAN Leon	24 + 5	6	2 + 1		3	1		
PISTONE Sandro	32 + 1		2 + 1		2 + 1			

Luis Boa Morte (Fulham)

	P/FL		FLC		FAC		Others	
	App	Goals	App	Goals	App	Goals	App	Goals
STUBBS Alan	29 + 2	1	2		3			
VAUGHAN James	0 + 2	1						
WATSON Steve	12 +13		3					
WEIR David	34	1	1		0 + 2			
WRIGHT Richard	6 + 1		3		2			
YOBO Joseph	19 + 8		3		3			
FULHAM (PREM: 13th)								
BOA MORTE Luis	29 + 2	8	3		5	1		
BOCANEGRA Carlos	26 + 2	1	3		4			
BUARI Malik			1					
CLARK Lee	15 + 2	1			4 + 1			
COLE Andy	29 + 2	12	3	1	5			
CROSSLEY Mark	5		3					
DIOP Pape	29	6	3		3	1		
FONTAINE Liam	0 + 1				1			
GOMA Alain	15 + 1		1		2 + 1			
GREEN Adam	4		1					
HAMMOND Elvis	0 + 1		0 + 1					
JENSEN Claus	10 + 2		1		0 + 2	1		
JOHN Collins	13 +14	4	0 + 2		1 + 4	2		
KNIGHT Zat	35	1	2		5	1		
LEGWINSKI Sylvain	13 + 2	1	1 + 1		5			
MALBRANQUE Steed	22 + 4	6	4	1	1			
McBRIDE Brian	15 +16	6	2 + 2	3	0 + 2			
McKINLAY Billy	1 + 1		1					
PEARCE Ian	11		1					
PEMBRIDGE Mark	26 + 2		3	1	2 + 1			
RADZINSKI Tomasz	25 +10	6	2	4	4	1		
REHMAN Zesh	15 + 2		4		2			
ROSENIOR Liam	16 + 1		1 + 1		4			
TIMLIN Michael			0 + 1					
VAN DER SAR Edwin	33 + 1		1		5			
VOLZ Moritz	31		3		2	1		
GILLINGHAM (CHAMP: 22nd)								
AGYEMANG Patrick	9 + 4	2	1					
ASHBY Barry	22		1		1			
BANKS Steve	26				1			
BECKWITH Dean	0 + 1				0 + 1			
BODKIN Matt	0 + 2				1			
BOSSU Bert	1 + 1							
BROWN Jason	16		1					
BYFIELD Darren	27 +11	6			1			
COX Ian	29 + 2	2	1		1			
CROFTS Andy	25 + 2	2			1			
DOUGLAS Jonathan	10							
FLYNN Mike	16	3						
GALLACHER Paul	3							
HENDERSON Darius	27 + 5	9			1			
HESSENTHALER Andy	14 + 3				1			
HILLS John	20 + 3							
HOPE Chris	35 + 2	2			0 + 1			
JARVIS Matt	12 +18	3	1					
JOHNSON Leon	6 + 2		1					
JOHNSON Tommy	2 + 6	2						
MARNEY Dean	3							
McEVELEY Jay	10	1						
NOSWORTHY Nyron	36 + 1							
NOWLAND Adam	3	1						
PERPETUINI David	3		1					
POUTON Alan	8 + 4		1					
ROBERTS Iwan	11 + 9	3	0 + 1		0 + 1			
ROBINSON John	2 + 2							
ROSE Richard	16 + 2		1		1			
SAUNDERS Mark	3							
SIDIBE Mamady	22 +13	2	1	1				
SMITH Paul	40 + 1	3	1		1			
SOUTHALL Nicky	30 + 3	1			1			
SPILLER Danny	19 + 3		0 + 1					
GRIMSBY TOWN (DIV 2: 18th)								
BULL Ronnie	22 + 5	2	0 + 1				1	
COLDICOTT Stacy	20 +12	1	0 + 1				1	
CRAMB Colin	7 + 4	2			0 + 1		1	1
CRANE Tony	2 + 1							
CROWE Jason	37	4	2		1			
DALY Jon	3	1						
DOWNEY Glen	0 + 1							
FLEMING Terry	43	2	2		1		0 + 1	
FORBES Terrell	33						1	
GORDON Dean	20	2	2		1			
GRITTON Martin	22 + 1	4						
HARROLD Matt	6	2						

	P/FL		FLC		FAC		Others	
	App	Goals	App	Goals	App	Goals	App	Goals
HEGARTY Nick	0 + 1							
HOCKLESS Graham	3 + 3		0 + 1				1	
JONES Rob	18 + 2	1			1		1	
MANSARAM Darren	3 + 5	1						
MARCELLE Clint	0 + 3		0 + 1				1	
McDERMOTT John	39	2	2		1			
NORTH Danny	0 + 1							
PARKINSON Andy	43 + 2	8	2	1	1			
PINAULT Thomas	32 +11	7	2		1		1	
RAMSDEN Simon	23 + 2		1					
REDDY Michael	24 +16	9	2		1		0 + 1	
ROBINSON Paul	1 + 1						1	
SESTANOVICH Ashley	17 + 5	2	2		1			
SOAMES David	0 + 4							
WHITTLE Justin	39 + 1	1	2		1			
WILLIAMS Anthony	46		2		1		1	
WILLIAMS Chris	1 + 2							
YOUNG Greg	2 + 4		1				1	
HARTLEPOOL UNITED (DIV 1: 6th)								
APPLEBY Andy	0 +15	2			1 + 2		0 + 1	
BARRON Mike	10 + 3				1		5	
BETSY Kevin	3 + 3	1	1					
BOYD Adam	43 + 2	22	2	1	6	3	4 + 1	
BRACKSTONE John	8 + 1				1		2	
BUTLER Thomas	5 + 4	1					1 + 1	
CLARK Ben	21 + 4				5 + 1		1	
CRADDOCK Darren	9 + 1		1				0 + 4	
DALY Jon	4 + 8	1					2 + 1	
FOLEY David	1 + 1				0 + 1		0 + 1	
GOBERN Lewis	1						0 + 1	
HOWEY Steve	0 + 1							
HUMPHREYS Richie	46	3	2		6		5 + 1	
ISTEAD Steven	0 +17		0 + 1		0 + 6		1 + 1	
KONSTANTOPOULOS Dimi	25		1		5		6	
MAIDENS Michael	0 + 1		0 + 1					
NELSON Michael	42 + 1	1	2		5		6	
PORTER Joel	36 + 3	14	1 + 1		5	1	4 + 2	
POUTON Alan	5						1	
PROVETT Jim	21		1		1			
ROBERTSON Hugh	17 + 3	2			4			
ROBSON Matty	22 + 5	2	2		1 + 1	1	5	
ROSS Jack	21 + 3				5 + 1		1	
STRACHAN Gavin	21 + 8	1	2		1 + 1		5	
SWEENEY Antony	44	13	2	1	6		5	
TINKLER Mark	30 + 3	2	2		5	1	2 + 2	
TURNBULL Stephen	0 + 2							
WESTWOOD Chris	36 + 1	4	2		6	2	5	
WILKINSON Jack	1 + 2							
WILLIAMS Eifion	31 + 7	5	0 + 2	1	2 + 1	1	4 + 1	
WOODS Martin	3 + 3		1				1	
HUDDERSFIELD TOWN (DIV 1: 9th)								
ABBOTT Pawel	36 + 8	26	1		1	1	0 + 1	
ADAMS Danny	5							
AHMED Adnan	16 + 2	1					0 + 2	
BECKETT Luke	7	6						
BOOTH Andy	25 + 4	10	1				1	
BRANDON Chris	42 + 2	6	1		1			
BROWN Nat	7 +10						1	
CARSS Tony	23 + 4	1	1				1	
CLARKE Nathan	37		1		1		1	
CLARKE Tom	12							
COLLINS Michael	7 + 1							
EDWARDS Rob	21 + 3	2	1					
FACEY Delroy	4							
FOWLER Lee	8 +12				0 + 1		2	
GRAY Ian	12		1					
HOLDSWORTH Andy	38 + 2		1		1		1	
LLOYD Anthony	10 + 1				1		2	
McALISKEY John	7 +11	2	0 + 1				1 + 1	
McCOMBE John	4 + 1						2	
MENDES Junior	13 +12	5	0 + 1		1		1	
MIRFIN David	38 + 3	4	1		1		1	
RACHUBKA Paul	29				1			
SCHOFIELD Danny	21 +12	5			1		2	
SENIOR Phil	5 + 1						2	
SODJE Akpo	1 + 6						1 + 1	
SODJE Efe	24 + 4	1	1				1	
WORTHINGTON Jon	39	3	1		1		1	
YATES Steve	15 + 2				1		1	
HULL CITY (DIV 1: 2nd)								
ALLSOPP Danny	14 +14	7			1 + 1			

	P/FL		FLC		FAC		Others	
	App	Goals	App	Goals	App	Goals	App	Goals
ANGUS Stev	1 + 1				1			
ASHBEE Ian	40	1	1		2		1	
BARMBY Nick	38 + 1	9			2			
BURGESS Ben	0 + 2							
CORT Leon	43 + 1	6	1		3			
DAWSON Andy	34		0 + 1		3			
DELANEY Damien	43	1	1		3			
DUKE Matt	1 + 1		1				0 + 1	
EDGE Roland	13 + 1		1				1	
ELLIOTT Stuart	35 + 1	27	0 + 1		2	1	0 + 1	1
ELLISON Kevin	11 + 5	1						
FACEY Delroy	12 + 9	4	1		2	2	1	
FAGAN Craig	11 + 1	4						
FRANCE Ryan	22 + 9	2	1	1	1 + 1	1		
FRY Russell	1				0 + 1			
GREEN Stuart	26 + 3	8	0 + 1		2	1	1	1
HESSENTHALER Andy	6 + 4							
HINDS Richard	6						1	
JOSEPH Marc	25 + 4		1		2			
KEANE Michael	12 + 8	3	1	1	3	1	1	
LEWIS Junior	31 + 8	2			1 + 1		1	
MYHILL Boaz	45				3		1	
PRICE Jason	6 +21	2	1		1 + 1		1	1
STOCKDALE Robbie	12 + 2							
THELWELL Alton	2 + 1						1	
WALTERS Jon	4 +17	1	1		0 + 2	1	1	
WILBRAHAM Aaron	10 + 9	2			1			
WISEMAN Scott	2 + 1				0 + 1		0 + 1	

IPSWICH TOWN (CHAMP: 3rd)

	P/FL		FLC		FAC		Others	
	App	Goals	App	Goals	App	Goals	App	Goals
BARRON Scott			1					
BENT Darren	45	20	2		1		2	
BOWDITCH Dean	6 +15	3	2				0 + 1	
COUNAGO Pablo	4 +15	3	2		0 + 1			
CURRIE Darren	19 + 5	3			1		1 + 1	
DAVIS Kelvin	39				1		2	
DE VOS Jason	45	3	1		1		2	
DIALLO Drissa	23 + 3		2				1	
DINNING Tony	3 + 4		2					
HORLOCK Kevin	33 + 8		0 + 1		1		1	
KARBASSIYOON Daniel	3 + 2				1			
KNIGHTS Darryl	0 + 1							
KUQI Shefki	40 + 3	19	0 + 2		1		2	1
MAGILTON Jim	33 + 6	3	2		1		2	
MILLER Tommy	45	13	0 + 2	1	0 + 1	1	2	
MITCHELL Scott			1		1			
NAYLOR Richard	46	6	2				2	
PRICE Lewis	7 + 1		2					
RICHARDS Matt	15 + 9	1	1		0 + 1		1 + 1	
SCOWCROFT Jamie	3 + 6							
UNSWORTH David	16	1						
WESTLAKE Ian	41 + 4	7	2	1	1		2	
WILNIS Fabian	40 + 1				1		2	

KIDDERMINSTER HARRIERS (DIV 2: 23rd)

	P/FL		FLC		FAC		Others	
	App	Goals	App	Goals	App	Goals	App	Goals
ADVICE-DESRUISSEAUX Frederic	9		1					
APPLEBY Richie	6 + 3	1	0 + 1					
BEARDSLEY Chris	15 +10	5						
BENNETT Tom	24				1			
BESWETHERICK Jon	10				1			
BIRCH Gary	11 + 3	4						
BROWN Simon	11 + 2		1	1			1	
BURNS Liam	0 + 1							
BURTON Steve	15 + 1		1		1		1	
CHAMBERS Adam	2							
CHRISTIANSEN Jesper	11 + 6		1		0 + 1		1	
CHRISTIE Iyseden	1 + 7							
CLARKE Ryan	6				1			
COOPER Shaun	10				1		1	
COZIC Bertrand	13 + 2							
DANBY John	37		1				1	
DIOP Youssou	7 + 3						0 + 1	
FOSTER Ben	2							
FOSTER Ian	15 +12	6	0 + 1		0 + 1		1	
GLEESON Jamie	2 + 5		0 + 1					
HATSWELL Wayne	38 + 2	1	1		1	1	1	
HOLLIS Jermain	0 + 1							
JACKSON Mark	13							
JENKINS Lee	31 + 1		1		0 + 1		0 + 1	
JONES Billy	10 + 2							
KEATES Dean	40 + 1	5	1		1		1	
KEENE James	5				1			
LANGMEAD Kelvin	9 + 1	1					1	
LEWIS Daniel	1							

	P/FL		FLC		FAC		Others	
	App	Goals	App	Goals	App	Goals	App	Goals
MATIAS Pedro	4 + 1	1						
McGRATH John	18 + 1							
McHALE Chris	11 + 3		1				1	
McMAHON Stephen	3 + 2						1	
MELLON Mickey	5 + 2		1					
MULLINS Johnny	21	2						
RAWLE Mark	5 + 6	3						
RICKARDS Scott	0 + 4							
ROBERTS Stuart	4 + 1	1	1					
RUSSELL Simon	18 +10	2			1			
SALL Abdou	13 + 1				1			
STAMP Darryn	4	1			1			
STURROCK Blair	17 + 5	5						
VIVEASH Adrian	7							
WEAVER Simon	22 + 1							

LEEDS UNITED (CHAMP: 14th)

	P/FL		FLC		FAC		Others	
	App	Goals	App	Goals	App	Goals	App	Goals
BAKKE Eirik	0 + 1							
BLAKE Nathan	2	1			1			
BUTLER Paul	39		2					
CADAMARTERI Danny			0 + 1					
CARLISLE Clarke	29 + 6	4	3					
CRAINEY Stephen	9		1					
DEANE Brian	23 + 8	6	1 + 1	1				
DERRY Shaun	7	2						
DUBERRY Michael	4				1			
EINARSSON Gylfi	6 + 2	1						
GRAY Michael	10							
GREGAN Sean	34 + 1		2		1			
GRIFFIT Leandre	0 + 1							
GUPPY Steve	1 + 2	1	1					
HEALY David	27 + 1	7			1			
HULSE Rob	13	6						
JOACHIM Julian	10 +17	2	3		0 + 1			
JOHNSON Seth	4 + 2	1						
JOHNSON Simon	1 + 1		1					
KELLY Gary	43		3		1			
KEOGH Andrew			0 + 1					
KILGALLON Matthew	26		1		1			
KING Marlon	4 + 5							
LENNON Aaron	19 + 8	1	0 + 1		1			
McMASTER Jamie	0 + 7		1 + 1					
MOORE Ian	4 + 2							
ORMEROD Brett	6							
OSTER John	8	1						
PUGH Danny	33 + 5	5	3	1	0 + 1			
RADEBE Lucas	1 + 2							
RICHARDSON Frazer	28 +10	1	2		1			
RICKETTS Michael	9 +12		2 + 1	1				
SPRING Matthew	4 + 9	1	2					
SULLIVAN Neil	46		3		1			
WALTON Simon	23 + 7	3	1 + 1		1			
WOODS Martin	0 + 1							
WRIGHT Jermaine	33 + 2	3	1		1			

LEICESTER CITY (CHAMP: 15th)

	P/FL		FLC		FAC		Others	
	App	Goals	App	Goals	App	Goals	App	Goals
BENJAMIN Trevor	2 + 8	2						
BLAKE Nathan	4 +10		1	1				
CANERO Peter	6							
CONNOLLY David	43 + 1	13			3 + 2			
DABIZAS Nicos	33	1	1		5	1		
DE VRIES Mark	9 + 7	1			2 + 2			
DUBLIN Dion	34 + 3	5			4 + 1	1		
ELLIOTT Matt	1 + 1		0 + 1					
GEMMILL Scot	11 + 6				1			
GILLESPIE Keith	19 +11	2	0 + 1		4			
GUDJONSSON Joey	26 + 9	2	1	1	5	1		
HARPER Kevin	2							
HEATH Matt	17 + 5	3	1		2			
HIRSCHFELD Lars	1							
HUGHES Stephen	13 + 3	1			1 + 1			
KENTON Darren	9 + 1				1			
KEOWN Martin	16 + 1				1			
MAKIN Chris	21		1		1			
MAYBURY Alan	17	2			4 + 1			
McCARTHY Paddy	12				0 + 1			
MOORE Stefan	2 + 5							
MORRIS Lee	2 + 8							
NALIS Lilian	32 + 7	5			1 + 4			
PRESSMAN Kevin	13		1		1			
SCOWCROFT Jamie	30 + 1	4	1		3	1		
SHEEHAN Alan	1							
STEARMAN Richard	3 + 5	1						
STEWART Jordan	33 + 2	1	1		4			

	P/FL		FLC		FAC		Others	
	App	Goals	App	Goals	App	Goals	App	Goals
TAYLOR Stuart	10							
TIATTO Danny	25 + 5	1	1		3			
WALKER Ian	22				4			
WILCOX Jason	11 + 3	1	0 + 1					
WILLIAMS Gareth	25 + 8	1	1		5	2		
WRIGHT Tommy	1 + 6		1		0 + 1			
LEYTON ORIENT (DIV 2: 11th)								
ALEXANDER Gary	25 + 3	9	0 + 1				1 + 1	1
BARNARD Donny	22 +11	1			1 + 1		4	
BARNARD Lee	3 + 5				1		1	
CARLISLE Wayne	24 + 4	3	1		2	1	3	1
CHILLINGWORTH Dan	8	2						
DUNCAN Derek	6 + 9				0 + 1		0 + 3	
ECHANOMI Efe	4 +14	5						
FITZGERALD Scott	1							
HARRISON Lee	34				2			
HUNT David	22 + 5		1		1	1	2 + 1	
IBEHRE Jabo	10 + 9	2	1		2		3	2
LOCKWOOD Matt	42 + 1	6	1		2	1	4	
MACKIE John	26 + 1	4			1		3	
McMAHON Daryl	22 + 2	3			0 + 1			
MILLER Justin	43		1		1		2	1
MORRIS Glenn	12		1				4	
NEWEY Tom	3 +17	1	0 + 1		0 + 2		3	
PALMER Aiden	3 + 2							
PETERS Mark	0 + 2						1	
PURSER Wayne	0 + 2	1						
SAAH Brian	9 + 3		0 + 1		1		3	1
SCOTT Andy	37 + 2	9	1		2		2 + 1	
SIMPSON Michael	45	2	1		2		3	
STEELE Lee	37 + 2	16	1	1	1		2	
WALLIS Scott	0 + 3							
WARDLEY Stuart	4 + 2				0 + 1		0 + 2	
WHITE Alan	26		1		2		2	
YOUNGS Tom	6 + 4	1						
ZAKUANI Gaby	32 + 1		1		1		1	
LINCOLN CITY (DIV 2: 6th)								
ASAMOAH Derek	8 + 2						1 + 2	
BEEVERS Lee	4 + 4						0 + 2	
BERMINGHAM Karl	0 + 2							
BLACKWOOD Michael	5 + 4		1					
BLOOMER Matt	31 + 6	2	2		1		0 + 2	
BUTCHER Richard	46	2	2		1		4	
CARRUTHERS Martin	7 + 4						1	
FOLKES Peter					0 + 1		1	
FRECKLINGTON Lee	0 + 3							
FUTCHER Ben	35	3	2		1		4	
GAIN Peter	36 + 4		2				4	
GREEN Francis	28 + 9	8	1 + 1				2 + 1	
HANLON Richie	6 + 6	1						
HOBBS Jack	0 + 1							
IPOUA Guy	0 + 6							
KERLEY Adam	0 + 1						0 + 1	
LITTLEJOHN Adrian	1 + 7				0 + 1			
MARRIOTT Alan	45		2		1		3	
McAULEY Gareth	32 + 5	3	2		1		4	2
McCOMBE Jamie	37 + 4	3	2	1	1		4	
McNAMARA Niall	0 + 1							
MORGAN Paul	39		1				3	
PEARSON Greg	1 + 2							
PEAT Nathan	6 + 4		1 + 1		1			
RAYNER Simon	1						1	
RICHARDSON Marcus	7 + 7	4	0 + 1		1			
RYAN Oliver	0 + 6				0 + 1			
SANDWITH Kevin	34 + 3	2			1		4	
TAYLOR-FLETCHER Gary	35 + 3	11	1 + 1	1	1		4	
TONER Ciaran	10 + 5	2	0 + 1				1	
WEAVER Simon	5		1					
WEST Dean	4							
WESTCARR Craig	5 + 1	1						
YEO Simon	38 + 6	21	2	2	1		3 + 1	
LIVERPOOL (PREM: 5th)								
ALONSO Xabi	20 + 4	2					7 + 1	1
BAROS Milan	22 + 4	9	1 + 3	2	0 + 1		13 + 1	2
BISCAN Igor	8 +11	2	4 + 2		1		8 + 1	
CARRAGHER Jamie	38		3				15	
CARSON Scott	4						1	
CISSE Djibril	10 + 6	4					4 + 5	1
DIAO Salif	4 + 4		3	1			1 + 2	
DUDEK Jerzy	24		6		1		10	
FINNAN Steve	29 + 4	1	4 + 1				12 + 2	
GARCIA Luis	26 + 3	8	2 + 1				12	5
GERRARD Steven	28 + 2	7	3	2			10	4
HAMANN Didi	23 + 7		3				8 + 2	1
HENCHOZ Stephane			3				1	
HYYPIA Sami	32	2	1		1		15	1
JOSEMI	13 + 2		1				5 + 2	
KEWELL Harry	15 + 3	1	1				7 + 5	
KIRKLAND Chris	10						4	
LE TALLEC Anthony	2 + 2						1 + 2	
MELLOR Neil	6 + 3	2	4	2	0 + 1		1 + 1	1
MORIENTES Fernando	12 + 1	3	2					
NUNEZ Antonio	8 +10		2 + 1	1	1		2 + 3	
PARTRIDGE Richie			0 + 2					
PELLEGRINO Mauricio	11 + 1		1					
POTTER Darren	0 + 2		3 + 1		1		1 + 2	
RAVEN David	0 + 1		1		1			
RIISE John Arne	34 + 3	6	3 + 2	1			15	1
SINAMA-PONGOLLE Florent	6 +10	2	4 + 1	1	1		0 + 4	1
SMICER Vlad	2 + 8						0 + 6	1
SMYTH Mark			0 + 1					
TRAORE Djimi	18 + 8		5		1		10	
WARNOCK Stephen	11 + 8		3 + 1		1		2 + 4	
WELSH John	2 + 1		0 + 2		1		0 + 1	
WHITBREAD Zak			3		1			
LUTON TOWN (DIV 1: 1st)								
ANDREW Calvin	2 + 6				0 + 2		1	
BARNETT Leon							1	
BAYLISS Dave					0 + 1		1	
BERESFORD Marlon	38		1		2			
BLINKHORN Matthew	0 + 2		0 + 1					
BRKOVIC Ahmet	39 + 3	15	1		3	1		
COYNE Chris	39 + 1	5	1		3			
DAVIES Curtis	44	1	1		3			
DAVIS Sol	45	2	1		3			
FEENEY Warren	1 + 5							
FOLEY Kevin	38 + 1	2			2			
HOLMES Peter	13 + 6	3					1	
HOWARD Steve	40	18	1		3	4		
HUGHES Paul							1	
KEANE Keith	11 + 6				1		1	
LEARY Michael	1 + 7							
MANSELL Lee	0 + 1		1				1	
McSHEFFREY Gary	1 + 4	1						
NEILSON Alan	6 + 3						1	
NICHOLLS Kevin	44	12	1	1	2	1		
O'LEARY Stephen	12 + 5	1			2		1	
PERRETT Russ	9 + 3	1					0 + 1	
ROBINSON Steve	28 + 3	4	1		2			
ROYCE Simon	2							
SEREMET Dino	6 + 1				1		1	
SHOWUNMI Enoch	7 +28	6	0 + 1	1	0 + 3		1	
UNDERWOOD Paul	37	5	1		3			
VINE Rowan	43 + 2	9	1		3			
MACCLESFIELD TOWN (DIV 2: 5th)								
BAILEY Mark	20 + 1	2	1				3	
BARRAS Tony	22 + 2	1	1		2		4	1
BOYD Marc	4 + 1							
BRIGHTWELL Ian	3 + 3				1 + 1			
BRISCOE Michael	12 + 2		1		0 + 1		1 + 2	
CARRAGHER Matthew	26 + 5				3		4 + 1	
FAYADH Jassim	0 + 1						0 + 1	
FETTIS Alan	28				1		4	
HARSLEY Paul	44 + 2	3	1		3		5	1
MacKENZIE Neil	16 + 2							
McINTYRE Kevin	21 + 2						2	
MILES John	14 +16	3			2 + 1		2 + 2	
MORLEY Dave	19	2					2	
NAVARRO Alan	11	1						
PARKIN Jon	42	22	1	1	3	1	5	2
POTTER Graham	39 + 2	6	1		3		2 + 1	
ROONEY Tommy	0 + 1				0 + 1			
SHERON Mike	14 +12	3	0 + 1		3	1	2 + 1	
STRONG Greg	4							
SWAILES Danny	17						2	
TEAGUE Andrew	5							
TIPTON Matthew	40 + 4	12	1		1 + 1		4 + 1	2
TOWNSON Kevin	2 + 4						1 + 1	
WEAVER Simon	7				2		2	
WELCH Michael	31	2	1		2		2	
WHITAKER Danny	26 +10	2	1		3	1	4 + 1	1
WIDDRINGTON Tommy	21 + 2		1		2		3	
WILSON Steve	18 + 1		1		2		1	

	P/FL App	P/FL Goals	FLC App	FLC Goals	FAC App	FAC Goals	Others App	Others Goals
MANCHESTER CITY (PREM: 8th)								
ANELKA Nicolas	18 + 1	7						
BARTON Joey	28 + 3	1	1	1	1			
BOSVELT Paul	28	2	1		1			
CROFT Lee	0 + 7							
DISTIN Sylvain	38	1	2		1			
D'LARYEA Jonathan			1					
DUNNE Richard	35	2			1			
FLOOD Willo	4 + 5	1	2	1	0 + 1			
FOWLER Robbie	28 + 4	11	1	1				
JAMES David	38				1			
JIHAI Sun	4 + 2		1					
JORDAN Steve	19		0 + 2					
MACKEN Jon	16 + 7	1	1	2	1			
McMANAMAN Steve	5 + 8				0 + 1			
MILLS Danny	29 + 3		2		1			
MUSAMPA Kiki	14	3						
NEGOUAI Christian	0 + 1		0 + 1					
ONUOHA Nedum	11 + 6		1					
REYNA Claudio	16 + 1	2						
SIBIERSKI Antoine	34 + 1	4	2	2	1			
SINCLAIR Trevor	2 + 2	1	1					
SOMMEIL David	1		0 + 1					
THATCHER Ben	17 + 1		2		1			
WATERREUS Ronald			2					
WEAVER Nicky	0 + 1							
WRIGHT-PHILLIPS Bradley	0 +14	1	0 + 2		1			
WRIGHT-PHILLIPS Shaun	33 + 1	10	2	1	1			
MANCHESTER UNITED (PREM: 3rd)								
BELLION David	1 + 9	1	3	1	1		3 + 1	2
BROWN Wes	18 + 3	1	3		6		6 + 1	
CARROLL Roy	26				3		5	
DJEMBA-DJEMBA Eric	3 + 2		4		2		6	
EAGLES Chris			1 + 2		1		1 + 2	
EBANKS-BLAKE Sylvan			0 + 1					
FERDINAND Rio	31		1		5		5	
FLETCHER Darren	18	3	3		1 + 2		3 + 3	
FORLAN Diego	0 + 1						0 + 2	
FORTUNE Quinton	12 + 5		4		5 + 1	1	4 + 2	
GIGGS Ryan	26 + 6	5	1	1	2 + 2		7	2
HEINZE Gabriel	26	1	2		4		7	
HOWARD Tim	12		5		4		6	
JONES David			0 + 1		1			
KEANE Roy	28 + 3	1	1		4	1	7	
KLEBERSON	6 + 2		3				2 + 1	
MILLER Liam	3 + 5		2	1	2 + 2		3 + 2	
NEVILLE Gary	22		1		4		8	1
NEVILLE Phil	12 + 7		3		4 + 1		1 + 6	
O'SHEA John	16 + 7	2	4		3 + 1	1	6	
PIQUE Gerard			0 + 1		1		0 + 1	
RICHARDSON Kieran	0 + 2		3	1	1		1 + 2	
RONALDO Cristiano	25 + 8	5	2		6 + 1	4	7 + 1	
ROONEY Wayne	24 + 5	11	1 + 1		6	3	6	3
ROSSI Giuseppe			0 + 2					
SAHA Louis	7 + 7	1	4	1	0 + 2		0 + 2	
SCHOLES Paul	29 + 4	9	1 + 1		5 + 1	3	8	
SILVESTRE Mikael	33 + 2	2	2		2 + 2		8 + 1	
SMITH Alan	22 + 9	6	1 + 1	1	0 + 3		4 + 2	3
SPECTOR Jonathan	2 + 1		0 + 1		1		1 + 2	
VAN NISTELROOY Ruud	16 + 1	6			3	2	6 + 1	8
MANSFIELD TOWN (DIV 2: 13th)								
ARTELL Dave	19	2	1		2		1	
ASAMOAH Derek	24 + 6	5			1		0 + 1	
BARKER Richard	28	10						
BARROWMAN Andrew	1 + 2							
BROWN Simon	16 + 5	2						
BUXTON Jake	29 + 1	1			2		1	
COKE Giles	7 + 2							
CORDEN Wayne	19 + 5	3	1		1		1	
CURLE Tom							2	
CURTIS Tommy	26 + 6		1		2			
DAY Rhys	11 + 7	3	1		0 + 1		1	
DIMECH Luke	19 + 6		1		2		2	
EATON Adam	2							
HERON Danny	1 + 2		0 + 1		0 + 1			
IPOUA Guy	4 + 1							
JELLEYMAN Gareth	14							
JOHN-BAPTISTE Alex	41	1	1		2	1	1 + 1	
KITAMIRIKE Joel	2							
LAMBU Goma	1							
LARKIN Colin	29 + 4	11	1		2		1 + 1	
LLOYD Callum	7 + 3	4			1		2	
LONSDALE Richard							0 + 1	
MacKENZIE Neil	9 + 6	1	1		2		2	
MAXWELL Leyton	1							
McINTOSH Austin	1				0 + 1			
McLACHLAN Fraser	16 + 5				1			
McNIVEN Scott	24 + 1						1	
MURRAY Adam	27 + 5	5	1		1 + 1		2	
NEIL Alex	40 + 1	1	1		1	1		
O'NEILL Joe	3 +12						2	
PILKINGTON Kevin	42		1		2		1	
RUNDLE Adam	18	4						
SMELTZ Shane	1 + 4							
TALBOT Jason	2							
TATE Chris	0 + 4		0 + 1					
WARNE Paul	7	1						
WHITE Jason	4						1	
WILLIAMSON Lee	3 + 1							
WOOD Chris	0 + 1				0 + 1			
WOODMAN Craig	8	1					1	
MIDDLESBROUGH (PREM: 7th)								
BATES Matthew	0 + 2							
BOATENG George	25	3					4	
CHRISTIE Malcolm	2	1					0 + 1	
COOPER Colin	11 + 4		2		1		3	
DAVIES Andrew	2 + 1		2					
DORIVA	15 +11		2		2	1	7 + 1	
DOWNING Stewart	28 + 7	5	2		2		8 + 1	1
EHIOGU Ugo	9 + 1		1		1			
GRAHAM Danny	0 +11	1	0 + 2	1	0 + 2		1 + 1	
HASSELBAINK Jimmy Floyd	36	13			2		5 + 2	3
JOB Joseph-Desire	10 +13	4	2		1 + 1	1	4 + 2	2
JOHNSON Adam							0 + 1	
JONES Brad	5							
KENNEDY Jason	0 + 1							
McMAHON Anthony	12 + 1		0 + 1		0 + 1		4	
MENDIETA-ZABALA Gaizka	7						0 + 1	
MORRISON James	4 +10		2	1	2		4 + 1	3
NASH Carlo	2		2					
NEMETH Szilard	18 +13	4	1	1			6 + 2	1
PARLOUR Ray	32 + 1				2		6	
PARNABY Stuart	16 + 3						4 + 1	
QUEUDRUE Franck	31	5	1		2		9	
REIZIGER Michael	15 + 3	1			2		4 + 1	
RIGGOTT Chris	20 + 1	2	2		1		8	1
SCHWARZER Mark	31				2		10	
SOUTHGATE Gareth	36				1		10	
VIDUKA Mark	15 + 1	5	1				3 + 1	2
WHEATER David							0 + 1	
WILSON Mark			1					
ZENDEN Bolo	36	5	1		1 + 1		10	3
MILLWALL (CHAMP: 10th)								
BRANIFF Kevin	1				1			
COGAN Barry	2 + 5						0 + 2	
CRAIG Tony	9 + 1							
DICHIO Danny	27 + 4	10					0 + 1	
DOBIE Scott	15 + 1	3						
DUNNE Alan	15 + 4	3	1		1			
ELLIOTT Marvin	32 + 9	1	1		1		2	
HARRIS Neil	5 + 7	1	1				2	
HAYLES Barry	28 + 4	12			1			
HEALY Joe	0 + 2		0 + 1		0 + 1			
IFILL Paul	9 + 9	4					1 + 1	
IMPEY Andy	0 + 5							
LAWRENCE Matt	40 + 4		1		1		2	
LIVERMORE David	41	2	1				2	
MARSHALL Andy	21 + 1							
MAY Ben	4 + 4	1						
McCAMMON Mark	5 + 3		0 + 1				0 + 1	
MOORE Stefan	3 + 3						1	
MORRIS Jody	35 + 2	5	1		1		2	
MUSCAT Kevin	25 + 1		1				2	
PEETERS Bob	0 + 3							
PHILLIPS Mark	25	1			1			
QUIGLEY Mark	4 + 4							
ROBINSON Anton					1			
ROBINSON Paul	7	1						
ROBINSON Trevor	1 + 1							
SERIOUX Adrian	10 + 9		1					
SIMPSON Josh	22 + 8	1			1		2	
STACK Graham	25 + 1		1		1		2	
SWEENEY Peter	23 + 1	2			1		0 + 1	

	P/FL		FLC		FAC		Others	
	App	Goals	App	Goals	App	Goals	App	Goals
TESSEM Jo	11 + 1	1	1					
WARD Darren	43		1				2	
WESTON Curtis	2 + 1				0 + 1			
WISE Dennis	16 + 9	3					2	2
MILTON KEYNES DONS (DIV 1: 20th)								
BAKER Matt	20							
BEVAN Scott	7		1				1	
CHORLEY Ben	41	2	2		2		2	
CROOKS Leon	15 + 2		1				1	
DANZE Anthony	2							
EDDS Gareth	37 + 2	5	2		2		1	
HARDING Ben	21 + 5	4						
HERVE Laurent	15 + 5		2		2		1 + 1	
HORNUSS Julien	0 + 3		0 + 1				0 + 1	
JOHNSON Richard	2						0 + 1	
KAMARA Malvin	16 + 9	1	0 + 1	1	2		1	
KOO-BOOTHE Nathan	1		1					
LEWINGTON Dean	43	2	1		3		1	1
MACKIE Jamie	0 + 3						1	
MAKOFO Serge	0 + 1						0 + 1	1
MARTIN David	15		1		3		1	
McCLENAHAN Trent	7 + 1							
McKOY Nick							0 + 1	
McLEOD Izale	39 + 4	16	2	2	2 + 1			
MITCHELL Paul	13				1			
NTIMBAN-ZEH Harry	11		2		1		1 + 1	
OYEDELE Shola	18 + 7		0 + 1		2		2	
PACQUETTE Richard	1 + 4						2	1
PALMER Steve	27 + 5	1	1		2 + 1		1	
PENSEE-BILONG Michel	18	1						
PLATT Clive	20	3						
PUNCHEON Jason	8 +17	1	1 + 1		1 + 1		2	
RACHUBKA Paul	4							
RIZZO Nicky	13 + 5	2			2			
SMALL Wade	41 + 3	10	2		3	1	1	1
SMART Allan	15 + 3	4	2	1	2	1		
SMITH Gary	20 + 3	1	0 + 1		3		1	
TAPP Alex	5 + 7	1			0 + 2		1	
WESTCARR Craig	0 + 4							
WILLIAMS Mark	11 + 2		1				1	
NEWCASTLE UNITED (PREM: 14th)								
AMBROSE Darren	8 + 4	3	1		0 + 1		2 + 2	
AMEOBI Shola	17 +14	2	1 + 1	1	3 + 2	3	6 + 1	1
BABAYARO Celestine	7				4	1	2	
BELLAMY Craig	21	7	1 + 1		1		5	3
BERNARD Olivier	19 + 2		2				5 + 1	
BOUMSONG Jean-Alain	14				4			
BOWYER Lee	26 + 1	3	0 + 1		2	1	8 + 1	3
BRAMBLE Titus	18 + 1	1	2		4		6 + 1	
BUTT Nicky	16 + 2	1	1		2		4 + 1	
CARR Steve	26	1			4		9	
CHOPRA Michael	0 + 1							
DYER Kieron	20 + 3	4	0 + 1		3		6 + 1	2
ELLIOTT Robbie	15 + 2	1					5	
FAYE Amdy	8 + 1				3		5	
GIVEN Shay	36		1		3		12	
GUY Lewis							0 + 1	
HARPER Steve	2		1		2		0 + 2	
HUGHES Aaron	18 + 4	1	1 + 1		1 + 1		9 + 1	
JENAS Jermaine	28 + 3	1	2	1	3 + 1		9 + 2	
JOHNSEN Ronny	3		2					
KLUIVERT Patrick	15 +10	6	2		3 + 1	2	5 + 1	5
MILNER James	13 +12	1	1		1 + 3		3 + 8	
N'ZOGBIA Charles	8 + 6				1 + 1		1 + 2	
O'BRIEN Andy	21 + 2	2	1		1 + 2		9 + 2	
RAMAGE Peter	2 + 2						0 + 1	
ROBERT Laurent	20 +11	3	2		4		8 + 2	2
SHEARER Alan	26 + 2	7	1		4	1	9	11
TAYLOR Steven	11 + 2				2		4 + 3	
NORTHAMPTON TOWN (DIV 2: 7th)								
ALSOP Julian	1 + 6	1			0 + 1		2	1
AMOO Ryan	2 + 3							
BARNARD Lee	3 + 2							
BENJAMIN Trevor	5	2			1			
BOJIC Pedj	25 +11		2		2 + 1		2	
CARRUTHERS Chris	0 + 1		0 + 1				0 + 1	
CHAMBERS Luke	19 + 8		1 + 1		1 + 1		3 + 1	
COZIC Bertrand	8 + 6		1		1 + 1		1 + 1	
CROSS Scott	0 + 1							
CROW Danny	4 + 6	2						
GALBRAITH David	9 +16	1	2		0 + 1		2	

	P/FL		FLC		FAC		Others	
	App	Goals	App	Goals	App	Goals	App	Goals
HARPER Lee	36		1		3		4	
HASLAM Steve	2 + 1							
HEARN Charley	21 + 3	1			1 + 1		2	
HICKS David	1 + 2		1				0 + 1	
HUGHES Mark	3							
HUNT David	2 + 2						0 + 1	
JASZCZUN Tommy	24 + 8		2		3		1	
KIRK Andy	8	7					2	
LOW Josh	33 + 1	7	2		2 + 1		2	
McGLEISH Scott	43 + 1	13	2	1	3	2	4	
MORISON Steve	1 + 3	1	0 + 2					
MURRAY Fred	38				2		4	
NOBLE Stuart	0 + 4							
RACHUBKA Paul	10		1					
REEVES Martin	0 + 1		0 + 1					
RICHARDS Marc	8 + 4	2	1				0 + 1	
ROWSON David	35 + 2	2			3		3	
SABIN Eric	28 +12	8	2	1	2 + 1		0 + 4	
SMITH Martin	31 + 3	10			3		2 + 1	
TOGWELL Sam	7 + 1						2	
WESTWOOD Ashley	19	2			1 + 1			
WILLIAMSON Lee	31 + 6		1		2	1	3	
WILLMOTT Chris	45		2		3		4	
YOUNGS Tom	4 + 5		1 + 1				1	
NORWICH CITY (PREM: 19th)								
ASHTON Dean	16	7						
BENTLEY David	22 + 4	2	0 + 1		1			
BRENNAN Jim	6 + 4				1			
CHARLTON Simon	22 + 2	1	1		1			
CROW Danny	0 + 3				0 + 1			
DOHERTY Gary	17 + 3	2	2		1			
DRURY Adam	31 + 2	1	2					
EDWORTHY Marc	27 + 1		1 + 1		1			
FLEMING Craig	38	1	2		1			
FRANCIS Damien	32	7	2		1			
GREEN Robert	38		2		1			
HELVEG Thomas	16 + 4		1 + 1		1			
HENDERSON Ian	0 + 3		0 + 1					
HOLT Gary	21 + 6		2					
HUCKERBY Darren	36 + 1	6	2	1	1			
JARVIS Ryan	1 + 3	1			0 + 1			
JONSON Mattias	19 + 9		1		1			
McKENZIE Leon	24 +13	7						
McVEIGH Paul	3 +14	1	1					
MULRYNE Phil	8 + 2				0 + 1			
SAFRI Youssef	13 + 5	1	1 + 1	1				
SHACKELL Jason	11		1					
STUART Graham	7 + 1							
SVENSSON Mathias	10 +12	4	1 + 1					
WARD Darren	0 + 1							
NOTTINGHAM FOREST (CHAMP: 23rd)								
BOPP Eugene	6 +12	3	0 + 1		1			
COMMONS Kris	19 +11	6	2 + 1		3	1		
CURTIS John	11				2			
DAWSON Michael	13 + 1	1	2		1			
DERRY Shaun	7				1			
DOBIE Scott	11 + 1	1						
DOIG Chris	20 + 1		1		4			
DOYLE Colin	2 + 1				1			
EVANS Paul	34 + 5	4	3		3			
FOLLY Yoann	0 + 1				1	1		
FRIIO David	5							
GARDNER Ross	9 + 5							
GERRARD Paul	42		4		3			
HARRIS Neil	5 + 8				0 + 2			
HJELDE Jon Olav	13 + 1		1					
IMPEY Andy	18 + 2		3					
JAMES Kevin	2 + 5							
JESS Eoin	16 + 4	2	3 + 1					
JOHNSON David	24 + 7	6	4		1 + 1			
KING Marlon	17 + 9	5	3	3	1 + 1	1		
LESTER Jack	3	1						
LOUIS-JEAN Mathieu	22 + 3		3		1			
MELVILLE Andy	13				2			
MORGAN Wes	42 + 1	1	4		4			
NOWLAND Adam	5				0 + 1			
PERCH James	17 + 5		2 + 1	1	2 + 1			
POWELL Darryl	11				2			
REID Andy	25	5	1	1	2	1		
ROBERTSON Gregor	13 + 7		1 + 1		2			
ROCHE Barry	2							
ROGERS Alan	32 + 1		4		2			

	P/FL App	P/FL Goals	FLC App	FLC Goals	FAC App	FAC Goals	Others App	Others Goals
TAYLOR Gareth	33 + 3	7	2 + 1	3	4	1		
THOMPSON John	14 + 6		1		1 + 2			
WALKER Des	0 + 1							
WESTCARR Craig	0 + 1							
NOTTS COUNTY (DIV 2: 19th)								
BAUDET Julien	38 + 1	5	1		2	1	1	
BOLLAND Paul	38 + 2	1	2		3			
DEENEY Saul	31 + 1		2		4			
EDWARDS Mike	8 + 1		2					
ELLIOT Rob	3 + 1							
FRIARS Emmet	4 + 5						1	
GILL Matthew	38 + 5		2		3 + 1		1	
GORDON Gavin	23 + 4	5			4	3	0 + 1	
HARRAD Shaun	4 +12	1			1 + 1			
HENDERSON Wayne	11						1	
HURST Glynn	36 + 5	14	2		2 + 1		1	1
KUDUZOVIC Fahrudin	0 + 3							
McFAUL Shane	17 + 7				2 + 1			
MILDENHALL Steve	1							
OAKES Stefan	28 + 3	5	0 + 1		2 + 1	1		
O'GRADY Chris	3 + 6				0 + 1		1	
PALMER Chris	23 + 2	4			4			
PEAD Craig	4 + 1						1	
PIPE David	38 + 3	2	2		4		1	
RICHARDSON Ian	10		2	2				
ROBINSON Marvin	1 + 1							
SCOFFHAM Steve	3 + 4							
SCULLY Tony	20 +11	2	2		2 + 2	1	0 + 1	
SOFIANE Youssef	2 + 2						1	1
STALLARD Mark	16	3						
ULLATHORNE Rob	34 + 2		2	1	1			
WHITLOW Mike	22 + 2		1		4		1	
WILLIAMS Matt	8 +10	1	1 + 1		2 + 1			
WILSON Kelvin	36 + 5	2	1 + 1	1	4		1	
ZADKOVICH Ruben	6 + 2	1						
OLDHAM ATHLETIC (DIV 1: 19th)								
APPLEBY Matty	9 + 8		1		1		2	1
ARBER Mark	13 + 1	1	2				1	
BARLOW Matty	1 + 8		0 + 2					
BECKETT Luke	9	6						
BEHARALL Dave	3		0 + 1		1		0 + 1	
BETSY Kevin	34 + 2	5			3		5	
BONNER Mark	15 + 4		1				2	
BOSHELL Danny	10 + 6	1	2		0 + 2			
BRANSTON Guy	6 + 1	1					1	
BRUCE Alex	8 + 4				2		2	
COOKSEY Ernie	1							
COOPER Kenny	5 + 2	3			0 + 1		1	
CROFT Lee	11 + 1				3	1	2	1
EYRE John	18 + 6	1	2	1	2		1 + 1	
EYRES David	40 + 2	4	2	1	4		4 + 1	2
FACEY Delroy	1 + 5							
GRIFFIN Adam	33 + 2	2	2		4		4 + 1	1
HAINING Will	34 + 1	5	2		3		4	
HALL Chris	2 + 4						0 + 2	
HALL Danny	20 + 1				4		4	
HOLDEN Dean	39 + 1	2	2		2		4	1
HUGHES Mark	25 + 2				3		1 + 3	
JACK Rodney	5 + 5	2	0 + 1					
JOHNSON Jermaine	13 + 6	4	2				1	
KILKENNY Neil	24 + 3	4			3		4	1
KILLEN Chris	25 + 1	10	2		2	4	1	1
LEE David	5 + 2				1		1	
LEE Rob							1	
LOMAX Kelvin	7 + 2				0 + 1		1 + 1	
MAWSON Craig	3 + 1		1					
MILDENHALL Steve	6							
OWEN Gareth	9							
POGLIACOMI Les	37		1		4		5	
SANOKHO Amadou	0 + 1							
STAM Stefan	11 + 2						0 + 1	
TIERNEY Marc	7 + 4							
VERNON Scott	13 + 9	7			2 + 1	1	2 + 2	2
WILBRAHAM Aaron	4	2					1	
WILKINSON Wes	0 + 1						0 + 1	
WINN Ashley	0 + 2							
WOLFENDEN Matty	0 + 1				0 + 1			
OXFORD UNITED (DIV 2: 15th)								
ALSOP Julian	3 + 2							
ASHTON Jon	30		1					
BASHAM Steve	29 +10	9	1		1		1	

	P/FL App	P/FL Goals	FLC App	FLC Goals	FAC App	FAC Goals	Others App	Others Goals
BEECHERS Billy	0 + 3							
BRADBURY Lee	39 + 2	4	1		1	1	1	
BROOKS Jamie	6 + 6	2			0 + 1			
BROWN Danny	3 + 1		1					
BURTON Paul	0 + 1		0 + 1					
CLARKE Bradie	3 + 1							
COMINELLI Lucas	11 + 5	1						
CORBO Mateo	13							
COX Simon	2 + 1							
DAVIES Craig	13 +15	6					0 + 1	
DIAZ Emiliano	2 + 5							
DOUDOU	0 + 1							
E'BEYER Mark	6 + 4	2			1			
HACKETT Chris	31 + 6	4			0 + 1		0 + 1	
HAND Jamie	11						1	1
JUDGE Alan	1							
KARAM Amine	0 + 2							
LOUIS Jefferson	0 + 1							
MACKAY David	44		1		1		1	
MOLYNEAUX Lee	6 +10						1	
MOONEY Tommy	42	15	1		1		1	
MORGAN Danny	0 + 3		0 + 1					
PARKER Terry	6 + 2		0 + 1					
QUINN Barry	34 + 2				1			
RAPONI Juan Pablo	5 + 5							
RAWLE Mark	0 + 6							
ROBINSON Matt	45	2	1		1		1	
ROGET Leo	35	2	1					
TARDIF Chris	40		1		1		1	
TOGWELL Sam	3 + 1				1			
WANLESS Paul	18 + 9	1	1		1		0 + 1	
WINTERS Tom	0 + 4						1	1
WOLLEASTON Robert	14 + 6		1				1	
WOOZLEY David	11 + 2	1			1		1	
PETERBOROUGH UNITED (DIV 1: 23rd)								
ARBER Mark	21				2	1		
BOUCAUD Andre	13 + 9	1			1		1	
BRANSTON Guy	4	1						
BURTON-GODWIN Sagi	16	1			3			
CASKEY Darren	2 + 2							
CLARKE Andy	13 +20	3	1		2 + 1		1	
CONSTANTINE Leon	5 + 6	1					1	
COULSON Mark	2 + 5							
DAY Jamie	0 + 1							
DEEN Ahmed	4 + 1							
FARRELL Dave	22 + 9	2	1		4			
FRY Adam	3						0 + 1	
HUKE Shane	6 + 2							
IRELAND Craig	22 + 1		1		1		1	
JELLEYMAN Gareth	11 + 3				2		1	
JENKINS Steve	5 + 1	1					1	
KANU Chris	9 + 4		1		0 + 1		0 + 1	
KENNEDY Peter	15 + 2	2	1		1 + 1	1		
LEGG Andy	38 + 1	5	1		3		1	
LOGAN Richard	15 +11	4			2 + 1	1		
McMASTER Jamie	3				1			
McSHANE Luke					1			
NEWTON Adam	27 + 3				3			
NOLAN Matt			0 + 1					
ONIBUJE Fola	0 + 2							
PLATT Clive	18 + 1	4	1		1			
PLUMMER Chris	21				1 + 2			
PURSER Wayne	15 +11	6						
REA Simon	13 + 1		1					
SEMPLE Ryan	2 + 6		0 + 1		1 + 2		0 + 1	
SONNER Danny	11 + 4		0 + 1				1	
ST LEDGER-HALL Sean	33				4		1	
THOMSON Steve	30 + 1	2	1		2			
TYLER Mark	46		1		3		1	
WILLOCK Calum	29 + 6	12			3	2		
WOODHOUSE Curtis	32 + 2	4	1		3	1	1	
PLYMOUTH ARGYLE (CHAMP: 17th)								
ADAMS Steve	17 + 3	1	1					
ALJOFREE Hasney	12	1						
BLACKSTOCK Dexter	10 + 4	4						
BUZSAKY Akos	14 + 1	1						
CAPALDI Tony	24 +11	2	1		1			
CHADWICK Nick	11 + 4	1						
CONNOLLY Paul	19				1			
COUGHLAN Graham	43	2	1		1			
CRAWFORD Stevie	19 + 7	6	1	1				
DICKSON Ryan	2 + 1							

	P/FL		FLC		FAC		Others	
	App	Goals	App	Goals	App	Goals	App	Goals
DODD Jason	4							
DOUMBE Mathias	24 + 2	2	0 + 1		1			
EVANS Mickey	33 + 9	4			1			
FRIIO David	23 + 5	6	0 + 1		1			
GILBERT Peter	38		1		1			
GUDJONSSON Bjarni	12 + 3				1	1		
HODGES Lee	11 + 8		1		1			
KEITH Marino	6 + 11	1	1		0 + 1			
LARRIEU Romain	23				1			
LASLEY Keith	14 + 10		1					
LOWNDES Nathan	1 + 3							
MAKEL Lee	13 + 6							
McCORMICK Luke	23		1					
MILNE Steven	0 + 12		0 + 1					
NORRIS David	33 + 2	3						
SUMMERFIELD Luke	0 + 1							
TAYLOR Scott	9 + 7	3						
WORRELL David	30		1					
WOTTON Paul	38 + 2	12	1	1	1			
YETTON Stewart	0 + 1							
PORT VALE (DIV 1: 18th)								
ABBEY George	16 + 2							
ARMSTRONG Ian	6 + 3	3	1		0 + 1		0 + 1	
BIRCHALL Chris	29 + 5	6	0 + 1		1 + 1		1 + 1	1
BRAIN Jonny	26 + 1		1		2		2	
BROOKER Steve	9	5	1				1	
BROWN Ryan	16 + 4		1		2		2	
COLLINS Sam	33	2	1		1		2	
CUMMINS Micky	39	2			2		2	
DINNING Tony	7	3						
ELDERSHAW Simon	5 + 8	1						
GOODFELLOW Marc	4 + 1							
GOODLAD Mark	20							
HANSON Christian	3 + 2							
HIBBERT Dave	2 + 7	2					1	
HULBERT Robin	23 + 1				1 + 1		1	
INNES Mark	2 + 3							
JAMES Craig	23 + 7	1	1				2	
LIPA Andreas	0 + 2							
LORAN Tyrone	6				1			
LOWNDES Nathan	7 + 5	1			2			
MATTHEWS Lee	21 + 10	10	1					
McMAHON Daryl	1 + 4						0 + 1	
O'CONNOR James	13						2	
PAYNTER Billy	43 + 2	10	1		2	2	2	1
PILKINGTON George	42 + 1		1		2		2	
PORTER Andy	0 + 2							
REID Levi	21 + 9		1		2	1	1	
ROWLAND Steve	17 + 7				0 + 2			
SMITH Dean	12 + 1		1	1			1	
SMITH Jeff	23 + 11	1	0 + 1		2		0 + 2	
SONNER Danny	13							
WALSH Michael	22 + 1				2			
WIDDRINGTON Tommy	2 + 4							
PORTSMOUTH (PREM: 16th)								
ASHDOWN Jamie	16		4		1			
BERGER Patrik	30 + 2	3	2 + 1		2			
BERKOVIC Eyal	6 + 5	1	2	1				
CHALKIAS Konstantinos	5				1			
CISSE Aliou	12 + 8		3 + 1		1			
CURTIS John	0 + 1							
DE ZEEUW Arjan	32	3	3		2			
FAYE Amdy	17 + 3		1					
FULLER Ricardo	13 + 18	1	3 + 1		1 + 1			
GRIFFIN Andy	18 + 4		3 + 1		1			
HARPER Kevin			0 + 1					
HISLOP Shaka	17							
HUGHES Richard	13 + 3		1 + 1		2			
KAMARA Diomansy	15 + 10	4	2	2	2			
KEENE James	1 + 1							
LUA-LUA Lumana	20 + 5	6	1					
MEZAGUE Valery	3 + 8		3					
O'NEIL Gary	21 + 3	2	2		2			
PRIMUS Linvoy	31 + 4	1	3		1 + 1			
PULIS Anthony			0 + 1					
QUASHIE Nigel	19		1		0 + 1			
RODIC Alexsander	1 + 3							
SKOPELITIS Giannis	9 + 4							
STEFANOVIC Dejan	32		1 + 1		2			
STONE Steve	22 + 1	3	1		0 + 1			
TAYLOR Matthew	21 + 11	1	4		1			
UNSWORTH David	15	2	3		1			
YAKUBU Ayegbeni	29 + 1	12	1 + 2	2	2	2		
PRESTON NORTH END (CHAMP: 5th)								
AGYEMANG Patrick	15 + 12	4			1		0 + 3	
ALEXANDER Graham	41 + 1	7	3	1	1		0 + 1	
BROOMES Marlon	8 + 3		1				0 + 2	
CRESSWELL Richard	46	16	3	4			3	1
CURTIS John	12							
DALEY Omar	1 + 13		1 + 2	1				
DAVIDSON Callum	16 + 3	1	1 + 1					
DAVIS Claude	21 + 11		3				3	
DAY Chris	6							
ETUHU Dickson	22 + 13	3	3		1		0 + 3	
FOLLY Yoann	0 + 2							
FULLER Ricardo	2	1						
GOULD Jonathan	4							
HEALY David	11	5	1					
HILL Matt	11 + 3						3	
JACKSON Mark	0 + 2		1 + 2		0 + 1			
KOZLUK Robbie	0 + 1				1			
LANGMEAD Kelvin	0 + 1							
LEWIS Eddie	37 + 3	4	2		1		3	
LONERGAN Andy	23	1	2		1			
LUCKETTI Chris	41	4	1		1		3	
LYNCH Simon	2 + 7		0 + 1	1				
MAWENE Youl	46	2	3		1		3	
McCORMACK Alan	0 + 3		0 + 1					
McKENNA Paul	37 + 2	3	2		1		3	
MEARS Tyrone	1 + 3				0 + 1			
NASH Carlo	7						3	
N'DUMBU-NSUNGU Guylain	4 + 2							
NEAL Chris	0 + 1							
NUGENT David	13 + 5	8					3	1
OLIVEIRA Filipe	1 + 4							
O'NEIL Brian	40 + 3	3	3				3	
O'NEILL Joe	0 + 2				1			
SEDGWICK Chris	24	3			1		3	
SKORA Eric	5 + 4		0 + 1					
SMITH Andy	3 + 11		2 + 1					
WARD Gavin	6 + 1		1					
QUEEN'S PARK RANGERS (CHAMP: 11th)								
AINSWORTH Gareth	14 + 8	2			1			
BAIDOO Shabazz	2 + 2							
BAILEY Stefan	1 + 1							
BEAN Marcus	13 + 7	1	0 + 1		1			
BEST Leon	2 + 3							
BIGNOT Marcus	41 + 2		2					
BIRCHAM Marc	32 + 3	1	0 + 1					
BRANCO Serge	3 + 4		1		1			
BROWN Aaron	0 + 1							
COOK Lee	38 + 4	2	1 + 1		1			
CURETON Jamie	18 + 12	4	2	1	1			
DAVIES Andrew	9							
DAY Chris	30		2		1			
DONNELLY Scott	0 + 2							
EDGHILL Richard	13 + 7		1		1			
FORBES Terrell	2 + 1		1					
FURLONG Paul	39 + 1	18	1 + 1					
GALLEN Kevin	46	10	2	1	1			
GNOHERE Arthur	3		1					
HAMILTON Lewis	0 + 1							
JOHNSON Richard	6		1					
KANYUKA Patrick	1							
McLEOD Kevin	4 + 20	1	1 + 1	1	1			
MILLER Adam	9 + 5							
MULHOLLAND Scott	0 + 1							
PADULA Gino	28 + 5		1		0 + 1			
ROSE Matthew	24 + 4	2						
ROSSI Generoso	3							
ROWLANDS Martin	31 + 4	3	2	1	1			
ROYCE Simon	13							
SANTOS Georges	39 + 4	5	1 + 1					
SHITTU Danny	33 + 1	4	2		1			
SIMEK Frankie	5							
STURRIDGE Dean	0 + 2							
THORPE Tony	4 + 6				0 + 1			
TOWNSEND Luke	0 + 2							
READING (CHAMP: 7th)								
BROOKER Paul	22 + 9		2		0 + 1			
CONVEY Bobby	4 + 14		1 + 1		2			
FERDINAND Les	4 + 8	1			2			
FORSTER Nicky	27 + 3	7	0 + 1		3	2		

	P/FL App	P/FL Goals	FLC App	FLC Goals	FAC App	FAC Goals	Others App	Others Goals
GOATER Shaun	2 + 7		2	1				
HAHNEMANN Marcus	46		2		3			
HARPER James	39 + 2	3	1 + 1		3			
HUGHES Andy	40 + 1		2	1	3			
INGIMARSSON Ivar	43 + 1	3	2		3	1		
KEOWN Martin	3 + 2							
KITSON Dave	37	19	1					
LITTLE Glen	29 + 6		1		3			
MORGAN Dean	10 + 8	2	0 + 1		0 + 1			
MURTY Graeme	41		2		2			
NEWMAN Ricky	11 + 6		1		1			
OWUSU Lloyd	14 +11	6	1 + 1		0 + 3			
SHOREY Nicky	44	3	1		3			
SIDWELL Steven	44	5	1		2			
SONKO Ibu	35 + 4	1			3			
WILLIAMS Adrian	11		2					
ROCHDALE (DIV 2: 9th)								
ATIENO Taiwo	6 + 7	2			1 + 1		1	
BERTOS Leo	33 + 9	4			2 + 1		1	
BRISCO Neil	6 + 5						0 + 1	
BROWN Gary	1							
BURGESS Daryl	19 + 2		1		1		2	
CASH Brian	6		1					
CLARKE Jamie	32 + 9	1	1		3		1 + 1	
COOKSEY Ernie	27 + 7	5			3		2	
EDWARDS Neil	16		1					
EVANS Wayne	40		1		3		1	
GALLIMORE Tony	32 + 2		1		2		2	
GILKS Matty	30				3		2	
GOODALL Alan	27 + 7	2			2		1	
GRIFFITHS Gareth	36 + 3	1			2		2	3
HEALD Greg	29	2	1		2			
HOLT Grant	40	17	1	1	3	5	1	1
JONES Gary	39	8	1		3		1	
KITCHEN Ben	0 + 1							
LAMBERT Rickie	15	6						
McCOURT Paddy	3 + 3		0 + 1				1	
McGIVERN Leighton	2 +23	1	0 + 1		0 + 2		0 + 2	
PROBETS Ashley	4 + 5		1				0 + 2	
RICHARDS Marc	4 + 1	2						
RICHARDSON Marcus	1 + 1							
TAIT Paul	27 + 9	2	1	1	3		2	
TOWNSON Kevin	1							
WARNER Scott	25 + 3				0 + 2		2	
WELLER Paul	5							
WILLIAMS Matt	0 + 1							
ROTHERHAM UNITED (CHAMP: 24th)								
BARKER Richie	16 + 1		2	1				
BARKER Shaun	30 + 3	2	1					
BURCHILL Mark	3	1						
BUTLER Martin	21	6			1			
CAMPBELL-RYCE Jamal	23 + 1				1			
DUNCUM Sam	1 + 1							
GARNER Darren	17 + 1		2					
GILCHRIST Phil	21 + 3	1	1		0 + 1			
GRIFFIT Leandre	1 + 1							
HOSKINS Will	6 +16	2	0 + 1		0 + 1			
HURST Paul	38 + 1		0 + 1		1			
JUNIOR	12	2						
KEANE Michael	9 + 1							
McINTOSH Martin	23	5			1			
McLAREN Paul	32 + 1	1			1			
MINTO Scott	13 + 1		2					
MONKHOUSE Andy	11 + 3	2			1			
MONTGOMERY Gary	1							
MULLIN John	26 + 5	1	2					
NEWSHAM Marc	0 + 4							
POLLITT Mike	45		2		1			
PROCTOR Michael	16 +12	1	2	1	1			
SCOTT Rob	17 + 7	2			1			
SEDGWICK Chris	19 + 1	2	2	1				
SHAW Paul	9	2						
STOCKDALE Robbie	27		2					
SWAILES Chris	37	2	2		1			
THORPE Tony	5	1						
VERNAZZA Paolo	14 +13		1 + 1		1			
WARNE Paul	13 +11	1	1					
RUSHDEN & DIAMONDS (DIV 2: 22nd)								
ALLEN Graham	25 + 1	1			2		1	
BELL David	39 + 1	3	1		0 + 1		1	
BLAYNEY Alan	4							

	P/FL App	P/FL Goals	FLC App	FLC Goals	FAC App	FAC Goals	Others App	Others Goals
BRANIFF Kevin	11 + 1	3	1				1	
BROUGHTON Drewe	20 + 1	6			1	1		
BURGESS Andy	42	1	1		2		1	
CONNELLY Sean	40 + 2		1		2		1	
DEMPSTER John	9 + 6							
DOVE Craig	31 + 5	6	0 + 1		2		1	
DUFFY Robert	0 + 1							
GIER Rob	30 + 2	2	1		0 + 1			
GRAY Stuart	37 + 1	1	1		2	1		
GULLIVER Phil	29 + 3		1		2		1	
HAWKINS Peter	41	1	1		2		1	
HAY Alex	29 +13	3	1		2		1	
HUNTER Barry	0 + 1							
JACKSON Simeon	0 + 3							
KELLY Marcus	3 + 8		0 + 1		0 + 1			
KENNEDY Luke	1 + 2						0 + 1	
LITTLEJOHN Adrian	8 + 7							
McCAFFERTY Neil	16							
MILLS Garry	7	1	1					
MULLIGAN Gary	12 + 1	3						
ROBINSON Marvin	0 + 2				2	1		
SAMBROOK Andy	3 + 5						1	
SHARP Billy	16	9						
SHEARER Scott	13							
TAYLOR Jason	4 +16	2			1			
TURLEY Billy	22		1		2		1	
WARK Scott	0 + 1							
WILLIAMS Mark	7							
WORGAN Lee	7							
SCUNTHORPE UNITED (DIV 2: 2nd)								
ANGUS Stev	9							
BAILEY Matt	2 + 2		1					
BARACLOUGH Ian	45	3	1		3	1		
BARWICK Terry							1	
BEAGRIE Peter	36	2	1		3			
BRIGHTON Tom	2 + 3						1	
BUTLER Andy	36 + 1	10	1		3			
BYRNE Cliff	24 + 5	1			3		1	
CORDEN Wayne	3 + 5							
CROSBY Andy	43 + 1	3	1		3			
EVANS Tom							1	
FEATHERSTONE Lee	0 + 1						1	
GRAVES Wayne							0 + 1	
HAYES Paul	41 + 5	18	1		3	2	0 + 1	
HINDS Richard	6 + 1							
JACKSON Mark	1 + 2						1	
KELL Richard	43	5	1		3			
KEOGH Andrew	13 +12	3						
MUSSELWHITE Paul	46		1		3			
PARTON Andy	0 + 1		0 + 1					
RANKINE Michael	1 +20	1			1 + 1		1	
RIDLEY Lee	43 + 1		1		3	1		
SHARP Kevin	4 + 2				0 + 1			
SPARROW Matt	35 + 9	5	0 + 1		3	1	1	
STANTON Nathan	18 + 3		1				1	
TAYLOR Cleveland	18 +26	6	1		0 + 3		1	
TEGGART Neil	1							
TORPEY Steve	33 + 1	12			2		1	1
WALTERS Jon	3							
WILLIAMS Marcus	0 + 4				0 + 1		0 + 1	
SHEFFIELD UNITED (CHAMP: 8th)								
BARNES Phil	1							
BECKETT Luke	1 + 4							
BENNETT Ian	5							
BLACK Tommy	3 + 1	1	1					
BROMBY Leigh	46	5	3		5			
CADAMARTERI Danny	14 + 7	1			0 + 1			
CULLIP Danny	11				4	1		
FORTE Jonathan	1 +21	1	2 + 1		0 + 2			
FRANCIS Simon	2 + 4				0 + 1			
GABRIELI Emanuele	0 + 1							
GEARY Derek	15 + 4	1			4 + 1			
GRAY Andy	41 + 2	15	2	2	5	1		
HARLEY Jon	44	2	3		5			
HAYLES Barry	4		1					
HURST Kevan	0 + 1		0 + 2					
JAGIELKA Phil	46		3	1	5	1		
JOHNSON David	0 + 4							
JOHNSON Tommy	1							
KABBA Steve	6 + 5	2						
KENNY Paddy	40		3		5			
KOZLUK Robbie	9							

	P/FL		FLC		FAC		Others	
	App	Goals	App	Goals	App	Goals	App	Goals
LESTER Jack	1 +11		1 + 1	1				
LIDDELL Andy	26 + 7	3	1		5	3		
McCALL Stuart			1 + 1					
MONTGOMERY Nick	16 + 9	1	3		4 + 1			
MORGAN Chris	40 + 1	2	3	1	3			
QUINN Alan	38 + 5	7	2		1 + 1			
SHARP Billy	0 + 2							
SHAW Paul	16 + 5	7	0 + 2		1 + 1			
THIRLWELL Paul	24 + 6	1	2 + 1		2 + 1			
TONGE Michael	33 + 1	2	1 + 1	1	5			
WARD Ashley	5 + 5	1	1					
WEBBER Danny	6 + 1	3						
WRIGHT Alan	11 + 3				1			
SHEFFIELD WEDNESDAY (DIV 1: 5th)								
ADAMS Steve	8 + 1						0 + 1	
ADAMSON Chris	1 + 1							
ALJOFREE Hasney	2						1	
ARANALDE Zigor	1 + 1							
BARRETT Graham	5 + 1	1						
BRANSTON Guy	10 + 1		1		1			
BRUCE Alex	5 + 1						3	
BRUNT Chris	27 +15	4	1 + 1		1		2 + 2	1
BULLEN Lee	46	7	2				4	
COLLINS Patrick	25 + 3	1	2		1		1 + 1	
GALLACHER Paul	8							
GREEN Adam	3							
GREENWOOD Ross	0 + 2		1				0 + 1	
HAMSHAW Matt	9 +11	1			0 + 1		2	
HECKINGBOTTOM Paul	37 + 1	4	1				3	
JONES Kenwyne	7	7						
LEE Graeme	19 + 3	1			1			
LUCAS David	34		2		1		4	
MacLEAN Steve	36	18	2		1		1 + 1	2
MARSDEN Chris	15		2				1	
McGOVERN Jon-Paul	46	6	2		1		4	2
McMAHON Lewis	13 + 2	2	1 + 1		1		1 + 1	
N'DUMBU-NSUNGU Guylain	4 + 7	1	0 + 1					
NEEDHAM Liam							0 + 1	
O'BRIEN Joey	14 + 1	2						
PEACOCK Lee	18 +11	4	1	1			3	1
PROUDLOCK Adam	11 + 3	6	1 + 1				1	
QUINN James	10 + 5	2					3	
ROCASTLE Craig	9 + 2	1					3	
SHAW Jon	1 + 2		0 + 1					
SMITH Paul	7 + 1		1				1	
TALBOT Drew	3 +18	4			1		0 + 3	1
TIDMAN Ola	3 + 1							
WHELAN Glenn	36	2	2		1	1	3	1
WOOD Richard	33 + 1	1			1		3	
SHREWSBURY TOWN (DIV 2: 21st)								
ADAGGIO Marco	0 + 5							
AISTON Sam	26 + 9	1	1		1		1	
ASHTON Neil	22 + 2							
BURNS Liam	1 + 1							
CHALLIS Trevor	38				1		1	
COWAN Gavin	5							
CRAMB Colin	0 + 2		0 + 1					
DARBY Duane	8 + 8	1					1	
EDWARDS David	16 +11	5	1		1		0 + 1	
FOX David	2 + 2	1					1	
GRANT John	10 + 9	2	1				0 + 1	
HART Joe	6							
HOWIE Scott	40		1		1		2	
LANGMEAD Kelvin	24 + 4	3						
LOGAN Richard	5	1					1	
LOWE Ryan	19 +11	3	1		1		0 + 2	1
LYNG Ciaran	0 + 4							
McGRATH John	7 + 1							
MOSS Darren	26	6	1				1	
O'CONNOR Martin	13 + 8				1			
RIDLER Dave	6 + 3		1				2	
RODGERS Luke	35 + 1	6	1	1	1		2	1
SEDGEMORE Jake	25 + 6	5			1		2	
SHERON Mike	6 + 1	2						
SMITH Ben	10 + 2	3	1				1	
STEPHENS Ross	0 + 2						1	
STREET Kevin	15 + 6	1			1		1 + 1	
TINSON Darren	42 + 1		1		1		1	
TOLLEY Jamie	33 + 3	4	0 + 1				2	1
WALTON Dave	20 + 2	2	1		0 + 1			
WHITEHEAD Stuart	37 + 3				1		2	
WILKINSON Andy	9							

	P/FL		FLC		FAC		Others	
	App	Goals	App	Goals	App	Goals	App	Goals
SOUTHAMPTON (PREM: 20th)								
BEATTIE James	11	3						
BERNARD Olivier	12 + 1				3			
BEST Leon	1 + 2		1 + 1					
BLACKSTOCK Dexter	8 + 1	1	0 + 2	4				
BLAYNEY Alan	1		1					
CAMARA Henri	10 + 3	4			2 + 1	2		
CRAINIE Martin	3		0 + 1		1 + 1			
CROUCH Peter	18 + 9	12	1		5	4		
DAVENPORT Calum	5 + 2				4 + 1			
DELAP Rory	34 + 3	2	2		4			
DODD Jason	4 + 1							
FERNANDES Fabrice	14 + 2		1 + 1					
FOLLY Yoann	1 + 2		0 + 1					
GRIFFIT Leandre	0 + 2		0 + 1					
HIGGINBOTHAM Danny	20 + 1	1	1		4			
JAKOBSSON Andreas	24 + 3	2	3		2 + 1			
JONES Kenwyne	1 + 1				0 + 1			
KELLER Kasey	4							
KENTON Darren	9		2					
LE SAUX Graeme	24 + 1	1			1			
LUNDEKVAM Claus	33 + 1		3		4			
McCANN Neil	5 + 6		2	1	1 + 3			
NIEMI Antti	28		2		2			
NILSSON Mikael	12 + 4		3		2			
OAKLEY Matthew	6 + 1	1			4 + 1	1		
ORMEROD Brett	5 + 4		2	1	0 + 1			
PHILLIPS Kevin	21 + 9	10	2	1	3 + 1	2		
PRUTTON David	19 + 4	1	2	1	3			
QUASHIE Nigel	13	1						
REDKNAPP Jamie	16				1	1		
SMITH Paul	5 + 1				3			
SVENSSON Anders	21 + 9	3	2		2			
TELFER Paul	26 + 4		1 + 1		4			
VAN DAMME Jelle	4 + 2		2 + 1					
SOUTHEND UNITED (DIV 2: 4th)								
BARRETT Adam	42 + 1	11	1		1		10	
BENTLEY Mark	35 + 4	5	1		0 + 1		10	1
BLEWITT Darren	0 + 1							
BRAMBLE Tes	10 +10	1	0 + 1		0 + 1		4	1
BROUGHTON Drewe	4 + 5		1				0 + 1	
CLARKE Ryan	1							
CORBETT Jimmy	1 + 5	1					0 + 2	
DUDFIELD Lawrie	16 +20	4	1				4 + 5	3
EASTWOOD Freddy	31 + 2	19			1		6 + 2	5
EDWARDS Andy	9 + 3	1	1		0 + 1		2 + 2	
FLAHAVAN Darryl	26 + 2						9	
GOWER Mark	32 + 6	6	1		1		7 + 1	1
GRAY Wayne	33 +11	11	0 + 1		1		6 + 4	2
GRIEMINK Bart	19		1		1		1	
GUTTRIDGE Luke	3 + 2						0 + 3	
HUNT Lewis	27 + 4				1		4 + 1	
HUSBANDS Michael	0 + 2							
JUPP Duncan	28 + 3		1		1		6	1
KIGHTLY Michael	0 + 1							
LAWSON James	0 + 1							
MAHER Kevin	42	1	1		1		10	
McCORMACK Alan	5 + 2	2					0 + 1	
NICOLAU Nicky	15 + 7	1	1				5 + 2	1
PETTEFER Carl	46		1		1		10	1
PRIOR Spencer	41	2			1		8	
WILSON Che	40				1		8	
STOCKPORT COUNTY (DIV 1: 24th)								
ADAMS Danny	27	1	1		2		1	
ALLEN Damien	14 + 7	1			1		1	
ARMSTRONG Chris	9 + 2	1						
BAILEY Matt	0 + 1						0 + 1	
BARLOW Stuart	11 +20	3			0 + 3		1 + 1	1
BECKETT Luke	15	7	1					
BRIDGE-WILKINSON Marc	19 + 3	2	1		2			
BRIGGS Keith	14 + 2	2						
CARTWRIGHT Lee	18 + 1	1	1		1		2	
CLARKE Darrell	1							
CUTLER Neil	22		1		1 + 1		2	
DALY Jon	10 + 4	3	1		2		1	1
DJE Ludovic	2 + 1							
DOLAN Joe	11	1						
FEENEY Warren	31	15			2	2		
GEARY Derek	12 + 1		1				1	
GOODWIN Jim	30 + 6		1		3		2	
GRIFFIN Danny	16				3	1	2	

	P/FL		FLC		FAC		Others	
	App	Goals	App	Goals	App	Goals	App	Goals
HADFIELD Jordan	1							
HARDIKER John	26 + 3		1		3		1	
HORWOOD Evan	10							
HURST Kevan	14	1						
ACKMAN Danny	24 + 9	2	1		1		2	
LAMBERT Rickie	27 + 2	4			1 + 1		1 + 1	
LE FONDRE Adam	11 + 9	4					1 + 1	1
MAIR Lee	9 + 5				1 + 1		1	
MORRISON Owen	0 + 1		0 + 1					
RAYNES Michael	15 + 4				0 + 1			
ROBERTSON Mark	18 + 2				3		1	
ROBINSON Marvin	3							
SINGH Harpal	5 + 1							
SMITH Andy	1				1			
SPENCER James	24				2			
TOMLINSON Ezekiel	2 + 3							
TURNBULL Paul	0 + 1							
WELSH Andy	4 + 9		0 + 1				1	
WILLIAMS Ashley	44	1	1		3	1	1	
WILLIAMS Chris	6 + 3		0 + 1		1 + 2			
STOKE CITY (CHAMP: 12th)								
AKINBIYI Ade	29	7			1			
ASABA Carl	14 +19	1	1	1	0 + 1			
BARKER Chris	4							
BRAMMER Dave	42 + 1	1	0 + 1					
BUXTON Lewis	14 + 2				1			
CLARK Chris	0 + 2							
CLARKE Clive	42	1	1		1			
DE GOEY Ed	17							
DICKINSON Carl	0 + 1							
DUBERRY Michael	25							
EUSTACE John	2 + 5				0 + 1			
GREENACRE Chris	18 +14	1	1		1			
GUDJONSSON Thordur	0 + 2							
GUPPY Steve	0 + 4							
HALL Marcus	19 + 1	1	1		1			
HALLS John	20 + 2		1		1			
HARPER Kevin	8 + 1							
HENRY Karl	14 +20		1		0 + 1			
HILL Clint	31 + 1	1	1					
ARRETT Jason	2				1			
ONES Kenwyne	13	3						
NEAL Lewis	10 +13	1	1					
NOEL-WILLIAMS Gifton	41 + 5	13	0 + 1					
OWEN Gareth	0 + 2							
PALMER Jermaine	0 + 1							
PATERSON Martin	0 + 3							
RICKETTS Michael	1 +10							
RUSSELL Darel	45	2	1		1			
SIMONSEN Steve	29 + 2		1		1			
TAGGART Gerry	31	2			1			
THOMAS Wayne	35	2	1		1	1		
WILKINSON Andy	0 + 1							
SUNDERLAND (CHAMP: 1st)								
ALNWICK Ben	3							
ARCA Julio	39 + 1	9	1		1			
BREEN Gary	40	2	1					
BRIDGES Michael	5 +14	1			0 + 2			
BROWN Chris	13 +24	5	1	2	0 + 2			
CALDWELL Steve	41	4	2	1	1			
CARTER Darren	8 + 2	1						
CLARK Ben	1 + 1		1					
COLLINS Danny	6 + 8				1			
COLLINS Neill	8 + 3		1		2			
DEANE Brian	0 + 4							
ELLIOTT Stephen	29 +13	15	0 + 2	1	2			
NGHAM Mike	1 + 1							
JOHNSON Simon	1 + 4							
KYLE Kevin	5 + 1		1	1				
LAWRENCE Liam	20 +12	7	1 + 1					
LEADBITTER Grant			1					
LYNCH Mark	5 + 6		2					
McCARTNEY George	35 + 1				2			
MYHRE Thomas	31		2		2			
OSTER John	6 + 3		2					
PIPER Matt	1 + 1				0 + 1			
POOM Mart	11		0 + 1					
ROBINSON Carl	40	4	1		2			
STEWART Marcus	40 + 3	16	1		2	1		
THORNTON Sean	3 +13	4	2		2			
WELSH Andy	3 + 4	1			1	1		
WHITEHEAD Dean	39 + 3	5	1 + 1		2			
WHITLEY Jeff	32 + 3							
WILLIAMS Darren	1		1					
WRIGHT Stephen	39	1	0 + 1		2			
SWANSEA CITY (DIV 2: 3rd)								
ANDERSON Ijah	8 + 5				1 + 1			
AUSTIN Kevin	41 + 1		1		5		2	
BEAN Marcus	6 + 2							
BRITTON Leon	16 +14	1	1		2 + 1		0 + 1	
CONNOR Paul	34 + 6	10			5	3	1	
FISKEN Gary	1 + 4		0 + 1		0 + 1			
FITZGERALD Scott	0 + 3						1	
FORBES Adrian	36 + 4	7	1		5		2	
GOODFELLOW Marc	6	3			1 + 1	1		
GUERET Willy	44		1		5		2	
GURNEY Andy	25 + 3	1			4		1	
IRIEKPEN Izzy	29	2			2		0 + 1	
JONES Stuart	2 + 2							
MARTINEZ Roberto	34 + 3				3		2	
MAYLETT Brad	4 +12		0 + 1		0 + 1		2	
McLEOD Kevin	7 + 4							
MONK Garry	34		1		4		2	
MURPHY Brian	2							
NUGENT Kevin	7 +12	3	1		0 + 1		0 + 2	1
O'LEARY Kris	32	1	1		3	1	2	
OLI Dennis	0 + 1							
RICKETTS Sam	42		1		5		2	1
ROBINSON Andy	29 + 8	8	1		3 + 1		1	
TATE Alan	17 + 6		1		2 + 1		1	
THOMAS James	0 + 2							
THORPE Lee	9 + 6	3						
TRUNDLE Lee	41 + 1	22	1		5	1	1	
SWINDON TOWN (DIV 1: 12th)								
BOOK Steve	1 + 1		1				2	
CATON Andy	1 + 7	1					1	
DUKE David	42 + 2	1	1		3	1	1	
EVANS Rhys	45		1		3		1	
FALLON Rory	12 +19	3	1 + 1		1 + 2		3	1
GARRARD Luke	8 + 1		1		1 + 1		2	
GURNEY Andy	6							
HENDERSON Darius	6	5						
HEWLETT Matt	30 + 1	1	2	1	2		2	
HEYWOOD Matt	28 + 4	1	0 + 1		3		3	
HOLGATE Ashan	0 + 2							
HOLMES Lee	14 + 1	1					1	
HOWARD Brian	28 + 7	5	2		3	1	1 + 1	
IFIL Jerel	31 + 4		2		2		3	
IGOE Sammy	42 + 1	4	1 + 1		3		1 + 1	
JENKINS Steve	24				2	1		
LAPHAM Kyle	2							
McMASTER Jamie	2 + 2	1						
MIGLIORANZI Stefani	16 + 5		1				1	
MITCHELL Paul	7							
NICHOLAS Andrew	8 + 8		1				2	1
O'HANLON Sean	40	3	1 + 1		3	1	1 + 1	
OPARA Lloyd			1					
PARKIN Sam	41	23	1 + 1		3		2 + 1	1
POOK Michael	3 + 2		0 + 1				1	
PROCTOR Michael	4	2						
REEVES Alan	6 + 2	1	1		1		2	
ROBERTS Chris	18 + 3	3			2	1		
ROBINSON Steve	11 + 7		2		1 + 1		1	
SLABBER Jamie	4 + 5						0 + 1	
SMITH Grant	23 + 7	10	2		0 + 2		2 + 1	
WELLS Ben	0 + 1							
YEATES Mark	3 + 1							
TORQUAY UNITED (DIV 1: 21st)								
ABBEY Zema	2 + 4	1						
AKINFENWA Adebayo	28 + 9	14	0 + 1		1		1 + 1	2
BARNES Phil	5							
BEDEAU Tony	31 + 4	2	1		1		0 + 2	1
BOARDLEY Stuart	2 + 4				0 + 1		2	
BOND Kain	0 + 1						0 + 1	
BOSSU Bert	2							
BROWN Aaron	5							
CANOVILLE Lee	29 + 2				1		2	
CONSTANTINE Leon	24 + 3	9			1			
DEARDEN Kevin	5						0 + 1	
FOWLER Jason	7 + 5		1		1		1	
GARNER Darren	8 + 1							
GOSLING Jamie	6 + 1	1						
GOTTSKALKSSON Ole	15				1		1	

	P/FL		FLC		FAC		Others	
	App	Goals	App	Goals	App	Goals	App	Goals
GRITTON Martin	16 + 3	6	1		0 + 1		1	
HILL Kevin	36 + 3	5			1		0 + 1	
HOCKLEY Matt	20 +14	1	1		1		2	
JARVIE Paul	1							
KEANE Kieron							1	
LOPES Osvaldo	1							
MARRIOTT Andy	11							
McGLINCHEY Brian	32 + 1		1		1		2	
MEIRELLES Bruno	5 + 4		1				1	
NOBLE Stuart	2 + 1		1					
OSEI-KUFFOUR Jo	26 + 8	6	1	1			1	1
OWEN Gareth	2 + 3		1					
PHILLIPS Martin	19 +11	2	0 + 1				2	
PULIS Anthony	1 + 2							
ROBINSON Paul	12							
RUSSELL Alex	38	3			1			
STORY Owen	0 + 2							
TAYLOR Craig	35 + 1				1		1	1

	P/FL		FLC		FAC		Others	
	App	Goals	App	Goals	App	Goals	App	Goa
VAN HEUSDEN Arjan	7		1				1	
VILLIS Matt	12 +10						2	
WARDLEY Stuart	5 + 2	2	0 + 1					
WOODMAN Craig	20 + 2	1						
WOODS Steve	36	2	1				1	
TOTTENHAM HOTSPUR (PREM: 9th)								
ATOUBA Thimothee	15 + 3	1	1		5			
BROWN Michael	20 + 4	1	3 + 1	1	6			
BUNJEVCEVIC Goran	2 + 1		2	2				
CARRICK Michael	26 + 3		2 + 1		5 + 1			
CERNY Radek	2 + 1							
DAVENPORT Calum	0 + 1							
DAVIES Simon	17 + 4		2 + 1		4 + 1			
DAVIS Sean	11 + 4		1					
DAWSON Michael	5							
DEFOE Jermain	28 + 7	13	2 + 2	5	5	4		
DOHERTY Gary	0 + 1							

Ledley King (Tottenham Hotspur)

	P/FL		FLC		FAC		Others	
	App	Goals	App	Goals	App	Goals	App	Goals
EDMAN Erik	28	1			2 + 1			
GARDNER Anthony	8 + 9		2	1	4 + 1			
IFIL Philip	2		0 + 1					
JACKSON Johnnie	3 + 5		1					
KANOUTE Fredi	22 +10	7	3 + 1	2	5			
KEANE Robbie	23 +12	11	3 + 1	3	3 + 3	3		
KELLER Kasey			2					
KELLY Stephen	13 + 4	2	1		5			
KING Ledley	38	2	4		5	1		
MABIZELA Mbulelo	1		1					
MARNEY Dean	3 + 2	2			0 + 3			
MENDES Pedro	22 + 2	1	2 + 2		2			
MIDO	4 + 5	2			0 + 2	1		
NAYBET Noureddine	27	1	2		2			
PAMAROT Noe	23	1	3		2	1		
REDKNAPP Jamie	9 + 5		1					
REID Andy	13	1						
RICKETTS Rohan	5 + 1		1 + 1					
ROBINSON Paul	36		2		6			
YEATES Mark	0 + 2				0 + 1			
ZIEGLER Reto	12 +11	1	3		5			
TRANMERE ROVERS (DIV 1: 3rd)								
ACHTERBERG John	39		2		1		4	
BERESFORD David	8 +11	2	1 + 1				0 + 3	1
BROWN Paul	1 + 3							
DADI Eugene	15 +16	9	1 + 1				1 + 3	
DAGNALL Chris	13 +10	6					1 + 1	
GOODISON Ian	43 + 1	1	1		1		5	
HALL Paul	40 + 6	11	2		1		5	1
HARRISON Danny	16 +16		0 + 1				3 + 1	
HAWORTH Simon	2 + 1							
HOWARTH Russell	7 + 1						1	
HUME Iain	40 + 2	15	2		1		5	1
JACKSON Michael	43	5	1		1		5	
JENNINGS Steve	4 + 7		0 + 1				1 + 1	
JONES Gary	5 + 5	1					0 + 1	
LINWOOD Paul	4 + 6						1	
LORAN Tyrone	0 + 2							
McATEER Jason	32 + 2	4	2	1	1		2	
RANKINE Mark	41		2		1		4	
ROBERTS Gareth	40	3	2		1		5	1
SHARPS Ian	44	1	2		1		4	
TAYLOR Ryan	43	8	2		1	1	5	1
TREMARCO Carl	2 + 1							
WHITMORE Theo	17 +16	5	1				2 + 1	
ZOLA-MAKONGO Calvin	7 + 8	2	1 + 1	1	1		1	1
WALSALL (DIV 1: 14th)								
ARANALDE Zigor	28 + 2		1		1		2	
ATIENO Taiwo	0 + 3		1					
BAZELEY Darren	7						1	
BENNETT Julian	30 + 1	2			1		3	
BEWERS Jon	1							
BIRCH Gary	11 + 2	2	1				2 + 1	
BRADLEY Mark	1							
BROAD Joe	5 + 5		1				1	
COLEMAN Dean	1 + 1							
DAKINAH Kofi	1		1					
DANN Scott	0 + 1							
EMBLEN Neil	34 + 2	2			1		2	
FRYATT Matt	22 +14	15			1		1 + 1	
GERRARD Anthony	8							
HARKNESS Jon	1							
HERIVELTO Moreira	0 + 1							
JOACHIM Julian	8	6						
KINSELLA Mark	21 + 1						1	
LEITAO Jorge	34 + 8	8			1		3	3
McDERMOTT David			0 + 1					
McKINNEY Richard	3							
McSHANE Paul	3 + 1	1						
MERSON Paul	31 + 5	2	1		1		2	
MURPHY Joe	25						2	
OAKES Andy	9							
OSBORN Simon	32 + 6				1		2	
PASTON Mark	8 + 1		1		1		1	
PEAD Craig	8							
PERPETUINI David	7							
ROBINSON Marvin	4 + 6	4						
ROPER Ian	25 + 1						1	
STANDING Michael	27 + 5	4	1		1		2	
SURMAN Andrew	10 + 4	2						
TAYLOR Daryl	10 + 9	3			0 + 1		0 + 2	
TAYLOR Kris	11 + 1	2	1				2	

	P/FL		FLC		FAC		Others	
	App	Goals	App	Goals	App	Goals	App	Goals
WILLETTS Ryan			1					
WILLIAMS Leroy	2 + 5	1	0 + 1		0 + 1		0 + 1	
WRACK Darren	43	7			1	1	3	
WRIGHT Mark	35 + 2	2	1		1		2	
WATFORD (CHAMP: 18th)								
ARDLEY Neal	28 + 2	4	5 + 1		1 + 1			
BANGURA Al	1 + 1							
BLIZZARD Dominic	12 + 5	1	2 + 2		1			
BOUAZZA Hameur	10 +18	1	4 + 2	2	2			
CHAMBERLAIN Alec	4 + 1				2			
CHAMBERS James	40		5	2	2			
COX Neil	38 + 1		6	1	2			
CULLIP Danny	4							
DARLINGTON Jermaine	25 + 1		7		2			
DE MERIT Jay	22 + 2	3	5 + 1		2			
DEVLIN Paul	15 + 2	1	3 + 1		2			
DOYLEY Lloyd	25 + 4		4					
DYCHE Sean	23		3					
DYER Bruce	21 +15	9	4 + 2	2	0 + 2			
EAGLES Chris	10 + 3	1						
FERRELL Andy			0 + 2	1				
FITZGERALD Scott	0 + 7		0 + 2					
GAYLE Marcus	0 + 3							
GUNNARSSON Brynjar	34 + 2	3	5		1 + 1			
HELGUSON Heidar	36 + 3	16	5	3	2	1		
JACKSON Johnnie	14 + 1							
JONES Paul	9		2					
LEE Richard	33		5					
MAHON Gavin	42 + 1		6		2			
MAYO Paul	13		2					
McNAMEE Anthony	1 +13		0 + 1		0 + 1			
OSBORNE Junior	0 + 1							
SMITH Jack	7		0 + 1					
WEBBER Danny	24 + 4	12	1 + 1		1 + 1			
YOUNG Ashley	15 +19		3 + 1					
WEST BROMWICH ALBION (PREM: 17th)								
ALBRECHTSEN Martin	20 + 4		1		3			
CAMPBELL Kevin	16	3			1 + 1			
CHAPLOW Richard	3 + 1							
CLEMENT Neil	35	3			3			
CONTRA Cosmin	5		1					
DOBIE Scott	1 + 4	1	1					
DYER Lloyd	0 + 4		1					
EARNSHAW Rob	18 +13	11			2 + 1	3		
GAARDSOE Thomas	25 + 4		1		1			
GERA Zoltan	31 + 7	6	1		3			
GREENING Jonathan	32 + 2		0 + 1		2			
HAAS Bernt	9 + 1							
HORSFIELD Geoff	18 +11	3	1	1	1 + 1			
HOULT Russell	36				3			
HULSE Rob	0 + 5		0 + 1		0 + 1			
INAMOTO Junichi	0 + 3							
JOHNSON Andy	22				1			
KANU Nwankwo	21 + 7	2			2	1		
KOUMAS Jason	5 + 5		1		1 + 1			
KUSZCZAK Tomasz	2 + 1		1		0 + 1			
MOORE Darren	10 + 6		1					
O'CONNOR James			0 + 1		0 + 1			
PURSE Darren	22				2			
RICHARDSON Kieran	11 + 1	3						
ROBINSON Paul	28 + 2	1			3			
SAKIRI Artim	2 + 1							
SCIMECA Riccy	27 + 6		1		2			
WALLWORK Ronnie	19 + 1	1			3			
WEST HAM UNITED (CHAMP: 6th)								
BREVETT Rufus	10	1	3					
BYWATER Steve	36				2		0 + 1	
CHADWICK Luke	22 +10	1	1		3			
COHEN Chris	1 +10		1 + 1		0 + 1			
DAILLY Christian	2 + 1						0 + 2	
DAVENPORT Calum	10							
ETHERINGTON Matthew	37 + 2	4	2				3	
FERDINAND Anton	24 + 5	1	1		3		3	
FLETCHER Carl	26 + 6	2			3		1	
GARCIA Richard	0 + 1							
HAREWOOD Marlon	45	17	3	2	3	2	3	1
HUTCHISON Don	2 + 3		0 + 1					
LOMAS Steve	18 + 5	1	2					
MACKAY Malky	17 + 1	2	1		3			
McANUFF Jobi	0 + 1							
McCLENAHAN Trent	0 + 2		1					

	P/FL		FLC		FAC		Others	
	App	Goals	App	Goals	App	Goals	App	Goals
MELVILLE Andy	3		0 + 1					
MULLINS Hayden	32 + 5	1	2		2 + 1		3	
NEWTON Shaun	11						2 + 1	
NOBLE Mark	10 + 3		0 + 2		3		0 + 3	
NOWLAND Adam	3 + 1	1	2					
POWELL Chris	35 + 1				3		3	
POWELL Darren	5	1						
REBROV Sergei	12 +14	1	2 + 1	1	1 + 1		0 + 1	
REO-COKER Nigel	34 + 5	3	3		1 + 1		3	
REPKA Tomas	42		3		3		3	
SHERINGHAM Teddy	26 + 7	20	0 + 1		2	1		
TARICCO Mauricio	1							
WALKER Jimmy	10		3		1		3	
WARD Elliott	10 + 1		1				3	
WILLIAMS Gavin	7 + 3	1						
ZAMORA Bobby	15 +19	7	2	2			3	4
WIGAN ATHLETIC (CHAMP: 2nd)								
BAINES Leighton	41	1	1					
BRECKIN Ian	42		1		0 + 1			
BULLARD Jimmy	46	3	1		0 + 1			
EADEN Nicky	33 + 6		1					
ELLINGTON Nathan	43 + 2	24						
FILAN John	46				1			
FLYNN Mike	1 +12	1			1			
FRANDSEN Per	9	1						
GRAHAM David	13 +17	1	1		1			
JACKSON Matt	35 + 1	1			1			
JARRETT Jason	4 +10							
JOHANSSON Andreas	0 + 1							
KAVANAGH Graham	11							
MAHON Alan	21 + 6	7	1		1	1		
McCULLOCH Lee	42	14	1					
McMILLAN Steve	5 + 3				1			
MITCHELL Paul	0 + 1		1					
ORMEROD Brett	3 + 3	2						
ROBERTS Jason	45	21			1			
ROBERTS Neil			1					
TEALE Gary	29 + 8	3	0 + 1		1			
THOME Emerson	11 + 4		1		1			
WALSH Gary			1					
WHALLEY Gareth	7 + 1				1			
WRIGHT David	19 +12				1			
WOLVERHAMPTON WANDERERS (CHAMP: 9th)								
ANDREWS Keith	14 + 6		2	1				
BISCHOFF Mikkel	9 + 2	1						
BJORKLUND Joachim	2 + 1		1		1			
CAMERON Colin	24 +13	3	1		0 + 2			
CLARKE Leon	11 +17	7	1 + 1	1	0 + 1			
CLYDE Mark	17 + 1		2		1			
COOPER Kevin	15 +15	6	1					
CORT Carl	34 + 3	15	1		2	1		
CRADDOCK Jody	40 + 2	1	2		2			
EDWARDS Rob	15 + 2		1					
INCE Paul	25 + 3	3	1	1	2			
JONES Paul	10							
KENNEDY Mark	27 + 3				2			
LESCOTT Jolean	41	4			2			
LOWE Keith	11		1 + 1					
MILLER Kenny	41 + 3	19	1	1	1 + 1			
MULLIGAN Gary	0 + 1							
MURRAY Matt	1				1			
NAYLOR Lee	36 + 2	1	1		2			
NEWTON Shaun	21 + 3	1	2		1 + 1			
OAKES Mike	35		2		1			
OLOFINJANA Seyi	41 + 1	5	1 + 1		2			
RICKETTS Rohan	3 + 4	1						
SEOL Ki-Hyeon	28 + 9	4	1	1	2	1		
STURRIDGE Dean	5 + 6	1						
WREXHAM (DIV 1: 22nd)								
ARMSTRONG Chris	18 +15	8	1		1 + 1		0 + 1	
BAKER Matt	11 + 2		1		2		3	
BENNETT Dean	7 + 7		2				1 + 1	
CAREY Brian	10		2					
CROWELL Matty	22 + 6				1		5 + 1	
DIBBLE Andy	15		1					
EDWARDS Carlos	18	1					3	
FERGUSON Darren	40	3	2	1	2		5 + 1	2
FOSTER Ben	17						4	
GREEN Scott	5 + 7				1		1 + 2	
HOLT Andy	45	6	2		2	1	6	
JONES Mark	17 + 9	3	0 + 1		1 + 1		6 + 1	1
JONES Michael	0 + 1							
LAWRENCE Denis	44	4			2	1	6	
LLEWELLYN Chris	45	7	1 + 1	1	2	1	7	
MACKIN Levi	5 + 5		0 + 1					
MORGAN Craig	18 + 8		1	1	1		6	
PEJIC Shaun	30 + 5		2		2		4 + 1	
ROBERTS Steve	34	3	1		1 + 1		5	
SAM Hector	19 +19	9	2	1	1 + 1	1	1 + 4	
SHAW Matt	0 + 1							
SMITH Alex	17 + 7		2		0 + 1		2 + 1	
SPENDER Simon	9 + 4		0 + 2		2		2	
UGARTE Juan	23 + 7	17			1 + 1		5 + 1	
VALERO Xavi	3							
WHITLEY Jim	13 + 3		0 + 1				2 + 1	
WILLIAMS Danny	21		2				3 + 1	
WYCOMBE WANDERERS (DIV 2: 10th)								
ABBEY Zema	3 + 2						1	
AHMED Shahed	0 + 4	1					0 + 1	
ANYA Ikechi	0 + 3						0 + 1	
BIRCHALL Adam	11 + 1	4	1				2	
BLOOMFIELD Matt	20 + 6	2			0 + 2		2	
BROUGHTON Drewe	2 + 1							
BURNELL Joe	23 + 1		1					
CACERES Adrian	1 + 2							
CLARIDGE Steve	14 + 5	4						
COMYN-PLATT Charlie	3 + 1						1	
COOKE Stephen	4 + 2							
CRAIG Tony	14				2		2	
CRONIN Lance	1							
DIXON Jonny	4 +12	1					0 + 1	
EASTON Clint	29 + 4	1	1				1	
FAULCONBRIDGE Craig	6 + 2				0 + 1		1	
GUPPY Steve	12 + 2	1			1		1	
JOHNSON Roger	40 + 2	6	1		2	1	2 + 1	
LEE Rob	6 + 1							
MARTIN Russell	1 + 6				1		2 + 1	
NETHERCOTT Stuart	27 + 2		1		0 + 1		1	
PERPETUINI David	1 + 1							
PHILO Mark	2 + 3							
REILLY Andy							1	
RYAN Keith	35 + 3	2			2			
SAVAGE Bas	2 + 2						1	
SENDA Danny	42 + 2	4	1		2		3	
SILK Gary	19 + 3		1		2		3	
STONEBRIDGE Ian	31 + 7	4	1		2		3	
TALIA Frank	45		1		2		2	
TYSON Nathan	40 + 2	22	1		2		0 + 2	
UHLENBEEK Gus	36 + 6	4	1		2		1	
WILLIAMS Steve	0 + 1						1	
WILLIAMSON Mike	32 + 5	2			2		2	
YEOVIL TOWN (DIV 2: 1st)								
AMANKWAAH Kevin	10 + 5							
BROWN Marvin	0 + 2							
CACERES Adrian	7 +14	3	2		0 + 2		1	1
COLLIS Steve	9						1	
DAVIES Arron	15 + 8	8			0 + 2	1		
FALLON Rory	2 + 4	1						
FONTAINE Liam	15		2				1	
GALL Kevin	30 +13	3	1 + 1		4 + 1		1	
GUYETT Scott	13 + 5	2			5			
IBE Kezie	0 + 3							
JEVONS Phil	45 + 1	27	2		4	2		
JOHNSON Lee	44	7	2	3	5	1	0 + 1	
LINDEGAARD Andy	19 +10	1			3 + 1		1	
LOCKWOOD Adam	6 + 4		1					
MILES Colin	20 + 1				3	1		
MIRZA Nicolas	0 + 3						1	
O'BRIEN Roy	10 + 4		1 + 1		0 + 1		1	
ODUBADE Yemi	0 + 4				0 + 1	1	0 + 1	
REED Steve	1 + 2						1	
RICHARDSON Marcus	2 + 2							
ROSE Michael	37 + 3	1	2		3 + 1		0 + 1	
SKIVERTON Terry	36 + 2	4	2		3			
SODJE Efe	6	2						
STOLCERS Andrejs	23 +13	5	1		4 + 1	1	1	1
TARACHULSKI Bartosz	27 +15	10	1 + 1		5	2	1	1
TERRY Paul	35 + 4	6	1 + 1		4	1	1	
WAY Darren	45	7	2		5	2		
WEALE Chris	37 + 1		2		5			
WEATHERSTONE Simon	0 + 6		0 + 1					
WILLIAMS Gavin	12 + 1	2	0 + 1		2			
WOOZLEY David	0 + 1							

Where Did They Go?

Below is a list of all players who were recorded in the previous edition as making a first-team appearance in 2003-2004, but failed to make the current book. They are listed alphabetically and show their last League club, their approximate leaving dates, as well as their next club, for which a minimum stay of three months is the requisite. Of course, they may well have moved on by now, but space does not allow further reference.

* Shows that the player in question is still with his named club but failed to make an appearance in 2004-2005, the most common reason being injury.

+ Players retained by Carlisle United and York City, who were relegated to the Conference.

Player	Last League club	Date	Next club
BIDALLAH Nabil	Ipswich T	03.04	Heerenveen (Netherlands)
LCOCK Danny	Barnsley	05.04	Accrington Stanley
LEXANDER John	Darlington	06.04	
LEXANDERSSON Niclas	Everton	03.04	IFK Göteborg (Sweden)
LLBACK Marcus	Aston Villa	08.04	Hansa Rostock (Germany)
LLEN-PAGE Danny	Brentford	03.04	Farnborough T
LPAY	Aston Villa	10.03	Incheon (Korea)
MBROSIO Marco	Chelsea	08.04	Grasshopper Zurich (Switzerland)
NDERSON Iain	Grimsby T	07.04	Dundee
NDRESEN Martin	Blackburn Rov	05.04	Stabaek (Norway)
NDREWS Lee	Carlisle U	+	
NGEL Mark	Boston U	06.04	Kings Lynn
NTOINE-CURIER Mickael	Grimsby T	05.04	Haugesund (Norway)
RASON Arni	Manchester C	05.04	Valerengen (Norway)
RMSTRONG Chris	Sheffield U	*	
RNDALE Neil	Bristol Rov	06.04	Clevedon T
RNISON Paul	Carlisle U	+	
RPEXHAD Pegguy	Coventry C	06.04	
RTHUR Adam	York C	+	
SHCROFT Kane	York C	+	
A Ibrahim	Bolton W	06.04	Djurgarden (Sweden)
ABB Phil	Sunderland	06.04	Retired
ABBEL Markus	Liverpool	07.04	VfB Stuttgart (Germany)
AGGIO Dino	Blackburn Rov	01.04	Ancona (Italy)
AIRD Chris	Southampton	*	
ALDACCHINO Ryan	Carlisle U	08.03	Gretna
ALDRY Simon	Notts Co	06.04	Retired
ALMER Stuart	Boston U	06.04	Clyde
ARDSLEY Phil	Manchester U	*	
ARNARD Darren	Grimsby T	06.04	Aldershot T
ARNES Paul	Doncaster Rov	12.03	Tamworth
ARRETT Paul	Wrexham	06.04	Blyth Spartans
ART-WILLIAMS Chris	Ipswich T	06.04	Apoel Nicosia (Cyprus)
ARTON Warren	Wimbledon	05.04	Dagenham & Redbridge
ARTRAM Vince	Gillingham	01.04	Retired
ASTOCK Paul	Boston U	10.04	St Albans C
ATTY David	Leeds U	06.04	Retired
AXTER Lee	Sheffield U	02.04	IFK Göteborg (Sweden)
EADLE Peter	Brentford	09.03	Barnet
ECK Dan	Brighton & Hove A	11.04	Eastbourne Borough
ECKWITH Robert	Luton T	*	
EECH Chris	Rochdale	06.04	Fleetwood T
ELL Andy	York C	05.04	Hednesford T
ENEFIELD Jimmy	Torquay U	06.04	Bath C
ENT Jason	Plymouth Arg	06.04	
ERNARD Narada	Torquay U	01.04	Welling U
ERTHE Sekou	West Bromwich A	*	
BERTHELIN Cedric	Crystal Palace	10.04	RAEC Mons (Belgium)
BETTS Robert	Kidderminster Hrs	03.04	RC Warwick
BIGGINS James	Nottingham F	*	
BILLY Chris	Carlisle U	+	
BIRCH Mark	Carlisle U	08.03	Gretna
BISHOP Andy	Walsall	06.04	York C
BLACK Chris	Doncaster Rov	04.04	
BLACKMAN Lloyd	Brentford	06.04	Farnborough T
BLONDEL Jonathan	Tottenham H	01.04	FC Brugge (Belgium)
BOLDER Chris	Grimsby T	05.04	Ossett T
BONNISSEL Jerome	Fulham	*	
BOOTY Martyn	Huddersfield T	06.04	Retired
BOSSY Fabien	Darlington	02.04	
BOUND Matt	Oxford U	06.04	Weymouth
BOUSSATTA Dries	Sheffield U	03.04	Retired
BOWEN Jason	Cardiff C	06.04	Newport Co
BOXALL Danny	Bristol Rov	06.04	Dublin C
BRACKENRIDGE Steve	Macclesfield T	*	
BRACKSTONE Steve	York C	05.04	Bishop Auckland
BRANNAN Ged	Wigan Ath	11.03	Accrington Stanley
BRASS Chris	York C	+	
BRAYSON Paul	Cheltenham T	06.04	Northwich Victoria
BRAZIER Matthew	Leyton Orient	06.04	Retired
BRIDGES David	Cambridge U	08.04	Latvia
BRILL Dean	Luton T	*	
BRISCOE Lee	Preston NE	06.04	Retired
BRITTAIN Martin	Newcastle U	*	
BROCK Stuart	Kidderminster Hrs	05.04	AFC Telford U
BROUGH Michael	Notts Co	03.04	Stevenage Borough
BROUGH Scott	Boston U	10.03	Barrow
BROWN Jermaine	Boston U	06.04	
BROWN Simon	Colchester U	06.04	Hibernian
BROWN Steve	Reading	10.04	Retired
BROWN Steve	Wycombe W	06.04	Retired
BROWNE Gary	York C	01.04	Volendam (Netherlands)
BRYANT Simon	Bristol Rov	05.04	Forest Green Rov
BULMAN Dannie	Wycombe W	06.04	Stevenage Borough
BURGESS Oliver	Northampton T	11.03	Basingstoke T
BURLEY Craig	Walsall	05.04	Retired
BURT Jamie	Chesterfield	08.03	Blyth Spartans
BURTON Steve	Doncaster Rov	06.04	Scarborough
BYRNE Danny	Manchester U	02.04	Weymouth
BYRNE Des	Carlisle U	11.03	St Patricks Ath
BYRNE Michael	Stockport Co	02.05	Northwich Victoria
BYRNE Shaun	West Ham U	06.04	Dublin C
CAIG Tony	Newcastle U	*	
CALDWELL Gary	Newcastle U	01.04	Hibernian
CALVO-GARCIA Alex	Scunthorpe U	06.04	Retired
CAMARA Zoumana	Leeds U	05.04	Saint Etienne (France)

CARNEY Dave	Oldham Ath	02.04	Sydney FC (Australia)
CAROLE Sebastien	West Ham U	05.04	AS Monaco (France)
CARR Chris	Sheffield Wed	12.04	Queen of South
CARR Michael	Macclesfield T	02.05	Northwich Victoria
CARSON Stephen	Hartlepool U	06.04	Coleraine
CAS Marcel	Grimsby T	01.04	Roesendal BC (Netherlands)
CHAPMAN Ben	Boston U	06.04	Alfreton T
CHAPUIS Cyril	Leeds U	01.04	Strasbourg (France)
CHARNOCK Phil	Bury	09.03	Linfield
CHEYROU Bruno	Liverpool	*	
CLANCY Sean	Blackpool	*	
CLARK Peter	Northampton T	07.04	Retired
CLARK Steve	Southend U	06.04	Hornchurch
CLARKE Chris	Cambridge U	06.04	Halifax T
CLARKE Matt	Crystal Palace	*	
CLEGG George	Bury	05.04	Worcester C
CLEGG Michael	Oldham Ath	*	
CLEVERLEY Ben	Cheltenham T	06.04	Forest Green Rov
CLIST Simon	Bristol C	01.04	Barnet
COAD Matthew	York C	+	
COATES Jonathan	Swansea C	06.04	Newport Co
COGHLAN Michael	Darlington	04.05	
COLEMAN Kenny	Kidderminster Hrs	05.04	Waterford U
COLLETT Andy	Darlington	06.04	Retired
COLLINS Wayne	Stockport Co	09.03	Retired
COMBE Alan	Bradford C	06.04	Kilmarnock
CONNELL Lee	Bury	06.04	Leigh RMI
CONNOLLY Karl	Swansea C	06.04	Prescot Cables
COOK Lewis	Wycombe W	06.04	Windsor & Eton
COOKE Terry	Sheffield Wed	06.04	Colorado Rapids (USA)
COOPER Richard	York C	05.04	Alfreton T
COOTE Adrian	Colchester U	11.03	Wivenhoe T
CORBETT Luke	Cheltenham T	*	
CORBISIERO Antonio	Swansea C	*	
CORICA Steve	Walsall	09.04	Sydney U (Australia)
CORNWALL Luke	Bradford C	03.04	Woking/Lewes
COSTA Candido	Derby Co	05.04	FC Porto (Portugal)
COWAN Tom	Carlisle U	+	
CRESPO Hernan	Chelsea	*	
CRITTENDEN Nick	Yeovil T	06.04	Aldershot T
CROPPER Dene	Boston U	06.04	Worksop T
CROWE Dean	Oldham Ath	05.04	Leek T
CRYAN Colin	Sheffield U	06.04	Scarborough
CULKIN Nick	Queens Park Rgrs	*	
DALMAT Stephane	Tottenham H	04.04	Toulouse (France)
DALY Wes	Queens Park Rgrs	06.04	Raith Rov
DAVIES Clint	Bradford C	06.04	Bristol C
DAVIES Sean	York C	+	
DAVIS Steve	Blackpool	05.04	York C
DAWS Nicky	Rotherham U	*	
DEENEY David	Luton T	*	
DELANY Dean	Port Vale	06.04	Shelbourne
DELGADO Agustin	Southampton	03.04	Pumas UNAM (Mexico)
DELL Steve	Wycombe W	02.04	Eastbourne Borough
DESAILLY Marcel	Chelsea	07.04	Al Ittihad (UAE)
DI CANIO Paolo	Charlton Ath	08.04	Lazio (Italy)
D'JAFFO Laurent	Mansfield T	06.04	Skonto Riga (Latvia)
DJETOU Martin	Fulham	06.04	OGC Nice (France)
DOBSON Craig	Cheltenham T	06.04	Grays Ath
DOHERTY Sean	Fulham	*	
DOMI Didier	Leeds U	05.04	Paris Saint Germain (France)
DONALDSON Clayton	Hull C	*	
DONOVAN Kevin	Rochdale	03.04	York C
DOUGHTY Matt	Rochdale	06.04	Halifax T
DOUGLAS Stuart	Boston U	06.04	RoPS (Finland)

DOWNER Simon	Leyton Orient	06.04	Retired
DOWNES Stephen	York C	05.04	Ossett A
DUFFIELD Peter	Carlisle U	06.04	Alfreton T
DUGARRY Christophe	Birmingham C	03.04	Qatar
DUGUID Karl	Colchester U	*	
DUNNING Darren	York C	+	
DURKAN Keiron	Swansea C	03.04	Runcorn Halton
DUTTON Brian	Cambridge U	06.04	Pickering T
DUXBURY Lee	Bury	09.04	Farsley Celtic
EBDON Marcus	Leyton Orient	11.03	Tamworth
EDWARDS Jake	Yeovil T	06.04	Exeter C
EDWARDS Paul	Crewe Alex	12.04	Gresley Rov
ELAM Lee	Yeovil T	05.04	Hornchurch
EMBERSON Carl	Southend U	04.04	Grays Ath
EVANS Paul	Rushden & Diamonds	12.03	Bath C
EVANS Richard	Sheffield Wed	*	
EVANS Steve	Brentford	06.04	Woking
FARRELL Craig	Carlisle U	+	
FARRELLY Gareth	Wigan Ath	06.04	Bohemians
FIELDWICK Lee	Brentford	06.04	Lewes
FIGUEROA Lucho	Birmingham C	01.04	Cruz Azul (Mexico)
FLEMING Craig	Oldham Ath	06.04	
FLITNEY Ross	Fulham	*	
FLO Tore Andre	Sunderland	08.03	Siena (Italy)
FLYNN Sean	Kidderminster Hrs	09.03	Evesham U
FOFANA Aboubaka	Millwall	05.04	PAOK Salonika (Gree
FORAN Richie	Carlisle U	07.04	Motherwell
FORBES Boniek	Leyton Orient	03.04	Ford U
FORD Simon	Grimsby T	05.04	Kilmarnock
FORSYTH Richard	Cheltenham T	06.04	Northwich Victoria
FOTIADIS Andy	Peterborough U	07.04	Retired
FOX Christian	York C	05.04	Wakefield & Emley
FOXE Hayden	Portsmouth	*	
FRANCIS Willis	Notts Co	06.04	Grantham T
FREESTONE Roger	Swansea C	06.04	Newport Co
FREUND Steffen	Tottenham H	06.03	Kaiserslautern (Germany)
FULLARTON Jamie	Chesterfield	05.04	Woodlands Wellingt (Singapore)
GABBIADINI Marco	Hartlepool U	02.04	Retired
GADSBY Matt	Kidderminster Hrs	06.04	Forest Green Rov
GANEA Ivo	Wolverhampton W	05.04	Retired
GARDEN Stuart	Notts Co	06.04	Ross Co
GEORGE Liam	York C	05.04	Grays Ath
GIBBS Paul	Barnsley	10.03	Canvey Island
GILES Chris	Yeovil T	03.04	Aldershot T
GILL Robert	Doncaster Rov	06.04	Scarborough
GILROY David	Bristol Rov	01.04	Weston-super-Mare
GLENNON Matty	Carlisle U	+	
GORDON Michael	Wimbledon	06.04	Havant & Waterloovi
GRABBI Ciccio	Blackburn Rov	01.04	Ancona (Italy)
GRAINGER Martin	Birmingham C	12.04	Retired
GRAND Simon	Rochdale	06.04	Carlisle U
GRAY Kevin	Carlisle U	+	
GRIFFIN Antony	Cheltenham T	06.04	Dorchester T
GROVES Paul	Scunthorpe U	06.04	York C
GUNBY Steve	Bury	01.04	Leigh RMI
HACKWORTH Tony	Notts Co	03.04	Scarborough
HADDRELL Matt	Macclesfield T	02.04	Leek T
HADJI Moustapha	Aston Villa	02.04	RCD Espanyol (Spain
HADLAND Phil	Colchester U	09.03	Leek T
HAMILTON Des	Grimsby T	03.04	
HANDYSIDE Peter	Barnsley	06.04	Northwich Victoria
HANKIN Sean	Torquay U	09.03	Crawley T

RDING Billy	Wycombe W	02.04	Carshalton Ath
RNWELL Jamie	Leyton Orient	09.03	Welling U
RRIS Richard	Wycombe W	06.04	Eastbourne Borough
RTE Ian	Leeds U	07.04	Levante (Spain)
W Robbie	York C	+	
WLEY Karl	Walsall	03.04	Carlisle U
Y Danny	Walsall	12.03	Auckland Kingz (NZ)
YWARD Steve	Barnsley	06.04	Retired
ZEL Reuben	Torquay U	06.04	Kidderminster Hrs
ALD Paul	Wimbledon	06.04	Retired
ALY Colin	Sunderland	*	
EROO Gavin	Crystal Palace	06.04	Grays Ath
NDERSON Kevin	Carlisle U	+	
NRIKSEN Bo	Bristol Rov	05.04	Koge BK (Denmark)
RRING Ian	Swindon T	12.03	Chippenham T
RZIG Nico	Wimbledon	06.04	Wacker Burghausen (Germany)
L Stephen	Rochdale	06.04	Radcliffe Borough
TON Kirk	Blackpool	06.04	Halifax T
CHEN Steve	Macclesfield T	01.04	Bangor C
BBS Shane	Bristol Rov	06.04	Mangotsfield U
CKING Matt	Boston U	06.04	Stevenage Borough
DGES Lee	Bristol Rov	06.04	Thurrock
EKSTRA Peter	Stoke C	06.04	Retired
GG Christopher	Ipswich T	01.05	Hibernian
LDSWORTH Dean	Wimbledon	06.04	Havant & Waterlooville
LE Stuart	Wycombe W	06.04	Chesham U
LLIGAN Gavin	Wycombe W	03.04	Havant & Waterlooville
LMES Shaun	Wrexham	06.04	Glentoran
WARD Michael	Swansea C	06.04	Morecambe
WELLS Lee	Cheltenham T	02.04	Merthyr Tydfil
WSON Stuart	Chesterfield	06.04	Accrington Stanley
GHES Ian	Huddersfield T	06.04	Bacup Borough
GHES Lee	West Bromwich A	08.04	
JGHES Steve	Brentford	06.04	Farnborough T
JNT Jonathan	Scunthorpe U	11.04	Guiseley
NT Warren	Portsmouth	06.04	Fareham T
DE Graham	Bristol Rov	06.04	Hereford U
LDGAARD Morten	Luton T	06.04	Brande IF (Denmark)
LTON Leon	Swansea C	01.05	Retired
NES Peter	Aston Villa	06.04	Dublin
WIN Denis	Wolverhampton W	05.04	Retired
ERSEN Steffen	Wolverhampton W	06.04	Valerengen (Norway)
ELUMO Chris	Brighton & Hove A	06.04	Alemannia Aachen (Germany)
CK Darren	Barnsley	03.04	Sligo Rov
CK Michael	Carlisle U	06.04	Kendal T
CKSON Kirk	Yeovil T	05.04	Hornchurch
RDEL	Bolton W	01.04	Ancona (Italy)
FFS Ian	Crewe Alex	02.04	IBV (Iceland)
NKINS Neil	Southend U	06.04	Crawley T
PHCOTT Avun	Coventry C	06.04	Nuneaton Borough
HNROSE Lenny	Burnley	06.04	Retired
NES Darren	Bristol C	02.04	Newport Co
NES Lee	Wrexham	06.04	Caernarfon T
NES Richard	Southampton	06.04	Llanelli
RDAN Andy	Hartlepool U	11.04	Retired
SEPH Matthew	Leyton Orient	06.04	Canvey Island
AN	Arsenal	01.04	Fluminense (Brazil)
DGE Matthew	Luton T	06.04	Dagenham & Redbridge
NINHO	Middlesbrough	08.04	Glasgow Celtic
ACHLOUL Hassan	Aston Villa	06.04	Livingston
EGAN Paul	Leeds U	*	
EN Peter	Carlisle U	09.04	Scarborough
ELLY Darren	Carlisle U	07.04	Portadown
KERR Brian	Newcastle U	06.04	Motherwell
KILFORD Ian	Scunthorpe U	06.04	Barrow
KILLOUGHERY Graham	Torquay U	11.03	
KIROVSKI Jovan	Birmingham C	02.04	Los Angeles Galaxy (USA)
KITSON Paul	Rushden & Diamonds	06.04	Retired
KOUMANTARAKIS George	Preston NE	06.04	RW Erfurt (Germany)
LABARTHE TOME Gianfranco	Derby Co	11.04	
LAW Graeme	York C	+	
LEWIS Matt	Kidderminster Hrs	12.03	Hinckley U
LIBURD Richard	Lincoln C	06.04	Eastwood T
LINCOLN Greg	Northampton T	06.04	Redbridge
LINDEROTH Tobias	Everton	07.04	FC Copenhagen (Denmark)
LITTLE Colin	Macclesfield T	03.04	Altrincham
LIVINGSTONE Steve	Carlisle U	01.04	Retired
LOCKETT Ryan	Cambridge U	*	
LOWE Onandi	Coventry C	05.04	
LUMSDON Chris	Barnsley	06.04	Carlisle U
LUZHNY Oleg	Wolverhampton W	06.04	Retired
LUZI-BERNARDI Patrice	Liverpool	*	
LYTTLE Des	Northampton T	06.04	Forest Green Rov
McALLISTER Gary	Coventry C	12.03	Retired
MACAULEY Steve	Macclesfield T	04.04	Bamber Bridge
McCANN Ryan	Hartlepool U	08.04	Linfield
MACCARONE Massimo	Middlesbrough	08.04	Parma (Italy)
McCARTHY Paul	Oxford U	06.04	Hornchurch
McCLARE Sean	Rochdale	06.04	Drogheda U
McDONAGH Will	Carlisle U	+	
McDONALD Scott	Wimbledon	11.03	Motherwell
McEVILLY Lee	Rochdale	06.04	Accrington Stanley
McGHEE Dave	Leyton Orient	03.04	Canvey Island
McGILL Brendan	Carlisle U	+	
McGOLDRICK David	Notts Co	06.04	Southampton
McHUGH Frazer	Notts Co	06.04	Hucknall T
McNULTY Jimmy	Wrexham	06.04	Caernarfon T
McPHEE Steve	Port Vale	07.04	Beira Mar (Portugal)
McSWEENEY Dave	Southend U	06.04	Billericay T
MADDISON Lee	Carlisle U	08.03	Gretna
MANANGU Eric	Rushden & Diamonds	*	
MANEL	Derby Co	05.04	
MANGAN Andrew	Blackpool	*	
MANSOURI Yazid	Coventry C	01.04	Chateauraux (France)
MAPES Charlie	Wycombe W	06.04	Crawley T
MARINELLI Carlos	Middlesbrough	11.03	Boca Juniors (Argentina)
MARLET Steve	Fulham	08.03	Marseilles (France)
MARNEY Danny	Brighton & Hove A	03.04	Crawley T
MARSHALL Lee	West Bromwich A	06.04	Retired
MARSHALL Scott	Wycombe W	06.04	Retired
MARTEINSSON Petur	Stoke C	08.03	Hammarby (Sweden)
MARTIN Ben	Swindon T	06.04	St Albans C
MASON Christopher	Darlington	06.04	Billingham T
MAY David	Burnley	06.04	Bacup Borough
MAY Rory	Lincoln C	06.04	Tamworth
MELLANBY Danny	Darlington	06.04	Crook T
MERRIS David	York C	+	
MITCHELL Craig	Mansfield T	06.04	Leigh RMI
MOLLOY David	Carlisle U	+	
MOORE Alan	Burnley	06.04	Shelbourne
MORENO Javi	Bolton W	05.04	Real Zaragoza (Spain)
MORGAN Lionel	Wimbledon	06.04	Retired
MORNAR Ivica	Portsmouth	08.04	Stade Rennais (France)
MORROW Sam	Ipswich T	04.04	Hibernian
MULLIGAN Lance	Mansfield T	11.03	Eastwood T

MUNROE Karl	Macclesfield T	06.04	Halifax T
MURPHY David	Middlesbrough	06.04	Hibernian
MURPHY Peter	Carlisle U	+	
MURRAY Paul	Oldham Ath	06.04	Beira Mar (Portugal)
MUSTOE Robbie	Sheffield Wed	06.04	Retired
NACCA Franco	Cambridge U	*	
NASH Gerard	Ipswich T	*	
NDIWA-LORD Kangana	Bolton W	06.04	Stalybridge Celtic
NDLOVU Peter	Birmingham C	07.04	Mamelodi Sundowners (South Africa)
N'DOUR Alassane	West Bromwich A	06.04	ES Troyes (France)
NICHOLSON Kevin	Notts Co	03.04	Scarborough
NIELSEN David	Norwich C	08.03	Aalborg (Denmark)
NIGHTINGALE Luke	Southend U	09.03	Weymouth
NIMMO Liam	Grimsby T	06.04	Spalding U
NIXON Eric	Sheffield Wed	05.04	Retired
NOGAN Lee	York C	+	
NOTMAN Alex	Norwich C	11.03	Retired
NYARKO Alex	Everton	01.05	
O'BRIEN Rob	Doncaster Rov	06.04	Gainsborough Trinity
O'Callaghan Brian	Barnsley	06.04	Worksop T
ODUNSI Leke	Southend U	05.04	Retired
OFFIONG Richard	Newcastle U	07.04	Istanbulspor (Turkey)
OKAI Parys	Luton T	06.04	Dunstable T
OKORONKWO Isaac	Wolverhampton W	06.05	Alania Vladikavkaz (Russia)
OKUONGHAE Magnus	Rushden & Diamonds	*	
OLDFIELD David	Oxford U	06.04	Retired
OLEMBE Salomon	Leeds U	01.04	Marseilles (France)
OLIVER Luke	Wycombe W	02.04	Woking
OLSEN James	Macclesfield T	05.04	Vauxhall Motors
OLSEN Kim	Sheffield Wed	10.04	Silkeborg (Denmark)
OLSZAR Sebastian	Portsmouth	06.04	Polonia Warsaw (Poland)
OLUGBODI Jide	Brentford	12.03	
OMOYINMI Manny	Oxford U	06.04	Gravesend & Northfleet
ONE Armand	Wrexham	10.03	Tamworth
O'NEILL Keith	Coventry C	10.03	Retired
ONUORA Iffy	Huddersfield T	06.04	Retired
O'SHAUGHNESSY Paul	Bury	06.04	
OVENDALE Mark	York C	06.04	Tiverton T
OWEN Michael	Liverpool	08.04	Real Madrid (Spain)
OYEN Davy	Nottingham F	03.04	Beringen HZ (Belgium)
PAHARS Marian	Southampton	*	
PAPADOPULOS Michal	Arsenal	06.04	Banik Ostrava (Czechoslovakia)
PARKER Sonny	Bristol Rov	*	
PARKER Wes	Grimsby T	06.04	Brigg T
PARRISH Sean	Kidderminster Hrs	05.04	AFC Telford U
PASANEN Petri	Portsmouth	05.04	Werder Bremen (Germany)
PATERSON Jamie	Doncaster Rov	06.04	Barrow
PATTERSON Rory	Rochdale	06.04	Radcliffe Borough
PATTERSON Simon	Watford	06.04	Maidenhead U
PAYNE Steve	Macclesfield T	04.05	Northwich Victoria
PEARCE Allan	Lincoln C	06.04	Bradford Park Avenue
PEARCE Dennis	Peterborough U	12.03	Stafford Rgrs
PEARSON Gary	Darlington	06.04	York C
PEMBERTON Martin	Stockport Co	11.04	Farsley Celtic
PERICARD Vincent	Portsmouth	*	
PETERS Mark	Brentford	03.04	Farnborough T
PETHICK Robbie	Brighton & Hove A	01.04	Weymouth
PETIT Manu	Chelsea	05.04	Retired
PETTERSON Andy	Walsall	05.04	Retired
PETTINGER Andy	Grimsby T	06.04	
PORTER Chris	York C	+	
POSTIGA Helder	Tottenham H	07.04	FC Porto (Portugal)
POULTER Robert	Sheffield Wed	*	
POYET Gus	Tottenham H	06.04	Retired
PREECE Andy	Carlisle U	+	
PRICE Michael	Darlington	*	
PRIEST Chris	Macclesfield T	06.04	Bangor C
PRITCHARD Mark	Swansea C	*	
PULLEN James	Peterborough U	11.04	Gravesend & Northfleet
QUINN Rob	Bristol Rov	06.04	Stevenage Borough
QUINN Wayne	West Ham U	06.04	
RAE Alex	Wolverhampton W	06.04	Glasgow Rangers
RAMMELL Andy	Bristol Rov	06.04	Nuneaton Griff
RAVEN Paul	Carlisle U	07.04	Barrow
REDFEARN Neil	Rochdale	05.04	Scarborough
REES Matt	Millwall	06.04	Newport Co
REEVES David	Chesterfield	06.04	Ards
REMY Ellis	Lincoln C	09.03	Grays Ath
REUSER Martijn	Ipswich T	07.04	Willem II Tilbury (Netherlands)
REVELL Alex	Cambridge U	06.04	Braintree T
REWBURY Jamie	Swansea C	01.05	
RHODES Chris	Notts Co	*	
RICHARDS Dean	Tottenham H	*	Retired
RICHARDSON Barry	Doncaster Rov	05.04	Retired
RICKERS Paul	Northampton T	02.04	Farsley Celtic
RILEY Paul	Notts Co	06.04	Matlock T
RITCHIE Paul	Walsall	06.04	Dundee U
RIX Ben	Crewe Alex	*	
ROBERTS Andy	Millwall	*	
ROBERTS Ben	Brighton & Hove A	*	
ROBINS Mark	Sheffield Wed	06.04	Burton A
ROBINSON James	Crewe Alex	03.05	
ROBINSON Mark	Hartlepool U	06.04	Hereford U
ROBINSON Neil	Macclesfield T	03.04	Southport
ROBINSON Paul	Hartlepool U	06.04	York C
ROBINSON Ryan	Southend U	06.04	Morecambe
ROBSON Glenn	Darlington	11.03	Durham C
ROCA Carlos	Oldham Ath	06.04	Carlisle U
RODGER Simon	Brighton & Hove A	07.04	Retired
RODRIGUES Hugo	Yeovil T	06.04	Portugal
ROGERS Kristian	Sheffield U	06.04	Worksop T
ROGERS Mark	Wycombe W	05.04	Stevenage Borough
ROQUE Junior Jose	Leeds U	01.04	Siena (Italy)
ROSS Neil	Macclesfield T	11.04	Halifax T
ROUGIER Tony	Bristol C	06.04	
ROWAN Jonny	Grimsby T	06.04	Kettering T
ROWETT Gary	Charlton Ath	05.04	Retired
RUSHBURY Andy	Chesterfield	03.04	Telford U
RUSTER Sebastien	Swindon T	01.04	Frejus (France)
SADLER Mat	Birmingham C	*	
SADLIER Richard	Millwall	01.04	Retired
SAKHO Lamine	Leeds U	05.04	Marseilles (France)
SAMPSON Ian	Northampton T	06.04	Retired
SAMWAYS Vinny	Walsall	05.04	Algeciras (Spain)
SAVA Facundo	Fulham	08.04	Celta Vigo (Spain)
SCHEMMEL Sebastien	Portsmouth	09.04	Le Harve (France)
SCOTT Paul	Burnley	*	
SCOTT Richard	Peterborough U	02.04	Cambridge C
SEAMAN David	Manchester C	01.04	Retired
SEARLE Damon	Chesterfield	10.03	Forest Green Rov
SEDDON Gareth	Bury	06.04	Rushden & Diamonds
SEDGEMORE Ben	Lincoln C	06.04	Canvey Island
SHEERAN Mark	Darlington	02.04	Whitby T
SHELLEY Brian	Carlisle U	+	

ㅓERIDAN Darren	Oldham Ath	06.04	Clyde
ㅓERIDAN John	Oldham Ath	04.04	Retired
ㅓIELDS Tony	Peterborough U	01.04	Waterford U
ㅓILTON Sam	Kidderminster Hrs	01.04	Burton A
GURDSSON Larus	West Bromwich A	11.04	Retired
LAS	Wolverhampton W	06.04	CS Maritimo (Portugal)
MPEMBA Ian	Wycombe W	06.04	Crawley T
MPKINS Mike	Rochdale	07.04	Burton A
MPSON Paul	Carlisle U	06.04	Retired
⟨OUBO Morten	West Bromwich A	05.04	Brondby (Denmark)
⟨ULASON Olafur-Ingi	Arsenal	*	
ΜITH Adie	Kidderminster Hrs	02.04	Tamworth
ΜITH Chris	York C	06.04	Stafford Rgrs
ΜITH Dave	Macclesfield T	04.04	Retired
ΜITH Jay	Southend U	*	
ΜITH Shaun	Rochdale	05.04	York C
ΜITH Stephen	Cambridge U	*	
⊃LSKJAER Ole Gunnar	Manchester U	*	
ℝNICEK Pavel	Portsmouth	06.04	Beira Mar (Portugal)
TAMPS Scott	Kidderminster Hrs	06.04	Tamworth
TANIC Mario	Chelsea	06.04	Retired
TANSFIELD Adam	Yeovil T	07.04	Hereford U
TEPHENS Kevin	Leyton Orient	02.04	Redbridge
TEVENSON Jon	Swindon T	06.04	Cambridge C
TEWART Bryan	York C	+	
TEWART Michael	Manchester U	*	
TOWELL Mike	Bristol C	*	Retired
TRACHAN Craig	Rochdale	11.03	Halesowen T
TUART Jamie	Southend U	06.04	Hornchurch
JMMERBELL Mark	Carlisle U	06.04	Spennymoor U
JTCH Daryl	Boston U	01.04	Retired
JTTON John	Millwall	*	
VENSSON Michael	Southampton	*	
YMONS Kit	Crystal Palace	06.04	Retired
ALBOT Daniel	Rushden & Diamonds	02.05	Woking
ALBOTT Nathan	Yeovil T	06.04	Stafford Rgrs
ARNAT Michael	Manchester C	06.04	Hannover 96 (Germany)
AVLARIDIS Stathis	Arsenal	01.04	Lille OSC (France)
AYLOR John	Northampton T	05.04	Retired
AYLOR Bob	Cheltenham T	06.04	Tamworth
EN HEUVEL Laurens	Sheffield U	10.03	De Graafschap (Netherlands)
HOMPSON Justin	Bury	12.03	Vancouver (Canada)
HOMPSON Tyrone	Huddersfield T	06.04	Scarborough
HOMSON Andy	Wycombe W	06.04	Forest Green Rov
HORNLEY Ben	Bury	11.03	Stalybridge Celtic
HORRINGTON John	Grimsby T	05.04	Chicago Fire (USA)
E Li	Everton	*	
LSON Steve	Southend U	05.04	Retired
NDALL Jason	Bournemouth	*	
ODOROV Svetoslav	Portsmouth	*	
OMLINSON Stuart	Crewe Alex	*	
OWNSEND Ryan	Burnley	*	
OWNSLEY Derek	Oxford U	01.04	Gretna
WIGG Gary	Derby Co	07.04	Derry C
'DDIN Anwar	Bristol Rov	06.04	Dagenham & Redbridge
AESEN Nico	Birmingham C	*	
ALAKARI Simo	Derby Co	03.04	Dallas Burn (USA)
AN BRONKHORST Gio	Arsenal	08.03	Barcelona (Spain)
AN BUYTEN Daniel	Manchester C	05.04	Hamburger SV (Germany)
ENUS Mark	Cambridge U	06.04	Hibernian
ERON Juan	Chelsea	07.04	Inter Milan (Italy)
IANA Hugo	Newcastle U	*	
IEIRA Magno	Wigan Ath	*	
INNICOMBE Chris	Wycombe W	06.04	Tiverton T

VOLMER Joost	West Bromwich A	06.04	Den Bosch (Netherlands)
WAKE Brian	Carlisle U	11.03	Gretna
WALES Gary	Gillingham	06.04	Kilmarnock
WALKER Rob	Oldham Ath	*	
WALKER Scott	Hartlepool U	06.04	Brechin C
WALLACE Rod	Gillingham	06.04	Retired
WANCHOPE Paulo	Manchester C	08.04	Malaga (Spain)
WAPENAAR Harald	Portsmouth	01.05	Vitesse Arnhem (Netherlands)
WARD Mitch	York C	05.04	Alfreton T
WARREN Mark	Southend U	06.04	Fisher Ath
WATERMAN Dave	Oxford U	06.04	Weymouth
WATTLEY David	Lincoln C	06.04	Yeading
WELLS Dean	Brentford	06.04	Hampton & Richmond Borough
WHELAN Noel	Derby Co	08.04	Aberdeen
WHITFIELD Paul	Wrexham	06.04	Bangor C
WIEKENS Gerard	Manchester C	06.04	Veendam (Netherlands)
WILFORD Aron	Lincoln C	06.04	Clyde
WILKINSON Shaun	Brighton & Hove A	11.03	Weymouth
WILLIAMS John	Kidderminster Hrs	06.04	Bath C
WILLIAMS Paul	Stoke C	02.05	Richmond Kickers (USA)
WILLIS Adam	Kidderminster Hrs	06.04	Hinckley U
WILLIS Scott	Lincoln C	06.04	Halifax T
WILLS Kevin	Torquay U	06.04	Tiverton T
WILSON Laurie	Sheffield Wed	06.04	Burton A
WILTORD Sylvain	Arsenal	08.04	Lyon (France)
WISE Stuart	York C	08.04	Gateshead
WOOD Leigh	York C	05.04	Harrogate T
WOODGATE Jonathan	Newcastle U	08.04	Real Madrid (Spain)
WOODMAN Andy	Oxford U	06.04	Stevenage Borough
YALCIN Lev	York C	+	
YATES Mark	Kidderminster Hrs	05.04	Retired
YOUNG Jamie	Reading	*	
ZAVAGNO Luciano	Derby Co	01.04	Ancona (Italy)
ZIEGE Christian	Tottenham H	06.04	Borussia München Gladbach (Germany)
ZIVKOVIC Boris	Portsmouth	01.04	VfB Stuttgart (Germany)

Jonathan Woodgate

PFA AWARDS 2005

Player of the Year
JOHN TERRY
(CHELSEA)

Young Player of the Ye
WAYNE ROONEY
(MANCHESTER UNITEC

Special Merit Award
SHAKA HISLOP
(PORTSMOUTH)

DIVISIONAL AWARDS

FA Barclaycard Premiership

Petr Cech	Chelsea
Gary Neville	Manchester United
John Terry	Chelsea
Rio Ferdinand	Manchester United
Ashley Cole	Arsenal
Frank Lampard	Chelsea
Steven Gerrard	Liverpool
Arjen Robben	Chelsea
Shaun Wright-Phillips	Manchester City
Thierry Henry	Arsenal
Andy Johnson	Crystal Palace

Coca Cola Championship

Kelvin Davis	Ipswich Town
Graham Alexander	Preston North End
Tom Huddlestone	Derby County
Gary Breen	Sunderland
George McCartney	Sunderland
Jimmy Bullard	Wigan Athletic
Steve Sidwell	Reading
Julio Arca	Sunderland
Inigo Idiakez	Derby County
Nathan Ellington	Wigan Athletic
Jason Roberts	Wigan Athletic

Coca Cola League Division One

Marion Beresford	Luton Town
Ryan Taylor	Tranmere Rovers
Curtis Davies	Luton Town
Chris Coyne	Luton Town
Warren Cummings	AFC Bournemouth
Stuart Elliott	Hull City
Paul Merson	Walsall
Ahmet Brkovic	Luton Town
Kevin Nicholls	Luton Town
Steve Howard	Luton Town
Leroy Lita	Bristol City

Coca League League Division Two

Chris Weale	Yeovil Town
Sam Ricketts	Swansea City
Adam Barrett	Southend United
Andy Crosby	Scunthorpe United
Michael Rose	Yeovil Town
Lee Johnson	Yeovil Town
Darren Way	Yeovil Town
Kevin Maher	Southend United
Peter Beagrie	Scunthorpe United
Phil Jevons	Yeovil Town
Lee Trundle	Swansea City

PFA Fans' Divisional Player of the Year Awards – Premiership: Frank Lampard (Chelsea). Championship: Paul McKenna (Preston North End). Division One: Keith Southern (Blackpool). Division Two: Adam Barrett (Southend United).

For information on how to vote during the season, go to the Official PFA website: www.givemefootball.cor